Pro SQL Server Relational Database Design and Implementation

Best Practices for Scalability and Performance

Sixth Edition

Louis Davidson

Apress®

Pro SQL Server Relational Database Design and Implementation: Best Practices for Scalability and Performance

Louis Davidson
Antioch, TN, USA

ISBN-13 (pbk): 978-1-4842-6496-6
https://doi.org/10.1007/978-1-4842-6497-3

ISBN-13 (electronic): 978-1-4842-6497-3

Managing Director, Apress Media LLC: Welmoed Spahr
Acquisitions Editor: Jonathan Gennick
Development Editor: Laura Berendson
Coordinating Editor: Jill Balzano

Cover image designed by Freepik (www.freepik.com)

Distributed to the book trade worldwide by Springer Science+Business Media LLC, 1 New York Plaza, Suite 4600, New York, NY 10004. Phone 1-800-SPRINGER, fax (201) 348-4505, e-mail orders-ny@springer-sbm.com, or visit www.springeronline.com. Apress Media, LLC is a California LLC and the sole member (owner) is Springer Science + Business Media Finance Inc (SSBM Finance Inc). SSBM Finance Inc is a **Delaware** corporation.

For information on translations, please e-mail booktranslations@springernature.com; for reprint, paperback, or audio rights, please e-mail bookpermissions@springernature.com.

Apress titles may be purchased in bulk for academic, corporate, or promotional use. eBook versions and licenses are also available for most titles. For more information, reference our Print and eBook Bulk Sales web page at http://www.apress.com/bulk-sales.

Any source code or other supplementary material referenced by the author in this book is available to readers on GitHub via the book's product page, located at www.apress.com/9781484264966. For more detailed information, please visit http://www.apress.com/source-code.

Printed on acid-free paper

This book is dedicated to my wife, who first and foremost waited until the sixth edition of this book because so many other people had passed away. But we are surviving together through these weird times!

—Louis

Table of Contents

About the Author

Louis Davidson has been working with databases (for what is starting to seem like a really long time) as a corporate database developer and architect. He has been a Microsoft MVP for 16 years, and this is the sixth edition of this database design book with Apress. Louis has been active speaking about database design and implementation at many conferences over the past 17 years, including SQL PASS, SQLRally, SQLSaturday events, CA World, Music City Data, and the devLink Technical Conference. Louis has worked for the Christian Broadcasting Network (CBN) as a developer, DBA (database administrator), and data architect for over 21 years. Louis has a bachelor's degree from the University of Tennessee at Chattanooga in computer science, which was a lot of work at the time, though he doesn't remember a whole lot about that time in the past because his head is in the future!

For more information, please visit his website at `www.drsql.org`.

About the Technical Reviewer

Aaditya Maruthi works as a senior database engineer for a reputed organization. Having over ten years of experience in RDBMSs (relational database management systems) like Microsoft SQL Server and Oracle, he worked extensively on Microsoft technologies like the SSAS, SSRS, SSIS, and Power BI.

Aaditya is also an AWS Certified Solutions Architect—Associate.

Acknowledgments

You are never too old to set another goal or to dream a new dream.

—C. S. Lewis

I am not a genius, nor am I some form of pioneer in the database design world. I am just a person who 18 or so years ago asked the question of a publisher: "Do you have any books on database design?" The reply was "No, why don't you write one?" So I did, and I haven't stopped writing since then, with this book now in its sixth edition. I acknowledge that the following "people" have been extremely helpful in making this book happen and evolve along the way. Some have helped me directly, while others probably don't even know that this book exists. Either way, they have all been an important part of the process:

Far above anyone else, Jesus Christ, without Whom I wouldn't have had the strength to complete the task of writing this book. I know I am not ever worthy of the love that You give me.

My wife, Valerie Davidson, for putting up with this craziness for yet another time, all while working on her doctorate in education.

Gary Cornell, for a long time ago giving me a chance to write the book that I wanted to write.

My current managers, Mark Carpenter, Andy Curley, and Keith Griffith, for giving me time to go to several conferences that really helped me to produce as good of a book as I did. And to all of my coworkers at CBN, who have provided me with many examples for this book and my other writing projects.

The PASS conferences (particularly SQLSaturday events), where I was able to hone my material and meet thousands of people over the past three years and find out what they wanted to know.

Jessica Moss, for teaching me a lot about data warehousing and taking the time to write what is now an appendix to this book that you can download. There is just so much to say about relational database design.

ACKNOWLEDGMENTS

Paul Nielsen, for challenging me to progress and think harder about the relational model and its strengths and weaknesses. During the writing of this book, he contracted COVID-19 and had a really rough time of it.

The MVP Program and, perhaps even more importantly, the MVPs and Microsoft folks I have come into contact with over the years. I have learned so much in the newsgroups, email lists, and, in particular, the MVP Summit that I could not have done half as well without them (check the first edition of this book for evidence that things got better after I became an MVP!).

The fantastic editing staff I've had, including Jonathan Gennick and Jill Balzano, who over the last four editions (figuratively) busted my lip a few times over my poor structure, use of the English language, and so on and without whom the writing would sometimes appear to come from an illiterate chimpanzee. Most of these people are included on the copyright page, but I want to say a specific thanks to them and to Tony Davis (who had a big hand in the 2005 version of the book) for making this book great, despite my frequently rambling writing style.

To the academics out there who have permeated my mind with database theory, such as E. F. Codd, Chris Date, Fabian Pascal, Joe Celko, my professors at the University of Tennessee at Chattanooga, and many others. I wouldn't know half as much without you. And thanks to Mr. Date for reviewing Chapter 1 a few editions ago; you probably did more for me than you will ever know, even if you probably hated every second. I still have your notes bundled up in printed copy of that Chapter 1 in my history box.

All of the people I have acknowledged in previous editions who were so instrumental in getting this book to where it is from all of the many changes and lessons over the years. I've built upon the help you've all provided over the past 15+ years.

—Louis Davidson

Introduction

Once upon a time, there lived a...

—Every Fairy-Tale Writer

These words start many a work of fiction and usually not the most believable works of fiction either. While this book is clearly, at its core, nonfiction, I felt the need to warn you that nearly every example in this book is fiction, carefully tailored to demonstrate some principle of database design. Why fictitious examples? My good friend, Jeremiah Peschka once explained it perfectly when he tweeted: "@peschkaj: I'm going to demo code on a properly configured server with best practices code. Then you're all going to [complain] that it takes too long." This book is already bursting at the seams from the examples I have attempted to provide. The most egregious work of fiction will be the chapter on requirements, as in most cases the document to describe where to find the actual requirements documents will be longer than the chapter where I describe the process and include several examples.

So don't expect that if you can understand all of the examples in the book, you can easily be an expert in a week. The fact is, the real-world problems you will encounter will be far more complex, and you will need lots of practice to get things close to right. Even worse, every single design will be a failure. Not a complete failure, but you will always have in the back of your head how you could have done things better. Failure is a tremendous teacher. It will teach you more than ten university degrees, though the parties will be a lot less fun.

The thing you will get out of my book is knowledge of how to get there, and ideals to follow. If you are lucky, you will have a mentor or two who already know a few things about database design to assist you with your first designs. I know that when I was first getting started, I learned from a few great mentors, and even today I do my best to bounce ideas off of others before I create my first table. (Note that you don't need an expert to help you validate designs. A bad design, like spoiled milk, always smells at least a little fonky, which is 3.53453 times worse than funky.)

What is definitely not fiction is my reason for writing, revising, and honing the material in this book: great design is still necessary no matter how much changes in development patterns. There is a sneaky principle among many programmers that as technology like CPU and disk improves, code needn't be written as well to get the job done fast enough. While there is a modicum of truth to that principle, consider just how wasteful this is. If you have to do the operation once, then getting it right that once in any method is fine. But programmers and architects don't generally write software to do something once. We write software to do repetitive tasks. Each execution of poorly written code wastes time and resources to get the job done. Now consider how many databases and how much code exist out there and guess what the impact to your slice of the world, and to the entire world, would be. "How good is good enough?" is a question one must ask, but if you aim for sleeping on the sidewalk, you are pretty much guaranteed not to end up with a mansion in Beverly Hills (swimming pools and movie stars!).

I cannot promise you the deepest coverage of the theory that goes into the database design process, nor do I want to. If you want to go to the next level, the latest edition of Chris Date's *An Introduction to Database Systems* (Addison-Wesley) is essential reading, and you'll find hundreds of other database design books listed if you search for "database design" on a book seller's website. The problem is that a lot of these books have far more theory than the average practitioner wants (or will take the time to read), and they don't really get into the actual implementation on an actual database system. Books that are implementation oriented often don't give you enough theory and focus solely on the coding and tuning aspects that one needs **after** the database is a mess. So, many years ago, I set out to write the book you have in your hands, and this is the sixth edition under the Apress banner. The song remains the same, but the instruments keep getting better.

This book's goal is simply to be a technique-oriented book that starts out with "why" to design like the founders suggested and then addresses "how" to make that happen using the features of SQL Server. I will cover many of the most typical features of the relational engine, giving you techniques to work with. I can't, however, promise that this will be the only book you need on your shelf on the subject of database design and particularly on SQL Server.

Oscar Wilde, the poet and playwright, once said, "I am not young enough to know everything." It is with some chagrin that I must look back at the past and realize that I thought I knew everything just before I wrote my first book, *Professional SQL Server 2000*

Database Design (Wrox Press, 2001). It was ignorant, unbridled, unbounded enthusiasm that gave me the guts to write the first book. In the end, I did write that first edition, and it was a decent enough book, largely due to the beating I took from my technical editing staff. And if I hadn't possessed such enthusiasm initially, I would not likely be writing this edition today. However, if you had a few weeks to burn and you went back and compared each edition of this book, chapter by chapter, section by section, to the current edition, you would notice a progression of material and a definite maturing of the writer.

There are a few reasons for this progression and maturity. One reason is the editorial staff I have had over the past three versions: first Tony Davis and now Jonathan Gennick for the fifth time. Both of them were very tough on my writing style and did wonders on the structure of the book (which is why this edition has only minor structural changes). Another reason is simply experience, as over 20 years have passed since I started the first edition. But most of the reason that the material has progressed is that it's been put to the test. While I have had my share of nice comments, I have gotten plenty of feedback on how to improve things (some of those were not nice comments!). And I listen very intently, keeping a set of notes that start on the release date. I am always happy to get any feedback that I can use (particularly if it doesn't involve any anatomical terms for where the book might fit). I will continue to keep my email address available (`louis@drsql.org`), and you can leave anonymous feedback on my website if you want (`www.drsql.org`). The code for the chapters and any addendums on features that cover material that I didn't have space for are located on my GitHub page here: (`www.github.com/drsqlgithub/dbdesignbook6`).

Purpose of Database Design

What is the purpose of database design? Why the heck should you care? The main reason is that a properly designed database is straightforward to work with, because everything is in its logical place, much like a well-organized cupboard. When you need paprika, it's easier to go to the paprika slot in the spice rack than it is to have to look for it everywhere until you find it, but many systems are organized just this way. Even if every item has an assigned place, of what value is that item if it's too hard to find? Imagine if a phone book wasn't sorted at all. What if the dictionary was organized by placing a word where it would fit in the text? With proper organization, it will be almost instinctive where to go to get the data you need, even if you have to write a join or two. I mean, isn't that fun after all?

You might also be surprised to find out that database design is quite a straightforward task and not as difficult as it may sound. Doing it right is going to take more up-front time at the beginning of a project than just slapping a database as you go along, but it pays off throughout the later lifecycle of a project, that time immediately after users begin to use it. Of course, because there's nothing visual to excite the client, database design is one of the phases of a project that often gets squeezed to make things seem to go faster. Even the least challenging or uninteresting user interface is still miles more interesting to the average customer than the most beautiful data model. Programming the user interface takes center stage, even though the data is generally why a system gets funded and finally created. It's not that your colleagues won't notice the difference between a cruddy data model and one that's a thing of beauty. They certainly will, but the amount of time required to decide the right way to store data correctly can be called into question when programmers need to code. I wish I had an answer for that problem, because I could sell a million books with just that. This book will assist you with some techniques and processes that will help you through the process of designing databases, in a way that's clear enough for novices and helpful to even the most seasoned professional.

This process of designing and architecting the storage of data belongs to a different role than that of database setup and administration. For example, in the role of data architect, I seldom create users, perform backups, or set up replication or clustering. Little is mentioned of these tasks, which are considered administration and the role of the DBA. It isn't uncommon to wear both a developer hat and a DBA hat (in fact, when you work in a smaller organization, you may find that you wear so many hats your neck tends to hurt), but your designs will generally be far better thought out if you can divorce your mind from the more implementation-bound roles that make you wonder how hard it will be to use the data. For the most part, database design looks harder than it is.

Who This Book Is For

This book is written for professional programmers and data architects who have the need to design a relational database using any of the Microsoft SQL Server family of technologies, or technology family, which includes the on-premises version that we used to get in a cool box. It includes SQL Server running on a virtual machine (VM), using Azure DB, and even Azure Managed Instance. The book is intended to be useful for the beginner to the advanced programmer, either strictly database programmers or a programmer who has never used a relational database product before to learn why relational databases are designed in the way they are and get some practical examples and advice for creating databases. Topics covered cater to the uninitiated to the experienced architect to learn techniques for solving database design issues, controlling concurrency, data protection and security, preemptive performance tuning, and more.

How This Book Is Structured

This book is composed of the following chapters, with the first five chapters being an introduction to the fundamental topics and processes that one needs to go through/know before designing a database. Chapters 6 and 7 are exercises in learning how a database is put together using scripts, and the rest of the book takes the topics of design and implementation and provides instructions and lots of examples to help you get started building databases:

> *Chapter 1, "The Fundamentals"*: This chapter provides a basic overview of essential terms and concepts necessary to get started with the process of designing a great relational database.

> *Chapter 2, "Introduction to Requirements"*: This chapter introduces how to gather and interpret requirements from a client. Even if it isn't your job to do this task directly from a client, you will need to extract some manner or requirements for the database you will be building from the documentation that an analyst will provide to you.

> *Chapter 3, "The Language of Data Modeling"*: This chapter serves as the introduction to the main tool of the data architect—the model. In this chapter, I introduce one modeling language (IDEF1X, Integration Definition for Information Modeling) in detail, as it's the modeling language that's used throughout this book to present database designs. I also introduce a few other common modeling languages for those of you who need to use these types of models for preference or corporate requirements.

Chapter 4, "Conceptual and Logical Data Model Production": In the early part of creating a data model, the goal is to discuss the process of taking a customer's set of requirements and to start the process of discovering the entities and attributes that will become the tables and columns along with relationships between objects and surrounding business rules. Implementability is less of a goal than is to faithfully represent the desires of the users. This chapter takes some brief requirements and puts them into a data model along with descriptions of the objects.

Chapter 5, "Normalization": The goal of normalization is to hone your data structures into objects that map to the relational model that the SQL Server engine was created for. To do this, we will take the set of tables, columns, relationships, and business rules and format them in such a way that every value is stored in one place and every table represents a single thing. Normalization can feel unnatural the first few times you do it, because instead of worrying about how you'll use the data, you must think of the data and how the structure will affect that data's quality. However, once you've mastered normalization, not to store data in a normalized manner will feel wrong.

Chapter 6, "Physical Model Case Study": In this chapter, we will walk through the process of taking a normalized model and translating it into a physical data model. The goal of this chapter is to go through the final steps that a data architect typically goes through before creating a live database (though this step is not done as its own distinct step in reality).

Chapter 7, "Physical Model Implementation": This is the point in the database design process in which we fire up SQL Server and start building scripts to implement the model we have labored over in previous chapters of the book. In this chapter, I cover writing the code to create most of the typical databases an average SQL Server data architect will go through.

Chapter 8, "Data Protection Patterns with Check Constraints and Triggers": Beyond the way data is arranged in tables and columns, other business rules need to be enforced. The front line of defense for enforcing data integrity conditions in SQL Server is formed by CHECK constraints and TRIGGER objects, as users cannot innocently avoid them. This chapter will walk through the typical patterns of implementing such data integrity checks.

Chapter 9, "Patterns and Anti-patterns": Beyond the basic set of techniques for table design, there are several techniques that I use to apply a common data/query interface for my future convenience in queries and usage. This chapter will cover several of the common useful patterns as well as take a look at some patterns that some people will use to make things easier to implement the interface that can be very bad for your query needs.

Chapter 10, "Database Security and Security Patterns": Security is high in almost every programmer's mind these days, or it should be. In this chapter, I cover the basics of SQL Server security and show how to employ strategies to use to implement data security in your system, such as employing views, triggers, encryption, row-level security (RLS), and using other tools that are a part of the SQL Server toolset.

Chapter 11, "Data Structures, Indexes, and Their Application": In this chapter, I show the basics of how data is stored internally in SQL Server, as well as some strategies for indexing data for better performance.

Chapter 12, "Matters of Concurrency": As part of the code that's written, some consideration needs to be given to actively sharing resources, if applicable. In this chapter, I describe several strategies for how to implement concurrency in your data access and modification code.

Chapter 13, "Coding Architecture": This chapter covers the concepts and concerns of choosing the storage engine and writing code that accesses SQL Server. I cover on-disk or in-memory, ad hoc SQL (Structured Query Language) vs. stored procedures (including all the perils and challenges of both, such as plan parameterization, performance, effort, optional parameters, SQL injection, etc.), and whether T-SQL (Transact-SQL) or CLR (Common Language Runtime) objects are best. In addition, there is a discussion on building reusable code to help you build applications.

Appendix A, "Scalar Datatype Reference": In this appendix, I present all of the types that can be legitimately considered scalar types, along with why to use them, their implementation information, and other details.

Prerequisites

The book assumes that the reader has some experience with SQL Server, particularly writing queries using existing databases. Beyond that, most concepts that are covered will be explained, and code should be accessible to anyone with experience in programming using any language.

Downloading the Code

A download will be available as individual files from the Apress download site. Files will also be available from my GitHub site, `github.com/drsqlgithub/dbdesignbook6`, as well as links to additional material I may make available between now and any future editions of the book.

Contacting the Author

Don't hesitate to give me feedback on the book, anytime, at my website (`www.drsql.org`) or my email (`louis@drsql.org`). I'll try to improve any sections that people find lacking in one of my blogs, or as articles, with links from my website, currently at `https://drsql.org/publications`, but if that direct link changes as it has in the past due to losing a web host, this book will feature prominently on my new website one way or another. I'll be putting more information there, if it becomes available, pertaining to new ideas, goof-ups I find, or additional material that I choose to publish because I think of them once this book is no longer a jumble of bits and bytes and is an actual instance of ink on paper.

CHAPTER 1

The Fundamentals

Get the fundamentals down and the level of everything you do will rise.

—Michael Jordan

Like almost anyone, I have a love–hate relationship with fundamentals. The easier the task *seems* to be, the less enjoyable I seem to find it, unless of course I already have a love for the topic. In elementary school, there were fun classes, like recess and lunch. But when handwriting class came around, very few kids really liked it, and a solid percentage of those who did just liked the taste of pencil lead. But handwriting class was an important part of childhood educational development. Without it, you wouldn't be able to write on a whiteboard, and without that skill, could you stay employed as a programmer? I know I personally am addicted to writing on whiteboards, and only a small fraction of that is the glorious smell of the markers.

Much like handwriting was an essential skill for life, database design has its own set of skills that you need if creating relational databases is part of your vocation. While database design is not a hard skill to learn, it is not exactly a completely obvious one either. In many ways, the fact that it isn't a hard skill makes it difficult to master. Databases are being designed all the time by people of limited understanding of what makes one "good." Administrative assistants build databases using Excel, kids make inventories of their video games on a sheet of paper, and newbie programmers do so with all sorts of database management tools. The problem is that in almost every case, the design produced is fundamentally flawed, not always so much that it is immediately obvious. However, the flaws are generally enough that it causes mistakes to manifest themselves in subtle, even dangerous ways. When you are finished with this book, you should be able to recognize many of the common fundamental blunders and design databases that avoid them in the first place. If a journey of a million miles starts with a

© Louis Davidson 2021
L. Davidson, *Pro SQL Server Relational Database Design and Implementation,*
https://doi.org/10.1007/978-1-4842-6497-3_1

single step, the first step in the process of designing a quality database is understanding why databases are designed the way they are, and this requires us to cover the fundamentals.

The first six chapters of this book are devoted to the fundamental tasks of relational database design and preparing your mind for the task at hand: implementing a relational database. The topics won't be particularly difficult in nature, and I will do my best to keep the discussion at the layman's level and not delve so deeply that you punch me if you pass me in the hall at the SQL PASS Summit [`https://www.pass.org/summit/`] or any of the technical conferences I try to get out to each year (assuming by the time you are reading this book, we are back to meeting in person again!).

For this chapter, we will start out looking at basic groundwork topics that help to align our thinking to someone designing and implementing with SQL Server's relational database engine:

- *"History"*: Where did all this relational database stuff come from? In this section, I will present some history, largely based on Codd's 12 rules as an explanation for why the RDBMS (relational database management system) is what it is.

- *"Recognizing Relational Data Structures"*: This section will provide introductions of some of the fundamental database objects, including the database itself, tables, columns, and keys. These terms are likely familiar to you, but there are some common misunderstandings in their definition that can make the difference between a mediocre design and an excellent one.

- *"Understanding Relationships"*: We will briefly survey the different types of relationships that can exist between the relational data structures introduced in the "Recognizing Relational Data Structures" section.

- *"Understanding Data Dependencies"*: The concept of dependencies between values and how they shape the process of relational database design will be discussed.

- *"Relational Programming"*: This section will cover the differences between procedural programming using C# or VB.NET (Visual Basic) and relational programming using SQL (Structured Query Language).

- *"Outlining the Database-Specific Project Phases"*: This section provides an overview of the major phases of relational database design: conceptual/logical, physical, and maintenance. For time and budgetary reasons, you might be tempted to skip the first database design phases and move straight to the physical implementation phase (coding). However, skipping any or all these phases can lead to an incomplete or incorrect design, as well as one that does not support high-performance querying and reporting.

At a minimum, this chapter on fundamentals should get us to a place where we have a set of common terms and concepts to use throughout this book when discussing and describing relational databases. Throughout my years of reading and research, I've noticed that lack of agreed-upon terminology is one of the biggest issues in the database community. Academics have multiple sets of terms to mean the same thing as people who develop code (who equally have several sets of terms, and sometimes overlapping terms have different meanings). Tradespeople (like myself and probably you the reader) have their own terminology, and it is usually used very sloppily. I am not immune to sloppy terminology myself when chatting about databases, but in this book, I do my best to try to be quite rigid to use proper terminology. Some might say that this is all semantics, and semantics aren't worth arguing about, but honestly, they are the *only* thing worth arguing about. Agreeing to disagree is fine if two parties understand one another, but the true problems in life tend to arise when people think they are in complete agreement about an idea but the words they are agreeing to have different meanings to the parties.

History

No matter what country you hail from, there is, no doubt, a point in history when your nation began. In the United States, that beginning came with the Declaration of Independence, followed by the Constitution of the United States (and the ten amendments known as the Bill of Rights). These documents are deeply ingrained in the experience of many citizens of the United States. We argue about them, we disagree on their meaning, but they are ours. For relational database design, we have three documents that are largely considered the foundations of relational databases.

The term "relational database" is always an interesting one for people, because it sounds like it has to do with the relationships between tables, but rather it is a term from mathematics. The word relation is rather about the relationship between a set of values (www.study.com/academy/lesson/relation-in-math-definition-examples.html), which is analogous to the set of columns in a table.

The people who formulated databases, especially Edgar F. Codd, were typically mathematicians. Hence, a lot of the terminology used by the theorists is from their math roots. This is a topic we will see later in the chapter, but the term "relational" stuck when in 1979, Codd, who worked for the IBM Research Laboratory at the time, wrote a paper entitled "A Relational Model of Data for Large Shared Data Banks," which was printed in *Communications of the ACM* ("ACM" is the Association for Computing Machinery [www.acm.org]). In this 11-page paper, Codd introduces a revolutionary idea for how to break the physical barriers of the types of databases in use at that time. At the time, most database systems were very structure oriented, requiring a lot of knowledge of how the data was organized in the storage. For example, to use indexes in the database, specific choices would be made, like only indexing one key, or if multiple indexes existed, the user was required to know the name of the index to use it in a query.

As almost any programmer knows, one of the fundamental tenets of good programming is to attempt low coupling of computer subsystems. Requiring a user to know about the internal structure of the data storage was obviously counterproductive. If you wanted to change or drop an index, the software and queries that used the database would also need to be changed. The first half of Codd's paper introduced a set of constructs that would be the basis of what we know as a relational database. Concepts such as tables, columns, keys (primary and candidate), indexes, and even an early form of normalization are be included. The second half of the paper introduced set-based logic, including joins. This paper was pretty much the database declaration of storage independence.

Moving six years in the future, after companies began to implement *supposed* relational database systems, Codd wrote a two-part article published by *Computerworld* magazine entitled "Is Your DBMS Really Relational?" and "Does Your DBMS Run by the Rules?" on October 14 and October 21, 1985. Though it is nearly impossible to get a copy of these original articles, many websites outline these rules, and I will too. These rules go beyond relational theory and define specific criteria that need to be met in an RDBMS, if it's to be truly considered relational even today.

Codd's Rules for an RDBMS

I feel it is useful to cover Codd's rules, because while these rules are well over 30 years old, they do probably the best job of setting up not only the criteria that can be used to measure how *relational* a database is but also the reasons why relational databases are implemented as they are. The neat thing about these rules is that they are seemingly just a formalized statement of the KISS manifesto for database users—keep it simple or keep it standard...stupid, either one. By establishing a formal set of rules and principles for database vendors, users could access data that not only was simplified from earlier data platforms but worked pretty much the same on any product that claimed to be relational. Every database vendor has a different version of a relational engine, and while the basics are the same, there are wild variations in how they are structured and used. The basics are the same, and for the most part, the SQL implementations are very similar (I will discuss very briefly the standards for SQL in the next section). The primary reason that these rules are so important for the person just getting started with design is that they elucidate why SQL Server and other relational engine–based database systems work the way they do. For another great overview of these rules from a person who has been involved at every level of the process, see Joe Celko's article "Codd's Twelve Rules" (`www. red-gate.com/simple-talk/homepage/codds-twelve-rules/`).

Rule 1: The Information Principle

> *All information in the relational database is represented in exactly one and only one way—by values in tables.*

While this rule might seem obvious after just a little bit of experience with relational databases, it really isn't. Designers of database systems could have used global variables to hold data or file locations or come up with any sort of data structure that they wanted. Codd's first rule set the goal that users didn't have to think about where to go to get data. One data structure—the table—followed a common pattern of rows and columns of data that users worked with.

Many different data structures were in use in the early days that required a lot of internal knowledge of data. Think about all the different data structures and tools you have used. Data could be stored in files, a hierarchy (like the file system), or any method that someone dreamed of. Even worse, think of all the computer programs you have used; how many of them followed a common enough standard that they worked just like everyone else's? Very few, and new innovations are coming every day.

While innovation is rarely a bad thing, innovation in relational databases is largely limited to the layer that is encapsulated from the user's view. The same database code that worked 20 years ago could easily work today with the simple difference that it now runs a great deal faster. There have been great advances in the language we use (T-SQL), but other than a few wonky bits of syntax that have been actually removed from the language (the most common example being *= for left join and =* for right [and there was not an operator like *=* for full outer join]), T-SQL written 20 years ago will work today, largely because data is stored in structures that appear to the user to be exactly the same as they did in SQL Server 1.0 even though the internals are vastly different.

Rule 2: Guaranteed Access

Each and every datum (atomic value) is guaranteed to be logically accessible by resorting to a combination of table name, primary key value, and column name.

This rule is an extension of the first rule's definition of how data is accessed. While all of the terms in this rule will be defined in greater detail later in this chapter, suffice it to say that columns are used to store individual points of data in a row of data and a primary key (PK) is a way of uniquely identifying a row using one or more columns of data. This rule defines that, at a minimum, there will be a non–implementation-specific way to access data in the database. The user can simply ask for data based on known data that uniquely identifies the requested data. "Atomic" is a term that will come up frequently; it simply means a value that cannot be broken down any further without losing its fundamental value. It will be defined later in this chapter and again in more depth in Chapter 5 when we cover normalization.

Together with the first rule, rule 2 establishes a kind of addressing system for data as well. The table name locates the container; the primary key value finds the row containing an individual data item of interest; and the column is used to address an individual piece of data.

Rule 3: Systematic Treatment of NULL Values

NULL values (distinct from the empty character string or a string of blank characters and distinct from zero or any other number) are supported in the fully relational DBMS for representing missing information in a systematic way, independent of datatype.

The NULL rule requires that the RDBMS support a method of representing "missing" data the same way for every implemented datatype. This is really important because it allows you to indicate that for any column you can consistently indicate the lack of a value, without resorting to tricks. For example, assume you are making a list of how many computer mice you have, and you think you still have an Arc mouse, but you aren't sure. You list Arc mouse to let yourself know that you are interested in such mice, and then in the count column, you put what? Zero? Does this mean you don't have one? You could enter –1, but what the heck does that mean? Did you loan one out? You could put "Not sure" in the list, but if you tried to programmatically sum the number of mice you have, 1 + "Not sure" does not compute.

To solve this problem, the placeholder NULL was devised to work regardless of datatype. For example, in string data, NULL values are distinct from an empty character string, and they are always to be considered a value that is unknown. Visualizing them as UNKNOWN is often helpful to understanding how they work in math and string operations. NULL values propagate through mathematic operations as well as string operations. NULL + <anything> = NULL, the logic being that NULL means UNKNOWN. If you add something known to something unknown, you still don't know what you have; it's still unknown. Throughout the history of relational database systems, NULL values have been implemented incorrectly or abused, so there are generally settings to allow you to ignore the properties of NULL column values. However, doing so is inadvisable. NULL values greatly affect how data is modeled, represented, coded, and implemented. NULL values are a concept that academics have tried to eliminate as a need for years and years, but no practical replacement has been created. I generally consider them a painful but necessary construct.

Rule 4: Dynamic Online Catalog Based on the Relational Model

> *The database description is represented at the logical level in the same way as ordinary data, so authorized users can apply the same relational language to its interrogation as they apply to regular data.*

This rule requires that a relational database be self-describing using the same tools that you store user data in. In other words, the database must contain tables that catalog and describe the structure of the database itself, making the discovery of the structure of the database easy for users, who should not need to learn a new language or method of accessing metadata. This trait is very common, and we will make use of the system catalog tables regularly throughout the latter half of this book to show how something we have just implemented is represented in the system and how you can tell what other similar objects have also been created.

Rule 5: Comprehensive Data Sublanguage Rule

A relational system may support several languages and various modes of terminal use. However, there must be at least one language whose statements are expressible, per some well-defined syntax, as character strings and whose ability to support all of the following is comprehensible: a. data definition, b. view definition, c. data manipulation (interactive and by program), d. integrity constraints, e. authorization, and f. transaction boundaries (begin, commit, and rollback).

This rule mandates the existence of a high-level relational database language, such as SQL, to manipulate data. The language must be able to support all the central functions of a DBMS: creating a database, retrieving and entering data, implementing database security, and so on. SQL as such isn't specifically required, and other experimental languages are in development all the time, but SQL is the de facto standard relational language and has been in use for well over 20 years.

Relational languages are different from procedural (and most other types of) languages in that you don't specify how things happen or even where. In ideal terms, you simply ask a question of the relational engine, and it does the work. You should at least, by now, be starting to realize that this encapsulation and relinquishing of responsibilities is a very central tenet of relational database implementations. Keep the interface simple and encapsulated from the realities of doing the hard data access. This encapsulation is what makes programming in a relational language very elegant but oftentimes frustrating. You are commonly at the mercy of the engine programmer, and you cannot implement your own access method, like you could in C# if you discovered an API that wasn't working well. On the other hand, the engine designers are like souped-up rocket scientists and, in general, do an amazing job of optimizing data access. The true hard part is understanding that usually the sooner you release responsibility and learn to follow the relational ways, the better. But the more you understand about what the engine is doing, the more you can help it.

Rule 6: View Updating Rule

All views that are theoretically updateable are also updateable by the system.

A table, as we briefly defined earlier, is a structure with rows and columns that represents data stored by the engine. A view is a stored representation of data that is technically a table too; it's commonly referred to as a virtual table. Views are generally allowed to be treated just like regular (sometimes referred to as materialized) tables, and you should be able to create, update, and delete data from a view just like from a table. This rule is quite hard to implement in practice because views can be defined in any way the user wants.

Rule 7: High-Level Insert, Update, and Delete

The capability of handling a base relation or a derived relation as a single operand applies not only to the retrieval of data but also to the insertion, update, and deletion of data.

This rule is probably the biggest blessing to programmers of them all. If you were a computer science student, an adventurous hobbyist, or just a programming sadist like the members of the Microsoft SQL Server Storage Engine team, you probably had to write some code to store and retrieve data from a file. You will probably also remember that it was very painful and difficult to do, as you had to manipulate data byte by byte, bit by bit, and usually you were just doing it for a single user at a time. Now, consider simultaneous access by hundreds or thousands of users to the same file and having to guarantee that every user sees and can modify the data concurrently and consistently. Only a truly excellent system programmer would consider that a fun challenge.

Yet, as a relational engine user, you write very simple statements using SELECT, INSERT, UPDATE, and DELETE statements that do this every day. Writing these statements is like shooting fish in a barrel—extremely easy to do (it's confirmed by *MythBusters* as easy to do, if you are concerned, but don't shoot fish in a barrel unless you are at least planning on having fish for dinner—it is not a nice thing to do). Simply by writing a single statement using a known table and its columns, you can put new data into a table that is also being used by other users to view, change data, or whatever. In Chapter 12, we will cover the concepts of concurrency to see how this multitasking of modification statements is done, but even the concepts we cover there can be mastered by common programmers who do not have a PhD from MIT because of the work of those who do have such deep mathematics and engineering knowledge.

Rule 8: Physical Data Independence

Application programs and terminal activities remain logically unimpaired whenever any changes are made in either storage representation or access methods.

Applications must work using the same syntax, even when changes are made to the way in which the database internally implements data storage and access methods. This rule basically states that the way the data is stored must be independent of the way it's used and the way data is stored is immaterial to the users. This rule will play a big part of our entire design process, because we will do our best to ignore implementation details and design for the data needs of the user. That way the folks who write the code for SQL Server's engine can add new fun features to the product, and we can use many of them without even knowing (or, at least, barely knowing) about them. For all we know, while the output of `SELECT * FROM <tablename>` would be the same in any version of SQL Server, the underlying code can be quite different (tremendously different when we look at how the new memory-optimized features will affect the internals and query processing!).

Rule 9: Logical Data Independence

Application programs and terminal activities remain logically unimpaired when information-preserving changes of any kind that theoretically permit unimpairment are made to the base tables.

While rule 8 is concerned with the internal data structures that interface the relational engine to the file system, this rule is more centered on things we can do to the table definition in SQL. Say you have a table that has two columns, A and B. User X makes use of A; user Y uses A and B. If the need for a column C is discovered, adding column C should not impair users' (X and Y) programs at all. If the need for column B was eliminated and hence the column was removed, it is acceptable that user Y would then be affected, yet user X, who only needed column A, would still be unaffected.

This principle, unlike physical data independence, does involve following solid programming practices. For example, consider the construct known as star (*) that is used as a wildcard for all the columns in the table (as in `SELECT * FROM <tablename>`).

Using this shorthand means that if a column is added to the table, the results will change in a way that might not be desirable. There are other places where this can cause issues (like using a column list in an INSERT statement), which we will cover throughout the book. Generally speaking, it is always a good idea to declare exactly the data you need for any operation that you expect to reuse.

Rule 10: Integrity Independence

Integrity constraints specific to a particular relational database must be definable in the relational data sublanguage and storable in the catalog, not in the application programs.

Another of the truly fundamental concepts is that data should have integrity; and in this case, the data subsystem should be able to protect itself from most common data issues. Predicates that state that data must fit into certain molds are to be implemented in the database. Minimally, the RDBMS must internally support the definition and enforcement of entity integrity (primary keys) and referential integrity (foreign keys). We also have unique constraints to enforce keys that aren't the primary key, NULL constraints to state whether or not a value must be known when the row is created, and check constraints that are simply table or column predicates that must be met. For example, say you have a column that stores employees' salaries. It would be good to add a condition to the salary storage location to make sure that the value is greater than or equal to zero, because you may have unpaid volunteers, but I can only think of very few jobs where you pay to work at your job.

Making complete use of the relational engine's integrity constraints can be controversial. Application programmers don't like to give up control of the management of rules because managing the general rules in a project must be done in multiple places (for user friendliness if for no other reason). At the same time, many types of constraints for which you need to use the engine are infeasible to implement in the application layer due to the desire to allow concurrent access. For example, uniqueness and referential integrity are extremely hard to implement from a client tool for reasons that probably are obvious in some respects but will be covered in some detail when we look at concurrency in depth in Chapter 12.

The big takeaway for this item should be that the engine provides tools to protect data, and in the least intrusive manner possible, you should use the engine to protect the integrity of the data.

Rule 11: Distribution Independence

The data manipulation sublanguage of a relational DBMS must enable application programs and terminal activities to remain logically unimpaired whether and whenever data are physically centralized or distributed.

This rule was exceptionally forward thinking in 1985 and is still only getting close to being realized for anything but the largest systems. It is an extension of the physical independence rule taken to a level that spans the containership of a single computer system. If the data is moved to a different location, the relational engine should recognize this and just keep working. With cloud computing exploding considerably in each of the last few editions of this book, we are just getting closer and closer to being a full reality.

Rule 12: Nonsubversion Rule

If a relational system has or supports a low-level (single-record-at-a-time) language, that low-level language cannot be used to subvert or bypass the integrity rules or constraints expressed in the higher-level (multiple-records-at-a-time) relational language.

This rule requires that methods of accessing data are not able to bypass everything that the relational engine has been specified to provide in the other rule, which means that users should not be able to violate the rules of the database in any way. At the time of this writing, most tools that are not T-SQL based do things like check the consistency of the data and clean up internal storage structures. There are also row-at-a-time operators called cursors that deal with data in a very nonrelational manner, but in all cases, they do not have the capability to go behind or bypass the rules of the RDBMS.

A common big (reasonable) cheat is to bypass rule checking when loading large quantities of data using bulk loading techniques. All the integrity constraints you put on a table generally will be quite fast and only harm performance an acceptable amount during normal operations. But when you must load millions of rows, doing millions of checks all at once can be very expensive, and hence there are tools to skip integrity checks. Using a bulk loading tool is a necessary evil, but it should never be an excuse to allow data with poor integrity into the system and just let it sit there.

SQL Standards

In addition to Codd's rules, one topic that ought to be touched on briefly is the SQL standards. Rules 5, 6, and 7 all pertain to the need for a high-level language that works on data in a manner that encapsulates the nasty technical details from the user. To fulfill this need, SQL was born. The language SQL was initially called SEQUEL (**S**tructured **E**nglish **Que**ry Language), but the name was changed to SQL for copyright reasons (though we still regularly pronounce it as "sequel" today). SQL had its beginnings in the early 1970s with Donald Chamberlin and Raymond Boyce (see `http://en.wikipedia.org/wiki/SQL`), but the path to get us to the place where we are now was quite a trip. Multiple SQL versions were spawned, and the idea of making SQL a universal language was becoming impossible. T-SQL is Microsoft's version of SQL that was borne of their partnering with Sybase in the 1990s, until they split around the time Microsoft rewrote the SQL Server core for version 7.0.

In 1986, the American National Standards Institute (ANSI) created a standard called SQL-86 for how SQL should be moved forward. This standard took features that the major players at the time had been implementing in an attempt to make code interoperable between these systems, with the engines being the part of the system that would be specialized. This early specification was tremendously limited and did not even include referential integrity constraints. In 1989, the SQL-89 specification was adopted, and it included referential integrity, which was a tremendous improvement and a move toward implementing Codd's twelfth rule (see *Handbook on Architectures of Information Systems* by Bernus, Mertins, and Schmidt [Springer 2006]).

Several more versions of the SQL standard have come and gone, with the latest being in 2016. For the most part, these documents are not exactly easy reading, nor do they truly mean much to the basic programmer/practitioner, but they can be quite interesting in terms of putting new syntax and features of the various database engines into perspective. The standard also helps you to understand what people are talking about when they talk about standard SQL and can help to explain some of the more interesting choices that are made by database vendors.

This brief history lesson was mostly for getting you started to understand why relational databases are implemented as they are today. In three papers, Codd took a major step forward in defining what a relational database is and how it is supposed to be used. In the early days, Codd's 12 rules were used to determine whether a database vendor could call itself relational and presented stiff implementation challenges for database developers. As you will see by the end of this book, even today, the implementation of the most complex of these rules is becoming achievable, though SQL Server and other RDBMSs still fall short of achieving their objectives.

Obviously, there is a lot more history between 1985 and today. Many academics, including Codd himself, have advanced the science of relational databases to the level we have now. Notable contributors include C. J. Date, Fabian Pascal (who has an interesting website: `www.dbdebunk.com`), Donald Chamberlin, and Raymond Boyce (who contributed to one of the normal forms, covered in Chapter 5), among many others. Some of their material is interesting only to academics, but it all has practical applications even if it can be very hard to understand and is very useful to anyone designing even a modestly complex model. I suggest reading all the other database design materials you can get your hands on after reading this book (after, read: after). In this book, I will keep everything at a very practical level that is formulated to cater to the general practitioner without dumbing it down to get down to the details that are most important and provide common useful constructs to help you start developing great databases quickly.

Recognizing Relational Data Structures

As a person reading this book, this is probably not your first time working with a database, and therefore, you will no doubt be somewhat familiar with some of the concepts I will be covering. However, you may find there are at least a few points presented here that you haven't thought about that might help you understand why I do things later—for example, the fact that a table consists of unique rows or that within a single row a column must represent only a single value. These points make the difference between having a database of data that the client relies on without hesitation and having one in which the data is constantly challenged.

This section introduces the following core relational database structures and concepts:

- Database and schema

- Tables, rows, and columns

- Missing values (nulls)

- Uniqueness constraints (keys)

Note too that in this section I will only be talking about items from the relational model. In SQL Server, you have a few layers of containership based on how SQL Server is implemented. For example, the concept of a server is analogous to a computer or a virtual machine perhaps. On a server, you may have multiple instances of SQL Server that can then have multiple databases. The terms "server" and "instance" are often misused as synonyms, mostly due to the original way SQL Server worked, allowing only a single instance per server (and since the name of the product is SQL *Server*, it is a natural mistake). For most of this book, we will not need to look at any higher level than the database, which I will introduce in the following section.

Introducing Databases and Schemas

The basic concept of a database is simply a collection of facts or data. It needn't be in electronic form; it could be a card catalog at a library, your checkbook, a set of words on a notepad, an Excel spreadsheet, or even just a simple text file. Typically, the point of any database is to arrange data for ease and speed of search and retrieval—electronic or otherwise.

For our purposes in relational design, the database is the highest-level container that you will use to colocate all the objects and code that serve a common purpose. On an instance of the database server, you can have many databases, but best practices suggest using as few as possible for your needs (but not fewer!). This container is often considered the level of consistency that is desired that all data is maintained at, but this can be overridden for certain purposes (one such case is that databases can be partially restored and be used to achieve quick recovery for highly available database systems). A database is also where the storage on the file system meets the logical implementation. Until very late in this book, we will treat the database as a logical container and ignore the internal properties of how data is stored; we will treat storage and optimization primarily as a post-relational structure implementation consideration. When I get to Chapter 11, I will start to talk more deeply about performance and physical characteristics you need to control.

The next level of containership is the schema. You use schemas to group objects in the database with common themes. All objects on a database server can be addressed by the server name, the database they reside on, and the schema, giving you what is known as the four-part name:

```
ServerName.DatabaseName.SchemaName.ObjectName
```

The only part of a name that is always required is the object name, but as we will see in Chapter 7 when a complete database is created, always including the schema name is generally desirable. Including the database name and server name typically is frowned upon in typical coding use where the code is to be reused. These naming parts are generally acquired by the context the user is in, to make code more portable. A three-part name would be used to access a resource outside of the database in context and a four-part name to access a database resource that is on another server. A goal in database development is to keep your code isolated in a single database if possible. Accessing a database on a different server is a practice disfavored by almost anyone who does database coding, first because it can be terrible for performance and second because it creates dependencies that are difficult to track and extremely hard to test.

The database functions as the primary container used to hold, back up, and subsequently restore data when necessary. It does not limit you to accessing data within only that one database; however, it should generally be the goal to keep your data access needs to one database.

Schemas are valuable not only for logical organization but also, as we will see later, to control access to the data and restrict permissions. In Chapter 10, we will discuss in some detail the methods, values, and problems of managing security of data in separate databases and schemas.

Note   The term "schema" has other common usages that you should realize: the entire structure for the database is referred to as schema, as are the Data Definition Language (DDL) statements that are used to create the objects in the database (such as CREATE TABLE and CREATE INDEX). Once we arrive to the point where we are talking about schemas in the database, I will clearly make that distinction.

Understanding Tables, Rows, and Columns

In a relational database, a table is used to represent some concept (generally a noun like a person, place, thing, or idea), and a column represents information about that concept (the name, address, descriptions, etc.). Getting the definitions of your tables correct is the most important part of database design and something we will discuss in more depth.

A table is the definition of the container for a concept. For instance, a table may represent a person. Each instance of a person "Fred Smith" or "Alice Smith" is represented as a "row" of data. So, in this table of people, one row would represent one person. Rows are further divided into columns that contain a single piece of information about whatever the row is representing. For example, the `FirstName` column of a row would contain "Fred" or "Alice." A table is not to be thought of as having any order and should not be thought of as a location in some type of storage. As previously discussed in the "History" section of this chapter, one of the major design concepts behind a relational database system is that it is to be encapsulated from the physical implementation.

The concept of "atomic" describes the type of data stored in a column. The meaning of "atomic" is pretty much the same as in physics as we understand it in the 21st century. Atomic values are values that cannot be broken up further without losing the original characteristics. In chemistry, molecules are made up of multiple atoms—H_2O can be broken down to two hydrogen atoms and one oxygen atom, but if you break the oxygen atom into smaller parts, you will no longer have oxygen (and your neighbors will not appreciate the massive crater where your house previously was).

In our data example, the name "Fred Smith" can be broken into "Fred" and "Smith" naturally, and we do not lose any meaning. It can also be further subdivided into "F", "re", "d", "Smit", and "h", but now the chunks of data make no sense anymore.

Hence, our goal in designing databases will be to find values that have a single meaning that is valuable to the common user, such as a single word or a number, or it can mean something like a whole chapter in a book stored in a binary or even a complex type, such as a point with longitude and latitude. The key is that the value represents a single message that resists being broken down to a lower level than what is needed when you start using the data. So having a scalar value defined as two dependent values, say X and Y, is perfectly acceptable because they are not independent of one another, while a value like `'Cindy,Leo,John'` would likely not be atomic, because that value can be broken down into three separate and independent values without losing any meaning. Keep in mind however that I said "would likely not be atomic," not "would definitely not be." Database design is a complex process because it matters what the customer means by `'Cindy,Leo,John'` and what you might do with them programmatically.

While you may be thinking that any programmer worth the price of a biscuit can split those values into three when they need to, our goal throughout the database design process is to do that work up front to provide the relational engine a consistent way of working with our data. It may also be that 'Cindy,Leo,John' is one complete value that should not be separated, despite what you think looking at it. Remember when I said that database design's simplicity makes it difficult. This is exactly why.

Before moving on, I would like to take a moment to discuss the complexities with the terms "table," "row," and "column." These terms are commonly used by tools like Excel, Word, and so on to mean a fixed structure for displaying data. For "table," Dictionary. com (www.dictionary.com) has the following definition:

> *An orderly arrangement of data, especially one in which the data are arranged in columns and rows in an essentially rectangular form.*

When data are arranged in a rectangular form, it has an order and very specific locations. A basic example of this definition of "table" that most people are familiar with is a Microsoft Excel spreadsheet, such as the one shown in Figure 1-1.

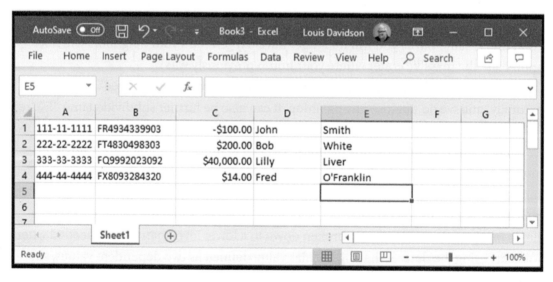

Figure 1-1.   *Excel table*

In Figure 1-1, the rows are numbered 1–4, and the columns are labeled A–E. The spreadsheet is a table of accounts. Every column represents some piece of information about an account: a Social Security number, an account number, an account balance, and the first and last names of the account holder. Each row of the spreadsheet represents one specific account. It is not uncommon to access data in a spreadsheet positionally (e.g., cell A1) or as a range of values (e.g., A1–A4) with no reference to the data's structure, something I have already mentioned several times as being against the principles of relational databases. This physical meaning of a table, row, and column gets mixed in with the more conceptual meaning that needs to be understood for relational databases.

In the next few tables (in the book—see, this term has lots of meanings!), I will present the terminology for tables, rows, and columns and explain how they will be used in this book. Understanding this terminology is a lot more important than it might seem, as using these terms correctly will point you down the correct path for using relational objects. Let's look at the different terms and how they are presented from the following perspectives (note that there are quite a few other terms that mean the same things too, but these are the most common that I see in mainstream discussions):

- *Relational theory*: This viewpoint is rather academic. It tends to be very stringent in its outlook on terminology and has names based on the mathematical origins of relational databases.

- *Logical/conceptual*: This set of terminology is used prior to the actual implementation phase. Basically, this is based on the concepts of Entity–Relationship (ER) modeling, which uses terms that are more generic than what you will use when working with your database.

- *Physical*: This set of terms is used for the implemented database. The word "physical" is a bit misleading here, because the physical database is really an abstraction away from the tangible, physical architecture. However, the term has been ingrained in the minds of data architects for years and is unlikely to change.

- *Record manager*: Early database systems required a lot of storage knowledge; for example, you needed to know where to go fetch a row in a file. The terminology from these systems has spilled over into relational databases, because the concepts are quite similar.

Table 1-1 shows the names that the basic data representations (e.g., tables) are given from the various viewpoints. These names have slightly different meanings but are often used as exact synonyms.

Table 1-1.   *Breakdown of Basic Data Representation Terms*

Viewpoint	Name	Definition
Relational theory	Relation	This term is seldom used by nonacademics, but some literature uses it exclusively to mean a strict version of what most programmers think of as a table. In set theory, it is a structure that is made up of tuples and attributes (which will be defined in greater detail later but share a lot in common conceptually with rows and columns.)
Logical/ conceptual	Entity	An entity represents a container for some "thing" you want to store data about. For example, if you are modeling a human resources application, you might have an entity for employees. During the logical modeling phase, many entities will be identified, some of which will become tables, and some will become several tables, based on the process known as normalization, which we'll cover extensively in Chapter 5. It should also be clear that an entity is not something that has an implementation but is a specification tool that will lead us to an implementation.
Physical	Table	A table is, at its heart, very similar to a relation and entity in that the goal is to represent some concept that you will store data about. The biggest difference between relations and tables is that tables technically may have duplication of data (even though they should not be allowed to in our implementations). A view is also considered a type of table, often a "virtual" table, since it has a structure that is considered permanent.
Record manager	File	In many nonrelational-based database systems (such as Microsoft FoxPro), each operating system file represents a table (and sometimes a table is referred to as a database, which is just way too confusing). Multiple files make up a database. SQL Server employs files, but at the engine level and may contain all or parts of one or more tables. As previously mentioned, regarding Codd's rules, how the data is stored should be unimportant to how it is used or what it is called.

(continued)

Table 1-1. *(continued)*

Viewpoint	Name	Definition
Physical	Recordset/ rowset	A recordset, or rowset, is data that has been retrieved for use, such as results sent to a client. Most commonly, it will be in the form of a tabular data stream that the user interfaces or middle-tier objects can use. Recordsets have some similarity to a normal table, but their differences are tremendous as well. Seldom will you deal with recordsets in the context of database design, but you will once you start writing SQL statements. A major difference between relations/tables and recordsets is that the former is considered "sets," which have no order, while recordsets are physical constructs used for communication.

Next up, we look at columns. Table 1-2 lists all the names that columns are given from the various viewpoints, several of which we will use in the different contexts as we progress through the design process.

Table 1-2. *Column Term Breakdown*

Viewpoint	Name	Definition
Logical/ conceptual	Attribute	The term "attribute" is common in the programming world. It basically specifies some information about an object. In modeling, this term can be applied to almost anything, and it may represent other entities. Just as with entities, in order to produce proper tables for implementation, normalization will change the shape of attributes until they are proper column material.
Relational theory	Attribute	When used in relational theory, an attribute takes on a strict meaning of a scalar value that describes the essence of what the relation is modeling.

(continued)

Table 1-2. *(continued)*

Viewpoint	Name	Definition
Physical	Column	A column is a single piece of information describing what a row represents. The position of a column within a table is strongly suggested to be unimportant to its usage, even though SQL does generally define a left-to-right order of columns in the catalog. All direct access to a column will be by name, not position. Each column value is expected to be, but isn't strictly enforced, an atomic value.
Record manager	Field	The term "field" has a couple of meanings in a database design context. One meaning is the intersection of a row and a column, as in a spreadsheet (this might also be called a cell). The other meaning is more related to early database technology: a field was the offset location in a record, which, as I will define in Table 1-3, is a location in a file on disk. There are no set requirements that a field store only scalar values, merely that it is accessible by a programming language.

Note   Datatypes like XML, spatial types (`geometry` and `geography`), `hierarchyId`, and even custom-defined CLR types really start to muddy the waters of atomic, scalar, and non-decomposable column values. Each of these has some implementational value, but in your design, the initial goal is to use a scalar type first and one of the commonly referred to as "beyond relational" types as a fallback for implementing structures that are overly difficult using scalars only. Additionally, some support for translating and reading JSON-formatted values was added to SQL Server 2016, though there is currently no formal datatype support.

Finally, Table 1-3 describes the different ways to refer to a row.

Table 1-3. *Row Term Breakdown*

Viewpoint	Name	Definition
Relational theory	Tuple	A tuple (pronounced "tupple," not "toople") is a finite unordered set of related and also unordered set of named value pairs, as in `ColumnName: Value`. By "named," I mean that each of the values is known by a name (e.g., `Name:Fred; Occupation:gravel worker`). "Tuple" is a term seldom used in a relational database context except in academic circles, but you should know it, just in case you encounter it when you are surfing the Web looking for database information. Note that tuple is used in cubes and MDX to mean pretty much the same concept, if things weren't confusing enough already. An important part of the definition of a relation is that no two tuples can be the same. This concept of uniqueness is a topic that is repeated frequently throughout the book because, while uniqueness is not a strict rule in the implementation of a table, it is a very strongly desired design characteristic.
Logical/ conceptual	Instance	Basically, as you are designing, you will think about what one version of an entity would look like, and this existence is generally referred to as an instance.
Physical	Row	A row is essentially the same as a tuple, with each column representing one piece of data in the row that represents one thing that the table has been modeled to represent.
Record Manager	Record	A record is a location in a file on disk. Each record consists of fields, which all have physical locations. Ideally, this term should not be used interchangeably with the term "row" because a row is not a physical location, but rather a structure that is accessed using data.

If this is the first time you've seen the terms listed in Tables 1-1 through 1-3, I expect that at this point you're banging your head against something solid (and possibly wishing you could use my head instead) and trying to figure out why such a variety of terms is used to represent pretty much the same things. Many a flame war has erupted over the difference between a field and a column, for example. I personally cringe whenever a person uses the term "record" when they really mean "row" or "tuple," but I also realize that misusing a term isn't the worst thing if a person understands everything about how a table should be dealt with in SQL.

Working with Missing Values (NULL)

In order to get the most heinous topics out of the way in the least amount of time, we move from terminology to the concept of NULL. The concept of NULL, and working with NULL values, is the source of a very large amount of issues in database code all over the world today.

In the previous section, we noted that columns are used to store a single value. The problem with this is that often you will want to store a value, but at some point in the process, you may not know the value. As mentioned earlier, Codd's third rule defined the concept of NULL values, which were different from an empty character string or a string of blank characters or zero, used for representing missing information in a systematic way, independent of datatype. All datatypes can represent a NULL, so any column may have the ability to represent that data is missing.

When representing missing values, it is important to understand what the value means. Since the value is missing, it is assumed that there may exist a value (even if that value is that there is specifically "no value"). Because of this, two values of NULL are not considered to be equal, and you must treat the value as UNKNOWN, as if it could be any value at all.

This brings up a few interesting properties of NULL that make it a pain to deal with, though it is very essential to express what you want to need to in a design without resorting to tricks that are even more troublesome to use:

- Any value concatenated with NULL is NULL. When NULL is present, it represents possibly every valid value, so if an unknown value is concatenated with a known value, the result is still an unknown value. If I add an unknown value to anything, I still have an unknown value.

- All math operations with NULL will evaluate to NULL, for the very same reason that any value +/- or any value in a mathematical equation will be unknown (though even 0 * NULL evaluates to NULL).

- Logical comparisons can get tricky when NULL is introduced. Consider the Boolean expression NULL <> NULL. The resulting Boolean value is NULL, not FALSE, since any unknown value might be equal to another unknown value, so it is unknown if they are not equal. Special care is required in your code to know if a conditional is looking for a TRUE or a non-FALSE (TRUE or NULL) condition. SQL CHECK constraints look for a non-FALSE condition to satisfy their predicate, whereas WHERE clauses look for TRUE conditions.

Let's expand this point on logical comparisons somewhat, as it is very important to understanding the complexities of NULL usage. When NULL is introduced into Boolean expressions, the truth tables get more complex. Instead of a simple two-condition Boolean value, when evaluating a condition with a NULL involved, there are three possible outcomes: TRUE, FALSE, or UNKNOWN. Only if a search condition evaluates to TRUE will a row appear in the results of a WHERE clause. As an example, if one of your conditions evaluates to NULL=1, you might be tempted to assume that the answer to this is FALSE, when in fact this resolves to UNKNOWN.

This is most interesting because of expressions such as the following in this SELECT statement:

```
SELECT CASE WHEN 1=NULL or NOT(1=NULL) THEN 'True' ELSE 'NotTrue' END;
```

Since you have two conditions and the second condition is the opposite of the first, it seems logical that either NOT(1=NULL) or (1=NULL) would evaluate to TRUE, but in fact, 1=NULL is UNKNOWN, and NOT(UNKNOWN) is also UNKNOWN. The opposite of UNKNOWN is not, as you might logically guess, known. Instead, since you aren't sure if UNKNOWN represents TRUE or FALSE, the opposite might also be TRUE or FALSE.

Table 1-4 shows the truth table for the NOT operator.

Table 1-4. *NOT Truth Table*

Operand	NOT(Operand)
TRUE	FALSE
UNKNOWN	UNKNOWN
FALSE	TRUE

Table 1-5 shows the truth tables for the AND and OR operators.

Table 1-5. *AND and OR Truth Tables*

Operand1	Operand2	Operand1 AND Operand2	Operand1 OR Operand2
TRUE	TRUE	TRUE	TRUE
TRUE	FALSE	FALSE	TRUE
TRUE	UNKNOWN	UNKNOWN	TRUE
FALSE	FALSE	FALSE	FALSE
FALSE	UNKNOWN	FALSE	UNKNOWN

In this introductory chapter, my main goal is to point out that the concept of NULL exists and is a part of the basic foundation of relational databases as we know them (along with giving you a basic understanding of why they can be troublesome); I don't intend to go too far into how to program with them unless it pertains strictly to a specific design issue I am covering.

The goal in your designs will be to minimize the use of any place where NULL is needed, but unfortunately, completely eliminating them is very nearly impossible, particularly because they begin to appear in your SQL statements even when you do an OUTER JOIN operation.

Defining Domains

The concepts discussed so far have one very important thing in common. They are established to help us end up with structures that store information. Just what can be considered information is our next consideration, and therefore we now need to define the *domain* of a structure. The domain is the set of valid values that can be stored. At the entity level, the domain is based on the definition of the object. For example, if you have a table of employees, each instance will represent an employee, not the parts that make up a ceiling fan or even the names of weasels, no matter your opinion of your coworkers. You generally will also define that we don't want the same employee represented multiple times, unless it makes sense in the design and there is another way to tell two rows apart. Unexpected duplicated data is one of the most troublesome things to deal with in a database. The only thing that is worse is the inability to store data that is legitimate because the data architect made up over-strict requirements.

While getting the domain of the entity is straightforward enough, defining the domain of attributes is a bit more work. For example, consider the following list of possible aspects of the domain that you might need to consider for an attribute for an `EmployeeDateOfBirth` column:

- The value must be a calendar date with no time value.

- The value must be a date prior to the current date (a date in the future would mean the person has not been born).

- The date value should evaluate such that the person is at least 16 years old, since you couldn't legally hire a 10-year-old, for example.

- The date value should usually be less than 70 years ago, since rarely will an employee (especially a new employee) be that age.

- The value must be less than 130 years ago, since we certainly won't have a new employee that old. Any value outside these bounds would clearly be in error.

As you define the domain of an attribute, the concepts of implementing a physical database aren't important; some parts of the domain definition may just end up just using them as warnings to the user. Starting with Chapter 7, we'll cover how you might implement this domain in code, but during the design phase, we at least need to start out by documenting it and then work toward making sure the data's domain is considered in the design. The most important thing to note here is that not all these rules are expressed as 100% required. For example, consider the statement that the date value should be less than 70 years old. This might just be an alert because it is so very rare and the times when it occurs tend to be in error. During your early design phase, it is best to define everything about your domains you can discover, so it may be implemented in some manner, even if it is just a message box asking the user "C'mon, really?" for values out of normal bounds.

As you start to create your first model, you will find a lot of commonality among attributes. As you start to build your second model, you will realize that you have done a lot of this before. After 100 models, trying to decide how long to make a person's first name in a customer table would be akin to reinventing sliced bread by discovering that wheat can be used as food. To make this process easier and to achieve some standards among your models, a great practice is to give common domain types names so you can associate them to attributes with common needs. For example, you could define the type we described at the start of this section as an `EmployeeBirthDate` domain. Every time an employee birth date is needed, it will be associated with this named domain.

Admittedly, as I go through the process, it will be clear that using a named domain in your models will not always be possible, particularly if you don't have a tool that will help you manage it. But I suggest that you at least take the time to start a document somewhere of datatypes for common usage: How long is a person's name? A phone number? An email address? Then standardize all usage. The ability to create reusable domain types is something I look for in a data modeling tool, but modeling tools can be hard on a small company's budget.

Domains do not have to be very specific, because often we just use the same kinds of values the same way. For example, if we have a count of the number of puppies, that data might resemble a count of bottles of hot sauce. Puppies and hot sauce don't mix (only older dogs use hot sauce after their palates have matured), but the domain for the value of how many of either you have is going to be very similar. Both will be cardinal numbers, but the upper bound may not be the same. For example, you might have the following named domains:

- `CardinalNumber`: Integer values 0 and greater

- `Date`: Any valid date value (with no time of the day value)

- `EmailAddress`: A string value that must be formatted as a valid email address

- `30CharacterString`: A string of characters that can be no longer than 30 characters

Keep in mind that if you define the domain of a string as any positive integer, the maximum is theoretically infinity. Today's hardware boundaries allow some pretty far-out maximum values (e.g., 2,147,483,647 for a regular integer; and Rodney Landrum, a technical editor for previous editions of this book, has this as a tattoo, if you were wondering), so it is useful to define how many is too many (can you really have a billion puppies or bottles of hot sauce?). It is fairly rare that a user will have to enter a value approaching 2 billion, but if you do not constrain the data within your domains, reports and programs will need to be able to handle such large data and possibly handle when two rows have 2 billion in them, leading to a sum that is greater than what can fit in a normal `int` datatype. In my experience, when there is not a domain set on such values, what happens is that someone accidentally keys in 1221404 instead of 12214.04 and 1.2 million is a real value that the system can handle, but is not a value that the company could ever handle and a lot of product shows up at the door. Without a defined domain limiting the value either in a hard manner (value must be less than 100000) or soft manner (warn user if value is greater than 100000 and require CEO approval if greater than 1000000), then to clean up from even one such mess can cost far more than it would cost to capture and implement a proper domain.

I will cover this more in Chapters 7 and 8 when we discuss data integrity as well as Chapter 9 when I will discuss patterns of implementation to meet requirements.

Metadata

Metadata is data used to describe other data. Knowing how to find information about the data stored in your system is a very important aspect of the documentation process. As previously mentioned in this chapter, Codd's fourth rule states that "The database description is represented at the logical level in the same way as ordinary data, so authorized users can apply the same relational language to its interrogation as they apply to regular data." This means you should be able to interrogate the system metadata using the same language you use to interrogate the user data (i.e., SQL).

In SQL Server, the catalog is a collective description of the heading of tables and other coded objects in the database. SQL Server exposes the heading information in a couple of ways:

- *In a set of views known as the information schema*: It consists of a standard set of views used to view the system metadata table and should exist on all database servers of any brand.

- *In the SQL Server-specific catalog (or system) views*: These views give you information about the implementation of your objects and many more properties of your system.

It is a very good practice to maintain your own metadata about your databases to further define a table's or column's purpose than just naming objects. This is commonly done in spreadsheets and data modeling tools, as well as using custom metadata storage, including those built into the RDBMS (e.g., extended properties in SQL Server).

Uniqueness Constraints (Keys)

As mentioned previously, in relational theory, a relation, by definition, cannot represent duplicate tuples. In RDBMS products, however, no enforced limitation says that there must not be duplicate rows in a table. However, it is the considered recommendation of myself and any reasonable data architect that practically every table needs at least one defined uniqueness criteria to fulfill the mandate that rows in a table are accessible by knowing the value of the key. Unless each row is unique from all other rows, there would be no way to effectively retrieve a single row.

To define the uniqueness criteria, we will define *keys*. Keys define uniqueness for an entity over one or more columns that will then be guaranteed as having distinct values from all other instances. Generically, a key is usually referred to as a candidate key, because you can have more than one key defined for an entity, and a key may play a few roles (primary or alternate) for an entity, as will be discussed in more detail later in this section.

Consider the following set of data, named T, with columns X and Y:

```
X     Y
---   ---
1     1
2     1
```

If you attempted to add a new row with values X:1, Y:1, there would then be two identical rows in the table. If this were allowed, it would be problematic for a couple of reasons:

- Rows in a table are unordered, so without keys, there would be no way to tell which of the rows with value X:1, Y:1 in the preceding table was which. Hence, it would be impossible to distinguish between these rows, meaning that there would be no logical method of accessing a single row. Using, changing, or deleting an individual row would be difficult without resorting to tricks with SQL (like using an ORDER BY with a TOP operator to access one row at a time).

- If more than one row has the same value, it describes the same thing, so if you try to change one of the rows, the other row should also change, which becomes a messy situation.

If we define a key on column X, the previous attempt to create a new row would fail, as would any other insert of a value of 1 for the X column, such as `X:1, Y:3`. Alternatively, if you define the key using both columns X and Y (known as a "composite" or "compound" key, i.e., a key that has more than one column, whereas a key with only one column is sometimes referred to as a "simple" key), the `X:1, Y:3` creation would be allowed, but attempting to create a row as `X:1, Y:1` would still be forbidden.

Note   In a practical sense, no two rows can be the same, because there are realities of the implementation, such as the location in the storage system where the rows are stored. However, this sort of thinking has no place in relational database design, where it is our goal to largely ignore the physical realities of the implementation.

So what is the big deal? If you have two rows with the same values for X and Y, what does it matter? Consider a table that has three columns:

MascotName	MascotSchool	PersonName
Smokey	UT	Bob
Smokey	UT	Fred

Now, you want to answer the question of who plays the part of Smokey for UT. If there is only one actual person who plays the part, you go to retrieve one row. Since we have stated that tables are unordered, you could get either row and hence either person. Applying a candidate key to `MascotName` and `MascotSchool` will ensure that a fetch to the table to get the mascot named Smokey that cheers for UT will get the name of only one person. (Note that this example is an oversimplification of what can be a very complicated issue, since you may or may not want to allow multiple people to play the part for a variety of reasons including time, stand-ins, backups, and so on. But we are currently defining a domain in which only one row should meet the criteria.)

Failure to identify the keys for a table is one of the largest blunders that a designer will make, mostly because during testing such issues may not be noticed because weaker testers tend to test with good data more than really messed up data. Add in the fact that deep testing is often the first cost to be cut when time is running out for a release and major blunders can persist until the real users start testing the database in production and just happen to enter the 20th Smokey in the database before it is noticed by the CEO in a report.

In summary, a candidate key (or simply "key" for short) defines the uniqueness of rows over a column or set of columns. In your logical designs, it will be essential for each entity to have one uniqueness criteria set, and it may have multiple keys to maintain the uniqueness of the data in the resulting tables and rows, and a key may have as many attributes as is needed to define its uniqueness.

Types of Keys

Two types of keys you will define on your objects are primary and alternate. (You may have also heard the term "foreign key," but this is a reference to a key and will be defined later in this chapter in the "Understanding Relationships" section.) A primary key (PK) is used as the primary identifier for an entity. Think of it like your company identification number in that it is the primary value you might use on things like your timesheet, your insurance forms, and so on. It is the primary way you are identified in the company systems. If you have more than one set of values that can perform the role of identifying an instance of your entity beyond the PK, each remaining candidate key would be referred to as an alternate key (AK). Your alternate keys at your company might be your government ID, driver's license number, and other pieces of data they know about you that must be considered unique, but that will not be the most prevalently used in the company to identify you regularly.

In theory, there is no difference in definition of an alternate or primary key, but in practice, SQL Server will not allow nullable columns in a PK as this ensures that at least one fully known key value will be available to fetch a row. Alternate keys do allow NULL values, but in SQL Server, a unique constraint (and unique index) will treat all NULL values as the same value and only a single instance of NULL may exist. In Chapter 7, we will discuss in more detail implementation patterns for implementing uniqueness conditions, and again in Chapter 8, we will revisit the methods of implementing the different sorts of uniqueness criteria that exist.

The choice of primary key is largely a matter of convenience and ease of use. We'll discuss primary keys later in this chapter in the context of relationships. The important thing to remember is that when you have values that should exist only once in the database, you need to protect against duplicates.

Choosing Key Attributes

While keys can consist of any number of columns, it is best to limit the number of columns in a key as much as possible. For example, you may have a Book entity with the attributes Publisher_Name, Publisher_City, ISBN_Number, Book_Name, and Edition. All of these together should be unique, so technically could be considered a key. But what you really want is the smallest subset of columns that can be considered unique in your object definition. From these attributes, the following three keys might be defined:

- Publisher_Name, Book_Name, Edition: A publisher will likely publish more than one book. Also, it is safe to assume that book names are *not* unique across all books. However, it is probably true that the same publisher will not publish two books with the same author, title, and edition. "Probably" however, does not a key make.

- ISBN_Number: The ISBN (International Standard Book Number) is the unique identification number assigned to a book when it is published.

- Publisher_City, ISBN_Number: Because ISBN_Number is unique, it follows that Publisher_City and ISBN_Number combined is also unique.

The choice of (Publisher_Name, Book_Name, Edition) as a composite candidate key seems valid, and the simple key ISBN_Number is a no-brainer. But consider the composite key (Publisher_City, ISBN_Number). The implication of this key is that in every city, ISBN_Number can be used again, a conclusion that is obviously not appropriate since we have already said that ISBN_Number must be unique on its own. This is a common problem with composite keys, which are often not thought out properly. In this case, you might choose ISBN_Number as the PK and (Publisher_Name, Book_Name) as the AK.

Note   Unique indexes should not be confused with uniqueness keys. There may be valid performance-based reasons to implement the Publisher_City, ISBN_Number unique index in your SQL Server database. However, this would not be identified as a key of an entity during design. In Chapter 7, we'll discuss implementing keys, and in Chapter 11 we'll cover implementing indexes for data access enhancement.

Having established what keys are, let's next discuss the two classes of keys:

- *Natural key*: The values that make up natural keys have some connection to the row data outside of the database context.

- *Surrogate key*: Usually a database-generated value that has no connection to the row data but is simply used as a stand-in for the natural key for complexity or performance reasons.

Natural Keys

A natural key is defined as an attribute that has a natural, or at least external to your system, connection with the entity in some manner. This means it wasn't just made up in the database where it is found. Natural keys are generally some attribute of an entity that the customer will enter or you will retrieve from a third party. From our previous examples, all our candidate keys so far—employee number, Social Security number (SSN), ISBN, and the (`Publisher_Name`, `Book_Name`, `Edition`) possible composite key—have been examples of natural keys. Of course, a number like an ISBN doesn't look like a natural number, as it is just 13 digits that are formatted like NNN-N-NN-NNNNNN-N and are managed by the International ISBN Agency to identify a book in a database and a store.

Natural keys are values that a user would recognize and would logically be presented to the user. Some common examples of natural keys are

- *For people*: Driver's license number + location of issue, company identification number, customer number, employee number, and so on

- *For transactional documents* (e.g., invoices, bills, and computer-generated notices): Usually assigned some sort of number when they are created

- *For products for sale*: Product numbers (product names are likely not unique), UPC (Universal Product Code), serial numbers

- *For buildings*: A complete street address, including the postal code, GPS coordinates

Be careful when choosing natural key column sets. Ideally, you are looking for something that is reasonably stable and most importantly that is going to allow you to uniquely identify every row in your table. A value that is not stable but is unique (say a security code for a user that is regenerated periodically) may not be a great key for a table that you may reference from another table, but it certainly should be tested for uniqueness in your structures.

One thing of interest here is that what might be considered a natural key in your database is often not actually a natural key in the place where it is defined—for example, the driver's license number of a person. In the example, this is a number that every person has (or may need before inclusion in our database). However, the value of the driver's license number can be a series of integers. This number did not appear tattooed on the back of the person's neck at birth. In the database where that number was created, it may be a random number created in some other database, but for your needs it will be a natural key as you don't have any control over it. In reality, it was possibly actually more of a smart key or possibly an artificial key, generated randomly and imparted value by being associated with that person in a database. Concepts which I will cover in a few pages.

Values for which you cannot guarantee uniqueness, no matter how unlikely the case, should not be considered as keys. With three-part people names that are common in the United States, it is very rare that you'll have two people working in the same company, attending the same school, or even living in the same city who have the same three name parts. (Have you ever wondered why they name serial killers with all three name parts?) Of course, as the number of people who work in the company increases, or the number of people who are related to one another live in the same area, the odds will certainly increase that you will have duplicates.

If you include prefixes and suffixes, duplicates get even more unlikely, but "rare" or even "extremely rare" cannot be implemented in a manner that makes a reasonable key. If you happen to hire two people called Sir Lester James Fredingston III (I know I work with three people with that name, because who doesn't, right?), the second of them probably isn't going to take kindly to being called Les for short just so your database system can store their name. (A user would, in fact, might do just that to get data to save in that "stupid" database system. It would not be the user's fault in that case.)

One notable profession where names must be unique is actors. No two actors who have their union cards can have the same name. Some change their names from Archibald Leach to something more cool sounding like Cary Grant, but in some cases, the person wants to keep their own name even though they are not the first Gary Grant, so in the actors' database, the Screen Actors Guild adds a uniquifier to the name to make it unique. A uniquifier is a nonmeaningful value (like a sequence number) that is added to values to produce uniqueness where it is required for a situation like this where names are very important to be dealt with as unique.

For example, 21 people (up from six in the last edition, just to prove I am diligent in giving you the most up-to-date information) are listed on the Internet Movie Database site (www.imdb.com) with the name Gary Grant (not Cary, but Gary). Each has a different number associated to make a unique Gary Grant. (Of course, none of these people have hit the big time yet, but watch out—it could be happening soon!)

Tip   While names are not reasonable keys, it is however useful to think of names as a kind of semi-unique natural key. This isn't good enough for identifying a single row, but it's great for a human to find a value. When someone calls your company to place an order, it is important not to just make a new row with John Smith every time without seeing if it is the same John Smith using other bits of data.

This semi-uniqueness is a very interesting attribute of an entity and should be documented for later use, but only in rare cases would you make a key from semi-unique values, probably by adding a uniquifier. In Chapter 9, we will cover the process of defining and implementing this case, which I refer to as "likely uniqueness." Likely uniqueness criteria basically states that you should ask for verification if you try to create very similar data that is likely to be the same, but may not be.

Finding and dealing with duplicate data is a lot harder once the data is stored and you have lost the connection to the source of the data.

A commonly occurring subclass of natural key in computer systems is a **smart**, or **intelligent**, key. Some identifiers will have additional information embedded in them, often as an easy way to build a unique value for helping a human identify some real-world thing. In most cases, the smart key can be disassembled into its parts, and typically the data will probably not jump out at you. Take the following example of the fictitious product serial number XJV102329392000123, which I have devised to be broken down into the following parts:

- *X*: Type of product (LCD television)

- *JV*: Subtype of product (32-inch console)

- *1023*: Lot that the product was produced in (batch number 1023)

- *293*: Day of year

- *9*: Last digit of year

- *2*: Original color

- *000123*: Order of production

The simpler-to-use smart key values serve an important purpose to the end user; the technician who is working on a product can decipher the value and see that, in fact, this product was built in a lot that contained defective whatchamajiggers, and he needs to replace it. The essential thing for us during the logical design phase is to find all the bits of information that make up the smart keys, because each of these values is almost certainly going to end up stored in its own column.

Smart keys, while useful as a human value that condenses a lot of information into a small location, definitely do not meet the criteria we originally set up as scalar earlier, and by the time when we start to implement database objects certainly should not be the only representation of these pieces of data, but rather implementing each bit of data as a single column with each of these values, and determine how best to make sure it matches the smart key if it is unavoidable.

A couple of big problems with smart keys are that you could run out of unique values for the constituent parts and some part of the key (e.g., the product type or subtype) may change. Being very careful and planning well are imperative if you use smart keys to represent multiple pieces of information. When you must change the format of smart keys, making sure that different values of the smart key are valid becomes a large validation problem. Note too that the color position can't indicate the current color, just the original color. This is common with automobiles that have been painted: the VIN includes color, but the color can change.

Note   Smart keys are useful tools to communicate a lot of information to the user in a single value instead of multiple attributes, which can be clunky to work with in the real world. However, all the bits of information that make up the smart key need to be identified, documented, and implemented in a straightforward manner. Optimum SQL code expects the data to all be stored in individual columns, and as such, it is of great importance that you needn't ever base computing decisions on decoding the value. We will talk more about the subject of choosing implementation keys in Chapter 7.

Surrogate Keys

Surrogate keys are kind of the opposite of natural keys. The word surrogate means "something that substitutes for," and in this case, a surrogate key serves as a substitute for a natural key. Sometimes, you may have no natural key that you think is stable or reliable enough to use as the primary key, or perhaps one that is too unwieldy to work with, in your model. Surrogate keys also make for a stable, common pattern for implementation, and this has made them desirable to many architects and programmers.

A surrogate key can give you a unique value for each row in a table, but it has no actual meaning about the data in the row other than to represent existence. Surrogate keys are usually manufactured by the system as a convenience to either the RDBMS, the modeler, or the client application or a combination of them. Common methods for creating surrogate key values are to use a monotonically increasing number, to use a random value, or even to use a globally unique identifier (GUID), which is a very long (16-byte) identifier that is unique on all machines in the world.

The concept of a surrogate key can be troubling to purists and may start an argument or two. Since the surrogate key is not really information, can it really be an attribute of the entity? The question is valid, but surrogate keys have several nice values for usage that make implementation easier:

- In the design phase of a project, the name of the surrogate key can simply be the name of the table, often suffixed with Id or Key. This makes it obvious what it is.

- An exceptionally nice aspect of a surrogate key is that the value of the key need never change, since the value has no meaning. Much like NULL, a value with no meaning + any value still has no real meaning. Since the value has no meaning, changing it makes no sense either. This, coupled with the fact that surrogate keys can always be a single column, makes several aspects of implementation far easier than they otherwise might be.

- For security purposes, since a surrogate key has no data in it, it means data is less duplicated in your database. We will talk more about personally identifiable information (PII) later in the book, but the fewer times you duplicate data that identifies whom data is about is a security win.

Ideally, a true surrogate key is never shared with any users. It will be a value generated on the computer system that is hidden from use, while the user directly accesses only the natural keys' values. Probably the best reason for this limitation is that once a user has access to a value, it may need to be modified. For example, customer 0000013 and customer 00000666 are requesting a change as I type this (and there are probably other customers requesting those same values).

Consider a driver's license; if the driver's license has just a single nonsensical alphanumeric value (the surrogate key) on it, how would Officer Reilly Tofast determine whether you were actually the person identified? He couldn't, so there are other attributes listed on the license, such as name, birth date, and your picture, which is an excellent unique key for a human to deal with (except for identical twins, of course). He can also go to the computer and enter the surrogate license number and get back all your details and history of driving too fast to get to work because you stayed up all night reading and writing books and didn't want to get out of bed.

Consider the earlier example of a product identifier consisting of seven parts:

- *X*: Type of product (LCD television)

- *JV*: Subtype of product (32-inch console)

- *1023*: Lot that the product was produced in (batch 1023)

- *293*: Day of year

- *9*: Last digit of year

- *2*: Original color

- *000123*: Order of production

A natural key would almost certainly consist of these seven parts since this is a smart key (it is possible that a subset of the values forms the key with added data, but we will assume all parts are needed for this example). There is also a product serial number, which is the concatenation of the values such as XJV102329392000123, to identify the row. Say you also have a surrogate key column in the table with a value of 10. If the only key defined on the rows is the surrogate, the following situation might occur if the same data is inserted other than the surrogate (which gets an automatically generated value of 3384):

SurrogateKey	ProductSerialNumber	ProductType	Lot	Date	ColorCode	
10	XJV102329392000123	X	1023	20091020	2	...
3384	XJV102329392000123	X	1023	20091020	2	...

The two rows are not technically duplicating each other due to the different SurrogateKey value, but since the surrogate key values have no real meaning, in essence these are duplicate rows—the user could not effectively tell them apart. This situation gets very troublesome when you start to work with relationships (which we cover in more detail later in this chapter). Once the values 10 and 3384 are stored in other tables as references to this table, it looks like two different products are being referenced when there is only one.

Note   When doing early design, I tend to model each entity with a surrogate primary key, letting it stand in for the as yet undetermined parts of the key during the design process, since I may not yet know what the keys will turn out to be until far later in the design process. In systems where the desired implementation does not include surrogates, the process of designing the system will eliminate the surrogates. This approach will become obvious throughout this book, starting with the conceptual model in Chapter 4.

Understanding Relationships

In the previous section, we established what an entity is and how entities are to be structured (especially with an eye on the future tables you will create), but an entity by itself is not terribly useful. To make entities more useful and to achieve some of the structural requirements to implement tables to meet your customers' requirements, you will need to link them together (sometimes even linking one entity to itself). Without the concept of a relationship, it would often be necessary to simply put all data into a single table when data was related to other data, which would be a very bad idea because of the need to repeat data over and over (repeating groups of data is a primary problem in a database design and much of what Chapter 5 will be about).

A term alluded to earlier that we need to establish is *"foreign key."* A foreign key, also known as a migrated key, is used to establish a link between two entities/tables by stating that a set of column values in one table is required to match a set of column values in a candidate key in another. The relationship is almost always with the primary key, but any declared candidate key is generally allowed, with some caveats having to do with NULL values that we will cover when we get to implementation sections of the book.

When defining the relationship of one entity to another, several factors are important:

- *Entity involvement*: Sometimes, just one entity is related to itself, such as an employee entity where you need to denote that one employee works for another. In this case, you treat the entity as two copies of itself for the operation. Sometimes, it is more than two entities; for example, Book Wholesalers, Books, and Book Stores are all common entities that would be related to one another in a complex relationship.

- *Ownership*: It is common that one entity will "own" the other entity. For example, an invoice will own the invoice line items. Without the invoice, there can logically exist no line items.

- *Cardinality*: Cardinality indicates the number of instances of one entity that can be related to another. For example, a person might be legally allowed to have only one spouse, but a person could have any number of children (still, I thought one was a good number there too!). In both cases, a negative number does not make sense (and the set of cardinal numbers is, by definition, 0 to infinity).

When we begin to implement tables, there will be a limitation that every relationship can only be between two tables. The relationship is established by taking the key columns and placing them in a different table. The table that provides the key that it migrated from is referred to as the parent in the relationship, and the one receiving the migrated key is the child.

For an example of a relationship between two tables with some representative data, consider the relationship between a `Parent` table, which stores the SSNs and names of parents, and a `Child` table, which does the same for the children, as shown in Figure 1-2. Bear in mind, this is a simple example that does not take into consideration even the most basic intricacies of storing people's names or the eventual discussion on the security aspects of handling personally identifiable information (PII). PII is different for every application, and what is acceptable in your modeling process may not be adequate (or even legal) in your actual implementation. People's names, for example, are far more interesting than what most people reading this book in English will likely expect. For an interesting list of considerations when storing a person's name, check out the article by Patrick McKenzie entitled "Falsehoods Programmers Believe About Names" (`www.kalzumeus.com/2010/06/17/falsehoods-programmers-believe-about-names/`); it is quite enlightening.

Parent

Parent SSN	Parent Name
111-11-1111	Larry Bull
222-22-2222	Fred Badezine

Child

Child SSN	Child Name	Parent's SSN
333-33-3333	Tay	111-11-1111
444-44-4444	Maya	222-22-2222
555-55-5555	Riely	222-22-2222

Figure 1-2. *Sample Parent and Child tables*

In the `Child` table, the `Parent's SSN` attribute is the foreign key (denoted in these little diagrams using a single underline, where the primary key is double underlined). It is used in a `Child` row to associate the child with the parent. From these tables, you can see that Tay's dad is Larry Bull, and the parent of Maya is Fred Badezine.

Cardinality is the next question. It is important when defining a relationship to know how many parent rows can relate to how many child rows. Based on the fact that the `Parent` entity has its key migrated to the `Child` entity, we have the following restriction: one parent can have any number of children, even zero, based on whether the relationship is considered optional (which we will get to later in the chapter). Of course, if this were really a parent–child human relationship, we could not limit parents to one, because every human (still) has two and only two biological parents, while the number of persons denoted as parents/caregivers/guardians can be far more varied. What makes the job of database design challenging and interesting is capturing all the realities of the world that don't always fit into nice neat molds, being able to record the data, and then later reporting it back to the user in the ways they need to see it. Cardinalities that are less than or greater than 1 add complexity to the job of working with data, but they are very much necessary to represent reality.

Relationships can be divided at this point into two basic types based on the number of entities involved in the relationship:

- *Binary relationships*: Those between two entities

- *Nonbinary relationships*: Those between more than two entities

The biggest difference between the two types of relationships is that the binary relationship is very straightforward to implement using foreign keys, as we have discussed previously. When more than two entities are involved, we will generally use modeling methods to break down the relationships into a series of binary relationships if it is possible, without losing fidelity or readability of the original relationship that your customer desired. More on this will be clarified in Chapter 5 as we get to the advanced normal forms.

When you are doing your early design, you need to keep this distinction in mind and learn to recognize each of the possible relationships. When I introduce data modeling techniques in Chapter 3, you'll learn how to represent relationships of many types in a structured representation.

Binary Relationships

The number of rows that may participate in each side of a relationship is known as the cardinality of the relationship. Different cardinalities of binary relationships will be introduced in this section, grouped into high-level distinctions:

- *One-to-many*: A relationship linking one instance of an entity with possibly multiple instances of another entity with a migrated key column. This is the only type of relationship that we will directly implement in our database's tables, with varying limits on the cardinality meant by "many."

- *Many-to-many*: Generally, a relationship where one instance of the first entity can be linked with multiple instances of the second entity and instances of the second entity can in turn be related to many instances of the first one. This is the most typical relationship type to occur naturally and will be implemented with two one-to-many relationships.

We will look at each of these relationship types and their different subtypes that have specific uses and specific associated challenges.

One-to-Many Relationships

One-to-many relationships are where one entity migrates its primary key to another as a foreign key. As discussed earlier, this is commonly referred to as a parent/child relationship and concerns itself only with the relationship between exactly two entities. A child may have, at most, one parent, but a parent may have one or more than one child instance. While the common name of a parent/child relationship is one-to-many, a more specific specification of cardinality is necessary to be technically correct, where the *one* part of the name really can mean zero or one (but never greater than one, as that would then be *many*) and *many* can mean zero, one, a specific number, or an unlimited number.

It should be immediately clear that when the type of relationship starts with "one-to-," such as "one-to-many," one row is related to some number of other rows. However, sometimes a child row can be related to zero parent row. This case is often referred to as an *optional* relationship. If you consider the earlier Parent/Child example, if this relationship were optional, a child might exist without a parent. In this case, it would be OK to have a child named Sonny who did not have a parent as far as the database knows, as shown in Figure 1-3.

Parent

Parent SSN	Parent Name
111-11-1111	Larry Bull
222-22-2222	Fred Badezine

Child

Child SSN	Child Name	Parent's SSN
333-33-3333	Tay	111-11-1111
444-44-4444	Maya	222-22-2222
555-55-5555	Riely	222-22-2222
666-66-6666	Sonny	

Figure 1-3. *Sample table including a parentless child*

The missing value would be denoted by NULL, so the row for Sonny would be represented as (ChildSSN:'666-66-6666', ChildName:'Sonny', Parent'sSSN:NULL). For the general case, it is typical to speak in terms of one-to-many relationships, just for ease of discussion. However, in more technical terms, the following is a list of several variations of the zero or one-to-(blank) theme that have different implications during implementation, that we will cover in this section:

- *One-to-many*: This is the general case, where "many" can be any cardinal number, that is, between zero and infinity.

- *One–to–exactly N*: In this case, one parent row is required to be related to a given number of child rows. For example, a child must have two biological parents, so it would be one–to–exactly two (though discussion about whether both parents must be known to record a child's existence is more of a topic for Chapter 2, when we discuss requirements; the common exact case is one-to-one).

- *One–to–between X and Y*: Usually, the case that X is 0 and Y is some boundary set up to make life easier. For example, a user may have between one and two usernames.

One-to-Many (The General Case)

The one-to-many relationship is the most common and important relationship type. For each parent row, there may exist between 0 and infinity child rows. An example one-to-many relationship might be Customer to Orders, as illustrated in Figure 1-4.

Customer Number	Name
1	Joe's Fisherteria
2	Betty's Bass Shop
3	Fred's Fish

Order Number	Customer Number	OrderDate
100002	1	2020-08-01
100003	1	2020-08-02
100005	2	2020-08-01
100012	2	2020-08-04
100022	2	2020-08-02
100029	3	2020-08-03

Figure 1-4. *One-to-many example*

A special type of one-to-many relationship is a "recursive relationship." In a recursive relationship, the parent and the child are from the same entity, and often the relationship is set up as a single entity. This kind of relationship is used to model a tree data structure. As an example, consider the classic example of a bill of materials. Take something as simple as a ceiling fan. In and of itself, a ceiling fan can be considered a thing for sale by a manufacturer, with its own product number, and each of its components is, in turn, also a product that has a different product or part number. Some of these components also consist of parts. In this example, the ceiling fan could be regarded as made up of each of its parts, and in turn, each of those parts consists of other parts, and so on. (Note that a bill of materials is a slice of a larger "graph" structure to document inventory, as each part can have multiple uses, and multiple parts. This structure type will be covered in more detail in Chapter 9.)

The following table is a small subset of the parts that make up a ceiling fan. Parts 2 - 5 are all parts of a ceiling fan. You have a set of blades and a light assembly (among other things). Part 4, the globe that protects the light, is part of the light assembly.

Part Number	Description	Used in Part Number
1	Ceiling Fan	NULL
2	White Fan Blade Kit	1
3	Light Assembly	1
4	Light Globe	3
5	White Fan Blade	2

To read this data, you would start at Part Number 1, and you can see what parts make up that part, which are a fan blade kit and a light assembly. Now, you have the parts with numbers 2 and 3, and you can look for parts that make them up, which gets you Part Numbers 4 and 5. (Note that the algorithm we just used is known as breadth-first, where you get all of the items on a level in each pass through the data. It's not terribly important at this point, but it will come up in Chapter 9 when we are discussing design patterns.)

One-to-N Relationship

Often, some limit to the number of children is required by the situation being modeled or a business rule. So rather than one-to-many (where many is infinity), you may say we only support a specific number of related items. A person playing poker is dealt five cards. Throughout the game, the player has between zero and five cards, but never more.

As another example, a business rule might state that a user must have exactly two email addresses so they can be more likely to answer one of the emails. Figure 1-5 shows an example of that one–to–exactly two relationship cardinality. It's not particularly a likely occurrence to have data specifically like this, but you never know whether you need a tool until a customer comes in with some wacky request that you need to fill.

Employee Reference Number	Name
5001	Bob
5002	Fred
5003	Jean

Employee Reference Number	Email Address
5001	dbo@apress.com
5001	dbo2@apress.com
5002	serveradmin@apress.com
5002	fred@apress.com
5003	md@apress.com
5003	jean@apress.com

Figure 1-5. *Example of a one-to-two relationship*

The most typical version of a one-to-N relationship type that gets used is a one-to-one relationship. This indicates that for any given parent, there may exist exactly one instance of the child. A one-to-one relationship may be a simple attribute relationship (e.g., a house has a location), or it may be what is referred to as an "is a" relationship. "Is a" relationships indicate that one entity is an extension of another.

For example, say there exists a person entity and an employee entity. Employees are all people (in most companies); thus, they need the same attributes as people, so we will use a one-to-one relationship: employee is a person. It would be illogical (if not illegal with the labor authorities) to say that an employee is more than one person or that one person is two employees. These types of "is a" relationships are often what are called subtype relationships, something we will cover again a few times later in the book.

Many-to-Many Relationships

The final type of binary relationship is the many-to-many relationship. Instead of a single parent and one or more children, you have two entities where each instance in both entities can be tied to any number of instances in the other. For example, continuing with the familial relationships, a child always has two biological parents—perhaps unknown, but they do exist. This mother and father may have more than one child, and each mother and father can have children from other relationships as well.

Many-to-many relationships make up a lot more of what we will model than you might immediately expect. Consider a car dealer. The car dealer sells cars. Inversely, pick nearly any single model of car, and you'll see that it is sold by many different car dealers.

Similarly, the car dealer sells many different car models. So many car models are sold by many car dealers and vice versa.

It may not always seem quite as obvious as these examples either. As another example, it initially seems that an album's relationship to a song is simply one-to-many when you begin defining an entity to catalog artists' music output, yet a song can be on many albums. Once you start to include concepts such as singers, musicians, writers, and so on into the equation, you will see that it requires a lot of many-to-many relationships to adequately model those relationships (many singers to a song, many songs to a singer, etc.). An important part of the design phase is going to be to examine the cardinality of your relationships and make sure you have considered how entities relate to one another in reality, as well as in your computer system.

The many-to-many relationship is not directly implementable using a simple SQL relationship but is typically implemented by introducing another structure. Instead of the key from one entity being migrated to the other, the keys from both objects in the relationship are migrated to a new entity that is used to implement the relationship (and will almost always record additional information about the nature of the connection of the specific two rows as well). In Chapter 3, I'll present more examples and discuss how to design the many-to-many relationship, and in Chapter 7, we will look at how to implement many-to-many relationships in some detail.

Many-to-many relationships are also the foundation of a type of structure known as a *graph* structure, which, for the purposes of this book, will be an extension of tables and relationships we have already introduced. Graph structures allow users to take many-to-many relationships and look at data in highly interconnected ways that more resemble how normal people think about data in the real world, rather than the somewhat rigidly structured manner that a relational database may lead to. In Chapter 9, we will look more at how we can mix graph structures with our relational database structures to expand the horizons of your typical relational database.

Nonbinary Relationships

Nonbinary relationships involve more than two entities in the relationship. Nonbinary relationships can be very problematic to discover and model properly, yet they are far more common than you might expect, for example:

A room is used for an activity in a given time period.

Publishers sell books through bookstores and online retailers.

Consider the first of these. We start by defining entities for each of the primary concepts mentioned—room, activity, and time period:

```
Room (room_number)
Activity (activity_name)
Time_Period (time_period_name)
```

Now, due to the way relational structures work, to relate these three entities together, we connect them together in one entity, forming one relationship between the three:

```
Room_Activity_TimePeriod (room number, activity_name, time_period_name)
```

We now have an entity that seemingly represents the relationship of room, activity, and time utilization. From there, it may or may not be possible to break down the relationships between these three entities (commonly known as a ternary relationship, because of the three entities, or even n-ary, because the max is not three related concepts) further into a series of relationships between the entities that will satisfy the requirements in an easy-to-use manner.

Often, what starts out as a complex relationship is discovered to be a series of binary relationships that are easy to work with. This is part of the normalization process that will be covered in Chapter 5 that will change our initial entities into something that can be implemented as tables in SQL. During the early, conceptual phases of design, it is enough to simply locate the existence of the different types of relationships. The ability (or nonability) to decompose entities to simpler pieces is largely dependent upon the concepts in the next section of this chapter on functional dependencies.

Understanding Data Dependencies

Beyond basic database concepts, I want to introduce a few other concepts now before they become necessary later. They center on the concept of that given one value (as defined earlier, a key value), you can definitively know some other related value or values. For a real-world example, take a person. If you can identify the person, you can also determine other information about the person (such as hair color, eye color, height, weight, driver's license number, home address). The values for each of these attributes may change over time, but when you ask the question, there should be one and only one answer to the question. For example, at any given instant, there can be only one answer to the question, "What is a person's eye color?"

We'll discuss two different concepts related to this in the sections that follow: functional dependencies and determinants. Each of these is based on the idea that one value depends on the value of another.

Functional Dependencies

Functional dependency is a very simple but important concept. It basically means that if you can determine the value of variable A given a value of variable B, B is functionally dependent on A. For example, you have a function, and you execute it with one value as a parameter (let's call it Value1), and the output of this function is always the same value (Value2). Then Value2 is functionally dependent on Value1. Then if you are certain that for every input to the function (Value1-1, Value1-2, ..., Value 1-N) you will always get back (Value2-1, Value2-2, ..., Value 2-N), the function that changes Value1 to Value2 is considered *deterministic*. On the other hand, if the value from the function can vary for each execution, it is *nondeterministic*. This concept is central to how we form a relational database to meet a customer's needs, along with the needs of the RDBMS engine.

In a table form, consider the functional dependency of non-key columns on key columns. For example, consider the following table T with a key of column X:

```
X    Y

---  ---

1    1
2    2
3    2
```

You can think of column Y as functionally dependent on the value in X, or fn(X) = Y. Clearly, Y may be the same for different values of X, but not the other way around (note that these functions are not strictly math; it could be IF X = (2 or 3) THEN 2 ELSE 1; that forms the function in question). This is a pretty simple yet important concept that needs to be understood.

Now, let's add in an additional attribute Z. You can see that in cases where Y = 2, Z = 4.

X	Y	Z
1	1	20
2	2	4
3	2	4

Determining what is a dependency and what is a coincidence is something to be careful of as well. In this example, fn(X) = Y and fn(X) = Z is certain (since that is the definition of a key), but looking at the data, there also appears to exist another dependency in this small subset of data, fn(Y) = Z.

If this is true, and in fact it is the case that fn(Y) = Z, you want to modify the Z value to 5 for the second row:

X	Y	Z
1	1	20
2	2	**5**
3	2	4

Now there is a problem with our proposed dependency of fn(Y) = Z because fn(2) = 5 AND fn(2) = 4. As you will see quite clearly in Chapter 5, poorly understood functional dependencies are at the heart of many database problems, because one of the primary goals of any database design is that to make one change to a piece of data, you should not need to modify data in more than one place. It is a lofty goal, but ideally, it is achievable with just a little bit of planning.

Finding Determinants

A term that is related to functional dependency is *determinant*, which can be defined as "any attribute or set of attributes on which any other attribute or set of attributes is functionally dependent." In our previous example, X would be considered the determinant. Two examples of this come to mind:

- Consider a mathematical function like 2 * X. For every value of X, a value will be produced. For 2, you will get 4; for 4, you will get 8. Anytime you put the value of 2 in the function, you will always return a 4, so 2 functionally determines 4 for function (2 * X). In this case, 2 is the determinant.

- In a more database-oriented example, consider the serial number of a product. From the serial number, additional information can be derived, such as the model number and other specific, fixed characteristics of the product. In this case, the serial number functionally determines the specific, fixed characteristics, and as such, the serial number is the determinant.

If this all seems familiar, it is because any key of an entity will functionally determine the other attributes of the entity, and each key will be a determinant, since it functionally determines the attributes of the entity. If you have two keys, such as the primary key and alternate key of the entity, each must be a determinant of the other.

Relational Programming

One of the more important aspects of Codd's rules was at least one language whose statements are expressible, per some well-defined syntax, as character strings and whose ability to support all of the following is comprehensive: data definition, view definition, data manipulation (interactive and by program), integrity constraints, authorization, and transaction boundaries (begin, commit, and rollback).

This language has been standardized over the years as the SQL we know (and love, or you will hopefully learn to love!). Throughout this book, we will use most of the capabilities of T-SQL (T-SQL is short for Transact-SQL, Microsoft's version of SQL that is in its relational database–oriented products) in some way, shape, or form, because any discussion of database design and implementation is going to be centered on using SQL to do all the things listed in the fifth rule and more.

There are two characteristics of SQL that are particularly important to understand. First, SQL is at its core a declarative language, which basically means that the goal is to describe what you want the computer to do for you, and the SQL engine works out the details.[1] So when you make the request "Give me all of the data about people," you ask SQL in a structured version of that very sentence, rather than describe each individual step in the process.

Second, as a relational language, you work at the relation (or table) level on sets of data at a time, rather than on one piece of data at a time. This is an important concept. Recall that Codd's seventh rule states "the capability of handling a base relation or a derived relation as a single operand applies not only to the retrieval of data but also to the insertion, update, and deletion of data."

What is amazingly cool about SQL as a language is that one very simple declarative statement almost always represents hundreds and thousands of lines of code being executed. Lots of this code execute in the hardware realm, accessing data on disk drives, moving that data into registers, and performing operations in the CPU, and now, 20 years removed from the first edition of this book, sometimes some of these operations are done thousands of miles away from each other, with data storage in one data center, processing in another, and the user sitting in yet another.

If you are already well versed as a programmer in a procedural language like C#, FORTRAN, VB.NET, and so on, SQL is a lot more restrictive in what you can do. You have two sorts of high-level commands:

- *Data Definition Language (DDL)*: SQL statements used to set up data storage (tables and the underlying storage), apply security, and so on.

- *Data Manipulation Language (DML)*: SQL statements used to create, retrieve, update, and delete data that has been placed in the tables. In this book, I assume you have used SQL before, so you know that almost everything done is handled by four statements: SELECT, INSERT, UPDATE, and DELETE.

As a relational programmer, your job is to work hard at giving up control of the details of storing data, querying data, modifying existing data, and so on. The system (commonly referred to as the relational engine) does the work for you—well, a lot of the work for you. There is talk after every version of every RDBMS released of the DBA

---

[1] For a nice definition of declarative languages, see www.britannica.com/technology/declarative-language.

becoming obsolete because the database system is so smart it tunes itself. Then users come along and demand more out of the platform without learning how to design or code well, and DBA futures look bright again.

Hence, it will probably always remain important as a relational database designer to make sure the database suits the needs of the RDBMS. Think of it like a chef in a kitchen. Producing wonderful food is what they do best, but if you arranged their utensils in a random order, it would take a lot longer for them to make dinner for you, and you just might end up with fingertip soup.

Dr. David DeWitt (a technical fellow in the Data and Storage Platform Division at Microsoft Corporation) said, during his PASS Keynote in 2010, that getting the RDBMS to optimize the queries you send isn't rocket science; it is far more difficult than that, mostly because people can send an almost infinite array of possible queries at the engine and expect perfection.

Microsoft SQL Server 2017 and 2019 have made many great strides since the previous version of this book, with new AI and Machine Learning features being integrated into query optimization under the heading of Intelligent Query Processing (`docs.microsoft.com/en-us/sql/relational-databases/performance/intelligent-query-processing`), moving closer and closer to this dream of self-tuning, letting us care less about common performance cases. The closer you design your database to the way the server wants it, the better.

The last point to make again ties back to Codd's rules, this time the twelfth, the nonsubversion rule. Basically, it states that the goal is to do everything in a language that can work with multiple rows at a time and that low-level languages shouldn't be able to bypass the integrity rules or constraints of the engine. In other words, leave the control to the engine and use T-SQL. Of course, this rule does not preclude other languages from existing. The twelfth rule does state that all languages that act on the data must follow the rules that are defined on the data. In some relational engines, it can be faster to work with rows individually rather than as sets in some scenarios. However, the creators of the SQL Server engine have chosen to optimize for set-based operations. This leaves the onus on the nonrelational programmer to play nice with the relational engine and let it do a lot of the work.

Outlining the Database-Specific Project Phases

As we go through the phases of a project, the phases of a database project have some very specific names and meanings that have evolved to describe the models that are created. Much like the phases of the entire project, the phases that you will go through when designing a database are defined specifically to help you think about only what is necessary to accomplish the task at hand.

Good design and implementation practices are essential for getting to the right result that the customer desires. Once that is done, we move on to implementation using proper fundamentals and, finally, tune the implementation to work in the real world by real people and processes.

The phases I outline here will steer us through creating a database by keeping the process focused on getting things done right, using terminology that is reasonably common in the general programmer community:

- *Conceptual*: During this phase, we are building a database sketch from requirements gathering and customer information. This sketch will consist of a data model with high-level entities and the relationships between them. In some respects, this is the hardest part of the design process because it requires understanding what the customer wants quite well. The name "conceptual" is based in finding concepts, not a design that is conceptual like building a cool concept car.

- *Logical*: The logical phase is an implementation-nonspecific refinement of the work done in the conceptual phase, transforming the concepts into a full-fledged database requirement that will be the foundation for the implementation design. During this stage, you flesh out the model that the system needs and capture the details that were missing from the conceptual model, like attributes, domains, and rules/predicates for data.

- *Physical*: In this phase, you adapt the logical model for implementation to the host RDBMS, in our case, SQL Server. For the most part, the focus in this phase is to build a solution to the design that matches the logical phase output while matching the needs of the SQL Server internals. It may also be decided that the design really should be done with a different engine altogether and to use

a completely different database management system, as I discussed
briefly in the "Introduction." Performance is certainly taken into
consideration as it meets the requirements, but the most important
thing is to make sure the requirements are met.

- *Maintenance*: This phase of the project is multifaceted and complex
  and is centered around surviving without changing the meaning of
  the code. For a vendor-oriented product, it starts when a company
  buys a product and installs it. You may need to add indexes, add
  hard drives, distribute data across multiple drives, add memory, add
  indexes, and so on to make the system run faster. For systems built
  in-house, this phase may start during implementation, but certainly
  runs longer than physical implementation.

You may be questioning at this point, "What about testing? Shouldn't there be a
testing phase?" No, there should not be a singular, independent, testing "phase." Every
phase of a project requires testing and multiple types of testing. This starts even before
code is written with the conceptual design to make sure it fits the requirements. You
test the logical design to make sure you have covered every data point that the user
requires. You test the physical design by building code and unit and scenario testing
it. You test how your code works in the engine by throwing more data at the database
than you will ever see in production and determining whether the engine can handle
it as is or requires adjustments. A specific testing phase is still necessary for the overall
application, but each of the database design/implementation phases should have testing
internally to the process (something that will equally be sewn into the rest of the book as
we cover the entire process).

In the book, I will mention testing in multiple places, but it is not covered nearly as
often as it needs to be done.

Conceptual

The conceptual design phase is essentially a process of analysis and discovery; the goal
is to define the organizational and user data needs of the system at a functional level.
Note that the overall design of an application goes beyond the needs of the database.
However, for much of this book, the design process will be discussed in a manner that
may make it sound as if the database is all that matters (as a reader of this book who is
actually reading this chapter on fundamentals, you probably already feel that way).

Over the years, I have discovered that the term "conceptual model" has several meanings depending on the person I interviewed about the subject. In some people's eyes, the conceptual model was very specifically only a diagram of entities and relationships. Others included attributes and keys as they were describing it. In early editions of this book, I leaned toward the latter, but shifted toward the former as I gained experience.

The core activity that defines the conceptual modeling process for every source I have found is discovering and documenting a set of entities and the relationships between them, the goal being to capture, at a high level, the fundamental concepts that are required to support the business processes and the users' needs. Entity discovery is at the heart of this process. Entities correspond to nouns (people, places, and things) that are fundamental to the business processes you are trying to improve by creating software. Once you understand the things your customer wants to store data about and how those things relate to one another, you are very close to understanding your customer's needs. Invariably, the closer I get to a correct conceptual model, the shorter the rest of the process is.

I personally find the discipline of limiting the model to entities and relationships to be an important first step, avoiding the technical arguments, things like whether the company name attribute needs to allow 100 Unicode characters or 75 ASCII characters to a time after we have the overall picture in mind. Those arguments may certainly matter, but doing them at the right time really helps.

Logical

The logical phase is a refinement of the work done in the conceptual phase. The output from this phase will be an essentially complete blueprint for the design of the relational database. During this stage, you should still think in terms of entities and their attributes, rather than tables and columns, though in the database's final state, there may be almost no difference. No consideration should be given at this stage to the exact details of how the system will be implemented.

As previously stated, a good logical design could be built on any RDBMS, or even in Excel for that matter. Core activities during this stage include the following:

- Drilling down into the conceptual model to identify the full set of entities that will be required to define the entire data needs of the user.

- Defining the attribute set for each entity. For example, an `Order` entity may have attributes such as `Order Date`, `Order Amount`, `Customer Name`, and so on.

- Identifying the attributes (or a set of attributes) that make up candidate keys. This includes primary keys, foreign keys, alternate keys, and so on.

- Defining relationships, their cardinalities, and whether they are optional or mandatory.

- Identifying an appropriate domain (which will become a datatype) for each table and attribute including whether values are required.

While the logical model continues like the conceptual model in that it is meant to give the involved parties a communication tool to discuss the data requirements and to start seeing a pattern to the eventual solution, the logical phase is also about applying proper design techniques. The finished logical modeling phase defines a blueprint for the database system, which can be handed off to someone else with little knowledge of the system to implement using a given technology (which in our case is going to be some version of Microsoft SQL Server).

Note   Before we begin to build the logical model, we need to introduce a complete data modeling language. In our case, we will be using the IDEF1X modeling methodology, described in Chapter 3.

Physical

During the physical implementation phase, you fit the logical design to the tool that is being used (in our case, the SQL Server RDBMS). This involves validating the design (using the rules of what is known as normalization, covered in Chapter 5), then choosing datatypes for columns to match the domains, building tables, applying constraints and occasionally writing triggers to implement business rules, and so on to implement the logical model in the most efficient manner. This is where reasonably deep platform-specific knowledge of SQL Server, T-SQL, and other technologies becomes essential.

Occasionally, this phase can entail some reorganization of the designed objects to make them easier to implement in the RDBMS. In general, I can state that for most designs there is seldom any reason to stray a great distance from a well-designed logical model, though the need to balance user load, concurrency needs, and hardware considerations can make for some changes to initial design decisions. Ultimately, one of the primary goals is that no data that has been specified or integrity constraints that have been identified in the logical model will be lost. Data points can (and will) be added, often to handle the process of writing programs to use the data, like data to know who created or was the last person to change a row. The key is to avoid affecting the designed meaning or, at least, not to take anything away from that original set of requirements.

At this point in the project, constructs will be applied to handle the business rules that were identified during the conceptual part of the design. These constructs will vary from the favored declarative constraints, such as DEFAULT and CHECK constraints, to less favorable but still useful TRIGGER and occasionally STORED PROCEDURE objects to make sure data meets certain rules. In Chapter 12, I discuss concurrency, where I will make it clear why many business rules cannot be effectively implemented outside of database engine code.

Finally, this phase includes designing the security for the data we will be storing (though to be clear, while we may design security late in the process, we shouldn't design it so late in the process that it gets shortchanged, especially in case it affects the desired design in some way).

Maintenance

The goal of the maintenance phase is really survival. The fact is, as an architect, I have built many databases, got them ready, and then pushed them to production; then you move along. From there, it becomes someone else's problem until new features are needed. In this phase, the goal of the DBA team is to manage the structures and data as they interact with the SQL Server engine and the hardware. The goal is to optimize how your design interacts with the relational engine with varying amounts of data, new versions of SQL Server, upgraded hardware, and newer versions of the query optimizer.

The most important point to understand about the maintenance phase is that all changes to optimize performance should be done *without* changing the meaning of the implemented database in any way. This goal embodies Codd's eleventh rule, which states that an RDBMS should have distribution independence. Distribution independence implies that users should not have to be aware of where the database is located or how it is physically implemented. Adding a non-unique index is not blocking, and adding a unique index that contains all the index keys of an existing uniqueness constraint is safe also. Equally safe is distributing data across different files, or even different servers, as long as the published interface object names do not change, since users will still access the data as columns in rows in tables in the same database. Using features such as Stretch DB, you can even have part of a table's data on-premises and part of it in Azure, and the user will be none the wiser.

Even as more and more data is piled into your database, ideally the only change you will need to make to your database (without changing requirements and functionality needs) is in this phase by adding indexes and newer, better hardware. This task is generally one for the production DBA, who is charged with maintaining the database environment. This is particularly true when the database system has been built by a third party, like in a packaged project or by a consultant.

When new features are needed, the process is started back over with the conceptual and logical phases (depending on how large or small the change may be) and iterated until the system is eventually retired.

Note   Our discussion of the storage model will be reasonably limited. We will start by looking at entities and attributes during conceptual and logical modeling. In implementation modeling, we will switch gears to deal with tables, rows, and columns. If you want a deeper understanding or how data is implemented internally, check out the latest in the Internals series by Kalen Delaney (`http://sqlserverinternals.com/`). To see where the industry is rapidly headed, look at the SQL Azure implementation, where the storage aspects of the implementation are very much removed from your control and even grasp.

Summary

In this chapter, I offered a quick overview of RDBMS history to provide context to the trip I will take you on in this book, along with some information on the basic concepts of database objects and some aspects of theory. It's very important that you understand most of the concepts discussed in this chapter, since from now on, I'll assume you understand them.

I introduced relational data structures and defined what a database is. Then, we covered tables, rows, and columns. From there, I explained the information principle (which states that data is accessible *only* in tables and that tables have no order), defined keys, and introduced NULL values and relationships. We also looked at a basic introduction to the impetus for how SQL works.

We discussed the concept of dependencies, which are concerned with noticing when the existence of a certain value requires the existence of another value. This information will be vital in Chapter 5 as we reorganize our data design for optimal usage in our relational engine.

In the next few chapters, as we start to formulate a conceptual and then a logical design, we will primarily refer to entities and their attributes. After we have logically designed what our data ought to look like, we'll shift gears to the implementation phase and speak of tables, rows, and columns. The terminology is not terribly important, and in the real world it is best not to be a terminology zealot, smacking your coworkers on the hand with a ruler when they call rows records and columns fields; but when learning, it is a good practice to keep the differences distinct. The exciting part comes as database construction starts, and our database starts to become real. After that, all that is left is to load our data into a well-formed, well-protected relational database system and set our users loose!

Everything starts with the fundamentals presented here, including understanding what a table is and what a row is (and why it differs from a record). As a last not-so-subtle-subliminal reminder, rows in tables have no order, and tables need natural keys.

The rest of the book will cover the process with the following phases in mind (the next chapter will be a short coverage of the project phase that comes just before you start the conceptual design requirements):

- *Conceptual*: Identify the concepts that the users expect to get out of the database system that you are starting to build.

- *Logical*: Document everything that the user will need in their database, including data, predicates/rules, and so on.

- *Physical:* Design and implement the database in terms of the tools used (in the case of this book, SQL Server), adjusting based on the realities of the current version of SQL Server/another RDBMS you are working with.

- *Maintenance*: Keep the system alive by adjusting and laying out data on storage based on actual usage patterns and what works best for SQL Server. Adjust the design such that it works well with the engine layers, both algorithms and storage layers. The changes made ought to only affect performance, not correctness or the meaning of the system that has been implemented.

Of course, the same person will not necessarily do every one of these steps. Some of these steps require different skill sets, and not everyone can know everything—or so I have been told.

Introduction to Requirements

The oldest, shortest words—"yes" and "no"—are those which require the most thought.

—Pythagoras

If there is anything worse than doing a simple task without fully understanding the requirements for success, it is doing a complex one. It happens every day; computer projects are created with only a shimmer of an idea of what the end goal is. Sometimes experimentation leads you to something interesting. What rarely happens though is that you experiment around and meet the actual goal of your customer who knew what they wanted but you just didn't take the time to ask. In every project, *someone* involved must take time to figure out what the customer wants before design begins (which also must precede coding!). If you are very lucky, the person who figures out what the customer wants will not be you, as capturing requirements is considerably more difficult than any task that will follow in later chapters. The name of this role is commonly known as a *business analyst*.

However, for the rest of this chapter, we are going to assume that we have been given a business analyst hat to wear, and we need to gather the requirements before we start to design a database. We will keep it very simple, covering only the bare minimum amount of detail that can be gotten away with as an illustration.

The first thing one generally does when starting a computer project is to interview users and ask a question along the lines of "What problem are you trying to solve?" And then listen, being mindful that users fall into many categories. Some are very technical. Some are not. Some think they are, but most certainly are not. Take the time to

© Louis Davidson 2021
L. Davidson, *Pro SQL Server Relational Database Design and Implementation*,
https://doi.org/10.1007/978-1-4842-6497-3_2

understand the customer's problems before you try to solve them. A major issue from my own history was that I would try to rapidly get past understanding the customer needs and right into designing the internals of a database.

Tip   It is important to realize the question was only "What problem are you trying to solve?" and did not end up "And how do you think the software should be built to solve it?" Some requirements may be technical, like requiring certain platforms or integrations, but the goal should be that the programmers build the technical solutions for the customers.

The problem lies in the fact that that users don't think about databases; they think about either the problem they need to solve or, if they are savvy with the tech, how they want things to look and feel in the user interfaces (UIs) and reports. Of course, a lot of what the user specifies for a UI or report format is actually going to end up reflected in the database design; it is up to you to be certain that there is enough in the requirements to design storage without too much consideration about how it will be displayed. The data has an essence of its own that must be obeyed at this point in the process, or you will find yourself in a battle with the structures you concoct. In this chapter, we will go through some of the basic types of information you want to gather and the locations to look to make sure you are getting all of the requirements necessary to do a proper database design.

Of course, if you are a newbie, as you work through this chapter, you are probably going to think that this all sounds like a lot of writing, not a lot of designing, and even less coding. No matter how you slice it, planning every project must start out like this to be successful in a smooth manner. As noted, typically as a data architect or programmer, analysts will do the lion's share of the requirements gathering, and you will design and code software. The most important thing is that you will need to at least read the requirements and judge whether they make sense, possibly compared to the artifacts the requirements are based on. The importance of making sure someone gathers requirements cannot be understated. During a software project, the following phases are common:

- *Requirements gathering*: Document what a system is to be and identify the criteria that will make the project a success.

- *Design*: Translate the requirements into a plan for implementation.

- *Implementation*: Code the software.

- *Testing*: Verify that the software does what it is supposed to do.

- *Maintenance*: Make changes to address problems not caught in testing.

Each phase of the project after requirements gathering relies on the requirements to make sure that the target is met. Trying to build your database without first outlining what you are trying to store is like taking a trip without a map. The journey may be fun, but you may find you should have taken that left turn at Albuquerque, so instead of sunning your feathers on Pismo Beach, you must fight an abominable snowman. Due to poor requirements, a very large percentage of projects fail to meet users' needs. A very reasonable discussion that needs to be considered is how detailed requirements need to be before moving forward with design. In the early days of software development, these phases were done one at a time for the entire project, so you gathered all requirements that would ever be needed and then designed the entire software project before any coding started and so on.

This method of arranging a project has been given the name of "waterfall method" because the output of one step flowed into another. Waterfall has been derided as a generally terrible idea, because each phase was done to completion before moving to the next. At a high level, it makes perfect sense to follow this pattern, but to do requirements for a reasonably sized website might take an entire year and then another year of design, and by that time, the rest of the world has moved on to using images on their web pages, and you are still employing flashing fonts.

So the concept of "agile" project development was developed, where small chunks of the process were done, in as short as a day or two, but typically between a week and a month. The phases are more or less the same as in the waterfall method, the major differences being that small, releasable chunks are gathered requirements for, designed, built, and tested, in a very short time frame, even daily. If the world changes between iterations, changing direction can be done quickly. Even still, it is essential to have an overall picture of where you are going and essential to know what is required of the software before you design, and to have the entire design done before you start to code is rather likely.

The important point I want to make clear in this rather long chapter introduction is simple: each of these phases will be performed whether you like it or not. I have been on projects where we started implementation almost simultaneously with the start of the project. Eventually, we had to go back to gather requirements to find out why the user wasn't happy with our output. The times when we jumped directly from gathering requirements to implementation were a huge mess, because every programmer did their own thing, and eventually every database, every object, and every interface in the system looked completely different and didn't work or make sense altogether. Some of these messes are probably still being dug out from today.

This book is truly about design and implementation, and after this chapter, I am going to assume requirements are finished, that you understand what the customer wants, and the design phase has begun properly. Many books have been written about the software requirements gathering and documenting process, so I am not going to even attempt to come up with a deep example of requirements. Rather, I'll just make a quick list of what I look for in requirements. As writer Gelett Burgess once said about art, "I don't know anything about art, but I know what I like," and the same can be quite true when it comes to requirements. And just like most art forms, when it is truly good, most people will like it.

Requirements should be captured and written down, and you can generally tell the good from the bad by a few key criteria:

- Requirements should include reasonably few unnecessary technical details about how a problem will be solved; they should contain only the definition of the problem and success criteria. For example, a good requirements document might say, "The clerks must do all their adding in their heads, and this is slow and error prone. For project success, we would prefer the math in a manner that avoids error." A poor requirements document would exchange the last phrase for "...we would prefer the math be done using an ACME QR3243 calculator." A calculator might be the solution, and that may be a great one, but the decision should be left to the technologist to avoid overly limiting the final solution. What if the WhatchaDooger 325 calculator is cheaper and has better ratings and battery life. Only when there is a very specific reason for a technology should technology show up in requirements.

- The language used should be as specific as it can without dictating a solution. As an example, consider a statement like "we only pay new-hire DBAs $20,000 a year, and the first raise is after six months." If this was the actual requirement, the company could never hire a

qualified DBA—ever. And if you implemented this requirement in
the software as is, the first time the company wanted to break the rule
(like if Paul Nielsen became available), that user would curse your
name; hire Paul as a CEO, in title only; and, after six months, change
his designation to DBA to get around silly software limitations. (Users
will find a way to get their job done!) If the requirement was written
specifically enough, it might have said, "We usually only…," which is
implemented much differently.

- Requirements should be easily read and validated by customers. Pure
  and simple, use language the users can understand, not technical
  jargon that they just gloss over, so they don't realize that you were
  wrong until their software fails to meet their needs. Simple diagrams
  and pictures also work nicely as communication devices.

For my mind, it really doesn't matter how you document requirements, just if they
get written down. Write them down. Write them down. Hopefully, if you forget the rest
of what I say in this chapter, you'll remember that. If you are married or have parents,
you have probably made the mistake of saying "Yes _____, I promise I will get that done
for you" and then promptly forgetting what was said exactly so an argument eventually
occurs. "Yes, you did say that you wanted the database blue!" you say to your customers.
At this point, you have just called them liars or stupid, and that is not a great business
practice. On the other hand, if you forward the document in which they agreed to color
the database blue, taking responsibility for their mistake is in their court. Besides, it is
rumored that mauve has more RAM.

Finally, how will we use written requirements in the rest of the software creation
process? In the design phase, requirements are your guide to how to mold your software.
The technical bits are yours (or corporate standards) to determine: two tables or three,
stored procedures or ad hoc access, C#, JavaScript, or Python? But the final output
should be verifiable by comparing the design to the requirements. And when it is time to
do the overall system tests, you will use the requirements as the target for success. As you
are building tests of your design and software, requirements should be the only place
you need to go to get the rules that your output needs to follow.

In this chapter, I will cover two parts of the requirements gathering process:

- *Documenting requirements*: I'll briefly introduce the types of concerns you'll have throughout the project process in terms of documenting requirements.

- *Gathering requirements*: Here, I'll talk about the places to find information and some techniques for mining that information.

Requirements are not a trivial part of a project and most certainly should not be omitted, but like anything, they can be overdone. This chapter will give you a bit of advice on where to look or, if you are in the happy programmer position of not being the one gathering requirements, what to make sure has been looked at. The sad reality of programming is that if the system you create stinks because the requirements that you were given stink, it won't be the requirements gatherer who has to do all that recoding and waking up at 3:00 AM because the software is crashing.

Documenting Requirements

If you've ever traveled to a place where no one speaks the same language as you, you know the feeling of being isolated based solely on communication. Everything everyone says sounds incomprehensible to you, and no matter how often you ask where the bathroom is, all you get is this blank look back no matter how desperate the look on your face may be getting. It has nothing to do with intelligence; it's because you aren't speaking the same language. This sounds obvious to say, but you can't expect the entire population of another country to learn your language perfectly just so you can get what you need. It works better if you learn their language. Even when two people speak the same basic language, often there can be dialects and phrasing that can be confusing. But that is what we expect of users of documentation we write.

Information technology professionals and our clients tend to have these sorts of communication issues, because frequently, we technology types don't speak the same dialect or even the same language as our clients. Clients tend to think in the language of their industry, and we tend to think in terms of computer solutions. For example, think about SQL Server's tools. We relational programmers have trouble communicating to the tool designers what we want in SQL Server's tools. They do an adequate job for most tasks, but clearly, they aren't completely on the same page as the users.

During the process of analysis, you should adopt one habit early on: document, document, document as much of the information that you acquire as reasonably possible. Sometimes people take vacations, departing with vast amounts of job knowledge that is in their heads only, and sometimes they don't come back from vacation (you know, because they get offered a job as a Jungle Cruise captain at Disney World; I know if I get that offer on my next trip, I won't be coming back!). Many variations on this scenario exist, not all as pleasant to contemplate or as possible to bribe for information about where and what the XRDCEIT object is. Without documentation, you will quickly risk losing vital details. It's imperative that you don't try to keep everything in your head, because even people with the best memories tend to forget the details of a project.

The following are a few helpful tips as you begin to take notes on users' needs:

- Try to maintain a set of documents that will share system requirements and specification information. Important documents to consider include design meeting notes, documents describing verbal change requests, and signoffs on all specifications, such as functional, technical, testing, and so on.

- Beyond formal documentation, it's important to keep the members of your design team up to date and fully informed. Develop and maintain a common repository for all the information and keep it up to date.

- Note anywhere that you add information that the users haven't given you and have specifically agreed to.

- Set the project's scope early on and do your best to scope the requirements the same. This will prevent the project from getting too big or diverse to be achievable within a reasonable time frame and within the budget. Hashing out changes that affect the budget, particularly ones that will increase the budget, early in the process will avoid future animosity.

- Be succinct, but thorough. Sometimes a document can be 100 pages or 10 and say the same thing. The big test: Can the users, architects, and programmers use it and produce the end goal?

Once you produce a document, a crucial step follows: make sure the client agrees with your version of their goals. As you go through the entire system design process, the clients will no doubt change their minds on entities, data points, business rules, user interface, or colors—just about anything they can—and you must prepare yourself for this. Whatever the client wants or needs is what you have to endeavor to accomplish, as they are ultimately in control of the project, which unfortunately often means communicating through a third party like a project manager and being flexible enough to run with any proposed changes, whether minor or major. This setup initially sounds great, because you think the project manager will translate for you and be on the side of quality and correctness, and sometimes this is true. But often, the manager will mistranslate a client desire into something quite odd and then insist that it is the client's desire. "I need all of the data on one screen" gets translated into "I need all of the data in one table." Best case is that the manager realizes who the technical people are and who have business needs. If you have a typical job, worst case is may be closer to reality.

In addition to talking to the client, it's important to acquire as many notes, printouts, screenshots, portable drives loaded with spreadsheets, database backups, Word documents, emails, handwritten notes, and so on that exist for any current solution to the problem. This data will be useful in the process of discovering data elements, screens, reports, and other elements that you'll need to design into your applications. Often, you'll find information in the client's artifacts that's invaluable when putting together the data model.

Tip   Throughout the process of design and implementation, you'll no doubt find changes to the original requirements. Make sure to continue to update and verify your documentation, because the most wonderfully written and formatted documentation in the world is sometimes worse than useless if it's out of date.

Gathering Requirements

No matter how you slice up the work, the eventual outcome should at least resemble the same set of desires of the customers (with allowances for change in technology and corporate needs). The important thing is that all development methodologies will tell you one thing: have an idea of a design from the requirements *before* you code.

For gathering requirements, there are many tools and methodologies for documenting processes, business rules, and database structures. The Unified Modeling Language (UML) is one possible choice; the Microsoft Solutions Framework (which employs UML) and Rational Unified Process are others. There are also several model types in the IDEF family of methods for business process modeling; we will cover their data modeling technique in Chapter 3. I'll employ the Entity–Relationship (ER) modeling method IDEF1X to model databases. I won't be covering any of the other modeling languages for the non–database structure parts of the project but will rather be using a simple manual spreadsheet method, which is by far the most common method of documenting requirements—even in medium-sized organizations where spending money on documentation tools can be harder than teaching your pet half-bee Eric to make good word choices when playing Scrabble ("Buzz...again?").

Regardless of the tools used to document the requirements, the needs for the database design process are the same. Specifications need to be acquired that will lead to you as the database designer to discover all the following:

- Entities and their relationships between each other

- Attributes

- Domain of entities and attributes

- Business rules that can be enforced in the database

- Processes that require the use of the database

Without these specifications, you'll either must constantly go back to the clients and ask a bunch of questions (which they will sometimes answer three different ways for every two times they are asked, teaching you discernment skills) or start making guesses. Some versions of Agile do have customers working with the team closely, which would seem like the same thing, though it is very unlikely that your customer will want to be at your team's beck and call 24 hours a day while you code. Note that there is a big difference between doing micro-designs and no design at all. If you have enough requirements that you can clearly understand where the requirements/design is leading you, that is fine. What you don't want to do is to be clueless as to what comes next and to be going back to the customer and asking "Now what are we doing again?" and then finding out that what you thought was a shipping container warehousing system is actually a cupcake bakery point of sale system.

Tip   During the early parts of a project, figure out the "what" and "why" first; then you can work on the "how." Once you know the details of what needs to be built, the process to get it built will be reasonably natural, and you can possibly apply preexisting patterns to the solution. Requirements are the whole essence of what the customer needs.

Vagueness may cause unnecessary discussions, fights, or even lawsuits later in the process. So make sure your clients understand what you're going to do for them, and use language that will be clearly understood and that's specific enough to describe what you learn in the information gathering process.

Throughout the process of discovery, *artifacts* will be gathered and produced that will be used throughout the process of implementation as reference materials. Artifacts are any kind of documents that will be important to the design, for example, interview notes, emails, sample documents, and so on. In this section, I'll discuss some of the main types of activities that you will need to be very interested in as a database architect:

- Interviewing clients

- Getting the answers to the right questions

- Finding obscure requirements

By no means will this chapter form an exhaustive list of tasks or questions for the process of finding and acquiring documentation; in fact, it's far from it. The goal is simply to get your mind clicking and thinking of information to get from the client so your job will be easier.

Interviewing People

As noted, it might be the case that the data architect will never meet the user, let alone be involved in formal interviews. The project manager, business analyst, and possibly the system architect might provide all the required information. Other projects might involve only a data architect or a single person wearing more hats than the entire Fourth Army on maneuvers. I've done it both ways: I've been in the early design sessions, and I've worked primarily from documentation. The better the people you work with, the more favorable the latter option is. In this section, I'll talk quickly about the basics of client interviews, because on almost any project, you may end up doing some amount of interviewing the client.

Interviewing the people who are going to use the final product is commonly where the project really gets started. It's where the free, unstructured flow of information starts. However, it's also where the communication gap starts to be a concern. Many people think visually—in terms of how they work, web pages they use, and perhaps simple user interfaces. Users also tend to think solely from their own perspective. For example, they may use the word "error" to denote why a process did not run as they expected. These error conditions may be not only actual errors but choices the user makes. A value like "scheduled maintenance" might be classified as an error condition. It is very much up to the people with "analyst" embroidered on the back of their hats to analyze what users are asking for.

As such, the job is to balance the customer's perceived wants and needs with their real need: a properly structured database that sits nicely behind a user interface and captures what they are after, information to make their business work well and to be more lucrative. Be careful of too quickly showing people you are interviewing something that looks like it might work. Doing so might give the user the false impression that creating the entire application is an easy process. If you want proof, make the foolish mistake of demonstrating a polished-looking prototype application with non–hard-coded values that makes the client think it actually works. The clients might be impressed that you've put together something so quickly and expect you to be nearly done. Rarely will they understand that what exists under the hood—namely, the database and other layers of business and interface objects—is where all the main work takes place.

Tip   While visual elements are great places to find a clue to what data a user will want as you go along in the process, you'll want to be careful not to let the customer think their database will mirror the interface. The structure of the data needs to be dictated by what the data means, not on how it will be presented. Presentation is more tailored to how the user typically uses the data; the database design will be more tailored to the overall meaning of the data.

Brainstorming sessions with users can also yield great results for gathering a lot of information at once, if the group doesn't grow too large (if your meeting requires an onsite caterer for lunch so you can keep working, you are probably not going to make a lot of monumental decisions). The key here is to make sure that someone is facilitating the meeting and preventing the "alpha" person from beating up on the others and giving only one loud opinion (it is even worse if you are that alpha person, which I tend to have a problem with myself!). Treat information from every person interviewed as important, because each person will likely have a different, yet valuable viewpoint. Sometimes (usually?) the best information comes not from the executive, but from the person who does the work. Don't assume that the first person speaks for the rest, even if they're all working on the same project or if this individual is the manager (or even president or owner of a major corporation, though a great amount of tact is required sometimes to walk that tight rope).

In many cases, when the dominant person cannot be controlled or the mousey person cannot be prodded into getting involved, one-on-one sessions should be employed to allow all clients to speak their minds, without untimely interruptions from stronger-willed (though perhaps not stronger-minded) colleagues. Be mindful of the fact that the loudest and boldest people might not have the best ideas and that the quiet person who sits at the back and says nothing might have the key to the entire project. Make sure to at least consider everybody's opinions.

This part of the book is written with the most humility, because I've made more mistakes in this part of the design process than any other (and like anyone with lots of experience, I have made my fair share of mistakes in all levels of the software engineering process). The client interview is one of the most difficult parts of the process that I've encountered. It might not seem a suitable topic for experienced analysts, but even the best of us need to be reminded that jumping the gun, bullying the clients, telling them what they want before they tell you, and even failing to manage the user's expectations can lead to the ruin of even a well-developed system. If you have a shaky foundation, the final product will likely be shaky as well.

Getting the Answers to the Right Questions

Before painting the interior of any house, there are a set of questions that the painting company's representative will ask every single one of their clients (colors to use, rooms to paint, children's room, write-on/wipe-off use). The same can go for almost any computer software project. In the following sections are some questions that are going to be important to the database design aspects of a system's development. Clearly, this is not going to be an exhaustive list, but it's certainly enough to get you started, so at a minimum, you won't have to sit in a room one day with no idea about what to say.

Tip   While this section is specifically speaking about questions you might ask people you are interviewing about a new system, they are also questions you are going to want to ask when you are looking over requirements that have been given to you to design a database.

What Data Is Needed?

Most users, at a high level, know what data they want to see out of the system. For example, if they're in accounting, they want to see dollars and cents summarized in very specific groupings. It will be very important at some time in your process to differentiate between what data is needed and what would just be nice to have. It is obviously a really straightforward question, and the customer may have no idea what they need, but many users already work with data, either on existing systems (they either hate these systems and will be glad you are replacing them, or they will hate you for changing things) or in a spreadsheet system that they have been using since VisiCalc.

How Will the Data Be Used?

Knowing what your client is planning to use the data in the system for is an important thing to know indeed. Not only will you understand the processes that you will be trying to model but you can also begin to get a good picture of the type of data that needs to be stored.

For example, imagine you're asked to create a database of contacts for a dental office. You might want to know the following:

- Will the contact names be used just to make phone calls, like a quick phone book?

- Will the client be sending email or posting to the members of the contact lists? Should the names be subdivided into groups for this purpose?

- Will the client be using the names to solicit a response from the mail, such as appointment reminders?

- Is it important to have family members documented? Do they want to send cards to the person on important dates?

Usage probably seems like it would be out of bounds early in the design process, but why capture any data if you don't have any idea how you might use it? Storage is cheap for sure. But why keep personal information about a person if you have no intention of using it?

Where usage information can be useful in your design later is how stringent to be with the data format. For example, take addresses. If you just capture them for infrequent usage, you might only need to give the user a single string to input an entire address. But if your business is mailing, you may need to format it to your post office's exact specifications, so you don't have to pay the same postage rates as the normal human beings.

What Rules Govern the Use of the Data?

Almost every piece of data you are going to want to store will have rules that govern how it is stored, used, and accessed. These rules will provide a lot of guidance to the model that you will produce. As an example, taking our previous example of contacts, you might discover the following:

- Every contact must have a valid email address.

- Every contact must have a valid street address.

- The client checks every email address using an email routine, and the contact isn't a valid contact until this routine has been successfully executed.

- Contacts must be subdivided by the type of issues they have.

- Only certain users can access the email addresses of the contacts.

It's important to be careful with the verbiage of the rules gathered early in the process. Many times, the kinds of rules you get seem pretty straightforward when they are written down, but the reality is quite often not so simple. It is important as you are reviewing rules to confirm them with the analyst and likely directly with the client before assuming them to be true.

As a case in point, what is a "valid" email address? Well, it's the email address that accurately goes with the contact. Sure, but how on earth do you validate that? The fact is that in many systems you don't. Usually, this is implemented to mean that the string meets the formatting for an email address, in that it has an ampersand character between other characters and a dot (.) between one or more alphanumeric values (such as %@%.%, plus all characters between A and Z and 0 and 9, an underscore, etc.), but the value is completely up to interpretation. On the other hand, in other types of systems, you require the user to pick up some information from the email to validate that it is, indeed, a working email address and that the person who entered the data has rights to it. It is very much up to the needs of the system, but the English question can easily be put using the exact same words.

The real problem comes when you too strictly interpret rules and your final product ends up unacceptable because you've placed an overly restrictive rule on the data that the client doesn't want or you've missed a rule that the client truly needs. I made this mistake in a big way once, which torpedoed a system for several weeks early in its life. Rules that the clients had seemingly wanted to be strictly enforced needed to be occasionally overridden on a case-by-case basis, based on the clients' desires. Unfortunately, our program didn't make it possible for the user to override these rules, and they never tried to simulate this condition in their user acceptance testing, so teeth were gnashed and sleep was lost fixing the problem.

Some rules might have another problem: the client wants the rule, but implementing it isn't possible or practical. For example, the client might request that all registered visitors of a website must insert a valid mobile phone number, but is it certain that visitors would provide this data? And what exactly is a valid mobile number? Can you validate that by format alone, or does the number have to be validated by calling it or checking with the phone company? What if users provide a landline instead? Implementability is of limited concern at this point in the process. Someone will have to enforce the rule, and that will be ironed out later in the process.

What Special Security Considerations Does the Data Require?

There are a plethora of data security regulations out there, including, but not limited to, Health Insurance Portability and Accountability Act (HIPAA), Sarbanes–Oxley (SOX) Act, General Data Protection Regulation (GDPR), California Consumer Privacy Act (CCPA), Children's Online Privacy Protection Act (COPPA), and Payment Card Industry (PCI) Data Security Standard. As a person gathering requirements and building code that stores data, you need to at least be aware of them. They are all acronyms for different security laws and protocols that govern how you can handle and store sensitive personal data. HIPAA is about medical data, COPPA is about child data, PCI is regarding payment forms, and GDPR and CCPA govern how you handle every piece of data your company stores about people from the European Union and California. And if by the time you are reading this book there aren't more of these governing more of your data, color me amazed.

Securing the personal and private data you capture about people has never been more scrutinized than it has been today. Part of the requirements gathering process needs to be understanding data that the customer wants to capture that may be sensitive in nature and how it needs to be safeguarded properly.

Throughout the book, I will mention this topic of handling sensitive data, but I am not going to dig into any specific details of any of the regulation because they are subject to change and are specific to specific industries. What is NOT subject to change is that we must understand the sensitivity of customer data, and the best possible place to start is before the system is created. There are tools that Microsoft and other vendors will provide to find and tag sensitive data, but during requirements gathering, you and your customers have a very good idea what data you would not like to just have sitting around for all of their employees to see. Couple that with whatever your company's security officer says about the laws that apply to your industry and do the right thing.

What Data Is Reported On?

There are typically two reasons we store data at all. First is to make something mechanical (or perhaps magical) happen—an order taken, invoice sent, payment recorded, or entry to a theme park recorded. Once the money is in the bank and the customer has their product, that is pretty much it for what a large majority of the common stakeholder cares about.

The second purpose is to report what has occurred, and this is where the true value of data really lies. It is where the things that have happened in the past start to inform us of what will happen in the future. Don't be misled by the word "reports" either; by this, I don't just mean some arcane spreadsheet–looking thing that could have been printed on a dot matrix printer. Those reports are more valuable and useful than they look, but reports can employ AI/Machine Learning built right into the tools today to give instant and valuable insights.

Many novice developers leave designing and implementing reports until the last minute (a mistake I've made more than once over the years and have suffered through many, many times). For the user, reports are where data becomes information and are used as the basis of vital decision making and can make or break a company. Note that it isn't a tools problem. Reporting Services, Power BI, Synapse, and so on all make the tasks easier. The problem lies in knowing what data to capture. If you need to know the temperature of a freezer over the last five days, a part of the initial design is to capture the temperature in a temporal manner, over at least five days. If you didn't know that requirement, you might just have a single value for the current freezer temperature and not be able to meet the reporting needs. That would be an easy problem to solve, but often there are many problems like this that come up late in the process that end up implemented in a less than awesome manner because it has to be done so late in the process. Getting it right the first time is better than not.

Looking back at the contact example, what name does the client want to see on the reports? The following items come to mind:

- First name, Last name

- First name, Middle name, Last name

- Last name, First name

- Nickname

It's important to try to nail down such issues early, no matter how small or silly they seem to you at this point. They're important to the client, who you should always remember is paying the bill. And frankly, the most important rule for reporting is that you cannot report on data that you do not capture. (And yes, that rule does collide nicely with the previous discussion of not capturing data unless you have some idea of how you would use it. Things like that are why requirements gathering is harder than designing and coding systems.)

From a database design standpoint, the content of reports is extremely important, because it will likely help to discover data requirements that aren't otherwise thought of. Avoid being concerned with the aesthetics of the reports yet if at all possible, because that might lead to the temptation of discussing implementation and away from the purpose of requirements: what the customer is trying to do.

Tip   Don't overlook any existing reports that might have a corresponding report in the new system. You may not want to duplicate old reports as was, but the content will likely include data that the client may never even think about when they're expressing needs. There will often be hundreds of reports currently in production, and in the new system, there is little doubt that the number will go up, unless many of the reports can be consolidated. Specific reporting architecture is covered in more detail in Appendix C, which will be available with the download for the book.

Where Is the Data Now?

It is nice occasionally to have the opportunity to create a totally new database with absolutely no preexisting data. This makes life easy and your job a lot of fun. Unfortunately, as years pass, finding a completely new system to implement is quite rare. The only likely exception is when building a product to be sold to end users in a turnkey fashion (then the preexisting data is their problem or yours if you also have to write the code to import data from your customers' systems). For almost every system I have worked on, I was creating a better version of an existing system, so we had to consider converting existing data that's important to the end users. (A rare few have been brand-new systems. These were wonderful experiences for many reasons; not only didn't we have to deal with data conversion but we didn't have to deal with existing processes, code, or expectations either.)

Every organization is different. Some have data in one centralized location, while others have it scattered in many (many) locations. Rarely, if ever, is all the related data already in well-structured database(s) that you can easily access and use. If that were the case, why would the client come to you at all? Clients typically have data in the following sundry locations:

- *Mainframe or legacy servers*: Millions of lines of active COBOL still power many corporations, even 20 years after the first edition of this book on relational databases.

- *Spreadsheets*: Spreadsheets are wonderful tools to view, slice, and dice data but are wildly inappropriate places to maintain complex data, especially by more than one person. Most users know how to use a spreadsheet as a database but, unfortunately, are not so experienced in ensuring the integrity of their data, so this data is undoubtedly going to give you a major headache.

- *Desktop databases such as Microsoft Access or SQL Server Express Edition*: Desktop databases are great tools and are easy to deploy and use. However, this ease of use often means that these databases are constructed and maintained by nontechnical personnel and are poorly designed, potentially causing many problems when the databases must be enlarged or modified. Both can be great products, but they are also often just data dumpsters where mounds of data are stored.

- *Filing cabinets*: Even now, in the twenty-first century, many companies still have few or no computers used for anything other than playing solitaire and instead maintain stockpiles of paper documents. Your project might simply be to replace a filing cabinet with a computer-based system or to supply a simple database that logs the physical locations of the existing paper documents.

- *The cloud*: There is nothing wrong with the cloud. Most of the code in this book will run in the cloud or on premises. But depending on where the data is and how it is formatted, the cloud can provide extra challenges. The name "the cloud" is there to give you a sense of grandeur, like anything is possible. Anything can be good... and anything can be the opposite of good.

Data that you need to include in the SQL Server database you're designing will come from these and other weird and wonderful sources that you discover from the client (truth is commonly stranger than fiction). Even worse, spreadsheets, filing cabinets, and poorly designed computerized databases don't enforce data integrity (and often desktop databases, mainframe applications, and even existing SQL Server databases don't necessarily do such a perfect job either), so always be prepared for freaky data that will have to be cleaned up before storage in your nice new database. Even more importantly, be ready to find out that what appears to be dirty data based on the original requirements is just wrong requirements.

Will the Data Need to Be Integrated with Other Systems?

Once you have a good idea of where the client's important data is located, you can begin to determine how the data in your new SQL Server solution will interact with the data that will stay in its original format. This might include building intricate gateway connections to mainframes; linking server connections to other SQL Servers, Oracle boxes, or Hadoop systems; or even linking to spreadsheets. You can't make too many assumptions about this topic at this point in your design. Just knowing the architecture you'll need to deal with can be helpful later in the process.

Tip   *Never* expect that the data you will be converting or integrating with is going to have *any* quality and plan accordingly. Too many projects get their start with poor guesses about the effort required, and data cleanup has been the least well-guessed part of them all. It will be hard enough to understand what is in a database to start with, but if the data is bad, it will make your job orders of magnitude more difficult.

How Much Is This Data Worth?

It's important to place value judgments on data. In some cases, data will have great value in the monetary sense. For example, in the dental office example that will be presented later in Chapter 4, the value lies in the record of what has been done to the patient and how much has been billed to the patient and their insurance company. Without this documentation, digging out this data to eventually get paid for the work done might take hours and days. This data has a specific monetary value; first, just to get paid at all is important. Then, perhaps temporally, the quicker the payment is received, the more interest is drawn, meaning more profits. If the client shifts the turnover of payments from one month to one week because of streamlining the process, this might be worth quite a bit more money over all the patients at a practice.

When considering keeping historical data, just because existing data is available doesn't necessarily mean that it should be included in the new database. The client needs to be informed of all the data that's available and should be provided with a cost estimate of transferring it into the new database. The cost of transferring legacy data can be high, and the client should be offered the opportunity to make decisions that might conserve funds for more important purposes.

Who Will Use the Data?

Who is going to use the data probably doesn't instantly jump out at you as a type of data that needs to be considered during the early stages of requirements gathering. When designing an interface, usually who is going to be clicking the button probably doesn't make a lot of difference to the button design (unless disabilities are involved in the equation perhaps, but UIs should be built that work for everyone, or morph to people's special needs). Yet, the answer to the question of "who" can start to answer several different types of questions:

- *Security*: "Who will use the data?" can be taken two ways. First, these are the only people who care about the data. Second, these are the only people who are allowed to use the data. The latter will require you to create boundaries to utilization. Add in the kinds of things the privacy regulations previously discussed in the "What Special Security Considerations Does the Data Require?" section earlier in this chapter, and this can be pretty complex at times.

- *Concurrency*: The design considerations for a system that has one user are different from those for a system that has ten simultaneous users, or a hundred, a thousand, or even more. The number of users should not considerably change our conceptual or logical designs, but it can certainly change how we design the physical layer and will definitely change how the hardware looks. Concurrency is something we won't make a lot of reference to until very late in this book (Chapter 12), but this is the point in time when you are doing the asking and likely specifying the future hardware/software (at least for cost estimates), so it doesn't hurt to find out now.

This choice of who will use the data goes hand in hand with all the other questions you have gotten answered during the process of gathering requirements. Of course, these questions are just the start of the information gathering process, but there is still a lot more work to go before you can start building a database, so you are going to have to cool your jets a bit longer.

Finding Obscure Requirements

This section contains a few locations where sneaky requirements may be found that you will not get from a user or an existing system. The problem with these locations is that they are not freely available to just anyone in an organization. The documents involved might include records of amounts of money paid to previous contractors for failed attempts to solve a problem, for example.

So apart from the obvious locations we have discussed such as talking to users and examining existing systems, there are some other more obscure locations you may wish to inquire about. Often, the project manager may be able to obtain these documents; sometimes, they will strictly not be available to you. Frequently you just must take someone else's word for what is said in them. In these cases, I find it best to put into writing your understanding and make sure it is clear who said what about the meaning of documentation you cannot see, because I have heard more than a few really weird requirements that supposedly came from contracts and one-tenth of the time they were actually true. As always, the following list is certainly not exclusive but should kick-start your thinking about where to get existing documentation for a system you are creating or replacing.

Early Project Documentation

If you work for a company that is creating software for other companies, you'll find that early in the project, there are often documents that get created to solicit costs and possible solutions, for example:

- *Request for quote (RFQ)*: A document with a fairly mature specification that an organization sends out to determine how much a solution would cost

- *Request for proposal (RFP)*: For less mature ideas for which an organization wants to see potential solutions and get an idea about costs

Each of these documents contains valuable information that can help you design a solution, because you can get an idea of what the client wanted before you got involved. Things change, of course, and not always will the final solution resemble the original request, but a copy of an RFP or an RFQ should be added to the pile of information that you'll have available later in the process. Although these documents generally consist of sketchy information about the problem and the desired solution, you can use them to confirm the original reason for wanting the system and for getting a firmer handle on what types of data are to be stored within it. A more interesting purpose may be to discover the underlying reason for a company wanting a new computer system. By the time programming starts, things often have a very single-minded focus toward delivering a solution and may miss that the most important part of the process is to be able to analyze some specific bit of data that may not seem essential to the primary purpose of the system.

No matter what, if you can get a copy of these documents (even redacted somewhat), you'll be able to see the client's thought pattern and why the client wants a system developed.

Contracts or Client Work Orders

Getting copies of the contract can seem like a radical approach to gathering design information, depending on the type of organization you're with. Frankly, in a corporate structure, you'll likely have to fight through layers of management to make them understand why you need to see the contract at all. Contracts can be inherently difficult to read because of the language they're written in (sort of like a terse version of a programming language, with intentional vagueness tossed in to give lawyers something to dispute with one another later). However, be diligent in filtering out the legalese, and you'll uncover what amounts to a high-level set of requirements for the system—often the requirements that you must fulfill exactly or not get paid. Even more fun is the stuff you may learn that has been promised that the implementation team has never heard of.

What makes the contract so attractive is simple: it is the target you'll be shooting at. No matter what the client says or what the existing system was, if the contract specifies that you deliver some sort of watercraft and you deliver a Formula 1 race car because the lower-level clients change their minds without changing the contract, you might not get paid because your project is deemed a failure (figuratively speaking, of course, since maybe they will let you keep the car?).

Level of Service Agreement

One section of legal documents that's important to the design process is the required level of service. This might specify the number of web pages per minute, the number of rows in the database, and so on. All this needs to be measured, stored, tested for, and so on. When it comes to the testing and optimization phases, knowing the target level of service can be of great value. You may also find some data that needs to be stored to validate that a service level is being met.

Audit Plans

Don't forget about audits. When you build a system, you must consider whether the system is likely to be audited in the future and by whom. Government agencies, ISO 9000 clients, and all of the regulations mentioned in the "What Special Security Considerations Does the Data Require?" section of this chapter are likely to have strict audit requirements. Certain types of clients may also have financial or oversight body audit processes. All of these will require not only that you follow rules that regulatory bodies set but that you document certain parts of your operation. These audit plans might contain valuable information that can be used in the design process.

Prototypes

A prototype is kind of a live document that gets created so that the user can get a feel for how software might work for them. Prototypes are fantastic communication devices, but they are focused on visuals, not internals. The real problem with prototypes is that if a database was created for the prototype, it is rarely going to be worth anything. So, by the time database design starts, you might be directed to take a prototype database that has been hastily developed and "make it work" or, worse yet, "polish it up." Indeed, you might inherit an unstructured, unorganized prototype, and your task will be to turn it into a production database in no time flat (loosely translated, that means to have it done early yesterday, or at least by late today).

It may be up to you, at times, to remind customers to consider prototypes only as interactive pictures to get the customer to try out a concept, often to get your company to sign a contract. As a data architect, you must work as hard as possible to use prototype code *only* as a working document that you use to inform your own design.

However, don't consider a prototype an enemy. What you see in the prototype is almost certainly very useful. The things the prototyper added to the screen and where they added them will not dictate the database design, but will inform it. Prototypes will almost certainly help you to be sure you're not going to miss out on any critical pieces of information that the users need—such as a name field, a search operation, or even a button (which might imply a data element)—just understand they don't dictate the future database design.

Best Practices

The following list of some best practices can be useful to follow when dealing with and gathering requirements:

- *Be diligent*: Look through everything to make sure that what's being said makes sense. Be certain to understand as many of the business rules that bind the system as possible before moving on to the next step. Mistakes made early in the process can mushroom later in the process.

- *Verify*: Whether gathering or interpreting requirements is your lot in life, make sure the requirements make sense. Too often I see where a requirement has been misinterpreted (or just mistyped) and a feature gets implemented to match the incorrect interpretation because that is what the requirement said, despite being illogical.

- *Document*: The format of the documentation isn't really all that important, only that you get documented as much of what the client wants as possible. Make sure that the documentation is understandable by all parties involved and that it will be useful going forward toward implementation.

- *Communicate*: Constant communication with clients is essential to keep the design on track. The danger is that if you start to get the wrong idea of what the client needs, every decision past that point might be wrong. Get as much face time with the client as possible.

- *Iterate*: Like a road trip, you always need to know where your destination is planned to be, but only make firm plans as far as the next stop. Make sure you firmly understand the requirements for each iteration of the system you are building and just enough of the overall picture to make sure you are still headed in the right direction.

Summary

In this chapter, I've touched on some of the basics of documentation and requirements gathering. This is one of the most important parts of the process of creating software, because it's the foundation of everything that follows. If the foundation is solid, the rest of the process has a chance. If the foundation is shoddy, the rest of the system that gets built will likely be the same. The purpose of this process is to acquire as much information as possible about what the clients want out of their system. As a data architect, this information might be something that's delivered to you, or at least most of it. Either way, the goal is to understand the users' needs.

Once you have as much documentation as possible from the users, the real work begins. Through all this documentation, the goal is to prepare you for the next step of producing a data model that will serve as the documentation of the following:

- Entities and relationships

- Attributes and domains

- Business rules that can be enforced in the database

- Processes that require the use of the database

From this, a conceptual data model will emerge that has many of the characteristics that will exist in the actual implemented database. In the upcoming chapters, the database design will certainly change from this conceptual model, but it will share many of the same characteristics.

CHAPTER 3

The Language of Data Modeling

A doctor can bury his mistakes, but an architect can only advise his clients to plant vines.

—Frank Lloyd Wright, Architect

In this chapter, I will introduce the basic process and concepts of *data modeling*, in which a representation of a database will be produced that shows the objects involved in the database design and how they interrelate. It is really a description of the exterior and interior parts of the database, with a graphical representation being a communication vehicle of the most important parts of the model (the graphical part of the model is probably the most interesting to the general audience, because it gives a very quick and easy-to-work-with user interface and overview of your objects and their relationships).

A data model is one of the most important tools in the design process, as if it isn't done well, you will pay for it until you replace the system. It starts as a sketch of the data requirements that you use to communicate with the customer and is refined over and over until you get it right and it becomes a real SQL Server (or perhaps another RDBMS) database. A common misconception is that a data model is a picture of a database. That is partly true, but a model is so much more. A true data model includes nongraphical representations of pretty much everything about a database and serves as the primary documentation for almost all aspects of the lifecycle of a database. Parts of the model will be useful to developers, users, and the database administrators (DBAs) who maintain the system.

© Louis Davidson 2021
L. Davidson, *Pro SQL Server Relational Database Design and Implementation*,
https://doi.org/10.1007/978-1-4842-6497-3_3

In the next section, I'll provide some basic information about data modeling and introduce the language I prefer for data modeling (and will use for many examples throughout this book): IDEF1X. I'll then cover how to use the IDEF1X methodology to model and document the following parts of the database (introduced in the first chapter):

- Entities/tables

- Attributes/columns

- Relationships

- Descriptive information

In the process of creating a database, we will start out modeling entities and attributes, which will start fairly loosely defined until we start to formalize tables and columns, which, as discussed in Chapter 1, have very formal definitions that we will continue to refine through Chapter 5. For this chapter and the next, I will primarily refer to entities during the modeling exercises, unless I'm trying to demonstrate something that would specifically be created in SQL Server. The same data modeling language will be used for the entire process of modeling the database, with some changes in terminology to describe an entity, changing to a table later in this book after we transform the model from requirements to an implementation tool.

After introducing IDEF1X, I will briefly introduce several other alternative modeling methodology styles, including Information Engineering (IE) (also known as "Crow's Feet") and the Chen Entity–Relationship Model (ERD) methodology because they both are very useful when looking for model examples in business and academic locations that do not use IDEF1X.

Note   This chapter mainly covers the mechanics and language of modeling. In the next chapter, we will apply these concepts to build a data model.

Introducing Data Modeling

Data modeling is a foundational skill of database design. In order to start designing databases, it is essential to effectively communicate the design to others by making it easier to visualize. Many of the concepts introduced in Chapter 1 have graphical representations that allow you to get an overview of a vast amount of database structures and metadata in a very small amount of space.

Note   There are many types of models or diagrams: process models, data flow diagrams, data models, sequence diagrams, and others. For our purpose of database design, however, I will focus specifically on data models.

Several popular modeling languages are available to use, and each is generally just as good as the others at the job of documenting a database design. The major difference will be some of the symbology that is used to convey the information. When choosing my data modeling methodology, I looked for one that was easy to read and could display and store everything required to implement very complex systems. The modeling language I use is Integration Definition for Information Modeling (IDEF1X). (It didn't hurt that the organization I have worked for over 20 years has used it for that amount of time too, but I definitely feel it to be at least as good as, if not slightly superior to, other modeling languages.)

IDEF1X is based on Federal Information Processing Standards (FIPS) Publication 184, published on September 21, 1993. To be fair, the other major mainstream methodology, Information Engineering, is good too, but I like the way IDEF1X works, and it is based on a publicly available standard. IDEF1X was originally developed by the US Air Force in 1985 to meet the following requirements:

1. Support the development of data models.

2. Be a language that is both easy to learn and robust.

3. Be teachable.

4. Be well tested and proven.

5. Be suitable for automation.

Note   At the time of this writing, the full specification for IDEF1X is available at `www.idef.com/idef1x-data-modeling-method/`. Wikipedia has a decent overview as well: `https://en.wikipedia.org/wiki/IDEF1X`.

While the selection of a data modeling methodology may be a personal choice, economics, company standards, or features usually influence tool choice. IDEF1X is implemented in many of the popular design tools, such as the following, which are just a few of the products available that claim to support IDEF1X (note that the URLs listed here were correct at the time of this writing, but are subject to change in the future, and most had changed since the last edition of this book):

- *SqlDBM:* `sqldbm.com/home/` *(This is the modeling tool that was used to draw the models in this book, with some modifications to keep more to the standard IDEF1X modeling language. Most deviations from the standards do not take away from a tool's ability to produce a working database.)*

- *erwin Data Modeler*: `erwin.com/products/data-modeler`

- *Toad Data Modeler*: `www.quest.com/products/toad-data-modeler/`

- *ER/Studio*: `www.idera.com/er-studio-enterprise-data-modeling-and-architecture-tools`

- *Visible Analyst DB Engineer*: `www.visiblesystemscorp.com/products/Analyst/`

Let's next move on to practice modeling and documenting, starting with entities.

Entities

In the IDEF1X standard, entities are modeled as rectangular boxes, as they are in most data modeling languages. Two types of entities can be modeled: identifier independent and identifier dependent, typically referred to as "independent" and "dependent," respectively. The difference between a dependent entity and an independent entity lies in how the primary key of the entity is structured. The independent entity is so named because it has no primary key dependencies on any other entity, or in other words, the primary key contains no foreign key columns from other entities.

Chapter 1 introduced the term foreign key, and the IDEF1X specification introduces an additional term: *migrated key.* If the attributes are migrated to the non–primary key attributes, they are independent of any other entities. All attributes that are not migrated as foreign keys from other entities are *owned*, as they have their origins in the current entity. Other methodologies and tools may use the terms "identifying" and "nonidentifying" instead of "dependent" and "independent." Another pair of terms that is commonly used for the same purposes is "strong" for identifying and "weak" for nonidentifying.

For example, consider an invoice that has one or more line items. The primary key of the Invoice entity might be `InvoiceNumber`. If the invoice has two line items, a reasonable choice for the primary key would be `InvoiceNumber` and probably some sequence attribute like `LineItemNumber` (you might consider a product identifier, but it is not uncommon to see two line items with the same product on each line), but since the primary key contains `InvoiceNumber`, it would be dependent on the `Invoice` entity. If you had an `InvoiceStatus` entity that was also related to `Invoice`, it would be independent, because an invoice's existence is not predicated on the existence of a status (even if a value for the `InvoiceStatus` to `Invoice` relationship *is* required—in other words, the foreign key column would not allow NULL values). We will see this more clearly later when we start to draw the relationships in the diagrams.

An independent entity is drawn with square corners, as shown here:

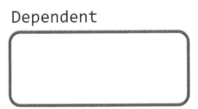

The dependent entity is drawn with rounded corners, as follows:

Note   The concept of dependent and independent entities leads us to a bit of a chicken and egg paradox (not to mention a fork in the road, also known as the don't write just before lunch principle). The dependent entity is dependent on a certain type of relationship. However, the introduction of entity creation can't wait until after the relationships are determined, since the relationships couldn't exist without entities. If this is the first time you've looked at data models, this chapter may require a reread to get the full picture, as the concept of independent and dependent objects is linked to relationships.

As we start to identify and model entities, we need to take a quick look at the topic of naming. One of the most important aspects of designing or implementing any system is how objects, variables, and so forth are named. Long discussions about names always seem like a waste of time, but if you have ever gone back to work on code that you wrote months ago, you understand what I mean. For example, @x might seem like a perfect, easy-to-type variable name when you first write some code, and it certainly saves a lot of keystrokes vs. typing @HoldEmployeeNameForCleaningInvalidCharacters, but the latter is much easier to understand after a period of time has passed (which, for some of us, is about the amount of time to grab something to drink).

Naming database objects is no different; actually, naming database objects is more important than naming other programming objects, as often *very* nontechnical end users will get used to these names—the names given to entities will be used as documentation and translated into table names that will be accessed by programmers and users alike. The conceptual and logical model will be considered your primary schematic of the data in the database and should be a living document that you change before changing any implemented structures.

Frequently, discussions on how objects should be named can get heated because there are several different schools of thought about how to name objects. A central concern is whether to use plural or singular entity/table names. Both have merit, but one style must be chosen and followed. I choose to follow the IDEF1X standard for object names, which says to use singular names. By this standard, the name itself doesn't name the container but, instead, refers to an instance of what is being modeled. Other standards use the table's name for the container/set of rows, which also makes sense from another reasonable standpoint. It truly matters how you use the names. Plural names tend to need to be constantly made singular. Say you have a table that represents donuts. To discuss it, you would need to say awkward-sounding things such as "I have a donuts table. I have a table of donuts. There are seven donuts rows. There are seven rows of donuts. One donuts row is related to one or more donut eaters rows." Singular names are appended to descriptions easily: "I have a donut table. I have seven donut rows. One donut row is related to one or more donut eater rows." By applying the pattern of adding the name to a scope, we can build up lots of documentation easily, and it is pretty readable by a normal person.

Each method has benefits and strong proponents, and plural or singular naming might be worth a few long discussions with fellow architects, but, honestly, it is certainly not something to get burned at the stake over. If the organization you find yourself beholden to uses plural names, that doesn't make it a bad place to work. The most important thing is to be consistent and not let your style go all higgledy-piggledy as you go along. Any naming standard is better than no standard at all, so if the databases you inherit use plural names, follow the "when in Rome" principle and use plural names so as not to confuse anyone else.

In this book, I will follow these basic guidelines for naming entities:

- *Entity names should never be plural.* The primary reason for this is that the name should refer to an instance of the object being modeled, rather than the collection.

- *The name given should directly correspond to the essence of what the entity is modeling.* For instance, if you are modeling a person, name the entity `Person`. If you are modeling an automobile, call it `Automobile`. Naming is not always this straightforward, but keeping the name simple and to the point is wise.

Entity names frequently need to be made up of several words. During the conceptual and logical modeling phases, including spaces, underscores, and other characters when multiple words are necessary in the name is acceptable but not required. For example, an entity that stores a person's addresses might be named `Person Address`, `Person_Address`, or, using the style I have recently become accustomed to and the one I'll use most frequently in this book, `PersonAddress`. This type of naming is known as *Pascal case* or *mixed case*. (When you don't capitalize the first letter, but capitalize the first letter of the second word, this style is known as *camelCase*.) Just as in the plural/singular argument, there really is no "correct" way; these are just the guidelines that I will follow to keep everything uniform.

Regardless of any style choices you make, very few abbreviations should be used in the logical naming of entities unless it is a universal abbreviation that every person reading your model will know (and you can actually be certain of that!). Every word ought to be fully spelled out, because abbreviations lower the value of the names as documentation and tend to cause confusion. Abbreviations may be necessary in the implemented model because of some naming standard that is forced on you or a very common industry standard term. Be careful of assuming the industry standard terms are universally known.

If you decide to use abbreviations in any of your names, make sure that you have a standard in place to ensure the same abbreviation is used every time. One of the primary reasons to avoid abbreviations is so you don't have to worry about different people using different abbreviations like Description, Descry, Desc, Descrip, and Descriptn for the same thing on different entities (or sometimes as a suffix on different attributes on the same entity!).

Often, novice database designers (particularly those who come from interpreted or procedural programming backgrounds) feel the need to use a form of *Hungarian notation* and include prefixes or suffixes in names to indicate the kind of object—for example, tblEmployee or tbl_Customer. Prefixes like this are generally considered a bad practice for entities (and tables), because names in relational databases are almost always used in an obvious context. Using Hungarian notation is often a good idea when writing procedural code (like Visual Basic or C#), since objects don't always have a very strict contextual meaning that can be seen immediately upon usage, especially if you are implementing one interface with many different types of objects. In SQL Server Integration Services (SSIS) packages, I commonly name each operator with a three- or four-letter prefix to help identify them in logs, and in PowerShell I name global variables G_ and parameters P_, for example. However, with database objects, questioning whether a name refers to a column or a table is rare. Plus, if the object type isn't obvious, querying the system catalog to determine it is easy. I won't go too far into implementation right now, but you can use the sys.objects catalog view to see the type of any object. For example, this query will list all of the different object types in the catalog (your results may vary; this query was executed against the WideWorldImporters database we will use for some of the examples in this book):

```
SELECT  DISTINCT type_desc
FROM    sys.objects
ORDER   BY type_desc;
```

Here's the result:

```
type_desc
---------------------------------------------
CHECK_CONSTRAINT
DEFAULT_CONSTRAINT
FOREIGN_KEY_CONSTRAINT
INTERNAL_TABLE
```

```
PRIMARY_KEY_CONSTRAINT
SECURITY_POLICY
SEQUENCE_OBJECT
SERVICE_QUEUE
SQL_INLINE_TABLE_VALUED_FUNCTION
SQL_SCALAR_FUNCTION
SQL_STORED_PROCEDURE
SYSTEM_TABLE
TYPE_TABLE
UNIQUE_CONSTRAINT
USER_TABLE
VIEW
```

We will use `sys.objects` and other catalog views throughout this book to view properties of objects that we create.

Attributes

All attributes in the entity must be uniquely named within it. They are represented by a list of names inside of the entity rectangle:

```
AttributeExample
┌─────────────────────┐
│  Attribute1         │
│  Attribute2         │
│                     │
└─────────────────────┘
```

Note   The preceding illustration shows a technically invalid entity, as there is no primary key defined (a requirement for a table and for IDEF1X). I'll cover the notation for keys in the following section.

At this point, you would simply enter all of the attributes that you discover from the requirements (the next chapter will demonstrate this process). As I will demonstrate in Chapter 5, the attributes will be transformed a great deal during the normalization process, but the process is iterative, and the goal will be to capture the details that are discovered. For example, the attributes of an `Employee` entity may start out as follows:

Employee

```
EmployeeNumber
FirstName
LastName
Address
PhoneNumber
```

During the normalization process, where we transform the table to work well with the relational engine, tables like this will often be broken down into many attributes (e.g., `Address` might, in an American company's database, be broken into `Number`, `Street Name`, `City`, `State`, `PostalCode`, etc.) and possibly multiple entities depending on your actual system's needs.

Note   Attribute naming is one place where I tend to deviate slightly from IDEF1X. The standard is that names are unique within a model, not just within a table. This tends to produce names that include the table name (or worse yet some table name abbreviation prefix) followed by the attribute name, which can result in unwieldy, long names that look archaic.

Just as with entity names, there is no need to include Hungarian notation prefixes or suffixes in names to let you know it is a column. However, there is value in structuring names in a very straightforward way to let the reader know what the column means. The implementation details of the attribute can be retrieved from the system catalog if there is any question about it.

The format I use is loosely based on the concepts in ISO 11179, though there really is not much freely available about this standard in a format that is worth referencing. Generally, the idea is that names include standard parts that are put together to form a standard-looking name. I will use the following parts in my names:

- *Role name*: Optionally explains a specific role the attribute/column plays

- *Attribute*: The primary purpose of the attribute being named. Optionally can be omitted, meaning the attribute/column name refers directly to the entity in the most obvious manner

- *Classword*: A required term that identifies the primary type of usage of the attribute/column, in non–implementation-specific terms

- *Scale*: Optional to tell the user what the scale of the data is in when it is not obvious from the context, like Minutes, Seconds, Dollars, Euros, and so on

Here are some examples of attribute names using some or all of the standard parts:

- Name: Simply uses a classword to denote a textual string that names the row value, but whether or not it is a varchar(30) or nvarchar(128) is immaterial (Without a role name, the name should apply directly to an instance of the entity. For example, Company.Name is the name of the company itself.)

- UserName: An attribute and a classword, where the attribute tells the more specific use of the Name classword to indicate what type of name. (For example, Company.UserName would be the username the company uses. More context would be acquired from the name and purpose of the database.)

- AdministratorUserName: A role name added to the UserName attribute, identifying the specific role the user plays that is being named. Specifically, this username is the username of the administrator.

- PledgeAmount: Here the attribute Pledge is coupled with a class I typically use for an amount of money, no matter the datatype which is used. The amount of money is assumed to be in the local currency that is typical for the database.

- PledgeAmountEuros: Indicates that for the PledgeAmount, this is an amount of money pledged, but with an atypical scale for the context of the database.

- `FirstPledgeAmountEuros`: Plays the role of the first `PledgeAmount` recorded in euros, unlike the previous which could be any pledge in order.

- `StockTickerCode`: Couples the `Code` classword (a short textual string) with the attribute part: `Ticker` and the role `Stock.` So this is a short textual string representing a stock ticker. Note that each part of the name need not be a single word; it is just important that the name flows in a way that feels the same to every user of your database.

- `EndDate`: The `Date` classword says that this will not include a time part, and the attribute is the ending date for the row.

- `SaveTime`: Much like the previous attribute, only now it is a time, which will be treated as a point in time.

Almost all the names used throughout the book will be in this format, unless I am explicitly attempting to demonstrate alternative naming. One of the most important parts of your database design is going to be consistent naming to assist users in understanding what you have built.

Next, we will go over the following aspects of attributes on your data model:

- Primary keys
- Alternate keys
- Foreign keys
- Domains
- Attribute naming

Primary Keys

An IDEF1X entity must have a primary key. This is convenient for us, because an entity is defined such that each instance must be unique (see Chapter 1). The primary key may be a single attribute, or it may be a composite of multiple attributes. A value is required for every attribute in the key (logically speaking, in the implementation, this means that no NULLs are allowed for column values for primary key columns).

The primary key is denoted by placing attributes above a horizontal line through the entity rectangle, as shown next:

PrimaryKeyExample

```
┌─────────────────────────┐
│ PrimaryKey              │
│ ─────────────────────   │
│ Attribute1              │
│ Attribute2              │
└─────────────────────────┘
```

Note that no additional notation is required to indicate that the value is the primary key, though sometimes you will see a key symbol or the letters PK on the diagram or even a tiny key glyph. As an example, consider the Employee entity from the previous section. The EmployeeNumber attribute is unique, and logically, every employee would have one, so this would be an acceptable primary key:

Employee

```
┌─────────────────────────┐
│ EmployeeNumber          │
│ ─────────────────────   │
│ FirstName               │
│ LastName                │
│ Address                 │
│ PhoneNumber             │
└─────────────────────────┘
```

The choice of primary key is an interesting one. In the early logical modeling phase, I generally do not like to spend time choosing the final primary key attribute(s) because it can easily change based on later findings. I tend to create a simple surrogate primary key to migrate to other entities to help me see when there is any ownership. In the current example, EmployeeNumber clearly refers to an employee, but not every entity will be so clear—not to mention that more advanced business rules may dictate that EmployeeNumber is not always unique or not always known. For example, the company also may have contractors in the table that have the same EmployeeNumber value, thus requiring EmployeeType as part of the key or some form of smart key that has an indicator of the person being a contractor or regular employee in the EmployeeNumber attribute value. That's not a good practice perhaps, but no matter how much I try to describe perfect databases in this book, the business world is full of weird, archaic, messy practices that you will have to incorporate into your models. Having to go back repeatedly and change the attribute used for the primary key in the logical model can be tiresome, particularly when you have a very large model with a lot of relationships.

It is also quite likely that you may have multiple column sets that uniquely identify a given instance of many of your entities. As an example, consider an entity that models a product manufactured by a company. The company may identify the product by the type, style, size, and series:

Product

```
┌─────────────────────────┐
│ Type                    │
│ Style                   │
│ Size                    │
│ Series                  │
│ ─────────────────────── │
│ ProductName             │
└─────────────────────────┘
```

The name may also be a good key, and more than likely, there is also a product code. Which attribute is the best key—or which is even truly a key—may not become completely apparent until later in the process. There are many ways to implement a good key, and the best way may not be recognizable right away.

Instead of choosing a primary key at this point, I add a value to the entity for identification purposes and then model all candidate keys as alternate keys (which I will discuss in the next section). As a result, the logical model clearly shows what entities are in an ownership role to other entities, since the key that is migrated contains the name of the modeled entity. I would model this entity as follows:

Product

```
┌─────────────────────────┐
│ ProductId               │
│ ─────────────────────── │
│ Type                    │
│ Style                   │
│ Size                    │
│ Series                  │
│ Name                    │
└─────────────────────────┘
```

Note   Using surrogate keys is certainly not a requirement in logical modeling; it is a personal preference that I have found a useful documentation method to keep models clean, and it corresponds to my method of implementation later. Not only is using a natural key as the primary key in the logical modeling phase reasonable but many architects find it preferable. Either method is perfectly acceptable (and just as likely to start a philosophical debate at a table of data modelers—you have been warned, so start the debate after the dessert course).

Alternate Keys

As defined in Chapter 1, an alternate key is a grouping of one or more attributes whose uniqueness needs to be guaranteed over all the instances of the entity. Alternate keys do not have specific locations in the entity graphics like primary keys, nor are they typically migrated for any relationship (you can reference an alternate key with a foreign key based on the SQL standards and in SQL Server, but this feature is seldom used, and when used, it often really confuses even the best DBAs). They are identified in the model in a very simple manner:

```
AlternateKeyExample
┌─────────────────────────────────┐
│ PrimaryKey                       │
├─────────────────────────────────┤
│ AlternateKey1             AK1    │
│ AlternateKey2Attribute1   AK2    │
│ AlternateKey2Attribute2   AK2    │
└─────────────────────────────────┘
```

In this example, there are two alternate *key groups*: group AK1, which has one attribute as a member, and group AK2, which has two attributes. There also is nothing wrong with overlapping alternate keys, which could be denoted as (AK1,AK2). Thinking back to the product example, the two keys could then be modeled as follows:

```
Product
┌─────────────────────────────┐
│ ProductId                   │
│ ─────────────────────────── │
│ Type              AK1       │
│ Style             AK1       │
│ Size              AK1       │
│ Series            AK1       │
│ Name              AK2       │
└─────────────────────────────┘
```

One extension that some data modeling tools may add to this notation is shown here:

```
AlternateKeyExample
┌─────────────────────────────────────────┐
│ PrimaryKey                              │
│ ─────────────────────────────────────── │
│ AlternateKey1              AK1.1        │
│ AlternateKey2Attribute1    AK2.1        │
│ AlternateKey2Attribute2    AK2.2        │
└─────────────────────────────────────────┘
```

A position number notation is tacked onto the name of each key (AK1 and AK2) to denote the position of the attribute in the key. In the logical model, technically, the order of attributes in the key should not be considered even if the tool does display them (unique is unique, regardless of key column order). Which attribute comes first in the key really does not matter; all that matters is that you make sure there are unique values across multiple attributes. When a key is implemented in the database, the order of columns *will almost certainly* become interesting for performance reasons, but uniqueness will be served no matter what the order of the columns of the key is.

Note   Primary and unique keys are implemented with indexes in SQL Server, but the discussion of index utilization for performance reasons is left to Chapter 11. Do your best to reasonably ignore performance tuning needs during the conceptual and logical design phases. Defer most performance tuning issues until you are coding and have enough data to really see what indexes are needed.

Foreign Keys

Foreign key attributes, as mentioned, are also referred to as migrated attributes. They are primary keys from one entity that serve as references to an instance in another entity. They are, again, a result of relationships (we'll look at their graphical representation later in this chapter). They are indicated, much like alternate keys, by adding the letters "FK" after the foreign key:

```
ForeignKeyExample

┌─────────────────────────┐
│ PrimaryKey              │
├─────────────────────────┤
│ ForeignKey      FK      │
└─────────────────────────┘
```

As an example of a table with foreign keys, consider an entity that is modeling a music album:

```
Album

┌──────────────────────────┐
│ AlbumId                  │
├──────────────────────────┤
│ Name           AK1       │
│ ArtistId       FK AK1    │
│ PublisherId    FK AK1    │
│ CatalogNumber  AK2       │
└──────────────────────────┘
```

The `ArtistId` and `PublisherId` represent migrated foreign keys from the `Artist` and `Publisher` entities. We'll revisit this example in the "Relationships" section later in this chapter.

One tricky thing about foreign keys is that diagrams don't generally show what entity the key is migrated from. This can tend to make things a little hard to follow, depending on how you choose and name your primary keys (and, as we will look at later, how you *role-name* your keys). This lack of clarity about what table a foreign key migrates from is a limitation of most modeling methodologies, because displaying the name of the entity where the key came from would be unnecessarily confusing for a couple of reasons:

- There is no limit (nor should there be) on how far a key will migrate from its original owner entity (the entity where the key value was not a migrated foreign key reference).

- It is not completely unreasonable that the same attribute might migrate from two separate entities with the same name, especially early in the logical design process. This is certainly not a best practice at all, but it is possible and can make for interesting situations.

As you can see, one of the reasons for the primary key scheme I will employ in logical models is to add a key named `<EntityName>Id` as the identifier for entities, so the name of the entity is easily identifiable and lets us easily know where the original source of the attribute is. Also, we can see the attribute migrated from entity to entity even without any additional documentation. For example, in the `Album` entity example, we instinctively know that the `ArtistId` attribute is a foreign key and most likely was migrated from the `Artist` entity just because of the name alone.

Domains

In Chapter 1, the term "domain" referred to a set of valid values for an attribute. In IDEF1X, you can formalize domains and define named, reusable specifications known as domains, for example:

- `String`: A character string

- `SocialSecurityNumber`: A character value with a format of `###-##-####`

- `PositiveInteger`: An integer value with an implied domain of `0-MAX(integer value)`

- `TextualFlag`: A five-character value with a domain of `('FALSE','TRUE')`

Domains in the specification not only allow us to define the valid values that can be stored by an attribute based on the domain but also can provide a form of inheritance in the datatype definitions. *Subclasses* can be defined of the domains that inherit the settings from the base domain. It is a good practice to build domains for any attributes that get used regularly, as well as domains that are base templates for infrequently used attributes. For example, you might have a character-type domain where you specify a basic length, like 60. Then, you may specify common domains, like name and description, to use in many entities. For these, you should choose a reasonable length for the values, plus you could include a requirement that the data in the column cannot be just space characters, to prevent a user from having one, two, or three spaces each looking like different values—except in the rare cases where that is desirable.

Note   In SQL Server, one space character (' ') in many situations is equivalent to multiple space characters, such as ('   ').

Regardless of whether you are using an automated tool for modeling or just a simple spreadsheet, try to define common domains that you use for specific types of things. For example, a person's first name might be a domain where you define at a corporate level that every column that stores a person's first name will allow up to 100 characters. This is cool because you don't have to answer more than once questions such as "Hmm, how long to make a person's name?" or "What is the format of our part numbers?" After you decide, you just use what you have used before.

If it sounds unreasonable that you might argue about a datatype length, it is likely that you don't get out much. Good programmers argue all the time about the details, so if you establish a standard after the first argument, you only have to have that argument once (until you hire a new employee, at least). Note too that almost everything you want to store data on has been done before, so look to standards documents on the Web. For example, how long might a dialable phone number column be? The answer is 15 characters based on ITU-T E.164 (`searchnetworking.techtarget.com/definition/E164`). So making it 100 characters "just in case one day it is 6.66 times longer than the current standard" is not only silly, but it is bad for data integrity.

Note   Defining common domains during design fights against another major terrible practice, the `string(2000)` syndrome (or similar string length), where every column in a database stores textual data in columns of exactly the same length. Putting in some early thought on the minimum and maximum lengths of data is easier than doing it when the project manager is screaming for results later in the process and the programmers are champing at the bit to get at your database and get coding. It is also one of the first steps in producing databases with data integrity.

Early in the modeling process, you'll commonly want to gather a few bits of information, such as the general type of the attribute: character, numeric, logical, or even binary data. Determining minimum and maximum lengths may or may not be possible, but the more information you can gather without crushing the process, the better. Another good thing to start is documenting the legal values for an attribute that is classified as being of the domain type. This is generally done using some pseudocode or in a textual manner, either in your modeling tool or even in a spreadsheet.

It is rather important to keep these domains as implementation independent as possible. For example, you might specify a domain of GloballyUniqueIdentifier, a value that will be unique no matter where it is generated. In SQL Server, a unique identifier could be used (GUID value) to implement this domain. Or you might use a SEQUENCE object that every user has to call to get a value from when needing a new value. In another database system (created by a company other than Microsoft, perhaps) where there is not exactly the same mechanism, it might be implemented differently; the point is that this value is statistically guaranteed to be unique every time it is generated. The conceptual/logical modeling phase should be done without too much thinking about what SQL Server can do, if for no other reason than to prevent you from starting to impose limitations on the future solution prior to understanding the actual problem. Another sort of domain might be a set of legal values, like if the business users had defined three customer types, you could specify the legal string values that could be used.

When you start the physical modeling of the physical relational structures, you will use the same domains to assign the implementation properties. This is the real value in using domains. By creating reusable template attributes that will also be used when you start creating columns, you'll spend less effort and time building simple entities, which makes up a lot of your work. Doing so also provides a way for you to enforce companywide standards, by reusing the same domains on all corporate models (predicated, of course, on your being diligent with your data modeling processes over time, something that is a lot more difficult than it initially sounds).

Later when you start designing the actual tables, implementation details such as exact datatypes, constraints, and so forth will be chosen, just to name a few of the more basic properties that may be inherited (and if Microsoft adds a more suitable datatype for a situation in the future, you can simply—at least from the model's standpoint—change all of the columns with that domain type to the new type). Since it is very likely that you will have fewer domains than implemented attributes, the double benefit of speedy and consistent model assembly is achieved. However, it is probably not overly reasonable or even useful to employ the inheritance mechanisms when building tables by hand. Implementation of a flat domain structure is enough work without a tool.

As an example of a domain hierarchy, consider this set of character string domains:

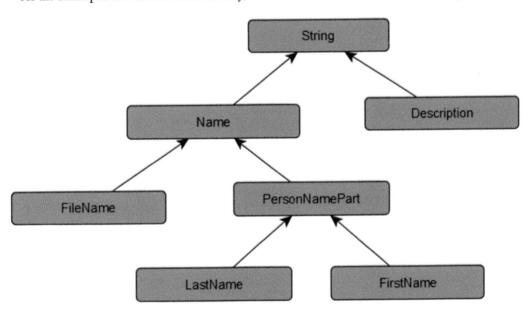

Here, String is the base domain from which you can then inherit Name and Description. String indicates that it is a typical character type, most likely a Unicode type; then the Name and Description domains have specific size, definition, and so on set. FileName and PersonNamePart are inherited from Name and FirstName and LastName from PersonNamePart. During logical modeling, this might seem like a lot of work for nothing, because most of these domains will share only a few basic details, such as not allowing NULL values or blank data. FileName may be optional, whereas LastName might be mandatory by default. FileName probably also starts to have rules like not allowing things like * in the value, all things that you need every time you have to store the name of a file.

Things get good when you need to change all of your datatypes for all string types, for example, if you decide to finally make that blanket change from ANSI character sets to Unicode or to implement encryption on all personal notes–type attributes but not name ones.

During logical modeling, domains might optionally be shown to the right of the attribute names in the entity (which is where you will eventually see the SQL Server datatype as well):

DomainExample

AttributeName	DomainName
AttributeName2	DomainName2

So, if I have an entity that holds domain values for describing a type of person, I might model it as follows:

Person

PersonId	SurrogateKey
Description	Description
Firstname	FirstName
LastName	LastName

To model this example, I defined four domains:

1. SurrogateKey: The surrogate key value (Implementation of the surrogate should not be implied by building a domain, so later, this can be implemented in any manner.)

2. Description: Holds the description of "something" (can be 60 characters maximum, cannot be blank or NULL)

3. FirstName: A person's first name (100 characters maximum, allows NULL values)

4. LastName: A person's last name (100 characters maximum, cannot be blank or NULL)

The choice of the length of name is an interesting one. I searched on Bing for "person first name varchar" and found lots of different possibilities: 10, 35, unlimited, 25, 20, and 15—all on the first page of the search! Just as you should use a consistent naming standard, you should use standard lengths every time that like data is represented, so when you hit implementation, the likelihood that two columns storing like data will have different definitions is minimized.

During the implementation phase, all the domains will get mapped to some form of datatype, check constraint, and so on in SQL Server. However, the future implementation isn't quite the point at this point of the process. The point of a domain in the logical model is to define common types of storage patterns that can be applied in a common manner, including all of the business rules that will govern their usage.

If you follow the naming standard I discussed earlier made up of Role name + Attribute + Classword + Scale, you may find that your domains often share a lot of similarity with that hierarchy. Name is a classword, and Name is in our domain list. FirstName is an attribute and classword that also ends up as a domain. Domains, however, as you get more and more specific in the deeper parts of the tree, will often include things like size. Name30Characters, Name60Characters, and so on may not be good classwords, but they can be perfectly acceptable domains with the size indicated in the name. This gives some clarity for cases where you just want a class of name attributes that are 30 characters, with others that are 60, and don't need to make one domain per specific attribute. Domains are there for your sake, to make things easier for you, so do what makes more sense.

Relationships

Up to this point, the visual constructs we have looked at have been pretty much the same across most visual data modeling languages. Entities are almost always signified by rectangles, and attributes are quite often words within the rectangles. Relationships are where things start to diverge greatly, as many of the different modeling languages approach representing relationships graphically a bit differently. To make the concept of relationships clear, I need to go back to the terms "parent" and "child." Consider the following definitions from the IDEF1X specification's glossary (as these are remarkably lucid definitions to have been taken straight from a government specification!):

- *Entity, Child*: The entity in a specific connection relationship whose instances can be related to zero or one instance of the other entity (parent entity)

- *Entity, Parent*: An entity in a specific connection relationship whose instances can be related to a number of instances of another entity (child entity)

- *Relationship*: An association between two entities or between instances of the same entity

In IDEF1X, every relationship is denoted by a line drawn between two entities, with a solid circle at one end of that line to indicate where the primary key attribute is migrated to as a foreign key. In the following image, the primary key of the parent will be migrated to the child.

Relationships come in several different flavors that indicate *how* the parent table is related to the child. We will look at examples of several different relationship concepts in this section:

- *Identifying:* Where the primary key of one table is migrated to the primary key of another. The child will be a dependent entity.

- *Nonidentifying:* Where the primary key of one table is migrated to the non–primary key attributes of another. The child will be an independent entity as long as no identifying relationships exist.

- *Optional nonidentifying:* When the nonidentifying relationship does not require a parent value.

- *Recursive relationships:* When a table is related to itself.

- *Subtype* or *categorization:* Which is a one-to-one relationship used to let one entity extend another.

- *Many-to-many:* Where an instance of an entity can be related to many in another and, in turn, many instances of the second entity can be related to multiples in the other.

We'll also cover the *cardinality* of the relationship (how many of the parent rows can relate to how many rows of the child table), *role names* (changing the name of a key in a relationship), and *verb phrases* (the name of the relationship). Relationships are a key topic in a database design diagram and not a completely simple one. A lot of information is related using a few dots, dashes, diamonds, and lines. Often it will help to look at the metadata that is represented in the graphical display to make sure it is clear (particularly if looking at a foreign modeling language!).

Note   Most of the relationships discussed in this section (except many-to-many) are of the one-to-many variety, which encompasses one-to-zero, one-to-one, one-to-many, or perhaps one–to–exactly *N* relationships. Technically, it is more accurately one–to–(from M to N), as this enables specification of the many in very precise (or very loose) terms as the situation dictates. However, the more common term is "one-to-many," and I will not try to make an already confusing term more so.

Identifying Relationships

The concept of a relationship being *identifying* is used to indicate containership that the essence (defined as the intrinsic or indispensable properties that serve to characterize or identify something) of the child instance is defined by the existence of a parent. Another way to look at this is that generally the child in an identifying relationship is an inseparable part of the parent. Without the existence of the parent, the child would make no sense.

The relationship is drawn as follows:

To implement this relationship in the model, the primary key attribute(s) is migrated to the primary key of the child. Hence, the key of a parent instance is needed to be able to identify a child instance record, which is why the name "identifying relationship" is used. In the following example, you can see that the `ParentId` attribute is a foreign key in the `Child` entity, from the `Parent` entity:

The child entity in the relationship is drawn as a rounded-off rectangle, which, as mentioned earlier in this chapter, means it is a dependent entity. A common example is an invoice and the line items being charged to the customer on the invoice:

It can also be said that the line items are part of the parent, much like in an object where you might have a property that is an array, but since all values are stored as atomic, independent units in SQL as columns or as tables, we end up with more tables instead of embedded arrays.

Nonidentifying Relationships

The *nonidentifying relationship* indicates that the parent represents a more informational attribute of the child. When implementing the nonidentifying relationship, the primary key attribute is migrated as a non–primary key attribute of the child. It is denoted by a dashed line between the entities. Note too that the rectangle representing the Child now has squared-off corners, since it stands alone, rather than being dependent on the `Parent`:

Now you can see that the attribute `ParentId` is migrated to the non-key attributes:

Taking again the example of an invoice, consider the vendor of the products that have been sold and documented as such in the line items. The product vendor does not define the existence of a line item, because with or without specifying the exact vendor the product originates from, the line item still makes sense.

The difference between identifying and nonidentifying relationships can sometimes be tricky but is essential to understanding the relationship between tables and their keys. If the parent entity defines the need for the existence of the child (as stated in the previous section), then use an identifying relationship. If, on the other hand, the relationship defines one of the child's attributes, use a nonidentifying relationship.

Here are some examples:

- *Identifying*: You have an entity that stores a contact and another that stores the contact's telephone number. The `Contact` entity identifies the phone number, and without the contact, there would be no need for a `ContactPhoneNumber` instance.

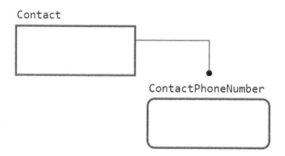

- *Nonidentifying*: Consider the entities that were defined for the identifying relationship, along with an additional entity called ContactPhoneNumberType. This entity is related to the ContactPhoneNumber entity, but in a nonidentifying way, and defines a set of possible phone number types (Voice, Fax, etc.) that a ContactPhoneNumber might be. The type of phone number does not identify the phone number; it simply classifies it. Even if the type didn't exist, recording the phone number would still be interesting, as the number still may have informational merit. However, a row associating a contact with a phone number would be useless information without the contact's existence.

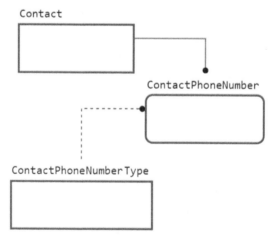

The ContactPhoneNumberType entity is commonly known as a *domain entity* or *domain table*, as it serves to implement an attribute's domain. Rather than having a fixed domain for an attribute, an entity is designed that allows programmatic changes to the domain with no recoding of constraints or client code. As a bonus, you can add columns to define, describe, and extend the domain values to implement business rules. It also allows the client user to build lists for users to choose values with very little programming. In logical modeling, often something like `ContactPhoneNumberType` may have been simply an attribute of `ContactPhoneNumber`, but later changed to a table in physical modeling.

While every nonidentifying relationship defines the domain of an attribute of the child table, sometimes when the row is created, the values don't need to be selected. For example, consider a database where you model houses, like for a neighborhood. Every house would have a color, a style, and so forth. However, not every house would have an alarm company, a mortgage holder, and so on. The relationship between the alarm company and bank would be optional in this case, while the color and style relationships could be mandatory. The difference in the implemented table will be whether or not the child table's foreign key columns will allow NULL values. If a value is required, then it is considered *mandatory*. If a value of the migrated key can be NULL, then it is considered *optional*.

The optional case is signified by an open diamond at the opposite end of the dashed line from the black circle, as shown here:

In the mandatory case, the relationship is drawn as before, without the diamond. Note that in an optional relationship, the cardinality may be zero or greater, but a mandatory relationship must have a cardinality of one or greater (as defined in Chapter 1, *cardinality* refers to the number of values that can be related to another value, and the concept will be discussed further in the next section as well).

Note   You might be wondering why there is not an optional identifying relationship. This is because you may not have any optional attributes in a primary key, which is true in relational theory and SQL Server as well.

For a one-to-many, optional relationship, consider the following:

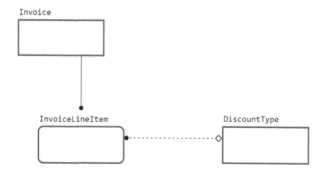

The InvoiceLineItem entity is where items are placed onto an invoice to receive payment. The user may sometimes apply a standard discount amount to the line item. The relationship, then, from the InvoiceLineItem to the DiscountType entity is an optional one, as no discount may have been applied to the line item.

For most optional relationships like this, there is another possible solution, which can be modeled as required, and in the implementation, a row can be added to the DiscountType table that indicates "none" or "unknown." An example of such a mandatory relationship could be genre to movie in a movie rental system database (even if the movies being rented are digital!):

The relationship is Genre <Classifies> Movie, where the Genre entity represents the "one" and Movie represents the "many" in the one-to-many relationship. Every movie being rented must have a genre, so that it can be organized in the inventory and then placed on the appropriate rental shelf. If the movie is new, but the genre isn't yet known, a row in the genre object with a genre of "New" or "Unknown" could be used.

Whether or not to use an optional relationship, or to manufacture a row that means the lack of a value, is discussed quite frequently. Generally, it is frowned upon in nonreporting databases to come up with a value that means "There is not a real related value" because it can cause confusion. Users who are writing a query and listing customer activity, for example, and end up seeing sales to a "Missing Customer" might not be sure if that is the name of a funky new restaurant or a manufactured row. In reporting, you generally are just looking at groupings, so it is less of an issue and you will design some way to make the row sort to the top or the bottom of the list.

Role Names

A *role name* is a more specific purpose name you can give an attribute when it is used as a foreign key. The purpose of a role name is to clarify the usage of a migrated key, because either the parent entity is generic and a more specific name is needed or the same entity has multiple relationships to the same entity. As attribute names must be unique, assigning different names for the child foreign key references is often necessary. Consider these tables:

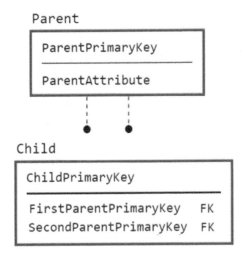

In this diagram, the `Parent` and `Child` entities share two relationships, and the migrated attributes have been role-named as `FirstParentPrimaryKey` and `SecondParentPrimaryKey`. In diagrams, you can indicate the original name of the migrated attribute after the role name, separated by a period (`.`), as follows (but usually it takes up too much space on the model):

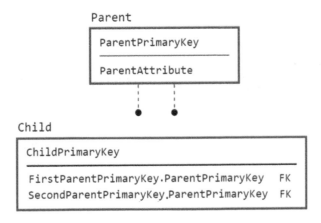

As an example, say you have a User entity and you want to store the name or ID of the user who created a DatabaseObject entity instance as well as the user that the DatabaseObject instance was created for. It would then end up as follows:

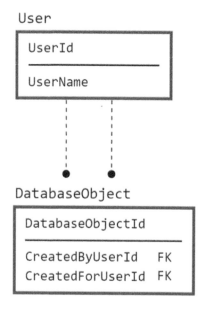

Note that there are two relationships to the DatabaseObject entity from the User entity. Due to the way the lines are drawn on a diagram, it is not clear from the diagram which foreign key goes to which relationship. Once you name the relationship (with a verb phrase, which will be covered later in this chapter), the key's relationships will be easier to determine, but often, determining which line indicates which child attribute is simply trial and error.

Relationship Cardinality

The *cardinality* of the relationship is the number of child instances that can be inserted for each parent instance of that relationship. A lot of people slough off this topic in requirements and design because it can be difficult to implement. However, our initial goal is to represent the requirements in our data models and leave discussion of data constraint implementation to later (we will start discussing implementation in Chapter 6 when we implement our first database and discuss it even more in Chapter 7, the data protection chapter, and throughout the latter half of the book). And the fact is if it is important to the customer that there should be no more than two child rows in a relationship, there should be no more than two child rows in a relationship.

Figures 3-1 through 3-6 show the six possible cardinalities that relationships can take. The cardinality indicators are applicable to either mandatory or optional relationships.

Figure 3-1. *One-to-zero or more—a parent row can but does not have to have one or more rows in Child. For child rows to exist, a corresponding parent row must exist*

Figure 3-2. *One-to-one or more (at least one), indicated by P—for a row to exist in Parent, at least one row must exist in Child and vice versa*

Figure 3-3. *One-to-zero or one (no more than one), indicated by Z—a parent row can have one or zero row in Child, but no more. For child rows to exist, a corresponding parent row must exist*

Figure 3-4. *One-to-some fixed range (in this case, between four and eight inclusive)—for a row to exist in Parent, between four and eight rows must exist in Child*

Figure 3-5. *One–to–exactly N (in this case, five, meaning each parent must have five children)—for a row to exist in Parent, exactly five rows must exist in Child*

Figure 3-6. *Specialized note describing the cardinality*

For example, a possible use for the one–to–one or more (see Figure 3-2) might be to represent the relationship between a guardian and a student in a high school:

This is a good example of a zero-or-one-to-one-or-more relationship, and an interesting one at that. It says that for a Guardian instance to exist, a related Student instance must exist, but a student need not have a guardian for us to wish to store the student's data, because the Guardian to Student relationship is optional.

Next, let's consider the case of a club that has members with certain positions that they should or could fill, as shown in Figures 3-7 through 3-9.

Figure 3-7. *One-to-many allows unlimited positions for the member*

Figure 3-8. *One-to-one allows only one position per member*

Figure 3-9. *A one-to-zero, one-to-one, or one-to-two relationship specifies a max limit of two positions per member*

Figure 3-7 shows that a member can take as many positions as are possible. Figure 3-8 shows that a member can serve in no position or one position, but no more. Finally, Figure 3-9 shows that a member can serve in zero, one, or two positions. They all look very similar, but the Z or 0–2 is important in signifying the cardinality.

Note   It is not an overly common occurrence that I have needed anything other than the basic one-to-many or one–to–zero or one relationship type, but your experience may lend itself to the specialized relationship cardinalities.

Recursive Relationships

One of the more difficult—and often important—relationship types to implement is the *recursive relationship*, also known as a *self-join, hierarchical, self-referencing,* or *self-relationship* (I have even heard them referred to as *fish hook relationships*, but that name always seems overly silly). It is used to model some form of hierarchy, where one row is related to one and only one parent. The "recursive" part of the name references the most common method of traversing the structure. In Chapter 9, we will look in more depth at hierarchies, looking at algorithms to manage using recursive relationships and some that do not.

The recursive relationship is modeled by drawing a nonidentifying relationship not to a different entity, but to the same entity. The migrated key of the relationship is given a role name. (In many cases, a naming convention of role-naming the attribute as "parent" or "referenced" is useful if no natural naming is available.)

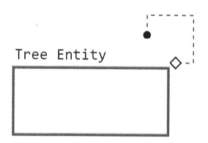

The recursive relationship is useful for creating tree structures, as in the following organizational chart:

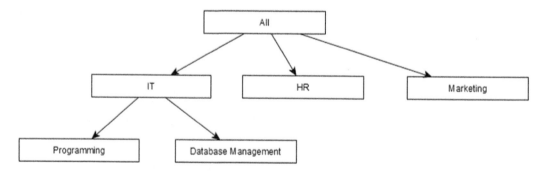

To explain this concept fully, I will show the data that would be stored to implement this hierarchy:

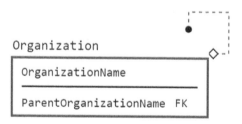

Here is the sample data for this table:

OrganizationName	ParentOrganizationName
ALL	
IT	ALL
HR	ALL
Marketing	ALL
Programming	IT
Database Management	IT

The organizational chart can now be traversed by starting at ALL and getting the children of ALL, for example, IT. Then, you get the children of those values, like for IT, one of the values is Programming.

As a final example, consider the case of a Person entity. If you wanted to associate a person with a single other person as the first person's current spouse, you might design the following:

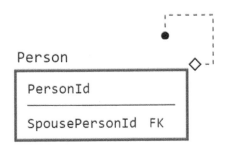

Notice that this is a one–to–zero or one relationship, since (in most places) a person may have no more than a single spouse but need not have one. If you require one person to be related as a child to two parents, another table entity is required to link two people together. Note that I said "current" spouse earlier in the section. If you need to know history of changes in the hierarchy, you will need some of the more complex versions of modeling hierarchies or temporal objects that we will look at in Chapter 9 when we discuss various modeling patterns and techniques for hierarchies. In this chapter, it is strictly important that you can grasp what the hierarchical relationship looks like on a data model.

Subtypes

Subtypes (also referred to as *categorization relationships*) are a special type of one-to-zero or one relationship used to indicate whether one entity is a specific type of a generic entity. It is similar to the concept of inheritance in object-oriented programming (if a lot clunkier to work with). Note in the following diagram that there are no black dots at either end of the lines; the specific entities are drawn with rounded corners, signifying that they are, indeed, dependent on the generic entity.

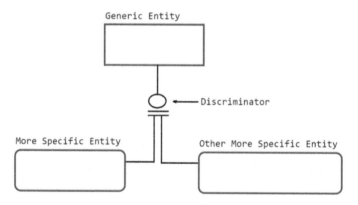

There are three distinct parts of the subtype relationship:

- *Generic entity*: This entity contains all the attributes common to all of the subtyped entities.

- *Discriminator*: This attribute acts as a switch to determine the entity where the additional, more specific information is stored.

- *Specific entity*: This is the place where the specific information is stored, based on the discriminator.

For example, consider an inventory of your home video library. If you wanted to store information about each of the videos that you owned, regardless of format, you might build a categorization relationship like the following:

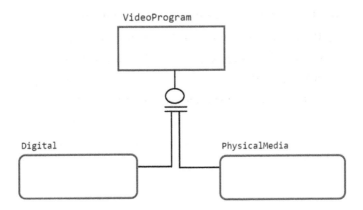

In this manner, you might represent each video's price, title, actors, length, and possibly description of the content in the VideoProgram entity, and then, based on format—which is the discriminator—you might store the information that is specific to Digital or PhysicalMedia in its own separate entity (e.g., physical location, special features, format [Blu-ray, DVD, associated digital copy] for physical-based video, and for digital, it might be the directory location of the files or services where you own them; it could also require another subtype relationship of Digital to implement DigitalLocal and DigitalStreamingService).

There are two distinct category types: complete and incomplete. The *complete* set of categories is modeled with a double line on the discriminator, and the *incomplete* set is modeled with a single line (see Figure 3-10).

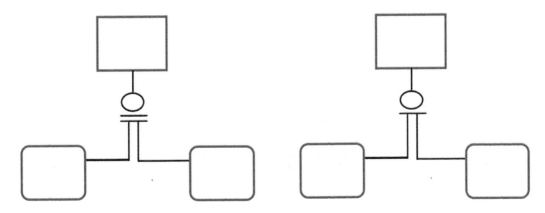

Figure 3-10. *Complete (left) and incomplete (right) sets of categories*

The primary difference between the complete and incomplete categories is that in the complete categorization relationship, each generic instance must have one specific instance, whereas in the incomplete case, this is not necessarily true. An instance of the generic entity can be associated with an instance of only one of the category entities, and each instance of a category entity is associated with exactly one instance of the generic entity. In other words, overlapping subentities are not allowed.

For example, you might have a complete set of categories like this:

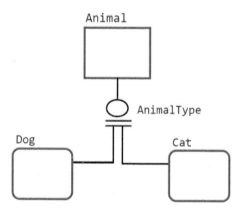

This relationship indicates that "An Animal *must* be either a Dog or a Cat." Clearly true only in the context of the requirements for this company, naturally. However, what it doesn't show us is, first, do we have to know that the animal type is known? There may be no rows in Dog or Cat at all, and animal type may be NULL.

However, what if this were modeled as an incomplete set of categories:

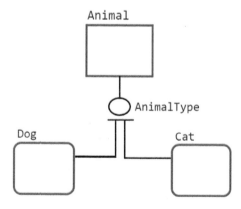

Now in our database, we may have values for AnimalType of 'Dog', 'Cat', 'Fish', 'Lizard', and so on, but we only have specific information recorded for 'Dog' and 'Cat' in their specific entities.

Additionally, a concept that is mentioned occasionally is whether a subclass is *exclusive* or not exclusive. For the animal, Animal can clearly only be a Dog, Cat, and so on, not both. But consider a common subclass of Person to Customer, Employee, and Manager. A person can be a manager, who is also an employee, and it may be advantageous to track their customer relationship in the same database from the subclass structure. This would not be an exclusive subtype.

Note   Not all tools will support subtypes, and implementing an enforced exclusive subtype is complex. The most important thing to realize when modeling is that you want to document what the data *should* be, not how it can be implemented. That is a task for another day, and making sure it is enforced is a job for coders (and perhaps more importantly testers).

Many-to-Many Relationships

The many-to-many relationship is also known as the *nonspecific relationship*, which is actually a better name, but far less well known. Having lots of many-to-many relationships in the data model is common, though they will look different as you progress further along in the process beyond early conceptual models. These relationships are modeled by a line with a solid black dot on both ends:

There is one real problem with modeling a many-to-many relationship, even in the logical model: it is often necessary to have more information about the relationship than that simply many EntityX instances are connected to many EntityY instances. For example, why are they connected, when were they connected, and, perhaps, by whom were they connected? So the relationship is usually modeled as follows very soon after its discovery:

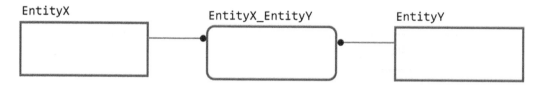

Here, the intermediate EntityX_EntityY entity is known as an *associative entity* (names like *bridge*, *tweener*, and *joiner* are not uncommon either, though I really find the tweener name very strange; I will commonly use the name *many-to-many junction table* also). In early modeling, I will often stick with the former representation when I haven't identified any extended attributes to describe the relationship and the latter representation when I need to add additional information to the model. To clarify the concept, let's look at the following example:

Here, I have set up a relationship where many customers are related to many products. This situation is common because in most cases, companies don't create specific products for specific customers; rather, any customer can purchase any of the company's products or certainly a subset of products that are also orderable by other customers. At this point in the modeling, it is likely reasonable to use the many-to-many representation.

I am generalizing the customer-to-product relationship. It is not uncommon to have a company build specific products for only one customer to purchase, making for a more interesting modeling requirement. Consider then the case where the Customer need only be related to a Product for a certain period of time, so now we have information about the relationship and need a place to put it. To implement this, you can use the following representation (Note that this implementation does not allow you to start and stop the relationship. That would require the time to be a part of the key.):

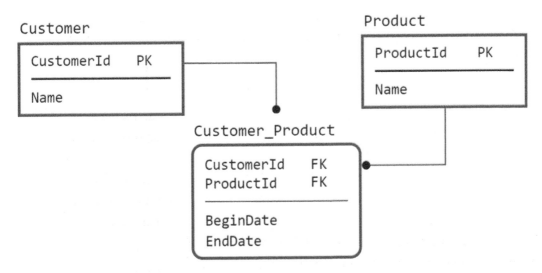

In fact, almost all of the many-to-many relationships tend to require some additional information like this to make them complete. It is not uncommon to have no many-to-many relationships modeled with the black circle on both ends in anything other than a simple conceptual model, so you will need to look for entities modeled like this to be able to discern them.

In Chapter 9, we will be introducing the concept of graph structures, and graph structures will be essentially system-managed many-to-many tables that implement connections between two tables (each table will be referred to as a *node*, and the associative entity will be known as an *edge*).

Note   You can't implement a many-to-many relationship without using an associative table for the resolution because there is no realistic way to migrate keys both ways.

Verb Phrases (Relationship Names)

In order to provide documentation for why a relationship is made between two entities, relationships are given names, called *verb phrases*. They are used to make the relationship between parent and child entities a readable sentence incorporating the entity names and the relationship cardinality. The name is usually expressed from parent to child, but it can be expressed in the other direction or even in both directions. The verb phrase is typically located on the graphical model somewhere close to the line that forms the relationship:

The relationship should be named such that it fits into the following general structure for reading the entire relationship: parent cardinality ➤ parent entity name ➤ relationship name ➤ child cardinality ➤ child entity name.

For example, consider the following relationship:

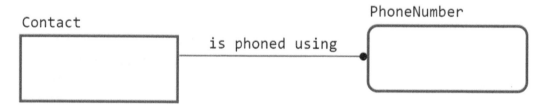

It would be read as "one Contact is phoned using zero, one, or more PhoneNumbers." Of course, the sentence may or may not make 100% perfect sense in normal conversational language; for example, this one brings up the question of how a contact is phoned using zero phone numbers. If presenting this phrase to a nontechnical person, it would make more sense to read it as follows: "Each contact can have either no phone number or one or more phone numbers" or perhaps "If the contact has a phone number, the contact can be phoned with one or more phone numbers." You don't want to simply use "have" for all verb phrases, as the goal of the verb phrase is to capture the essence of how the data will be used and provide documentation that doesn't need editing to be semantically understandable (even if not tremendously impressive prose).

Being able to read the relationship helps you to notice obvious problems. For instance, consider the following relationship:

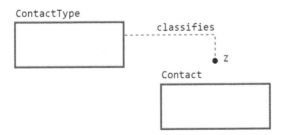

It looks fine at first glance, but when read as "one ContactType classifies zero or one Contact," it doesn't make logical sense (since Contact requires a ContactType, you would need the same number of or more rows in a ContactType table). This would be properly modeled as simply

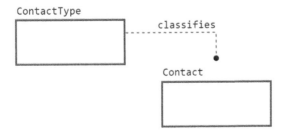

which now reads, "one ContactType classifies zero or more Contacts." Note that the type of relationship, whether it is identifying, nonidentifying, optional, or mandatory, makes no difference when reading the relationship.

You can also include a verb phrase that reads from child to parent as well as parent to child. For a one-to-many relationship, this would be of the following format: "One child instance (relationship) one parent instance."

In the case of the first example, you could have added an additional verb phrase:

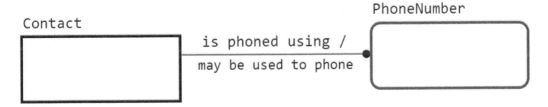

The parent-to-child relationship again is read as "one Contact is phoned using zero, one, or more PhoneNumbers." You can then read the relationship from child to parent. Note that, when reading in this direction, you are in the context of zero or one phone number to one and only one contact: "zero or one PhoneNumber may be used to phone one Contact."

Since this relationship is going from many to one, the parent in the relationship is assumed to have one related value, and since you are reading in the context of the existence of the child, you can also assume that there is zero or one child record to consider in the sentence.

Note   Taking the time to define verb phrases can be a hard sell, because they are not actually used in a substantive way in the implementation of the database, and often people consider doing work that doesn't produce code directly to be a waste of time. However, well-defined verb phrases make for great documentation, giving the reader a good idea of why the relationship exists and what it means. I usually use the verb phrase when naming the foreign key constraints too, which you will see in Chapter 7 when we create a database with foreign keys.

Descriptive Information

Take a picture of a beautiful mountain, and it will inspire thousands of words about the beauty of the trees, the plants, and the babbling brook (my ability to describe a landscape being one of the reasons I write technical books). What it *won't* tell you is how to get there yourself, what the temperature is, and whether you should bring a sweater and mittens or your swim trunks.

Data models are the same way. So far, we have only really discussed things you can see in the graphical part of the model. You can get a great start on understanding the database from the picture, as I have discussed in the previous sections of this chapter. We started the documentation process by giving good names to entities, attributes, and the relationships, but even with well-formed names, there will still likely be confusion as to what exactly an attribute is used for and how it might be used.

For this, we need to add our own thousand words (give or take) to the pictures in the model. When sharing the model, descriptions will let the eventual reader—and even a future version of yourself—know what you originally had in mind. Remember that not everyone who views the models will be on the same technical level; some will be nonrelational programmers or indeed users or (nontechnical) product managers who have no modeling experience.

Descriptive information need not be in any special format. It simply needs to be detailed, up to date, and capable of answering as many questions as can be anticipated. Each bit of descriptive information should be stored in a manner that makes it easy for users to quickly connect it to the part of the model where it was used, and it should be stored as metadata either in a modeling tool (preferably) or in some sort of document that will be easy to maintain in the future. (If documentation is not reasonably easy to use, it will be very quickly forgotten.)

You should start creating this descriptive text by asking questions such as the following:

- What is the object supposed to represent?

- How will the object be used?

- Who might use the object?

- What are the future plans for the object?

- What constraints are not specifically implied by the model?

The scope of the descriptions should not extend past the object or entities that are affected. For example, the entity description should refer only to the entity and not any related entities, relationships, or even attributes unless completely necessary. An attribute definition should only speak to the single attribute and where its values might come from. It is also a good idea to avoid a lot of examples that happen in the real world, as they may change, while the model itself may not need to change. If you need examples, make the data up (perhaps based on real data, but changed to protect the innocent).

Maintaining good descriptive information is roughly equivalent to putting decent comments in code. As the eventual database that you are modeling is usually the central part of any computer system, comments at this level are more important than at any others. For most people, being able to go back and review notes that were taken about each object and why things were implemented is invaluable, which is especially true for organizations that hire new employees and need to bring them up to speed on complex systems.

For example, say the following two entities have been modeled:

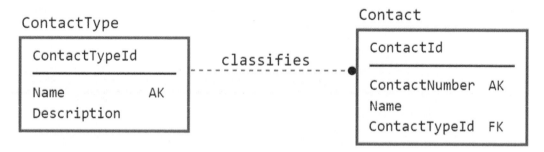

The very basic set of descriptive information in Tables 3-1 and 3-2 could be captured to describe the attributes created.

Table 3-1. *Entities and Attributes from the model*

Entity	Attribute	Description
Contact		Persons who can be contacted to do business with.
	ContactId	Surrogate key representing a Contact.
	ContactNumber	A ten-digit/numeric code assigned to the contact that will be how they identify themselves uniquely.
	Name	The full name of a contact.
	ContactTypeId	Primary key reference for a ContactType, classifies the type of contact.
ContactType		Domain of different contact types.
	ContactTypeId	Surrogate key representing a ContactType.
	Name	The name that the contact type will be uniquely known as.
	Description	The description of exactly how the contact should be used.

Table 3-2. *Relationships*

Parent Entity Name	Phrase	Child Entity Name	Definition
ContactType	Classifies	Contact	Contact-type classification

Alternative Modeling Methodologies

In this section, I will briefly describe a few of the other modeling methodologies that you will likely run into with tools you may use when looking for database information on the Web.

While the examples in this book will be done in IDEF1X, knowing about the other methodologies may be helpful when you are surfing around the Internet, looking for sample diagrams to help you design the database you are working on. (Architects are often particularly bad about not looking for existing designs, because frankly, solving the problem at hand is one of the best parts of the job even if it has already been solved 113 times before.)

I will briefly discuss the following:

- *Information Engineering (IE)*: The other main methodology, which is commonly referred to as the *Crow's Feet* method

- *Chen Entity–Relationship Model (ERD)*: The methodology used mostly by academics, though you can run into these models online

You will see a lot of similarities among them—for example, both of these alternate methodologies use a rectangle to represent a table and a line to indicate a relationship. You will also see some big differences among them, such as how the cardinality and direction of a relationship is indicated.

Note   This list is by no means exhaustive. For example, several variations loosely based on the Unified Modeling Language (UML) class modeling methodology are not listed. These types of diagrams are common, particularly with people who use the other components of UML, but these models really have no standards. Some further reading on UML data models can be found in Clare Churcher's book *Beginning Database Design* (Apress, 2007) and on Scott Ambler's Agile Data site (www.agiledata.org/essays/umlDataModelingProfile.html), among others. SSMS includes some rudimentary modeling capabilities that can show you the model of a physical database as well.

Information Engineering

The *Information Engineering (IE)* methodology is well known and widely used (it would be a tossup as to which methodology is most common, IE or IDEF1X). Like IDEF1X, it does a very good job of displaying the necessary information in a clean, compact manner that is easy to follow. The biggest difference is in how this method denotes relationship cardinalities: it uses a crow's foot looking symbol instead of a dot and lines and uses dashes instead of diamonds and some letters.

Tables in this method are denoted as rectangles, basically the same as in IDEF1X. According to the IE standard, attributes are not shown on the model, but most models show them the same as in IDEF1X—as a list, although the primary key is often denoted by underlining the attributes, rather than the position in the table. (I have seen other ways of denoting the primary key, as well as alternate/foreign keys, but they are all typically clear.) Where things get very different using IE is when dealing with relationships.

Just like in IDEF1X, IE has a set of symbols that must be understood to indicate the cardinality and ownership of the data in the relationships. By varying the basic symbols at the end of the line, you can arrive at all the various possibilities for relationships. Table 3-3 shows the different base symbols that can be employed to build relationship representations.

Table 3-3. *Base Information Engineering Relationship Symbols*

Symbol	Meaning
—+—	One row
>—	Many rows
—O—	Zero row

The symbols in Table 3-3 can be used as they are or combined to make other meaningful phrases, as shown in Table 3-4.

Table 3-4. *Common Combinations of IE Symbols*

Symbol	Meaning
$\dashv\!\!\ominus\!-$	Zero or one (optional)
$\succ\!\!\ominus\!-$	Zero to many (optional)
$\succ\!\!\!\dashv\!-$	One to many (mandatory)
$\dashv\!\!\dashv\!-$	One and only one (mandatory)

Figures 3-11 through 3-14 show some examples of relationships in IE, with explanations of what each of the cardinalities indicates.

Figure 3-11. *One–to–at least one or many: Specifically, one row in Table A must be related to one or more rows in Table B. A related row must exist in Table B for a row to exist in Table A and vice versa*

Figure 3-12. *One–to–zero, one, or many: Specifically, one row in Table A may be related to one or more rows in Table B. A value is required for a foreign key from Table A in Table B*

Figure 3-13. *One-to-zero, one, or many: Specifically, one row in Table A may be related to one or more rows in Table B. A value is optional for a foreign key from Table A in Table B*

Figure 3-14. *One-to-zero or one: Specifically, one row in Table A can be related to zero or one row in Table B. A row needn't exist in Table B for a row to exist in Table A, but the key value in Table A is not optional in Table B*

Figure 3-15. *Many-to-many relationship: The same as the many-to-many relationships I have previously covered*

IE conveys the information well and is likely to be used in some of the documents that you will come across in your work as a data architect or developer. IE is also not typically fully or strictly implemented in tools; however, usually the circles, dashes, and crow's feet of the relationships are implemented properly.

Note   You can find far more details about the Information Engineering methodology in the book *Information Engineering, Books 1, 2, and 3*, by James Martin (Prentice Hall, 1990).

Chen ERD

The Chen Entity–Relationship Model (ERD) methodology is very different from IDEF1X, but it's pretty easy to follow and largely self-explanatory. You will seldom see this methodology used in a corporate setting, as it is mainly used in the academic world, but since quite a few of these types of diagrams are on the Internet, it's good to understand the basics of the methodology. In Figure 3-16 is a very simple Chen ERD diagram showing the basic constructs.

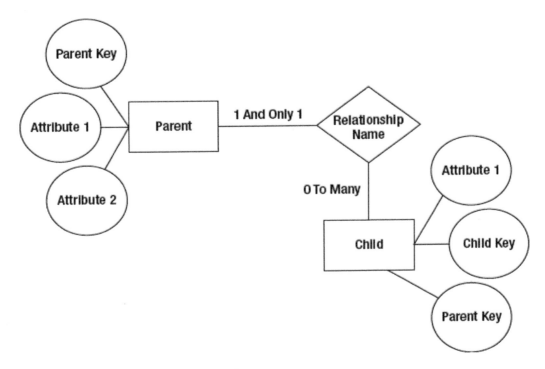

Figure 3-16. *Example Chen ERD diagram*

Each entity is again a rectangle; however, the attributes are not shown in the entity but are instead attached to the entity in circles. The primary key either is not denoted or, in some variations, is underlined. The relationship is denoted by a rhombus, or diamond shape.

The cardinality for a relationship is denoted in text. In the example, it is 1 and Only 1 Parent row <relationship name> 0 to Many Child rows. The primary reason for including the Chen ERD format is for contrast. Several other modeling methodologies— for example, Object Role Modeling (ORM) and Bachman—implement attributes in this style, where they are not displayed in the rectangle.

While I understand the logic behind this approach (entities and attributes are separate things), I have found that models I have seen using the format with attributes attached to the entity like this seemed overly cluttered, even for small diagrams. The methodology does, however, do an admirable job with the logical model of showing what is desired and does not rely on overcomplicated symbology to describe relationships and cardinality (I have a difficult time with the IE symbols in each and every edition of this book because I do not use them very often).

Note   You can find further details on the Chen ERD methodology in the paper "The Entity–Relationship Model—Toward a Unified View of Data" by Peter Chen (it can be found by performing an Internet search for the title of the paper on many academic websites).

Also, note that I am not saying that such a tool to create Chen diagrams does not exist; rather, I personally have not seen the Chen ERD methodology implemented in a mainstream database design tool other than some earlier versions of Microsoft Visio. Quite a few of the diagrams you will find on the Internet will be in this style, however, so understanding at least the basics of the Chen ERD methodology is useful.

Best Practices

The following are some basic best practices that can be very useful to follow when doing data modeling:

- *Modeling language*: If possible, pick a model language, understand it, and use it correctly and to express your models graphically and internally. This chapter has been a basic coverage of much of the symbology of the IDEF1X modeling language, but clearly IDEF1X is not the only modeling language. After using one style a few times, it is likely you will develop a favorite flavor and not like the others. The plain fact is that almost all the modeling options have some merit. The important thing is that you understand your chosen language and can use it to communicate with users and programmers at the levels they need and can explain the intricacies as necessary.

- *Entity names*: There are two ways you can go with these: plural or singular. I follow a style where entity names are singular (meaning that the name describes a single instance, or row, of the entity, much like an OO object name describes the instance of an object, not a group of them), but many highly regarded data architects and authors feel that the table name refers to the set of rows and should be plural. Whichever way you decide to go, it's most important that you are consistent. Anyone reading your model shouldn't have to guess why some entity names are plural and others aren't.

- *Attribute names*: While it is perfectly acceptable as a practice, it is generally not necessary to repeat the entity name in the attribute name, except for the primary key and some common terms. The entity name is implied by the attribute's inclusion in the entity. The attribute name should reflect precisely what is contained in the attribute and how it relates to the entity. And as with entities, abbreviations ought to be used extremely sparingly in naming of attributes and columns; every word should be spelled out in its entirety. If any abbreviation is to be used, because of some naming standard currently in place, for example, a method should be put into place to make sure the abbreviation is used consistently.

- *Relationships*: Name relationships with verb phrases, which make the relationship between a parent and a child entity a readable sentence. The sentence expresses the relationship using the entity names and the relationship cardinality. The relationship sentence is a very powerful tool for communicating the purpose of the relationships with technical and nontechnical members of the project team alike.

- *Defined datatype domains*: Using defined, reusable domains for columns gives you a set of standard templates to apply when building databases to ensure consistency across your database and, if the templates are used extensively, all your databases. Implement type inheritance wherever possible to take advantage of domains that are similar and maximize reusability.

- *Consistency*: Not to beat this drum until you are deaf, consistency is key. Don't make abrupt changes in your designs, tools, and so on just because you read a book, take a class, and so on. Make changes gradually and as widespread as possible. Having 15 naming standards, 3 different modeling standards, and 12 coloring schemes that are all great on their own molded together is not going to be better than poor, well-understood design scheme.

Summary

One of the primary tools of a database designer is the data model. It's such a great tool because it can describe not only the details of a single table at a time but the relationships between several entities at a time. Add in the graphical view of the model, and you have a picture that you can share with users that can communicate a lot of information in a very small space.

Of course, a formal data model in a formal data modeling language is not the only way to document a database; each of the following is useful, but not nearly as useful as a full-featured data model:

- Often a product that features a database as the central focus will include a document that lists all tables, datatypes, and relationships in its own format.

- Every good DBA has a script of the database saved and ideally in source control for re-creating every database.

- SQL Server's metadata includes ways to add properties to the database to describe the objects.

A good data modeling tool will do all of these things and more for you. I won't give you any guidance as to which tool to purchase, as this is not an advertisement for any tool. Clearly, you need to do a bit of research to find a tool that suits your needs and (perhaps more importantly) that you can afford on an ongoing basis that meets your needs. Some of the more expensive modeling tools have rich tools that use the metadata you painstakingly enter and make creating the database that much easier later.

In this chapter, I presented the basic building blocks of graphically documenting the objects that were introduced in Chapter 1. I focused heavily on the IDEF1X modeling methodology, taking a detailed look at the symbology that will be used through database designs. The base set of symbols outlined here will enable us to fully model logical databases (and later physical databases) in detail.

All it takes is a little bit of training, and the rest is easy. For example, take the model in Figure 3-17.

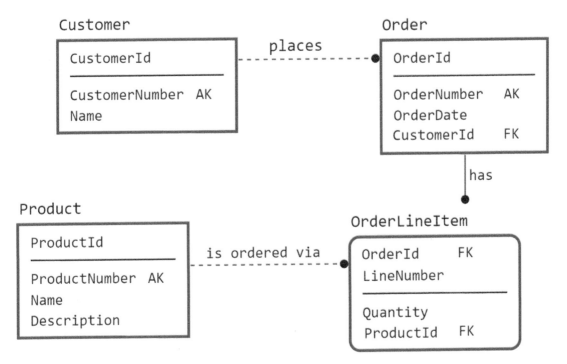

Figure 3-17. *Reading this basic model is not difficult at all, if you simply apply the explanations from this chapter*

Customers place orders. Orders have line items. The line items are used to order products. With very little effort, nontechnical users can start to understand what the data is, how the data is related, and so on allowing you to communicate data structures very easily, rather than using large spreadsheets as your primary communication method. The finer points of cardinality and ownership might not be completely clear, but usually, those technical details are not as important as the larger picture of knowing which entities relate to which.

Now that we've considered the symbology required to model a database, I'll frequently make use of data models throughout this book to describe the entities, starting with conceptual and logical models in Chapter 4, and many other models throughout this book as shorthand to give you an overview of the scenario I am setting up, often in addition to scripts to demonstrate how to create the tables in the model.

CHAPTER 4

Conceptual and Logical Data Model Production

I never design a building before I've seen the site and met the people who will be using it.

—Frank Lloyd Wright, Architect

In this chapter, we are going to really wind things up and begin to apply the skills that were covered in the previous chapters and create a data model from a set of requirements. The data model I create will not be ready to be implemented by any means, as there are more refinement steps to come in the next couple of chapters, but the goal of this model will be to serve as the basis for the eventual model that will get implemented. Personally, I both love and loathe this particular step in the process because this is where things get complicated. All the requirements and documents need to be considered, which hopefully reflect a complete understanding and desires of the people who actually want your software.

The architects and programmers from all disciplines, ideally, will be collaborating to achieve not only a data model but also designs for the user experience and the rest of the system architecture. It is a step where you get to be somewhat artistic, looking for unique and interesting solutions, but need to be careful not to make the output about your hopes and dreams either. It is more like a commissioned piece of art where you have been given lots of strict details to replicate with only hints of your personal style. Obviously, for this chapter's content, we will solely focus on producing the data model and ignore the rest of the application. Even with a short set of requirements that is less than one page, you will note that this chapter is over 60 times that length.

© Louis Davidson 2021
L. Davidson, *Pro SQL Server Relational Database Design and Implementation*,
https://doi.org/10.1007/978-1-4842-6497-3_4

For the book's purposes, the process of requirements gathering is 100% complete and as good as it gets before starting the conceptual data model. Someone has interviewed all the relevant clients (and documented the interviews) and gathered artifacts ranging from previous system documentation to sketches of what the new system might look like to prototypes to whatever is available and then has summarized everything needed in a short, one-page document. In other projects, you may have to model to keep up with your agile team members, and much of the process may get done mentally and verbally. In either case, the exhilarating part of the process starts now: sifting through all these artifacts and documents (or sometimes dealing with human beings directly) and discovering a database from within the cacophony.

Note   The process of discovery is rarely over in a real project before it is released to production. It is very difficult to get requirements perfect from any human being, much less a group of them. In this chapter, I am going to assume the requirements are both simple and perfect, but expect requirements to shift, and you'll discover requirements that were never captured in almost every project you work on.

The goal at this point in the process of creating a data model is to take the requirements and distill out the stuff that has a relationship to data that will be reflected in the database you are architecting and take the first two steps toward turning the requirements into a relational database. In this chapter, I'll introduce the following two main processes:

- *Building the conceptual model*: Get the base concepts and relationships identified in the system.

- *Building the logical model*: Starting with the conceptual model, flesh out the details that are needed to express the information to describe and identify all of the data points the customer desires.

I will go through the steps required to produce a simple logical model using a one-page set of requirements as the basis of our project. For those readers who are new to database design, this deliberate method of working though the design to build this model is a great way to help you through the steps. Take care that I said "new to database design," not "new to creating and manipulating tables in SQL Server." Although these two things are interrelated, they are distinct and different steps of the same process. We will cover creating the database objects, but first we will cover how to interpret the data requirements.

After some experience, you will likely not always take the time to produce a model exactly like the one I will discuss in this chapter. In all likelihood, you may perform some of these steps mentally and will combine them with some of the refinement processes we will work on in later chapters. Such an approach is natural and a very normal thing at times.

You should know, however, that working though the database design process is a lot like working through a complex math problem in that you are solving a messy problem and showing your work is never a bad thing. As a student in a lot of math classes, I was always amazed that showing one's work is usually done more by the advanced mathematician than by anyone else. They realized that writing things down avoided errors, and when errors do occur, you can look back and figure out why. The more you know about the proper process of designing a database, the less likely you are to try to force the next model into a certain mold, sometimes without listening to what the customer needs first.

Example Scenario

The following example documentation will be used as the basis of the database we will build throughout the chapter. In a real system, this might be just a tiny part of the documentation that has been gathered. (It always amazes me how much useful information you can get from a few paragraphs, though to be fair, I did write—and rewrite—this example more than a couple of times.)

> *The client manages a couple of dental offices. One is called the Chelsea Office and the other the Downtown Office. The client needs the system to manage its patients and appointments, alerting the patients when and where their appointments occur, either by email or by phone, and then assisting in the selection of new appointments. The client wants to be able to keep up with the records of all the patients' appointments without having to maintain lots of files. The dentists might spend time at each of the offices throughout the week.*
>
> *For each appointment, the client needs to have everything documented that went on and then invoice the patient's insurance, if they have insurance (otherwise, the patient pays). Invoices should be sent within one week after the appointment. Each patient should be able to be associated with other patients in a family for insurance and appointment purposes. We will need to have an address, a phone number (home, mobile, and/or office), and*

optionally an email address associated with each family and possibly each patient if the client desires. Currently, the client uses a patient number in its computer system that corresponds to a particular folder that has the patient's records.

The system needs to track and manage several dentists and quite a few dental hygienists whom the client needs to allocate to each appointment as well. The client also wants to keep up with its supplies, such as sample toothpastes, toothbrushes, and floss, as well as dental supplies. The client has had problems in the past keeping up with when it's about to run out of supplies and wants this system to take care of this for both locations. For the dental supplies, we need to track usage by employee, especially any changes made in the database to patient records.

Through each of the following sections, our goal will be to acquire all the pieces of information that need to be stored in our new database system. Sounds simple enough, right? Well, although it's much easier than it might seem, it takes time and effort (two things every technology professional has in abundance...in addition to sarcasm).

In the coming chapters, I will present smaller examples to demonstrate independent concepts in modeling that have been trimmed down to only the concepts needed.

Building the Conceptual Model

The conceptual model is all about the big picture of the model. What is being modeled? At a high level, what should the resulting database look? Details like how data will be stored should be left alone for now. We want to know "what are the concepts the customer wants to store data about." Customers, dentists, insurance policies, and so on and how they are related are the essential parts of this process. Customers have insurance policies, and other relationships give you the skeleton of the database.

If you have ever been involved with building a building of some sort, there are many iterations in the process. You start by sketching out the basic structure that the customer wants and refine it over and over until you have a solid understanding of what the customer wants. Everything is changeable, but usually once the design shows the concepts and the customer approves it, the foundation for success has been laid.

In the database design process, our goal will be to understand the types of data the customer needs to store and how things are related to one another. When we complete the conceptual model, we will have the framework of our database completed and will be ready to fill in the details.

In this section, we will cover the following steps of the process:

- *Identifying entities*: Looking for all the concepts that need to be modeled in the database.

- *Identifying relationships between entities*: Looking for natural relationships between high-level entities. Relationships between entities are what make entities useful.

Tip   You don't have to get things perfect at any step of a software project, but the sooner you find problems, the better. Finding a design issue before you code is a lot cheaper than once code has been written. Typically, as soon as you create a table, there will be other people attaching code to it who will not want you to change your design.

Identifying Entities

Entities generally represent people, places, objects, ideas, or things, referred to grammatically as nouns. While it isn't really necessary for the final design to put every noun into a specific grouping, doing so can be useful in identifying patterns of attributes later. People usually have names, phone numbers, and so on. Places have an address that identifies an actual location. It isn't so much so you can add details for the customer later in the process, but rather so you know where to look for those details and to ask questions like "Nowhere is it specified that you want to know the name of the dentist. Is this correct?"

In the next major section of this chapter, we will use these entity types as clues to some attribute needs and to keep you on the lookout for additional bits of information along the way. So I try to make a habit of classifying entities as people, places, and objects for later in the process. For example, our dental office includes the following:

- *People*: A patient, a doctor, a hygienist

- *Places*: Dental office, patient's home, hospital

- *Objects*: A dental tool, stickers for the kids, toothpaste

- *Ideas*: A document, insurance, a group (such as a security group for an application), the list of services provided, and so on

There's clearly overlap in several of the categories (e.g., a building is a "place" and an "object"). Don't be surprised if some objects fit into several of the subcategories below them that I will introduce. Let's look at each of these types of entities and see what kinds of things can be discovered from the documentation sample for each of the aforementioned entity types.

Tip   The way an entity is implemented in a table might be different from your initial expectation. When building the initial design, you want the document to come initially from what the user wants. Then, you'll fit what the user wants into a proper table design later in the process. Especially during the conceptual modeling phase, a change in the design is still a click and drag, or eraser drag even, away.

Persons

Nearly every database needs to store information about people. Most databases have at least some notion of user (generally thought of as people, though not always, so don't assume and end up with your actual users required to create a user with a first name of "Alarm" and last name "System"). Additionally, as far as real people are concerned, a database might need to store information about many different types of people. For instance, a school's database might have a Student entity, a Teacher entity, and an Administrator entity.

In our example, three people-type entities can be found by reading through our example scenario—patients, dentists, and hygienists:

> ...the system to manage its ___patients___...

and

> ...manage several ___dentists___ and quite a few dental ___hygienists___...

Patients are clearly people, as are dentists and hygienists (yes, that crazy person wearing a mask not during a pandemic and digging into your gums with a pitchfork is *actually* a person). One additional person-type entity is also found here:

> ...we need to track usage by ___employee___...

Dentists and hygienists have already been mentioned. It's clear that they'll be employees as well. For now, unless you can clearly discern that one entity is exactly the same thing as another, just document that there are four entities: patients, hygienists, dentists, and employees. Our model then starts out as shown in Figure 4-1.

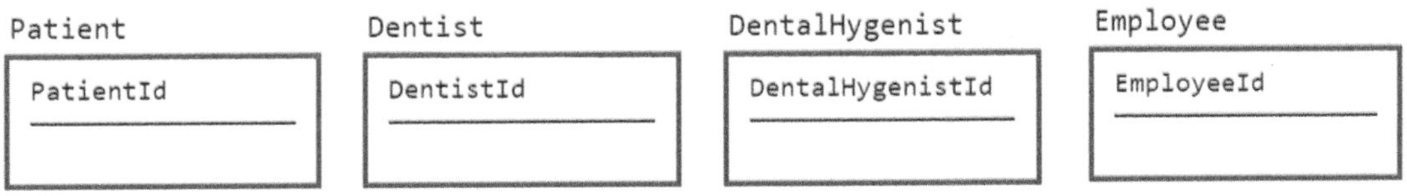

Patient	Dentist	DentalHygenist	Employee
PatientId	DentistId	DentalHygenistId	EmployeeId

Figure 4-1. *Four entities that make up our initial model*

Tip   Note that I have started with giving each entity a simple surrogate key attribute. In the conceptual model, we don't care about the existence of a key, but as we reach the next step with regard to relationships, the surrogate key will migrate from table to table to give a clear picture of the lineage of ownership in the model. Feel free to leave the surrogate key off if you want, especially if it gets in the way of communication, because laypeople sometimes get hung up over keys and key structures.

Along the way, as you create a new entity, take a moment to write down a definition of each, either in your data modeling tool or even in a spreadsheet. For space reasons, I will not list the definitions in each section, but they will be presented at intervals in the chapter.

Places

Users will want to store information relative to many different types of places. One obvious place entity is in our sample set of notes:

> *...manages a couple of **dental offices...***

From the fact that dental offices are places, later we'll be able to expect that there's address information about the offices and probably phone numbers, staffing concerns, and so on that the user may be interested in capturing information about. We also get the idea from the requirements that the two offices aren't located very close to each other, so there might be business rules about having appointments at different offices or to prevent the situation in which a dentist might be scheduled at two offices at one time. "Expecting" is just slightly informed guessing, so verify all expectations with the client.

I add the `Office` entity to the model, as shown in Figure 4-2.

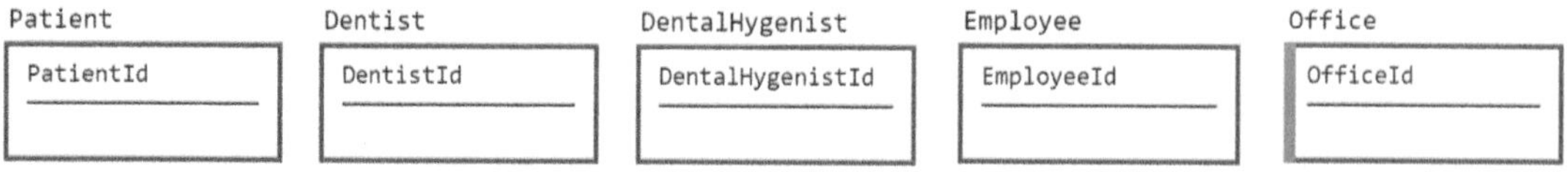

Patient	Dentist	DentalHygenist	Employee	Office
PatientId	DentistId	DentalHygenistId	EmployeeId	OfficeId

Figure 4-2. *Added Office as an entity*

Note   To show progress in the model as it relates to the narrative in the book, in the models, things that have changed from the previous step in the process are lightly highlighted with a bar to the left of the entity.

Objects

Objects refer primarily to physical items. In our example, there are a few objects:

> ...*with its **supplies**, such as sample toothpastes, toothbrushes, and floss, as well as* dental supplies...

Supplies, such as sample toothpastes, toothbrushes, and floss, as well as dental supplies, are all things that the client needs to run its business. Obviously, most of the supplies will be simple, and the client won't need to store a large amount of descriptive information about them. For example, it's possible to come up with a pretty intense list of things you might know about something as simple as a tube of toothpaste:

1. *Tube size*: Perhaps the length of the tube or the amount in grams

2. *Brand*: Colgate, Crest, or some other brand/lack of brand (which should not feel slighted by the lack of inclusion in my book)

3. *Format*: Metal or plastic tube, pump, and so on

4. *Flavor*: Mint, bubble gum (the nastiest of all flavors), cinnamon, and orange

5. *Manufacturer information*: Batch number, price, expiration date, and so on

We could go on and on coming up with more and more attributes of a tube of toothpaste, but it's unlikely that the users will have a business need for this information, because they probably just have a box of whatever samples they have been bribed with from the dental supply companies and give them out to their patients (to make them feel better about the metal against enamel experience they have just gone through).

One of the first, extremely important lessons about overengineering starts right here. At this point, we need to apply *selective ignorance* to the process and ignore the different attributes of things that have no specifically stated business interest. If you think that the information is useful, it is probably a good idea to drill into the client's process to make sure what they actually want, but don't assume that just because you could design the database to store something that it makes it necessary or that the client will change their processes to match your design. If you have good ideas, they might change, but most companies have what seem like insane business rules for reasons that make sense to them, and (sometimes) they can reasonably defend them.

Only one entity is necessary—Supply—but document that "Examples given were sample items, such as toothpaste or toothbrushes, plus there was mention of dental supplies. These supplies are the ones that the dentists and hygienists use to perform their job." This documentation you write will be important later when you are wondering what kind of supplies are being referenced.

Catching up, I add the Supply entity to the model, as shown in Figure 4-3.

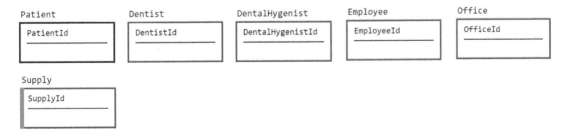

Figure 4-3. *Added the Supply entity*

Ideas

One thing to be on the lookout for in the requirements are concepts that don't stand out directly as nouns. More or less, we would be looking for data that seems necessary to support some idea or concept found in the document.

For example, consider the following:

> *...and then invoice the patient's insurance, if they have insurance (otherwise, the **patient pays**)...*

Insurance is an obvious important entity as the medical universe rotates around it (at least in the United States, where I am located). Another entity name looks like a verb rather than a noun in the phrase "patient pays." From this, we can infer that there might be some form of Payment entity to deal with.

Tip   Not all entities will obviously be an entity from the requirements. A lot of the time, you'll have to read what has been documented over and over and infer what is desired. The conceptual modeling process is, if you do it right, the most iterative of the modeling steps.

The model now looks like Figure 4-4.

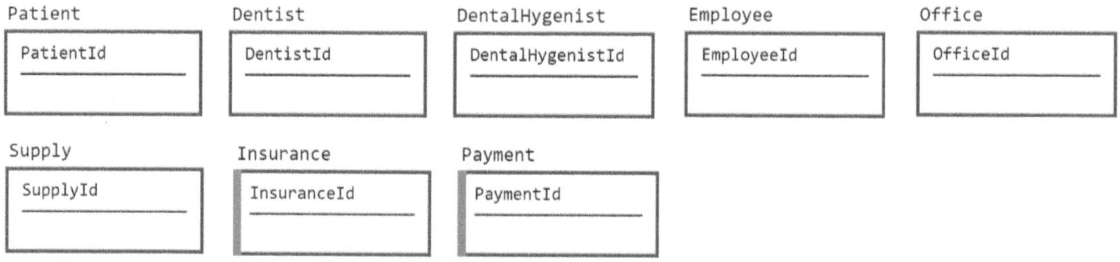

Patient	Dentist	DentalHygenist	Employee	Office
PatientId	DentistId	DentalHygenistId	EmployeeId	OfficeId

Supply	Insurance	Payment
SupplyId	InsuranceId	PaymentId

Figure 4-4. *Added the Insurance and Payment entities*

Documents

A document represents some piece of information that is captured and transported in one package. The classic example is a piece of paper that has been written on documenting a bill that needs to be paid. If you have a computer and/or have used the Internet at all, you probably know that the notion that a document has to be a physical piece of paper is as antiquated as borrowing a cup of sugar from your neighbor to make cupcakes to take to a child's school (have some birthday celery, classmates!). And even for a paper document, what if someone makes a copy of the piece of paper? Does that mean there are two documents, or are they both the same document? Usually, it isn't the case, but sometimes people do need to track physical pieces of paper and, just as often, versions and revisions of a document.

In the requirements for our new system, we have a few examples of documents that need to be dealt with. First up, we have the following:

> *...and then **invoice** the patient's insurance, if they have insurance (otherwise, the patient pays)...*

Invoices are pieces of paper (or emails) that are sent to a customer after the services have been rendered. However, no mention was made as to how invoices are delivered. They could be emailed or postal mailed—it isn't clear—nor would it be prudent for the database design to force it to be done either way unless there is a specific business rule governing the method of or tracking the delivery (and even still things change faster than database implementations, so be wary of hard-coding business rules in a non-changeable manner). At this point, just identify the entities (Invoice in this instance) and move along.

Next up, we have the following:

> *...appointments, **alerting** the patients when and where their appointments occur, either by email or by phone...*

This type of document almost certainly isn't delivered by paper but by an email message or phone call. The email is also used as part of another entity, Alert. The alert can be either an email or a phone alert. You may also be thinking, "Is the alert really something that is stored?" Maybe or maybe not, but it is probably likely that when the administrative assistants call and alert the patient that they have an appointment, a record of this interaction would be made. Then, when the person misses their appointment, they can say, "We called you, emailed you, and texted you on June 14 to no avail using the details that you provided us!" It is generally important that you track the addresses that are used for alerts, in case the primary numbers change so you can know what address was actually alerted, but more on that later in the chapter.

Note   If you are alert, you probably are thinking that Appointment, Email, and Phone are all entity possibilities, and you would be right. In my teaching process here, I am looking at the types one at a time to make a point. In the real process, you would just look for nouns linearly through the text, enhancing in a very set manner so this chapter isn't larger than my allocation of pages for the entire book.

Next, we add the `Invoice` and `Alert` entities to the model, as shown in Figure 4-5.

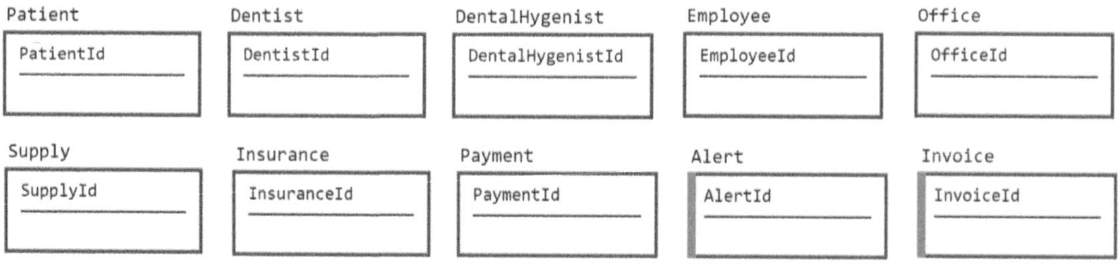

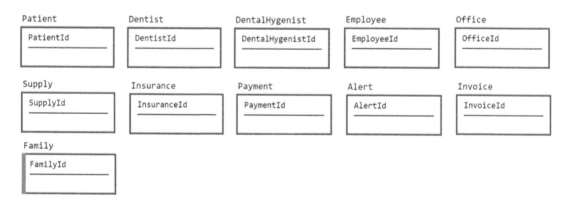

Figure 4-5. *Added the Alert and Invoice entities*

Groups

Another idea-type entity is a group of things or, more technically, a grouping of entities. For example, you might have a club that has members or certain types of products that make up a grouping that seems more than just a simple attribute. In our sample, we have one such entity:

> *Each patient should be able to be associated with other patients in a* family *for insurance and appointment purposes.*

Although a person's family could be an attribute of the person, it's likely more than that. So we add a `Family` entity, as shown in Figure 4-6. Remember that anything added to the conceptual model can be removed later.

Figure 4-6. *Added the Family entity*

Other Entities

The following sections outline some additional common objects that are perhaps not as obvious as the ones that have been presented. They don't always fit a simple categorization, but they're pretty straightforward.

Audit Trails

Audit trails, generally speaking, are used to track changes to the database. You might know that the RDBMS uses a log to track changes, but this is off-limits to the average user. So, in cases where the user wants to keep up with who does what, entities need to be modeled (or sometimes database features used) to represent these logs. They could be analogous to a sign-in/sign-out sheet, an old-fashioned library card in the back of the book, or just a list of things that went on in any order.

Consider the following example:

> *For the dental supplies, we need to **track usage** by employee,*
> *especially any changes made in the database to the patient records.*

In this case, the client clearly is keen to keep up with the kinds of materials that are being used by each of its employees. Perhaps a guess can be made that the user needs to be documented when dental supplies are taken (the difference between dental supplies and nondental supplies will certainly have to be discussed in due time). Also, it isn't necessary at this time that the needed logging eventually be done totally on a computer or even by using a computer at all. We document at this point that it needs to be done, if it likely will be done by computer, and work from there.

Another example of an audit trail is as follows:

> *For the dental supplies, we need to track usage by employee,*
> ***especially any changes made in the database to the patient***
> ***records.***

A typical entity that you need to define is the audit trail or a log of database activity, and this entity is especially important when the data is sensitive. An audit trail isn't a normal type of entity in that it stores no data that the user directly manipulates, and the final design will generally be deferred to the implementation design stage, although it is common to have specific requirements for what sorts of information need to be captured in the audit. Generally, the primary kinds of entities to be concerned with at this point are those that users wish to store in directly.

Events

Event entities generally represent verbs or actions:

> For each **appointment**, the client needs to have everything
> documented that went on...

An appointment is an event in that it's used to record information about when patients come to the office to be tortured for not flossing regularly enough. For most events, appointments included, it's important to have a schedule of where and when the event is supposed to occur and where it did occur, if it did. It's also not uncommon to want to have data that documents an event's occurrence (what was done, how many people attended, etc.). Hence, many event entities will be tightly related to some form of document entity. In our example, appointments are more than likely scheduled for the future, along with information about the expected activities (cleaning, x-rays, etc.), and once the appointment occurs, a record is made of what services were actually performed so that the dentist can get paid. Generally speaking, there are all sorts of events to look for in any system, such as meter readings for a utility company, weather readings for a sensor, equipment measurements, phone calls, and so on.

Records and Journals

The last of the entity types I will suggest is a record or journal of activities (and remember this is not an exhaustive list by any means, just a short list of places to consider when starting a database design!). A record could be any kind of activity that a user might previously have recorded on paper. In our example, the user wants to keep a record of each visit:

> The client wants to be able to keep up with the **records of all the**
> **patients' appointments without having to maintain lots of files**.

Keeping information in a centralized database is one of the main advantages of building database systems: eliminating paper files and making data more accessible, particularly for future data mining. Note that the database we are building may not be the database where the data mining actually occurs, but having clean, well-understood data structures will greatly assist in the future. In a database of any real size and heavy usage, a data warehouse will be built that offloads data for reporting. Appendix C, available for download, covers that pattern of design in more detail.

A well-designed database helps to alleviate problems for the customer, like eliminating the number of times I must tell the doctor what medicines I'm taking, all because their files are insane clutters used to cover the billing process, rather than being a useful document of my history. What if I forget one what another doctor prescribed and it interacts strongly with another drug? All of this duplication of asking me what drugs I take is great for covering the doctor's and pharmacy's backsides, but by leveraging an electronic database that is connected to other doctor and pharmacy records, the information that people are constantly gathering comes alive, and trends can be seen instantly in ways it would take hours to see on paper. "Hmm, after your primary doctor started you on vitamin Q daily, when the time between cleanings is more than 10 months, you have gotten a cavity!" Or perhaps even more importantly, given enough data from enough people, we can finally get a good idea of what course of drugs cures diseases, even further beyond the data from the original experiments.

Keep in mind that the more data you can get into your database *in a usable fashion*, the more likely that data can be used for data mining at some time in the future. Of course, putting too much information in a centralized location makes security all that much more important as well, so it is a double-edged sword as well. We will talk about security in Chapter 10, but suffice it to say that it is not a trivial issue, which is why so often you hear of data breaches.

The model after this last round of changes looks like Figure 4-7.

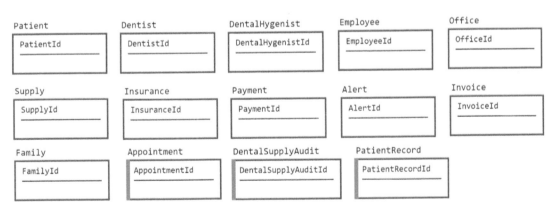

Figure 4-7. *Added the Appointment, DentalSupplyAudit, and PatientRecord entities*

Careful now, as you are probably jumping to a quick conclusion that a patient's record is just an amalgamation of their invoices, insurance information, x-rays, and so on. This is 100% possible, and I will admit right now that the `PatientRecord` table is *probably* a screen in the application where each of the related rows would be located. During early conceptual modeling, assuming you are working like we are, on an isolated island away from your customer, it is generally best to just put it on the model as you have found it and do the refinement later during customer or analyst review and get some clarity as to what is being requested.

Entity Recap

So far, we've discovered the list of preliminary entities shown in Table 4-1. It makes a pretty weak model so far, but this will change in the next few sections as we begin adding relationships between entities and the attributes. At this point, it is a good time to review the definitions of the items that are in the model after you have identified all of the entities, as shown in Table 4-1.

Table 4-1. *Entity Listing*

Entity	Type	Description
Patient	People	The people who are the customers of the dental office. Services are performed, supplies are used, and patients are billed for them.
Family	Idea	Patients grouped together for convenience of billing, alerting, insurance, and so on.
Dentist	People	People who do the most important work at the dental office. Several dentists are working for the client's practice.
DentalHygienist	People	People who do the routine work for the dentist. There are quite a few more hygienists than dentists. *(Note: Check with the client to see whether there are guidelines for the number of hygienists per dentist. It might be needed for setting appointments.)*
Employee	People	Any person who works at the dental office. Dentists and dental hygienists are clearly types of employees.

(continued)

Table 4-1. (*continued*)

Entity	Type	Description
Office	Places	Locations where the dentists do their business. They have multiple offices to deal with and schedule patients for.
Supply	Objects	Supplies for the running of the dental operations of the office. Examples given were sample items, such as toothpaste or toothbrushes, plus there was mention of dental supplies as the supplies that the dentists and hygienists use to perform their jobs.
Insurance	Idea	Used by patients to pay for the dental services rendered.
Payment	Idea	Money received from insurance or patients (or both) to pay for services.
Invoice	Document	A document sent to the patient or insurance company explaining how much money is required to pay for services.
Alert	Document	A communication made to tell a patient of an impending appointment.
DentalSupplyAudit	Audit trail	Used to track the usage of dental supplies.
Appointment	Event	The event of a patient coming in and having some dental work done.
PatientRecord	Record	All the pertinent information about a patient, much like a patient's folder in any doctor's office.

Implementation modeling note: Log any changes to sensitive/important data.

The descriptions are based on the facts that have been derived from the preliminary documentation. Note that the entities that have been specified are directly represented in the customer's documentation.

Are these all of the entities? Maybe, maybe not, but it is the set we have discovered after the first design pass. During a real project, you will frequently discover new entities and delete an entity or two that you thought would be necessary. It is not a clean, single-pass process, because you will be constantly learning the needs of the users.

Note   The conceptual modeling phase is where knowledge of your clients' type of business can easily help and hinder you. On one hand, it helps you see what they want quickly and lets you speak their language. On the other, it can lead you to jump to conclusions based on "how things were done when I did something similar." Every project is unique and may or may not have its own way of doing stuff. The most important design tools are your eyes and ears.

Identifying Relationships Between Entities

Next, we will look for the ways that the entities relate to one another, which will then be translated to relationships between the entities on the model. The idea here is to find how each of the entities will work with one another to solve the client's needs. I'll start first with the one-to-N type of relationships and then cover the many-to-many. It's also important to consider obvious relationships from the base understanding of common data structures that aren't directly mentioned in your requirements. Relationships are somewhat safer than entities, because you are connecting objects they have specified, not creating new objects they haven't.

Just realize that the user knows how they want the system, and you are going to go back over their requests and fill in the blanks and review with them multiple times before the process is complete and point out things you did not see in the requirements but added because it felt natural and explain why in some detail.

One-to-N Relationships

In each of the one-to-N relationships, the table that is the "one" table in the relationship is considered the parent, and the "N" is the child or children rows. While the one-to-N relationship is going to be the only relationship you will implement in your relational model, a lot of the natural relationships you will discover in the model may in fact turn out to be many-to-many relationships. It is important to really scrutinize the cardinality of all relationships you model so as not to limit future design considerations by missing something that is very natural to the process. To make it more real, instead of thinking about a mechanical term like one-to-N, we will break it down into a couple of types of relationships:

Simple: One instance is related to one or more child instances. The primary point of identifying relationships this way is to form an association between two entity rows.

Is a: Unlike the previous classification, when we think of an "is a" relationship, usually the two related items are the same thing, often meaning that one table is a more generic version of the other. A manager is an employee, for example. In Chapter 3, we referred to this type of relationship as a subtype or categorization relationship.

I'll present examples of each type in the next couple sections.

Simple Relationships

In this section, I discuss some of the types of associations that you might uncover along the way as you are modeling relationships. Another common term for a simple relationship is a "has-a" relationship, so named because as you start to give verb phrases/names to relationships, you will find it very easy to say "has a" for almost every relationship. In fact, a common lazy move by modelers is to end up using "has a" as the verb phrase for too many of their parent–child relationships, which degrades the value of the verb phrase (sometimes, however, it really just is the best verb phrase).

In this section, I will discuss a few examples of simple relationships that you will come in contact with quite often. The following are different types of simple relationships:

- *Connection*: An association between two things. You could even think of it as a bond that holds two things together, like a person and their driver's license or car. This is the most generic of all relationships and will generally cover any sort of ownership or association between entities.

- *Transaction*: More generically, this could be thought of as an interaction relationship where you are capturing some interaction between two entities. For example, a customer pays a bill or makes a phone call, so an account is credited/debited money through transactions.

- *Multivalued attribute*: In an object implemented in an object-oriented language, one can have arrays for attributes, but in a relational database, as discussed in Chapter 1, all attributes must be atomic/scalar values (or at least should be) in terms of what data we will use in relational queries. So, when we design, say, an invoice entity, we don't put all the line items in the same table; we make a new table, commonly called `InvoiceLineItem`. Another common example is storing customers' preferences. Unless they can only have a single preference, at least one new table is required, and possibly more.

- *Domain*: A type of relationship that you may possibly uncover in early modeling is a domain type. It is used to implement the domain for an attribute where more than a single attribute seems useful. I will not demonstrate this relationship type in this chapter, but we will look at domain relationships in later chapters (they are most commonly used as an implementation tool).

In the next few sections, I will use the first three types of relationships to classify and pick out the relations discovered in our dental office example.

Connection

In our example requirements paragraph, consider the following:

> ...then invoice the **patient's insurance, if they have insurance**...

In this case, the relationship is between the `Patient` and `Insurance` entities. It's an optional relationship, because it says "if they have insurance." Add the following relationship to the model, as shown in Figure 4-8.

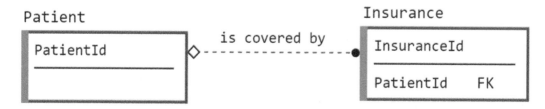

Figure 4-8. *Added the optional relationship between the Patient and Insurance entities (additional relationships between Patient, Insurance, and Invoice will be added later in the process)*

Another example of a has-a relationship follows:

> Each **patient should be able to be associated with other patients
> in a** family for insurance and appointment purposes.

In this case, we identify that a family has patients. Although this sounds a bit odd, it makes perfect sense in the context of a medical office. Instead of maintaining ten different insurance policies for each member of a family of ten, the client wants to have a single one where possible. So we add a relationship between Family and Patient, stating that a family instance may have multiple patient instances. Note too that we make it an optional relationship because a patient isn't required to have insurance.

That the family is covered by insurance is also a possible relationship added in Figure 4-9. It has already been specified that patients have insurance. This isn't unlikely, because even if a person's family has insurance, one of the members might have an alternative insurance plan. It also doesn't contradict our earlier notion that patients have insurance, although it does give the client two different paths to identify the insurance. This isn't necessarily a problem, but when two insurance policies exist, you might have to implement business rule logic to decide which one takes precedence. Again, this is something to discuss with the client, and in a real modeling session, you would flag this for more discussion when you meet with the client.

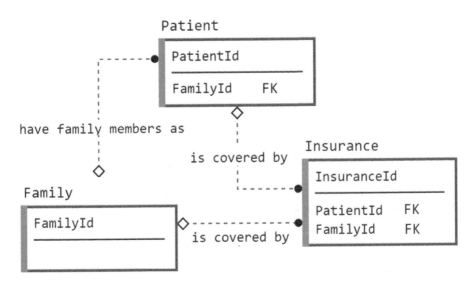

Figure 4-9. *Relationships added among the Patient, Insurance, and Family entities*

Here's another example of connective relationship, shown in Figure 4-10:

> ... *dental offices... The client needs the system to manage its*
> *patients and* appointments...

In this case, make note that each dental office will have appointments. Clearly, an appointment can be for only a single dental office, so this is not a many-to-many relationship. One of the attributes of an event type of entity is often a location. It's unclear at this point whether a patient comes to only one of the offices or whether the patient can float between offices. However, it is certain that appointments must be made at the office, so the relationship between Office and Appointment is required. Now add the relationship as shown in Figure 4-10.

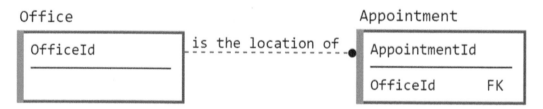

Figure 4-10. *Relationship added between the Office and Appointment entities*

Transactions

Transactions are seemingly the most common type of relationships in a business database (hence the name Online Transaction Processing or OLTP is often used). Almost every database will have some way of recording interactions with an entity instance. For example, some very common transactions are simply customers making purchases, payments, and so on. I can't imagine a terribly useful database that only has customer and product data with no transactional information.

In our database, we have one very obvious transaction:

> ...*if they have insurance (otherwise, the patient pays). Invoices*
> *should be sent...*

We identified Patient and Payment entities earlier, so we add a relationship to represent a patient making a payment. Figure 4-11 shows the new relationship.

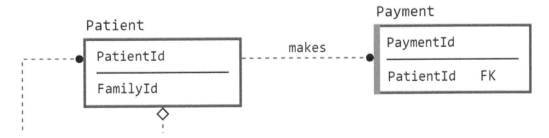

Figure 4-11. *Relationship added between the Patient and Appointment entities*

Multivalued Attributes and Domains

During the early phases of modeling, it is far less likely to discover multivalued attribute and domain relationships naturally than any other types. The reason is our goal is to keep them focused on the big picture. But in some cases, attributes and domains are more naturally part of the model than simply being a multivalued attribute like email or phone number. In our model, so far, we identified several places where we are likely to expand the entities to cover array types that may not strictly be written in requirements, particularly true when the requirements are written by end users.

For example, in terms of multivalued attributes, invoices have invoice line items; appointments have lists of actions that will be taken such as cleaning, taking x-rays, and the ever-popular drilling out cavities; payments can have multiple payment sources. For domain relationships, you can think of status values for most of the aforementioned entities. While a domain of "Active" and "Inactive" may not elevate to the need of a domain entity in the conceptual or logical model, if we also want to associate a description with this value in the database ("Active patients get better goodies") or perhaps include some process to take when the patient is in the status, having a table of possible status values would make that possible, which then might elevate them to be included in the conceptual model. Just be careful that during conceptual modeling in particular, when adding entities to your models, they should have real customer-understood value, rather than cluttering up the model.

As such, I won't come up with any examples of domain or multivalued attribute relationships from the example requirements, but we will cover this topic in more depth in Chapter 9 when I cover modeling patterns for implementation.

The "Is A" Relationship

The major idea behind an "is a" relationship is that the child entity in the relationship *extends* the details of the parent. For example, cars, trucks, RVs, and so on are all types of vehicles, so a car *is a* vehicle. The cardinality of this type of relationship is always one-to-one, because the child entity simply contains more specific information that qualifies this extended relationship. There would be some information that's common to each of the child entities (stored as attributes of the parent entity) but also other information that's specific to each child entity (stored as attributes of the child entity).

In our example text, the following snippets exist:

> *...manage several **dentists** and quite a few **dental hygienists** whom the client...*

and

> *...track usage by **employee**, especially...*

From these statements, you can reasonably infer that there are three entities, and there's a relationship between them. A dentist is an employee, as is a dental hygienist. There are possibly other employees for whom the system needs to track supply usage as well, but none listed at this point. Figure 4-12 represents this relationship, which is modeled using the subtype relationship type. Note that this is modeled as a complete subtype, meaning every Employee instance would either have a corresponding Dentist or DentalHygenist instance. It is likely that there are other employee types, so this part of the model might change, but this is the documentation we currently have.

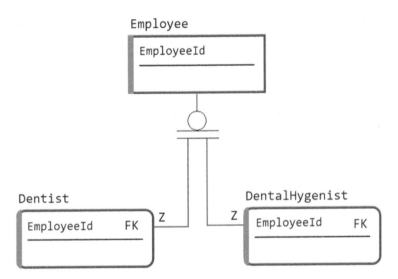

Figure 4-12. *Identified subtype relationship between the Employee, Dentist, and DentalHygienist entities*

Note   Because the subtype manifests itself as a one-to-one identifying relationship (recall from Chapter 3 that the Z on the relationship line indicates a one-to-zero-or-one relationship), separate named keys for the Dentist and DentalHygienist entities aren't needed. Having the same key name makes it easier for the customer to know they can join each of these three tables to any table with an EmployeeId attribute, and it would limit your results to only rows of that certain type without using the discriminator of the subtype relationship.

Many-to-Many Relationships

As you refine a data model, a great number of relationships may end up being many-to-many relationships as the real relationship between entities is realized. However, early in the design process, only a few obvious many-to-many relationships might be recognized. In our example, one is obvious:

> *The **dentists might spend time at each of the offices** throughout the week.*

In this case, each of the dentists can work at more than one dental office. A one-to-many relationship won't suffice; it's wrong to state that one dentist can work at many dental offices, because this implies that each dental office has only one dentist. The opposite, that one office can support many dentists, implies dentists work at only one office. Hence, this is a many-to-many relationship (see Figure 4-13).

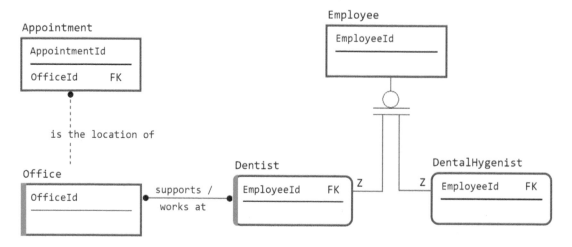

Figure 4-13. *Added a many-to-many relationship between Dentist and Office*

This brings up the question, "What about dentists being associated with appointments and the same for dental hygienists?" When conferring with your client, you probably will want to discuss that issue with them. It could be that, in this iteration of the product, they just want to know where the dentist is so they can use that information as the dentist is not scheduled with the patients, but one just has to be at the office to do a final check at the end of each cleaning. Again, we are not to read minds but to do what the client wants in the best way possible.

There is an additional many-to-many relationship that can be identified:

> *...dental supplies, we need to track usage by employee...*

This quote says that multiple employees can use different types of supplies, and for every dental supply, multiple types of employees can use it. However, it's possible that controls might be required to manage the types of dental supplies that each employee might use, especially if some of the supplies are regulated in some way (such as narcotics).

The relationship shown in Figure 4-14 is added.

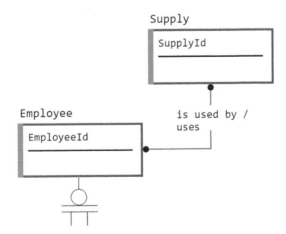

Figure 4-14. *Added a many-to-many relationship between the Supply and Employee entities*

I'm also going to remove the DentalSupplyAudit entity, because it's becoming clear that this entity is a report, and we will figure out how to solve this need later in the process. What we know from here is that employees use supplies, and we need to capture that that is happening.

Listing Relationships

Figure 4-15 shows the model so far.

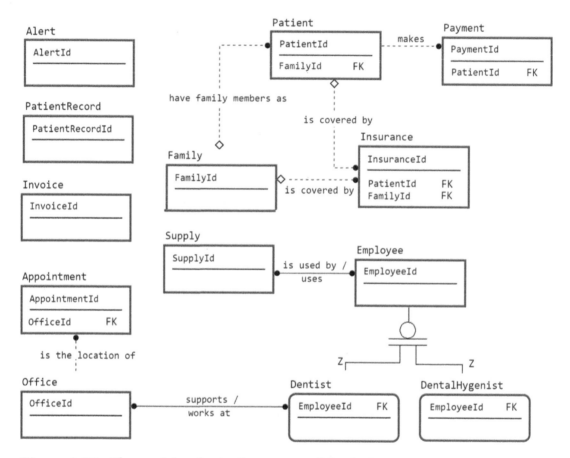

Figure 4-15. *The model so far in the process of the design*

There are other relationships in the text that I won't cover explicitly, but I've documented them in the descriptions in Table 4-2, which is followed by the model with relationships identified and the definitions of the relationships in our documentation (note that the relationship is documented at the parent only).

Table 4-2. *Initial Relationship Documentation*

Entity	Type	Description
Patient	People	The people who are the customers of the dental office. Services are performed, supplies are used, and the patient is billed for these services.
	Relationships	
	Is covered by (0-to-many) Insurance (Instances)	Identifies when the patient has personal insurance.
	Is reminded by (1-to-many) Alert (Instances)	Alerts are sent to patients to remind them of their appointments.
	Is scheduled via (1-to-many) Appointment (Instances)	Appointments need to have one patient.
	Is billed with (1-to-many) Invoice (Instances)	Patients are charged for appointments via an invoice.
	Makes (1-to-many) Payment (Instances)	Patients make payments for invoices they receive.
	Has activity listed in (1-to-many) PatientRecord (Instances)	Activities that happen in the doctor's office.
Family	Idea	A group of patients grouped together for convenience.
	Relationships	
	Has family members as (0-to-many) patients (Instances)	A family consists of multiple patients.
	Is covered by (0-to-many) Insurance (Instances)	Identifies when there's coverage for the entire family.

(*continued*)

Table 4-2. (*continued*)

Entity	Type	Description
Dentist	People	People who do the most skilled work at the dental office. Several dentists work for the client's practice.
	Relationships	
	Works at many Office (Instances)	Dentists can work at multiple offices.
	Is (0-to-1) Employee (Instances)	Dentists have some of the attributes of all employees.
	Works during (0-to-many) Appointment (Instances)	Appointments might require the services of one dentist.
DentalHygienist	People	People who do the routine work for the dentist. There are quite a few more hygienists than dentists. *(Note: Check with the client to see if there are guidelines for the number of hygienists per dentist. It might be needed for setting appointments.)*
	Relationships	
	Is (0-to-1) Employee (Instance)	Hygienists have some of the attributes of all employees.
	Has (0-to-many) Appointment (Instances)	All appointments need to have at least one hygienist.
Employee	People	Any person who works at the dental office. Dentists and hygienists are clearly types of employees.
	Relationships	
	Uses (many) Supply (Instances)	Employees use supplies for various reasons.

(continued)

Table 4-2. (*continued*)

Entity	Type	Description
Office	Places	Locations where the dentists do their business. They have multiple offices to deal with and schedule patients for.
	Relationships	
	Is the location of (0-to-many) Appointments (Instances)	Appointments are made for a single office.
	Supports (many) Dentist (Instances)	
Supply	Objects	Supplies for the running of the dental operations of the office. Examples given were sample items, such as toothpaste or toothbrushes, plus there was mention of dental supplies as the supplies that the dentists and hygienists use to perform their jobs.
	Relationships	
	Are used by (many) Employees (Instances)	Employees use supplies for various reasons.
Insurance	Idea	Used by patients to pay for the dental services rendered.
	Relationships	
	Is billed with (0-to-many) Invoice (Instances)	If the patient has insurance, an invoice will go to the insurance company, as well as the patient.
Payment	Idea	Money received from insurance or patients (or both) to pay for services.

(*continued*)

Table 4-2. (*continued*)

Entity	Type	Description
Invoice	Document	A document sent to the patient or insurance company explaining how much money is required to pay for services.
	Relationships	
	Is paid with (0-to-many) Payment (Instances)	Payments are usually made to cover costs of the invoice (some payments are for other reasons).
Alert	Document	Email or phone call made to tell a patient of an impending appointment.
Appointment	Event	The event of a patient coming in and having some dental work done.
PatientRecord	Record	All the pertinent information about a patient, much like a patient's chart in any doctor's office.

Figure 4-16 shows how the model has progressed after filling in the details that were added but not gone through step by step in the text.

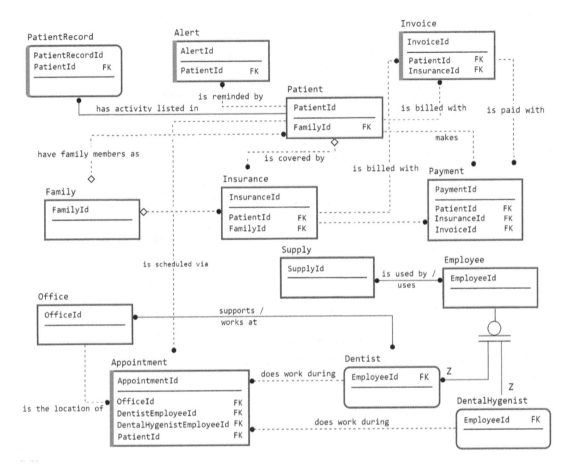

Figure 4-16. *The final conceptual model*

You can see, at this point, that the conceptual model has really gelled, and you can get a feel for what the final model might look like. In the next section, we will start adding attributes to the tables, and the model will truly start to take form. It is not 100% complete, and you could probably find a few things that you really want to add or change. However, note that for this exercise we are trying our best to avoid adding value/ information to the model as we do not have access to a client. In a real project, it is best to avoid adding stuff to your model, but also don't go through the entire design if you are confused with what something means and waste a lot of time messing around. Ask as many questions as you reasonably need to as soon as you reasonably can.

The only attributes that I have included in this model were used as a method to show lineage. The only time I used any role names for attributes was in the final model, when I related the two subtypes of Employee to the Appointment entity, as shown in Figure 4-17.

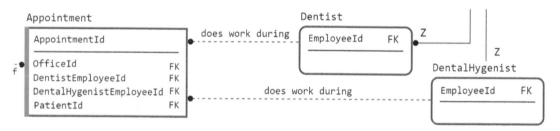

Figure 4-17. *Appointment entity with a role named EmployeeRelationship*

I related the two subtypes to the `Appointment` entity to make it clear what the role of each relationship was for, rather than having the generic `EmployeeId` in the table for both relationships. Again, even the use of any sort of key is not a standard conceptual model construct, but without relationship attributes, the model seems sterile and also tends to hide lineage from entity to entity.

The `Appointment` entity is the best example in my tiny example diagram of how the model shows you some basic makeup of the entity, as we can now see that for an appointment, we need an office, a patient, a hygienist, and sometimes a dentist available (since the relationship is optional). None of these things really define an appointment, so it is still an independent entity, but those attributes are critical.

Testing the Conceptual Model

Before stamping "done" on the conceptual model and doing a celebration lap around the conference room for that last stale doughnut, this is the time to take a validation pass through the requirements and make sure that they can be met by the entities in your model. We will not spend too much time here in the text covering what this means, because it is exactly the same process you have already gone through, iterating until you don't find anything that needs to be changed.

Seeing that every requirement can be met by your conceptual model will help you see if your model is prepared to move on to the logical modeling phase of the project. It is possible that you may have changed an entity to something that will no longer meet the requirements, but you are still at a great place in the process where changes require zero coding.

Building the Logical Model

With the conceptual model completed and validated as well as possible, the next steps in the modeling process are going to be progressively easier, though don't take the term "easier" to mean "take less time." Unlike the conceptual model, where you focus on the big picture, now we want to focus on the details which can take a lot of time to get right. For the most part, the most difficult part of the data modeling process is really understanding what the customer's needs are.

In this section, we will continue the model we started in the main section of the chapter with the following steps to build the logical model:

- *Identifying attributes and domains*: Looking for the individual data points that describe the entities and how to constrain them to only real/useful values

- *Identifying business rules*: Looking for the boundaries that are applied to the data in the system that go beyond the domains of a single attribute

- *Identifying fundamental processes*: Looking for different processes (code and programs) that the client tends to execute that are fundamental to its business

- *Finalizing the logical model*: Tasks needed to make sure the process is complete ready to start the process of making an implementable database

Identifying Attributes and Domains

As we start creating the logical model, the goal is to look for items that identify and describe the entities from the conceptual model. For example, if the entity is a person, attributes might include a driver's license number, Social Security number, hair color, eye color, weight, spouse, children, mailing address, and/or email address. Each of these values serves to provide details about the entity that the customer you are building the database for might be desiring for their needs.

Identifying which attributes to associate with an entity requires a similar approach to identifying the entities themselves. You can frequently find attributes by noting adjectives that are used to describe an entity you have previously found. Some attributes will simply be discovered because of the type of entity they are (person, place, etc., which was part of the reason we used that method of classifying the entities in the conceptual model part of the chapter).

Domain information for an attribute is generally discovered at the same time as the attribute, so at this point, you should identify domains whenever you can conveniently locate them. The following is a list of some of the common types of attributes to look for during the process of identifying attributes and their domains:

- *Identifiers*: Any information used to identify a single instance of an entity. This will be loosely analogous to a key, though identifiers won't always make for proper keys so much as identifying ways that a user may search for a particular instance.

- *Descriptive information*: Information used to describe something about the entity, such as color, status, name, description, and so on.

- *Locators*: Identify how to locate what the entity is modeling, both physically in the real world, such as a mailing address, and on a technical scale, a position on a computer screen and so on.

- *Values*: Things that quantify something about the entity, such as monetary amounts, counts, and so on.

- *Points in time*: When something that has occurred or will occur is one of the most important things we capture in data.

As was true during our entity search, these aren't the only places to look for attributes, but they're just a few common places to start. The most important thing for now is that you'll look for values that make it clearer *what* the entity is modeling. Also, it should be noted that all of these have equal merit and value, and groupings may overlap. Lots of attributes will not fit into these groupings (even if my example attributes all too conveniently will). These are just a set of ideas to give you help when looking for attributes.

Identifiers

In this section, we will consider elements used to identify one instance of an entity from another. Every entity needs to have at least one identifying set of attributes. Without identifiers, there's no way that different instances can be identified later in the process. These identifiers are likely to end up being used as candidate keys of the entity, but not always (sometimes you may not be able to guarantee uniqueness or even guarantee each instance will have a value). Here are some common examples of good identifiers:

- *For people*: Social Security and tax identification numbers (in the United States), full names (not generally a perfect computing identifier, but something to narrow down identification), or other IDs (such as customer numbers, employee numbers, etc.)

- *For transactional documents (invoices, bills, computer-generated notices)*: Some sort of number generally assigned for tracking purposes

- *For books*: The ISBN (titles aren't unique, not even always by author, but are still identifying information)

- *For products*: Product numbers for a manufacturer (product names aren't unique), Universal Product Code, and so on

- *For companies that clients deal with*: Commonly assigned a customer/client number for tracking that probably wouldn't change even if the client changed names

- *For buildings*: Building given a name to be referred to

- *For mail*: The addressee's name and address and the date it was sent

This is not by any means an exhaustive list, but this representative list will help you understand what identifiers mean. Think back to the relational model overview in Chapter 1—each instance of an entity must be unique. Identifying unique natural keys in the data is a very important step in implementing a design.

Take care to really discern whether what you think of as a unique item is actually unique. Look at people's names. At first glance, they almost seem unique, and in real life you will personally use them as keys (and if you know two people named Louis Davidson, heaven help you, you would morph the name to be Louis Davidson the author, or the Disney nut, and Louis Davidson the other guy who isn't those things), but in a database, doing so becomes problematic. For example, there are thousands, if not millions, of people named John Smith out there! Even extending to middle name, title, and so on, absolute uniqueness is not guaranteed. For these cases, you may want to identify in the documentation what I call "likely uniqueness."

In your model and eventually in your applications, you will most likely want to identify data that is not actually a legitimate key (like first, middle, and last names) but that is very likely unique, so that while you can't enforce uniqueness, you can use this to let the UI identify likely matching people when you put in first and last names and then ask for a known piece of information rather than expecting that it is a new customer. Usually, the process will then include not only the given name but the address, phone number, email address, and so on to start to increase the probability of a match. (In Chapter 9, we will discuss the different ways we can implement uniqueness criteria; for now, it is important to contemplate and document the cases.)

In our example, the first such example of an identifier is found in this phrase:

> *The client manages a couple of dental offices. One is called the*
> **Chelsea Office** *and the other the* **Downtown Office**.

In many entities you will design, there will be some sort of a name that a company has given something, and in most cases, it's a good attribute to identify the entity. In this case, a Name attribute for the Office entity. This makes it a likely candidate for a key because it's unlikely that the client has two offices that it refers to as "Downtown Office," because that would be silly and lead to a lot of confusion. So I add the Name attribute to the Office entity in the model (shown in Figure 4-18).

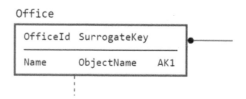

Figure 4-18. *Added the Name attribute to the Office entity*

I'll create a generic domain for these types of generic names, for which I generally choose 60 characters as a reasonable length. This isn't a replacement for customer validation, because the client might have specific size requirements for attributes, though most of the time the client will not really give a thought to lengths nor care initially until reports are created and the values must be displayed. I use 60 because that is well over half of the number of characters that can be displayed in the width of a normal document or form in a reasonable font. This following string of characters is 60 monospaced characters, and it is almost the entire width of the page:

```
123456789012345678901234567890123456789012345678901234567890
```

The actual default length can easily be changed. That is the point of using domains. It may also be clear that the office name is actually a domain of its own.

Tip   Report formatting and print systems can often vary what your model can handle, but be careful about letting it be the complete guide. If 200 characters are needed to form a good name, use 200, and then create attributes that shorten the name where needed. When you get to testing, if 200 is the maximum length and no shortened version is available, then all forms, reports, queries, and so on should be tested for the full-sized attribute's size, hence the desire to keep things to a reasonable length. Just because the max current value length is 10 is meaningless if the next second, a 200-character string could be input and destroy your formatting.

When I added the Name attribute to the Office entity in Figure 4-18, I also set it to require unique values, because it would be really awkward to have two offices named the same name, unless you are modeling a dentist/carpentry office for Moe, Larry, and Curly.

Another identifier is found in this text:

> *Currently, the client uses a* **patient number** *in its computer system that corresponds to a particular folder that has the patient's records.*

Hence, the system needs a patient number attribute for the Patient entity. I'll create a specific domain for the patient number that can be tweaked if needed. After further discussion, we learn that the client is using eight-character patient numbers from the existing system (see Figure 4-19).

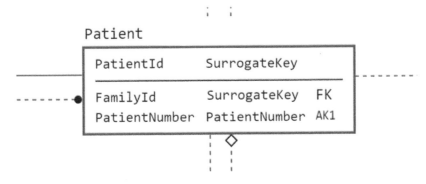

Figure 4-19. *Added the PatientNumber attribute to the Patient entity*

Note   I used the name `PatientNumber` in this entity even though it includes the name of the table as a prefix (something I previously suggested should be done sparingly). I did this because it's a common term to the client. It also gives clarity to the name that `Number` would not have. Other examples might be terms like `PurchaseOrderNumber` or `DriversLicenseNumber`, where the meaning sticks out to the client. No matter what your naming standards, it's generally best to make sure that terms that are common to the client appear as the client normally uses them.

For the most part, it's usually easy to discover an entity's identifier, and this is especially true for the kinds of naturally occurring entities that you find in user-based specifications. Almost everything that exists naturally has some sort of way to differentiate itself, although differentiation can become harder when you start to dig deeper into the customers' actual business practices.

A common contrapositive to the statement about everything being identifiable is things that are managed in bulk. Take our dentist office—although it's easy to differentiate between toothpaste and floss, how would you differentiate between two tubes of toothpaste? And does the customer really care? It's probably a safe enough bet that no one cares which exact toothbrush and tube of toothpaste are given to little Mortimer for taking his scraping like a trooper, but this specificity might be very important when it comes to some implant that the dentist uses to replace Ben's tooth when he fails to adequately use the sample toothbrush and toothpaste between this visit and the next. More discussion with the client would be necessary, but my point is that differentiation and uniqueness aren't always simple.

During the early phase of logical design, the goal is to do the best you can. Some details like this can become implementation details. For implants, there are almost certainly serial numbers. Perhaps for medicines like narcotics, we might require a label be printed with a code and maintained for every bottle that is distributed. For toothbrushes and toothpastes, you may have one row and an estimated inventory amount. In the former, the key might be the code you generate and print, and in the latter, the name "dental samples" might be the key, regardless of the actual brand and type of sample.

Descriptive Information

Descriptive information refers to the common types of adjectives used to describe things that have been previously identified as entities and will usually point directly to an attribute. In our example, different types of supplies are identified, namely, sample and dental:

> *...their supplies, such as **sample toothpastes, toothbrushes, and floss, as well as dental supplies**.*

Another thing you can identify is the possible domain of an attribute. In this case, the attribute is "Type of Supply," and the domain seems to be "Sample" and "Dental." Hence, I create a specific special domain: SupplyType (see Figure 4-20).

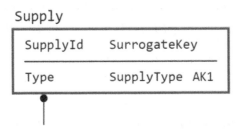

Figure 4-20. *Added the Type attribute to the Supply entity*

Locators

The concept of a locator is not unlike the concept of a key, except that instead of talking about locating something within the electronic boundaries of our database, the locator finds the geographic location, physical position, or even electronic location of something.

For example, the following are examples of locators:

- *Mailing address*: Every address leads us to some physical location on Earth, such as a mailbox at a house or even a post office box in a building.

- *Geographical references*: These are things such as longitude and latitude or even textual directions on how to get to some place.

- *Phone numbers*: Although you can't always pinpoint a physical location using the phone number, you can use it to locate a person for a conversation.

- *Email addresses*: As with phone numbers, you can use these to locate and contact a person.

- *Websites, FTP sites, or other assorted web resources*: You'll often need to identify the website of an entity or the URL of a resource that's identified by the entity; such information would be defined as attributes.

- *Coordinates of any type*: These might be a location on a shelf, pixels on a computer screen, an office number, and so on.

The most obvious location we have in our example is an office, going back to the text we used in the previous section:

> *The client manages a couple of dental offices. One is called the* **Chelsea Office** *and the other the* **Downtown Office***.*

It is reasonably clear from the names that the offices are not located together (like in the same building that has 100 floors, where one office is a posher environment or something), so another identifier we should add is the building address. A building will be identified by its geographic location because a nonmoving target can always be physically located with an address or geographic coordinates. Figure 4-21 shows the Office entity after adding the Address attribute:

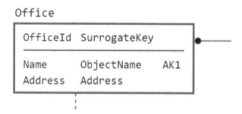

Figure 4-21. *Added an Address attribute to the Office entity*

Each office can have only one address that identifies its location, so the Address attribute initially can go directly in the Office entity. Also important is that the domain for this address be a physical address, not a post office box. Don't get hung up on the fact that you know addresses are more complex than a simple value... How you end up implementing addresses is beyond the scope of the conversation. We will discuss the details of how the address is implemented more later in the process, depending on how addresses will be used by the user.

Immovable places aren't the only things you can locate. A location can be a temporary location or a contact that can be made with the locator, such as addresses, phone numbers, or even something like GPS coordinates, which might change quite rapidly (consider how companies may want to track physical assets, like taxi cabs, tools, etc.). In this next example, there are three typical locators:

> *...have an **address**, a phone number (home, mobile, and/or office),*
> *and optionally an **email address associated with each family***
> ***and possibly each patient if the client desires**...*

Most customers, in this case the dental patients, have phone numbers, addresses, and/or email address attributes. The dental office uses these to locate and communicate with the patient for many different reasons, such as billing, making and canceling appointments, and so on. Note also that often families don't live together, because of college, divorce, and so on, but you might still have to associate them for insurance and billing purposes. From these factors, you get the sets of attributes on families and patients that are shown in Figure 4-22. None of these will generally be an adequate key either, because they could easily be shared with other people or even family units (e.g., an adult child who manages elderly parents who live in a different household, but uses the same email address and perhaps phone number; in other cases, email addresses or phone numbers may make adequate keys).

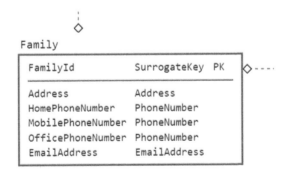

Figure 4-22. *Added location-specific attributes to the Family entity*

The same is found for the patients, as shown in Figure 4-23.

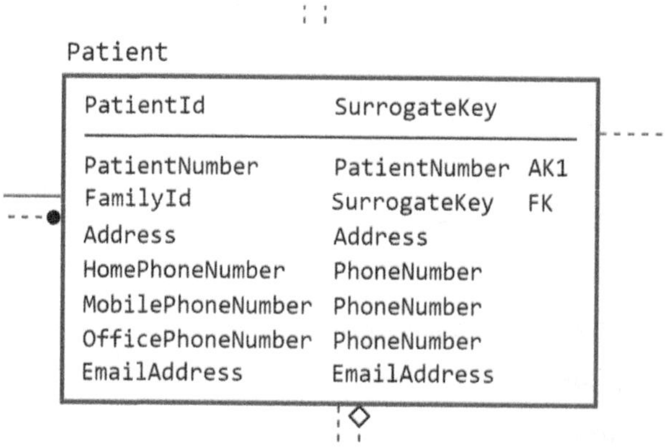

```
Patient

┌─────────────────────────────────────────────────┐
│ PatientId            SurrogateKey                │
│ ───────────────────────────────────────         │
│ PatientNumber        PatientNumber  AK1          │
│ FamilyId             SurrogateKey   FK           │
│ Address              Address                     │
│ HomePhoneNumber      PhoneNumber                 │
│ MobilePhoneNumber    PhoneNumber                 │
│ OfficePhoneNumber    PhoneNumber                 │
│ EmailAddress         EmailAddress                │
└─────────────────────────────────────────────────┘
```

Figure 4-23. *Added location-specific attributes to the Patient entity*

This is a good place to reiterate one of the major differences between a column that you are intending to implement and an attribute in your early modeling process. An attribute needn't follow any specific requirement for its shape. It might be a simple atomic value; it might be an array; and it might end up being an entire set of tables in and of itself. A column in the physical database you implement needs to fit a certain mold of being an atomic value and nothing else. The normalization process, which will be covered in Chapter 5, completes the process of shaping all the attributes into the proper shape for implementation in our relational database.

Since I know the goal is to make atomic-valued attributes, I do tend to break down attributes in the logical model if I am fairly certain they will be in the physical model. But consider the phone number attributes in this table. It is useful to represent them as three attributes in this model, even though for a US-based company that does a lot of phone dialing work, I might have area code, exchange, and suffix as individual columns. That would make nine columns here. I also know that I more than likely will make a specific PhoneNumber table in my database for normalization reasons, so this representation is perfectly adequate to tell the customer, "I know you need to store the home, mobile, and office phone numbers of the patient."

Values

Numbers are some of the most powerful attributes, because often, math is performed with them to get your client paid or to calculate or forecast revenue. Get the number of dependents wrong for a person, and their taxes will be messed up. Or get your wife's weight wrong in the decidedly wrong direction on a form, and she might just beat you with some sort of cooking device (which is not as funny when Rapunzel isn't doing it in *Tangled!*).

Values are generally numeric, such as the following examples:

- *Monetary amounts*: Financial transactions, invoice line items, and so on

- *Quantities*: Weights, number of products sold, counts of items (e.g., number of pills in a prescription bottle), number of items on an invoice line item, number of calls made on a phone, and so on

- *Other*: Wattage for light bulbs, dimensions of a TV screen, RPM rating of a good old-fashioned hard disk, maximum speed on tires, and so on

Numbers are used all around as attributes and are generally going to be rather important. They're also likely candidates to have domains chosen for them to make sure their values are reasonable.

If you were writing a package to capture tax information about a person, you would almost certainly want a domain to state that the count of dependents must be greater than or equal to zero. You might also want to set a likely maximum value, such as 10. It would not be a hard and fast rule, but it would be a sanity check, because most people don't have ten dependents, so it would be good to add a "Did you type this number correctly?" check to the application, and maybe there is an upper value set by law (certainly isn't 2 billion like an integer datatype allows!). Domains don't have to be hard and fast rules at this point (only the hard and fast rules will likely end up as database DDL, but they must be implemented somewhere, or users can and will put in whatever they feel like at the time). It is nice to establish a sanity value, so one doesn't accidentally type 100 when meaning 10 and get audited.

In our example paragraphs, there's one such attribute:

> *The client manages a **couple of dental offices**.*

The question here is what attribute this would be. In this case, it turns out it won't be a numeric value, but instead some information about the cardinality of the dental Office entity. There would be others in the model once we dug deeper into invoicing and payments, but I specifically avoided having monetary values to keep things simple in the model.

193

Times and Dates

The last, and not least, significant type of attribute I will cover is when things occur. I can't imagine only the simplest of databases that would not include attributes of the point in time something has or will take place. When you start to work on reporting, when things occur will almost certainly become the most important thing.

For example, the fact that a customer purchased a product is interesting, but when they purchased it is often just as interesting. The time of day, the month of the year, advertisements that had been sent out or that they might have seen—all these things can be stitched together to start to determine if a company's marketing campaigns are working to bring customers in the store who actually spend money.

In our dental requirements, a few dates are specifically called out that we will cover, and there are far more that would be added to the final product to cover not only when the appointment was but when it was cancelled or rescheduled, how long between cleanings, overdue payments, and so on. I specifically will cover these two. First is in this sentence:

Invoices should be sent within one week after the appointment

From this, we can discern that the date when the invoice is sent has meaning. For this attribute, as shown in Figure 4-24, I specify a domain of date, which will indicate a date, not in the future, with no time component. Typically (and likely for a small dental office), they would not want to know that they wrote the invoice on May 1, 2020 13:43:45.0393532; just May 1, 2020, would suffice.

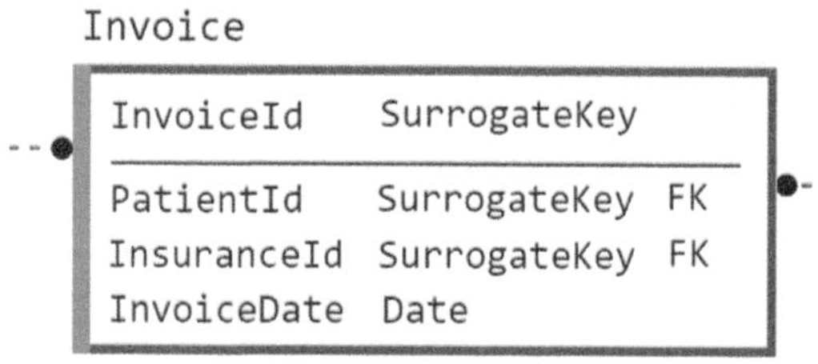

```
Invoice

  InvoiceId     SurrogateKey
  ─────────────────────────────────
  PatientId     SurrogateKey   FK
  InsuranceId   SurrogateKey   FK
  InvoiceDate   Date
```

Figure 4-24. Invoice entity with the added InvoiceDate Attribute

Next, we have the Appointment entity, which is referenced here in the following sentence:

...alerting the patients when and where their appointments occur...

Appointments occur, and we know that appointments occur at some point in time—most typically on the hour, half hour, or 15-minute mark. I set the domain to `PointInTime` for the model now, but as you worked through the exercise with the client, determining whether it should be more granular at the database level would be important, and you might want to refine that to an `AppointmentTime` domain that rounded to a certain time frame.

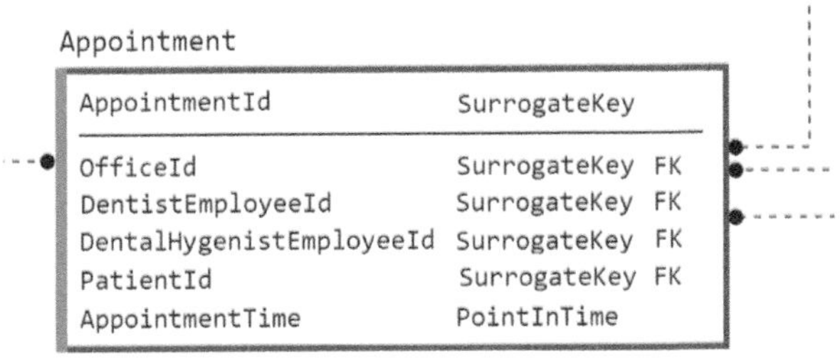

```
Appointment
┌─────────────────────────────────────────────────────────┐
│ AppointmentId               SurrogateKey                 │
│─────────────────────────────────────────────────────────│
│ OfficeId                    SurrogateKey  FK             │
│ DentistEmployeeId           SurrogateKey  FK             │
│ DentalHygenistEmployeeId    SurrogateKey  FK             │
│ PatientId                   SurrogateKey  FK             │
│ AppointmentTime             PointInTime                  │
└─────────────────────────────────────────────────────────┘
```

Figure 4-25. *Appointment entity with time attribute*

For brevity's sake, we won't cover it too much more, but time also will carry along with it a set of rules that you may wish to consider. New appointments typically should not be in the past (typically, as they may need to be allowed to record an appointment that was not properly recorded), appointments should not overlap one another with the same dental hygienist, and so on. The overlapping time frame is an example I will present code for in Chapter 8, but suffice it to say it is important to recognize concerns with dates while doing your logical model.

Tip   Don't fret too hard that you might miss something essential early in the design process. Often, the same entity, attribute, or relationship will crop up in multiple places in the documentation, and your clients will also recognize many bits of information that you miss as you review things with them over and over as well as when you are running through tests until you are happy with your design and move past the logical model and start to produce a physical one.

Many-to-Many Relationships

In the model, we have a few many-to-many relationships that had been modeled, the assignment of Office to Dentist, and Supply usage to Employee. In the original model, they had been drawn as a single line with dots on each end. The problem with this is twofold. First, it can't be implemented this way, so it doesn't look right to most programmers and users. Second, in almost every case, when you have a many-to-many relationship, the relationship between the two entities implies data exists between the entities.

As an example, take Office to Dentist, in Figure 4-26. The table DentistOffice between the Office and Dentist is where details such as when the dentist is available, what duties they might perform, and so on would be placed.

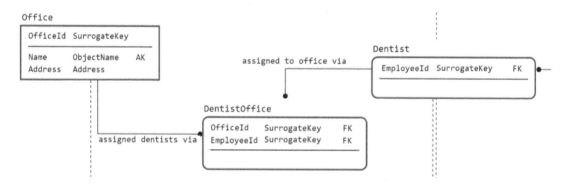

Figure 4-26. *Office to Dentist many-to-many relationship reworked*

In Figure 4-27, Employee to Supply has been remodeled, and in this case, the key of the table probably grows beyond just EmployeeId and SupplyId to include the date of use and then an attribute of quantity perhaps. This would then track the usage of supplies by the Employee. This is conjecture, and in a chapter that is already large, hopefully the point that expanding the many-to-many entities we find out thusly will help us in our next round of model review with the customer is clear enough.

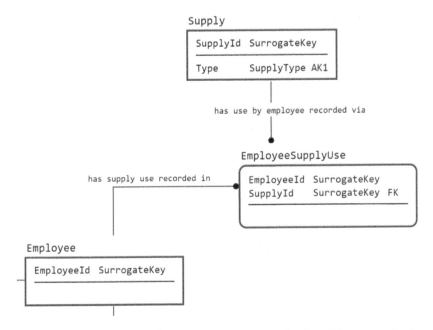

Figure 4-27. *Employee to Supply many-to-many relationship reworked*

The List of Entities, Attributes, and Domains

Figure 4-28 shows the logical graphical model as it stands now (I've removed the relationship verb phrases found in the previous diagram for clarity).

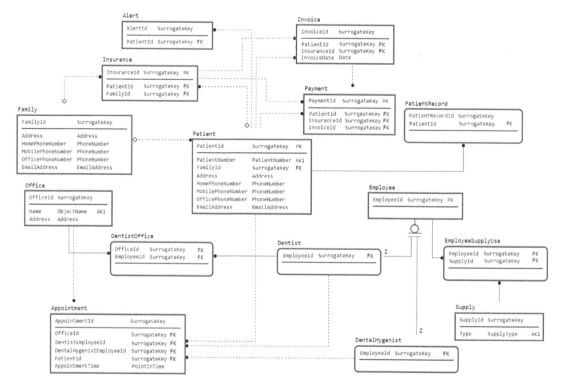

Figure 4-28. *Graphical model of the patient system so far (without verb phrases for simplicity)*

In Table 4-3, there is a subset (for space reasons) of the entities, along with their descriptions, as well as attribute domain descriptions. The more documentation you can accomplish during this phase of the project, the better, because it will afford your customer more details to read, rather than to interpret from your code. It will not be perfect any more than your final database will, so set yourself a reasonable time limit and stick with it (both in filling the time and not going far beyond it as well).

Table 4-3. *Final Model for the Dental Office Example*

Entity/Attribute	Description	Column Description	Column Domain
Patient	The people who are the customers of the dental office. Services are performed, supplies are used, and patients are billed for them.		
	PatientNumber	Used to identify a patient's records in the computer.	Unknown, generated by the current computer system.
	HomePhoneNumber	Phone number to call patient at home.	Any valid phone number.
	MobilePhoneNumber	Phone number to call patient away from home.	Any valid phone number.
	OfficePhoneNumber	Phone number to call patient during work hours. *(Note: Do we need to know work hours for the patient?)*	Any valid phone number.
	Address	Postal address of the family.	Any valid address.
	EmailAddress	Electronic mail address of the family.	Any valid email address.

(continued)

Table 4-3. (*continued*)

Entity/Attribute	Description	Column Description	Column Domain
Family	Groups of persons who are associated, likely for insurance purposes.		
	HomePhoneNumber	Phone number to call patient at home.	Any valid phone number.
	MobilePhoneNumber	Phone number to call patient away from home.	Any valid phone number.
	OfficePhoneNumber	Phone number to call patient during work hours. (*Note: Do we need to know work hours for the patient?*)	Any valid phone number.
	Address	Postal address of the family.	Any valid address.
	EmailAddress	Electronic mail address of the family.	Any valid email address.
	FamilyMembers	Patients that make up a family unit.	Any patients. (*Note: Can a patient be a member of only one family?*)
Dentist	Persons who do the most skilled work at the dental office. Several dentists work for the client's practice.		

(*continued*)

Table 4-3. (*continued*)

Entity/Attribute	Description	Column Description	Column Domain
DentalHygienist	People who do the routine work for the dentist. There are quite a few more hygienists than dentists. *(Note: Check with the client to see if there are guidelines for the number of hygienists per dentist. It might be needed for setting appointments.)*		
Employee	Any person who works at the dental office. Dentists and hygienists are clearly types of employees.		
Office	Locations where the dentists do their business. They have multiple offices to deal with and schedule patients for.		
	Address	Physical address where the building is located.	Address that is not a PO box.
	Name	The name used to refer to a given office.	Unique.

(*continued*)

Table 4-3. (*continued*)

Entity/Attribute	Description	Column Description	Column Domain
Supply	Supplies for the running of the dental operations of the office. Examples given were sample items, such as toothpastes or toothbrushes; plus there was mention of dental supplies as the supplies that the dentists and hygienists use to perform their jobs.		
	Type	Classifies supplies into different types.	"Sample" or "Dental" identified.

Implementation modeling note: Log any changes to sensitive or important data. The relationship between employees and supplies will likely need additional information to document the purpose for the usage.

The biggest concern with the documentation I provided is the use of the phrase "any valid" or any of its derivatives. It is certainly okay as you get started in the process, but as you work with the customer, narrowing down the scope of these statements is a key part of the process. In other words, what does "valid" mean? The phrase "valid dates" indicates that there must be something that could be considered invalid. This, in turn, could mean the "November 31st" kind of invalid or that it isn't valid to schedule an appointment during the year 3000, which is a valid year, just probably not for Myrtle who is already cresting 90 in the year 2020.

At this point, the entities and attributes have been defined. Note that little beyond addresses and phone numbers has been added to the design that wasn't directly impliable from the single requirement artifact we started with.

Identifying Business Rules

Business rules can be defined as statements that govern and shape business behavior. Depending on an organization's methodology, these rules can be in the form of bulleted lists, simple text diagrams, or other formats or perhaps too often stored only in a key employee's head who is off until the week you were planning to be on vacation after finishing the model.

The goal is to get down all data-oriented rules for use later in the process, though a business rule's existence doesn't imply the ability to implement it in the database. It will often become an argument about why we are discussing such things, but it will pay off later when someone is required to write reports and the meetings start to discuss how it was allowed that $100000 was an acceptable charge for a patient's semiannual cleaning and x-rays.

When defining business rules, there might be some duplication of rules and attribute domains, and you may even find new attributes needed to support the business rules, but this isn't a problem. Get as many rules as possible documented, because missing business rules will hurt you more than missing attributes, relationships, or even tables. You'll frequently find new tables and attributes when you're implementing the system, but missing business rules can ruin data quality for reporting or even wreck an entire design, forcing an expensive rethink or an ill-advised kludge to shoehorn data in while tens or hundreds of thousands of dollars are wasted every hour while you are coding the fix. There are better ways to spend a Tuesday morning when you were supposed to be on vacation (sort of a true story...though not sure it was actually Tuesday; it could have been a Thursday).

Recognizing business rules isn't generally a difficult process, but it is time-consuming and fairly tedious. Unlike entities, attributes, and relationships, there's no straightforward, specific grammar-oriented clue for identifying all the business rules (certainly none that is regularly followed by a large number of organizations).

However, my general practice when I have to look for business rules is to read documents line by line, looking for sentences including language such as "once... occurs," "...have to... ," "...must...," "...will... ," and so on. Unfortunately for you, documents don't usually include every business rule, and it is just as great a folly to expect that your clients will remember all of them right off the top of their heads. You might look through a hundred or a thousand invoices and not see a single instance where a client is credited money, but this doesn't mean it never happens. In many cases, you have to mine business rules from three places:

- *Old code*: It's the exception, not the rule, that an existing system will have great documentation (or even documentation at all). Even the ones that start out with wonderful system documentation tend to have their documentation grow worse and worse as time grows shorter and client desires grow. It isn't uncommon to run into poorly written spaghetti code that needs to be analyzed (made worse when it is code that you personally wrote 10 years ago).

- *Client experience*: Using human memory for documentation can be as hard as asking college students what they did the night before. Forgetting important points of the story or simply making up stuff that they think you want to hear so they can get to what they want to be doing is just part of human nature. I've already touched on how difficult it is to get requirements from users, but when you get into rules, this difficulty grows by at least an order of magnitude because most humans don't think in details, and a good portion of the business rules hunt is about minute details.

- *Your experience*: Or at least the experience of one member of your team. Like the invoice example, you might ask questions like "Do you ever...?" to jog the customer's memory. Just be careful that you use your experience to inform your questions, not force the answers.

If you're lucky, you'll be blessed with a business analyst who will take care of this process, but in a lot of cases, the business analyst won't have the experience to think in code-level details and to ferret out subtle business rules from code, so a programmer may have to handle this task. That's not to mention that it's hard to get to the minute details until you understand the system, something you can do only by spending lots of time thinking, considering, and digesting what you are reading. Rare is the occasion going to be afforded you to spend enough time to do a good enough job in that regard.

In our "snippet of notes from the meeting" example, an additional few business rules need to be documented. For example, I've already discussed the need for a customer number attribute but was unable to specify a domain for the customer number. Take the following sentence:

> *For each appointment, the client needs to have everything*
> *documented that went on...*

From it, you can derive a business rule such as this:

> *For every appointment, it is required to document every action on*
> *the patient's chart.*

Note that this rule brings up the likelihood that there exists yet another attribute of a patient's chart—Activity—and another attribute of the activity—ActivityPrice (since most dentists' offices don't work for free). This concept of implementing a relationship between Patient, PatientRecord, Activity, and ActivityPrice gives you a feeling that it might be wrong. The process of normalization covered in the next chapter will work to correct complex relationships, and it's logical that there exists an entity for activities with attributes of `name` and `price` that relate back to the `PatientRecord` entity that has already been specified. Either way is acceptable before calling an end to the modeling process, as long as it makes sense to the readers of the documents.

Another sentence in our example suggests a further possible business rule:

> *The dentists might spend time at each of the offices throughout the week.*

Obviously, a doctor cannot be in two different locations at one time. Hence, we have the following rule:

> *Doctors must not be scheduled for appointments at two locations at one time.*

Another rule that's probably needed is one that pertains to the length of time between appointments for doctors:

> *The length of time between appointments for dentists at different offices can be no shorter than X.*

Not every business rule will manifest itself within the database, even some that specifically deal with a process that manages data. For example, consider this rule:

> *Invoices should be sent within one week after the appointment.*

This is great and everything, but what if it takes a week and a day or even two weeks? Can the invoice no longer be sent to the patient? Should there be database code to chastise the person if there was a holiday or someone was sick and it took a few hours longer than a week? No. Although this seems much like a rule that could be implemented in the database, it isn't. This rule will be given to the people doing system documentation and UI design for use when designing the rest of the system, and as such it might manifest itself as a report or an alert in the UI.

The specifics of some types of rules will be dealt with later in Chapters 7 and 8 and often throughout the book, as we implement various types of tables and integrity constraints.

Identifying Fundamental Processes

A process is a sequence of steps undertaken by a user/program that uses the data that has been identified to do something. It might be a computer-based process, such as "process daily receipts," where some form of report is created or possibly a deposit is created to send to the bank. It could be something manual, such as "creating a new patient," which details that this is the first time the patient fills out a set of forms, then the receptionist asks many of the same questions, and, finally, the hygienist and dentist ask the same questions again once arriving in the room. Then, some of this information is keyed into the computer after the patient leaves so the dental office can send a bill. If you are familiar with UML diagrams, these might be called out as a key term.

You can figure out a lot about your client by studying their processes. Often, a process that you guess should take two steps and ten minutes can drag on for months and months. The hard part will be determining why. Is it for good, sometimes security-oriented reasons? Or is the long process the result of historical inertia? Or just because they are clueless? There are good reasons for a lot of the bizarre corporate behaviors out there, and you may or may not be able to figure out why it is as it is and possibly make changes. At a minimum, the processes will be a guide to some of the data you need, when it is required, and who uses the data in the organization operationally.

As a reasonable manual process example, consider the process of getting your first driver's license, ignoring the case of failure at any step along the way (at least in Tennessee for a new driver; there are other processes that are followed if you come from another state, are a certain age, are not a citizen, etc.):

1. Fill out learner's permit forms.

2. Obtain learner's permit.

3. Practice.

4. Fill out license forms.

5. Pass eye exam.

6. Pass written exam.

7. Pass driving exam.

8. Have picture taken.

9. Receive license.

10. Drive safe out there.

In the license process, you have not only an explicit order that some tasks must be performed but other rules too, such as that you must be 15 to get a learner's permit, you must be 16 to get the license, you must pass the exam with a certain grade, practice must be with a licensed driver, and so on (and there are even exceptions to some of these rules, like getting a license earlier than 16 if you are a hardship case). Some steps might also be able to be done out of order or concurrently. If you were the business analyst helping to design a driver's license project, you would have to document this process in greater detail, likely with some form of flowchart at some point.

Identifying processes (and the rules that govern them) is relevant to the task of data modeling because many of these processes will require manipulation of data. Each process usually translates into one or more queries or stored procedures, which might require more data than has been specified, particularly to store state information throughout the process.

In our example, there are a few examples of such processes:

The client needs the system to manage its patients and appointments...

This implies that the client needs to be able to make appointments, as well as manage the patients—presumably the information about them. Making appointments is one of the most central things our system will do, and you will need to answer questions like these: What appointments are available during scheduling? When can appointments be made?

This is certainly a process that you would want to go back to the client and understand:

...and then invoice the patient's insurance, if they have insurance (otherwise, the patient pays).

I've discussed invoices already, but the process of creating an invoice might require additional attributes to identify that an invoice has been sent electronically or in printed form (possibly reprinted). Document control is an important part of many processes when helping an organization that's trying to modernize a paper system. Note that sending an invoice might seem like a pretty inane event—click a button on a screen, and paper pops out of the printer. All this requires is selecting some data from a table, so what's the big deal? However, when a document is printed, we might have to record the fact that the document was printed, who printed it, and what the use of the document is. We might also need to indicate that the documents are printed during a process that includes closing out and totaling the items on an invoice. Electronic signatures may need to be registered as well. The most important point here is that you should assume that it is dangerous to make major assumptions.

Here are other processes that have been listed:

- *Track and manage dentists and hygienists*: From the sentence "The system needs to track and manage several dentists and quite a few dental hygienists whom the client needs to allocate to each appointment as well."

207

- *Track supplies*: From "The client has had problems in the past keeping up with when it's about to run out of supplies and wants this system to take care of this for both locations. For the dental supplies, we need to track usage by employee, especially any changes made in the database to the patient records."

- *Alert patient*: From "...alerting the patients when and where their appointments occur, either by email or by phone..."

Each of these processes identifies a unit of work that you must deal with during the implementation phase of the database design procedure.

Finalizing the Logical Model

There is an old and reviled saying, "Better is the enemy of good enough." It is a very true saying admittedly, but one of the most difficult parts of the design process is to know when things are good enough. There's a sweet spot when it comes to the amount of design needed. If you don't do enough, blindly believing that you have all the details you need from a team that your client has put together that really couldn't care less about the project, abject failure is pretty certain.

At the same time though, there is a point in time where your design is good enough to move past the logical model and start creating database code that the customer can use. If you go too far past this, you move to a condition commonly known as *"analysis paralysis."* Finding this sweet spot requires experience. Most of the time, a little bit too little design occurs, usually because of a deadline that was set without any understanding of the realities of what the customer really wanted. On the other hand, without strong management, I've found that I easily get myself into analysis paralysis. (Hey, this book focuses on design for a reason. To me it's the second most fun part of the project; users and the realities of life definitely complicate things. Keep it to yourself, but the most fun part of any project is the short period of time after deployment where people say how they love what you have created, that all the work you have done is worth it. It only lasts a few minutes until they want something else, but it is glorious!)

There are a few more things left to do, before starting to write code:

1. Identify obvious additional data needs.

2. Continue to test your model, making sure the requirements that have been identified can be met.

3. Review with the customer.

4. The customer is happy and signs off on what has been designed (or not, in which case you loop back to a previous step).

These steps are part of any system design, not just the data-driven parts.

Identifying Obvious Additional Data Needs

Up to this point, I've been reasonably careful not to broaden the information that was included from the discovery phase. The purpose has been to achieve a baseline to our documentation, staying faithful to the piles of documentation that were originally gathered (and will be far more complete than my requirements were in any case). At this point in the design, you need to change direction and begin to add the attributes that come naturally to fill in any gaps. Usually there's a large set of obvious attributes and, to a lesser extent, business rules that haven't been specified by any of the users or initial analysis.

Ideally, this is done in a series of discussions with the business analysts and, if they don't know the answers, the customers—iterating though the requirements, looking for gaps, and pointing out things you don't quite understand about their processes. If you add any entities to the model without direct links to requirements, make these entities, attributes, relationships, and so on stand out from what you have gotten from the documentation. Colors, notes, tags, and so on will be very useful.

Testing the Logical Model

Just like the conceptual model, it is very much worth it to again test that everything your requirements required is still possible based on the model you are putting out. This step will help you not miss any detail. We won't spend any more text on this concept, as it is simply doing exactly what we have already done for the conceptual model, with more focus spent on whether we have the attributes to support the stated needs.

As an example, consider the following requirement we picked out:

> ...and then invoice the patient's insurance, if they have insurance (otherwise, the patient pays) ...

When I read this and look carefully at the diagram, I notice that the relationship between Insurance and Invoice I added to the diagram is mandatory. But it is clearly stated that insurance is optional for the patient (in the diagram, the patient is optional for insurance, but that is because the family could be the one with insurance, not the specific patient), as you can see in Figure 4-29. The relationship is highlighted in the picture.

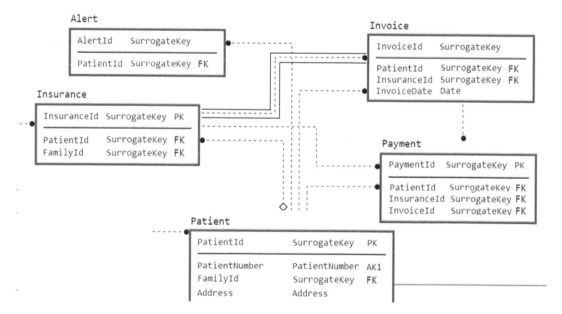

Figure 4-29. *Model subset, with the problematic Insurance to Invoice relationship highlighted*

To rectify this one problem, I would need to make this an optional relationship. The model we have ended up with is flawed in other ways for sure, and I found the lack of a relationship from `Insurance` to `Invoice` working on this testing section revising the last edition of this book.

Note   My goal in making this chapter's example not completely trivial was to make sure this process did not seem easy. You can look at the resulting model and feel a dental office database coming together, but it certainly isn't complete. We are quite a few iterations away from success, if for nothing more than identifiers, handling things like patients inheriting and overriding details from their family, and so on.

All of this rolls into the process of test-driven development. The concept is that the earlier you catch defects, the cheaper they are to mitigate. The idea is errors are easier to fix before code is deployed, and imagine how much easier it is to fix before the code is written! Finding bugs in the logical model before you build the physical model is ideal. Once your data structures, code, and then customer data are employed for business purposes, forget about fixing some problems. You may just have to work around some of the issues. Plus, the tests you do now in words will translate to the tests that are performed in code as well.

Final Review with the Client

Once you've finished putting together this first draft document, it's time to meet with the client to explain where you've gotten to in your design and have the client review every bit of this final logical model and associated documents. Make sure the client understands the solution that you're beginning to devise. This may be the business analyst and/or system architect representing the customer, and then relaying the information to the customer, it could be the CEO of the firm directly. That is totally up to the customer. But you want to cover your bases as much as possible such that you feel confident that the design is well understood.

Customer Agrees with Your Model and Signs Document (or Not)

It isn't likely you'll get everything right in this phase of the project and certainly not on the first try. The most important thing is to get as much correct as you can and get it in front of the customer to agree on. Of course, it's unlikely that the client will immediately agree with everything you say, even if you're the greatest data architect in the world. It is also true that often the client will know what they want just fine but cannot express it in a way that gets through your thick skull. In either event, it usually takes several attempts to get the model to a place where everyone agrees, and each iteration should move you and the client closer to your goal.

There will be many times later in the project that you might have to revisit this part of the design and find something you missed or something the client forgot to share with you. As you get through more and more iterations of the design, it becomes increasingly important to make sure you have your client sign off at regular times; you can point to these documents when the client changes their mind later.

If you don't get agreement, often in writing or in a public forum, such as a meeting with enough witnesses, things can get complicated. This is especially true when you don't do an adequate job of handling the review and documentation process and there's no good documentation to back up your claim vs. the client's. I've worked on consulting projects where the project was well designed and agreed on but documentation of what was agreed wasn't done too well (a lot of handshaking at a higher level to "save" money). As time went by and thousands of dollars were spent, the client reviewed the agreement document, and it became obvious that we didn't agree on much at all. Needless to say, that whole project worked out about as well as a hydrogen-filled, thermite-coated dirigible.

Note   I've been kind of hard on customers in this chapter, making them out to be conniving folks who will cheat you at the drop of a hat. This is seldom the case, but it takes only one. The truth is that almost every client will appreciate your keeping them in the loop and getting approval for the design at reasonable intervals, because clients are only as invested in the process as they must be. You might even be the 15th consultant performing these interviews because the previous 14 were tremendous failures.

Best Practices

The following list of some best practices can be useful to follow when doing conceptual and logical modeling:

- *Be patient*: The way in which I present the process in this book is intended to encourage you to follow a reasonably linear process rather than starting out with a design and looking for a problem to solve with it. I am also aware that reality will be more compressed than this, but keeping the discipline to follow the steps quickly in your head will be beneficial.

- *Be diligent*: Look through everything to make sure that what's being said makes sense. Be certain to understand as many of the business rules that bind the system as possible before moving on to the next step. Mistakes made early in the process can fester later.

- *Document*: The point of this chapter has been just that—document every entity, attribute, relationship, business rule, and process identified (and anything else you discover, even if it won't fit neatly into one of these buckets). The format of the documentation isn't really all that important, only that the information is there, that it's understandable by all parties involved, and that it will be useful going forward toward implementation.

- *Communicate*: Constant, typically written, communication with clients is essential to keep the design on track. The danger is that if you start to get the wrong idea of what the client needs, every decision past that point might be wrong. Get as much face time with the client as possible. It is a great practice to continually update your client on your design and make sure that the requirements of the client haven't changed.

Note   This mantra of "review with client, review with client, review with client" is probably starting to get a bit old at this point (it is as the writer of the chapter, because I am somewhat preaching to myself). This is one of the last times I'll mention it, but it's so important that I hope it has sunk in. The following chapters are going to start back down the hill toward producing output without thinking about how we got the requirements.

Summary

In this chapter, I've presented the process of discovering the structures that should eventually make up a simple dental office database solution. We've waded through all the documentation that had been gathered during the information gathering phase, doing our best not to add our own contributions to the solution without input from the customer. This is no small task; in our initial example, we had only three paragraphs to work with, yet we ended up with quite a few pages of documentation from it.

Through all this documentation, the goal is to discover as many of the following as possible:

- Entities and relationships

- Attributes and domains

- Business rules that can be enforced in the database

- Processes that require the use of the database

From this, a logical data model will emerge that has most of the characteristics that will exist in the actual implemented database. Pretty much all that is left after this is to mold the design into a shape that fits the needs of the RDBMS to provide maximum ease of use. In the upcoming chapters, the database design will certainly change in various ways (e.g., to fit SQL Server and to meet requirements that were missed) from the model we have just produced, but unless your team does a terrible job of gathering requirements and modeling, it will not be so different that even the nontechnical layperson who has to approve your designs will understand it. (And if you do a terrible job of it now and again, it happens to everyone. Failure is the best teacher!)

In Chapters 6 and 7, we will apply the skills covered in this chapter for translating requirements to a data model and those for normalization from Chapter 5 to produce portions of data models that demonstrate the many ways you can take these very basic skills and create complex, interesting models.

CHAPTER 5

Normalization

We are mistaken when we compare war with "normal life." Life has never been normal. Even those periods which we think most tranquil, like the nineteenth century, turn out, on closer inspection, to be full of cries, alarms, difficulties, emergencies.

—C. S. Lewis, "Learning in Wartime"

The most personal part of this book has come to be the quotes that start each chapter. As I write this, we are semi-quarantined from a pandemic, not going out except for exercise and basics, but that is not the main meaning to garner from this quote. The main thing I want you to get from this quote is that life is always insane and, learning and doing the best job, you should not be constantly put on hold for every insane cry you will receive. In fact, for the users and administrators of the databases you will create, the architect of the healthy or sick database is, or someday will be, you.

By now, you should have built the conceptual and logical model that covers the data requirements for your database system. As we have discussed over the previous four chapters, our design so far needn't follow any strict format or method (even if it probably will as you practice the craft over time); the main thing it must do right now is reflect the customer's data-related requirements for the system that needs to be built in a manner that is clear to you and your customer.

At this point, we are going to shift into the process of turning our entities and attributes into strictly formatted tables and columns, ready for the Data Definition Language (DDL) of SQL Server. To make this transformation, we are going to look at the most hyped (or perhaps most despised) topic in all relational database–dom: *normalization.* It is where the theory meets reality and we translate the model from something loosely structured to something that is very structured to follow a certain pattern. Normalization is a process

© Louis Davidson 2021
L. Davidson, *Pro SQL Server Relational Database Design and Implementation,*
https://doi.org/10.1007/978-1-4842-6497-3_5

by which redundancies are removed and objects shaped in a manner that the relational engine has been designed to work with. Once you are done with the process, working with the data will be (for the most part) natural using SQL.

T-SQL is a language designed to work with sets of atomic values. To review, in computer science terms, *atomic* means that a value should not be broken down into smaller parts. Our eventual goal is to break down the entities and attributes into atomic units; that is, break them down to the lowest form that will need to be accessed in T-SQL code.

The phrase "lowest form" can be dangerous for newbies and seasoned veterans alike because one must resist the temptation to go too far. At the correct atomic level, using the database will be a natural process, but at the wrong level of atomicity (too much or too little), you will find yourself struggling against the design by needing to disassemble data values into the bit of data that you need or, conversely, reassemble data from parts that have no actual use to your users.

Some joke that if most developers had their way, every database would have exactly one table with two columns. The table would be named `"Object"`, and the columns would be `"Pointer"` and `"Contents"`. But this desire is usurped by a need to satisfy the customer with searches, reports, and consistent results from their data being stored, and it will no doubt take you quite a few tries before you start realizing just how true this is.

The process of normalization is based on a set of levels, each of which achieves a level of correctness or adherence to a set of "rules." The rules are formally known as *forms*, as in the *normal forms*. Quite a few normal forms have been theorized and postulated, but I'll focus on the four most important, commonly known, and often applied. I'll start with First Normal Form (1NF), which eliminates data redundancy (such as a name being stored in two separate places), and continue through to Fifth Normal Form (5NF), which deals with the decomposition of ternary relationships. (One of the normal forms I'll present isn't numbered; it's named for the people who devised it and encompasses two of the numbered forms.) Each level of normalization indicates an increasing degree of adherence to the recognized standards of database design. As you increase the degree of normalization of your data, you'll naturally tend to create an increasing number of tables of decreasing width (fewer columns).

The problem with this view of normalization is that it leads to the view that if you can't precisely achieve a lower level, why even try to achieve the higher ones? This is the kind of thinking that creates real problems. The rules are all valuable to understand and either attempt to achieve or at least to understand what the purpose is and how to mitigate failing to meet their (rarely lofty) goals.

In this chapter, I will present the different normal forms defined not so much by their numbers but by the problems they were designed to solve. For each, I will include examples, describe the programming anomalies they help you avoid, and identify the telltale signs that your relational data is breaking that normal form. It might seem out of place to show programming anomalies at this point, since we clearly have not stated that we are ready to start coding, but the point of normalization is to transform the entities we have started with into something that is implementable as tables. It is an iterative process, honing the structures to be what is needed, something you can do with any design to see if it is as right as necessary. It is very important to start thinking as a programmer so you can reconcile *why* having data in each normal form can make the tables easier to work with in T-SQL. Otherwise, all this stuff tends to just look like more work for the sake of some arcane practices come up by people who write academic articles who haven't actually coded database code in 40 years. In reality, some of these academics haven't built real systems in a long time, but the theory is still sound and valuable for the normal programmer.

The Process of Normalization

The process of normalization is generally straightforward: take entities that are overly complex and extract simpler entities from them with the goal of ending up with entities that express fewer concepts than before until every entity/table expresses one and only one concept. The process continues until we produce a model such that, in practical terms, every table in the database will represent one thing and every column in each table represents one thing about what the table is modeling. This will become more apparent throughout the chapter as I work through the different normal forms.

Note   There is a theorem called "Heath's Theorem" that can explain the process of normalization in more mathematical terms. You can read about it in *Database Systems: A Pragmatic Approach, Second Edition*, by Elvis Foster (`www.apress.com/9781484211922`) or in Professor William Perrizo's online notes for a college database design class (`www.cs.ndsu.nodak.edu/~perrizo/classes/765/nor.html`). It may make you a little dizzy if you have my personal tolerance for relational algebra. You have been warned.

I'll break down normalization into three general categories:

- Table and column shape

- Relationships between columns

- Multivalued and join dependencies in tables

Note that the conditions mentioned for each should be considered for every entity you design, because each normal form is built on the precept that the lower forms have been complied with. The reality is that few designs, and even fewer implementations, meet any of the normal forms perfectly, and just because you can't meet one set of criteria doesn't mean you should chuck the more advanced. Just like breaking down and having a donut on a diet doesn't mean you should go ahead and eat the entire box, imperfections are a part of the reality of database design.

As an architect, you will strive for perfection, but it is largely impossible to achieve, if for no other reason than the fact that users' needs change frequently and impatient project managers demand completion dates far in advance of realistic time frames. In agile projects, I simply try to do the best I can to meet the demanding schedule requirements, but minimally, I try to at least document and know what the design should be because the perfect design matches the real world in a way that makes it natural to work with (if sometimes a bit tedious). What you design and what actually gets implemented will always be a trade-off with your skills and schedule, but the more you know about what correct is, the more likely you will be able to eventually achieve a solid output regardless of artificial schedule milestones.

Table and Column Shape

The first step in the process of producing a normalized database is to deal with the "shape" of the data. To produce well-performing SQL Server code, it is minimally important to understand how SQL Server's relational engine wants the data shaped for simple searching and indexing. Recall from Chapter 1 that the first two of Codd's rules are the basis for the definition of a table. The first states that data is to be represented only by values in tables, and the second states that any piece of data in a relational database is guaranteed to be logically accessible by knowing its table name, primary key value, and column name. This combination of rules sets forth the requirements that

- All columns must be atomic; that is, only a single value is represented in a single column in a single row of a table. Otherwise, the column name is no longer the end of the address of a value, but a position in the value is required.

- All rows of a table must be different. This is for the same addressing reasons as before. If you can't tell one row from another by a key value, it means there is more work to pick a row than using a key value.

To strengthen this stance, the First Normal Form was specified to require that a value would not be extended to implement arrays or, even worse, position-based fields (yes, in this case, *field* is the right term since it would be positional) having multiple values would be allowed. Hence, First Normal Form states that

> *Every row should contain the same number of values or, in other words, no arrays, subtables, or repeating groups.*

This rule centers on making sure the implemented tables and columns are shaped properly for the relational languages that manipulate them (most importantly for you and me, T-SQL). "Repeating groups" is an odd term that is not used often these days that references having multiple values of the same type in a row, rather than splitting the repeating groups into multiple rows.

Violations from the three presented criteria generally manifest themselves in the implemented model requiring suboptimal data handling, usually because of having to decode multiple values stored where a single one should be. This might be too many independent values in a row, multiple values in a column, or one row value duplicated in multiple rows.

In this book, we are generally speaking of OLTP solutions where we desire data to be modified at any location, by multiple users, sometimes attempting to do so simultaneously. It is interesting to note that for the most part, even data warehousing databases typically follow First Normal Form in order to make queries work with the engine optimally. The later normal forms are less applicable to data warehousing situations because they are more concerned with redundancies in the data that make it harder to modify data, which is handled specially in data warehouse solutions.

All Columns Must Be Atomic

The goal of this requirement is that each column should represent only one type of value and every column value should have one and only one value represented by it. This means there should be nothing like an array, no delimited lists, and no other types of multivalued columns that you could dream up represented by a single column. For example, consider a data value like '1, 2, 3, 6, 7'. This likely represents five separate values. It may not, though whether or not it is five different values will be up to the context of the customer's needs (as we covered during design, the hardest part of the entire database design and implementation processes is that you have to be able to separate what something looks like vs. what it means).

It also means that if you have a value like '1, 2, 3, Bob, 6, 7' that does represent six different values, the integer values you see in the list should be of the same type of data as 'Bob', in the context of the system if you end up storing them in the same column. Perhaps these are nicknames of people, like the *Peanuts* character named 5? Either way, context is important to normalization.

One good way to think of atomicity of a columnar value is to consider whether you would ever need to deal with part of a column without the other parts of the data in that same column. If the list previously mentioned—'1, 2, 3, 6, 7'—is always treated as a single value by the client and, in turn, WHERE ColumnName = '1, 2, 3, 6, 7'; in the T-SQL code, it might be acceptable to store the value in a single column. However, if you might need to deal with the value 3 individually in any substantial manner, the value is not in First Normal Form. It is okay to occasionally search for a value LIKE '%3%' because sometimes you don't remember the entire value. For example, if you are thinking, "I remember the name of that speaker was something ending in 'sen,' 'son'... something like that," then SpeakerName LIKE '%s_n' is fine—just not as a regular part of a process.

One variation on atomicity is for complex datatypes such as a point in a graph like (X, Y). Complex datatypes can contain more than one value, if

- There is always the same number of values.

- The values are dependent on each other.

- The values are rarely, if ever, dealt with individually.

- The values make up some atomic thing/attribute that only makes sense as a single value and could not be fully expressed with a single value.

For example, consider geographic location. Two values are generally used to locate something on Earth, these being the longitude and the latitude. Most of the time, either of these, considered individually, has some (if incomplete) meaning, but taken together, they pinpoint an exact position on Earth. Implementing as a complex type can give us some ease of implementing data protection schemes and can make using the types in formulas easier. It could also be something more complex like an entire shape in a value as well.

When it comes to testing atomicity, the test of reasonability is left up to the designer and the customer need. However, the goal is that any data you ever need to deal with as a single value is modeled as its own column, so it's stored in a column of its own (e.g., as a search argument or a join criterion). As an example of taking atomicity to the extreme, consider a text document with ten paragraphs. A table to store the document might easily be implemented that would require ten different rows (one for each paragraph), but in the *typical case,* there's likely little reason to design like that, because you'll be unlikely to deal with a paragraph as a single value in the T-SQL language.

Of course, when you are building your physical designs, the real-world typical cases are meaningless; all that matters is meeting the requirements of your current design. If your T-SQL is often counting the paragraphs in documents, an approach with a paragraph per row might just be the solution you are looking for (never let anyone judge your database without knowledge of your requirements!). And why stop at paragraphs? Why not sentences, words, letters, or even bits that make up the characters? Each of those breakdowns may actually make sense in some extreme context, so understanding the context is key to normalization.

Note   While you can normalize pretty much any data structure, there are other technologies that can be used to implement a database, such as Hadoop, NoSQL, DocumentDB, and so on, that, even at this point in the process, may actually make more sense for your implementation. Just because all you own is a hammer doesn't make every problem solvable with a nail.

As examples, consider some of the common locations where violations of this rule of First Normal Form often can be found:

1. Email addresses

2. Names

3. Telephone numbers

Each of these gives us a slightly different kind of issue with atomicity that needs to be considered when designing columns.

Email Addresses

In an email message, the To address is typically stored in a format such as the following, using encoding characters to enable you to put multiple email addresses in a single value:

```
name1@domain1.com;name2@domain2.com;name3@domain3.com
```

In the data storage tier of an email engine, this is the optimum format. The email address columns follow a common format that allows multiple values separated by semicolons. However, if you need to store the values in a relational database, storing the data in this format is going to end up being a problem because it represents more than one email address in a single column and leads to difficult utilization in your T-SQL. In Chapter 11, it will become more apparent from an internal engine standpoint why this is, but here, we will look at a practical example of how this will be bothersome when working with the data in T-SQL.

If users can have more than one email address, the value of an email column might look like this: `tay@bull.com;norma@liser.com`. Consider too that several users in the database might use the `tay@bull.com` email address (e.g., if it were the family's shared email account).

Note   In this chapter, I will use the character = to underline the key columns in a table of data and the − character for the non-key attributes in order to make the representation easier to read without explanation.

The following is an example of some unnormalized data. In the following table, PersonId is the key column, while FirstName and EmailAddresses are the non-key columns (not likely good enough for a real table, of course, but good enough for this specific discussion):

```
PersonId    FirstName   EmailAddresses
==========  ----------  ------------------------------------------------
0001003     Tay         tay@bull.com;taybull@hotmail.com;tbull@gmail.com
0003020     Norma       norma@liser.com
```

Consider the situation when one of the addresses changes. For example, we need to change all occurrences of tay@bull.com to family@bull.com. You could execute code such as the following to update every person who references the tay@bull.com address:

```
UPDATE Person
SET    EmailAddress =
            REPLACE(EmailAddresses,'tay@bull.com','family@bull.com')
WHERE  ';' + emailAddress + ';' like '%;tay@bull.com;%';
```

This code might not seem like that much trouble to write and execute, and while it is pretty messy compared to the proper solution (a table with one row per email address for each person), it is very similar to what one might write in a language like C# one row at a time. However, there are problems first with dealing with the true complex nature of data formats. For example, "email;"@domain.com is, in fact, a valid email address based on the email standard (www.lifewire.com/elements-of-email-address-1166413). However, the biggest issue is going to be in how the relational engine works with the data. Comparisons on entire column values (or at least partial values that include the leading characters) can be optimized well by the engine using indexes. Any other comparisons can mean touching every row of a table.

Consider other common operations, such as counting how many distinct email addresses you have. With multiple email addresses inline, using SQL to get this information is painful at best. But, as mentioned, you should implement the data correctly with each email address represented individually in a separate row. Reformat the data as two tables, one for the `Person`

```
PersonId         FirstName
==============   ----------------------
0001003          Tay
0003020          Norma
```

and another table for `PersonEmailAddress`:

```
PersonId         EmailAddress
==============   =========================
0001003          tay@bull.com
0001003          taybull@hotmail.com
0001003          tbull@gmail.com
0003020          norma@liser.com
```

Now, an easy query determines how many email addresses there are per person:

```
SELECT PersonId, COUNT(*) AS EmailAddressCount
FROM   PersonEmailAddress
GROUP BY PersonId;
```

And the previous update we wrote is now simply written as

```
UPDATE PersonEmailAddress
SET    EmailAddress = 'family@bull.com'
WHERE  EmailAddress = 'tay@bull.com';
```

Looking at the structure of an email address, you might notice that beyond being broken down into individual rows, each email address can be broken down into two or three obvious parts based on their format. A common way to break up these values is into the following parts:

- AccountName: name1

- Domain: domain1.com

Whether storing the data as multiple parts is desirable will usually come down to whether you intend to access the individual parts separately in your code. For example, if all you'll ever do is send email, a single column (with a formatting constraint so you don't get "This is my @ email address" as a value!) is perfectly acceptable. However, if you need to consider what domains you have email addresses stored for, then it's a completely different matter. You might think, "What if an entire domain were to change like when `bull.com` becomes `bul.com`." Yet, something like this happens almost never and could be done as a one-off maintenance operation and probably would not make sense as a reason to break data down beyond its natural format.

Finally, a domain consists of two parts: `domain1` and `com`. So you might end up with this:

PersonId	Name	Domain	TopLevelDomain	EmailAddress (calc)
0001003	tay	bull	com	tay@bull.com
0001003	taybull	hotmail	com	taybull@hotmail.com
0001003	tbull	gmail	com	tbull@gmail.com
0003020	norma	liser	com	norma@liser.com

At this point, you might be saying, "What? Who would do that?" First off, I hope your user interface wouldn't force the users to enter their addresses one section at a time in either case, since parsing into multiple values is something the code can do easily (and needs to do at least somewhat to validate the format of the email address). Having the interface that is validating the email addresses do the splitting is natural (as is having a calculated column to reconstitute the email for normal usage).

The purpose of separating email addresses into sections is another question. First off, you can start to be sure that all email addresses are at least somewhat legally formatted. The second answer is that if you ever need to field questions like "What are the top ten services our clients are using for email?" you can execute a query such as the following with relative ease and decent performance:

```
SELECT TOP 10 Domain, TopLevelDomain AS Domain, COUNT(*) AS DomainCount
FROM   PersonEmailAddress
GROUP BY Domain, TopLevelDomain
ORDER BY DomainCount;
```

Is this sort of data understanding necessary to your system? Perhaps and perhaps not. The point of this exercise is to help you understand that if you get the data broken down to the level in which you will query it, life will be easier, SQL will be easier to write, and your client will be happier.

Keep in mind, though, as the database designer, you can name a column singularly and ask the user nicely to put in proper email addresses, but if you don't protect the format, you will likely end up with your email address table looking like this, which is actually worse than what you started because the same email address is duplicated multiple times for person '0001003'!

PersonId	EmailAddress
==========	==============
0001003	tay@bull.com
0001003	tay@bull.com;taybull@hotmail.com;tbull@gmail.com
0001003	tbull@gmail.com
0003020	norma@liser.com

Email address values are unique in this example, but clearly do not represent single email addresses. Every user represented in this data will now get lies as to how many addresses are in the system, and Tay is going to get duplicate emails, making your company look either desperate or stupid (and possibly hurting your corporate email reputation making you look like a spammer).

Names

Names are a special case, as people in the Western culture generally have three parts to their names. Not every culture follows this same pattern, and how much you need to try to fit names into your database properly (as always) depends on what you will do with the data. In a database, the name is often used in many ways: first and last names when greeting someone we don't know, first name only when we want to sound cordial, and all three when we need to make our child realize we are serious.

Consider the name Rei Leigh Badezine. The first name, middle name, and last name (sometimes all the database cares about is a middle initial) could be stored in a single column and used. Using string parsing, you could get the first name and last name if you needed them on occasion. Parsing seems simple, assuming every name is formatted with precisely one first name, one middle name, and one last name. Add in names that have even slightly more complexity though, and parsing becomes a nightmare.

Consider the following list of names:

```
PersonId       FullName
==========     ---------------------------
00202000       R. Lee Ermey
02300000       John Ratzenberger
03230021       Javier Fernandez Pena
```

This "one, big column" initially seems to save a lot of formatting work, but it has a lot of drawbacks particularly for searching. The problem with this approach is that it is hard to figure out what the first and last names are, because we have three different sorts of names formatted in the list. The best we could do is parse out the first and last parts of the names for reasonable searches (assuming no one has only one name!).

Consider you need to find the person with the name John Ratzenberger. This is easy:

```
SELECT  FullName
FROM    Person
WHERE   FullName = 'John Ratzenberger';
```

But what if you need to find anyone with a last name of Ratzenberger? This gets more complex, not so much in the coding, rather for the relational engine that works best with atomic values:

```
SELECT  FullName
FROM    Person
WHERE   FullName LIKE '% Ratzenberger';
```

But what about Mr. Fred Ratzenberger Jr.? Starting the process to remove Jr./Junior (except where Junior is the actual last name, which it can be) is very complicated. Add in that some last names are also first names (Lee Ermey's first name of Lee being a very common example). Consider next the need of searching for someone with a middle name of Fernandez. This is where things get muddy and very difficult to code correctly and achieve with great performance. So instead of just one big column, consider instead the following, more proper method of storing names. This time, each name part gets its own column:

PersonId	FirstName	MiddleName	LastName	FullName (calc)
==========	===========	============	==========	=================
00202000	R.	Lee	Ermey	R. Lee Ermey
02300000	John	NULL	Ratzenberger	John Ratzenberger
03230021	Javier	Fernandez	Pena	Javier Fernandez Pena

I included a calculated column that reconstitutes the name like it starts and included the period after R. Lee Ermey's first name because it is an abbreviation. Names like his can be tricky, because you have to be careful as to whether this should be "R. Lee" as a first name or managed as two names. I would also advise you that, when creating interfaces to save names, it is almost always going to be better to minimally provide the user with first, middle, and last name fields to fill out. Then allow the user to decide which parts of a name go into which of those columns. Leonardo Da Vinci is generally considered to have two names, not three. But Fred Da Bomb (who is also an artist, just not up to Leonardo's quality) considers Da as a middle name.

The prime value of doing more than having a blob of text for a name is in search performance. Instead of doing some wacky parsing on every usage and hoping everyone paid attention to the formatting, you can query by name using the following simple, easy-to-understand approach:

```
SELECT  FirstName, LastName
FROM    Person
WHERE   LastName = 'Ratzenberger';
```

Not only does this code look a lot simpler than the code presented earlier; it works tremendously better in almost every possible case. Because we are using the entire column value, indexing operations can be used to make searching easier (and even without indexes, statistics can help SQL Server have a good guess on how many rows will be returned before the query is executed). What of the case where we are looking for John Ratzenberger only?

```
SELECT   FirstName, LastName
FROM     Person
WHERE    FirstName = 'John'
  AND    LastName = 'Ratzenberger';
```

If there are only a few persons named John in the database or only a few persons with a last name of Ratzenberger (perhaps far more likely unless this is the database for the Ratzenberger family reunion), the optimizer can determine the best way to search.

Finally, the reality of a customer-oriented database may be that you need to store seemingly redundant information in the database to store different/customizable versions of the name, each manually created. For example, you might store versions of a person's name, like how they prefer to be addressed in correspondence:

PersonId	FirstName	MiddleName	LastName	CorrespondenceName
00202000	R.	Lee	Ermey	R. Lee Ermey
02300000	John	NULL	Ratzenberger	John Ratzenberger
03230021	Javier	Fernandez	Pena	Javier Pena

Is this approach a problem with respect to normalization? Absolutely not. The name used to talk to the person might be Q-dog and the given name Leonard. Duplication of data is only going to be an issue when there is a direct functional dependency with no possibility of variation.

The problem is that the approach is not a design problem, so much as a data management one. In the normal case, if the FirstName value changes, the CorrespondenceName value *probably* needs to change as well. It *definitely* should be reviewed. So we will want to document the dependencies that naturally exist, even if the dependencies are not truly functional dependencies in that they can be overridden, and perhaps even create additional columns that indicate to external software to rewrite the value in the default way if the CorrespondenceNameOverrideFlag = 0 and leave it whatever it is if it = 1 (perhaps adding a warning to the UI in that case to review the CorrespondenceName value).

Note that no matter how well you think this design works, there are still problems with it if getting everyone's name correct exists. As stated, while it is common in many Western cultures for people to have three-part names, it is not true for everyone here (e.g., some married persons keep their original name and their spouse's name, so they have four names) and is certainly not the case for all cultures. What to do if a person has ten words to their name? Stuff eight of the names in the MiddleName column? If you want to get it perfectly right (as you may need to do if you are doing certain types of applications), you need to allow for as many words as might ever be necessary (note that we also get some level of metadata now about each part of the name). Of course, this sort of solution is very rare and usually unneeded for almost all implementations, but if you needed to store an unlimited number of name parts for a person, this would be the best way to go:

PersonId	NamePart	Type	Sequence
============	-----------	-------------	--------
00202000	R.	First	1
00202000	Lee	Middle	2
03230021	Javier	Lastname	3
03230021	Fernandez	First	1
00202000	Ermey	Lastname	2

Tip   Names are an extremely important part of many customer systems. There is at least one hotel in Chicago I would hesitate to go back to because of what they called me in a very personal-sounding thank-you email, and when I responded that it was wrong, they did not reply.

Telephone Numbers

Telephone numbers where I am located are of the form 1-888-555-1212, plus some possible extension number. From our previous examples, you can guess that several potential columns are probably present in the telephone number value. However, complicating matters is that frequently the need exists to store more than just telephone numbers from one numbering plan in a database. The decision on how to handle this situation is usually based on how often the users store phone numbers in other formats and how important phone numbers are to the purpose of the customer storing them. It would be a very messy set of tables to handle every possible phone format well enough and certainly more difficult than most clients will support paying you for.

For a North American Numbering Plan (NANP) phone number (America, Canada, and several other countries, but not Mexico), you can represent the standard phone number with three different columns for each of the three following parts, AAA-EEE-SSSS (the country is always 1):

- *AAA (area code)*: Indicates a calling area located within a region
- *EEE (exchange)*: Indicates a set of numbers within an area code
- *SSSS (suffix)*: Number used to make individual phone numbers unique

Whether you make three columns for the NANP phone numbers in your database can be a tricky decision. If every phone number fits this format because you only permit calling to numbers in the United States, for example, having three columns to represent each number is generally the best solution for all the same reasons mentioned in the "Email Addresses" and "Names" sections. You might want to include extension information in an additional column too. The problem is that all it takes is a single need to allow a phone number of a different format to make the pattern fail. So what do you do? Have a single column and just let anyone enter anything they want? That is the common solution, but a step back in data integrity as you will all too frequently get users actually entering anything they want like {PhoneNumber:"Doesn't have a phone number"} and some stuff they will swear they didn't actually enter. Should you build some tools to constrain values at the database level? That will make things better in some respects, but sometimes you lose that battle because the errors you get back when you violate a CHECK constraint aren't very nice (a problem that will be discussed in more detail in Chapter 8).

Why does it matter? Well, if a user misses a digit, you no longer will be able to call your customers to thank them or to tell them their products will not be on time. In addition, new area codes are showing up all the time, and in some cases, phone companies split an area code and reassign certain exchanges to a new area code. The programming logic required to change part of a multipart value can be confusing. Take for example the following set of phone numbers:

```
PhoneNumber
==============
615-555-4534
615-434-2333
```

The code to modify an existing area code to a new area code is messy and certainly not the best performer. Usually, when an area code splits, it is for only certain exchanges. Assuming a well-maintained format of AAA-EEE-NNNN where AAA equals area code, EEE equals exchange, and NNNN equals the phone number, the code looks like this:

```
UPDATE PhoneNumber
SET PhoneNumber = '423' + SUBSTRING(PhoneNumber,4,8)
WHERE SUBSTRING(PhoneNumber,1,3) = '615'
    AND SUBSTRING(PhoneNumber,5,3) IN ('232','323',...,'989');
    --area codes generally change for certain exchanges
```

This code requires perfect formatting of the phone number data to work, and unless the formatting is forced on the users in some manner, perfection is unlikely to be the case. Consider even a slight change, as in the following values that have an extra space character thrown in for your programming amusement (not to mention when a user feels the need to prefix a phone number with a 1- on occasion):

```
PhoneNumber
==============
 615-555-4534
615- 434-2333
```

You are not going to be able to deal with this data simply, because neither of these rows would be updated by the previous UPDATE statement. TRIM might help the first, but not the second. And you could use REPLACE to remove spaces, but plugging holes in poorly formatted data is more complicated than plugging holes in a dam with chewing gum.

Changing the area code is much easier if all values are stored in single, atomic, strongly domained containers, as shown here (each container only allowing the exact number of characters that the real world allows, no more and no less, which in the NANP phone number is three, three, and four characters, respectively):

```
AreaCode  Exchange    Suffix
========= ==========  ==============
615         555         4534
615         434         2333
```

Now, updating the area code takes a single, easy-to-follow SQL statement such as

```
UPDATE PhoneNumber
SET    AreaCode = '423'
WHERE  AreaCode = '615'
  AND  Exchange IN ('232','323',...,'989');
```

How you represent phone numbers in a database is a case-by-case decision driven by requirements. Using three separate values is easier for some purposes and, as a result, will be the better performer in almost all cases where you deal with primarily only this single type of phone number. The one-value approach (with some version of enforced formatting) has merit and will work, especially when you have to deal with multiple formats (be careful to have a key for what different formats mean and know that some countries have a variable number of digits in some positions). Note that it probably won't matter for searches if you have your numbers stored all in one value since searches would generally be on the entire value. And you would not call part of a phone number.

Dealing with multiple international telephone number formats complicates matters greatly, since other major countries don't use the same format as in the United States and Canada. In addition, they all have the same sorts of telephone number concerns as we do with the massive proliferation of telephone number–addressed devices. Much like mailing addresses will be, how you model phone numbers is heavily influenced by how you will use them and especially how valuable they are to your organization. For example, a call center application might need deep control on the format of the numbers since the company makes its money making calls to people. Getting the right phone number is ultra-important as the value of a call can be calculated.

An application to provide simple phone functionality for an office might be different in that the onus may be placed more on the customer to get it right. It might be legitimate to just leave it up to the user to fix numbers as they call them, rather than worry about how the numbers can be accessed programmatically.

A solution that I have used is to have two sets of columns, with a column implemented as a calculated column that uses either the three-part number or the alternative number. The following is an example:

AreaCode	Exchange	Suffix	AlternativePhoneNumber	FullPhoneNumber (calc)
615	555	4534	NULL	615-555-4534
615	434	2333	NULL	615-434-2333
NULL	NULL	NULL	01100302030324	01100302030324

Then, on occasion I may write a CHECK constraint to make sure data follows one format or the other. In Chapter 8, I will demonstrate techniques to build such CHECK constraints. This approach allows the interface to present the formatted phone number but provides an override as well. The fact is, with any concerns on the shape of the data, you have to make value calls on how important the data is and whether or not values that are naturally separable should be broken down in your actual storage. You could go much farther with your design and have a subclass for every possible phone number format on Earth, ending up with many many tables, but this is likely overkill for all but the most telephony-specific systems. Just be sure to consider how likely you are to have to do searches, such as on an area code or the exchange, and design accordingly. If you have millions or billions of phone numbers, it can make quite a difference.

All Rows Must Contain the Same Number of Values

The First Normal Form says that every row in a table must have the same number of values. There are two interpretations of this, both very important to how relational tables are constructed:

- Tables must have a fixed number of columns.

- Tables need to be designed such that every row has a fixed number of values associated with it.

The first interpretation is simple and goes back to the nature of relational databases. You cannot have a table with a varying format with one row such as {Name, Address, HairColor} and another with a different set of columns such as {Name, Address, PhoneNumber, EyeColor}. This kind of implementation was common with record-based implementations (and still is with JSON and XML) but isn't strictly possible with a relational database table. Internally, of course, the storage of data may look a lot like this because taking up space for EyeColor when there is not an EyeColor value is wasteful. But in our view of the data, when a column is implemented, it will be in every row of the table. The goal of T-SQL is to make it easy to work with data and leave the hard part to the engine.

The second interpretation, however, is more about how you use the tables you create. As an example, if you are building a table that stores a person's name and you have a column for the first name, then all rows must have only one first name. If they might have two, all rows must have precisely two (not one sometimes and certainly never three). If they may have a different number, it's inconvenient to deal with using T-SQL statements, which is the main reason a database is being built in an RDBMS!

The most obvious violation of this rule is where people make up several columns to hold multiple values of the same type. An example is a table that has several columns with the same base name suffixed (or prefixed) with a number, such as Payment1, Payment2, and so on. As an example, consider the following set of data:

CustomerId	Name	Payment1	Payment2	Payment3
================	-----------------	-------------	-------------	----------
0000002323	Joe's Fish Market	100.03	23.32	120.23
0000230003	Fred's Cat Shop	200.23	NULL	NULL

Each column represents one payment, which makes things easy for a programmer to make a screen, but consider how we might add the next payment for Fred's Cat Shop. We might use some SQL code along these lines (we could do something that is simpler looking, but it would do the same logically):

```
UPDATE Customer
SET Payment1 = CASE WHEN Payment1 IS NULL THEN 1000.00 ELSE Payment1 END,
    Payment2 = CASE WHEN Payment1 IS NOT NULL AND Payment2 IS NULL
                    THEN 1000.00 ELSE Payment2 END,
    Payment3 = CASE WHEN Payment1 IS NOT NULL
                    AND Payment2 IS NOT NULL
                    AND Payment3 IS NULL
                    THEN 1000.00 ELSE Payment3 END
WHERE CustomerId = '0000230003';
```

Of course, if there were already three payments, like for Joe's, you would not have made any changes at all, losing the change you expected to make and not registering the update. Obviously, a setup like this is far more optimized for manual modification, but our goal should be to eliminate places where people do manual tasks and get them back to doing what they do best, uploading cat pictures to Twitter or perhaps even doing actual business. Of course, even if the database is just used like a big spreadsheet, the preceding is not a great design. In the rare cases where there's always precisely the same number of values, then there's technically no violation of the definition of a table, or the First Normal Form. In that case, you could state a business rule that "each customer has exactly two payments, the first and the last." The values could be NULL; there isn't a need for both values to be known, just that they are distinctly different things.

Allowing multiple values of the same type in a single row still isn't generally a good design decision, because users change their minds frequently as to how many of whatever there are, as well as other processing concerns. For payments, if the person paid full in payment 1 or only paid half of their expected payment, what would that mean?

To overcome these sorts of problems, you should create a child table to hold the values from the repeating payment columns. The following is an example. There are two tables. The first table holds customer details like name. The second table holds payments by customer. I've added a PaymentNumber column as part of the key. It could have easily been the Date value, if you wanted to limit people to one payment (and perhaps have another table that indicated how it was being paid, so the value for the date was a sum of all money brought in for the day).

PaymentNumber could be a column that is manually filled in by the customer, but ideally you could calculate the payment number from previous payments, which is far easier to do using a set-based T-SQL statement. Of course, the payment number could be based on something in the documentation accompanying the payment or even on when the payment is made—it really depends on the desires of the business whose design you are trying to implement. If you aren't doing something hokey and fragile, it is generally not an issue:

```
CustomerId          Name
================    ------------------
0000002323          Joe's Fish Market
0000230003          Fred's Cat Shop
```

CustomerId	PaymentNumber	Amount	Date
0000002323	1	100.03	2020-08-01
0000002323	2	23.32	2020-09-12
0000002323	3	120.23	2020-10-04
0000230003	1	200.23	2020-12-01

Now adding a payment to the table is simple in one statement:

```
INSERT CustomerPayment (CustomerId, PaymentNumber, Amount, Date)
VALUES ('0000230003',2, 1000,'2021-02-15');
```

As in earlier examples, notice that I was able to add an additional column of information about each payment with relative ease—the date each payment was made. What is worse is that, initially, the design may start out with a column set like Payment1, Payment2, but it is not uncommon to end up with a table that looks like this, with repeating groups of columns about the already repeated columns:

CustomerId	Payment1	Payment1Date	Payment1MadeBy	Payment1Returned
0000002323	100.03	2020-08-01	Spouse	NULL
0000230003	200.23	2020-12-01	Self	NULL

It wasn't that long ago, longer now than it seems, that I actually had to implement such a design to deal with the status and purpose of a set of columns that represented multiple email addresses for a customer, because the original design I inherited already had columns EmailAddress1, EmailAddress2, and EmailAddress3.

In the properly designed table, you could also easily make additions to the customer payment table to indicate if payment was late, whether additional charges were assessed, whether the amount was correct, whether the principal was applied, and more. Even better, this new design also allows us to have virtually unlimited payment cardinality, whereas the previous solution had a finite number (three, to be exact) of possible configurations. The fun part is designing the structures to meet requirements that are strict enough to constrain data to good values but loose enough to allow the user to innovate agilely (within reason).

Beyond allowing you to add data naturally, designing row-wise rather than repeating groups clears up multiple annoyances, such as relating to the following tasks:

- *Deleting a payment*: Much like the update that had to determine what payment slot to fit the payment into, deleting anything other than the last payment required shifting. For example, if you delete the payment in Payment1, then Payment2 needs to be shifted to Payment1, Payment3 to Payment2, and so on.

- *Updating a payment*: Say Payment1 equals 10 and Payment2 equals 10. Which one should you modify if you must modify one of them because the amount was incorrect? Does it matter? The extra information about the time of the payment, the check number, and so on would likely clear this up too.

If your requirements actually allow three payments, it is easy enough to specify and then implement a limit on cardinality of the table of payments (e.g., with a UNIQUE constraint and a CHECK constraint PaymentNumber BETWEEN 1 and 3). As discussed in Chapter 3 for data modeling, we control the number of allowable child rows using relationship cardinality. You can restrict the number of payments per customer using constraints or triggers (which will be described in more detail in Chapter 8), but whether or not you can implement something in the database is somewhat outside of the bounds of the current portion of the database design process.

Caution   Another common (mildly horrifying) design uses columns such as UserDefined1, UserDefined2, …, UserDefinedN to allow users to store their own data that was not part of the original design. This practice is heinous for many reasons, one of them related to the proper application of First Normal Form. Moreover, using such column structures is directly against the essence of Codd's fourth rule involving a dynamic online catalog based on the relational model. That rule states that the database description is represented at the logical level in the same way as ordinary data so that authorized users can apply the same relational language to its interrogation that they apply to regular data.

Putting data into the database in such columns requires extra knowledge about the system beyond what's included in the system catalogs which then makes usage far more complicated. In Chapter 9, when I cover storing user-specified data (allowing user extensibility to your schema without changes in design), I will discuss more reasonable methods of giving users the ability to extend the schema at will.

All Rows Must Be Different

One of the most important things you must take care of when building a database is to make sure to have keys on tables to be able to tell rows apart. Although having a completely meaningful key isn't reasonable 100% of the time, exceptions are quite uncommon and must stand up to simple reasoning. An example is a situation where you cannot tell the physical items apart, such as perhaps cans of corn, bags of Legos, and so on, at the local department store. You cannot tell two cans of corn apart based on their packaging, so you might be tempted to assign a value that has no meaning as part of the key, along with the things that differentiate the can from other similar objects, such as large cans of corn or small cans of spinach. Generally, if you can't tell two items apart in the real world, don't endeavor to make them distinguishable in your database. It will be perfectly acceptable to assign a key to the class of items "cans of Brand X corn" and then keep up with the changes of cans in inventory through sales to customers and orders from vendors. (If this sounds like a foreign concept, consider the cash that customers use to purchase things with. Other than special circumstances, even though paper money has unique serial numbers written on it, cashiers do not save those values on each transaction, just the amount of the transaction.)

The goal in all cases is to find the lowest granular level where a user may want to distinguish between one thing and another. For example, in retail, it is common to allow returns of items. If a person wants to return a $10 DVD, the retailer will make sure that the item being returned is simply the same thing that the person purchased. On the other hand, if the person has purchased a $20,000 diamond ring, there will likely be a serial number to make sure that it is the same ring and not a ring of lesser value (or even a fake).

Often, database designers (such as myself) are keen to automatically add an artificial key value to their table to distinguish between items, but as discussed in Chapter 1, adding an artificial key alone might technically make the table comply with the letter of the rule, but it certainly won't comply with the purpose. The purpose is that no two rows represent the same thing. You could have two rows that represent the same thing because every meaningful value has the same value, with the only difference between rows being a system-generated value. As mentioned in Chapter 1, another term for such a key is a *surrogate key*, so named because it is a surrogate (or a stand-in) for the real key.

Another common approach that can be concerning is to use a date and time value to differentiate between rows. If the date and time value is part of the row's logical identification, such as a calendar entry or a row that's recording/logging some event, this is ideal. Conversely, simply tossing on a date and time value to force uniqueness is worse than just adding a random number or GUID on the row when time is not part of what identifies the item being modeled. This is the blue Ford C-Max I purchased on December 22, 2014, at 12:23 PM...or was it the 23rd at 12:24 PM? What if the client registered the purchase twice, at different times? Or you actually purchased two similar vehicles? Either way would be confusing! Ideally in that case, the client would use the vehicle identification number (VIN) as the key, which is guaranteed to be unique. (Strictly speaking, using the VIN does violate the atomic principle since it loads multiple bits of information in that single value. Smart keys, as they are called, are useful for humans but should not be the sole source of any data you need that might be embedded in the value, like what color is the vehicle, based on the rules we have already stated.)

As an example of how generated values lead to confusion, consider the following subset of a table with school mascots:

MascotId	Name
===========	------------------
1	Smokey
112	Smokey
4567	Smokey
979796	Smokey

Taken as presented, there is no obvious clue as to which of these rows represents the real Smokey or if there needs to be more than one Smokey or if the data entry person just goofed up. It could be that the school name ought to be included to produce a key or perhaps names are supposed to be unique or even this table should represent the people who play the role of each mascot at a certain school during different time periods. It is the architect's job to make sure that the meaning is clear and that keys are enforced to prevent, or at least discourage, alternative (possibly incorrect) interpretations.

Of course, the reality of life is that users will do what they must to get their job done. Take for example the following table of data that represents books:

BookISBN	BookTitle	PublisherName	Author
111111111	Normalization	Apress	Louis
222222222	SQL Tacklebox	Simple Talk	Rodney

The users go about life, entering data as needed. Nevertheless, when users realize that more than one author needs to be added per book, they will figure something out. What a user might figure out might look as follows (this is a contrived example, but I have heard from more than one person that this has occurred in real databases):

444444444	DMV Book	Simple Talk	Tim
444444444-1	DMV Book	Simple Talk	Louis

The user has done what was needed to get by, and assuming the domain of the column BookISBN allows multiple formats of data (ISBNs do have a specific format), the approach works with no errors. However, *DMV Book* looks like two books with the same title. Now, your support programmers are going to have to deal with the fact that your data doesn't mean what they think it does.

The proper solution is to have a table to represent each individual thing you are trying to express: a book and a book's author. So we now have the following two tables:

BookISBN	BookTitle	PublisherName
111111111	Normalization	Apress
222222222	SQL Tacklebox	Simple Talk
333333333	Indexing	Microsoft
444444444	DMV Book	Simple Talk

```
BookISBN     Author
==========   =========
111111111    Louis
222222222    Rodney
333333333    Kim
444444444    Tim
444444444    Louis
```

Just looking at this solution, you can feel why it was not the immediately chosen answer. It is more difficult to work with when you just want to answer a quick question. But it is important to make sure that getting the most correct answer comes first, before worrying about performance and simplicity of writing the code, or you will end up short cutting yourself to death.

Now, if you need information about an author's relationship to a book (chapters written, pay rate, etc.), you can add columns to the second table without harming the current uses of the system. Yes, you end up having more tables, and yes, you must do more coding up front, but if you get the design right, it just plain works. The likelihood of discovering all data cases such as this case with multiple authors to a book before you have "completed" your design is low, so don't immediately think it is your fault. Requirements are often presented that are not fully thought through, such as claiming only one author per book. Sometimes it isn't that the requirements were faulty so much as the fact that requirements change over time. In this example, it could have been that during the initial design phase, the reality at the time was that the system was to support only a single author. Ever-changing realities are what make software design such a delightful task at times.

Caution   Key choice is one of the most important parts of your database design. Duplicated data causes tremendous and obvious issues to anyone who deals with it. It is particularly bad when you do not realize you have the problem until it is too late.

Clues That an Existing Design Is Not in First Normal Form

When you are looking at a database of data to evaluate it, you can look quickly at a few basic things to see whether the data is in First Normal Form. In this section, we'll look at some of these ways to recognize whether data in a database is already likely to be in First Normal Form. None of these clues is, by any means, a perfect test. They are only clues that you can look for in data structures for places to dig deeper. While the normal forms themselves are very strict, the process of normalizing a database is a process based on the content and requirements/use of your data.

The following sections describe a couple of data characteristics that suggest that the data isn't in First Normal Form:

- "String Data Containing Separator-Type Characters"

- "Column Names with Numbers at the End"

- "Tables with No or Poorly Defined Keys"

This is not an exhaustive list, of course, but these are a few places to start.

String Data Containing Separator-Type Characters

Separator-type characters include commas, brackets, parentheses, semicolons, and pipe characters. These act as warning signs that the data is likely a multivalued column. Obviously, these same characters can be found in correct columns. So you need not go too far. As mentioned earlier, if you're designing a solution to hold a block of text, you've probably normalized too much if you have a word table, a sentence table, and a paragraph table. This clue is aligned to tables that have structured, delimited lists stored in a single column rather than broken out into multiple rows.

Column Names with Numbers at the End

An obvious example would be finding tables with Child1, Child2, and similar columns or, my least favorite, UserDefined1, UserDefined2, and so on. These kinds of tables are usually messy to deal with and should be considered for transformation into a new, related table. They don't have to be wrong; for example, your table might need exactly two values to always exist. In that case, it's perfectly allowable to have the numbered columns, but be careful that what's thought of as "always" is actually always. Too often, exceptions cause this solution to fail. "A person always has two forms of identification noted in fields `ID1` and `ID2`." In this case, "always" may not mean always; and in reality, the requirement probably should have continued like this: "And you may want to record a third item of ID in case one that is provided is not valid." Always must mean always.

These kinds of columns are a common holdover from the days of flat-file databases. Multi-table/multirow data access was costly, so developers put many fields in a single file structure. Doing this in a relational database system is a waste of the power of the relational programming language. They are equally the result of trying not to have to join two tables together to deal with multiple values that don't seem that complicated to deal with on the surface, until a search for an email address becomes three queries instead of one, with duplicates returned because enforcing uniqueness across three columns was "too hard to be worth the time."

`Coordinate1` and `Coordinate2` might be acceptable in cases that always require two coordinates to find a point in a two-dimensional space, never any more or never any less (though something more like `CoordinateX` and `CoordinateY` would likely be better column names).

Tables with No or Poorly Defined Keys

As noted in the early chapters several times, key choice is very important. Almost every database will be implemented with some primary key (though even this is not a given in a few valid cases). However, all too often the only key a person will implement will simply be a GUID or a sequence/identity-based value that originates in that table and has no other meaning.

It might seem like I am picking on sequential numbers and GUIDs, and for good reason, I am. While I will usually suggest you use surrogate keys in your designs (and a sequential number is generally the perfect choice), too often people use them incorrectly and forget that such values have no meaning to the user. If customer 1 could inadvertently be the same as customer 2, you are not doing it right. Keeping row values unique is a big part of First Normal Form compliance and is something that should be high on your list of important activities.

Non–Key Column Relationships

The next set of normal forms I will cover are concerned with the relationships between key attributes in a table and the non-key attributes of the table. We have established key attributes as the set of attributes that can be used to identify an instance of an entity and now, as we move to tables, the set of columns that can be used to locate a row in a table. This group of normal forms deal with making sure that all functional dependencies between the non-key attributes are on the key(s) of the table. As discussed in Chapter 1, being functionally dependent implies that when running a function on one value (call it Value1), if the output of this function is *always* the same value (call it Value2), then Value2 is functionally dependent on Value1.

The normal forms we will look at are defined as follows:

- *Second Normal Form (2NF)*: Each column must be a fact describing the entire primary key (and the table is in First Normal Form).

- *Third Normal Form (3NF)*: Non–primary key columns cannot describe other non–primary key columns (and the table is in Second Normal Form).

- *Boyce-Codd Normal Form (BCNF)*: All columns are fully dependent on a key. Every determinant is a key (and the table is in First Normal Form, not Second or Third, since BCNF itself is a more strongly stated version that encompasses both).

I am going to focus on BCNF because it encompasses the other forms, and it is the clearest and makes the most sense based on today's typical database design patterns (specifically the use of surrogate keys and natural keys). I will note in the examples which issue falls in the domain of Second and Third Normal Forms.

BCNF Defined

BCNF is named after Ray Boyce, one of the creators of the SQL language, and Edgar Codd, whom I introduced in Chapter 1 as the father of relational databases. It's a better-constructed replacement for both the Second and Third Normal Forms, and it takes the meanings of the Second and Third Normal Forms and restates them in a more general way. The BCNF is defined as follows:

- The table is already in First Normal Form.

- All columns are fully dependent on a key.

- A table is in BCNF if every determinant is a key.

BCNF encompasses 2NF and 3NF and changed the definition from the "primary key" to simply all defined keys. With today's relatively common practice of using a surrogate key for most primary keys, as well as the reality that a table may then also have more than one natural key identified, BCNF is a far better definition of how a properly designed database might be structured. It is my opinion that *most* of the time, in the twenty-first century, when someone says "Third Normal Form," they are referencing something closer to BCNF.

An important part of the definition of BCNF is that "every determinant is a key." I introduced determinants back in Chapter 1, but as a quick review, consider the following table of rows, with X defined as the key:

X	Y	Z
=============	-------------	-----------------
1	1	2
2	2	4
3	2	4

X is unique and defined as the primary key of this set. Because it is a determinant, given a value of X, you can determine the values of Y and Z. Now, given a value of Y, you can't determine the value of X, but you seemingly can determine the value of Z. When Y = 1: Z = 2, and when Y = 2: Z = 4. Now before you pass judgment and start adding the Y table, this appearance of determinism can simply be a coincidence. It is very much up to the requirements to help us decide if this is determinism or happenstance. If the values of Z were arrived at by a function of Y*2, then Y would determine Z and really wouldn't need to be stored or would require its own table.

When a table is in BCNF, any update to a non-key column requires updating one and only one value. By discovering that Y is the determinant of Z, you have discovered that YZ should be its own independent table. So instead of the single table we had before, we have two tables that express the previous table without invalid functional dependencies, like this:

X	Y
=============	-------------
1	1
2	2
3	2

```
Y                   Z
=============   ----------------
1                   2
2                   4
```

For a somewhat less abstract example, consider the following set of data, representing book information:

```
BookISBN       BookTitle        PublisherName    PublisherLocation
===========    -------------    ---------------  --------------------
111111111      Normalization    Apress           United States
222222222      SQL Tacklebox    Simple Talk      England
444444444      DMV Book         Simple Talk      England
```

BookISBN is the defined key, so every one of the columns should be completely dependent on this value. The title of the book is dependent on the book ISBN and the publisher too. The concern in this table is the PublisherLocation. A book doesn't have a publisher location; a publisher does. Therefore, if you needed to change the publisher, you would also need to change the publisher location in multiple rows.

To correct this situation, you need to create a separate table for publisher. The following is one approach you can take:

```
BookISBN       BookTitle        PublisherName
===========    -------------    ---------------
111111111      Normalization    Apress
222222222      SQL Tacklebox    Simple Talk
444444444      DMV Book         Simple Talk

Publisher      PublisherLocation
=============  --------------------
Apress         United States
Simple Talk    London
```

Now, a change of publisher for a book requires only changing the publisher value in the Book table, and a change to publisher location requires only a single update to the Publisher table.

Of course, there is always a caveat. Consider the following table of data:

BookISBN	BookTitle	PublisherName	PublisherLocation
===========	============	===============	===================
111111111	Normalization	Apress	California
222222222	SQL Tacklebox	Simple Talk	New York
444444444	DMV Book	Simple Talk	London

Now Simple Talk has two locations. Wrong? Or a different meaning that we expected? If the column's true meaning is "Location of Publisher at Time of Book Publishing," then (other than a truly poorly named column) the design isn't wrong. Or perhaps Apress has multiple offices and that is what is being recorded? So it is important to understand what is being designed, to name columns correctly, and to document that purpose of the column as well to make sure meaning is not lost.

Partial Key Dependency

In the original definitions of the normal forms, we had Second Normal Form that dealt with partial key dependencies. In BCNF, this is still a concern when you have defined composite keys (more than one column making up the key). Most of the cases where you see a partial key dependency in an example are pretty contrived (and I will certainly not break that trend, though don't be fooled into believing that the real scenarios will be quite so obvious). Partial key dependencies deal with the case where you have a multicolumn key and, in turn, columns in the table that reference only part of the key.

As an example, consider a car rental database and the need to record driver information and type of cars the person will drive. Consider you are reviewing the following table that was designed to meet those requirements:

Driver	VehicleStyle	Height	EyeColor	ExampleModel	DesiredModelLevel
========	==============	========	==========	==============	===================
Louis	CUV	6'0"	Blue	Edge	Premium
Louis	Sedan	6'0"	Blue	Fusion	Standard
Ted	Coupe	5'8"	Brown	Camaro	Performance

The key of `Driver` plus `VehicleStyle` means that all the columns of the table should reference the combination of these values. Consider the following columns:

- `Height`: Unless this is the height of the car as it adjusts once the driver enters the vehicle, this apparently references the driver and not car style. If it is the height of the car, it is still wrong!

- `EyeColor`: Clearly, this references the driver only, unless we rent cars in Radiator Springs. Either way it's not referencing the combination of `Driver` and `VehicleStyle`.

- `ExampleModel`: This references the `VehicleStyle`, providing a model for the person to reference so they will know approximately what they are getting.

- `DesiredModelLevel`: This represents the model of vehicle that the driver wants to get. This is the only column that is correct in that it applies both to the vehicle and to the driver.

To transform the initial one table into a proper design, we will need to split the one table into three. The first one defines the driver and just has the driver's physical characteristics:

```
Driver    Height   EyeColor
========  -------  ---------
Louis     6'0"     Blue
Ted       5'8"     Brown
```

The second one defines the car styles and model levels the driver desires:

```
Driver    Car Style          DesiredModelLevel
========  ================   -------------------
Louis     CUV                Premium
Louis     Sedan              Standard
Ted       Coupe              Performance
```

Finally, we need one table to define the types of car styles available (and I will add a column to give an example model of the style of car):

```
Car Style          ExampleModel
================   ----------
CUV                Edge
Sedan              Fusion
Coupe              Camaro
```

Note that, since the driver was repeated multiple times in the original poorly designed sample data, I ended up with only two rows for the driver as the Louis entry's data was repeated twice. It might seem like I have just made three shards of a whole table, without saving much space, and ultimately will need costly joins to put everything back together. There are two things to note here. First, the integrity of the data means more than any space savings. If one of the EyeColor values was updated because it was originally entered incorrectly, but the other rows were left incorrect, the customer would probably get very frustrated when their rental was denied since they didn't match the physical description listed and eventually give up and use a different company.

Second, the reality is that in a real database, the driver table would have many, many rows and several more columns; the table assigning drivers to car styles would be thin (have a small number of columns); and the car style table would be very small in number of rows and columns. The savings from not repeating so much data will more than overcome the overhead of doing joins.

Entire Key Dependency

Where Second Normal Form dealt with partial key dependencies on the primary key, Third Normal Form dealt with the case where all columns need to be dependent on the entire key.

In our previous example, we ended up with a Driver table. That same developer, when we stopped watching, made some additions to the Driver table to get an idea of what the driver currently drives:

Driver	Height	EyeColor	VehicleOwned	VehicleDoorCount	WheelCount
Louis	6'0"	Blue	Hatchback	3	4
Ted	5'8"	Brown	Coupe	2	4
Rob	6'8"	NULL	Tractor trailer 2		18

To our trained eye, it is pretty clear almost immediately that the vehicle columns aren't quite right, but what to do? You could make a row for each vehicle or each vehicle type, depending on how specific the need is for the usage. Since we are trying to gather demographic information about the user, I am going to choose vehicle type to keep things simple (and it is a great segue to the next section). The vehicle type now gets a table of its own, and we remove from the driver table the entire vehicle pieces of information and create a key that is a coagulation of the values for the data in row:

VehicleTypeId	VehicleType	DoorCount	WheelCount
3DoorHatchback	Hatchback	3	4
2DoorCoupe	Coupe	2	4
TractorTrailer	Tractor trailer	2	18

And the driver table now references the vehicle type table using its key:

Driver	VehicleTypeId	Height	EyeColor
Louis	3DoorHatchback	6'0"	Blue
Ted	2DoorCoupe	5'8"	Brown
Rob	TractorTrailer	6'8"	NULL

Note that for the vehicle type table in this model, I chose to implement a smart key/code for simplicity and because it is a common method that people use. A short code is concocted to give the user a bit of readability; then the additional columns are there to use in queries, particularly when you need to group or filter on some value (like if you wanted to send an offer to all drivers of three-door cars to drive a luxury car for the weekend!). It has drawbacks that are the same as the normal form we are working on if you aren't careful (the smart key has redundant data in it), so using a smart key like this is a bit dangerous. But what if we decided to use the natural key? We would end up with two tables that look like this:

```
Driver    Height  EyeColor  Vehicle Owned      VehicleDoorCount
========  ------- --------- ----------------- ----------------
Louis     6'0"    Blue      Hatchback          3
Ted       5'8"    Brown     Coupe              2
Rob       6'8"    NULL      Tractor trailer   2

VehicleType          VehicleDoorCount WheelCount
================ ================= --------------
Hatchback            3                4
Coupe                2                4
Tractor trailer  2                18
```

The driver table now has almost the same columns as it had before (e.g., less the WheelCount, which does not differ from a three- or five-door hatchback), referencing the existing table columns, but it is still a far better, more flexible solution. If you want to include additional information about given vehicle types (like towing capacity), you could do it in one location and not in every single row, and users entering driver information could only use data from a given domain that is defined by the vehicle type table. Note too that the two solutions proffered are semantically equivalent but have two different solution implementations that will influence implementation, but not the meaning of the data in actual usage. In the next section, we will take this even farther to encompass surrogate keys and their effect on the dependencies.

Surrogate Keys' Effect on Dependency

When you use a surrogate key, it is used as a stand-in for other existing keys. To our previous example of driver and vehicle type, let's make one additional example table set, using a meaningless surrogate value for the vehicle type key, knowing that the natural key of the vehicle type set is VehicleType and DoorCount (the AK denoted by ~):

Driver	VehicleTypeId	Height	EyeColor
========	===============	========	==========
Louis	1	6'0"	Blue
Ted	2	5'8"	Brown
Rob	3	6'8"	NULL

VehicleTypeId	VehicleType	DoorCount	WheelCount
===============	=============	===========	============
1	Hatchback	3	4
2	Coupe	2	4
3	Tractor trailer	2	18

The design is perfectly acceptable too if you want to include the codes from earlier as a key (3DoorHatchback, 2DoorCoupe, TractorTrailer) or any other value. I am going to cover key choices a bit more in Chapter 7 when I discuss the process of implementing the various uniqueness patterns, but suffice it to say that, for design and normalization purposes, using surrogates doesn't change anything except the amount of work it takes to validate the model. Everywhere the VehicleTypeId of 1 is referenced, it is semantically the same as using the natural key of VehicleType, DoorCount; and you must take this into consideration. The benefits of surrogates are more for programming convenience and performance, but they do not take onus away from you as a designer to expand them for normalization purposes.

For an additional example involving surrogate keys, consider the case of an employee database that records the driver's license of the person. We normalize the table and create a table for driver's license, and we end up with the model snippet in Figure 5-1. Now, as you are figuring out whether the Employee table is in proper BCNF, you check out the columns, and you come to DriversLicenseNumber and DriversLicenseStateCode. Does an employee have a DriversLicenseStateCode? Not exactly, but a driver's license does, and a person may have a driver's license. When columns are part of a foreign key, you must consider the entire foreign key. So can an employee have a driver's license? Absolutely. You must think of the foreign key values as a single cluster of dependent values.

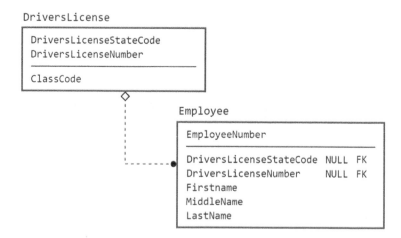

Figure 5-1.   *DriversLicense and Employee tables with natural keys*

What about using surrogate keys? Well, this is where the practice comes with additional cautions. In Figure 5-2, I have remodeled the table using surrogate keys for each of the tables.

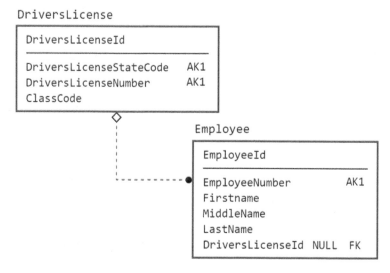

Figure 5-2.   *DriversLicense and Employee tables with surrogate keys*

This design looks cleaner in some ways, and with the very well-named columns from the natural key, it is a bit easier to see the relationships in these tables, and it is not always possible to name the various parts of the natural key as clearly as I did. In fact, the state code likely would have a domain of its own and might be named StateCode. The major con is that there is a hiding of implementation details that can lead to insidious multi-table normalization issues. For example, take the addition to the model shown in Figure 5-3.

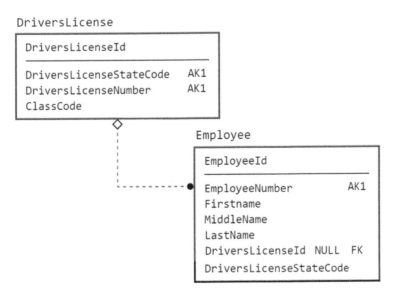

Figure 5-3.   *DriversLicense and Employee tables with improper normalization*

The users wanted to know the state code from the driver's license for the employer, so the programmer simply added it to the Employee table because it wasn't easily visible in the table. Now in essence, here is what we have in the Employee table once we expand the columns from the natural key of the DriversLicense table:

- EmployeeNumber

- FirstName

- MiddleName

- LastName

- DriversLicenseStateCode (DriversLicense)

- DriversLicenseNumber (DriversLicense)

- DriversLicenseStateCode

The state code is duplicated just to save a join to the table where it existed naturally, so the fact that we are using surrogate keys to simplify some programming tasks is complicated by the designer's lack of knowledge (or possibly care) for why we use surrogates.

While the DriversLicense example is a simplistic case, in a real model, the parent table could be five or six joins away from the child, and with all tables using single-key surrogates, lots of natural relationships could be hidden. It looks initially like the relationships are simple one-table relationships, but a surrogate key takes the place of the natural key, so in a model like in Figure 5-4, the keys are more complex than it appears.

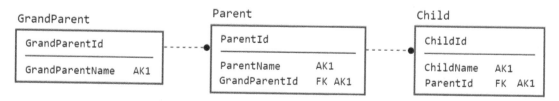

Figure 5-4.   *Tables chained to show key migration*

The full key for the GrandParent table is obvious, but the key of the Parent table is a little bit less so. Where you see the surrogate key of GrandParentId in the Parent table, you need to also logically replace it with a natural key from GrandParent. So the key to Parent is ParentName, GrandParentName. Then with child, it is the same thing, so the key becomes ChildName, ParentName, GrandParentName. This is the key you need to compare your other attributes against to make sure that it is correct.

Note   A lot of purists really hate surrogates because of how much they hide the interdependencies, and I would avoid them if you are unwilling to take the time to understand (and document) the models you are creating using them. But the performance benefits, the read-only nature of surrogates, and data safety issues of not duplicating personally identifiable data outweigh the purist concerns.

Dependency Between Rows

A consideration when discussing non-key column relationships is data that is dependent on data in a different row, possibly even in a different table. A common example of this is summary data. It is an epidemic among row-by-row–thinking programmers who figure that it is very costly to calculate values. Say you have objects for invoice and invoice line items like the following tables of data, the first being an invoice and the second being the line items of the invoice:

InvoiceNumber	InvoiceDate	InvoiceAmount
000000000323	2011-12-23	100

InvoiceNumber	ItemNumber	InvoiceDate	Product	Quantity	(Continued)
000000000323	1	2011-12-23	KL7R2	10	
000000000323	2	2011-12-23	RTCL3	10	

ProductPrice	OrderItemId
8.00	1232322000000000323
2.00	1232323

There are two issues with this data arrangement.

- InvoiceAmount is just the calculated value of SUM(Quantity * ProductPrice).

- InvoiceDate in the line item is just repeated data from Invoice.

Now, your design has become a lot more brittle, because if InvoiceDate changes, you will have to change all the line items. The same is likely true for the InvoiceAmount value as well. However, be careful if you see data like this. You must question whether or not the InvoiceAmount is a true calculation or a value that has to be balanced against. The value of 100 may be manually set as a check to make sure that no items are changed on the line items. The requirements (and ideally a very specific naming standard) must always be your guide when deciding what is and isn't wrong in normalizations and all of database/software design.

Clues That Your Database Is Not in BCNF

In this section, I will present a few of the flashing red lights that can tell you that your design isn't in BCNF:

- Multiple columns with the same prefix

- Repeating groups of data

- Summary data

Of course, these are only the truly obvious issues with tables, but they are very representative of the types of problems that you will frequently see in designs that haven't been done well.

Multiple Columns with the Same Prefix

The situation of repeating column prefixes is one of the dead giveaways that your design isn't in BCNF. Let's go back to our earlier example table:

```
BookISBN      BookTitle       PublisherName    PublisherLocation
===========   -------------   ---------------  --------------------
111111111     Normalization   Apress           California
222222222     T-SQL           Apress           California
444444444     DMV Book        Simple Talk      England
```

The problem identified was in the PublisherLocation column that is functionally dependent on PublisherName. Prefixes like "Publisher" in these two column names are a rather common tip-off, especially when designing new systems. Of course, having such an obvious prefix on columns such as Publisher% is awfully convenient, but it isn't always the case in real-life examples that weren't conjured up as an illustration.

Sometimes, rather than having a single table issue, you find that the same sort of information is strewn about the database, over multiple columns in multiple tables. For example, consider the tables in Figure 5-5.

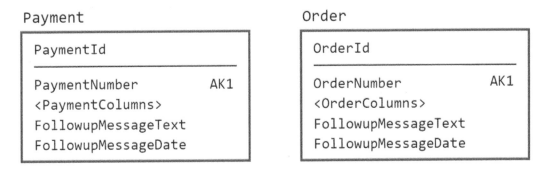

Figure 5-5.   *Payment and Order with errant Followup columns*

The tables in Figure 5-5 are a glowing example of information being wasted by not having it consolidated in the same table. Most likely, you want to be reasonable with the number of messages you send to your customers. Send too few and they forget you and too many and they get annoyed by you. By consolidating the data into a single table, it is far easier to manage. Figure 5-6 shows a better version of the design.

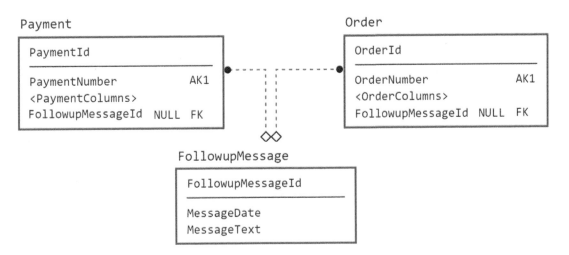

Figure 5-6.   *Payment and Order with added Followup object*

This design in Figure 5-6 allows you to tag a given message to multiple payments and orders and use that information to form more information (for customers who made an order and were sent a follow-up message in N days, they were P% more likely to purchase...). The FollowupMessage table needs more work to be a complete table, but the issue with the duplicated dependency is gone now.

Repeating Groups of Data

More difficult to recognize are the repeating groups of data, often because the names given to columns generally won't be as obviously telling that there is an issue in all cases you encounter. Imagine executing multiple SELECT statements on a table, each time retrieving all rows (if possible), ordered by each of the important columns. If there's a functionally dependent column, you'll see that in the form of the dependent column taking on the same value Y for a given column value X.

Look at some example entries for the tables we just used in previous sections:

BookISBN	BookTitle	PublisherName	PublisherLocation
111111111	Normalization	Apress	California
222222222	SQL Tacklebox	Simple Talk	London
444444444	DMV Book	Simple Talk	London

The repeating values (Simple Talk and London) are a clear example of something that is likely amiss. It isn't a guarantee, of course, since (as mentioned earlier) it may be the publisher's location at the time of the order. It can be beneficial to use a data profiling tool and look for these dependencies not as absolutes, but as percentages, because if there are a million rows in this table, you are very likely to have some inconsistent dependent data no matter how good the code is that manipulates this data. Profile your data to identify suspicious correlations that deserve a closer look. Sometimes, even if the names are not so clearly obvious, finding ranges of data such as in the preceding example can be very valuable.

Summary Data

One of the most common data dependency issue that might not seem obvious is summary data. Summary data has been one of the most frequently necessary evils that we've had to deal with throughout the early history of the relational database server. There might be cases where calculated data needs to be stored in a table in violation of Third Normal Form, but usually there is very little place for it. Not only is summary data not functionally dependent on non-key columns; it's dependent on columns from a different table altogether. Summary data should be reserved either for dealing with extreme performance tuning, much later in the database design process, or ideally for reporting/data warehousing databases.

Take the example of an auto dealer, as shown in Figure 5-7. The dealer system has a table that represents all the types of automobiles it sells, and it has a table recording each automobile sale.

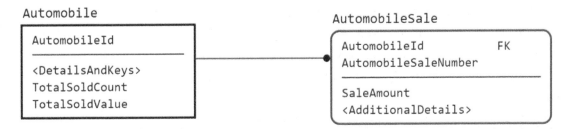

Figure 5-7.   *The auto dealer submodel*

Instead of accepting that the total number of vehicles sold and their value is available, the designer has decided to add columns in the parent table that refer to the child rows and summarize them. Just to constantly remind you that nothing is necessarily 100% wrong, if you included a `PreviouslySoldCount` on `Automobile` that contained sales that had been archived off, it would not be a normalization issue. A common phrase that is mentioned around this is "single source of the truth." The old saying goes, "A person with one watch knows what time it is, and a person with two has no idea," as you can practically never get two watches to match, even with electronics these days. Best to calculate the values as much as possible, until there is absolutely zero chance of the data changing.

The point is that including summary data in the model isn't generally desirable, because the data modeled in the total column exists in the `Sales` table. Data that we identify in our databases should be modeled to exist in only one place, and any values that could be calculated from other values shouldn't be represented on the model. This aids in keeping the integrity of the design of the data at its highest level possible. There are definitely performance reasons to precalculate data in some extremely high-read, low-latency applications, which I will touch on in the "Denormalization" section later in this chapter. However, it is rarely the place where you want to start and rarer still before you have uncovered a performance issue in testing.

Tip   One way of dealing with summary data is to use a view. An automobile view might summarize the automobile sales. In some cases, you can index the view, and the summary data is automatically maintained for you. The summarized data is easier to maintain using the indexed view, though it can have negative performance repercussions on modifications but positive ones on reads. Only testing your actual situation will tell, but this is not quite the implementation part of the book! I'll discuss indexes in some detail in Chapter 11.

Positional Meaning

The last point I want to make about dependency issues is that you must be truly careful where it makes sense. For example, consider the following table of data—about the meaning of the data you are normalizing, because as you get closer and closer to the goal of one table having one meaning, almost every column will have one place:

CustomerId	Name	EmailAddress1	EmailAddress2	AllowEmailMarketingFlag
A0000000032	Fred	fred@email.com	fr2@email.com	1
A0000000033	Sally	sally@email.com	NULL	0

To get this table into First Normal Form, you should immediately recognize that we need to implement a table to hold the email address for the customer. The questionable attribute is AllowEmailMarketingFlag, which denotes whether we wish to market to this customer by email. Is this an attribute about the email address? Or the customer?

Without additional knowledge from the client, it must be assumed that the AllowMarketingByEmailFlag column applies to how we will market to the customer, so it should remain on the customer table like this:

CustomerId	Name	AllowEmailMarketingFlag
A0000000032	Fred	1
A0000000033	Sally	0

CustomerId	EmailAddress	EmailAddressNumber
===============	================	=====================
A0000000032	fred@email.com	1
A0000000032	fred2@email.com	2
A0000000033	sally@email.com	1

You will also notice that I made the key of the customer email address table CustomerId, EmailAddressNumber and not EmailAddress. Without further knowledge of the system, it would be impossible to know if it was acceptable to have duplication in the two columns. It really boils down to the original purpose of having multiple EmailAddress values, and you must be careful about what the customers may have been using the values for. In a project I recently was working on, half of the users used the latter addresses as history of old email addresses and the other half as a backup email for contacting the customer. For the historic email address values, it certainly could make sense to add start and end date values to tell when and if the address is still valid, particularly for customer relationship management systems. However, at the same time, it could make sense to have only current customer information in your OLTP system and move history to an archival or data warehouse database instead.

Finally, consider the following scenario. A client sells an electronic product that is delivered by email. Sometimes, it can take weeks before the order is fulfilled and shipped. The designer of the system created the following solution (less the sales order line item information about the product that was ordered):

CustomerId	Name	AllowMarketingByEmailFlag
===============	===========	==========================
A0000000032	Fred	1

CustomerId	EmailAddress	EmailAddressNumber
===============	================	=====================
A0000000032	fred@email.com	1
A0000000032	fred2@email.com	2

SalesOrderId	OrderDate	ShipDate	CustomerId	(Continued)
===============	===========	===========	============	-------------
1000000242	2012-01-01	2012-01-02	A0000000032	

```
EmailAddressNumber   ShippedToEmailAddress
------------------   ---------------------
1                    fred@email.com
```

What do you figure the purpose is of the redundant email address information? Is it a normalization issue? In this case, no, because although the `ShippedToEmailAddress` may always be exactly the same as the email address for the email address table row with the related email address number in the existing data (even over millions of rows), the value is to capture the data at the point of the shipment, so if the customer changes their email addresses and then call in to ask where you sent the email, you have where the information was sent. If you only maintained the link to the customer's current email address, you wouldn't be able to know what the email address was when the product shipped.

The point of this section has been to think before you eliminate what seems like redundant data. Good naming standards, such as spelling out `ShippedToEmailAddress` during the logical database design phase, are a definite help to make sure other developers/architects know what you have in mind for a column that you create.

Key Column Relationships

Assuming you (A) have done some work with databases before getting this deep in the book and (B) haven't been completely self-taught while living underneath 100,000 pounds of granite, you may have wondered why this chapter on normalization did not end with the last section. You probably have heard that Third Normal Form (or maybe you may have heard of BCNF in these modern times) is far enough to take your designs. That is often true, but not because the higher normal forms are useless or completely esoteric, but because once you have really done justice to First Normal Form and BCNF, you quite likely have it right. All your keys are defined, and all the non-key columns properly reference them.

However, now we need to look at the keys you have defined to make sure they properly match up with the requirements that have been set, to determine if the key properly identifies one real concept or if it could be broken down into smaller atomic pieces that have meaning in and of themselves. Fourth and Fifth Normal Forms now focus on the relationships between key columns to make sure the keys truly do have a singular meaning. If the natural composite keys for your tables have no more than two independent key columns, you are guaranteed to be in Fourth and Fifth Normal Forms if you are in BCNF as well.

According to the Fourth Normal Form article in Wikipedia (https://en.wikipedia.org/wiki/Fourth_normal_form), there was a paper done back in 1992 by Margaret S. Wu that claimed that more than 20% of all databases had issues with Fourth Normal Form. And back in 1992, people spent a lot of time doing design for months on end, unlike today when we erect databases like reverse implosions. However, the normal forms we will discuss in this section are truly interesting in many designs, because they center on the relationships between key columns and are very business rule driven, meaning often it takes more than just the table and column names to know if there is an issue or not. The same table can be a horrible mess to work with in one case, and in the next, it can be exactly the correct answer. The only way to know is to spend the time validating the relationship against what it is supposed to mean. In the next two sections, I will give an overview of Fourth and Fifth Normal Forms and what they mean to your designs.

Fourth Normal Form: Independent Multivalued Dependencies

Fourth Normal Form deals with multivalued dependencies (MVDs). When we discussed dependencies in the previous sections, we discussed the case where fn(x) = y, where both x and y were scalar values. For a multivalued dependency, the y value in a table is essentially an unorder set of atomic values. So fn(key) = fn(nonkey1, nonkey2, . . . , nonkeyN) is an acceptable multivalued dependency. For a table to be in Fourth Normal Form, it needs to be in BCNF first, and then, there must not be more than one independent multivalued dependency (MVD) between the key columns.

As an example, recall a previous example table we used for a rental car database:

Driver	VehicleStyle	DesiredModelLevel
========	================	------------------
Louis	CUV	Premium
Louis	Sedan	Standard
Ted	Coupe	Performance

Think about the key columns. The relationship between `Driver` and `VehicleStyle` represents a multivalued dependency for the `Driver` and the `VehicleStyle` entities. A driver such as Louis will drive either CUV- or Sedan-style vehicles, and Louis is the only driver currently configured to drive the CUV style (and Louis is the only driver configured for Sedan, Ted is the only driver configured for Coupe, etc.). As we add more data, each vehicle style will have many drivers who choose the type as a preference. A table such as this one for `DriverVehicleStyle` is used frequently to resolve a many-to-many relationship between two tables, in this case, the `Driver` and `VehicleStyle` tables.

The modeling problem comes when you need to model a relationship between three (or more) entities, modeled as three columns in a key from three separate table types. As an example, consider the following table representing the assignment of a trainer to a type of class that is assigned to use a certain book. The model snippet in Figure 5-8 is how the model would look, just thinking of surrogate keys, with all the implementation details hidden in additional tables.

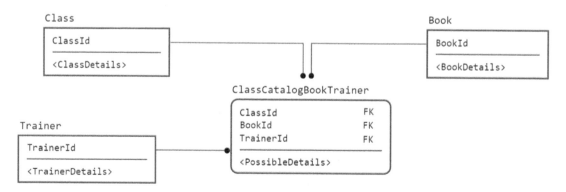

Figure 5-8.   *The ClassCatalogBookTrainer model snippet*

But for simplicity of display, for this example, we will use textual values for the keys that should suffice to let us see the issues in a smaller amount of text space. So we have this table, and it says that for each class, these are the trainers and books used. The class could be a class given at a specific point in time. Hence, the possible details in the model could represent the room and time the class is taught or just a catalog of classes, trainers, and books that can be used. For the first pass, assume the latter, that this is a catalog of possible combinations of these three items:

Trainer	Class	Book
=========	=======	======
Louis	Normalization	DB Design & Implementation
Chuck	Normalization	DB Design & Implementation
Fred	Implementation	DB Design & Implementation
Fred	Golf	Topics for the Non-Technical

To decide if this table is acceptable, we will look at the relationship of each key column to each of the others to determine how they are related. If any two columns are not directly related to one another, there will be an issue with Fourth Normal Form for the design of the table. Here are the possible combinations and their relationships:

- Class and Trainer are related, based on the skill of being able to train for a certain type of class. A class may have multiple trainers.

- Book and Class are related. You can't use just any book to teach any class. A book may be used for multiple classes.

- Trainer and Book are not directly related, because the requirement is simply to assign to the class both books and trainers.

Hence, what we really have here are two independent pieces of information being represented in a single table, rather than each row having only one single meaning. You can see from the sample data that we ended up with duplicated data because the class 'Normalization' has the book 'DB Design & Implementation' recorded twice. To deal with this, I will split the table on the column that is common to the two dependent relationships. Now, take this one table and make two tables, the first recording the trainers for a class and the other essentially representing the Class entity with a Book attribute (note the key is now the Class and not Class and Book). These two tables are equivalent to the initial table with the following three-part key:

Class	Trainer
=======	=========
Normalization	Louis
Normalization	Chuck
Implementation	Fred
Golf	Fred

Class	Book
===============	----------------------------
Normalization	DB Design & Implementation
Implementation	DB Design & Implementation
Golf	Topics for the Non Technical

While you can join these two tables together on Class, it generally does not make sense because there is no criteria to connect trainer to book.

A solid test for your tables and keys is considering what attributes you could add to the table without duplicating data. Of course, the problem typically arises because one designs a table and really doesn't think about higher-cardinality cases than the one-to-one-to-one, in this case. For example, let's consider the original set of data:

Trainer	Class	Book
==========	==============	============================
Louis	Normalization	DB Design & Implementation
Chuck	Normalization	DB Design & Implementation
Fred	Implementation	DB Design & Implementation
Fred	Golf	Topics for the Non-Technical

Defined as it was, just a catalog of classes with possible books and trainers, this made no sense; and there really aren't any attributes that make sense for the entire key. (Remember this is a contrived example, as will be almost any other example you find on the Web or in textbooks. Real situations will be more complex and more nuanced.) But that exact set of data could just as easily have been defined as Class Offerings by One and Only One Trainer with One and Only One Book. Then this is a perfectly acceptable table. Attributes can easily be added like time, room number, and so on or related via another table. Requirements matter.

As an alternate scenario, consider the following table of data, which might be part of the car rental system that we have used for examples before. This table defines the brand of vehicles that the driver will drive:

Driver	VehicleStyle	VehicleBrand
====================	===========================	=================
Louis	Station Wagon	Ford
Louis	Sedan	Hyundai
Ted	Coupe	Chevrolet

- VehicleStyle and VehicleBrand are related, defining the styles of vehicles the brand offers.

- Driver is related to VehicleStyle and VehicleBrand directly, representing the brand of vehicle the driver will drive.

This table defines the types of vehicles that the driver will take. Each of the columns has a relationship to the other, so it *is* in Fourth Normal Form. In the next section, I will use this table again to assist in identifying Fifth Normal Form issues with a different take on the requirements for the same columns and data.

Of considerable concern from an architectural standpoint is how this plays out when using surrogate keys. Most often, a designer would have noted that VehicleStyle and VehicleBrand are related and thus would have created the following:

VehicleStyleBrandId	VehicleStyle	VehicleBrand
1	Station Wagon	Ford
2	Sedan	Hyundai
3	Coupe	Chevrolet

Which would be related to:

Driver	VehicleStyleBrandId
Louis	1
Louis	2
Ted	3

It is important to understand that this table has the same key (Driver, VehicleStyle, VehicleBrand) as the original table and the same checks ought to be carried out no matter how the table is defined. Of course, the relationship between VehicleStyle and VehicleBrand in that case would be explicit, rather than implicit, making our decisions far easier. Moreover, the determination that VehicleStyle and VehicleBrand are related to one another is up to interpretation of business rules.

It might also be that you could independently pick brands and styles that are matched to inventory, even if they are not logical (e.g., `Ford, Motorcycle`). This is the primary reason why these rules are very business rule oriented. Slight variations of user requirements can make the same table design right or wrong (and consequently end up driving your users bananas when they expect one interpretation and get a different one to work with).

Fifth Normal Form

Fifth Normal Form is a rule that breaks out any improper key data dependencies that were not specifically culled out by Fourth Normal Form. The idea is that if you can break a table with three (or more) dependent keys into three (or more) individual tables and be guaranteed to get the original table by joining them together, the table is not in Fifth Normal Form. An alternate name of this normal form is *Project-Join Normal Form*, where project means to take a set of attributes, like in a `SELECT` statement. In this case, it will be to take subsets of columns from a table's key and then try to join them back together to safely get the same data.

Fifth Normal Form is an esoteric rule that is seldom violated, but it is interesting nonetheless because it does have some basis in reality and is a good exercise in understanding how to work through intercolumn dependencies. In the previous section, I presented the following table of data:

Driver	VehicleStyle	VehicleBrand
==================	============================	================
Louis	Station Wagon	Ford
Louis	Sedan	Hyundai
Ted	Coupe	Chevrolet

We defined in the previous section that the table was in Fourth Normal Form because the columns in this key were dependent upon one another in either of the sets of requirements we chose for the table (which will be reiterated in the section as well). At this point, Fifth Normal Form would suggest that it is best to break down any existing ternary (three) or greater key relationships into binary relationships if possible. To determine if breaking down tables into smaller tables will be lossless (i.e., not changing the meaning of the data storage), you need the requirements that were used to create the table and the data.

Let's consider the requirements that stated that the relationship between `Driver`, `VehicleStyle`, and `VehicleBrand` meant that the data in the table indicated that

- Louis is willing to drive any `Station Wagon` or Sedan.
- Louis is willing to drive vehicles from `Ford` or `Hyundai`.
- Ted is willing to drive any `Coupe`.
- `Ted is willing to drive vehicles from Chevrolet.`

Then, we can infer from this definition of the table that the following dependencies exist:

- `Driver` determines `VehicleStyle`.
- `Driver` determines `VehicleBrand`.
- `VehicleBrand` determines `VehicleStyle`.

The issue here is that if you wanted to express that Louis is now willing to drive Volvos and that Volvo has station wagons and sedans, you would need to add multiple rows, in this case the two bolded rows:

Driver	VehicleStyle	VehicleBrand
==================	==============================	================
Louis	Station Wagon	Ford
Louis	Sedan	Hyundai
Louis	**Station Wagon**	**Volvo**
Louis	**Sedan**	**Volvo**
Ted	Coupe	Chevrolet

In these two rows, you are expressing several different pieces of information. `Volvo` presumably has `Station Wagons` and `Sedans` that could possibly be driven. Louis is willing to drive Volvos (which you have repeated multiple times). If other drivers will drive Volvos, you will have to repeat the information that Volvo has station wagons and sedans repeatedly.

At this point, you probably now see why ending up with tables with redundant data like in our previous example is such an unlikely mistake to make—not impossible, but not probable by any means, assuming any testing goes on with actual data in your implementation process. Once the user must query (or, worse yet, update) a million rows to express a very simple thing like the fact Volvo is now offering a sedan-class automobile, changes will be made. The fix for this situation is to break the table into the following three tables, each representing the binary relationship between two of the columns of the original table:

Driver	VehicleStyle
Louis	Station Wagon
Louis	Sedan
Ted	Coupe

Driver	VehicleBrand
Louis	Ford
Louis	Hyundai
Louis	**Volvo**
Ted	Chevrolet

VehicleStyle	VehicleBrand
Station Wagon	Ford
Sedan	Hyundai
Coupe	Chevrolet
Station Wagon	**Volvo**
Sedan	**Volvo**

I included the additional row that says that Louis will drive Volvo vehicles and that Volvo has station wagon– and sedan-style vehicles. Joining these rows together will give you the table I had originally created:

Driver	VehicleStyle	VehicleBrand
Louis	Sedan	Hyundai
Louis	Station Wagon	Ford
Louis	Sedan	Volvo
Louis	Station Wagon	Volvo
Ted	Coupe	Chevrolet

I mentioned earlier that the meaning of the table makes a large difference. As in the "Fourth Normal Form: Independent Multivalued Dependencies" section, the alternate interpretation of the table is that instead of giving the users such a weak way of choosing their desired rides (maybe Volvo has the best station wagons and Ford the best sports cars), the table just presented might be interpreted as

- Louis is willing to drive Ford sports cars, Hyundai sedans, and Volvo station wagons and sedans.

- Ted is willing to drive a Chevrolet coupe.

In this case, the original table is in Fifth Normal Form because instead of VehicleStyle and VehicleBrand being loosely related, they are directly related and can be thought of as a single value rather than two independent ones. Now a dependency is Driver to VehicleStyle plus VehicleBrand. This was the solution we arrived at previously, noting that in most cases, the designer would have likely already noted that VehicleStyle and VehicleBrand should be an entity of its own and the key would be migrated to our table to form a three-part composite key, either using natural keys or perhaps via a surrogate from VehicleStyleBrandId and Driver.

As our final example, consider the following table of Books along with Authors and Editors:

Book	Author	Editor
Design	Louis	Jonathan
Design	Jeff	Leroy
Golf	Louis	Steve
Golf	Fred	Tony

There are two possible interpretations that would (hopefully) be made clear in the requirements and ideally reflected in the name of the table:

- This table is not even in Fourth Normal Form if it represents the following:

  - The Book *Design* has Authors Louis and Jeff and Editors Jonathan and Leroy.

  - The Book *Golf* has Authors Louis and Fred and Editors Steve and Tony.

- This table is in Fifth Normal Form if it represents the following:

  - For the Book *Design*, Editor Jonathan edits Louis's work and Editor Leroy edits Jeff's work.

  - For the Book *Golf*, Editor Steve edits Louis's work and Editor Tony edits Fred's work.

In the first case, the author and editor are independent of each other, meaning that technically you should have a table for the Book to Author relationship and another for the Book to Editor relationship. In the second case, the author and editor are directly related to the book. Hence, all three of the values are required to express the single thought of "for book X, only editor Y edits Z's work."

Note I hope the final sentence of that previous paragraph makes it clear the point that permeates this entire chapter—that tables should mean one thing and, since a key represents one row in the table, a key value must strictly represent one thing. This is the goal that is being pressed by each of the normal forms. First required row uniqueness, BCNF worked through non-key dependencies to make sure the key references were correct, and Fourth and Fifth Normal Forms made sure that the key identified expressed a single thought.

What can be gleaned from Fourth and Fifth Normal Forms, and indeed all the normal forms, is that when you think you can break down a table into smaller parts with different natural keys, which then have different meanings without losing the essence of the solution you are going for, then it is almost certainly better to do so for the integrity of your data.

The most important thing to take note of is the phrase "different natural keys," or you can easily take this too far. For example, one might do something like the following to their customer table:

CustomerNumber	FirstName
000000001	Bob

CustomerNumber	LastName
000000001	Jones

In the general case, this is not desirable because both tables have the same natural key and they both represent the same thing. The atomic unit of customer is not split into two pieces, and for the user to fetch the thing that they need to fetch to do some basic unit of work, they need to go to two tables to fetch it is wasted work.

There are valid reasons to vertically partition a table like this, but they are performance oriented and generally for very high–performance purposes where one slice of the table might be locked differently than the other.

Denormalization

Denormalization is the practice of taking a properly normalized set of tables and selectively undoing some of the changes in the resulting tables made during the normalization process for performance. Bear in mind that I said "properly normalized." I'm not talking about skipping normalization and just saying the database is denormalized. Denormalization is a process that requires you to understand the requirements, design the proper database, normalize, ideally test the database, and then selectively pick out data issues that you are willing to code protection for rather than using normalized structures to prevent data anomalies. Too often, the term "denormalization" is used as a synonym for "work of an ignorant or, worse, lazy designer."

Back in the good old days, there was a saying: "Normalize 'til it hurts; denormalize 'til it works." In those early days, hardware was a lot less powerful, and some of the dreams of using the relational engine to encapsulate away performance issues were hard to achieve. I was reminiscing in a conference the other day of a server my first organization ran its worldwide accounting systems on that had 1 MB of RAM. In the current hardware and software reality, there are only a few reasons to denormalize your transactional systems when normalization has been done based on requirements and user need.

Denormalization should be used primarily to improve performance in cases where normalized structures are causing overhead to the query processor and, in turn, other processes in SQL Server or to tone down some complexity to make things easy enough to implement. This, of course, introduces risks of data anomalies or even making the data less appropriate for the relational engine. Any additional code written to deal with these anomalies must be duplicated in every application that uses the database, thereby increasing the likelihood of human error. The judgment call that needs to be made in this situation is whether a slightly slower (but 100% accurate) application is preferable to a faster application of lower accuracy.

Denormalization should *not* be used as a crutch to make implementing the user interfaces easier. For example, suppose the user interface in Figure 5-9 was fashioned for a book inventory system.

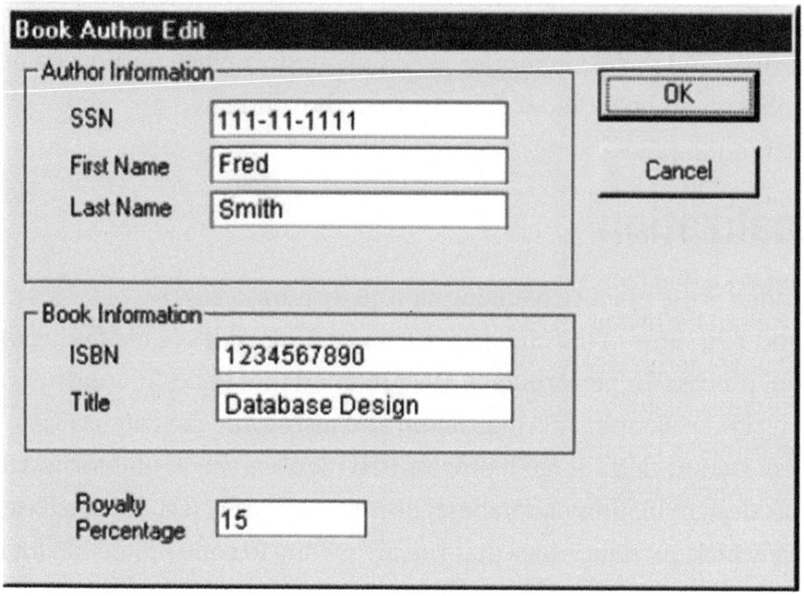

Figure 5-9.   *A possible graphical front end to our example*

Does Figure 5-9 represent a bad user interface (aside from my ancient Windows ME–style interface aspects, naturally)? Not in and of itself. If the design calls for the data you see in the figure to be entered most of the time and the client wants the design to look like this, fine. However, this requirement to see certain data on the screen together is clearly a UI design concern, not a question of data structure. Don't let the user interface dictate the data structure any more than the data structures should dictate the UI. When the user figures out the problem with expecting a single author for every book, you won't have to change the underlying database design.

Note   It might also be that Figure 5-9 represents the basic UI and a button is added to the form to implement the multiple-cardinality situation of more than one author in the "expert" mode, since a large majority of all books for your client have one author.

UI design and database design are separate things. The power of the UI comes with focusing on making the top 80% of use cases easier, and some processes can be left to be difficult if they are done rarely. The database can only have one way of looking at the problem, and it must be as complicated as the most complicated case, even if that case happens just .001% of the time. If it is legal to have multiple authors, the database must support that case, and the queries and reports that make use of the data must support that case as well.

It's my contention that during the modeling and implementation process, we should rarely step back from our normalized structures to performance-tune our applications proactively—that is, before a performance issue is felt/discovered and found to be non-tunable using available technology. This advice would change for something that might run on lightweight hardware like the upcoming Azure Edge platform that runs on a Raspberry Pi or something that needs to ingest millions of transactions per second, but even these designs ought to know what the normalized database would look like before starting to tear the design down for performance.

Because this book is centered on OLTP database structures, the most important part of our design effort is to make certain that the tables we create are well formed for the relational engine and can be equated to the requirements set forth by the entities and attributes of the logical model. Once you start the process of physical storage modeling/integration (which should be analogous to performance tuning, using indexes, partitions, etc.), there might well be valid reasons to denormalize the structures, either to improve performance or to reduce implementation complexity, but neither of these pertains to the model that represents the world that our customers live in. You will always have fewer problems if you implement physically what is true logically. For almost all cases, I always advocate waiting until you find a compelling reason to denormalize (such as if some part of your system is failing and you find it impossible to tune) before you denormalize.

There is, however, one major caveat to the "normalization at all costs" model. Whenever the read/write ratio of data is nearly infinite, meaning whenever data is essentially read only, it can be advantageous to store some calculated values for easier usage. For example, consider the following scenarios:

- *Balances or inventory as of a certain date*: Look at your bank statement. At the end of every banking day, it summarizes your activity and uses that value as the basis of your bank balance. The bank never goes back and makes changes to the history but instead debits or credits the account.

- *Calendar table, table of integers, or prime numbers*: Certain values are fixed by definition. For example, take a table with dates in it. Storing the name of the day of the week rather than calculating it every time can be advantageous, and given a day like May 4, 2020, you can always be sure it is a Monday, and every May the 4th will always be *Star Wars* Day. A calendar table will be demonstrated in Chapter 13.

When the writes are guaranteed to be zero after row creation, denormalization by duplication can be an easy choice, but you still need to make sure that data is in sync and cannot be made out of sync. Even minimal numbers of writes can make your implementation way too complex because, again, you cannot just code for the 99.9% case when building a noninteractive part of the system. If someone updates a value, its copies will have to be dealt with, and usually it is far easier, and not that much slower, to use a query to get the answer than it is to maintain lots of denormalized data when it is rarely used.

One suggestion that I make to people who use denormalization as a tool for tuning an application is to always include queries to verify the data. Take the following table of data:

InvoiceNumber	InvoiceDate	InvoiceAmount
=============	----------------	---------------
000000000323	2015-12-23	100

InvoiceNumber	ItemNumber	Product	Quantity	ProductPrice	OrderItemId
=============	===========	---------	----------	-------------	-----------
000000000323	1	KL7R2	10	8.00	1232322
000000000323	2	RTCL3	10	2.00	1232323

If the InvoiceAmount (the denormalized version of the summary of line item prices) is to be kept in the table, you build tests that run a query such as the following on a regular basis during off-hours to make sure that something hasn't gone wrong:

```
SELECT Invoice.InvoiceNumber
FROM   Invoice
         JOIN InvoiceLineItem
           ON Invoice.InvoiceNumber = InvoiceLineItem.InvoiceNumber
```

```
GROUP  BY Invoice.InvoiceNumber, InvoiceLineItem.InvoiceAmount
HAVING  SUM(InvoiceLineItem.Quantity * InvoiceLineItem.ProductPrice)
                                        <> Invoice.InvoiceAmount;
```

Alternatively, you can feed output from such a query into the WHERE clause of an UPDATE statement to fix the data if it isn't super-important that the data is maintained perfectly on a regular basis.

Note At last year's PASS Summit, a presenter I respect argued that in some architectures it can be better to optimize for reads, whereas a normalized database optimizes for writes. I personally still would argue that point, but this point is not arguable: data correctness and integrity are the most important thing. Normalization is for data integrity, and you cannot protect data integrity or denormalize without normalizing first. If you understand normalization and do it well, you are probably qualified to denormalize your data as well. If you don't quite understand normalization, you are bound to make big mistakes.

Best Practices

The following are a few guiding principles that I use when normalizing a database. If you understand the fundamentals of why to normalize, these five points pretty much cover the entire process:

- *Normalization is not an academic process*: It is a programming process. A value like 'a,b,c,d,e' stored in a single column is not in and of itself incorrect. Only when you understand the context of such a value can you know if it needs one or five columns or one or five rows to store. The value from the decomposition is to the programming process, and if there is no value, it is not worth doing.

- *Follow the rules of normalization as closely as possible to meet the customer's requirements*: This chapter's "Summary" section summarizes these rules. These rules are optimized for use with relational database management systems such as SQL Server. Keep in mind that SQL Server now has, and will continue to add, tools that will not necessarily be of use for normalized structures, because the goal of SQL Server is to be all things to all people. The principles of normalization are 30-plus years old and are still valid today for maximizing utilization of the core relational engine.

- *All columns must describe the essence of what's being modeled in the table*: Be certain to know what that essence or exact purpose of every table is. For example, when modeling a person, only things that describe or identify a person should be included. Anything that is not directly reflecting the essence of what the table represents should be removed and placed in a different table.

- *At least one key must uniquely identify what the table is modeling*: Uniqueness alone isn't enough criterion for being a table's only key. It isn't wrong to have a meaningless uniqueness-only surrogate key, but it shouldn't be the only key.

- *Choice of primary key isn't necessarily important*: Keep in mind that the primary key is changeable at any time with any candidate key. It isn't until you start to build real code and create real data that making changes becomes hard. As long as the values in the primary key column set are all not nullable, they will do just fine, though a surrogate key does have value.

- *Data integrity and correctness are the reasons we do this*: Pure and simple. Normalization is about making data structures that resist data integrity issues by reducing redundancy and uncomfortable processing.

Summary

In this chapter, I've presented the criteria for normalizing databases so they'll work properly with SQL Server. At this stage, it's pertinent to summarize quickly the nature of the main normal forms we've outlined in this chapter and the preceding chapter; see Table 5-1.

Table 5-1. *Normal Form Recap*

Form	Rules
Definition of a table	All columns must be atomic—only one value per column. All rows of a table must contain the same number of values.
First Normal Form	Every row should contain the same number of values or, in other words, no arrays, subtables, or repeating groups.
BCNF	All columns are fully dependent on a key; all columns must be a fact about a key and nothing but a key. A table is in BCNF if every determinant is a key.
Fourth Normal Form	There must not be more than one independent multivalued dependency represented by the table, meaning all key columns should be dependent upon one another.
Fifth Normal Form	All relationships and keys are broken down to binary relationships when the decomposition is lossless.

It is not necessary to go through the steps one at a time in a linear fashion. Once you have designed databases quite a few times, you'll usually realize when your model is not quite right instinctively. It is still very useful to go back over your work in case you have missed something before you progress to making tables in a database, but ideally you will have very little to do.

The following list is the shorthand version of normalization I use when building systems that correspond to the normal forms we have covered in this chapter:

- *Columns*: One column, one value.

- *Table/row uniqueness*: Tables have independent meaning; rows are distinct from one another.

- *Proper relationships between columns*: Columns either are a key or describe something about the row identified by the key.

- *Key column dependencies*: Make sure key column relationships between three values or tables are correct. Reduce all relationships to binary relationships if possible.

There is also one truth that I feel the need to slip into this book right now. You are not done. Basically, we are just refining the blueprints to get them closer to something we can hand off to an programmer to build. The blueprints can and almost certainly will change because of any number of things. You may miss something the first time around, or you may discover a technique for modeling something that you didn't know before (maybe from reading the rest of this book!). Now it is time to do some real work and build what you have designed (well, after an extra example and a section that kind of recaps the first chapters of the book, but then we get rolling, I promise).

Still not convinced? Consider the following list of pleasant side effects of normalization:

- *Eliminating duplicated data*: Any piece of data that occurs more than once in the database is an error waiting to happen. No doubt you've been beaten by this once or twice in your personal life: your address is stored in multiple places, and then you move and try to change your address in the multiple places where it is stored. In my last move, it took over two years to eliminate old copies of my address. Additionally, a side effect of eliminating duplicated data is that less data is stored on disk or in memory, which can be among the biggest bottlenecks.

- *Avoiding unnecessary coding*: Extra programming in triggers, in stored procedures, or even in the business logic tier can be required to handle poorly structured data, and this, in turn, can impair performance significantly. Extra coding also increases the chance of introducing new bugs by causing a labyrinth of code to be needed to maintain redundant data.

- *Keeping tables thin*: When I refer to a "thin" table, the idea is that a relatively small number of columns are in the table. Thinner tables mean more data fits on a given page, therefore allowing the database server to retrieve more rows for a table in a single read than would otherwise be possible. This all means that there will be more tables in the system when you're finished normalizing.

- *Maximizing clustered indexes*: Clustered indexes order a table natively in SQL Server. Clustered indexes are special indexes in which the physical storage of the data matches the order of the indexed data, which allows for better performance of queries using that index. Each table can have only a single clustered index. The concept of clustered indexes applies to normalization in that you'll have more tables when you normalize. The increased numbers of clustered indexes increase the likelihood that joins between tables will be efficient.

CHAPTER 6

Physical Model Case Study

The way to get started is to quit talking and begin doing.

—Walt Disney, Visionary Who Started My Happy Place,
Walt Disney World

Once the normalization task is complete, pretty much everything is ready to start the implementation process. In this chapter, I will go through the process that will turn the normalized model into a physical data model that I will use to create a SQL Server database in the next chapter. At a minimum, between normalization and actual implementation, take plenty of time to review the model to make sure you are completely happy with it.

Even starting from the same base data model, different people tasked with implementing a database may take subtly (or even dramatically) different approaches to the process. The final physical design will always be, to some extent, a reflection of the person/organization who designed it, although each of the solutions should strongly resemble one another at its core.

The models we have built so far in the book have been pretty much implementation agnostic and unaffected by whether the final implementation would be on Microsoft SQL Server, Microsoft Access, Oracle, Sybase, or any RDBMS. (You should expect some serious changes if you end up implementing with a nonrelational engine, naturally.) However, during this stage, in terms of the naming conventions that are defined, the domain chosen, and so on, the design is geared specifically for implementation on SQL Server. Each of the relational engines has its own intricacies and quirks, so it is helpful to understand how to implement on the system you are tasked with. In this book, we

© Louis Davidson 2021
L. Davidson, *Pro SQL Server Relational Database Design and Implementation*,
https://doi.org/10.1007/978-1-4842-6497-3_6

will stick with SQL Server 2019, noting where you would need to adjust if using one of the more recent previous versions of SQL Server, such as SQL Server 2016 or SQL Server 2017.

We will go through the following steps to transform the blueprint of a database into an actual functioning database:

- *Choosing names*: We'll finalize naming concerns for tables and columns started in previous chapters.

- *Choosing key implementation*: Throughout the earlier bits of the book, we've made several types of key choices. In the "Choosing Key Implementation" section, we will go ahead and finalize the implementation keys for the model, discussing the merits of the different implementation methods.

- *Determining column domain implementation*: We'll cover the basics of choosing datatypes, choosing whether a column allows NULL values, and computed columns. Other choices include determining the default value for a column and choosing between using a domain table or a column with a CHECK constraint for types of values where you want to limit column values to a given set.

- *Setting up schemas*: The "Setting Up Schemas" section provides some basic guidance in creating and naming your schemas. Schemas allow you to set up groups of objects that provide groupings for usage and security.

- *Adding implementation columns*: We'll consider columns that can be common to almost every database that are not part of the logical design and that do not provide value to the corporate user, but rather to the technology user.

The main example in this chapter (and the next) is based on a simple messaging database that a hypothetical company is building for its hypothetical upcoming online-only conference. Any similarities to other systems are purely coincidental, and the model is specifically created not to be overly functional but to be very, very small. The following are the simple requirements for the database:

- Messages can be 200 characters of Unicode text. Messages can be sent privately to one user, to everyone, or both. The user cannot send a message with the exact same text more than once per hour (to cut down on mistakes where users click <Send> too often).

- Users will be identified by a handle that must be 5–20 characters and that uses their conference attendee number and the key value on their badges to access the system. To keep up with your own group of people, apart from other users, users can connect themselves to other users. Connections are one-way, allowing users to see all the speakers' information without the reverse being true.

Figure 6-1 shows the logical database design for this application, on which I'll base the physical design.

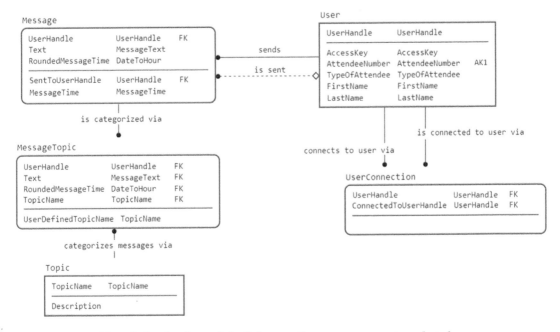

Figure 6-1. *Simple logical model of the conference messaging database*

The following is brief documentation of the tables and columns in the model. To keep things simple, I will expound on the needs as we get to each of them.

- User: Represents a user of the messaging system, which will be preloaded from another system with attendee information:

    - UserHandle: The name the user wants to be known as, initially preloaded with a value based on the person's first and last names, plus an integer value, changeable by the user

    - AccessKey: A password-like value given to the users on the back of their badges to gain access

    - AttendeeNumber: The number that the attendees are given to identify themselves, printed on the front of their badges

    - TypeOfAttendee: Used to give the user special privileges, such as access to speaker materials, vendor areas, and so on

    - FirstName, LastName: Name of the user printed on the badge for people to see

- UserConnection: Represents the connection of one user to another in order to filter results to a given set of users:

    - UserHandle: Handle of the user who is going to connect to another user

    - ConnectedToUser: Handle of the user who is being connected to

- Message: Represents a single message in the system:

    - UserHandle: Handle of the user sending the message

    - Text: The text of the message being sent

    - RoundedMessageTime: The time of the message, rounded to the hour

    - SentToUserHandle: The handle of the user that is being sent a message

    - MessageTime: The time the message is sent, to the second

- `MessageTopic`: Relates a message to a topic:
  - `UserHandle`: User handle of the user who sent the message
  - `RoundedMessageTime`: The time of the message, rounded to the hour
  - `TopicName`: The name of the topic being sent as seen by the user
  - `UserDefinedTopicName`: Allows the users to type their own message topic, when the proper topic value is set
- `Topic`: Predefined topics for messages:
  - `TopicName`: The name of the topic
  - `Description`: Description of the purpose and utilization of the topics

---

Note   The UserConnection table is a prime example of a table that could be implemented using a graph table to provide additional value. In this chapter, I will leave it in a strictly relational table for simplicity, but in Chapter 9, we will be covering graph tables in SQL Server 2017 and later.

Choosing Names

The target database for our model is (obviously) SQL Server, so our table and column naming conventions must adhere to the rules imposed by this database system, as well as being consistent and logical. In this section, I'll briefly cover some of the different concerns when naming tables and columns. All the system constraints on names have been the same for versions of SQL Server going back to SQL Server 7.0.

Names of columns, tables, procedures, and so on are referred to technically as *identifiers*. Identifiers in SQL Server are stored in a system datatype of `sysname`. It is defined as a 128-character (or less, of course) string using Unicode characters and does not allow `NULL` values by default. SQL Server's rules for identifiers consist of two distinct naming methods:

- *Regular identifiers*: Identifiers that need no delimiter but have a set of rules that govern what can and cannot constitute a name. This is the preferred method, with the following rules:

  - The first character must be a letter as defined by Unicode Standard 3.2 (generally speaking, Roman letters A–Z, uppercase and lowercase, as well as letters from other languages) or the underscore character (_). You can find the Unicode Standard at `home.unicode.org`.

  - Subsequent characters can be Unicode letters, numbers, the "at" sign (@), or the dollar sign ($).

  - The name must not be a SQL Server reserved word. You can find a large list of reserved words in SQL Server 2019 documentation here: `docs.microsoft.com/en-us/sql/t-sql/language-elements/reserved-keywords-transact-sql`. Some of these are tough, like user, `transaction`, and `table`, as they do often come up in typical, real-world designs. (Note that our original model includes the name User, which we will have to correct.) Some words are considered keywords but not reserved (such as `description`) and may be used as identifiers. (Some, such as int, would make terrible identifiers!) Reserved words and keywords are colored in SSMS, which can be confusing to some programmers and users, so it is good to beware of this.

  - The name cannot contain spaces.

- *Delimited identifiers:* These identifiers must be surrounded by either square brackets ([ ]) or double quotes ("") which are allowed only when the SET QUOTED_IDENTIFIER option is set to ON. By placing delimiters around an object's name, you can use *any* string as the name, for example, [Table Name], [3232 fjfa*&(&^(], and [Drop Database HR;]. Or even [ ] would be legal (but really annoying and dangerous) names. Even things like emojis, if they can be represented in Unicode, can be in object names.

If you need to put a closing square bracket (]) or even a double quote character in the name, you must include two of the characters, such as two closing square brackets (]]), just like when you need to include a single quote within a string. So the name `fred]olicious` would have to be delimited as `[fred]]olicious]`. For the most part, delimited names should be avoided when at all possible. However, they can be necessary for interacting with data from other environments. While names that require delimiters should be avoided, when you write tools to script SQL code, delimiters should always be used because a name like `[;Drop Database HR;]` can cause "problems" if you don't. Creating output for some applications, like Excel, can be made easier by using names with spaces in them, but should not be a primary practice.

If you determine after some thinking that you do believe that using names with spaces in them is a best practice, please ask someone else for help naming your objects, or email me at `louis@drsql.org`. This is a pretty horrible thing to do to your fellow human and will make working with your objects very cumbersome. Even just including space characters is a bad enough practice that you and your users will regret for years. Note too that `[name]` and `[name ]` are treated as different names in some contexts (see the embedded space) as will `[ name ]` for sure.

Note   Using policy-based management, you can create naming standard checks for whenever a new object is created. Policy-based management is a management tool rather than a design one, though it could pay to create naming standard checks to make sure you don't accidentally create objects with names you won't accept. In general, I find doing things that are way far too restrictive, because there are always exceptions to the rules, and automated policy enforcement only works with a dictator's hand. (Have you met Darth Development Manager? He is nice!)

Table Naming

While the rules for creating an object name are straightforward, the more important question is, "What kind of names should be chosen?" The answer I generally give is: "Whatever you feel is best, as long as others can read it and it follows the local naming standards." This might sound like a cop-out, but there are more naming standards than there are data architects. (On the day this paragraph was originally written, I had two independent discussions about how to name several objects, and neither person wanted to follow the same standard.) The standard I generally go with is the standard that was used in the logical model, that being Pascal-cased names, little if any abbreviation, and as descriptive as necessary. With space for 128 characters, there's little reason to do much abbreviating (thank goodness for IntelliSense and Redgate's SQL Prompt tool). A Pascal-cased name is of the form `PartPartPart`, where words are concatenated with nothing separating them. Camel-cased names do not start with a capital letter, such as `partPartPart`.

Caution   Because most companies have existing systems, it's a must to know the shop standard for naming objects so that it matches existing systems and so that new developers on your project will be more likely to understand your database and get up to speed more quickly. The key thing to make sure of is that you keep your full logical names intact for documentation purposes.

As an example, let's consider the name of the `UserConnection` table we will be building later in this chapter. The following list shows several different ways to build the name of this object:

- `user_connection` (*or sometimes, by some awful mandate, an all-caps version* `USER_CONNECTION`): Use underscores to separate values. Most programmers aren't big friends of underscores, because they're cumbersome to type until you get used to them. Plus, they have a COBOLesque quality that rarely pleases anyone.

- `[user connection]` *or* `"user connection"`: This name is delimited by brackets or quotes. Being forced to use delimiters is annoying, and many other languages use double quotes to denote strings. (In SQL, you always use single quotes for strings.) On the other hand, the brackets [and] don't denote strings, although they are a Microsoft-only convention that will not port well if you need to do any kind of cross-platform programming.

- `UserConnection` *or* `userConnection`: Pascal case or camel case (respectively), using mixed case to delimit between words. I'll use Pascal style in most examples, because it's the style I like.

- usrCnnct *or* usCnct: The abbreviated forms are problematic, because you must be careful always to abbreviate the same word in the same way in all your databases. You must maintain a dictionary of abbreviations, or you'll get multiple abbreviations for the same word—for example, getting "description" as "desc," "descr," "descrip," and/or "description." Some applications that access your data may have limitations like 30 characters that make abbreviations necessary, so understand the need.

One specific place where abbreviations do make sense is when abbreviation is *very* standard in the organization. As an example, if you were writing a purchasing system and you were naming a purchase order table, you could name the object PO, because this is widely understood. Often, users will desire this, even if some abbreviations don't seem that obvious. Just be 100% certain, so you don't end up with PO also representing disgruntled customers along with purchase orders.

Choosing names for objects is ultimately a personal choice but should never be made arbitrarily and should be based first on existing corporate standards, then existing software, and finally legibility and readability. The most important thing to try to achieve is internal consistency. Your goal as an architect is to ensure that your users can use your objects easily and with as little thinking about structure as possible. Even most bad naming conventions will be better than having ten different good ones being implemented by warring architect/developer factions.

A particularly hideous practice that is somewhat common with people who have grown up working with procedural languages (particularly interpreted languages) is to include something in the name to indicate that a table is a table, such as tblSchool or tableBuilding. Please don't do this (really...I beg you). It's clear by the context what is a table. This practice, just like the other Hungarian-style notations, makes good sense in a procedural programming language where the type of object isn't always clear just from context, but this practice is never needed with SQL tables. Note that this dislike of prefixes is just for names that are used by users. I will quietly establish prefixes and naming patterns for non–user-addressable objects as the book continues.

Note   There is something to be said about the quality of corporate standards as well. If you have an archaic standard, like one that was based on the mainframe team's standard back in the 19th century, you really need to consider trying to change the standards when creating new databases so you don't end up with names like HWWG01_TAB_USR_CONCT_T just because the shop standards say so (and yes, I do know when the 19th century was).

Naming Columns

The naming rules for columns are the same as for tables as far as SQL Server is concerned—names must be legal identifiers. As for how to choose a name for a column, again, it's one of those tasks for the individual architect, based on the same sorts of criteria as before (shop standards, best usage, etc.). This book follows this set of guidelines:

- Other than the primary key, my feeling is that the table name should only be included in the column name when it *feels necessary*. For example, in an entity named Person, it isn't necessary to have columns called PersonName or PersonSocialSecurityNumber. Most columns should not be prefixed with the table name other than with the following two exceptions:

  - A surrogate key such as PersonId. This reduces the need for role naming (modifying names of attributes to adjust meaning, especially used in cases where multiple migrated foreign keys exist), making joins a lot easier to code.

  - Columns that are naturally named with the entity name in them, such as PersonNumber, PurchaseOrderNumber, or something that's common in the language of the client and used as a domain-specific term.

- The name should be as descriptive as possible. Use few abbreviations in names, except for the very common abbreviations, as well as generally pronounced abbreviations where a value is read naturally as the abbreviation. For example, I always use Id instead of

Identifier, first because it's a common abbreviation that's known to most people and second because the surrogate key of the Widget table is naturally pronounced Widget Eye-Dee, not Widget Identifier.

- Follow a common pattern if possible. As a review from the naming topic in Chapter 3, names should preferably have four parts:

  - *Role name [optional]*: When you need to explain the purpose of the attribute in the context of the table.

  - *Attribute [optional]*: The primary purpose of the column being named. If omitted, the name refers to the entity purpose directly.

  - *Classword*: A general suffix that identifies the usage of the column, in non–implementation-specific terms. It should not be the same thing as the datatype. For example, Id is a surrogate key, not IdInt or IdGUID. (If you need to expand or change types but not purpose, it should not affect the name.)

  - *Scale [optional]*: Tells the user what the scale of the data is when it is not easily discerned, like minutes or seconds, or when the typical currency is dollars and the column value represents euros.

  - Some example names might be

  - Store**Id** is the identifier for the store.

  - User**Name** is a textual string, but whether or not it is a varchar(30) or nvarchar(128) is immaterial.

  - End**Date** is the date when something ends and does not include a time part.

  - Save**Time** is the point in time when the row was saved.

  - Pledge**Amount** is an amount of money (using a decimal(12,2) or money or any sort of types).

  - Pledge**AmountEuros** is an amount of money in euros.

  - Distribution**Description** is a textual string that is used to describe how funds are distributed.

- **TickerCode** is a short textual string used to identify a ticker row.

- **OptInFlag** is a two-value column (or three including NULL) that indicates a status, such as in this case if the person has opted in for some reason.

Many possible classwords could be used, and this book is not about giving you all the standards to follow at that level. Too many variances from organization to organization make that too difficult. The most important thing is that if you can establish a standard, make it work for your organization and follow it.

Note   Just as with tables, avoid prefixes like col_ to denote a column, as it is a messy practice that doesn't look great in the final object.

I'll use the same naming conventions for the implementation model as I did for the logical model: Pascal-cased names with a few abbreviations (with the primary abbreviation that I ever use of "Id" for "Identifier," and I generally use the term "identifier" to mean a generic value that can be used to identify a row). Later in the book, I will use a Hungarian-style prefix for objects other than tables, such as constraints, and other technical-looking naming patterns for coded objects such as procedures. This is mostly to keep the names unique and avoid clashes with the table names. Tables, columns, and, to a similar extent, views are commonly used directly by users. They write queries and build reports directly using database object names and shouldn't need to change the displayed name of every column and table.

Model Name Adjustments

In our demonstration model, the first thing we will do is to rename the User table to MessagingUser because "User" is a SQL Server reserved keyword. While User is the more natural name than MessagingUser, it is one of the trade-offs we must make because of the legal values of names. In rare cases, when a suitable name can't be created that says what the keyword says, I may use a bracketed name, but even if it took me four hours to redraw graphics and undo my original choice of User as a table name when I first built this example before realizing what I had done, I don't want to give you that as a typical practice. If you find you have used a reserved keyword in your model (and you are not writing a chapter in a book that is over 50 pages long about it), it is usually a very minor change.

In the model snippet in Figure 6-2, I have made that change.

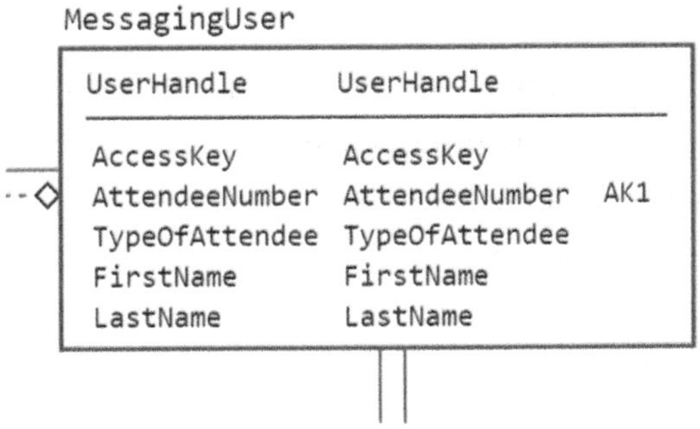

MessagingUser

UserHandle	UserHandle	
AccessKey	AccessKey	
AttendeeNumber	AttendeeNumber	AK1
TypeOfAttendee	TypeOfAttendee	
FirstName	FirstName	
LastName	LastName	

Figure 6-2. *Table User has been changed to MessagingUser*

The next change we will make will be to a few of the columns in this table. We will start off with the TypeOfAttendee column. The standard we discussed is to use a classword at the end of the column name. In this case, Type will make an acceptable class, as when you see AttendeeType, it will be clear what it means. The implementation will be a value that will be an up to 20-character value.

Another change will be to the AccessKey column. Key itself would be acceptable as a classword, but it will give the implication that the value is a key in the database (a standard I have used in my data warehousing dimensional database designs). So suffixing Value to the name will make the name clearer and distinctive. Figure 6-3 reflects the change in name.

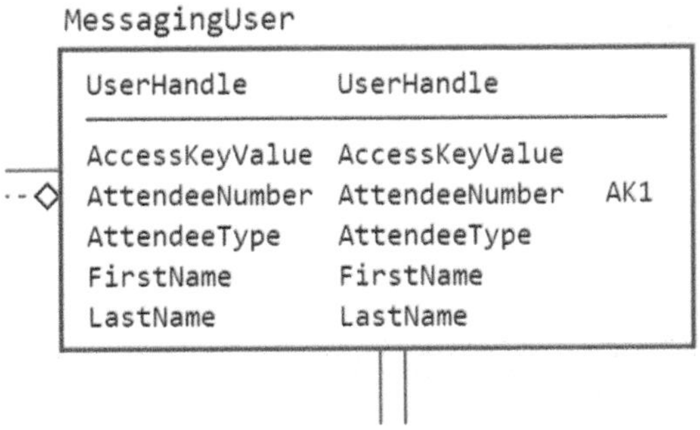

MessagingUser

UserHandle	UserHandle	
AccessKeyValue	AccessKeyValue	
AttendeeNumber	AttendeeNumber	AK1
AttendeeType	AttendeeType	
FirstName	FirstName	
LastName	LastName	

Figure 6-3. *MessagingUser table after change to AccessKey column name*

Choosing Key Implementation

The next step in the process is to choose how to implement the keys for the table. In the model at this point, tables have a natural key identified for the primary key. In this section, we will look at the issues surrounding key choice and, in the end, will set the keys for the demonstration model. We will look at choices for implementing primary keys and then note the choices for creating alternate keys as needed.

Primary Key

Choosing the style of implementation for primary keys is an important step. Depending on the style you go with, the look and feel of the rest of the database project will be affected, because whatever method you go with, the primary key value will be migrated to other tables as a reference to the row. In this book, I'll be reasonably agnostic about the whole thing, and I'll present several methods for choosing the implemented primary key throughout the book. In the designs in this chapter and the next, I will use a very specific method for all the tables, of course.

Presumably, during the logical phase, you've identified the different ways to uniquely identify a row. Hence, there should be several choices for the primary key, including the following:

- Using an existing column (or set of columns)

- Deriving a new surrogate column to represent the row

Each of these choices has pros and cons for the implementation. I'll look at them in the following sections.

Basing a Primary Key on Existing Columns

In many cases, a table will have an obvious, easy-to-use primary key. This is especially true when talking about independent entities. For example, take a table such as Product. It would often have a ProductNumber defined. A person usually has some sort of identifier, either government or company issued. (For example, my company has an EmployeeNumber that I have to put on all documents, particularly when the company needs to write me a check.)

For example, I used to have a Ford SVT Focus, made by the Ford Motor Company, so to identify this particular model, I might have a row in the `Manufacturer` table for the Ford Motor Company (e.g., as opposed to GM). Then, I'd have an `AutomobileMake` row with a key value of `ManufacturerName` = `'Ford Motor Company'` and `MakeName` = `'Ford'` (as opposed to Lincoln), `style` = `'SVT'`, and so on for the other values. This can get a bit messy to deal with, because the key of the `AutomobileModelStyle` table would be used in many places to describe which products are being shipped to which dealership. Note that this isn't generally about the size in terms of the performance of the key, just the number of values that make up the key. Performance will be better the smaller the key, as well, but this is true not only of the number of columns, but this also depends on the size of the value or values that make up a key. Using five 2-byte values could be better than one 15-byte value, though it is a lot more cumbersome to join on five columns.

Note that the complexity in a real system such as this would be compounded by the realization that you must be concerned with model year, possibly body style, different prebuilt packages of options, and so on. The key of the table may frequently have many parts, particularly in tables that are the child of a child of a child and so on.

Basing a Primary Key on a New, Surrogate Value

The other common key style is to use only a single column for the primary key, regardless of the size of the other keys. In this case, you'd specify that every table will have a single artificially generated primary key column and implement alternate keys to protect the uniqueness of the natural keys in your tables, as shown in Figure 6-4.

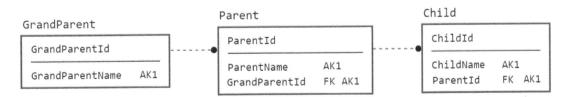

Figure 6-4. *Single-column key example*

Note that in this scenario, all your relationships will be implemented in the database as nonidentifying-type relationships, though you will implement them to all be required values (no `NULL` values). Functionally, this is the same as if the `GrandParentName` was migrated from `GrandParent` through `Parent` and down to `Child`, though it makes it harder to see in the model.

In the model in Figure 6-4, the most important thing you should notice is that each table has not only the primary key but also an alternate key. The "surrogate" key that each table has serves only as a stand-in for the natural key(s). The surrogate key for the parent object of ParentName can be used as a substitute for the defined key, in this case GrandParentName.

This method does have some useful implementation advantages:

- *Every table has a single-column primary key*: It's much easier to develop applications that use this key, because every table will have a key that follows the same pattern. It also makes code generation easier to do, because it is always understood how the table will look, relieving you from having to deal with all the other possible permutations of key setups.

- *The primary key index will be as small as possible*: If you use numbers, you can use the smallest integer type possible. If you have a max of 200 rows, you can use a tinyint; 2 billion rows, a 4-byte integer. Operations that use the index to access a row in the table will be faster. Most update and delete operations will likely modify the data by accessing the data based on simple primary keys that will use this index. (Some use a 16-byte GUID for convenience to the UI code, but GUIDs have their downfall, as we will discuss.)

- *Joins between tables will be easier to code*: That's because all migrated keys will be a single column. Plus, if you use a surrogate key that is named TableName + Suffix (always Id in my examples), there will be less thinking to do when setting up the join. Less thinking equates to less errors as well.

- *Security*: Consider our tables. The UserHandle column of the MessagingUser table has meaning, so if you select out a list of messages, it will automatically include the name of the user. If you need to delete that user, because a customer asks to be forgotten, you may only need to change the value of UserHandle and blank out some messages. If that user value is on every related table, cleaning out a user's details could take a very long time.

There are also disadvantages to this method, such as always having to join to a table to find out the meaning of the surrogate key value. In our example table in Figure 6-4, you would have to join from the Child table through the Parent table to get even key values from GrandParent. Another issue is that some parts of the self-documenting nature of relationships are eliminated, because using only single-column keys eliminates the obviousness of all identifying relationships. In order to know that the logical relationship between GrandParent and Parent is actually identifying, you will have to trace the relationship and look at the uniqueness constraints and foreign keys carefully.

Assuming you have chosen to use a surrogate key, the next choice is to decide what values to use for the key. Let's look at two methods of implementing the surrogate key, either by deriving the key from some other data or by using a meaningless surrogate value.

A popular way to define a primary key is to use a column with the IDENTITY property or generated from a SEQUENCE object, which can automatically generate a unique value. In this case, you rarely let the user have access to the value of the key but use it primarily for programming, providing the user with only natural key values.

It's exactly what was done for most of the entities in the logical models worked on in previous chapters: simply employing the surrogate key while we didn't know what the actual value for the primary key would be.

Once the key is generated for a row, it never changes, even if all the data changes (though ideally not so much data that the meaning of the surrogate is different on different uses!). This is an especially nice property when you need to do analysis over time. No matter what any of the other values in the table have been changed to, if the row's surrogate key value (as well as the row) represents the same thing, you can still relate it to its usage in previous times. (This is something you must be clear about with the DBA/programming staff as well. Sometimes, they may want to delete all data and reload it, but if the surrogate changes, your link to the unchanging nature of the surrogate key is broken.) Consider the case of a row that identifies a company. If the company is named Bob's Car Parts and it's located in Topeka, Kansas, but then it hits it big, moves to Detroit, and changes the company name to Car Parts Amalgamated, only one row is touched: the row where the name is located. Just change the name, address, and so on and it's done. Key values in the natural keys may change, but not the surrogate primary key values. Also, if the method of determining uniqueness changes for the object, the structure of the database needn't change beyond dropping one UNIQUE constraint and adding another.

Using a surrogate key value doesn't in any way prevent you from creating additional keys, like we did in the previous section. In fact, it demands it. For most tables, having a small code value is likely going to be a desired thing. Many clients hate long values, because they involve "too much typing." For example, say you have a value such as "Fred's Car Mart." You might want to have a code of "FREDS" for it as the shorthand value for the name. Some people are even so programmed by their experiences with ancient database systems that had arcane codes that they desire codes such as "XC10" to refer to "Fred's Car Mart."

In the demonstration model, I set all of the keys to use natural keys based on how one might do a logical model, so a table like MessagingUser in Figure 6-5 uses a key of the entire handle of the user, as well as having two other key values defined.

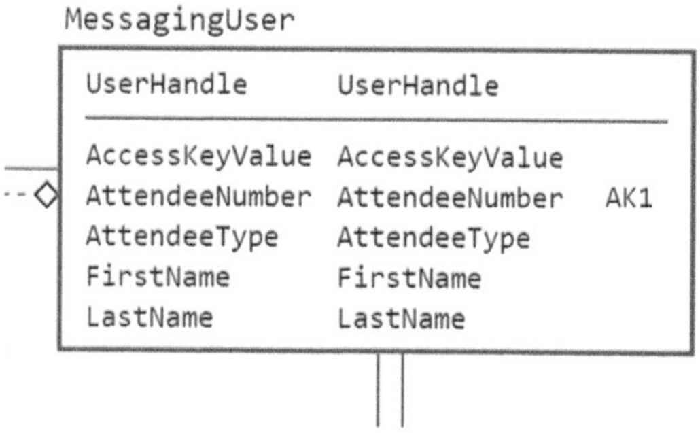

MessagingUser

UserHandle	UserHandle	
AccessKeyValue	AccessKeyValue	
AttendeeNumber	AttendeeNumber	AK1
AttendeeType	AttendeeType	
FirstName	FirstName	
LastName	LastName	

Figure 6-5. *MessagingUser table before changing model to use surrogate key*

This value is the most logical, but this name, based on the requirements (current and future), can change. Changing this to a surrogate value will make it easier to make the name change, and we will not have to worry about existing data in this table and related tables. Making this change to the model results in the change shown in Figure 6-6, and now, the key is a value that is clearly recognizable as being associated with the MessagingUser, no matter what the uniqueness of the row may be. Note that I made the UserHandle an alternate key as I switched it from primary key.

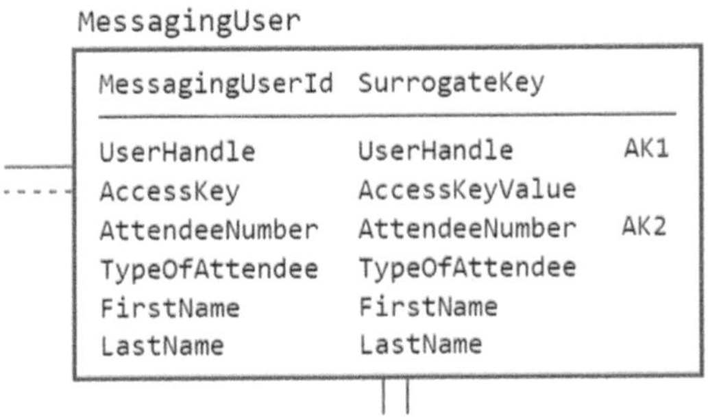

```
MessagingUser

  MessagingUserId  SurrogateKey
  ──────────────────────────────────────────
  UserHandle        UserHandle          AK1
  AccessKey         AccessKeyValue
  AttendeeNumber    AttendeeNumber      AK2
  TypeOfAttendee    TypeOfAttendee
  FirstName         FirstName
  LastName          LastName
```

Figure 6-6. *MessagingUser table after changing model to use surrogate key*

Next up, we will look at the `Message` table shown in Figure 6-7. Note that the two columns that were named `UserHandle` and `SentToUserHandle` have had their role names changed to indicate the change in names from when the key of `MessagingUser` was `UserHandle`.

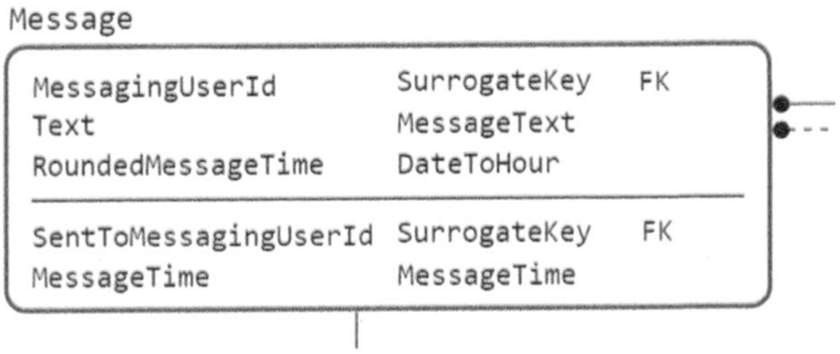

```
Message

  MessagingUserId            SurrogateKey    FK
  Text                       MessageText
  RoundedMessageTime         DateToHour
  ──────────────────────────────────────────────
  SentToMessagingUserId      SurrogateKey    FK
  MessageTime                MessageTime
```

Figure 6-7. *Message table before changing model to use surrogate key*

We will transform this table to use a surrogate key by moving all three columns to non-key columns, placing them in a uniqueness constraint, and adding the new `MessageId` column. Notice too in Figure 6-8 that the table is no longer modeled with rounded corners, because the primary key no longer is modeled with any migrated keys in the primary key.

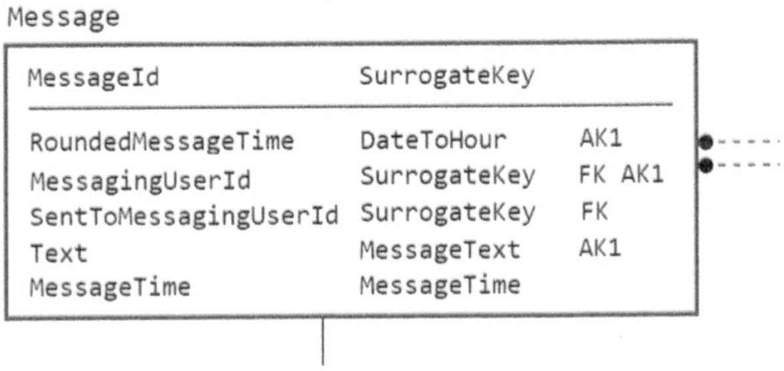

```
Message

  MessageId                   SurrogateKey
  ──────────────────────────────────────────────────
  RoundedMessageTime          DateToHour      AK1
  MessagingUserId             SurrogateKey    FK AK1
  SentToMessagingUserId       SurrogateKey    FK
  Text                        MessageText     AK1
  MessageTime                 MessageTime
```

Figure 6-8. *Message table after changing model to use surrogate key*

Note once more that nothing should be lost when you use surrogate keys, because a surrogate of this style only stands in for an existing natural key. Many of the object-relational mapping (ORM) tools that are popular (if sometimes controversial in the database community) require a single-column integer PRIMARY KEY constraint as part of their implementation pattern. I don't favor forcing the database to be designed in any manner to suit client tools, but sometimes, what is good for the database is the same as what is good for the tools, making for a relatively happy ending, at least.

By implementing tables using this pattern, I'm covered in two ways: I always have a single primary key value, but I always have a key that cannot be modified, which eases the difficulty for loading a secondary copy like a data warehouse. No matter the choice of human-accessible key, surrogate keys are the style of key that I use for nearly all tables in databases I create (and *always* for tables with user-modifiable data, which I will touch on when we discuss "domain" tables later in this chapter). In Figure 6-9, I have completed the transformation to using surrogate keys.

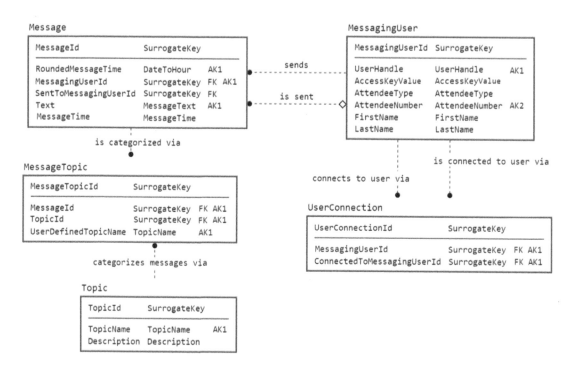

Figure 6-9. *Messaging database model progression after surrogate key choices*

Keep in mind that I haven't specified any sort of implementation details for the surrogate key at this point, and clearly, in a real system, I would already have done this during the transformation. For this chapter example, I am using a deliberately detailed process to separate each individual step, so I will put off that discussion until the "Choosing the Datatype" section of this chapter, where I will present code to build this database.

Alternate Keys

In the model so far, we have already identified alternate keys as part of the model creation (MessagingUser.AttendeeNumber was our only initial alternate key), but I wanted to just take a quick stop on the model and make it clear in case you have missed it. Every table should have a minimum of one natural key, that is, a key that is tied to the meaning of what the table is modeling.

A primary key that's manufactured or especially one that is meaningless in the logical model shouldn't be your only defined key. One of the ultimate mistakes made by people using such keys is to ignore the fact that two rows whose only difference is a system-generated value are not different. With only an artificially generated value as your key, it becomes impossible to tell one row from another.

For example, take Table 6-1, a snippet of a Part table, where PartID is an IDENTITY column and is the primary key for the table.

Table 6-1. *Sample Data to Demonstrate How Surrogate Keys Don't Make Good Logical Keys*

PartID	PartNumber	Description
1	XXXXXXXX	The X part
2	XXXXXXXX	The X part
3	YYYYYYYY	The Y part

How many individual items are represented by the rows in this table? Well, there seem to be three, but are rows with PartIDs 1 and 2 actually the same row, duplicated? Or are they two different rows that should be unique but were keyed in incorrectly? You need to consider at every step along the way whether a human being could not pick a desired row from a table without knowledge of the surrogate key. Therefore, there should be a key of some sort on the table to guarantee uniqueness, in this case likely on PartNumber.

Caution   As a rule, each of your tables should have a natural key that means something to the user and that can uniquely identify each row in your table. In the very rare event that you cannot find a natural key (perhaps, e.g., in a table that provides a log of events that could occur in the same .000001 of a second), then it is acceptable to make up some uniquifier value that is part of a larger key that helps you tell two rows apart.

In a well-designed and normalized model, you should not have anything to do at this point with keys that protect the uniqueness of the data from a requirements standpoint. The architect (probably yourself) has already determined some manner of uniqueness that can be implemented. For example, in Figure 6-10, a MessagingUser row can be identified by either the UserHandle or the AttendeeNumber.

MessagingUser

MessagingUserId	SurrogateKey	
UserHandle	UserHandle	AK1
AccessKeyValue	AccessKeyValue	
AttendeeType	AttendeeType	
AttendeeNumber	AttendeeNumber	AK2
FirstName	FirstName	
LastName	LastName	

Figure 6-10. MessagingUser table for review

A bit more interesting is the Message table, shown in Figure 6-11. The key is the RoundedMessageTime, which is the time, rounded to the hour, the text of the message, and the UserId.

Message

MessageId	SurrogateKey		
RoundedMessageTime	DateToHour	AK1	
MessagingUserId	SurrogateKey	FK	AK1
SentToMessagingUserId	SurrogateKey	FK	
Text	MessageText	AK1	
MessageTime	MessageTime		

Figure 6-11. Message table for review

In the business rules, it was declared that the user could not post the same message more than once an hour. Constraints such as this are not terribly easy to implement in a simple manner, but breaking it down to the data you need to implement the constraint can make it easier. In our case, by putting a key on the message, the user sending the message, and the time rounded to the hour (which we will find some way to implement later in the process), configuring the structures is quite easy.

Of course, by putting this key on the table, if the UI sends the same data twice, an error will be raised when a duplicate message is sent. This error will need to be dealt with at the client side, typically by translating the error message to something nicer.

The last table I will cover here is the MessageTopic table, shown in Figure 6-12.

MessageTopic

MessageTopicId	SurrogateKey	
MessageId	SurrogateKey	FK AK1
TopicId	SurrogateKey	FK AK1
UserDefinedTopicName	TopicName	AK1

Figure 6-12. *MessageTopic table for review*

What is interesting about this table is the optional UserDefinedTopicName value. Later, when we are creating this table, we will load some seed data that indicates that the TopicId is 'UserDefined', which means that the UserDefinedTopicName column can be used. Along with this seed data, on this table will be a CHECK constraint that indicates whether the TopicId value represents the user-defined topic. I will use a 0 surrogate key value. Later, we will create a CHECK constraint to make sure that all data fits the required criteria.

At this point, to review, we have the model in Figure 6-13.

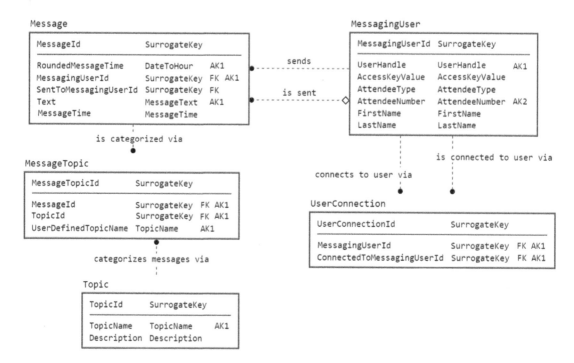

Figure 6-13. *Messaging model for review*

Determining Column Domain Implementation

In our model, the concept of domains has been used to specify a template for datatypes and column properties that are used repeatedly. Now, we need to use the domain to choose the datatype to use and give us a guide as to the validations we will need to implement.

For example, in a typical logical modeling exercise, domains are defined for such columns as name and description, which occur regularly across a database/enterprise. The reason for defining domains might not have been completely obvious at the time of logical design (it can seem like work to be a pompous data architect, rather than a get it done right enough and fast enough programmer), but it becomes clear during physical modeling if it has been done well up front. During implementation, domains serve several purposes:

- *Consistency*: We have used TopicName twice as a domain. This reminds us to define every column of type TopicName in precisely the same manner; there will never be any question about how to treat the column. In a larger database, columns like FirstName, EmailAddress,

City, PostalCode, and so on all benefit from having a standard picked so you don't have to think about it every single time.

- *Documentation*: Even if every column used a different domain and there was no reuse, the column/domain documentation would be very useful for programmers to be able to see what datatype to use for a given column and variables that correspond to that column type. In the final section of the next chapter, I will include the domain as part of the metadata I will add to the extended properties of the implemented columns.

Domains aren't a requirement of logical or physical database design, nor does SQL Server actually make it easy for you to use them, but even if you just use them in a spreadsheet or design tool, they can enable easy and consistent design and are a great idea, if only for important things like lengths of names or email addresses. I personally have seen a column type implemented in four different ways in five different columns when proper domain definitions were not at least documented. So, tool or not, having domains documented in a data dictionary that identifies columns that share a common type definition is extremely useful.

For example, for the TopicName domain that's used often in the Topic and MessageTopic tables in our ConferenceMessage model, the domain may have been specified by the contents of Table 6-2.

Table 6-2. Sample Domain: TopicName

Property	Setting
Name	TopicName.
Optional	No.
Datatype	Unicode text, 30 characters.
Value limitations	Must not be empty string or only space characters.
Default value	N/A.

I'll defer the CHECK constraint and DEFAULT bits until the next chapter, where I discuss implementation in more depth. Several tables will have a TopicName column, and you'll use this template to build every one of them in the model, which will ensure that every time you build one of these columns, it will have a type of nvarchar(30). We will discuss datatypes and their usages later in this chapter.

Another domain that is used very often in our model is SurrogateKey, shown in Table 6-3.

Table 6-3. *Sample Domain: SurrogateKey*

Property	Setting
Name	SurrogateKey.
Optional	When used for primary key, not optional, typically auto-generated. When used as a non-key, foreign key reference, optionality determined by utilization in the relationship.
Datatype	int.
Value limitations	N/A.
Default value	N/A.

This domain is a bit different in that it will be implemented exactly as specified for a primary key attribute, but when it is migrated for use as a foreign key, some of the properties will be changed. First, if using identity columns for the surrogate, the migrated copy won't have the IDENTITY property set. Second, an optional relationship will allow nulls in the migrated key, but when used as the primary key, it will not allow them.

Finally, let's set up one more domain definition to our sample, the UserHandle domain, shown in Table 6-4.

Table 6-4. *Sample Domain: UserHandle*

Property	Setting
Name	UserHandle.
Optional	No.
Datatype	Basic character set, 20 characters maximum.
Value limitations	Must be 5–20 simple alphanumeric characters and must start with a letter.
Default value	N/A.

In the next four subsections, I'll discuss several topics concerning the implementation of domains:

- *Implementing as a column or table*: You need to decide whether a value should simply be entered as a value in a column or whether to implement a new table to manage the values.

- *Choosing the datatype*: SQL Server gives you a wide range of datatypes to work with, and I'll discuss some of the issues concerning making the right choice.

- *Choosing nullability*: In the "Setting Nullability" section, I will demonstrate how to implement the nullability choices for the columns.

- *Choosing the collation and code page of character data*: Collation of character determines how data is sorted and compared, based on character set and language used. The code page of an 8-bit character set determines how the characters look when displayed.

Getting the domain of a column implemented correctly is an important step in getting the implementation correct. Too many databases end up with all columns with the same datatype and size, allowing NULL values (except for primary keys, if they have them), and lose the integrity of having properly sized and constrained constraints.

Enforce Domain in the Column or With a Table?

Although many domains have only minimal limitations on values, often a domain will specify a fixed set of named values that a column might have that is less than what can be fit into one of the base datatypes. For example, in the demonstration table MessagingUser shown in Figure 6-14, a column AttendeeType has a domain of AttendeeType.

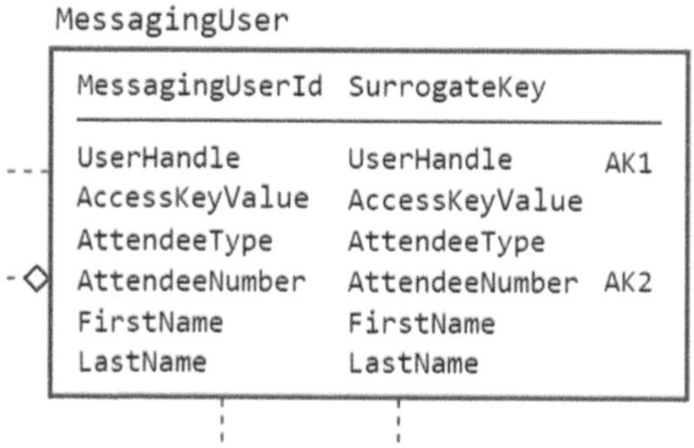

MessagingUser

MessagingUserId	SurrogateKey	
UserHandle	UserHandle	AK1
AccessKeyValue	AccessKeyValue	
AttendeeType	AttendeeType	
AttendeeNumber	AttendeeNumber	AK2
FirstName	FirstName	
LastName	LastName	

Figure 6-14. *MessagingUser table for reference*

This domain might be specified as in Table 6-5.

Table 6-5. *Genre Domain*

Property	Setting
Name	AttendeeType.
Optional	No.
Datatype	Basic character set.
Value limitations	Regular, Volunteer, Speaker, Administrator.
Default value	Regular.

The value limitation limits the values to a fixed list of values. We could choose to implement the column using a declarative control (a CHECK constraint) with a predicate of AttendeeType IN ('Regular', 'Volunteer', 'Speaker', 'Administrator') and a literal default value of 'Regular'. There are a couple of minor annoyances with this method:

- *There is no place for table consumers to know the domain*: Unless you have a row with one of each of the values, it isn't easy to know what the possible values are without either having foreknowledge of the system or looking in the metadata. If you're doing conference messaging system utilization reports by `AttendeeType`, it won't be easy to find out what attendee types had no activity for a time period, certainly not using a simple, straightforward SQL query that has no hard-coded values.

- *It is typically handy to be able to associate additional information with values such as in the given list*: For example, this domain might have information about actions that a given type of user could do. For example, if a `Volunteer` attendee is limited to using certain topics, you would have to manage the types in a different table. Ideally, if you define the domain value in a table, any other uses of the domain are easier to maintain.

I regularly include tables for all domains that are essentially "lists" of items, as it is just far easier to manage, even if it requires more tables. It is especially valuable as the UI developer can provide a list to choose from.

While a domain table is a table like any other, the choice of key for a domain table can be a bit different than that for other tables. Sometimes, I use a surrogate key for the actual primary key, and other times, I use a natural key that corresponds to the value that was already in the table.

The general difference is whether the values are user manageable and if the programming tools require the integer/GUID approach (e.g., if the front-end code uses an enumeration that is being reflected in the table values). In the model, I have two examples of such types of domain implementations. In Figure 6-15, I have added a table to implement the domain for attendee types, and for this table, I will use the natural key.

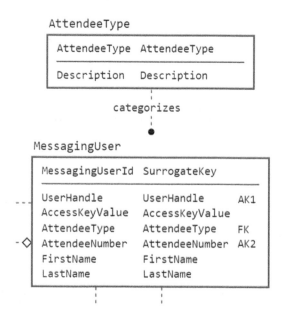

Figure 6-15. *AttendeeType domain implemented as a table*

This lets an application treat the value as if it is a simple value just like if this was implemented without the domain table. So, if the application wants to manage the value as a simple string (or integer) value, I don't have to know about it from the database standpoint. I still get the value and validation that the table implementation affords me, plus the ability to have a Description column, plus any other columns describing what each of the values actually means (which really comes in handy at 12:10 AM on December 25 when the system is crashing and needs to be fixed all while you are really thinking about the bicycle you haven't finished putting together).

In the original model, we had the Topic table, shown in Figure 6-16, which is a domain like the AttendeeType but is designed to allow a user to make changes to the topic list. Domains where the user can manage the data are more likely to have been defined during the logical modeling process because the user will have been thinking about them as needing to be maintained.

Topic

TopicId	SurrogateKey	
TopicName	TopicName	AK
Description	Description	

Figure 6-16. *Topic table for reference*

In our design, we will initialize the table with a row that represents the user-defined topic that allows the user to enter their own topic in the MessageTopic table.

Choosing the Datatype

Choosing proper datatypes to match the domain chosen during logical modeling is an important task. One datatype might be more efficient than another of a similar type, but not every datatype is suitable for every usage. For example, you can store integer data in an int datatype, a numeric datatype, a floating-point datatype, or even a varchar(10) type, but these datatypes are certainly not alike in implementation or performance. It is not, however, unlikely that two or more of them may have valid reasons to be used to store an integer value in some situations.

Note   I have broken up the discussion of datatypes into two parts. First, there is this section which offers basic guidance on the types of datatypes that exist in SQL Server and some light discussion on what to use. Second, Appendix A at the end of this book is an expanded look at all the datatypes and is dedicated to giving examples and example code snippets with all the types.

It's important to choose the best possible datatype when building the column. The following list contains the intrinsic datatypes (built-in types that are installed when you install SQL Server) and a brief explanation of each of them. As you are translating domains to implementation, step 1 will be to see which of these types matches the need best first; then we will look to constrain the data even further with additional techniques.

The following list contains the primary datatypes and an overview of their purposes:

- *Precise numeric data*: Stores numeric data with no loss of precision:

  - bit: Stores either 1, 0, or NULL; frequently used for Boolean-like columns (1 = True, 0 = False, NULL = Unknown). Up to 8-bit columns can fit in 1 byte. Some typical integer operations, like basic math, and some aggregations cannot be performed.

  - tinyint: Nonnegative values between 0 and 255 (0 to $2^8 - 1$) (1 byte).

- `smallint`: Integers between $-32,768$ and $32,767$ (-2^{15} to $2^{15} - 1$) (2 bytes).

- `int`: Integers between $-2,147,483,648$ and $2,147,483,647$ (-2^{31} to $2^{31} - 1$) (4 bytes).

- `bigint`: Integers between $9,223,372,036,854,775,808$ and $9,223,372,036,854,775,807$ (-2^{63} to $2^{63} - 1$) (8 bytes).

- `decimal` (or `numeric`, *which is functionally the same in SQL Server, but decimal is generally preferred for portability*): All numbers between $-10^{38} + 1$ and $10^{38} - 1$ (between 5 and 17 bytes, depending on precision). Allows for fractional numbers, unlike integer-suffixed types.

- *Approximate numeric data*: Stores approximations of numbers, typically for scientific usage. Gives an extremely large range of values with a high amount of precision, but with only up to 53 significant digits:

  - `float(N)`: Values in the range from $-1.79E + 308$ through $1.79E + 308$ (storage varies from 4 bytes for N between 1 and 24 to 8 bytes for N between 25 and 53).

  - `real`: Values in the range from $-3.40E + 38$ through $3.40E + 38$. `real` is an ISO synonym for a `float(24)` datatype and hence is equivalent (4 bytes).

- *Date and time*: Stores values that deal with temporal data:

  - `date`: Date-only values from January 1, 0001, to December 31, 9999 (3 bytes).

  - `time`: Time-of-day-only values to .0000001 second, which is the same as 100 nanoseconds (3–5 bytes).

  - `datetime2(N)`: Despite the maclunky name, this type will store a point in time from January 1, 0001, to December 31, 9999, with accuracy ranging from 1 second where N = 0 to .0000001 second where N = 7 (6–8 bytes).

- datetimeoffset: Same as datetime2 but includes an offset from the UTC time zone (8–10 bytes). This is a great datatype to allow you to store data that looks like the time from whence it came from and still be able to tell exactly when it occurred.

- smalldatetime: A point in time from January 1, 1900, through June 6, 2079, with accuracy to 1 minute (4 bytes). (Note: It is suggested to phase out usage of this type and use the more standards-oriented datetime2, though smalldatetime is not deprecated.)

- datetime: Points in time from January 1, 1753, to December 31, 9999, with accuracy to 3.33 milliseconds (8 bytes). (Note: It is suggested to phase out usage of this type and use the more standards-oriented datetime2, though datetime is not deprecated.)

- *Binary data*: Strings of bytes, for example, files or images. Storage for these datatypes is based on the size of the data stored:

  - binary(N): Fixed-length binary data up to 8,000 bytes long.

  - varbinary(N): Variable-length binary data up to 8,000 bytes long.

  - varbinary(max): Variable-length binary data up to $2^{31} - 1$ bytes (2 GB) long.

- *Character (or string) data*:

  - char(N): Fixed-length ASCII (or, in SQL Server 2019, UTF8) character data up to 8,000 bytes long.

  - varchar(N): Variable-length character data up to 8,000 bytes long.

  - varchar(max): Variable-length character data up to $2^{31} - 1$ bytes (2 GB) long.

  - nchar, nvarchar, nvarchar(max): UTF16 encoded Unicode equivalents of char, varchar, and varchar(max). Sizes provided to nchar *and* nvarchar specify double bytes of storage.

- Note: More details on character data, especially Unicode, UTF8, UTF16, and character sizes, will be covered in the "Collation and Code Page of Character Data" section later in this chapter.

- *Other datatypes*:

  - `sql_variant`: Stores (pretty much) any datatype, other than CLR-based datatypes (`hierarchyId`, spatial types) and any types with a max length of over 8,016 bytes. (CLR is a topic I won't hit on too much, but it allows Microsoft and you to program SQL Server objects in a .NET language. For more information, check `https://msdn.microsoft.com/en-us/library/ms131089.aspx`). It's generally a bad idea to use `sql_variant` for all but a few fringe cases. It is usable in cases where you don't know the datatype of a value before storing. The only use of this type in the book will be in Chapter 9 when we create user-extensible schemas (which is itself a fringe pattern).

  - `rowversion` (`timestamp` is a synonym that will seemingly never go away): Used for optimistic locking to version-stamp a row. It changes on every modification. The name of this type was `timestamp` in all SQL Server versions before 2000, but in the ANSI SQL standards, the `timestamp` type is equivalent to the `datetime` datatype. I'll make further use of the `rowversion` datatype in more detail in Chapter 12, which is about concurrency. (Sixteen years later, it is still referred to as `timestamp` very often, so this may never actually go away completely.)

  - `uniqueidentifier`: Stores a GUID value.

  - XML: Allows you to store an XML document in a column. The XML type gives you a rich set of functionality when dealing with structured data that cannot be easily managed using typical relational tables. You shouldn't use the XML type as a crutch to violate First Normal Form by storing multiple values in a single column. I will not use XML specifically in any of the designs in this book.

- Spatial types (geometry, geography, circularString, compoundCurve, and curvePolygon): Used for storing spatial data, like for maps. I will not be using these types in this book.

- hierarchyId: Used to store data about a hierarchy, along with providing methods for manipulating the hierarchy. We will cover more about manipulating hierarchies in Chapter 9 on storing graph data.

Choice of datatype is a tremendously important part of the process, but if you have defined the domain well, it is not that difficult of a task. In the following sections, we will look at a few of the more important parts of the choice. A few of the considerations we will include are

- Deprecated or bad choice types

- Common datatype configurations

- Large-value datatype columns

- Complex datatypes

I didn't use too many of the different datatypes in the sample model, because my goal was to keep the model very simple and not try to be AdventureWorks-esque who tries to show every possible type of SQL Server in one model (or even the newer WideWorldImporters database, which is slightly less unrealistically complex than AdventureWorks and will be used in several chapters later in the book).

Deprecated or Bad Choice Types

I didn't include several datatypes in the previous list because they have been deprecated for quite some time, and it wouldn't be surprising if they are actually completely removed from a version of SQL Server sometime eventually (even though backward compatibility is a big feature that they promise and there is a lot of legacy code still using the datatypes we will mention). Their use was common in versions of SQL Server before 2005, but they've been replaced by types that are *far* easier to use:

- image: Replaced with varbinary(max)

- text *or* ntext: Replaced with varchar(max) and nvarchar(max)

If you have ever tried to use the text datatype in SQL code, you know it is not a pleasant thing. Few of the common text operators were implemented to work with it, and in general, it just doesn't work like the other native types for storing string data. The same can be said with image. Changing from text to varchar(max), and image to varbinary(max), is definitely a no-brainer choice.

The next types that are generally advised against being used are the two money types:

- money: −922,337,203,685,477.5808 through 922,337,203,685,477.5807 (8 bytes)

- smallmoney: Money values from −214,748.3648 through 214,748.3647 (4 bytes)

In general, the money datatype sounds like a good idea, but using it has some confusing consequences. In Appendix A, I spend a bit more time covering these consequences, but here are two problems:

- There are issues with rounding off, because intermediate results for calculations are calculated using only four decimal places.

- Money data input allows for including a monetary sign (such as $ or £), but inserting $100 and £100 results in the same value being represented in the variable or column.

Hence, it's generally accepted that it's best to store monetary data in decimal datatypes. This also gives you the ability to assign the numeric types to sizes that are reasonable for the situation. For example, in a grocery store, having the maximum monetary value of a grocery item over 200,000 dollars is probably unnecessary, even figuring for a heck of a lot of inflation. Note that in the appendix, I will include a more thorough example of the types of issues you could see.

Common Datatype Configurations

In this section, I will briefly cover concerns and issues relating to Boolean/logical values, large datatypes, and complex types and then summarize datatype concerns in order to discuss the most important thing you need to know about choosing a datatype.

Boolean/Logical Values

Boolean values (TRUE or FALSE) are another of the hotly debated choices that are made for SQL Server data. There's no Boolean type in standard SQL, since every type must support NULL, and a NULL Boolean makes life far more difficult for the people who implement SQL, so a suitable datatype needs to be chosen through which to represent Boolean values. Truthfully, though, what we really want from a Boolean is the ability to say that the property of the modeled entity "is" or "is not" for some basic setting.

There are three common choices to implement a value of this sort:

- *Using a* bit *datatype where a value of* 1: True *and* 0: False: This is, by far, the most common datatype because it works directly with programming languages such as the .NET language with no translation. The check box and option controls can directly connect to these values, even though languages like VB.NET use -1 to indicate True. It does, however, draw the ire of purists, because it is too much like a Boolean. I typically use a name suffixed with "Flag" as a classword, like for a special sale indicator: SpecialSaleFlag. Some people who don't do the suffix thing as a rule often start the name off with Is, like IsSpecialSale. Microsoft uses the prefix in the catalog views quite often, like in sys.databases: is_ansi_nulls_on, is_read_only, and so on.

- *A* char(1) *value with a domain of* 'Y', 'N', 'T', 'F', *or other values*: This is the easiest for ad hoc users who don't want to think about what 0 or 1 means, but it's generally the most difficult from a programming standpoint. Sometimes, a varchar(3) is even better to go with 'yes' and 'no'. Usually, this is named the same as the bit type, but just having a slightly more attractive-looking output.

- *A full, textual value that describes the need*: For example, a preferred customer indicator, instead of PreferredCustomerFlag, PreferredCustomerIndicator, with values 'Preferred Customer' and 'Not Preferred Customer'. Popular for reporting types of databases, for sure, it is also more flexible for when there become more than two values, since the database structure needn't change

if you need to add 'Sorta Preferred Customer' to the domain of
PreferredCustomerIndicator. (This is generally more common as a
reporting value, where you need to group on descriptive values more
frequently.)

As an example of a Boolean column in our messaging database, I'll add a simple flag
to the MessagingUser table that tells whether the account has been disabled, as shown
in Figure 6-17. As before, we are keeping things simple, and in simple cases, a simple
flag generally will do it. But of course, in a sophisticated system, you would probably
want to have more information, like who did the disabling, why they did it, when it took
place, and perhaps even when it takes effect (these are all questions for design time, but
it doesn't hurt to be thorough). You might even want to log the changes in another table
(or using a temporal table—see Chapter 9 for more on temporal tables).

```
MessagingUser
┌─────────────────────────────────────────────┐
│ MessagingUserId  int                         │
├─────────────────────────────────────────────┤
│ UserHandle       varchar(20)  AK1            │
│ AccessKeyValue   char(10)                    │
│ AttendeeNumber   char(8)      AK2            │
│ FirstName        varchar(50)                 │
│ LastName         varchar(50)                 │
│ AttendeeType     varchar(20)  FK             │
│ DisabledFlag     bit                         │
└─────────────────────────────────────────────┘
```

Figure 6-17. *MessagingUser table with DisabledFlag bit column*

Large-Value Datatype Columns

In SQL Server 2005, dealing with large datatypes changed quite a bit (and hopefully
someday Microsoft will kill the text and image types for good). By using the max specifier
on varchar, nvarchar, and varbinary types, you can store far more data than was
possible in previous versions using a "normal" type while still being able to deal with the
data using the same functions and techniques you can on a simple varchar(10) column,
though performance will differ slightly.

As with all datatype questions, use the varchar(max) types only when they're
required; always use the smallest types possible. The larger the datatype, the more data
possible, and the more trouble it can be to get optimal storage retrieval times. In cases

where you know you need large amounts of data or in the case where you sometimes need greater than 8,000 bytes in a column, the max specifier is a fantastic thing.

Note   Keep on the lookout for uses that don't meet the normalization needs as you start to implement. Most databases have a "comments" column somewhere that morphed from comments to a semistructured mess that your DBA staff then needs to dissect using SUBSTRING and CHARINDEX functions.

There are two special concerns when using these types:

- There's no automatic datatype conversion from the normal character types to the large-value types.

- Updating such values can be costly when they are very large. Because of this, a special clause is added to the UPDATE statement to allow partial column modifications.

The first issue is pretty simple, but it can be a bit confusing at times. For example, concatenate '12345' + '67890'. You've taken two char(5) scalar expressions, and the result will be contained in a value that is automatically recast as a char(10) expression. But if you concatenate two varchar(8000) values, you don't get a varchar(16000) value, nor do you get a varchar(max) value. The values get truncated to a varchar(8000) value. This isn't always intuitively obvious. For example, consider the following code:

```
SELECT    LEN( CAST(REPLICATE ('a',8000) AS varchar(8000))
            + CAST(REPLICATE('a',8000) AS varchar(8000))
          );
```

It returns 8000, as the two columns concatenate to a type of varchar(8000). If you cast one of the varchar(8000) values to varchar(max), then the result will be 16,000:

```
SELECT    LEN(CAST(REPLICATE('a',8000) AS varchar(max))
            + CAST(REPLICATE('a',8000) AS varchar(8000))
          )
```

Second, because the size of columns stored using the varchar(max) datatype can be so huge, it wouldn't be favorable to always pass around these values just like you do with smaller values. Because the maximum size of a varchar(max) value is 2 GB, imagine having to update a value of this size in its entirety. Such an update would be nasty, because the client would need to get the whole value, make its changes, and then send the value back to the server. Some client machines may only have 2 GB of physical RAM, and many even today may not have that much free RAM, so paging would likely occur on the client machine, and the whole process would crawl and more than likely crash occasionally. So you can do what are referred to as *chunked* updates. These are done using the .WRITE clause in the UPDATE statement, for example:

```
UPDATE TableName
SET    VarcharMaxCol.WRITE('the value', <offset>, <expression>)
WHERE  . . .
```

One important thing to note is that varchar(max) values will easily cause the size of rows to be quite large. In brief, a row that fits into 8,060 bytes can be stored in one physical unit. If the row is larger than 8,060 bytes, string data can be placed on what are called *overflow pages*. Overflow pages are not terribly efficient because SQL Server must go fetch extra pages that will not be in line with other data pages. (Physical structures, including overflow pages, are covered more in Chapter 11 when the physical structures are covered.)

I won't go over large types in any more detail at this point. Just understand that you might have to treat the data in the (max) columns differently if you're going to allow huge quantities of data to be stored. And if you really only need to allow 8020 characters, use the varchar(max), and put a CHECK constraint on with (LEN(ColumnName) <= 8020) as the definition.

The main point to understand here is that having a datatype with relatively unlimited storage comes at a price. SQL Server does allow you some additional freedom when dealing with varbinary(max) data by placing it in the file system using what is called *filestream storage*. I will discuss large object storage in Chapter 9 in more detail, including filetables. In Chapter 11, the physical structures of objects and indexes will be covered, including how large objects change the physical storage. For now, the point to get across is that use the smallest type possible and then work out the performance details.

User-Defined Type/Alias

One excellent-*sounding* feature that you can use to help make your code cleaner is a user-defined type (UDT), which is really an alias to a type. You can use a datatype alias to specify a commonly used datatype configuration that's used in multiple places using the following syntax:

```
CREATE TYPE <typeName>
        FROM <intrinsic type> --any type that can be used as a column of a
                              --table, with precision and scale or length,
                              --as required by the intrinsic type
        [NULL | NOT NULL];
```

When declaring a table, if nullability isn't specified, then NULL or NOT NULL is based on the setting of ANSI_NULL_DFLT_ON, except when using an alias type (variables will always allow NULL values). In general, it is best to always specify the nullability in the table declaration, and something I will do always in the book, though I do sometimes forget in real life.

As an example, consider the UserHandle column. Earlier, we defined its domain as being varchar(20), not optional, and alphanumeric, with the data required to be between 5 and 20 characters. The datatype alias would allow us to specify

```
CREATE TYPE UserHandle FROM varchar(20) NOT NULL;
```

Then, in the CREATE TABLE statement, we could specify

```
CREATE TABLE MessagingUser
...
UserHandle UserHandle,
```

By declaring that the UserHandle type will be varchar(20), you can ensure that every time the type of UserHandle is used in table and variable declarations, the effective datatype will be varchar(20), and as long as you don't specify NULL or NOT NULL, the column will not allow NULL values. It is not possible to implement the requirement that data be between 5 and 20 characters or any other constraints on the type, other than the NULL specification.

For another example, consider an SSN type. It's char(11), so you cannot put a 12-character value in, sure. But what if the user had entered 234433432 instead of including the dashes? The datatype would have allowed it, but it isn't what's desired. The data will still have to be checked in other methods such as CHECK constraints.

I am personally not a user of these types. I have never really used these kinds of types because you cannot do anything with these other than simply alias a basic datatype. Any changes to the type also require removal of all references to the type making a change to the type a two-step process. Hence, it is easier to me to define domains outside of the server, so if you need to change a datatype, you have to alter the type from the alias to the regular type, then change the alias type, and then change the datatype again.

I will note, however, that I have a few architect friends who make extensive use of them to help keep data storage consistent. I have found that using domains and a data modeling tool serves me better, but I do want to make sure that you have at least heard of them and know the pros and cons.

Complex CLR Datatypes

In SQL Server 2005 and later, we can build our own datatypes using the SQL CLR (Common Language Runtime). Unfortunately, they are quite cumbersome, and the implementation of these types does not lend itself to the types behaving like the intrinsic types. Utilizing CLR types for any interesting case will require you to install the type on the client for them to get the benefit of the type being used.

For the most part, you should use CLR types only in the cases where it makes a very compelling reason to do so. There are a few different possible scenarios where you could reasonably use user-defined types to extend the SQL Server type system with additional scalar types or different ranges of data of existing datatypes. Some potential uses of UDTs might be

- Complex types that are provided by an owner of a format, such as a media format that could be used to interpret a varbinary(max) value as a movie or an audio clip. This type would have to be loaded on the client to get any value from the datatype.

- Complex types for a specialized application that has complex needs, when you're sure your application will be the only user.

Although the possibilities are virtually unlimited, I suggest that CLR UDTs be considered only for specialized circumstances that make the database design extremely more robust and easier to work with. CLR UDTs are a nice addition to the DBA's and developer's toolkit, but they should be reserved for those times when adding a new scalar datatype solves a complex business problem.

Microsoft has provided several intrinsic types based on the CLR to implement hierarchies and spatial datatypes. I point this out here to note that if Microsoft is using the CLR to implement complex types (and the spatial types at the very least are pretty darn complex), the sky is the limit. The spatial and hierarchyId types push the limits of what should be in a type, and some of the data stored (like a polygon) is an array of connected points. For more details, see the Microsoft Docs article "CLR User-Defined Types" at docs.microsoft.com/en-us/sql/relational-databases/clr-integration-database-objects-user-defined-types/clr-user-defined-types.

Choosing the Right Datatype

SQL Server gives you a wide range of datatypes, and many of them can be declared in a wide variety of sizes. I never cease to be amazed by the number of databases around in which every single column is either an integer or a varchar(N) (where N is the same for every single string column, sometimes in the 8000 range) and varchar(max). One particular example I've worked with had everything, including GUID-based primary keys, all stored in nvarchar(200) columns! It is bad enough to store your GUIDs in a varchar column at all, since they can be stored as a 16-byte binary value, whereas if you use a varchar column, it will take 36 bytes; however, store it in an nvarchar (Unicode) column, and now it takes 72 bytes, plus 2 more bytes for variable-sized column overhead! What a terrible waste of space. Even worse, someone could put in a non-GUID value up to 200 characters wide. Now, people using the data will feel like they need to allow for 200 characters on reports and such for the data. Time wasted, space wasted, money wasted.

As another example, say you want to store a person's name and date of birth. You could choose to store the name in an nvarchar(max) column and the date of birth in a varchar(max) column. In all cases, these choices would certainly store the data that the user wanted, but they wouldn't be good choices at all. The name should be in something such as an nvarchar(50) column and the date of birth in a date column. Notice that I used a variable-sized type for the name. This is because you don't know the length, and not all names are the same size. Because most names aren't nearly 50 characters/100 bytes wide, using a variable-sized type will save space in your database. I used a Unicode type because persons' names do fit the need of allowing nontypical Latin characters.

Of course, seldom would anyone make such poor choices of a datatype as putting a date value in a varchar(max) column. Most choices are reasonably easy. However, it's important to keep in mind that the datatype is the first level of domain enforcement. Thinking back to our domain for UserHandle, we had the datatype definition and value limitations specified in Table 6-6.

Table 6-6. *Sample Domain: UserHandle*

Property	Setting
Name	UserHandle.
Optional	No.
Datatype	Basic character set, maximum of 20 characters.
Value limitations	Must be 5–20 simple alphanumeric characters and start with a letter.
Default value	N/A.

You can enforce the first part of this at the database level by declaring the column as a varchar(20). A column of type varchar(20) won't even allow a 21-character or longer value to be entered. It isn't possible to enforce the rule of greater than or equal to five characters using only a datatype. I'll discuss more about how to enforce simple domain requirements later in this chapter and even more in the next chapter as we implement this database. In this case, I do use a simple ASCII character set because the requirements called for simple alphanumeric data.

Initially, we had the model in Figure 6-18 for the MessagingUser table.

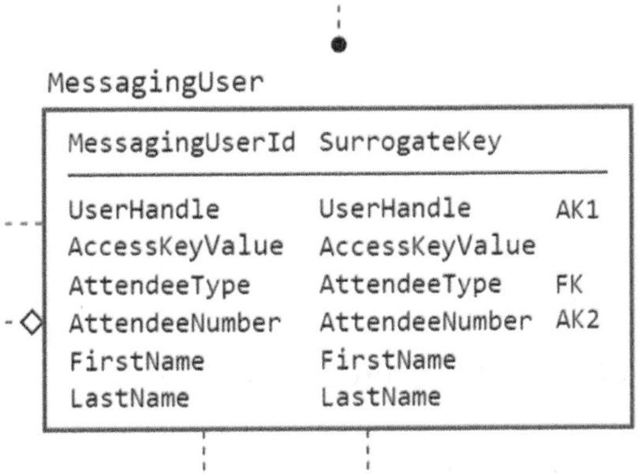

MessagingUser

MessagingUserId	SurrogateKey	
UserHandle	UserHandle	AK1
AccessKeyValue	AccessKeyValue	
AttendeeType	AttendeeType	FK
AttendeeNumber	AttendeeNumber	AK2
FirstName	FirstName	
LastName	LastName	

Figure 6-18. *MessagingUser table before choosing exact datatypes*

Choosing types, we will use an `int` for the surrogate key; and in the DDL, we will set the implementation of the rest of the optionality rule set in the domain—"Not optional, auto-generated for keys, optionality determined by utilization for non-key"—but will replace items of `SurrogateKey` domain with `int` types. `UserHandle` was discussed earlier in this section. In Figure 6-19, I chose some other basic types for `Name`, `AccessKeyValue`, and `AttendeeType` columns.

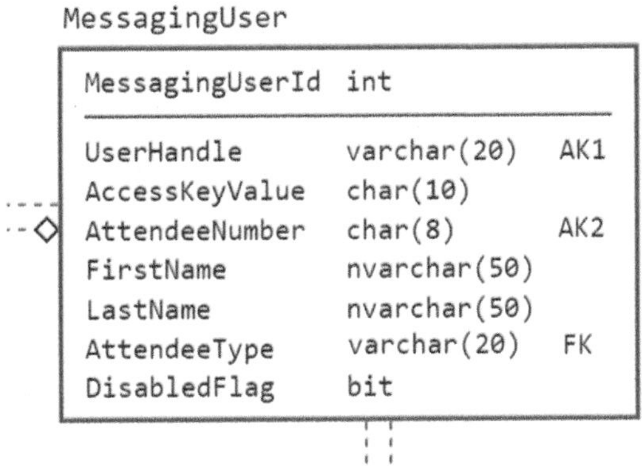

MessagingUser

MessagingUserId	int	
UserHandle	varchar(20)	AK1
AccessKeyValue	char(10)	
AttendeeNumber	char(8)	AK2
FirstName	nvarchar(50)	
LastName	nvarchar(50)	
AttendeeType	varchar(20)	FK
DisabledFlag	bit	

Figure 6-19. *MessagingUser after datatype choice*

Sometimes, you won't have any real domain definition, and you will use common sizes. For these, I suggest either using a standard type (if you can find them, like on the Internet) or looking through data you have in your system. Until the system gets into production, changing types is easy from a database standpoint, but the more code that accesses the structures, the more difficult it gets to make changes.

For the Message table in Figure 6-20, we will choose types.

```
Message
┌─────────────────────────────────────────────────────────────┐
│ MessageId                      SurrogateKey                  │
├─────────────────────────────────────────────────────────────┤
│ RoundedMessageTime             DateToHour     AK1           ●--│
│ MessagingUserId                SurrogateKey  FK AK1          │
│ SentToMessagingUserId  SurrogateKey  FK                      │
│ Text                           MessageText    AK1          ●--│
│ MessageTime                    MessageTime                   │
└─────────────────────────────────────────────────────────────┘
```

Figure 6-20. *Message table before datatype choice*

The Text column isn't datatype text but is the text of the message, limited to 200 characters. For the time columns, in Figure 6-21, I choose datetime2(0) for the MessageTime, since the requirements specified time down to the second. For RoundedMessageTime, it will be a computed column based on the MessageTime value. Hence, MessageTime and RoundedMessageTime are two views of the same data value.

```
Message
┌─────────────────────────────────────────────────────────────┐
│ MessageId                      int                          │
├─────────────────────────────────────────────────────────────┤
│ RoundedMessageTime             (computed)           AK1    ●---│
│ MessagingUserId                int                 FK  AK1 ●---│
│ SentToMessagingUserId  int                 FK               │
│ Text                           nvarchar(200)        AK1     │
│ MessageTime                    datetime2(0)                 │
└─────────────────────────────────────────────────────────────┘
```

Figure 6-21. *Message table after datatype choice, with calculated column denoted*

So I am going to use a computed column as shown in Figure 6-21. I will specify the type of RoundedMessageTime as a nonexistent datatype (so if I try to create the table, it will fail). A calculated column is a special type of column that isn't directly modifiable, as it is based on the result of an expression.

I will leave the actual implementation until the next chapter when I build the database, but for now, we basically just set a placeholder. Of course, I would specify the implementation immediately, but again, for this first learning process, I am doing things in this deliberate manner to keep things orderly. So, in Figure 6-22, I have the model with all the datatypes set.

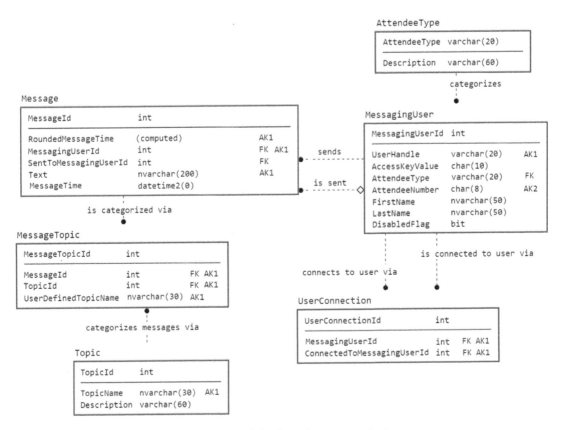

Figure 6-22. *Messaging system model after datatype choices*

Setting Nullability

The next step in the process is to set nullability of columns. In our domains, we specified whether data for the columns were optional, so this will generally be a simple task. For the Message table in Figure 6-23, I have chosen the nullability settings for the columns. (Only columns that allow NULL values have additional details on this diagram.)

Message

MessageId	int	
RoundedMessageTime	(computed)	AK1
MessagingUserId	int	FK AK1
SentToMessagingUserId	int	NULL FK
Text	nvarchar(200)	AK1
MessageTime	datetime2(0)	

Figure 6-23. *Message table for review*

The interesting choice was for the two MessagingUserId columns. In Figure 6-24, you can see the full model, but note the relationships from MessagingUser to Message. The relationship for the user that sent the message (MessagingUserId) is NOT NULL, because every message is sent by a user. However, the relationship representing the user the message was sent to allows NULL values, since not every message is sent to a user.

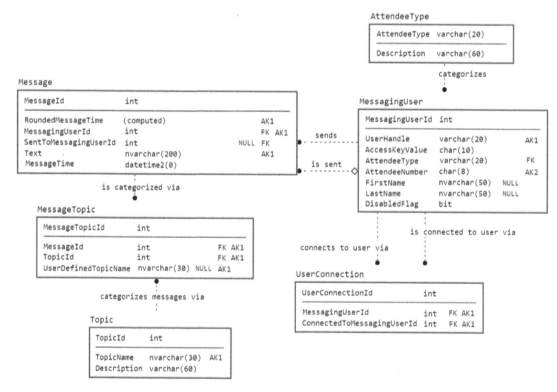

Figure 6-24. *Messaging system model, with NULL specifications chosen*

At this point, our model is very nearly done and very much resembles a database that could be built and employed in an application. Just a bit more information is needed to finish out the model.

Collation and Code Page of Character Data

When you install SQL Server, there is a choice that you need to make that is called the collation of the server. This seemingly simple choice is a very important choice, because it determines a lot about your server metadata, and unless you override the collation in your databases and/or tables, it will affect a lot about how all of your character data is managed on your server.

The collation of a character value sets up the way one character value is compared with another, how values are sorted, and what characters can be represented. Many character sets are used by the many different cultures around the world. While you can choose a Unicode datatype if you need to store the characters for almost any character set, there still is the question of how data is sorted and compared (accent sensitive, case sensitive, or not, for starters). SQL Server and Windows provide a tremendous number of collation types to choose from, many very similar, with just very minor differences. The collation is specified at many locations, starting with the server. The server collation determines how the system metadata is stored. Then the database has a collation, and finally, each character column may have a different collation.

Collations specify how Unicode data is sorted and compared and whether it is compared as

- *Binary*: Using the byte value of how a value is stored. For example, 'h' is 104 in Unicode, and 'H' is 72, and hence, HI would sort before hi. Binary sorting and comparisons stand alone and do not mix with the rest of the list. Use the _BIN2 version of the collation, as it does a better job of sorting the data on the Unicode values of the characters properly (for more detail, see this blog by Solomon Ruzky www. sqlservercentral.com/blogs/differences-between-the-various-binary-collations-cultures-versions-and-bin-vs-bin2).

- *Case sensitivity*: Either sensitive or insensitive. With insensitive sorting and comparisons, case is ignored, and 'hi' and 'HI' will match and will sort randomly. With sensitive set, 'hi' would come first.

- *Accent sensitivity*: Either sensitive or insensitive. With insensitive sorting and comparisons, accent marks on characters are ignored, and 'ápple' and 'apple' will match and will sort randomly. With sensitive settings, 'apple' would come first.

- *Width sensitivity–accent sensitivity*: Either sensitive or insensitive. With insensitive sorting and comparisons, case is ignored, and '10022' and '100²²' will match and will sort randomly. With sensitive settings, '10022' would come first.

- *Kana sensitivity*: Used to make comparisons and sorts to differentiate between two types of Japanese kana characters: Hiragana and Katakana.

The collation also determines what kind of data can be stored in columns. All collations can store basic 2-byte Unicode data in nvarchar-type columns in the UTF16 format. But there are two additional values in the collation specification to understand:

- *Version*: A collation with version 90 or 100 in the name can support supplemental character sets, which are characters beyond 2 bytes, up to 4 bytes each.

- *Code page for 8-bit columns*: For char and varchar columns, which use 8 bits per character, that is, by default, only 256 characters. In order to be able to output the many different characters that existed, there were different code pages that swapped different character sets. New for 2019 is a code page that enables UTF8 data to be stored.

SQL Server has had UTF16 support for Unicode since SQL Server 2005 via the nvarchar datatype. The general advice has been to use this datatype where possible for storing textual data to match both users' needs and the applications. However, UTF8 is a very popular implementation of Unicode, and while they both can store the same character set, there are differences in how data is encoded. Translating from one format to another when modifying data can be costly. By adding UTF8 support to the char datatype, this data can be stored without transformation in an 8-bit format.

While UTF8 is not implemented as a method to save space, UTF8 can save considerable space when storing Unicode data that is comprised of mostly characters that are the typical ASCII character set including numerals and the Latin alphabet characters, as they use only 1 byte. However, UTF8 may not save space if you use many characters in the code point 2048–65535 range of Unicode characters, as they use 3 bytes each, but only 2 bytes each in UTF16. UTF8 and UTF16 both use 4 bytes each for characters in code points 65536–1114111 (commonly referred to as the supplemental character set).

With this change to the 8-byte character datatypes, it is important to make sure that you understand that for varchar data, like for a varchar(30), the (30) does not represent the number of characters, but instead the maximum number of bytes the character string may contain. For a UTF8 string, this could be as few as 7 if all values are 4-byte supplemental characters or as many as 30. For an nvarchar(30), it is double bytes, so it is 60 bytes. So, if characters are what you are concerned with, it is important to define the type large enough for the largest value and use a check constraint to limit the number of characters.

With all these choices, how to set your collation may seem like a very complicated discussion. It generally isn't. Most organizations will pick a base character set that they work in. I am writing this book in American English and as such will use a Latin1 collation. I use a 100 version, case-, width-, and kana-insensitive, but accent-sensitive collation. For most servers, a case-insensitive collation allows that when doing comparisons and sorts, 'A' = 'a' and N'A' = N'a'. Of course it is also true that N'A' = 'a', though when you see this comparison, in the query plan there will be an implicit data conversion, which can be negative for performance.

I only use an alternative collation occasionally for columns where case sensitivity is desired (one time was so that a client could force more four-character codes into a four-character column than a case-insensitive collation would allow!). If you use case sensitivity at the server or database level, a good amount of your metadata will be case sensitive. So, if you have a table named Schema.TableName, you could not query it as SELECT * FROM schema.tableName; even if you were in a bit of a hurry. The error message would not kindly tell you that it was the case of the name either, but rather that the table did not exist (leading to a bit of fear to work through the first few times). You could still use SeLeCt * fRoM Schema.TableName; as system commands are not affected by the collation.

To see the current collation type for the server and database, you can execute the following commands:

```
SELECT SERVERPROPERTY('collation');
SELECT DATABASEPROPERTYEX('DatabaseName','collation');
```

On most systems installed in English-speaking countries, the default collation type is SQL_Latin1_General_CP1_CI_AS, where Latin1_General represents the normal Latin alphabet, CP1 refers to code page 1252 (the SQL Server default Latin1 ANSI character set), and the last parts represent case insensitive and accent sensitive, respectively. You can find full coverage of all collation types in the SQL Server documentation. However, the default is rarely the desired collation to use and is set to that older (as in pre–SQL Server 2005) collation for backward compatibility. Ideally, you will use a Windows collation, and as stated, I have used Latin1_General_100_CI_AS for my example database, which will be what I have installed my server as.

You can list all of the possible collations on a server using the following query:

```
SELECT name, description,
       COLLATIONPROPERTY(name, 'CodePage') AS AsciiCodePage
FROM ::fn_helpcollations();
```

On the computer on which I do testing, this query returned more than 5,500 rows (up from 3800 in SQL Server 2016), but usually, you don't need to change from the default that the database administrator initially chooses. To set the collation sequence for a char, varchar, text, nchar, nvarchar, or ntext column when creating a column, you specify it using the COLLATE clause of the column definition, like so:

```
CREATE TABLE alt.OtherCollate
(
    OtherCollateId int IDENTITY
        CONSTRAINT PKAlt_OtherCollate PRIMARY KEY ,
    Name varchar(30) COLLATE Latin1_General_100_CI_AS_SC_UTF8 NOT NULL,
    FrenchName nvarchar(30) COLLATE French_CI_AS_WS NULL,
    SpanishName nvarchar(30) COLLATE Modern_Spanish_CI_AS_WS NULL
);
```

Now, when you sort output by FrenchName, it's case insensitive, but arranges the rows according to the order of the French character set. The same applies with Spanish, regarding the SpanishName column. The Name column is an 8-byte character set, but it will be Unicode in the UTF8 format, so it can store the same data the other columns in the table can. For most of the book, we will stick with the server default in almost all cases as you will for most of your databases.

The only "typical" variation from the default collation of the database is if you need a different case sensitivity for a column, in which case you might use a binary collation or a case-sensitive one. Some companies may build key columns that use a surrogate key system that includes binary, upper, and lowercase letters to pack more details into a single character value. It can be effective, if more confusing to the user than using something like a bigint value.

As a side note, in your code, if you need to specify a change in collation, like to make a WHERE clause case sensitive, you can code the WHERE clause using the COLLATE keyword:

```
SELECT Name
FROM alt.OtherCollate
WHERE Name COLLATE Latin1_General_CS_AI
          LIKE N'[A-Z]%' COLLATE Latin1_General_CS_AI;
                    --case sensitive and accent insensitive
```

It is important to be careful when choosing a collation that is different from the default, because at the server level it is extremely hard to change and at the database level it is no picnic. You can change the collation of a column with an ALTER command, but it can't have constraints, indexes, or any schema-bound code referencing it, and you may need to recompile all of your objects that reference the column after the change.

If you do find yourself on a server with multiple collations and need to query data across databases, a handy collation setting to use can be database_default, which uses the default for the context of the database you are executing from. However, much of the performance optimizations that SQL Server uses need collations of columns to be the same, because the collation determines how columns compare to one another.

Setting Up Schemas

A *schema* is a namespace: a container where database objects are contained, all within the confines of a database. We will use schemas to gather our tables and eventually views, procedures, functions, and so on into functional groups. By default, objects in a SQL Server database go into a schema named dbo that matches the built-in owner of the database, the dbo user. Ideally, objects should not be placed in the dbo schema, for several reasons, the first of which is documentation. Hence, the goal when creating a database is to create named schema containers to put your objects in that have a similar purpose. Also, by creating your own schemas, your objects can be grouped more clearly, and as you will see in Chapter 10, you can give a user rights to an entire schema to read, write, or even modify the objects in the schema without providing them superpowers on the server or even the database. Schemas also give you a logical grouping of objects when you view them within a list, such as in Management Studio.

Naming schemas is a bit different than naming tables or columns. Schema names should sound right, so sometimes, they make sense to be plural and other times singular. It depends on how they are being used. I find myself using plural names most of the time because they sound better and because, sometimes, you will have a table named the same thing as the schema if both are singular.

In our model in Figure 6-25, we will put the tables that are used to represent messages in a Messages schema and the ones that represent Attendees and their relationships to one another in a schema we will name Attendees.

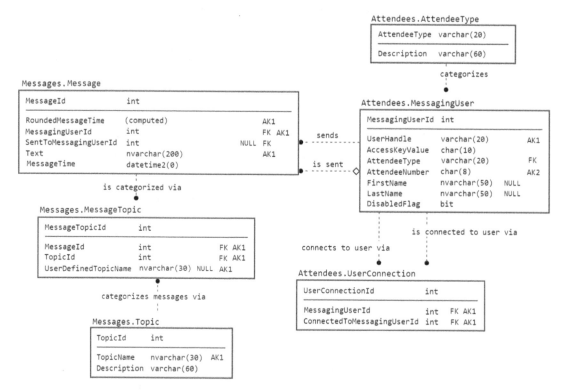

Figure 6-25. *Messaging model with schemas assigned*

Note too that I often will set up schemas late in the process, and it might seem more correct to start there. I find that it is often easier to discover the different areas of the implementation and that schemas aren't necessarily easy to start with, but that different areas come and go until I get to the final solution. Sometimes, it is by necessity because you have multiple tables with the same name, though this can be a sign of a bad design (or a very compartmental one for security reasons). Much like all tasks in each phase of a design, order doesn't make any difference as long as the outcome is correct. In this manufactured solution, I simply did it last to make the point that it could be last.

I'm not going to go any further into the security aspects of using schemas at this point in the book, but understand that schemas are not just for aesthetics. Throughout this book, I'll always name the schema that a table is in when doing examples. Schemas will be part of any system I design in this book, simply because it's going to be best practice to do so. On a brief trip back to the land of reality, I said in the previous editions of this book that beginning to use schemas in production systems will be a slow process, and it still can be jarring to some users 11+ years later. Chapter 10 will discuss using schemas for security in more detail.

Adding Implementation Columns

Finally, I will add one more thing to the database before we start to code: columns to support the implementation of the code only (and not to support a user requirement directly). A very common need is to have columns that indicate when the row was created, when it was updated, and perhaps by whom. In our model, I will stick to the simple case of the times mentioned and in the next chapter will demonstrate how to implement this in the database. A lot of implementers like to leave these values to the client, but I very much prefer using the database code because then I have one clock managing times, rather than multiples. (I once managed a system that used two clocks to set row times, and occasionally a row was created years after it was last updated!)

In Figure 6-26, I add two NOT NULL columns to every table for the RowCreateTime and RowLastUpdateTime, except for the AttendeeType table, which we specified to be not user manageable, so I chose not to include the modified columns for that table. Of course, you might want to do this to let your development team know when the row was first available. I also left off columns to denote who changed the row for simplicity.

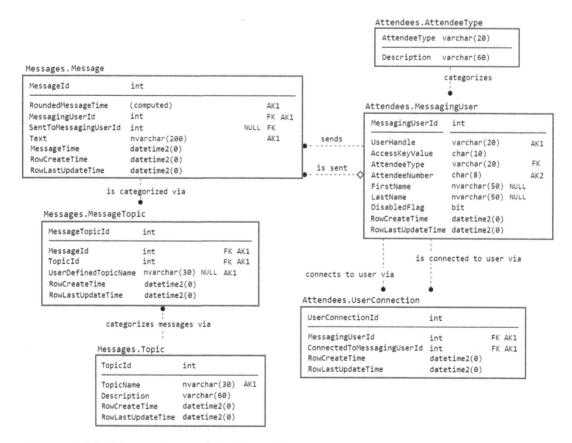

Figure 6-26. *Messaging model after adding RowCreateTime and RowLastUpdateTime to tables*

As a final note, it is generally best to only use these implementation columns strictly for metadata purposes. For example, consider the Messages.Message table. If you need to know when the message was created, you should use the MessageTime column as that value may represent the time when the user clicked the create button, captured from a different clock source, even if it took five minutes to actually store the data. Plus, if you need to load the data into a new table, the row may have been created in 2020, but the thing that data is representing is in 2000, so not using these columns as user data means you can truthfully reflect when the row was created. It is also a decent sanity check for the other clocks that data may use to set values. If the MessageTime column was created after the RowCreateTime, that is good. If after, then something is wrong somewhere.

That is why I use such clunky names for the implementation column. Many tables will include a column like CreateTime as part of the table, but even that data may be modifiable, like if you determine that the customer was actually created a year earlier than you believed it was. I don't want users changing the time when the row was created for any reason at all, so the name notes that the time of creation is strictly for the row, and I don't allow this column to be modified by anyone.

Sometimes, I will use these columns in concurrency control to denote when a row was changed, but when I have control over the design, I will use a `rowversion` type if the client can (and will) make use of it. Concurrency control is a very important topic that I will spend a full chapter on in Chapter 12.

The model presented in Figure 6-26 is the model that will be used to write the code in the next chapter. Not every detail has been covered in this chapter like you should in a real database design, for brevity's sake (something that is semi-difficult to say about a nearly 60-page chapter covering the creation of six tables, but there is a lot that goes into preparing to write the code for those six tables and equally so to actually write the code.)

Best Practices

The following are a set of some of the most important best practices when designing your physical database. Pay attention to the advice about UNIQUE constraints. Just having a surrogate key on a table is one of the worst mistakes made when implementing a database:

- *Invest in database generation tools*: Do this after you know what the tool should be doing. Implementing tables, columns, relationships, and so on is a tedious and painful task when done by hand. There are many great tools that double as logical data modeling tools and also generate these objects, as well as sometimes the objects and code to be covered in the upcoming three chapters. A list of such tools that support IDEF1X was presented in the intro of Chapter 3, but it is not exhaustive in any means.

- *Maintain the logical design and normalization*: As much as possible, try to maintain the integrity of the original design and the normalizations that were designed in Chapter 5. It will help keep the data better protected and will be more resilient to change.

- *Develop a real strategy for naming objects*: Keep the basics in mind:

- Give all objects reasonably user-friendly names. Make sure that it's obvious—at least to support personnel—what the purpose of every object, column, and so on is without digging into documentation, if at all possible.

- Have either all plural or all singular names for tables. Consistency is the key. I use singular to match the IDEF1X standard.

- Have all singular names for columns to make the atomic nature of columns.

- *Develop and use the template domains*: Reuse in every case where a similar datatype is needed. This cuts down on time spent implementing and makes users of the data happy, because every time they see a column called WhatsitDescription, it's likely that it will have the same characteristics of other like columns.

- *Carefully choose the datatype and nullability for each column*: These are the first level of data protection to keep your data clean and pure. Also, improper datatypes can cause precision difficulties with numbers and even performance issues.

- *Define the domain of each column carefully*: For example, don't simply allow a column to be of type integer when the range of values is from –2,147,483,648 to 2,147,483,647 unless that really is the allowable range of values. If the logical range of the value is 0–1,000,000, use an integer and make sure you have a CHECK constraint specified for whomever is writing the code.

- *Make certain that every table has at least one uniqueness constraint that doesn't include an artificial value*: It's a good idea to consider using an IDENTITY column as the primary key. However, if that is the only uniqueness constraint on the table, then there can (and usually will) be duplication in the *real* columns of the table—a bad idea.

Summary

In this chapter, we have worked through the process to transform the normalized, mostly platform-agnostic model created in the previous chapter into the full-on blueprint for the database code that will be written in Chapter 7. This has been a long chapter covering a large amount of ground. Understanding how to build tables, and how they're implemented, is the backbone of every database designer's knowledge.

Choosing decent names, this time for our actual tables, was again covered, and to be fair, naming things in our database will certainly come up again. A rose by any other name may smell as sweet, but a table named `tbl_X` is not likely going to win you any friends.

Picking and setting keys for your implementation was discussed and finalized, with a major emphasis on being sure that at least one set of column values uniquely identifies a row in your table.

Probably the most important discussion in the chapter was about how to define and model a column's domain. We looked at the concept of a domain table (or a table that is specifically built to enforce a column domain, not for any particular user request), as well as using constraints and proper datatypes, allowing `NULL` values, and collation support, including (new to SQL Server 2019) support for UTF8 Unicode in the 8-byte character datatypes.

Next, I finished up the data model by separating the tables into schemas and added some columns that are there for programming processes only, not for the customer's needs, like to tell when the row was last modified.

In the next chapter, we will take this model and write the code to create an actual database.

The Story of the Book So Far

This is the "middle" of the process of designing a database, so I want to take a page here and recap the process we have covered:

- You've spent time gathering information, doing your best to be thorough. You know what the client wants, and the client knows that you know what they want (and you have their written-down agreement that you do understand their needs!).

- Next, you looked for entities, attributes, business rules, and so on in this information and drew a picture, creating a model that gives an overview of the structures in a graphical manner.

- You broke down these entities and turned them into basic functional relational tables such that every table relays a single meaning. One noun equals one table, pretty much.

- Lastly, the physical blueprint for the database was created, and you are ready to write the code for what could be your first SQL Server database.

If you're reading this book in one sitting (and I *hope* you aren't doing it in the bookstore without buying it, if bookstores even still exist these days), be aware that we're about to switch gears. We're turning away from the theory, modeling, and such topic; and most of the rest of the book is going to focus on applying and optimizing designs, beginning with the simplistic requirements from this chapter and then building SQL Server 2019 objects in a real SQL Server instance.

In short, we will be writing code. (Most examples will work in 2012 and earlier without change. I will note in the text when using specifically new features along with comments in the code as to how to make something work in pre-2019 versions if possible.) Likely, writing code could be what you thought you were getting when you first chunked down hard-earned money for this book (ideally your employer's (or parent's) money for a full-priced edition).

If you don't have a SQL Server to play with, this would be a great time go ahead and get one (ideally, the Developer edition on a machine you have complete control over). You can download the Developer edition for free from `www.microsoft.com/en-us/sql-server/sql-server-editions-developers`, or you could use any SQL Server system you have access to (just don't do this on a production server unless you have permission). Almost everything done in this book will work on all editions of SQL Server, in both Windows and Linux versions of SQL Server, and Azure SQL Database and Azure Managed Instances also. A few examples will not work on Linux or the Azure platforms, and I will note where that is the case. They are not of major consequence to the overall topic of database design and implementation. Installing much with the default database engine will be adequate if you are installing this on the same computer where you will be running the toolset. We will not be using advanced features of SQL Server, just the relational engine.

You can install SQL Server Management Studio (SSMS) from `https://docs.microsoft.com/en-us/sql/ssms/sql-server-management-studio-ssms` or use Azure Data Studio (ADS) from `https://docs.microsoft.com/en-us/sql/azure-data-studio/download-azure-data-studio`. SSMS is the more administrative tool, and ADS is used by more user/analyst types. Most of the examples in the book will be simply presented in the T-SQL language and as such will execute in either tool adequately. Some differences in performance output may be noticeable depending on the tool you use, but the differences are not tremendous.

If you would prefer not to install SQL Server on any of your own machines, you can use a virtual machine (you can get one with SQL Server preinstalled) from Microsoft Azure, or you can also use Azure SQL DB or even an Azure Managed Instance if you have one available for usage. Check `azure.microsoft.com` for details. At the time of writing, they had some great deals that would more than get you through the examples in this book.

To do some of the upcoming examples, you will also need the latest `WideWorldImporters` sample database installed, of which as of this writing you can find the latest version at `github.com/Microsoft/sql-server-samples/releases/tag/wide-world-importers-v1.0`. I do try my best to maintain proper casing of object names, so if you decide to use a case-sensitive version of the code, it will work.

The code and any extra code I add to the code for the book will be available on GitHub at `https://github.com/drsqlgithub/dbdesignbook6`.

Tip   I will not be covering much about installation or configuration for the on-premises or cloud versions of SQL Server. The fact is that a simple installation is indeed quite simple and a complex installation can be very complex indeed. If you need a book on this topic, I would suggest Peter Carter's *Pro SQL Server Administration* (Apress, 2015), a book I helped tech edit, which taught me a lot along the way about how to set up SQL Server in various configurations.

CHAPTER 7

Physical Model Implementation

The quality of your work, in the long run, is the deciding factor on how much your services are valued by the world.

—Orison Swett Marden, American Inspirational Author

While I am a firm and solid believer in the importance of fundamentals and doing things right, I am no different than any other programmer at heart. I am far happier when I am writing code at my desk. In this chapter, we finally reach that segment of the process. The data model is prepared and ready to be turned into code.

In this chapter, we will look at the following steps in the process:

- *Choosing the engine for your tables*: In the "Choosing the Engine for Your Tables" section, I will briefly introduce the choice of engine models that are available to your implementation.

- *Using Data Definition Language (DDL) to create database objects*: In this step, we will go through the common DDL that is needed to build tables, constraints, and so on for almost every database you will encounter.

- *Baseline testing your creation*: Because it is a great practice to load some data and test your complex constraints, the "Unit Testing Your Structures" section offers guidance on how you should approach and implement testing.

© Louis Davidson 2021
L. Davidson, *Pro SQL Server Relational Database Design and Implementation*,
https://doi.org/10.1007/978-1-4842-6497-3_7

- *Deploying your database*: As you complete the DDL and at least some
  of the testing, you need to create the database for users to use for
  more than just unit tests. The "Deployment Lifecycle" section offers a
  short introduction to the process.

To do this, we'll continue work on the complete (if small) database example from
Chapter 6. The example database is tailored to keeping the chapter simple and to avoid
too many difficult design decisions, the kind which we will flesh out more deeply in
the next few chapters with more pointed, specific examples. The data model for this
database is presented in Figure 7-1, with the details that were filled out in the previous
chapter.

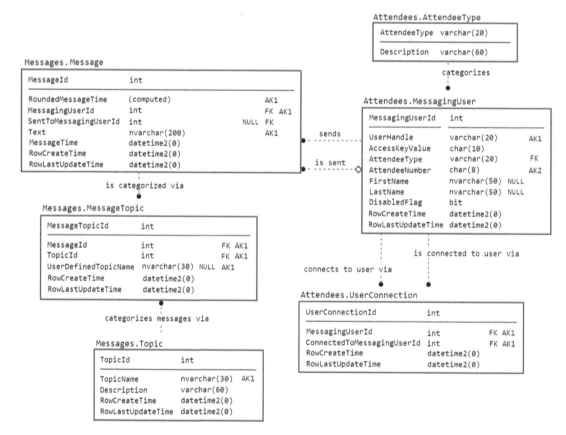

Figure 7-1. *Messaging model after adding RowCreateTime and
RowLastUpdateTime to tables*

Note   For this and subsequent chapters, I'll assume that you have access to a SQL Server where you have access to create a database. The ideal configuration is SQL Server 2019 and SQL Server Management Studio (SSMS) installed on your machine. Where to acquire a free version for developers was covered in the pages between this and the previous chapter.

Choosing the Engine for Your Tables

Prior to SQL Server 2014, there was simply one relational database engine housed in SQL Server. Every table worked the same way (and we liked it—consarn it!). In 2014, a second "*in-memory* OLTP" engine (also referred to as "memory optimized") was introduced, which works very differently than the original engine internally but, for SQL programmers, works in basically the same, declarative manner. In this section, I will introduce some of the differences at a high level and will cover the differences in more detail in later chapters. (Also, the database and objects created in this chapter will be reproduced with memory-optimized tables and code in the downloads.)

Briefly, there are two engines that you can choose for your objects:

- *On-disk*: The classic model that has been incrementally improved since SQL Server 7.0 was rewritten from the ground up. Data is housed on disk until needed. When the query processor uses the data, it is brought into memory, housed in pages that mimic the disk structures. Changes are written to memory and the transaction log and then persisted to the physical disk structures asynchronously. Concurrency/isolation controls are implemented by blocking resources from affecting another connection's resources by using locks (to signal to other processes that you are using a resource, like a table, a row, etc.) and latches (which are locks, used mostly for physical resources).

- *Memory optimized*: Also referred to as "*in-memory OLTP*" or simply "*in-memory.*" Data is first and foremost in RAM, in structures that are natively compiled (if you do some digging into the SQL Server directories, you can find the C code for tables and other objects). As data is changed, it is written to memory and the transaction log first and asynchronously written to a delta file that is used to load memory if you restart the server (there is an option to make a table nondurable; that is, if the server restarts, the data goes away, which is also referred to as "log-less"). Concurrency/isolation controls are implemented using versioning (MVCC, multiversion concurrency control), so instead of locking a resource, most concurrency collisions are signaled by an isolation-level failure, rather than blocking. The 2014 edition was very limited, with tables allowing just one unique constraint and no foreign keys or check constraints. The 2016 edition was much improved with support for most needed constraint types, and 2017 added new features like allowing more than eight indexes and computed columns.

What is awesome about the engine choice is that you make the setting at a table level, so you can have tables in each model, and those tables can interact in joins, as well as interpreted T-SQL (as opposed to natively compiled T-SQL objects, which will be noted later in this section). The memory-optimized engine is purpose built for much higher-performance scenarios than the on-disk engine can generally handle, because it uses neither latches nor locks/blocking operations for concurrency control. Despite how great it can be, it has two major concerns for most common usage:

- All your data in this model must reside in RAM, and servers with hundreds of gigabytes or terabytes are still quite expensive.

- MVCC is a *very* different concurrency model than many SQL Server applications are built for, and this can lead to big changes in code depending on how your application is built.

The differences mean that using the memory-optimized model is not typically a simple "go faster" button. Since objects using both engines can reside in the same database, you can take advantage of both as it makes sense. For example, you could have a table of products that uses the on-disk model because it is a very large table with very little write contention, but the table of orders and their line items may need to support tens of thousands of write operations per second. This is just one simple scenario where it may be useful for you to use the in-memory model.

In addition to tables being in-memory, there are stored procedures, functions, and triggers that are natively compiled at create time (using T-SQL DDL, compiled to native code) as well that can reference the memory-optimized tables (but cannot reference on-disk tables or interpreted code). They are, even in SQL Server 2019, limited in programming language surface but can certainly be worth it for many scenarios.

There are several scenarios in which you might apply the in-memory model. The Microsoft In-Memory OLTP web page (docs.microsoft.com/en-us/sql/relational-databases/in-memory-oltp/overview-and-usage-scenarios) recommends this model for multiple purposes, including the following:

- *High data read or insertion rate*: Because there is no structure contention, the memory-optimized model can handle far more concurrent operations than the on-disk model, for example, when rapidly ingesting large amounts of Internet-of-Things (IOT) data from many different devices.

- *Intensive processing*: If you are doing a lot of business logic that can be compiled into native code, code will perform far better than the interpreted version. For example, using log-less in-memory tables for temporary storage can be tremendously beneficial to processing times.

- *Low latency*: Since all data is contained in RAM and the code can be natively compiled, the amount of execution time can be greatly reduced, particularly when milliseconds (or even microseconds) count for an operation.

- *Scenarios with high-scale load*: Such as session state management, which has very little contention and may not need to persist for long periods of time (particularly not if the SQL Server machine is restarted).

So, when you are plotting out your physical database design, it is useful to consider which model is needed for your design. In most cases, the on-disk model will be the one that you will want to use (and if you are truly unsure, start with on-disk and adjust from there). It has supported some extremely large data sets in a very efficient manner and will handle an amazing amount of throughput when you design your database properly. However, as memory becomes cheaper and the engine approaches coding parity with the interpreted model we have had for 20+ years, this model may become the default model. For now, databases that need very high throughput (e.g., like ticket brokers back when the force awakened) are going to be candidates for employing this model.

If you start out with the on-disk model for your tables and during testing determine that there are hot spots in your design that could use in-memory, SQL Server provides tools to help you decide if the in-memory engine is right for your situation, which are describe in the page named "Determining if a Table or Stored Procedure Should Be Ported to In-Memory OLTP" (docs.microsoft.com/en-us/sql/relational-databases/in-memory-oltp/determining-if-a-table-or-stored-procedure-should-be-ported-to-in-memory-oltp).

The bottom line at this early part of the implementation chapters of the book is that you should be aware that there are two query processing models available to you as a data architect and understand the basic differences so throughout the rest of the book when the differences are explained more, you understand the basics.

The examples in this chapter will be done solely in the on-disk model, because it would be the most typical place to start, considering the requirements will be for a small user community. If the user community was expanded greatly, the in-memory model would likely be useful, at least for the highest-contention areas such as creating new messages.

Note   Throughout the book, there will be small asides to how things may be affected if you were to employ in-memory tables, but the subject is not a major one throughout the book. The topic is covered in greater depth in Chapter 11, because the internals of how these tables are indexed are important to understand; in Chapter 12, because concurrency is the biggest difference; and somewhat again in Chapter 13, as we will discuss a bit more about when to choose the engine and coding using it.

Using DDL to Create the Database

In the previous chapter, I went through the process to make the model ready to implement. We added columns, added tables, and specified constraints. In this chapter, what's left is to implement the tables we have spent so much time designing. The blueprints have been drawn up, and now, we can finally grab a hammer and start driving nails.

For all of the book, I will do the work of creating objects manually using DDL, because it will help you understand what a tool is building for you. It's also a good exercise for any database architect or DBA to use and understand the T-SQL syntax; I personally wouldn't suggest building a database with 300 tables without a data modeling tool, but I definitely do know people who do and wouldn't consider using a tool to create any of their database objects. On the other hand, the same data modeling tools that could be used to do the logical modeling can usually create the tables and often some of the associated code, saving your fingers from added wear and tear, plus giving you more time to help Mario save the princess or vice versa.

Ideally, don't just throw the scripts away that you write or a tool generates; keep scripts of your database structures in a source control system too. There are various ways of source controlling your databases, using Visual Studio Data Tools (docs.microsoft. com/en-us/sql/ssdt/download-sql-server-data-tools-ssdt) or Redgate SQL Source Control (www.red-gate.com/products/sql-development/sql-source-control/) or just checking in scripts into source control as I will in this chapter into something like GitHub. (The code for this chapter and the rest of the book can be found here on GitHub: https://github.com/drsqlgithub/dbdesignbook6.)

In this book, I am going to create a database directly one command at a time in T-SQL. Such scripts can be executed using any SQL Server tool, but I will generally just use a query window in SSMS or sometimes the SQLCMD.exe command-line tools when executing multiple scripts.

Before starting to build anything else, you'll need a database. I'll create this database using all default values, and my installation is very generic on any desktop computer (almost any VM technology will do), or you can install on most modern versions of Windows or several distros of Linux. I use the Developer edition, and I used most of the default settings when installing (other than setting up mixed mode for security to allow for some security testing later and the collation, which I will set to Latin1_General_100_ CI_AS), but whatever collation you have for your location will suffice. This may not be enough of an installation if you want to test features like Always On, Replication, and so on but is more than enough to create a relational database with all the features you will need for this book.

If you are using a shared server, such as a corporate development server, you'll need to do this with an account that has rights to create a database or will need to have a database created for you where you have full control (this will not be adequate for some later security examples, as they require us to do some things that are not ideal to show why they are not ideal!). If you install your server yourself, part of the process will be to set up logins so the server will be accessible for your use.

Choosing a database name is in the same level of importance as naming of other objects, and I tend to take the same sort of naming stance. Keep it as simple as possible to differentiate between all other databases and follow the naming standards in place for your organization. I would try to be careful to try to standardize names across instances of SQL Server to allow moving of databases from server to server.

The steps I'll take along the way are as follows:

- *Creating the database*: Creating the default database and finding some of the metadata about the database.

- *Creating the basic table structures*: Building the base schemas and the tables and columns contained in them.

- *Adding uniqueness constraints*: Using primary and unique constraints to enforce uniqueness between rows in the table.

- *Building default constraints*: Assisting users in choosing proper values when it isn't obvious.

- *Adding relationships*: Defining how tables relate to one another (foreign keys).

- *Implementing basic check constraints*: Some domains need to be implemented a bit more strictly than using a simple datatype.

- *Documenting the database*: Including documentation directly in the SQL Server objects.

- *Validating the dependency information*: Using the catalog views and dynamic management views (DMVs), you can validate that the objects you expect to depend on the existence of one another do, in fact, exist, keeping your database cleaner to manage.

Creating the Database

To get the database created, I will use the simplest version of a CREATE DATABASE statement. Basically, it inherits all the settings from the model database, including initial size and so on. This is not typically the method you will want to create a real database, as you will want to lay out your files in specific locations, at least for size purposes, but also for performance reasons. This will be covered more in Chapter 11, but this is an adequate way to start a database for testing purposes.

```
CREATE DATABASE ConferenceMessaging;
```

You can see where the database files were placed by running the following statement (note that size is presented in 8 KB pages—more on the internal structures of the database storage in Chapter 11):

```
SELECT type_desc, size * 8 / 1024 AS size_MB, physical_name
FROM    sys.master_files
WHERE   database_id = DB_ID('ConferenceMessaging');
```

This returns

type_desc	size (MB)	physical_name
ROWS	8	C:\Progr...SQL\DATA\ConferenceMessaging.mdf
LOG	8	C:\Progr...SQL\DATA\ConferenceMessaging_log.ldf

Next, we want to deal with the owner of the database. The database is initially owned by the user who created the database, as you can see from the following query:

```
USE ConferenceMessaging;


--determine the login that is linked to the dbo user in the database
SELECT   SUSER_SNAME(sid) AS databaseOwner
FROM     sys.database_principals
WHERE    name = 'dbo';
```

On my instance, I created the database using a user named drsql with a machine named DESKTOP-1E29384:

databaseOwner
Domain\drsql

You can see the owner of all databases on an instance using the following query (and a lot more metadata about the database is available in the sys.databases catalog view as well):

```
--Get the login of owner of the database from all database
SELECT SUSER_SNAME(owner_sid) AS databaseOwner, name
FROM    sys.databases;
```

On a typical corporate production server, I almost always will set the owner of the database to be the system administrator account so that all databases are owned by the same users. A common reason I may not do this is when you are sharing databases or when you have implemented cross-database security that needs to be different for multiple databases (more information about security in Chapter 10). You can change the owner of the database by using the ALTER AUTHORIZATION statement:

```
ALTER AUTHORIZATION ON DATABASE::ConferenceMessaging TO SA;
```

Going back and using the code to see the database owner, you will see that the owner is now SA.

Tip   Placing a semicolon at the end of every statement in your T-SQL is fast becoming a standard that will possibly be required in a future version of SQL Server. It is always a good idea.

Creating the Basic Table Structures

The next step is to create the tables of the database. In this section, we will form CREATE TABLE statements to create the tables. The following is the basic syntax for the CREATE TABLE statement:

```
CREATE TABLE [<database>.][<schema>.]<tablename>
(
        <column specification>
);
```

If you look in Microsoft Docs for the CREATE TABLE statement article, you will see a lot of additional settings that allow you to use either an on-disk or in-memory configuration, place the table on a filegroup, partition the table onto multiple filegroups, control where maximum/overflow data is placed, and so on. Some of this will be discussed in Chapter 11 on table structures and indexing. As will be the typical norm for most databases created, we will be using on-disk tables for the examples in this book unless otherwise specified.

Tip   Don't make this your only source of information about DDL in SQL Server. Microsoft Docs (docs.microsoft.com) is another great place to get exhaustive coverage of the DDL statements I will cover, and other sorts of books will cover the physical aspects of table creation in detail. Many of the remaining chapters of the book will delve into some of the other usage patterns, but even then, we will not cover every possible, nor even every useful, setting that exists.

The base CREATE clause is straightforward:

```
CREATE TABLE [<database>.][<schema>.]<tablename>
```

I'll expand on the items between the angle brackets (< and >). Anything in square brackets ([and]) is optional:

- <database>: If not specified, this defaults to the current database where the statement is being executed. Specifying the database means that the script will only be able to create objects in a single database, which precludes us from using the script unchanged to build alternately named databases on the same server, should the need arise.

- <schema>: This is the schema to which the table will belong. We specified a schema in our model, and we will create schemas as part of this section. By default, the schema will be dbo (or the default schema set for the database principal...however, it's better to always specify the schema).

- <tablename>: This is the name of the table.

For the table name, if the first character is a single # symbol, the table is a temporary table. If the first two characters of the table name are ##, it's a global temporary table. Temporary tables are not so much a part of database design as a mechanism to hold intermediate results in complex queries, so they don't really pertain to the database design. You can also declare a local variable table that has the same scope as a variable by using an @ in front of the name, which can be used to hold small sets of data.

The combination of schema and tablename must be unique in a database, and tablename must be unique from any other objects in the schema, including tables, views, procedures, constraints, and functions, among other things. It is why I will suggest a prefix or naming pattern for objects other than tables. Some things that look like objects are not, such as indexes. This will all be clearer as we progress through the book.

Schema

As discussed in the previous chapter where we defined schemas for our database, a *schema* is a namespace/container for database objects in a database. A schema is owned by a user, and tables (and all other objects) are contained in a schema. Changing owners of the schema changes owners of the objects within the schema.

You address objects using the same three-part naming method as described when using the CREATE TABLE statement (there is a fourth part, which is a server name, which we will ignore for the purposes of this chapter):

```
[<databaseName>.][<schemaName>.]objectName
```

As a note, it is suggested to always specify the two-part name for objects in code. Including the database name makes code less portable, so it is ideally left out. Including the schema name is safer, because you know what schema it is using, and it doesn't need to check the default on every execution. However, for ad hoc (one-time) access, it can be burdensome to type the schema if you are commonly using a certain schema. You can set a default schema for a user in the CREATE and ALTER USER statements, like this:

```
CREATE USER <schemaUser>
        FOR LOGIN <schemaUser>
        WITH DEFAULT SCHEMA = schemaname;
```

The ALTER USER command allows the changing of the default schema for existing users (and in SQL Server 2012 and later, it works for Windows group–based users as well; for 2005-2008R2, it only worked for standard users).

Note   Unless otherwise specified, it is assumed that the user executing this code has full control over the database and is a member of the db_owner database role in the ConferenceMessaging database and likely the sysadmin server role. This is not atypical for a user that is making changeset to a development database and then for the process that makes changes to production systems using well-tested code.

Schemas are of great use to segregate objects within a database for clarity of use. In our database, we specified two schemas: Messages and Attendees. The basic syntax to create a schema is simple, just CREATE SCHEMA <schemaName> (it must be the first statement in the batch). So I will create them using the following commands.:

```
CREATE SCHEMA Messages; --tables pertaining to the messages being sent
GO
CREATE SCHEMA Attendees; --tables pertaining to the attendees
                         --and how they can send messages
```

The CREATE SCHEMA statement has another variation where you create the objects that are contained within the schema that is rarely used, as in the following example:

```
CREATE SCHEMA Example
    CREATE TABLE ExampleTableName ...   --no schema name on the object
    CREATE TABLE ExampleTableName2 ... ; --no schema name on the object
```

The schema will be created, as well as any objects you include in the script, which will be members of that schema. If you need to drop a schema (like if you created the Example schema to try out the syntax like I did!), use DROP SCHEMA Example;. You will need to drop everything in the schema first or you will receive an error message.

You can view the schemas that have been created using the sys.schemas catalog view:

```
SELECT name, USER_NAME(principal_id) AS principal
FROM    sys.schemas
WHERE   name <> USER_NAME(principal_id); --don't list user schemas
```

This returns

name	principal
Messages	dbo
Attendees	dbo

Sometimes, schemas end up owned by a user other than dbo, like when a developer without db_owner privileges creates a schema. Or sometimes a user will get a schema with the same name as their user built by some of the SQL Server tools (which is the purpose of WHERE name <> USER_NAME(principal_id) in the schema query). You can change the ownership using the ALTER AUTHORIZATION statement much like for the database:

```
ALTER AUTHORIZATION ON SCHEMA::Messages TO dbo;
```

Columns and Base Datatypes

The next part of the CREATE TABLE statement is for the column specifications:

```
CREATE TABLE [<database>.][<schema>.]<tablename>
(
    <columnName> <datatype> [<NULL specification>]
                                    [IDENTITY [(seed,increment)]]
    --or
    <columnName> AS <computed definition>
);
```

The <columnName> placeholder is where you specify the name of the column. There are two types of columns:

- *Implemented*: This is an ordinary column, in which physical storage is always allocated and data is stored for the value.

- *Computed (or virtual/calculated)*: These columns are made up by a calculation derived from any of the physical columns in the table. These may be stored or calculated only when accessed.

Most of the columns in any database will be implemented columns, but computed columns have some pretty cool uses, so don't think they're of no use just because they aren't talked about much. You can avoid plenty of code-based denormalizations by using computed columns. In our example tables, we specified one computed column, shown in Figure 7-2.

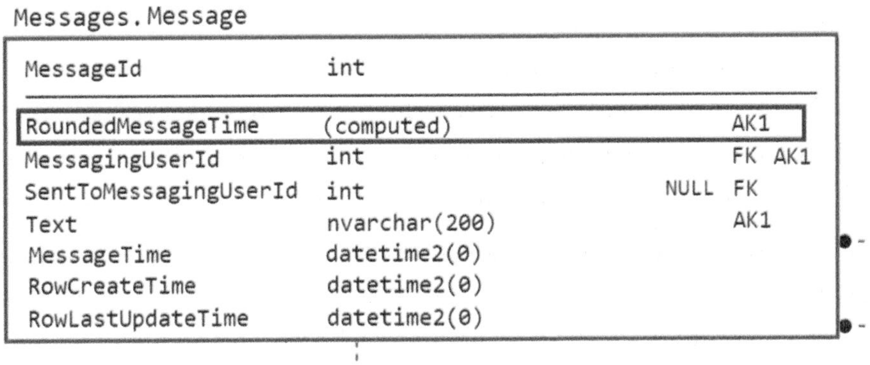

Messages.Message

MessageId	int		
RoundedMessageTime	(computed)		AK1
MessagingUserId	int		FK AK1
SentToMessagingUserId	int	NULL	FK
Text	nvarchar(200)		AK1
MessageTime	datetime2(0)		
RowCreateTime	datetime2(0)		
RowLastUpdateTime	datetime2(0)		

Figure 7-2. *Message table with computed column highlighted*

So the basic columns (other than the computed column) are fairly simple, just name and datatype:

```
MessageId               int,
SentToMessagingUserId   int,
MessagingUserId         int,
Text                    nvarchar(200),
MessageTime             datetime2(0),
RowCreateTime           datetime2(0),
RowLastUpdateTime       datetime2(0)
```

The requirements called for the person to not send the same message more than once an hour. So we construct an expression that takes the MessageTime in datetime2(0) datatype. That time is at a level of seconds, and we need the data in the form of hours. I start out with a variable of the type of the column we are deriving from and then set it to some value. I start with a variable of datetime2(0) and load it with the time from SYSDATETIME():

```
DECLARE @pointInTime datetime2(0);
SET @pointInTime = SYSDATETIME();
```

Next, I write the following expression:

```
SELECT DATEADD(HOUR,DATEPART(HOUR,@pointInTime),
               CAST(CAST(@PointInTime AS date) AS datetime2(0)) )
```

You will see the output is the current time, rounded to the hour, like 2020-05-13 23:00:00, as I am writing this. The code can be broken down fairly simply, but basically takes the number of hours since midnight and adds that to the date-only value by casting it to a date and then to a datetime2, which allows you to add hours to it. Once the expression is tested, you replace the variable with the RoundedMessageTime column, and we define our calculated column as follows:

```
,RoundedMessageTime AS DATEADD(HOUR,DATEPART(HOUR,MessageTime),
                    CAST(CAST(MessageTime AS date) AS datetime2(0)) )
                                                          PERSISTED
```

The PERSISTED specification indicates that the value will be calculated and saved as when the row is changed. This means reading the data will not incur a performance hit because the value looks to be a normal, stored column, but any update to the MessageTime column will be like updating two columns, plus the calculation, albeit a very simple calculation. In order to be persisted, the expression must be deterministic, which basically means that for the same input, you will always get the same output (much like what we covered in normalization back in Chapter 5). You can also use a computed column based on a deterministic expression as a column in an index or even a UNIQUE or PRIMARY KEY constraint (as we will do for this table). So while an expression like SYSDATETIME() is certainly possible to use in (or even AS) the expression of a computed column, you could not persist or index it, since the value would change for every execution.

NULL Specification

In the column creation phrase, simply change the <NULL specification> in your physical model to NULL to allow NULLs or NOT NULL to not allow NULLs:

```
<columnName> <data type> [<NULL specification>]
```

There's nothing particularly surprising here. For the noncomputed columns in the Messages.Message table back in Figure 7-2, we will specify the following NULL specifications:

MessageId	int	**NOT NULL,**
SentToMessagingUserId	int	**NULL ,**
MessagingUserId	int	**NOT NULL ,**
Text	nvarchar(200)	**NOT NULL ,**
MessageTime	datetime2(0)	**NOT NULL ,**
RowCreateTime	datetime2(0)	**NOT NULL ,**
RowLastUpdateTime	datetime2(0)	**NOT NULL**

Note   Leaving off the NULL specification altogether, the SQL Server default is used, which is governed by the ANSI_NULL_DFLT_OFF and ANSI_NULL_ DFLT_ON database properties (see https://msdn.microsoft.com/en-us/library/ms187356.aspx for more details). It is a definite best practice to always specify the NULL specification of a column, and I won't attempt to demonstrate how those settings work, as they are fairly confusing, which should be expected based on the diametrically opposed names.

For the computed column, you can also specify a NULL specification, when the column is persisted. In our example, we will declare it as NOT NULL, because it should never be null, assuming our calculation is correct:

```
,RoundedMessageTime AS DATEADD(HOUR,DATEPART(HOUR,MessageTime),
                    CAST(CAST(MessageTime AS date) AS datetime2(0)) )
                                               PERSISTED NOT NULL
```

Note that the data that the computation is based on does not need to not allow NULL values. For example, take the following simplest case:

```
CREATE SCHEMA DemoNull;
GO
CREATE TABLE DemoNull.ComputedColumn
(
    BaseColumn int NULL,
    ComputedColumn AS BaseColumn PERSISTED NOT NULL
);
```

The computed column expression is exactly the value of a column, but that column allows NULL values. But the ComputedColumn is declared as NOT NULL. To see this work, I insert two rows:

```
INSERT INTO DemoNull.ComputedColumn(BaseColumn)
VALUES (1);
```

The first statement works, because BaseColumn is not NULL, but when it is NULL

```
INSERT INTO DemoNull.ComputedColumn(BaseColumn)
VALUES (NULL);
```

the following error occurs:

```
Msg 515, Level 16, State 2, Line 76
Cannot insert the value NULL into column 'ComputedColumn', table 'tempdb.
DemoNull.ComputedColumn'; column does not allow nulls. INSERT fails.
```

Managing Non-Natural Primary Keys

Finally, before getting too excited and completing the table creation script, there's one more thing to discuss. In several chapters so far in this book, including the prior chapter, I have talked about picking primary keys. In this section, I'll present the method that I typically use to implement surrogate keys. I break down surrogate key values into the types that I use:

- Automatically generated as part of the definition of the column using the IDENTITY property.

- Automatically generated, but applied programmatically, often including using a DEFAULT constraint. This method allows you to override values if it is desirable. For this, you might use a GUID using the NEWID() or NEWSEQUENTIALID() function or a value generated based on a SEQUENCE object's values.

Generation Using the IDENTITY Property

Most of the time, tables are created to allow users to create, modify, and delete rows. Implementing a surrogate key on these tables can be done using (what are commonly referred to as) identity columns, but more technically columns with the IDENTITY property set. For any of the precise numeric datatypes, there's an option to create an automatically incrementing (or decrementing, depending on the increment value) column. The identity value adds or subtracts some amount automatically on each insert based on what you set when you create it, and it works as an autonomous transaction that is outside of the normal transaction, so it works extremely fast and doesn't lock other connections from anything other than the generation of a new sequential value.

The column that implements this IDENTITY column should also be defined as NOT NULL. From the "Columns and Base Datatypes" section, I had this for the column specification:

```
<columnName> <data type> [<NULL specification>]
                    IDENTITY [(SEED,INCREMENT)]
```

The SEED portion specifies the number that the column values will start with, and the INCREMENT is how much the next value will increase. For example, take the Movie table created earlier, this time implementing the IDENTITY-based surrogate key:

```
MessageId  int  NOT NULL IDENTITY(1,1)
```

To the column declaration for the MessageId column of the Message table we have been using in the past few sections, I've added the IDENTITY property. The seed of 1 indicates that the values will start at 1, and the increment says that the second value will be 1 greater, in this case 2, the next 3, and so on. You can set the seed and increment to any value that is of the datatype of the column it is being applied to. For example, you could declare the column as IDENTITY(1000,-50), and the first value would be 1000, the second 950, the third 900, and so on.

The IDENTITY property is useful for creating a surrogate primary key that's small and fast. The int datatype requires only 4 bytes and is ideal because most tables will have fewer than 2 billion rows. There are, however, a couple of *major* caveats that you have to understand about IDENTITY values:

- IDENTITY values are apt to have holes in the sequence. For example, if an error occurs when creating new rows, the IDENTITY value that is going to be used will be lost from the sequence. This is one of the things that allows them to be good performers when you have heavy-concurrency needs. Because IDENTITY values aren't affected by transactions, other connections don't have to wait until another's transaction completes.

- If a row gets deleted, the deleted value won't be reused unless you insert a row manually.

- The value of a column with the IDENTITY property cannot be updated. You can insert your own value by using SET IDENTITY_ INSERT <tablename> ON, but for the most part, you should use this only when starting a table using values from another table.

- You cannot alter a column to turn on the IDENTITY property, but you can add an IDENTITY column to an existing table.

Keep in mind the fact (I hope I've said this enough) that the surrogate key should not be the only key on the table or that the only uniqueness is a more or less random value!

Automatically Generated, Programmatically Applied Value

Using identity values, you get a very strict surrogate key management system, where you must use special syntax (SET IDENTITY_INSERT) to add a new row to the table. Instead of using a strict key generation tool like the identity, there are a couple of things you can use in a DEFAULT constraint to set values when a value isn't provided.

First, if using GUIDs for a key, you can simply default the column to NEWID(), which will generate a random GUID value. Or you can use NEWSEQUENTIALID() in a DEFAULT constraint, which will generate a GUID with a higher value each time it is called. (There is a caveat with NEWSEQUENTIALID() that upon reboot there is a chance the new value will not be greater than existing values. Having a monotonically increasing sequence of values has benefits to indexes, something we will discuss more in Chapter 11.)

A second method of generating an integer value for a surrogate is to use a SEQUENCE object to generate new values for you. Like an identity column, it is not subject to the primary transaction, so it is fast, but a rollback will not recover a value that is used, leaving gaps on errors/rollbacks.

For our database, I will use a SEQUENCE object with a default constraint instead of the identity column for the key generator of the Topic table. Users can add new general topics, but special topics will be added manually with a specific value. The only real concern with using a SEQUENCE-based surrogate key is that you are not limited to using the values the SEQUENCE object generates. So, if someone enters a value of 10 in the column without getting it from the SEQUENCE object, you may get a key violation. SEQUENCE objects have techniques to let you allocate (or sometimes referred to as *burn*) sets of data (which I will cover in a few pages).

I will start the user-generated key values at 10000, since it is unlikely that 10,000 specially coded topics will be needed:

```
CREATE SEQUENCE Messages.TopicIdGenerator
AS INT
MINVALUE 10000 --starting value
NO MAXVALUE --technically will max out at max int
START WITH 10000 --value where the sequence will start,
                 --differs from min based on cycle property
INCREMENT BY 1 --number that is added to the previous value
NO CYCLE    --if setting is cycle, when it reaches max value it starts over
CACHE 100;  --Use adjust number of values that SQL Server caches.
            --Cached values would be lost if the server is restarted,
            --but keeping them in RAM makes access faster;
```

You can get the first two values using the NEXT VALUE statement for sequence objects:

```
SELECT NEXT VALUE FOR Messages.TopicIdGenerator AS TopicId;
SELECT NEXT VALUE FOR Messages.TopicIdGenerator AS TopicId;
```

This returns

```
TopicId
-----------
10000

TopicId
-----------
10001
```

One interesting thing about the NEXT VALUE FOR syntax is that if you repeat the same call multiple times in a statement (or in multiple DEFAULT constraints), only one value is fetched per call. For example, execute the following statement:

```
SELECT NEXT VALUE FOR Messages.TopicIdGenerator AS TopicId,
       NEXT VALUE FOR Messages.TopicIdGenerator AS TopicId2,
       NEXT VALUE FOR Messages.TopicIdGenerator AS TopicId3;
```

And the output will be something like

```
TopicId   TopicId   TopicId
--------  --------  --------
10002     10002     10002
```

Note   The default datatype for a SEQUENCE object is `bigint` and the default starting point is the smallest number that the SEQUENCE supports. So, if you declared CREATE SEQUENCE `dbo.test` and fetched the first value, you would get -9223372036854775808, which is an annoying starting place for most usages. Like almost every DDL you will use in T-SQL, it is generally desirable to specify most settings, especially those settings that control or affect the way the object works for you.

You can then reset the sequence to the original START WITH value using the ALTER SEQUENCE statement with a RESTART clause:

```
--To start a certain number add WITH <starting value literal>
ALTER SEQUENCE Messages.TopicIdGenerator RESTART;
```

For the Topic table, I will use the following column declaration to use the SEQUENCE object in a default. This is the first time I use a DEFAULT constraint, so I will note that the name I gave the default object starts with a prefix of DFLT, followed by the table name, underscore, and then the column the default pertains to. This will be enough to keep the names unique and to identify the object in a query of the system catalog:

```
TopicId int NOT NULL
        CONSTRAINT DFLTTopic_TopicId DEFAULT
            (NEXT VALUE FOR  Messages.TopicIdGenerator),
```

In the final section of this chapter, I will load some data for the table to give an idea of how all the parts work together. One additional super-nice property of SEQUENCE objects is that you can pre-allocate values to allow for bulk inserts. This way, if you want to load 100 topic rows, you can get the values for use, build your set, and then do the insert. The allocation is done using a system stored procedure:

```
DECLARE @range_first_value sql_variant, @range_last_value sql_variant,
        @sequence_increment sql_variant;

EXEC sp_sequence_get_range @sequence_name = N'Messages.TopicIdGenerator'
    , @range_size = 100
    , @range_first_value = @range_first_value OUTPUT
    , @range_last_value = @range_last_value OUTPUT
    , @sequence_increment = @sequence_increment OUTPUT;

SELECT CAST(@range_first_value AS int) AS FirstTopicId,
        CAST(@range_last_value AS int) AS LastTopicId,
        CAST(@sequence_increment AS int) AS Increment;
```

Since our object was just reset, the first 100 values are allocated and returned, along with the increment (which you should not assume when you use these values; also, you want to follow the rules of the object):

```
FirstTopicId LastTopicId Increment
------------ ----------- -----------
10000        10099       1
```

If you want to get metadata about the SEQUENCE objects in the database, you can use the sys.sequences catalog view:

```
SELECT start_value, increment, current_value
FROM sys.sequences
WHERE SCHEMA_NAME(schema_id) = 'Messages'
    AND name = 'TopicIdGenerator';
```

For the TopicGenerator object we set up, this returns

```
start_value     increment       current_value
--------------  --------------  ----------------------
10000           1               10099
```

Using a SEQUENCE object can be a great improvement on identity-based columns, especially whenever you have any need to control the values in the surrogate key (like having unique values across multiple tables). They are a bit more work than identity values, but the flexibility is worth it when you need it. I foresee identity columns to remain the standard way of creating surrogate keys for most purposes, as their inflexibility offers some protection against having to manage data in the surrogate key, since you have to go out of your way to insert a value other than what the next identity value is with SET IDENTITY_INSERT ON.

The Actual DDL to Build Tables

We have finally reached the point where we are going to create the basic table structures we have specified, including generating the primary keys and the calculated column that we created. Note that we have already created the SCHEMA and SEQUENCE objects earlier in the chapter. I will start the script with a statement to drop the objects if they already exist (my favorite feature added to SQL Server 2016!), as this lets you create and try out the code in a testing manner. At the end of the chapter, I will discuss strategies for versioning your code, keeping a clean database from a script, either by dropping the objects or by dropping and recreating a database:

```
--Make the tables able to be dropped and recreated in our test scenario
DROP TABLE IF EXISTS Attendees.UserConnection,
                     Messages.MessageTopic,
                     Messages.Topic,
                     Messages.Message,
                     Attendees.AttendeeType,
                     Attendees.MessagingUser;
--create all of the objects
CREATE TABLE Attendees.AttendeeType (
        AttendeeType            varchar(20)  NOT NULL ,
        Description             varchar(60)  NOT NULL
);
--As this is a non-editable table, we load the data here to
--start with as part of the create script
INSERT INTO Attendees.AttendeeType
VALUES ('Regular', 'Typical conference attendee'),
        ('Speaker', 'Person scheduled to speak'),
        ('Administrator','Manages System');

CREATE TABLE Attendees.MessagingUser (
        MessagingUserId         int NOT NULL IDENTITY ( 1,1 ) ,
        UserHandle              varchar(20)  NOT NULL ,
        AccessKeyValue          char(10)   NOT NULL ,
        AttendeeNumber          char(8)   NOT NULL ,
        FirstName               nvarchar(50)   NULL ,
        LastName                nvarchar(50)   NULL ,
        AttendeeType            varchar(20)   NOT NULL ,
        DisabledFlag            bit  NOT NULL ,
        RowCreateTime           datetime2(0)   NOT NULL ,
        RowLastUpdateTime       datetime2(0)   NOT NULL
);
```

```
CREATE TABLE Attendees.UserConnection
(
        UserConnectionId       int NOT NULL IDENTITY ( 1,1 ) ,
        ConnectedToMessagingUserId int   NOT NULL ,
        MessagingUserId        int   NOT NULL ,
        RowCreateTime          datetime2(0)  NOT NULL ,
        RowLastUpdateTime      datetime2(0)  NOT NULL
);

CREATE TABLE Messages.Message (
        MessageId              int NOT NULL IDENTITY ( 1,1 ) ,
        RoundedMessageTime  as
            (DATEADD(hour,DATEPART(hour,MessageTime),
             CAST(CAST(MessageTime AS date) AS datetime2(0)) ))
                                    PERSISTED NOT NULL,
        SentToMessagingUserId int   NULL ,
        MessagingUserId        int   NOT NULL ,
        Text                   nvarchar(200)  NOT NULL ,
        MessageTime            datetime2(0)  NOT NULL ,
        RowCreateTime          datetime2(0)  NOT NULL ,
        RowLastUpdateTime      datetime2(0)  NOT NULL
);
CREATE TABLE Messages.MessageTopic (
        MessageTopicId         int NOT NULL IDENTITY ( 1,1 ) ,
        MessageId              int   NOT NULL ,
        UserDefinedTopicName nvarchar(30)  NULL ,
        TopicId                int   NOT NULL ,
        RowCreateTime          datetime2(0)  NOT NULL ,
        RowLastUpdateTime      datetime2(0)  NOT NULL
);

CREATE TABLE Messages.Topic (
        TopicId int NOT NULL
           CONSTRAINT DFLTTopic_TopicId
               DEFAULT(NEXT VALUE FOR  Messages.TopicIdGenerator),
        TopicName              nvarchar(30)  NOT NULL ,
```

```
    Description             varchar(60)  NOT NULL ,
    RowCreateTime           datetime2(0)  NOT NULL ,
    RowLastUpdateTime       datetime2(0)  NOT NULL
);
```

After running this script, I actually have a real database where work *could* actually take place, but there are still quite a few steps to go before we get the finished product that we took the time to design. Sometimes, this is as far as people go when building a "small" system, to the detriment of integrity. It is important to do the steps in this chapter for almost every database you create to maintain a reasonable level of data integrity.

Note   If you are trying to create a table (or any object, setting, security principal [user or login], etc.) in SQL Server, SSMS will almost always have tooling to help. For example, right-clicking the Tables node under Databases\ ConferenceMessaging\ in Management Studio will give you a New Table menu (as well as some other specific table types that we will look at later in the book). If you want to see the script to build an existing table, right-click the table and select Script Table As and then CREATE to and choose how you want it scripted. I use these options very frequently to see the structure of a table, and I expect you will too.

Adding Uniqueness Constraints

As I've mentioned several (and, perhaps if you are the type of person who reads the entire book carefully, many many) times, it's important that every table has at least one constraint that prevents duplicate rows from being created. In this section, I'll introduce the following tasks, plus a topic (indexes) that inevitably comes to mind when I start talking about keys that are implemented with indexes:

- Adding PRIMARY KEY constraints
- Adding UNIQUE (alternate key) constraints
- Viewing uniqueness constraints
- Where other indexes fit in

Both PRIMARY KEY and UNIQUE constraints are implemented using unique indexes to do the enforcing of uniqueness. It's conceivable that you could use unique indexes instead of constraints, but I specifically use constraints because of the meaning that they suggest: constraints are intended to semantically represent and enforce some limitation on data, whereas indexes (which are covered in detail in Chapter 10) are intended to speed access to data.

It doesn't matter how the uniqueness is implemented, but it is necessary to have either unique indexes or UNIQUE constraints in place. Usually an index will be useful for performance as well, as usually when you need to enforce uniqueness, it's also the case that a user or process will be searching for a reasonably small number of values in the table.

Adding PRIMARY KEY Constraints

The first set of constraints we will add to the tables will be PRIMARY KEY constraints. The syntax of the PRIMARY KEY declaration is straightforward:

```
[CONSTRAINT constraintname] PRIMARY KEY [CLUSTERED | NONCLUSTERED]
```

As with all constraints, the constraint name is optional, but you should never treat it as such. I'll name PRIMARY KEY constraints using a name like PK<tablename>. Generally, you will want to make the primary key clustered for the table, as normally the column(s) of the primary key will be the most frequently used for accessing rows. This is definitely not always the case and will usually be something discovered later during the testing phase of the project. In Chapter 11, I will give more indications of when you might alter from the clustered primary key path.

Tip   The PRIMARY KEY constraint and other constraints of the table will be members of the table's schema, so you don't need to name your constraints for uniqueness over all objects in the database, just those in the schema.

You can specify the PRIMARY KEY constraint when creating the table, just as we did the default for the SEQUENCE object. If it is a single-column key, it can be added to the statement at the end of the column declaration, and constraints can be stacked, as I have done for this table:

```
CREATE TABLE Messages.Topic (
        TopicId int NOT NULL
                CONSTRAINT DFLTTopic_TopicId
                        DEFAULT(NEXT VALUE FOR dbo.TopicIdGenerator)
                --makes the TopicId the PK
                CONSTRAINT PKTopic PRIMARY KEY,
        TopicName               nvarchar(30)  NOT NULL ,
        Description             varchar(60)   NOT NULL ,
        RowCreateTime           datetime2(0)  NOT NULL ,
        RowLastUpdateTime       datetime2(0)  NOT NULL
);
```

For a multiple-column key, you can specify it inline with the columns enumerated like the following example:

```
CREATE TABLE Examples.ExampleKey
(
        ExampleKeyColumn1 int NOT NULL,
        ExampleKeyColumn2 int NOT NULL,
        CONSTRAINT PKExampleKey
                PRIMARY KEY (ExampleKeyColumn1, ExampleKeyColumn2)
);
```

Another common method is to use an ALTER TABLE statement and simply modify the table to add the constraint, like the following, which is the code in the downloads that will add the primary keys. (CLUSTERED is optional for a PRIMARY KEY constraint, and where there is not currently a clustered index on the table, it will make it a clustered index and nonclustered otherwise. I will typically add it to my CREATE TABLE statements for emphasis and to make sure that I haven't accidentally forgotten that another index was chosen at some other point in time.)

```
ALTER TABLE Attendees.AttendeeType
    ADD CONSTRAINT PKAttendeeType PRIMARY KEY CLUSTERED (AttendeeType);

ALTER TABLE Attendees.MessagingUser
    ADD CONSTRAINT PKMessagingUser
            PRIMARY KEY CLUSTERED (MessagingUserId);
```

```
ALTER TABLE Attendees.UserConnection
    ADD CONSTRAINT PKUserConnection
            PRIMARY KEY CLUSTERED (UserConnectionId);

ALTER TABLE Messages.Message
    ADD CONSTRAINT PKMessage PRIMARY KEY CLUSTERED (MessageId);

ALTER TABLE Messages.MessageTopic
    ADD CONSTRAINT PKMessageTopic PRIMARY KEY CLUSTERED (MessageTopicId);

ALTER TABLE Messages.Topic
    ADD CONSTRAINT PKTopic PRIMARY KEY CLUSTERED (TopicId);
```

Tip   If you skip the CONSTRAINT <constraintName> part of any constraint declaration, SQL Server will assign a name for you, and it will be ugly and will be different each and every time you execute the statement. This will make it harder to compare to multiple databases created from the same script, like for dev, test, and prod. For example, create the following object in tempdb:

```
CREATE TABLE dbo.TestConstraintName (   TestConstraintNameId int
PRIMARY KEY);
```

Look at the object name with this query:

```
SELECT constraint_name FROM information_schema.table_constraints WHERE
table_schema = 'dbo'  AND  table_name = 'TestConstraintName';
```

You see the name chosen is something hideous like PK__TestCons__BA850E1F4E8FA3CF. Drop the table, execute the statement a second time, and it will have a different name.

Adding UNIQUE Constraints

Enforcing alternate keys is probably more important than for primary keys, especially when using an artificial key. When implementing alternate keys, it's best to use a UNIQUE constraint. These are very similar to PRIMARY KEY constraints (other than they can have columns that allow NULL values) and can even be used as the target of a relationship (relationships are covered later in the chapter).

The syntax for their creation is as follows:

```
[CONSTRAINT constraintname] UNIQUE [CLUSTERED | NONCLUSTERED]
[(ColumnList)]
```

Just like the PRIMARY KEY, you can declare a UNIQUE constraint during table creation or using an ALTER statement:

```
ALTER TABLE Messages.Message
    ADD CONSTRAINT AKMessage_TimeUserAndText UNIQUE
    (RoundedMessageTime, MessagingUserId, Text);

ALTER TABLE Messages.Topic
    ADD CONSTRAINT AKTopic_Name UNIQUE (TopicName);

ALTER TABLE Messages.MessageTopic
    ADD CONSTRAINT AKMessageTopic_TopicAndMessage UNIQUE
    (MessageId, TopicId, UserDefinedTopicName);

ALTER TABLE Attendees.MessagingUser
    ADD CONSTRAINT AKMessagingUser_UserHandle UNIQUE (UserHandle);

ALTER TABLE Attendees.MessagingUser
    ADD CONSTRAINT AKMessagingUser_AttendeeNumber UNIQUE
    (AttendeeNumber);

ALTER TABLE Attendees.UserConnection
    ADD CONSTRAINT AKUserConnection_Users UNIQUE
    (MessagingUserId, ConnectedToMessagingUserId);
```

The only interesting tidbit here is in the Messages.Message declaration. Remember in the table declaration this was a computed column, so now, by adding this constraint, we have prevented the same message from being entered more than once per hour. This should show you that you can implement some complex constraints using the basic building blocks we have covered so far. I will note again that the computed column you specify must be based on a deterministic expression to be used in an index. Declaring the column as PERSISTED is a good way to know if it is deterministic or not. Note that we declared the computed column as NOT NULL, and as such it could have even been part of the PRIMARY KEY if it was so desired.

In the next few chapters, we will cover many different patterns for using these building blocks in very interesting ways. Now, we have covered all the uniqueness constraints that are needed in our ConferenceMessaging database.

What About Indexes?

The topic of indexes is one that generally begins to be discussed before the first row of data is loaded into the first table. Indexes that you will add to a table other than uniqueness constraints will generally have a singular responsibility for increasing performance. At the same time, they must be maintained, so they decrease performance too, though in most cases considerably less than they increase it. This conundrum is the foundation of the "science" of performance tuning. Generally, it is best to leave any discussion of adding indexes until data is loaded into tables and queries are executed that show the need for indexes or at least understand the most common search patterns during implementation of the external interfaces.

In the previous section, we created uniqueness constraints whose purpose is to constrain the data in some form to make sure integrity is met. These uniqueness constraints we have just created are built using unique indexes and will also incur some performance penalty just as any index will. However, while they will also likely have a positive performance value, the premier value of the uniqueness constraint is to enforce the uniqueness contract for a set of columns. If they harm performance by never being used in queries, it is enough that they protect against duplication.

To see the indexes that have been created for your constraints, you can use the sys. indexes catalog view (with some shortened data to fit in the book)

```
SELECT CONCAT(OBJECT_SCHEMA_NAME(object_id),'.',
              OBJECT_NAME(object_id)) AS object_name,
              name as index_name, is_primary_key as PK,
              is_unique_constraint as UQ
FROM    sys.indexes
WHERE   OBJECT_SCHEMA_NAME(object_id) <> 'sys'
  AND   (is_primary_key = 1
         OR is_unique_constraint = 1)
ORDER BY object_name, is_primary_key DESC, name;
```

which, for the constraints we have created so far, returns

object_name	index_name	PK	UC
Attendees.AttendeeType	PKAttendees_AttendeeType	1	0
Attendees.MessagingUser	PKAttendees_MessagingUser	1	0
Attendees.MessagingUser	AKAttendees_MessagingUser_A...	0	1
Attendees.MessagingUser	AKAttendees_MessagingUser_U...	0	1
Attendees.UserConnection	PKAttendees_UserConnection	1	0
Attendees.UserConnection	AKAttendees_UserConnection_...	0	1
Messages.Message	PKMessages_Message	1	0
Messages.Message	AKMessages_Message_TimeUser...	0	1
Messages.MessageTopic	PKMessages_MessageTopic	1	0
Messages.MessageTopic	AKMessages_MessageTopic_Top...	0	1
Messages.Topic	PKMessages_Topic	1	0
Messages.Topic	AKMessages_Topic_Name	0	1

As you start to do index tuning, one of the major tasks is to determine whether indexes are being used and to eliminate the indexes that are never (or very rarely) used to optimize queries, but you will not want to remove any indexes that show up in the results of the previous query, because they are there for data integrity purposes.

Building DEFAULT Constraints

If a user doesn't know what value to enter into a column and then leaves the column out of an INSERT statement, by default, the value will be NULL. However, if you omit a column in an INSERT statement, you can create a DEFAULT constraint that will let the value be set to a preconfigured value. This helps in that you help users avoid having to make up illogical, inappropriate values if they don't know what they want to put in a column, yet they need to create a row. However, the true value of defaults is lost in most applications, because the user interface would have to honor this default and not reference the column in an INSERT operation (or use the DEFAULT keyword for the column value for a DEFAULT constraint to matter).

We used a DEFAULT constraint earlier to implement the primary key generation, but here, I will spend a bit more time describing how it works. The basic syntax for the default constraint is

```
[CONSTRAINT constraintname] DEFAULT (<scalar expression>)
```

The scalar expression must be a literal or an expression that returns a scalar, even one that uses a function (even a user-defined one that accesses a table.) Table 7-1 has sample literal values that can be used as defaults for a few datatypes.

Table 7-1. *Sample Default Values*

Datatype	Sample Default Value
int	1
varchar(10)	'Value'
binary(2)	0x0000
datetime2(7)	'20080101 23:54:33.0000234'

As an example, in the database I am building, we have the DisabledFlag on the Attendees.MessagingUser table. I'll set the default value to 0 for this column here:

```
ALTER TABLE Attendees.MessagingUser
   ADD CONSTRAINT DFLTMessagingUser_DisabledFlag
   DEFAULT (0) FOR DisabledFlag;
```

Beyond literals, it is very common to use system functions to implement DEFAULT constraints. In our model, we will use a default on all the table's RowCreateTime and RowLastUpdateTime columns. To create these constraints, I will demonstrate one of the most useful tools in a DBA's toolbox: using the system views to generate code. Since we have to do the same code over and over, I will query the metadata in the INFORMATION_ SCHEMA.COLUMN view and put together a query that will generate the DEFAULT constraints (you will need to set your output to text and not grids in SSMS to use this code):

```
SELECT CONCAT('ALTER TABLE ',TABLE_SCHEMA,'.',TABLE_NAME,CHAR(13),CHAR(10),
              '     ADD CONSTRAINT DFLT', TABLE_NAME, '_' ,
           COLUMN_NAME, CHAR(13), CHAR(10),
        '   DEFAULT (SYSDATETIME()) FOR ', COLUMN_NAME,';')
```

```
FROM    INFORMATION_SCHEMA.COLUMNS
WHERE   COLUMN_NAME in ('RowCreateTime', 'RowLastUpdateTime')
  and   TABLE_SCHEMA in ('Messages','Attendees')
ORDER BY TABLE_SCHEMA, TABLE_NAME, COLUMN_NAME;
```

This code will generate the code for ten constraints:

```
ALTER TABLE Attendees.MessagingUser
    ADD CONSTRAINT DFLTMessagingUser_RowCreateTime
    DEFAULT (SYSDATETIME()) FOR RowCreateTime;

ALTER TABLE Attendees.MessagingUser
    ADD CONSTRAINT DFLTMessagingUser_RowLastUpdateTime
    DEFAULT (SYSDATETIME()) FOR RowLastUpdateTime;

ALTER TABLE Attendees.UserConnection
    ADD CONSTRAINT DFLTUserConnection_RowCreateTime
    DEFAULT (SYSDATETIME()) FOR RowCreateTime;

ALTER TABLE Attendees.UserConnection
    ADD CONSTRAINT DFLTUserConnection_RowLastUpdateTime
    DEFAULT (SYSDATETIME()) FOR RowLastUpdateTime;

ALTER TABLE Messages.Message
    ADD CONSTRAINT DFLTMessage_RowCreateTime
    DEFAULT (SYSDATETIME()) FOR RowCreateTime;

ALTER TABLE Messages.Message
    ADD CONSTRAINT DFLTMessage_RowLastUpdateTime
    DEFAULT (SYSDATETIME()) FOR RowLastUpdateTime;

ALTER TABLE Messages.MessageTopic
    ADD CONSTRAINT DFLTMessageTopic_RowCreateTime
    DEFAULT (SYSDATETIME()) FOR RowCreateTime;

ALTER TABLE Messages.MessageTopic
    ADD CONSTRAINT DFLTMessageTopic_RowLastUpdateTime
    DEFAULT (SYSDATETIME()) FOR RowLastUpdateTime;
```

```
ALTER TABLE Messages.Topic
    ADD CONSTRAINT DFLTTopic_RowCreateTime
    DEFAULT (SYSDATETIME()) FOR RowCreateTime;

ALTER TABLE Messages.Topic
    ADD CONSTRAINT DFLTTopic_RowLastUpdateTime
    DEFAULT (SYSDATETIME()) FOR RowLastUpdateTime;
```

Obviously, it's not the point of this section, but generating code with the system metadata is a very useful skill to have, particularly when you need to add some type of code over and over.

Adding Relationships (Foreign Keys)

Adding relationships is perhaps the trickiest of the constraints to code because both the parent and child tables need to exist to create the constraint. Hence, it is more common to add FOREIGN KEY constraints using the ALTER TABLE statement, but you can also do this using the CREATE TABLE statement if you have the tables in the right order. Creating FOREIGN KEY objects in the CREATE TABLE statement is certainly more common when adding a new table than when creating an entire new database of tables.

The typical FOREIGN KEY constraint is implemented as the columns from the PRIMARY KEY constraint of one table migrated to another table (it could be the same table, playing a different role) to establish a relationship between the tables. You can also reference a UNIQUE constraint, but it is a pretty rare implementation (and gets really tricky when the columns in the UNIQUE constraint allow NULL values too). An example of referencing a UNIQUE constraint I have used a few times is a table with an identity key and a textual code. I referenced the textual code for an older reference that could not be changed to meet the new standard at the time.

The syntax of the statement for adding FOREIGN KEY constraints is straightforward:

```
ALTER TABLE TableName [WITH CHECK | WITH NOCHECK]
    ADD [CONSTRAINT <constraintName>]
    FOREIGN KEY REFERENCES <referencedTable> (<referencedColumns>)
    [ON DELETE <NO ACTION | CASCADE | SET NULL | SET DEFAULT> ]
    [ON UPDATE <NO ACTION | CASCADE | SET NULL | SET DEFAULT> ];
```

The components of this syntax are as follows:

- `<referencedTable>`: The parent table in the relationship.

- `<referencedColumns>`: A comma-delimited list of columns in the child table in the same order as the columns in the primary key of the parent table. They don't have to have the same names, but they have to have the exact same datatypes.

- ON DELETE *or* ON UPDATE *clause*: Specifies what to do when a row is deleted or updated. Options are as follows:

  - NO ACTION: Raises an error if you end up with a child with no matching parent after the statement completes.

  - CASCADE: Applies the action on the parent to the child; either updates the migrated key values in the child to the new parent key value or deletes the child row.

  - SET NULL: If you delete or change the value of the parent, the child key will be set to NULL. Note I said *or change*; if the parent key value changes from 1 to 2, the reference is invalidated and the child set to NULL, not changed.

  - SET DEFAULT: If you delete or change the value of the parent, the child key is set to the default value from the default constraint or NULL if no constraint exists.

If you are using surrogate keys, you will very rarely need either of the ON UPDATE options, since the value of a surrogate is rarely editable. For deletes, 98.934% of the time you will use NO ACTION, because most of the time, you will simply want to make the user manually delete the children rows first to avoid accidentally deleting data.

The most common of the actions to see used is ON DELETE CASCADE, which is frequently useful for table sets where the child table is, in essence, just a part of the same object as the parent table (and in your original diagrams would have been designed as a dependent entity). For example, Invoice <-- InvoiceLineItem. Usually, if you are going to delete the invoice, you are doing so because it needs deleting, and you will want the line items to go away too because they don't make sense to exist anymore either, automatically. On the other hand, you want to avoid it for relationships like Customer <-- Invoice. Deleting a customer who has invoices as a general rule is probably not desired, and automatically deleting all of the customer's invoices, sales orders, messages, notes, contacts, and so on on the occasion that you do wish to eliminate a customer from your database is typically not desired. So you will want client code to need to be executed that specifically chooses to delete the Invoice rows before deleting the Customer rows on the rare occasion that you do wish to delete a customer that already has activity in your database.

Note too the optional [WITH CHECK | WITH NOCHECK] specification. When you create a constraint, the WITH NOCHECK setting gives you the opportunity to create the constraint without checking existing data. Using NOCHECK and leaving the values unchecked is a generally bad thing to do because if you try to resave the exact same data that existed in a row, you could get an error. Also, if the constraint is built using WITH CHECK, the query optimizer can possibly make use of this fact when building a query plan by knowing that a row with a certain key value in the parent table must exist for the corresponding column value to exist in the child table. Chapter 8 will cover more on enabling and checking constraints.

Thinking back to our modeling discussions, there were optional and required relationships such as the one in Figure 7-3.

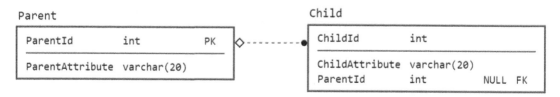

Figure 7-3. *Optional parent-to-child relationship indicates NULL on the migrated key*

The Child.ParentId column needs to allow NULLs (which it does on the model). For a required relationship, the Child.ParentId does not allow NULL values, like in Figure 7-4.

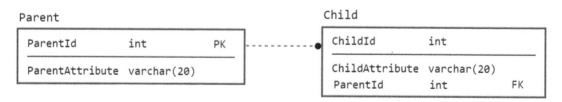

Figure 7-4. *Required parent-to-child relationship requires NOT NULL on the migrated key*

This is all you need to do, because SQL Server knows that when the referencing key allows a NULL, the relationship value is optional. In our model, represented in Figure 7-5, we have seven relationships modeled.

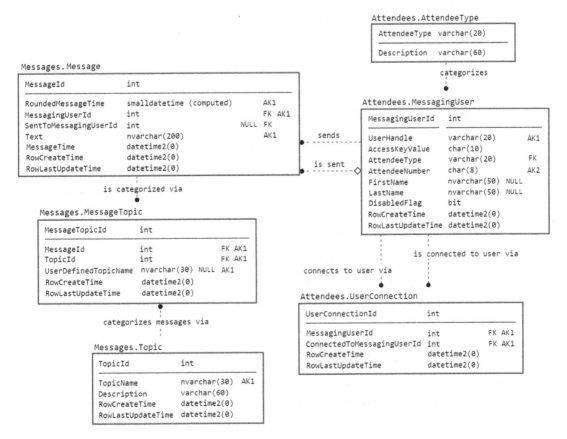

Figure 7-5. *Messaging model for reference*

As you can see in Figure 7-5, we have given relationships a verb phrase, which is used to read the name. For example, between MessagingUser and Message, we have two relationships. One of them was verb phrased as "Is Sent" as in MessagingUser-Is Sent-Message. In order to get interesting usage of these verb phrases, I will use them as part of the name of the constraint, so that constraint will be named

FKMessagingUser$IsSent$Messages_Message

Doing this greatly improves the value of the names for constraints, particularly when you have more than one foreign key going between the same two tables. Now, let's go through the seven constraints and decide the options to use on the FOREIGN

KEY constraints to implement the relationships. First up is the relationship between AttendeeType and MessagingUser. Since it uses a natural key, it is a target for the UPDATE CASCADE option. However, note that if you have a lot of MessagingUser rows, this operation can be very costly, so it should be done during off-hours. And, if it turns out it is done very often, the choice to use a nonvolatile natural key value ought to be reconsidered. We will use ON DELETE NO ACTION, because we don't usually want to cascade a delete from a table that is strictly there to implement a domain:

```
ALTER TABLE Attendees.MessagingUser
      ADD CONSTRAINT FKMessagingUser$IsSent$Messages_Message
            FOREIGN KEY (AttendeeType)
                  REFERENCES Attendees.AttendeeType(AttendeeType)
            ON UPDATE CASCADE
            ON DELETE NO ACTION;
```

Next, let's consider the two relationships between the MessagingUser table and the UserConnection table. If one of the users in the connection relationship is deleted (as opposed to being disabled by the DisabledFlag), then we would need to delete all connections to and from the MessagingUser table. Hence, you might consider implementing both as DELETE CASCADE. However, if you execute the statements

```
ALTER TABLE Attendees.UserConnection
      ADD CONSTRAINT
        FKMessagingUser$ConnectsToUserVia$Attendees_UserConnection
      FOREIGN KEY (MessagingUserId)
            REFERENCES Attendees.MessagingUser(MessagingUserId)
      ON UPDATE NO ACTION
      ON DELETE CASCADE;

ALTER TABLE Attendees.UserConnection
      ADD CONSTRAINT
        FKMessagingUser$IsConnectedToUserVia$Attendees_UserConnection
      FOREIGN KEY  (ConnectedToMessagingUserId)
            REFERENCES Attendees.MessagingUser(MessagingUserId)
      ON UPDATE NO ACTION
      ON DELETE CASCADE;
```

you will receive the following error message from the second ALTER TABLE statement:

```
Introducing FOREIGN KEY constraint 'FKMessagingUser$IsConnectedToUserVi
a$Attendees_UserConnection' on table 'UserConnection' may cause cycles
or multiple cascade paths. Specify ON DELETE NO ACTION or ON UPDATE NO
ACTION, or modify other FOREIGN KEY constraints.
```

In this case, this message is stating that you cannot have two CASCADE operations to the same table. This even more limits the value of the CASCADE operations. Instead, we will use NO ACTION for the DELETE and will just have to implement the cascade in the client code or using a TRIGGER object (which I will do as an example).

I will also note that, in many ways, having these limitations on cascading operations is probably a good thing. Too much automatically executing code that you didn't write yourself explicitly can be troublesome. I will change the constraints to NO ACTION and recreate (dropping the one that was created first):

```
ALTER TABLE Attendees.UserConnection
        DROP CONSTRAINT IF EXISTS --works on some DDL also!
            FKMessagingUser$ConnectsToUserVia$Attendees_UserConnection;
GO

ALTER TABLE Attendees.UserConnection
        ADD CONSTRAINT
            FKMessagingUser$ConnectsToUserVia$Attendees_UserConnection
        FOREIGN KEY (MessagingUserId)
                REFERENCES Attendees.MessagingUser(MessagingUserId)
        ON UPDATE NO ACTION
        ON DELETE NO ACTION;

ALTER TABLE Attendees.UserConnection
        ADD CONSTRAINT
            FKMessagingUser$IsConnectedToUserVia$Attendees_UserConnection
        FOREIGN KEY  (ConnectedToMessagingUserId)
                REFERENCES Attendees.MessagingUser(MessagingUserId)
        ON UPDATE NO ACTION
        ON DELETE NO ACTION;
GO
```

Next, I will add the following INSTEAD OF trigger that will go ahead and delete the rows before the actual operation that the user tried is executed (note, Chapter 8 will cover writing triggers in more detail and Appendix B has details on the template that this trigger was created from):

```
CREATE TRIGGER MessagingUser$InsteadOfDeleteTrigger
ON Attendees.MessagingUser
INSTEAD OF DELETE AS
BEGIN
   DECLARE @msg varchar(2000),      --used to hold the error message
   --use inserted for insert or update trigger, deleted for
   --update or delete trigger count instead of @@rowcount due to merge
   --behavior that sets @@rowcount to a number that is equal to number of
   --merged rows, not rows being checked in trigger
          @rowsAffected int = (select count(*) from deleted);

   --no need to continue on if no rows affected
   IF @rowsAffected = 0 RETURN;

   SET NOCOUNT ON; --to avoid the rowcount messages
   SET ROWCOUNT 0; --in case the client has modified the rowcount

   BEGIN TRY
          --[validation section]
          --[modification section]

          --implement multi-path cascade delete in trigger
          DELETE FROM Attendees.UserConnection
          WHERE  MessagingUserId IN (SELECT MessagingUserId FROM DELETED);

          DELETE FROM Attendees.UserConnection
          WHERE  ConnectedToMessagingUserId IN (SELECT MessagingUserId
                                                FROM DELETED);

          --<perform action>
          DELETE FROM Attendees.MessagingUser
          WHERE  MessagingUserId IN (SELECT MessagingUserId FROM DELETED);
   END TRY
   BEGIN CATCH
```

```
        IF @@trancount > 0
            ROLLBACK TRANSACTION;
        THROW;
    END CATCH;
END;
```

For the two relationships between MessagingUser and Message, it may seem like we want to use cascade operations, but in this case, since we implemented a disabled indicator in the MessagingUser table, we would probably not use cascade operations. If the MessagingUser had not created message rows yet, it could be deleted; otherwise, it would usually be disabled (and the row would not be deleted, which would cause the previous trigger to fail and leave the connection rows alone too).

Tip   Data such as this is a concern for GDPR requests, like "right to be forgotten," but you must decide how to best implement. Delete the user, and you must delete the messages. This can make your data look really messed up for other users. Or you can just blank out that user's data in some cases (but then you have the concern that the messages have PII in them as well!). How you build your system is up to the need at hand, but be sure to consider that as you do the design and write the code.

If a system administrator wants to remove the user completely, a module would likely be created to manage this operation, as it would be the exception rather than the rule. For this example, we will implement NO ACTION on DELETE:

```
ALTER TABLE Messages.Message
    ADD CONSTRAINT FKMessagingUser$Sends$Messages_Message FOREIGN KEY
        (MessagingUserId) REFERENCES Attendees.MessagingUser(MessagingUserId)
            ON UPDATE NO ACTION
            ON DELETE NO ACTION;

ALTER TABLE Messages.Message
    ADD CONSTRAINT FKMessagingUser$IsSent$Messages FOREIGN KEY
        (SentToMessagingUserId) REFERENCES
                                Attendees.MessagingUser(MessagingUserId)
            ON UPDATE NO ACTION
            ON DELETE NO ACTION;
```

CASCADE operations (including SET NULL and SET DEFAULT, which give you additional possibilities for controlling cascading operations) are powerful tools to make coding easier, but can easily wipe out a lot of data. For example, if you cascade from MessagingUser to Message and UserConnection and then execute DELETE MessagingUser;, your data can be gone in a hurry.

The next relationship we will deal with is between Topic and MessageTopic. Deleting a Topic row, which likely is not a typical task anyhow, would not be a good candidate for deleting all of the messages that have used that topic, so hence set to DELETE NO ACTION and UPDATE NO ACTION:

```
ALTER TABLE Messages.MessageTopic
      ADD CONSTRAINT
        FKTopic$CategorizesMessagesVia$Messages_MessageTopic FOREIGN KEY
          (TopicId) REFERENCES Messages.Topic(TopicId)
      ON UPDATE NO ACTION
      ON DELETE NO ACTION;
```

The last relationship to implement is the MessageTopic to Message relationship. Just like the Topic to MessageTopic relationship, there is no need to automatically delete messages if the topic is deleted:

```
ALTER TABLE Messages.MessageTopic
      ADD CONSTRAINT FKMessage$isCategorizedVia$MessageTopic FOREIGN KEY
          (MessageId) REFERENCES Messages.Message(MessageId)
      ON UPDATE NO ACTION
      ON DELETE NO ACTION;
```

One of the other limitations on constraint-based FOREIGN KEY constraints that comes into play occasionally is that the tables participating in the relationship cannot span different databases (or different engine model transaction containers in that a memory-optimized table's FOREIGN KEY constraints cannot reference an on-disk table's constraints). When this situation occurs, these relationship types need to be implemented via triggers from the on-disk table or interpreted T-SQL stored procedures for in-memory tables.

While cross-container (as the memory-optimized and on-disk storage/transaction engines are commonly referred to) relationships may be useful at times (more on this in later chapters), it is considered a bad idea to design databases with cross-database relationships. A database should be considered a unit of related tables that are always kept in sync. When designing solutions that extend over different databases or even servers, carefully consider how spreading around references to data that isn't within the scope of the database will affect your solution. You need to understand that SQL Server cannot guarantee the existence of the value, and another user could restore a database with improper values, even an empty database, and the cross-database integrity of the data would be invalidated. Of course, as is almost always the case with anything that isn't best-practice material, there are times when cross-database relationships are unavoidable; and I'll demonstrate building triggers to support this need in the next chapter on data protection, and in Chapter 11, we will discuss more about how to secure cross-database access, but it is generally considered a less than optimal configuration.

Composite FOREIGN KEY Constraints and NULL Values

I haven't included any composite keys in this design, and I rarely do. However, one property of using composite keys is an essential topic when learning to use FOREIGN KEY constraints. I have noted that for optional relationships, the child columns are left as null. Constraints fail when their comparison is false, but what happens when there are NULL values in the child table because of that can be confusing, leaving you with data that looks wrong, but is allowed based on the table configuration.

For example, consider the following tables:

```
--table with a compound key
CREATE TABLE dbo.TwoPartKey
(
        Column1 int NOT NULL,
        Column2 int NOT NULL,
        CONSTRAINT PKTwoPartKey
          PRIMARY KEY (Column1,Column2)
);
--a row to reference
INSERT INTO dbo.TwoPartKey(Column1, Column2)
VALUES(1,1);
```

```
--table that references the two part key
CREATE TABLE dbo.TwoPartReference
(
        TwoPartReferenceId int NOT NULL
            CONSTRAINT PKTwoPartReference PRIMARY KEY,
        CONSTRAINT FKTwoPartReference$references$TwoPartKey
            FOREIGN KEY (Column1, Column2) REFERENCES
                dbo.TwoPartKey (Column1,Column2),
        Column1 int NULL,
        Column2 int NULL
);
```

The first table has two columns, Column1 and Column2, and the one row has a value of 1 for both columns. So if you insert a referencing row where both values are 1, it will succeed:

```
INSERT INTO dbo.TwoPartReference(TwoPartReferenceId, Column1, Column2)
VALUES(1,1,1);
```

Try to insert a row where Column1 and Column2 are not NULL values, but not both 1, and you will get an error:

```
INSERT INTO dbo.TwoPartReference(TwoPartReferenceId, Column1, Column2)
VALUES(2,1,2);
```

This is the error you will receive:

```
Msg 547, Level 16, State 0, Line 29
The INSERT statement conflicted with the FOREIGN KEY constraint "FKTwoP
artReference$references$TwoPartKey". The conflict occurred in database
"ConferenceMessaging", table "dbo.TwoPartKey".
```

But if one column has a NULL value, the other column can have any value legal for the column to hold, even if it does not exist in the parent table, for example:

```
INSERT INTO dbo.TwoPartReference(TwoPartReferenceId, Column1, Column2)
VALUES(3,237209334,NULL);
```

This will succeed and you can see the row in the table:

```
SELECT *
FROM dbo.TwoPartReference;
```

TwoPartReferenceId	Column1	Column2
1	1	1
3	237209334	NULL

Hence, you would need to add a CHECK constraint to the child table to check either both values are NULL or neither value is NULL.

Adding Basic CHECK Constraints

In our database, we have specified a couple of domains that need to be implemented a bit more strictly that a simple datatype can be used to implement. In most cases, to implement a column domain, we can use a simple CHECK constraint. CHECK constraints are simple, single-row predicates that can be used to validate the data in a row. The basic syntax is

```
ALTER TABLE <tableName> [WITH CHECK | WITH NOCHECK]
   ADD [CONSTRAINT <constraintName>]
   CHECK <BooleanExpression>
```

One thing interesting about CHECK constraints is how the <BooleanExpression> is evaluated. The <BooleanExpression> component is like the WHERE clause of a typical SELECT statement, but with the caveat that no subqueries are allowed. (Subqueries are allowed in standard SQL but not in T-SQL. In T-SQL, you must use a function to access other tables.)

CHECK constraints can reference system and user-defined functions (UDFs) and use the name or names of any columns in the table. However, they any row other than the current row being modified (except through a function and the row values you will be checking must already exist in the table). If multiple rows are modified, each row is checked against this expression individually.

The interesting thing about this expression is that, unlike a WHERE clause, the condition is checked for falseness rather than truthness (just as described earlier for FOREIGN KEY constraints). If the result of a Boolean expression is UNKNOWN because of any NULL comparison, the row will pass the CHECK constraint and be entered. Even if this isn't immediately confusing, it is often confusing when figuring out why an operation on a row did or did not work as you might have expected. For example, consider a possible CHECK constraint Boolean expression Value <> 'fred'. If Value is NULL, this is accepted, because NULL <> 'fred' evaluates to UNKNOWN. If Value is 'fred', it fails because 'fred' <> 'fred' evaluates to False. Where this truly gets complicated is when your CHECK constraint references multiple columns and/or has multiple expressions and just one of the column's values is NULL.

The reason for the way CHECK constraints work with Booleans is that if the column is defined as NULL, it is assumed that you wish to allow a NULL value for the column value. You can force the Boolean expression to return False by explicitly checking for NULL values using IS NULL or IS NOT NULL. This is useful when you want to ensure that a column that technically allows NULL values does not allow NULL values if another column has a given value. As an example, if you have a column defined as name varchar(10) NULL, having a CHECK constraint that says Value = 'fred' technically says Value = 'fred' or Value IS NULL. If you want to ensure it is not null if the column ValueIsNotNullFlag = 1, you would state ((ValueIsNotNullFlag = 1 and Value is not null) or (ValueIsNotNullFlag = 0)). This is the same as the compound foreign key concern, where you would want to make sure that either all referencing columns are NULL or none of them is.

Note that the [WITH CHECK | WITH NOCHECK] specification works just as it did for FOREIGN KEY constraints, so even if the CHECK constraint says Value <> 'fred', that is only guaranteed if you declare the constraint using WITH CHECK. Chapter 8 will cover more on enabling and checking constraints.

In our model, we had two domain predicates specified in the text that we will implement here. The first is the TopicName, which called for us to make sure that the value is not an empty string or all space characters. I repeat it here in Table 7-2 for review.

Table 7-2. *Domain: TopicName*

Property	Setting
Name	TopicName.
Optional	No.
Datatype	Unicode text, 30 characters.
Value limitations	Must not be an empty string or only space characters.
Default value	N/A.

The maximum length of 30 characters was handled by the datatype nvarchar(30) we used, but now we will implement the rest of the value limitations. The method I will use for this is to do a TRIM on the value and then check the length. If it is 0, it is either all spaces or empty. We used the TopicName domain for two columns, the TopicName column from Messages.Topic and the UserDefinedTopicName column from the Messages.MessageTopic table:

```
ALTER TABLE Messages.Topic
    ADD CONSTRAINT CHKTopic_TopicName_NotEmpty
        CHECK (LEN(TRIM(TopicName)) > 0); --NOTE: TRIM introduced in 2017
                                    --Use RTRIM(LTRIM in earlier
versions

ALTER TABLE Messages.MessageTopic
    ADD CONSTRAINT CHKMessageTopic_UserDefinedTopicName_NotEmpty
        CHECK (LEN(TRIM(UserDefinedTopicName)) > 0);
```

The other domain we specifically mentioned was for the UserHandle, as repeated in Table 7-3.

Table 7-3. *Domain: UserHandle*

Property	Setting
Name	UserHandle.
Optional	No.
Datatype	Basic character set, maximum of 20 characters.
Value limitations	Must be 5–20 simple alphanumeric characters and start with a letter.
Default value	N/A.

To implement this domain, things get a bit more interesting:

```
ALTER TABLE Attendees.MessagingUser
  ADD CONSTRAINT CHKMessagingUser_UserHandle_LengthAndStart
    CHECK (LEN(TRIM(UserHandle)) >= 5
            AND TRIM(UserHandle) LIKE '[a-z]' +
                    REPLICATE('[a-z1-9]',LEN(RTRIM(UserHandle)) -1));
--Note, this REPLICATE expression only works as is for case
--insensitive collation, more ranges needed for case sensitive ones
--and you could use an accent sensitive collation if you wanted to include
--accented characters.
```

The first part of the CHECK constraint Boolean expression simply checks to see if the string is longer than five characters. The second part creates a LIKE expression that checks that the name starts with a letter and that the following characters are only alphanumeric. It looks like it might be slow, based on the way we are taught to write WHERE clause expressions, but in this case, you aren't searching but are working on a single row already in memory.

Finally, we have one other predicate that we need to implement. Back in the requirements, it was specified that in the MessageTopic table, we need to make sure that the UserDefinedTopicName is NULL unless the Topic that is chosen is the one set up for the UserDefined topic. So we will create a new row. Since the surrogate key of MessageTopic is a default constraint using a sequence, we can simply enter the row specifying the TopicId as 0:

```
INSERT INTO Messages.Topic(TopicId, TopicName, Description)
VALUES (0,'User Defined','User Enters Their Own User Defined Topic');
```

Then, we add the constraint, checking to make sure that the UserDefinedTopicId is NULL if the TopicId = 0 and vice versa:

```
ALTER TABLE Messages.MessageTopic
  ADD CONSTRAINT CHKMessageTopic_UserDefinedTopicName_NullUnlessUserDefined
    CHECK ((UserDefinedTopicName IS NULL and TopicId <> 0)
                OR (TopicId = 0 AND UserDefinedTopicName IS NOT NULL));
```

Be sure to be as specific as possible with your predicate, as it will make implementation a lot safer. Now, we have implemented all the CHECK constraints we are going to for our demonstration database. In the "Unit Testing Your Structures" section later in this chapter, one of the most important things to test are the CHECK constraints (and if you have done any advanced data integrity work in triggers, which we will leave to later chapters).

Triggers to Maintain Automatic Values

For all our tables, I included two columns that we are going to implement as automatically maintained columns. These columns are the RowCreateTime and RowLastUpdateTime columns. These columns are useful to help us get an idea of some of the actions that have occurred on our row. Automatically generated values are not limited to implementation columns like these Row%-prefixed columns, but most often, we are implementing them strictly for software's sake, hence the reason that we will implement them in such a manner that the client cannot modify the values. A big difference between implementation columns and user-facing columns is that we will code our triggers to ensure that the data in the column cannot be overridden without disabling the trigger.

I will do this with an INSTEAD OF trigger, which will, for the most part, be a very smooth way to manage automatic operations on the base table, but it does have a few downsides:

- SCOPE_IDENTITY() will no longer return the identity value that is set in the row, since the actual insert will be done in the trigger, outside of the scope of the code. @@IDENTITY will work, but it has its own issues, particularly with triggers that perform cascading operations.

- An OUTPUT clause on a modification DML statement will not work if you have triggers on the table.

The SCOPE_IDENTITY() issue can be gotten around by using an AFTER trigger for an INSERT (which I will include as a sample in this section). I personally suggest that you consider using a SEQUENCE-based key or use one of the natural keys you have implemented to get the inserted value if you are inserting a single row. I only made one table use a SEQUENCE because so many tables will use an IDENTITY column for surrogate keys because they are easy to implement, and many tools will use that method.

One of the downsides of TRIGGER objects can be performance, so sometimes, automatically generated values will simply be maintained by the SQL code that uses the tables, or perhaps the columns are simply removed. I far prefer a server-based solution, because clock synchronization can be an issue when even two distinct servers are involved with keeping time. So, if an action says it occurred at 12:00 AM by the table, you look in the log and, at 12:00 AM, everything looks fine, but at 11:50 PM there was a glitch of some sort. Are they related? It is not possible to know to the degree you might desire because the client's clock may be off by 10 minutes.

As it is my favored mechanism for maintaining automatically maintained columns, I will implement triggers for tables, other than Attendees.AttendeeType, because, you should recall, we will not enable end users to make changes to the data, so tracking changes will not be needed.

To build the triggers, I will use the trigger templates that are included in Appendix B as the basis for the triggers. If you want to know more about the basics of triggers and how these templates are constructed, check Appendix B. The basics of how the triggers work should be very self-explanatory. The code added to the base trigger template from the appendix will be highlighted in bold.

In the following INSTEAD OF INSERT TRIGGER object, we will replicate the operation of INSERT on the table, passing through the values from the user insert operation, but replacing the RowCreateTime and RowLastUpdateTime with the function SYSDATETIME(). One quick topic I should briefly mention about triggers is multirow operations. Well-written triggers take into consideration that any INSERT, UPDATE, or DELETE statement may affect multiple rows in one execution. The inserted and deleted virtual tables house the rows that have been created or removed by the operation. (For an update, think of rows as being deleted and then inserted, at least logically.)

```
CREATE TRIGGER MessageTopic$InsteadOfInsertTrigger
ON Messages.MessageTopic
INSTEAD OF INSERT AS
BEGIN
```

```
DECLARE @msg varchar(2000),      --used to hold the error message
--use inserted for insert or update trigger, deleted for update or
--delete trigger count instead of @@rowcount due to merge behavior that
--sets @@rowcount to a number that is equal to number of merged rows,
--not rows being checked in trigger
        @rowsAffected int = (select count(*) from inserted)

--no need to continue on if no rows affected
IF @rowsAffected = 0 RETURN;

SET NOCOUNT ON; --to avoid the rowcount messages
SET ROWCOUNT 0; --in case the client has modified the rowcount

BEGIN TRY
   --[validation section]
   --[modification section]
   --<perform action>
   INSERT INTO Messages.MessageTopic (MessageId, UserDefinedTopicName,
                         TopicId,RowCreateTime,RowLastUpdateTime)
   SELECT MessageId, UserDefinedTopicName, TopicId,
          SYSDATETIME(), SYSDATETIME()
   FROM   inserted ;
END TRY
BEGIN CATCH
   IF @@trancount > 0
       ROLLBACK TRANSACTION;

   THROW; --will halt the batch or be caught by the caller's catch block

   END CATCH;
END;
```

For the UPDATE operation, we will do very much the same thing, only when we replicate the UPDATE operation, we will make sure that the RowCreateTime stays the same, no matter what the user might send in the update, and the RowLastUpdateTime will be replaced by SYSDATETIME():

```
CREATE TRIGGER Messages.MessageTopic$InsteadOfUpdateTrigger
ON Messages.MessageTopic
INSTEAD OF UPDATE AS
BEGIN

    DECLARE @msg varchar(2000),     --used to hold the error message
    --use inserted for insert or update trigger, deleted for update or
    --delete trigger count instead of @@rowcount due to merge behavior that
    --sets @@rowcount to a number that is equal to number of merged rows,
    --not rows being checked in trigger
            @rowsAffected int = (select count(*) from inserted)
            --@rowsAffected = (select count(*) from deleted)

    --no need to continue on if no rows affected
    IF @rowsAffected = 0 RETURN;

    SET NOCOUNT ON; --to avoid the rowcount messages
    SET ROWCOUNT 0; --in case the client has modified the rowcount

    BEGIN TRY
            --[validation section]
            --[modification section]
            --<perform action>
        UPDATE MessageTopic
        SET    MessageId = Inserted.MessageId,
               UserDefinedTopicName = Inserted.UserDefinedTopicName,
               TopicId = Inserted.TopicId,
               --no changes allowed
               RowCreateTime = MessageTopic.RowCreateTime,
               RowLastUpdateTime = SYSDATETIME()
        FROM   inserted
                   JOIN Messages.MessageTopic
                       ON inserted.MessageTopicId =
                                         MessageTopic.MessageTopicId;
```

```
END TRY
BEGIN CATCH
   IF @@TRANCOUNT > 0
       ROLLBACK TRANSACTION;

   THROW; --will halt the batch or be caught by the caller's catch block

  END CATCH;
 END;
```

If you find using an INSTEAD OF INSERT TRIGGER object too invasive of a technique, particularly due to the loss of SCOPE_IDENTITY(), you can change to using an after trigger. For an after trigger, you only need to update the columns that are important. For example, we could have created the INSERT TRIGGER like this (both of the following objects are commented out in the downloads)

```
CREATE TRIGGER MessageTopic$InsertRowControlsTrigger
ON Messages.MessageTopic
AFTER INSERT AS
BEGIN

   DECLARE @msg varchar(2000),     --used to hold the error message
   --use inserted for insert or update trigger, deleted for update or
   --delete trigger count instead of @@rowcount due to merge behavior that
   --sets @@rowcount to a number that is equal to number of merged rows,
   --not rows being checked in trigger
          @rowsAffected int = (select count(*) from inserted)
          --@rowsAffected = (select count(*) from deleted)

   --no need to continue on if no rows affected
   IF @rowsAffected = 0 RETURN;

   SET NOCOUNT ON; --to avoid the rowcount messages
   SET ROWCOUNT 0; --in case the client has modified the rowcount

   BEGIN TRY
      --[validation section]
      --[modification section]
     UPDATE Messages.MessageTopic
```

```
    SET     RowCreateTime = SYSDATETIME(),
            RowLastUpdateTime = SYSDATETIME()
    FROM    inserted
                JOIN Messages.MessageTopic
                ON inserted.MessageTopicId = MessageTopic.MessageTopicId;
END TRY
BEGIN CATCH
    IF @@trancount > 0
        ROLLBACK TRANSACTION;

    THROW; --will halt the batch or be caught by the caller's catch block

  END CATCH;
END;
```

and the update as

```
CREATE TRIGGER MessageTopic$UpdateRowControlsTrigger
ON Messages.MessageTopic
AFTER UPDATE AS
BEGIN

  DECLARE @msg varchar(2000),     --used to hold the error message
  --use inserted for insert or update trigger, deleted for update or
  --delete trigger count instead of @@rowcount due to merge behavior that
  --sets @@rowcount to a number that is equal to number of merged rows,
  --not rows being checked in trigger
          @rowsAffected int = (select count(*) from inserted)
          --@rowsAffected = (select count(*) from deleted)

  --no need to continue on if no rows affected
  IF @rowsAffected = 0 RETURN;

  SET NOCOUNT ON; --to avoid the rowcount messages
  SET ROWCOUNT 0; --in case the client has modified the rowcount

  BEGIN TRY
      --[validation section]
      --[modification section]
```

```
    UPDATE Messages.MessageTopic
    SET     RowCreateTime = deleted.RowCreateTime,
            RowLastUpdateTime = SYSDATETIME()
    FROM    inserted
                JOIN deleted
                  ON inserted.MessageTopicId = deleted.MessageTopicId
                JOIN Messages.MessageTopic
                  ON inserted.MessageTopicId = MessageTopic.MessageTopicId;
  END TRY
  BEGIN CATCH
     IF @@trancount > 0
         ROLLBACK TRANSACTION;

     THROW; --will halt the batch or be caught by the caller's catch block

   END CATCH;
 END;
```

It is a bit slower because it is updating the row after the operation has already occurred to the row(s) in the table, but not so much slower that it is worth the support time determining why the main process is broken. The most interesting part of the UPDATE TRIGGER object is that you need to make sure that you don't skip the RowCreateTime, but instead set it to the value in the deleted virtual object, so it is the value that it was originally, even if the data is updated by the user.

Another reason why an "instead of" trigger may not be allowed is if you have a cascade operation. For example, consider our relationship from MessagingUser to AttendeeType:

```
ALTER TABLE Attendees.MessagingUser
    ADD  CONSTRAINT FKMessagingUser$IsSent$Messages_Message
            FOREIGN KEY(AttendeeType)
            REFERENCES Attendees.AttendeeType (AttendeeType)
ON UPDATE CASCADE;
```

If you tried to create an INSTEAD OF TRIGGER object on this table with a CASCADE FOREIGN KEY object, you would see the following message:

```
Msg 2113, Level 16, State 1, Procedure MessagingUser$UpdateRowControlsTri
gger, Line 2 [Batch Start Line 663]
Cannot create INSTEAD OF DELETE or INSTEAD OF UPDATE TRIGGER 'Messaging
User$UpdateRowControlsTrigger' on table 'Attendees.MessagingUser'. This
is  because the table has a FOREIGN KEY with cascading DELETE or UPDATE.
```

I will not create a trigger for this table because this table doesn't need updates from a user, but it was there to give me the error message to show.

The Chapter 7.sql download for this chapter will have only the code found in the book, but in the "Chapter 7 - Database Create Objects.sql" file, I will include triggers for all the tables in our database. They will follow the same basic pattern, and because of this, I will almost always use some form of code generation tool to create these triggers. We discussed code generation earlier for building default constraints for these same columns, and you could do the very same thing for building triggers. I generally use a third-party tool to do code generation, but it is essential to the learning process that you code the first ones yourself, so you know how things work.

Documenting Your Database

In the modeling process, one of the things that has been emphasized has been to create descriptions, notes, and various pieces of data to help the other developers (and future you) understand the whys and wherefores of using the tables you've created. A great way to share this data is using SQL Server extended properties that allow you to store specific information about objects. Extended properties allow you to extend the metadata of your tables in ways that can be used by your applications using simple SQL statements.

By creating extended properties, you can build a repository of information that the application developers can use to do the following:

- Understand what the data in the columns is used for.

- Store information to use in applications, such as the following:

  - Captions to show on a form when a column is displayed

  - Advanced error messages to display when a constraint is violated

- Formatting rules for displaying or entering data

- Domain information, like the domain you have chosen for the column during design

To maintain extended properties, the following functions and stored procedures are provided:

- `sys.sp_addextendedproperty`: Used to add a new extended property

- `sys.sp_dropextendedproperty`: Used to delete an existing extended property

- `sys.sp_updateextendedproperty`: Used to modify an existing extended property

- `fn_listextendedproperty`: A system-defined function that can be used to list extended properties

- `sys.extendedproperties`: Can be used to list all extended properties in a database, less friendly than `fn_listextendedproperty`

The first four stored procedures and the table-valued function have an interface that has the parameters that follow this explanation. These parameters are fairly cryptic in nature, but not terribly complicated to understand once you use them a few times (I typically have made `STORED PROCEDURE` objects or scripts that wrap the stored procedures up into packages that use more straightforward variable names, when I have used them not from generated code):

- `@name`: The name of the user-defined property.

- `@value`: What to set the value to when creating or modifying a property. The datatype is `sql_variant`, with a maximum length limitation of 7500.

- `@level0type`: Top-level object type, often `'Schema'`, especially for most objects that users will use (tables, procedures, etc.).

- `@level0name`: The name of the object of the type that's identified in the `@level0type` parameter.

- `@level1type`: The name of the type of object such as `'Table'`, `'View'`, and so on.

- @level1name: The name of the object of the type that's identified in the @level1type parameter.

- @level2type: The name of the type of object that's on the level 2 branch of the tree under the value in the @level1Type value.
  For example, if @level1type is Table, then @level2type might be 'Column','Index','Constraint' or 'Trigger'.

- @level2name: The name of the object of the type that's identified in the @level2type parameter.

For simplicity's sake, I will just be adding a property with a description of the schema and Messages tables from the model, but you can add whatever bits of information you may want to enhance the schema, both in usage and for management tasks. For example, you might add an extended property to tell the reindexing schemes when or how to reindex a table's indexes. To document this table, let's add a property to the table and columns named Description. You execute the following script after creating the table (note that I used the descriptions as outlined in the start of the chapter for the objects):

```
--Messages schema
EXEC sp_addextendedproperty @name = 'Description',
   @value = 'Messaging objects',
   @level0type = 'Schema', @level0name = 'Messages';

--Messages.Topic table
EXEC sp_addextendedproperty @name = 'Description',
   @value = ' Pre-defined topics for messages',
   @level0type = 'Schema', @level0name = 'Messages',
   @level1type = 'Table', @level1name = 'Topic';

--Messages.Topic.TopicId
EXEC sp_addextendedproperty @name = 'Description',
   @value = 'Surrogate key representing a Topic',
   @level0type = 'Schema', @level0name = 'Messages',
   @level1type = 'Table', @level1name = 'Topic',
   @level2type = 'Column', @level2name = 'TopicId';
```

```
--Messages.Topic.Name
EXEC sp_addextendedproperty @name = 'Description',
   @value = 'The name of the topic',
   @level0type = 'Schema', @level0name = 'Messages',
   @level1type = 'Table', @level1name = 'Topic',
   @level2type = 'Column', @level2name = 'TopicName';

--Messages.Topic.Description
EXEC sp_addextendedproperty @name = 'Description',
   @value = 'Description of the purpose and utilization of the topics',
   @level0type = 'Schema', @level0name = 'Messages',
   @level1type = 'Table', @level1name = 'Topic',
   @level2type = 'Column', @level2name = 'Description';

--Messages.Topic.RowCreateTime
EXEC sp_addextendedproperty @name = 'Description',
   @value = 'Time when the row was created',
   @level0type = 'Schema', @level0name = 'Messages',
   @level1type = 'Table', @level1name = 'Topic',
   @level2type = 'Column', @level2name = 'RowCreateTime';

--Messages.Topic.RowLastUpdateTime
EXEC sp_addextendedproperty @name = 'Description',
   @value = 'Time when the row was last updated',
   @level0type = 'Schema', @level0name = 'Messages',
   @level1type = 'Table', @level1name = 'Topic',
   @level2type = 'Column', @level2name = 'RowLastUpdateTime';
```

Now, when you go into Management Studio, right-click the Messages.Topic table, and select Properties. Choose Extended Properties, and you see your description, as shown in Figure 7-6.

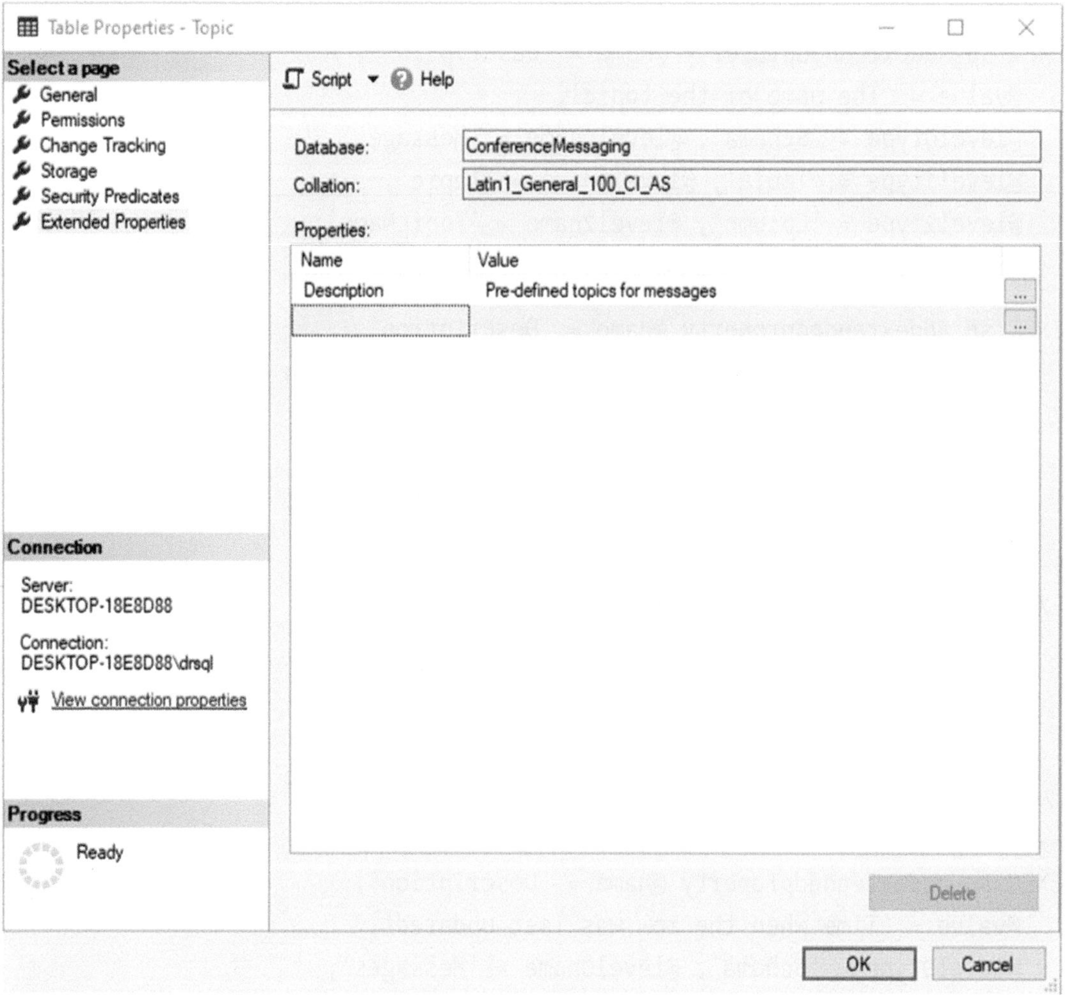

Figure 7-6. *Descriptions in Management Studio (reward for hard work done)*

The fn_listExtendedProperty object is a system-defined function you can use to fetch the extended properties (the parameters are as discussed earlier—the name of the property and then each level of the hierarchy):

```
SELECT objname, value
FROM   sys.fn_listExtendedProperty ( 'Description',
                                     'Schema','Messages',
                                     'Table','Topic',
                                      'Column',null);
```

This code returns the following results:

```
objname                 value
-------------------     ------------------------------------------------
TopicId                 Surrogate key representing a Topic
Name                    The name of the topic
Description             Description of the purpose and utilization of …
RowCreateTime           Time when the row was created
RowLastUpdateTime       Time when the row was last updated
```

In the code download, I have included descriptions for all the columns in the database. You aren't limited to tables, columns, and schemas either. Constraints, databases, and many other objects in the database can have extended properties.

Note   As of SQL Server 2019, extended properties are not available on memory-optimized tables.

Viewing the Basic System Metadata

In the process of implementing a database, knowing where to look in the system metadata for descriptive information about the model is extremely useful. Futzing around in the UI will give you a headache and is certainly not the easiest way to see all the objects at once, particularly to make sure everything seems to make sense. It is nice to have a set of queries you have at your fingertips to run and see the data in a query form.

There is a plethora of objects in the sys schema that will provide you details about the system. However, they can be a bit messier to use and aren't based on a standard that is generally applied to SQL Server, Oracle, and so on, so they're apt to change in future versions of SQL Server, just as these views replaced the system tables from versions of SQL Server before 2005. Of course, with the changes in 2005, it also became a lot easier to use the sys schema objects (the subset of which we are discussing now are commonly referred to as the system catalog which is data about data structures; other areas include dynamic management views to get data about the state of the system) to get metadata as well.

First, let's get a list of the schemas in our database. To view these, use the INFORMATION_SCHEMA.SCHEMATA view:

```
SELECT SCHEMA_NAME, SCHEMA_OWNER
FROM    INFORMATION_SCHEMA.SCHEMATA
WHERE   SCHEMA_NAME <> SCHEMA_OWNER;
```

Note that I limit the schemas to the ones that don't match their owners. SQL Server tools automatically create a schema for every user that gets created:

```
SCHEMA_NAME       SCHEMA_OWNER
---------------   -----------------

Messages          dbo
Attendees         dbo
```

Note   Why use the INFORMATION_SCHEMA views instead of the sys.
schema catalog views? I tend to use the INFORMATION_SCHEMA views as the INFORMATION_SCHEMA views have a lot of niceties that are useful for reporting on metadata that I want to view, such as returning readable names for all of the layers of database structure I am interested in, and the INFORMATION_SCHEMA views are based on standards so are less likely to change from version to version. The catalog views in the sys schema are more convenient for programming tasks like seeing if a schema exists or finding implementation details. One example is that indexes are not reflected in the INFORMATION_SCHEMA views, because indexes are a physical-only construct.

For tables and columns, we can use INFORMATION SCHEMA.COLUMNS, and with a little massaging, you can see the table, the column name, and the datatype in a format that is easy to use (neither the catalog views nor the INFORMATION_SCHEMA views do a good job of outputting the datatype in the proper compact format normally desired):

```
SELECT table_schema + '.' + TABLE_NAME as TABLE_NAME, COLUMN_NAME,
            --types that have a character or binary length
        case WHEN DATA_TYPE IN ('varchar','char','nvarchar',
```

```
                              'nchar','varbinary')
        THEN DATA_TYPE + CASE WHEN character_maximum_length = -1
                             THEN '(max)'
                             ELSE '('
                             + CAST(character_maximum_length as
                                            varchar(4)) + ')' END
          --types with a datetime precision
          WHEN DATA_TYPE IN ('time','datetime2','datetimeoffset')
              THEN DATA_TYPE +
                  '(' + CAST(DATETIME_PRECISION as varchar(4)) + ')'
          --types with a precision/scale
          WHEN DATA_TYPE IN ('numeric','decimal')
              THEN DATA_TYPE
                + '(' + CAST(NUMERIC_PRECISION as varchar(4)) + ','
                    + CAST(NUMERIC_SCALE as varchar(4)) +  ')'
          --timestamp should be reported as rowversion
          WHEN DATA_TYPE = 'timestamp' THEN 'rowversion'
          --and the rest. Note, float is declared with a bit length,
          --but is represented as either float or real in types
          else DATA_TYPE END AS DECLARED_DATA_TYPE,
      COLUMN_DEFAULT
FROM    INFORMATION_SCHEMA.COLUMNS
ORDER BY TABLE_SCHEMA, TABLE_NAME,ORDINAL_POSITION;
```

To see the constraints we have added to these objects (other than NULL specification and defaults, which were included in the previous results), you can use this code:

```
SELECT TABLE_SCHEMA, TABLE_NAME, CONSTRAINT_NAME, CONSTRAINT_TYPE
FROM    INFORMATION_SCHEMA.TABLE_CONSTRAINTS
WHERE   CONSTRAINT_SCHEMA IN ('Attendees','Messages')
ORDER   BY  CONSTRAINT_SCHEMA, TABLE_NAME;
```

To see the a list of triggers that have been created on the tables and what they will fire on, this statement will do it (note that triggers are not covered by the INFORMATION_SCHEMA views, as they too are part of the code, not part of the details that you would share with the users):

```
SELECT OBJECT_SCHEMA_NAME(parent_id) + '.'
                          + OBJECT_NAME(parent_id) AS TABLE_NAME,
           name AS TRIGGER_NAME,
           CASE WHEN is_instead_of_trigger = 1
                   THEN 'INSTEAD OF'
           ELSE 'AFTER' END AS TRIGGER_FIRE_TYPE
FROM    sys.triggers
WHERE   type_desc = 'SQL_TRIGGER' --not a clr trigger
     --DML trigger on a table or view
   AND   parent_class_desc = 'OBJECT_OR_COLUMN'
ORDER BY TABLE_NAME, TRIGGER_NAME;
```

Finally, if you need to see the CHECK constraints in the database, you can use the following:

```
SELECT   TABLE_SCHEMA + '.' + TABLE_NAME AS TABLE_NAME,
         TABLE_CONSTRAINTS.CONSTRAINT_NAME, CHECK_CLAUSE
FROM     INFORMATION_SCHEMA.TABLE_CONSTRAINTS
             JOIN INFORMATION_SCHEMA.CHECK_CONSTRAINTS
               ON TABLE_CONSTRAINTS.CONSTRAINT_SCHEMA =
                             CHECK_CONSTRAINTS.CONSTRAINT_SCHEMA
               AND TABLE_CONSTRAINTS.CONSTRAINT_NAME =
                             CHECK_CONSTRAINTS.CONSTRAINT_NAME
```

This is just a taste of the metadata available, and we will make use of the information schema and other catalog views throughout this book, rather than give you any screenshots of SSMS or any other query tools.

Tip   The INFORMATION_SCHEMA and catalog views are important resources for the DBA to find out what is in the database. Throughout this book, I will try to give insight into some of them, but there is another book's worth of information out there on the metadata of SQL Server.

Unit Testing Your Structures

Coding tables (and other bits of database code that we will look at in Chapter 13) is a lot of fun, but is not the end of the process as a programmer. Now that you have structures created, you need to create unit test scripts to make sure that what you expect out of your code is in fact the truth. For example, you need to insert good and bad data into your tables to make sure that they accept the good and reject the bad. There are some automated tools that are set up to help you with this task (a cursory search for "T-SQL testing" shows you testing tools and training classes to expand on the processes I will cover in this section).

Many people have different ideas of testing, particularly trying to treat a database like it is a normal coded object and set up a state for the objects (create or read in some data), try their code—perhaps a stored procedure, function, or trigger—and then delete the data once the test is complete. This technique works when you are trying to test a single module of code, but it is quite tedious when you want to test the entire database and you have to load 20 tables to test one procedure, one constraint, and so on as well as test that reports give you back respectable answers.

In this section, I will give you a simplistic version of testing your database structures that you can easily do for free. In it, I will use a single script that will run and basically insert data into your database and then test one or more situations with that data.

So far in this chapter, we have created a script to create a completely empty database. This is the database that we will use for our testing. Performance is of no concern, nor is concurrency. (Admittedly, if it takes 10 minutes to execute any of our tiny scripts, you should investigate the cause. But even if you have somehow loaded Windows and SQL Server onto a Raspberry Pi or Apple Watch, all the test scripts should still take considerably less than a second each).

For this pass of testing, we want to make sure that the database will save and deal with data and will catch data outside of the reasonable norm. I say "reasonable" because unless we have a real reason to do so, we won't be testing minimum and maximum values for a datatype, since we will trust that SQL Server can handle minimum and maximum values. We will also assume that FOREIGN KEY constraints work to validate INSERT, UPDATE, and DELETE statements and will not take time seeing what happens when we violate a constraint with an invalid key value. We will check that a delete operation with a cascading operation works where it needs to and not where it does not. In my real systems, we do include test scripts to verify the existence of the constraints we expect to have, but trust that if they are there and enabled, they work. For example, you

413

could create the following to check that a certain CHECK constraint still exists (this code is easy to generate as well):

```
IF NOT EXISTS (SELECT *
                FROM  sys.check_constraints
                WHERE OBJECT_SCHEMA_NAME(check_constraints.parent_object_id)
                                                         = 'Messages'
                  AND sys.check_constraints.name =
                                        'CHKTopic_TopicName_NotEmpty'
                  --be aware that SQL Server may reformat your constraint
                  AND   check_constraints.definition =
                                        '(LEN(Trim([TopicName]))>(0))'
                  AND check_constraints.is_disabled = 0)
  THROW 50000,'Check constraint CHKTopic_TopicName_NotEmpty does not exist
  or is disabled',1;
```

In the scripts I will build, I will be testing any CHECK constraints we have built because these are apt to be an issue, and we will check to make sure that triggers we have created work as well other than the basic RowCreated/RowLastModify ones that we will have unit tested as they were created.

Note   A comprehensive discussion of testing is beyond the scope I am going for with this book because complete testing requires involvement of the entire team. The unit test is generally the first of several testing steps, which include integration testing, user testing, performance testing, and so on. These will flow out of the application implementation that will be tested simultaneously. During unit testing our database structures, the goal will be simply to prove to ourselves that the code we created minimally performs the individual task that we expect it to.

The Chapter 7.sql download for this chapter will have only the code found in the book, but in the "Chapter 7 - Test Script" file, I will include these tests and a few others to test the database structures.

We will work with two types of scenarios: those we expect to work and those we expect to fail. For the scenarios we expect to succeed, we will check the row count after the statement and see if it is what we expect. If an error is raised, that will be self-explanatory. The tests follow the pattern

```
DECLARE @TestName nvarchar(100) = 'What we are doing';
BEGIN TRY
        <statement to test>;
        --if statement was expected to fail, then a THROW to say
        --that it should have failed
        THROW 50000,'No error raised',1;
END TRY
BEGIN CATCH
        DECLARE @msg nvarchar(4000) = CONCAT(@Testname,
          '; ErrorNumber:',ERROR_NUMBER(),' ErrorMessage:',ERROR_MESSAGE());
        --if error expected check error message not like some text
        IF ERROR_MESSAGE() NOT LIKE '%<constraint being violated>%'
                  --or if it wasn't supposed to fail this too.
                  THROW 50000,@msg,1;
END CATCH
```

The preceding example is a very minimalist method to test your structures, but even this will take quite a while to build, even for a smallish database. As the number of tables and columns climbs, the complexity rises exponentially. The goal is to build a test script that gradually loads up a database full of data and tests failures along the way (using our technique to quash errors that are expected) and ends up with a full database.

Note   In the download/GitHub repository, I have included a script file named Chapter 7 - Database Create Objects.sql that includes the minimal script to create the database and return the metadata. This will allow you to start with a clean database over and over without working through the entire chapter script if you modify something and things get out of sync.

The first step is to include DELETE statements to clear out all the data in the database, except for any data that is part of the base load. The goal here is to make your test script repeatable so you can run your script over and over, particularly if you get an error that you don't expect and you have to fix your structures:

```
SET NOCOUNT ON;
USE ConferenceMessaging;
GO
DELETE FROM Messages.MessageTopic ;
DELETE FROM Messages.Message;
DELETE FROM Messages.Topic WHERE TopicId <> 0; --Leave the User Defined Topic
DELETE FROM Attendees.UserConnection;
DELETE FROM Attendees.MessagingUser;
```

By deleting the data in the table, you will reset the data, but you won't reset the identity values and the sequence objects. This will help you to make sure that you aren't relying on certain identity values to test with. Next, I will add a legal user to the MessagingUser table:

```
DECLARE @TestName nvarchar(100) = 'Attendees.MessagingUser Single Row';
BEGIN TRY
        INSERT INTO [Attendees].[MessagingUser]
                            ([UserHandle],[AccessKeyValue],[AttendeeNumber]
                            ,[FirstName],[LastName],[AttendeeType]
                            ,[DisabledFlag])
        VALUES ('SamJ','0000000000','00000000','Sam',
                                        'Johnson','Regular',0);
END TRY
BEGIN CATCH
        DECLARE @msg nvarchar(4000) = CONCAT(@Testname,
                                        '; ErrorNumber:',ERROR_NUMBER(),
                                        ' ErrorMessage:',ERROR_MESSAGE());
        THROW 50000, @msg,16;
END CATCH;
```

Next, I will test entering data that fails one of the check constraints. In the next statement, I will enter data with a user handle that is too small. If there is no error, we throw an error. If the error message doesn't match the constraint name we expect, then we get the failure message too:

```
DECLARE @TestName nvarchar(100) =
            'Check CHKMessagingUser_UserHandle_LengthAndStart';
BEGIN TRY
        INSERT INTO [Attendees].[MessagingUser]
                              ([UserHandle],[AccessKeyValue],[AttendeeNumber]
                              ,[FirstName],[LastName],[AttendeeType]
                              ,[DisabledFlag])
        VALUES ('Wil','0000000000','00000001','Wilma',
                                        'Johnson','Regular',0);
        THROW 50000,'No error raised',1;
END TRY
BEGIN CATCH
        DECLARE @msg nvarchar(4000) = CONCAT(@Testname,
                                '; ErrorNumber:',ERROR_NUMBER(),
                                ' ErrorMessage:',ERROR_MESSAGE());
        IF ERROR_MESSAGE() NOT LIKE
                    '%CHKMessagingUser_UserHandle_LengthAndStart%'
            THROW 50000,@msg,1;
END CATCH;
```

When you execute this batch, you won't get an error if the constraint you expect to fail is mentioned in the error message (and it will be if you have built the same database I have, which I know is hard when following along in the text of a book when you want to try things... hence the file that just has table created separately). Then, I will enter another row that fails the check constraint due to the use of a nonalphanumeric character` in the handle:

```
DECLARE @TestName nvarchar(100) =
            'Check CHKMessagingUser_UserHandle_LengthAndStart';
BEGIN TRY --Check UserHandle Check Constraint
        INSERT INTO [Attendees].[MessagingUser]
                              ([UserHandle],[AccessKeyValue],[AttendeeNumber]
```

```
                       ,[FirstName],[LastName],[AttendeeType]
                       ,[DisabledFlag])
        VALUES ('Wilma@','0000000000','00000001',
                'Wilma','Johnson','Regular',0);
        THROW 50000,'No error raised',1;
END TRY
BEGIN CATCH
        DECLARE @msg nvarchar(4000) = CONCAT(@Testname,
                              '; ErrorNumber:',ERROR_NUMBER(),
                              ' ErrorMessage:',ERROR_MESSAGE());

        IF ERROR_MESSAGE() NOT LIKE
             '%CHKMessagingUser_UserHandle_LengthAndStart%'
                THROW 50000,@msg,1;
END CATCH;
```

Tip   In the previous block of code, the statement fails, but no error is returned. The goal is that you can run your test script over and over and get no output other than seeing rows in your tables. If you would prefer, add more output to your test script as best suits your desire.

Skipping some of the simpler test items, we now arrive at a test of the UNIQUE constraint we set up based on the RoundedMessageTime that rounds the MessageTime to the hour. (Some of the data to support these tests are included in the sample code.) To test this, I will enter a row into the table and then immediately enter another at the same time. If you happen to run this on a slow machine right at the turn of the hour, although it is extremely unlikely, the two statements execute in the same second (probably even the same millisecond):

```
DECLARE @TestName nvarchar(100) = 'Messages.Messages Single Insert';
BEGIN TRY
        INSERT INTO [Messages].[Message]
            ([MessagingUserId]
                    ,[SentToMessagingUserId]
            ,[Text]
            ,[MessageTime])
```

```
    VALUES
      ((SELECT MessagingUserId FROM Attendees.MessagingUser
        WHERE UserHandle = 'SamJ')
      ,(SELECT MessagingUserId FROM Attendees.MessagingUser
        WHERE UserHandle = 'WilmaJ')
      ,'It looks like I will be late tonight'
        ,SYSDATETIME());
END TRY
BEGIN CATCH
      DECLARE @msg nvarchar(4000) = CONCAT(@Testname,
                        '; ErrorNumber:',ERROR_NUMBER(),
                        ' ErrorMessage:',ERROR_MESSAGE());
      THROW 50000, @msg,16;
END CATCH;
```

Then, this statement will cause an error that should be caught in the CATCH block:

```
DECLARE @TestName nvarchar(100) = 'AKMessage_TimeUserAndText';
BEGIN TRY
  INSERT INTO [Messages].[Message]
                ([MessagingUserId]
                ,[SentToMessagingUserId]
                ,[Text]
                ,[MessageTime])
      VALUES
        --Row1
        ((SELECT MessagingUserId FROM Attendees.MessagingUser
          WHERE UserHandle = 'SamJ')
        ,(SELECT MessagingUserId FROM Attendees.MessagingUser
          WHERE UserHandle = 'WilmaJ')   --
        ,'It looks like I will be late tonight',SYSDATETIME()),

        --Row2
        ((SELECT MessagingUserId FROM Attendees.MessagingUser
          WHERE UserHandle = 'SamJ')
        ,(SELECT MessagingUserId FROM Attendees.MessagingUser
          WHERE UserHandle = 'WilmaJ')   --
```

```
            ,'It looks like I will be late tonight',SYSDATETIME());
        THROW 50000,'No error raised',1;
END TRY
BEGIN CATCH
        DECLARE @msg nvarchar(4000) = CONCAT(@Testname,
                        '; ErrorNumber:',ERROR_NUMBER(),
                        ' ErrorMessage:',ERROR_MESSAGE());
    IF ERROR_MESSAGE() NOT LIKE '%AKMessage_TimeUserAndText%'
                THROW 50000, @msg,16;
END CATCH;
```

If the error occurs, it is trapped, and we know the constraint is working. If no error occurs, then the no error THROW will. Finally, I will show in the text the most complicated error checking block we have to deal with for this database. This is the message and the message Topic. In the download, I insert the two successful cases, first for a specific topic and then with a user-defined topic.

In the next block, I will show the failure case:

```
DECLARE @TestName nvarchar(100) =
        'CHKMessageTopic_UserDefinedTopicName_NullUnlessUserDefined';
--Usually the client would pass in these values
DECLARE @messagingUserId int, @text nvarchar(200),
        @messageTime datetime2, @RoundedMessageTime datetime2(0);

SELECT @messagingUserId = (SELECT MessagingUserId
                            FROM Attendees.MessagingUser
                            WHERE UserHandle = 'SamJ'),
        @text = 'Oops Why Did I say That?', @messageTime = SYSDATETIME();

--uses same algorithm as the check constraint to calculate part of the key
SELECT @RoundedMessageTime = (
        DATEADD(HOUR,DATEPART(HOUR,@MessageTime),
            CONVERT(datetime2(0),CONVERT(date,@MessageTime))));

IF NOT EXISTS (SELECT * FROM  Messages.Topic WHERE Name = 'General Topic')
    INSERT INTO Messages.Topic(Name, Description)
    VALUES('General Topic','General Topic');
```

```
BEGIN TRY
   BEGIN TRANSACTION;
   --first create a new message
   INSERT INTO Messages.Message
            (MessagingUserId, SentToMessagingUserId, Text,MessageTime)
   VALUES (@messagingUserId,NULL,@text, @messageTime);

   --then insert the topic, but this will fail because General topic is not
   --compatible with a UserDefinedTopicName value
   INSERT INTO Messages.MessageTopic
                (MessageId, TopicId, UserDefinedTopicName)
   VALUES(       (SELECT MessageId
                 FROM    Messages.Message
                 WHERE   MessagingUserId = @messagingUserId
                   AND   Text = @text
                   AND   RoundedMessageTime = @RoundedMessageTime),
                                (SELECT TopicId
                                 FROM Messages.Topic
                                 WHERE Name = 'General Topic'),
                                'Stupid Stuff');
   COMMIT TRANSACTION;
END TRY
BEGIN CATCH
        IF @@TRANCOUNT > 0
              ROLLBACK;

        DECLARE @msg nvarchar(4000) = CONCAT(@Testname,
                            '; ErrorNumber:',ERROR_NUMBER(),
                            ' ErrorMessage:',ERROR_MESSAGE());
     IF ERROR_MESSAGE() NOT LIKE
              '%CHKMessageTopic_UserDefinedTopicName_NullUnlessUserDefined%'
          THROW 50000,@msg,1;
END CATCH;
```

The test script provided with the download is just a very basic example of a test script, and it will take a while to get a good unit test script created. It took me several hours to create this one for this simple six-table database, to nail down the places where

421

I had not quite gotten things right as I was putting together the chapter. However, once you get a template down that works for your needs, it is a matter of naming each test and coding the statement to test. Some of the statements can get complex, as I have demonstrated, but the process is generally not difficult.

Once the process of building your unit tests is completed, you will find that it will have helped you find issues with your design and any problems with constraints. In many cases, you may not want to put certain constraints on the development server immediately and work with developers to know when they are ready. As a database developer, and a lapsed UI developer, I personally liked it when the database prevented me from breaking a fundamental rule, so your mileage may vary as to what works best with the people you work with/against. I will say this, as I created this script, I discovered a few semi-significant issues with the demo design I created for this chapter that wouldn't have likely been noticed by simple observation, without actually taking the time to test the code.

Best Practices

The following are a set of some of the most important best practices when implementing your database structures. Pay attention to the advice about UNIQUE constraints. Just having a surrogate key on a table is one of the worst mistakes made when implementing a database:

- *Understand the relational engines and choose wisely*: With the classic on-disk engine model and the in-memory model coexisting in SQL Server, you have more choices than ever to produce highly concurrent database solutions. Most relational database projects do not need the in-memory model, but for those that do, you can get tremendous performance for some or all the tables in your database.

- *Implement foreign keys using foreign key constraints*: They're fast, and no matter what kind of gaffes a client makes, the relationship between tables cannot be messed up if a foreign key constraint is in place.

- *Maintain your naming standards*: Just because the database is being created is no reason to toss your naming conventions aside. Continue to be diligent, naming objects following an easy to remember standard that works for you (just leave off the tbl_ prefix!)

- *Document and maintain scripts of* everything: Using extended properties to document your objects can be extremely valuable. Most of all, when you create objects in the database, keep scripts of the T-SQL code for later use when moving to the QA and production environments. Keeping your scripts versioned in a source control repository is a definite good next step as well so you can see where you are, where you are going, and where you have been in one neat location.

- *Test your database, at least with a simple test script*: Test your structures as much as possible. Testing is often the forgotten step in database implementation, leaving it until the UI is created to let them test out the structures, but early testing is very useful to know that your design works.

Deployment Lifecycle

As you complete the DDL and complete as much of the unit testing as you can, usually there are other people who are waiting to build UIs, reports, object models, and so on. So, when you arrive at that point in the dev process that your DDL is ready to go, things get real.

The next step is to provide a real database for your teammates to work with, one that you don't drop and recreate over and over. There are two steps to deploying a database script:

- *Brand-new database*: This is easy. Simply use the script you used for testing. Sadly, this usually only works once per database, out of the 100s to 1000s of times you will need the following step. The biggest difference will likely be that the DBA will want to locate the database on standard drive locations. Physical structures are covered more in Chapter 11.

- *Subsequent builds of the database*: Databases are different from most other types of software programming because tables have state information. If you change the design, you must retrofit the data into the new objects. The method I have adopted is to generate the database that I test with and consider it the "model" database. No code, no data (other than model/domain data like was included in the Messaging database for type of messaging user and topic), just what was in the design. From there I use a comparison tool to generate the differences between the model and the live database, verify the script, and apply.

I need to describe just a bit more about the second step of the process. What is described is rather simplified from the myriad of possible methods of applying changes. I use the mentioned process of creating a model database, and then I compare it to a database that is mirrored in source control using Redgate's SQL Source Control tool and apply the changes. (Microsoft's Visual Studio Data Tools Extension has similar functionality as part of the tools as well.) After checking in the changes, this is used with Redgate's SQL Compare tools to apply structure changes to multiple developer servers and then to dev, test, and finally prod servers.

Visual Studio has lifecycle steps built in, and that tool works a lot more like what Visual Studio programmers are used to, if that suits you. And other companies have other tools to help manage the database lifecycle as well.

The primary idea that I am advocating here in this section is that you keep a pristine copy of your database that has the objects as you designed them from a modeling tool or script set and then run your unit tests on it. From there, figure out a method of getting your changes to the other members of your team that works for you.

Summary

Understanding how to build tables, and how they're implemented, is the backbone of every database designer's knowledge. After getting satisfied that a model was ready to implement in the previous chapter, I went through the process of creating the database using the CREATE TABLE and ALTER TABLE syntax for adding and creating tables, adding constraints and modifying columns, and even creating triggers to manage automatically maintained columns.

At this point in the process, you have created a database, one that could actually do the job of implementing a solution to solve a real-world problem if one was so inclined. While it was a very small example, it had all the pieces and parts that you need in a fully working database (and the code for the entire system is included in the downloads for the book, in both on-disk and in-memory versions).

In the rest of the book, we will continually expand on the topics of this and the previous chapter. Taking the simplistic example, building more and more complex objects, and digging deeper into the behaviors of SQL Server will take your designs from the simplicity of this chapter and allow you to create complex, high-performance database solutions.

CHAPTER 8

Data Protection Patterns with Check Constraints and Triggers

The world will not be destroyed by those who do evil, but by those who watch them without doing anything.

—Albert Einstein

One of the weirdest things I see in database implementations is that people spend tremendous amounts of time designing the correct database storage (or, at least, what seems like tremendous amounts of time to them designing something that is as good as they can) and then just leave the data unprotected with tables being more or less buckets that will accept anything, opting to let code outside of the database layer to do all of the data protection aside from perhaps using an integer datatype to hold whole numbers. Honestly, I do understand the allure in that the more constraints you apply, the harder development is in the early stages of the project, and the programmers honestly do believe that they will catch everything. The problem is there is rarely a way to be 100% sure that all code written will always enforce every rule.

A particularly interesting argument against using automatically enforced data protection is that programmers want complete control over the errors they will get back and over what events may occur that can change data. I am for this also, as I don't want to use a "dumb" client server application in the year 2020. The UI should catch all the errors it can before starting a transaction with the server, but UI code can never really be 100% trustworthy, for matters of concurrency. In the moments from the time the UI checks for the existence of a customer to the time the invoices are saved, anything can happen.

© Louis Davidson 2021
L. Davidson, *Pro SQL Server Relational Database Design and Implementation*,
https://doi.org/10.1007/978-1-4842-6497-3_8

When the table itself says no bad data, you can be completely sure that it contains no bad data (as much as you have designed and implemented what "bad data" means). The UI needs to duplicate some of the rules that have been specified to provide a good experience to the user. The data layer's error messaging is atrocious, even using a few techniques to map error messages to descriptions. Even if you could make sure that every possible interface that accesses that database implements every rule (even the DBA doing an import, which is oddly a very common source of data), the problem is there are data issues that simply cannot be caught anywhere other than the data layer (certainly without holding locks on all of the data in the database).

No matter how many times I've forgotten to apply a UNIQUE constraint in a place where one should be, data duplications would start to occur, even if the other layers of the application were theoretically protecting against the very same duplication of data. Ultimately, user perception is governed by the reliability and integrity of the data that users retrieve from your database. If they detect data anomalies in their data sets (usually in skewed report values or duplicated query results), their faith in the whole application plummets faster than a skydiving elephant who packed lunch instead of a parachute, and the pretty UI they use is not getting the blame.

One of the things I hope you will feel as you read this chapter is that, if possible, the data storage layer should own protection of the fundamental data integrity. We started in the previous chapter with FOREIGN KEY, UNIQUE, and a few basic CHECK constraints. One of those CHECK constraints was to make sure required input wasn't skipped past with a value like ' '. If this is violated, you will get a rather ugly error message; then the UI programmer gets a ticket to make sure that doesn't happen again.

This leads to a very specific argument that arises regarding the concept of putting code in multiple in that it's both

- Bad for performance

- More work

As C. S. Lewis had one of his evil characters in *The Screwtape Letters* note, "By mixing a little truth with it they had made their lie far stronger." The fact of the matter is that these are, in fact, true statements from one perspective, but these two arguments miss the point.

The first is that data can come from multiple locations:

- Users using custom, very well-built front-end tools

- Users using generic data manipulation tools, such as Microsoft Access

- Routines that import data from external sources

- Raw queries executed by data administrators to fix problems caused by user error

Each of these poses different issues for your integrity scheme. What's most important is that each of these scenarios (except for the second, perhaps) forms part of nearly every database system developed. To best handle each scenario, the data must be safeguarded, using mechanisms that work without the responsibility of the user, even the DBA fixing data who is very careful. If you decide to implement your fundamental data logic in a different tier other than directly in the database, you must make sure that you implement it—and, far more importantly, implement it *correctly*—in every single one of those clients/scenarios. If you update the rules, you must make sure they are changed in every location.

The second concern is really the most important. Because of concurrency, data validated in the UI typically is not guaranteed to in the same state as it was when you do the next step of a process, even milliseconds later. In Chapter 12, we will cover concurrency, but suffice it to say that errors arising from issues in concurrency are often exceedingly random in appearance and must be treated as occurring at any time. Concurrency is the final nail in the coffin of using a client tier as the single tier for integrity checking. Unless you elaborately single-thread access to the database objects you are using, the state could change, and a database error or inconsistency could occur. Are database errors annoying? Yes, they are, but they are the last line of defense between having excellent data integrity and something quite the opposite.

In this chapter, I will present more complex examples of using two building blocks of enforcing data integrity in SQL Server, first using declarative CHECK constraints, which allow you to define fairly complex predicates on new and modified rows in a table, and TRIGGER objects, which are stored procedure–style objects that can fire after a table's contents have changed and let you build insanely complex data checks, if they are necessary.

In SQL Server 2014 and later (with incremental improvements in later versions), the native compilation model that works with in-memory objects supports CHECK constraints and TRIGGER objects. In this chapter, I will focus only on interpreted code and on-disk objects. In Chapter 14, when we discuss creating code to access the tables we have created, I will cover some of the differences in code for interpreted and natively compiled modules, and the difference is great and figures into what can be coded in TRIGGER objects and CHECK constraints. Native compilation may improve more in upcoming versions, but as of 2019, it still has plenty of limitations. In the downloadable Appendix B, I will include a section on writing natively compiled TRIGGER objects as well as interpreted ones. And in the downloads for Chapter 7, there is a complete example of using memory-optimized tables to replicate the chapter-long database example that was implemented using on-disk tables.

CHECK Constraints

CHECK constraints are part of a class of the declarative data protection options. Basically, constraints are SQL Server devices that are used to enforce data integrity automatically on a single column or row. You should use constraints as extensively as possible to protect your data, because they're simple and, for the most part, have minimal overhead. This is particularly true of CHECK constraints, as they operate only on one row that is already in memory.

One of the greatest aspects of all of SQL Server's constraints (other than DEFAULT constraints) is that the query optimizer can use them to optimize queries, because the constraints can tell the optimizer some quality aspects of the data. For example, say you place a CHECK constraint on a column that requires that all values for a column must fall between 5 and 10. If a query is executed that asks for all rows with a value greater than 100 for that column, the optimizer will know without even looking at the data that no rows meet the criteria.

SQL Server has five kinds of declarative constraints:

- NULL: Determines if a column will accept NULL for its value. Though NULL constraints aren't technically named constraints you add on, they are generally regarded as, and referred to as, constraints.

- PRIMARY KEY *and* UNIQUE *constraints*: Used to make sure your rows contain only unique combinations of values over a given set of key columns.

- FOREIGN KEY: Used to make sure that any migrated keys have only valid values that match the key columns they reference.

- DEFAULT: Used to set an acceptable default value for a column when the user doesn't provide one. (Some people don't count defaults as constraints, because they don't constrain updates.)

- CHECK: Used to limit the values that can be stored in a single column or an entire row.

We have covered NULL, PRIMARY KEY, UNIQUE, and DEFAULT constraints in enough detail in Chapter 7; they are straightforward enough for their primary usage without a lot of variation in the ways you will use them. In this section, I will focus the examples on the various ways to use CHECK constraints to implement data protection patterns for your columns/rows. CHECK constraints are executed after DEFAULT constraints (so you cannot specify an expression in a DEFAULT constraint that would contradict a CHECK constraint, or at least if you do, you won't be able to insert a row!) and INSTEAD OF TRIGGER objects (covered later in this chapter) but before AFTER TRIGGER objects. CHECK constraints cannot affect the values being inserted or deleted.

The biggest complaint that is often lodged against constraints is about the horrible error messages you will get back. It is one of my biggest complaints as well, and there is very little you can do about it, although I will posit a solution to the problem later in this chapter that will at least help out when the error precedes implementation of a proper UI catch of a condition. It will behoove you to understand one important thing: all DML (and DDL) statements you execute from an application should have error handling as if the database might give you back an error—because it might. There are many different reasons, system issues, connectivity issues, concurrency issues like deadlocks, and so on. Having code to properly handle deadlocks will have you almost ready to use memory-optimized tables. So best to be prepared.

There are two flavors of CHECK constraint: *column* and *table*. Column CHECK constraints reference a single column and are used when an individual column is referenced in a modification. CHECK constraints are considered table constraints when more than one column is referenced in the criteria. Fortunately, you don't have to worry about declaring a constraint as either a column constraint or a table constraint, and it really doesn't make that much difference except for a little bit of metadata. When SQL Server compiles the constraint, it verifies whether it needs to check more than one column and sets the proper internal values.

We'll be looking at building CHECK constraints using two methods:

- Simple expressions

- Complex expressions using user-defined functions

The two methods are similar, but you can build more complex constraints using functions, though the code in a function can be more complex and difficult to manage. In this section, we'll look at some examples of CHECK constraints built using each of these methods; then we'll look at a scheme for dealing with errors from constraints. First, though, let's set up a simple schema that will form the basis of the examples in this section.

The examples in this section on creating CHECK constraints use the sample tables shown in Figure 8-1.

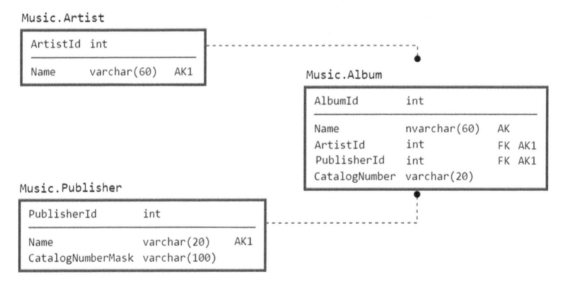

Figure 8-1. *The example schema*

To create and populate the tables, execute the following code (in the downloads, I include a simple CREATE DATABASE for a database named Chapter8 and will put all objects in that database):

```
CREATE SCHEMA Music;
GO
CREATE TABLE Music.Artist
(
    ArtistId int NOT NULL,
    Name varchar(60) NOT NULL,
```

```
   CONSTRAINT PKArtist PRIMARY KEY CLUSTERED (ArtistId),
   CONSTRAINT PKArtist_Name UNIQUE NONCLUSTERED (Name)
);
CREATE TABLE Music.Publisher
(
        PublisherId int CONSTRAINT PKPublisher PRIMARY KEY,
        Name varchar(20) NOT NULL,
        CatalogNumberMask varchar(100) NOT NULL
            CONSTRAINT DFLTPublisher_CatalogNumberMask DEFAULT ('%'),
        CONSTRAINT AKPublisher_Name UNIQUE NONCLUSTERED (Name),
);

CREATE TABLE Music.Album
(
        AlbumId int NOT NULL,
        Name varchar(60) NOT NULL,
        ArtistId int NOT NULL,
        CatalogNumber varchar(20) NOT NULL,
        PublisherId int NOT NULL,

        CONSTRAINT PKAlbum PRIMARY KEY CLUSTERED(AlbumId),
        CONSTRAINT AKAlbum_Name UNIQUE NONCLUSTERED (Name),
        CONSTRAINT FKArtist$records$Music_Album
            FOREIGN KEY (ArtistId) REFERENCES Music.Artist(ArtistId),
        CONSTRAINT FKPublisher$Published$Music_Album
            FOREIGN KEY (PublisherId)
                REFERENCES Music.Publisher(PublisherId)
);
```

Then seed the data with the following:

```
INSERT  INTO Music.Publisher (PublisherId, Name, CatalogNumberMask)
VALUES (1,'Capitol',
        '[0-9][0-9][0-9]-[0-9][0-9][0-9a-z][0-9a-z][0-9a-z]-[0-9][0-9]'),
        (2,'MCA', '[a-z][a-z][0-9][0-9][0-9][0-9][0-9]');

INSERT  INTO Music.Artist(ArtistId, Name)
VALUES (1, 'The Beatles'),(2, 'The Who');
```

```
INSERT INTO Music.Album (AlbumId, Name, ArtistId, PublisherId,
CatalogNumber)
VALUES (1, 'The White Album',1,1,'433-43ASD-33'),
       (2, 'Revolver',1,1,'111-11111-11'),
       (3, 'Quadrophenia',2,2,'CD12345');
```

A likely problem with this design is that it isn't normalized well enough for a complete solution. Publishers usually have a mask that's valid at a given point in time, but everything changes. If the publishers lengthen the size of their catalog numbers or change to a new format, what happens to the older data? For a functioning system, it would be valuable to have a release date column and catalog number mask that is valid for a given range of dates. Of course, if you implemented the table as presented, the enterprising user, to get around the improper design, would create publisher rows such as 'MCA 1989-1990', 'MCA 1991-1994', and so on and mess up the data for future reporting needs, because then, you'd have work to do to correlate values from the MCA company (and your table would be not even technically in First Normal Form!). The catalog mask format could easily be moved into its own table that had a from and to effective dates, but that would complicate the example too much.

CHECK Constraints Based on Simple Expressions

By far, most CHECK constraints are simple expressions that just test some characteristic of a value in a column or columns. These constraints often don't reference any data other than a single column, but can reference any of the columns in a single row.

As a few examples, consider the following:

- *Empty strings*: Prevent users from inserting one or more space characters to avoid any real input into a column, such as CHECK(LEN(ColumnName) > 0). This constraint is on 90% of the character columns in databases I design, to avoid the space character entry that drives you crazy when you don't expect it.

- *Date range checks*: Make sure a reasonable date is entered, for example:

    - The date a rental is required to be returned should be greater than one day after the RentalDate (assume the two columns are implemented with the date datatype): CHECK (ReturnDate > DATEADD(DAY,1,RentalDate)).

- The date of some event that's supposed to have occurred already in the past: CHECK(EventDate <= GETDATE()). Nothing better than finding out that the payment was sent out on January 12, 3020.

- *Value reasonableness*: Make sure some value, typically a number of some sort, is reasonable for the situation. "Reasonable," of course, does not imply that the value is necessarily correct for the given situation, which is usually the domain of the middle tier of objects— just that it is within a reasonable domain of values, for example:

  - Values needing to be a nonnegative integer: CHECK(MilesDriven >= 0). This constraint is commonly needed, because there are often columns where negative values don't make sense (hours worked, miles driven, etc.), but the intrinsic type will allow it (and it is the best type other than negative values).

  - Royalty rate for an author that's less than or equal to 30%. If this rate ever could be greater, it isn't a CHECK constraint. So, if 15% is the typical rate, the UI might warn that it isn't normal, but if 30% is the absolute ceiling, it would be a good CHECK constraint: CHECK (RoyaltyRate <= .3). I might lobby for that percentage to be a bit higher personally!

CHECK constraints of this variety are always a good idea when you have situations where there are data conditions that *must* always be true. Another way to put this is that the very definition of the data is being constrained, not just a convention that could change often or even be situationally different. These CHECK constraints are generally extremely fast and won't appreciably affect performance except in extreme situations. As a first example, consider the empty string check.

To avoid letting a user get away with a blank column value, you can add the following constraint. For example, in the Album table, the Name column doesn't allow NULLs. The user must enter something, but what about when the enterprising user realizes that ' ' is not the same as NULL? What will be the response to an empty string? Ideally, of course, the UI wouldn't allow such nonsense for a column that had been specified as being required, but the user just hits the space bar, but to make sure, we will want to code a constraint to avoid it.

The constraint simply works by using the LEN function that does a trim by default, eliminating any space characters, and checking the length:

```
ALTER TABLE Music.Album WITH CHECK
    ADD CONSTRAINT CHKAlbum$Name$noEmptyString
            CHECK (LEN(Name) > 0); --note,len does a trim by default, so
                            --any string of all space characters will return 0
```

Testing this with data that will clash with the new constraint

```
INSERT INTO Music.Album ( AlbumId, Name, ArtistId,
                            PublisherId, CatalogNumber )
VALUES ( 4, '', 1, 1,'dummy value' );
```

you get the following error message:

```
Msg 547, Level 16, State 0, Line 1
The INSERT statement conflicted with the CHECK constraint
"CHKAlbum$Name$noEmptyString". The conflict occurred in database
"Chapter8", table "Music.Album", column 'Name'.
```

All too often, nonsensical data is entered just to get around your warning, but that is more of a UI or managerial oversight problem than a database design concern, because the check to see whether 'ASDFASDF' is a reasonable name value is definitely not of the definite true/false variety (for example, Genesis's "Abacab" could look like gibberish, though it was a section progression through the song at one time).

What's generally the case is that the user interface might try to use some form of intelligence to prevent such data from being created, but the CHECK constraint is there to prevent other processes from putting in completely invalid data, no matter what the source of data. Realistically, what ends up happening is when garbage data like 'ASDFASDF' (assuming it is garbage) is manually handled, either by terminating employees who don't do a good job or deleting customers who weren't really customers, just someone on your website trying to get a free sample of software without sharing their personal data.

As a bit more complex example of a CHECK constraint, consider if you had a business rule that no artist with a name that contains the word 'Pet' *followed by the word* 'Shop' is allowed. You could code the rule as follows (note all examples assume a case-insensitive collation, which is almost certainly the normal; and we do not need to remove the empty string CHECK constraint either):

```
ALTER TABLE Music.Artist WITH CHECK
    ADD CONSTRAINT CHKArtist$Name$NoPetShopNames
            CHECK (Name NOT LIKE '%Pet Shop%');
```

Then, test by trying to insert a new row with an offending value:

```
INSERT INTO Music.Artist(ArtistId, Name)
VALUES (3, 'Pet Shop Boys');
```

This returns the following result, keeping my music collection database safe from at least one 1980s band.

```
Msg 547, Level 16, State 0, Line 1
The INSERT statement conflicted with the CHECK constraint "CHKArtist$Na
me$NoPetShopNames". The conflict occurred in database "Chapter8", table
"Music.Artist", column 'Name'.
```

When you create a CHECK constraint, the WITH NOCHECK setting (the default is WITH CHECK) gives you the opportunity to add the constraint without checking the existing data in the table.

Let's add a row for another musician whom I don't necessarily want in my table:

```
INSERT INTO Music.Artist(ArtistId, Name)
VALUES (3, 'Madonna');
```

Later in the process, it is desired that no artists with the word "Madonna" will be added to the database, but if you attempt to add a CHECK constraint to stop that name from being created, you will not get the "Commands completed successfully" message you so desire to see.

```
ALTER TABLE Music.Artist WITH CHECK
    ADD CONSTRAINT CHKArtist$Name$noMadonnaNames
            CHECK (Name NOT LIKE '%Madonna%');
```

Rather, you will see the following error message:

```
Msg 547, Level 16, State 0, Line 1
The ALTER TABLE statement conflicted with the CHECK constraint "CHKArtist$
Name$noMadonnaNames". The conflict occurred in database "Chapter8", table
"Music.Artist", column 'Name'.
```

Ideally, you will then change the contents of the table such that it will meet the requirements of the constraint. In order to allow the constraint to be added, you might specify the constraint using WITH NOCHECK rather than WITH CHECK because you now want to allow this new constraint, but there's data in the table that conflicts with the constraint, and it is deemed too costly to fix or clean up the existing data:

```
ALTER TABLE Music.Artist WITH NOCHECK
    ADD CONSTRAINT CHKArtist$Name$noMadonnaNames
            CHECK (Name NOT LIKE '%Madonna%');
```

The statement is executed to add the CHECK constraint to the table definition, and using NOCHECK means that the invalid value does not affect the creation of the constraint. This is OK in some cases but can be very confusing because any time a modification statement references the column, the CHECK constraint is fired. If you tried to add a row where the name was "Madonna Nash," it would fail, as desired, based on the criteria. (I just found this artist and am listening as I edit, and she is a country artist, which I like more than new wave!)

What is weird about this scenario is that the next time you try to set the value of the table to the same bad value, an error occurs. In the following statement, I simply set every row of the table to the same name it has stored in it:

```
UPDATE Music.Artist
SET Name = Name;
```

This produces the following error message:

```
Msg 547, Level 16, State 0, Line 1
The UPDATE statement conflicted with the CHECK constraint "CHKArtist$Na
me$noMadonnaNames". The conflict occurred in database "Chapter8", table
"Music.Artist", column 'Name'.
```

"What?" most users will exclaim (well, unless they are the support person at 3:00 AM wondering what is going on, in which case they will upgrade it to "WHAT?!?!"). "If the value was in the table, shouldn't it already be good?" The user is correct. A strategy to deal with changes in format or allowing older data to meet one criterion while new data fits a different one can be to include a time range for the values. CHECK Name NOT LIKE '%Madonna%' OR RowCreateDate < '20141131' could be a reasonable compromise—if the users understand what is going on with their queries, naturally.

Using NOCHECK and leaving the values unchecked is almost worse than leaving the constraint off in many ways.

Tip   If a data value could be right or wrong, based on external criteria, it is best not to be overzealous in your enforcement. The fact is, unless you can be 100% sure, when you use the data later, you will still need to make sure that the data is correct before usage.

If a constraint is built with WITH CHECK, it's considered trusted, because the optimizer can trust that all values conform to the CHECK constraint. You can determine whether a constraint is trusted by using the sys.check_constraints catalog object:

```
SELECT definition, is_not_trusted
FROM    sys.check_constraints
WHERE   object_schema_name(object_id) = 'Music'
  AND   name = 'CHKArtist$Name$noMadonnaNames';
```

This returns the following results (with some minor formatting, of course):

definition	is_not_trusted
(NOT [Name] like '%Madonna%')	1

Make sure, if possible, that is_not_trusted = 0 for all rows so that the system trusts all your CHECK constraints and the optimizer can use the information when building plans.

> **Caution**   Creating check constraints using the CHECK option (instead of NOCHECK) on a tremendously large table can take a very long time to apply, so often, you'll feel like you need to cut corners to get it done fast. The problem is that the shortcut on design or implementation often costs far more in later maintenance or, even worse, in the user experience. If at all reasonable, it's best to try to get everything set up properly, so there is no confusion.

To make the constraint trusted, you will need to clean up the data and use

```
ALTER TABLE <tableName> WITH CHECK CONSTRAINT ConstraintName;
```

This will have SQL Server check the constraint and set it to trusted. Of course, this method suffers from the same issues as creating the constraint with NOCHECK in the first place (mostly, it can take forever!). But without checking the data, the constraint will not be trusted, not to mention that forgetting to re-enable the constraint is too easy. For our constraint, we can try to check the values:

```
ALTER TABLE Music.Artist
    WITH CHECK CHECK CONSTRAINT CHKArtist$Name$noMadonnaNames;
```

And it will return the following error (as it did when we tried to create it the first time):

```
Msg 547, Level 16, State 0, Line 1
The ALTER TABLE statement conflicted with the CHECK constraint "CHKArtist$
Name$noMadonnaNames". The conflict occurred in database "Chapter8", table
"Music.Artist", column 'Name'.
```

Delete the row with the name Madonna.

```
DELETE FROM  Music.Artist
WHERE  Name = 'Madonna';
```

Now try to check the constraint again. The ALTER TABLE statement will be executed without error, and the constraint will be trusted (and all will be well with the world!). One last thing you can do is to disable a constraint, using NOCHECK:

```
ALTER TABLE Music.Artist NOCHECK CONSTRAINT CHKArtist$Name$noMadonnaNames;
```

Now, you can see that the constraint is disabled by adding an additional object property:

```
SELECT definition, is_not_trusted, is_disabled
FROM    sys.check_constraints
WHERE   OBJECT_SCHEMA_NAME(object_id) = 'Music'
  AND   name = 'CHKArtist$Name$noMadonnaNames';
```

This will return

definition	is_not_trusted	is_disabled
(NOT [Name] like '%Madonna%')	1	1

Then, rerun the statement to enable the statement before we continue:

```
ALTER TABLE Music.Artist
      WITH CHECK CHECK CONSTRAINT CHKArtist$Name$noMadonnaNames;
```

After that, checking the output of the sys.check_constraints query, you will see that it has been enabled.

These CHECK constraints are very useful when you are loading data into the table from an outside source. Often, when data is imported from a file, like from the SSMS Import Wizard, blank data will be propagated as blank values, and the programmers involved might not think to deal with this condition. The "Check constraints" setting makes sure that the data is put in correctly. And as long as you are certain to go back and recheck the trusted status and values, their existence helps to remind you even if they are ignored, like using SSIS's bulk loading features. In Figure 8-2, you will see that you can choose to (or choose not to) check constraints on the OLE DB destination output. In this case, it may either disable the constraint or set it to not trusted to speed loading, but it will limit the data integrity and optimizer utilization of the constraint until you reset it to trusted as was demonstrated in the previous section.

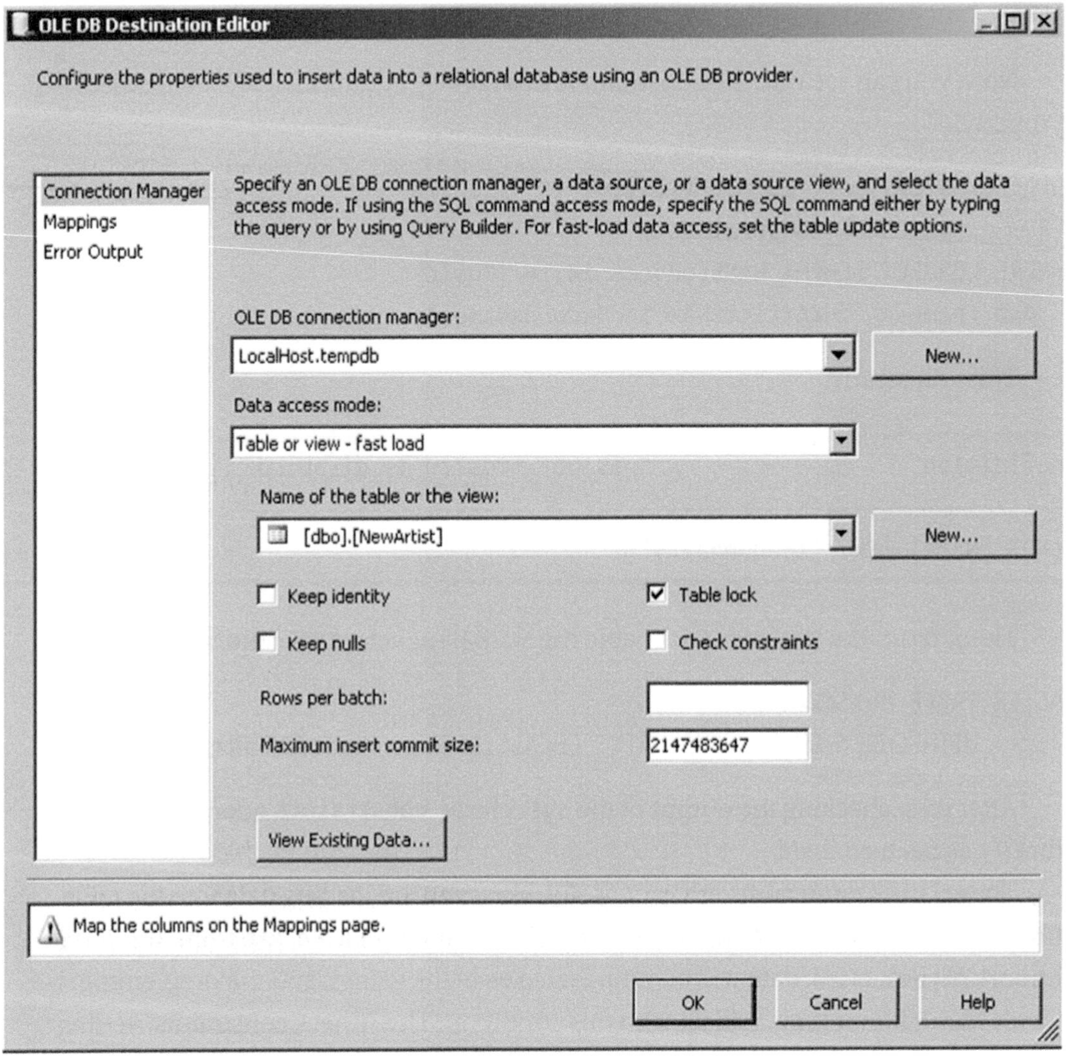

Figure 8-2. *Example SSIS OLE DB output with check constraints deselected*

CHECK Constraints Using Functions

Sometimes, you really need to implement a complex data check where a simple Boolean expression using the columns in the table and base T-SQL scalar functions just won't do. In the SQL standard, it is allowed to use a subquery in a constraint, but in SQL Server, subqueries are not allowed. However, you can use a scalar T-SQL function, even if it accesses tables.

In general, using functions is a fairly atypical solution to ensuring data integrity, but it can be powerful and, in many ways, quite useful when you need to build slightly complex data integrity protection. For the most part, CHECK constraints usually consist of the simple task of checking a stable format or value of a single column, and for this task, a standard CHECK constraint using the simple <BooleanExpression> is perfectly adequate.

However, a CHECK constraint need not be so simple. A user-defined function (UDF) can be complex and might touch several tables in the instance. Here are some examples:

- *Complex scalar validations (often using CLR functions)*: For example, in a situation where a regular expression would be easier to use than a LIKE comparison, you could create a CLR function that implemented regular expressions and use it to validate some data. (Phil Factor, on Simple Talk, has the code to implement just such a solution at this URL: www.red-gate.com/simple-talk/sql/t-sql-programming/clr-assembly-regex-functions-for-sql-server-by-example/.)

- *Validations that access other tables*: For example, to check a domain that is based on values in several tables, rather than a simple foreign key. In the example, I will implement an entry mask that is table based, so it changes based on a related table's value.

I should warn you that calling a UDF has a lot more overhead than a simple expression when you are accessing a table (SQL Server 2019 introduces *scalar function inlining* that will greatly improve performance of scalar functions in some utilizations).

As we have mentioned, CHECK constraints are executed once per row that is affected by the DML modification statement, and this extra cost will be compounded for every row affected by the modification query. I realize that this can be counterintuitive to a good programmer thinking that encapsulation is one of the most important goals of programming, but SQL is quite different from other types of programming in many ways because of the fact that you are pushing so much of the work to the engine, and the engine has to take what you are doing and find the best way of executing the code.

Hence, it's best to try to express your Boolean expression without a UDF unless it's entirely necessary to access additional tables or to do something more complex than a simple expression can. In the following examples, I'll employ UDFs to provide powerful rule checking, which can implement complex rules that would prove difficult to code using a simple Boolean expression.

You can implement the UDFs in either T-SQL (interpreted or natively compiled) or even a .NET language (VB .NET, C#, or any .NET language that lets you exploit the capabilities of SQL Server 2005 and later to write CLR-based objects in the database). In many cases, especially if you aren't doing any kind of table access in the code of the function, the CLR will perform better than the T-SQL version, but will be a lot more complicated to manage and maintain. In practice, CLR implementation is seemingly quite rare, though very much available for use if you need high performance. Native compilation can be great, but the programming interface is quite complex.

For my mask validation example, I first want to start by validating something that sounds easy but isn't exactly. I want to make sure that the catalog number is all numbers and capital letters and dashes, with no spaces, from 5 characters to 20 characters long. It is easy to do a fixed character size like this, for 5 characters. The collation makes the expression case sensitive, and the ESCAPE lets you look for the – and also use it in the two 0–9 and A–Z:

```
ALTER TABLE Music.Album
    WITH CHECK ADD CONSTRAINT
        CHKAlbum$CatalogNumber$CatalogNumberValidate
            CHECK (CatalogNumber LIKE
                    '[0-9A-Z`-][0-9A-Z`-][0-9A-Z`-][0-9A-Z`-][0-9A-Z`-]'
                        COLLATE Latin1_General_100_CS_AS ESCAPE '`')
```

But since we need to vary the size for the size of the data, we need to vary the mask to the data size. For this, we will use a REPLICATE function, to replicate the [0-9A-Z`-] part of the expression as many times as there are characters in the expression. It also checks to make sure the CatalogNumber value is 5 characters or longer:

```
ALTER TABLE Music.Album
  WITH CHECK ADD CONSTRAINT
  CHKAlbum$CatalogNumber$CatalogNumberValidate
    CHECK (LEN(CatalogNumber) >= 5
            AND
          CatalogNumber LIKE REPLICATE('[0-9A-Z`-]',LEN(CatalogNumber))
              COLLATE Latin1_General_100_CS_AS ESCAPE '`');
```

Now, if the person tries to insert a new album, but doesn't know the CatalogNumber value and puts in garbage, it might help:

```
INSERT  Music.Album(AlbumId, Name, ArtistId, PublisherId, CatalogNumber)
VALUES  (4,'Who''s Next',2,2,'?No idea?');
```

This causes the following error:

```
Msg 547, Level 16, State 0, Line 12
The INSERT statement conflicted with the CHECK constraint "CHKAlbum$Ca
talogNumber$CatalogNumberValidate". The conflict occurred in database
"tempdb", table "Music.Album", column 'CatalogNumber'.
```

But we all know that sooner or later, users will figure out how to get around simple policies if they try hard enough:

```
INSERT  Music.Album(AlbumId, Name, ArtistId, PublisherId, CatalogNumber)
VALUES  (4,'Who''s Next',2,2,'NOIDEA');
```

While this mask validation will do to make sure that we only use acceptable characters (sometimes half the battle), the next step in this section is to take the mask validation example to the next level. For this I need to access values in a different table where I will store the proper way to format a catalog number for each publisher, so I'm going to build an example that implements an entry mask that varies based on the parent of a row. Consider that it's desirable to validate that catalog numbers for albums are of the proper format. However, different publishers have different catalog number masks for their clients' albums. (More realistic, yet distinctly more complex examples would be phone numbers and perhaps address parts (like postal code formats) from around the world.)

For this example, I will continue to use the tables from the previous section. Note that the mask column, `Publisher.CatalogNumberMask`, needs to be considerably larger (five times larger in my example code) than the actual `CatalogNumber` column, because some of the possible masks use multiple characters to indicate a single character.

To do this, I build a T-SQL function that accesses this column to check that the value matches the mask, as shown (note that we'd likely build this constraint using T-SQL rather than by using the CLR, because it accesses a table in the body of the function):

```
CREATE FUNCTION Music.Publisher$CatalogNumberValidate
(
    @CatalogNumber varchar(20),
    @PublisherId int --now based on the Artist Id
)
```

```
RETURNS bit
AS
BEGIN
    DECLARE @LogicalValueFlag bit, @CatalogNumberMask varchar(100);

    SELECT @LogicalValueFlag = CASE WHEN @CatalogNumber
                                            LIKE CatalogNumberMask
                                            THEN 1
                                    ELSE 0   END
    FROM    Music.Publisher
    WHERE   PublisherId = @PublisherId;

    RETURN @LogicalValueFlag;
END;
```

When I loaded the data in the start of this section, I preloaded the data with valid values for the CatalogNumber and CatalogNumberMask columns:

```
SELECT Album.CatalogNumber, Publisher.CatalogNumberMask
FROM    Music.Album
        JOIN Music.Publisher as Publisher
            ON Album.PublisherId = Publisher.PublisherId;
```

This returns the following results:

CatalogNumber	CatalogNumberMask
433-43ASD-33	[0-9][0-9][0-9]-[0-9][0-9][0-9a-z][0-9a-z][0-9a-z]-…
111-11111-11	[0-9][0-9][0-9]-[0-9][0-9][0-9a-z][0-9a-z][0-9a-z]-…
CD12345	[a-z][a-z][0-9][0-9][0-9][0-9][0-9]

Now, let's change the constraint to use the table, as shown here:

```
ALTER TABLE Music.Album
    DROP CONSTRAINT IF EXISTS CHKAlbum$CatalogNumber$CatalogNumberValidate;
GO
ALTER TABLE Music.Album
    WITH CHECK ADD CONSTRAINT
```

```
CHKAlbum$CatalogNumber$CatalogNumberValidate
        CHECK (Music.Publisher$CatalogNumberValidate
                    (CatalogNumber,PublisherId) = 1);
```

If the constraint gives you errors because of invalid data existing in the table (because you were adding data, trying out the table, or in real development, this often occurs with test data from trying out the UI that they are building), you can use a query like the following to find them:

```
SELECT Album.Name, Album.CatalogNumber, Publisher.CatalogNumberMask
FROM Music.Album
        JOIN Music.Publisher
          ON Publisher.PublisherId = Album.PublisherId
WHERE Music.Publisher$CatalogNumberValidate
                    (Album.CatalogNumber,Album.PublisherId) <> 1;
```

Now, let's attempt to add a new row with an invalid value:

```
INSERT  Music.Album(AlbumId, Name, ArtistId, PublisherId, CatalogNumber)
VALUES  (4,'Who''s Next',2,2,'NOIDEA');
```

This causes the following error, because the catalog number of '1' doesn't match the mask set up for PublisherId number 2:

```
Msg 547, Level 16, State 0, Line 1
The INSERT statement conflicted with the CHECK constraint "CHKAlbum$Ca
talogNumber$CatalogNumberValidate". The conflict occurred in database
"Chapter8", table "Music.Album".
```

Now, change the catalog number to something that matches the entry mask the constraint is checking:

```
INSERT  Music.Album(AlbumId, Name, ArtistId, CatalogNumber, PublisherId)
VALUES  (4,'Who''s Next',2,'AC12345',2);

SELECT * FROM Music.Album;
```

This returns the following results, which as you can see match the '[a-z][a-z][0-9][0-9][0-9][0-9][0-9]' mask set up for the publisher with PublisherId = 2:

AlbumId	Name	ArtistId	CatalogNumber	PublisherId
1	The White Album	1	433-43ASD-33	1
2	Revolver	1	111-11111-11	1
3	Quadrophenia	2	CD12345	2
4	Who's Next	2	AC12345	2

Using this kind of approach, you can build any single-row validation code for your tables. As described previously, each UDF will fire once for each row when a column the CHECK constraint references was modified by the UPDATE statement. If you are making large numbers of inserts, performance might suffer, but having data that you can trust is worth it. Along the lines of performance, using a UDF in a CHECK constraint will limit the query plan of the modification queries on the table to not allow parallelism, so this could be an issue for performance as well.

We will talk about TRIGGER objects later in this chapter, but alternatively, you could create a TRIGGER object that checks for the existence of any rows returned by a query, based on the query used earlier to find improper data in the table:

```
SELECT *
FROM    Music.Album AS Album
           JOIN Music.Publisher AS Publisher
               ON Publisher.PublisherId = Album.PublisherId
WHERE   Music.Publisher$CatalogNumberValidate
                       (Album.CatalogNumber, Album.PublisherId) <> 1;
```

There's one drawback to this type of constraint, whether implemented in a constraint or trigger. As it stands right now, the Album table is protected from invalid values being entered into the CatalogNumber column, but it doesn't say anything about what happens if a user changes the CatalogEntryMask on the Publisher table. If this is a concern, you'd need to add a TRIGGER object to the Publisher table that validates changes to the mask against any existing data.

> **Caution**   Using user-defined functions that access other rows in the same table is dangerous, because while the data for each row appears in the table as the function is executed, if multiple rows are updated simultaneously, those rows do not appear to be in the table, so if an error condition exists only in the rows that are being modified, your final results could end up in error.

Enhancing Errors Caused by Constraints

The real downside to CHECK constraints is the error messages they produce upon failure. The error messages are certainly things you don't want to show to a user, if for no other reason than they will generate service desk calls at least the first time a typical user sees them. Dealing with these errors is one of the more annoying parts of using constraints in SQL Server.

Whenever a statement fails a constraint requirement, SQL Server provides you with an ugly message and offers no real method for displaying a clean message automatically. In this section, I'll briefly detail a way to refine the ugly constraint error messages you get, much like the error from the previous statement:

```
Msg 547, Level 16, State 0, Line 1
The INSERT statement conflicted with the CHECK constraint "CHKAlbum$Ca
talogNumber$CatalogNumberValidate". The conflict occurred in database
"Chapter8", table "Music.Album".
```

I'll show you how to map this to an error message that at least makes some sense. First, the parts of the error message are as follows:

- Msg 547: The error number that's passed back to the calling program. In some cases, this error number is significant; however, in most cases it's enough to say that the error number is nonzero.

- Level 16: A severity level for the message. Levels 0–18 are generally considered to be user messages, with 16 being the default. Levels 19–25 are severe errors that cause the connection to be severed (with a message written to the log). Level 10 is an informational message.

- State 0: A value from 0 to 127 that represents the state of the process when the error was raised. This value is rarely used by any process, but is there to let an error message send an encoded message.

- Line 1: The line in the batch or object where the error is occurring. This value can be extremely useful for debugging purposes. In some situations, you may also get a location in the batch as well to help find the error.

- *Error description*: A text explanation of the error that has occurred.

In its raw form, this is the exact error that will be sent to the client, and basically the details you get are only that the constraint was violated, even if 100,000 rows were inserted and only one column value in one row violated the constraint condition leading to the error message. In this section, I will provide a simple pattern for helping you document your error messages. This can also help you provide details to your clients when they occur if the UI hasn't captured the message first.

First, let's create a mapping table where we put the name of the constraint that we've defined and a message that explains what the constraint means. The MetaData schema would be the entryway for customers and code to get details about data:

```
CREATE SCHEMA MetaData; --used to hold objects to provide users
                        --extra system details
GO
CREATE TABLE MetaData.ConstraintDetail --constraint is not a legal name
(                                       --and prefer no [] names
    SchemaName      sysname NOT NULL,
    ConstraintName sysname NOT NULL,
    Message         nvarchar(2000) NOT NULL,
    Description     nvarchar(4000) NULL,
    CONSTRAINT PKConstraint PRIMARY KEY
        (SchemaName, ConstraintName)
);
GO
INSERT MetaData.ConstraintDetail(SchemaName,ConstraintName,
                                Message, Description)
VALUES ('Music',
        'CHKAlbum$CatalogNumber$CatalogNumberValidate',
```

```
         'The catalog number does not match the proper publisher format',
         'Used to prevent new data from breaking the current format rule');
GO
```

Using this data (and it doesn't just have to be CHECK constraints, though you will notice that the use of single and double quotes in error messages seems pretty random at times), we can create tools that use this information to make life easier for the users. The following maps a check constraint to a clearer message so the developer/user can figure out what went wrong:

```
CREATE OR ALTER PROCEDURE MetaData.CheckConstraintMessage$Help
(
        @ErrorMessage nvarchar(4000)
)
AS
 BEGIN
   DECLARE @ConstraintName sysname= SUBSTRING( @ErrorMessage,
                    CHARINDEX('constraint "',@ErrorMessage) + 12,
                    CHARINDEX('"',substring(@ErrorMessage,
                    CHARINDEX('constraint "',@ErrorMessage) + 12,4000))-1),
           @SchemaName nvarchar(257) = SUBSTRING( @ErrorMessage,
                    CHARINDEX('table "',@ErrorMessage) + 7,
                    CHARINDEX('.',substring(@ErrorMessage,
                    CHARINDEX('table "',@ErrorMessage) +  7,4000))-1)

      DECLARE @constraintType sysname =
      (SELECT type_desc FROM sys.objects WHERE name = @constraintName),
                @Message nvarchar(2000), @Description nvarchar(4000)

     SELECT @Message = Message, @Description = Description
     FROM   MetaData.ConstraintDetail
     WHERE  SchemaName = @SchemaName
       AND  ConstraintName = @ConstraintName

    IF @ConstraintType <> 'CHECK_CONSTRAINT'
        THROW 50000,'This error message is not from a CHECK constraint',1;
```

```
    SELECT @constraintName AS ConstraintName,
           @Message AS ClearMessage,
           @Description AS ConstraintDescription
  END
GO
```

Then, if you document all your CHECK constraints, a programmer (or user, doing ad hoc work) could use the tools to decode the message into more interesting details:

```
EXEC MetaData.CheckConstraintMessage$Help @ErrorMessage = 'The INSERT
statement conflicted with the CHECK constraint "CHKAlbum$CatalogNumber$Ca
talogNumberValidate". The conflict occurred in database "Chapter8", table
"Music.Album".';
```

This returns (though all in one result set)

```
ConstraintName
---------------------------------------------------
CHKAlbum$CatalogNumber$CatalogNumberValidate

ClearMessage
-----------------------------------------------------------------
The catalog number does not match the proper publisher format

ConstraintDescription
-----------------------------------------------------------------
Used to prevent new data from breaking the current format rule
```

If your organization would prefer to rely on the error messages that come from SQL Server, we can create a STORED PROCEDURE object to do the actual mapping by taking the values that can be retrieved from the ERROR_%() procedures that are accessible in a CATCH block and using them to look up the value in the ConstraintDetail table:

```
CREATE OR ALTER PROCEDURE
                    Metadata.CheckConstraintDetail$ReformatErrorMessage
(
    @ErrorNumber  int = NULL,
    @ErrorMessage nvarchar(2000) = NULL,
```

```
    @ErrorSeverity INT= NULL,
    @AppendOriginalMessageFlag bit = 1
) AS
  BEGIN
    SET NOCOUNT ON

    --use values in ERROR_ functions unless the user passes in values
    SET @ErrorNumber = COALESCE(@ErrorNumber, ERROR_NUMBER());
    SET @ErrorMessage = COALESCE(@ErrorMessage, ERROR_MESSAGE());
    SET @ErrorSeverity = COALESCE(@ErrorSeverity, ERROR_SEVERITY());

    --strip the constraint name out of the error message
    DECLARE @ConstraintName sysname= SUBSTRING( @ErrorMessage,
                   CHARINDEX('constraint "',@ErrorMessage) + 12,
                   CHARINDEX('"',substring(@ErrorMessage,
                   CHARINDEX('constraint "',@ErrorMessage) + 12,4000))-1),
            @SchemaName nvarchar(257) = SUBSTRING( @ErrorMessage,
                   CHARINDEX('table "',@ErrorMessage) + 7,
                   CHARINDEX('.',substring(@ErrorMessage,
                   CHARINDEX('table "',@ErrorMessage) +  7,4000))-1)

    --store off original message in case no custom message found
    DECLARE @originalMessage nvarchar(2000);
    SET @originalMessage = ERROR_MESSAGE();

    IF @ErrorNumber = 547 --constraint error
      BEGIN
        SET @ErrorMessage =
                        (SELECT Message
                             FROM   MetaData.ConstraintDetail
                             WHERE  SchemaName = @SchemaName
                               AND  ConstraintName = @ConstraintName
                        );
      END

        SET @ErrorMessage = CONCAT(@ErrorMessage,
            CASE WHEN @AppendOriginalMessageFlag = 0 THEN NULL ELSE '' END
```

```
             + '   (Original Error: ' + CAST(@ErrorNumber AS nvarchar(10))
             + ':' + @originalMessage + 'Severity: '
             + CAST(@ErrorSeverity AS varchar(10)) +')') ;
      THROW  50000, @ErrorMessage, 1;
   END;
```

Using TRY-CATCH error handling, we can build a simple error handler that uses the preceding STORED PROCEDURE object (you can do much the same thing in client code as well for errors that you just cannot prevent from the user interface). Part of the reason we name constraints is to determine what the intent was in creating the constraint in the first place. In the following code, we'll implement a very rudimentary error-mapping scheme by parsing the text of the name of the constraint from the message, and then we'll look up this value in a mapping table. It isn't a "perfect" scheme, but it does the trick when using constraints as the only data protection for a situation (it is also helps you to document the errors that your system may raise as well).

Now, see what happens when we enter an invalid value for an album catalog number:

```
BEGIN TRY
     INSERT  Music.Album(AlbumId, Name, ArtistId,
                         CatalogNumber, PublisherId)
     VALUES  (5,'who are you',2,'badnumber',2);
END TRY
BEGIN CATCH
     EXEC Metadata.CheckConstraintDetail$ReformatErrorMessage;
END CATCH;
```

The error message is as follows:

```
Msg 50000, Level 16, State 1, Procedure ErrorMap$mapError, Line 24
The catalog number does not match the proper publisher format   (Original
Error: 547:The INSERT statement conflicted with the CHECK constraint "CH
KAlbum$CatalogNumber$CatalogNumberValidate". The conflict occurred in
database "Chapter8", table "Music.Album".Severity: 16)
```

This is a little better than the original error message, for sure:

```
Msg 547, Level 16, State 0, Line 1
The INSERT statement conflicted with the CHECK constraint "CHKAlbum$Ca
talogNumber$CatalogNumberValidate". The conflict occurred in database
"Chapter8", table "Music.Album".
```

DML Triggers

It is, perhaps, the primary theme of this book that getting the data right is the most important thing about designing and implementing a database. What TRIGGER objects do for the database implementation experience is provide the ability to code complex data protections that cannot be done in any other manner. Performance is important, and ease of management is desirable, as is ease of programming. However, TRIGGER objects are honestly going to be somewhat negative for all of these aspects of the development experience; their only positive is that they can validate certain things and cause certain side effects in a manner that no other tool can.

A TRIGGER object is a type of coded module, like a STORED PROCEDURE object, but instead of being something you manually execute, it is attached to a TABLE or VIEW object and is executed automatically when an INSERT, UPDATE, or DELETE statement is executed. While triggers share the ability to enforce data protection, they differ from constraints in being far more flexible because you can code them like stored procedures and you can introduce side effects like formatting input data or cascading any operation to another table. You can use triggers to enforce almost any business rule, and they're especially important for dealing with situations that are too complex for a CHECK constraint to handle. We used triggers in Chapter 7 to automatically manage row modification time values.

Triggers often get a bad name because they can be quirky, especially because they degrade performance noticeably as the number of rows increases when you are dealing with large modifications. For example, if you have a trigger on a table and try to update a million rows, you are likely to have issues (a lot depends on the server you are working on, naturally). However, for most operations in a typical OLTP database, operations shouldn't be touching more than a handful of rows at a time. Trigger usage does need careful consideration, but there are places where they are essential tools to guarantee certain types of operations are handled correctly. In this chapter, I will discuss a few uses of triggers that can't be done automatically in T-SQL code any other way nearly as safely:

- Perform cross-database referential integrity.

- Check inter-row rules, where just looking at the current row isn't enough for the constraints.

- Check inter-table constraints, when rules require access to data in a different table.

- Introduce desired side effects to your data modification queries, such as maintaining required denormalizations.

- Guarantee that no INSERT, UPDATE, or DELETE operations can be executed on a table, even if the user does have rights to perform the operation.

Some of these operations could also be done in an application layer, but for the most part, these operations are far safer (particularly for data integrity due to concurrency concerns) when done automatically using a TRIGGER object. When it comes to data protection, the primary advantages that triggers have over application code are being able to access any data in the database to do the verification without sending it to a client. In this chapter, I am going to create DML triggers to handle typical business needs.

There are two different types of DML triggers that we will make use of in this chapter. Each type can be useful in its own way, but they are quite different in why they are used:

- AFTER: These triggers fire after the DML statement (INSERT/UPDATE/DELETE) has affected the table. AFTER triggers are usually used for handling rules that won't fit into the mold of a constraint, for example, rules that require data to be stored, such as a logging mechanism. You may have a virtually unlimited number of AFTER triggers that fire on INSERT, UPDATE, and DELETE or any combination of them.

- INSTEAD OF: These triggers operate "instead of" the built-in command (INSERT, UPDATE, or DELETE) affecting the table or view. In this way, you can do whatever you want with the data, either doing exactly what was requested by the user or doing something completely different (you can even just ignore the operation altogether). You can have a maximum of one INSTEAD OF INSERT, UPDATE, and DELETE trigger of each type per table. It is allowed (but not always a good idea) to combine all three into one and have a single trigger that fires for all three operations.

This section will be split into these two types of triggers because they have two mostly distinct sets of use cases. Since coding triggers is not one of the more well-trod topics in SQL Server, in Appendix B, I will introduce coding techniques for TRIGGER objects and provide a template that we will use throughout this chapter (it's the template we used in Chapter 7 too). I will also discuss in more detail the mechanics of writing triggers and their various limitations.

Natively compiled triggers are available in SQL Server, but are limited to AFTER triggers, as well as being subject to the current limitations on natively compiled modules.

AFTER TRIGGER Objects

An AFTER TRIGGER object fires after one of the three modification DML statements (INSERT, UPDATE, or DELETE) has completed. Though triggers may not seem like they could be used to do much, back in SQL Server 6.0 and earlier, there were no CHECK constraints, and even FOREIGN KEYS had just been introduced, so all data protection was managed using triggers, and we did actually validate data to much the same level as I try to today. Other than being quite cumbersome to maintain, some fairly complex systems were created using hardware that in some ways wasn't even comparable to my Nintendo Switch.

In this section, I will present examples that demonstrate several forms of triggers that I use to solve problems that are reasonably common. I'll give examples of the following types of triggers:

- Range checks on multiple rows

- Cascading inserts

- Child-to-parent cascades

- Relationships that span databases and servers

From these examples, you should be able to extrapolate almost any use of an AFTER TRIGGER object. Just keep in mind that triggers, although not inherently *terrible* for performance, should be used no more than necessary because they are far more of a drag on performance than a CHECK or FOREIGN KEY constraint.

Note   For another example, check the "Uniqueness Techniques" section in Chapter 9, where I will implement a type of uniqueness based on ranges of data using a trigger-based solution. In Appendix B (available as a download), the example is based on maintaining summary values (something that is generally frowned upon but is a good example of building a complex trigger).

Range Checks over Multiple Rows

The first type of check we'll look at is the range check, in which we want to make sure that a column is within some specific range of values. You can do a simple, single-row range check using a CHECK constraint to validate the data in a single row (e.g., Column > 10) quite easily. However, you can't use this to validate conditions based on aggregate conditions (like SUM(Column) > 10) because the CHECK constraint can only access data in the current row (and using a UDF, you can't see the new data either).

If you need to check that a row or set of rows doesn't violate a given condition, usually based on an aggregate like a SUM or AVG, you use an AFTER TRIGGER object. As an example, I'll look at a simple accounting system. As users deposit and withdraw money from accounts, you may wish to make sure that the balances never dip below zero. All transactions for a given account must be considered.

First, we create a schema for the accounting objects:

```
CREATE SCHEMA Accounting;
```

Then, we create a table for an account and then one to contain the activity for the account:

```
CREATE TABLE Accounting.Account
(
        AccountNumber char(10) NOT NULL
                CONSTRAINT PKAccount PRIMARY KEY
        --would have other columns
);
```

```
CREATE TABLE Accounting.AccountActivity
(
        AccountNumber char(10) NOT NULL
            CONSTRAINT FKAccount$has$Accounting_AccountActivity
                FOREIGN KEY REFERENCES Accounting.Account(AccountNumber),
        --this might be a value that each ATM/Teller generates
        TransactionNumber char(20) NOT NULL,
        Date  datetime2(3) NOT NULL,
        Amount numeric(12,2) NOT NULL,
        CONSTRAINT PKAccountActivity
                    PRIMARY KEY (AccountNumber, TransactionNumber)
);
```

Now, we add a TRIGGER object to the Accounting.AccountActivity table that checks to make sure that when you sum together the transaction amounts for an Account, the sum is greater than zero:

```
CREATE TRIGGER Accounting.AccountActivity$InsertTrigger
ON Accounting.AccountActivity
AFTER INSERT AS
BEGIN
   SET NOCOUNT ON;
   SET ROWCOUNT 0; --in case the client has modified the rowcount
   --use inserted for insert or update trigger, deleted for update
   --or delete trigger count instead of @@ROWCOUNT due to merge behavior
   -- that sets @@ROWCOUNT to a number that is equal to number of merged
   -- rows, not rows being checked in trigger
   DECLARE @msg varchar(2000),     --used to hold the error message
   --use inserted for insert or update trigger, deleted for update
   --or delete trigger count instead of @@ROWCOUNT due to merge behavior
   --that sets @@ROWCOUNT to a number that is equal to number of merged
   --rows, not rows being checked in trigger
          @rowsAffected int = (SELECT COUNT(*) FROM inserted);

   --no need to continue on if no rows affected
   IF @rowsAffected = 0 RETURN;

   BEGIN TRY
```

```
    --[validation section]
    --disallow Transactions that would put balance into negatives
    IF EXISTS ( SELECT AccountNumber
                FROM Accounting.AccountActivity AS AccountActivity
                WHERE EXISTS (SELECT *
                              FROM    inserted
                              WHERE   inserted.AccountNumber =
                                AccountActivity.AccountNumber)
                GROUP BY AccountNumber
                HAVING SUM(Amount) < 0)
      BEGIN
        IF @rowsAffected = 1
            SELECT @msg = CONCAT('Account: ', AccountNumber,
              ' TransactionNumber:',TransactionNumber, ' for amount: ',
              Amount, ' would cause a negative balance.')
            FROM    inserted;
        ELSE
          SELECT @msg = 'One of the rows caused a negative balance.';
          THROW  50000, @msg, 1;
      END

    --[modification section]
    END TRY
    BEGIN CATCH
        IF @@TRANCOUNT > 0
            ROLLBACK TRANSACTION;

        --will halt the batch or be caught by the caller's catch block
        THROW;

    END CATCH
END;
```

The key to this type of TRIGGER object is to look for the existence of rows in the base table, not the rows in the inserted table, because the concern is how the inserted rows affect the overall status for an Account.

Note   As you are writing your validations in TRIGGER objects, it is important to consider how much data is locked when you do so. In Appendix B in the section "Trigger Validations and Isolation Levels," I will show a case where too little data may be locked, such that at the end of your transaction, the database state is actually incorrect when you COMMIT your transaction. None of the examples in this chapter have these issues, and most validations will not.

The base of the query is a query one might run to check the status of the table without a trigger. Is there an account where the sum of their transactions is less than 0?

```
SELECT AccountNumber
FROM Accounting.AccountActivity AS AccountActivity
GROUP BY AccountNumber
HAVING SUM(Amount) < 0;
```

Then we include a correlation to the rows that have been created since this is an insert trigger:

```
SELECT AccountNumber
FROM  Accounting.AccountActivity AS AccountActivity
WHERE EXISTS(SELECT *
             FROM    inserted
             WHERE   inserted.AccountNumber = AccountActivity.AccountNumber)
GROUP BY AccountNumber
HAVING SUM(TransactionAmount) < 0;
```

The WHERE clause simply makes sure that the only rows we consider are for accounts that have new data inserted. This way, we don't end up checking all rows, including rows that we know our query hasn't touched. Note too that I don't use a JOIN operation. By using an EXISTS criteria in the WHERE clause, we don't affect the cardinality of the set being returned in the FROM clause, no matter how many rows in the inserted table have the same AccountNumber. Now, this is placed into the trigger using an IF EXISTS control of flow statement, which is then followed by the error handling stuff:

```
IF EXISTS ( SELECT AccountNumber
               FROM Accounting.AccountActivity AS AccountActivity
               WHERE EXISTS (SELECT *
                            FROM    inserted
                            WHERE   inserted.AccountNumber =
                               AccountActivity.AccountNumber)
               GROUP BY AccountNumber
               HAVING SUM(TransactionAmount) < 0)
    BEGIN            --error handling stuff
```

To see it in action, use this code:

```
--create some set up test data
INSERT INTO Accounting.Account(AccountNumber)
VALUES ('1111111111');

INSERT INTO Accounting.AccountActivity(AccountNumber, TransactionNumber,
                                    Date, Amount)
VALUES ('1111111111','A0000000000000000001','20050712',100),
       ('1111111111','A0000000000000000002','20050713',100);
```

Now, let's see what happens when we violate this rule:

```
INSERT  INTO Accounting.AccountActivity(AccountNumber, TransactionNumber,
                                    Date, Amount)
VALUES ('1111111111','A0000000000000000003','20050713',-300);
```

Here's the result:

```
Msg 50000, Level 16, State 16, Procedure AccountActivity$insertTrigger
Account: 1111111111 TransactionNumber:A0000000000000000003 for amount:
-300.00 cannot be processed as it will cause a negative balance
```

The error message is the custom error message that we coded in the case where a single row was modified. Now, let's make sure that the trigger works when we have greater than one row in the INSERT statement:

```
--create new Account
INSERT  INTO Accounting.Account(AccountNumber)
VALUES ('2222222222');
GO
--Now, this data will violate the constraint for the new Account:
INSERT  INTO Accounting.AccountActivity(AccountNumber, TransactionNumber,
                                        Date, Amount)
VALUES ('1111111111','A0000000000000000004','20050714',100),
       ('2222222222','A0000000000000000005','20050715',100),
       ('2222222222','A0000000000000000006','20050715',100),
       ('2222222222','A0000000000000000007','20050715',-201);
```

This causes the following error:

```
Msg 50000, Level 16, State 16, Procedure AccountActivity$insertUpdateTrigger
One of the rows caused a negative balance
```

The multirow error message is much less informative, though you could expand it to include information about a row (or all the rows) that caused the violation with some more text, even showing the multiple failed values with a bit of work if that was an issue. Usually a simple message is enough to deal with, because generally if multiple rows are being modified in a single statement, it's a batch process, and the complexity of building error messages is way more than its worth.

Tip   Error handling will be covered in more detail in the "Dealing with TRIGGER and Constraint Errors" section later in this chapter. I have used a very simple error model for these triggers that simply rethrows the error that occurs in the trigger after rolling back the transaction.

If this is a real accounting-oriented table, then an INSERT trigger may be enough, as a true accounting system handles modifications with offsetting entries (delete a $100 charge with a –$100 charge). However, if you did need to process deletes, in a DELETE TRIGGER object, you would change the base query to

```
SELECT AccountNumber
FROM Accounting.AccountActivity AS AccountActivity
WHERE EXISTS (SELECT *
              FROM    deleted
              WHERE   deleted.AccountNumber = AccountActivity.AccountNumber)
GROUP BY AccountNumber
HAVING SUM(TransactionAmount) < 0;
```

For an UPDATE trigger, we need to check both virtual tables for activity by
AccountNumber (in case someone updates data if that is allowed, or perhaps change this
to check for changes and fail if changes have occurred):

```
SELECT AccountNumber
FROM Accounting.AccountActivity AS AccountActivity
WHERE EXISTS (SELECT *
              FROM    (SELECT AccountNumber
                        FROM    deleted
                        UNION ALL
                        SELECT AccountNumber
                        FROM    inserted) AS CheckThese
              WHERE   CheckThese.AccountNumber =
                                        AccountActivity.AccountNumber)
GROUP BY AccountNumber
HAVING SUM(TransactionAmount) < 0;
```

Note too that this would handle cases where an AccountNumber column value was
modified as well. Changeable keys such as an account number that can be modified on a
transaction trip up a lot of people when implementing data checking that spans multiple
rows because it is easy to see that you need to catch that the AccountNumber you updated
needs to be recalculated, but the one you changed may not be remembered so quickly,
so the other AccountNumber may be left in deficit and cause issues.

VIEWING TRIGGER EVENTS

To see the events for which a trigger fires, you can use the following query:

```
SELECT trigger_events.type_desc
FROM sys.trigger_events
         JOIN sys.triggers
                 ON sys.triggers.object_id = sys.trigger_events.object_id
WHERE  triggers.name = 'AccountActivity$InsertTrigger';
```

Cascading Inserts

A cascading insert refers to the opposite situation of a cascading delete, whereby after an operation occurs on one table (often an INSERT operation), one or more other new rows are automatically created in other tables. This is frequently done when you need to initialize a row in another table, quite often a status of some sort, or to try to enforce a 1–1 relationship by automatically creating the child or parent row upon creation of one or the other.

For this example, we're going to build a small system to store URLs for a website-linking system. During low-usage periods, an automated browser connects to the URLs so that they can be verified (the goal being to limit broken links on a web page aggregator).

To implement this, I'll use the set of tables shown in Figure 8-3 and the following code.

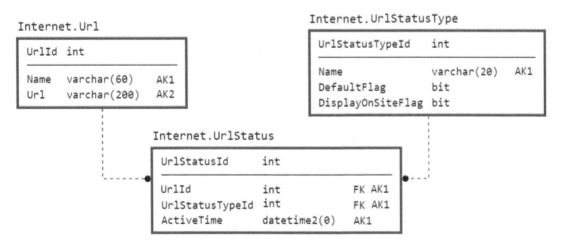

Figure 8-3. *Storing URLs for a website-linking system*

```
CREATE SCHEMA Internet;
GO
CREATE TABLE Internet.Url
(
    UrlId int NOT NULL IDENTITY(1,1) CONSTRAINT PKUrl primary key,
    Name  varchar(60) NOT NULL CONSTRAINT AKUrl_Name UNIQUE,
    Url   varchar(200) NOT NULL CONSTRAINT AKUrl_Url UNIQUE
);

--Not a user manageable table, so not using identity key (as discussed in
--Chapter 6 when I discussed choosing keys) in this one table.  Others are
--using identity-based keys in this example.
CREATE TABLE Internet.UrlStatusType
(
        UrlStatusTypeId  int NOT NULL
                    CONSTRAINT PKUrlStatusType PRIMARY KEY,
        Name varchar(20) NOT NULL
                    CONSTRAINT AKUrlStatusType UNIQUE,
        DefaultFlag bit NOT NULL,
        DisplayOnSiteFlag bit NOT NULL ,
        INDEX AKOnlyOneDefaultFlag UNIQUE (DefaultFlag)
                                    WHERE (DefaultFlag=1)
);

CREATE TABLE Internet.UrlStatus
(
        UrlStatusId int NOT NULL IDENTITY(1,1)
                    CONSTRAINT PKUrlStatus PRIMARY KEY,
        UrlStatusTypeId int NOT NULL
                    CONSTRAINT
                FKUrlStatusType$defines_status_type_of$Internet_UrlStatus
                    REFERENCES Internet.UrlStatusType(UrlStatusTypeId),
        UrlId int NOT NULL
          CONSTRAINT FKUrl$has_status_history_in$Internet_UrlStatus
                    REFERENCES Internet.Url(UrlId),
```

```
        ActiveTime        datetime2(0),
        CONSTRAINT AKUrlStatus_statusUrlDate
                      UNIQUE (UrlStatusTypeId, UrlId, ActiveTime)
);

--set up status types
INSERT  Internet.UrlStatusType (UrlStatusTypeId, Name,
                                    DefaultFlag, DisplayOnSiteFlag)
VALUES (1, 'Unverified',1,0),
       (2, 'Verified',0,1),
       (3, 'Unable to locate',0,0);
```

The Url table holds URLs to different sites on the Web. When someone enters a URL, we initialize the status to 'Unverified'. A process should be in place in which the site is checked often to make sure nothing has changed.

You begin by building a trigger that inserts a row into the UrlStatus table on the INSERT operation that creates a new row with the UrlId and the default UrlStatusType based on DefaultFlag having the value of 1:

```
CREATE TRIGGER Internet.Url$insertTrigger
ON Internet.Url
AFTER INSERT AS
BEGIN
   SET NOCOUNT ON;
   SET ROWCOUNT 0; --in case the client has modified the rowcount
   --use inserted for insert or update trigger, deleted for update
   --or delete trigger count instead of @@ROWCOUNT due to merge behavior
   -- that sets @@ROWCOUNT to a number that is equal to number of merged
   -- rows, not rows being checked in trigger
   DECLARE @msg varchar(2000),    --used to hold the error message
   --use inserted for insert or update trigger, deleted for update
   --or delete trigger count instead of @@ROWCOUNT due to merge behavior
   --that sets @@ROWCOUNT to a number that is equal to number of merged
   --rows, not rows being checked in trigger
          @rowsAffected int = (SELECT COUNT(*) FROM inserted);
   --no need to continue on if no rows affected
```

```
    IF @rowsAffected = 0 RETURN;

    BEGIN TRY

        --[validation section]

        --[modification section]
        --add a row to the UrlStatus table to tell it that the new row
        --should start out as the default status
        INSERT INTO Internet.UrlStatus (UrlId, UrlStatusTypeId, ActiveTime)
        SELECT inserted.UrlId, UrlStatusType.UrlStatusTypeId, SYSDATETIME()
            FROM inserted
                CROSS JOIN (SELECT UrlStatusTypeId
                            FROM    UrlStatusType
                            WHERE  DefaultFlag = 1)  as UrlStatusType;
                                --use cross join to apply this one row to
                                --rows in inserted
    END TRY
    BEGIN CATCH
        IF @@TRANCOUNT > 0
            ROLLBACK TRANSACTION;
        --will halt the batch or be caught by the caller's catch block
        THROW;
    END CATCH;
END;
```

The idea here is that for every row in the inserted table, we'll get the single row from the UrlStatusType table that has DefaultFlag equal to 1. So let's try it:

```
INSERT  Internet.Url(Name, Url)
VALUES ('Author''s Website',
        'http://drsql.org');
```

```
SELECT Url.Url,Url.Name,UrlStatusType.Name as Status, UrlStatus.ActiveTime
FROM    Internet.Url
            JOIN Internet.UrlStatus
                ON Url.UrlId = UrlStatus.UrlId
            JOIN Internet.UrlStatusType
                ON UrlStatusType.UrlStatusTypeId = UrlStatus.UrlStatusTypeId;
```

This returns the following results:

Url	Name	Status	ActiveTime
http://drsql.org	Author's Website	Unverified	2020-05-19 22:49:42

Tip   It's easier if users can't modify the data in tables such as the UrlStatusType table, so there cannot be a case where there's no status set as the default (or too many rows, which is why I included the UNIQUE filtered index on the table).

Cascading from Child to Parent

All the cascade operations on updates that you can do with constraints (CASCADE or SET NULL) are strictly from parent to child. Sometimes, you want to go the other way around and delete the parent of a row when you delete the child. Typically, you do this when the child is what you're interested in and the parent is simply maintained as an attribute of the child that is only desired when one or more child rows exist. Also typical of this type of situation is that you want to delete the parent if and only if all children rows have been deleted.

In our example, we have a small model of my game collection. I have several game systems and quite a few games. Often, I have the same game on multiple platforms, so I want to track this fact, especially if I want to trade a game that I have on multiple platforms for something else. So I have a table for the GamePlatform (the system) and another for the actual Game itself. This is a many-to-many relationship, so I have an associative entity called GameInstance to record ownership, as well as when the game was purchased for the given platform. Each of these tables has a DELETE CASCADE relationship, so all instances are removed. What about the games, though? If all GameInstance rows are removed for a given game, in this database, I want to delete the game from the database. The tables are shown in Figure 8-4.

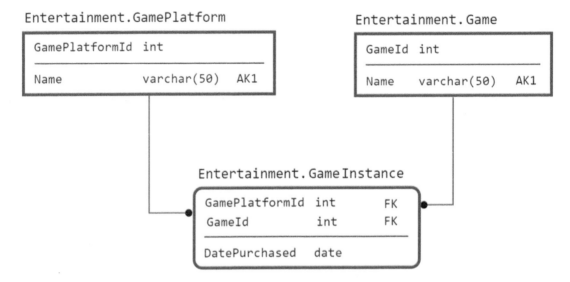

Figure 8-4. *The game tables*

```
--start a schema for entertainment-related tables
CREATE SCHEMA Entertainment;
GO
CREATE TABLE Entertainment.GamePlatform
(
    GamePlatformId int NOT NULL CONSTRAINT PKGamePlatform PRIMARY KEY,
    Name  varchar(50) NOT NULL CONSTRAINT AKGamePlatform_Name UNIQUE
);
CREATE TABLE Entertainment.Game
(
    GameId  int NOT NULL CONSTRAINT PKGame PRIMARY KEY,
    Name    varchar(50) NOT NULL CONSTRAINT AKGame_Name UNIQUE
    --more details that are common to all platforms
);

--associative entity with cascade relationships back to Game and
GamePlatform
CREATE TABLE Entertainment.GameInstance
(
    GamePlatformId int NOT NULL,
    GameId int NOT NULL,
```

```
    PurchaseDate date NOT NULL,
    CONSTRAINT PKGameInstance PRIMARY KEY (GamePlatformId, GameId),
    CONSTRAINT FKGame$is_owned_on_platform_by$EntertainmentGameInstance
          FOREIGN KEY (GameId)
              REFERENCES Entertainment.Game(GameId) ON DELETE CASCADE,
    CONSTRAINT FKGamePlatform$is_linked_to$EntertainmentGameInstance
          FOREIGN KEY (GamePlatformId)
              REFERENCES Entertainment.GamePlatform(GamePlatformId)
                                                    ON DELETE CASCADE
);
```

Then, I insert a sampling of data:

```
INSERT  Entertainment.Game (GameId, Name)
VALUES (1,'Legend of Zelda'),
       (2,'Super Mario Bros');

INSERT  Entertainment.GamePlatform(GamePlatformId, Name)
VALUES (1,'Nintendo Switch'),    --Yes, as a matter of fact I am still a
       (2,'Nintendo 3DS');       --Nintendo Fanboy, why do you ask?

INSERT  Entertainment.GameInstance(GamePlatformId, GameId, PurchaseDate)
VALUES (1,1,'20190804'),
       (1,2,'20190810'),
       (2,2,'20180604');

--the full outer joins ensure that all rows are returned from all
--sets, leaving nulls where data is missing
SELECT  GamePlatform.Name as Platform, Game.Name as Game,
        GameInstance.PurchaseDate
FROM    Entertainment.Game as Game
            FULL OUTER JOIN Entertainment.GameInstance as GameInstance
                ON Game.GameId = GameInstance.GameId
            FULL OUTER JOIN Entertainment.GamePlatform
                ON GamePlatform.GamePlatformId =
                                    GameInstance.GamePlatformId;
```

As you can see, I have two games for the Switch and only a single one for Nintendo 3DS:

Platform	Game	PurchaseDate
Nintendo Switch	LegendOfZelda	2019-08-04
Nintendo Switch	Super Mario Bros	2019-08-10
Nintendo 3DS	Super Mario Bros	2018-06-04

So I create an AFTER DELETE TRIGGER object on the table to do the "reverse" cascade operation:

```
CREATE TRIGGER Entertainment.GameInstance$deleteTrigger
ON Entertainment.GameInstance
AFTER DELETE AS
BEGIN
   SET NOCOUNT ON;
   SET ROWCOUNT 0; --in case the client has modified the rowcount
   --use inserted for insert or update trigger, deleted for update
   --or delete trigger count instead of @@ROWCOUNT due to merge behavior
   -- that sets @@ROWCOUNT to a number that is equal to number of merged
   -- rows, not rows being checked in trigger
   DECLARE @msg varchar(2000),    --used to hold the error message
   --use inserted for insert or update trigger, deleted for update
   --or delete trigger count instead of @@ROWCOUNT due to merge behavior
   --that sets @@ROWCOUNT to a number that is equal to number of merged
   --rows, not rows being checked in trigger
         @rowsAffected int = (SELECT COUNT(*) FROM deleted);

   --no need to continue on if no rows affected
   IF @rowsAffected = 0 RETURN;

   BEGIN TRY
      --[validation section]
      --[modification section]
                   --delete all Games
      DELETE Game    --where the GameInstance was deleted
```

```
    WHERE   GameId IN (SELECT deleted.GameId
                       FROM    deleted   --and no GameInstances left
                       WHERE   NOT EXISTS (SELECT  *
                                           FROM    GameInstance
                                           WHERE   GameInstance.GameId =
                                                        deleted.GameId));
    END TRY
    BEGIN CATCH
        IF @@TRANCOUNT > 0
            ROLLBACK TRANSACTION;
        --will halt the batch or be caught by the caller's catch block
        THROW;
    END CATCH;
END;
```

It's as straightforward as that. Just delete the games, and let the trigger cover the rest. Delete the row for the Switch:

```
DELETE  Entertainment.GameInstance
WHERE   GamePlatformId = 1;
```

Next, check the data:

```
SELECT  GamePlatform.Name AS Platform, Game.Name AS Game,
        GameInstance. PurchaseDate
FROM    Entertainment.Game AS Game
            FULL OUTER JOIN Entertainment.GameInstance AS GameInstance
                ON Game.GameId = GameInstance.GameId
            FULL OUTER JOIN Entertainment.GamePlatform
                ON GamePlatform.GamePlatformId =
                                GameInstance.GamePlatformId;
```

You can see that now I have only a single row in the Game table:

platform	Game	PurchaseDate
Nintendo 3DS	Super Mario Bros	2018-06-04
Nintendo Switch	NULL	NULL

This shows us that the Game row was deleted when all instances were removed, but the platform remains. (The technique of using a query with a FULL OUTER JOIN operation like this will help you to be able to see permutations of rows that have, and do not have, matches in a set of tables that are related to one another in a many-to-many relationship.) You could also easily expand the trigger to delete the game system when you get rid of all the games for a system as well.

Relationships

In the Jurassic period (when the movie *Jurassic Park* came out in 1993 at least), we did not have FOREIGN KEY constraints, and all relationships were enforced by triggers. This is not one of those stories where any one of us looks back fondly on those days at all. Thankfully, in terms of relationship enforcement, triggers are now relegated to enforcing special cases, such as when you have relationships between tables that are on different databases or if you want to only partially implement a relationship.

For the most part, it is somewhat more of an academic exercise at this point, as for most readers this will not occur. However, it is a good academic exercise because it helps you to think about all of the different directions that changes come in that you may need to protect against when you implement data protection in triggers.

To implement a relationship using triggers, you need several triggers:

- Parent:

  - UPDATE: Disallow the changing of keys if child values exist, or cascade the update.

  - DELETE: Prevent or cascade the deletion of rows that have associated parent rows.

- Child:

  - INSERT: Check to make sure the key exists in the parent table.

  - UPDATE: Check to make sure the "possibly" changed key exists in the parent table.

To begin this section, I will present templates to use to build these triggers, and then in the final section, I will code a complete trigger for demonstration. For these snippets of code, I refer to the tables as *parent* and *child*, with no schema or database named. Replacing the bits that are inside these greater than and less than symbols with appropriate code and table names that include the database and schema gives you the desired result when plugged into the trigger templates we've been using throughout this chapter.

Parent Update

Note that you can omit the parent update step if using surrogate keys based on identity property columns, because they aren't editable and hence cannot be changed.

There are a few possibilities you might want to implement:

- Cascading operations to child rows

- Preventing updating parent if child rows exist

If your table does allow changing of keys, then cascading operations is not possible from a proper generic trigger-coding standpoint. The problem is that if you modify the key of one or more parent rows in a statement that fires the trigger, there is not necessarily any way to correlate rows in the inserted table with the rows in the deleted table, leaving you unable to know which row in the inserted table is supposed to match which row in the deleted table. So I would not implement the cascading of a parent key change in a trigger; I would do this in your external code if you find the need for editable keys that cascade where a FOREIGN KEY constraint is not allowed (which should be pretty uncommon).

Preventing an update of parent rows where child rows exist is very straightforward. The idea here is that you want to take the same restrictive action as the NO ACTION clause on a relationship, for example:

```
--UPDATE() function is true if the column is referenced in an UPDATE
--statement SET clause or always true for DELETE or INSERT action
IF  UPDATE(<parent_key_column>) or UPDATE(<parent_key_column2>)
   BEGIN
       IF EXISTS ( SELECT   *
                   FROM    deleted
                           JOIN <child>
                               ON <child>.<parent_keys> =
                                           deleted.<parent_keys>
                 )
       BEGIN
```

```
        IF @rowsAffected = 1
                SELECT @msg = 'one row message' + inserted.somedata
                FROM    inserted;
        ELSE
                SELECT @msg = 'multi-row message';
            THROW 50000, @msg, 1;
    END;
END;
```

Parent Delete

Like the update, when a parent table row is deleted, we can either

- Cascade the delete to child rows.

- Prevent deleting parent rows if child rows exist.

Cascading is very simple. For the DELETE action, you simply use a correlated EXISTS subquery to get matching rows in the child table to the parent table:

```
DELETE <child>
WHERE  EXISTS ( SELECT *
                FROM    <parent>
                WHERE   <child>.<parent_key> = <parent>.<parent_key>);
```

To prevent the DELETE operation from happening when a child row exists, here's the basis of code to prevent deleting rows that have associated parent rows:

```
IF EXISTS ( SELECT  *
            FROM    deleted
                        JOIN <child>
                            ON <child>.<parent_key> = deleted.<parent_key>
            )
    BEGIN
        IF @rowsAffected = 1
            SELECT @msg = 'one row message' + inserted.somedata
            FROM    inserted;
        ELSE
```

```
        SELECT @msg = 'multi-row message';

      THROW 50000, @msg, 1;
  END;
END;
```

Child Insert and Child Update

On the child table, the goal will basically be to make sure that for every value you create in the child table, there exists a corresponding row in the parent table. The following snippet does this and takes into consideration the case where NULL values are allowed as well:

```
--@rowsAffected is part of the standard template
DECLARE @nullcount int, --you can omit if nulls are not allowed
        @validcount int;

IF UPDATE(<parent_key>)
  BEGIN
     --you can omit this check if nulls are not allowed
     SELECT  @nullcount = COUNT(*)
     FROM    inserted
     WHERE   inserted.<parent_key> is null;

     --does not count null values
     SELECT  @validcount = COUNT(*)
     FROM    inserted
                JOIN <parent> as Parent
                    ON  inserted.<parent_keys> = Parent.<parent_keys>;
     --If the null rows plus the valid ones don't equal the number of row
     --modified, it is a problem
     IF @validcount + @nullcount != @rowsAffected
       BEGIN
          IF @rowsAffected = 1
             SELECT @msg = 'The inserted <parent_key_name>: '
                            + CAST(parent_key as varchar(10))
                            + ' is not valid in the parent table.'
               FROM    inserted;
```

477

```
        ELSE
            SELECT @msg = 'Invalid <parent key column> inserted in rows.'
            THROW 50000, @msg, 16;
      END
  END
```

Example Trigger

Using basic blocks of code such as these, you can validate almost any foreign key relationship using triggers. For example, say you have a table in your PhoneData database called Logs.Call, with a primary key of CallId. In the CRM database, you have a Contacts.Journal table that stores contacts made to a person. To implement the child insert trigger, just fill in the blanks. The update trigger will be identical in the code as well and could be combined if only one trigger will ever be needed. This code will not execute as is; this is just for illustration purposes:

```
CREATE TRIGGER Contacts.Journal$insertTrigger
ON Contacts.Journal
AFTER INSERT AS
BEGIN
   SET NOCOUNT ON;
   SET ROWCOUNT 0; --in case the client has modified the rowcount
   --use inserted for insert or update trigger, deleted for update
   --or delete trigger count instead of @@ROWCOUNT due to merge behavior
   -- that sets @@ROWCOUNT to a number that is equal to number of merged
   -- rows, not rows being checked in trigger
   DECLARE @msg varchar(2000),     --used to hold the error message
   --use inserted for insert or update trigger, deleted for update
   --or delete trigger count instead of @@ROWCOUNT due to merge behavior
   --that sets @@ROWCOUNT to a number that is equal to number of merged
   --rows, not rows being checked in trigger
         @rowsAffected int = (SELECT COUNT(*) FROM inserted);

   --no need to continue on if no rows affected
   IF @rowsAffected = 0 RETURN;
```

```
BEGIN TRY

   --[validation section]
   --@rowsAffected is part of the standard template
   DECLARE @nullcount int,
           @validcount int;

   IF UPDATE(CallId)
    BEGIN
       --omit this check if nulls are not allowed
       --(left in here for an example)
       SELECT  @nullcount = COUNT(*)
       FROM    inserted
       WHERE   inserted.CallId IS NULL;

       --does not include null values
       SELECT  @validcount = count(*)
       FROM    inserted
                   JOIN PhoneData.Logs.Call AS Parent
                        on  inserted.CallId = Parent.CallId;

       IF @validcount + @nullcount != @rowsAffected
         BEGIN
             IF @rowsAffected = 1
                SELECT @msg = 'The inserted CallId: '
                                + cast(CallId AS varchar(10))
                                + ' is not valid in the'
                                + ' PhoneData.Logs.Call table.'
                 FROM    inserted;
             ELSE
                SELECT @msg = 'Invalid CallId in the inserted rows.';

             THROW  50000, @Msg, 1;

         END
    END
   --[modification section]
```

```
    END TRY
    BEGIN CATCH
        IF @@TRANCOUNT > 0
            ROLLBACK TRANSACTION;
        --will halt the batch or be caught by the caller's catch block
        THROW;
    END CATCH;
END;
```

INSTEAD OF Triggers

As explained in the introduction to the "DML Triggers" section, INSTEAD OF triggers fire before the DML action being affected by the SQL engine, rather than after it for AFTER triggers. In fact, when you have an INSTEAD OF trigger on a table, it's the first thing that's done when you INSERT, UPDATE, or DELETE from a table, because, as they are named, they fire *instead of* the native action the user executed. Inside the trigger, you perform the action—either the action that the user performed or some other action. You could make the DELETE action just insert the same row again, so instead of deleting a row, it replicates itself. Things like that are why I noted early in the chapter that triggers are not the best-loved devices. What they can do, not what they should do.

Tip   INSTEAD OF TRIGGER objects are notoriously dangerous for being forgotten and losing data when poor unit testing practices are employed. Because they replicate the statement being executed on a table, adding a new column to a table requires two steps, first to add the column and then to add the column to any INSTEAD OF TRIGGER objects.

Probably the most obvious limitation of INSTEAD OF triggers is that you can have only one for each action (INSERT, UPDATE, and DELETE) on the table. It is also possible to combine triggered actions just as you can for AFTER triggers, like having one INSTEAD OF trigger for INSERT and UPDATE (something I even more strongly suggest against for almost all uses of INSTEAD OF triggers). We'll use a slightly modified version of the same trigger template that we used for the T-SQL AFTER triggers, covered in more detail in Appendix B (available as a download).

One thing that makes these triggers extra useful is that you can use them on VIEW objects to make what would otherwise be noneditable views editable. Doing this, you encapsulate calls to all the affected tables in the trigger, much as you would a stored procedure, except now this view has all the external properties of a physical table, hiding the actual implementation from users.

I most often use INSTEAD OF triggers to set or modify values automatically so that the values are set to what I want, no matter what the client sends in a statement, much like we did in the previous chapter with the RowLastModifiedTime and RowCreatedTime columns. If you record last update times through client calls, it can be problematic if one of the client's clocks is a minute, a day, or even a year off. (You can extend the paradigm of setting a value to formatting any data, such as if you wanted to make all data that was stored lowercase.)

In this section, I'll demonstrate a few common ways you can use INSTEAD OF TRIGGER objects:

- Redirecting invalid data to an exception table

- Forcing no action to be performed on a table, even by someone who technically has proper rights

- Making a complex view modifiable as if it was a table

It's generally a best practice not to use INSTEAD OF triggers to do error raising validations such as we did with AFTER triggers unless you specifically need to. Typically, an INSTEAD OF trigger is employed to make things happen in the background in a silent manner.

Redirecting Invalid Data to an Exception Table

On some occasions, instead of returning an error when an invalid value is set for a column, you simply want to ignore it and log that an error had occurred. Generally, this wouldn't be used for bulk loading data (using SSIS's facilities to do this is a much better idea), but some examples of why you might do this follow:

- *Heads-down key entry*: In many shops where customer feedback forms or payments are received by the hundreds or thousands, there are people who open the mail, read it, and key in what's on the page. These people become incredibly skilled in rapid entry and generally make few mistakes. The mistakes they do make don't raise an error on their screens; rather, they fall to other people—exception handlers—to fix. You could use an INSTEAD OF trigger to redirect the wrong data to an exception table to be handled later.

- *Values that are read in from devices*: An example of this is on an assembly line, where a reading is taken but is so far out of range it couldn't be true, because of the malfunction of a device or just a human moving a sensor. Too many exception rows would require a look at the equipment, but only a few might be normal and acceptable. Another possibility is when someone scans a printed page using a scanner and inserts the data. Often, the values read are not right and have to be checked manually.

For our example, I'll design a table to take weather readings from a single thermometer. Sometimes, this thermometer sends back bad values that are impossible because it is starting to fail. We need to be able to put in readings, sometimes many at a time, because the device can cache results for some time if there is signal loss, but it tosses off the unlikely rows.

We build the following table, initially using a constraint to implement the simple sanity check. In the analysis of the data, we might find anomalies, but in this process, all we're going to do is look for the "impossible" cases:

```
CREATE SCHEMA Measurements;
GO
CREATE TABLE Measurements.WeatherReading
(
    WeatherReadingId int NOT NULL IDENTITY
          CONSTRAINT PKWeatherReading PRIMARY KEY,
    ReadingTime    datetime2(3) NOT NULL
          CONSTRAINT AKWeatherReading_Date UNIQUE,
    Temperature     float NOT NULL
          CONSTRAINT CHKWeatherReading_Temperature
                    CHECK(Temperature BETWEEN -80 and 150)
                    --raised from last edition for global warming
);
```

Then, we go to load the data, simulating what we might do when importing the data all at once:

```
INSERT  INTO Measurements.WeatherReading (ReadingTime, Temperature)
VALUES ('20200101 0:00',82.00), ('20200101 0:01',89.22),
       ('20200101 0:02',600.32),('20200101 0:03',88.22),
       ('20200101 0:04',99.01);
```

As we know with CHECK constraints, this isn't going to fly:

```
Msg 547, Level 16, State 0, Line 741
The INSERT statement conflicted with the CHECK constraint
"CHKWeatherReading_Temperature". The conflict occurred in database
"Chapter8", table "Measurements.WeatherReading", column 'Temperature'.
```

Select all the data in the table, and you'll see that this data never gets entered. Does this mean we have to dig through every row individually? Yes, in the current scheme. Or you could insert each row individually, which would take a lot more work for the server, but if you've been following along, you know we're going to write an INSTEAD OF TRIGGER to do this for us. First, we add a table to hold the exceptions to the Temperature rule:

```
CREATE TABLE Measurements.WeatherReading_exception
(
    WeatherReadingId  int NOT NULL IDENTITY
          CONSTRAINT PKWeatherReading_exception PRIMARY KEY,
    ReadingTime       datetime2(3) NOT NULL,
    Temperature       float NULL,
    ErrorNumber       int NOT NULL,
    ErrorMessage      nvarchar(2000) NOT NULL
);
```

Then, we create the trigger:

```
CREATE TRIGGER Measurements.WeatherReading$InsteadOfInsertTrigger
ON Measurements.WeatherReading
INSTEAD OF INSERT AS
BEGIN
```

```
SET NOCOUNT ON;
SET ROWCOUNT 0; --in case the client has modified the rowcount
--use inserted for insert or update trigger, deleted for update
--or delete trigger count instead of @@ROWCOUNT due to merge behavior
-- that sets @@ROWCOUNT to a number that is equal to number of merged
-- rows, not rows being checked in trigger
DECLARE @msg varchar(2000),    --used to hold the error message
--use inserted for insert or update trigger, deleted for update
--or delete trigger count instead of @@ROWCOUNT due to merge behavior
--that sets @@ROWCOUNT to a number that is equal to number of merged
--rows, not rows being checked in trigger
        @rowsAffected int = (SELECT COUNT(*) FROM inserted);

--no need to continue on if no rows affected
IF @rowsAffected = 0 RETURN;

BEGIN TRY
        --[validation section]
        --[modification section]

        --<perform action>

         --BAD data
        INSERT Measurements.WeatherReading_exception
                            (ReadingTime, Temperature)
        SELECT ReadingTime, Temperature
        FROM   inserted
        WHERE  NOT(Temperature BETWEEN -80 and 150);

         --GOOD data
        INSERT Measurements.WeatherReading (ReadingTime, Temperature)
        SELECT ReadingTime, Temperature
        FROM   inserted
        WHERE  (Temperature BETWEEN -80 and 150);
END TRY
BEGIN CATCH
```

```
IF @@TRANCOUNT > 0
    ROLLBACK TRANSACTION;

--will halt the batch or be caught by the caller's catch block
THROW;

END CATCH
END;
```

Now, we try to insert the rows with the bad data still in there:

```
INSERT  INTO Measurements.WeatherReading (ReadingTime, Temperature)
VALUES ('20200101 0:00',82.00), ('20200101 0:01',89.22),
        ('20200101 0:02',600.32),('20200101 0:03',88.22),
        ('20200101 0:04',99.01);

SELECT *
FROM Measurements.WeatherReading;
```

The good data is in the following output:

WeatherReadingId	ReadingTime	Temperature
4	2020-01-01 00:00:00.000	82
5	2020-01-01 00:01:00.000	89.22
6	2020-01-01 00:03:00.000	88.22
7	2020-01-01 00:04:00.000	99.01

The nonconforming data can be seen by viewing the data in the exception table:

```
SELECT *
FROM   Measurements.WeatherReading_exception;
```

This returns the following result:

WeatherReadingId	ReadingTime	Temperature
1	2020-01-01 00:02:00.000	600.32

Now, it might be possible to go back and work on each exception, perhaps extrapolating the value it should have been, based on the previous and the next measurements taken:

```
(88.22 + 89.22) /2 = 88.72
```

Of course, if we did that, we would probably want to include another attribute that indicated that a reading was extrapolated rather than an actual reading from the device. This is obviously a very simplistic example, and you could even make the functionality a lot more interesting by using previous readings to determine what is reasonable.

One note about INSTEAD OF TRIGGER objects: If you are doing a singleton insert, you may be inclined to use SCOPE_IDENTITY() to fetch the row that is inserted. If you have an INSTEAD OF trigger on the table, this will not give you the desired value:

```
INSERT  INTO Measurements.WeatherReading (ReadingTime, Temperature)
VALUES ('20160101 0:05',93.22);

SELECT SCOPE_IDENTITY();
```

This returns NULL, regardless of whether or not the row goes into one table or the other. If you need the last created identity value, you can use the alternate key for the row (in this case the ReadingTime, which may feel wrong, but for a reading, it would be logical to not accept > 1 reading at the same point in time) or use a SEQUENCE generator as we did in Chapter 7 for one of the tables which provides control over the value that is used.

Forcing No Action to Be Performed on a Table

This example deals with what's almost a security issue. Often, users have *too* much access, and this includes administrators who generally use sysadmin privileges to look for problems with systems. Some tables we simply don't ever want to be modified. We might implement triggers to keep any user—even a system administrator—from changing the data.

In this example, we're going to implement a table to hold the version of the database. It's a single-row "table" that behaves more like a global variable. It's here to tell the application which version of the schema to expect, so it can tell the user to upgrade or lose functionality:

```
CREATE SCHEMA System;
GO
CREATE TABLE System.Version
(
    DatabaseVersion varchar(10)
);
INSERT  INTO System.Version (DatabaseVersion)
VALUES ('1.0.12');
```

Our application always looks to this value to see what objects it expects to be there when it uses them. We clearly don't want this value to get modified, even if someone has db_owner rights in the database. So we might apply an INSTEAD OF TRIGGER object (no need for all the template stuff—we just want to fail immediately in this case):

```
CREATE TRIGGER System.Version$InsteadOfInsertUpdateDeleteTrigger
ON System.Version
INSTEAD OF INSERT, UPDATE, DELETE AS
BEGIN
    SET NOCOUNT ON;

    --No error handling necessary, just the message.
    --We just put the kibosh on the action.
    THROW 50000, 'Rows in System.Version table may not be modified', 1;
END;
```

attempts to delete the value, like so

```
UPDATE System.Version
SET     DatabaseVersion = '1.1.1';
GO
```

This will result in the following:

```
Msg 50000, Level 16, State 1, Procedure Version$InsteadOfInsertUpdateDele
teTrigger, Line 15
Rows in System.Version table may not be modified
```

Checking the data, you will see that it remains the same:

```
SELECT *
FROM    System.Version;
```

Returns:
```
DatabaseVersion
---------------
1.0.12
```

The administrator, when doing an upgrade, would then have to take the conscious step of running the following code:

```
ALTER TABLE System.Version
    DISABLE TRIGGER Version$InsteadOfInsertUpdateDeleteTrigger;
```

Now, you can run the UPDATE statement:

```
UPDATE System.Version
SET     DatabaseVersion = '1.1.1';
```

Check the data again

```
SELECT *
FROM    System.Version;
```

and you will see that it has been modified:

```
DatabaseVersion
---------------
1.1.1
```

Re-enable the trigger using ALTER TABLE...ENABLE TRIGGER:

```
ALTER TABLE System.Version
    ENABLE TRIGGER Version$InsteadOfInsertUpdateDeleteTrigger;
```

Using a trigger like this enables you to "close the gate," keeping the data safely in the table, even from accidental changes. You can also add an AFTER UPDATE TRIGGER object such as the following to re-enable the INSTEAD OF TRIGGER after the modification and get a lot more complex with the data checking, depending on how complex your needs are:

```
CREATE TRIGGER System.Version$AfterUpdateTrigger
ON System.Version
AFTER UPDATE AS
BEGIN
  ALTER TABLE System.Version
    ENABLE TRIGGER Version$InsteadOfInsertUpdateDeleteTrigger;
END;
```

This is a nice method to build a simple solution for an administrator to have a gate to make sure they open and close the gate on a table like this, but it is best to not get overly tricky with too many solutions such as this, or it can get confusing when too many things just happen in your databases.

Making a Complex View Modifiable

The final trigger example using an INSTEAD OF TRIGGER object is to make a complex VIEW object updatable. The example code will be rather abstract to keep things simple, but a decent use of this technology is to vertically partition a table where either part of the table is accessed frequently, so keeping the size down is useful, or to vertically partition one or more very large columns that are rarely used.

The latter case is the example we will implement. Say you have the following table, loaded with three rows. The ValueB column is very large and rarely used, but when it is used, it is quite large compared to the rest of the data:

```
--say you have a simple enough table...
CREATE SCHEMA Alt;
GO
CREATE TABLE Alt.TableName
(
        TableNameId int PRIMARY KEY,
        ValueA varchar(10) NOT NULL,
        ValueB varchar(4000) NULL
)
```

```
GO
--with some simple enough data
INSERT INTO Alt.TableName(TableNameId, ValueA, ValueB)
VALUES (1, 10, NULL);
INSERT INTO Alt.TableName(TableNameId, ValueA, ValueB)
VALUES (2, '20', REPLICATE('A',4000));
INSERT INTO Alt.TableName(TableNameId, ValueA, ValueB)
VALUES (3, '30', NULL);
GO

SELECT TableName.TableNameId, TableName.ValueA, TableName.ValueB
FROM    Alt.TableName;
```

The data in the table looks like this:

TableNameId	ValueA	ValueB
1	10	NULL
2	20	AAAAAAAAAAAAAAAAAAAAAAAAAAAAAAAAAAAAAAAAAAAAAAAAAA...
3	30	NULL

The customer rarely uses ValueB, but this column is taking up space in the primary table, not allowing some highly concurrent queries to process in a timely manner due to using a lot of extra memory. One thing that could be done is to make this into a view that looks like Alt.TableName. So we use the following script to create two TABLE objects and a VIEW object:

```
CREATE TABLE Alt.TableNameA
(
    TableNameId int NOT NULL PRIMARY KEY,
    ValueA  varchar(10) NOT NULL

);
CREATE TABLE Alt.TableNameB
(
    TableNameId int NOT NULL PRIMARY KEY,
    ValueB  varchar(4000) NOT NULL
);
```

```
GO
--split the data...Only put rows that are non-null...
INSERT INTO Alt.TableNameA
SELECT TableName.TableNameId, TableName.ValueA
FROM    Alt.TableName;

INSERT INTO Alt.TableNameB
SELECT TableName.TableNameId, TableName.ValueB
FROM    Alt.TableName
WHERE   ValueB IS NOT NULL;
GO

SELECT TableNameA.TableNameId, TableNameA.ValueA
FROM    Alt.TableNameA;

SELECT TableNameB.TableNameId, TableNameB.ValueB
FROM    Alt.TableNameB;
```

The output of the SELECT statements shows you the partitioned data:

```
TableNameId ValueA

----------- ----------
1           10
2           20
3           30

TableNameId ValueB

----------- -----------------------------------------------------
2           AAAAAAAAAAAAAAAAAAAAAAAAAAAAAAAAAAAAAAAAAAAAAAAAAAAAA...
```

With the table partitioned, we can now drop the original table (in practice, I typically would suggest renaming the table for safety's sake if you are doing this in a live setting and then dropping it after you are comfortable that the changes have been completely made). We will also create the VIEW:

```
DROP TABLE Alt.TableName;
GO
CREATE VIEW Alt.TableName
```

```
AS
SELECT TableNameA.TableNameId, TableNameA.ValueA, TableNameB.ValueB
FROM   Alt.TableNameA --this is the primary table
       LEFT JOIN Alt.TableNameB
           ON TableNameA.TableNameId = TableNameB.TableNameId;
GO
```

For users reading this data, they would not be able to tell the difference between this VIEW and the original TABLE. Users that query the TABLE or VIEW without referencing ValueB would see performance gains because the query processor will not access TableNameB. However, query writers who need to change data in the TABLE would not have such luck. If you try to execute an INSERT statement, like we used to load data previously, you will see a failure:

```
INSERT INTO Alt.TableName(TableNameId, ValueA, ValueB)
VALUES (4, NULL, '10');
```

This will cause the following error:

```
Msg 4405, Level 16, State 1, Line 57
View or function 'Alt.TableName' is not updatable because the modification
affects multiple base tables.
```

To change this, you can create an INSTEAD OF TRIGGER object that splits the operation and does the INSERT operation:

```
CREATE TRIGGER Alt.TableName$InsteadOfInsertTrigger
ON Alt.TableName
INSTEAD OF INSERT AS
BEGIN
    SET NOCOUNT ON;
    SET ROWCOUNT 0; --in case the client has modified the rowcount
    --use inserted for insert or update trigger, deleted for update
    --or delete trigger count instead of @@ROWCOUNT due to merge behavior
    -- that sets @@ROWCOUNT to a number that is equal to number of merged
    -- rows, not rows being checked in trigger
    DECLARE @msg varchar(2000),     --used to hold the error message
```

```
--use inserted for insert or update trigger, deleted for update
--or delete trigger count instead of @@ROWCOUNT due to merge behavior
--that sets @@ROWCOUNT to a number that is equal to number of merged
--rows, not rows being checked in trigger
        @rowsAffected int = (SELECT COUNT(*) FROM inserted);

--no need to continue on if no rows affected
IF @rowsAffected = 0 RETURN;

BEGIN TRY
        --[validation section]
        --[modification section]

        --<perform action>

        INSERT INTO Alt.TableNameA(TableNameId,ValueA)
        SELECT TableNameId, ValueA
        FROM inserted;

        INSERT INTO Alt.TableNameB(TableNameId,ValueB)
        SELECT TableNameId, ValueB
        FROM inserted
        WHERE ValueB IS NOT null
    END TRY
    BEGIN CATCH
        IF @@TRANCOUNT > 0
            ROLLBACK TRANSACTION;

        --will halt the batch or be caught by the caller's catch block
        THROW;

    END CATCH
END;
```

Now you can insert just like a normal TABLE object:

```
INSERT INTO Alt.TableName(TableNameId, ValueA, ValueB)
VALUES (4, '40', NULL);
INSERT INTO Alt.TableName(TableNameId, ValueA, ValueB)
VALUES (5, '50',REPLICATE('B',4000));
```

You can query the data just like a normal TABLE object as well:

```
SELECT *
FROM   Alt.TableName;
```

This returns the data that looks just like the original table plus some new rows we have added:

```
TableNameId ValueA    ValueB
----------- --------- -------------------------------------------------
1           10        NULL
2           20        AAAAAAAAAAAAAAAAAAAAAAAAAAAAAAAAAAAAAAAAAAAAAAAA…
3           30        NULL
4           40        NULL
5           50        BBBBBBBBBBBBBBBBBBBBBBBBBBBBBBBBBBBBBBBBBBBBBBBB…
```

And of course, you can query/manipulate the data in the individual objects separately. If you want to be able to do DELETE and UPDATE operations, the very same process is required. An INSTEAD OF TRIGGER object does the work that is not allowed by SQL Server.

Dealing with TRIGGER and Constraint Errors

One important thing to consider about TRIGGER objects and CHECK (and FOREIGN KEY) constraints is how you need to deal with the error handling errors violating their rules. One of the drawbacks to using TRIGGER objects is that the state of the database after an error is different from when you have a constraint error. We need to consider two situations when we do a ROLLBACK in a trigger, using an error handler as we have in this chapter:

- *You aren't using a* TRY-CATCH *block*: This situation is simple. The batch stops processing in its tracks. SQL Server handles cleanup for any transaction you were in.

- *You* are *using a* TRY-CATCH *block*: This situation can be a bit tricky and will depend on what you want to occur.

Take a TRY-CATCH block such as this one:

```
BEGIN TRY
    <DML STATEMENT>
END TRY
BEGIN CATCH
    <handle it>
END CATCH;
```

If the T-SQL trigger rolls back and an error is raised, when you get to the <handle it> block, you won't be in a transaction. (For the rare use of CLR triggers, you're in charge of whether the connection ends.) When a CHECK constraint causes the error or the caller manually executes a simple THROW or RAISERROR, you'll still be in a transaction context. Generically, here's the CATCH block that I use (as I have used in the triggers written so far in this chapter):

```
    BEGIN CATCH
            IF @@TRANCOUNT > 0
                ROLLBACK TRANSACTION;

            --will halt the batch or be caught by the caller's catch block
            THROW;
    END CATCH;
```

In almost every case, I roll back any transaction, possibly log the error (though I haven't done this in the primary chapters of the book, it is outlined in Appendix B, available in the downloads for the book), and then reraise the error. It is simpler to do as a rule and is 99.997% of the time what will be desired. In order to show the different scenarios that can occur, I will build the following abstract tables for demonstrating TRIGGER and constraint error handling:

```
CREATE TABLE Alt.ErrorHandlingTest
(
    ErrorHandlingTestId   int CONSTRAINT PKErrorHandlingTest PRIMARY KEY,
    CONSTRAINT CHKErrorHandlingTest_ErrorHandlingTestId_GreaterThanZero
          CHECK (ErrorHandlingTestId > 0)
);
```

Note that if you try to put a value greater than 0 into the ErrorHandlingTestId, it will cause a constraint error. In the TRIGGER object, the only statement we will implement in the TRY section will be to raise an error. So, no matter what input is sent to the table, it will be discarded and an error will be raised; and, as we have done previously, we will use ROLLBACK if there is a transaction in progress and then execute a THROW:

```
CREATE TRIGGER Alt.ErrorHandlingTest$InsertTrigger
ON Alt.ErrorHandlingTest
AFTER INSERT
AS
 BEGIN
    BEGIN TRY
        THROW 50000, 'Test Error',16;
    END TRY
    BEGIN CATCH
        IF @@TRANCOUNT > 0
              ROLLBACK TRANSACTION;
        THROW;
    END CATCH;
 END;
```

The first thing to understand is that when a normal constraint causes the DML operation to fail, the batch will continue to operate:

```
--NO Transaction, Constraint Error
INSERT Alt.ErrorHandlingTest
VALUES (-1);
SELECT 'continues';
```

You will see that the error is raised and then the SELECT statement is executed:

```
Msg 547, Level 16, State 0, Line 913
The INSERT statement conflicted with the CHECK constraint
"CHKErrorHandlingTest_ErrorHandlingTestId_GreaterThanZero". The conflict
occurred in database "Chapter8", table "Alt.ErrorHandlingTest", column
'ErrorHandlingTestId'.
```

The statement has been terminated.

----

continues

However, do this with a trigger error:

```
--NO Transaction, Trigger Error
INSERT Alt.ErrorHandlingTest
VALUES (1);
SELECT 'continues';
```

This returns the following and does not get to the SELECT 'continues' line at all:

```
Msg 50000, Level 16, State 16, Procedure ErrorHandlingTest$AfterInsertTrigg
er, Line 6
Test Error
```

This fairly elegant stoppage occurs using THROW because THROW stops the batch. However, using RAISERROR, the batch will still stop, but it will give you an extra message about stopping the trigger. As I will show, if you just use THROW to throw an error in the trigger, it will still end up ending as well, in a far less elegant manner.

There are also differences in dealing with errors from constraints and TRIGGER objects when you are using TRY-CATCH and transactions. Take the following batch. The error will be a constraint type. The big thing to understand is the state of a transaction after the error. This is definitely an issue that you have to be careful with:

```
-- Transaction, Constraint Error
BEGIN TRY
    BEGIN TRANSACTION
    INSERT Alt.ErrorHandlingTest
    VALUES (-1);
    COMMIT;
END TRY
BEGIN CATCH
    SELECT  CASE XACT_STATE()
                WHEN 1 THEN 'Committable'
                WHEN 0 THEN 'No transaction'
                ELSE 'Uncommitable tran' END as XACT_STATE
```

```
            ,ERROR_NUMBER() AS ErrorNumber
            ,ERROR_MESSAGE() as ErrorMessage;
    IF @@TRANCOUNT > 0
          ROLLBACK TRANSACTION;
END CATCH;
```

This returns the following:

XACT_STATE	ErrorNumber	ErrorMessage
Committable	547	The INSERT statement conflicted with the…

When you reach the CATCH block, the transaction is still in force and in a stable state. If you want to continue on in the batch doing whatever you need to do, it is certainly fine to do so. However, if you end up using any TRIGGER objects to enforce data integrity, the situation will be different (and not entirely obvious to the programmer). In the next batch, we will use 1 as the value, so we get a TRIGGER error instead of a constraint one:

```
-- Transaction, Trigger Error
BEGIN TRANSACTION
    BEGIN TRY
          INSERT Alt.ErrorHandlingTest
          VALUES (1);
          COMMIT TRANSACTION;
    END TRY
BEGIN CATCH
    SELECT  CASE XACT_STATE()
                 WHEN 1 THEN 'Committable'
                 WHEN 0 THEN 'No transaction'
                 ELSE 'Uncommitable tran' END as XACT_STATE
            ,ERROR_NUMBER() AS ErrorNumber
            ,ERROR_MESSAGE() as ErrorMessage;
    IF @@TRANCOUNT > 0
          ROLLBACK TRANSACTION;
END CATCH;
```

This returns the following:

```
XACT_STATE          ErrorNumber ErrorMessage
----------------    ----------- --------------------------------------------
No transaction      50000       Test Error
```

In the error handler of our batch, the session is no longer in a transaction, since we rolled the transaction back in the trigger. However, unlike the case without an error handler, we continue on in the batch rather than the batch ending. Note, however, that there is no way to recover from an issue in a TRIGGER object without resorting to trickery (like storing status in a temporary variable table (which is not subject to transactions) instead of throwing an error or rolling back, but this is discouraged unless you really need it for a specific need; it really gets messy to keep up with as you nest triggers).

The unpredictability of the transaction state is why we check the @@TRANCOUNT to see if we need to do a rollback. In this case, the error message in the TRIGGER was bubbled up into this CATCH statement, so we are in an error state that is handled by the CATCH BLOCK.

As a final demonstration, let's look at one other case, and this is where you raise an error in a TRIGGER without rolling back the transaction:

```
ALTER TRIGGER Alt.ErrorHandlingTest$InsertTrigger
ON Alt.ErrorHandlingTest
AFTER INSERT
AS
    BEGIN TRY
        THROW 50000, 'Test Error',16;
    END TRY
    BEGIN CATCH
        --Commented out for test purposes
        --IF @@TRANCOUNT > 0
        --    ROLLBACK TRANSACTION;

        THROW;
    END CATCH;
```

Now, causing an error in the trigger

```
--Transaction, Special Trigger
BEGIN TRY
    BEGIN TRANSACTION
    INSERT Alt.errorHandlingTest
    VALUES (1);
    COMMIT TRANSACTION;
END TRY
BEGIN CATCH
    SELECT  CASE XACT_STATE()
                WHEN 1 THEN 'Committable'
                WHEN 0 THEN 'No transaction'
                ELSE 'Uncommitable tran' END as XACT_STATE
            ,ERROR_NUMBER() AS ErrorNumber
            ,ERROR_MESSAGE() as ErrorMessage;
    IF @@TRANCOUNT > 0
        ROLLBACK TRANSACTION;
END CATCH;
```

the result will be as follows:

XACT_STATE	ErrorNumber	ErrorMessage
Uncommitable tran	50000	Test Error

You get an uncommittable transaction, also referred to as a *doomed* transaction. An uncommittable transaction is still in force but can never be committed and must eventually be rolled back.

The point of all of this is that you need to be careful when you code your error handling to do a few things:

- *Keep things simple*: Do only as much handling as you need, and generally treat errors as unrecoverable unless recovery is truly necessary. The key is to deal with the errors and get back out to a steady state so that the client can know what to try again.

- *Keep things standard*: Set a standard and follow it. Always use the same handler for all your code in all cases except where you have a specific need to do something special. It is important to realize that your code may be called by other code as part of a transaction that has already millions of changes, which complicates matters greatly.

- *Test well*: The most important bit of information is to test and test again all the possible paths your code can take.

To always get a consistent situation in my code, I pretty much always use a standard handler as I will demonstrate in the following code block. Basically, before every data manipulation statement, I set a manual message in a variable that says what I was doing, use it as the first half of the message to know what was being executed, and then append the system message to know what went wrong, sometimes using a constraint mapping function as mentioned earlier, although usually that is overkill since the UI traps all errors and knows what it was attempting to do when the error occurred:

```
BEGIN TRY
    BEGIN TRANSACTION;
    DECLARE @errorMessage nvarchar(4000) =
            N'Error inserting data into Alt.ErrorHandlingTest';
    INSERT Alt.ErrorHandlingTest
    VALUES (-1);
    COMMIT TRANSACTION;
END TRY
BEGIN CATCH
    IF @@TRANCOUNT > 0
        ROLLBACK TRANSACTION;

    --I also add in the stored procedure or trigger where the error
    --occurred also when in a coded object
    SET @errorMessage = CONCAT( COALESCE(@errorMessage,''),
                ' ( System Error: ', ERROR_NUMBER(),':',ERROR_MESSAGE(),
                ' : Line Number:',ERROR_LINE()));
        THROW 50000,@errorMessage,16;
END CATCH;
```

Now, this returns the following:

```
Msg 50000, Level 16, State 16, Line 18
Error inserting data into alt.errorHandlingTest ( System Error:
547:The INSERT statement conflicted with the CHECK constraint "chkAlt_
errorHandlingTest_errorHandlingTestId_greaterThanZero".
The conflict occurred in database "Chapter8", table "alt.
errorHandlingTest", column 'errorHandlingTestId': Line Number:4)
```

This returns the manually created message and the system message, as well as where the error occurred. In Appendix B, I outline some additional methods you might take to log errors, using a stored procedure I call ErrorHandling.ErrorLog$Insert, depending on whether the error is something that you expected to occur on occasion or is something (as I said about triggers) that really shouldn't happen. If I was implementing the code in such a way that I expected errors to occur, I might also include a call to something like the ErrorHandling.ErrorMap$MapError procedure that was discussed earlier in the chapter to beautify the error message value for the system error.

Error handling is definitely a place where SQL Server's T-SQL language lacks in comparison to almost any other language, but took leaps of improvement in 2005 with TRY...CATCH, with a few improvements continued in 2012 with the ability to rethrow an error using THROW, which we have used in the standard trigger template. Of course, the most important part of writing error handing code is the testing you do to make sure that it works!

Best Practices

The main best practice is to protect the integrity of your data at all costs, using the right tool for the job. There are many tools in (and around) SQL Server to use to protect the data. Picking the right tool for a given situation is essential. For example, every column in every table could be defined as nvarchar(max). Using CHECK constraints, you could then constrain the values to look like almost any datatype. It sounds silly perhaps, but it is possible. But you know better after reading Chapter 7 and now this chapter, right?

When choosing your method of protecting data, it's best to apply the following types of objects, in this order:

- *Datatypes*: Choosing the right type is the first line of defense. If all your values need to be integers between 1 and 100,000, just using an `integer` datatype takes care of one part of the rule immediately, but it doesn't take care of cases where the value is set to 100000000.

- *Defaults*: Though you might not think defaults can be considered data protection resources, you should know that you can use them to automatically set column values where the purpose of the column might not be apparent to the user (and the database adds a suitable value for the column).

- *Simple* `CHECK` *constraints*: These are important in ensuring that your data is within specifications. The performance implications of simple `CHECK` constraints are minimal. In the constraint definition, you can use almost any system scalar functions with no concern for performance.

- *Complex* `CHECK` *constraints using user-defined scalar functions*: These can be very interesting parts of an implementation to meet some complex need for a design but should be used sparingly, and you should rarely use a function that references the same table's data due to inconsistent results. The performance implications of such constraints can be considerable, depending on what is in the code of the functions.

- *Triggers*: Triggers allow you to build pieces of code that fire automatically `INSTEAD OF` or `AFTER` any `INSERT`, `UPDATE`, and `DELETE` operation that's executed against a single table. These are used to enforce rules that are too complex for `CHECK` constraints and to introduce desired side effects to a DML operation.

Don't be afraid to enforce rules in more than one location. Although having rules as close to the data storage as possible is essential to trusting the integrity of the data when you use the data, there's no reason why the user needs to suffer through a poor user interface with a bunch of simple text boxes with no validation, just to have to fix ten errors, one at a time. The database checks are there to make sure the integrity is preserved no matter how the data is loaded into the table, but the UI is there for the user.

Or course, not all data protection can be done at the object level, and some will need to be managed using client code or even asynchronous processes that execute long after the data has been entered. The major difference between user code and the methods we have discussed so far in the book is that SQL Server-based enforced integrity is automatic and cannot (accidentally) be overridden. It also is far better in terms of dealing with concurrent users making frequent changes to data.

Summary

Now that we have covered all of the major topics of implementing a simple database, you should be able to build databases to serve the majority of needs. And as we have seen in this chapter, if you take the time to build data protection into your database, the only bad data that can get into your system has nothing to do with the design (if a user wants to type the name John as "Jahn" or even "IdiotWhoInsultedMe"—stranger things *have* happened!—there's nothing much that can realistically be done in the database server to prevent it). As an architect or programmer, you can't possibly stop users from putting the names of pieces of equipment in a table named Employee. There's no semantic checking built in, and it would be impossible to do so without some form of external processes to check data to see that the name Mr. TwoDoor Ford isn't caused by a parent with different tastes in child names. Only users using the database as it is designed can take care of this. Of course, it helps if you've given the users the right set of tables to store all their data, but still, users will be users.

The most we can do in SQL Server is to make sure that design is fundamentally sound, such that the data minimally makes sense without knowledge of decisions that were made by the users that, regardless of whether they are correct, are legal values. If your HR employees keep trying to pay your new programmers minimum wage, the database likely won't care, but if they try to say that new employees make a negative salary, actually owing the company money for the privilege to come to work, well, that is probably unacceptable. (This is true even if the job is doughnut tester or some other highly desirable occupation.)

- Use CHECK constraints to protect data in a single row. You can access any column in the table, but only the data in that one row. You can access data in other tables using user-defined functions, if you so desire, but note that just like building your own foreign key checking, you need to consider what happens in the table you are checking and the table you are referencing.

- Use TRIGGER objects to do most complex checking, especially when you need to reference rows in the same table, like checking balances. Triggers can also introduce side effects, like maintaining denormalized data if it is needed or even calling other procedures like sp_db_sendmail if it is truly needed.

- Avoid using triggers to do anything that could be safely done elsewhere, if possible, as they are not the best-performing tool in your toolbox. And always keep in mind that the most important part of writing a TRIGGER object is understanding that it executes once per DML execution, no matter if one row was affected or 1 billion rows. Understand what happens if you use a CURSOR to send email one row at a time for those billion rows that were modified. (Cue the *Jeopardy!* music on a long loop.)

Once you've built and implemented a set of appropriate data-safeguarding resources, you can then trust that the data in your database has been validated. You should never need to revalidate keys or values in your data once it's stored in your database, but it's never a bad idea to do such testing regularly, so you know that no integrity gaps have slipped by you, particularly when a DBA had to do an import from a spreadsheet and forgot to turn back on a constraint because a manager was breathing fire down their neck to finish immediately!

CHAPTER 9

Patterns and Anti-patterns

A designer has a duty to create timeless design. To be timeless you have to think really far into the future, not next year, not in two years but in 20 years minimum.

—Philippe Starck, Designer, Architect

There is an old saying that you shouldn't try to reinvent the wheel, and honestly, in essence it is a very good saying. But with all such sayings, a modicum of common sense is required for its application. If everyone down through history took the saying literally, your car would have wheels made out of the trunk of a tree (which the *MythBusters* proved you could do in their "Good Wood" episode), since that clearly could have been one of the first wheel-like machines that was used. If everyone down through history had said "that's good enough," driving to Walley World in the family truckster would be a far less comfortable experience.

Over time, however, the basic concept of a wheel has been intact, from rock wheel to wagon wheel, to steel-belted radials, and even a wheel of cheddar. Each of these is round and able to move by rolling from place A to place B. Each solution follows that common pattern but diverges to solve a unique, specific instance of a problem. The goal of a software programmer should be to first try understanding existing techniques and then either use or improve them. Solving the same problem over and over without any knowledge of the past is nuts.

One of the neat things about software design, including database design, is that there are base patterns, such as normalization, that we will build upon. That is what this chapter is about, taking the basic structures we have built so far, and taking more and more complex groupings of structures, we will produce more complex, interesting solutions to problems.

© Louis Davidson 2021
L. Davidson, *Pro SQL Server Relational Database Design and Implementation*,
https://doi.org/10.1007/978-1-4842-6497-3_9

Of course, in as much as there are positive patterns that work, there are also negative patterns that have failed over and over down through history. Take personal flight. For many, many years, truly intelligent people tried over and over to strap wings on their arms and fly. They were close in concept, but just doing the same thing over and over was folly. Once it was understood how to apply Bernoulli's principle to building wings and what it would truly take to fly, the Wright brothers applied these principles to produce the first manned flying machine. If you ever happen by Kitty Hawk, North Carolina, you can see the plane and location of that flight. Not an amazing amount has changed between that airplane and today's airplanes in basic principle. They weren't required to have their entire body scanned and patted down for that first flight, but the wings worked the same way.

Throughout this book, we have covered the basic implementation tools that you can use to assemble solutions that meet your real-world needs. In this chapter, I am going to extend this notion and present a few deeper examples where we assemble a part of a database that deals with common problems that show up in almost any database solution. The chapter is broken up into two major sections, starting with the larger topic, patterns that are desirable to use. The other major section discusses anti-patterns, or patterns that you may frequently see that are not desirable to use (along with the preferred method of solution, naturally).

Desirable Patterns

In this section, I am going to cover a variety of implementation patterns that can be used to solve very common problems. By no means should this be confused with a comprehensive list of the types of problems you may face; think of it instead as a sampling of methods to show how to solve specific problems.

The patterns and solutions that I will present in the following subsections are as follows:

- *Uniqueness*: Moving beyond the simple uniqueness we covered in the first chapters of this book, we'll look at some very realistic patterns of solutions that cannot be implemented with a simple uniqueness constraint.

- *Data-driven design*: The goal of data-driven design is to never hard-code values that don't have a fixed meaning. You break down your programming needs into situations that can be based on sets of data values that can be modified without affecting code.

- *Historical/temporal*: At times it can be very desirable to look at previous versions of data that has changed over time. I will present strategies you can use to view your data at various points in history.

- *Images, documents, and other files*: There is, quite often, a need to store documents in the database, like a web user's avatar picture, the movie *Avatar*, a security photo to identify an employee, or even documents of many types. We will look at some of the methods available to you in SQL Server and discuss the reasons you might choose one method or another.

- *Generalization*: We will look at some ways that you need to be careful with how specific you make your tables so that you fit the solution to the needs of the user.

- *Storing user-specified data*: You can't always design a database to cover every known future need. I will cover some of the possibilities for letting users extend their database themselves in a manner that can be somewhat controlled by the administrators.

- *Graph data in SQL Server*: Storing loosely interconnected data has always been a desire when building relational databases but has always been somewhat complicated. SQL Server 2017 introduced, and 2019 improved, graph objects to SQL Server, and in this section, we will cover their usage.

Uniqueness Techniques

Throughout this book, you probably have noted that uniqueness of data is a major concern for your design. The fact is uniqueness is one of the largest problems you will tackle when designing a database, because figuring out how to tell two rows apart from one another can be a very difficult task in some cases. It will also be one of the most difficult tasks you will encounter if you do any support as well, trying to fix the cases where rows actually are not unique.

In this section, we will explore how you can implement more advanced types of uniqueness than what simple PRIMARY KEY and UNIQUE constraints will afford you. Each of these scenarios hits at the heart of the common problems you will come across:

- *Selective*: Sometimes, we won't have information for all rows, but the rows where we do have data need to be unique. As an example, consider the driver's license numbers of employees. No two people can have the same information, but not everyone will necessarily have one, at least not recorded in the database.

- *Bulk*: Sometimes, we need to inventory items where some of the items are equivalent to the human eye. For example, cans of corn in the grocery store. You can't tell each item apart, but you do need to know how many you have.

- *Range*: Instead of a single value of uniqueness, we often need to make sure that ranges of data don't overlap, like appointments. For example, take a hair salon. You don't want Mrs. McGillicutty to have an appointment at the same time as Mrs. Mertz, or no one is going to end up happy. Things are even more important when you are controlling something like a transportation system.

- *Likely*: The most difficult case is the most common in that it can be difficult to tell two people apart who come to your company for service. Did two persons with the name Louis Davidson purchase toy airplanes yesterday? Possibly. At the same phone number and address, with the same last four digits of a credit card number? Probably not. But another point I have worked to death in this book is that in the database you can't enforce *likely*...only *definitely*.

Uniqueness is one of the biggest struggles in day-to-day operations, as it is essential to not offend customers nor ship them 100 orders of Legos when they actually only placed a single order. We need to make sure that we don't end up with ten employees with the same tax identification number (prompting a not so friendly visit from the tax man), far fewer cans of corn than we expected, ten appointments at the same time, and so on.

Selective Uniqueness

We previously discussed PRIMARY KEY and UNIQUE constraints, but neither of these will fit the scenario where you need to make sure some subset of the data, rather than every row, is unique. For example, say you have a table of employees, and each employee can possibly have an insurance policy. The policy numbers must be unique, but the user might not have a policy.

Three of the best solutions to this problem are the following:

- *Filtered indexes*: This feature was new in SQL Server 2008. The CREATE INDEX command syntax has a WHERE clause so that the index pertains only to certain rows in the table.

- *Indexed view*: In versions prior to 2008, the way to implement this was to create a VIEW object with a WHERE clause and then index the view. This method can still have value if you need the view for other reasons.

- *Separate table for the data pertaining to the selective uniqueness*: A solution that needs noting is to make a separate table for the lower-cardinality uniqueness items. So, for example, you might have a table for employees' insurance policy numbers. In some cases, this may be the best solution, but it can lead to proliferation of tables that never really are accessed alone, making more work than needed. If you designed properly, you would have decided on this in the design phase of the project.

As a demonstration, I will create a schema and table for the human resources' employee table with a column for employee number and a column for insurance policy number as well. I will use a database named Chapter9 with default settings for the examples unless otherwise noted:

```
CREATE SCHEMA HumanResources;
GO
CREATE TABLE HumanResources.Employee
(
    EmployeeId int IDENTITY(1,1) CONSTRAINT PKEmployee PRIMARY KEY,
```

```
    EmployeeNumber char(5) NOT NULL
            CONSTRAINT AKEmployee_EmployeeNumber UNIQUE,
    --skipping other columns you would likely have
    InsurancePolicyNumber char(10) NULL
);
```

Filtered unique indexes are useful for performance-tuning situations where only a few values are selective, but I find I use them more often to eliminate values for data protection (which in turn has performance value). Everything about the index is the same as a normal index (indexes will be covered in greater detail in Chapter 11) save for the WHERE clause. So you add an index like this:

```
--Filtered Alternate Key (AKF)
CREATE UNIQUE INDEX AKFEmployee_InsurancePolicyNumber ON
        HumanResources.Employee(InsurancePolicyNumber)
                WHERE InsurancePolicyNumber IS NOT NULL;
```

Then, create an initial sample row:

```
INSERT INTO HumanResources.Employee (EmployeeNumber, InsurancePolicyNumber)
VALUES ('A0001','1111111111');
```

If you attempt to give another employee row the same InsurancePolicyNumber value

```
INSERT INTO HumanResources.Employee (EmployeeNumber, InsurancePolicyNumber)
VALUES ('A0002','1111111111');
```

it fails with the following error message:

```
Msg 2601, Level 14, State 1, Line 29
Cannot insert duplicate key row in object 'HumanResources.Employee' with
unique index 'AKFEmployee_InsurancePolicyNumber'. The duplicate key value
is (1111111111).
```

Adding the row with the corrected value will succeed:

```
INSERT INTO HumanResources.Employee (EmployeeNumber, InsurancePolicyNumber)
VALUES ('A0002','2222222222');
```

However, adding two (or two hundred) rows with a value of NULL for InsurancePolicyNumber will work fine:

```
INSERT INTO HumanResources.Employee (EmployeeNumber, InsurancePolicyNumber)
VALUES ('A0003','3333333333'),
       ('A0004',NULL),
       ('A0005',NULL);
```

You can see that this

```
SELECT *
FROM   HumanResources.Employee;
```

returns the following:

EmployeeId	EmployeeNumber	InsurancePolicyNumber
1	A0001	1111111111
3	A0002	2222222222
4	A0003	3333333333
5	A0004	NULL
5	A0005	NULL

The NULL example is the classic example, because it is common to desire this functionality. However, this technique can be used for more than just NULL exclusion. As another example, consider the case where you want to ensure that only a single row is set as primary for a group of rows, such as a primary contact for an account:

```
CREATE SCHEMA Account;
GO
CREATE TABLE Account.Contact
(
    ContactId    varchar(10) NOT NULL,
    AccountNumber    char(5) NOT NULL, --would be FK in full example
    PrimaryContactFlag bit NOT NULL,
    CONSTRAINT PKContact PRIMARY KEY(ContactId, AccountNumber)
);
```

Again, create an index, but this time, choose only those rows with PrimaryContactFlag = 1. The other values in the table could have as many other values as you want (of course, in this case, since it is a bit, the values could be only 0 or 1):

```
CREATE UNIQUE INDEX AKFContact_PrimaryContact
            ON Account.Contact(AccountNumber) WHERE PrimaryContactFlag = 1;
```

If you try to insert two rows that are primary, as in the following statements that will set both contacts 'fred' and 'bob' as the primary contact for the account with account number '11111'

```
INSERT INTO Account.Contact
VALUES ('bob','11111',1);
GO
INSERT INTO Account.Contact
VALUES ('fred','11111',1);
```

the following error is returned after the second insert:

```
Msg 2601, Level 14, State 1, Line 73
Cannot insert duplicate key row in object 'Account.Contact' with unique
index 'AKFContact_PrimaryContact'. The duplicate key value is (11111).
```

To insert the row with 'fred' as the name and set it as primary (assuming the 'bob' row was inserted previously), you will need to update the other row to be not primary and then insert the new primary row:

```
--Using very simplistic error handling
BEGIN TRY
  BEGIN TRANSACTION;

  UPDATE Account.Contact
  SET PrimaryContactFlag = 0
  WHERE  accountNumber = '11111';
```

```
    INSERT Account.Contact
    VALUES ('fred','11111', 1);

    COMMIT TRANSACTION;
END TRY
BEGIN CATCH
    ROLLBACK TRANSACTION;
    THROW; --just show the error that occurred
END CATCH;
```

A side effect of the filtered index is that it (like the uniqueness constraints we have used previously) has a very good chance of being useful for searches against the table where you are looking just for rows that have values or rows that have the special value, like these contacts are primary. The only downside is that the error comes from an index rather than a constraint, so it does not fit into our existing paradigms for error handling and reporting.

Bulk Uniqueness

Sometimes, we need to inventory items where some of the items are equivalent in the physical world, for example, bags of salad in the grocery store. Generally, you can't even tell the bags apart by looking at them (unless they have different expiration dates, perhaps), but knowing how many are in stock is a very common need. Implementing a solution that has a row for every packaged produce item in a corner market would require a very large database even for a very small store. This would be really quite complicated and would require a lot of basically useless rows and data manipulation. It would, in fact, make some queries easier, but it would make data storage a lot more difficult.

Instead of having one row for each individual item, you can implement a row per type of item. This type would be used to store inventory and utilization, which would then be balanced against one another. Figure 9-1 shows a very simplified model of such activity.

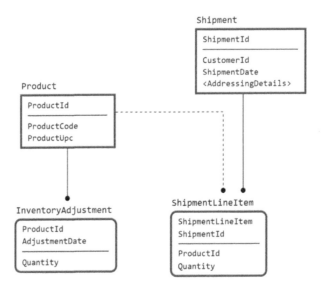

Figure 9-1. *Simplified inventory model*

In the InventoryAdjustment table, you would record shipments coming in, items stolen, changes to inventory after taking inventory (could be more or less, depending on the quality of the data you had), and so forth, and in the ShipmentLineItem table, you would record when a product is shipped to a customer.

The sum of the InventoryAdjustment.Quantity value less the sum of the ShipmentLineItem.Quantity value should tell you the amount of product on hand (or perhaps the amount of product you have oversold and need to order posthaste!). In the more realistic case, you would have a lot of complexity for back orders, future orders, returns, and so on, but the base concept is basically the same. Instead of each row representing a single item, each represents a handful of items.

The following miniature design is an example I give to students when I give my daylong seminar on database design. It is referencing a collection of toys, many of which are exactly alike:

> *A certain person was obsessed with his Lego collection. He had thousands of them and wanted to catalog his Legos both in storage and in creations where they were currently located and/or used. Legos are either in the storage "pile" or used in a set. Sets can either be purchased, which will be identified by an up to five-digit numeric code, or personal, which have no numeric code. Both styles of sets should have a name assigned and a place for descriptive notes.*

Legos come in many shapes and sizes, with most measured in two or three dimensions, first in width and length based on the number of studs on the top and then sometimes in a standard height (e.g., bricks have height; plates are fixed at one-third of one brick height unit). Each part comes in many different standard colors as well. Beyond sized pieces, there are many different accessories (some with length/width values), instructions, and so on that can be catalogued.

Example pieces and sets are shown in Figure 9-2.

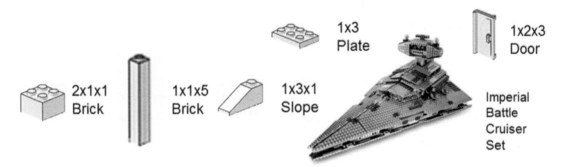

Figure 9-2. *Sample Lego parts for a database*

To solve this problem, I will create a table for each set of Legos I own (which I will call Build, since "set" is a bad word for a SQL name and "build" is better anyhow to encompass a personal creation):

```
CREATE SCHEMA Lego;
GO
CREATE TABLE Lego.Build
(
        BuildId int CONSTRAINT PKBuild PRIMARY KEY,
        Name     varchar(30) NOT NULL CONSTRAINT AKBuild_Name UNIQUE,
        LegoCode varchar(5) NULL, --five character set number
        InstructionsURL varchar(255) NULL
        --where you can get the PDF of the instructions
);
```

Then, I'll add a table for each individual instance of that build, which I will call BuildInstance:

```
CREATE TABLE Lego.BuildInstance
(
        BuildInstanceId int CONSTRAINT PKBuildInstance PRIMARY KEY ,
        BuildId int CONSTRAINT FKBuildInstance$isAVersionOf$LegoBuild
                        REFERENCES Lego.Build (BuildId),
        BuildInstanceName varchar(30) NOT NULL, --brief description of item
        Notes varchar(1000)  NULL,
        --longform notes. These could describe modifications
                                --for the instance of the model
        CONSTRAINT AKBuildInstance UNIQUE(BuildId, BuildInstanceName)
);
```

The next task is to create a table for each individual piece type. I used the term "piece" as a generic version of the different sorts of pieces you can get for Legos, including the different accessories:

```
CREATE TABLE Lego.Piece
(
        PieceId int CONSTRAINT PKPiece PRIMARY KEY,
        Type    varchar(15) NOT NULL,
        Name    varchar(30) NOT NULL,
        Color   varchar(20) NULL,
        Width int NULL,
        Length int NULL,
        Height int NULL,
        LegoInventoryNumber int NULL,
        OwnedCount int NOT NULL,
        CONSTRAINT AKPiece_Definition
                    UNIQUE (Type,Name,Color,Width,Length,Height),
        CONSTRAINT AKPiece_LegoInventoryNumber UNIQUE (LegoInventoryNumber)
);
```

Note that I implement the owned count as an attribute of the piece and not as a multivalued attribute to denote inventory change events. In a fully fleshed-out sales model, this might not be enough, but for a personal inventory, it would be a reasonable solution. The likely use here will be to update the value as new pieces are added to inventory and possibly to count loose pieces later and add that value to the ones in sets (which we will have a query for later).

Next, I will implement the table to allocate pieces to different builds:

```
CREATE TABLE Lego.BuildInstancePiece
(
        BuildInstanceId int NOT NULL,
        PieceId int NOT NULL,
        AssignedCount int NOT NULL,
        CONSTRAINT PKBuildInstancePiece
                    PRIMARY KEY (BuildInstanceId, PieceId)
);
```

From here, I can load some data. I will load a true Lego item that is available for sale and that I have often given away during presentations. It is a small, black, one-seat car with a little guy in a sweatshirt:

```
INSERT Lego.Build (BuildId, Name, LegoCode, InstructionsURL)
VALUES  (1,'Small Car','3177',
'https://www.brickowl.com/catalog/lego-small-car-set-3177-instructions/
viewer');
```

I will create one instance for this, as I personally have only one in my collection (plus some boxed ones to give away):

```
INSERT Lego.BuildInstance
        (BuildInstanceId, BuildId, BuildInstanceName, Notes)
VALUES (1,1,'Small Car for Book',NULL);
```

Then, I load the table with the different pieces in my collection, in this case the types of pieces included in the set, plus some extras thrown in. (Note that in a fully fleshed-out design, some of these values would have domains enforced, as well as validations to enforce the types of items that have height, width, and/or length. This detail is omitted partially for simplicity of demonstrating the underlying principle of bulk uniqueness in the most compact possible manner.)

```
INSERT Lego.Piece (PieceId, Type, Name, Color, Width, Length, Height,
                   LegoInventoryNumber, OwnedCount)
VALUES (1,  'Brick','Basic Brick','White',1,3,1,'362201',20),
        (2,  'Slope','Slope','White',1,1,1,'4504369',2),
        (3,  'Tile','Groved Tile','White',1,2,NULL,'306901',10),
        (4,  'Plate','Plate','White',2,2,NULL,'302201',20),
        (5,  'Plate','Plate','White',1,4,NULL,'371001',10),
        (6,  'Plate','Plate','White',2,4,NULL,'302001',1),
        (7,  'Bracket','1x2 Bracket with 2x2','White',2,1,2,'4277926',2),
        (8,  'Mudguard','Vehicle Mudguard','White',2,4,NULL,'4289272',1),
        (9,  'Door','Right Door','White',1,3,1,'4537987',1),
        (10,'Door','Left Door','White',1,3,1,'45376377',1),
        (11,'Panel','Panel','White',1,2,1,'486501',1),
        (12,'Minifig Part',
            'Minifig Torso , Sweatshirt','White',NULL,NULL,
            NULL,'4570026',1),
        (13,'Steering Wheel','Steering Wheel','Blue',1,2,NULL,'9566',1),
        (14,'Minifig Part',
            'Minifig Head, Male Brown Eyes','Yellow',NULL, NULL,
            NULL,'4570043',1),
        (15,'Slope','Slope','Black',2,1,2,'4515373',2),
        (16,'Mudguard','Vehicle Mudgard',
            'Black',2,4,NULL,'4195378',1),
        (17,'Tire',
            'Vehicle Tire,Smooth','Black',NULL,NULL,NULL,'4508215',4),
        (18,'Vehicle Base','Vehicle Base','Black',4,7,2,'244126',1),
        (19,'Wedge','Wedge (Vehicle Roof)','Black',1,4,4,'4191191',1),
        (20,'Plate','Plate','Lime Green',1,2,NULL,'302328',4),
        (21,'Minifig Part','Minifig Legs',
            'Lime Green',NULL,NULL,NULL,'74040',1),
        (22,'Round Plate','Round Plate','Clear',1,1,NULL,'3005740',2),
        (23,'Plate','Plate','Transparent Red',1,2,NULL,'4201019',1),
        (24,'Briefcase','Briefcase',
            'Reddish Brown',NULL,NULL,NULL,'4211235', 1),
        (25,'Wheel','Wheel',
```

```
         'Light Bluish Gray',NULL,NULL,NULL,'4211765',4),
     (26,'Tile','Grilled Tile','Dark Bluish Gray',1,2,NULL,
         '4210631', 1),
     (27,'Minifig Part','Brown Minifig Hair',
         'Dark Brown',NULL,NULL,NULL,
         '4535553', 1),
     (28,'Windshield','Windshield',
         'Transparent Black',3,4,1,'4496442',1),
     --and a few extra pieces to make the queries more interesting
     (29,'Baseplate','Baseplate','Green',16,24,NULL,'3334',4),
     (30,'Brick','Basic Brick','White',4,6,NULL,'2356',10);
```

Next, I will assign the 43 pieces that make up the first set:

```
INSERT INTO Lego.BuildInstancePiece
      (BuildInstanceId, PieceId, AssignedCount)
VALUES (1,1,2),(1,2,2),(1,3,1),(1,4,2),(1,5,1),(1,6,1),(1,7,2),
      (1,8,1),(1,9,1),(1,10,1),(1,11,1),(1,12,1),(1,13,1),(1,14,1),
      (1,15,2),(1,16,1),(1,17,4),(1,18,1),(1,19,1),(1,20,4),(1,21,1),
      (1,22,2),(1,23,1),(1,24,1),(1,25,4),(1,26,1),(1,27,1),(1,28,1);
```

Next, I will set up two other minimal builds to make the queries more interesting:

```
INSERT Lego.Build (BuildId, Name, LegoCode, InstructionsURL)
VALUES   (2,'Brick Triangle',NULL,NULL);
GO
INSERT Lego.BuildInstance (BuildInstanceId, BuildId,
                           BuildInstanceName, Notes)
VALUES (2,2,'Brick Triangle For Book','Simple build with 3 white bricks');
GO
INSERT INTO Lego.BuildInstancePiece (BuildInstanceId, PieceId,
                                     AssignedCount)
VALUES (2,1,3);
GO
INSERT Lego.BuildInstance (BuildInstanceId, BuildId, BuildInstanceName,
                           Notes)
VALUES (3,2,'Brick Triangle For Book2','Simple build with 3 white bricks');
```

```
GO
INSERT INTO Lego.BuildInstancePiece (BuildInstanceId, PieceId,
                                     AssignedCount)
VALUES (3,1,3);
```

After the mundane (and quite tedious when done all at once) business of setting up the data, we can count the types of pieces we have in our inventory and the total number of pieces we have using a query such as this:

```
SELECT COUNT(*) AS PieceCount, SUM(OwnedCount) AS InventoryCount
FROM  Lego.Piece;
```

This query returns the following, with the first column giving us the different types:

PieceCount	InventoryCount
30	111

Here, you start to get a feel for how this is going to be a different sort of solution than the basic relational inventory solution. Instinctively, one expects that a single row represents one thing, but here, you see that, on average, each row represents four different pieces. Following this train of thought, we can group based on the generic type of piece using a query such as

```
SELECT Type, COUNT(*) AS TypeCount, SUM(OwnedCount) AS InventoryCount
FROM  Lego.Piece
GROUP BY Type;
```

In these results, you can see that we have two types of brick but 30 bricks in inventory, one type of baseplate but 4 of them in inventory, and so on:

Type	TypeCount	InventoryCount
Baseplate	1	4
Bracket	1	2
Brick	2	30
Briefcase	1	1
Door	2	2

Minifig Part	4	4
Mudguard	2	2
Panel	1	1
Plate	5	36
Round Plate	1	2
Slope	2	4
Steering Wheel	1	1
Tile	2	11
Tire	1	4
Vehicle Base	1	1
Wedge	1	1
Wheel	1	4
Windshield	1	1

The biggest concern with this method is that users must know the difference between a row and an instance of the thing the row is modeling. And it gets more interesting where the cardinality of the type is very close to the number of physical items on hand. With 30 types of item and only 111 actual pieces, users querying may not immediately see that they are getting a wrong count. In a system with 20 different products and 1 million pieces of inventory, it will be a lot more obvious.

In the next two queries, I will expand on actual interesting queries that you will likely want to use. First, I will look for pieces that are assigned to a given set, in this case the small car model that we started with. To do this, we will just join the tables, starting with Build and moving on to BuildInstance, BuildInstancePiece, and Piece. All these joins are inner joins, since we want items that are included in the set. I use grouping sets (another wonderful feature that comes in handy to give us a very specific set of aggregates—in this case, using the () notation to give us a total count of all pieces):

```
SELECT CASE WHEN GROUPING(Piece.Type) = 1
            THEN '--Total--' ELSE Piece.Type END AS PieceType,
       Piece.Color,Piece.Height, Piece.Width, Piece.Length,
       SUM(BuildInstancePiece.AssignedCount) AS AssignedCount
FROM   Lego.Build
                JOIN Lego.BuildInstance
                    ON Build.BuildId = BuildInstance.BuildId
                JOIN Lego.BuildInstancePiece
```

```
                        ON BuildInstance.BuildInstanceId =
                                    BuildInstancePiece.BuildInstanceId
              JOIN Lego.Piece
                        ON BuildInstancePiece.PieceId = Piece.PieceId
WHERE   Build.Name = 'Small Car'
  AND   BuildInstanceName = 'Small Car for Book'
GROUP BY GROUPING SETS((Piece.Type,Piece.Color,
                          Piece.Height, Piece.Width, Piece.Length),
            ());
```

This returns the following, where you can see that 43 pieces go into this set:

PieceType	Color	Height	Width	Length	AssignedCount
Bracket	White	2	2	1	2
Brick	White	1	1	3	2
Briefcase	Reddish Brown	NULL	NULL	NULL	1
Door	White	1	1	3	2
Minifig Part	Dark Brown	NULL	NULL	NULL	1
Minifig Part	Lime Green	NULL	NULL	NULL	1
Minifig Part	White	NULL	NULL	NULL	1
Minifig Part	Yellow	NULL	NULL	NULL	1
Mudguard	Black	NULL	2	4	1
Mudguard	White	NULL	2	4	1
Panel	White	1	1	2	1
Plate	Lime Green	NULL	1	2	4
Plate	Transparent Red	NULL	1	2	1
Plate	White	NULL	1	4	1
Plate	White	NULL	2	2	2
Plate	White	NULL	2	4	1
Round Plate	Clear	NULL	1	1	2
Slope	Black	2	2	1	2
Slope	White	1	1	1	2
Steering Wheel	Blue	NULL	1	2	1
Tile	Dark Bluish Gray	NULL	1	2	1
Tile	White	NULL	1	2	1

Tire	Black	NULL	NULL	NULL	4
Vehicle Base	Black	2	4	7	1
Wedge	Black	4	1	4	1
Wheel	Light Bluish Gray	NULL	NULL	NULL	4
Windshield	Transparent Black	1	3	4	1
--Total--	NULL		NULL	NULL	NULL	43

The final query in this section is the more interesting one. A very common question would be, "How many pieces of a given type do I own that are not assigned to a set?" For this, I will use a common table expression (CTE) that gives me a sum of the pieces that have been assigned to a BuildInstance and then use that set to join to the Piece table:

```
WITH AssignedPieceCount
AS (
SELECT PieceId, SUM(AssignedCount) AS TotalAssignedCount
FROM   Lego.BuildInstancePiece
GROUP  BY PieceId )

SELECT Type, Name,  Width, Length,Height,
       Piece.OwnedCount - Coalesce(TotalAssignedCount,0) AS AvailableCount
FROM   Lego.Piece
                LEFT OUTER JOIN AssignedPieceCount
                        on Piece.PieceId = AssignedPieceCount.PieceId
WHERE Piece.OwnedCount - Coalesce(TotalAssignedCount,0) > 0;
```

Because the cardinality of the AssignedPieceCount to the Piece table is zero or one to one, we can simply do an outer join and subtract the number of pieces we have assigned to sets from the amount owned. This returns

Type	Name	Width	Length	Height	AvailableCount
Brick	Basic Brick	1	3	1	12
Tile	Groved Tile	1	2	NULL	9
Plate	Plate	2	2	NULL	18
Plate	Plate	1	4	NULL	9
Baseplate	Baseplate	16	24	NULL	4
Brick	Basic Brick	4	6	NULL	10

You can expand this basic pattern to almost any bulk uniqueness situation you may have. The calculation of how much inventory you have may be more complex and might include inventory values that are stored daily to avoid massive recalculations (think about how your bank account balance is set at the end of the day, and then daily transactions are added/subtracted as they occur until they too are posted and fixed in a daily balance).

Range Uniqueness

In some cases, uniqueness isn't uniqueness on the values of a single column set, but rather over the ranges of values. Very common examples of this include appointment times, class times, or even employees who can only be assigned to one location at a time (which was part of the model we created with the dentist office example that ran the length of Chapter 4).

For example, consider an appointment time. It has a start and an end, and the start and end ranges of two appointments should not overlap. Suppose we have an appointment with start and end times defined with precision to the second, starting at `'20200712 1:00:00PM'` and ending at `'20200712 1:59:59PM'`. To validate that this data does not overlap other appointments, we need to look for rows where any of the following conditions are met, indicating we are double-booking appointment times:

- The start or end time for the new appointment falls between the start and end for another appointment.

- The start time for the new appointment is before and the end time is after the end time for another appointment.

We can protect against situations such as overlapping appointment times by employing a `TRIGGER` object that uses a query that checks for range overlapping. If the conditions are not met, the new row is acceptable. We will implement a simplistic example of assigning a doctor to an office. Clearly, other parameters need to be considered, like office space, assistants, and so on, but I don't want this section to be larger than the allotment of pages for the entire book. First, we create a table for the doctor and another to set appointments for the doctor:

```
CREATE SCHEMA Office;
GO
CREATE TABLE Office.Doctor
(
        DoctorId         int NOT NULL CONSTRAINT PKDoctor PRIMARY KEY,
        DoctorNumber char(5) NOT NULL
                           CONSTRAINT AKDoctor_DoctorNumber UNIQUE
);
CREATE TABLE Office.Appointment
(
        AppointmentId    int NOT NULL CONSTRAINT PKAppointment PRIMARY KEY,
        --real situation would include room, patient, etc,
        DoctorId         int NOT NULL,
        StartTime        datetime2(0), --precision to the second
        EndTime          datetime2(0),
        CONSTRAINT
              AKAppointment_DoctorStartTime UNIQUE (DoctorId,StartTime),
        CONSTRAINT AKAppointment_DoctorEndTime UNIQUE (DoctorId,EndTime),
        --this covers one very specific requirement Starts before Ends
        CONSTRAINT CHKAppointment_StartBeforeEnd
                                        CHECK (StartTime <= EndTime),
        CONSTRAINT FKDoctor$IsAssignedTo$OfficeAppointment
                FOREIGN KEY (DoctorId) REFERENCES Office.Doctor (DoctorId)
);
```

Next, we will add some data to our new table. The AppointmentId value 5 will include a bad date range that overlaps another row for demonstration purposes:

```
INSERT INTO Office.Doctor (DoctorId, DoctorNumber)
VALUES (1,'00001'),(2,'00002');

INSERT INTO Office.Appointment
VALUES (1,1,'20200712 14:00','20200712 14:59:59'),
       (2,1,'20200712 15:00','20200712 16:59:59'),
       (3,2,'20200712 8:00','20200712 11:59:59'),
       (4,2,'20200712 13:00','20200712 17:59:59'),
       (5,2,'20200712 14:00','20200712 14:59:59');
       --offensive item for demo, conflicts with 4
```

As far as the declarative constraints can tell, everything is okay, but the following query will check for data conditions between each group of rows in the table to every other row in the table:

```
SELECT Appointment.AppointmentId,
       Acheck.AppointmentId AS ConflictingAppointmentId
FROM   Office.Appointment
         JOIN Office.Appointment AS ACheck
           ON Appointment.DoctorId = ACheck.DoctorId
    /*1*/    AND Appointment.AppointmentId <> ACheck.AppointmentId
    /*2*/    AND (Appointment.StartTime BETWEEN ACheck.StartTime AND
                                                        ACheck.EndTime
    /*3*/          OR Appointment.EndTime BETWEEN ACheck.StartTime AND
                                                        ACheck.EndTime
    /*4*/          OR (Appointment.StartTime < ACheck.StartTime
                      AND Appointment.EndTime > ACheck.EndTime));
```

In this query, I have highlighted four points:

1. Make sure that we don't compare the current row to itself, because an appointment will always overlap itself.

2. Here, we check to see if the StartTime of one appointment is between the StartTime and EndTime of another, inclusive of the actual values.

3. This is same as 2, except checking for EndTime issues.

4. Finally, we check to see if any appointment is engulfing another appointment.

Running the query, we see that

AppointmentId	ConflictingAppointmentId
5	4
4	5

The interesting part of these results is that where there is one offending row, there will also be the inverse. If one row is offending in one way, like starting before and ending after another appointment, the conflicting row will have a start and end time between the first appointment's time. This won't be a problem, and to be fair, when you query for the rows to handle, you will need both rows to see their start and end times.

Next, we remove the bad row for now:

```
DELETE FROM Office.Appointment WHERE AppointmentId = 5;
```

We will now implement a TRIGGER object (using the template as defined in Appendix B, available for download) that will check for this condition based on the values in new rows being inserted or updated. There's no need to check deleted rows because all deleted rows can do is help the situation (even in the case of the update, where you may move an appointment from one doctor to another).

Note that the basis of this trigger is the query we used previously to check for bad values (I usually implement this as two triggers, one for insert and another for update, both having the same code to start with, but it is shown here as one for simplicity of demonstration):

```
CREATE TRIGGER Office.Appointment$InsertAndUpdate
ON Office.Appointment
AFTER UPDATE, INSERT AS
BEGIN
   DECLARE @msg varchar(2000),      --used to hold the error message
   --use inserted for insert or update trigger, deleted for
   --update or delete trigger count instead of @@rowcount due to merge
   --behavior that sets @@rowcount to a number that is equal to number of
   --merged rows, not rows being checked in trigger
         @rowsAffected int = (SELECT COUNT(*) FROM inserted);

   --no need to continue on if no rows affected
   IF @rowsAffected = 0 RETURN;

   SET NOCOUNT ON; --to avoid the rowcount messages
   SET ROWCOUNT 0; --in case the client has modified the rowcount

   BEGIN TRY
      --[validation section]
```

```
--if this is an update, but they don't change times or doctor,
--don't check the data. UPDATE is always true for INSERT action
IF UPDATE(StartTime) OR UPDATE(EndTime) OR UPDATE(DoctorId)
BEGIN
IF EXISTS ( SELECT *
            FROM   Office.Appointment
                    JOIN Office.Appointment AS ACheck
                      ON Appointment.doctorId = ACheck.doctorId
                         AND Appointment.AppointmentId <>
                                                ACheck.AppointmentId
                         AND (Appointment.StartTime BETWEEN
                                 Acheck.StartTime AND Acheck.EndTime
                              OR Appointment.EndTime BETWEEN
                                 Acheck.StartTime AND Acheck.EndTime
                              OR (Appointment.StartTime <

                                               Acheck.StartTime
                         AND Appointment.EndTime > Acheck.EndTime))
                    WHERE   EXISTS (SELECT *
                                    FROM   inserted
                                    WHERE  inserted.DoctorId =
                                              Acheck.DoctorId))
          BEGIN
            IF @rowsAffected = 1
               SELECT @msg = 'Appointment for doctor '
                       + doctorNumber
                       + ' overlapped existing appointment'
               FROM   inserted
                        JOIN Office.Doctor
                          ON inserted.DoctorId = Doctor.DoctorId;
            ELSE
               SELECT @msg = 'One of the rows caused '
                       + ' an overlapping appointment time '
                       + ' a doctor.';
            THROW 50000,@msg,1;
```

```
                END;
        END;
        --[modification section]
    END TRY
    BEGIN CATCH
        IF @@trancount > 0
            ROLLBACK TRANSACTION;
        THROW;
    END CATCH;
END;
```

This time, we try to add an appointment for DoctorId number 1:

```
INSERT INTO Office.Appointment
VALUES (5,1,'20200712 14:00','20200712 14:59:59');
```

This first attempt is blocked because the row is an exact duplicate of the start time value. The most common error that will likely occur in a system such as this is trying to duplicate something, usually by accident. This case is handled by the UNIQUE constraint:

```
Msg 2627, Level 14, State 1, Line 2
Violation of UNIQUE KEY constraint 'AKOfficeAppointment_DoctorStartTime'.
Cannot insert duplicate key in object 'Office.Appointment'. The duplicate
key value is (1, 2020-07-12 14:00:00).
```

Next, we check the case where the appointment fits wholly inside of another appointment:

```
INSERT INTO Office.Appointment
VALUES (5,1,'20200712 14:30','20200712 14:40:59');
```

This fails and tells us the doctor for whom the failure occurred:

```
Msg 50000, Level 16, State 16, Procedure appointment$InsertAndUpdate
Appointment for doctor 00001 overlapped existing appointment
```

Then, we test for the case where the entire appointment engulfs another appointment:

```
INSERT INTO Office.Appointment
VALUES (5,1,'20200712 11:30','20200712 17:59:59');
```

This quite obediently fails, just like the other case:

```
Msg 50000, Level 16, State 16, Procedure appointment$InsertAndUpdate
Appointment for doctor 00001 overlapped existing appointment
```

And, just to drive home the point of always testing your code extensively, you should always test the greater-than-one-row case, and in this case, I included rows for both doctors:

```
INSERT into Office.Appointment
VALUES (5,1,'20200712 11:30','20200712 15:59:59'),
       (6,2,'20200713 10:00','20200713 10:59:59');
```

This time, it fails with our multirow error message:

```
Msg 50000, Level 16, State 16, Procedure Appointment$InsertAndUpdate
One of the rows caused an overlapping appointment time for a doctor
```

Whether it makes sense to implement a preventative solution like this using a TRIGGER object is going to be determined by exactly what it is you are doing. Sometimes in a system like this, you want to be able to temporarily have bad data exist in the system during intermediate steps along the process. It may be that you want to alert the user to the overlap using a query like the one we started with, maybe in a daily report of upcoming appointment overlaps.

Instead of blocking the operation, the trigger could update a status on the row to tell the user that it overlaps. Or you might even get more interesting and let the algorithms involve prioritizing certain conditions above other appointments. Maybe a checkup gets bumped for a surgery, marked to reschedule. In this section, I've shown you the basis of a pattern to apply to locate and/or prevent range overlaps if that is the desired result. It is up to the requirements to lead you to exactly how to implement.

Likely Uniqueness

The most difficult case of uniqueness is actually quite common, and it is usually the most critical to get right. It is also a topic far too big to cover with a coded example, because it is more of a political question than a technical one. For example, if two people call in to your company from the same phone number and say their name is Abraham Lincoln, are they the same person, or are they two different people with a unique name? Or one alias and one real name? What if Abraham provides you with an address and phone number (both located in Gettysburg!)?

Whether you can call them the same person is a very important decision and one that is based largely on the industry you are in, made especially tricky due to privacy laws (if you give one person who claims to be Abraham Lincoln the data of the real person with that name, well, that just isn't going to be good no matter what your privacy policy is or which laws that govern privacy apply). I don't talk deeply about privacy laws in this book, mostly because that subject is very messy and ever changing, but also because dealing with privacy concerns is

- Largely just an extension of the principles I have covered so far and will cover in the next chapter on security

- Widely varied by industry and type of data you need to store

- Changing faster than a printed book can cover

- Different depending on what part of the world you are reading this book in

The principles of privacy are part of what makes the process of identification so difficult. At one time, companies would just ask for an American customer's Social Security number and use that as identification in a very trusting manner. Of course, no sooner does some value become used widely by lots of organizations than it begins to be abused. (Chapter 10 will expand a little bit on this topic as we talk about encryption technologies, but encryption is another wide topic for which the best advice is to make sure you are doing as much or more than is required.)

So the goal of your design is to work at getting your customer to use an identifier to help you distinguish them from another customer. This customer identifier will be used, for example, as a login to the corporate website, for the convenience card that is being used by so many businesses, and likely on any correspondence. The problem is how to gather this information. When a person calls a bank or doctor, the staff member answering the call always asks some random questions to better identify the caller. For many companies, it is impossible to force the person to give information, so it is not always possible to force customers to uniquely identify themselves. You can entice them to identify themselves, such as by issuing a customer savings card, or you can just guess from bits of information that can be gathered from a web browser, telephone number, and so on. Even worse, what if someone signs up twice for a customer number? Can you be sure that it is the same person, then?

The challenge becomes to match people to the often-limited information they are willing to provide. You can try to gather as much information as possible from people, such as

- Name

- Address, even partial like city and/or state

- Phone number(s)

- Payment method

- Email address(es)

The list goes on. Then, depending on the industry, you determine levels of matching that work for you. Lots of methods and tools are available to you, from standardization of data to make direct matching possible, fuzzy matching, and even third-party tools that will help you with the matches. The key, of course, is that if you are going to send a message alerting of a sale to repeat customers, only a slight bit of a match might be necessary, but if you are sending personal information, like how much money they have spent, a very deterministic match ought to be done. Identification of multiple customers in your database that are legitimately the same customer is the holy grail of marketing, but it is achievable given you respect your customer's privacy and use their data in a safe manner. I will submit to you that just making a new customer row every time the same person comes in is just as good as not having a customer row at all, but getting even somewhat matched data is very useful.

Data-Driven Design

One of the worst practices I see some programmers get in the habit of doing is programming using specific values to force a specific action. For example, they will get requirements that specify that for customers 1 and 2, we need to do action A and for customer 3, we need to do action B. So they go in and code something very close to the following:

```
IF @customerId in ('1', '2')
    Do ActionA(@customerId);
ELSE IF @customerId in ('3')
    Do ActionB(@customerId);
```

It works, meets the requirements to the letter, so they breathe a sigh of relief and move on. But the next day, they get a request that customer 4 should be treated in the same manner as customer 3. They don't have time to do this request immediately because it requires a code change, which requires testing. So, a month later, they add '4' to the code, test it, deploy it, and perhaps claim it required 40 hours of IT time.

This is clearly not optimal. The point of this section is that we want to look to push as much repeatable actions from the customer into repeatable automatable chunks. Then, once something has been done once, it can be done again. For example, in this case, if, as an analyst, we can determine why we are doing ActionA or ActionB, we can make this process repeatable.

For example, say we determine that for CustomerType: 'Great', we do ActionA, but for 'Good' we do ActionB and for all other values of CustomerType no action is needed. The following could be coded:

```
IF @customerType = 'Great'
    Do ActionA(@customerId);
ELSE IF @customerType = 'Good'
    Do ActionB(@customerId);
```

Now adding another customer to these groups is trivial enough. You set the value of the CustomerType column on the Customer table to Great or Good, and one of these actions occurs in you code automatically. But (as you might hear on any infomercial) you can do better! The shortcoming in this design now is: How do you change the treatment of good customers if you want to have them do ActionA temporarily? In some cases, the answer is to add to the definition of the CustomerType table and add a column to indicate what action to take:

```
--In real table, expand ActionType to be a more descriptive value
--or a domain of its own
CREATE SCHEMA Customers;
GO
CREATE TABLE Customers.CustomerType
```

```
(
        CustomerType      varchar(20) NOT NULL
                          CONSTRAINT PKCustomerType PRIMARY KEY,
        Description       varchar(1000) NOT NULL,
        ActionType        varchar(30) NOT NULL
);
```

Now, the treatment of this `CustomerType` can be set at any time to whatever the user decides. The only time you may need to change code (requiring testing, downtime, etc.) is if you need to change what an action means or add a new one. Adding different types of customers, or even changing existing ones, would be a nonbreaking change, so no testing is required. If you also need to add to the `Customers.Customer` table an `OverrideActionType` column to allow special cases, that too is perfectly fine because it is still data driven, and customer 1 isn't hard-coded in a place where it requires a release to be changed.

The basic goal should be that the structure of data should represent the requirements, so rules are enforced by varying data, not by having to hard-code special cases. Flexibility at the code level is ultra-important, particularly to your support staff. In the end, the goal of a design should be that changing configuration should not require code changes, so create attributes that will allow you to configure your data and usage.

Historical/Temporal Data

One pattern that is quite often useful is to be able to see how a row looked at a previous point in time. For example, when did Employee 100001's salary change? When did Employee 2010032's insurance start? In some cases, you need to capture changes using a column in a table. For example, take the `Employee` table we used in the "Selective Uniqueness" section (if you are following along, this table already exists in the database, so you don't need to recreate it):

```
CREATE SCHEMA HumanResources;
GO
CREATE TABLE HumanResources.Employee
(
    EmployeeId int IDENTITY(1,1) CONSTRAINT PKEmployee primary key,
    EmployeeNumber char(5) NOT NULL
```

```
          CONSTRAINT AKEmployee_EmployeeNummer UNIQUE,
    InsurancePolicyNumber char(10) NULL
);
CREATE UNIQUE INDEX AKFEmployee_InsurancePolicyNumber ON
HumanResources.Employee(InsurancePolicyNumber)
                              WHERE InsurancePolicyNumber IS NOT NULL;
```

One method of answering the question of when the insurance number changed would be to add a column to the table that captures the time when the policy changed such as the following:

```
ALTER TABLE HumanResources.Employee
    ADD InsurancePolicyNumberChangeTime datetime2(0);
```

You might also want to add a table where you can capture all the different insurance changes that an employee has had over time as well. For this sort of need, a standard design and solution is in order, as the user should be able to modify both the table with the employee details and the history table to adjust history when it is discovered that the employee got the details wrong and they really did have insurance on a certain date.

However, while there is a value to being able to accurately reflect the true reality that existed by updating historical data, this opens other doors to (best case) accidental changes and (worst case) fraud. So in this section we are going to focus on being able to see the history of changes to a table as it looked based on system time using two techniques in T-SQL:

- *Using a trigger*: Using a simple trigger, we can capture changes to the row and save them in a separate table. The benefit of this method over the next method is that it does not need to capture change for all columns and you can set your own time of change.

- *Using temporal extensions*: These were made available in SQL Server 2016 and allow you to let the engine capture the changes to a table. The major benefit is that there is syntax that allows you to query the changed data in a quite simple manner.

Note that neither version of this pattern is generally a version of strict auditing. In Chapter 10, the SQL Audit feature will be covered that will let you capture activity to a table outside of the relational mode. This pattern is specifically set up to show changes in data, and it is not beyond reasonability that you might change history to fix mistakes that were data related. Audits should *never* be changed, or they will quickly be considered unreliable. Any events where you need to do something out of the ordinary would need to be captured (and documented) for the audit as well.

Using a Trigger to Capture History

While temporal support was a new feature of SQL Server 2016 that is used to capture system time–based changes in a table's data pretty easy, it does not take away the value of using a trigger to capture history (the temporal feature will be covered in detail in the next section).

In this section, our goal is simply to see a log of modified rows, or rows that have been deleted from the table. For this exercise, we will start by resetting the data in the Employee table:

```
TRUNCATE TABLE HumanResources.Employee;

INSERT INTO HumanResources.Employee (EmployeeNumber, InsurancePolicyNumber)
VALUES ('A0001','1111111111'),
       ('A0002','2222222222'),
       ('A0003','3333333333'),
       ('A0004',NULL),
       ('A0005',NULL),
       ('A0006',NULL);
```

Next, I will create a schema for the history that corresponds to the name of the schema that owns the data but is not the same schema. This will allow you to manage security at the schema level for history different than for the base table. So giving the user SELECT rights to the HumanResources schema where the base Employee table exists will not automatically give them rights to see the history data. This will be a separate action. However, the trigger will be able to insert the history rows because it will be part of the HumanResources schema, and it and the HumanResourcesHistory schema will be owned by the same database principal:

```
CREATE SCHEMA HumanResourcesHistory;
```

Next, we will create a parallel history table in the new schema that has all the columns of the original table, along with a few management columns, which have explanations in the following code. The table needn't include every column from the source table, so if you only wanted to capture changes to the InsurancePolicyNumber column, for example, that would be easy to do:

```
CREATE TABLE HumanResourcesHistory.Employee
(
    --Original columns
    EmployeeId int NOT NULL,
    EmployeeNumber char(5) NOT NULL,
    InsurancePolicyNumber char(10) NULL,

    --WHEN the row was modified
    RowModificationTime datetime2(0) NOT NULL,
    --WHAT type of modification
    RowModificationType varchar(10) NOT NULL CONSTRAINT
                CHKEmployeeSalary_RowModificationType
                    CHECK (RowModificationType IN ('UPDATE','DELETE')),

    --tiebreaker for seeing order of changes, if rows were modified rapidly
    --use to break ties in RowModificationTime
    RowSequencerValue bigint IDENTITY(1,1)
);
```

Next, we create the following trigger. The basic flow is to determine the type of operation and then write the contents of the deleted table to the history table we have previously created:

```
CREATE TRIGGER HumanResources.Employee$HistoryManagementTrigger
ON HumanResources.Employee
AFTER UPDATE, DELETE AS --usually duplicate code in two triggers to allow
BEGIN                   --future modifications;

   DECLARE @msg varchar(2000),    --used to hold the error message
   --use inserted for insert or update trigger, deleted for
   --update or delete trigger count instead of @@rowcount due to merge
   --behavior that sets @@rowcount to a number that is equal to number of
   --merged rows, not rows being checked in trigger
          @rowsAffected int = (SELECT COUNT(*) FROM deleted);
```

```
   --no need to continue on if no rows affected
   IF @rowsAffected = 0 RETURN;

   SET NOCOUNT ON; --to avoid the rowcount messages
   SET ROWCOUNT 0; --in case the client has modified the rowcount

   DECLARE @RowModificationType char(6);
   SET @RowModificationType = CASE WHEN EXISTS (SELECT * FROM inserted)
                                      THEN 'UPDATE' ELSE 'DELETE' END;

   BEGIN TRY
       --[validation section]
       --[modification section]
       --write deleted rows to the history table
       INSERT   HumanResourcesHistory.Employee
                (EmployeeId,EmployeeNumber,InsurancePolicyNumber,
                 RowModificationTime,RowModificationType)
       SELECT EmployeeId,EmployeeNumber,InsurancePolicyNumber,
              SYSDATETIME(), @RowModificationType
       FROM    deleted;
   END TRY
   BEGIN CATCH
          IF @@trancount > 0
              ROLLBACK TRANSACTION;
          THROW;
     END CATCH;
END;
```

Now let's make a few changes to the data in the table. First, update `EmployeeId` = 4 and set that it has insurance:

```
UPDATE HumanResources.Employee
SET    InsurancePolicyNumber = '4444444444'
WHERE  EmployeeId = 4;
```

You can see the change and the history here:

```
SELECT *
FROM   HumanResources.Employee
WHERE  EmployeeId = 4;
```

```
SELECT *
FROM    HumanResourcesHistory.Employee
WHERE   EmployeeId = 4;
```

```
EmployeeId  EmployeeNumber  InsurancePolicyNumber
----------- --------------- ---------------------
4           A0004           4444444444
```

```
EmployeeId  EmployeeNumber  InsurancePolicyNumber  RowModificationTime
----------- --------------- ---------------------  -------------------------
4           A0004           NULL                   2020-05-07 20:26:38
```

```
RowModificationType RowSequencerValue
------------------- --------------------
UPDATE              1
```

Now let's update all of the rows where there is an insurance policy to a new format and delete EmployeeId = 6. I updated all rows so we can see in the history what happens when a row is updated and does not actually change:

```
UPDATE HumanResources.Employee
SET   InsurancePolicyNumber = 'IN' + RIGHT(InsurancePolicyNumber,8);

DELETE HumanResources.Employee
WHERE EmployeeId = 6;
```

Then check out the data:

```
SELECT *
FROM    HumanResources.Employee
ORDER BY EmployeeId;

--limiting output for formatting purposes
SELECT EmployeeId, InsurancePolicyNumber,
       RowModificationTime, RowModificationType
FROM    HumanResourcesHistory.Employee
ORDER  BY EmployeeId,RowModificationTime,RowSequencerValue;
```

These queries return

EmployeeId	EmployeeNumber	InsurancePolicyNumber
1	A0001	IN11111111
2	A0002	IN22222222
3	A0003	IN33333333
4	A0004	IN44444444
5	A0005	NULL

EmployeeId	InsurancePolicyNumber	RowModificationTime	RowModificationType
1	1111111111	2020-05-07 20:27:59	UPDATE
2	2222222222	2020-05-07 20:27:59	UPDATE
3	3333333333	2020-05-07 20:27:59	UPDATE
4	4444444444	2020-05-07 20:26:38	UPDATE
4	4444444444	2020-05-07 20:27:59	UPDATE
5	NULL	2020-05-07 20:27:59	UPDATE
6	NULL	2020-05-07 20:27:59	UPDATE
6	NULL	2020-05-07 20:27:59	DELETE

Using this data, you can see the progression of what has happened to the data, starting from the time the trigger was added, including seeing rows that have been deleted. It is a well-worn method to capture history, but it is very hard to work with in your queries to look back on history.

Using Temporal Extensions to Manage History

SQL Server 2016 introduced a very useful feature for capturing changes to data in a table, allowing you to see how a table looks at any point in time, called temporal tables, or more specifically "system-versioned temporal tables" in that they only track changes using system time.

Temporal extensions will provide the same basic information that we provided using a TRIGGER object in the previous section, but there is one major difference: integrated query support. If you want to see the current data, there is no change to your query. But if you want to see how the data looked at a particular point in time, the only change to your query is to specify the time (or time range) for which you want to see history.

One of the biggest limitations on temporal tables over using a build-your-own trigger solution is that the history copy must version all columns in the table. So if you are using columns with a varchar(max) or an nvarchar(max) datatype, it will work, but you could incur massive storage costs or performance issues if your values are very large because every modification will duplicate these large values. In-memory tables support temporal extensions, but the version data will be stored in an on-disk table. In Chapter 8, we covered using INSTEAD OF TRIGGER objects to make a view updatable, and one method of reducing the columns that are in the temporal view is to split out the columns you want to track into their own table and use a view that puts the tables together to look like the original table.

There are other limitations, such as requiring a PRIMARY KEY, TRUNCATE TABLE no longer being allowed on your base table, INSTEAD OF TRIGGER objects not allowed on the table, replication use being limited, and DROP TABLE not working without removing the temporal extensions. Several other configuration limitations are included in this more complete list of considerations and limitations from Microsoft: https://docs.microsoft.com/en-us/sql/relational-databases/tables/temporal-table-considerations-and-limitations. However, the limitations are not terribly constraining if you can make use of the DML extensions described later in the section.

I will continue to use the HumanResources schema and objects we used in the previous section, but I will reset the data and drop the history table from the previous section:

```
TRUNCATE TABLE HumanResources.Employee;

INSERT INTO HumanResources.Employee (EmployeeNumber, InsurancePolicyNumber)
VALUES ('A0001','1111111111'),
       ('A0002','2222222222'),
       ('A0003','3333333333'),
       ('A0004',NULL),
       ('A0005',NULL),
       ('A0006',NULL);
GO
DROP TABLE IF EXISTS HumanResourcesHistory.Employee;
DROP TRIGGER IF EXISTS HumanResources.Employee$HistoryManagementTrigger;
```

In the following subsections, I will cover configuring temporal extensions, along with how you can coordinate changes to multiple rows and how you can change history if needed.

Configuring Temporal Extensions

The first step to using temporal tables is to add the required temporal extensions to the table, in this case the HumanResources.Employee table. To do this, you are required to have two columns in the table, one for a start time, which you will see often in the documentation as SysStartTime, and one for an end time, usually named SysEndTime. I will use a naming standard that matches my normal standard. These time range columns must be datetime2, but they can be any precision from 0 to 7. These values are used to denote the start and end times that the row is valid, so when we query the rows using temporal extensions, the one (or zero, if the row had been deleted at the time) active row can be picked.

The precision of the start and end time columns will determine how many active versions you can have per second (there can be unlimited rows with the exact same time, but only the last entered will be used in normal queries). If datetime2(0) is used, then you can have one version per second and if datetime2(7) then ~9999999 versions per second. While it is not likely that many readers will have such needs to track changes to this deep level, I tend to use (7) just because it feels like it is safer, if more difficult to type. (For this book, I will use datetime2(1) to allow for the limited amount of text real estate I have available.)

The following code snippet adds the columns and the settings that we will use once we turn on system versioning (then drops the temporary constraints):

```
ALTER TABLE HumanResources.Employee
ADD
    RowStartTime datetime2(1) GENERATED ALWAYS AS ROW START NOT NULL
        --HIDDEN can be specified
        --so temporal columns don't show up in SELECT * queries
        --This default will start the history of all existing rows at the
        --current time (system uses UTC time for these values)
        --this default sets the start to NOW... use the best time
        --for your need. Also, you may get errors as SYSUTCDATETIME()
        --may produce minutely future times on occaions
        CONSTRAINT DFLTDelete1 DEFAULT (SYSUTCDATETIME()),
    RowEndTime datetime2(1) GENERATED ALWAYS AS ROW END NOT NULL --HIDDEN
        --data needs to be the max for the datatype
        CONSTRAINT DFLTDelete2
```

```
        DEFAULT (CAST('9999-12-31 23:59:59.9' AS datetime2(1)))
  , PERIOD FOR SYSTEM_TIME (RowStartTime, RowEndTime);
GO
```

```
--DROP the constraints that are just there to backfill data
ALTER TABLE HumanResources.Employee DROP CONSTRAINT DFLTDelete1;
ALTER TABLE HumanResources.Employee DROP CONSTRAINT DFLTDelete2;
```

The GENERATED ALWAYS AS ROW START and END pair tells the system to set the value when the table is completely configured for temporal support. If you are creating a new table and want to turn on temporal extensions, you will use the same columns and settings in the CREATE TABLE statement, but you won't need the DEFAULT constraints. Unfortunately, this only works for temporal tables, so you still need triggers to set your own values for row created and modified times in other cases.

The next step is to create a table to hold the versions. There are two ways to do this. The easiest is to just let SQL Server build it for you. You can either specify a name or let SQL Server pick one for you. For example, if we want SQL Server to create the history table, we will just use

```
ALTER TABLE HumanResources.Employee
        SET (SYSTEM_VERSIONING = ON);
```

Now you can look in the system metadata and see what has been added:

```
SELECT  tables.object_id AS BaseTableObject,
        CONCAT(historySchema.name,'.',historyTable.name) AS HistoryTable
FROM    sys.tables
          JOIN sys.schemas
            ON schemas.schema_id = tables.schema_id
          LEFT OUTER JOIN sys.tables AS historyTable
              JOIN sys.schemas AS historySchema
                    ON historySchema.schema_id = historyTable.schema_id
            ON TABLES.history_table_id = historyTable.object_id
WHERE   schemas.name = 'HumanResources'
  AND   tables.name = 'Employee';
```

This returns something like the following, with almost certainly a different base table object_id:

```
BaseTableObject HistoryTable
--------------- ----------------------------------------------------------
1330103779      HumanResources.MSSQL_TemporalHistoryFor_581577110
```

This leads to a predictable but ugly name. The table will have the same columns as the base table but will have a few differences that we will look at later when we cover creating our own table and then when I modify the data in the table to use previous historical data you have saved off.

While there may not be a reason all that often to look at the history table itself, it will be useful to be able to correlate the names of the tables without knowing the object_id. Let's go ahead and name the table ourselves in the DDL. First, we need to disconnect the history table that was created and drop it. Before you can do much to the base table, in fact, you will have to turn off the system versioning:

```
ALTER TABLE HumanResources.Employee
    SET (SYSTEM_VERSIONING = OFF); --your history table will be different
DROP TABLE HumanResources.MSSQL_TemporalHistoryFor_581577110;
```

Now let's specify a table name. If it is an existing table, there will be more to do in that you may want to backfill up history (like if you were using the previous section's TRIGGER object to capture history). Just like in the trigger method, I will use a different schema for the history table, but you can put it in the same schema if so desired (you always have to specify the schema in the HISTORY_TABLE clause):

```
ALTER TABLE HumanResources.Employee --must be in the same database
SET (SYSTEM_VERSIONING = ON (HISTORY_TABLE =
                                  HumanResourcesHistory.Employee));
```

Taking a look at the metadata query we ran earlier, you can see that the history table has been set to a much better table name:

```
BaseTableObject HistoryTable
--------------- -------------------------------------
1330103779      HumanResourcesHistory.Employee
```

Now you have configured the HumanResources.Employee table to capture history, starting with the time period of your ALTER statement to add the columns to the table. Check the table's content using a SELECT statement (condensing the output for space):

```
SELECT Employee.EmployeeId, Employee.InsurancePolicyNumber AS PolicyNumber,
       Employee.RowStartTime, Employee.RowEndTime
FROM   HumanResources.Employee;
```

This returns

EmployeeId	PolicyNumber	RowStartTime	RowEndTime
1	1111111111	2020-05-27 23:51:51.9	9999-12-31 23:59:59.9
2	2222222222	2020-05-27 23:51:51.9	9999-12-31 23:59:59.9
3	3333333333	2020-05-27 23:51:51.9	9999-12-31 23:59:59.9
4	NULL	2020-05-27 23:51:51.9	9999-12-31 23:59:59.9
5	NULL	2020-05-27 23:51:51.9	9999-12-31 23:59:59.9
6	NULL	2020-05-27 23:51:51.9	9999-12-31 23:59:59.9

You can see the columns added for RowStartTime and RowEndTime. Using these time frames, you will be able to see the data at given points in time. So if you wanted to see how the table would have looked on May 28 (at 0:00 UTC), use the FOR SYSTEM_TIME clause on the table in the FROM clause using AS OF a current point in time, in our case where RowStartTime >= PassedValue > RowEndTime. There are four others: FROM, BETWEEN, CONTAINED IN, and ALL. I will mostly make use of AS OF and ALL in the book, as usually I want to see data at a point in time or I want to see all history to show you what has changed.

```
SELECT *
FROM   HumanResources.Employee FOR SYSTEM_TIME AS OF '2020-05-27';
```

This returns nothing, as the RowStartTime and RowEndTime do not include that time period for any row in the table, since all the data starts at 23:51 on the 27th. The following query will (based on the data as I have it in my sample table) return the same as the previous query to get all rows in the base table, since May 28, 2020, is after all of the RowStartTime values in the base table:

```
SELECT *
FROM   HumanResources.Employee FOR SYSTEM_TIME AS OF '2020-05-28';
```

If you want to work in your own time zone values, you can use AT TIME ZONE to translate the dates. AT TIME ZONE changes a date value with no time zone information to a datetimeoffset type with the offset for the time zone passed in. When the value is a datetimeoffset type, it will change the time value to the time zone passed in and with the new offset (the point in time is the same, just the different offset from UTC). For example, to see the data on May 28, 2020, midnight in the Eastern Standard Time (it does honor Daylight Saving Time, but is always named standard), you can use the following code:

```
DECLARE @asOfTime datetime2(1) = '2020-05-28';

SET @asOfTime = @asOfTime
        --first set the variable to the time zone you are in
        AT TIME ZONE 'Eastern Standard Time'
        AT TIME ZONE 'UTC' --then convert to UTC

SELECT EmployeeId, RowStartTime,
        CAST(RowStartTime AT TIME ZONE 'UTC' --set to UTC, then Local
            AT TIME ZONE 'Eastern Standard Time' AS datetime2(1))
            AS RowStartTimeLocal
FROM    HumanResources.Employee FOR SYSTEM_TIME AS OF @asOfTime;
```

Dealing with Temporal Data One Row at a Time

When your application modifies a single row in a table that has temporal extensions enabled, there really isn't much you need to consider in your application. Every INSERT, UPDATE, and DELETE operation will just capture changes and let you query each table that is involved in the operation at a point in time. You can use the FROM FOR SYSTEM_TIME clause on any statement where a FROM clause makes sense. And you can use it on all tables that are used in a query or just some. For example, the following is perfectly acceptable:

```
FROM  Table1
        JOIN Table2 FOR SYSTEM_TIME AS OF <Time  Value>
                    ON ...
        JOIN Table3 FOR SYSTEM_TIME AS OF <Time  Value>
                    ON ...
```

And you can even do this:

```
FROM   Table1 FOR SYSTEM_TIME AS OF <Time  Value>
          JOIN Table1 as DifferentLookAtTable1
                          FOR SYSTEM_TIME AS OF <Time  Value 2>
             ON ...
```

In the next section, we will look more at coordinating modifications on multiple rows (in the same or multiple tables), but in this section, let's look at the basic mechanics.

First, let's modify some data, to show what this looks like:

```
UPDATE HumanResources.Employee
SET    InsurancePolicyNumber = '4444444444'
WHERE  EmployeeId = 4;
```

So let's look at the data:

```
SELECT Employee.EmployeeId, Employee.InsurancePolicyNumber AS PolicyNumber,
       Employee.RowStartTime, Employee.RowEndTime
FROM   HumanResources.Employee
WHERE  Employee.EmployeeId = 4;
```

As expected:

EmployeeId	PolicyNumber	RowStartTime	RowEndTime
4	4444444444	2020-05-28 00:11:07.1	9999-12-31 23:59:59.9

But check just before the RowStartTime (.1 second to be precise):

```
SELECT Employee.EmployeeId, Employee.InsurancePolicyNumber AS PolicyNumber,
       Employee.RowStartTime, Employee.RowEndTime
FROM   HumanResources.Employee FOR SYSTEM_TIME AS OF '2020-05-28 00:11:07'
WHERE  Employee.EmployeeId = 4;
```

Now you will see that the data looks just the same as it did pre-UPDATE execution:

EmployeeId	PolicyNumber	RowStartTime	RowEndTime
4	NULL	2020-05-27 23:51:51.9	2020-05-28 00:11:07.1

This is where ALL comes in handy, so you can see almost all of the changes:

```
SELECT *
FROM    HumanResources.Employee FOR SYSTEM_TIME ALL
ORDER   BY EmployeeId, RowStartTime;
```

This returns all the valid history rows (ones where RowStartTime <> RowEndTime, a situation that I will cover in a moment), including previous versions of data:

EmployeeId	PolicyNumber	RowStartTime	RowEndTime
1	1111111111	2020-05-27 23:51:51.9	9999-12-31 23:59:59.9
2	2222222222	2020-05-27 23:51:51.9	9999-12-31 23:59:59.9
3	3333333333	2020-05-27 23:51:51.9	9999-12-31 23:59:59.9
4	NULL	2020-05-27 23:51:51.9	2020-05-28 00:11:07.1
4	4444444444	2020-05-28 00:11:07.1	9999-12-31 23:59:59.9
5	NULL	2020-05-27 23:51:51.9	9999-12-31 23:59:59.9
6	NULL	2020-05-27 23:51:51.9	9999-12-31 23:59:59.9

Now, let's delete EmployeeId = 6 (we are not a fan after they ate the last non–gluten-free cupcake):

```
DELETE HumanResources.Employee
WHERE  EmployeeId = 6;
```

Then check out the data:

```
SELECT *
FROM    HumanResources.Employee FOR SYSTEM_TIME ALL
WHERE   EmployeeId = 6
ORDER   BY EmployeeId, RowStartTime;
```

Now you can see that the RowEndTime value is not '9999-12-31 23:59:59.9' but is set to the time of the DELETE operation:

EmployeeId	PolicyNumber	RowStartTime	RowEndTime
6	NULL	2020-05-27 23:51:51.9	2020-05-28 00:29:25.6

The reason is that at that point in time, it *did* exist, but now it doesn't, so if you were looking at the data as of May 27, 2020, 23:51:51.9, you would need to see the row. However, if (EmployeeId = 6) apologizes and brings proper cupcakes and gets added back with the same surrogate key value, there would be a gap in time sequence that would correspond to the time when the row was removed so you could query at May 28, 2020, 00:29:25.6 and not see the Employee row with EmployeeId = 6.

A word of caution about versions: When the table has SYSTEM_VERSIONING ON, every update will cause a new version, even if no data changes. So execute the following query:

```
UPDATE HumanResources.Employee
SET    InsurancePolicyNumber = InsurancePolicyNumber
WHERE  EmployeeId = 4;
```

You will find another version with the same data as the previous version:

```
SELECT Employee.EmployeeId, Employee.InsurancePolicyNumber AS PolicyNumber,
       Employee.RowStartTime, Employee.RowEndTime
FROM   HumanResources.Employee FOR SYSTEM_TIME ALL
WHERE  EmployeeId = 4
ORDER  BY EmployeeId, RowStartTime;
```

This returns

EmployeeId	PolicyNumber	RowStartTime	RowEndTime
4	NULL	2020-05-27 23:51:51.9	2020-05-28 00:11:07.1
4	4444444444	2020-05-28 00:11:07.1	2020-05-28 00:31:27.6
4	4444444444	2020-05-28 00:31:27.6	9999-12-31 23:59:59.9

You can see that there is no difference between the second row in the output and the third (I assure you there is nothing different between the EmployeeNumber column value either). Now, let's do five updates, immediately following one another using SSMS's GO # extension:

```
UPDATE HumanResources.Employee
SET    EmployeeNumber = EmployeeNumber
WHERE  EmployeeId = 4;
GO 5
```

Then run the following query to the historical data:

```
SELECT Employee.EmployeeId, Employee.InsurancePolicyNumber AS PolicyNumber,
       Employee.RowStartTime, Employee.RowEndTime
FROM   HumanResources.Employee FOR SYSTEM_TIME ALL
WHERE  EmployeeId = 4
ORDER  BY EmployeeId, RowStartTime;
```

As you look at the data, it may look off in that you probably only see a row or two added. In my case I only saw four rows (just one more than the previous execution), but there should be more, right? In this case, some rows were updated within what the system registered as the same time, so they are hidden. You can only see them in the history table; you can query it using

```
SELECT Employee.EmployeeId, Employee.InsurancePolicyNumber AS PolicyNumber,
       Employee.RowStartTime, Employee.RowEndTime
FROM   HumanResourcesHistory.Employee
WHERE  EmployeeId = 4
  AND  RowStartTime = RowEndTime;
```

Here you see the remaining four rows:

EmployeeId	PolicyNumber	RowStartTime	RowEndTime
4	4444444444	2020-05-28 00:33:38.0	2020-05-28 00:33:38.0
4	4444444444	2020-05-28 00:33:38.0	2020-05-28 00:33:38.0
4	4444444444	2020-05-28 00:33:38.0	2020-05-28 00:33:38.0
4	4444444444	2020-05-28 00:33:38.0	2020-05-28 00:33:38.0

If your application is very chatty and updates the same row over and over, you could end up with a lot of useless version rows, based on the granularity of your start and end time values.

Tip   Another way you end up with start and end times that are the same is when you modify the same row multiple times in the same transaction. Every modification you make will get a row in the history table, but each will have the same start and end times, down to all places in a `datetime2(7)` value. All of these modifications are hidden to the `FOR SYSTEM_TIME` but can be seen in the history table.

Now that you have started accumulating history, you are free to query your data at any point in time, down to whatever your precision is set to. How did the data look yesterday at this point in time? Or the previous day at 11:00 AM? Compared to now? The value of this could be enormous. However, as we will dig deeper in the next section, it brings up a problem. Now you can't limit your thinking to just one point in time. Every time slice should be synchronized.

What if you accidentally set the `InsurancePolicyNumber` to NULL? Or you set it to an incorrect value? In a regular situation, you update the row, and all is great. But if you are using your temporal versions to look back at your database at a point in time, reports may not look correct. You cannot simply update the history table, but rather must turn off versioning, fix the history, and turn versioning back on. I will cover the process in the forthcoming section "Setting/Rewriting History," but it is something to be done after hours when no one can access the table, which is not optimal.

Dealing with Multiple Rows in One or More Tables

At the end of the previous section, I started the discussion about thinking temporally with one row at a time. Versions throughout history need coordinated data that does not tell any falsehoods (even if you have cleared them up later in your base table). In this section, we will extend the concept to multiple rows. If you change two rows in a table, the only easy way to make sure their historical time values are the same if you are building your own using triggers is to make sure you do your update in a single statement. The temporal extensions give you a much better method of synchronizing changes. Basically, the start and end time columns are set at `COMMIT` time in the transaction.

If you want to update all of the InsurancePolicyNumber values to include the letters 'IN' as a prefix and, for some reason, you were unable to do this in a single statement (not every example can be realistic!), you wrap the change into a BEGIN and COMMIT transaction:

```
BEGIN TRANSACTION;
UPDATE HumanResources.Employee
SET    InsurancePolicyNumber = CONCAT('IN',RIGHT(InsurancePolicyNumber,8))
WHERE  EmployeeId = 1;

WAITFOR DELAY '00:00:01';


UPDATE HumanResources.Employee
SET    InsurancePolicyNumber = CONCAT('IN',RIGHT(InsurancePolicyNumber,8))
WHERE  EmployeeId = 2;

WAITFOR DELAY '00:00:01';


UPDATE HumanResources.Employee
SET    InsurancePolicyNumber = CONCAT('IN',RIGHT(InsurancePolicyNumber,8))
WHERE  EmployeeId = 3;

WAITFOR DELAY '00:00:01';


UPDATE HumanResources.Employee
SET    InsurancePolicyNumber = CONCAT('IN',RIGHT(InsurancePolicyNumber,8))
WHERE  EmployeeId = 4;

COMMIT TRANSACTION;
```

Then check out the data in the table:

```
SELECT *
FROM   HumanResources.Employee
WHERE  InsurancePolicyNumber IS NOT NULL
ORDER BY EmployeeId;
```

Looking at the data in the results, you can see that the RowStartTime value for every row that was updated is exactly the same, even if the UPDATE statements weren't actually executed at the same point in time (which I made sure of in this example by using the WAITFOR command and putting a 1-second delay between each execution of each statement):

EmployeeId	PolicyNumber	RowStartTime	RowEndTime
1	IN11111111	2020-05-28 00:51:35.6	9999-12-31 23:59:59.9
2	IN22222222	2020-05-28 00:51:35.6	9999-12-31 23:59:59.9
3	IN33333333	2020-05-28 00:51:35.6	9999-12-31 23:59:59.9
4	IN44444444	2020-05-28 00:51:35.6	9999-12-31 23:59:59.9

For simplicity's sake, I won't try to show multiple tables as an example, but the same thing holds true across multiple tables. Every row in a temporal table that is affected in a transaction will have the same start time (and end time) in the corresponding history table.

Setting/Rewriting History

History rows cannot be modified at all if the table is connected to a table to represent historical rows, but there are two major places where you may need to change history rows:

- *Major mistakes*: As alluded to previously, if you make a mistake and correct it in the base table, it will still be reflected as wrong in the history table. Sometimes, it may be advantageous to fix history, so it reflects what was really true. (As I noted in the intro to the main "Historical/Temporal Data" section, temporal tables are probably not where you want to audit changes for security purposes, but rather audit changes for business reasons.)

- *Upgrading a previous solution to use temporal extensions*: Since this is a still a relatively new feature and not even somewhat a new need, many people have already built solutions that keep history using some other techniques (like the trigger we have already covered). You can load your own data into the historical table if you need to.

As a very simple example, let's change our history to go back to the start of the year 2020. It is not something that is built into your code, so this is really an administrative task for a DBA. First, let's find the time we started keeping temporal data on the HumanResources.Employee table:

```
SELECT MIN(RowStartTime)
FROM    HumanResources.Employee FOR SYSTEM_TIME ALL;
```

This returns (for me, on my 100th+ time of running this script to get it just right)

```
--------------------------
2020-05-27 23:51:51.9
```

This is the time value we will need to create new version rows later. Next, we will turn off versioning, which will turn HumanResourcesHistory.Employee into a regular table that can be modified:

```
ALTER TABLE HumanResources.Employee
        SET (SYSTEM_VERSIONING = OFF);
```

The next step is to update all the rows that have '2020-05-10 02:35:49.1' as their start time to '2020-01-01'. You will not want to do this for all row's minimum row, because that means they were started after versioning was turned on, just the cases where the rows were started at the initial time the table was created (it won't hurt to carefully check the data to determine if someone made multiple starting points). In a real case, you will want to do a lot of research to determine what times make sense for all the rows, as you will want to figure out what their actual first time of existence was:

```
--Rows that have been modified
UPDATE HumanResourcesHistory.Employee
SET    RowStartTime = '2020-01-01 00:00:00.0'
WHERE  RowStartTime = '2020-05-10 02:35:49.1';
--value from previous select if you are following along in the home game
```

Additionally, you will need to generate history rows for rows that had not been modified yet, as you cannot change the RowStartTime in the HumanResources.Employee table:

```
INSERT INTO HumanResourcesHistory.Employee (EmployeeId, EmployeeNumber,
                        InsurancePolicyNumber,RowStartTime, RowEndTime)
SELECT EmployeeId, EmployeeNumber, InsurancePolicyNumber,
       '2020-01-01 00:00:00.0', RowStartTime
    --use the rowStartTime in the row for the endTime of the history
FROM   HumanResources.Employee
WHERE  NOT EXISTS (SELECT *
                   FROM   HumanResourcesHistory.Employee AS HistEmployee
                   WHERE  HistEmployee.EmployeeId = Employee.EmployeeId);
```

If you have done it correctly, you will have one row per Employee row that you want
to go back to January 1 returned in the following query:

```
SELECT Employee.EmployeeId, Employee.RowEndTime
FROM   HumanResourcesHistory.Employee
WHERE  RowStartTime = '2020-01-01 00:00:00.0'
ORDER BY EmployeeId;
```

And we do, including deleted rows:

```
EmployeeId  RowEndTime
----------  ---------------------------
1           2020-05-28 00:51:35.6
2           2020-05-28 00:51:35.6
3           2020-05-28 00:51:35.6
4           2020-05-28 00:11:07.1
5           2020-05-27 23:51:51.9
6           2020-05-28 00:29:25.6
```

Then turn back on system versioning:

```
ALTER TABLE HumanResources.Employee
       SET (SYSTEM_VERSIONING = ON
               (HISTORY_TABLE = HumanResourcesHistory.Employee));
```

Next, execute the following to see the data at the start of 2020:

```
SELECT *
FROM  HumanResources.Employee FOR SYSTEM_TIME AS OF '2020-01-01 00:00:00.0'
ORDER BY EmployeeId;
```

You can see that now your data seems to have existed since the start of 2020, instead of when I was writing this chapter:

EmployeeId	PolicyNumber	RowStartTime	RowEndTime
1	1111111111	2020-01-01 00:00:00.0	2020-05-28 00:51:35.6
2	2222222222	2020-01-01 00:00:00.0	2020-05-28 00:51:35.6
3	3333333333	2020-01-01 00:00:00.0	2020-05-28 00:51:35.6
4	NULL	2020-01-01 00:00:00.0	2020-05-28 00:11:07.1
5	NULL	2020-01-01 00:00:00.0	2020-05-27 23:51:51.9
6	NULL	2020-01-01 00:00:00.0	2020-05-28 00:29:25.6

You can make other changes to the history while the tables are not paired, but this is definitely one of the easiest. In the downloadable code, I have an additional example that will change EmployeeNumber 'A0005' to have had insurance since the start of March. This will entail splitting a history in two, so you have one history row for the before image and another for the after image. It is messy and tedious, so you will want to set up repeatable code processes if you must modify history in anything other than a very simple manner on a repeating process.

Note that when you turn system versioning on, a set of system consistency checks takes place to make sure that everything is configured correctly for the data in your history table and that you have not violated any of the rules for the schema of a history table. For more details, go to Microsoft Docs article "Temporal Table System Consistency Checks" (docs.microsoft.com/en-us/sql/relational-databases/tables/temporal-table-system-consistency-checks).

Maintaining History

By default, your history table will start out with no history (or the history that you add to it), but then grow unchecked forever. There are a few methods to keep it from growing out of control in your database. In this section, I will summarize the approaches and provide a link to the deeper setup details:

- *Using a temporal history retention policy*: In SQL Server 2017 and later, in the same syntax for `SYSTEM_VERSIONING = ON`, you can set a `HISTORY_RETENTION_PERIOD`. This time period will tell SQL Server how much history to keep before purging old history using a background task.

- *Stretch Database*: In SQL Server 2019, you can use Stretch Database to migrate some or all of the historical data for your temporal table(s) to Azure.

- *Table partitioning*: Using a sliding window approach, moving out partitions of the oldest portions of the historical data.

- *Custom cleanup script*: Turning of SYSTEM_VERSIONING periodically and performing maintenance much like what was performed in the "Setting/Rewriting History" section of this chapter.

For more details on each of these topics, see the "Manage retention of historical data in system-versioned temporal tables" article on Microsoft Docs: `docs.microsoft.com/en-us/sql/relational-databases/tables/manage-retention-of-historical-data-in-system-versioned-temporal-tables`.

Images, Documents, and Other Files

Storing large binary objects, such as PDFs, images, and really any kind of object you might find in your Windows file system, is generally not the historic domain of the relational database. As time has passed, however, it is becoming more and more commonplace.

When discussing how to store large objects in SQL Server, generally speaking this would be in reference to data that is (obviously) large but usually in some form of binary format that is not naturally modified using common T-SQL statements, for example, a picture or a formatted document. Most of the time, this is not simple text data or even formatted, semistructured text or even highly structured text such as XML. SQL Server has an XML type for storing XML data (including the ability to index fields in the XML document), and it also has `varchar(max)`/`nvarchar(max)` types for storing very large "plain" text data. Of course, sometimes you will want to store text data in the form of a

Windows text file to allow users to manage the data naturally. When deciding on a way to store binary data in SQL Server, there are two broadly characterizable ways that are available:

- Storing a path reference to the file data

- Storing the binaries using SQL Server's storage engine

In early editions of this book, the question was pretty easy to answer indeed. Almost always, the most reasonable solution was to store files in the file system and just store a path to the data in an nvarchar column. In SQL Server 2008, Microsoft implemented a type of binary storage called *filestream*, which allows binary data to be stored in the file system as actual files, which makes accessing this data from a client much faster than if it were stored in a binary column in SQL Server. In SQL Server 2012, the picture improved even more to give you a method to store any file data in the server that gives you access to the data using what looks like a typical network share. In all cases, you can deal with the data in T-SQL as before, and even that may be improved, though you cannot do partial writes to values as you can in a basic varbinary(max) column.

Since SQL Server 2012, the picture hasn't changed terribly. I generally choose between the two possible ways to store binaries according to one primary simple reason: transactional integrity. If you require transaction integrity, you use SQL Server's storage engine, regardless of the cost you may incur. If transaction integrity isn't tremendously important, you probably will want to use the file system. For example, if you are just storing an image that a user could go out and edit, leaving it with the same name, the file system is perfectly natural.

If you are going to store large objects in SQL Server, you will usually want to use filestream, particularly if your files are of fairly large size. It is suggested that you consider filestream if your binary objects will be greater than 1 MB, but recommendations change over time. Setting up filestream access is pretty easy; first, you enable filestream access for the server. For deeper details on this process, check the Microsoft Docs topic "Enable and Configure FILESTREAM" (docs.microsoft.com/en-us/sql/relational-databases/blob/enable-and-configure-filestream).

The basics to enable filestream (if you did not already do this during the process of installation) are to go to SQL Server Configuration Manager and choose the SQL Server instance in SQL Server Service. Open Properties, and choose the FILESTREAM tab, as shown in Figure 9-3.

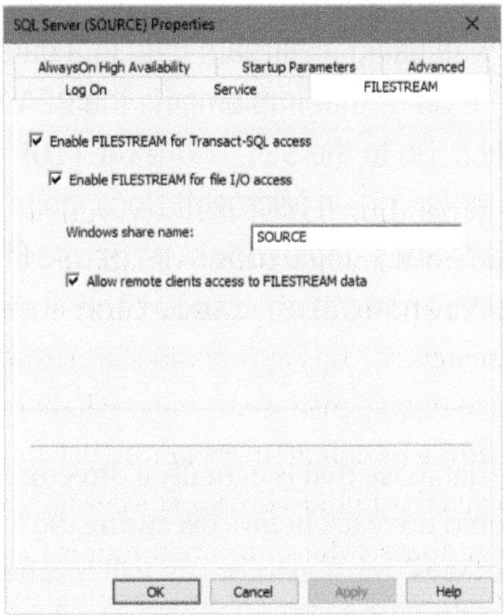

Figure 9-3. *Configuring the server for filestream access*

The Windows share name will be used to access filestream data via the API, as well as using a filetable later in this chapter. Later in this section, there will be additional configurations based on how the filestream data will be accessed. Start by enabling filestream access for the server using sp_configure filestream_access_level of either 1 (T-SQL access) or 2 (T-SQL and Win32 access). We will be using both methods, and here I will use the latter:

```
EXEC sp_configure 'filestream_access_level', 2;
RECONFIGURE;
```

Next, we create a sample database:

```
CREATE DATABASE FileStorageDemo; --uses basic defaults from model database
GO
USE FileStorageDemo;
GO
--will cover filegroups more in the chapter 11 on structures
ALTER DATABASE FileStorageDemo ADD
        FILEGROUP FilestreamData CONTAINS FILESTREAM;
```

Tip   There are caveats with using filestream data in a database that also needs to use snapshot isolation level or that implements the READ_COMMITTED_ SNAPSHOT database option. Go to the SET TRANSACTION ISOLATION LEVEL statement (covered in Chapter 12). In Microsoft Docs, go to the "SET TRANSACTION ISOLATION LEVEL (Transact-SQL)" topic (docs.microsoft.com/en-us/sql/t-sql/statements/set-transaction-isolation-level-transact-sql) for more information.

Next, add a "file" to the database that is actually a directory for the filestream files (note that the directory should not exist before executing the following statement, but the directory, in this case, c:\sql, must exist or you will receive an error):

```
ALTER DATABASE FileStorageDemo ADD FILE (
      NAME = FilestreamDataFile1,
      FILENAME = 'c:\sql\filestream')
   --directory cannot yet exist and SQL account must have access to drive.
TO FILEGROUP FilestreamData;
```

Now, you can create a table and include a varbinary(max) column with the keyword FILESTREAM after the datatype declaration. Note too that we need a unique identifier column with the ROWGUIDCOL property that is used by some of the system processes as a kind of special surrogate key.

```
CREATE SCHEMA Demo;
GO
CREATE TABLE Demo.TestSimpleFileStream
(
        TestSimpleFilestreamId INT NOT NULL
                    CONSTRAINT PKTestSimpleFileStream PRIMARY KEY,
        FileStreamColumn VARBINARY(MAX) FILESTREAM NULL,
        RowGuid uniqueidentifier NOT NULL ROWGUIDCOL DEFAULT (NEWID())
                    CONSTRAINT AKTestSimpleFileStream_RowGuid UNIQUE
)       FILESTREAM_ON FilestreamData;
```

It is as simple as that. You can use the data exactly like it is in SQL Server, as you can create the data using a simple query

```
INSERT INTO Demo.TestSimpleFileStream
                            (TestSimpleFilestreamId,FileStreamColumn)
SELECT 1, CAST('This is an exciting example' AS varbinary(max));
```

and see it using a typical SELECT:

```
SELECT TestSimpleFilestreamId,FileStreamColumn,
       CAST(FileStreamColumn AS varchar(40)) AS FileStreamText
FROM   Demo.TestSimpleFilestream;
```

I won't go any deeper into filestream manipulation here, because all of the more interesting bits of the technology from here are external to SQL Server in API code, which is well beyond the purpose of this section, which is to show you the basics of setting up the filestream column in your structures.

In SQL Server 2012, we got a new feature for storing binary files called a filetable. A filetable is a special type of table that you can access using T-SQL or directly from the file system using the share we set up earlier in this section, named MSSQLSERVER. One of the nice things for us is that we will be able to see the file that we create in a very natural manner that is accessible from Windows Explorer.

Enable and set up filetable-style filestream in the database as follows:

```
ALTER DATABASE FileStorageDemo
        SET FILESTREAM (NON_TRANSACTED_ACCESS = FULL,
                        DIRECTORY_NAME = N'ProSQLServerDBDesign');
```

The setting NON_TRANSACTED_ACCESS lets you set whether users can change data when accessing the data as a Windows share, such as opening a document in Word. The changes are not transactionally safe (meaning they aren't written to the log), so data stored in a filetable is not as safe as using a simple varbinary(max) with or without the filestream attribute. It behaves pretty much like data on any file server, except that it will be backed up with the database, and you can easily associate a file with other data in the server using common relational constructs. The DIRECTORY_NAME parameter is there to add to the path you will access the data (this will be demonstrated later in this section).

The syntax for creating the filetable is straightforward:

```
CREATE TABLE Demo.FileTableTest AS FILETABLE
  WITH (
        FILETABLE_DIRECTORY = 'FileTableTest',
        FILETABLE_COLLATE_FILENAME = database_default
        );
```

The FILETABLE_DIRECTORY is the final part of the path for access, and the FILETABLE_COLLATE_FILENAME determines the collation that the filenames will be treated as. It must be case insensitive, because Windows directories are case insensitive. I won't go in depth with all of the columns and settings, but suffice it to say that a filetable is based on a fixed table schema, and you can access it much like any other table. While you cannot change the structure of a filetable, you can add constraints and indexes. For more details, go to Microsoft Docs topic "Create, Alter, and Drop FileTables" (docs.microsoft.com/en-us/sql/relational-databases/blob/create-alter-and-drop-filetables).

There are two types of rows, directories, and files. Creating a directory is easy. For example, you wanted to create a directory for Project 1:

```
INSERT INTO Demo.FiletableTest(name, is_directory)
VALUES ( 'Project 1', 1);
```

Then, you can view this data in the table:

```
SELECT stream_id, file_stream, name
FROM   Demo.FileTableTest
WHERE  name = 'Project 1';
```

This will return (though with a different stream_id)

stream_id	file_stream	name
9BCB8987-1DB4-E011-87C8-000C29992276	NULL	Project 1

The stream_id column is a unique key that you can relate to with your other tables, allowing you to simply present the user with a "bucket" for storing data. Note that the primary key of the table is the column path_locator which is of datatype hierarchyId, which is a modifiable value. The stream_id value shouldn't ever change, though the file or directory could be moved. Before we go check it out in Windows, let's add a file to the directory. We will create a simple text file, with a small amount of text:

```
INSERT INTO Demo.FiletableTest(name, is_directory, file_stream)
VALUES ( 'Test.Txt', 0, CAST('This is some text' AS varbinary(max)));
```

Then, we can move the file to the directory we just created using the path_locator hierarchyId functionality:

```
UPDATE Demo.FiletableTest
SET    path_locator =
         path_locator.GetReparentedValue( path_locator.GetAncestor(1),
                                    (SELECT path_locator
                                     FROM Demo.FiletableTest
                                     WHERE name = 'Project 1'
                                         AND parent_path_locator IS NULL
                                         AND is_directory = 1))
WHERE name = 'Test.Txt';
```

Now, go to the share that you have set up and view the directory in Windows. Using the function FileTableRootPath(), you can get the filetable path for the database; in my case, the name of my VM is WIN-8F59B05AP, so the share is \\WIN-8F59B05AP\ MSSQLSERVER\ProSQLServerDBDesign, which is my computer's name, the MSSQLSERVER we set up in Configuration Manager, and ProSQLServerDBDesign from the ALTER DATABASE statement turning on filestream.

Now, concatenate the root to the path for the directory, which can be retrieved from the file_stream column (yes, the value you see when querying it is NULL, which is a bit confusing). Now, execute this:

```
SELECT  CONCAT(FileTableRootPath(),
                        file_stream.GetFileNamespacePath()) AS FilePath
FROM    Demo.FileTableTest
WHERE   name = 'Project 1'
  AND   parent_path_locator is NULL
  AND   is_directory = 1;
```

This returns the following:

```
FilePath
-----------------------------------------------------------------------
\\WIN-8F59BO5AP\MSSQLSERVER\ProSQLServerDBDesign\FileTableTest\Project 1
```

You can then enter this into Explorer to see something like what's shown in Figure 9-4 (assuming you have everything configured correctly, of course). Note that security for the Windows share is the same as for the filetable through T-SQL, which you administer the same as with any regular table, and you may need to set up your firewall to allow access as well.

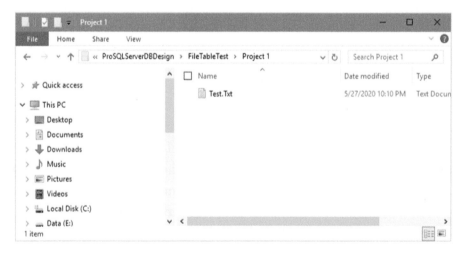

Figure 9-4. *Filetable directory opened in Windows Explorer*

From here, I would suggest you drop a few files in the directory from your local drive and check out the metadata for your files in your newly created filetable. It has a lot of possibilities. I will touch more on security in Chapter 10, but the basics are that security is based on Windows Authentication as you have it set up in SQL Server on the table, just like any other table.

Note   If you try to use Notepad to access the text file on the same server as the share is located, you may receive an error due to the way Notepad accesses files locally. Accessing the file from a remote location using Notepad will work fine.

I won't spend any more time covering the particulars of implementing with filetables. Essentially, with very little trouble, any programmer could provide a directory per client to allow the user to navigate to the directory and get the customer's associated files. And the files can be backed up with the normal backup operations.

So, mechanics aside, consider the four various methods of storing binary data in SQL tables:

- Store a UNC path in a simple character column.

- Store the binary data in a simple `varbinary(max)` column.

- Store the binary data in a `varbinary(max)` using the filestream type.

- Store the binary data using a filetable.

Tip   There is one other method of storing large binary values using what is called the Remote Blob Store (RBS) API. It allows you to use an external storage device to store and manage the images. It is not a typical case, though it will definitely be of interest to people building high-end solutions needing to store blobs on an external device. For more information, see Microsoft Docs topic "Remote Blob Store (RBS) (SQL Server)" (`docs.microsoft.com/en-us/sql/relational-databases/blob/remote-blob-store-rbs-sql-server`).

For three quick examples, consider a movie delivery database (online these days, naturally). We have a `MovieDeliveryFormat` table that represents a particular packaging of a movie for digital delivery. Because this is just the picture/packaging of a movie, it is a perfectly valid choice to store a path to the picture of the movie cover. This data will simply be used to present electronic browsing of the store's stock, so if it turns out to not work one time, that is not a big issue. Have a column for the `PictureUrl` that is `varchar(500)`, as shown in Figure 9-5.

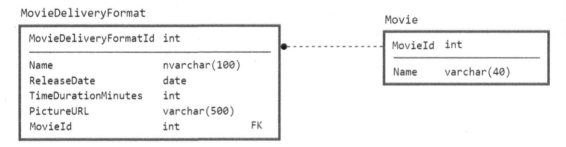

Figure 9-5. *MovieDeliveryFormat table with PictureUrl datatype set as a path to a file*

This path might even be on an Internet source where the filename is an HTTP:// address and be located in a web server's image cache and could be replicated to other web servers. The path may or may not be stored as a full UNC location; it really would depend on your infrastructure needs. The goal will be, when the page is fetching data from the server, to be able to build a bit of HTML such as this to get the picture that you would display for the movie's catalog entry:

```
SELECT '<img src = "' + MovieDeliveryFormat.PictureUrl + '">', ...
FROM    Movies.MovieDeliveryFormat
WHERE   MovieDeliveryFormatId = @MovieDeliveryFormatId;
```

If this data were stored in the database as a binary format, it would need to be materialized onto disk as a file first and then used in the page, which is going to be far slower than doing it this way, no matter what your architecture. This is probably not a case where you would want to go through the hoops necessary for filestream access, since transactionally speaking, if the picture link is broken, it would not invalidate the other data, and it is probably not very important (i.e., other than making a customer more interested in purchasing or renting the item). Plus, you will probably want to access this file directly, making the main web screens very fast and easy to code.

An alternative example might be accounts and associated users (see Figure 9-6). To fight fraud, a car rental chain may decide to start taking digital photos of customers and comparing the photos to the customers whenever they rent an item. This data is far more important from a security standpoint and has privacy implications. For this, I'll use a varbinary(max) for the person's picture in the database.

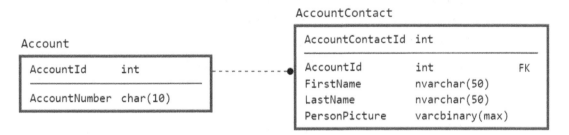

Figure 9-6. Customer table with picture stored as data in the table

At this point, assume you have definitely decided that transactional integrity is necessary and that you want to retrieve the data directly from the server. The next thing to decide is whether to employ a filestream storage method. The big question regarding this decision is whether your API supports the filestream feature. If so, this would likely be a very good place to make use of it. Size could play a part in the choice too, though security pictures could likely be less than 1 MB anyhow.

Overall, speed probably isn't a big deal, and even if you needed to take the binary bits and stream them from SQL Server's normal storage into a file, it would probably still perform well enough since only one image needs to be fetched at a time, and performance will be adequate as long as the image displays before the rental transaction is completed. Don't get me wrong; the varbinary(max) types aren't that slow, but performance would be acceptable for these purposes even if they were.

Finally, consider the case where a client wants to implement a file system to store scanned images pertaining to their customers, for example, a copy of the rental agreement, any late notices, and so on. Not enough significance is given to the data to require it to be managed in a structured manner, but they simply want to be able to create a directory to hold scanned data. The data does need to be kept in sync with the rest of the database. So you could extend your table to include a filetable (AccountFileDirectory in Figure 9-7, with stream_id modeled as primary key; even though it is technically a unique constraint in implementation, you can treat it as a primary key for all intents and purposes).

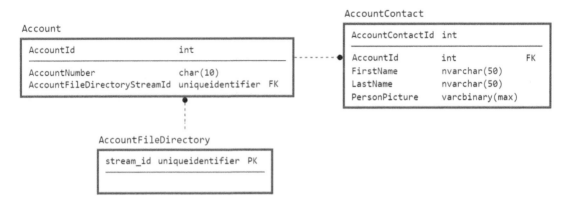

Figure 9-7. *Account model extended with an AccountFileDirectory*

In this manner, you have included a directory for the account's files that can be treated like a typical file structure but will be securely located with the account information. This not only will be very usable for the programmer and user alike but will also give you the security of knowing the data is backed up with the account files and treated in the same manner as the account information.

Generalization

Designing is often discussed as an art form, and that is what this topic is about. When designing a set of tables to represent some real-world activity, how specific should your tables be? For example, if you were designing a database to store information about camp activities, it might be tempting to have an individual table for the archery class, another for the swimming class, and so on, modeling with detail each camp activity. If there were 50 activities at the camp, you might have 50 tables, plus a bunch of other tables to tie these 50 together, so you could assign campers for each session and schedule activities. In the end though, while these tables may not look the same, you would start to notice that every table is used for basically the same thing: assign an instructor, sign up kids to attend, add a description, and so forth.

Rather than the system being about each activity, requiring you to model each of the different activities as being different from one another, what you would truly need to do is model the *abstraction* of a camp activity. So then you might end up with just one table for all 50 activities. This simplifies some parts of the process, and now the primary focus of the design is the management of an activity. You might discover that some extended information is needed about some or all the types of classes. Generalization is about making objects as general as possible, employing a pattern like subclassing to tune in the best possible solution where the broad, common tasks are easy; and the detailed tasks are as well.

During design, it is useful to look for similarities in utilization, columns, and so on, in a set of tables that serve a common purpose, and consider collapsing multiple tables into one, ending up with a generalization/abstraction of what is truly needed to be modeled. Clearly, however, the biggest problem is that sometimes you do need to store different information about some of the things your original tables were modeling. In our example, if you needed special information about the snorkeling class, you might lose that if you just created one activity abstraction, and heaven knows the goal is *not* to end up with a table with 200 columns all prefixed with what ought to have been a table in the first place (or, even worse, one general-purpose bucket of a table with a varchar(max) column where all of the desired information is shoveled into).

In those cases, you can consider using a subclassed entity for certain entities. Take the camp activity model. You could include the generalized table for the generic CampActivity, in which you would associate students and teachers who don't need special training, and in the subclassed tables, you would include specific information about the snorkeling and archery classes, likely along with the teachers who meet specific criteria (in unshown related tables), as shown in Figure 9-8.

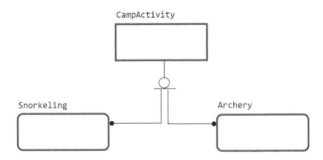

Figure 9-8. *Extending generalized entity with specific details as required*

As a coded example, we will look at a home inventory system. Suppose we have a client who wants to create an inventory of the various types of stuff in their house, or at least everything valuable, for insurance purposes. So should we simply design a table for each type of item? That seems like too much trouble, because for almost everything the client will simply have a description, picture, value, and receipt. On the other hand, a single table, generalizing all the items in the client's house down to a single list, seems like it might not be enough for items that they need specific information about, like appraisals and serial numbers. For example, some jewelry probably ought to be appraised and have the appraisal listed. Electronics and appliances ought to have brand, model, and possibly serial numbers captured. So the goal is to generalize a design to the level where the client has a basic list of the home inventory but can also print a list of jewelry alone with extra detail or print a list of electronics with their identifying information.

A method to implement this is to build tables such as the following. First, create the generic table that holds item descriptions:

```
CREATE SCHEMA Inventory;
GO
CREATE TABLE Inventory.Item
(
        ItemId  int NOT NULL IDENTITY CONSTRAINT PKItem PRIMARY KEY,
        Name    varchar(30) NOT NULL CONSTRAINT AKItemName UNIQUE,
        Type    varchar(15) NOT NULL,
        Color   varchar(15) NOT NULL,
        Description varchar(100) NOT NULL,
        ApproximateValue   numeric(12,2) NULL,
        ReceiptImage    varbinary(max) NULL,
        PhotographicImage varbinary(max) NULL
);
```

As you can see, I included two columns for holding an image of the receipt and a picture of the item. As discussed in the previous section, you might want to use a filetable construct to just allow various electronic items to be associated with this data, but it would probably be sufficient to simply have a picture of the receipt and the item minimally attached to the row for easy use. In the sample data, I always load the varbinary data with a simple hex value of 0x001 as a placeholder:

```
INSERT INTO Inventory.Item
VALUES ('Den Couch','Furniture','Blue',
        'Blue plaid couch, seats 4',450.00,0x001,0x001),
       ('Den Ottoman','Furniture','Blue',
        'Blue plaid ottoman that goes with couch',
         150.00,0x001,0x001),
```

```
('40 Inch Sorny TV','Electronics','Black',
 '40 Inch Sorny TV, Model R2D12, Serial Number XD49292',
 800,0x001,0x001),
('29 Inch JQC TV','Electronics','Black',
 '29 Inch JQC CRTVX29 TV',800,0x001,0x001),
('Mom''s Pearl Necklace','Jewelry','White',
 'Appraised for $1300 June of 2003. 30 inch necklace, was Mom''s',
 1300,0x001,0x001);
```

Check out the data using the following query:

```
SELECT Name, Type, Description
FROM   Inventory.Item;
```

Looking at the output, we see that we have a good little system, though data isn't organized how we really need it to be, because in realistic usage, we will probably need some of the specific data from the descriptions to be easier to access:

Name	Type	Description
Den Couch	Furniture	Blue plaid couch, seats 4
Den Ottoman	Furniture	Blue plaid ottoman that goe...
40 Inch Sorny TV	Electronics	40 Inch Sorny TV, Model R2D...
29 Inch JQC TV	Electronics	29 Inch JQC CRTVX29 TV
Mom's Pearl Necklace	Jewelry	Appraised for $1300 in June...

At this point, we look at our data and reconsider the design. The two pieces of furniture are fine as listed. We have a picture and a brief description. For the other three items, however, using the data becomes trickier. For electronics, the insurance company is going to want model and serial number for each, but the two TV entries use different formats, and one of them doesn't capture the serial number. Did the client forget to capture it? Or does it not exist?

So we add subclasses for cases where we need to have more information, to help guide the user as to how to enter data:

```
CREATE TABLE Inventory.JewelryItem
(
        ItemId  int CONSTRAINT PKJewelryItem PRIMARY KEY
                   CONSTRAINT FKJewelryItem$Extends$InventoryItem
                                REFERENCES Inventory.Item(ItemId),
        QualityLevel   varchar(10) NOT NULL,
        --a case might be made to store the appraisal document, and
        --possibly a new table for appraisals. This will suffice for
        --the current example set
        AppraiserName   varchar(100) NULL,
        AppraisalValue numeric(12,2) NULL,
        AppraisalYear  char(4) NULL
);
GO
CREATE TABLE Inventory.ElectronicItem
(
        ItemId         int        CONSTRAINT PKElectronicItem PRIMARY KEY
                       CONSTRAINT FKElectronicItem$Extends$InventoryItem
                                REFERENCES Inventory.Item(ItemId),
        BrandName   varchar(20) NOT NULL,
        ModelNumber varchar(20) NOT NULL,
        SerialNumber varchar(20) NULL
);
```

Now, we adjust the data in the tables to have names that are meaningful to the family, but we can create views of the data that have technical information to provide to other people—first, the two TVs. Note that we still don't have a serial number, but now, it would be simple to find the electronics for which the client doesn't have a serial number listed and needs to provide one:

```
UPDATE Inventory.Item
SET    Description = '40 Inch TV'
WHERE  Name = '40 Inch Sorny TV';
GO
```

```
INSERT INTO Inventory.ElectronicItem
            (ItemId, BrandName, ModelNumber, SerialNumber)
SELECT ItemId, 'Sorny','R2D12','XD49393'
FROM    Inventory.Item
WHERE   Name = '40 Inch Sorny TV';
GO
UPDATE Inventory.Item
SET     Description = '29 Inch TV'
WHERE   Name = '29 Inch JQC TV';
GO
INSERT INTO Inventory.ElectronicItem
            (ItemId, BrandName, ModelNumber, SerialNumber)
SELECT ItemId, 'JVC','CRTVX29',NULL
FROM    Inventory.Item
WHERE   Name = '29 Inch JQC TV';
```

Finally, we do the same for the jewelry items, adding the appraisal value from the text:

```
UPDATE Inventory.Item
SET     Description = '30 Inch Pearl Necklace'
WHERE   Name = 'Mom''s Pearl Necklace';
GO

INSERT INTO Inventory.JewelryItem
      (ItemId, QualityLevel, AppraiserName, AppraisalValue,AppraisalYear )
SELECT ItemId, 'Fine','Joey Appraiser',1300,'2003'
FROM    Inventory.Item
WHERE   Name = 'Mom''s Pearl Necklace';
```

Looking at the data now, we see the more generic list with names that are more specifically for the person maintaining the list:

```
SELECT Name, Type, Description
FROM    Inventory.Item;
```

This returns

Name	Type	Description
Den Couch	Furniture	Blue plaid couch, seats 4
Den Ottoman	Furniture	Blue plaid ottoman that goes w...
40 Inch Sorny TV	Electronics	40 Inch TV
29 Inch JQC TV	Electronics	29 Inch TV
Mom's Pearl Necklace	Jewelry	30 Inch Pearl Necklace

And to see specific electronic items with their information, we can use a query such as this, with an inner join to the parent table to get the basic nonspecific information:

```
SELECT Item.Name, ElectronicItem.BrandName, ElectronicItem.ModelNumber,
        ElectronicItem.SerialNumber
FROM    Inventory.ElectronicItem
          JOIN Inventory.Item
                ON Item.ItemId = ElectronicItem.ItemId;
```

This returns

Name	BrandName	ModelNumber	SerialNumber
40 Inch Sorny TV	Sorny	R2D12	XD49393
29 Inch JQC TV	JVC	CRTVX29	NULL

Finally, it is also quite common to want to see a complete inventory with the specific information, since this is truly the natural way to think of the data and is why the typical designer will design the table in a single table no matter what. We return an extended description column this time by formatting the data based on the type of row:

```
SELECT Name, Description,
        CASE Type
            WHEN 'Electronics'
                THEN CONCAT('Brand:', COALESCE(BrandName,'_____'),
                        ' Model:',COALESCE(ModelNumber,'_____'),
                        ' SerialNumber:', COALESCE(SerialNumber,'_____'))
```

```
        WHEN 'Jewelry'
          THEN CONCAT('QualityLevel:', QualityLevel,
                ' Appraiser:', COALESCE(AppraiserName,'_____'),
                ' AppraisalValue:',
              COALESCE(Cast(AppraisalValue as varchar(20)),'_____'),
                ' AppraisalYear:', COALESCE(AppraisalYear,'____'))
          ELSE '' END as ExtendedDescription
FROM    Inventory.Item --simple outer joins because every not item will have
              -- extensions but they will only have one if any extension
          LEFT OUTER JOIN Inventory.ElectronicItem
            ON Item.ItemId = ElectronicItem.ItemId
          LEFT OUTER JOIN Inventory.JewelryItem
            ON Item.ItemId = JewelryItem.ItemId;
```

This query will return a formatted description and visually shows missing information. The point of this section on generalization really goes back to the basic precepts that you design for the user's needs. If we had created a table per type of item in the house—Inventory.Lamp, Inventory.ClothesHanger, and so on—the process of normalization would normally get the blame. But the truth is, if you really listen to the user's needs and model them correctly, you will naturally generalize your objects until you have blanks to fill in for every piece of information that the customer needs to keep track of. However, it is still a good thing to look for commonality among the objects in your database, looking for cases where you could get away with less tables rather than more.

Tip   It may seem unnecessary, especially for a simple home inventory system, to take these extra steps in your design. However, the point I am trying to make here is that if you have rules about how data should look, having a column for that data almost certainly is going to make more sense, even if it takes making a few more tables. Even if your business rule enforcement is as minimal as just using the final query, it will be far more obvious to the end user that the SerialNumber: _____ value is a missing value that probably needs to be filled in.

Storing User-Specified Data

Try as one might, it is nearly impossible to get a database design that can store every single piece of data that every one of your customers wants to store, especially for unseen future needs. Users need to be able to morph their schema slightly at times to add some bit of information that they didn't realize would exist and doesn't meet the bar of making a change to the schema and user interfaces. So we need to find some way to provide a method of tweaking the schema without changing the interface that does the best job at meeting the normal forms that were established in Chapter 5. The biggest issue is the integrity of the data that users want to store in this database in that it is very rare that they'll want to store data and not use it to make decisions. In this section, I will explore a couple of the common methods for enabling the end user to expand the data catalog.

As I have established throughout the book so far, relational databases are not fundamentally meant to be flexible. T-SQL as a language is not made for flexibility (at least not from the standpoint of producing reliable databases that produce expected results with acceptable performance and quality data, which, as I have said many times, is almost always the most important thing). Unfortunately, users need flexibility; you can't tell users that they can't get what they want, when they want it, and continue to get paid for long.

As an architect, I want to give the users what they want, within the confines of reality and sensibility, so it is necessary to ascertain some method of giving the users the flexibility they demand, along with methods to deal with this data in a manner that feels good to them.

Note   I will specifically speak only of methods that allow you to work with the relational engine in a reasonably relational manner. One method I won't cover is using a basic XML data in an `xml` datatype or even a column with JSON-structured text in an `nvarchar` datatype. This is available, but is very messy to handle in T-SQL code.

The methods I will demonstrate are as follows:

- Entity-attribute-value (EAV)

- Adding columns to the table, likely using sparse columns

The last time I had this type of need was to gather the properties on networking equipment. Each router, modem, and so on for a network has various properties (and hundreds or thousands of them at that). While the usage of a solution for a problem like that would be generally different than a problem where you want to let a customer add custom attributes to some object because of the sheer number of attributes, the foundations are basically the same.

The basis of this example will be a simple table called Hardware.Equipment. It will have a surrogate key and a tag that will identify it. It is created using the following code:

```
CREATE SCHEMA Hardware;
GO
CREATE TABLE Hardware.Equipment
(
    EquipmentId int NOT NULL
        CONSTRAINT PKEquipment PRIMARY KEY,
    EquipmentTag varchar(10) NOT NULL
        CONSTRAINT AKEquipment UNIQUE,
    EquipmentType varchar(10)
);
GO
INSERT INTO Hardware.Equipment
VALUES (1,'CLAWHAMMER','Hammer'),
       (2,'HANDSAW','Saw'),
       (3,'POWERDRILL','PowerTool');
```

By this point in this book, you should know that this is not how the whole table would look in the actual solutions, but these three columns will give you enough to see the one concept I am demonstrating. One anti-pattern I won't demonstrate is what I call the "Big Ol' Set of Generic Columns." Basically, it involves adding multiple columns to the table as part of the design, as in the following variant of the Equipment table:

```
CREATE TABLE Hardware.Equipment
(
    EquipmentId int NOT NULL
        CONSTRAINT PKHardwareEquipment PRIMARY KEY,
    EquipmentTag varchar(10) NOT NULL
        CONSTRAINT AKHardwareEquipment UNIQUE,
```

```
    EquipmentType varchar(10),
    UserDefined1 sql_variant NULL,
    UserDefined2 sql_variant NULL,
    ...
    UserDefinedN sql_variant NULL
);
```

I don't favor such a solution because it hides what kind of values are in the added columns and is often abused because the UI is built to have generic labels as well. Such implementations rarely turn out well for the person who needs to use these values at a later point in time. It is definitely possible to extend this by adding additional tables for metadata about the UserDefined columns, but as we will see, it is far easier to use the metadata built into SQL Server to capture the metadata.

Entity-Attribute-Value (EAV)

The first recommended method of implementing user-specified data is the entity-attribute-value (EAV) method. This is also known by a few different names, such as property tables, loose schemas, or open schema. This technique is often considered the default method of implementing a table to allow users to configure their own storage.

The basic idea is to have another related attribute table associated with the table you want to add information about. Then, you can either include the name of the attribute in the property table or (as I will do) have a table that defines the basic properties of a property.

Considering our needs with equipment, I will use the model shown in Figure 9-9.

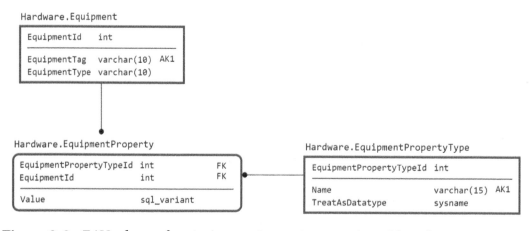

Figure 9-9. *EAV schema for storing equipment properties with unknown attributes*

If you as the architect know that you want to allow only three types of properties, you should almost never use this technique because it is almost certainly better to add the three known columns, possibly using the techniques for subtyped entities presented earlier in the book to implement the different tables to hold the values that pertain to only one type or another. The goal here is to build loose objects that can be expanded on by the users, but still have a modicum of data integrity. In our example, it is possible that the people who develop the equipment you are working with will add a property that you want to then keep up with. In one of my real-life usage of this technique, there were hundreds of properties added as different equipment was brought online, and each device was interrogated for its properties.

What makes this method desirable to programmers is that you can create a user interface that is just a simple list of attributes to edit. Adding a new property is simply another row in a table. Even the solution I will provide here, with some additional data control, is easy to provide a UI for.

To create this solution, I will create an EquipmentPropertyType table and add a few types of properties:

```
CREATE TABLE Hardware.EquipmentPropertyType
(
    EquipmentPropertyTypeId int NOT NULL
        CONSTRAINT PKEquipmentPropertyType PRIMARY KEY,
    Name varchar(15)
        CONSTRAINT AKEquipmentPropertyType UNIQUE,
    TreatAsDatatype sysname NOT NULL
);

INSERT INTO Hardware.EquipmentPropertyType
VALUES(1,'Width','numeric(10,2)'),
      (2,'Length','numeric(10,2)'),
      (3,'HammerHeadStyle','varchar(30)');
```

Then, I create the EquipmentProperty table, which will hold the actual property values. I will use a sql_variant type for the Value column to allow any type of data to be stored, but it is also typical either to use a character string–type value (requiring the caller/user to convert to a string representation of all values) or to have multiple columns, one for each possible/supported datatype. Both of these options and using sql_variant all have slight difficulties, but I tend to use sql_variant for truly unknown types of data because data is stored in its native format (though in many cases you will need to cast the data to some datatype to use it). In the definition of the property, I include the datatype that I expect the data to be, and in my insert procedure, I will test the data to make sure it meets the requirements for a specific datatype:

```
CREATE TABLE Hardware.EquipmentProperty
(
    EquipmentId int NOT NULL
      CONSTRAINT
          FKEquipment$hasExtendedPropertiesIn$HardwareEquipmentProperty
          REFERENCES Hardware.Equipment(EquipmentId),
    EquipmentPropertyTypeId int
      CONSTRAINT
        FKEquipmentPropertyTypeId$definesTypesFor$HardwareEquipmentProperty
          REFERENCES Hardware.EquipmentPropertyType
                                    (EquipmentPropertyTypeId),
    Value sql_variant,
    CONSTRAINT PKEquipmentProperty PRIMARY KEY
                          (EquipmentId, EquipmentPropertyTypeId)
);
```

Then, I need to load some data. For this task, I will build a procedure that can be used to insert the data by name and, at the same time, will validate that the datatype is right. That is a bit tricky because of the sql_variant type, and it is one reason that property tables are sometimes built using character values. Since everything has a textual representation and it is easier to work with in code, it can make things simpler for the code but often far worse for the storage engine to maintain.

In the procedure, I will insert the row into the table and then use dynamic SQL to validate the value by casting it to the datatype the user configured for the property. (Note that the procedure follows the standards that I will establish in later chapters for transactions and error handling. I don't always do this in all examples in the book, to keep the samples cleaner, but this procedure deals with validations.)

```
CREATE PROCEDURE Hardware.EquipmentProperty$Insert
(
    @EquipmentId int,
    @EquipmentPropertyName varchar(15),
    @Value sql_variant
)
AS
 BEGIN
    SET NOCOUNT ON;
    DECLARE @entryTrancount int = @@trancount;

    BEGIN TRY
        DECLARE @EquipmentPropertyTypeId int,
                @TreatAsDatatype sysname;

        SELECT @TreatAsDatatype = TreatAsDatatype,
               @EquipmentPropertyTypeId = EquipmentPropertyTypeId
        FROM   Hardware.EquipmentPropertyType
        WHERE  EquipmentPropertyType.Name = @EquipmentPropertyName;

      BEGIN TRANSACTION;
        --insert the value
        INSERT INTO Hardware.EquipmentProperty
                (EquipmentId, EquipmentPropertyTypeId, Value)
        VALUES (@EquipmentId, @EquipmentPropertyTypeId, @Value);

        --Then get that value from the table and cast it in a dynamic SQL
        -- call.  This will raise a trappable error if the type is
        --incompatible
        DECLARE @validationQuery  varchar(max) =
          CONCAT(' DECLARE @value sql_variant
                   SELECT  @value = CAST(VALUE AS ', @TreatAsDatatype, ')
                   FROM    Hardware.EquipmentProperty
                   WHERE   EquipmentId = ', @EquipmentId, '
                     and   EquipmentPropertyTypeId = ' ,
                                @EquipmentPropertyTypeId);
```

```
        EXECUTE (@validationQuery);
      COMMIT TRANSACTION;
    END TRY
    BEGIN CATCH
        IF @@TRANCOUNT > 0
            ROLLBACK TRANSACTION;

        DECLARE @ERRORmessage nvarchar(4000)
        SET @ERRORmessage = CONCAT('Error occurred in procedure ''',
                OBJECT_NAME(@@procid), ''', Original Message: ''',
                ERROR_MESSAGE(),''' Property:''',@EquipmentPropertyName,
                ''' Value:''',cast(@Value as nvarchar(1000)),'''');
      THROW 50000,@ERRORMessage,1;
      RETURN -100;

    END CATCH;
  END;
```

So, if you try to put in an invalid piece of data such as

```
--width is numeric(10,2)
EXEC Hardware.EquipmentProperty$Insert 1,'Width','Claw';
```

you will get the following error:

```
Msg 50000, Level 16, State 1, Procedure EquipmentProperty$Insert
Error occurred in procedure 'EquipmentProperty$Insert', Original Message:
'Error converting data type varchar to numeric.'. Property:'Width'
Value:'Claw'
```

Now, I create some proper demonstration data:

```
EXEC Hardware.EquipmentProperty$Insert @EquipmentId =1 ,
        @EquipmentPropertyName = 'Width', @Value = 2;
EXEC Hardware.EquipmentProperty$Insert @EquipmentId =1 ,
        @EquipmentPropertyName = 'Length',@Value = 8.4;
EXEC Hardware.EquipmentProperty$Insert @EquipmentId =1 ,
        @EquipmentPropertyName = 'HammerHeadStyle',@Value = 'Claw';
```

```
EXEC Hardware.EquipmentProperty$Insert @EquipmentId =2 ,
        @EquipmentPropertyName = 'Width',@Value = 1;
EXEC Hardware.EquipmentProperty$Insert @EquipmentId =2 ,
        @EquipmentPropertyName = 'Length',@Value = 7;
EXEC Hardware.EquipmentProperty$Insert @EquipmentId =3 ,
        @EquipmentPropertyName = 'Width',@Value = 6;
EXEC Hardware.EquipmentProperty$Insert @EquipmentId =3 ,
        @EquipmentPropertyName = 'Length',@Value = 12.1;
```

To view the data in a raw manner, I can simply query the data as such:

```
SELECT Equipment.EquipmentTag,Equipment.EquipmentType,
      EquipmentPropertyType.name, EquipmentProperty.Value
FROM   Hardware.EquipmentProperty
          JOIN Hardware.Equipment
            on Equipment.EquipmentId = EquipmentProperty.EquipmentId
          JOIN Hardware.EquipmentPropertyType
            on EquipmentPropertyType.EquipmentPropertyTypeId =
                          EquipmentProperty.EquipmentPropertyTypeId;
```

This is usable but not very natural as results:

EquipmentTag	EquipmentType	name	Value
CLAWHAMMER	Hammer	Width	2
CLAWHAMMER	Hammer	Length	8.4
CLAWHAMMER	Hammer	HammerHeadStyle	Claw
HANDSAW	Saw	Width	1
HANDSAW	Saw	Length	7
POWERDRILL	PowerTool	Width	6
POWERDRILL	PowerTool	Length	12.1

To view this in a natural, tabular format along with the other columns of the table, I could use PIVOT, but the "old"-style method to perform a pivot, using MAX() aggregates, works better here because I can fairly easily make the statement dynamic (which is the next query sample):

```
SET ANSI_WARNINGS OFF; --eliminates the NULL warning on aggregates.
SELECT  Equipment.EquipmentTag,Equipment.EquipmentType,
   MAX(CASE WHEN EquipmentPropertyType.name = 'HammerHeadStyle'
       THEN Value END) AS 'HammerHeadStyle',
   MAX(CASE WHEN EquipmentPropertyType.name = 'Length'
       THEN Value END) AS Length,
   MAX(CASE WHEN EquipmentPropertyType.name = 'Width'
       THEN Value END) AS Width
FROM   Hardware.EquipmentProperty
         JOIN Hardware.Equipment
           on Equipment.EquipmentId = EquipmentProperty.EquipmentId
         JOIN Hardware.EquipmentPropertyType
           on EquipmentPropertyType.EquipmentPropertyTypeId =
                          EquipmentProperty.EquipmentPropertyTypeId
GROUP BY Equipment.EquipmentTag,Equipment.EquipmentType;
SET ANSI_WARNINGS OFF; --eliminates the NULL warning on aggregates.
```

This returns the following:

EquipmentTag	EquipmentType	HammerHeadStyle	Length	Width
CLAWHAMMER	Hammer	Claw	8.4	2
HANDSAW	Saw	NULL	7	1
POWERDRILL	PowerTool	NULL	12.1	6

If you execute this on your own in the "Results to Text" mode in SSMS, what you will quickly notice is how much editing I had to do to the data. Each sql_variant column will be formatted for a huge amount of data. And you have to manually set up each column ahead of execution time. In the following extension, I have used XML PATH to output the different properties to different columns, starting with MAX. (This is a common SQL Server 2005 and later technique for converting rows to columns. Do a web search for "convert rows to columns in SQL Server," and you will find the details.)

```
DECLARE @query varchar(8000);
SELECT  @query = 'SELECT Equipment.EquipmentTag,Equipment.EquipmentType ' +
(
                SELECT DISTINCT
                    ',MAX(CASE WHEN EquipmentPropertyType.name = ''' +
                        EquipmentPropertyType.name + '''
                        THEN CAST(Value AS ' +
                        EquipmentPropertyType.TreatAsDatatype + ') END) AS
                        [' +
                        EquipmentPropertyType.name + ']' AS [text()]
                FROM
                    Hardware.EquipmentPropertyType
                FOR XML PATH('') , type ).value('.', 'NVARCHAR(MAX)') + '
                FROM  Hardware.EquipmentProperty
                    JOIN Hardware.Equipment
                        ON Equipment.EquipmentId =
                                    EquipmentProperty.EquipmentId
                    JOIN Hardware.EquipmentPropertyType
                        ON EquipmentPropertyType.EquipmentPropertyTypeId
                            = EquipmentProperty.EquipmentPropertyTypeId
        GROUP BY Equipment.EquipmentTag,Equipment.EquipmentType  '
EXEC (@query);
```

Executing this will get you the following (which is exactly what was returned in the last results, plus a warning that looks like this: "Warning: Null value is eliminated by an aggregate or other SET operation"; but you will notice a major difference if you execute this code yourself):

EquipmentTag	EquipmentType	HammerHeadStyle	Length	Width
CLAWHAMMER	Hammer	Claw	8.40	2.00
HANDSAW	Saw	NULL	7.00	1.00
POWERDRILL	PowerTool	NULL	12.10	6.00

I won't pretend that I didn't have to edit the results to get them to fit, but each of these columns was formatted as the datatype specified in the `EquipmentPropertyType` table, not as 8,000-character values (that is a lot of little minus signs under each heading to delete). You could expand this code further if you wanted to limit the domain further than just by datatype (like to make sure length is only a positive value), but it definitely will complicate matters beyond what I have space for in this book.

Adding Columns to a Table

Next, consider the idea of using the facilities that SQL Server gives us for implementing columns, rather than implementing your own metadata system. In the previous examples, it was impossible to use the table structures in a natural way, meaning that if you wanted to query the data, you had to know what was meant by interrogating the metadata. As I demonstrated, using the EAV pattern, a normal `SELECT` statement is not possible, but can be simulated with a dynamic stored procedure, or you could possibly create a hard-coded view (completely defeating the purpose of the flexible EAV pattern), but it certainly would not be easy for the typical end user without the aid of a programmer.

Tip   If you build products to ship to customers, you should produce an application to validate the structures against before applying a patch or upgrade or even allowing your tech support to help with a problem. Although you cannot stop a customer from making a change to your SQL Server database (like a new column, index, trigger, or whatever), you don't want the change to cause an issue that your tech support won't immediately recognize.

The key to this method is to use SQL Server more or less in a natural manner (there may still be some metadata required to manage data rules, but it is possible to use native SQL commands with the data). Instead of all the stuff we went through in the previous section to save and view the data, just use `ALTER TABLE` and add the column.

To implement this method, for the most part we will make use of *sparse columns*, a type of column storage where a column that is NULL takes no storage at all after the first one is added (normal NULL columns require space to indicate that they are NULL, but sparse columns, once configured, take no extra space for new null columns).

Internally, the data is stored as a form of an EAV/XML that is associated with each row in the table. Sparse columns are added and dropped from the table using the same DDL statements as normal columns (with the added keyword of SPARSE on the column create statement). You can also use the same DML operations on the data as you can for regular tables. However, since the purpose of having sparse columns is to allow you to add many columns to the table (sparse columns increase the maximum number of columns on a table to 30,000, though this should probably not be a personal goal), you can also work with sparse columns using a *column set*, which gives you the ability to retrieve and work with only the sparse columns that you desire to or that have values in the row. Because of the concept of a column set, this solution will allow you to build a UI that doesn't know all the structure along with a typical SQL solution.

Sparse columns are slightly less efficient in many ways when compared to normal columns, so the idea would be to add non-sparse columns to your tables when they will be used quite often, and if they will pertain only to rare or certain types of rows, then you could use a sparse column. Several types cannot be stored as sparse:

- The spatial types
- rowversion/timestamp
- User-defined datatypes
- text, ntext, and image (Note that you shouldn't use these anyway; use varchar(max), nvarchar(max), and varbinary(max) instead.)

Returning to the Equipment example, all I'm going to use this time is the single table. Note that the data I want to produce looks like this:

EquipmentTag	EquipmentType	HammerHeadStyle	Length	Width
CLAWHAMMER	Hammer	Claw	8.40	2.00
HANDSAW	Saw	NULL	7.00	1.00
POWERDRILL	PowerTool	NULL	12.10	6.00

To add the Length column to the Equipment table, use this:

```
ALTER TABLE Hardware.Equipment
    ADD Length numeric(10,2) SPARSE NULL;
```

If you were building an application to add a column, you could use a procedure like the following to give the user ability to add a column without getting all the other control types over the table. Note that if you are going to allow users to remove columns they add, you will want to use some mechanism to prevent them from dropping primary system columns, such as a naming standard or extended property. You also may want to employ some manner of control to prevent them from doing this at just any time they want:

```
CREATE PROCEDURE Hardware.Equipment$AddProperty
(
    @propertyName     sysname, --the column to add
    @datatype         sysname, --the datatype as it appears in declaration
    @sparselyPopulatedFlag bit = 1 --Add column as sparse or not
)
WITH EXECUTE AS OWNER --provides the user the rights of the
--owner of the object when executing this code
AS
 BEGIN

   --note: I did not include full error handling for clarity
   DECLARE @query nvarchar(max);

  --check for column existence
  IF NOT EXISTS (SELECT *
                 FROM    sys.columns
                 WHERE   name = @propertyName
                   AND   OBJECT_NAME(object_id) = 'Equipment'
                   AND   OBJECT_SCHEMA_NAME(object_id) = 'Hardware')
    BEGIN
       --build the ALTER statement, then execute it
       SET @query = 'ALTER TABLE Hardware.Equipment ADD '
               + quotename(@propertyName) + ' '
               + @datatype
               + case when @sparselyPopulatedFlag = 1 then ' SPARSE ' end
               + ' NULL ';
```

```
    EXEC (@query);
  END
 ELSE
    THROW 50000, 'The property you are adding already exists',1;
END;
```

Now, any user to whom you give rights to run this procedure can add a column to the table:

```
--Previously Added
--EXEC Hardware.Equipment$AddProperty 'Length','numeric(10,2)',1;
EXEC Hardware.Equipment$AddProperty 'Width','numeric(10,2)',1;
EXEC Hardware.Equipment$AddProperty 'HammerHeadStyle','varchar(30)',1;
```

View the table with the following SELECT statement:

```
SELECT EquipmentTag, EquipmentType, HammerHeadStyle,Length,Width
FROM   Hardware.Equipment;
```

This returns the following (I will use this SELECT statement several times):

EquipmentTag	EquipmentType	HammerHeadStyle	Length	Width
CLAWHAMMER	Hammer	NULL	NULL	NULL
HANDSAW	Saw	NULL	NULL	NULL
POWERDRILL	PowerTool	NULL	NULL	NULL

Now, you can treat the new columns just like they were normal columns. You can update them using a normal UPDATE statement:

```
UPDATE Hardware.Equipment
SET    Length = 7.00,
       Width =  1.00
WHERE  EquipmentTag = 'HANDSAW';
```

Checking the data, you can see that the data was updated:

EquipmentTag	EquipmentType	HammerHeadStyle	Length	Width
CLAWHAMMER	Hammer	NULL	NULL	NULL
HANDSAW	Saw	NULL	7.00	1.00
POWERDRILL	PowerTool	NULL	NULL	NULL

One thing that is so much more powerful about this method of user-specified columns is validation. Because the columns behave just like columns should, you can use a CHECK constraint to validate row-based constraints:

```
ALTER TABLE Hardware.Equipment
  ADD CONSTRAINT CHKEquipment$HammerHeadStyle CHECK
        ((HammerHeadStyle is NULL AND EquipmentType <> 'Hammer')
        OR EquipmentType = 'Hammer');
```

Note   You could easily create a procedure to manage a user-defined check constraint on the data just like I created the columns.

Now, if you try to set an invalid value, like a saw with a HammerHeadStyle, you get an error:

```
UPDATE Hardware.Equipment
SET    Length = 12.10,
       Width =  6.00,
       HammerHeadStyle = 'Wrong!'
WHERE  EquipmentTag = 'HANDSAW';
```

This returns the following:

```
Msg 547, Level 16, State 0, Line 1
The UPDATE statement conflicted with the CHECK constraint
"CHKEquipment$HammerHeadStyle". The conflict occurred in database
"Chapter8", table "Hardware.Equipment".
```

Setting the rest of the values, I return to where I was in the previous section's data, only this time the SELECT statement could have been written by a novice:

```
UPDATE Hardware.Equipment
SET    Length = 12.10,
       Width = 6.00
WHERE  EquipmentTag = 'POWERDRILL';

UPDATE Hardware.Equipment
SET    Length = 8.40,
       Width = 2.00,
       HammerHeadStyle = 'Claw'
WHERE  EquipmentTag = 'CLAWHAMMER';

GO
SELECT EquipmentTag, EquipmentType, HammerHeadStyle ,Length,Width
FROM   Hardware.Equipment;
```

This returns that result set I was shooting for:

EquipmentTag	EquipmentType	HammerHeadStyle	Length	Width
CLAWHAMMER	Hammer	Claw	8.40	2.00
HANDSAW	Saw	NULL	7.00	1.00
POWERDRILL	PowerTool	NULL	12.10	6.00

Now, up to this point, it really did not make any difference if this was a sparse column or not. Even if I just used a SELECT * from the table, it would look just like a normal set of data. Pretty much the only way you can tell is by looking at the metadata:

```
SELECT name, is_sparse
FROM   sys.columns
WHERE  OBJECT_NAME(object_id) = 'Equipment'
```

This returns the following:

name	is_sparse
EquipmentId	0
EquipmentTag	0
EquipmentType	0
Length	1
Width	1
HammerHeadStyle	1

But there is a different way of working with this data that can be much easier to deal with if you have many sparse columns with only a few of them filled in or if you are trying to build a UI that morphs to the data. You can define a *column set*, which will let you work with sparse columns using an XML representation. With a column set defined, you can access XML that manages the sparse columns and works with it directly. This is handy for dealing with tables that have a lot of empty sparse columns, because NULL sparse columns do not show up in the XML, allowing you to pass very small amounts of data to the user interface, though it will have to deal with it as XML rather than in a tabular data stream.

Tip   You cannot add or drop the column set once there are sparse columns in the table, so decide which to use carefully.

For our table, I will drop the CHECK constraint and sparse columns and add a column set (you cannot modify the column set when any sparse columns exist in the table):

```
ALTER TABLE Hardware.Equipment
    DROP CONSTRAINT IF EXISTS CHKEquipment$HammerHeadStyle;
ALTER TABLE Hardware.Equipment
    DROP COLUMN IF EXISTS HammerHeadStyle, Length, Width;
```

Now, I add a column set, which I will name SparseColumns:

```
ALTER TABLE Hardware.Equipment
  ADD SparseColumns XML COLUMN_SET FOR ALL_SPARSE_COLUMNS;
```

Next, I add back the sparse columns and constraints using my existing procedure:

```
EXEC Hardware.Equipment$addProperty 'Length','numeric(10,2)',1;
EXEC Hardware.Equipment$addProperty 'Width','numeric(10,2)',1;
EXEC Hardware.Equipment$addProperty 'HammerHeadStyle','varchar(30)',1;
GO
ALTER TABLE Hardware.Equipment
 ADD CONSTRAINT CHKEquipment$HammerHeadStyle CHECK
        ((HammerHeadStyle is NULL AND EquipmentType <> 'Hammer')
         OR EquipmentType = 'Hammer');
```

Now, I can still update the columns individually using the UPDATE statement:

```
UPDATE Hardware.Equipment
SET    Length = 7,
       Width =  1
WHERE  EquipmentTag = 'HANDSAW';
```

But this time, using SELECT * does not return the sparse columns as normal SQL columns; it returns them as XML:

```
SELECT *
FROM   Hardware.Equipment;
```

This returns the following:

```
EquipmentId EquipmentTag EquipmentType (continued)
----------- ------------ -------------
1           CLAWHAMMER    Hammer
2           HANDSAW       Saw
3           POWERDRILL    PowerTool

SparseColumns
--------------------------------------------
NULL
<Length>7.00</Length><Width>1.00</Width>
NULL
```

You can also update (or also insert) the SparseColumns column directly using the XML representation:

```
UPDATE Hardware.Equipment
SET    SparseColumns = '<Length>12.10</Length><Width>6.00</Width>'
WHERE  EquipmentTag = 'POWERDRILL';

UPDATE Hardware.Equipment
SET    SparseColumns = '<Length>8.40</Length><Width>2.00</Width>
                        <HammerHeadStyle>Claw</HammerHeadStyle>'
WHERE  EquipmentTag = 'CLAWHAMMER';
```

Enumerating the columns (which every application should be doing in every case anyhow) gives us the output that matches what we expect:

```
SELECT EquipmentTag, EquipmentType, HammerHeadStyle, Length, Width
FROM   Hardware.Equipment;
```

Finally, we're back to the same results as before:

EquipmentTag	EquipmentType	HammerHeadStyle	Length	Width
CLAWHAMMER	Hammer	Claw	8.40	2.00
HANDSAW	Saw	NULL	7.00	1.00
POWERDRILL	PowerTool	NULL	12.10	6.00

Sparse columns can be indexed, but you will likely want to create a filtered index in many cases (discussed earlier in this chapter for selective uniqueness). The WHERE clause of the filtered index could be used either to associate the index with the type of row that makes sense (like in our HAMMER example's CHECK constraint, you would likely want to include EquipmentTag and HammerHeadStyle) or to simply ignore NULL. So, if you wanted to index the HammerHeadStyle for the hammer type rows, you might add the following index (preceded by the settings that must be turned on before creating an index on the XML-based column set):

```
SET ANSI_PADDING, ANSI_WARNINGS, CONCAT_NULL_YIELDS_NULL, ARITHABORT,
QUOTED_IDENTIFIER, ANSI_NULLS ON
GO
```

```
CREATE INDEX HammerHeadStyle_For_ClawHammer ON Hardware.Equipment
(HammerHeadStyle) WHERE EquipmentType = 'Hammer';
```

In comparison to the methods used with property tables, this method is going to be tremendously easier to implement, and if you are able to use sparse columns, this method is faster and far more natural to work with in comparison to the EAV method. It is going to feel strange allowing users to change the table structures of your main data tables, but with proper coding, testing, and security practices (and perhaps a DDL trigger monitoring your structures for changes to let you know when these columns are added), you will end up with a far better-performing and more flexible system.

Storing Graph Data in SQL Server

When used in a database, a graph records the relationship of things to other things. If you have ever modeled a many-to-many relationship in a relational database, you have already modeled something analogous to a graph. The graph is one of the most natural data structures you will work with in computing, though definitely not natural in the sense that it is easy to work with in a relational data. In this section, I will look at how to use the graph tables in SQL Server to implement a few common shapes of graphs, and I will touch on some alternate implementations of graphs as well.

Note   Graphs are an expansive topic and cannot be served completely in a section of a book on relational database design. This topic will be covered in greater detail in my forthcoming book on graph structures in T-SQL.

There are many examples of graphs, but the most common example that almost everyone these days is aware of is a social network, where we are recording things like the relationship from one person to another on Twitter, Facebook, and so on and then more structured relationships like manager to employee, sales regions, and so on. Possibly the most famous graph that most people will have heard of is the basis of the parlor game "Six Degrees of Kevin Bacon" which suggests that everyone is no more than six connections away from anyone else, including Kevin Bacon (and not just that your favorite breakfast meat is bacon).

The definition of a graph is very simple, based on two primary structures: nodes and edges. Nodes represent something that one might care about, much like any table in a relational database. Edges establish a connection between exactly two nodes (the nodes can be the exact same node, meaning the node is related to itself, but in this case the node plays two roles). An edge is basically the same as a many-to-many resolution table we created in earlier chapters. Figure 9-10 shows a simple graph.

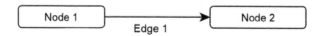

Figure 9-10. Simple graph with two nodes connected by one edge

The edge is drawn with an arrow from Node 1 to Node 2. This says that Node 1 is connected to Node 2, but not vice versa. This is considered a directed graph, and all graphs you implement with SQL Server will be directed. If you want the graph to be undirected, where a connection between Node 1 and Node 2 says that both Node 1 is connected to Node 2 and Node 2 is connected to Node 1, then you must implement two edges (as you will see in Figure 9-11).

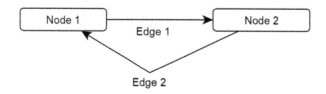

Figure 9-11. Simple graph with a cyclic relationship between Node 1 and Node 2

As you add more nodes to your graph, there are a few more distinctions to be made between graph types. If your graph can have a cycle in it, something like Figure 9-11, then it is considered a *cyclic* graph.

A graph where you do not have cycles is called *acyclic*. Using the two patterns of cyclic and acyclic graphs, you can put together the common types of graphs that can be implemented in SQL Server. Processing a cyclic graph can be distinctly different than a acyclic one because in an acyclic graph you are guaranteed to be able to go from node to node and never repeat nodes, meaning all paths are finite. The graph in Figure 9-11 has an infinite path, because you can keep taking the path from Node 1 to Node 2 and vice versa forever.

In the following subsections, I will introduce the basics of graph tables in SQL Server and then show a few examples of acyclic and cyclic graphs.

Graph Table Basics

Graph tables were first implemented in SQL Server 2017, but they really became quite usable in 2019 with some big improvements. They are more or less just regular SQL Server tables, with some extra tooling, metadata, internal configuration, and special syntax. At their core the implementation is just a many-to-many junction table that allows connections between one or more other tables. However, there is some powerful syntax you get with these tables that helps you implement very complicated, highly interconnected relationships that have always been very messy to implement using T-SQL (or any other version of the SQL relational language).

As described in the introduction, a graph structure is made up of two object types, nodes and edges. A node is analogous to a typical relational table. It represents something and can have one or more columns to store data about the object. The edge is analogous to a many-to-many junction table and captures the node that it is related from and to.

In this section, I will demonstrate the bare necessities of graph objects, and I will extend the details in each of the following examples. To start, I will create the node tables, each with one column for the primary key value that one would use to access nodes in relational queries (a practice that is suggested when creating a node much like for any table so the user can tell one node from another).

```
CREATE SCHEMA Basics;
GO
CREATE TABLE Basics.Node1
(
        Node1Id int NOT NULL CONSTRAINT PKNode1 PRIMARY KEY
) AS NODE;
CREATE TABLE Basics.Node2
(
        Node2Id int NOT NULL CONSTRAINT PKNode2 PRIMARY KEY
) AS NODE;
```

The only difference between the TABLE declaration and any other is the AS NODE clause. This adds internal columns that handle the graph implementation, while you can still use any of the relational constructs you desire with the rest of the table.

Insert a few rows into the table as you would with any table:

```
INSERT INTO Basics.Node1(Node1Id)
VALUES(1001),(1002);
INSERT INTO Basics.Node2(Node2Id)
VALUES(2011),(2012),(2020);
```

Then you can query the table, using SELECT *, and see what is in the table:

```
SELECT *
FROM    Basics.Node1
WHERE   Node1.Node1Id = 1001;
```

You will see something like the following:

$node_id_54F4C9AFD0BF49F2A7A9D292BA5E9450	Node1Id
{"type":"node","schema":"Basics","table":"Node1","id":0}	101

The column that starts $node_id is a textual representation of the object's position in the graph structures. Users see and manipulate the data as an nvarchar(2000) value, but it is technically implemented internally as bigint. The id value in the JSON can be useful if you see an error message that includes this internal value, because it will show up as part of the value. You can use the shorthand $node_id to represent the value in a query, such as

```
SELECT *
FROM    Basics.Node1
WHERE   $node_id =
                '{"type":"node","schema":"Basics","table":"Node1","id":0}';
```

Next, I will create an edge that we will use to connect the two nodes with:

```
CREATE TABLE Basics.Edge1
(
    ConnectedSinceTime datetime2(0) NOT NULL
        CONSTRAINT DFLTEdge1_ConnectedSinceTime DEFAULT (SYSDATETIME()),
    CONSTRAINT EC_Edge1_Node1_to_Node2
            CONNECTION (Basics.Node1 TO Basics.Node2) ON DELETE NO ACTION
) AS EDGE
```

Note the CONSTRAINT object that limits the types of nodes that can be connected with the edge. Edges, by default, can connect nodes of any types in the same edge. You could connect a dog to its owner, a frying pan to lunch, and a person to a plane seat, all in the same edge table. This is one of the things that set them apart from basic relational constructs. They are made to implement highly connected data sets, so the limitation is not to relate one table to another. It is also the reason the JSON of a $node_id includes so many details about the node that is being connected.

ON DELETE NO ACTION means that you cannot delete either of the rows that are connected without deleting the edge first. If you include ON DELETE CASCADE, then deleting a node deletes all of the connected edges. You can include more than one set of nodes in the CONNECTION clause, such as (Basics.Node1 TO Basics.Node2, Basics. Node2 TO Basics.Node1), for example, to let the relationship be bidirectional.

To insert an edge, you get the $node_id JSON for two nodes and insert them into the table. I will generally use a stored procedure for this operation because it is kind of a tedious process, and I usually just want to work with the key values of rows. (I wrote a blog about an alternative method using VIEW and INSTEAD OF TRIGGER objects to manage nodes using regular DDL here: www.red-gate.com/simple-talk/blogs/how-to-modify-a-sql-server-graph-edge-with-t-sql/.)

Just as the node table had a $node_id, the edge table has its own special columns that have long, ugly physical names and pseudo-column names of $from_id and $to_id. I will use these in the following STORED PROCEDURE object to insert the node:

```
CREATE OR ALTER PROCEDURE Basics.Edge1$Insert
(
        @From_Node1Id int,
        @To_Node2Id int,
        @OutputEdgeFlag bit = 0
) AS
  BEGIN
      --full procedure should have a TRY..CATCH and a THROW

      --get the node_id values from the table to use in the insert
      DECLARE @from_node_id nvarchar(2000), @to_node_id nvarchar(2000)
      SELECT @from_node_id = $node_id
      FROM   Basics.Node1
      WHERE Node1.Node1Id = @From_Node1Id;
```

```
SELECT @to_node_id = $node_id
FROM   Basics.Node2
WHERE Node2.Node2Id = @To_Node2Id;

--insert the from and to nodes, let the ConnectedSinceTime default
INSERT INTO Basics.Edge1($from_id, $to_id)
VALUES(@from_node_id, @to_node_id);

--show the edge that was created if desired
IF @OutputEdgeFlag = 1
    SELECT CONCAT('From:', $from_id, ' To:', $to_id,
            ' ConnectedSinceTime:', Edge1.ConnectedSinceTime)
    FROM   Basics.Edge1
    WHERE  $from_id = @from_node_id
      AND  $to_id = @to_node_id
END;
```

Now, I will insert my first edge:

```
EXEC Basics.Edge1$Insert @From_Node1Id = 1001, @To_Node2Id = 2011,
                    @OutputEdgeFlag = 1;
```

The output of this code shows the two nodes that were created and the
ConnectedSinceTime value. I included a column on the edge, though it isn't necessary.
You can use the edge column as a filter or display it on the output:

```
From:{"type":"node","schema":"Basics","table":"Node1","id":0} To
:{"type":"node","schema":"Basics","table":"Node2","id":0}
ConnectedSinceTime:2020-08-05 20:47:13
```

Next, add two more edges:

```
EXEC Basics.Edge1$Insert @From_Node1Id = 1001, @To_Node2Id = 2012;
EXEC Basics.Edge1$Insert @From_Node1Id = 1002, @To_Node2Id = 2020;
```

You can use the pseudo-columns in your queries and join the tables as you would
with any many-to-many relationship like this:

```
SELECT Node1.Node1Id, Node2.Node2Id AS ConnectedNode1
FROM    Basics.Node1
           JOIN Basics.Edge1
                ON Node1.$node_id = Edge1.$from_id
              JOIN Basics.Node2
                ON Node2.$node_id= Edge1.$to_id;
```

But this is not the syntax that is desirable to use with graph tables. Rather, there is a graph function named MATCH that is used. To join the two nodes together, you use the following syntax:

```
SELECT Node1.Node1Id,   Node2.Node2Id
          --MATCH is not compatible with ANSI join syntax
FROM    Basics.Node1, Basics.Edge1, Basics.Node2
WHERE   MATCH(Node1-(Edge1)->Node2);
```

The result of this query, as it was for the join example, is:

Node1Id	Node2Id
1001	2011
1001	2012
1002	2020

In this operation, the MATCH criteria breaks down like this. Return Node1 rows that connect to Node2 through Edge1 in the direction of the >. If you changed it to MATCH(Node1<-(Edge1)-Node2), then it would return no rows, because I did not create any edge rows that were from Node2 to Node1 (and could not, since the CONNECTION CONSTRAINT object did not allow that direction).

As your graph objects grow larger, you may also need to add indexes to your objects. In particular, even for smaller objects, one particular unique constraint\index is generally useful and one that makes sure you only have unique nodes:

```
ALTER TABLE Basics.Edge1
   ADD CONSTRAINT AKEdge1_UniqueNodes UNIQUE ($from_id, $to_id);
```

You can also include regular columns in your query, if you have an attribute of the edge like EdgeType (e.g., if this were a superhero database, you might have an edge Connection and EdgeType of Friend or Foe). This index will also help with the MATCH criteria going from node to node, since the internal algorithm will be basically like any other query, get the initial set of rows, and fetch all rows where the $from_id matches the $to_id of the initial set of rows. In later sections, a more iterative approach will be demonstrated using the SHORTEST_PATH variant of the MATCH criteria.

Acyclic Graphs

Acyclic graphs are the typical kind of graphs that have been implemented in SQL Server for many years, even before graph tables were introduced. In our original models, they might have been implemented with a table that had columns like

```
CREATE TABLE Employee (
    EmployeeId int PRIMARY KEY,
    ManagerId int REFERENCES Employee(EmployeeId)
);
```

This implementation is called an *adjacency list* (as would the graph table structure as well) and, with the uniqueness constraint on the EmployeeId column, implements what is called a tree structure. Variants of this can store any form of graph structure. For example, if you remove the PRIMARY KEY from the EmployeeId column and store the adjacency list external to the table, it is no longer acyclic and implements a network. Processing the data in the structures was too difficult to get out interesting information unless it was implementing a tree, so for the most part a tree structure was the limitation for storing graph data prior to SQL Server 2017.

When storing the graph structure external to the base table, one of the common checks is to check to make sure that you have no cycles in the structure, because you don't want to have Bob managing Betty who manages Fred who manages Bob (the same Bob as we started with), since this would be illogical. When storing some kinds of acyclic graphs, like a bill of materials, the goal is to make sure that a product doesn't end up containing itself in the data, because that is physically and logically impossible.

In this section, I will show two design snippets of how acyclic graphs can be effectively implemented using graph tables. The first design will be a tree and the second a directed acyclic graph (DAG) where we still can't have cycles, but items can have more than one parent in the structure.

Tree Structures

A tree structure is a special case of a directed acyclic graph (DAG) where a node can have only one predecessor in the structure, but more than one child row (variants of trees are things like *binary trees*, where each item can only have zero, one, or two child items). Tree structures were discussed back in Chapter 4, and at the time we modeled them just like the Employee object in the introduction to this section. However, in SQL Server 2017 and later, we can alter the physical implementation of the graph structure to use graph tables.

Note   Tree structures have more solutions than I will present in detail in this book, but I will describe some of those possible solutions in the section "Alternative Tree Implementations."

To demonstrate this, I will create tables that implement a corporate hierarchy with just a few basic attributes in one node table and one edge table. The goal will be to implement a corporate structure like the one shown in Figure 9-12. Note that a typical requirement of tree structures is to have only one root node. An alternative name for a tree is a *directed rooted acyclic graph* structure, but tree is much easier to say. A rooted structure has only one root node. Technically, you could implement more than one rooted graph structure in the same table, but this is generally not the expectation when you are building a tree structure like a corporate hierarchy.

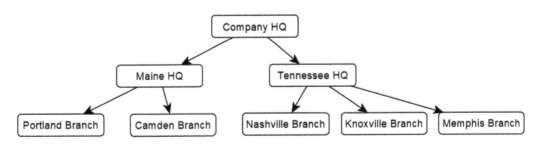

Figure 9-12. *Demonstration company hierarchy*

The most important thing to understand when dealing with trees in SQL Server is that the most efficient way to work with adjacency list–based trees and graphs in a procedural language is not the most efficient way to work with data in a set-based relational language. Both methods employ a form of recursion, but in very different ways.

If you were searching a tree in a procedural language, a very common algorithm would be to traverse the tree one node at a time, from the topmost item down to the lowest in the tree, and then work your way around to all of the nodes. This is generally done using a recursive algorithm, diving down into the structure in a similar manner to what you see in Figure 9-13, iterating down and going back up the recursive stack when you reach the end of the children to a node.

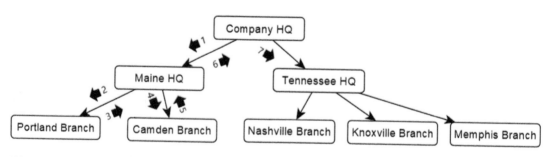

Figure 9-13. *Sample tree structure searched depth first*

This is referred to as a depth-first search and is fast when the language is optimized for single-instance-at-a-time access, particularly when you can load the entire tree structure into RAM. If you attempted to implement this using T-SQL, you would find that it is obnoxiously slow, as most any iterative processing can be. In relational programming, we use what is called a breadth-first search that can be scaled to many more nodes, because the number of queries is limited to the number of levels in the hierarchy. The limitations here pertain to the size of the temporary storage needed and how many rows you end up with on each level. Joining to an unindexed temporary set is bad in your code, and it is not good in SQL Server's algorithms either.

A tree can be broken down into levels, from the parent row that you are interested in. From there, the levels increase as you are one level away from the parent, as shown in Figure 9-14.

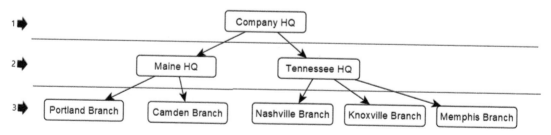

Figure 9-14. *Sample tree structure with levels*

In Figure 9-14, level 1 is commonly referred to as the root node, and the third-level nodes (those without children) are the leaf nodes.

Now, working with this structure will deal with each level as a separate set, joined to the matching results from the previous level. You iterate one level at a time, matching rows from one level to the next. This reduces the number of queries to use this sample tree down to three, rather than a minimum of eight, plus the overhead of going back and forth from parent to child. In SQL, there are two ways to process a tree: either using a recursive CTE (common table expression), fetching one level at a time, or, when working with SQL Server 2019, using a MATCH clause with the SHORTEST_PATH extension. SHORTEST_PATH is one of the most complicated bits of syntax I have seen in the T-SQL language. It is even more complex than some of the stuff you see with the windowing functions and grouping sets, but just like these extensions, the payoff of learning the syntax is well worth it.

To implement our tree structure, I will create the following objects:

```
USE Chapter9;
GO

CREATE SCHEMA TreeInGraph;
GO

CREATE TABLE TreeInGraph.Company
(
    CompanyId int NOT NULL IDENTITY(1, 1)
            CONSTRAINT PKCompany PRIMARY KEY,
    Name varchar(20) NOT NULL CONSTRAINT AKCompany_Name UNIQUE
) AS NODE;

CREATE TABLE TreeInGraph.CompanyEdge
(
        CONSTRAINT EC_CompanyEdge$DefinesParentOf
            CONNECTION (TreeInGraph.Company TO TreeInGraph.Company)
                ON DELETE NO ACTION,
        --enforces the one unique parent in the tree
        CONSTRAINT AKCompanyEdge_ToId UNIQUE ($to_id),
        --performance of fetching parent nodes
        INDEX FromIdToId ($from_id, $to_id)
)
AS EDGE;
GO
```

It is semi-tricky to insert nodes in the tree, since we need to get the parent node's $node_id before inserting the data, so I will use the following stored procedure that includes comments to note what is being done:

```
CREATE OR ALTER PROCEDURE TreeInGraph.Company$Insert
(
    @Name               varchar(20),
    @ParentCompanyName varchar(20)
)
AS
BEGIN
    SET NOCOUNT ON;
    SET XACT_ABORT ON; --will stop the operation if an error occurs
    BEGIN TRANSACTION;
    -- implement error handling if done for real

    --Get the node id of the paren
    DECLARE @ParentNode nvarchar(2000) =
                    (SELECT $node_id
                     FROM TreeInGraph.Company
                     WHERE name = @ParentCompanyName);

    IF @ParentCompanyName IS NOT NULL AND @ParentNode IS NULL
        THROW 50000, 'Invalid parentCompanyName', 1;
    ELSE
      BEGIN
          --insert done by simply using the Name of the parent to get
          --the key of the parent...
          INSERT INTO TreeInGraph.Company(Name)
          SELECT @Name;

        IF @ParentNode IS NOT NULL --then we need an edge inserted
            BEGIN
              DECLARE @ChildNode nvarchar(1000) =
                    (SELECT $node_id
                     FROM TreeInGraph.Company
                     WHERE name = @Name);
```

```
        INSERT INTO TreeInGraph.CompanyEdge ($from_id, $to_id)
        VALUES (@ParentNode, @ChildNode);
      END;
    END
  COMMIT TRANSACTION;
END;
```

Next, insert the nodes of the tree we had designed using a set of insert statements:

```
EXEC TreeInGraph.Company$Insert @Name = 'Company HQ',
                                @ParentCompanyName = NULL;
EXEC TreeInGraph.Company$Insert @Name = 'Maine HQ',
                                @ParentCompanyName = 'Company HQ';
EXEC TreeInGraph.Company$Insert @Name = 'Tennessee HQ',
                                @ParentCompanyName = 'Company HQ';
EXEC TreeInGraph.Company$Insert @Name = 'Nashville Branch',
                                @ParentCompanyName = 'Tennessee HQ';
EXEC TreeInGraph.Company$Insert @Name = 'Knoxville Branch',
                                @ParentCompanyName = 'Tennessee HQ';
EXEC TreeInGraph.Company$Insert @Name = 'Memphis Branch',
                                @ParentCompanyName = 'Tennessee HQ';
EXEC TreeInGraph.Company$Insert @Name = 'Portland Branch',
                                @ParentCompanyName = 'Maine HQ';
EXEC TreeInGraph.Company$Insert @Name = 'Camden Branch',
                                @ParentCompanyName = 'Maine HQ';
```

From here, we can view the data using a query such as the following, which will include comments on all the different pieces that are not typical T-SQL:

```
DECLARE @CompanyId int = 1;

--First SELECT is to get the node that we are starting from as it
--is not connected to itself, it would not be included in the SHORTEST_PATH
--output.
SELECT  CompanyId AS ParentCompanyId,
        CompanyId AS CompanyId, Name,
        1 AS TreeLevel, CAST(CompanyId AS varchar(10)) AS Hierarchy
FROM    TreeInGraph.Company
```

```
WHERE   Company.CompanyId = @CompanyId
UNION ALL
        --FromCompany is the root node in the set starting with @CompanyId
SELECT FromCompany.CompanyId AS ParentCompanyId,

        --Gives you the last value that is connected to the From node
        --in the path of connections between the node
        LAST_VALUE(ToCompany.CompanyId) WITHIN GROUP (GRAPH PATH)
                                                            AS CompanyId,
        LAST_VALUE(ToCompany.Name) WITHIN GROUP (GRAPH PATH) AS Name,

        --Counting the nodes that were touched along the path gives you
        --the level in the tree from the parameter node
        1+COUNT(ToCompany.Name) WITHIN GROUP (GRAPH PATH) AS TreeLevel,

        --the first CompanyId of the from company
        CAST(FromCompany.CompanyId as NVARCHAR(10)) +
          --Then STRING_AGG aggregates along the path, each company id
          '\' + STRING_AGG(CAST(ToCompany.CompanyId AS nvarchar(10)), '\')
                         WITHIN GROUP (GRAPH PATH) AS Hierarchy
FROM TreeInGraph.Company AS FromCompany,
     --FOR PATH required in the declaration for nodes and edges that will
     --be used recursively
     TreeInGraph.CompanyEdge FOR PATH AS CompanyEdge,
     TreeInGraph.Company FOR PATH AS ToCompany

     --SHORTEST PATH starts with the anchor node, then the recursed nodes
     --in parenthesis. SHORTEST_PATH(Anchor(Matching Criteria)+)
     --+ indicates unlimited levels, replace with {0,1} to get 1 level
WHERE MATCH(SHORTEST_PATH(FromCompany(-(CompanyEdge)->ToCompany)+))
  AND FromCompany.CompanyId = @CompanyId
ORDER BY Hierarchy;
```

It is a lot to take in in one query but this is basically all of the syntax needed to first see the hierarchy:

ParentCompanyId	CompanyId	Name	TreeLevel	Hierarchy
1	1	Company HQ	1	1
1	2	Maine HQ	2	1\2
1	7	Portland Branch	3	1\2\7
1	8	Camden Branch	3	1\2\8
1	3	Tennessee HQ	2	1\3
1	4	Nashville Branch	3	1\3\4
1	5	Knoxville Branch	3	1\3\5
1	6	Memphis Branch	3	1\3\6

If you want to get the parent hierarchy of a row, that can be achieved by changing the direction of the arrow in the SHORTEST_PATH expression like this:

```
WHERE MATCH(SHORTEST_PATH(FromCompany(<-(CompanyEdge)-ToCompany)+))
```

Now on each iteration of the code, the FromCompany is the child, and the query is looking for the parent of that company, instead of the child.

Due to space limitations, this is the extent of the example in the text. In the downloads, I will include the code to the following:

- *Using a CTE to get children of a node or see all paths, not just the shortest one:* If you are not using SQL Server 2019 or later or if you are implementing your tree using relational tables, SHORTEST_PATH will not be available. A recursive CTE is used to iterate through the levels in that case. This will be demonstrated.

- *Aggregating over a node*: One of the main reasons to have a tree structure in a business database is to sum up activity of a node's children. For example, the HQ node needs to sum up sales over the other nodes. Tennessee HQ needs to sum the sales of Nashville, Knoxville, and Memphis.

- *Reparenting a node*: Moving the child of one node to be the child of another node.

- *Deleting a node*: How to handle removing a node, especially a node that is not a leaf node.

Each of these options is very important in the implementation of a proper tree structure, and the latter two will usually apply to the other two graph examples I will present as well.

Alternative Tree Implementations

Dealing with hierarchies in relational data has long been a well-trod topic. As such, a lot has been written on the subject of hierarchies, and quite a few other techniques have been implemented. In this section, I will give an overview of three other ways of dealing with hierarchies that have been and will continue to be used in designs:

- *Path technique*: In this method, you store the path from the child to the parent in a formatted text string. This is a very simple to query, but moderately hard to maintain method that provides amazing performance.

- *HierarchyId*: Using the internal datatype that was built to implement tree data. This datatype is *fairly complicated, but useful to learn, especially if you start to use filetables, where the directory structure is represented using it.*

- *Nested sets*: Use the position in the tree to allow you to get children or parents of a row very quickly. This is generally regarded as the fastest method to manipulate nodes for reading (e.g., fetching the child rows of a node), but by far the costliest to maintain and slowest to load.

- *Kimball helper table*: Designed for ease of reporting data that is stored in a tree, this stores a row for every single path from parent to child. It's great for reads but tough to maintain and was developed for read-only situations, like read-only databases.

Each of these methods has benefits. Each is more difficult to maintain than a simple adjacency model but can offer benefits in different situations. In the following sections, I am going to give a brief illustrative overview of each.

Path Technique

The path technique takes the same path representation we have been generating in our graph queries to show the user the hierarchy and stores it to make accessing data quick. Using our hierarchy that we have used so far, to implement the path method, we could use the set of data in Figure 9-12. Note that each of the tags in the hierarchy will use the surrogate key for the key values in the path, so it will be essential that the surrogate value is immutable. In Figure 9-15, I have included a diagram of the hierarchy implemented with the path value set for our design.

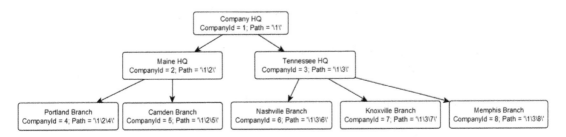

Figure 9-15. *Sample hierarchy diagram with values for the path technique*

With the path in this manner, you can find all of the children of a row using the path in a like expression. For example, to get the children of the Main HQ node, you can use a WHERE clause such as WHERE Path LIKE '\1\2\%', and the path to the parents is directly in the path too. So the parents of the Portland Branch, whose path is '\1\2\4\', are '\1\2\' and '\1\'. (Using STRING_SPLIT in SQL Server 2016 and later, this is a fairly easy process as well.)

One of the great things about the path method is that it readily uses indexes, because most of the queries you will make will use the left side of a string or the values from the primary key of the actual row. So up to SQL Server 2014, as long as your path could stay below 900 bytes, your performance is generally awesome. In 2016, the max key length of a nonclustered rowstore index was increased to 1,700 bytes, which is great, but once your paths are in this range of length, you will only end up with four keys per page, which is not going to give amazing performance. (Indexes are covered in Chapter 11.)

Using HierarchyId Datatype

In addition to the fairly standard adjacency list implementation, there is also a datatype called hierarchyId that is a proprietary CLR-based datatype that can be used to do some of the heavy lifting of dealing with hierarchies. It has some definite benefits in that it makes queries on hierarchies fairly easier, but it has some difficulties as well.

The primary downside to the hierarchyId datatype is that it is not as simple to work with for some of the basic tasks as is the self-referencing column. Putting data in this table will not be as easy as it was for that method. The representation of this column is very similar to the path method, but the textual hierarchy does not reference the surrogate key values. You have to use the methods of the type to make positional space in the hierarchy, for example.

It is worth a look if you are considering building filetable structures, as the Windows hierarchy is managed as a hierarchy using this datatype.

Nested Sets

One of the cleverer methods of dealing with hierarchies was created in 1992 by Michael J. Kamfonas. It was introduced in an article titled "Recursive Hierarchies: The Relational Taboo!" in *the Relational Journal*, October/November 1992. It is also a favorite method of Joe Celko, who has written a book about hierarchies titled *Joe Celko's Trees and Hierarchies in SQL for Smarties* (Morgan Kaufmann, 2004); check it out (now in its second edition, 2012) for further reading about this type of hierarchies.

The basics of the method are that you organize the tree by including pointers to the left and right of the current node, enabling you to do math to determine the position of an item in the tree. Again, going back to our company hierarchy, the structure would be as shown in Figure 9-16.

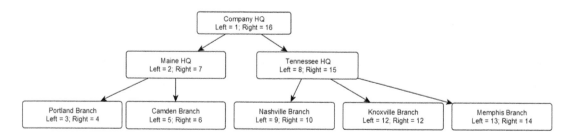

Figure 9-16. *Sample hierarchy diagram with values for the nested sets technique*

This has the value of now being able to determine children and parents of a node very quickly. To find the children of Maine HQ, you would say WHERE Left > 2 and Right < 7. No matter how deep the hierarchy, there is no traversing the hierarchy at all, just simple integer comparisons. To find the parents of Maine HQ, you simply need to look for the case WHERE Left < 2 and Right > 7.

Adding a node has a rather negative effect of needing to update all rows to the right of the node, increasing their Right value, since every single row is a part of the structure. Deleting a node will require decrementing the Right values. Even reparenting becomes a math problem, just requiring you to update the linking pointers. Probably the biggest downside is that it is not a very natural way to work with the data, since you don't have a link directly from parent to child to navigate. There is a method of relieving the costs of managing nodes by leaving space for nodes to be added, but it adds even more complexity to the management of the graph.

Kimball Helper Table

Finally, you can use a method that Ralph Kimball created for dealing with hierarchies, particularly in a data warehousing/read-intensive setting, a method that is going to be relatively simple to implement, but the most costly to manage (but, in most cases, the fastest to query). Even though it was designed for fairly static data, it can be useful in an OLTP setting if the hierarchy is not modified too often.

Going back to our graph implementation, shown in Figure 9-17 with edge data, assume we already have this implemented in SQL. (For simplicity, assume the surrogate key of each item matches the $edge_id which is also the $from_id of the item.)

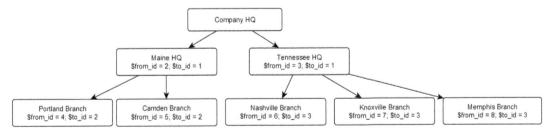

Figure 9-17. *Sample hierarchy diagram with values for the adjacency list technique repeated for the Kimball helper table method*

To implement this method, you will use a table of data that describes the hierarchy with one row per parent-to-child relationship, for every level of the hierarchy. So there would be a row for Company HQ to Maine HQ, Company HQ to Portland Branch, and so on. The helper table provides the details about distance from parent, if it is a root node or a leaf node. So, for the leftmost four items (1, 2, 4, 5) in the tree, we would get the following table:

ParentId	ChildId	Distance	ParentRootNodeFlag	ChildLeafNodeFlag
1	2	1	1	0
1	4	2	1	1
1	5	2	1	1
2	4	1	0	1
2	5	1	0	1

The power of this technique is that now you can simply ask for all children of 1 by looking for WHERE ParentId = 1, or you can look for direct descendants of 2 by saying WHERE ParentId = 2 and Distance = 1. And you can look for all leaf nodes of the parent by querying WHERE ParentId = 1 and ChildLeafNode = 1. The code to implement this structure is basically a slightly modified version of the SHORTEST_PATH expression used in our tree structure example where you do not constrain the query to just one parent. For our earlier example, you can use the following code:

```
WITH BaseRows AS (
--Fetch every row as its own row
SELECT Company.CompanyId AS ParentCompanyId,
       Company.CompanyId AS ChildCompanyId, 1 AS Distance,
       $node_id AS parent_node_id, $node_id AS child_node_id
FROM   TreeInGraph.Company
UNION ALL
--expand every row's child rows as rows in the output
SELECT FromCompany.CompanyId AS ParentCompanyId,
       LAST_VALUE(ToCompany.CompanyId) WITHIN GROUP (GRAPH PATH)
                                                          AS ChildCompanyId,
       1+COUNT(ToCompany.NAME) WITHIN GROUP (GRAPH PATH) AS Distance,
       FromCompany.$node_id AS parent_node_id,
       LAST_VALUE(ToCompany.$node_id) WITHIN GROUP (GRAPH PATH)
                                                          AS child_node_id
FROM
            TreeInGraph.Company AS FromCompany,
            TreeInGraph.CompanyEdge FOR PATH AS CompanyEdge,
            TreeInGraph.Company FOR PATH AS ToCompany
WHERE MATCH(SHORTEST_PATH(FromCompany(-(CompanyEdge)->ToCompany)+))
)

SELECT ParentCompanyId, ChildCompanyId, Distance,
       --calculate parent and child nodes
       CASE WHEN NOT EXISTS (SELECT * FROM TreeInGraph.CompanyEdge
                             WHERE BaseRows.parent_node_id = $to_id)
     THEN 1 ELSE 0 END AS ParentRootNodeFlag,
       CASE WHEN NOT EXISTS (SELECT * FROM TreeInGraph.CompanyEdge
```

```
                        WHERE BaseRows.parent_node_id = $from_id)
        THEN 1 ELSE 0 END AS ChildLeafNodeFlag
FROM BaseRows
ORDER BY ParentCompanyId, ChildCompanyId;
```

It may take a few minutes to rebuild for millions of nodes and may require additional indexes in some cases, but the performance of querying with a structure like this is generally worth it.

The obvious downfall of this method is simple. It is costly to maintain and if the structure is modified frequently could not be a reasonable general-purpose solution. To be honest, Kimball's purpose for the method was to optimize relational usage of hierarchies in the data warehouse, which is maintained by ETL and refreshed daily. For this sort of purpose, this method should be the quickest, because all queries will be almost completely based on simple relational queries. Of all of the methods, this one will be the most natural for users while being less desirable to the team that has to maintain the data. I have known people who have used just such a solution for corporate hierarchies, for example, for row-level security, since that data changes very rarely.

Directed Acyclic Graph

A directed acyclic graph (DAG) is a data structure where all edges are directed and cycles are prohibited. The definition of a DAG includes trees, but in this section we will briefly discuss a DAG example that is not as strict as trees in that you do need to have a root node and nodes can have more than one parent. Since they are directed and acyclic, their processing when working from parent to child node is not terribly complex because from any single node, you can follow the parentage down through the child nodes just like a tree.

A common use of such a DAG is for a bill of materials of goods for a company. For example, in Figure 9-18, you can see that the Snurgle Mounting Kit is made up of a screwdriver, mounting bracket, 100-feet roll of wire, and electrical tape roll, which you would get using a simple single-level MATCH expression. If you want to know what each item is made up of in the structure, you follow the path down the section of the graph by changing the MATCH to use the SHORTEST_PATH, which in a DAG will always be a straight line down the structure.

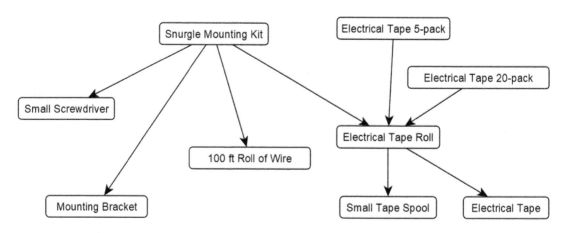

Figure 9-18. *Example bill of materials*

Processing the DAG is exactly like the code for the tree implementation, so I will not present it here in the text, but the code to create and view this tree will be found in the downloads, including a trigger for protecting against cycles, since there is no easy index method for handling this situation.

Cyclic Graphs

Cyclic graphs are graphs that allow cycles to exist in the data between nodes. For example, "Fred is a friend of Cindy who's a friend of Jack who is a friend of Fred" is a perfectly reasonable scenario. Until SQL Server 2017, it was very rare to attempt to store such highly connected data in SQL Server—even more unlikely to try to process it, because while using a CTE on a tree structure can be quite fast, when you introduce cycles into the data, it complicates the processing greatly (it is not impossible, but the growing number of relationships you discover even in a small graph structure can be amazingly large).

Using graph and edge tables in SQL Server 2019, the processing can be far simpler and faster because using SHORTEST_PATH handles the complexity of cycles for you under the covers. In my example for this section, I am going to set up a small social network that implements a set of Account rows, each with just an AccountHandle attribute for simplicity, but a node can represent anything a relational table can. With these accounts, I will connect them to one another via an edge that says that one account follows another account. I will also set up an Interest node that lets accounts be connected with an interest that they may hold. These are the objects:

```
CREATE SCHEMA SocialGraph;
GO

--table for accounts. Could have more attributes
CREATE TABLE SocialGraph.Account (
     AccountHandle nvarchar(30) CONSTRAINT AKAccount UNIQUE
) AS NODE;

--Holds the details of who follows whom
CREATE TABLE SocialGraph.Follows (
  FollowTime datetime2(0) NOT NULL
    CONSTRAINT DFLTFollows_FollowTime DEFAULT SYSDATETIME(),
    CONSTRAINT AKFollows_UniqueNodes UNIQUE ( $from_id, $to_id),
    CONSTRAINT ECFollows_AccountToAccount
       CONNECTION (SocialGraph.Account TO SocialGraph.Account)
                                             ON DELETE NO ACTION
) AS EDGE;
GO
--Cannot use $from_id and $to_id in a CHECK CONSTRAINT, so using
--TRIGGER to avoid self reference
CREATE TRIGGER SocialGraph.Follows_IU_Trigger ON SocialGraph.Follows
AFTER INSERT, UPDATE
AS
BEGIN
    --for real object, use full template/error handling
    IF EXISTS (SELECT *
               FROM    inserted
               WHERE   $from_id = $to_id)
      BEGIN
        ROLLBACK;
        THROW 50000,'Modified data introduces a self reference',1;
      END;
END;
```

```
GO
--table of things an account could be interested in
CREATE TABLE SocialGraph.Interest (
    InterestName nvarchar(30) CONSTRAINT AKInterest UNIQUE
) AS NODE;

--edge to connect people to those interests
CREATE TABLE SocialGraph.InterestedIn
(
        CONSTRAINT AKInterestedIn_UniqueNodes UNIQUE ($from_id, $to_id),
        CONSTRAINT ECInterestedIn_AccountToInterestBoth
            CONNECTION (SocialGraph.Account TO SocialGraph.Interest)
                                                ON DELETE NO ACTION
) AS EDGE;
```

In the downloads, there are two stored procedures and a set of calls to load the data into the table. The data will implement the data from Figure 9-19 that shows which account follows which other account and Figure 9-20 that shows which accounts are interested in which interests.

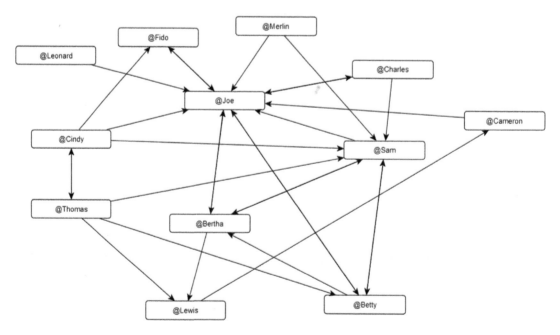

Figure 9-19. *Sample Social Graph Data*

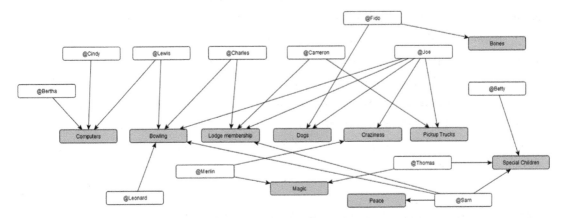

Figure 9-20. *Sample structure for which accounts are interested in what*

Using the tables we have created and the data that matches the graph charts in Figures 9-19 and 9-20, we can ask interesting questions, such as the following:

```
-- what is @Joe interested in?
SELECT Account.AccountHandle, Interest.InterestName
FROM   SocialGraph.Account, SocialGraph.Interest, SocialGraph.InterestedIn
       --literally, what account is linked to interest through interestedIn
WHERE  MATCH(Account-(InterestedIn)->Interest)
  AND  Account.AccountHandle = '@Joe';
```

This returns the following set of data

AccountHandle	InterestName
@Joe	Bowling
@Joe	Craziness
@Joe	Dogs
@Joe	Lodge Membership
@Joe	Pickup Trucks

```
--Who is @Joe connected to?
 SELECT FromAccount.AccountHandle AS FromAccountHandle, ToAccount.
AccountHandle AS ToAccountHandle
FROM    SocialGraph.Account AS FromAccount, SocialGraph.Follows AS Follows,
            SocialGraph.Account AS ToAccount
```

621

```
WHERE   MATCH(FromAccount-(Follows)->ToAccount)
  AND   FromAccount.AccountHandle = '@Joe'
  ORDER BY FromAccountHandle, ToAccountHandle;
```

which returns the following data:

FromAccountHandle	ToAccountHandle
@Joe	@Bertha
@Joe	@Betty
@Joe	@Charles
@Joe	@Fido

```
--Who shares an interest with @Joe, and what interests are they?
SELECT Account1.AccountHandle AS FromAccountHandle,
       Account2.AccountHandle AS ToAccountHandle,
       Interest.InterestName AS SharedInterestName
FROM   SocialGraph.Account AS Account1
         ,SocialGraph.Account AS Account2
         ,SocialGraph.Interest AS Interest
         ,SocialGraph.InterestedIn
         ,SocialGraph.InterestedIn AS InterestedIn2

         --Account1 is interested in an interest, and Account2 is also
         --note the arrows show linkage, and we are navigating both
         --account nodes to the Interest node (you cannot reuse the
         --the same edge in your queries)
WHERE   MATCH(Account1-(InterestedIn)->Interest<-(InterestedIn2)-Account2)
  AND   Account1.AccountHandle = '@Joe'
     --ignore stuff you share with yourself
  AND   Account1.AccountHandle <> Account2.AccountHandle
ORDER BY FromAccountHandle, ToAccountHandle, SharedInterestName;
```

The output of this query shows that @Joe shares interests with several other persons in this social group:

```
FromAccountHandle   ToAccountHandle   SharedInterestName
-----------------   ---------------   ------------------------------

@Joe                @Cameron          Lodge Membership
@Joe                @Cameron          Pickup Trucks
@Joe                @Charles          Bowling
@Joe                @Charles          Lodge Membership
@Joe                @Fido             Dogs
@Joe                @Leonard          Bowling
@Joe                @Lewis            Bowling
@Joe                @Merlin           Craziness
@Joe                @Sam              Bowling
@Joe                @Sam              Lodge Membership
```

So far, the connections have been one single MATCH, but they can be far more interesting, like the following:

```
--Who is @Joe connected who also shares a common interest?
SELECT Account1.AccountHandle AS FromAccountHandle, Account2.AccountHandle
AS ToAccountHandle, Interest.InterestName AS SharedInterestName
FROM    SocialGraph.Account AS Account1
        ,SocialGraph.Account AS Account2
        ,SocialGraph.Interest AS Interest
        ,SocialGraph.InterestedIn
        ,SocialGraph.InterestedIn AS InterestedIn2
        ,SocialGraph.Follows
        --Account1 is interested in an interest, and Account2 is also
WHERE   MATCH(Account1-(InterestedIn)->Interest<-(InterestedIn2)-Account2)
        --Account1 is connected to Account2
   AND  MATCH(Account1-(Follows)->Account2)
   AND  Account1.AccountHandle = '@Joe'
ORDER BY FromAccountHandle, ToAccountHandle, SharedInterestName;
```

This returns the following:

FromAccountHandle	ToAccountHandle	SharedInterestName
@Joe	@Cameron	Lodge Membership
@Joe	@Cameron	Pickup Trucks
@Joe	@Fido	Dogs

One thing to note is that you cannot use OR in a predicate with MATCH, or you will receive the following error:

```
Msg 13905, Level 16, State 1, Line 106
A MATCH clause may not be directly combined with other expressions using
OR or NOT.
```

Any need to do MATCH() OR-type queries would require using multiple queries and a UNION operator.

If you want to see who is connected to @Joe and whom they are connected to, you can use the following MATCH criteria:

```
--Who is connected to @Joe, and who they are connected to
SELECT  Account1.AccountHandle AS FromAccountHandle,
        ThroughAccount.AccountHandle AS ThroughAccountName,
        Account2.AccountHandle AS ToAccountHandle
FROM    SocialGraph.Account AS Account1,
        SocialGraph.Follows AS Follows,
        SocialGraph.Account AS Account2,
        SocialGraph.Follows AS Follows2,
        SocialGraph.Account AS ThroughAccount
WHERE   MATCH(Account1-(Follows)->ThroughAccount-(Follows2)->Account2)
  AND   Account1.AccountHandle = '@Joe'
  AND   Account2.AccountHandle <> Account1.AccountHandle
ORDER BY FromAccountHandle, ToAccountHandle;
```

You can see from the output of this query that @Joe is second level connected to @Sam through three other connections:

FromAccountHandle	ThroughAccountName	ToAccountHandle
@Joe	@Betty	@Bertha
@Joe	@Bertha	@Betty
@Joe	@Bertha	@Lewis
@Joe	@Bertha	@Sam
@Joe	@Betty	@Sam
@Joe	@Charles	@Sam

You could continue adding more copies of the Account node and Follows edge to the query to get people further away in the structure, but you can also use SHORTEST_PATH as discussed in the section "Tree Structures" and see all the accounts that @Joe is connected to:

```
--Who is @Joe connected to via follows, and how far away are they
SELECT COUNT(Account2.AccountHandle) WITHIN GROUP (GRAPH PATH) AS Distance,
       LAST_VALUE(Account2.AccountHandle) WITHIN GROUP (GRAPH PATH)
                                                          AS ConnectedTo,
       STRING_AGG(Account2.AccountHandle, '->') WITHIN GROUP (GRAPH PATH)
                                                          AS Path
FROM    SocialGraph.Account AS Account1,
            SocialGraph.Follows FOR PATH AS Follows,
            SocialGraph.Account  FOR PATH AS Account2
WHERE MATCH(SHORTEST_PATH(Account1(-(Follows)->Account2)+))
   AND Account1.AccountHandle = '@Joe';
```

In the results, you will notice that you see the same connections, but now you see only one way each person is connected and the path that was chosen. Each of the accounts that @Joe was connected to via two follows steps is there, but only one connection to @Sam, and @Betty and @Bertha show up as direct connections only:

Distance	ConnectedTo	Path
1	@Bertha	@Bertha
1	@Betty	@Betty
1	@Charles	@Charles
1	@Fido	@Fido
2	@Joe	@Bertha->@Joe
2	@Sam	@Charles->@Sam
2	@Lewis	@Bertha->@Lewis
3	@Cameron	@Bertha->@Lewis->@Cameron

The last example I will show in this book is connecting through more than just one edge. In this next query, we will look at accounts that are connected to @Joe through common interests. So take the following subgraph as seen in Figure 9-21.

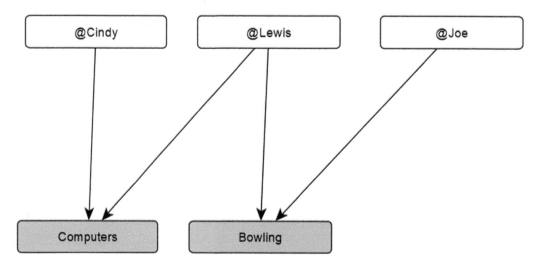

Figure 9-21. *Subgraph showing connections from @Joe to @Cindy through interests and other accounts*

The MATCH comparison uses a SHORTEST_PATH in this example that constructs a link from @Joe to @Lewis through Bowling and then iterates from @Lewis to @Cindy through Computers:

```
--How is @Joe connected to @Cindy through the shortest path
--including interests
WITH BaseRows AS (
  SELECT  LAST_VALUE(Account2.AccountHandle) WITHIN GROUP (GRAPH PATH)
                                          AS ConnectedToAccountHandle,
        Account1.AccountHandle + '->' +
            STRING_AGG(CONCAT(Interest.InterestName,'->',
            Account2.AccountHandle), '->') WITHIN GROUP (GRAPH PATH)
                                          AS ConnectedPath
  FROM    SocialGraph.Account AS Account1
            ,SocialGraph.Account FOR PATH AS Account2
            ,SocialGraph.Interest FOR PATH AS Interest
            ,SocialGraph.InterestedIn FOR PATH AS InterestedIn
            ,SocialGraph.InterestedIn FOR PATH AS InterestedIn2

  WHERE   MATCH(SHORTEST_PATH(Account1(-(InterestedIn)->Interest<-
                                          (InterestedIn2)-Account2)+))
      AND  Account1.AccountHandle = '@Joe'
)
SELECT *
FROM    BaseRows
WHERE   ConnectedToAccountHandle = '@Cindy';
```

In the output, you can see the output that was described in Figure 19-18.

ConnectedToAccountHandle	ConnectedPath
@Cindy	@Joe->Bowling->@Lewis->Computers->@Cindy

One last construct that I want to cover in this overview of basic data manipulation is heterogeneous nodes and edges. You can create a VIEW object (or use a derived table) that takes multiple nodes and edges and allows you to treat them as one. For the nodes and edges in our SocialGraph schema, this would look like the following:

```
CREATE OR ALTER VIEW SocialGraph.AllNodes AS
     SELECT Account.AccountHandle AS Display, 'Account' AS NodeType
     FROM   SocialGraph.Account
     UNION ALL
     SELECT Interest.InterestName AS Display, 'Interest' AS NodeType
     FROM   SocialGraph.Interest;
GO

CREATE OR ALTER VIEW SocialGraph.AllEdges AS
     SELECT 'Follows' AS EdgeType
     FROM   SocialGraph.Follows
     UNION ALL
     SELECT 'InterestedIn' AS EdgeType
     FROM   SocialGraph.InterestedIn;
GO
```

Note that I did not include the $node_id, $from_id, or $to_id in the queries for the view. You cannot return them in a query of the view, but they do exist. With this construct, you can now query nodes in a polymorphic style, with a query such as the following:

```
SELECT AllNodes.Display,
       AllEdges.EdgeType,
       AllNodes2.Display
FROM   SocialGraph.AllNodes,
       SocialGraph.AllEdges,
       SocialGraph.AllNodes AS AllNodes2
WHERE  MATCH(AllNodes-(AllEdges)->AllNodes2)
  AND  AllNodes.Display = '@Joe';
```

Naturally SQL is still a very rigid language, so you won't get a variable output, but for the columns you have defined in the view and the metadata you output (like EdgeType), you can get answers like the following that tell us who @Joe follows and what @Joe's interests are:

Display	EdgeType	Display
@Joe	Follows	@Bertha
@Joe	Follows	@Betty
@Joe	Follows	@Charles
@Joe	Follows	@Fido
@Joe	InterestedIn	Bowling
@Joe	InterestedIn	Craziness
@Joe	InterestedIn	Dogs
@Joe	InterestedIn	Lodge Membership
@Joe	InterestedIn	Pickup Trucks

With graph tables, you can extend your designs to connect various types of data with one another, and this is not all you can do, but this brief overview of graph structures will hopefully give you ideas about how you might extend your databases with graph structures (even if you just create nodes that are simply in a 1–1 relationship with your relational tables, but you use them to capture the connectedness of your data).

For more technical details about graph databases, see the Microsoft Docs article "Graph processing with SQL Server and Azure SQL Database" here: `docs.microsoft.com/en-us/sql/relational-databases/graphs/sql-graph-overview`.

Anti-patterns

For every good practice put forth to build awesome structures, there come many that fail to meet the level of awesome or even adequate. In this section, I will outline four of these practices that are often employed by designers and implementers, some novice and some experienced, and explain why I think they are such bad ideas:

- *Undecipherable data*: You are looking at the data in a table, and you see a column with a name like Status. Then you find the values 1, 2, and 49 in the column with no idea what any of these values actually means without looking into copious amounts of code, likely not even in any of the database code.

- *One-size-fits-all domain*: One domain table is used to implement all domains rather than using individual tables that are smaller and more precise.

- *Generic key references*: In this anti-pattern, you have one column where the data in the column might be the key from any number of tables, requiring you to decode the value rather than know what it is.

- *Overusing unstructured data*: This is the bane of existence for DBAs—the blob-of-text column that the users swear they put well-structured data in for you to parse out. You can't eliminate a column for notes here and there, but overuse of such constructs leads to lots of user pain in the future trying to find and use the data again.

There are a few other problematic patterns I need to reiterate (with chapter references), in case you have read only this chapter so far. My goal in this section is to hit upon some patterns that would not come up in the "right" manner of designing a database but are common ideas that designers get when they haven't gone through the heartache of these patterns:

- *Poor normalization*: Normalization is an essential part of the process of OLTP database design, and it is far easier to achieve than it will seem when you first start. And don't be fooled by people who say that Third Normal Form is the ultimate level; Fourth Normal Form is very important and common as well. Fifth is rare to violate, but if you do you will know why it is interesting as well. (Chapter 5 covers normalization in depth.)

- *Poor domain choices*: Lots of database designers just use varchar(50) for every non-key column (or varchar(max)!), rather than taking the time to determine proper domains for their data. Sometimes, this is even true of columns that are related via foreign key and primary key columns, which makes the optimizer work harder. (See Chapters 5, 6, and 7.)

- *No standardization of datatypes*: It is a good idea to make sure you use the same sized/typed column whenever you encounter like typed things. For example, if your company's account number is always exactly nine ASCII characters long, it is best to use a char(9) column to store that data. Too often a database might have it 20 different ways: varchar(10), varchar(20), nchar(9), char(15), and so on. All of these will store the data in a lossless manner, but only char(9) will be best and will help keep your users from needing to think about how to deal with the data. (See Chapters 6 and 7 for more discussion of choosing a datatype and Appendix A for a more detailed list and discussion of all the intrinsic relational types. In Chapter 12, when we discuss matters of indexing and performance, it will also become clear that mixing certain datatypes (like Unicode and ASCII character sets), or even different collations, can have negative effects on performance.)

And yes, there are many more things you shouldn't do, but this section has listed some of the bigger design-oriented issues that really drive you crazy when you have to deal with the aftermath of their use.

Undecipherable Data

One of the most annoying things when dealing with a database is values that make no sense without (and sometimes with) context. Code such as WHERE status = 1 that peppers code you discover will have you scratching your head in wonderment as to what 1–8 and then 10 represent. Is 9 a value that rarely occurs, or did 7 actually eat 9 as the joke goes? Of course, the reason for this is that the developers in question did not think of the database as a primary data resource to not only store data but also to be queried by people other than the code they have written. It is simply thought of as the place where they hold state for their objects.

Of course, they are probably doing a decent job of presenting the meaning of the values in *their* coding. They aren't dealing with a bunch of numbers in their code; they have a constant structure, such as

```
CONST (CONST_Active = 1, CONST_Inactive = 2, CONST_BarelyActive = 3, CONST_
DoNotUseAnymore = 4, CONST_Asleep = 5, CONST_Dead = 282);
```

So the code they are using to generate the T-SQL code makes sense when looking at it because they have said "WHERE status = " & CONST_Active. This is clear in the usage but not clear at the database level (where the values are seen and used by everyone else!). From a database standpoint, we have a few possibilities:

- Use descriptive values such as "Active" and "Inactive" rather than integer values that don't need decoding at all. This makes the data more decipherable but doesn't provide a domain of possible values. If you have no inactive values, you will not know about its existence at the database.

- As described in Chapter 6, model and implement a domain table that mirrors the CONST structure. Have a table with all possible values.

For the latter, your table could use the descriptive values as the domain key value, or you could use the integer values that the programmer likes as well. Yes, there will be double definitions of the values (one in the table, one in the constant declaration), but since domains such as this rarely change, it is generally not a terrible issue. And if the values DO change, this should make it more obvious to the database users.

In your source control, you would check in a script such as the following, with not only the table structure but the code also:

```
CREATE SCHEMA Status;
GO
CREATE TABLE Status.StatusCode(
    StatusCodeId int NOT NULL CONSTRAINT PKStatusCode PRIMARY KEY,
    Name  varchar(20) NOT NULL CONSTRAINT AKStatusCode UNIQUE
);
INSERT INTO Status.StatusCode
VALUES (1,'Active'),(2,'Inactive'),(3,'BarelyActive'),
       (4,'DoNotUseAnyMore'),(5,'Asleep'),(6,'Dead');
```

The principles I tend to try to design by follow:

- Only have values that can be deciphered using the database:

  - Foreign key to a domain table.

  - Human-readable values with no expansion in CASE expressions.

  - No bitmasks unless it provides an AMAZING benefit! A bitmask is using the storage of an integer value as 1s and 0s to make each bit mean something. 01001010 not only translates to a number value; it could be eight different bit values. We are not writing machine code, and loading 31 values into an integer does save space, but it is very frustrating to work with. It is actually how SQL Server internally stores `bit` columns, so it has benefit internally, but is terrible for users.

- Don't be afraid to have lots of small tables. Joins generally cost a lot less than the time needed to decipher a value, measured in programmer time, ETL time, and end user frustration. Even if you had to spend $20,000 on hardware upgrades (which you would not!), how many hours of worker time does that need to save to be worth it? Not many.

One-Size-Fits-All Key Domain

Relational databases are based on the fundamental idea that every object represents one and only one thing. There should never be any doubt as to what a piece of data refers. By tracing through the relationships, from column name to table name to primary key, it should be easy to examine the relationships and know exactly what a piece of data means.

However, oftentimes, it will seem reasonable that, since domain-type data looks the same (or at least looks the same shape) in many cases, creating just one such table and reusing it in multiple locations would be a great idea. This is an idea from people who are architecting a relational database who don't really understand relational database architecture (me included, early in my career)—that the more tables there are, the more complex the design will be. It is a bit more complex to actually model. It certainly was the case as I was building the example diagrams for this chapter, but the old saying of "pay me now, or pay me later" is very appropriate.

As an example, consider that I am building a database to store customers and orders. I need domain values for the following:

- Customer credit status

- Customer type

- Invoice status

- Invoice line item back order status

- Invoice line item ship via carrier

Why not just use one generic table to hold these domains, as indicated in Figure 9-22?

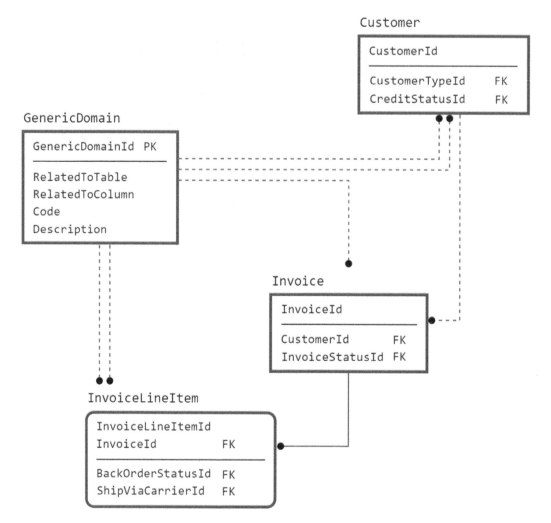

Figure 9-22. *One multiuse domain table*

The problem from a relational coding/implementation standpoint is that it is just not natural to work with in T-SQL. In many cases, the person who does this does not even think about T-SQL access. Domain tables should be purpose built to validate a value in a table in a more configurable, extensible way than using a CHECK constraint.

For example, say the report writer wants to get the domain values for the `Customer` table:

```
SELECT *
FROM Customer
  JOIN GenericDomain as CustomerType
    ON Customer.CustomerTypeId = CustomerType.GenericDomainId
  JOIN GenericDomain as CreditStatus
    ON  Customer.CreditStatusId = CreditStatus.GenericDomainId

--NOTE: This code is not part of the downloads, nor are the tables for the
--examples in this anti-pattern section.
```

But what if the `GenericDomainId` value isn't actually of the right type? You could change the key of the `GenericDomain` table to include the table it can be related to, but then every one of the child tables would need to be included in the join, like this:

```
SELECT *
FROM Customer
  JOIN GenericDomain as CustomerType
    ON Customer.CustomerTypeId = CustomerType.GenericDomainId
      and CustomerType.RelatedToTable = 'Customer'
      and  CustomerType.RelatedToColumn = 'CustomerTypeId'
  JOIN GenericDomain as CreditStatus
    ON  Customer.CreditStatusId = CreditStatus.GenericDomainId
      and CreditStatus.RelatedToTable = 'Customer'
      and CreditStatus.RelatedToColumn = 'CreditStatusId';
```

But now, what if a domain can be used across multiple tables? The crux of the problem is that relational tables should not mix different types of things. At first glance, domain tables are just an abstract concept of a container that holds text. And from an implementation-centric standpoint, this is quite true, but it is not the correct way to build a database because we never want to mix the rows together as the same thing ever in a query.

In a database, the process of normalization is a means of breaking down and isolating data by taking every table to the point where one table represents one type of thing and one row represents the existence of one of those things. Every independent domain of values should be thought of as a distinctly different thing from all the other domains (unless, as we explored when defining domains, it is the same domain used in multiple places, in which case one table will suffice). We did, even in the book, notably add domain tables after the formal normalization step and note that domain tables weren't so much entities that the customer cared about as physical constructs for the user. This stays true. But it doesn't mean the same principles do not apply.

So what you do is normalize the data over and over on each usage, spreading the work out over time, rather than doing the task once and getting it over with. Instead of a single table for all domains, you should model it as shown in Figure 9-23.

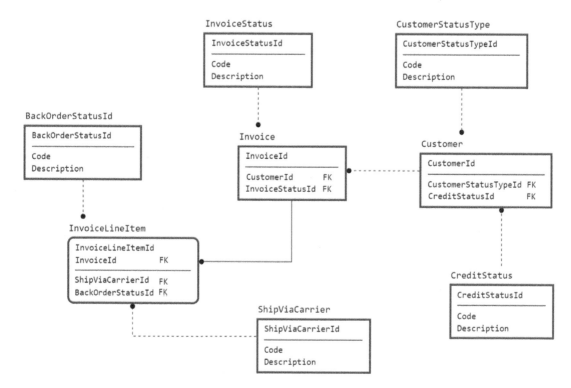

Figure 9-23. *One domain table per purpose*

That looks harder to do, right? Well, it is initially (like for the 5 or 10 minutes it takes to create a few tables). But now you are able to implement FOREIGN KEY constraints to protect the values in the tables. The fact is there are quite a few tremendous gains to be had:

- *Using the data in a query is much easier and self-documenting:*

```
SELECT *
FROM Customer
  JOIN CustomerType
    ON Customer.CustomerTypeId = CustomerType.CustomerTypeId
  JOIN CreditStatus
    ON  Customer.CreditStatusId = CreditStatus.CreditStatusId
```

- *Data can be completely validated using simple FOREIGN KEY constraints*: This was something not feasible for the one-table solution.

- *Expandability and control*: If it turns out that you need to keep more information in your domain row, it is as simple as adding a column or two to the specific domain. For example, if you have a domain of shipping carriers, you might define a ShipViaCarrier in your master domain table. In its basic form, you would get only one column for a value for the user to choose. But if you wanted to have more information—such as a long name for reports, as in "United Parcel Service," a description, and some form of indication when to use this carrier—you would be forced to change your implementation including all the references to the domain values.

Generic Key References

In an ideal situation, one table is related to another via a key. However, it is entirely possible to have a table that has a foreign key value (albeit one not enforced using a FOREIGN KEY constraint) that can be a value from several different tables, instead of just one.

For example, consider the case where you have several objects, all of which need a reference to one table. In our sample, say you have a customer relationship management system with a SalesOrder and a TroubleTicket table. Each of these objects has the need to reference to a JournalEntry row, outlining the user's contact with the customer (e.g., in the case where you want to make sure not to overcommunicate with a customer!). You might logically draw it up like in Figure 9-24.

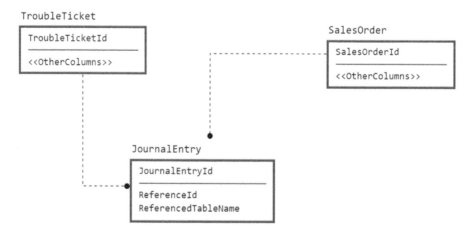

Figure 9-24. *Multiple tables related to the same key*

You might initially consider modeling it like a classic subtype relationship, but it really doesn't fit that mold because you probably can have more than one journal entry per sales order and trouble ticket. Fair enough, each of these relationships is 1–*N*, where *N* is between 0 and infinity (though the customer with infinite journal entries must really hate you). Having all parents relate to the same column is a possible solution to the problem but not a very favorable one. For our table in this scenario, we build something like this:

```
CREATE TABLE SalesOrder
(
    SalesOrderId <int or uniqueidentifier> PRIMARY KEY,
    <other columns>
)
CREATE TABLE TroubleTicket
(
    TroubleTicketId <int or uniqueidentifier> PRIMARY KEY,
    <other columns>
)
CREATE TABLE JournalEntry
(
    JournalEntryId <int or uniqueidentifier>,
    ReferenceId  <int or uniqueidentifier>,
```

```
    RelatedTableName sysname,
    PRIMARY KEY (JournalEntryId)
    <other columns>
)
```

Now, to use this data, you must indicate the table you want to join to, which is very much an unnatural way to do a join. You can use a universally unique GUID key so that all references to the data in the table are unique, eliminating the need for the specifically specified related table name. However, I find when this method is employed if the RelatedTableName is actually used, it is far clearer to the user what is happening.

A major concern with this method is that you cannot use constraints to enforce the relationships; you need either to use TRIGGER objects or to trust the middle layers to validate data values, which definitely increases the costs of implementation/testing, since you have to verify that it works in all cases, which is something we can simply trust for constraints.

You might also be thinking that from the graph section, this looks a bit like what we can do with an edge table in that an edge can contain connections from and to multiple types of objects. It is certainly similar in implementation and in some cases may actually turn out to be something to build into a graph depending on the purpose of the relationships.

One reason this method is employed is that it is very easy to add new references to one table. You just put the key value and table name in there, and you are done. Unfortunately, for the people who have to use this for years and years to come, it would have just been easier to spend a bit longer and do some more work, because the generic relationship means that using a constraint is not possible to validate keys, leaving open the possibility of orphaned data.

So, when the need isn't really graph-like, the better idea is to model it more like Figure 9-25.

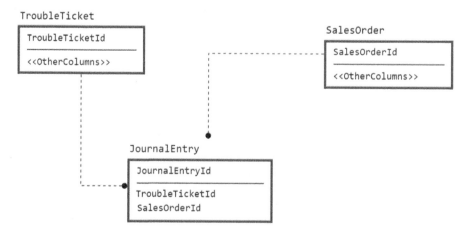

Figure 9-25. *Objects linked for maximum usability/flexibility*

```
CREATE TABLE SalesOrder
(
    SalesOrderId <int or uniqueidentifier> PRIMARY KEY,
    <other columns>
);
CREATE TABLE TroubleTicket
(
    TroubleTicketId <int or uniqueidentifier> PRIMARY KEY,
    <other columns>
);
CREATE TABLE JournalEntry
(
    JournalEntryId <int or uniqueidentifier> NOT NULL PRIMARY KEY,
    TroubleTicketId <int or uniqueidentifier> NULL
          REFERENCES TroubleTicket (TroubleTicketId),
    SalesOrderId <int or uniqueidentifier> NULL,
          REFERENCES SalesOrder (SalesOrderId),
    --make sure 1 and only 1 of the two references is not null
    CHECK ( (TroubleTicketId IS NULL OR SalesOrderId IS NULL)
          AND (TroubleTicketId IS NOT NULL OR SalesOrderId IS NOT NULL)))
);
```

While this table structure is definitely clunky feeling, because the reference is explicitly named, using the table is very natural, and it doesn't matter if there is any overlap in the surrogate values for the `SalesOrderId` or `TroubleTicketId`, because they are distinctly in two different values and both are protected by proper `FOREIGN KEY` constraints.

Overusing Unstructured Data

As much as I would like to deny it, and would love to find some way to avoid it, people need to have unstructured notes to store various unstructured pieces of information about their data. I will confess that many of the systems I have created in my career included some column that allowed users to insert freeform text. In the early days, it was a `varchar(256)` column and then `varchar(8000)` or `varchar(max)`. It is not something that you can get away from, because users need this scratchpad just slightly more than Linus needs his security blanket. And if used properly, it is not such a terrible practice, to be honest. What is the harm in letting the user have a place to note some bit of information about their data? I know I personally have tons of OneNote notebooks with lots of unstructured data, and if I had to design a database to store it, the output would be kind of insane, with tables created often for one concept and then abandoned. Yet, if I look at my collection of OneNote notebooks, the answer is right there, staring at me in the face. It easily becomes a total freaking mess.

Given too many generic buckets for text in a database, what happens is that notes become a replacement for doing actual design. The notes section becomes a replacement for things that ought to be a full-blown column. Should we have a column for special dietary restrictions? "Nah, no time for that, just put it in the notes column." Once the users do something once and particularly find it useful, they will do it again. And they tell their buddies, "Hey, I have started using notes to indicate that the order needs processing. Saved me an hour yesterday." And then it costs the programmers hundreds of hours sorting out unstructured data. (Hundreds is really not an exaggeration; it probably isn't nearly enough in many organizations.)

Probably the most common use of this I have seen that concerns me is contact notes. I have done this myself in the past, where I had a column that contained formatted text something like the following on a `Customer` table:

ContactNotes

2008-01-11 – Stuart Pidd -Spoke to Fred on the phone. Said that his wangle
was broken, referencing Invoice 20001. Told him I would check and call
back tomorrow.
2008-02-15 – Stuart Pidd – Fred called back, stating his wangle was still
broken, and now it had started to dangle. Will call back tomorrow.
2008-04-12 – Norm Oliser – Stu was fired for not taking care of one of our
best customers.

The proper solution is almost certainly to take this data that is being stored into this text column and apply the rigors of normalization to it. Clearly, in this example, you can see three "rows" of data, with at least three "columns." Eventually the users start asking things like "Can you tell us when the first and last times we spoke to our customers?" Given enough time, anything is possible.

However, instead of having a Customer table with a ContactNotes column, implement the tables like this:

```
CREATE TABLE Customer
(
     CustomerId   int   CONSTRAINT PKCustomer PRIMARY KEY
     <other columns>
)
CREATE TABLE CustomerContactNotes
(
     CustomerId   int,
     NoteTime     datetime,
     UserId  datatype, --references the User table
     Notes varchar(max),
     CONSTRAINT PKCustomerContactNotes PRIMARY KEY (CustomerId, NoteTime)
)
```

You might even stretch this to the model we discussed earlier with the journal entries where the notes are a generic part of the system and can refer to the customer, multiple customers, and other objects in the database. This might even link to a reminder system to remind Stu to get back to Fred, and he would not be jobless—though one probably should have expected such out of a guy with a first name of Stu and a last name of Pidd (obviously). You might even consider implementing this as graph nodes, where you could attach notes to multiple customer edges.

Even using XML to store the notes in a more structured manner would be an amazing improvement. You could then determine who entered the notes, what the day was, and what the notes were, and you could fashion a UI that allowed the users to add new fields to the XML, right on the fly. What a tremendous benefit to your users and, let's face it, to the people who must go in and answer questions like this, "How many times have we talked to this client by phone?"

The point of this section is simply this: educate your users. Give them a place to write the random note/comment, but teach them that when they start to use notes to store the same specific sorts of things over and over, their jobs could be easier if you gave them a place to store their values that would be searchable, repeatable, and so on. Plus, never again would you have to write queries to "mine" information from notes.

Tip   SQL Server provides a tool to help search text called Full-Text Search. It can be very useful for searching textual data in a manner much like a typical web search. However, it is no replacement for proper design that makes a different column and row from every single data point that the users are typically interested in.

Summary

This chapter was dedicated to expanding the way you think about tables and to giving you some common solutions to problems that are themselves common. The point was simply to cover some solutions that are a bit beyond the basic table structures I covered in earlier chapters.

The following are the "good" patterns we covered:

- *Uniqueness*: Simple uniqueness constraints are often not enough to specify uniqueness for "real" data. We discussed going deeper than basic implementation and working through uniqueness scenarios where you exclude values (selective uniqueness), bulk object uniqueness, and the real-world example of trying to piece together uniqueness where you can't be completely sure (like visitors to a website).

- *Data-driven design*: The goal is to build your databases to be flexible enough that adding new data to the database that looks and acts like previous values does not require code changes. You do this by attempting to avoid hard-coded data that is apt to change and making columns for typical configurations.

- *Historical/temporal*: Often the user needs to be able to see their data at previous points in time as it has changed over time. I presented strategies you can use to view your data at various points in history. Using a TRIGGER object gives you a lot of control, but temporal extensions are awesome if you can live with some of their constraints.

- *Large binary data*: This often pertains to images but could refer to any sort of file that you might find in a Windows file system. Storing large binary values allows you to provide your users with a place to extend their data storage.

- *Generalization*: Although this is more a concept than a pattern, we discussed why we need to match the design to the users' realistic needs by generalizing some objects to the system needs.

- *Storing graph data in SQL Server*: This section explored some of the ways you can model and create interconnected data in a different way than foreign keys in SQL Server, to build rich interconnected data sets.

We finished up with a section on anti-patterns and poor design practices, including some pretty heinous ones:

- *Undecipherable data*: All data in the database should have some sort of meaning. Users should not have to wonder what a value of 1 means.

- *One domain table to cover all domains*: This is yet another issue that can be traced to concepts in normalization, because the overarching goal of a normalized database is to match one table with one need. Domain values may seem like one thing, but the goal should be that every row in a table is usable in any table it is relatable to.

- *Generic key references*: It is a very common need to have multiple tables relate to another. It can also be true that only one table should be related at a time. However, every column should contain one and only one type of data. Otherwise, users have no idea what a value is unless they go hunting.

- *Overusing unstructured data*: Like so many other concerns in a database design, this too hearkens back to normalization, where we desire to store one value per column. Users are given a generic column for notes regarding a given item, and because they also have unplanned-for needs for additional data storage, they use the notes instead. The mess that ensues, particularly for the people who need to report on this data, is generally the fault of the architect at design time to not give the users a place to enter whatever they need or, to be fair, the users changing their needs over time and adapting to the situation rather than consulting the IT team to adjust the system to their ever-changing needs.

Of course, these lists are not exhaustive of all the possible patterns out there that you should use or not use, respectively. The goal of this chapter was to help you see some of the common usages of objects so you can begin to put together models that follow a common pattern where it makes sense. Feedback, particularly ideas for new sections, is always desired at `louis@drsql.org`.

CHAPTER 10

Database Security and Security Patterns

Do not think because an accident hasn't happened to you that it can't happen.

—Safety Saying, Circa Early 1900s

There are so many threats to your security that it is essential to remain ever vigilant—though not so vigilant that you end up with your server in a bunker of lead, wearing a tinfoil hat and keeping data completely inaccessible to even your users. Business needs connectivity to customers, and customers need connectivity to their data. With that having been said, security is a very important task when setting up and deploying a new application, yet it is often overlooked and dealt with late in the application building process. Whether or not this is acceptable is generally up to your requirements, the sensitivity of your data, and how your application will be built; but at one point or another, your application team must take the time to get serious about security. Over and over, news stories report data being stolen, and the theft is inevitably due to poor security. Several editions of this book ago, I used an example of an election official's stolen laptop in my then home city of Nashville, Tennessee; names, addresses, and partial Social Security numbers being stolen. It was mildly shocking at the time, but by now we all just roll our eyes at such things because of the continual stream of such stories, be them from financial institutions or adultery-oriented websites.

If you haven't received an email purporting to have pictures of you in compromising situations because a website has stolen a copy of your email address and one of the hopefully many passwords you use, you may be in the minority. The threat is a hoax, but only because they have not found any other use for the password (for me it was extra use of my Hulu account before I learned my lesson!).

© Louis Davidson 2021
L. Davidson, *Pro SQL Server Relational Database Design and Implementation*,
https://doi.org/10.1007/978-1-4842-6497-3_10

Note   There is a saying that "data is the new oil," which is flawed in some ways, mostly because it is a lot harder to steal and exploit oil.

Every company these days has a privacy policy, and as a database designer/programmer, meeting that policy is going to be partially your responsibility. Sometimes you will be the only person who seems to care about the privacy policy, and your calls for strict security will make you sound like your tinfoil hat is not for aesthetic reasons only. There are many laws that will govern how well you need to protect various types of data and which data you can share with the customer, with other customers, with agencies, and even with people in the same company who work in offices in different locations. I will not even somewhat try to specifically cover these broad privacy and legal topics more than what I did in Chapter 2 because of their fluidity over time, but the foundations of them all will basically be the same: limit access to data to only authorize persons, obfuscate certain data unless it is read by the right people, and delete data that you don't need to store.

Instead, I will cover some of the tools you can use to secure your data so that you have the technical knowledge to meet any privacy policy or law that applies to your employer or client. If you implement these security techniques correctly, at least you will not end up being the cause of your customers' passwords, credit card numbers, and even personal proclivities being shared on the Internet for all to know.

In this chapter, I will cover the following security-based topics:

- *Database access*: The fundamentals that you need to understand about how a person or process gets access to a SQL Server instance and into a database.

- *Database object securables*: Once the user is in the context of a database, you have a lot of built-in controls to manage what the user can access. We will cover what they are and how to use and test them.

- *Row-level security*: We will explore how to use SQL Server's row-level security tools to limit access to certain rows in a table, with limited if any changes to the underlying application.

- *Controlling access to data via T-SQL coded objects*: We will look beyond direct access to data, at how you can restrict access to data in more granular ways using T-SQL procedures, views, and so on.

- *Crossing database lines*: Databases ideally are independent containers, but on occasion, you will need to access data that is not stored within the confines of the database. We will cover some of the caveats when implementing cross-database access.

- *Obfuscating data*: While the only reason to store data is (unsurprisingly) to be able to read it, you want the program to be able to decode some data only when needed and by the right people. This is particularly important for personally identifiable data (PII) or financial data, so we obfuscate the data to keep eyes out except where allowable.

- *Auditing*: Turning on a "security camera" to watch what people are doing with data is sometimes the only real way to verify that you can provide adequate security. In most cases, you will do this *and* the aforementioned items so that only the right people can do certain actions, and those people have their actions tracked.

Overall, we will cover a deep sampling of what you need to do during database design and implementation to secure your data, but we won't cover the complete security picture, especially if you start to use some of the features of SQL Server that we are not covering in this book (Service Broker to name one). The goal of this chapter is to help you architect a security solution for your relational database by showing you what is available, demonstrating some of the implementation patterns you may use, and then letting you dig in for your exact needs.

One bit of terminology clarification is important to understand. When you think of SQL Server architecture, you should think of three layers, each involved in the security (and code execution) of data:

- *Host/server*: The machine (physical, virtual, or cloud) that the software runs on. SQL Server typically runs on a Windows Server platform, but also several distros of Linux and Docker and Kubernetes containers, and also in a hosted platform where the operating system is invisible to you as a designer/administrator. The host server provides authentication of the identity trying to access SQL Server.

- *Instance/SQL Server*: The SQL Server installation (often referred to as just "server" because old habits are hard to break...and the fact that the product is not called SQL Instance). You can have multiple instances on a host server. The instance can provide authentication services of its own. SQL Server is basically an operating system of its own, interacting with the host operating system to perform some of its tasks.

- *Database*: The container for data that the users will access. Databases can also contain authentication information.

These concepts will show up in both the on-premises and cloud versions of SQL Server. Luckily for developers, security *inside* the database container will behave pretty much the same on-premises and in the cloud. This chapter will mostly center on database security because this is a database design book, and the external layers of security vary wildly by organization, platform, and how you use the product. Another book I contributed to, *SQL Server 2019 Administration Inside Out* (2020, Pearson), is a great resource for setting up and configuring SQL Server in the various platforms it is available on.

In terms of users accessing data, the application layer is commonly left to implement much of the security alone, by simply showing or hiding functionality from the user. This approach is common, but it can leave gaps in security, especially when you have to give users ad hoc access to the data or you have multiple user interfaces that have to implement different methods of security. My advice is to make use of the facilities in the database server as much as possible. Having the application layer control security isn't a tremendous hole in the security of the organization, as long as the data is accessed using Windows Authentication using adequate security policies. If the application has complete access to all data and it is broken into, then all data is lost.

Tip   The examples in this chapter will all be of the interpreted T-SQL variety. CLR and native objects generally follow the same patterns of security with some minor differences, mostly limitations on what can be done.

Database Security Prerequisites

In this initial section, we are going to cover a few prerequisites that we will need to access the database container, starting with connecting to the server and gaining access to a database. In this section, I will cover the following topics:

- *Guidelines for host server security configuration*: Some considerations to make sure your server is configured to protect against outside harm.

- *Principals and securables*: Security in SQL Server is centered on principals (loosely, logins and users) and securables (stuff that you can limit access to).

- *Connecting to the server*: With changes that started in SQL Server 2012, along with Azure products, there are multiple ways to access a server and then the database. We will touch on the various methods.

- *Impersonation*: Using the EXECUTE AS statement, you can "pretend" you are a different security principal to use the other user's security. It is a very important concept for testing security that we will use often in this chapter.

Guidelines for Host Server Security Configuration

It is very important to configure the host server to be as secure as possible based on how your server will be used. Very few servers these days are completely cut off from the Internet (and the scum-sucking nerf-herding hacker types who lurk there). As an application/data architect/programmer, I have generally only been an advisor on how to configure most of the servers I work with, beyond the confines of the individual database, and deep details on configuration are outside of the scope of this book anyhow. However, it is worth a few pages to make it clear that the host server is the linchpin to the matter of securing your data. The following list contains some high-level characteristics you will want to use to validate the security of the server to protect your on-premises system from malicious hackers. If you are using one of the Azure products, some of the same advice still holds, particularly if you use an Azure SQL Server VM-based approach.

It is not an exhaustive list, just a list of almost universally required considerations for configuring the Windows Server and the SQL Server instance that we will be using to house our databases:

- *Passwords*: Strong passwords are applied to all accounts that can access the host server, and very strong passwords are applied to all universally known system accounts. Certainly, there are no blank passwords for any accounts! (The same will apply to accounts that can access SQL Server, both from Windows Authentication and, if you must use it, standard accounts.)

- *Network access*: The host server isn't sitting unguarded on the Web, using standard ports or no firewall for access and/or not logging failed login attempts. (Honestly, what makes Azure products so appealing is that it is Microsoft's job to make sure of this and your VM starts completely locked down and you have to allow access to what you need.)

- *Access codes encrypted*: Application passwords are secured/encrypted and put where they can be seen only by people who need to see them (such as the DBA and the application programmers who use them in their code). The password is encrypted into application code modules when using application logins. Connections to server using such passwords are encrypted as well.

- *Limited file system access*: Very few people have file-level access to the server where the data is stored and, probably more important, where the backups are stored. If one malicious user has access to unencrypted backups in whatever form you have them in, that person has access to your data by simply restoring that file to a different server, and you can't stop access to the data (and even encryption isn't 100% secure if the hacker has virtually unlimited time and the value of cracking it is high enough; just ask the CIA, FBI, or Apple).

- *Physical access*: Your host server is in a very secure location. A Windows or Linux server, just like your laptop, is only as secure as the physical box. Just like on any spy TV show, if the bad guys can access your physical hardware, they could boot to a CD or USB device and gain access to your hard disks (note that using Transparent Data Encryption [TDE] can help in this case if you don't keep everything to decrypt it right on the same server). This is even more important as virtualization is becoming the de facto standard. The files for the VM or container image are a lot easier to smuggle out of the office than a 50-pound machine with disk arrays dragged along behind. Again, another way the Azure offerings excel is that their security is probably better than yours unless you work for a bank...or the CIA.

- *Limited software surface area*: All features that you are not using are turned off. This pertains both to the Windows Server components (if you are not using the web server services, turn them off) and to the SQL Server installations. Windows helps by not turning on everything by default, as does SQL Server. For example, remote administrator connections, Database Mail, CLR programming, and other features are all off by default. You can enable these features and others by using the `sp_configure` stored procedure.

- *Accessing SQL Server with the correct protocols for your scenario*: You have chosen proper protocols for accessing the server. Of greatest importance is to use an encrypted connection when your application transmits sensitive data (as defined by laws, privacy policies, requirements, and just plain being a good steward of your customers' data). It is best that the new intern doesn't discover that they can see all of the customer's credit card and personal information using free software on the Internet because you didn't encrypt the connection.

The bottom line is that most of what you will do at the database level is intended to keep your mostly honest users from seeing and doing things that they shouldn't (other than some forms of encryption, at least) and isn't nearly as important as keeping the data safe from malicious outsiders. For most of your user community, you could leave all the data unprotected, and like Dorothy and her magical shoes, they wouldn't know what they can do, and they won't take your data and go back to Kansas.

But that kind of thinking, which permeates many information technology groups across the world, is seriously flawed because of the hackers we mentioned earlier. If you watch your personal router at home, you will no doubt see people trying to access your local network if you are directly on the Internet. Bots are out there looking for a way into every network in the world, seeing what they can find, and they will exploit any opening. It doesn't have to be a large opening, and you are in trouble. But keeping the openings sealed up is not as difficult as it may seem either.

If you aren't convinced that people are out to get your information, go to account. live.com if you have a Microsoft account and go to Security and Sign-in activity. See how many unsuccessful attempts there have been to access your account in the past and possibly the past few minutes. (Then turn on two-factor authentication immediately if you haven't already!)

Security Principals

At the very core of security in SQL Server are the concepts of principals and securables. *Principals* are those identities that may be granted permission to access resources, while *securables* are things to which access can be controlled. Principals can represent a specific persona, a role that may be adopted by multiple personas, or an application, certificate, and more. The following is a list of the essential constructs you may encounter:

- *Instance-level principals*: These represent some way of accessing the SQL Server from the outside of the instance. There are several kinds, but two main types that you will deal with for SQL Server instances both on a local machine or in a VM:

    - *Windows principals*: These connect to Windows user accounts or groups, authenticated using Windows security. SQL Server trusts Windows to determine who has been authenticated as known and allowable to connect to the server, and when Windows passes an identifier to SQL Server, it trusts that if the identifiers match what is expected, things are great.

    - *SQL Server principals*: These are logins that are authenticated using SQL Server–based authentication, which is implemented through storage and algorithms located in the software of the SQL Server instance. It is best to avoid if possible, but if not, use best practices for choosing usernames (e.g., don't use the built-in SA account or consider renaming it first and use very complex passwords).

For Azure SQL DB and Managed Instance, you will also encounter another type of principal that will allow you to access a database from outside of the server:

- *Azure Active Directory* principals: These are principals that are part of Microsoft's cloud-based identity system that you can use to access Microsoft 365 and Azure resources, such as Azure Virtual Machines (Azure VM), Azure SQL DB, and Azure Managed Instance.

Finally, once you are in the context of a database, there are

- *Database principals*: These include users (usually mapped to a server principal, but can be mapped to other items, such as certificates), roles (groups of users and other roles to give access to en masse), and application roles (a special type of role that can be used to let an application have different rights than the user has normally). Most of this chapter will focus on database principal configuration.

Granting and Denying Access to Securables

Securables are the things to which you can control access on all parts of the instance and database and to which you can grant principals permissions. SQL Server distinguishes between three scopes at which different objects can be secured:

- *Server scoped*: Securables that are at the scope of the entire server, which generally affect all server principals, including logins, HTTP endpoints, availability groups, and databases. These are items that exist at the server level, outside of any individual database, and to which access is controlled on a server-wide basis.

- *Database scoped*: Securables with database scope are objects such as schemas, users, roles, CLR assemblies, DDL triggers, and so on, which exist inside a database but not within a schema.

- *Schema scoped*: This group includes those objects that reside within a schema in a database, such as tables, views, and stored procedures.

These concepts will come into play in the rest of the chapter as we walk through the different ways that you will need to secure the data in the database. You can then allow, or disallow, usage of these objects to the roles that have been created. SQL Server uses three different security statements to give rights to or take away rights from each of your roles:

- GRANT: Allows access to an object. A principal can be granted the same right multiple times, through role memberships and directly.

- DENY: Forcibly removes access to an object, regardless of whether the user has been granted the privilege from any other GRANT. A principal can be granted and denied the same right multiple times, but one DENY overrides any number of GRANT privileges that have been applied for the denied right.

- REVOKE: Essentially a DELETE statement for security. Removes a GRANT or DENY permission that has been applied to an object.

Typically, you'll simply use GRANT to give permissions to a principal to perform tasks. DENY is then used only in "extreme" cases, because no matter how many other times the principal has been granted privileges to an object, the principal won't have access to it while there's one DENY, which actually makes for a confusing security scenario when you are trying to work out why user X can't access object Y.

For a right that pertains to the entire database or server, you will use syntax like

```
GRANT <privilege> TO <principal> [WITH GRANT OPTION];
```

Including the WITH GRANT OPTION will allow the principal to grant the privilege to another principal, something that should be used sparingly, lest you have users sprawling permissions for you, instead of DBAs and developers carefully creating and testing privileges and then checking them into source control and releasing them through proper channels.

For the most part, this book will deal primarily with privileges that operate on schema-scoped objects, as database- and server-type privileges are largely administrative. They allow you to let principals create objects, drop objects, do backups, change settings, view metadata, and so on. The users who can do these operations are largely administrators.

For database objects, there is a minor difference in the syntax from what was previously demonstrated in that a securable that you will be granting rights to will be specified. For example, to grant a privilege on a securable in a database, the command would be as follows:

```
GRANT <privilege> ON <securable> TO <principal> [WITH GRANT OPTION];
```

Next, if you want to remove the privilege, use REVOKE on the permission, which will delete the granted access:

```
REVOKE <privilege> ON <securable> FROM <principal>;
--Can also be TO instead of FROM to make code generation easier
```

If you want to prevent the principal from using the securable, no matter any role membership, you use DENY:

```
DENY <privilege> ON <securable> FROM <principal>;
--Can also be TO instead of FROM to make code generation easier
```

To remove the DENY, you would again use the REVOKE command, and you needn't tell whether you are revoking a GRANT or a DENY. Another bit of notation you will see quite often is to denote the type of securable before the securable where it is not the default. For objects that show up in sys.objects that have security granted to them (table, view, table-valued function, stored procedure, extended stored procedure, scalar function, aggregate function, service queue, or synonym), you can simply reference the name of the object:

```
GRANT <privilege> ON <securable> TO <database principal>;
```

Or you can use

```
GRANT <privilege> ON OBJECT::<securable> TO <database principal>;
```

For other types of objects, such as schemas, assemblies, and so on, you will specify the type in the name. For example, for a GRANT on a schema securable, the syntax is

```
GRANT <privilege> ON SCHEMA::<schema securable> TO <database principal>;
```

Connecting to a SQL Server Database

Before we get to database security, we need to cover accessing the server. In the first several editions of this book, there was one SQL Server, it ran on Windows, and it worked one way. Today, connecting to a SQL Server database is often the exact same experience, but it can also be a lot different. You can access different kinds of SQL Servers:

- *Local instance*: Includes SQL Server instances installed locally on any Windows or Linux computer, a VM, or a container like Docker or Kubernetes in your enterprise. Typically, this is a server, but it can also be a user's laptop.

- *SQL Server on Azure VM*: The cloud version of the local instance, where you have basically the same Windows or Linux OS and SQL Server binaries as the local instance, but integrated security is handled through Azure Active Directory instead of local Windows Active Directory.

- *Docker/Kubernetes container*: A lightweight UI-less VM-like server that can run SQL Server either locally or in the cloud.

- *Azure SQL DB*: An Azure database offering that provides you, in its typical format, with a SQL Server database to work with. Much of the management of the platform is done for you, and is greenfield, in that it is always on the very latest version of SQL Server.

- *Azure Managed Instance*: An Azure database offering that provides many of the managed features of Azure SQL DB, but mimics many of the features of a local instance for users that want the assistance with maintaining their estate (e.g., automated backups), but have historical work tied up in their local instances.

In the next few pages, I am going to go over the basics of accessing the local instance using a login principal that is defined which allows a principal to access the server. The login is then typically mapped to a user within the database to gain access.

I will also discuss an additional method using the concept of a contained database (CDB). I will cover the broader picture and a bit of the management of CDBs as a whole later in the chapter when I cover cross-database security, but I do need to introduce the syntax and creation of the database here because it is, from a coding standpoint, largely a security question.

Linux has some slight differences in how you configure it to do Windows Authentication, but most of what is covered for instances is applicable. The Azure offerings are quite different because they use Azure Active Directory and how they are configured changes quite often. They do have tools that will help you get things configured for your usage, and many of the same concepts of logins and users do apply, depending on the offering. Managed Instance for example is very similar.

Connecting to a Database Using a Login and a Database User

To access a SQL Server instance and a database on that instance, we will create a server principal commonly referred to as a *login*. There are two typical methods that you will use to create almost all common logins (and all that we will need for this book). The first method is to map a login to a Windows Authentication principal (either a local login or an Active Directory login). This is done using the CREATE LOGIN statement. The following example would create the login I have on my laptop for writing content (of course, this user probably was created when you installed SQL Server if you are using a local Developer edition):

```
--square brackets required for WinAuth login because of the bracket
CREATE LOGIN [DomainName\drsql] FROM WINDOWS
      WITH DEFAULT_DATABASE=tempdb, DEFAULT_LANGUAGE=us_english;
```

The name of the login is the same as the name of the Windows principal, which is how they map together when using the FROM WINDOWS syntax. On my local virtual machine (the name of which I will replace with DomainName), I have a user named drsql. The Windows principal can be a single user or a Windows group. For a group, all users in the group will gain access to the server in the same way and have the same permission set afforded them from being given access through this group, though some logins could acquire more though other groups (as could the group itself). This is, generally speaking, the most convenient method of creating and giving users rights to SQL Server.

If you are using Azure SQL DB or Managed Instance, you can use Azure Active Directory Authentication to do something very similar. For more details, see the Microsoft Docs article "Authentication AAD Overview" (docs.microsoft.com/en-us/azure/azure-sql/database/authentication-aad-overview).

The second way is to create a login with a password:

```
CREATE LOGIN Fred WITH PASSWORD=N'password' MUST_CHANGE, DEFAULT_
DATABASE=tempdb,
     DEFAULT_LANGUAGE=us_english, CHECK_EXPIRATION=ON, CHECK_POLICY=ON;
```

If you set the CHECK_POLICY setting to ON, the password will need to follow the password complexity rules of the server it is created on, and CHECK_EXPIRATION, when set to ON, will require the password to be changed based on the policy of the Windows Server as well, and 'password' is not likely to pass, even on a simple machine you have created just for trying out this code, so pick something that will meet your requirements. Typical password requirements are as follows:

- Should be very long

- Should be varied in values. Certainly not just one character from each of the following bullets

- Should contain uppercase letters (A–Z)

- Should contain lowercase letters (a–z)

- Should contain numbers (0–9)

- Should contain at least one symbol from this list: _, @, *, ^, %, !, #, $, or &

For more ideas, consider the article "Password Size Does Matter" from InfoWorld: www.infoworld.com/article/2655121/security/password-size-does-matter.html.

Generally speaking, the most desirable method is to use Windows Authentication for the default access to the server where possible, since keeping the number of passwords a person has to a minimum makes it less likely they will tape a list of passwords to the wall for all to see and makes them have a really complex one they will remember (and actually use two-factor authentication!). Of course, using Windows Authentication can be troublesome in some cases where SQL Server is located in a DMZ with no trust between domains, so you have to resort to SQL Server Authentication, so use complex passwords and (ideally) change them often.

In both syntax examples of login creation, I defaulted the database to tempdb, because it requires a conscious effort to go to a user database and start building, or even dropping, objects. However, any work done in tempdb is deleted when the server is stopped. This is one of those things that may save you more times than you might imagine. Often, a script gets executed and the database is not specified and a bunch of objects get created—usually in master (the default, default database if you haven't set one explicitly). I have built more test objects on my local SQL Server in master over the years than I can count.

Once you have created the login, you will need to do something with it. If you want to make it a system administrator–level user, you could add it to the sysadmin server role, which is something that you will want to do on your local machine with your login that you will be doing your test database design work with. You probably already did this when you were installing the server and working though the previous chapters during the installation process, likely without even realizing that was what you were doing:

```
ALTER SERVER ROLE sysadmin ADD MEMBER [Domain\drsql];
```

Tip   Members of the sysadmin role basically bypass almost all rights checks on the server and can do anything ("almost all" because they will be subject to row-level security, data masking, and anything you code in a coded object). It is important to make sure you always have one sysadmin user that someone has the credentials for. It may sound obvious, but many a server has been reinstalled after all sysadmin users have been dropped or lost their passwords. True story.

You can give users rights to do certain actions using server permissions. For example, if Fred works in support, you may want to give read-only access to a server (without rights to change anything). First off, say you want Fred to be able to run DMVs (dynamic management views, which are sometimes technically functions, but table-valued functions are more or less parameterized views, hence the name DMV) to see the state of the server. You would grant the Fred user VIEW SERVER STATE permission using

```
GRANT VIEW SERVER STATE to Fred;.
```

You can also create your own user-defined server roles. For example, say you want to set up a role to let a login view the server settings and data on the instance, but not be able to make any changes. You could give the following rights:

- VIEW SERVER STATE: Access DMVs (previously mentioned).

- VIEW ANY DATABASE: See the structure of all databases.

- CONNECT ANY DATABASE: Connect to any existing and future database.

- SELECT ALL USER SECURABLES: View all data in databases the login can connect to.

To create a server role for these items, you could use

```
CREATE SERVER ROLE SupportViewServer;
```

Grant the role the rights desired as follows:

```
GRANT  VIEW SERVER STATE to SupportViewServer; --run DMVs
GRANT  VIEW ANY DATABASE to SupportViewServer; --see any database
--set context to any database
GRANT  CONNECT ANY DATABASE to SupportViewServer;
--see any data in databases
GRANT  SELECT ALL USER SECURABLES to SupportViewServer;
```

And add the login to the server role:

```
ALTER SERVER ROLE SupportViewServer ADD MEMBER Fred;
```

Once you have created your login, the next step is to access a database (unless you used sysadmin, in which case you have unfettered access to everything on the server). For the first examples in this chapter, create a database called ClassicSecurityExample, as shown next. (For the remainder of this chapter, as I have for the previous chapters, I will expect that you are using a user who is a member of the sysadmin server role as the primary user, except when we are testing some code and I specify a different user in the text.)

```
CREATE DATABASE ClassicSecurityExample;
```

Next, create another login that uses SQL Server Authentication. Most logins we will create in the book will use SQL Server Authentication to make it easier to test. DO NOT use these examples on a server that is not a private test server with no data that matters on it. I will delete the logins along the way, but these settings are not meant to be worthy of proper security (you know, mostly because the password is printed in this book and this book will definitely end up on the Internet!):

```
CREATE LOGIN Barney WITH PASSWORD=N'MyPa$$werdIsAWESum3',
          DEFAULT_DATABASE=[tempdb], DEFAULT_LANGUAGE=[us_english],
          CHECK_EXPIRATION=OFF, CHECK_POLICY=OFF;
```

Log in using the user in SSMS into a query window, as shown in Figure 10-1.

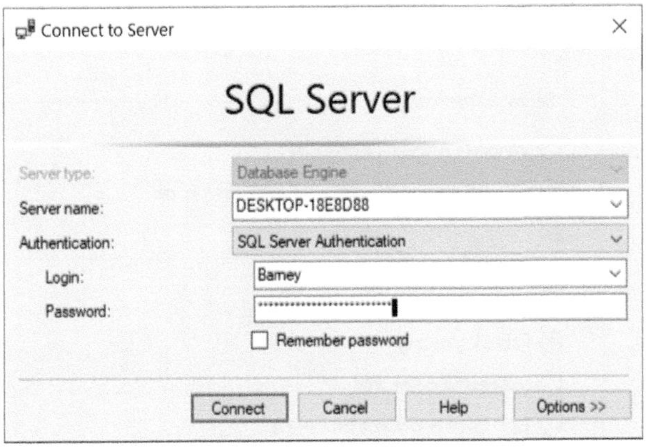

Figure 10-1. *Logging in using test user*

Your server needs to allow SQL Server Authentication to log in with this user. To check and change the setting, right-click your server in the Object Explorer and choose Properties. Choose the Security page. In Figure 10-2, you can see what this dialog looks like, and make sure SQL Server and Windows Authentication mode is set. Most examples in the chapter do not need this setting, but I did want to demonstrate how this worked in a "normal" fashion. For testing security, there are easier ways to achieve this.

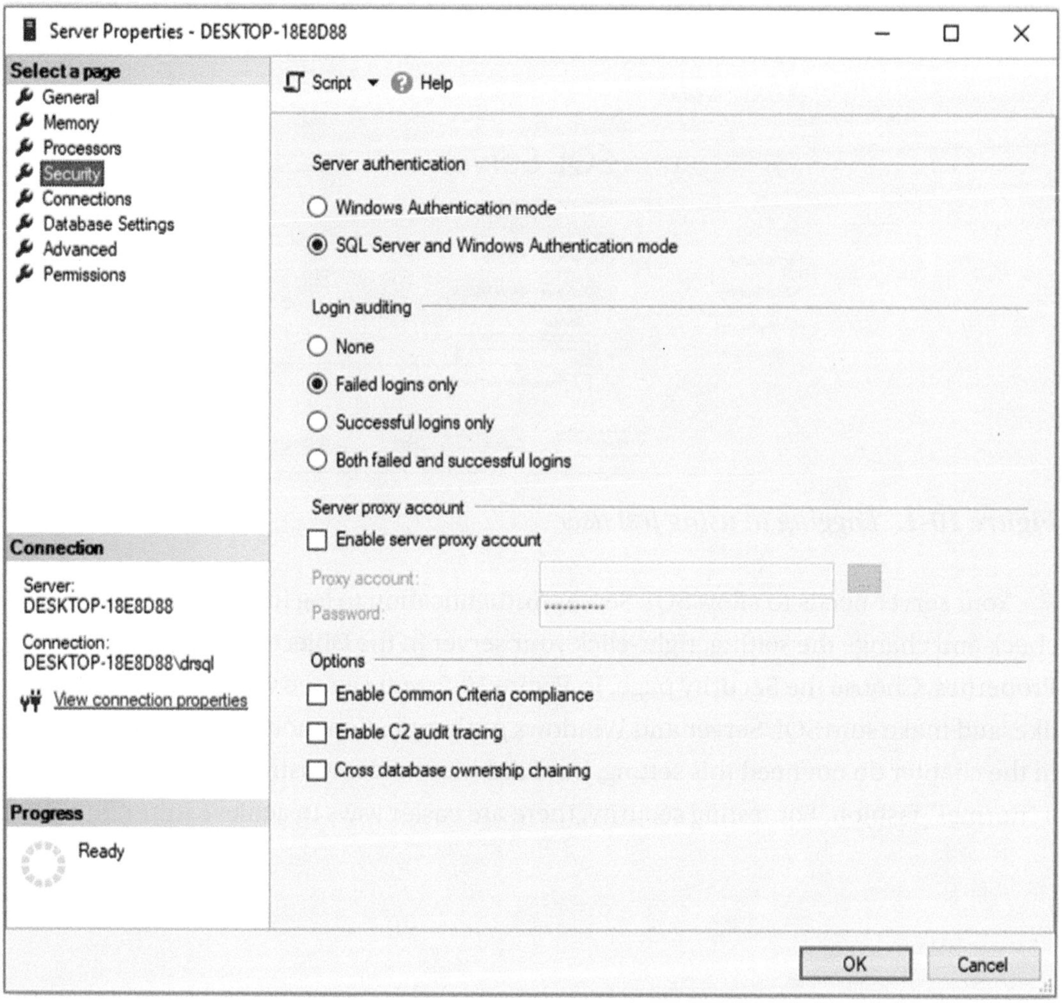

Figure 10-2. *Configuring the instance for SQL Server Authentication mode*

After logging in as Barney, try to execute a USE statement to change context to the ClassicSecurityExample database:

```
USE ClassicSecurityExample;
```

You will receive the following error:

```
Msg 916, Level 14, State 1, Line 1
The server principal "Barney" is not able to access the database
"ClassicSecurityExample" under the current security context.
```

Your database context will remain in tempdb, since this is the default database you set up for the user. Going back to the window where you are in the sysadmin user context, you need to enable the user to access the database. There are two ways to do this, the first being to give the guest user rights to connect to the database (back as the sysadmin user, naturally). The guest user is a built-in user that every database has. It equates to "anyone who connects," basically. Note that this is not an endorsement for using the guest user in any database unless you have seriously considered the ramifications. It is just a demonstration of how it works, so you know what the guest user is:

```
USE ClassicSecurityExample;
GO
GRANT CONNECT TO guest;
```

If you go back to the connection where the user Barney is logged in, you will find that Barney can now access the ClassicSecurityExample database—as can any other login in your system. You can apply this strategy if you have a database that you want all users to have access to, but it is generally not the best idea under most circumstances.

So remove this right from the guest user using the REVOKE statement:

```
REVOKE CONNECT TO guest;
```

Going back to the window where you have connected to the database as Barney, you will find that executing a statement like SELECT 'hi'; is still allowed, but if you disconnect and reconnect, you will not be able to access the database. Finally, to give server principal Barney access to the database, create a user in the database linked to the login and grant it the right to connect:

```
USE ClassicSecurityExample;
GO
CREATE USER BarneyUser FROM LOGIN Barney;
GO
GRANT CONNECT to BarneyUser;
```

Going back to the query window in the context of Barney, you will find that you can connect to the database and, using a few system functions, see your server and database security contexts in each:

```
USE ClassicSecurityExample;
GO
SELECT SUSER_SNAME() AS server_principal_name,
       USER_NAME() AS database_principal_name;
```

This will return

server_principal_name	database_principal_name
Barney	BarneyUser

Executing this in your system administrator connection, you will see something like the following (depending on what you used to log in to the server):

server_principal_name	database_principal_name
DomainName\drsql	dbo

The server principal will be the login you used, and the database principal will always be dbo (the database owner) user, as the system administrator user will always be mapped to the database owner. Now, this is the limit of what we are covering in this section, as you are now able to connect to the database. We will cover what you can do in the database after we cover connecting to the database with a contained database.

Using the Contained Database Model

A tremendous paradigm shift has occurred since I first started writing about database design and programming: virtualization. One of the many tremendous benefits of virtualization is that you can move around your virtual computer and/or servers within your enterprise to allow optimum use of hardware. With this new edition of the book, virtualization has expanded further to include Docker and Kubernetes containers, and if it hasn't expanded further by the next edition to some paradigm I haven't heard of yet, I will be amazed.

Another paradigm shift that changed security has been cloud computing. Azure DB databases typically behave like self-contained database servers. When you connect to one, you see a version of a master database, a tempdb, and a database container. Logins do not reside at the server level but instead are contained in the database. In the on-premises product, we can do the same thing using the "containment" model. The idea behind containment is that everything your database needs (jobs, ETL, tempdb objects, etc.) will begin to be a part of the database directly. Where applicable, I will note some of the places where contained database security is different from the classic model, which is mostly in the context of accessing external objects.

Your first step is to create a new database in which you will set containment = partial. For SQL Server 2012–2019 (in other words, up until what I know about as I write this sixth edition), there are two models: OFF, which I am referring to as the classic model, and PARTIAL, which will give you a few portability benefits (like principals to access the server and database contained in the database and temporary object collation defaulting to the partially contained database's collation setting rather than the server). Not much has changed in containment since 2012, but the hopeful eventual promise of the containment feature is SQL Server including a fully contained model that would be almost completely isolated from other databases in most ways.

The way you will connect to the database is a fundamental change, and just like filestream discussed in Chapter 9, this means a security point that is going to be turned off by default. Hence, the first thing you will do is configure the server to allow new connections using what is called "contained database authentication" using sp_configure:

```
EXECUTE sp_configure 'contained database authentication', 1;
GO
RECONFIGURE WITH OVERRIDE;
```

You should get a message telling you that the value was changed, either from 0 to 1 or 1 to 1, depending on if the server is already set up for the contained authentication. Next, create the database. You can set the containment properties in the CREATE DATABASE statement:

```
CREATE DATABASE ContainedDBSecurityExample CONTAINMENT = PARTIAL;
```

Or you can set them for an existing database using the ALTER DATABASE statement:

```
-- set the contained database to be partial
ALTER DATABASE ContainedDBSecurityExample SET CONTAINMENT = PARTIAL;
```

Next, you will create a user, which in this context is referred to as a "contained user." Contained users are basically a hybrid of login and user, created using the CREATE USER statement, which is a bit regrettable that it is the same statement, as the syntax is quite overloaded, but you will be warned if you obviously try to use the wrong syntax for the wrong type of user. In the "CREATE USER (Transact-SQL)" topic, Microsoft Docs lists at least 11 variations of the CREATE USER syntax, so you should check it out for more details (docs.microsoft.com/en-us/sql/t-sql/statements/create-user-transact-sql).

The first case I will use is a new SQL Server Authentication user that logs into the database directly with a password that exists in the system catalog tables in the database. You must be in the context of the database (which you set earlier), or you will get an error telling you that you can only create a user with a password in a contained database:

```
USE ContainedDBSecurityExample;
GO
CREATE USER WilmaContainedUser WITH PASSWORD = 'p@sasdfaerord1';
```

You can also create a Windows Authentication user in the following manner (it could be a role as well) as long as a corresponding login (server principal) does not exist. So the following syntax is correct, but on my computer, this fails because that user already has a login defined, since it is the system administrator:

```
CREATE USER [DomainName\drsql];
```

Since that user already has a login, I get the following error:

```
Msg 15063, Level 16, State 1, Line 1
The login already has an account under a different user name.
```

During the testing phase, we will be using SQL Server Authentication to make the process easier, because creating Windows users to authenticate with is time consuming and doesn't add anything to the demonstration of the capabilities of contained database users.

Next, connect to the database in SSMS using the contained user you previously created named WilmaContainedUser with password p@sasdfaerord1. To do this, specify the server name, choose SQL Server Authentication, and set the username and password, as shown in Figure 10-3.

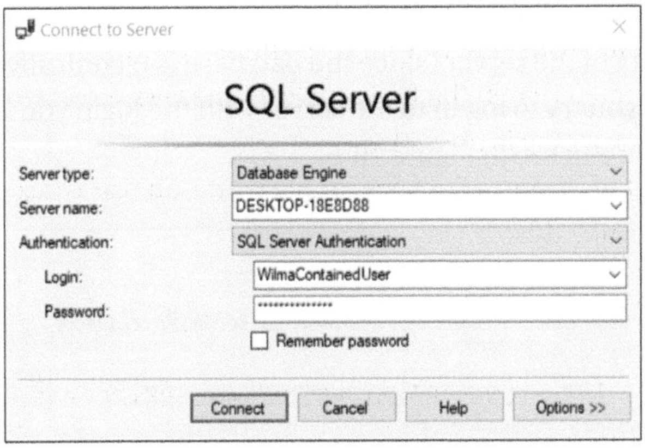

Figure 10-3. *Demonstrating logging in to a contained user*

Next, click the Options button. Go to the Connection Properties tab and enter the name of the contained database as shown in Figure 10-4.

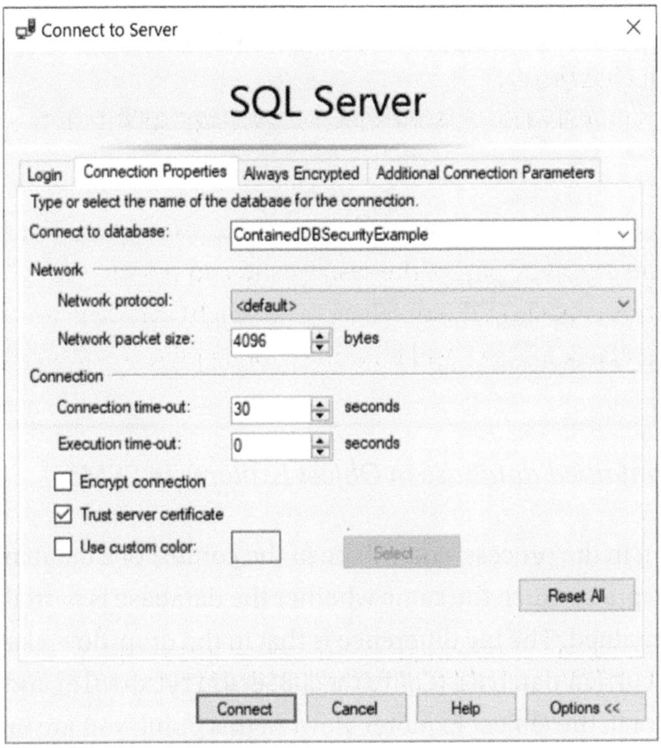

Figure 10-4. *Enter the name of the database in the blank*

You will need to know the name since the security criteria you are using will not have rights to the metadata of the server (since the database is technically the server you are connecting to), so if you try to log in to the server with the login you have supplied, it will give you the error you can see in Figure 10-5.

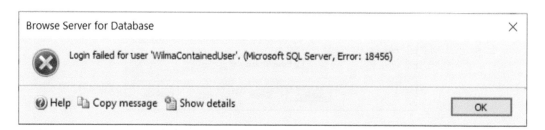

Figure 10-5. *Error trying to browse for name of contained database*

Now, if you connect to the Object Explorer, the server seems like it is made up of a single database, as shown in Figure 10-6.

Figure 10-6. *Contained database in Object Explorer in SSMS*

After this point in the process, you will be in the context of a database, and everything will be pretty much the same whether the database is partially contained or completely uncontained. The big difference is that in the drop-down list of databases, you will have the current database (`ContainedDBSecurityExample`) and `master` and `tempdb`, though not in the Object Explorer view. At this point, you are in the context of the database just like in the classic security model covered in the previous section.

You cannot create a contained user in an uncontained database, but you can still create a user linked to a login in a contained database. For example, you could create a new login:

```
CREATE LOGIN Pebbles WITH PASSWORD = 'BamBam01$';
```

Then link that user to the login you have created:

```
CREATE USER PebblesUnContainedUser FROM LOGIN Pebbles;
```

Obviously, this begins to defeat the overarching value of a contained database, which is to make the database portable without the need to reconcile logins on one server to a login on another, but rather to be immediately usable with the same users (with the caveat that the Windows Authentication user will have to be able to connect to the authenticating server to be authenticated, whereas the standard user will have all details contained in the database, for better and worse).

Note that you can switch a contained database back to not being contained, but you cannot have any contained database principals in it. Let's see what happens if you try to set the ContainedDbSecurityExample database back to uncontained (after disconnecting all users from the database). (You can use the following command to do this if you are sure of what you are doing: ALTER DATABASE ContainedDbSecurityExample SET SINGLE_USER WITH ROLLBACK IMMEDIATE;. That will set the database to single-user mode and kill all existing connections. Revert back to normal when done, using ALTER DATABASE ContainedDbSecurityExample SET MULTI_USER;.)

```
ALTER DATABASE ContainedDbSecurityExample   SET CONTAINMENT = NONE;
```

This will fail. In SQL Server 2012, you get a confusing error message:

```
Msg 33233, Level 16, State 1, Line 1
You can only create a user with a password in a contained database.
Msg 5069, Level 16, State 1, Line 1
ALTER DATABASE statement failed.
```

But in SQL Server 2016 and later, the error message is very clear:

```
Msg 12809, Level 16, State 1, Line 103
You must remove all users with password before setting the containment
property to NONE.
Msg 5069, Level 16, State 1, Line 1
ALTER DATABASE statement failed.
```

If you need to make this database uncontained, you will need to drop the contained users, which you can identify with the following list:

```
SELECT name
FROM    ContainedDBSecurityExample.sys.database_principals
--3 part name since you are outside of db to make this change.
WHERE   authentication_type_desc = 'DATABASE';
```

In our example, this returns

```
Name
---------------------------
WilmaContainedUser
```

Drop this user, and you would then be able to turn containment off for this database. Later in this chapter, we will come back to the topic of containment when we cover cross-database access (and in the case of containment, working to protect against it to keep databases more portable).

Impersonation

The ability to pretend to be another user or login is a very important tool when it comes to security. It has two main uses, the first and lesser of which is in code to let one principal impersonate another to temporarily gain access to their privileges. This usage is typically a dangerous one that, while very useful, must be treated with the utmost care. This will be covered more in this chapter, as well as Chapter 13, when we talk about building code.

The second purpose is arguably the most important security tool for a developer/ DBA for testing that security is properly configured. After you set up security in dev and again after some code has been migrated to production, it is not an uncommon occurrence to get a call from users who claim that they cannot do something that you think they really ought to be able to do. Since all system problems are inevitably blamed on the database first, it is a useful trick to impersonate the user and then try the questioned code in a query tool to see whether it is a security problem. If the code works for you, your job is almost certainly done from a database standpoint, and you can tell the support team to look at some other part of the system. You can do all of this without knowing their passwords, as you are either the sysadmin user or should have been granted rights to impersonate users that you are supporting. (There is a server-scoped permission IMPERSONATE ANY LOGIN that was added to SQL Server 2014 to make this easier for a semi-sysadmin type to do; however, it gives you the ability to impersonate any login, even SA. So be careful. You can deny impersonation of SA easily, but what about any other sysadmin-level login?)

To demonstrate security in a reasonable manner on a single SQL Server connection, use the EXECUTE AS command to impersonate different security principals, both database and server.

Note   Prior to 2005, the command to impersonate was SETUSER. Some use of that command in legacy code is still possible, as it still works. SETUSER is limited in comparison to EXECUTE AS but is similar.

As an example of how powerful impersonation can be, I'll show a way that you can have a user impersonating a member of the server-system sysadmin role. Using impersonation in such a way takes some getting used to, but it certainly makes it easier to have full sysadmin power only when it's needed. As said previously, there are lots of server privileges, so you can mete out rights that are needed on a day-to-day basis and reserve the "dangerous" ones like DROP DATABASE only for logins that you have to impersonate.

In this example, I use a SQL Server Authentication login, but you would typically map it to a Windows user in normal scenarios or even a certificate, key, or whatever works and is deemed secure. The thing that makes standard logins easier to use in test situations and learn from (they're self-contained) is part of what makes them less secure for production use! Then, I add the login to the sysadmin role. You probably also want to use a name that isn't so obviously associated with system administration. If a hacker got into your list of users somehow, the name 'itchy' wouldn't so obviously be able to do serious damage to your database server, but maybe not a name like 'Merlin' or 'Harry':

```
USE master;
GO
CREATE LOGIN SlateSystemAdmin
    WITH PASSWORD = 'weqc33(*hjnNn3202x2x89*6(6';

ALTER SERVER ROLE sysadmin ADD MEMBER SlateSystemAdmin;
```

Then, I create a regular login and give rights to impersonate the system_admin user:

```
CREATE LOGIN Slate with PASSWORD = 'different-afal230920j8&^^3',
                                DEFAULT_DATABASE=tempdb;

--Must execute in master Database
GRANT IMPERSONATE ON LOGIN::SlateSystemAdmin TO Slate;
```

I log in as Slate and try to run the following code (in SSMS, you can just right-click in the query window to use the Connection/Change Connection context menu and use a standard login):

```
USE ClassicSecurityExample;
```

The following error is raised:

```
Msg 916, Level 14, State 1, Line 1
The server principal "Slate" is not able to access the database
"ClassicSecurityExample" under the current security context.
```

Now, I change security context to the system_admin-level user (note that you cannot use EXECUTE AS LOGIN when you are in the context of a contained database user):

```
EXECUTE AS LOGIN = 'SlateSystemAdmin';
```

I now have control of the server in that window as the system_admin user! To look at the security context, I can use several variables/functions (note the functions USER and SYSTEM_USER are niladic scalar functions, which take no parameters and have no parentheses; USER_NAME() and SUSER_SNAME () return the same output as USER and SYSTEM_USER):

```
USE     ClassicSecurityExample;
GO
SELECT USER AS UserName, SYSTEM_USER AS SystemUserName,
       ORIGINAL_LOGIN() AS OriginalLoginName;
```

This returns the following result:

UserName	SystemUserName	OriginalLoginName
dbo	SlateSystemAdmin	Slate

The columns mean the following:

- UserName: The database principal name of context for the user in the database.

- SystemUserName: The server principal name of context for the login.

- OriginalLoginName: The login name of the server principal who actually logged in to start the connection. (ORIGINAL_LOGIN() is an important function that you should use when logging which login performed an action so when the DBA is testing something and impersonates Sally, Sally doesn't get blamed for trying to look at data that Sally should not ought to look at...which was what the DBA was testing.)

Then, I execute the following code:

```
REVERT; --go back to previous security context
```

I see the following result:

```
Msg 15199, Level 16, State 1, Line 1
The current security context cannot be reverted. Please switch to the
original database where 'Execute As' was called and try it again.
```

I started in `tempdb`, so I use the following code:

```
USE     tempdb;
GO
REVERT;
SELECT USER AS UserName, SYSTEM_USER AS SystemUserName,
       ORIGINAL_LOGIN() AS OriginalLoginName;
```

This now returns the following result:

UserName	SystemUserName	OriginalLoginName
guest	Slate	Slate

Impersonation gives you a lot of control over what a principal can do and allows you to situationally play one role or another, giving that principal a completely different permission set.

Note   The user here is `guest`, which is a user I recommend that you consider disabling in every non-system database unless it is specifically needed. Disable `guest` by executing REVOKE CONNECT FROM GUEST. However, guest is enabled on `tempdb` or `master` database so everyone has access, because users must have access to these databases to do any work. Trying to disable `guest` in these databases will result in the following message: `Cannot disable access to the guest user in master or tempdb.`

Using impersonation, you can write your code as a member of the `sysadmin` server role or db_owner database role and then test your code as a typical user without opening multiple connections (and this technique makes the sample code considerably easier to follow).

Note that I have only demonstrated impersonating a login, but you can also impersonate users, which we will use along with impersonating a login throughout the rest of this chapter. Note that there are limitations on what you can do when using impersonation. For a full treatment of the subject, check in Microsoft Docs in the "EXECUTE AS (Transact-SQL)" topic (https://docs.microsoft.com/en-us/sql/t-sql/statements/execute-as-transact-sql).

Database Object Securables

Now that we have covered giving your users access to the server and/or database, they are going to need the ability to do something in the database. In this section, we are going to cover the different ways that the database principals you have created can access resources in the database.

At the database level, there are two main types of principals: the *user* and the *role*. We covered the basic user principal in the previous section and whether you use Windows Authentication or SQL Server standard authentication; and if you use the classic or the containment model, the database security aspects will be essentially the same.

The other principal we will establish as extremely important is a role, which is used to set up different functional roles and then assign a user or another role to them. The very best practice for assigning security to database principals is to always use roles, even if you have only a single user in a role. This practice may sound like more work, but in the end, it helps keep rights straight between your development and production environments (and all environments in between) and helps avoid users who end up with god-like powers from getting one permission here, another there, and so on. The roles will be the same in all areas, allowing most of your security code to be checked into source control and be testable. The only differences you should have between different environments come down to the different users who are associated with the roles in production, test, and so on. The roles remain the same, just who can see test data and who can drop a test table is usually very different from who can see production data and who can drop a production table.

Note   Most examples will not take the space to create a role to demonstrate what can be granted or denied to and from a principal. In every example, all permissions can be granted to a user or role server principal in exactly the same way, with the exact same result (the role can simply confer the rights to more than one additional principal).

In this section, I'll cover the following topics, which revolve around giving users permissions to use securables in a database:

- *Grantable permissions*: The different sorts of permissions you can grant to database resources and how to grant and revoke permissions on these securables.

- *Roles and schemas*: Groups of uses and groups of groups to grant rights efficiently to database securables.

These two topics will give you most of the information you need to get started setting up your database-level security.

Grantable Permissions

You can control rights to almost every object type in SQL Server. For our purposes of database design, I'll cover data-oriented security specifically, limited to the objects and the actions you can give or take away access to (see Table 10-1). There are also rights you can use to allow a user to make changes to a table (ALTER) or do anything that is available (CONTROL). If you want to give all of the listed permissions to a principal, use ALL instead of the permission name.

Table 10-1. *Database Objects and Permissions*

Object Type	Permission Type
Tables, views	SELECT, INSERT, UPDATE, DELETE, REFERENCES
Columns (view and table)	SELECT, INSERT, UPDATE, DELETE
Scalar functions	EXECUTE, REFERENCES
Table-valued functions (not all will apply in all functions)	SELECT, UPDATE, DELETE, INSERT, REFERENCES
Stored procedures	EXECUTE

Most of these are straightforward and probably are familiar if you've done any SQL Server administration, although perhaps REFERENCES isn't familiar as it is not used very often. Briefly, SELECT allows you to read data using a SELECT statement; INSERT allows you to add data, UPDATE to modify, and DELETE to remove data from a table. EXECUTE lets you execute coded objects, and REFERENCES allows objects that one user owns to reference another object owned by another via a foreign key or to be used by a schema-bound object, like a view or user-defined function. For 99.5% of databases that you will design for users, all objects should be owned by the same user, so REFERENCES is not needed but good to know about. For the other .5% of cases, the objects might be owned by different users, but you would probably not want to implement FOREIGN KEY constraints or use SCHEMABINDING between the tables. Hence, we will largely ignore the REFERENCES permission, but it is available.

As briefly mentioned earlier in this chapter for server and database permissions, you will use one of the three different statements to give rights to or take away rights from each of your roles:

- GRANT: Gives a right

- DENY: Disallows access to an object, regardless of any other associated grants

- REVOKE: Deletes a previously applied GRANT or DENY permission

To see the user's specific rights they have been granted in a database, you can use the sys.database_permissions catalog view. For example, use the following code to see all the rights that have been granted in the database:

```
SELECT  class_desc AS PermissionType,
        OBJECT_SCHEMA_NAME(major_id) + '.' + OBJECT_NAME(major_id)
                                                AS ObjectName,
        permission_name, state_desc, USER_NAME(grantee_principal_id)
                                                AS Grantee
FROM    sys.database_permissions;
```

Using that query in the master database, you will be able to see users that have CONNECT rights, as well as the different stored procedures and tables that you have access to.

If you want to see your or any user's effective rights in a database, the query for this is a bit more complicated and uses a system function fn_my_permissions. You can see this query in a blog I wrote in 2018 here: www.red-gate.com/simple-talk/blogs/calculating-a-security-principals-complete-effective-rights/.

Table Security

As already mentioned, for tables at an object level, you can grant principal rights to INSERT and UPDATE data in a table or DELETE or SELECT (or rarely REFERENCES) data from a table. This is the most basic form of security when dealing with data. The goal when using table-based security is to keep users looking at, or modifying, the entire set of data, rather than specific rows. We'll progress to the specific security types as we move through the chapter.

Note   In the context of security, a VIEW object will be treated just like a table in that you can grant INSERT, UPDATE, DELETE, and/or SELECT rights to the view, whether or not data represented by it is technically modifiable. Views have other considerations that will be covered later in this chapter.

As an example of table security, I will create a new TABLE object and demonstrate, through the use of a new user, what the user can and cannot do:

```
USE ClassicSecurityExample;
GO
--start with a new schema for this test and create a
--table for our demonstrations
CREATE SCHEMA TestPerms;
GO

CREATE TABLE TestPerms.TableExample
(
    TableExampleId int IDENTITY(1,1)
                CONSTRAINT PKTableExample PRIMARY KEY,
    Value   varchar(10)
);
```

Next, I create a new user, without associating it with a login. You won't need a login for many of the examples, because you'll use impersonation to pretend to be the user without logging in:

```
CREATE USER Tony WITHOUT LOGIN;
```

Note   The ability to have a user without login privileges allows you to have objects in the database that aren't actually associated with a login, making managing objects cleaner, particularly when you drop a login that was connected to a user or when you restore a database that has existing users but no login on the server.

I impersonate the user Tony and try to create a new row:

```
EXECUTE AS USER = 'Tony';

INSERT INTO TestPerms.TableExample(Value)
VALUES ('a new row');
```

Well, as you would (or, at least, will come to) expect, here's the result:

```
Msg 229, Level 14, State 5, Line 154
The INSERT permission was denied on the object 'TableExample', database
'ClassicSecurityExample', schema 'TestPerms'.
```

Now, I go back to the security context of the dbo using the REVERT command, giving the user rights to insert rows into the table:

```
REVERT; --return to admin user context
GRANT INSERT ON TestPerms.TableExample TO Tony;
GO
```

Then, I return to the security context of Tony and try to execute the INSERT statement again:

```
EXECUTE AS USER = 'Tony';

INSERT INTO TestPerms.TableExample(Value)
VALUES ('a new row');
```

No errors here. Now, because Tony just created the row, the user should be able to select the row, right?

```
SELECT TableExampleId, Value
FROM   TestPerms.TableExample;
```

No, creating some resource in SQL Server does not imply any ownership to the resource. The user had rights only to INSERT data, not to view it, so the following error will be raised:

```
Msg 229, Level 14, State 5, Line 168
The SELECT permission was denied on the object 'TableExample', database
'ClassicSecurityExample', schema 'TestPerms'.
```

Now, I can give the user Tony rights to SELECT data from the table using the following GRANT statement:

```
REVERT;
GRANT SELECT ON TestPerms.TableExample TO Tony;
```

Now that Tony has rights, I can successfully run the following:

```
EXECUTE AS USER = 'Tony';

SELECT TableExampleId, Value
FROM   TestPerms.TableExample;
```

```
REVERT;
```

The SELECT statement works and does return 'a new row' the user created. At the table level, you can do this individually for each of the four DML statement permission types INSERT, UPDATE, DELETE, and SELECT (or you can use GRANT ALL ON <objectName> TO <principal> to give all rights to the <objectName> to the <principal>). The goal is to give the users only what they need. For example, if the user happened to represent a device that was inserting readings, it wouldn't need to be able to read, modify, or destroy data, just create new rows.

Column-Level Security

For the most part, it's enough simply to limit a user's access at the level of either being able to use (or not use) the entire TABLE or VIEW object, but as the next two major sections of the chapter will discuss, sometimes the security needs to be more granular. Sometimes you need to restrict users to using merely part of a table. In this section, I'll present the security syntax that SQL Server provides at a basic level to grant rights at a column level. Later in this chapter, I'll present other methods that use VIEW or STORED PROCEDURE objects.

For our example, we'll create a couple of database users:

```
CREATE USER Employee WITHOUT LOGIN;
CREATE USER Manager WITHOUT LOGIN;
```

Then, we'll create a table to use for our column-level security examples—Product table. This Product table has the company's products, including the current price and the cost to produce this product:

```
CREATE SCHEMA Products;
GO
CREATE TABLE Products.Product
(
    ProductId    int NOT NULL IDENTITY CONSTRAINT PKProduct PRIMARY KEY,
    ProductCode varchar(10) NOT NULL
                                CONSTRAINT AKProduct_ProductCode UNIQUE,
    Description varchar(20) NOT NULL,
    UnitPrice   decimal(10,4) NOT NULL,
    ActualCost  decimal(10,4) NOT NULL
);
INSERT INTO Products.Product(ProductCode, Description,
                             UnitPrice, ActualCost)
VALUES ('widget12','widget number 12',10.50,8.50),
       ('snurf98','snurfulator',99.99,2.50);
```

Now, we want our employees to be able to see all the products, but we don't want them to see what each product costs to manufacture. The syntax is the same as using GRANT on a table, but we include in parentheses a comma-delimited list of the columns to which the user is being denied (or granted) access. In the next code block, we grant

SELECT rights to both users but take away these rights on the ActualCost column from the Employee user (in the real world, Employee would be a role with multiple users most likely):

```
GRANT SELECT on Products.Product to Employee,Manager;
DENY SELECT on Products.Product (ActualCost) to Employee;
```

To test our security, we impersonate the user Manager:

```
EXECUTE AS USER = 'Manager';
SELECT  *
FROM    Products.Product;
```

This returns all columns with no errors:

ProductId	ProductCode	Description	UnitPrice	ActualCost
1	widget12	widget number 12	10.5000	8.5000
2	snurf98	Snurfulator	99.9900	2.5000

Tip You may be thinking that it's bad practice to use SELECT * in a query. It's true that using SELECT * in your permanent code is a bad idea, but generally speaking, when writing ad hoc queries, almost everyone uses the * shorthand for all columns, and it is perfectly acceptable to do so. (It can save a trip to an occupational therapist for pain from too much typing, even using IntelliSense.)

The user Manager worked fine; what about the user Employee?

```
REVERT;--revert back to SA level user or you will get an error that the
        --user cannot do this operation because the Manager user doesn't
        --have rights to impersonate the Employee
GO
EXECUTE AS USER = 'Employee';
GO
SELECT *
FROM    Products.Product;
```

This returns the following result:

```
Msg 230, Level 14, State 1, Line 1
The SELECT permission was denied on the column 'ActualCost' of the object
'Product', database 'ClassicSecurityExample', schema 'Products'.
```

"Why did I get this error?" the user first asks. Then (and this is harder to explain), they ask, "How do I correct it?" You might try to explain to the user, "Well, just list all the columns you *do* have access to, without the columns you cannot see, like this":

```
SELECT ProductId, ProductCode, Description, UnitPrice
FROM    Products.Product;
REVERT;
```

This returns the following results for the user Employee:

```
ProductId    ProductCode Description           UnitPrice
-----------  ----------- --------------------- ----------------------------
1            widget12    widget number 12      10.5000
2            snurf98     Snurfulator           99.9900
```

The answer, although technically correct, isn't even vaguely what the user wants to hear. "So," the user asks, in a not exactly patient tone of voice, "every time I want to build an ad hoc query on the Product table which has 87 columns, I have to type out all the columns?"

This is why, for the most part, column-level security is rarely used as a primary security mechanism. You don't want users getting error messages when they try to run a simple query on a table. You might add column-level security to the table "just in case," but for the most part, use coded objects such as stored procedures or views to control access to certain columns. I'll discuss these solutions in the next section.

Roles

Core to the process of granting rights is determining whom to grant rights to and how to effectively grant them for easiest maintenance. The user is the lowest level of security principal in the database and can be mapped to a single login, certificate, or asymmetrical key or, as we have used already in examples, not mapped to anything.

(Users not mapped to anything can occur because either a user was created with the WITHOUT LOGIN option specifically for impersonation or they can be orphaned by dropped logins.)

Database roles are groups of database principals (users and other database roles) that allow you to grant object access to multiple database principals at once. Every user in a database is a member of at least the public role, which will be mentioned again in the "Built-in Database Roles" section, but may be a member of multiple roles. Roles themselves may be members of other roles. Roles provide us with a method of building reusable security grouping to make things that are similar in all environments the same without duplicating work.

In this section, I'll discuss the following types of roles:

- *Built-in database roles*: Roles that are provided by Microsoft as part of the system

- *User-defined database roles*: Roles, defined by you, that group Windows users together in a user-defined package of rights

- *Application roles*: Roles that are used to give an application specific rights, rather than giving rights to a group or individual user

Each of these types of roles is used to give rights to objects in a more convenient manner than granting them directly to an individual user. Many of the possible ways to implement roles (and all security, really) are based on the politics of how you get to set up security in your organization. There are many different ways to get it done, and a lot of it is determined by who will do the actual work. End users may need to give another user right to do some things, as a security team, network administrators, DBAs, and so on also dole out rights. The whole idea of setting up roles to group users is to lower the amount of work required to get things done and managed correctly.

Built-In Database Roles

As part of the basic structure of the database, Microsoft provides a set of nine built-in database roles that give a user a special set of rights at a database level. Note that none of these roles, including db_owner, prohibits the user from a DENY being used to prevent any right in the database. Users that are mapped to the dbo user in the database cannot be denied any action, but even membership in the db_owner role does not:

- db_owner: Users associated with this role can perform any activity in the database.

- db_accessadmin: Users associated with this role can add or remove users from the database.

- db_backupoperator: Users associated with this role are allowed to back up the database.

- db_datareader: Users associated with this role are allowed to read any data in any table.

- db_datawriter: Users associated with this role are allowed to write any data in any table.

- db_ddladmin: Users associated with this role are allowed to add, modify, or drop any objects in the database (in other words, execute DDL statements).

- db_denydatareader: Users associated with this role are denied the ability to see any data in the database, though they may still see the data through stored procedures through ownership chaining, which will be discussed later in the chapter.

- db_denydatawriter: Much like the db_denydatareader role, users associated with this role are denied the ability to modify any data in the database, though they still may modify data through stored procedures.

- db_securityadmin: Users associated with this role can modify and change permissions and roles in the database.

Of particular interest in these groups to many DBAs and developers are the db_datareader and db_datawriter roles. All too often these roles (or, unfortunately, the db_owner role) are the only permissions ever used (possibly with the addition of the database-level EXECUTE permission too). For almost any database, this should rarely be the case. Even when the bulk of the security is being managed by the user interface, there are going to be objects that you may not want users, or even the application, to be able to access. As an example, in my databases, I almost always have Utility and Monitoring schemas that I place objects in to implement certain database-level utility tasks. If I wanted to keep up with the counts of rows in tables on a daily basis, I would create a row in a table in the Monitoring schema each day with the row count of each table. If I wanted a procedure to drop all the constraints on a database for a given process, I would have a procedure in the Utility schema as well. If users accidentally execute that procedure instead of the benign query procedure they were trying to click, it is as much your fault as it is theirs.

The point is that security should be well planned out and managed in a thoughtful manner, not just managed by giving full access and hoping for the best from the user interface standpoint. As I will note in the upcoming "Schemas" section, instead of using the db_datareader fixed role, consider granting permissions at the schema level, like SELECT to give a principal rights to see all the data in all TABLE, table-valued USER DEFINED FUNCTION, and VIEW objects in a schema. If you do, any new schema added for some purpose will not automatically be accessible to everyone, but all of the objects in that schema (even new ones) will automatically get the existing schema permission. My goal is to limit fixed role use to utility users, perhaps an admin type, or on a rare occasion an ETL program's access that will not be doing any ad hoc queries that could be in error (after considerable testing, naturally).

User-Defined Database Roles

Just as you could at the server level, you can create your own database roles to grant rights to database objects. To a role, you can grant or deny the right to use tables and code in the database, as well as database-level rights such as ALTER, ALTER ANY USER, DELETE (from one table, a schema's tables, or any table in the database), CREATE ROLE, and so on. You can control rights to database management and data usage together in the same role package, rather than needing to grant users ownership of the database where they have unlimited power to make your day busy restoring from backups and fixing stuff that has been "inexplicably broken."

Roles should be used to create a set of database rights for a job description or perhaps an aspect of a job description. Take, for example, any typical human resources system that has employee information such as name, address, position, manager, pay grade, and so on. We'll likely need several roles, such as the following to cover all the common roles that individuals and some processes need to do their job:

- Administrators: Should be able to do any task with data, including ad hoc access; will also need rights to back up and restore the database on occasion (using a user interface, naturally).

- HRManagers: Should be able to do any task in the system with data.

- HRWorkers: Can maintain any attribute in the system, but approval rows are required to modify salary information.

- Managers: All managers in the company might be in a role like this, which might give them view rights to high-level corporate information. You can then limit them to only the ability to see the details for their own workers, using further techniques I'll present in the section "Using Specific-Purpose Views to Provide Row-Level Security" later in this chapter.

- Employees: Can see only their own information and can modify only their own personal address information.

Each of the roles would then be granted access to all the resources that they need. A member of the Managers role would likely also be a member of the Employees role. That way, the managers could see the information for their employees and also for themselves. Users can be members of multiple roles, and roles can be members of other roles.

Tip   Another method I have used is to have roles by database function, like SchemaName_Read SchemaName_Modify, and then push similarly named, role-oriented groups into the ActiveDirectory layer. Then I allow the ActiveDirectory management to grant database rights to different environments via Windows group membership.

Permissions are additive, so if a user is a member of three roles, the user has an effective set of permissions that's the union of all permissions of the groups, for example:

- Managers: Can view the Employees table

- Employees: Can view the Product table

- HRWorkers: Can see employment history

If the Managers role were a member of the Employees role, a member of the Managers role could do activities that were enabled by either role. If a user were a member of the HRWorkers role and the Employees role, the user could see employment history and the Product table (it might seem logical that users could see the Employees table, but this hasn't been explicitly set in our tiny example). If a manager decides that making the lives of others miserable is no longer any fun, as part of the demotion, that user would be removed from the Managers role.

I won't do it in this example, but you may then want to create a role titled TypeOfManager that is a member of all three roles. This would allow you to define the roles in the company to the level of employee is a member of TypeOfManager, and it covers all that you need. A SecondTypeOfManager may have several of the same role memberships, but also have a few more. Crafting a security configuration is complex, but once it is created and tested, it is a wonderful thing.

Programmatically, you can determine some basic information about a user's security information in the database with the following functions (we already mentioned the synonymous USER and USER_NAME() previously):

- IS_MEMBER('<role>'): Tells you whether the current user is the member of a given role. This is useful for building security-based views. You can also pass in a Windows group to see if the user is a member of that group.

- HAS_PERMS_BY_NAME: Lets you interrogate the security system to see what rights a user has. This function has a complex public interface, but it's powerful and useful.

You can use these functions in applications and T-SQL code to determine at runtime what the user can do. For example, if you wanted only HRManager members to execute a procedure, you could check this:

```
SELECT IS_MEMBER('HRManager');
```

A return value of 1 means the user is a member of the role (0 means not a member, and NULL means the role doesn't exist). A procedure might start out like the following:

```
IF (SELECT IS_MEMBER('HRManager')) = 0 or (SELECT IS_MEMBER('HRManager'))
IS NULL
        SELECT 'I..DON''T THINK SO!';
```

This prevents even the database owner from executing the procedure, though dbo users can obviously get the code for the procedure and execute it if they're desirous enough (the "Auditing SQL Server Use" section of this chapter covers some security precautions to handle nosy DBA types), though this is generally a hard task to make bulletproof enough, so it is best to have more than one DBA if you really need to keep things safe.

For example, in our HR system, if you wanted to remove access to the SalaryHistory table just from the Employees role, you wouldn't deny access to the Employees role, because managers are employees also and would need to have rights to the SalaryHistory table. To deal with this sort of change, you might have to revoke rights to the Employees role and then give rights to the other groups, rather than deny rights to a group that has lots of members.

As an example, consider that you have three users in the database:

```
CREATE USER Addi WITHOUT LOGIN;
CREATE USER Aria WITHOUT LOGIN;
CREATE USER Amanda WITHOUT LOGIN;
```

Aria and Amanda are members of the HRWorkers role, so you add the following:

```
CREATE ROLE HRWorkers;

ALTER ROLE HRWorkers ADD MEMBER Aria;
ALTER ROLE HRWorkers ADD MEMBER Amanda;
```

Tip   In SQL Server 2012, ALTER ROLE replaced sp_addrolemember, which was deprecated. Use ALTER ROLE as you write new code not just because sp_addrolemember is deprecated, but because it is much easier to remember syntax.

Next, you have a Payroll schema, and in this is an EmployeeSalary table:

```
CREATE SCHEMA Payroll;
GO
CREATE TABLE Payroll.EmployeeSalary
(
    EmployeeId  int NOT NULL CONSTRAINT PKEmployeeSalary PRIMARY KEY,
    SalaryAmount decimal(12,2) NOT NULL
);
GRANT SELECT ON Payroll.EmployeeSalary to HRWorkers;
```

Next, test the users:

```
EXECUTE AS USER = 'Addi';

SELECT *
FROM    Payroll.EmployeeSalary;
```

This returns the following error, because Addi isn't a member of this group:

```
Msg 229, Level 14, State 5, Line 253
The SELECT permission was denied on the object 'EmployeeSalary', database
'ClassicSecurityExample', schema 'Payroll'.
```

However, change over to Aria:

```
REVERT;
EXECUTE AS USER = 'Aria';

SELECT *
FROM    Payroll.EmployeeSalary;
```

You will find that Aria can view the data of tables in the Payroll schema because Aria is a member of the role that was granted SELECT permissions to the table:

```
EmployeeId  SalaryAmount
----------- ---------------------------------------
```

Roles are almost always the best way to apply security in a database because they can be tested and made the same in different environments. To keep this section reasonable, I won't extend the example to include multiple roles, but a user can be a member of many roles, and the user gets the cumulative effect of the chosen rights.

There's one notable exception: one DENY operation prevents another's GRANT operations from applying. Say Amanda has had rights to the EmployeeSalary table denied:

```
REVERT; --back to admin rights
DENY SELECT ON Payroll.EmployeeSalary TO Amanda;
```

If Amanda now tried to execute a SELECT statement on the data in the EmployeeSalary table

```
EXECUTE AS USER = 'Amanda';
SELECT *
FROM    Payroll.EmployeeSalary;
```

access would be denied:

```
Msg 229, Level 14, State 5, Line 2
The SELECT permission was denied on the object 'EmployeeSalary', database
'ClassicSecurityExample', schema 'Payroll'.
```

This denial of access is true even though Amanda was granted rights via the HRWorkers group. This, plus what you will see when we reach the T-SQL coded objects section, adds up to why DENY is generally not used much. Rarely will you use DENY because it is almost punitive, rather than a control, if for no other reason than keeping up with the rights can be too difficult. You might apply DENY to a sensitive table or procedure to be certain it wasn't used, but only in limited cases.

If you want to know from which tables the user can SELECT, you can use a query such as the following while in the context of the user. Reverting to your sysadmin login-based user, executing this query will return the three tables we have created so far in this database. A bit more interesting is what happens when I check the permissions when the user is Aria:

```
REVERT ;
EXECUTE AS USER = 'Aria';

--note, this query only returns rows for tables where the user has SOME
rights
SELECT   TABLE_SCHEMA + '.' + TABLE_NAME AS tableName,
         HAS_PERMS_BY_NAME(TABLE_SCHEMA + '.' + TABLE_NAME,
                            'OBJECT', 'SELECT') AS AllowSelect,
         HAS_PERMS_BY_NAME(TABLE_SCHEMA + '.' + TABLE_NAME,
                            'OBJECT', 'INSERT') AS AllowInsert
FROM     INFORMATION_SCHEMA.TABLES;
REVERT ; --so you will be back to sysadmin rights for next code
```

This returns

TableName	AllowSelect	AllowInsert
Payroll.EmployeeSalary	1	0

User `Aria` has rights to see the tables we have created and has only `SELECT` rights (you can easily extend this for `UPDATE` and `DELETE` rights as well, not to mention `EXECUTE` for coded objects). Applications that use direct access to the tables can use a query such as this to determine what actions users can do and adjust the user interface to match their rights. Finally, you will need to use `REVERT` to go back to the security context of the power user to continue to the next examples.

Tip   `HAS_PERMS_BY_NAME` can be used to see if a user has rights to a column as well. If you choose to use column-level security, you could use this to generate `SELECT` statements for your user.

Application Roles

Developers commonly like to set up applications using a single login and then manage security in the applications. This can be an adequate way to implement security, but it requires you to recreate all the login stuff, when you could use simple Windows Authentication to check whether a user can execute an application. Application roles let you use the SQL Server login facilities to manage who a person is and if that person has rights to the database and then let the application perform the finer points of security.

To be honest, this can be a nice mix, because the hardest part of implementing security isn't restricting a person's ability to do an activity; it's nicely letting them know by hiding actions they cannot do. I've shown you a few of the security catalog views already, and there are more in the Microsoft Docs article "System Catalog Views (Transact-SQL)" located here: `docs.microsoft.com/en-us/sql/relational-databases/system-catalog-views/security-catalog-views-transact-sql`. Using them, you can query the database to see what a user can do to help facilitate this process. However, it isn't a trivial task and is often considered too much trouble, especially for homegrown applications.

An application role is almost analogous to using EXECUTE AS to set rights to another user, but instead of a person, the user is an application. You change to the context of the application role using sp_setapprole. You grant the application role permissions just like any other role, by using the GRANT statement.

As an example of using an application role, create both a user named Bob and an application role and give them totally different rights. The TestPerms schema was created earlier, so if you didn't create it before, go ahead and do so:

```
CREATE TABLE TestPerms.BobCan
(
    BobCanId int NOT NULL IDENTITY(1,1) CONSTRAINT PKBobCan PRIMARY KEY,
    Value varchar(10) NOT NULL
);
CREATE TABLE TestPerms.AppCan
(
    AppCanId int NOT NULL IDENTITY(1,1) CONSTRAINT PKAppCan PRIMARY KEY,
    Value varchar(10) NOT NULL
);
```

Now, create the user Bob to correspond to the BobCan table:

```
CREATE USER Bob WITHOUT LOGIN;
```

Next, give the user Bob SELECT rights to the BobCan table:

```
GRANT SELECT on TestPerms.BobCan to Bob;
GO
```

Finally, create an application role, and give it rights to its table:

```
CREATE APPLICATION ROLE AppCan_application with password =
'39292LjAsll2$3';
GO
GRANT SELECT on TestPerms.AppCan to AppCan_application;
```

One of the drawbacks to using an application role is that it requires a password. This password is passed in clear text to the SQL Server, so make sure that, first, the password is complex and, second, you encrypt any connections that might be using this. There is an encryption option that will obfuscate the password, but it is only available with an ODBC or OLE DB client.

CHAPTER 10   DATABASE SECURITY AND SECURITY PATTERNS

Next, set the user you're working as to Bob and try to retrieve data from the BobCan table:

```
EXECUTE AS USER = 'Bob';
SELECT * FROM TestPerms.BobCan;
```

It works with no error:

```
BobCanId      Value
-----------   ----------
```

However, try retrieving data from the AppCan table:

```
SELECT * FROM TestPerms.AppCan;
```

The following error is returned:

```
Msg 229, Level 14, State 5, Line 315
The SELECT permission was denied on the object 'AppCan', database
'ClassicSecurityExample', schema 'TestPerms'.
```

This isn't surprising, because Bob has no permissions on the AppCan table. Next, still in the context of user Bob, use the sp_setapprole procedure to change the security context of the user to the application role, and the security is reversed. You can execute this in the same connection, but you cannot easily unset the approle. These next few statements can also be done from a different connection:

```
EXECUTE sp_setapprole 'AppCan_application', '39292LjAsll2$3';
GO
SELECT * FROM TestPerms.BobCan;
```

This returns the following error:

```
Msg 229, Level 14, State 5, Line 1
The SELECT permission was denied on the object 'BobCan', database
'ClassicSecurityExample', schema 'TestPerms'.
```

That's because you're now in the context of the application role, and the application role doesn't have rights to the table. Finally, the application role can read from the AppCan table:

```
SELECT * from TestPerms.AppCan;
```

This doesn't return an error:

```
AppCanId     Value
----------- ----------
```

When you're in the application role context, you look to the database as if you're the application, not your user, as evidenced by the following code:

```
SELECT USER AS UserName;
```

This returns the following result:

```
UserName
--------------------
AppCan_application
```

Once you've executed sp_setapprole, the security stays as this role until you disconnect from the SQL Server or execute sp_unsetapprole. However, sp_unsetapprole doesn't work nearly as elegantly as REVERT, because you need to have a "cookie" value stored to be able to go back to your previous database security context.

Note   If you have been following along with the code, you will likely need to disconnect and reconnect at this point, because you will be stuck in the application role state.

To demonstrate, log back in as your sysadmin role user:

```
USE ClassicSecurityExample;
--Note that this must be executed as a single batch because of the variable
--for the cookie
DECLARE @cookie varbinary(8000);
```

```
EXECUTE sp_setapprole 'AppCan_application', '39292LjAsll2$3'
                , @fCreateCookie = true, @cookie = @cookie OUTPUT;

SELECT @cookie as Cookie;
SELECT USER as BeforeUnsetApprole;

EXEC sp_unsetapprole @cookie;

SELECT USER as AfterUnsetApprole;

REVERT; --done with this user
```

This returns the following results:

```
Cookie
-------------------------------------------------------------------
0x39881A28E9FB46A0A002ABA31C11B7F4C149D8CB2BCF99B7863FFF729E2BE48F...

BeforeUnsetApprole
---------------------------------------------------AppCan_application

AfterUnsetApprole
---------------------------------------------------------------dbo
```

The cookie is an interesting value, much larger than a GUID—it is declared as varbinary(8000) in Books Online, even though the current value is considerably less wide. It does change for each execution of the batch. The fact is it is fairly unlikely to want to unset the application role for most usages.

Schemas

Schemas were introduced and used heavily in the previous chapters, and up to this point, they've been used merely as a method to group like objects. Logical grouping is an important usage of schemas, but it is only the first step. Using these logical groups to apply security is where they really pay off. A user owns a schema, and a user can also own multiple schemas. For almost any database that you'll develop for a system, the best practice is to let all schemas be owned by the dbo system user, but put none of the objects in the dbo schema.

Now, instead of the reasonably useless dbo prefix being attached to all objects representing the owner, you can nicely group together objects of a common higher purpose and then (because this is a security chapter) grant rights to users at a schema level, rather than at an individual object level.

For our database design purposes, we will typically assign rights for users to use the following:

- Tables

- Views

- Synonyms (which can represent any of these things and more)

- Functions

- Procedures

You can grant rights to other types of objects, including user-defined aggregates, queues, and XML schema collections, but I won't cover them here. As an example, in the WideWorldImporters database, use the following query of the sys.objects catalog view (which reflects schema-scoped objects):

```
USE WideWorldImporters; --or whatever name you have given it
GO
SELECT  SCHEMA_NAME(schema_id) AS schema_name, type_desc, COUNT(*)
FROM    sys.objects
WHERE   type_desc IN ('SQL_STORED_PROCEDURE','CLR_STORED_PROCEDURE',
                      'SQL_SCALAR_FUNCTION','CLR_SCALAR_FUNCTION',
                      'CLR_TABLE_VALUED_FUNCTION','SYNONYM',
                      'SQL_INLINE_TABLE_VALUED_FUNCTION',
                      'SQL_TABLE_VALUED_FUNCTION','USER_TABLE','VIEW')
GROUP BY  SCHEMA_NAME(schema_id), type_desc
ORDER BY schema_name;
GO
USE ClassicSecurityExample;
```

This query shows how many of each object can be found in the version of the WideWorldImporters database in each schema you have on your development machine. As shown in syntax previously in this chapter, to grant privileges to a schema to a role or user, you prefix the schema name with SCHEMA:: to indicate the type of object you are granting to. To give the users full usage rights to all these, you can use the following command:

```
GRANT EXECUTE, SELECT, INSERT, UPDATE, DELETE ON
                          SCHEMA::<schemaname> to <database_principal>;
```

By using schemas and roles liberally, the complexity of granting rights to users on database objects can be reduced. That's because, instead of having to make sure rights are granted to 10 or even 100 stored procedures to support your application's Customer section, you need just a single line of code:

```
GRANT EXECUTE on SCHEMA::Customer to CustomerSupport;
```

Bam! Every user in the CustomerSupport role now can execute all stored procedures in this schema. Nicer still is that even new objects added to the schema at a later date will be automatically accessible to people with rights at the schema level. Naturally this does take some care to make sure that any sensitive data in the schema isn't given out accidentally because of this setup, so make sure and design the security you need and not just follow the simplest pattern you come across.

For example, create a user named Tom; then, grant user Tom SELECT rights on the TestPerms schema created in a previous section:

```
CREATE USER Tom WITHOUT LOGIN;
GRANT SELECT ON SCHEMA::TestPerms TO Tom;
```

Immediately, Tom has rights to view data from the tables that have been created:

```
EXECUTE AS USER = 'Tom';
GO
SELECT * FROM TestPerms.AppCan;
GO
REVERT;
```

But also, Tom gets rights to the new table that we create here:

```
CREATE TABLE TestPerms.SchemaGrant
(
    SchemaGrantId int CONSTRAINT PK SchemaGrant PRIMARY KEY
);
```

```
GO
EXECUTE AS USER = 'Tom';
GO
SELECT * FROM TestPerms.SchemaGrant;
GO
REVERT;
```

Essentially, a set statement like GRANT SELECT ON SCHEMA::SchemaName is a much better way to give a user read rights to the database than using the db_datareader fixed database role, especially if you use schemas. This ensures that if a new schema is created and some users shouldn't have access, they will not automatically get access, but it also ensures that users get access to all new tables that they should get access to.

Controlling Access to Data via T-SQL Coded Objects

Just using database-level security DDL in SQL Server allows you to give a user rights to access only certain objects, but it doesn't give you fine-grained control. For example, if you want to let a user join to a table to get a value but not to browse the entire table using a SELECT statement, this would be very difficult using table-/object-level and even row-level security alone. However, by using T-SQL coded objects in a very similar manner as we have already done using views for row-level security, it is very possible.

Now, we get down to the business of taking complete control over database access by using the following types of objects:

- *Stored procedures and scalar functions*: These objects give users an API to the database, and then, the DBA can control security based on what the procedure does.

- *Views and table-valued functions*: In cases where the tools being used can't use stored procedures, you can still use views to present an interface to the data that appears to the user as a normal table would. In terms of security, views and table-valued functions can be used for partitioning data vertically by hiding columns or, as seen earlier, horizontally by providing row-level security.

I put stored procedures together with views and functions in this section because whichever option you choose, you will still have accomplished the separation of interface from implementation. As long as the contract between the stored procedure or view is what the developer or application is coding or being coded to, the decision of which option to select will offer different sorts of benefits.

One fundamental concept that we need to introduce at this point is *ownership chaining*. Controlling security with coded objects requires an understanding of how ownership affects rights to objects. For example, if a user owns a SCHEMA and in the SCHEMA there is a STORED PROCEDURE object and it uses other objects that are in the same SCHEMA or another one that is owned by the same database principal, any user that the owner gives rights to to execute the STORED PROCEDURE doesn't need direct rights to the other objects.

As long as the owner or the object owns all the schemas for all the objects that are referenced, the ownership chain isn't broken, and any user granted rights to use the object can see any referenced data. If you break the ownership chain and reference data in a schema not owned by the same user, the user will require rights granted directly to the referenced object, instead of the object being created. This concept of the ownership chain is at the heart of why controlling object access via coded objects is so nice.

For example, say we have table S.T and a view that is defined as CREATE VIEW S.V AS SELECT C FROM S.T;. If a user has rights to view S.V, as long as the tables referenced in the view (in this case S.T) are owned by the same database principal, no rights are needed on the objects used. This allows us to use coded objects to control access to objects situationally.

Stored Procedures and Scalar Functions

Security in STORED PROCEDURE and FUNCTION objects is always at the object level (though the row-level security policies that we will cover later in the chapter will be enforced). Using STORED PROCEDURE and SCALAR FUNCTION objects to apply security is quite nice because you can give the user rights to do many operations without the user having rights to do the same operations on their own or even knowing how they're done.

In some companies, STORED PROCEDURE objects are used as the primary security mechanism, requiring that all access to the server be done without executing a single ad hoc or "raw" DML statement against the database. By building code that encapsulates all functionality, you then can apply permissions to the stored procedures to restrict what the user can do.

In security terms only, this allows you to have *situational control* over access to a table. This means that you might have two different procedures that functionally do the same operation, but giving a user rights to one procedure doesn't imply rights to the other. (I will discuss more about the pros and cons of different access methods in Chapter 13, but in this chapter, I will limit the discussion to the security aspects.)

Take, for example, the case where a form is built using one procedure. The user might be able to do an action, such as deleting a row from a specific table, but when the user goes to a different application window that allows deleting 100 rows, that ability might be denied. What makes this even nicer is that with decent naming of your objects, you can give end users or managers rights to dole out security based on actions they want their employees to have, without needing the IT staff to handle it.

I will create a new SCHEMA and TABLE object for this demonstration:

```
CREATE SCHEMA ProcTest;
GO
CREATE TABLE ProcTest.Misc
(
    GeneralValue varchar(20),
    SecretValue varchar(20)
);
GO
INSERT INTO ProcTest.Misc (GeneralValue, SecretValue)
VALUES ('somevalue','secret'),
       ('anothervalue','secret');
```

Next, we will create a STORED PROCEDURE object to return the values from the GeneralValue column in the table, not the SecretValue column, and then grant rights to the ProcUser user to execute the procedure:

```
CREATE PROCEDURE ProcTest.Misc$Select
AS
    SELECT GeneralValue
    FROM   ProcTest.Misc;
GO
```

Now I will create a new user for the demonstration and grant rights to execute the new procedure:

```
CREATE USER ProcUser WITHOUT LOGIN;
GRANT EXECUTE on ProcTest.Misc$Select to ProcUser;
```

After that, we change the context to the ProcUser user and try to SELECT from the table:

```
EXECUTE AS USER = 'ProcUser';
GO
SELECT GeneralValue , SecretValue
FROM    ProcTest.Misc;
```

We get the following error message, because the user hasn't been given rights to access this table:

```
Msg 229, Level 14, State 5, Line 768
The SELECT permission was denied on the object 'Misc', database
'ClassicSecurityExample', schema 'ProcTest'.
```

Next, execute the following procedure:

```
EXECUTE ProcTest.Misc$Select;
```

This returns the expected result that the user does have access to execute the procedure, and executing it does allow us to see the data in the table:

```
GeneralValue
--------------------
somevalue
anothervalue
```

This is one of the best ways to architect a database solution, both for security and for performance. It leaves a well-named, manageable surface area, providing a lot of control over what T-SQL is executed in the database (much easier to performance tune!), and lets you control security nicely. (For performance, it allows caching of complex plans and having a known set of queries to tune, but more on that in Chapter 13.)

You can see what kinds of access a user has to STORED PROCEDURE objects by executing the following statement:

```
SELECT SCHEMA_NAME(schema_id) +'.' + name AS ProcedureName
FROM    sys.procedures;

REVERT;
```

While in the context of the ProcUser, you will see the one row for the ProcTest. Misc$Select procedure returned. If you were using only stored procedures to access the data, this query could be executed by the application programmer to know everything the user can do in the database.

Tip If you don't like using stored procedures as your access layer, I know you can probably make a list of reasons why you disagree with this practice. However, as I mentioned, this is largely considered a best practice in the SQL Server community because of not only the security aspects of stored procedures but also the basic encapsulation reasons I will discuss in Chapter 13. A lot of applications using object-relational mapping layers will not work with stored procedures, at least not in "easy" mode, which would mean a noticeable drop-off in coding performance, leading to unhappy managers, no matter what the future benefit may be.

Impersonation Within Objects

I already talked about the EXECUTE AS statement, and it has some great applications, but there is a WITH EXECUTE clause that you can use on an object declaration which you can use to get incredible flexibility to give the executer greater powers than might not have been possible otherwise, certainly not without granting additional rights. Instead of changing context before an operation, you can change context as part of the DML declaration for a STORED PROCEDURE, SCALAR FUNCTION, or DML TRIGGER object (plus queues for Service Broker, but I won't be covering that topic). Unfortunately, the WITH EXECUTE clause is not available for views, because they are not technically executable objects (hence the reason why you grant SELECT rights and not EXECUTE ones).

By adding the following clause to the object, you can change the security context of a procedure to a different server or database principal when the execution begins:

```
CREATE <objectType> <schemaName>.<objectName>
WITH EXECUTE AS <'UserName' | CALLER | SELF | OWNER >;
```

The different options for whom to execute as are as follows:

- 'UserName': This is a specific database user principal.

- CALLER: The context of the user who called the procedure. This is the default security context you get when executing an object.

- SELF: It's in the context of the user who created the procedure. You can see who self will represent by looking in sys.sql_modules at the execute_as_principal_id column.

- OWNER: It's executed in the context of the owner of the module or schema.

Note that using EXECUTE AS doesn't affect the ownership chaining of the call. The security of the statements in the object is still based on the security of the schema owner. Only when the ownership chain is broken will the EXECUTE AS setting come into play. The following statements go along with the EXECUTE AS clause:

- EXECUTE AS CALLER: If you are using a security context other than EXECUTE AS CALLER, you can execute this in your code to go back to the default, where access is as the user who actually executed the object.

- REVERT: This reverts security to the security specified in the WITH EXECUTE AS clause.

Basic Impersonation Example

As an example, I'll show you how to build a scenario where one schema owner contains a table and another schema owner has a table and a procedure that the schema owner wants to use to access the first user's table. Finally, the scenario has an average user who wants to execute the stored procedure.

This first example is not intended as a "best practice," but rather as an example of how ownership chaining and impersonation work with objects. Ideally, all objects are owned by the database owner for typical databases. Of course, not all databases are typical, so your usage may differ. Also note that I switch context of user several times to get different kinds of ownership chaining to occur. It can be tricky, which is why the first sentence of this paragraph is what it is!

First, create a few users and give them rights to create objects in the database. The three users are named as follows:

- SchemaOwner: This user owns the schema where one of the objects resides.

- ProcedureOwner: This user is owner of a table and a stored procedure.

- AveSchlub: This is the average user who finally wants to use ProcedureOwner's stored procedure.

So now create these users and grant them rights:

```
--this will be the owner of the primary schema
CREATE USER SchemaOwner WITHOUT LOGIN;
GRANT CREATE SCHEMA TO SchemaOwner;
GRANT CREATE TABLE TO SchemaOwner;

--this will be the procedure creator
CREATE USER ProcedureOwner WITHOUT LOGIN;
GRANT CREATE SCHEMA TO ProcedureOwner;
GRANT CREATE PROCEDURE TO ProcedureOwner;
GRANT CREATE TABLE TO ProcedureOwner;
GO

--this will be the average user who needs to access data
CREATE USER AveSchlub WITHOUT LOGIN;
```

Then, change to the context of the main object owner, create a new SCHEMA, and create a TABLE object with some rows:

```
EXECUTE AS USER = 'SchemaOwner';
GO
CREATE SCHEMA SchemaOwnersSchema;
GO
CREATE TABLE SchemaOwnersSchema.Person
```

```
(
    PersonId    int NOT NULL CONSTRAINT PKPerson PRIMARY KEY,
    FirstName   varchar(20) NOT NULL,
    LastName    varchar(20) NOT NULL
);
GO
INSERT INTO SchemaOwnersSchema.Person
VALUES (1, 'Phil','Mutayblin'),
       (2, 'Del','Eets');
```

Next, this user gives SELECT permissions to the ProcedureOwner user:

```
GRANT SELECT ON SchemaOwnersSchema.Person TO ProcedureOwner;
```

After that, set context to the secondary user to create the TABLE and PROCEDURE object:

```
REVERT;--we can step back on the stack of principals,
       --but we can't change directly to ProcedureOwner without giving
       --ShemaOwner impersonation rights. Here I step back to the db_owner
       --user you have used throughout the chapter
GO
EXECUTE AS USER = 'ProcedureOwner';
```

Then, create a SCHEMA and another TABLE object, owned by the ProcedureOwner user, and add some simple data for the demonstration:

```
CREATE SCHEMA ProcedureOwnerSchema;
GO
CREATE TABLE ProcedureOwnerSchema.OtherPerson
(
    PersonId    int NOT NULL CONSTRAINT PKOtherPerson PRIMARY KEY,
    FirstName   varchar(20) NOT NULL,
    LastName    varchar(20) NOT NULL
);
GO
INSERT INTO ProcedureOwnerSchema.OtherPerson
VALUES (1, 'DB','Smith');
```

```
INSERT INTO ProcedureOwnerSchema.OtherPerson
VALUES (2, 'Dee','Leater');
```

You can see the owners of the objects and their schema using the following query of the catalog views:

```
REVERT;

SELECT tables.name AS TableName, schemas.name AS SchemaName,
       database_principals.name AS OwnerName
FROM   sys.tables
          JOIN sys.schemas
            ON tables.schema_id = schemas.schema_id
          JOIN sys.database_principals
            ON database_principals.principal_id = schemas.principal_id
WHERE  tables.name IN ('Person','OtherPerson');
```

This returns the following:

TableName	SchemaName	OwnerName
OtherPerson	ProcedureOwnerSchema	ProcedureOwner
Person	SchemaOwnersSchema	SchemaOwner

Next, create two STORED PROCEDURE objects as the ProcedureOwner user, one for the WITH EXECUTE AS CALLER, which is the default, and then another for SELF, which puts it in the context of the creator, in this case ProcedureOwner:

```
EXECUTE AS USER = 'ProcedureOwner';
GO

CREATE PROCEDURE ProcedureOwnerSchema.Person$asCaller
WITH EXECUTE AS CALLER --this is the default
AS
BEGIN
   SELECT  PersonId, FirstName, LastName
   FROM    ProcedureOwnerSchema.OtherPerson; --<-- ownership same as proc
```

```
   SELECT  PersonId, FirstName, LastName
   FROM    SchemaOwnersSchema.Person;  --<-- breaks ownership chain
END;
GO

CREATE PROCEDURE ProcedureOwnerSchema.Person$asSelf
WITH EXECUTE AS SELF --now this runs in context of procedureOwner,
                    --since it created it
AS
BEGIN
   SELECT  PersonId, FirstName, LastName
   FROM    ProcedureOwnerSchema.OtherPerson; --<-- ownership same as proc

   SELECT  PersonId, FirstName, LastName
   FROM    SchemaOwnersSchema.Person;  --<-- breaks ownership chain
END;
```

Next, grant rights on the procedure to the AveSchlub user:

```
GRANT EXECUTE ON ProcedureOwnerSchema.Person$asCaller TO AveSchlub;
GRANT EXECUTE ON ProcedureOwnerSchema.Person$asSelf TO AveSchlub;
```

Then, change to the context of the AveSchlub:

```
REVERT; EXECUTE AS USER = 'AveSchlub'; --If you receive error about not
                         --being able to impersonate another user, it means
                         --you are not executing as dbo..
```

Finally, execute the procedure:

```
--this proc is in context of the caller, in this case, AveSchlub
EXECUTE ProcedureOwnerSchema.Person$asCaller;
```

This produces the following output, because the ownership chain is fine for the ProcedureOwnerSchema object, but not for the SchemaOwnersSchema:

PersonId	FirstName	LastName
1	DB	Smith
2	Dee	Leater

```
Msg 229, Level 14, State 5, Procedure person$asCaller, Line 7
The SELECT permission was denied on the object 'Person', database
'ClassicSecurityExample', schema 'SchemaOwnersSchema'.
```

Next, execute the asSelf variant:

```
--procedureOwner, so it works
EXECUTE ProcedureOwnerSchema.Person$asSelf;
```

This returns two result sets:

PersonId	FirstName	LastName
1	DB	Smith
2	Dee	Leater

PersonId	FirstName	LastName
1	Phil	Mutayblin
2	Del	Eets

What makes this different is that when the ownership chain is broken, the security context you're in is the ProcedureOwner, not the context of the caller, AveSchlub. Using EXECUTE AS to change security context is a cool, powerful feature. Now, you can give users temporary rights that won't even be apparent to them and won't require granting any permissions.

However, EXECUTE AS isn't a feature that should be overused, and its use should definitely be monitored during code reviews! It can be all too easy just to build your procedures in the context of the dbo and forget about decent security altogether. And that is the "nice" reason for taking care in using the feature. Another reason to take care is that a malicious programmer could (if they were devious or stupid) include dangerous code that would run as if it were the database owner, which could certainly cause undesired effects.

For example, using impersonation is a simple way to implement dynamic SQL calls without having to worry about ownership chaining (I will discuss this more in Chapter 13 when I discuss code-level design, but generally these are calls that are formed as textual queries in your stored procedures, rather than being compiled), but if you aren't careful to secure your code against an injection attack, the attack might just be in the context of the database owner rather than the basic application user that *should* have only limited rights if you have listened to anything I have said so far in this chapter.

Temporary Rights Elevation

One thing that you can do with this EXECUTE AS technique is to give a user super-rights temporarily in a database. For example, consider the following procedure:

```
REVERT;
GO
CREATE PROCEDURE dbo.TestCreateTableRights
AS
 BEGIN
    DROP TABLE IF EXISTS dbo.Test;
    CREATE TABLE dbo.Test
    (
        TestId int
    );
 END;
```

This procedure isn't executable by any users other than one who has CREATE TABLE rights in the database, even if they have rights to execute the procedure. Say we have the following USER and give rights to execute the STORED PROCEDURE object:

```
CREATE USER Leroy WITHOUT LOGIN;
GRANT EXECUTE on dbo.TestCreateTableRights to Leroy;
```

Note that you grant *only* rights to the dbo.TestCreateTableRights procedure. The user Leroy can execute the one STORED PROCEDURE object:

```
EXECUTE AS USER = 'Leroy';
EXECUTE dbo.TestCreateTableRights;
```

The result is as follows, because creating a table is a database permission that Leroy doesn't have, either explicitly granted or as a member of a db_owner's role:

```
Msg 262, Level 14, State 1, Procedure testDboRights, Line 5
CREATE TABLE permission denied in database 'ClassicSecurityExample'.
```

To make the procedure work, you could use EXECUTE AS 'dbo', which would give the procedure right to do anything in the database, or you could create a user and give it rights to do what you want, for example:

```
REVERT;
CREATE USER DboTableCreator WITHOUT LOGIN;
GRANT CREATE TABLE TO DboTableCreator; --lets user create a table at all
GRANT ALTER ON SCHEMA::dbo TO DboTableCreator; -- allows them to in dbo
```

Now, recreate the stored procedure with EXECUTE AS 'DboTableCreator', and when the procedure is executed, the result is that the table is dropped and recreated:

```
ALTER PROCEDURE dbo.TestCreateTableRights
WITH EXECUTE AS 'DboTableCreator'
AS
 BEGIN
    DROP TABLE IF EXISTS dbo.Test;
    CREATE TABLE dbo.Test
    (
        TestId int
    );
 END;
```

Now, you can execute this procedure and have it create the table. Run the procedure twice, and it will drop the existing table and recreate it. For more detailed information about the EXECUTE AS clause, check the "EXECUTE AS Clause (Transact-SQL)" topic in Microsoft Docs (docs.microsoft.com/en-us/sql/t-sql/statements/execute-as-clause-transact-sql).

Tip   As will be discussed in the "Crossing Database Lines" section later in this chapter, to use external resources (like a table in a different database) using impersonation of a database principal, you need to set TRUSTWORTHY to ON using the ALTER DATABASE command.

Views and Table-Valued Functions

Views and table-valued functions share security aspects with executable coded objects but behave in most contexts like tables. Views, as discussed in previous chapters, allow you to form pseudotables from other table sources, sometimes by adding tables together and sometimes by splitting a table up into smaller chunks. You can use views to provide an encapsulation layer that looks like tables to the user (and using triggers as we discussed in Chapter 7 can almost always be programmed to behave like actual tables with enough work). Table-valued functions are very similar to views, but the data they return cannot be modified even when they are of the simple, single-statement, single-table variety.

In this section, I'll briefly discuss a few ways for views and table-valued functions to encapsulate data in a manner that leaves the data in table-like structures. You might use views and table-valued functions in concert with, or in lieu of, a full stored procedure approach to application architecture. In this section, the goal is to "hide" data, like a column, from users or hide certain rows in a table, providing data security by keeping the data out of the view of the user in question.

Instead of the more up-front programming-heavy stored procedure methods from the previous section, in this section, I will discuss simply accessing VIEW and TABLE VALUED FUNCTION objects.

We'll use two properties of VIEW objects to build a more secure database. The first is to assign privileges to users such that they can use a view, though not the underlying tables. For example, let's go back to the Products.Product table used earlier in this chapter. As a reminder, execute this statement (after executing REVERT, if you haven't already, from the previous example):

```
SELECT *
FROM    Products.Product;
```

The following data is returned (if you have additional rows from testing, delete them now; a statement to do so is provided in the download):

This returns all columns with no errors:

ProductId	ProductCode	Description	UnitPrice	ActualCost
1	widget12	widget number 12	10.5000	8.5000
2	snurf98	Snurfulator	99.9900	2.5000

We could construct a VIEW object such as

```
CREATE VIEW Products.AllProducts
AS
SELECT ProductId,ProductCode, Description,
       UnitPrice, ActualCost
FROM   Products.Product;
```

Selecting data from either the table or the view returns the same data. However, they're two separate structures to which you can separately assign access privileges, and you can deal with each separately. If you need to tweak the table, you might not have to modify the VIEW object either. Of course, in practice, the view won't usually include the same columns and rows as the base table, but as an example, it is interesting to realize that if you build the view in this manner, there would be little, if any, difference with using the two objects, other than how the security was set up. As the view is made up of one table, you can execute INSERT, UPDATE, or DELETE as you can against the table as well.

One of the most important things that make views useful as a security mechanism is the ability to partition a table structure, by limiting the rows or columns visible to the user. First, I'll look at using views to implement *column-level security*, which is also known as *projection* or *vertical partitioning* of the data, because you'll be dividing the view's columns. For example, consider that the users in a WarehouseUsers role need only to see a list of products, not how much they cost and certainly not how much they cost to produce. You might create a view like the following to vertically partition the columns accordingly:

```
CREATE VIEW Products.WarehouseProducts
AS
SELECT ProductId,ProductCode, Description
FROM   Products.Product;
```

In the same manner, you can use TABLE VALUED FUNCTION objects, though you can do more with them, including forcing some form of filter on the results. A simple TABLE-VALUED FUNCTION will have performance characteristics like a VIEW object as well, or a multistatement TABLE-VALUED FUNCTION will allow you to validate parameters (e.g., make sure the unit price is < 100 or the product is in a certain type only). For example, you might code the following function to list all products that are less than some price:

```
CREATE FUNCTION Products.ProductsLessThanPrice
(
    @UnitPrice  decimal(10,4)
)
RETURNS table
AS
    RETURN ( SELECT ProductId, ProductCode, Description, UnitPrice
             FROM   Products.Product
             WHERE  UnitPrice <= @UnitPrice);
```

This can be executed like the following:

```
SELECT * FROM Products.ProductsLessThanPrice(20);
```

This returns the following result:

ProductId	ProductCode	Description	UnitPrice
1	widget12	widget number 12	10.5000

Now for each of these views and functions, you can simply GRANT SELECT rights to a user to use them, and almost all tools would be able to use them more or less like tables.

Row-Level Security

So far, we have discussed methods of securing data at the object level. If you have access to Table A, you have access to all of the rows of Table A. If you execute Stored Procedure A that returns all of the data in Table A, that is what you got. In this section, we will look at several methods of securing the rows of the table, letting a user see only part of the rows in the table. In SQL Server 2016, a feature was added called row-level security, but row-level security is something that has been needed for 20+ years, and the methods previously used are still interesting for now and years to follow.

We will look at three methods for performing row-level security, including the feature:

- *Specific-purpose views*: Creating a view that represents a specific subset of rows in a table.

- *Row-level security feature*: There are several ways this feature will work, allowing you to show a subset to a user with very few changes to your application architecture.

- *Data-driven security views*: Basically, the precursor to the row-level security feature.

For the examples in this section, we will continue using the `Products.Product` table that was created back in the "Column-Level Security" section. To remind you of the structure, it is repeated here:

```
CREATE SCHEMA Products;
GO
CREATE TABLE Products.Product
(
    ProductId    int NOT NULL IDENTITY CONSTRAINT PKProduct PRIMARY KEY,
    ProductCode varchar(10) NOT NULL
                                CONSTRAINT AKProduct_ProductCode UNIQUE,
    Description varchar(20) NOT NULL,
    UnitPrice   decimal(10,4) NOT NULL,
    ActualCost  decimal(10,4) NOT NULL
);
```

To extend the example, I am going to add a categorization column that our security examples will use to partition the security on and set the values to our usual generally silly values to keep the examples small and nothing like anyone's real work data:

```
ALTER TABLE Products.Product
    ADD ProductType varchar(20) NOT NULL
                CONSTRAINT DFLTProduct_ProductType DEFAULT ('not set');
GO
UPDATE Products.Product
SET    ProductType = 'widget'
WHERE  ProductCode = 'widget12';
```

```
GO
UPDATE  Products.Product
SET     ProductType = 'snurf'
WHERE   ProductCode = 'snurf98';
```

Looking at the data in the table, you can see the following contents that we will work with, giving a database principal access to a given product type:

ProductId	ProductCode	Description	UnitPrice	ActualCost	ProductType
1	widget12	widget n...er 12	10.5000	8.5000	widget
2	snurf98	Snurfulator	99.9900	2.5000	snurf

In this section, we will use views to limit access to a table, and the user will have rights to the view only.

Using Specific-Purpose Views to Provide Row-Level Security

The absolute simplest version of row-level security is just building views to partition the data in some form, such as all products of a given type, employees in Division X, and so on. Whether or not this makes sense for your usage is really up to how the data will be used. Usually this is not going to be flexible enough for your needs, but it really depends on how deep the domain is you are working with.

As an example, our Products table is a case where, assuming the range of values supported by ProductType isn't large, simple row-level security may make sense. So let's configure a view that allows you to just see one particular type of product. You can build the following view:

```
CREATE VIEW Products.WidgetProduct
AS
SELECT ProductId, ProductCode, Description,
       UnitPrice, ActualCost, ProductType
FROM   Products.Product
WHERE  ProductType = 'widget'
WITH   CHECK OPTION; --This prevents the user from INSERTING/UPDATING
                     --data that would not match the view's criteria
```

Note a few important things about this view. First, I named it like it was a table. Usually when I use a VIEW object for row-level security, I want it to seem like a table to the user. Second, I included the ProductType column. We would need that column if we wanted to allow the user to INSERT new rows into the table using the view, even though we have limited the rows to only "widget"-type rows. Using an INSTEAD OF trigger, we could get around the need to include missing columns, if desired, but this is a lot easier to build. Finally, the CHECK OPTION says that if someone inserts data using the view, the ProductType would have to be set to 'widget' or it would fail.

To show this working, I will create a user Andrew whom I will give access to the view:

```
CREATE USER Andrew WITHOUT LOGIN;
GO
GRANT SELECT ON Products.WidgetProduct TO Andrew;
```

Now the user comes in, does their query, and only sees the subset of rows:

```
EXECUTE AS USER = 'Andrew';
SELECT *
FROM    Products.WidgetProduct;
```

This returns the following result:

ProductId	ProductCode	Description	UnitPrice	ActualCost	ProductType
1	widget12	widget n...er 12	10.5000	8.5000	widget

However, just to make sure, try to SELECT rows from the Product table:

```
SELECT *
FROM    Products.Product;
GO
REVERT;
```

This returns the following error message:

```
Msg 229, Level 14, State 5, Line 423
The SELECT permission was denied on the object 'Product', database
'ClassicSecurityExample', schema 'Products'.
```

You can grant INSERT, UPDATE, and DELETE rights to the user to modify the view as well, because it's based on one table; and since we set the WITH CHECK OPTION, there is no way they can put in any data that doesn't match the definition of the view. This view can then have permissions granted to let only certain people use it. This is a decent technique when you have an easily described set, or possibly few types to work with, but can become a maintenance headache for more complex scenarios.

In the next step, let's build in some more flexible security to a view, allowing everyone to see any ProductType other than 'snurf' and only members of a certain group ('SnurfViewer', naturally) to view the snurf products:

```
CREATE VIEW Products.ProductSelective
AS
SELECT ProductId, ProductCode, Description, UnitPrice, ActualCost,
ProductType
FROM    Products.Product
WHERE   ProductType <> 'snurf'
   or   (IS_MEMBER('SnurfViewer') = 1)
   or   (IS_MEMBER('db_owner') = 1) --can't add db_owner to a role
WITH CHECK OPTION;
```

I called this ProductSelective, but here is where the naming gets tricky. If this is a reporting view, I might call it ProductView. In this case, I am treating it like it is meant to be used like a normal table. I will set the view to be usable by anyone who has access to the database (good for demo, perhaps less good for production work!). Note that you are not limited to such a simple predicate for the view, but the more complex the need, the more taxing it might be on performance:

```
--Granting to public for demo purposes only. Public role should be limited
--to only utility type objects that any user could use, much like there are
--system objects that are available to guest
GRANT SELECT ON Products.ProductSelective to public;
```

Next, add a new SNURFVIEWER role. Note that I did not add this user to the group yet; I'll do that later in the example:

```
CREATE ROLE SnurfViewer;
```

Then, change security context to Amanda and select from the view:

```
EXECUTE AS USER = ' Andrew ';
SELECT * FROM Products.ProductSelective;
REVERT;
```

This returns the one row to which Amanda has access:

ProductId	ProductCode	Description	UnitPrice	ActualCost	ProductType
1	widget12	widget n...er 12	10.5000	8.5000	widget

Next, add Andrew to the SnurfViewer group, go back to context as this user, and run the statement again:

```
ALTER ROLE SnurfViewer ADD MEMBER Andrew;
GO

EXECUTE AS USER = 'Andrew';
SELECT *
FROM Products.ProductSelective;

REVERT;
```

Now, you see all the rows:

ProductId	ProductCode	Description	UnitPrice	ActualCost	ProductType
1	widget12	widget n...er 12	10.5000	8.5000	widget
2	snurf98	Snurfulator	99.9900	2.5000	snurf

This technique of using specific, hard-coded views is the simplest to configure, but lacks some level of elegance and ends up being very difficult to manage. The next methods will take this concept to a deeper level.

Using the Row-Level Security Feature

Row-level security (RLS) was a new feature available as of SQL Server 2016 that provides highly configurable methods of securing rows in a table in a manner that may not require any changes to an application. Basically, you configure one or more predicate functions (a simple `TABLE VALUED FUNCTION` that returns either something or nothing) to indicate that a user can or cannot see or modify a row in the table. I will note too that, depending on how much access a user has to a server, there are a few side channel ways a user might be able to infer the data in the table. RLS is designed to block these side channels, but they exist. For more information, check the "Row-Level Security" topic in Microsoft Docs: `docs.microsoft.com/en-us/sql/relational-databases/security/row-level-security`.

In the following example, we will continue with the same scenario from the previous section, but instead of creating a `VIEW` object, we will apply the security to the table itself (you can apply row-level security to a schema-bound view just like you can a full table).

To start with, we will reset things from the previous scenario by giving a user rights to read and modify the rows of the `Products.Product` table. In order to make security easier to manage, we will put all of the row-level security objects in a separate schema. Unlike the separate schemas we created for the temporal feature in Chapter 9, no users will need access to the objects in this schema other than when we are testing the functionality, so we will just create one schema:

```
CREATE SCHEMA RowLevelSecurity;
```

Next, we will create a simple `TABLE VALUED FUNCTION` object that provides the exact same security configuration as we used in the previous section for a view. Every user can see all rows except the ones of product type `'snurf'`, and the db_owner role members can see everything. The database principal will also need `SELECT` rights to the table we will apply this to:

```
CREATE FUNCTION RowLevelSecurity.Products_Product$SecurityPredicate
                                        (@ProductType AS varchar(20))
RETURNS TABLE
WITH SCHEMABINDING --not required, but a good idea nevertheless
AS
    RETURN (SELECT 1 AS Products_Product$SecurityPredicate
            WHERE  @ProductType <> 'snurf'
```

```
OR (IS_MEMBER('snurfViewer') = 1)
OR (IS_MEMBER('db_owner') = 1));
```

Unlike most security features in SQL Server, sa and dbo users are subject to the row-level security predicates that are configured. Most of the time, for supportability, you will want to not make that the case, but it can be useful. Another difference between this and other security features is how they behave in coded objects. By default, even when using the base table in an object like a procedure, rows will be filtered by row-level security. I will show this later in the chapter when I discuss impersonation in objects.

While you will not generally want to grant rights to the security function, when testing it is useful to make sure how the function will behave on its own. So we start by creating and granting a new user rights to select from the function:

```
CREATE USER Valerie WITHOUT LOGIN;
GO
GRANT SELECT ON RowLevelSecurity.Products_Product$SecurityPredicate
                                                        TO Valerie;
```

Now we test to see what the output will be:

```
EXECUTE AS USER = 'Valerie';
GO
SELECT 'snurf' AS ProductType,*
FROM    rowLevelSecurity.Products_Product$SecurityPredicate('snurf')
UNION ALL
SELECT 'widget' AS ProductType,*
FROM    rowLevelSecurity.Products_Product$SecurityPredicate('widget');

REVERT;
```

This returns just the one row for the widget type of row:

```
ProductType Products_Product$SecurityPredicate
----------- ----------------------------------
widget         1
```

When we feel confident that the function is correct, we remove user access from the row-level security function:

```
REVOKE SELECT ON RowLevelSecurity.Products_Product$SecurityPredicate
                                                    TO Valerie;
```

Now that we have the function created, we apply it using the CREATE SECURITY POLICY statement. You can create two kinds of predicates: FILTER, which filters out viewing rows, and BLOCK, which disallows certain operations. We will start with a simple filter. The user will need to have access to SELECT from the table already, and then this security policy will take away access to certain rows within.

The following command adds a filter predicate that will pass in the ProductType value to the function and see if it returns anything. Because this is row-level security, this function will be "executed" once per row, so keep the function as simple as possible to limit the overhead. Technically, because it is a simple table-valued function, it will be integrated into your queries like you joined it in yourself, so as long as the query isn't terribly complex, the drag on performance is generally not great, but it is always possible:

```
CREATE SECURITY POLICY RowLevelSecurity.Products_Product_SecurityPolicy
ADD FILTER PREDICATE rowLevelSecurity.Products_Product$SecurityPredicate
                                                    (ProductType)
    ON Products.Product WITH (STATE = ON, SCHEMABINDING = ON);
```

State=ON turns on the policy to be checked. SCHEMABINDING=ON says that the predicate functions must all be schema bound. Not having the function schema bound would allow you to access objects in a different database if you needed to and change the rules without changing the policy, but generally it is considered a bad idea. You can only have one enabled filter predicate per table. If you try to put another in the same policy, you get an error message, depending on if you try to create two in the same policy or different policies, for example:

```
CREATE SECURITY POLICY RowLevelSecurity.Products_Product_SecurityPolicy2
    ADD FILTER PREDICATE RowLevelSecurity.Products_Product$SecurityPredicate
                                                    (ProductType)
    ON Products.Product WITH (STATE = ON, SCHEMABINDING= ON);
```

This will cause the following message:

```
Msg 33264, Level 16, State 1, Line 607
The security policy 'RowLevelSecurity.Products_Product_SecurityPolicy2'
cannot be enabled with a predicate on table 'Products.Product'. Table
'Products.Product' is already referenced by the enabled security policy
'RowLevelSecurity.Products_Product_SecurityPolicy'
```

We start by giving the user all rights on the table, to enable the rest of the demos. We will limit the user's ability to perform these tasks using row-level security:

```
GRANT SELECT, INSERT, UPDATE, DELETE ON Products.Product TO Valerie;
```

Now, with the policy in place, let's see what the user can see:

```
EXECUTE AS USER = 'Valerie';

SELECT *
FROM    Products.Product;

REVERT;
```

ProductId	ProductCode	Description	UnitPrice	ActualCost	ProductType
1	widget12	widget n...er 12	10.5000	8.5000	widget

We have filtered the rows down to the non-snurf rows. The filter works not just for SELECT, but for DELETE and UPDATE too. For example, we know that there are snurf rows, but executing as user Valerie, they can't be modified because Valerie cannot see them:

```
EXECUTE AS USER = 'Valerie';

DELETE Products.Product
WHERE   ProductType = 'snurf';

REVERT;
```

```
--back as dbo user
SELECT *
FROM    Products.Product
WHERE   ProductType = 'snurf';
```

ProductId	ProductCode	Description	UnitPrice	ActualCost	ProductType
2	snurf98	Snurfulator	99.9900	2.5000	snurf

However, just because we can't see a row doesn't mean we can't create a row of that type:

```
EXECUTE AS USER = 'Valerie';

INSERT INTO Products.Product (ProductCode, Description, UnitPrice,
ActualCost,ProductType)
VALUES  ('test' , 'Test' , 100 , 100  , 'snurf');

SELECT *
FROM    Products.Product
WHERE   ProductType = 'snurf';

REVERT;

SELECT *
FROM    Products.Product
WHERE   ProductType = 'snurf';
```

This returns the following, because user Valerie cannot see any snurf rows, but could create the new row with ProductCode Test:

ProductId	ProductCode	Description	UnitPrice	ActualCost	ProductType

ProductId	ProductCode	Description	UnitPrice	ActualCost	ProductType
2	snurf98	Snurfulator	99.9900	2.5000	snurf
3	test	Test	100.0000	100.0000	snurf

To block actions from occurring (either creating a new row or doing something to a row we can see), you use a BLOCK predicate. There are two block types:

- AFTER: If the row does not match the security predicate after the operation, it will fail. So, if you can see A, but not B, you could not change A to B. But you could change B to A, if you could see it.

- BEFORE: If the row does not match the security predicate before the operation, you cannot perform the operation. If you can modify A, but not B, you could update A to B, but no longer be able to modify the row again.

We are going to set one of the seemingly obvious sets of row-level security predicates that one might set in a realistic scenario for a "managed by user type" column: BLOCK AFTER INSERT. If you can't see the row, then you can't create a new row. We will leave the FILTER predicate on for now:

```
--Note that you can alter a security policy, but it seems easier
--to drop and recreate in most cases.
DROP SECURITY POLICY RowLevelSecurity.Products_Product_SecurityPolicy;

CREATE SECURITY POLICY RowLevelSecurity.Products_Product_SecurityPolicy
    ADD FILTER PREDICATE RowLevelSecurity.Products_Product$SecurityPredicate
                                                             (ProductType)
                                                 ON Products.Product,
    ADD BLOCK PREDICATE RowLevelSecurity.Products_Product$SecurityPredicate
                                                             (ProductType)
    ON Products.Product AFTER INSERT WITH (STATE = ON, SCHEMABINDING = ON);
```

Next, we will test this by trying to create a new row of ProductType of 'snurf':

```
EXECUTE AS USER = 'Valerie';

INSERT INTO Products.Product (ProductCode, Description, UnitPrice,
                              ActualCost,ProductType)
VALUES  ('test2' , 'Test2' , 100 , 100  , 'snurf');

REVERT;
```

```
Msg 33504, Level 16, State 1, Line 696
The attempted operation failed because the target object
'ClassicSecurityExample.Products.Product' has a block predicate that
conflicts with this operation. If the operation is performed on a view,
the block predicate might be enforced on the underlying table. Modify the
operation to target only the rows that are allowed by the block predicate.
```

There's one last configuration to demonstrate. In cases where the principal can see the row, we use the BEFORE type of predicate. In the following configuration, we will let the user see all rows, but only INSERT, UPDATE, or DELETE rows that meet the predicates:

```
DROP SECURITY POLICY RowLevelSecurity.Products_Product_SecurityPolicy;

CREATE SECURITY POLICY RowLevelSecurity.Products_Product_SecurityPolicy
        ADD BLOCK PREDICATE RowLevelSecurity.Products_Product$SecurityPredicate
                    (ProductType) ON Products.Product AFTER INSERT,
        ADD BLOCK PREDICATE RowLevelSecurity.Products_Product$SecurityPredicate
                    (ProductType) ON Products.Product BEFORE UPDATE,
        ADD BLOCK PREDICATE RowLevelSecurity.Products_Product$SecurityPredicate
                    (ProductType) ON Products.Product BEFORE DELETE
        WITH (STATE = ON, SCHEMABINDING = ON);
```

First, let's see what the data looks like to us now:

```
EXECUTE AS USER = 'Valerie';
GO

SELECT *
FROM    Products.Product;
```

ProductId	ProductCode	Description	UnitPrice	ActualCost	ProductType
1	widget12	widget n...er 12	10.5000	8.5000	widget
2	snurf98	Snurfulator	99.9900	2.5000	snurf
3	test	Test	100.0000	100.0000	snurf

Without changing back to the previous security context, try to DELETE the last row created, which user Valerie can see:

```
DELETE Products.Product
WHERE  ProductCode = 'test';
```

This fails:

```
Msg 33504, Level 16, State 1, Line 731
The attempted operation failed because the target object
'ClassicSecurityExample.Products.Product' has a block predicate that
conflicts with this operation. If the operation is performed on a view,
the block predicate might be enforced on the underlying table. Modify the
operation to target only the rows that are allowed by the block predicate.
```

Now, since we used BEFORE UPDATE in our predicate, we can update a row to a value that we may not be able to see after the update:

```
UPDATE Products.Product
SET    ProductType = 'snurf'
WHERE  ProductType = 'widget';
```

```
--But we cannot update the row back, even though we can see it:
```

```
UPDATE Products.Product
SET    ProductType = 'widget'
WHERE  ProductType = 'snurf';
```

```
REVERT;
```

This returns

```
Msg 33504, Level 16, State 1, Line 731
The attempted operation failed because the target object
'ClassicSecurityExample.Products.Product' has a block predicate that
conflicts with this operation. If the operation is performed on a view,
the block predicate might be enforced on the underlying table. Modify the
operation to target only the rows that are allowed by the block predicate.
```

Obviously, we have just scratched the surface with the row-level security feature, but you should be able to see that from here, you could create a very tight layer of row-level security if needed.

Tip   If you are using a single user to connect to the server, you can use the new `sys.sp_set_session_context` system procedure to save a security context to the connection metadata and the `SESSION_CONTEXT` system function to retrieve it, for example:

```
EXEC sys.sp_set_session_context @key = N'SecurityGroup',
@value = 'Management';
```

And then you can use

```
SELECT SESSION_CONTEXT(N'SecurityGroup');
```

in your predicate function instead of `IS_MEMBER`, for example. Be sure that the actual user doesn't have ad hoc access to execute `sys.sp_set_session_context`, or they can set whatever they want and circumvent security.

Using Data-Driven Row-Level Security

In this section, I want to expand on the predicate possibilities for both the view driven and row-level security feature driven row-level security implementation. Instead of embedding access through the code, you can create a rich layer of user-configurable row-level security using a table that maps database role principals with some data in the table. In the case of our example scenarios, different types of products can be expanded and configured over time without any code needing to be released, giving total control to the process.

To start the process, we will create the following table that will hold the set of product types that a database role can see:

```
CREATE TABLE Products.ProductSecurity
(
    ProductType varchar(20), --at this point you probably will create a
                             --ProductType domain table, but this keeps the
                             --example a bit simpler
```

```
DatabaseRole    sysname,
    CONSTRAINT PKProductsSecurity PRIMARY KEY(ProductType, DatabaseRole)
);
```

Then, we insert a row that will be used to give everyone with database rights the ability to see widget-type products:

```
INSERT INTO Products.ProductSecurity(ProductType, DatabaseRole)
VALUES ('widget','public');
```

Next, we create a VIEW object named ProductsSelective to show only rows to which the user has rights, based on row security:

```
ALTER VIEW Products.ProductSelective
AS
SELECT Product.ProductId, Product.ProductCode, Product.Description,
       Product.UnitPrice, Product.ActualCost, Product.ProductType
FROM   Products.Product as Product
          JOIN Products.ProductSecurity as ProductSecurity
            ON (Product.ProductType = ProductSecurity.ProductType
                AND IS_MEMBER(ProductSecurity.DatabaseRole) = 1)
                OR IS_MEMBER('db_owner') = 1; --don't leave out the dbo!
```

This exact same thing is available to the row-level security feature as well. The predicate function can access tables as well. You could create the TABLE VALUED FUNCTION object as follows (after dropping the policy that is using it, or you will get an error stating that you can't alter this function):

```
ALTER FUNCTION RowLevelSecurity.Products_Product$SecurityPredicate
                                          (@ProductType AS varchar(20))
RETURNS TABLE
WITH SCHEMABINDING --not required, but a good idea nevertheless
AS
    RETURN (SELECT 1 AS Products_Product$SecurityPredicate
             WHERE is_member('db_owner') = 1
               OR  EXISTS (SELECT 1
                            FROM   Products.ProductSecurity
                            WHERE  ProductType = @ProductType
                              AND  IS_MEMBER(DatabaseRole) = 1));
```

731

The primary limitations are performance. Even with this being a relatively new feature, I have heard of people using this feature with lots of rows in their row-level security tables, even using hierarchical data. While the sky is the limit, it is highly recommended before endeavoring to make heavy use of any row-level technique that you test heavily and with multiple users.

Row-Level Security and Impersonation

Starting with SQL Server 2016, the row-level security feature started throwing a bit of a spanner into how this all works. Usually, when you execute a coded object (or use a view), you get access to everything the owner of the object provided you. However, for row-level security, when executing as the caller, the caller's information is provided to the predicate function (the same is true for a VIEW object doing the same sort of code). When executing as a different user, that user's information is used.

As an example, create the following table, with a few rows:

```
CREATE SCHEMA RLSDemo;
GO
CREATE TABLE RLSDemo.TestRowLevelChaining
(
        Value     int CONSTRAINT PKTestRowLevelChaining PRIMARY KEY
)
INSERT RLSDemo.TestRowLevelChaining (Value)
VALUES  (1),(2),(3),(4),(5);
```

Then set up a filtering predicate that returns values > 3 if you are not the dbo and apply it:

```
CREATE FUNCTION RowLevelSecurity.dbo_TestRowLevelChaining$SecurityPredicate
                                    (@Value AS int)
RETURNS TABLE WITH SCHEMABINDING
AS RETURN (SELECT 1 AS dbo_TestRowLevelChaining$SecurityPredicate
           WHERE  @Value > 3 OR  USER_NAME() = 'dbo');
GO

CREATE SECURITY POLICY
    RowLevelSecurity.dbo_TestRowLevelChaining_SecurityPolicy
    ADD FILTER PREDICATE
```

```
RowLevelSecurity.dbo_TestRowLevelChaining$SecurityPredicate (Value)
ON RLSDemo.TestRowLevelChaining WITH (STATE = ON, SCHEMABINDING = ON);
```

Then set up two STORED PROCEDURE objects, one that executes as caller and the other that executes as the dbo user:

```
CREATE PROCEDURE RLSDemo.TestRowLevelChaining_asCaller
AS
SELECT * FROM RLSDemo.TestRowLevelChaining;
GO

CREATE PROCEDURE RLSDemo.TestRowLevelChaining_asDbo
WITH EXECUTE AS 'dbo' --keeping it simple for demo.. not best practice
AS                    --but you can be sure has full rights
SELECT * FROM RLSDemo.TestRowLevelChaining;
```

Create a new USER, and grant it rights to execute both procedures:

```
CREATE USER Bobby WITHOUT LOGIN;
GRANT EXECUTE ON RLSDemo.TestRowLevelChaining_asCaller TO Bobby;
GRANT EXECUTE ON RLSDemo.TestRowLevelChaining_asDbo TO Bobby;
```

Now, executing as the new user Bobby, you will see that the asCaller variant only returns the two rows that are greater than 3:

```
EXECUTE AS USER = 'Bobby'
GO
EXECUTE  RLSDemo.TestRowLevelChaining_asCaller;
```

```
Value
-----------
4
5
```

But the asDbo variant is now executing as if the dbo user is the one executing it, even for the row-level security access:

```
 EXECUTE  RLSDemo.TestRowLevelChaining_asDbo;
```

This returns all the data in the table:

```
Value
-----------
1
2
3
4
5
```

This is a very useful thing, first, that the normal case allows you to largely ignore row-level security when writing your objects and, second, that you can apply it to objects that already exist. It is essential to understand how row-level security applies to cases when you are using impersonation, so as to not expect to be giving access to an object and accidentally grant rights to a lot more data than you are expecting.

Crossing Database Lines

So far, most of the code and issues we've discussed have been concerned with everything owned by a single owner and everything within a single database. This will almost always be the desired pattern of development, but sometimes it is not possible to achieve. When our code and/or relationships must go outside the database limits, the complexity is greatly increased. This is because in SQL Server architecture, databases are generally designed to be thought of as independent containers of data, and this is becoming more and more the expectation with Azure SQL DB, contained databases, and even the developer tools that are shipped with SQL Server. (Azure SQL DB does allow some cross-database queries with its elastic database query features, which you can read about here: docs.microsoft.com/en-us/azure/azure-sql/database/elastic-query-overview. However, it is very much not the same thing as what you will get in the SQL Server product that runs on-premises, in a VM, or in a Managed Instance.) Sometimes, however, you need to share data from one database to another, often for some object that's located in a third-party system your company has purchased. This can be a real annoyance for the following reasons:

- FOREIGN KEY constraints cannot be used to handle referential integrity needs (I covered in Chapter 8 how you implement relationships using triggers to support this).

- Backups must be coordinated, or your data could be out of sync with a restore. You lose some of the protection from a single database backup scenario. This is because when, heaven forbid, a database restore is needed, it isn't possible to make certain that the data in the two databases is in sync.

A typical example of cross-database access might be linking an off-the-shelf system into a homegrown system. The off-the-shelf package may have requirements that you not make any changes or additions to its database schema. So you create a database to bolt on functionality. Another scenario could be a hosted server with databases from many clients, but clients need access to more than one database without gaining access to any other client's data.

Beyond the coding and maintenance aspects of cross-database access, which aren't necessarily trivial, the most complex consideration is security. As mentioned in the first paragraph of this section, databases are generally considered independent in the security theme of how SQL Server works. This causes issues when you need to include data outside the database, because by default, users are scoped to a database. UserA in database1 is not exactly the same as UserA in database2, even in an uncontained database mapped to the same login.

The ownership chain inside the boundaries of a database is relatively simple. If the owner of the object refers only to other objects owned by that user, then the chain isn't broken. Any user to whom the object's owner grants rights can use the object. However, when leaving the confines of a single database, things get more complex. Even if a database is owned by the same system login, the ownership chain is (by default) broken when an object references data outside the database, even owned by the same login. So not only does the object creator need to have access to the objects outside the database; the caller needs rights also.

This section demonstrates four different concepts for the on-premises version of SQL Server when building T-SQL coded objects that need to access data outside of a single database while seeking to limit the rights of the caller of the coded objects:

- Using cross-database chaining

- Using impersonation to implement cross-database connections

- Using a certificate-based trust

- Accessing data outside of the server

Ideally, you will seldom, if ever, need to access data that is not within the boundaries of a single database, but when you do, you will want to choose the method that is the most secure for your needs.

If you are a person who is doing ad hoc querying of data in a server, the problem is considerably easier. The login of that person is typically given rights to access the databases that they need access to, via being mapped by one or more users (possibly mapped to a Windows Authentication group). If the LOGIN has rights to the databases and objects that are accessed, there are no issues.

Using Cross-Database Chaining

The cross-database chaining solution is to tell the database to recognize that if the owners of database1 and database2 are the same, it should not let ownership chaining be broken when crossing database boundaries. Then, if you, as system administrator, want to allow users to use your objects seamlessly across databases, that's fine. However, a few steps and requirements need to be met:

- Each database that participates in the chaining relationship must be owned by the same server principal.

- The DB_CHAINING database option (set using ALTER DATABASE) must be set to ON for each database involved in the relationship. It's OFF by default. One of the largest issues is that DB_CHAINING cannot be set to chain to only a specific database.

- The database where the object uses external resources must have the TRUSTWORTHY database option set to ON; it's OFF by default. (Again, set using ALTER DATABASE.)

- The users who use the objects need to have a matching user in the database where the external resources reside based on the same login.

I often will use the database chaining approach to support a reporting solution for an internal server. For example, in a reporting system I built, we have several databases that make up a complete solution in our production system. We have a single database with views of each system to provide a single database for reporting from the OLTP databases (for real-time reporting needs only; other reporting needs come from an integrated copy of the database and a data warehouse, as will be described in more detail in Appendix C available as a download).

Caution   If I could put this caution in a flashing font, I would, but my editor would probably say it wasn't cost effective or something silly like that. It's important to understand the implications of the database chaining scenario. You're effectively opening up the external database resources completely to the users in the database who are members of the db_owner database role, even if they have no rights in the external database. Because of the last two criteria in the bulleted list, chaining isn't necessarily a bad thing to do for most corporate situations where you simply have to retrieve data from another database. However, opening access to the external database resources can be especially bad for shared database systems, because this can be used to get access to the data in a chaining-enabled database. All that may need to be known is the username and login name of a user in the other database.

Note that if you need to turn chaining on or off for all databases, you can use sp_ configure to set 'Cross DB Ownership Chaining' to '1', but this is not considered a best practice. Use ALTER DATABASE to set chaining *only* where absolutely required, though it is still not a targeted command where you specify chaining from a specific database to another specific database.

As an example, the following scenario creates two databases with a TABLE object in each database and then a STORED PROCEDURE object. First, create the new database and add the simple table. You don't need to add any rows or keys, because this isn't important to this demonstration. Note that you have to create a LOGIN for this demonstration, because the user must be based on the same login in both databases. I will start with this database in an uncontained model and then switch to a contained model to show how it affects the cross-database access:

```
CREATE DATABASE ExternalDb;
GO
USE ExternalDb;
GO
```

```
CREATE LOGIN Paul WITH PASSWORD = 'H(*3n1923cjqp9232';
CREATE USER  Paul FROM LOGIN Paul;
CREATE TABLE dbo.Table1 ( Value int );
```

Next, create a local database, the one where you'll be executing your queries. You add the login you created as a new user and again create a table:

```
CREATE DATABASE LocalDb;
GO
USE LocalDb;
GO
CREATE USER Paul FROM LOGIN Paul;
```

Another step that's generally preferred is to have all databases owned by the same server_principal. I will create a login to own these two databases that is purpose built, that is, designed to never be used (I will disable the login, and I temporarily set my server to Windows Authentication only to be 100% sure of this solution as well):

```
CREATE LOGIN ExternalLocalDbOwner WITH PASSWORD = 'kjfk34iu39zskcnn4x';
ALTER LOGIN ExternalLocalDbOwner DISABLE;
```

You can also use the sa account to own your database, which would be typical for a database in which you were not using trusts. If you are using these techniques on a shared server, using sa would definitely not be the preferred method, and you could use different database owners for different users. Do this with the ALTER AUTHORIZATION DDL statement:

```
ALTER AUTHORIZATION ON DATABASE::ExternalDb TO ExternalLocalDbOwner;
ALTER AUTHORIZATION ON DATABASE::LocalDb TO ExternalLocalDbOwner;
```

To check the owner of the database, use the sys.databases catalog view:

```
SELECT name, SUSER_SNAME (owner_sid) AS owner
FROM   sys.databases
WHERE  name IN ('ExternalDb','LocalDb');
```

This should return the following, as it is essential that the databases are owned by the same server principal for the upcoming examples:

```
name                owner
----------------    ------------------
ExternalDb          ExternalLocalDbOwner
LocalDb             ExternalLocalDbOwner
```

Next, create a simple STORED PROCEDURE object, still in the LocalDb context, selecting data from ExternalDb, with the objects being owned by the same dbo owner. You then give rights to your new user:

```
CREATE PROCEDURE dbo.ExternalDb$TestCrossDatabase
AS
SELECT Value
FROM    ExternalDb.dbo.Table1;
GO
GRANT EXECUTE ON dbo.ExternalDb$TestCrossDatabase TO Paul;
```

Now, try it as the sysadmin user:

```
EXECUTE dbo.ExternalDb$TestCrossDatabase;
```

And it works fine, because the sysadmin user is basically implemented to ignore all security. Execute as the user Paul that is in the LocalDb:

```
EXECUTE AS USER = 'Paul';
GO
EXECUTE dbo.ExternalDb$TestCrossDatabase;
GO
REVERT;
```

This will give you the following error:

```
Msg 916, Level 14, State 1, Procedure externalDb$testCrossDatabase, Line 3
The server principal "Paul" is not able to access the database
"ExternalDb" under the current security context.
```

You then set the chaining and trustworthy attributes for the LocalDb and chaining for the ExternalDb (making these settings requires sysadmin rights):

```
ALTER DATABASE LocalDb
    SET DB_CHAINING ON;
ALTER DATABASE LocalDb
    SET TRUSTWORTHY ON;

--It does not need to be TRUSTWORTHY since it is not reaching out
ALTER DATABASE externalDb
    SET DB_CHAINING ON;
```

Now, if you execute the procedure, you will see that it returns a valid result. This is because

- The owner of the objects and databases is the same, which you set up with the ALTER AUTHORIZATION statements.

- The user has access to connect to the external database, which is why you created the user when you set up the ExternalDb database. (You can also use the guest user to allow any user to access the database as well, though as mentioned, this is not a best practice.)

You can validate the metadata for these databases by using the sys.databases catalog view:

```
SELECT name, is_trustworthy_on, is_db_chaining_on
FROM   sys.databases
WHERE  name IN ('ExternalDb','LocalDb');
```

This returns the following results:

name	is_trustworthy_on	is_db_chaining_on
ExternalDb	0	1
LocalDb	1	1

I find that the biggest issue when setting up cross-database chaining is the question of ownership of the databases involved. The owner changes sometimes because users create databases and leave them owned by their security principals. Note that this is the only method I will demonstrate that doesn't require stored procedures to work. You can also use basic queries and views using this method, as they are simply stored queries that you use as the basis of a SELECT statement. STORED PROCEDURE objects are executable code modules that allow them a few additional properties, which I will demonstrate in the next two sections.

Now check how this will be affected by setting the database to use the containment model:

```
ALTER DATABASE LocalDB SET CONTAINMENT = PARTIAL;
```

Then, connect to the server as user Paul using SSMS and default database to LocalDb and try to run the procedure. You will notice that the connection isn't to the contained database; it is to the server and you are in the context of the contained database. Using EXECUTE AS will give you the same effect, because user Paul is not a contained user:

```
EXECUTE AS USER = 'Paul';
go
EXECUTE dbo.ExternalDb$TestCrossDatabase;
GO
REVERT;
GO
```

You will see that it behaves the exact same way and gives you a result to the query. However, connecting with a contained user is a different challenge. First, create a contained user, and then give it rights to execute the procedure:

```
CREATE USER ContainedPaul WITH PASSWORD = '2k23k49(H23H2';
GO
GRANT EXECUTE ON dbo.ExternalDb$TestCrossDatabase to ContainedPaul;
```

Next, change to the database security context of the new contained user and try to change context to the ExternalDb:

```
EXECUTE AS USER = 'ContainedPaul';
GO
USE ExternalDb;
```

This will give you the following error (plus or minus some characters in that server principal moniker, naturally):

```
Msg 916, Level 14, State 1, Line 1
The server principal "S-1-9-3-3326261859-1215110459-3885819776-190383717."
is not able to access the database "ExternalDb" under the current security
context.
```

Obviously the "server principal" part of the error message could be confusing, but it is also true because in this case, the database will behave as a server to that user. Executing the following code will give you the exact same error:

```
EXECUTE dbo.ExternalDb$TestCrossDatabase;
GO
REVERT;
GO
```

When turning on containment, you will note that since the maximum containment level is PARTIAL, some code you have written may not be containment safe. To check, you can use the sys.dm_db_uncontained_entities dynamic management view. To find objects that reference outside data, you can use the following query:

```
SELECT  OBJECT_NAME(major_id) AS object_name, statement_line_number,
        statement_type, feature_name, feature_type_name
FROM    sys.dm_db_uncontained_entities
WHERE   class_desc = 'OBJECT_OR_COLUMN';
```

For our database, it will return the following, which corresponds to the procedure and the query that used a cross-database reference:

object_name	statement_line_number	statement_type
ExternalDb$TestCrossDatabase	3	SELECT

feature_name	feature_type_name
Server or Database Qualified Name	T-SQL Syntax

The object will also return uncontained users:

```
SELECT   USER_NAME(major_id) AS USER_NAME
FROM     sys.dm_db_uncontained_entities
WHERE    class_desc = 'DATABASE_PRINCIPAL'
  AND    USER_NAME(major_id) <> 'dbo';
```

And you created one already in this chapter:

```
USER_NAME
---------------------
Paul
```

Note   One additional very interesting (albeit non–security-related) feature of contained databases is that the collation of the `tempdb` as seen from the contained user will be that of the contained database. While this is not frequently an issue for most databases, it will make life easier for moving databases around to servers with different collations. I won't cover that feature in any other location in this book.

Finally, to do a bit of housekeeping and remove containment from the database, delete the contained user you created and turn off containment (you have to drop the user or, as previously mentioned, you would receive an error stating that uncontained databases cannot have contained users):

```
DROP USER ContainedPaul;
GO
USE Master;
GO
ALTER DATABASE LocalDB  SET CONTAINMENT = NONE;
GO
USE LocalDb;
GO
```

Using Impersonation to Cross Database Lines

Impersonation can be an alternative to using the DB_CHAINING setting. Now, you no longer need to set the chaining to ON; all you need is to set it to TRUSTWORTHY, since you will be executing code that reaches out of the current database:

```
ALTER DATABASE LocalDb
    SET DB_CHAINING OFF;
ALTER DATABASE LocalDb
    SET TRUSTWORTHY ON;

ALTER DATABASE ExternalDb
    SET DB_CHAINING OFF;
```

Now, you can rewrite the procedure like this, which lets the person execute in the context of the owner of the schema that the procedure is in:

```
CREATE PROCEDURE dbo.ExternalDb$testCrossDatabase_Impersonation
WITH EXECUTE AS SELF
--as procedure creator, who is the same as the db owner
AS
SELECT Value
FROM    ExternalDb.dbo.Table1;
GO
GRANT EXECUTE ON dbo.ExternalDb$TestCrossDatabase_Impersonation to Paul;
```

If the login of the owner of the database, and it follows the dbo schema (in this example ExternalLocalDbOwner, because I set the owner of both databases to ExternalLocalDbOwner in the previous section to cordon them off for safer cross-database access), has access to the other database, you can impersonate dbo in this manner. In fact, you can access the external resources seamlessly. This is probably the simplest method of handling cross-database chaining for some corporate needs. Of course, impersonation should be used very carefully and raise a humongous flag if you're working on a database server that's shared among many different companies.

Setting TRUSTWORTHY to ON requires sysadmin privileges, but note that the members of the sysadmin role aren't required to understand the implications if one of their users calls up and asks for TRUSTWORTHY to be turned on for them.

Now, when you execute the procedure as Paul user, it works:

```
EXECUTE AS USER = 'Paul';
GO
EXECUTE dbo.ExternalDb$TestCrossDatabase_Impersonation;
GO
REVERT;
```

If you toggle TRUSTWORTHY to OFF and try to execute the procedure

```
ALTER DATABASE localDb  SET TRUSTWORTHY OFF;
GO
EXECUTE dbo.ExternalDb$TestCrossDatabase_Impersonation;
```

you'll receive the following error, no matter what user you execute as:

```
Msg 916, Level 14, State 1, Procedure ExternalDb$TestCrossDatabase_
Impersonation, Line 4
The server principal "sa" is not able to access the database "ExternalDb"
under the current security context.
```

This is clearly another of the confusing sorts of error messages you get on occasion, since the server principal sa ought to be able to do anything, but it is what it is. Next, go back to the containment method. Turn back on TRUSTWORTHY, set the containment, and recreate the ContainedPaul user, giving rights to the impersonation procedure:

```
ALTER DATABASE LocalDb  SET TRUSTWORTHY ON;
GO
ALTER DATABASE LocalDB  SET CONTAINMENT = PARTIAL;
GO
CREATE USER ContainedPaul WITH PASSWORD = 'Nasty1$';
GO
GRANT EXECUTE ON
    ExternalDb$TestCrossDatabase_Impersonation TO ContainedPaul;
```

Now execute the procedure in the context of the contained user:

```
EXECUTE AS USER = 'ContainedPaul';
GO
EXECUTE dbo.ExternalDb$TestCrossDatabase_Impersonation;
GO
REVERT;
```

This time, you will see that no error is raised, because the procedure is in the context of the owner of the procedure and is mapped to a server principal that owns the database and the object you are using. Note that this breaks (or, really, violates) containment because you are using external data, but it is important to understand what can be done, especially what to watch out for in implementations you work with.

Finally, clean up the users and containment as you have done before:

```
DROP USER ContainedPaul;
GO
USE Master;
GO
ALTER DATABASE LocalDB  SET CONTAINMENT = NONE;
GO
USE LocalDb;
```

Using a Certificate-Based Trust

The final thing I'll demonstrate around cross-database access is using a single certificate installed in two databases to let the code access data across database boundaries. You'll use it to sign the stored procedure and map a user to this certificate in the target database. This is a straightforward technique and is really the best way to do cross-database security chaining when the system isn't a dedicated corporate resource where you have complete control.

It requires a bit of atypical setup, but it isn't overwhelmingly difficult. What makes using a certificate nice is that you don't need to open the hole left in the system's security by setting the database to TRUSTWORTHY. This is because the user who will be executing the procedure is a user in the database, just as if the target login or user were given rights in the ExternalDB. Because the certificate matches, SQL Server knows that this cross-database access is acceptable.

First, turn off the TRUSTWORTHY setting:

```
USE LocalDb;
GO
ALTER DATABASE LocalDb
    SET TRUSTWORTHY OFF;
```

Check the status of your databases as follows:

```
SELECT name,
       SUSER_SNAME(owner_sid) AS owner,
       is_trustworthy_on, is_db_chaining_on
FROM    sys.databases
WHERE name IN ('LocalDb','ExternalDb');
```

This should return the following results (if not, go back and turn off TRUSTWORTHY and chaining for the databases where necessary):

name	owner	is_trustworthy_on	is_db_chaining_on
ExternalDb	sa	0	0
LocalDb	sa	0	0

Now, I will create another STORED PROCEDURE object and give the user Paul rights to execute it, just like the others (which won't work now because TRUSTWORTHY is turned off):

```
CREATE PROCEDURE dbo.ExternalDb$TestCrossDatabase_Certificate
AS
SELECT Value
FROM    ExternalDb.dbo.Table1;
GO
GRANT EXECUTE on dbo.ExternalDb$TestCrossDatabase_Certificate to Paul;
```

Then, create a certificate:

```
CREATE CERTIFICATE ProcedureExecution
                        ENCRYPTION BY PASSWORD = 'jsaflajOIo9jcCMd;SdpSljc'
    WITH SUBJECT =
            'Used to sign procedure:ExternalDb$TestCrossDatabase_Certificate';
```

Add this certificate as a signature on the procedure:

```
ADD SIGNATURE TO dbo.ExternalDb$TestCrossDatabase_Certificate
    BY CERTIFICATE ProcedureExecution
        WITH PASSWORD = 'jsaflajOIo9jcCMd;SdpSljc';
```

Finally, make an OS file out of the certificate, so a certificate object can be created in the ExternalDb based on the same certificate (choose a directory that works best for you):

```
BACKUP CERTIFICATE ProcedureExecution
                TO FILE = 'c:\temp\procedureExecution.cer';
```

This completes the setup of the LocalDb. Next, you have to apply the certificate to the ExternalDb:

```
USE ExternalDb;
GO
CREATE CERTIFICATE ProcedureExecution
                FROM FILE = 'c:\temp\procedureExecution.cer';
```

After that, map the certificate to a user, and give that user rights to the Table1 that the user in the other database is trying to access:

```
CREATE USER ProcCertificate FOR CERTIFICATE ProcedureExecution;
GO
GRANT SELECT on dbo.Table1 TO ProcCertificate;
```

Now, you're good to go. Change back to the LocalDb and execute the procedure:

```
USE LocalDb;
GO
EXECUTE AS LOGIN = 'Paul';
EXECUTE dbo.ExternalDb$TestCrossDatabase_Certificate;
```

The STORED PROCEDURE object has a signature that identifies it with the certificate, and in ExternalDb, it connects with this certificate to get the rights of the certificate-based user. So, since the certificate user can view data in the table, your procedure can use the data.

The certificate-based approach isn't as simple as the other possibilities, but offers far tighter control. Pretty much the major downside to this is that it does not work with VIEW or TABLE VALUED FUNCTION objects. However, now you have a safe way of crossing database boundaries that doesn't require giving the user direct object access and doesn't open up a hole in your security. Hence, you could use this solution on any server in any situation. Make sure to secure or destroy the certificate file once you've used it, so no other user can use it to gain access to your system.

This method does not work when using containment, unless you use impersonation, since the user will not have any way to access the other database.

Finally, clean up the databases used for the examples and move back to the ClassicSecurityExample database you have used throughout this chapter:

```
REVERT;
GO
USE MASTER;
GO
DROP DATABASE ExternalDb;
DROP DATABASE LocalDb;
GO
USE ClassicSecurityExample;
```

Accessing Data on a Different Server

Sometimes, you not only need to go past the lines of the database but all the way past the lines of the server. Due to some new tools in recent versions of SQL Server, accessing data on a different server needs to be broken down into two different needs: read-only and read-write.

Read-Only

When you need read-only access to data on another server, the best method for many years has been to copy data to the server you are on using SSIS or a similar ETL tool. In SQL Server 2016, SQL Server added a feature that made this slightly less necessary called PolyBase. It allowed you to access data in SQL Server directly that was housed in Hadoop, Azure Blob Storage, or Azure Data Lake Store. In SQL Server 2019, it was greatly improved to include SQL Server data, as well as Oracle, MongoDB, and other data sources using an ODBC driver. This will be a much better method of accessing data on other servers for read-only access than any other method.

Read-Write

For read-write access, it is generally better to use a method like an external application to do the access in the two SQL Server databases whenever possible. However, if you do actually need to do cross-server access in T-SQL code directly, you can use either of a few methods:

- *Linked servers*: You can build a connection between two servers by registering a "server" name that you then access via a four-part name (`<linkedServerName>.<database>.<schema>.<objectName>`) or through the `OPENQUERY` interface. The linked server name is the name you specify using `sp_addlinkedserver`. This could be a SQL Server or anything that can be connected to via OLE DB. For more details on linked servers, go to Microsoft Docs article "Linked Servers (Database Engine)" (`docs.microsoft.com/en-us/sql/relational-databases/linked-servers/linked-servers-database-engine`).

- *Ad hoc connections*: Using the `OPENROWSET` or `OPENDATASOURCE` interfaces, you can return and modify data from any OLE DB source. For more details, see Microsoft Docs articles "OPENROWSET (Transact-SQL)" (`docs.microsoft.com/en-us/sql/t-sql/functions/openrowset-transact-sql`) and "OPENDATASOURCE (Transact-SQL)" (`docs.microsoft.com/en-us/sql/t-sql/functions/opendatasource-transact-sql`).

- *Service Broker to do asynchronous access*: Service Broker allows you to do asynchronous access between resources, both inside a SQL Server and outside. For example, Database Mail is implemented using Service Broker so you can ask it to send an email without waiting for it to complete. More details in Microsoft Docs on the "SQL Server Service Broker" topic here: `docs.microsoft.com/en-us/sql/database-engine/configure-windows/sql-server-service-broker`.

No matter the method you use, the security chain will be broken from the executing user when crossing SQL Server instance connections. Using linked servers, you could be in the context of the Windows login you are logged in with, a SQL Server standard login on the target machine, or even a single login that everyone uses to "cross over" to the other server depending on how you configure it.

As I mentioned briefly in the previous section, one use for EXECUTE AS could be to deal with the case where you're working with distributed databases. One user might be delegated to have rights to access the distributed server, and then, you execute the procedure as this user to give access to the linked server objects.

Using linked servers or ad hoc connections will both break the containment model. Linked servers are defined in the master database.

Obfuscating Data

We database administrator types all too often have unfettered access to entire production systems with far too much personal data. Even with well-designed security granularity, a few users will still need to have rights to run as a member of the sysadmin server role, giving them access to *all* data.

On the more administrative side of things, if DBAs have access to unencrypted backups of a database, they may be able to easily access any data in a database by simply restoring it to a different server where they are administrators. If you're dealing with sensitive data, you need to be wary of how you deal with this data:

- Do you back up the database? Where are these backups?

- Do you send the backups to an offsite safe location? Who sends or takes them there?

- Who has access to the servers where data is stored? Do you trust the fate of your company in their hands? Could these servers be hacked?

When data is at rest in the database and users have access to the data, it is also important that we obfuscate some data such that a user cannot tell what it is exactly. This is one of the main ways that we can protect data from casual observers, especially those like us DBA types who generally have full control over the database (in other words, way too much power in the database). In this section, we will look at two methods of obfuscating data:

- *Encryption*: Encrypting the data so no one without the certificates, passwords, and so on can reasonably access the data. (Encryption isn't perfect, given enough time, computing power, and know-how to crack it.)

- *Dynamic data masking*: A new feature as of 2016 that allows you to mask over data in given scenarios.

Neither of these techniques is perfect, but together you can provide a very solid obfuscation layer over your data.

Encrypting Data

Way back in Chapter 2, when introducing the concept of requirements, I discussed "special security considerations," which, loosely speaking, meant legal and regulatory requirements that exist in the world to protect your privacy, and there are lots of them that cover a wide variety of the personal data you let others have access to. As a data architect, the best way to design a database to protect the private data of your customers is to simply not include columns that capture the private data of your customers. Where possible, see if a third-party service is available to handle things like credit card numbers for you. There are banking systems that will store credit card information for you and provide you a token that looks like a credit card that your organization and only that specific bank can make use of.

Unfortunately, it is not realistic to just say "Our company is not going to store any private data of our customers." When you do need to capture the private data of your customers, you need to protect that data in one of several ways, depending upon the actual sensitivity requirements of your data. The following are several tools in the SQL Server kit to provide encryption for your data. I will not cover any of them in detail, but if you are architecting a database solution, it is fairly essential that you know about these technologies:

- *Encrypted backups*: SQL Server provides methods using the BACKUP command to make backups encrypted. This is like the "least you can do" encryption, but definitely valuable for most of your databases to use if you have any data in a database that could be identified as from a person who does business with your company or if the data could be identified as coming from your company if someone got a hold of the data—in other words, any database ("Backup Encryption": docs.microsoft.com/en-us/sql/relational-databases/backup-restore/backup-encryption).

- *Transparent Data Encryption (TDE)*: A feature that will encrypt the data and log files during I/O so that you don't have to change your code, but anytime the data is at rest, it will stay encrypted (including when it is backed up, including the files for memory-optimized tables in SQL Server 2016 and later). It is more secure than encrypting backups, but every reader with SELECT rights can read the data, so TDE encrypts your data from the database files from being stolen, not from prying, authenticated eyes ("Transparent Data Encryption": docs.microsoft.com/en-us/sql/relational-databases/security/encryption/transparent-data-encryption).

- *Encryption functions*: Functions that let you encrypt values using SQL Server function calls. They are very simple to use, but their biggest downfall is that all the data needed to decrypt the data is stored locally to SQL Server. There is one function that allows you to encrypt by a passcode, allowing a user to encrypt data such that no other user can read the data without knowing the passcode, even the system administrator ("Cryptographic Functions (Transact-SQL)": docs.microsoft.com/en-us/sql/t-sql/functions/cryptographic-functions-transact-sql).

- *Always Encrypted*: A feature added in SQL Server 2016 that is somewhat external to the database engine. Unlike the encryption functions, the information needed to decrypt the data is not stored in SQL Server. This technology is coordinated in the database and the application layer, and even if your server was stolen from you with all the files, data encrypted using Always Encrypted would not be accessible ("Always Encrypted": docs.microsoft.com/en-us/sql/relational-databases/security/encryption/always-encrypted-database-engine). SQL Server 2019 added secure enclaves, which can decrypt textual data in the SQL Server engine to make searches faster, without revealing data to even administrators to increase performance without reducing security.

The biggest "key" to any encryption strategy that is intended to obfuscate important data is that you don't store all the information to decrypt data together with the data or with the backup. It would be just as silly as taking the time to install deadbolt locks and then leaving a key on the outside of what you are protecting under one of those little fake-looking rocks that every criminal knows what is.

I am not going to go any deeper into the concepts of encryption, because it is far too complex to cover in one section of a chapter and the most complicated parts on the database side are about configuration, which you can get from the links.

My big concern for the section is that you understand the need to consider two things when considering your encryption needs: First, "Who can decrypt the data and how?" SQL Server's basic encryption uses certificates and keys that are all on the local server. This can keep employees' eyes off sensitive data, but if a person got the entire database and a `sysadmin` role user, they could get to everything. The best method is to implement your decryption engine on a different server that is not linked to the database engine at all, and using Always Encrypted will allow you to do that for your sensitive data. If you don't have any very sensitive data, then just using TDE or backup encryption may be enough. (Note that it is equally important to understand how you will make sure that you will be *able* to decrypt the data in a few months as it is to make sure that a bad actor will *not* be able to decrypt it. If your server crashes and you have backups, but not a copy of the certificates that were used to encrypt the data…you are as good off as if the data was never stored in the first place.)

Second, if someone gets the data, how easily could they decrypt it with unlimited computing power and time? Some encryption is deterministic in that every time value 'A' is encrypted, the same binary string is output. This can make things like searching for encrypted values faster but makes it easier to break. Probabilistic encryption schemes output different values every time but will be much costlier to search for an encrypted value.

In the end, if your data is stolen, the goal needs to be that the data is worthless, so that all your press release needs to say is "Company X regrets to say that some financial data was stolen from our vaults. All data was encrypted at this level; hence, there is little chance any usable data was acquired and so on." And you, as DBA, will be thanked (as long as it wasn't your fault that the data was stolen; if that is the case, you are still boned).

Using Dynamic Data Masking to Hide Data from Users

Dynamic data masking is used to obfuscate data from users, most typically when using a user interface, but will do nothing for the security of your data if it is stolen. (There is another concept called "static data masking," which you may find references to that was almost in SQL Server 2019, based on releases of SSMS 18, that actually changes the data in the table permanently. The idea is that you mask data to make it safe to use for developers in a way that should not give away personal details, but as of the writing of this book, it has not been released, though some other companies may have tools to do the static masking process.)

What dynamic data masking does is allow you to show a user a column, but instead of showing them the actual data, mask the data from their view. As an example, consider a table that has email addresses. You might want to mask the data so most users can't see the actual data when they are querying the data, but rather just show them the first letter of the email address and a bit of data that looks like an email address that follows.

Dynamic data masking falls under the head of Security Center features in Microsoft Docs (docs.microsoft.com/en-us/sql/relational-databases/security/dynamic-data-masking), but as we will see, it doesn't behave like classic security features, as you will be adding some code to the DDL of the table. It is not a general-purpose feature, due to some fairly large limitations, which we will see, but it can be very useful for building a user interface where data needs to be masked.

There are a couple of serious limitations to understand. First, masks only pertain to SELECT operations. If a user can INSERT, UPDATE, or DELETE the row, they still can even if the data is masked. Hence, this feature is generally going to be used strictly for read operations. The second, fairly huge limitation with this feature is that there is only one right to allow unmasked viewing of all masked data, and it is at the database level (not the column level nor the table level nor the schema level).

To demonstrate, consider the following table (including my favorite column I have ever included in a demo, YachtCount!):

```
CREATE SCHEMA Demo;
GO
CREATE TABLE Demo.Person
--warning, I am using very small column datatypes in this
--example to make looking at the output easier, not as proper sizes
```

```
(
    PersonId     int NOT NULL CONSTRAINT PKPerson PRIMARY KEY,
    FirstName    nvarchar(10) NULL,
    LastName     nvarchar(10) NULL,
    PersonNumber varchar(10) NOT NULL,
    StatusCode   varchar(10) CONSTRAINT DFLTPersonStatus DEFAULT ('New')
         CONSTRAINT CHKPersonStatus
                        CHECK (StatusCode in ('Active','Inactive','New')),
    EmailAddress nvarchar(40) NULL,
    InceptionTime date NOT NULL, --Time we first saw this person. Usually
                                 -- the row create time, but not always
    -- YachtCount is a number that I didn't feel could insult anyone of any
    -- origin, ability, etc that I could put in this table
    YachtCount   tinyint NOT NULL
                        CONSTRAINT DFLTPersonYachtCount DEFAULT (0)
                        CONSTRAINT CHKPersonYachtCount CHECK (YachtCount >= 0),
);
```

Some of this data we will want to keep hidden from viewers. The PersonNumber, StatusCode, EmailAddress, InceptionTime, and YachtCount values all need to be hidden away. There are four types of built-in masks that we can use:

- *Default*: Takes the default mask of the datatype (*not* the default of the column, which would actually be kind of nice, but each datatype has an output that replaces the values from the column)

- *Email*: Masks the email so you only see a few meaningful characters to give you an idea of what the email address is, but not the full address

- *Random*: Puts a random number in place of an actual number (which can actually be kind of weird, as we will see)

- *Custom string (partial value, similar to SUBSTRING)*: Basically gives you control over what characters to keep and what to replace them with

Dynamic data masking becomes part of the table definition, so you use ALTER COLUMN to add this to the columns mentioned, starting with using default for each of the columns. Dynamic data masking can be added at table create time as well:

```
ALTER TABLE Demo.Person ALTER COLUMN PersonNumber
    ADD MASKED WITH (Function = 'default()');
ALTER TABLE Demo.Person ALTER COLUMN StatusCode
    ADD MASKED WITH (Function = 'default()');
ALTER TABLE Demo.Person ALTER COLUMN EmailAddress
    ADD MASKED WITH (Function = 'default()');
ALTER TABLE Demo.Person ALTER COLUMN InceptionTime
    ADD MASKED WITH (Function = 'default()');
ALTER TABLE Demo.Person ALTER COLUMN YachtCount
    ADD MASKED WITH (Function = 'default()');
```

Next, we add a few rows:

```
INSERT INTO Demo.Person (PersonId,FirstName,LastName,PersonNumber,
                    StatusCode, EmailAddress, InceptionTime,YachtCount)
VALUES(1,'Fred','Washington','0000000014','Active',
       'frew@ttt.net','1/1/1959',0),
(2,'Barney','Lincoln','0000000032','Active','barl@aol.com',
'8/1/1960',1),
(3,'Wilma','Reagan','0000000102','Active',NULL, '1/1/1959', 1);
```

Next, we create a user that will see the data as masked and give the user SELECT rights to the table:

```
CREATE USER MaskedMarauder WITHOUT LOGIN;
GRANT SELECT ON Demo.Person TO MaskedMarauder;
```

Then, we select the data as the administrative user and select it again impersonating the MaskedMarauder:

```
SELECT PersonId, PersonNumber, StatusCode, EmailAddress,
       InceptionTime, YachtCount
FROM   Demo.Person;
```

```
EXECUTE AS USER = 'MaskedMarauder';

SELECT PersonId, PersonNumber, StatusCode, EmailAddress,
       InceptionTime, YachtCount
FROM   Demo.Person;

REVERT;
```

This returns two result sets, the first unmasked and the second masked:

PersonId	PersonNumber	StatusCode	EmailAddress	InceptionTime	YachtCount
1	0000000014	Active	frew@ttt.net	1959-01-01	0
2	0000000032	Active	barl@aol.com	1960-08-01	1
3	0000000102	Active	NULL	1959-01-01	1

PersonId	PersonNumber	StatusCode	EmailAddress	InceptionTime	YachtCount
1	xxxx	xxxx	xxxx	1900-01-01	0
2	xxxx	xxxx	xxxx	1900-01-01	0
3	xxxx	xxxx	NULL	1900-01-01	0

A few initial notes: First, the data looks like regular, real data in some cases. YachtCount = 0 is the data for at least one row. Second, NULL data is still shown as NULL. Some defaults work well enough for the general case, like string being 'xxxx'. However, we probably want a bit more information in some cases (EmailAddress, PersonNumber), and sometimes you may want to use a random value, so I will use one for YachtCount.

First, we will change the EmailAddress masking. Instead of default, we will use email() as the masking function:

```
ALTER TABLE Demo.Person ALTER COLUMN EmailAddress
    ADD MASKED WITH (Function = 'email()');
```

Selecting out the data as the MaskedMarauder (a name which is not getting old to type), we see that email address gives us enough information to perhaps verify with a customer (note that all masked email addresses end in .com):

PersonId	PersonNumber	StatusCode	EmailAddress	InceptionTime	YachtCount
1	XXXX	XXXX	fXXX@XXXX.com	1900-01-01	0
2	XXXX	XXXX	bXXX@XXXX.com	1900-01-01	0
3	XXXX	XXXX	NULL	1900-01-01	0

But we can do better. Next, we will try the random masking function, with YachtCount. Random only works with numeric data:

```
ALTER TABLE Demo.Person ALTER COLUMN YachtCount
    ADD MASKED WITH (Function = 'random(1,100)');
    --makes the value between 1 and 100.
```

Viewing the masked versions of the data now shows the following nonsensical, definitely noncontroversial, data:

PersonId	PersonNumber	StatusCode	EmailAddress	InceptionTime	YachtCount
1	XXXX	XXXX	fXXX@XXXX.com	1900-01-01	35
2	XXXX	XXXX	bXXX@XXXX.com	1900-01-01	47
3	XXXX	XXXX	NULL	1900-01-01	25

Finally, we will use the custom string masking function, partial(). This lets you mask all or some of the data in a string-based column using a function: partial (number of characters to keep at the start of the string, string to be replaced, number of characters to keep on the end of the string). So we are going to mask the person number to show the first and last characters and then all status codes with 'Unknown':

```
ALTER TABLE Demo.Person ALTER COLUMN PersonNumber
    ADD MASKED WITH (Function = 'partial(1,"-------",2)');
    --note double quotes on the text

ALTER TABLE Demo.Person ALTER COLUMN StatusCode
    ADD MASKED WITH (Function = 'partial(0,"Unknown",0)');
```

Here is our final output, though the YachtCount may change:

PersonId	PersonNumber	StatusCode	EmailAddress	InceptionTime	YachtCount
1	0-------14	XXXX	fXXX@XXXX.com	1900-01-01	12
2	0-------32	XXXX	bXXX@XXXX.com	1900-01-01	43
3	0-------02	XXXX	NULL	1900-01-01	42

As mentioned earlier in the section, if we want to allow a user to see the unmasked data, there are two ways. First, we can grant the UNMASK permission at the database level. This means the user will be able to see all data in the database unmasked. The second is basically using impersonation. Create a user that has UNMASK rights, and use impersonation in a STORED PROCEDURE object to let the user see the data that way.

While it is limited in general-purpose value, dynamic data masking may come in handy in some situations where you want to hide the actual values of columns in tables in a user interface most of the time, particularly when you want to show the user partial values.

The real downside to this feature (and the reason I said that it is useful mainly for a user interface) comes with how it works with a WHERE clause. If you see the final output, you can see the value has a person number of '0-------14'. The problem is the user sort of has access to the value, if they have any idea of what to search for. For example, this following T-SQL statement returns 0 row:

```
EXECUTE AS USER = 'MaskedMarauder';

SELECT PersonId, PersonNumber, StatusCode, EmailAddress,
       InceptionTime, YachtCount
FROM   Demo.Person
WHERE  Person.PersonNumber = '0-------14';
```

But the following statement does return data, so while the user could not search for the existence of a certain piece of data, it would be possible to verify the existence of a piece of data very easily. This is something you would desire from a UI, but not so much from a user, poking around with enough time to randomly try all values:

```
SELECT PersonId, PersonNumber, StatusCode, EmailAddress,
       InceptionTime, YachtCount
FROM   Demo.Person
WHERE  Person.PersonNumber = '0000000014';

REVERT;
```

Auditing SQL Server Use

Keeping up with what your customers are doing with their data sounds nefarious, and it can be. But the opposite direction, making sure your employees aren't poking around in your customers' data, is actually quite essential. Sometimes, a client won't care too much about security in that employees do have valid reasons to view every bit of data in a database, at the proper time, in the proper context. For example, if they have issues to troubleshoot or are working on a specific customer's data, then accessing it is fine. Just bored and poking around, not so much. Hence, they cannot have any real limits on what can be done in the database. Yet at the same time, it is important to be able to know what these super-users have done, so they don't abuse their rights.

Auditing is not an alternative to implementing a full-blown security system, but simply to watch what users do, in case they do something out of the ordinary that they should not have done. To implement auditing, I'll configure a server and database audit using SQL Server's audit features. (SQL Server Audit works with SQL Server and Azure Managed Instance. If you are using Azure SQL DB, there is a different method that you can read about in Microsoft Docs: docs.microsoft.com/en-us/azure/azure-sql/database/auditing-overview. Managed Instance has some additional auditing information covered here as well: docs.microsoft.com/en-us/azure/azure-sql/managed-instance/auditing-configure.)

SQL Server Audit is a tremendously cool feature that will allow you to implement detailed monitoring in a declarative manner and will make the process of meeting auditing requirements reasonably straightforward. Instead of lots of code to pour through, you can just print the audits that you are enforcing, and you are done. Using SQL Server Audit, you will be able to watch what users are doing. While you will not be able to see the changes that are made, if you want to capture what is changing in the data, you can use the temporal feature (SQL Server 2016 or later) or a DML trigger, as we discussed in Chapter 9.

Note   As usual, there are graphical user interface (GUI) versions of almost everything I discuss, and I imagine that many programmers/DBAs (even some hardcore ones) will probably use the GUI for the most part, but as with everything else in this book, I want to show the syntax because it will make using the GUI easier.

Auditing is file based in that you don't do your logging to a database; rather, you specify a directory on your server (or off your server if you so desire). When auditing is turned on, each operation will be queued for audit or not executed. It doesn't write directly to the file; for maximum performance, SQL Server Audit uses Service Broker queues under the covers, so it doesn't have to write audit data to the file as part of each transaction. Instead, queue mechanisms make sure that the data is written asynchronously. (There is a setting to force an audit trail to be written in some amount of time or synchronously if you need it to be guaranteed 100% up to date. You will want to make sure that the directory is a very fast-access location to write to if you use a synchronous mode because completion of the audit write will then be part of the transactions you execute.).

The audit structures consist of three basic layers of objects:

- *Server audit*: Top-level object that defines where the audit file will be written to and other essential settings

- *Server audit specification*: Defines the actions at the server level that will be audited

- *Database audit specification*: Defines the actions at the database level that will be audited (Prior to SQL Server 2016, SP1, Database Auditing, was an Enterprise edition–only feature. It is available in all editions now.)

In the following sections, we will go through the steps to define an audit specification, enable the audit, and then view the audit results.

Defining an Audit Specification

As an example, we will set up an audit on our test server/security database to watch for logins to be changed (such as a new login created or one changed/dropped), watch for the Employee or Manager user to execute a SELECT statement against the Products. Product table, and watch for SELECT statements by anyone on the Sales.Invoice table. First, we define the SERVER AUDIT:

```
USE master;
GO
CREATE SERVER AUDIT ProSQLServerDatabaseDesign_Audit TO FILE
--choose your own directory, I expect most people
--have a temp directory on their system drive of their demo machine
(      FILEPATH = N'c:\temp\'
      ,MAXSIZE = 15 MB --of each file
      ,MAX_ROLLOVER_FILES = 0 --unlimited
)
WITH
(
      ON_FAILURE = SHUTDOWN --if the file cannot be written to,
                            --shut down the server
);
```

Note   The audit is created in a disabled state. You need to start it once you have added audit specifications.

The next step is to define an audit specification to set up the container to hold a list of related items to audit. This container-based approach lets you easily enable or disable auditing for the entire group of related features. Create the container by defining a SERVER AUDIT SPECIFICATION:

```
CREATE SERVER AUDIT SPECIFICATION ProSQLServerDatabaseDesign_Server_Audit
    FOR SERVER AUDIT ProSQLServerDatabaseDesign_Audit
    WITH (STATE = OFF); --disabled. I will enable it later
```

The next step is to add things to the specification to audit. There are lots of different things you can audit. You can find the list in Microsoft Docs on the "SQL Server Audit Action Groups and Actions" topic (docs.microsoft.com/en-us/sql/relational-databases/security/auditing/sql-server-audit-action-groups-and-actions).

At the server level, you can watch for changes to the configuration of your server. In the example, we are going to watch for server principals to change:

```
ALTER SERVER AUDIT SPECIFICATION ProSQLServerDatabaseDesign_Server_Audit
    ADD (SERVER_PRINCIPAL_CHANGE_GROUP);
```

Next, we will go through the same process for the database that we did for the server, setting up the container for the audit using the DATABASE AUDIT SPECIFICATION command for the table we created earlier. At the database level, we can look for configuration changes, but perhaps more interestingly, we can audit people accessing tables. In this example, we will monitor the one thing that is pretty difficult to do with any other method (impossible without requiring STORED PROCEDURE object access only), auditing certain users executing a SELECT statement that references a table (and we could look for modification DML as well, just keeping this simple for the example):

```
USE ClassicSecurityExample;
GO
CREATE DATABASE AUDIT SPECIFICATION
                ProSQLServerDatabaseDesign_Database_Audit
    FOR SERVER AUDIT ProSQLServerDatabaseDesign_Audit
    WITH (STATE = OFF);
```

This time, we will audit the Employee and Manager database users' use of the Products.Product table and the Products.AllProducts view (created earlier in this chapter). Here is how we add those items to the specification:

```
ALTER DATABASE AUDIT SPECIFICATION
    ProSQLServerDatabaseDesign_Database_Audit
    ADD (SELECT ON Products.Product BY Employee, Manager),
    ADD (SELECT ON Products.AllProducts BY Employee, Manager);
```

Enabling an Audit Specification

Next, we enable the two AUDIT SPECIFICATION objects that we've just created and the SERVER AUDIT itself:

```
USE master;
GO
ALTER SERVER AUDIT ProSQLServerDatabaseDesign_Audit
    WITH (STATE = ON);

ALTER SERVER AUDIT SPECIFICATION ProSQLServerDatabaseDesign_Server_Audit
    WITH (STATE = ON);
GO

USE ClassicSecurityExample;
GO
ALTER DATABASE AUDIT SPECIFICATION ProSQLServerDatabaseDesign_Database_
Audit
    WITH (STATE = ON);
```

At this point, the audits are enabled, and the system is being watched for suspicious activity.

Viewing the Audit Trail

Now that our audits are enabled, we can monitor the usage of the features and functionality that we're auditing. The following code executes some actions that will be audited as a result of the specifications we've just created. The following script will do a few actions that will be audited by the audit objects we have set up in the previous sections:

```
CREATE LOGIN MrSmith WITH PASSWORD = 'A very g00d password!';
GO
USE ClassicSecurityExample;
GO
EXECUTE AS USER = 'Manager'; --existed from earlier examples
GO
SELECT *
FROM    Products.Product;
```

```
GO
SELECT  *
FROM    Products.AllProducts; --Permissions will fail
GO
REVERT
GO
EXECUTE AS USER = 'Employee'; --existed from earlier examples
GO
SELECT  *
FROM    Products.AllProducts; --Permissions will fail
GO
REVERT;
GO
```

The following query will let us view the log that was set up with the CREATE SERVER AUDIT command in the first step of the process. Execute the following query:

```
SELECT event_time, succeeded,
       database_principal_name, statement
FROM sys.fn_get_audit_file ('c:\temp\*', DEFAULT, DEFAULT);
```

The results show the different statements that were executed (note the two statements where the permission failed; the passwords in the CREATE LOGIN statements were replaced with ****** as well):

event_time	succeeded	user_name	statement
01:16:49	1	dbo	CREATE LOGIN MrSmith WITH PASSWORD ...
01:17:53	1	Manager	SELECT * FROM Products.Product
01:17:53	0	Manager	SELECT * FROM Products.AllProducts
01:18:06	0	Employee	SELECT * FROM Products.AllProducts

There are lots of other pieces of information returned by the sys.fn_get_audit_file function that are very useful, especially the server principal information. Using a few of the catalog views, you can get a picture of what is captured by the audits. Note that the query I built works only at an object (table, view, etc.) level. It could be extended if you wanted to do column-level audits.

Viewing the Audit Configuration

Finally, once you have set up the audit trail, it is often important to find out what is being audited. You can do this using several of the catalog views:

- sys.server_audits: One row per server audit

- sys.server_audit_specifications: Details about the audits that have been configured for this server, such as when it was started, the last time it was modified, and so on

- sys.server_audit_specification_details: Links the objects being audited and actions being audited

The following query, using these catalog views, will get you the definition of what is being audited at a server level:

```
SELECT   sas.name AS audit_specification_name,
         audit_action_name
FROM     sys.server_audits AS sa
            JOIN sys.server_audit_specifications AS sas
               ON sa.audit_guid = sas.audit_guid
            JOIN sys.server_audit_specification_details AS sasd
               ON sas.server_specification_id = sasd.server_specification_id
WHERE    sa.name = 'ProSQLServerDatabaseDesign_Audit';
```

By executing this, given all the audit stuff we had set up, the following is returned:

audit_specification_name	audit_action_name
ProSQLServerDatabaseDesign_Server_Audit	SERVER_PRINCIPAL_CHANGE_GROUP

Digging deeper, to get the objects and actions, the following query will get you the database-level actions that are being audited:

```
SELECT audit_action_name,dp.name AS [principal],
       SCHEMA_NAME(o.schema_id) + '.' + o.name AS object
FROM   sys.server_audits AS sa
          JOIN sys.database_audit_specifications AS sas
             ON sa.audit_guid = sas.audit_guid
```

```
        JOIN sys.database_audit_specification_details AS sasd
            ON sas.database_specification_id =
                          sasd.database_specification_id
        JOIN sys.database_principals AS dp
            ON dp.principal_id = sasd.audited_principal_id
        JOIN sys.objects AS o
            ON o.object_id = sasd.major_id
WHERE   sa.name = 'ProSQLServerDatabaseDesign_Audit'
  and   sasd.minor_id = 0; --need another query for column level audits
```

This query returns the following:

```
audit_action_name    principal      object
-------------------   -------------  -------------------------------
SELECT                Employee       Products.Product
SELECT                Manager        Products.Product
SELECT                Employee       Products.allProducts
SELECT                Manager        Products.allProducts
```

Quite a few more catalog views pertain to the server and database facilities of SQL Server, certainly more than is necessary in this chapter for me to cover. The basic setup of auditing is quite straightforward, and auditing is a nice feature that is useful for DBAs/ architects who have the need to audit the activities of their users and administrators.

Best Practices

Security is always one of the most important tasks to consider when implementing a system. Storing data could be worse than not storing it, if it can be used for improper purposes:

- *Secure the server first*: Although this topic is outside the scope of this book, be certain that the server is secure. If a user can get access to unencrypted data or backup files and take them home, all the database security in the world won't help.

- *Grant rights to roles rather than users*: Roles should be the same in DEV, QA, and PROD and need to be tested, but the security principals that fill those roles will be different. If you have tested that adding a user to the Manager role in DEV gives them access to everything they need to do their job, granting actual users to that role will definitely work.

- *Use schemas to simplify security*: Because you can grant rights at a schema level, you can grant rights to SELECT, INSERT, UPDATE, DELETE, and even EXECUTE everything within a schema. Even new objects that are added to the schema after the rights are granted are usable by the grantees.

- *Consider security using stored procedures as the access layer*: Using stored procedures as the only way for a user to get access to the data presents the user with a nice interface to the data. If procedures are well named, you can also easily apply security to match up with the interfaces that use them. Chapter 13 will advance this concept further.

- *Don't overuse the impersonation features*: EXECUTE AS is a blessing, and it opens up a world of possibilities. It does, however, open up security holes without careful consideration of its use. Add a database with TRUSTWORTHY access set to ON, and a procedure can be written to do dangerous things on a server, which could be exploited as a big security hole by a devious programmer.

- *Encrypt sensitive data*: SQL Server has several means of encrypting data, and there are other methods available to do it off the SQL Server box with Always Encrypted (with performance improvements in its use with secure enclaves in SQL Server 2019), or you can use some tool that SQL Server has no idea about. Use it as much as necessary, but make sure not to store everything needed to decrypt the data with the encrypted data, in case someone gets hold of the data. Use Transparent Data Encryption to secure important files from exploit if they fall into the wrong hands. (And if some encrypted data gets re-encrypted, that will not be the worst thing.)

- *Segregate security between environments*: Security in development environments will be very different. Take care not to end up with developers having the same rights to production data as they have in development, because you use the same security script to create your development servers as you do in production. Developers generally should be given very few rights to production data, to limit access to sensitive data. All it takes is one production support issue where a connection is left open to a production server for bad things to occur (true story).

Summary

Security is a large topic, and understanding all the implications requires way more information than we covered in this chapter. I discussed some of the ways to secure your data inside a single SQL Server database. This isn't an easy subject, but it's far easier than dealing with securing the computer and instance that SQL Server resides on. Fortunately, in the database we're usually looking to protect ourselves from ordinary users, though doing a good job of encryption is a good barricade to keep most thieves at bay.

We discussed a range of topics for when we need to design security into our database usage:

- The basics of permissions-based security using SQL Server DDL statements and how this security works on SQL Server objects. This included using principals of several types—logins, users, roles, certificates, and application roles—and then applying different security criteria to the base tables and columns in a database.

- Using coded objects to encapsulate statements that can limit the queries that users can execute. We discussed using several types of objects:

  - *Stored procedures and scalar functions*: Giving advanced usages to users without letting them know how they're doing it. Included in this section was how security works across database lines and server lines.

- *Views and table-valued functions*: Used to break tables up in a simple manner, either row- or column-wise. The goal is to make security seamless, such that the users feel that only this database has the data to which they have rights.

- We looked at obfuscating data to make it hard to view the data unless you specifically try to, generally by using encryption to make the data unreadable without a key.

- Next, we discussed using an audit trail to give the user an audit of what goes on in given rows and columns in the database. This is the typical method when it comes to most data, because it's easy to give the users access to the lists of what has changed (and why, if the application asks for a reason with certain types of changes).

Of course, make sure that you understand that there is a lot more to security than just security on the database. The biggest task is limiting the people/processes that can even connect to the server, the instance, and the database to the correct set of users, and that means working with the administrators of your network, websites, and applications to make sure to limit the threat surface as much as possible.

CHAPTER 11

Data Structures, Indexes, and Their Application

The best index to a person's character is how he treats people who can't do him any good, and how he treats people who can't fight back.

— Abigail Van Buren, aka Dear Abby

To me, the true beauty of the relational database engine comes from its declarative nature. As a programmer, I simply ask the engine a question, and it answers it. The questions I ask are usually pretty simple; just give me some data from a few tables, correlate it based on a column or two, do a little math perhaps, and give me back information (and naturally do it incredibly fast, if you don't mind, regardless of the fact that there are 10 billion rows involved). While simple may not actually be the right single-word description for what I have asked, the engine usually obliges with an answer pretty quickly when the database is designed well enough. Usually, but not always. This is where the DBA and data programmers must figure out what the optimizer is doing and help it along.

If you are not a particularly deep technical person, you probably think of query tuning as a kind of magic. It is not. What it is is a lot of complex code implementing complex algorithms that allow the engine to educatedly guess the best way to answer your query in a timely manner. And, with every passing version of SQL Server, that code gets better at it than the last. To prove it isn't magic, these operations can be shown to you on a query plan, which is a blueprint of the algorithms used to execute your query. I will use query plans in this chapter to show you how your design choices can affect the way work gets done.

Our part in the process of getting back lightning-fast answers to complex questions is to assist the query optimizer (which takes your query and turns it into a plan of how to run the query), the query processor (which takes the plan and uses it to do the actual

773

© Louis Davidson 2021
L. Davidson, *Pro SQL Server Relational Database Design and Implementation*,
https://doi.org/10.1007/978-1-4842-6497-3_11

work), and the storage engine (which manages IO for the whole process). We do this first by designing and implementing as close to a normalized relational model as possible, using good set-based code, following best practices with coding T-SQL, and so on.

This is obviously still a design book, so I won't cover a lot about T-SQL coding, but it is a skill you should master. Consider Apress's *Beginning T-SQL, Third Edition,* by Kathi Kellenberger and Scott Shaw, or perhaps one of Itzik Ben-Gan's Inside SQL books on T-SQL for some deep learning on the subject. Once we have built our systems correctly, the next step is to help out by adjusting the physical structures using proper hardware laid out well on disk subsystems, filegroups, and files, partitioning, and configuring our hardware to work best with SQL Server and with the load we will be, are, and have been placing on the server. This is yet another book's worth of information, for which I will direct you to a book I reviewed an earlier edition as a technical editor, Peter Carter's *Pro SQL Server Administration 2019* (Apress, 2019).

In this chapter, much of what we are going to cover will concern the structures that you will be adding and subtracting on a semi-regular basis: indexes. Indexing is a constant balance of helping performance vs. harming performance, ideally a lot of help and a little harm. If you don't use indexes enough, queries will be slow, as the query processor has to read every row of your tables (which, even if it seems fast on your test machine, can cause the concurrency issues we will cover in the next chapter by forcing the query processor to lock a lot more of a table than ought to be necessary as it touches every row of the structure it is scanning). Use too many indexes, and modifying data could take too long, as indexes have to be maintained. Balance is the key, kind of like matching the amount of fluid to the size of the glass so that you will never have to answer that annoying question about a glass that has half as much fluid as it can hold. (The answer is that the glass is always completely full...of some part liquid and some part air.)

Most of the query plans that I present will be obtained using the SET SHOWPLAN_TEXT ON statement. When you're doing this locally, it is almost always easier to use the graphical showplan from SSMS (or one of the better free tools out there, SentryOne Plan Explorer available here at www.sentryone.com/plan-explorer which provides a few views of the query plan that can be very helpful when dealing with very huge and complex plans). However, when you need to post the plan or include it in a document, using one of the SET SHOWPLAN_TEXT statements can make it far easier to format and see some of the important details. You can read about this more in Microsoft Docs at "SET SHOWPLAN_ TEXT (Transact-SQL)" (docs.microsoft.com/en-us/sql/t-sql/statements/set-showplan-text-transact-sql). Note that using SET SHOWPLAN_TEXT (or the other versions of SET SHOWPLAN that are available, such as SET SHOWPLAN_XML) commands does not actually execute the statement/batch; rather, they output the estimated plan when you execute the statement. If you need to execute the statement and get the textual actual query plan (like to get some dynamic SQL statements to execute to see the plan), you can use SET STATISTICS PROFILE ON to get the plan and some other pertinent information about what has been executed. Each of these session settings will need to be turned OFF explicitly once you have finished, or they will continue returning plans where you don't want so.

Everything we have done so far in the book has been centered on the idea that the quality of the data is the number one concern. This is the foundation of what I try to teach in this book, and it will not change. At this point in the process, I am going to assume that the job of designing and implementing quality database that houses your data is done and done well. I also ask that we agree that slow and right is *always* better than fast and wrong. How would you like to get paid a week early, but only get half your money? Paid late isn't ideal either, so the obvious goal of building a computer system is to do things right *and* fast enough.

We have already added indexes in previous chapters, as a side effect of adding PRIMARY KEY and UNIQUE constraints (in that a UNIQUE INDEX is built by SQL Server to implement the uniqueness condition). In many cases, those indexes will turn out to be almost all of what you need to make normal OLTP queries run nicely, since the most common searches that people will do will be on identifying information.

One thing that complicates all of our performance choices at this point in the process is that Microsoft has added an additional engine to the mix. I have noted in Chapter 7 and onward that these different versions exist and that some of the sample code from those chapters will have downloaded versions to show how it might be coded with the different engines. But the differences are more than code. The design of the logical database isn't different at all, and what is put into the physical database design generally isn't going to change considerably, if at all, either. But there are internal differences to how indexes work that will change some of the implementation, which I will explore in this chapter. Chapter 12 will discuss how these changes affect concurrency and isolation, and finally, Chapter 13 will discuss changes in coding you will see. For now, we will start with the more common on-disk indexes, and then we will look at the memory-optimized index technologies, including indexes on memory-optimized tables and columnstore indexes (which will be discussed in more detail in Appendix C as well, available to download).

Indexing Overview

Indexes allow the SQL Server engine to perform fast, targeted data retrieval rather than simply scanning though the entire table. A well-placed index can speed up data retrieval by orders of magnitude, while a haphazard approach to indexing can actually have the opposite effect when creating, updating, or deleting data, particularly if you are creating a lot more data than you are reading.

Indexing your data effectively requires a working knowledge of how that data will change over time, the sort of questions that will be asked of it, and the volume of data that you expect to be dealing with. Unfortunately, this is what makes any topic about physical tuning so challenging. To index effectively, you need real history or the nonexistent psychic ability to foretell the future of your exact data usage patterns. When deciding to (or not to) use an index to improve the performance of one query, you have to consider the effect on the overall performance of the system.

In the upcoming sections, I'll do the following:

- Introduce the basic structure of rowstore indexes.

- For on-disk tables, discuss the two fundamental types of indexes and how their structure determines the structure of the table.

- Do the same for memory-optimized tables, which have quite different physical structures, with very similar syntax.

- Demonstrate basic index usage, introducing you to the basic syntax and usage of indexes.

- Show you how to determine whether SQL Server is likely to use your index and how to see if SQL Server has used your index.

- Introduce some basic management concepts.

If you are producing a product for sale that uses SQL Server as the backend, indexes are truly going to be something that ideally your customers can manage, unless you can truly effectively constrain how users will use your product. For example, if you sell a product that manages customers and your basic expectation is that they will have around 1,000 customers, what happens if one wants to use it with 100,000 customers? Or 1 million customers? Do you not take their money? Of course you do and charge them more, but what about performance? Hardware improvements generally can barely come close to linear improvements in performance. So, if you get hardware that is 100 times "faster," you would be extremely fortunate to get close to 100 times improvement (and that would require 100 times faster CPU, disk, and RAM capability or increases in each). However, adding a simple index can provide 100,000 times improvement on a large data set that may not even make a noticeable difference on the smaller data set. (This is not to pooh-pooh the value of faster hardware either. The point is that, situationally, you get far greater gain from writing better code than you do from just throwing hardware at a problem. The ideal situation is adequate hardware and excellent code.)

Note   One bit of terminology that comes up is rowstore and columnstore indexes. Most indexes in SQL Server are called rowstore indexes because they store data from each row together. The term rowstore is not always used except when in contrast to columnstore indexes, which we will cover briefly later in the chapter.

Basic Index Structure

An index is a structure that SQL Server uses to optimize access to the physical data in a table. An index can be on one or more columns of a table. In essence, an index in SQL Server works on the same principle as the index of a book. It organizes the data from the column (or columns) of data in a manner that's conducive to fast, efficient searching, so you can find a row or set of rows without looking at an entire set of data. It provides a means to jump quickly to a specific piece of data, rather than just starting on row one each time you search the table and scanning through until you find what you're looking for. Even worse, when you are looking for one specific value, unless SQL Server knows that is has every single row with that value, it has no way to know if it can stop scanning data when rows have been found.

As an example, consider that you have a completely unordered list of employees and their details in a book. If you had to search this list for persons named "Davidson," you would have to look at every single name on every single page. Assuming you weren't paid by the hour, soon after trying this once, you would start trying to devise some better manner of searching. On first pass, you would probably sort the list alphabetically. But what happens if you needed to search for an employee by their employee identification number? Well, you would spend a bunch of time searching through the list sorted by last name for the employee number. Eventually, you could create a list of last names and the pages you could find them on and another list with the employee numbers and their pages. Following this pattern, you would build sorted lists for any other type of search you'd regularly perform on the list. In this analogy, the sorted list is an index. Of course, SQL Server is a lot faster at scanning through the list one name or employee ID at a time than you are, so if you need to scan a table occasionally, it isn't such a bad thing, but looking at two or three names per search is always more efficient than 2 or 3 million.

Now, consider this in terms of a table like an Employee table. You might execute a query such as the following:

```
SELECT LastName, <EmployeeDetails>
FROM Employee
WHERE LastName = 'Davidson';
```

In the absence of an index to rapidly search, SQL Server will perform a scan of the data in the entire (referred to as a *table scan*) Employee table, looking for rows that satisfy the query predicate. A full table scan generally won't cause you too many problems with small tables, but it can cause poor performance for large tables with many *pages* of data, much as it would if you had to manually look through 20 names vs. 2,000. A page of data, as we will cover later in this chapter, is an 8 KB unit of storage that SQL Server uses to store data.

Of course, on your development box with a few hundred or maybe a few hundred thousand test rows, you probably won't be able to discern the difference between a seek and a scan (or even hundreds of scans). Only when you are experiencing a reasonably heavy load will the difference be noticed. (And as we will notice in the next chapter, the more rows SQL Server needs to touch, the more blocking you may do to other users.)

If we instead created an index on the LastName column, the index would create a structure to allow searching for the rows with the matching LastName in a logical fashion, and the database engine could move directly to rows where the last name is Davidson and retrieve the required data quickly and efficiently. And even if there are ten people with the last name of 'Davidson', SQL Server knows to stop when it hits 'Davidtown'.

Of course, as you might imagine, the engineer types who invented the concept of indexing and searching data structures don't simply make lists to search through. Instead, most indexes are implemented using what is known as a *balanced tree* (B-tree) structure (some others are built using *hash* structures, as we'll cover when we get to the "Memory-Optimized Indexes and Data Structures" section, but B-trees will be overwhelmingly the norm, so they get the primary introduction). The B-tree index is made up of index pages structured, again, much like an index of a book or a phone book. Each index page contains the first value in a range and a pointer to the next lower page in the index. The pages on the last level in the index are referred to as the *leaf pages*, which contain the actual data values that are being indexed, plus either the data for the row or pointers to the data. This allows the query processor to go directly to the data it is searching for by checking only a few pages, even when there are millions of values in the index.

Figure 11-1 shows an example of the type of B-tree that SQL Server uses for on-disk indexes (memory-optimized indexes are different and will be covered later). Each of the outer rectangles is an 8 KB index page, just as we mentioned earlier. The three values— 'A', 'J', and 'P'—are the *index keys* in this top-level page of the index. The index page has as many index keys as will fit physically on the page. To decide which path to follow to reach the lower level of the index, we have to decide if the value requested is between two of the keys: 'A' to 'I', 'J' to 'P', or greater than 'P'. For example, say the value we want to find in the index happens to be 'I'. We go to the first page in the index. The database determines that 'I' doesn't come after 'J', so it follows the 'A' pointer to the next index page. Here, it determines that 'I' comes after 'C' and 'G', so it follows the 'G' pointer to the leaf page.

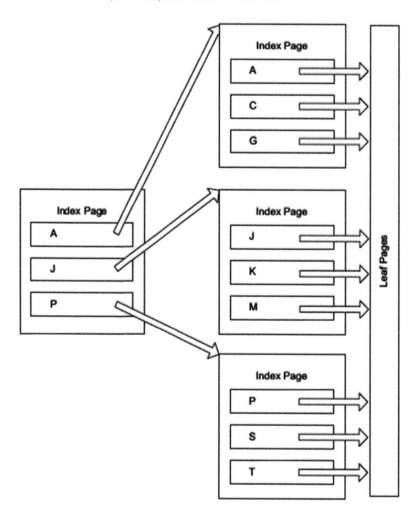

Figure 11-1. *Basic index structure*

Each of these pages is 8 KB in size. Depending on the size of the key (determined by summing the data lengths of the columns in the key, up to a maximum of 1,700 bytes for some types of indexes), it's possible to have anywhere from 4 entries to over 1,000 on a single page. The more keys you can fit onto a single index page, the more child nodes it allows that page to support. The more pages are linked from each level to the next, finally, the fewer numbers of steps from the top page of the index to reach the leaf.

B-tree indexes are extremely efficient, because for an index that stores only 500 different values on a page, it has 500 pointers to the next level in the index, and the next level has 500 pages with 500 values each. That makes 250,000 different pointers on that level, and the next level has up to 250,000 × 500 pointers. That's 125,000,000 different values in just a three-level index. At 16 bytes, just over 500 unique identifiers will fit into 8060 bytes, and while that is a very optimistic number, because there's overhead to an index key, this is just a rough estimation of the number of levels in the index, but certainly if the index key is an integer or even a bigint, these numbers are more than achievable.

Another concept to understand is how balanced the tree is. If the tree is perfectly balanced, every index page would have exactly the same number of keys on it. Once the index has lots of data on one end or data gets moved around on it for insertions or deletions, the tree becomes ragged, with one end having one level and another many levels. This is why you have to do some basic maintenance on the indexes, something we will discuss further at the end of the chapter.

This is just a general overview of what an index is, and there are several variations of types of indexes in use with SQL Server. The most important aspect to understand at this point is that indexes speed access to rows by giving you quicker access to some part of the table so that you don't have to look at every single row and inspect it individually.

On-Disk Indexes

To understand indexes on on-disk objects, it helps to have a working knowledge of the physical structures of a database. At a high level, the storage component of the on-disk engine works with a hierarchy of structures, starting with the database, which is broken down into filegroups (with one PRIMARY filegroup always existing), with each filegroup containing a number of files. As we discussed in Chapter 9 in the sections about storing large binary items, a filegroup can contain files for filestream, which in-memory OLTP also uses; but we are going to keep this simple and just talk about simple files that store basic data. This is shown in Figure 11-2.

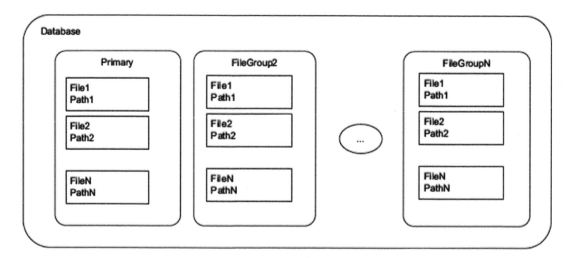

***Figure 11-2.** Simplified database and filegroup structure*

You control the placement of objects that store physical data pages at the filegroup level (code and metadata is always stored on the primary filegroup, along with all the system objects). New objects created are placed in the *default* filegroup, which is the PRIMARY filegroup (every database has one as part of the CREATE DATABASE statement, or the first file specified is set to primary) unless another filegroup is specified in any CREATE <object> commands. For example, to place an object in a filegroup other than the default, you need to specify the name of the filegroup using the ON clause of the table or index creation statement:

```
CREATE TABLE <tableName>
(...)  ON <fileGroupName>
```

The ON <fileGroupName> clause of the CREATE TABLE statement assigns the table to the filegroup, but not to any particular file. There are clauses on statements to place indexes and constraints that are backed with unique indexes on a different filegroup as well. An important part of tuning can be to see if there is any pressure on your disk subsystems and, if so, possibly redistribute data to different disks using filegroups. If you want to see what files you have in your databases, you can query the sys.filegroups and sys.master_files catalog views, which are both system-level objects. This will show you all the files and filegroups for all databases on an instance:

```
SELECT DB_NAME(df.database_id) AS DatabaseName,
        CASE WHEN fg.name IS NULL
        --other, such as logs
        THEN CONCAT('OTHER-',df.type_desc COLLATE database_default)
                    ELSE fg.name END AS FileGroup,
        df.name AS LogicalFileName,
        df.physical_name AS PhysicalFileName
FROM    sys.filegroups AS fg
        RIGHT JOIN sys.master_files AS df
            ON fg.data_space_id = df.data_space_id
ORDER BY DatabaseName, CASE WHEN fg.name IS NOT NULL THEN 0 ELSE 1 END,
            fg.name, df.type_desc;
```

As shown in Figure 11-3, files are further broken down into a number of extents, each consisting of eight separate 8 KB pages where tables, indexes, and so on are physically stored. SQL Server only allocates space in a database in extents. When files grow, you will notice that the size of files will be incremented only in 64 KB increments.

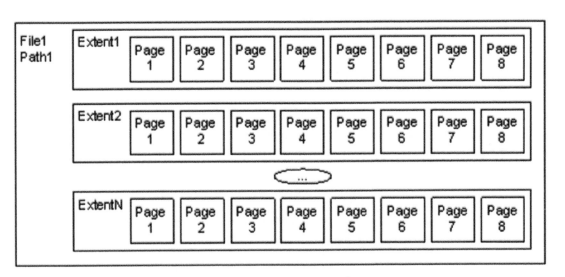

Figure 11-3. *Files and extents*

Each extent in turn has eight pages that hold one specific type of data each:

- *Data*: Table data.

- *Index*: Index data.

- *Overflow data:* Used when a row is greater than 8,060 bytes or for varchar(max), varbinary(max), text, or image values.

- *Allocation map*: Information about the allocation of extents.

- *Page free space*: Information about what different pages are allocated for.

- *Index allocation*: Information about extents used for table or index data.

- *Bulk changed map*: Extents modified by a bulk INSERT operation.

- *Differential changed map*: Extents that have changed since the last database backup command. This is used to support differential backups.

In larger databases, most extents will contain just one type of page, but in smaller databases, SQL Server can place any kind of page in the same extent. When all data is of the same type, it's known as a *uniform* extent. When pages are of various types, it's referred to as a *mixed* extent.

There are two kinds of pages in the database that are used to help manage allocation of extents in the database: GAM (Global Allocation Map, for uniform extents) and SGAM (Shared Global Allocation Map, for mixed extents). These pages have a bit for every extent, and if the extent is available, the bit is 0, 1 if the extent is in use.

As of SQL Server 2016, mixed extents are turned off in tempdb, but are on by default in user databases. Mixed extents were created to save space, but for most user databases, it can be better to turn off mixed extents using the following command:

```
ALTER DATABASE <DatabaseName>
    SET MIXED_PAGE_ALLOCATION OFF;
```

SQL Server places all on-disk table data in pages, with a header that contains metadata about the page (object ID of the owner, type of page, etc.), as well as the rows of data, which is what we typically care about as programmers.

Figure 11-4 shows an example data page from a table. The header of the page contains identification values such as the page number, the object ID of the object the data is for, compression information, and so on. (Compression will be covered in more detail later in the chapter.) The data rows hold the actual data. Finally, there's an allocation block that has the offsets/pointers to the row data.

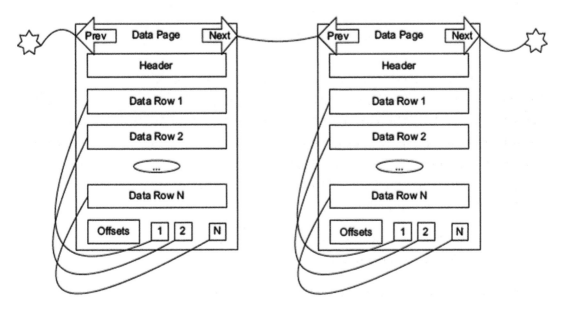

Figure 11-4. *Data pages*

Figure 11-4 also shows that there are doubly linked pointers from the next to the previous rows. These pointers are added when pages are ordered, such as in the pages of an index. Heap objects (tables with no clustered index) are not ordered. This will be clearer as I cover the types of indexes in the next two sections.

The other kind of page that is frequently used that you need to understand is the *overflow page*. It is used to hold row data that won't fit on the basic 8,060-byte page. There are two reasons an overflow page is used:

- The combined length of all data in a row grows beyond 8,060 bytes. In this case, data goes on an overflow page automatically, allowing you to have virtually unlimited row sizes (with the obvious performance concerns that go along with that, naturally).

- By setting the sp_tableoption setting on a table for large value types out of row to 1, all the (max) and XML datatype values are immediately stored out of row on an overflow page. If you set it to 0, SQL Server tries to place all data on the main page in the row structure, if it fits into the 8,060-byte row. The default is 0, because this is typically the best general setting when the most column set values are short enough to fit on a single page. Your mileage may vary, as very large rows that need scanning can be quite costly.

For example, Figure 11-5 depicts the type of situation that might occur for a table that has the large value types out of row set to 1. Here, Data Row 1 has two pointers to support two varbinary(max) columns: one that spans two pages and another that spans only a single page. Using all of the data in Data Row 1 will now require up to four reads (depending on where the actual page gets stored in the physical structures), making data access far slower than if all of the data were on a single page. This kind of performance problem can be easy to overlook, but on occasion, overflow pages will really drag down your performance, especially when other programmers use SELECT * on tables where they don't really need all of the data.

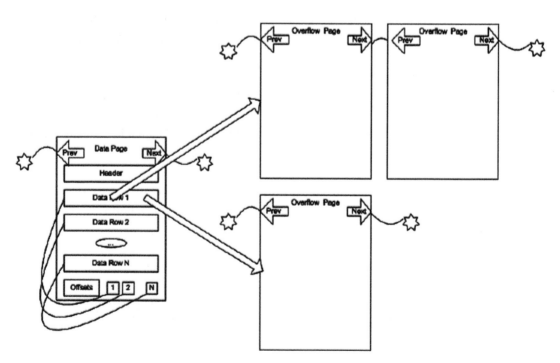

Figure 11-5. *Sample overflow pages*

The overflow pages are linked lists that can accommodate up to 2 GB of storage in a single column. Generally speaking, it isn't really a very good idea to store 2 GB in a single column (or even a row) if you want even somewhat quick reaction times, but the ability to do so is available if needed.

Storing large values that are placed off of the main page will be far costlier when you need these values than if all of the data can be placed in the same data page. On the other hand, if you seldom use the data in your queries, placing them off the page can give you a much smaller footprint for the important data, requiring far less disk access on average. It is a balance that you need to consider, as you should be able to envision how much more costly a table scan of columns that are on the overflow pages is going to be than if data is self-contained. Not only will you have to read extra pages; you'll have to be redirected to the overflow page for every row that's overflowed.

When you get down to the row level, the data is laid out with metadata, fixed-length fields, and variable-length fields, as shown in Figure 11-6. (Note that this is a generalization and the storage engine does a lot of stuff to the data for optimization, especially when you enable compression.)

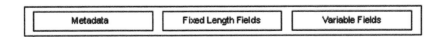

Figure 11-6. *Data row*

The metadata describes the row, gives information about the variable-length fields, and so on. Generally speaking, since data is dealt with by the query processor at the page level, even if only a single row is needed, data can be accessed very rapidly no matter the exact physical representation.

The maximum amount of data that can be placed on a single page (including overhead from variable-length fields) is 8,060 bytes. As illustrated in Figure 11-5, when a data row grows larger than 8,060 bytes, the data in variable-length columns can spill out onto an overflow page. A 16-byte pointer is left on the original page and points to the page where the overflow data is placed. (Yes, that is correct; it costs 16 bytes of overhead to point to the overflow page, in addition to size of the data!)

One last concept we need to discuss is page splits. When inserting or updating rows, SQL Server might have to rearrange the data on the pages due to the pages being filled up. Such rearranging can be a particularly costly operation. Consider the situation from our example shown in Figure 11-7, assuming that only three values can fit on a page.

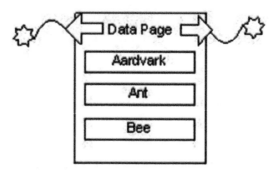

Figure 11-7. *Sample data page before page split*

Say we want to add the value Bear to the page. If that value won't fit onto the page, the page will need to be reorganized. Pages that need to be split are split into two, generally with 50% of the data on one page and 50% on the other (there are usually more than three values on a real page). Once the page is split and its values are reinserted, the new pages would end up looking something like Figure 11-8.

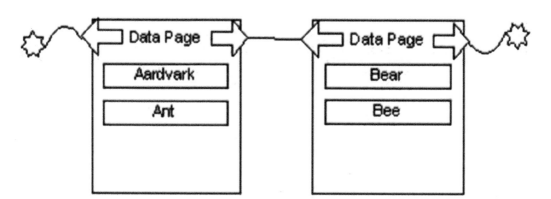

Figure 11-8. *Sample data page after page split*

Page splits are costly operations and ,when using physical spinning media, can be terrible for performance, because after the page split, data won't be located on successive physical pages. This condition is commonly known as *fragmentation*. Page splits occur in a normal system and are simply a part of adding data to your table. However, they can occur extremely rapidly and seriously degrade performance if you are not aware and do not maintain your physical structures. When using solid-state media, fragmentation is less of a concern in terms of and heads moving around spinning disks to read data, but as mentioned before, it can make the B-tree less balanced, causing a larger number of reads than necessary. Understanding the effect that page splits can have on your data and indexes is important as you tune performance on tables that have large numbers of inserts or updates.

To tune your tables and indexes to help minimize page splits, you can use the FILL FACTOR of the index. When you build or rebuild an index or a table (using ALTER TABLE <tablename> REBUILD), the fill factor indicates how much space is left on each page for future data. If you are inserting random values all over the structures (e.g., a common situation that occurs when you use a nonsequential uniqueidentifier for a primary key), you will want to leave adequate space on each page to cover the expected number of rows that will be created in the future. During a page split, the data page is always split approximately fifty-fifty, and it is left half empty on each page, and even worse, the structure is becoming, as mentioned, fragmented.

Now that we have looked at the basic physical structures of an index, let's look at the base index structures that we will commonly work with. There are two different types of indexes:

- *Clustered*: This type of index orders the physical table in the order of the index. You can have only one, and the choice of clustered index will greatly affect the performance of your system.

- *Nonclustered*: These are completely separate structures that simply speed access.

The examples in this section on indexes will mostly be based on tables from the WideWorldImporters database you can download from Microsoft in some manner (as I was writing this chapter, it was located on GitHub). I drop and recreate this database regularly when trying out concepts.

Clustered Indexes

The name *clustered index* in SQL Server has the specific meaning that it is an index that becomes the physical structure of a table. There are two types of clustered indexes, a clustered rowstore index and a clustered columnstore index. The key of a clustered index is referred to as the *clustering key*. The columnstore version is used primarily for reporting purposes and will be discussed a bit more later in the chapter.

Clustered rowstore indexes are B-tree indexes where the leaf pages of the index are also the data pages of the table. The leaf pages of a B-tree index are ordered, so each of the data pages is then linked to one or two other pages in a doubly linked list to provide two-directional ordered scanning. Tables with a clustered rowstore index are referred to as *clustered tables*.

In the following sections, I will discuss the structure of a rowstore clustered index, followed by showing the usage patterns and examples of how these indexes are used.

Index Structure

Say you have an index that is defined as

```
CREATE CLUSTERED INDEX IndexName ON
                SchemaName.TableName (ColumnName1, ColumnName2);
```

In this example, the key is Column1, Column2, and it would be the clustering key of SchemaName.TableName, no matter what the PRIMARY KEY constraint's columns were or if there was a PRIMARY KEY constraint.

The clustered index, since it becomes the physical structure of the table, needs to have a way to locate the physical row in the structure. Since the index I defined isn't defined as UNIQUE, each record in the physical structure will also have a 4-byte value (commonly known as a *uniquifier*) added to each value in the index where a duplicate value exists (what the value is is not important, just that it is there to let us tell two rows apart that have the same key value). For example, if the values were A, A; A, B; and A, C, you would be fine. But, if you added another key combination A, A, the value internally would be A, A + 4ByteValue. Typically, it is not optimal to get stuck with 4 bytes on top of the other value you are dealing with in every level of the index, so in general, you should try to define the key columns of the clustered index on column(s) where the values are unique, and the smaller the better, as I will cover next, since the clustering key will be employed in every other index that you place on a table that has a clustered index.

Figure 11-9 shows, at a high level, what a clustered index might look like for a table of animal names. (Note that this is just a partial example; there would likely be more second-level pages for Horse and Python at a minimum.)

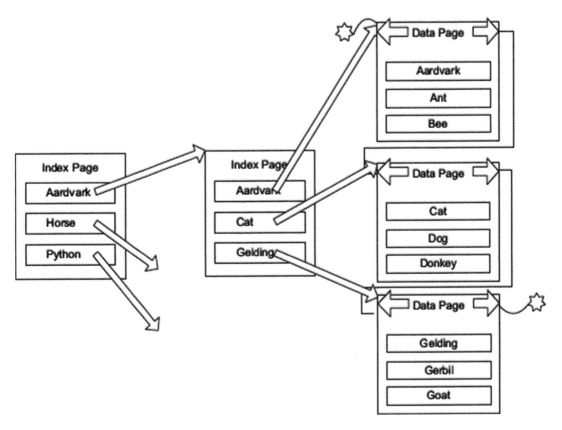

Figure 11-9. *Clustered index example*

You can have only one clustered index on a table, because the leaf pages of a table cannot be ordered on more than one set of columns. (Remember this; it is one of the most fun interview questions. Answering anything other than "one clustered index per table" leads to a fun line of follow-up questioning.)

A good real-world example of a clustered index would be a set of old-fashioned encyclopedias. Each book is a level of the index, and on each page, there is another level that denotes the things you can find on each page (e.g., Office–Officer). Then each topic is the leaf level of the index. These books are clustered on the topics in the encyclopedia, just as the example is clustered on the name of the animal. In essence, the entire set of books is a table of information in clustered order. And indexes can be partitioned as well. The encyclopedias are partitioned by letter into multiple books.

Now, consider a dictionary. Why are the words sorted, rather than just having a separate index with the words not in order? I presume that at least part of the reason is to let the readers scan through words they don't know exactly how to spell, checking the definition to see if the word matches what they expect. SQL Server does something like this when you do a search. For example, back in Figure 11-9, if you were looking for a cat named George, you could use the clustered index to find rows where Animal = 'Cat' and then scan the data pages for the matching pages for any rows where Name = 'George'.

I must caution you that although it's true, physically speaking, that tables are stored in the order of the clustered index, logically speaking, tables must be thought of as having no order. This lack of order is a fundamental truth of relational programming: *you aren't required to get back data in the same order when you run the same query twice.* The ordering of the physical data can be used by the query processor to enhance your performance, but during intermediate processing, the data can be moved around in any manner that results in faster processing of the answer to your query. It's true that you do almost always get the same rows back in the same order, mostly because the optimizer is almost always going to put together the same plan every time the same query is executed under the same conditions. However, load up the server with many requests, and the order of the data might change so SQL Server can best use its resources, regardless of the data's order in the structures. If order matters, use ORDER BY clauses to make sure that data is returned as you want.

Using the Clustered Index

As mentioned earlier, the clustering key you choose has implications for the rest of your physical design. The column you use for the clustered index will become a part of every index for your table, so it has heavy implications for all indexes. Because of this, for a typical OLTP system, a very common practice is to choose a surrogate key value, often the columns of the PRIMARY KEY constraint for a table, since the surrogate can be kept very small.

Using the surrogate key as the clustering key is usually a great decision, not only because it is a small key (most often, the datatype is an integer that requires only 4 bytes or possibly less using compression) but also because it's always a unique value. As mentioned earlier, a non-unique clustering key has a 4-byte uniquifier tacked onto its value when keys are not unique. It also helps the optimizer that an index has only unique values, because it knows immediately that for an equality operator, either 1 or 0 values will match. Because the surrogate key is often used in joins, it's helpful to have smaller keys for the primary key.

Caution   Using a GUID for a surrogate key is common but be careful. GUIDs are 16 bytes wide, which is a fairly large amount of space, but that is really the least of the problem. GUIDs are random values in that they generally aren't monotonically increasing, and a new GUID could sort anywhere in a list of other GUIDs and end up causing page splits. The only way to make GUIDs a reasonably acceptable type is to use the NEWSEQUENTIALID() function (or one of your own) to build sequential GUIDS, but it only works with unique identifier columns in a default constraint and may not always provide a larger sequential value than existing data after a reboot.

And realistically, seldom will the person architecting a solution that is based on GUID surrogates want to be tied down to using a default constraint to generate surrogate values. The ability to generate GUIDs from anywhere and ensure their uniqueness is part of the lure of the siren call of the 16-byte value. In SQL Server 2012 and later, the SEQUENCE object to generate guaranteed unique values could be used in lieu of GUIDs.

The clustered index won't always be used for the surrogate key or even the primary key, especially in cases where the system is used for reporting. The value of the clustered key is as a primary access point, particularly for more than a few rows. Some possible reasons you might use the clustered index for something other than for a surrogate key typically fall under the following:

- *Range queries*: Having all of the data in the table in a certain order usually makes sense when there's data for which you often need to get a range, such as from A to F.

- *Data that's always accessed sequentially*: Obviously, if the data needs to be accessed in a given order, having the data already sorted in that order will significantly improve performance.

- *Queries that return large result sets*: This point will make more sense once I cover nonclustered indexes, but for now, note that having the data on the leaf index page saves overhead.

- *For an identifying relationship key*: In some cases, a table like
  InvoiceLineItem with basic structure (InvoiceLineItemId PK,
  InvoiceId FK, LineNumber, UNIQUE(InvoiceId, LineNumber))
  may benefit greatly by clustering on the InvoiceId, or likely in this
  case change the UNIQUE constraint to be clustered. First, you fetch
  the Invoice and then the InvoiceLineItem rows. Important to note
  is that sometimes you will end up using the surrogate key to fetch
  rows more than seems logical, so empirical testing and watching
  usage are important.

The choice of how to pick the clustered index depends on several factors, such as how many other indexes will be derived from this index, how big the key for the index will be, and how often the value will change. When a clustered index value changes, as we will see in an upcoming section, every index on the table must also be touched and changed, and if the value can grow larger, well, then we again might be talking page splits. This goes back to understanding the users of your data and testing the heck out of the system to verify that your index choices don't hurt overall performance more than they help. Speeding up one query by using one clustering key could hurt all queries that use the nonclustered indexes, especially if you chose a large or non-unique key for the clustered index.

Frankly, in an OLTP setting, in all but the most unusual cases, I stick with a surrogate key for my clustering key, usually one of the integer types or sometimes even the unique identifier (GUID) type. I use the surrogate key because so many of the queries you do for modification (the general goal of the OLTP system) will access the data via the primary key. You then just have to optimize retrievals, which should also be of generally small numbers of rows, and doing so is usually pretty easy.

Another thing that is good about using the clustered index on a monotonically increasing value is that page splits over the entire index are greatly decreased. Of course, as insert frequency increases, contention grows on the one page of the index, so Microsoft added a new setting called OPTIMIZE_FOR_SEQUENTIAL_KEY to address throughput issues dealing with latch (lightweight locks on hardware resources) contention. For more details than I can cover, check out this great article by Pam Lahoud at Microsoft "Behind the Scenes on OPTIMIZE_FOR_SEQUENTIAL_KEY" (techcommunity.microsoft.com/t5/sql-server/behind-the-scenes-on-optimize-for-sequential-key/ba-p/806888).

The table grows only on one end of the index, and while it does need to be rebuilt occasionally using ALTER INDEX REORGANIZE or ALTER INDEX REBUILD, you don't end up with page splits all over the table. Maintaining your indexes is generally fairly easy. You can do this with maintenance plans that are similar to SSIS packages (docs.microsoft.com/en-us/sql/relational-databases/maintenance-plans/maintenance-plans). Use one of the great free tools out there that will do this for you like the one from Ola Hallengren (ola.hallengren.com/). In the last main section of the chapter, I will show you where to find metadata on fragmentation and some other details on indexes.

Now, let's look at an example of a clustered index in use. If you select all of the rows in a clustered table, you'll see a Clustered Index Scan in the plan. For this we will use the Application.Cities table from WideWorldImporters, with the following structure:

```
CREATE TABLE Application.Cities
(
    CityID int NOT NULL
        CONSTRAINT PK_Application_Cities PRIMARY KEY CLUSTERED,
    CityName nvarchar(50) NOT NULL,
    StateProvinceID int NOT NULL  CONSTRAINT
        FK_Application_Cities_StateProvinceID_Application_StateProvinces
            REFERENCES Application.StateProvinces (StateProvinceID),
    Location geography NULL,
    LatestRecordedPopulation bigint NULL,
    LastEditedBy int NOT NULL,
    ValidFrom datetime2(7) GENERATED ALWAYS AS ROW START NOT NULL,
    ValidTo datetime2(7) GENERATED ALWAYS AS ROW END NOT NULL,
    PERIOD FOR SYSTEM_TIME (ValidFrom, ValidTo)
) ON USERDATA TEXTIMAGE_ON USERDATA --These are the filegroups
WITH (SYSTEM_VERSIONING = ON (HISTORY_TABLE = Application.Cities_Archive))
```

This table has temporal extensions added to it, as covered in Chapter 9. In this version of the example database, there is currently also an index on the StateProvince column, which we will use later in the chapter:

```
CREATE NONCLUSTERED INDEX FK_Application_Cities_StateProvinceID
                                            ON Application.Cities
(
        StateProvinceID ASC
)
ON USERDATA; --This is the filegroup
```

There are 37,940 rows in the `Application.Cities` table. Execute the following batch:

```
SET SHOWPLAN_TEXT ON;
GO
SELECT *
FROM    Application.Cities;
GO
SET SHOWPLAN_TEXT OFF;
```

The estimated plan for this query is as follows (for the rest of the cases in this chapter where I use the textual query plan using SET SHOWPLAN_TEXT, I will not include these statements, though I will include them for you in the downloads if you are following along):

```
|--Clustered Index Scan
   (OBJECT:([WideWorldImporters].[Application].[Cities].
                                       [PK_Application_Cities]))
```

If you query on a value of the clustered index key, the scan will almost certainly change to a seek. Although a scan touches all the data pages, a clustered index seek probes the index structure to find a starting place for the scan, and then it can tell just how far to scan. For a unique index with an equality operator, a seek would be used to touch one page in each level of the index to find (or not find) a single value on a single data page, for example:

```
SELECT *
FROM    Application.Cities
WHERE   CityID = 23629; --Hot Chicken capital of the world.
```

The plan for this query now does a seek:

```
|--Clustered Index Seek
   (OBJECT:([WideWorldImporters].[Application].[Cities].
                                       [PK_Application_Cities]),
      SEEK:([WideWorldImporters].[Application].[Cities].[CityID]=
                       CONVERT_IMPLICIT(int,[@1],0)) ORDERED FORWARD)
```

Note the CONVERT_IMPLICIT of the @1 value. This shows the query is being parameterized for the plan, and the variable is cast to an int type. In this case, you're seeking in the clustered index based on the SEEK predicate of CityID = 23629. SQL Server will create a reusable plan by default for simple queries. Any queries that are executed with the same exact format and a simple integer value would use the same plan. You can let SQL Server parameterize more complex queries as well, something I cover more about in Chapter 13.

You can eliminate the CONVERT_IMPLICIT by explicitly applying a CAST OR CONVERT in your query to the value in your WHERE as WHERE CityID = CAST(23629 AS int):

```
|--Clustered Index Seek
   (OBJECT:([WideWorldImporters].[Application].[Cities].
                                    [PK_Application_Cities]),
    SEEK:([WideWorldImporters].[Application].[Cities[CityID]=[@1])
                                            ORDERED FORWARD)
```

Though this is not typically done when it is a complementary literal type in the WHERE clause, it can be an issue when you use noncomplementary types, like when mixing a Unicode value and non-Unicode value, which we will see later in the chapter. Increasing the complexity, now, we search for two rows:

```
SELECT *
FROM    Application.Cities
WHERE   CityID IN (23629,334);
```

And in this case, pretty much the same plan is used, except the seek criteria now has an OR in it:

```
|--Clustered Index Seek
   (OBJECT:([WideWorldImporters].[Application].[Cities].
                                    [PK_Application_Cities]),
    SEEK: ([WideWorldImporters].[Application].[Cities].[CityID]=(334)
              OR
          [WideWorldImporters].[Application].[Cities].[CityID]=(23629))
                                            ORDERED FORWARD)
```

Note that it did not create a parameterized plan this time, but a fixed one with literals for 334 and 23629. Also note that this plan indicates that the query processor will execute the query using two separate seek operations. If you turn on SET STATISTICS IO before running the query

```
SET STATISTICS IO ON;
GO
SELECT *
FROM   [Application].[Cities]
WHERE  CityID IN (23629,334);
GO
SET STATISTICS IO OFF;
```

you will see that it did two "scans," which using STATISTICS IO generally means any operation that probes the table, so a seek or scan would show up the same:

```
Table 'Cities'. Scan count 2, logical reads 4, physical reads 0, read-
ahead reads 0, lob logical reads 0, lob physical reads 0, lob read-ahead
reads 0.
```

But whether any given query uses a seek or scan, or even two seeks, can be a pretty complex question. Why it is so complex will become slightly clearer over the rest of the chapter, and it will become instantly clearer how useful a clustered index seek is in the next section on nonclustered indexes. The other interesting part of this is the logical reads. This is telling us that each of the seeks did two logical reads (reading data that is in RAM, if it was not in cache yet, there could also have been four physical reads): one read for the root of the B-tree structure and one for the leaf page. There would not be intermediate pages on such a small table clustered on a 4-byte integer.

Entire books have been written on query plans and indexes, such as Jason Strate's *Expert Performance Indexing in SQL Server 2019* (www.apress.com/gp/book/9781484254639) and Grant Fritchey's *SQL Server Execution Plans* (www.red-gate.com/simple-talk/books/sql-server-execution-plans-third-edition-by-grant-fritchey/), so my goal is not to teach you everything there is to know about using indexes in SQL Server, but rather the index building blocks that you can apply to your designs as you are creating them, and I expect that as your designs grow to be used in very large, highly concurrent systems, you will expand beyond what I can teach you here.

Nonclustered Indexes

Unlike clustered indexes, for on-disk tables, nonclustered index structures are independent of the underlying table. Like clustered indexes, there are nonclustered rowstore B-tree and columnstore indexes that you can have on a table that are used to enhance performance. Just like for the clustered case, the term nonclustered index is used interchangeably with a nonclustered rowstore index for historical and simplification reasons.

The organization of a clustered rowstore index is synonymous with the way an encyclopedia is organized with the table of contents physically linked to the table (since the leaf pages of the index are a part of the table). Nonclustered rowstore indexes are more like indexes of a book like this one. Instead of the leaf page having the data, they have a way to find the data you are looking for. For an index, this means the index key values and a pointer to the data you are looking for. (The leaf pages may have additional data, called *included values*, which I will cover later in the section as well. Consider it like a synopsis in a web search where you might get your answer without going to the actual page.).

Each leaf page in a nonclustered index contains some form of link to the rows on the data page. The link from the index to a data row is known as a *row locator*. Exactly how the row locator of a nonclustered index is structured is based on whether the underlying table has a clustered index and what type of clustered index it has.

In this section, I will start with the structure of nonclustered indexes and then look at how these indexes are used.

Index Structure

The base B-tree of the nonclustered index is the same as the B-tree of the clustered index. The difference will be when you reach the leaf node of the tree. First, we will look at an abstract representation of the nonclustered index and then show the differences between the implementation of a nonclustered index when you do and do not also have a clustered index. At an abstract level, all nonclustered indexes follow the basic form shown in Figure 11-10.

Index leaf pages

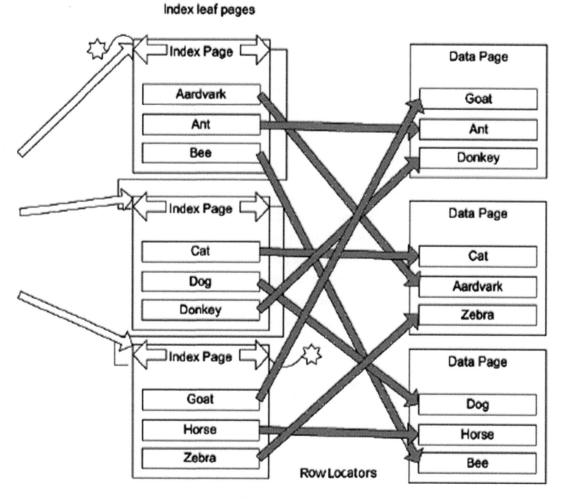

Figure 11-10. *Sample nonclustered index*

The major difference between the two possibilities comes down to the row locator being different based on whether the underlying table has a clustered index. There are two different types of pointer that will be used:

- *Tables with a clustered index*: Clustering key

- *Tables without a clustered index*: Pointer to physical location of the data, commonly referred to as a row identifier (RID)

In the next two sections, I'll explain these in more detail.

Tip   You can place nonclustered indexes on a different filegroup than the data
pages to maximize the use of your disk subsystem in parallel.

Nonclustered Index on a Clustered Table

When a clustered index exists on the table, the row locator for the leaf node of any
nonclustered index is the clustering key from the clustered index. In Figure 11-11, the
structure on the right side represents the clustered index, and the structure on the
left represents the nonclustered index. To find a value, you start at the leaf node of the
nonclustered index and traverse to the leaf pages. The result of the index traversal is one or
more clustering keys, which you then use to traverse the clustered index to reach the data.

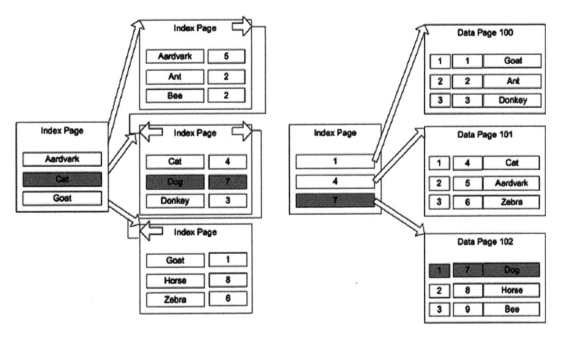

Figure 11-11. Nonclustered index on a clustered table

The overhead of the operation I've just described is minimal as long as you keep your
clustering key optimal and the index well maintained. While having to use two indexes
is more work than just having a pointer to the physical location, you have to think of
the overall picture. Overall, it's better than having direct pointers to the table, because
only minimal reorganization is required for any modification of the values in the table.

801

Consider if you had to maintain a book index manually. If you used the book page as the way to get to an index value and subsequently had to add a page to the book in the middle, you would have to update all of the page numbers. But if all of the topics were ordered alphabetically and you just pointed to the topic name, adding a topic would be easy.

The same is true for SQL Server, and the structures can be changed thousands of times a second or more. Since there is very little hardware-based information in the structure when built this way, data movement is easy, and maintaining indexes is a generally trouble-free process. Early versions of SQL Server used physical location pointers for indexes, and this led to frequent corruption in our indexes and tables. (Note that in the next section, without a clustering key, pointers are still employed, but with a format that reduces corruption at the cost of performance).

The primary benefit of the key structure becomes more obvious when we you consider modification operations. Because the clustering key is the same regardless of physical location, only the lowest levels of the clustered index need to know where the physical data is. Add to this that the data is organized sequentially, and the overhead of modifying indexes is significantly lowered, making all of the data modification operations far faster. Of course, this benefit is only true if the clustering key rarely, or never, changes. Therefore, the general suggestion is to make the clustering key a small, nonchanging value, such as an identity column (but I will discuss more about how to employ nonclustered indexes in the section "Using the Nonclustered Index").

Nonclustered Indexes on a Heap

A *heap* data structure in computer science is a generally unordered binary tree structure. In SQL Server, when a table does not have a clustered index, the table is physically referred to as a heap. A more practical definition of a heap is "a group of things placed or thrown one on top of the other." This is a great way to explain what happens in a table when you have no clustered index: SQL Server simply puts every new row on the end of the last page for the table. Once that page is filled up, it puts data on the next page or a new page as needed.

When building a nonclustered index on a heap, the row locator is a pointer to the physical page and row that contains the row. As an example, take the example structure from the previous section with a nonclustered index on the name column of an animal table, represented in Figure 11-12.

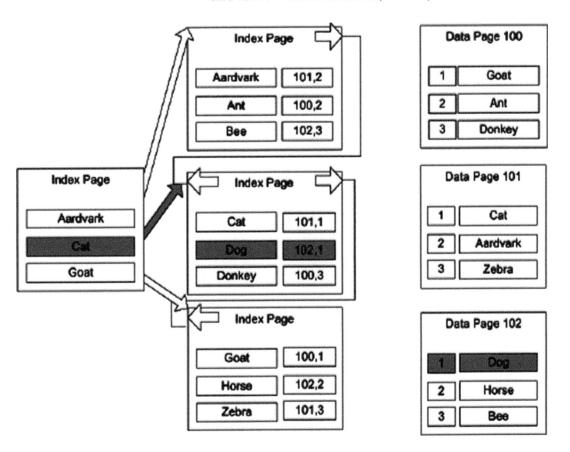

Figure 11-12. *Nonclustered index on a heap*

If you want to find the row where Animal = 'Dog', you first find the path through the index from the top-level page to the leaf page. Once you get to the leaf page, you get a pointer to the page that has a row with the value, in this case page 102, row 1. This pointer consists of the page location and the record number on the page to find the row values. The most important fact about this pointer is that it points directly to the row on the page that has the values you're looking for. The pointer for a table with a clustered index (a clustered table) is different, and this distinction is important to understand because it affects how well the different types of indexes perform.

To avoid the types of physical corruption issues that I previously mentioned can occur when you are constantly managing pointers and physical locations, heaps use a very simple method of keeping the row pointers from getting corrupted: they never change until you rebuild the table. Instead of reordering pages or changing pointers if the data for a row no longer fits on the page, it moves data to a different page, and a *forwarding pointer* is left to point to the new page where the data is now. So if the row where `Animal = 'Dog'` had moved (e.g., perhaps due to a `varchar(3000)` value being updated from a data length of 10 to 3,000), you might end up with a situation to extend the number of steps required to pick up the data. In Figure 11-13, a forwarding pointer is illustrated.

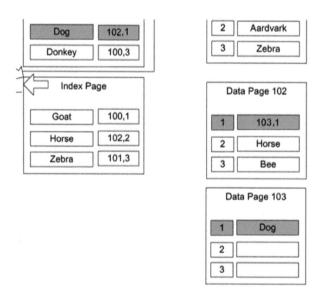

Figure 11-13. *Forwarding pointer*

All existing indexes that have the old pointer simply go to the old page and follow the forwarding pointer on that page to the new location of the data. If the value on page 103 no longer fits, it could be moved again and then have multiple forwarding pointers, and then the row can even be deleted, but the forwarding pointers still have to be traversed to discover that fact. Since there is no order in the heap, it doesn't matter what the data is.

If you are using heaps, which should be rare (rapid data loading is generally the main reason that I do), it is important to be careful with your structures to make sure that data should rarely be moved around within a heap. For example, you have to be careful if you're often updating data to a larger value in a variable-length column that's used as an index key, because it's possible that a row may be moved to a different page. This adds another step to finding the data and, if the data is moved to a page on a different extent, adds another read to the database. This forwarding pointer is immediately followed when scanning the table, eventually causing terrible performance over time if it's not removed from the structure during maintenance.

Space is typically not reused in the heap without rebuilding the table (either by selecting into another table or by using the ALTER TABLE command with the REBUILD option). In the section "Indexing Dynamic Management View Queries" later in this chapter, I will provide a query that will give you information on the structure of your index, including the count of forwarding pointers in your table.

Using the Nonclustered Index

After you have made the ever-important choice of what to use for the clustered index, all other indexes will be nonclustered. In this section, I will cover some of the choices of how to apply nonclustered indexes in the following areas:

- General considerations

- Composite index considerations

- Nonclustered indexes with clustered tables

- Nonclustered indexes on heaps

In reality, many of the topics in this section pertain to clustered indexes as well—things such as composite indexes, statistics, uniqueness, and so on, for certain. I am covering them here because you will typically make these decisions for nonclustered indexes, and choose the clustered index based on patterns of usage as the PRIMARY KEY, though not always.

General Considerations

We generally start to get the feeling that indexes are needed because queries are (or seem) slow. Naturally though, lack of indexes is clearly not the only reason that queries are slow. Here are some of the obvious reasons for slow queries:

- Extra heavy user load

- Hardware load

- Network load

- Poorly designed database, though some of that can be the lack of indexes!

- Concurrency configuration issues (as covered in Chapter 12, though some of this too can be the lack of indexes!)

After looking for the existence of the preceding reasons, we can pull out SSMS and start to look at the plans of the slow queries. Most often, slow queries are apparent because either |--Clustered Index Scan or |--Table Scan shows up in the query plan, and those operations take a large percentage of time to execute. Simple, right? Essentially, it is a true enough statement that index and table scans are time consuming, but unfortunately, that really doesn't give a full picture of the process. It's hard to make specific indexing changes before knowing about usage, because the usage pattern will greatly affect these decisions, for example:

- Is a query executed once a day, once an hour, or once a minute?

- Is a background process inserting into a table rapidly? Or perhaps inserts are taking place during off-hours?

Using Extended Events, the Query Store, and the dynamic management views (DMVs), you can watch the usage patterns of the queries that access your database, looking for slowly executing queries, poor plans, and so on. After you do this and you start to understand the usage patterns for your database, you need to use that information to consider where to apply indexes—the final goal being that you use the information you can gather about usage and tailor an index plan to solve the overall picture.

It is important to be careful not to just throw around indexes to fix individual queries constantly. Nothing comes without a price, and indexes definitely have a cost. You need to consider how indexes help and hurt the different types of operations in different ways:

- SELECT: Indexes can only have a beneficial effect on SELECT queries.

- INSERT: An index can only hurt the process of inserting new data into the table. As data is created in the table, there's a chance that the indexes will have to be modified and reorganized to accommodate the new values. Indexes on other tables may help when enforcing constraints or executing triggers, naturally.

- UPDATE: An update physically requires two or three steps: find the row(s) and change the row(s), or find the row(s), delete it (them), and reinsert it (them). During the phase of finding the row, the index is beneficial, just as for a SELECT. How much it hurts during the second phase depends on several factors, for example:

- Did the index key value change such that it needs to be moved around to different leaf nodes?

- Will the new value fit on the existing page of any index the values are used in, or will it require a page split?

- DELETE: Requires two steps: to find the row and to remove it. Indexes are beneficial to find the row, but on deletion, you might have to do some reshuffling to accommodate the deleted values from the indexes.

You should also realize that for INSERT, UPDATE, or DELETE operations, if TRIGGER objects on the table exist and FOREIGN KEY constraints or even CHECK constraints exist that execute functions that reference tables, indexes will affect those operations in the same ways as in the list. For this reason, I'm going to shy away from any generic advice about what types of columns to index. In practice, there are just too many variables to consider. Testing, with real users, in an environment where the users know that they are being tested on is the best way to start finding what may need indexing, and then watching production loads will really give you an understanding of what needs tuned.

For a good idea of how your current indexes and/or tables are currently being used, you can query the dynamic management view sys.dm_db_index_usage_stats:

```
SELECT CONCAT(OBJECT_SCHEMA_NAME(i.object_id),'.',OBJECT_NAME(i.object_id))
                                                            AS ObjectName
        , CASE WHEN i.is_unique = 1 THEN 'UNIQUE ' ELSE '' END +
                i.TYPE_DESC AS IndexType
        , i.name AS IndexName
        , user_seeks AS UserSeeks, user_scans AS UserScans
        , user_lookups AS UserLookups, user_updates AS UserUpdates
FROM  sys.indexes AS i
        LEFT OUTER JOIN sys.dm_db_index_usage_stats AS s
            ON i.object_id = s.object_id
                AND i.index_id = s.index_id
                AND database_id = DB_ID()
WHERE  OBJECTPROPERTY(i.object_id , 'IsUserTable') = 1
ORDER  BY ObjectName, IndexName;
```

This query will return the name of each object, an index type, an index name, plus the number of user seeks, updates, and lookups. I will cover this more in the "Indexing Dynamic Management View Queries" section, but it is very useful to help you see how nonclustered indexes work. User seeks and scans are the number of times the index was used for a query that a non-system process executed, updates are how many times it was modified in your query, and lookups pertain to clustered indexes and record the number of times the index was used to resolve the row locator of a nonclustered index search.

This information is very important when trying to get a feel for which indexes are valuable and not so valuable. Even worse are the indexes that are not useful and are mostly getting updated. A particularly interesting thing to look at in an OLTP system is the user_scans on a clustered index. For example, thinking back to our queries of the Application.Cities table, we only have a clustered index on the PRIMARY KEY column CityID. So if we query

```
SELECT *
FROM   Application.Cities
WHERE  CityName = 'Nashville';
```

the plan will be a scan of the clustered index:

```
|--Clustered Index Scan (OBJECT:([WideWorldImporters].[Application].
        [Cities].[PK_Application_Cities]),
WHERE:([WideWorldImporters].[Application].[Cities].[CityName]
                                        =(N'Nashvile')));
```

Execute the query on sys.dm_db_index_usage_stats from earlier, and you will see the user_scans value increases every time you run this query for the PK_Application_Cities index (without outputting the estimated plan using SHOWPLAN_TEXT). This is something we can reconcile by adding a nonclustered index to this column, locating it in the USERDATA filegroup, since that is where other objects were created in the DDL I included earlier:

```
CREATE INDEX CityName ON Application.Cities(CityName) ON USERDATA;
```

Of course, there are plenty more settings when creating an index, some we will cover and some we will not. If you need to manage indexes, it certainly is a great idea to read the Microsoft Docs article "CREATE INDEX (Transact-SQL)" (docs.microsoft.com/

en-us/sql/t-sql/statements/create-index-transact-sql) for the wider variety of information on the topic.

Tip   You can create indexes inline with the CREATE TABLE statement starting with SQL Server 2014.

Now check the plan of the query again, and you will see

```
|--Nested Loops(Inner Join,
OUTER REFERENCES:([WideWorldImporters].[Application].[Cities].[CityID]))
   |--Index Seek (OBJECT:([WideWorldImporters].[Application].[Cities]
      .[CityName]),
   SEEK:([WideWorldImporters].[Application].
      [Cities].[CityName]=N'Nashville')  ORDERED FORWARD)

   |--Clustered Index Seek (OBJECT: ([WideWorldImporters].
      [Application].[Cities].[PK_Application_Cities]),
         SEEK:([WideWorldImporters].[Application].
         [Cities].[CityID]=[WideWorldImporters].
         [Application].[Cities].[CityID]) LOOKUP ORDERED FORWARD)
```

This not only is more to format, but it looks like it should be a lot more to execute. However, this plan illustrates nicely the structure of a nonclustered index on a clustered table. The second |-- points at the improvement. To find the row with CityName of Nashville, it sought in the new index. Once it had the index keys for Nashville rows, it took those and joined them together like two different tables, using a nested loops join type. Look back to the DMV query. You should see UserSeeks on the CityName index and now the same number of UserLookups values on the PK_Application_Cities index as well.

For more information about nested loops and other join operators, check Microsoft Docs for "Showplan Logical and Physical Operators Reference" (docs.microsoft.com/ en-us/sql/relational-databases/showplan-logical-and-physical-operators-reference).

Determining Index Usefulness

It might seem at this point that all you need to do is look at the plans of queries, look for the search arguments, and put an index on the columns and then things will improve. There's a bit of truth to this in a lot of cases, but indexes have to be useful to be used by a query. What if the index of a 418-page book has two entries:

General Topics 1

Determining Index Usefulness 417

This means that pages 1–416 cover general topics and pages 417–418 are about determining index usefulness. This would be useless to you, unless you needed to know about index usefulness. Another thing we all do with the index of a book to see if the index is useful is to take a value and look it up in the index. If what you're looking for is in there (or something close), you go to the page and check it out.

SQL Server determines whether or not to use your index in much the same way. It has two specific measurements that it uses to decide if an index is useful: the *density* of values (also referred to as the *selectivity*) and a histogram of a sample of values in the table to check against.

You can see these in detail for indexes by using DBCC SHOW_STATISTICS, and look at the details of the index we just created:

```
DBCC SHOW_STATISTICS('Application.Cities', 'CityName') WITH DENSITY_VECTOR;
DBCC SHOW_STATISTICS('Application.Cities', 'CityName') WITH HISTOGRAM;
```

This returns the following sets (truncated for space). The first tells us the size and density of the keys. The second shows the histogram of where the table was sampled to find representative values.

All density	Average Length	Columns
4.297009E-05	17.17427	CityName
2.635741E-05	21.17427	CityName, CityID

RANGE_HI_KEY	RANGE_ROWS	EQ_ROWS	DISTINCT_RANGE_ROWS	AVG_RANGE_ROWS
Aaronsburg	0	1	0	1
Addison	123	11	70	1.757143
Albany	157	17	108	1.453704

Alexandria	90	13	51	1.764706
Alton	223	13	122	1.827869
Andover	173	13	103	1.679612
....	...	..	...	....
White Oak	183	10	97	1.886598
Willard	209	10	134	1.559701
Winchester	188	18	91	2.065934
Wolverton	232	1	138	1.681159
Woodstock	137	12	69	1.985507
Wynnewood	127	2	75	1.693333
Zwolle	240	1	173	1.387283

I won't cover the DBCC SHOW_STATISTICS command in great detail, but there are several important things to note from this output. First, consider the density of each column set. The CityName column is the only column that is actually declared in the index, but note that it includes the density of the index column and the clustering key as well.

All the density is calculated approximately by 1/number of distinct rows, as shown here for the same columns as I just checked the density on:

```
--Used ISNULL as it is easier if the column can be null
--value you translate to should be impossible for the column
--ProductId is an identity with seed of 1 and increment of 1
--so this should be safe (unless a dba does something weird)
SELECT 1.0/ COUNT(DISTINCT ISNULL(CityName,'NotACity')) AS Density,
       COUNT(DISTINCT ISNULL(CityName,'NotACity')) AS DistinctRowCount,
       1.0/ COUNT(*) AS UniqueDensity,
       COUNT(*) AS AllRowCount
FROM   Application.Cities;
```

This returns the following:

Density	DistinctRowCount	UniqueDensity	AllRowCount
0.000042970092	23272	0.000026357406	37940

You can see that the densities match. (The query's density is in a numeric type, while the DBCC is using a float, which is why they are formatted differently, but they are the same value!) The smaller the number, the better the index, and the more likely it will be easily chosen for use. There's no magic number, per se, but this value fits into the calculations of which way is best to execute the query. The actual numbers returned from this query might vary slightly from the DBCC value, as a sampled number might be used for the distinct count.

The second thing to understand in the DBCC SHOW_STATISTICS output is the histogram. Even if the density of the index isn't low, SQL Server can check a given value (or set of values) in the histogram to see how many rows will likely be returned. SQL Server keeps statistics about columns in a table as well as in indexes, so it can make informed decisions as to how to employ indexes or table columns. For example, consider the following rows from the histogram (I have faked some of these results for demonstration purposes):

RANGE_HI_KEY	RANGE_ROWS	EQ_ROWS	DISTINCT_RANGE_ROWS	AVG_RANGE_ROWS
Aaronsburg	111	58	2	55.5
Addison	117	67	2	58.5
...	...	...	...	...

In the second row, the row values tell us the following:

- RANGE_HI_KEY: The sampled CityName values are Aaronsburg and Addison.

- RANGE_ROWS: There are 117 rows where the value is between Aaronsburg and Addison (excluding the upper value, in this case Addison). These values other than Aaronsburg are not to be known. However, if a user uses Acronsville as a search argument, the optimizer can now guess that a maximum of 117 rows would be returned. This is one of the ways that the query plan gets the estimated number of rows for each step in a query and is one of the ways to determine if an index will be useful for an individual query.

- EQ_ROWS: There were exactly 67 rows where CityName = Addison when the sample was taken.

- DISTINCT_RANGE_ROWS: For the row with the value of Addison, it is estimated that there are two distinct values between Aaronsburg and Addison. Since the high value is not included, there is expected to be one other value in the range. So, if it was scanning for Acronsville, if it was in this range, it is expected to be the only other value.

- AVG_RANGE_ROWS: This is the average number of duplicate values in the range, excluding the upper and lower bounds. This value is what the optimizer can expect to be the average number of rows. Note that this is calculated by RANGE_ROWS/DISTINCT_RANGE_ROWS.

One thing that having this histogram can do is allow a seemingly useless index to become valuable in some cases. For example, say you want to index a column with only two values. If the values are evenly distributed, the index would be useless. However, if there are only a few of a certain value, it could be useful (using tempdb):

```
USE tempdb;
GO
CREATE SCHEMA Demo;
GO
CREATE TABLE Demo.TestIndex
(
    TestIndex int IDENTITY(1,1) CONSTRAINT PKTestIndex PRIMARY KEY,
    BitValue bit,
    Filler char(2000) NOT NULL
      CONSTRAINT DFLTTestIndex_Filler DEFAULT (REPLICATE('A',2000))
);
CREATE INDEX BitValue ON Demo.TestIndex(bitValue);
GO

SET NOCOUNT ON; --or you will get back 50100 1 row affected messages
INSERT INTO Demo.TestIndex(BitValue)
VALUES (0);
GO 50000 --runs current batch 50000 times in Management Studio.

INSERT INTO Demo.TestIndex(BitValue)
VALUES (1);
GO 100 --puts 100 rows into table with value 1
```

You can guess that few rows will be returned if the only value desired is 1. Check the plan for bitValue = 0 (again using SET SHOWPLAN ON or using the GUI):

```
SELECT *
FROM    demo.testIndex
WHERE   bitValue = 0;
```

This shows a clustered index scan:

```
|--Clustered Index Scan(OBJECT:([tempdb].[demo].[testIndex].
                        [PKtestIndex]),
   WHERE:([tempdb].[demo].[testIndex].[bitValue]=(0)))
```

However, change the 0 to a 1, and the optimizer chooses an index seek. This means that it performed a seek into the index to the first row that had a 1 as a value and worked its way through the values:

```
|--Nested Loops(Inner Join, OUTER REFERENCES: ([tempdb].[demo].
        [testIndex].[testIndex], [Expr1003]) WITH UNORDERED PREFETCH)
   |--Index Seek(OBJECT:([tempdb].[demo].[testIndex].[bitValue]),
              SEEK:([tempdb].[demo].[testIndex].[bitValue]=(1))
                                               ORDERED FORWARD)
   |--Clustered Index Seek(OBJECT:([tempdb].[demo].[testIndex].
                                              [PKtestIndex]),
       SEEK:([tempdb].[demo].[testIndex].[testIndex]=
       [tempdb].[demo].[testIndex].[testIndex]) LOOKUP ORDERED FORWARD)
```

As we saw earlier, this better plan looks more complicated, but it hinges on now only needing to touch a 100 rows, instead of 50,100, using the index seek operator (and then again with the clustered index seek to get the rest of the columns because we chose to do SELECT *; we will discuss more on how to avoid the clustered seek in the section "Covering Indexes").

You can see why in the histogram:

```
DBCC SHOW_STATISTICS('Demo.TestIndex', 'BitValue')  WITH HISTOGRAM;
```

This returns the following results in my test. Your actual values will likely vary:

RANGE_HI_KEY	RANGE_ROWS	EQ_ROWS	DISTINCT_RANGE_ROWS	AVG_RANGE_ROW
0	0	49976.95	0	1
1	0	123.0454	0	1

The statistics gathered estimated that about 123 rows match for bitValue = 1. That's because statistics gathering isn't an exact count unless you ask it to touch every row—it uses a sampling mechanism rather than checking every value (your values might vary as well).

Tip You can use the same sampling technology in your queries using the TABLESAMPLE clause. For more information, see the Microsoft Docs topic "FROM clause plus JOIN, APPLY, PIVOT (Transact-SQL)—Tablesample Clause" (docs.microsoft.com/en-us/sql/t-sql/queries/from-transact-sql#tablesample-clause-1).

The optimizer knew that it would be advantageous to use the index when looking for BitValue = 1, because approximately 123 rows are returned when the index key with a value of 1 is desired, but 49,977 are returned for 0. (Your try will likely return a different value. For the rows where the bitValue was 1, I got 80 in the previous edition and 137 in a different set of tests. They are all approximately the 100 that you should expect, since we specifically created 100 rows when we loaded the table.)

This simple demonstration of the histogram is one thing, but in practice, actually building a filtered index to optimize this query is a generally better practice. You might build an index such as this:

```
CREATE INDEX BitValueOneOnly
     ON Demo.TestIndex(BitValue) WHERE BitValue = 1;
```

The histogram for this index is definitely by far a clearer good match:

RANGE_HI_KEY	RANGE_ROWS	EQ_ROWS	DISTINCT_RANGE_ROWS	AVG_RANGE_ROWS
1	0	100	0	1

Whether or not the query actually uses this index will likely depend on how badly another index would perform, if the other index would be useful in other ways (again, such as covering parts of the query or other needs) which can also be dependent on a myriad of other SQL Server internals. The histogram is, however, another tool that you can use when optimizing your SQL to see what the optimizer is using to make its choices.

Tip   Whether or not the histogram includes any data where the `BitValue` = `1` is largely a matter of chance. I have run this example many times, and one time, no rows were shown unless I used the `FULLSCAN` option on the `UPDATE` `STATISTICS` command (which isn't feasible on very large tables unless you have quite a bit of time).

Indexing and Multiple Columns

So far, the indexes I've talked about were simple indexes (on single columns), but it isn't always what you need—performance-enhancing indexes only on single columns. When multiple columns are included in the `WHERE` clause of a query on the same table, there are several possible ways you can enhance your queries:

- Having one composite index on all columns

- Creating *covering indexes* by including all columns that a query touches

- Having multiple indexes on separate columns

- Adjusting key sort order to optimize sort operations

Composite Indexes

When you include more than one column in an index, it's referred to as a *composite index*. As the number of columns grows, the effectiveness of the index is reduced for the general case. The reason is that the index is sorted by the first column values first and then the second column. So the second column in the index is generally only useful if you need the first column as well (the section "Covering Indexes" demonstrates a way that this may not be the case, however). Even so, you will very often need composite indexes to optimize common queries when predicates on all of the columns are involved.

The order of the columns in a query is important with respect to whether a composite index can and will be used. There are a couple of important considerations:

- *Which column is most selective?* If one column includes unique or mostly unique values, it is likely a good candidate for the first column. The key is that the first column is the one by which the index is sorted. Searching on the second column only is less valuable (though queries using only the second column can scan the index leaf pages for values).

- *Which column is used most often without the other columns?* One composite index can be useful to several different queries, even if only the first column of the index is all that is being used in those queries.

For example, consider this query (StateProvince is probably a more obvious choice of column, but it has an index that we will be using in a later section):

```
SELECT *
FROM   Application.Cities
WHERE  CityName = 'Nashville'
  AND  LatestRecordedPopulation = 601222;
```

The index on CityName we had is useful, but an index on LatestRecordedPopulation might also be good. It may also turn out that neither column alone provides enough of an improvement in performance. Composite indexes are great tools, but just how useful such an index will be is completely dependent on how many rows will be returned by CityName = 'Nashville' and LatestRecordedPopulation = 601222.

The preceding query uses existing indexes (non-unique, nonclustered index named CityName and clustered primary key named PK_Application_Cities on CityId) and is optimized with the previous plan, with the extra population predicate:

```
|--Nested Loops(Inner Join, OUTER REFERENCES:([WideWorldImporters].
            [Application].[Cities].[CityID]))
   |--Index Seek(OBJECT:([WideWorldImporters].[Application].
      [Cities].[CityName]), SEEK:([WideWorldImporters].
      [Application].[Cities].[CityName]=N'Nashville')
                         ORDERED FORWARD)
```

```
|--Clustered Index Seek (OBJECT:([WideWorldImporters].
   [Application].[Cities].[PK_Application_Cities]),
      SEEK:([WideWorldImporters].[Application].[Cities].[CityID]=
            [WideWorldImporters].[Application].[Cities].[CityID]),
      WHERE:([WideWorldImporters].[Application].
            [Cities].[LatestRecordedPopulation]=(601222))
                                    LOOKUP ORDERED FORWARD)
```

Adding an index on CityName and LatestRecordedPopulation seems like a good way to further optimize the query, but first, you should look at the data for these columns (consider future usage of the index too, but existing data is a good place to start):

```
SELECT CityName, LatestRecordedPopulation, COUNT(*) AS [Count]
FROM   Application.Cities
GROUP BY CityName, LatestRecordedPopulation
ORDER BY CityName, LatestRecordedPopulation;
```

This returns partial results:

CityName	LatestRecordedPopulation	Count
Aaronsburg	613	1
Abanda	192	1
Abbeville	419	1
Abbeville	2688	1
Abbeville	2908	1
Abbeville	5237	1
Abbeville	12257	1
Abbotsford	2310	1
Abbott	NULL	2
Abbott	356	3
Abbottsburg	NULL	1
...	...	...

Of course, you can't always look at all the rows like this, so another possibility is to do a little data profiling to see which of the columns has more distinct values, and look for NULL values when columns are nullable:

```
SELECT COUNT(DISTINCT CityName) AS CityName,
       SUM(CASE WHEN CityName IS NULL THEN 1 ELSE 0 END) AS NULLCity,
       COUNT(DISTINCT LatestRecordedPopulation)
                                        AS LatestRecordedPopulation,
       SUM(CASE WHEN LatestRecordedPopulation IS NULL THEN 1 ELSE 0 END)
                                        AS NULLLatestRecordedPopulation
FROM   Application.Cities;
```

This query returns the following:

```
CityName NULLCity LatestRecordedPopulation NULLLatestRecordedPopulation
-------- -------- ------------------------ ----------------------------
23272    0        9324                     11048
```

The column CityName has the most unique values, which kind of runs counter to what you would expect. However, lots of NULL column values will do that. So we add the following index:

```
CREATE INDEX CityNameAndLastRecordedPopulation
       ON Application.Cities (CityName, LatestRecordedPopulation);
```

Now, reevaluate the query plan of the query:

```
SELECT *
FROM   Application.Cities
WHERE  CityName = 'Nashville'
  AND  LatestRecordedPopulation = 601222;
```

The plan changes to the following, using the new index, as well as the clustered index to fetch the rest of the data in the row due to the * in the query needing all of the data in the row:

```
|--Nested Loops(Inner Join,OUTER REFERENCES:([WideWorldImporters].
               [Application].[Cities].[CityID]))
    |--Index Seek
        (OBJECT:([WideWorldImporters].[Application].
        [Cities].[CityNameAndLastRecordedPopulation]),
        SEEK:([WideWorldImporters].[Application].[Cities].
           [CityName]=N'Nashville' AND [WideWorldImporters].
           [Application].[Cities].[LatestRecordedPopulation]=(601222))
                                          ORDERED FORWARD)
    |--Clustered Index Seek (OBJECT:([WideWorldImporters].
         [Application].[Cities].[PK_Application_Cities]),
              SEEK:([WideWorldImporters].[Application].[Cities].[CityID]
              =[WideWorldImporters].[Application].[Cities].[CityID])
                                    LOOKUP ORDERED FORWARD)
```

Keep in mind too, exactly how the indexes will be used. If your queries mix equality comparisons and inequality comparisons, you will likely want to favor the columns you are using in equality comparisons first. Of course, your selectivity estimates also need to be based on how selective the index will be for your situations. For example, if you are doing small ranges on very selective data in each column, that could be the best first column in the index. If you have a question about how you think an index can help, test multiple cases and see how the plans and costs change. If you have questions about why a plan is behaving as it is, use the statistics to get more deep ideas about why an index is chosen.

In the next section, I will show how you can eliminate the clustered index seek, but in general, having the seek isn't the worst thing in the world unless you are matching lots of rows. In this case, for example, the two single-column seeks would result in better performance than a full scan through the table or using the techniques in the next section to cover the query, but then needing to maintain an extra index to save a few reads per query. When the number of rows found using the nonclustered index grows large, however, a plan such as the preceding one can become very costly.

Covering Indexes

When you are only retrieving data from a table, if an index exists that has all the data values that are needed for a query, the base table needn't be touched. Back in Figure 11-10, there was a nonclustered index on the type of animal. If the name of the animal was the only data the query needed to use, the data pages of the table wouldn't need to be accessed directly. The index *covers* all the data needed for the query and is commonly referred to as a *covering index*. The ability to create covering indexes is an essential performance-tuning feature, and the approach even works with clustered indexes, although with clustered indexes, SQL Server scans the lowest index structure page, because scanning the leaf nodes of the clustered index is the same as a table scan.

From our previous examples, if, instead of returning all columns in the table, we just returned CityName and LatestRecordedPopulation

```
SELECT CityName, LatestRecordedPopulation
FROM   Application.Cities;
```

the resulting plan would not be complex at all—just a simple scan for the rows, using just the index, because all of the data that the query needed was right in the index:

```
|--Index Scan (OBJECT:([WideWorldImporters].[Application].
   [Cities].[CityNameAndLastRecordedPopulation]))
```

But what if we also needed the LastEditedBy column in the output? We could add the column to the index as an index key, but if it isn't needed for the search, that is wasteful because the index keys would then bloat all of the non-leaf pages of the index and could also require maintaining if the values were volatile.

Instead, there is a feature of an index to improve the ability to implement covering indexes—the INCLUDE (<columns>) clause of the CREATE INDEX statement. The included columns can be almost any datatype, even large (max)-type columns. In fact, the only types that aren't allowed are text, ntext, and image datatypes, which you should not use because they are very outdated/deprecated anyhow.

Using the INCLUDE clause gives you the ability to add columns to cover a query without including those columns in the index pages and thus without causing overhead in the use of the index. Instead, the data in the INCLUDE columns is added only to the leaf pages of the index. The INCLUDE columns won't help in index seeking, but they do eliminate the need to go to the data pages to get the data being sought.

To demonstrate, first, check the plan on the following query:

```
SELECT CityName, LatestRecordedPopulation, LastEditedBy
FROM   Application.Cities;
```

It is a scan through the clustered index:

```
|--Clustered Index Scan (OBJECT:([WideWorldImporters].[Application].
  [Cities].[PK_Application_Cities]))
```

Now let's modify the index on city name and population and include the LastEditedBy column:

```
DROP INDEX CityNameAndLastRecordedPopulation
        ON Application.Cities;

CREATE INDEX CityNameAndLastRecordedPopulation
        ON Application.Cities (CityName, LatestRecordedPopulation)
                INCLUDE (LastEditedBy);
```

Now, the query goes back to only touching the index, because it has all the data in the index, and this time, it doesn't even need to go to the clustered index to pick up the name column:

```
|--Index Scan (OBJECT:([WideWorldImporters].[Application].
  [Cities].[CityNameAndLastRecordedPopulation]))
```

This ability to include columns only in the leaf pages of covering indexes is incredibly useful in a lot of situations. Too many indexes with overly large keys are created to cover a query to avoid accessing the base table and end up being only good for one situation, which ends up wasting valuable resources. Using INCLUDE, you get the benefits of a covering index without the overhead of bloating the non-leaf pages of the index.

Be careful not to go crazy with covering indexes unless you can see a large benefit from them. The INCLUDE feature costs less to maintain than including the values in the index structure, but it doesn't make the index structure free to maintain as you are duplicating data. It can be very costly to maintain if it references a varchar(max) column, as but one example. One thing you will likely notice when looking at query plans or the missing index DMVs is that indexes using the INCLUDE feature are commonly suggested, because quite often, the key lookup is the costliest part of queries. I must include a caution about going too far and abusing covering indexes, because their use does incur a fairly heavy modification/disk space cost. Be careful to test that the additional overhead of duplicating data in indexes doesn't harm performance more than it helps it.

Columns that are a part of the INCLUDE clause are sometimes for scans too. This is because if the leaf page of the nonclustered index has a piece of data that is needed to answer a query, it may determine that the leaf page of the index is smaller (and, hence, less IO) than the clustered index (or heap) and use the index, even if the column is just included. For example, execute the following query and check out the plan:

```
SELECT LatestRecordedPopulation, LastEditedBy
FROM   Application.Cities;
```

Paired together, or either of the columns alone, end up with the CityNameAndLastRecordePopulation index being used that we created and included LastEditedBy. Things like this can make reading your query plan "interesting" because you start to find things that don't pop out as obvious, but you can see that SQL Server is using every bit of smarts that it has to get you the best performance possible.

Multiple Indexes

Sometimes, we might not have a single index on a table that meets the given situation for the query optimizer to do an optimum job. In this case, SQL Server can sometimes use two or more indexes to meet the need. When processing a query with multiple indexes, SQL Server uses the indexes as if they were tables, filters the results to the values it can, then joins the sets together, and returns a set of rows. The more indexes used, the larger the cost, but if each query eliminates enough rows or is smaller than the alternatives available, the overall cost can be very useful for handling ad hoc queries that are very unpredictable.

Multiple indexes aren't usually something to rely on to optimize known queries that are executed frequently. It's almost always better to support a specific query with a single index. However, if you need to support ad hoc queries that cannot be foretold as a system designer, having several indexes that are useful for multiple situations might be the best idea.

For example, assume you want data from four columns in a table that contains telephone listings. You might create a table for holding phone numbers called PhoneListing with these columns: PhoneListingId, FirstName, LastName, ZipCode, AreaCode, Exchange, and Number (assuming US-style phone numbers).

You have a CLUSTERED PRIMARY KEY constraint index on PhoneListingId and nonclustered composite indexes on LastName and FirstName, one on AreaCode and Exchange, and another on ZipCode. From these indexes, you can effectively perform a large variety of searches, though generally speaking, none of these will be perfect alone, but with one or two columns considered independently, it might be adequate.

For less typical names (e.g., such as Leroy Shlabotnik), a person can find this name without knowing the location. For other names, hundreds and thousands of other people have the same first and last names. (I always thought I was the only schmuck with the name Louis Davidson, but it turns out that there are quite a few others!)

You could build a variety of indexes on these columns, such that SQL Server would only need a single index. However, not only would these indexes have a lot of columns in them but you'd need several indexes. As I covered in the previous section, a composite index can be useful for searches on the second and third columns, but if the first column is not included in the filtering criteria, it will require a scan, rather than a seek, of the index. Instead, for large sets, if you have multiple indexes on multiple columns (or sets of columns), SQL Server can find the set of data that meets one index's criteria and then join it to the set of rows that matches the other index's criteria.

As an example, using the table we have been working with, I want to search for the Nashville in StateProvince 44 (Tennessee). There is an index on the CityName column, and there is one on the StateProvince table as part of the table as it was created. Checking the plan on the following query

```
--limiting output to make the plan easier to follow
SELECT CityName, StateProvinceID
FROM   Application.Cities
WHERE  CityName = 'Nashville'
  AND  StateProvinceID = 44;
```

produces the following plan:

```
|--Merge Join(Inner Join,
        MERGE:([WideWorldImporters].[Application].[Cities].[CityID])=
            ([WideWorldImporters].[Application].[Cities].[CityID]),
      RESIDUAL:([WideWorldImporters].[Application].[Cities].[CityID] =
              [WideWorldImporters].[Application].[Cities].[CityID]))
```

```
|--Index Seek(OBJECT:([WideWorldImporters].[Application].
          [Cities].[CityName]),
    SEEK:([WideWorldImporters].[Application].[Cities].
       [CityName]=N'Nashville')  ORDERED FORWARD)

|--Index Seek (OBJECT:([WideWorldImporters].[Application].
        [Cities].[FK_Application_Cities_StateProvinceID]),
      SEEK:([WideWorldImporters].[Application].
        [Cities].[StateProvinceID]=(44)) ORDERED FORWARD)
```

Looking at the plan for this query, you can see that there are two index seeks to find rows where CityName = 'Nashville' and StateProvince = 44. These seeks would be fast on even a very large set, as long as the index was reasonably selective. Then, a merge join is done between the sets, because the sets can be ordered by the clustered index. (There's a clustered index on the table, so the clustering key is included in the index keys.)

Sort Order of Index Keys

While SQL Server can traverse an index in either direction (since it is a doubly linked list), sometimes sorting the keys of a composite index to match the sort order of some desired output can be valuable. For example, consider the case where you want to look at the CityName values in alphabetical order, but then ordered by LastRecordedPopulation in descending order:

```
SELECT CityName, LatestRecordedPopulation
FROM   Application.Cities
ORDER BY CityName ASC, LatestRecordedPopulation DESC;
```

The plan for this query follows:

```
|--Sort(ORDER BY:([WideWorldImporters].[Application].
    [Cities].[CityName] ASC, [WideWorldImporters].[Application].
    [Cities].[LatestRecordedPopulation] DESC))
      |--Index Scan (OBJECT:([WideWorldImporters].[Application].
         [Cities].[CityNameAndLastRecordedPopulation]))
```

But change the index to match the sort order that we are using, keeping the INCLUDE column:

```
DROP INDEX CityNameAndLastRecordedPopulation
        ON Application.Cities;
```

```
CREATE INDEX CityNameAndLastRecordedPopulation
        ON Application.Cities (CityName, LatestRecordedPopulation DESC)
                INCLUDE (LastEditedBy);
```

Rechecking the plan, you will see that the plan changes to an index scan (since it can use the index to cover the query), and it no longer requires a sort operation:

```
|--Index Scan (OBJECT:([WideWorldImporters].[Application].[Cities].
                [CityNameAndLastRecordedPopulation]), ORDERED FORWARD)
```

Now, change the sort orders of the query, and it has to be exactly opposite the sort orders of this query that produced the previous plan:

```
SELECT CityName, LatestRecordedPopulation
FROM   Application.Cities
ORDER BY CityName DESC, LatestRecordedPopulation ASC;
```

And it will still use the more optimal plan, but there will be one difference:

```
|--Index Scan (OBJECT:([WideWorldImporters].[Application].[Cities].
                [CityNameAndLastRecordedPopulation]), ORDERED BACKWARD)
```

An on-disk B-tree index can be scanned forward and backward, so it doesn't really matter which direction you set a simple index, nor does it matter for composite index, as long as the descending and ascending or opposite match the order the query needs.

In a specifically OLTP database, tweaking index sorting is not generally the best thing to do just to tune a single query unless it is a very important query. Doing so creates an index that will need to be maintained, which, in the end, may cost more than just paying the cost of the index scan. Creating an index in a sort order to match a query's ORDER BY clause is, however, another tool in your belt to enhance query performance. Consider it when an ORDER BY operation is done frequently enough and at a cost that is otherwise too much to bear.

Nonclustered Indexes on a Heap

Although there are rarely compelling use cases for leaving a table as a heap structure in a production OLTP database, I do want at least to show how this works. As an example of using a nonclustered index with a heap, we'll make a copy of the table we have been working with and make the primary key a nonclustered one:

```
SELECT *
INTO    Application.HeapCities
FROM    Application.Cities;

ALTER TABLE Application.HeapCities
    ADD CONSTRAINT PKHeapCities PRIMARY KEY NONCLUSTERED (CityID);

CREATE INDEX CityName ON Application.HeapCities(CityName) ON USERDATA;
```

Now, we look for a single value in the table:

```
SELECT *
FROM    Application.HeapCities
WHERE   CityID = 23629;
```

The following plan will be used to execute the query:

```
|--Nested Loops(Inner Join, OUTER REFERENCES:([Bmk1000]))
    |--Index Seek (OBJECT:([WideWorldImporters].[Application].
        [HeapCities].[PKHeapCities]),
      SEEK:([WideWorldImporters].[Application].[HeapCities].[CityID]=
            CONVERT_IMPLICIT(int,[@1],0)) ORDERED FORWARD)
    |--RID Lookup(OBJECT:([WideWorldImporters].[Application].
        [HeapCities]),
      SEEK:([Bmk1000]=[Bmk1000]) LOOKUP ORDERED FORWARD)
```

First, we probe the index for the value; then, we have to look up the row from the row ID (RID) in the index (the RID lookup operator). You can see the lookup where it says Bmk1000 = Bmk1000. The RID lookup operator is the most important thing I wanted to show in this section, so you can identify this on a plan and understand what is going on. This RID lookup operator is very similar to the CLUSTERED INDEX seek or row lookup operator. However, instead of using the clustering key, it uses the physical location of the row in the table. (As discussed earlier in this chapter, keeping this physical pointer stable is why the heap structure uses forwarding pointers instead of page splits and why it is generally considered best practice to have every table be a clustered table.)

Unique Indexes

An important index setting is UNIQUE, and not simply to enforce uniqueness. In the design of the tables, UNIQUE and PRIMARY KEY constraints were created to enforce keys, and behind the scenes, SQL Server employs unique indexes to enforce uniqueness over a column or group of columns. SQL Server uses them for this purpose because to determine if a value is unique, you have to look it up in the table. Because SQL Server uses indexes to speed access to the data, you have the perfect match.

Enforcing uniqueness is a business rule, and as I covered in Chapter 8, the rule of thumb is to use UNIQUE or PRIMARY constraints to enforce uniqueness on a set of columns. Now, as you're improving performance, use unique indexes when the data you're indexing allows them.

For example, say you're building an index that happens to include all the columns that are already a part of another unique index. Another possibility might be if you're indexing a column that's naturally unique, such as a GUID. It's up to the designer to decide if this GUID is a key or not, and that depends completely on what it's used for. But if the data is definitively unique, using a unique index lets the optimizer determine more easily the number of rows it has to deal with in an equality operation.

Note that it's important for the performance of your systems that you use unique indexes whenever possible, as they enhance the SQL Server optimizer's chances of predicting how many rows will be returned from queries that use these indexes. If the index is unique, the maximum number of rows that can be returned from a query that requires equality is one. This is common when working with joins. Do however be careful not to use a unique index where you cannot be completely sure that the data is unique. Note that, just like a uniqueness constraint, if you attempt to insert non-unique data into a unique index, an error will be raised.

Memory-Optimized Indexes and Data Structures

In SQL Server 2012, Microsoft started implementing what have been known as memory-optimized indexes with read-only nonclustered columnstore indexes. These indexes use a columnar approach to data storage that, instead of storing rows together, stores each column together. This is further enhanced by an engine called xVelocity that provides excellent compression and enhanced performance for some uses.

In 2014, while enhancing columnstore indexes to include a writable clustered version (though without the ability to have additional row-based indexes), Microsoft added something else that we have alluded to many times already in this book: memory-optimized tables (also known as in-memory OLTP and Hekaton…a term that you may see when doing searches about this technology; plus sometimes XTP shows up in the metadata for extreme processing). Originally memory-optimized tables were very limited at a table level (no CHECK or FOREIGN KEY constraints, only a single PRIMARY KEY constraint, etc.) and worked primarily for cases where an application treats SQL Server as just an optimized data storage bucket.

In 2016, Microsoft enhanced both technologies, allowing nonclustered indexes on columnstore clustered tables, allowing updateable nonclustered columnstore indexes, and giving in-memory OLTP tables check constraints, FOREIGN KEY constraints between in-memory tables, and up to eight uniqueness indexes/constraints. All this to say… memory-optimized technologies are still fairly new, very specific in what they are used for, and changing very fast. In SQL Server 2017, Microsoft increased the number of indexes to an unlimited amount. (I haven't tested what unlimited actually means, but unlimited is what it says in the documentation!)

In this section, I will start with an overview of memory-optimized tables and indexes and then provide an overview of the basic structure of a columnstore index. For the columnstore index, I will only provide some base examples and will leave deeper discussion to Appendix C (Available in the downloads), where reporting is covered in more detail, since columnstore indexes are much more aligned to either reporting databases or a few new reporting scenarios that allow you to report right off of your OLTP database using an asynchronously maintained index.

One major difference between on-disk and in-memory indexes is that in-memory indexes are not logged and are not stored anywhere. When you shut down the server, they are gone. When you restart the server, the indexes are rebuilt as the data is read in from the disk files that back up the memory structures. As such, changes to in-memory tables do not log changes to the indexes, so you pay a cost during startup, but there is a great benefit during normal operations.

Memory-Optimized Tables

While programming with memory-optimized tables is very much the same T-SQL code you already know, internally things are very different. Data resides in-memory as its home, rather than on disk, and while there is still an internal record size limitation of 8060 bytes (and still the ability to have large objects using the varbinary(max) and varchar(max) types), memory is not organized to match on-disk files, nor is data saved to files in the same format as it is for on-disk tables. While it is in a different format, data is still persisted to disk in a very similar pattern to on-disk tables. Just like for on-disk tables, when you make a change to data, the changes are written to memory and to the log (if you have specified the table to be durable), and before the transaction completes, data is written to the transaction log (unless you have DELAYED_DURABILITY enabled for the database, in which case the transaction log write is done asynchronously).

Tip   You can use temporal extensions with in-memory tables, but the history table will be an on-disk table.

Similarities generally end there. The structure of the rows is different, and indexes are very different, as is what happens during an UPDATE or DELETE. In this section, we will discuss the general structure of in-memory objects and indexes, and then we will take a look at the two types of indexes, including one that is very new to the SQL Server engine.

General Table Structure

Memory-optimized TABLE objects use a temporal-style internal structure that is the basis of multiversion concurrency control (MVCC) internal structures. Every change to the database results in a new row in a structure and/or an update to an effective timestamp in the data structure. Locks and latches are not employed to enable consistent modification of resources, and no connection ever waits for anything other than hardware busy doing work for another connection.

The basic structure of a record in the table is shown in Figure 11-14. Nothing too interesting in the basic structure. However, the row is limited to 8060 bytes, and data that takes more space than this is stored in its own internal table. For most cases, a row size that approaches 8060 bytes may not be great for usage in memory, particularly if you have a lot of rows (be sure and test it out in any case). Where things get interesting is in the Record Header, as shown in Figure 11-15.

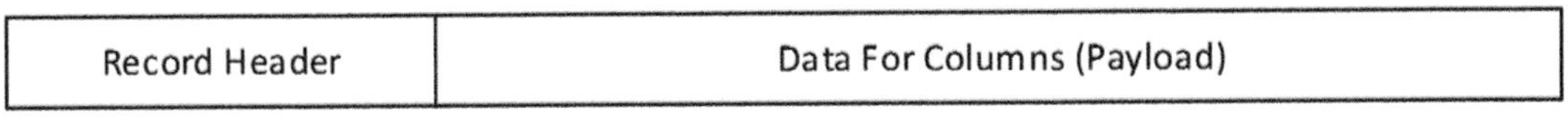

Record Header	Data For Columns (Payload)

Figure 11-14. *Basic row structure*

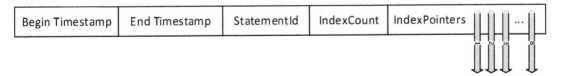

Figure 11-15. *In-memory Record Header*

The Begin Timestamp and End Timestamp represent a time frame in which the row is valid (Time >= [Begin Timestamp] and Time < [End Timestamp]). This timestamp is used by transactions that have started to let the connection know what rows in the structure it can see. All concurrency (covered in Chapter 12 in greater detail) is handled using SNAPSHOT isolation level in that a transaction will always see its distinct view of the database as of the start of its transaction.

As an example, say we have a partial table with two columns, AddressId, a unique integer value, and Country, with the name of a country. From timestamp 0 to 100, it looked like

AddressId	Country	Value
1	USA	T
2	USA	D
3	Canada	D
4	Colombia	D

Then, at timestamp 100, it changed to the following, with address 2 now being a Canadian one:

AddressId	Country	Value
1	USA	T
2	Canada	D
3	Canada	D
4	Colombia	D

However, a connection still has a transaction open at timestamp 50, so the old view of the structure needs to remain. Figure 11-16 shows how this would look (technically, memory-optimized tables need a unique index in order to connect rows together in a linked list, but this is an abstract example of the basic structure).

Start	End	Index		AddessId	Country	Value
0	∞	Φ	Φ	1	USA	T
0	100	Φ	Φ	2	USA	D
100	∞	Φ	Φ	2	Can ada	D
0	∞	Φ	Φ	3	Can ada	D
0	∞	Φ	Φ	4	Colom bia	D

***Figure 11-16.** Sample table structure*

By filtering on the two time frames, you can see one of the rows where AddressId = 2 falls out, leaving us with the two tables of the data.

The other very different part of the structure is how indexes work. The arrows in Figure 11-17 are index pointers. Every table must have at least one index, because this is how rows are connected (there are no page to page pointers, and index pointes are one way, meaning that if you need the ability to traverse the keys of an index in two directions, you need two indexes with the same keys, but different orders). The part of the structure to find the first row is always a separate structure, but the physical record pointer just points to one row in the table. From there, all values that meet the criteria for a level in the index become a chain of rows.

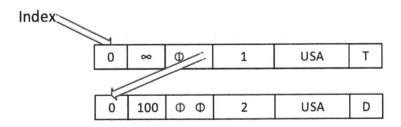

Figure 11-17. *Index pointers*

In the example, one row from an index would point to the first row in the image, and the pointer would be followed for the second row. For the unique index, you instinctively might think there would never be a chain of rows, but this is not the case. For updates, you end up with multiple rows until the old rows are removed. Also, if using a hash index (which is implemented in a very different way than B-tree indexes), it does not have uniqueness in the way it is implemented; it still needs to look for uniqueness. For any of the index types, the goal is generally to have no more than an average of 100 values in this chain to be scanned. If this is the case, it will be best to choose your index key columns so they are more unique (this should not be an issue with indexes you are using for a PRIMARY KEY/UNIQUE constraint).

The index pointer structure is pretty amazing because the leaf node of every index is the table's data. So the primary benefit of a clustered index, that of not having to go fetch the rest of the data from a separate structure, is there for all memory-optimized indexes because of how they are structured.

Conceptually and structurally, things are very different, but for the most part, assuming you are designing and implementing memory-optimized tables, the most important thing is to understand the basic versioning structure to understand which index to choose when and to really grok the differences in how concurrency is implemented.

Index Structure

When Microsoft created the memory-optimized engine, they didn't just create one type of index as we had in the on-disk structures. There are two types of rowstore indexes (and you can use columnstore indexes as well). B-tree–based indexes are awesome structures, but they can be overkill when you simply need to do a single-row lookup. So Microsoft has given us (for memory-optimized objects only, so far) a new index type, a *hash index*.

In this section, we will look at the B-tree–based Bw-tree indexes, as well as hash index types that are used for the in-memory OLTP structures.

Bw-Tree Indexes

The Bw-tree index is, for all intents and purposes, very similar to the B-tree indexes that we have had in SQL Server since the very beginning. In this section, I will look at the conceptual implementation and usage patterns for Bw-tree indexes. In Figure 11-18, you can see the base structure of the index. There is a page mapping layer that contains the memory addresses of the pages of the index and a B-tree structure that conceptually is the same as on on-disk B-tree, except the lower values of the tree are less than the key (rather than greater than for the on-disk counterpart) on the parent page. So, because page 0 has C as the first entry, all values on the leftmost node will be C or less.

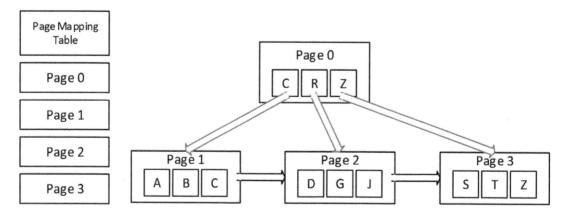

Figure 11-18. *Bw-tree index node pages*

The values in the nodes of the index are not timestamped and are maintained for all values. The values on the leaf nodes point to actual rows in the table. In our example table, this node set is an index that includes the Value column from the rows in our sample structure, as shown in Figure 11-19.

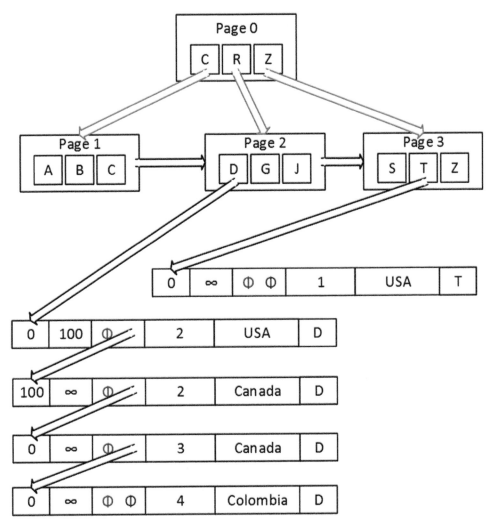

Figure 11-19. *Bw-tree index node pages linked to data*

As shown in the start of the "Memory-Optimized Tables" section, once you reach the value in the leaf node, it is the entry point into the internal linked list of index pointers. So all of the D values and versions we have are chained together row by row, and any older transactions are cleaned up as the engine can get to it.

Hash Indexes

Hashing is a well-tested concept in computer science and has been used by the optimizer since SQL Server 7.0 to do joins on unindexed, unordered sets. The idea is that you create a function that takes (more or less) an infinite number of inputs and outputs a finite, manageable "bucket" to match them in. For example, suppose you have the following data, and the ellipsis represents approximately 100 rows:

Name
Amanda
Emma
Aria
Andrew
Addison
...
Jim
Linda
Max

Say all you ever need to do is find a name in the list. In a Bw-tree, you would have the overhead of sorting the data and perhaps also duplicating the data in the leaf pages of the index. In a hash index, you simply devise a function that will let you separate things into piles. As a human, you might use the first letter or letters of the name, or perhaps the length of the name, which gives you the following:

Name	HashBucket
Amanda	6
Emma	4
Aria	4
Andrew	6
Addison	7
...	
Jim	3
Linda	5
Max	3

You sort the data by the HashBucket and then scan the bucket. This is very similar to what SQL Server will do with hash index structures, only with a hash function that will produce a lot greater variety in hash bucket values (details of the hashing algorithm are not shared, but there is one hash algorithm for all datatypes). In this section, I will look at conceptually how this is applied to hash indexes and then cover some of the basics of creating and using hash indexes.

SQL Server basically implements hash buckets as one might do manually, using an algorithm to do the hashing that you have no control over. You simply choose a number of buckets based on the expected number of unique values × approximately 2, which will be internally rounded up to the next highest power of 2. Then create the index and it does the work. Each bucket takes 8 bytes upon creation (or index rebuild) and does not change on its own. You have to resize the bucket count manually if your estimated number of unique values changes. Bear in mind that it is far better to have too many hash buckets than too few. If too many values are placed in the chain to scan, performance will degrade. The larger the number of hash buckets, the less likely this scenario will become.

As an example, in Figure 11-20, I have the structure that I started with earlier in this section, but now I have a hash index on the Country column. Note that two of the values hashed to the same value (how convenient for the example!). While you won't see the internals, there are DMVs that will tell you the average bucket length, and it will almost never be 1, even when the index key is unique.

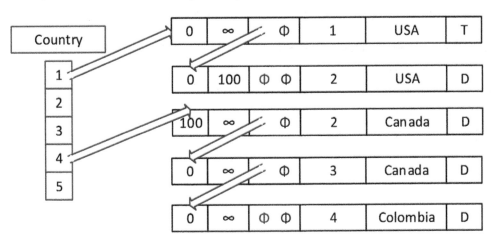

Figure 11-20. Sample hash index

In the data, USA hashes to bucket 1, and Canada and Colombia hash to 5. When SQL Server does a lookup in the index, it uses the same hash function that it used to put up the value; then it goes to the first row in the hash bucket and scans all the rows. So it would be three memory reads for Colombia, or Canada, or any other value that hashes to 4.

Indexing Memory-Optimized Tables

Microsoft's current prescription as of this book writing for indexing in-memory OLTP tables is to start with the Bw-tree–based nonclustered indexes for pretty much all primary keys, unique keys, and all other indexes one might need. They are easier to create and have less maintenance, and they work well for most of the use cases one will have for in-memory OLTP tables. For more details, see the Microsoft Docs article "Indexes for Memory-Optimized Tables: Comparing when to use each index type" (docs.microsoft.com/en-us/sql/relational-databases/in-memory-oltp/indexes-for-memory-optimized-tables#comparing-when-to-use-each-index-type).

It must be noted, however, that hash indexes will perform better if your use case is 100% single-value lookups like a typical PRIMARY KEY constraint on a surrogate key value might be used for. This is largely due to fixed memory sizing and less processing needed to get to the head of the linked list of rows. But even then, how well the hashing function performs will depend on how many rows will end up needing scanned, as opposed to a nonclustered Bw-Tree, where the scanned rows will be based strictly on all rows having the same index key value. Be certain that your bucket sizes are at least twice the number of unique values you have/expect and watch the chain length as previously mentioned. A very large number of values in a chain will start to degrade performance. Also remember that both indexes will have in their index chains data for expired rows that have not been cleaned up because transactions haven't ended or the cleanup routines have not removed them from memory yet due to contention.

In the WideWorldImporters sample database, there are a few in-memory tables. We will use Warehouse.VehicleTemperatures in this section for a few plan demonstrations. It has the following structure:

```
CREATE TABLE Warehouse.VehicleTemperatures
(
    VehicleTemperatureID bigint IDENTITY(1,1) NOT NULL
        CONSTRAINT PK_Warehouse_VehicleTemperatures  PRIMARY KEY NONCLUSTERED,
    VehicleRegistration nvarchar(20) COLLATE Latin1_General_CI_AS NOT NULL,
    ChillerSensorNumber int NOT NULL,
    RecordedWhen datetime2(7) NOT NULL,
    Temperature decimal(10, 2) NOT NULL,
    FullSensorData nvarchar(1000) COLLATE Latin1_General_CI_AS NULL,
    IsCompressed bit NOT NULL,
```

```
CompressedSensorData varbinary(max) NULL
) WITH ( MEMORY_OPTIMIZED = ON , DURABILITY = SCHEMA_AND_DATA );
```

It comes with 65,998 rows and does not have any other indexes or foreign keys defined on the table itself other than the primary key.

The first thing you will notice is that not much is different in using these tables in simple queries (larger differences show up more in the next chapter with explicit transactions and concurrency and even more when we get to Chapter 13 and I discuss a bit about native code vs. interpreted T-SQL). Take the following query:

```
SELECT *
FROM    Warehouse.VehicleTemperatures;
```

The query plan is very much what you would expect:

```
|--Table Scan(OBJECT:([WideWorldImporters].[Warehouse].
  [VehicleTemperatures]))
```

Add in a primary key value:

```
SELECT *
FROM    Warehouse.VehicleTemperatures
WHERE   VehicleTemperatureID = 2332;
```

Now the plan will indicate that you get an index seek and a parameterized plan:

```
|--Index Seek (OBJECT:([WideWorldImporters].[Warehouse].
        [VehicleTemperatures].[PK_Warehouse_VehicleTemperatures]),
    SEEK:([WideWorldImporters].[Warehouse].[VehicleTemperatures].
        [VehicleTemperatureID]=CONVERT_IMPLICIT(bigint,[@1],0))
                                        ORDERED FORWARD)
```

One difference you may see is a plan making more use of an index. For example, the query

```
SELECT *
FROM    Warehouse.VehicleTemperatures
WHERE   VehicleTemperatureID <> 0;
```

looks like a definite case for a full table scan. VehicleTemperature = 0 could only return one row, so the opposite must return at a minimum the number of rows in the table—one, but the plan here uses the index, because less memory will be scanned since all indexes include all row data.

```
|--Index Seek (OBJECT:([WideWorldImporters].[Warehouse].
      [VehicleTemperatures].[PK_Warehouse_VehicleTemperatures]),
  SEEK:([WideWorldImporters].[Warehouse].[VehicleTemperatures].
      [VehicleTemperatureID] < (0)
      OR    [WideWorldImporters].[Warehouse].[VehicleTemperatures].
      [VehicleTemperatureID] > (0))
                                          ORDERED FORWARD)
```

One of the reasons that the prescription is to use Bw-tree indexes first is that hash indexes have only one purpose: single-row lookups. So, if you need to do any sort of range query, hash indexes will not be helpful. For example, let's add one to the RecordedWhen column:

```
ALTER TABLE Warehouse.VehicleTemperatures ADD INDEX RecordedWhen
--33000 distinct values, values are in powers of 2
    HASH (RecordedWhen) WITH (BUCKET_COUNT = 64000);
```

Use an equality operator

```
SELECT *
FROM    Warehouse.VehicleTemperatures
WHERE   RecordedWhen = '2016-03-10 12:50:22.0000000';
```

and the index is used:

```
|--Index Seek(OBJECT:([WideWorldImporters].[Warehouse].
      [VehicleTemperatures].[RecordedWhen]),
  SEEK:([WideWorldImporters].[Warehouse].[VehicleTemperatures].
      [RecordedWhen]=CONVERT_IMPLICIT(datetime2(7),[@1],0))
                                          ORDERED FORWARD)
```

But even if the plan clearly can only return the same row(s), if the comparison is not converted to an equality operator, it will use a scan and filter:

```
SELECT *
FROM    Warehouse.VehicleTemperatures
WHERE   RecordedWhen BETWEEN
           '2016-03-10 12:50:22.0000000' AND '2016-03-10 12:50:22.0000000';
```

This results in the following plan:

```
|--Filter(WHERE:([WideWorldImporters].[Warehouse].[VehicleTemperatures].
      [RecordedWhen]>=CONVERT_IMPLICIT(datetime2(7),[@1],0)
                AND
      [WideWorldImporters].[Warehouse].[VehicleTemperatures].
      [RecordedWhen]<= CONVERT_IMPLICIT(datetime2(7),[@2],0)))
      |--Table Scan(OBJECT:([WideWorldImporters].[Warehouse].
            [VehicleTemperatures])) ORDERED FORWARD)
```

If you have throughput needs that merit the use of the memory-optimized engine, you need to do testing to make sure that everything is working as you expect. In Chapter 12, we will see how even fast-looking queries can have a negative impact on concurrency when you don't get your indexes right. The memory-optimized engine is built for specific scenarios and has quite a few differences, but it can provide tremendous improvements in performance.

Columnstore Indexes

Columnstore indexes are, for the reporting specialist, an amazing tool. In this section, I just want to give a very brief introduction to the structures so you can see conceptually the difference between columnstore indexes and the rowstore indexes we have been covering. A columnstore index is a form of columnar index. Columnar databases have been around for quite a while, so named because instead of keeping entire rows together, they keep entire columns of data together. They have generally been great at implementing reporting solutions where you have to scan a lot of rows for every query, especially when dealing with lots of duplicate data, and are particularly useful when processing aggregates on large sets. The more columns in the object and the fewer you need to use in the query, the greater the performance benefit. Figure 11-21 shows a conceptual diagram of the structure of a columnstore index.

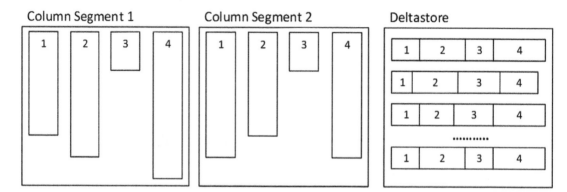

Figure 11-21. *Conceptual view of a columnstore index*

In SQL Server, the column segment blocks are ideally 1,048,576 rows each with each of the numbered sections representing a column, with each segment ordered by the rows in the table. They are different sized because each of the segments is compressed, much like you can compress normal data on a page, but instead of an 8 KB page, over 1 million rows are compresses in a blob-style storage.

Data in a columnstore index is not ordered and can be scanned for all usage in what is called "batch mode," which processes data in ~900 at once, instead of the "row" mode used for typical rowstore indexes (SQL Server 2019 enables batch mode processing on rowstore indexes in some cases as well). In practice I have found in extreme cases (like a data warehouse fact table that has 120 columns and you are aggregating on 3) query performance can be several orders of magnitude faster to process.

Note   SQL Server 2019 enables batch mode processing on rowstore indexes in some cases as well as part of the Intelligent Query Processing feature set. For more details, go to the Microsoft Docs article "Batch Mode on Rowstore" (docs. microsoft.com/en-us/sql/relational-databases/performance/ intelligent-query-processing#batch-mode-on-rowstore).

The Deltastore column segment in Figure 11-21 comes into play when you are modifying a table with a columnstore index on it, and new rows are dropped into the deltastore until you reach the 1,048,576-row threshold. The deltastore is basically a rowstore heap structure that will be scanned for the contents to satisfy queries. Using the REBUILD or REORGANIZE commands of the ALTER INDEX command, you can manually push rows into the column segments also. I won't delve into the management of columnstore indexes in this book.

Updates to rows in a columnstore index are a delete from the columnstore index, and then the row is added to either the deltastore for a clustered columnstore or to the last columnstore segment for a nonclustered version. So it will behoove you to avoid doing a lot of modifications if possible.

As of SQL Server 2016, there are clustered and nonclustered columnstore indexes, and both are updateable, and both can be mixed with rowstore indexes. This improvement enables some very advanced scenarios, such as adding a columnstore index on a table that is heavily modified, where the columnstore index is maintained asynchronously, allowing data that is being actively modified to stay in the deltastore longer where it is cheaper to modify. This allows you to put a columnstore index on an active OLTP table so real-time reporting can occur without interfering with real-time data capture. This will be discussed more in Appendix C which is available as a download. The most important benefit of mixing the indexes is that columnstore indexes are horrible at single-row lookups. This is because there is no uniqueness declared or enforced. This leads to every query being a scan of the structure.

Common OLTP Patterns of Index Usage

In this section, I have gathered a few topics that are important to cover but did not fit the flow of the previous sections (sometimes because they needed multiple sections to be completed).

We will look at these topics:

- *Indexing foreign keys*: Foreign keys almost always represent a common path to retrieve data from a table, but do they always need indexed? Do they ever?

- *Indexed views*: So far, we have limited discussion to indexing tables, but you can index views in some cases to give you fast answers maintained by SQL Server's code instead of yours.

- *Compression*: Fitting more data onto disk means less reads from disk, which is still the slowest part of a computer.

- *Partitioning*: Partitioning breaks up a table or index physically but still makes it look like one object to the end user. This allows for some coding and maintenance scenarios to be easier.

Indexing Foreign Keys

Foreign key columns are a special case where we often need an index that may or may not be of immediate general usefulness to end user queries. This is true both in on-disk and memory-optimized tables. We build foreign keys so we can match up rows in one table to rows in another. For this, we have to take a value in one table and match it to another.

Any time you have a FOREIGN KEY constraint declared, there's the potential for need of an index. Often when you have a parent table with specific values, you may want to see the children of the row. A special and important case where this type of access is essential is when you have to delete the parent row in any relationship, even one of a domain type that has a very low cardinality. If in doubt, it is not a terrible practice to add indexes to foreign keys by default, and during testing use one of the queries in the upcoming "Indexing Dynamic Management View Queries" section to identify how or if indexes are being used.

Say you have five values in the parent table and 500 million in the child. For example, consider the case of a click log for a sales database, a snippet of which is shown in Figure 11-22.

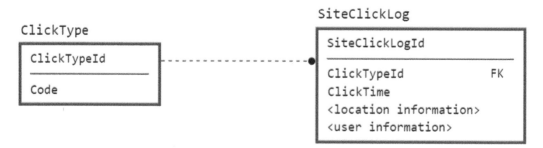

Figure 11-22. *Sample foreign key relationship*

Consider that you want to delete a ClickType row that someone added inadvertently. Creating the row took no more than a millisecond or two. Deleting it shouldn't take long at all, right? Well, even if there isn't a matching value in the table, if you don't have an index on the foreign key in the SiteClickLog table, it may take just over 10 seconds longer than eternity to try to delete this row. Even though the value doesn't exist in the table, the query processor would need to touch and check all 500 million rows for the value. From the statistics on the column, the query processor can guess how many rows might exist, but it can't definitively know that there is or is not a value because statistics are maintained asynchronously and rows are stored unsorted. (Ironically, because it is an existence search, the query processor could fail quickly on the first row it checked, but to successfully delete the row, every child row must be touched.)

If you have an index on the foreign key columns, deleting the row (or knowing that you can't delete it) will take a very short period of time, because in the upper pages of the index, you'll have all the unique values in the index, in this case, five values. There will be a fairly substantial set of leaf pages for the index, but only one page in each index level; usually no more than three or four pages will need to be touched before the query processor can determine the existence of a row out of millions of rows. When NO ACTION is specified for the relationship, if just one row is found, the operation could be stopped. If you have cascading operations enabled for the relationship, the cascading options will need the index to find the rows to cascade to.

This adds more decisions when building indexes. Is the cost of building and maintaining the index during creation of millions of SiteClickLog rows justified, or do you just bite the bullet and do deletes during off-hours? Add a SoftDeleteFlag column to ClickType and a trigger such as the following, ignoring schemas and error handling in this example for brevity:

```
CREATE TRIGGER ClickType$InsteadOfDeleteTrigger
ON ClickType
INSTEAD OF DELETE
AS
    UPDATE ClickType
    SET    SoftDeleteFlag = 1
    FROM   ClickType
              JOIN deleted
                ON deleted.ClickTypeId = ClickType.ClickTypeId;
```

Then, let your queries that return lists of `ClickType` rows check this table when presenting rows to the users (ideally by changing the code to use a view that uses the following code, but the more change you make, the harder these changes are):

```
SELECT Code, Description, ClickTypeId
FROM   ClickType
WHERE  SoftDeleteFlag = 0;
```

Now, assuming all code follows this pattern (you could change the table to a different name and use a VIEW object to encapsulate the query), the users will never see the value, so it won't be an issue (at least not in terms of values being used; performance will suffer obviously). Then, you can delete the row in the wee hours of the morning without building the index. Whether or not an index proves useful generally depends on the purpose of the FOREIGN KEY constraint. I'll mention specific types of foreign keys individually, each with their own signature usage:

- *Domain tables*: Used to implement a defined set of values and their descriptions

- *Ownership relationships*: Used to implement a multivalued attribute of the parent

- *Many-to-many resolution table relationships*: Used to implement a many-to-many relationship physically

- *One-to-one relationships*: Cases where a parent may have only a single value in the related table

We'll look at examples of these types of relationships and discuss when it's typically appropriate to index them before trial-and-error performance tuning, where the rule of thumb is to add indexes to make queries faster while not slowing down other operations that create data.

In all cases, deleting the parent row requires a table scan of the child if there's no index on the child row. This is an important consideration if there are deletes.

Domain Tables

You use a domain table to enforce a domain using a table, rather than using a scalar value with a constraint. This is often done to enable a greater level of data about the domain value, such as a descriptive value. For example, consider the tables in Figure 11-23.

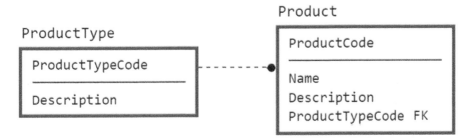

Figure 11-23. *Sample domain table relationship*

In this case, there are a small number of rows in the ProductType table. It's unlikely that an index on the Product.ProductTypeCode column would be of any value in a join, because you'll generally be getting a ProductType row for every row you fetch from the Product table.

What about the other direction, when you want to find all products of a single type? This can be useful if there aren't many products, but in general, domain-type tables don't have enough unique values to merit an index due to the high cardinality of the values. The general advice is that tables of this sort don't need an index on the foreign key values, by default. Of course, deleting ProductType rows would need to scan the entire ProductType. But, since this is a domain table, where ideally we don't let users do such operations, any changes to the data are more of a release situation than a normal update, so disabling a relationship might be the smarter way to handle this.

On the other hand, as discussed earlier in the chapter, sometimes an index can be useful when there are limited numbers of some value. For example, consider a User to UserStatus relationship illustrated in Figure 11-24.

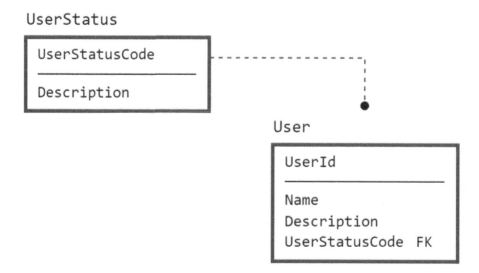

Figure 11-24. *Sample domain table relationship with low cardinality*

In this case, most users would be in the database with an "active" status. However, when a user is deactivated, you might need to do some action for that user. Since the number of inactive users would be far fewer than active users, it might be useful to have an index (possibly a filtered index) on the UserStatusCode column for that purpose.

Ownership Relationships

Some tables have no meaning without the existence of another table and pretty much exist as part of another table (due to the way relational design works with all atomic column values). When I am thinking about an ownership relationship, I am thinking of relationships that implement multivalued attributes for a row, just as an array in a procedural language does for an object. The main performance characteristic of this situation is that most of the time when the parent row is retrieved, the child rows are retrieved as well. You'll be less likely to need to retrieve a child row and then look for the parent row.

For example, take the case of an invoice and its line items in Figure 11-25.

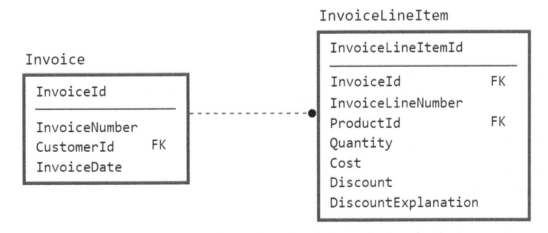

Figure 11-25. *Sample ownership relationship*

In this case, it's essential to have an index on the InvoiceLineItem.InvoiceId column, almost certainly as part of a UNIQUE constraint with InvoiceLineNumber. A large amount of access to the InvoiceLineItem table results from a user's need to get an invoice first. This situation is also ideal for an index because, usually, it will turn out to be a very selective index (unless you have large numbers of items and few sales).

Note that you should already have a UNIQUE constraint (and a unique index because of this) on the alternate key for the table—in this case, InvoiceId and InvoiceLineNumber. Therefore, you probably wouldn't need to have an index on just InvoiceId. What might be in question would be whether the index on InvoiceId and InvoiceLineNumber ought to be clustered, as I noted in the previous section about when to cluster on a non-surrogate value. If you do most of your SELECT operations using the InvoiceId, this can be a good idea. However, you should be careful in this case because you can actually do a lot more fetches on the primary key value, since UPDATE and DELETE operations start out performing like a SELECT before the modification. For example, the application may end up doing one query to get the invoice line items and then update each row individually. So always watch the activity in your database and tune accordingly.

Many-to-Many Resolution Table Relationships

When we have a many-to-many relationship, there certainly needs to be an index on the two migrated keys from the two parent tables. Using an example that we used in Chapter 8, with a many-to-many relationship between tables that hold games a person owns, the relationship between GamePlatform and Game is shown in Figure 11-26.

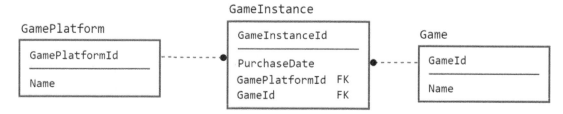

Figure 11-26. *Sample many-to-many relationship*

In this case, you should already have a unique constraint on GamePlatformId and GameId, and one of the two will necessarily be first in the composite index. If you need to search for both keys independently of one another, you may want to create an index on each column individually (or at least the column that is listed second in the uniqueness constraint's index).

Take this example. If we usually look up a game by name (which would probably be an alternate key index in the fully fleshed-out design) and then get the platforms for this game, an index only on GameInstance.GameId would be much more useful and two-thirds the size of the alternate key index (assuming a clustering key of GameInstanceId).

In some cases, with a many-to-many relationship, it could be that not only do you need an index for the attributes in one order but in both. So, in this case, you could have a UNIQUE constraint on (GamePlatformId, GameId), but also a UNIQUE INDEX or CONSTRAINT on (GameId, GamePlatformId) to support searches in either direction quickly.

One-to-One Relationships

One-to-one relationships generally require some form of unique index on the key in the parent table as well as on the migrated key in the child table. For example, consider the subclass example of a BankAccount, shown in Figure 11-27.

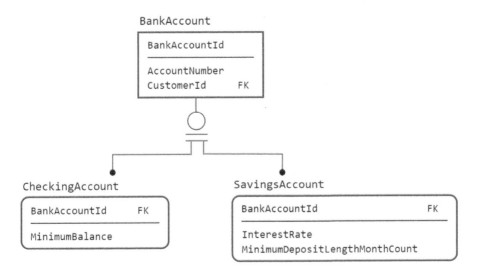

Figure 11-27. *Sample one-to-one relationship*

In this case, because these are one-to-one relationships and there are already indexes on the primary key of each table, no other indexes would need to be added to effectively implement the relationship.

Indexed Views

I mentioned the use of persisted calculated columns in Chapter 7 for optimizing denormalizations for a single row, but sometimes, your denormalizations need to span multiple rows and include things like summarizations. In this section, I will introduce a way to take precalculated values to the next level, using *indexed views*.

Indexing a view basically takes the virtual structure of the view and makes it a physical entity, managed completely by the SQL Server infrastructure. The data to resolve queries with the view is generated as data is modified in the table, so access to the results from the view is just as fast as if it were an actual table (because internally it physically is). Creating indexed views is (more or less) as easy as writing a query and building a table.

The benefits are twofold when using indexed views. First, when you use an indexed view directly in any edition of SQL Server, it does not have to do any calculations (editions less than Enterprise must specify NOEXPAND as an option hint to use the precalculated data, and if you have need to ignore the precalculated data, you can use the EXPAND VIEWS option hint). Second, in Enterprise edition (including Developer edition which is functionally equivalent to Enterprise edition), SQL Server automatically considers the use of an indexed view whenever you execute any query, even if the query doesn't reference the view but the code you execute uses the same aggregates. SQL Server accomplishes this by matching the executed query to each indexed view to see whether that view already has the answer to something you are asking for.

For example, we could create the following view on the product and sales tables in the WideWorldImporters database. Note that only schema-bound views can be indexed as this makes certain that the tables and structures that the index is created upon won't change underneath the view. (A more complete list of requirements is presented after the example.)

```
CREATE VIEW Warehouse.StockItemSalesTotals
WITH SCHEMABINDING --schemabinding required
AS
SELECT StockItems.StockItemName,
        --ISNULL because expression can't be nullable
        SUM(OrderLines.Quantity * ISNULL(OrderLines.UnitPrice,0))
                                                AS TotalSalesAmount,
        --must use COUNT_BIG for indexed view
        COUNT_BIG(*) AS TotalSalesCount
FROM   Warehouse.StockItems
            JOIN Sales.OrderLines
                ON  OrderLines.StockItemID = StockItems.StockItemID
GROUP  BY StockItems.StockItemName;
```

This would do the calculations at execution time. We run the following query:

```
SELECT *
FROM   Warehouse.StockItemSalesTotals;
```

The estimated plan looks like...well, six operators that have a lot of detail in the textual plan. An image is provided in Figure 11-28 from the estimated plan (you can get this from SSMS menu Query ➤ Display Estimated Execution Plan). Though it loses a lot of fidelity from the textual plans, it might save a tree.

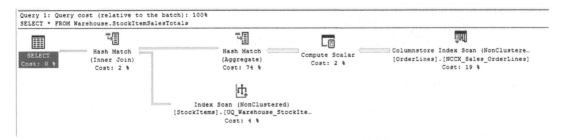

Figure 11-28. *Estimated query plan image from using the view*

Sometimes you might see something like the following plan be generated. Instead of the hash join, it does an adaptive join, which means it decides how to execute the query at runtime, depending on which method is best for the query processor at runtime. You can see this plan in Figure 11-29.

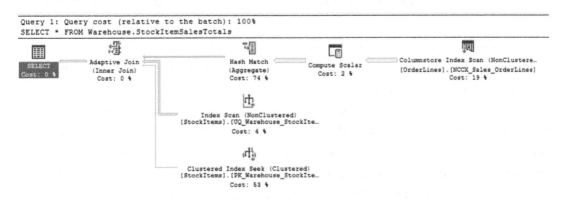

Figure 11-29. *Estimated query plan image from using the view using an adaptive join*

When you execute the query and turn on the actual query plan (you can get this from the SSMS menu Query ➤ Include Actual Execution Plan), this will return a view like the following that shows you the same things that you can get from the estimated plan, but now it has the time each step takes and the number of rows that were processed, along with the estimated number of rows to be processed. For this query the estimate is perfect, but that is only semi-rarely the case. Usually the estimate is close, but sometimes it can be way off, often due to stale statistics. For our query, you can see that Figure 11-30.

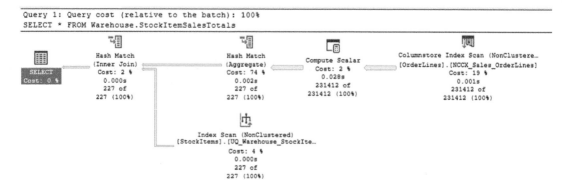

```
Query 1: Query cost (relative to the batch): 100%
SELECT * FROM Warehouse.StockItemSalesTotals
```

Figure 11-30. *Actual query plan image from using the view*

In any case, this is a big plan for such a small query, for sure. It scans the OrderLines columnstore index, computes our scalar values, and then does a hash match aggregate to compute the SUM and the COUNT_BIG values. From there, it gets to use a Hash Match (Inner Join) to join the StockItems rows to the aggregated OrderLines. For further reading on the join types, again consider Grant Fritchey's Apress book, *SQL Server Query Performance Tuning*. This is a good plan for the query, but if you are doing this many times a day, using an indexed view can help.

One last query tuning note: You can watch as data moves around a query plan using live statistics. Our query isn't terribly interesting in this way, but if you choose Query ➤ Include Live Statistics, you can see the actual query plan with the adaptive join method chosen and the number of rows moving through the query. This is very useful if you are waiting forever for a query to complete and you want to see what is taking so long.

The query only returns 227 rows in this sample database, but say this query wasn't fast enough or it used too many resources to execute or it was used extremely often. In this case, we might add an index on the view. Note that it must be a clustered index, as it will create a physical structure from the query data, and the data pages will be ordered based on the key we chose:

```
CREATE UNIQUE CLUSTERED INDEX XPKStockItemSalesTotals on
                    Warehouse.StockItemSalesTotals(StockItemName);
```

SQL Server then materializes the view and stores it. Now, our queries to the view will be *very* fast. However, although we've avoided all the coding issues involved with storing summary data, the data has to be kept up to date. Every time data changes in the underlying tables, the index on the view changes its data, so there's a performance hit in maintaining the index for the view. Hence, indexing views means that performance is great for reading but not necessarily for updating, and the update costs will be considerably higher than for normal indexes.

Now, run the query again, and the plan is just a simple scan of the physical structure since we asked for the entire table to be returned:

```
|--Clustered Index Scan
  (OBJECT:([WideWorldImporters].[Warehouse].
  [StockItemSalesTotals].[XPKStockItemSalesTotals]))
```

We expected this result because we directly queried the view. On Enterprise edition, to get the previous plan, change the query to use OPTION(EXPAND VIEWS), and it will ignore the stored data and use the text of the VIEW object. This can be handy in some cases when the query will integrate with your overall query better than using the table:

```
SELECT *
FROM    Warehouse.StockItemSalesTotals
OPTION (EXPAND VIEWS);
```

For standard edition, to get the clustered index scan result, change EXPAND VIEWS to NOEXPAND. Kind of clunky, but still can be worth it if you can change code.

On my test system, running Developer edition (which is functionally comparable to Enterprise edition), you get a great insight into how cool this feature is by running the following query, which is basically our original query with a division operator between the two factors:

```
SELECT StockItems.StockItemName,
       SUM(OrderLines.Quantity * ISNULL(OrderLines.UnitPrice,0)) /
                          COUNT_BIG(*) AS AverageSaleAmount
FROM   Warehouse.StockItems
          JOIN Sales.OrderLines
                  ON  OrderLines.StockItemID = StockItems.StockItemID
GROUP  BY StockItems.StockItemName;
```

We'd expect the plan for this query to be the same as the first query of the view was, because we haven't referenced anything other than the base tables, right? I already told you the answer, so here's the plan:

```
|--Compute Scalar(DEFINE:([Expr1006]=[Expr1004]/
                    CONVERT_IMPLICIT(decimal(19,0),[Expr1005],0)))
     |--Clustered Index Scan(OBJECT:([WideWorldImporters].[Warehouse].
                    [StockItemSalesTotals].[XPKStockItemSalesTotals]))
```

There is a scalar compute that does our math, but instead you will notice that the plan references the StockItemSalesTotals indexed view, and we did not reference it directly in our query. The ability to use the optimizations from an indexed view indirectly when the algorithms match up is a neat feature that allows you to build in some guesses as to what ad hoc users will be doing with the data and give them performance they didn't even ask for.

Tip   The indexed view feature in Enterprise edition can also come in handy for tuning third-party systems that work on an API that is not tunable in a direct manner (i.e., to change the text of a query to make it more efficient).

As alluded to earlier in the section, there are some pretty heavy caveats, though. The restrictions on what can be used in a view, prior to it being indexed, are fairly tight. The most important things that *cannot* be done are as follows:

- Use the SELECT * syntax—columns must be explicitly named.
- Use a CLR user-defined aggregate.
- Use UNION, EXCEPT, or INTERSECT in the view.
- Use any subqueries.
- Use any outer joins or recursively join back to the same table.
- Specify TOP in the SELECT clause.
- Use DISTINCT.
- Include a SUM() function if it references more than one column.

- Use COUNT(*), though COUNT_BIG(*) is allowed.

- Use almost any aggregate function against a nullable expression.

- Reference any other views, or use CTEs or derived tables.

- Reference any nondeterministic functions.

- Reference data outside the database.

- Reference tables owned by a different owner.

- FOR SYSTEM_TIME temporal extension cannot be used.

And this isn't all. You must meet several pages of requirements, documented in Microsoft Docs in the topic "Create Indexed Views" (docs.microsoft.com/en-us/sql/relational-databases/views/create-indexed-views). However, these are the most significant ones that you need to consider before using indexed views.

Indexed views are particularly useful when you have a VIEW object that's costly to run but the data on which it's based doesn't change a tremendous amount. As a last example, consider a decision support system where you load data once a day. There's overhead either maintaining the index or, possibly, just rebuilding it, but if you can build the index during off-hours, you can omit the cost of redoing joins and calculations for every view usage.

Compression

I mentioned compression when we looked at columnstore indexes. In a normal index (which includes clustered tables, heaps, and B-trees), SQL Server can save space by storing all of your data like it was a variable-sized type, yet in usage, the data will appear and behave like a fixed-length type. In Appendix A, I will note how compression will affect each datatype individually, or if you want to see a list that may show any recent changes, you can check SQL Server Books Online for the topic "Row Compression Implementation" (docs.microsoft.com/en-us/sql/relational-databases/data-compression/row-compression-implementation).

For example, if you stored the value of 100 in an int column, SQL Server needn't use all 4 bytes; it can store the value 100 in the same amount of space as a tinyint. So instead of taking a full 4 bytes, SQL Server can simply use 8 bits (1 byte). Another case is when you use a fixed-length type like a char(30) column but store only two characters; 28 characters could be saved and the data padded as it is used.

This datatype-level compression is part of *row compression*, where each row in the table will be compressed as datatypes allow, shrinking the size on disk, but not making any major changes to the page structure. Row compression is a very interesting option for many databases that use lots of fixed-length data (e.g., integers, especially for surrogate keys).

SQL Server also includes an additional level of compression capability called *page compression*. With page compression, first, the data is compressed in the same manner as row compression, and then, the storage engine does a couple of interesting things to compress the data on a page:

- *Prefix compression*: The storage engine looks for repeated values in a value (like '0000001') and compresses the prefix to something like 6-0 (six zeros).

- *Dictionary compression*: For all values on the page, the storage engine looks for duplication, stores the duplicated value once, and then stores pointers to the data pages where the duplicated values originally resided.

You can apply data compression to your tables and indexes with the CREATE TABLE, ALTER TABLE, CREATE INDEX, and ALTER INDEX syntaxes. As an example, I will create a simple table, called TestCompression, and enable page compression on the table, row compression on a clustered index, and page compression on another index:

```
USE Tempdb
GO
CREATE SCHEMA Demo;
GO
CREATE TABLE Demo.TestCompression
(
    TestCompressionId int,
    Value  int
)
WITH (DATA_COMPRESSION = ROW) -- PAGE or NONE;

--change compression to PAGE
ALTER TABLE Demo.TestCompression REBUILD WITH (DATA_COMPRESSION = PAGE);
```

```
CREATE CLUSTERED INDEX Value
   ON Demo.TestCompression (Value) WITH ( DATA_COMPRESSION = ROW );

ALTER INDEX Value   ON Demo.TestCompression
           REBUILD WITH ( DATA_COMPRESSION = PAGE );
```

Note   The syntaxes of the CREATE INDEX and CREATE TABLE commands allow for compression of the partitions of an index in different manners. I mention partitioning in the next section of the chapter. For full syntax, refer to SQL Server Books Online.

Giving advice on whether to use compression is not really possible without knowing the factors that surround your actual situation, though I have started to use it more and more as a default in my recent databases. If you are wondering if a table or index would benefit from compression, a tool you should use is the system procedure—sp_estimate_data_compression_savings—to check existing data to see just how compressed the data in the table or index would be after applying compression, but it won't tell you how the compression will positively or negatively affect your performance.

There are trade-offs to any sorts of compression. CPU utilization will go up in most cases, because instead of directly using the data right from the page, the query processor will have to translate the values from the compressed format into the uncompressed format that SQL Server will use. On the other hand, if you have a lot of data that would benefit from compression, you could likely lower your I/O enough to make doing so worth the cost. Frankly, with CPU power continuing to grow and I/O still the most difficult to tune, even with modern hardware, compression can definitely be a great thing for many systems, and more and more I have started to apply compression as a default for many tables I have created recently.

Partitioning

Partitioning allows you to break an index/table into multiple physical structures that look to the end user to be only one by breaking them into more manageable chunks. Partitioning can allow SQL Server to scan data from different processes, enhancing opportunities for parallelism.

Partitioning allows you to define physical divisions within your table structure. Instead of making a physical table for each partition, you define, at the DDL level, the different partitions of the table. Internally, the table is broken into the partitions based on a scheme that you set up.

At query time, SQL Server can dynamically scan only the partitions that need to be searched, based on the criteria in the WHERE clause of the query being executed. I am not going to describe partitioning too much, but I felt that it needed a mention in this book as a tool at your disposal with which to design and tune your databases at the physical level, particularly if they are very large or very active. Memory-optimized tables can participate in a partitioning scheme, and not every partition needs to be in-memory to do so. For deeper coverage, I would suggest you consider one of Kalen Delaney's *SQL Server Internals* books. They are the gold standard in understanding the internals of SQL Server.

I will, however, present the following basic example of partitioning. Use whatever database you desire. The example is that of a sales order table. I will partition the sales into three partitions based on the order date. One is for sales before 2014, another for sales between 2014 and 2015, and the last for 2015 and later. The first step is to create a partitioning function. You must base the function on a list of values, where the VALUES clause sets up partitions that the rows will fall into based on the date values that are presented to it, for our example:

```
USE Tempdb;
GO
--Note that the PARTITION FUNCTION is not a schema owned object
CREATE PARTITION FUNCTION PartitionFunction$Dates (date)
AS RANGE LEFT FOR VALUES ('20140101','20150101');
                    --set based on recent version of
                    --WideWorldImporters.Sales.Orders table to show
                    --partition utilization
```

Specifying the function as RANGE LEFT says that the values in the comma-delimited list should be considered the boundary on the side listed. So in this case, the ranges would be as follows:

- value <= '20131231'

- value >= '20140101' and value <= '20141231'

- value >= '20150101'

Next, use that partition function to create a partitioning scheme:

```
CREATE PARTITION SCHEME PartitonScheme$Dates
                AS PARTITION PartitionFunction$Dates ALL to ( [PRIMARY] );
```

This will let you know

Partition scheme 'PartitonScheme$Dates' has been created successfully. 'PRIMARY' is marked as the next used filegroup in partition scheme 'PartitonScheme$Dates'.

With the CREATE PARTITION SCHEME command, you can place each of the partitions you previously defined on a specific filegroup. I placed them all on the same filegroup for clarity and ease, but in practice, you may want them on different filegroups, depending on the purpose of the partitioning. For example, if you were partitioning just to keep the often-active data in a smaller structure, placing all partitions on the same filegroup might be fine. But if you want to improve parallelism or be able to just back up one partition with a filegroup backup, you would want to place your partitions on different filegroups.

Next, you can apply the partitioning to a new table. You'll need a clustered index involving the partition key. You apply the partitioning to that index. The following is the statement to create the partitioned table:

```
CREATE SCHEMA Processing;
GO
CREATE TABLE Processing.SalesOrder
(
    SalesOrderId    int,
    CustomerId  int,
    OrderDate   date,
    CONSTRAINT PKOrder PRIMARY KEY
                NONCLUSTERED (SalesOrderId) ON [Primary],
    CONSTRAINT AKOrder UNIQUE CLUSTERED (SalesOrderId, OrderDate)
) ON PartitonScheme$Dates (OrderDate);
```

Next, load some data from the WideWorldImporters.Sales.Orders table to make looking at the metadata more interesting. You can do that using an INSERT statement such as the following:

```
INSERT INTO Processing.SalesOrder (SalesOrderId, CustomerId, OrderDate)
SELECT OrderId, CustomerId, OrderDate
FROM  WideWorldImporters.Sales.Orders;
```

You can see what partition each row falls in using the $partition function. You suffix the $partition function with the partition function name and the name of the partition key (or a partition value) to see what partition a row's values are in, for example:

```
SELECT *, $partition.PartitionFunction$dates(OrderDate) as Partition
FROM  Processing.SalesOrder;
```

You can also view the partitions that are set up through the sys.partitions catalog view. The following query displays the partitions for our newly created table:

```
SELECT  partitions.partition_number, partitions.index_id,
        partitions.rows, indexes.name, indexes.type_desc
FROM    sys.partitions as partitions
          JOIN sys.indexes as indexes
            on indexes.object_id = partitions.object_id
              and indexes.index_id = partitions.index_id
WHERE   partitions.object_id = object_id('Processing.SalesOrder');
```

This will return the following:

partition_number	index_id	rows	name	type_desc
1	1	19547	AKSalesOrder	CLUSTERED
2	1	21198	AKSalesOrder	CLUSTERED
3	1	32850	AKSalesOrder	CLUSTERED
1	2	73595	PKSalesOrder	NONCLUSTERED

Partitioning is not a general-purpose tool that should be used on every table. However, partitioning can solve a good number of problems for you, if need be:

- *Performance*: If you only ever need the past month of data out of a table with three years' worth of data, you can create partitions of the data where the current data is on a partition and the previous data is on a different partition.

- *Rolling windows*: You can remove data from the table by dropping a partition, so as time passes, you add partitions for new data and remove partitions for older data (or move to a different archive table). Multiple uniqueness constraints can be difficult using rolling windows, so be sure to cover all of your uniqueness needs in some manner.

- *Maintenance*: Some maintenance can be done at the partition level rather than for the entire table, so once partition data is read-only, you may not need to maintain any longer. Some caveats do apply that are subject to change, so I will leave it to you to check the documentation.

Indexing Dynamic Management View Queries

In this section, I want to provide several queries that use the DMVs that you may find handy when you are tuning your system or trying to determine index usage. In SQL Server 2005, Microsoft added a set of objects (views and table-valued functions) to SQL Server that gave us access to some of the deep metadata about the performance of the system. A great many of these objects are useful for managing and tuning SQL Server, and I would suggest you do some reading about these objects. (Not to be overly self-serving, but the book *Performance Tuning with SQL Server Dynamic Management Views (High Performance SQL Server)* by Tim Ford and myself, published by Simple-Talk in 2010, is *my* favorite book on the subject, even though it is kind of old at this point. Most of the queries in the book are still useful to this day.) I do want to provide you with some queries that will likely be quite useful for you when doing any tuning using indexes.

Missing Indexes

The first query we'll discuss provides a peek at what indexes the optimizer thought might be useful for queries (on-disk and in-memory). It can be very helpful when tuning a database, particularly a very busy database executing thousands of queries a minute. I have personally used this query to tune third-party systems where I didn't have a lot of access to the queries in the system and using Extended Events was simply far too cumbersome with too many queries to effectively tune manually.

This query uses three of the DMVs that are part of the missing index family of objects:

- `sys.dm_db_missing_index_groups`: This relates missing index groups with the indexes in the group.

- `sys.dm_db_missing_index_group_stats`: This provides statistics of how much the indexes in the group would have helped (and hurt) the system.

- `sys.dm_db_missing_index_details`: This provides information about the index that the optimizer would have chosen to have available.

The query is as follows. I won't attempt to build a scenario where you can test this functionality in this book, but run the query on one of your development servers and check the results. The results will likely make you want to run it on your production server:

```
SELECT ddmid.statement AS object_name, ddmid.equality_columns,
       ddmid.inequality_columns, ddmid.included_columns,
       ddmigs.user_seeks, ddmigs.user_scans,
       ddmigs.last_user_seek, ddmigs.last_user_scan,
       ddmigs.avg_total_user_cost,
       ddmigs.avg_user_impact, ddmigs.unique_compiles
FROM   sys.dm_db_missing_index_groups AS ddmig
         JOIN sys.dm_db_missing_index_group_stats AS ddmigs
              ON ddmig.index_group_handle = ddmigs.group_handle
         JOIN sys.dm_db_missing_index_details AS ddmid
              ON ddmid.index_handle = ddmig.index_handle
ORDER BY ((user_seeks + user_scans) * avg_total_user_cost *
          (avg_user_impact * 0.01)) DESC;
```

The query returns the following information about the structure of the index that might have been useful:

- object_name: This is the database- and schema-qualified object name of the object that the index would have been useful on. The data returned is for all databases on the entire server.

- equality_columns: These are the columns that would have been useful, based on an equality predicate. The columns are returned in a comma-delimited list.

- inequality_columns: These are the columns that would have been useful, based on an inequality predicate (which as we have discussed is any comparison other than column = value or column in (value, value1)).

- included_columns: These columns, if added to the index via an INCLUDE clause, would have been useful to cover the query results and avoid a key lookup operation in the plan. Ignore these for in-memory queries as all columns are essentially included due to the structure of these tables.

As discussed earlier, the equality columns would generally go first in the index column definition, but it isn't guaranteed that that will make the correct index. These are just guidelines, and using the next DMV query I will present, you can discover if the index you create turns out to be of any value, because it will have a set of columns that look just like the next columns for real indexes to show how those indexes are actually being used:

- user_seeks: The number of seek operations in user queries that might have used the index

- user_scans: The number of scan operations in user queries that might have used the index

- last_user_seek: The last time that a seek operation might have used the index

- last_user_scan: The last time that a scan operation might have used the index

- `avg_total_user_cost`: Average cost of queries that could have been helped by the group of indexes

- `avg_user_impact`: The percentage of change in cost that the index is estimated to make for user queries

- `unique_compiles`: The number of plans that have been compiled that might have used the index

Note that I sorted the query results as `(user_seeks + user_scans) * avg_total_user_cost * (avg_user_impact * 0.01)` based on the initial blog article I read about using the missing indexes, "Fun for the Day—Automated Auto-Indexing" (`blogs.msdn.microsoft.com/queryoptteam/2006/06/01/fun-for-the-day-automated-auto-indexing/`). I generally use some variant of that to determine what is most important. For example, I might use `ORDER BY (user_seeks + user_scans)` to see what would have been useful the most times. It really just depends on what I am trying to scan; with all such queries, it pays to try out the query and see what works for your situation.

To use the output, you can create a `CREATE INDEX` statement from the values in the four structural columns. Say you received the following results:

object_name	equality_columns
databasename.schemaname.tablename	columnfirst, columnsecond

inequality_columns	included_columns
columnthird	columnfourth, columnfifith

You could build the following index to satisfy the need:

```
CREATE INDEX XName ON databaseName.schemaName.tableName(columnfirst,
columnsecond, columnthird) INCLUDE (columnfourth, columnfifith);
```

Next, see if it helps out performance in the way you believed it might. And even if you aren't sure of how the index might be useful, create it and just see if it has an impact. Also look at your other indexes and make sure there aren't very similar indexes too.

Microsoft Docs (`docs.microsoft.com/en-us/previous-versions/sql/sql-server-2005/ms345485%28v%3dsql.90%29`) lists the following limitations to consider:

- It is not intended to fine-tune an indexing configuration.

- It cannot gather statistics for more than 500 missing index groups.

- It does not specify an order for columns to be used in an index.

- For queries involving only inequality predicates, it returns less accurate cost information.

- It reports only include columns for some queries, so index key columns must be manually selected.

- It returns only raw information about columns on which indexes might be missing. This means the information returned may not be sufficient by itself without additional processing before building the index.

- It does not suggest filtered indexes.

- It can return different costs for the same missing index group that appears multiple times in XML showplans.

- It does not consider trivial query plans.

Probably the biggest concern is that it can specify a lot of overlapping indexes, particularly when it comes to included columns, since each entry could have been specifically created for distinct queries. For very busy systems, you may find a lot of the suggestions include very large sets of included columns that you may not want to implement.

However, limitations aside, the missing index DMVs are amazingly useful to help you see places where the optimizer would have liked to have an index and one didn't exist. This can greatly help diagnose very complex performance/indexing concerns, particularly ones that need a large amount of included columns to cover complex queries. This feature is turned on by default and can only be disabled by starting SQL Server with a command-line parameter of –x. This will, however, disable keeping several other statistics like CPU time and cache hit ratio stats.

Using this feature and the query in the next section that can tell you what indexes have been used, you can use these index suggestions in an experimental fashion, just building a few of the indexes and see if they are used and what impact they have on your performance-tuning efforts.

Fragmentation

One of the biggest tasks for the DBA of a system is to make sure that the structures of
indexes and tables are within a reasonable tolerance for the physical structures. You can
decide whether to reorganize or to rebuild using the criteria stated by Microsoft Docs
in the "sys.dm_db_index_physical_stats (Transact-SQL)" topic (docs.microsoft.com/
en-us/sql/relational-databases/system-dynamic-management-views/sys-dm-db-
index-physical-stats-transact-sql).

Using this DMV, you can check the FragPercent column and REBUILD indexes with
greater than 30% fragmentation and REORGANIZE those that are just lightly fragmented.
As a warning, this can be a very slow query to run, no matter what settings you choose:

```
SELECT  s.[name] AS SchemaName,
        o.[name] AS TableName,
        i.[name] AS IndexName,
        f.[avg_fragmentation_in_percent] AS FragPercent,
        f.fragment_count ,
        f.forwarded_record_count --heap only
FROM sys.dm_db_index_physical_stats(DB_ID(), NULL, NULL, NULL, DEFAULT) f
        JOIN sys.indexes i
            ON f.[object_id] = i.[object_id]
                AND f.[index_id] = i.[index_id]
        JOIN sys.objects o
            ON i.[object_id] = o.[object_id]
        JOIN sys.schemas s
            ON o.[schema_id] = s.[schema_id]
WHERE o.[is_ms_shipped] = 0
  AND i.[is_disabled] = 0; -- skip disabled indexes
```

sys.dm_db_index_physical_stats will give you a lot more information about the
internal physical structures of your tables and indexes than I am making use of here.

If you find you are having a lot of fragmentation, adjusting the fill factor of your tables
or indexes (specified as a percentage of page size to leave empty for new rows) in CREATE
INDEX and PRIMARY KEY and UNIQUE constraint CREATE/ALTER DDL statements can help
tremendously. How much space to leave will largely depend on your exact situation,
but minimally, if you are going to leave space via FILL FACTOR, you need to leave
approximately enough space for one full additional row to be added to each page.

On-Disk Index Statistics

This next query gives statistics on how an index has been used to resolve queries using `sys.dm_db_index_usage_stats` and was previously used when demonstrating how nonclustered indexes work. Most importantly, it tells you the number of times a query was used to find a single row (`user_seeks`), a range of values, or to resolve a non-unique query (`user_scans`), if it has been used to resolve a bookmark lookup (`user_lookups`), and how many changes to the index (`user_updates`). If you want deeper information on how the index was modified, check `sys.dm_db_index_operational_stats,` as it shows a great deal of detail of what has happened to the index at a low level with columns such as `leaf_insert_count`, `range_scan_count`, `singleton_lookup_count`, `forwarded_fetch_count`, `row_lock_count`, and so on:

```
SELECT OBJECT_SCHEMA_NAME(indexes.object_id) + '.' +
        OBJECT_NAME(indexes.object_id) AS objectName,
        indexes.name,
        CASE when is_unique = 1 THEN 'UNIQUE '
                else '' END + indexes.type_desc AS index_type,
        ddius.user_seeks, ddius.user_scans, ddius.user_lookups,
        ddius.user_updates, last_user_lookup, last_user_scan, last_user_
        seek,last_user_update
FROM    sys.indexes
            LEFT OUTER JOIN sys.dm_db_index_usage_stats ddius
                ON indexes.object_id = ddius.object_id
                    AND indexes.index_id = ddius.index_id
                    AND ddius.database_id = DB_ID()
WHERE OBJECT_SCHEMA_NAME(indexes.object_id)
                            NOT IN ('sys','INFORMATION_SCHEMA')
ORDER  BY ddius.user_seeks + ddius.user_scans + ddius.user_lookups DESC;
```

The query (as written) is database dependent in order to look up the name of the index in `sys.indexes`, which is a database-level catalog view. The `sys.dm_db_index_usage_stats` object returns all indexes that have been used in some way since the last server restart (including heaps and the clustered index) from the entire server. The query will return all indexes for the current database (since the DMV is filtered on `DB_ID()` in the join criteria) and will return

- `object_name`: Schema-qualified name of the table.

- `index_name`: The name of the index (or table) from `sys.indexes`.

- `index_type`: The type of index, including uniqueness and clustered/nonclustered.

- `user_seeks`: The number of times the index has been used in a user query in a seek operation (one specific row).

- `user_scans`: The number of times the index has been used by scanning the leaf pages of the index for data.

- `user_lookups`: For clustered indexes only, this is the number of times the index has been used in a bookmark lookup to fetch the full row. This is because nonclustered indexes use the clustered index key as the pointer to the base row.

- `user_updates`: The number of times the index has been modified due to a change in the table's data.

- `last_user_seek`: The date and time of the last user seek operation.

- `last_user_scan`: The date and time of the last user scan operation.

- `last_user_lookup`: The date and time of the last user lookup operation.

- `last_user_update`: The date and time of the last user update operation.

There are also columns for system utilizations of the index in operations such as automatic statistics operations: `system_seeks`, `system_scans`, `system_lookups`, `system_updates`, `last_system_seek`, `last_system_scan`, `last_system_lookup`, and `last_system_update`.

This is one of the most interesting views that I often use in performance tuning. It gives you the ability to tell when indexes are and, perhaps more importantly, are *not* being used. It is easy to see when an index is being used by a query by simply looking at the plan. But now, using this dynamic management view, you can see over time what indexes are used, not used, and, probably more importantly, updated many, many times without ever being used.

Memory-Optimized Table Index Stats

In this section, I want to briefly point out a few DMVs that you can use with in-memory tables to get some general-purpose information about your objects.

The first is sys.dm_db_xtp_table_memory_stats, and it will provide you information about how much memory is being tied up by your in-memory objects (note the xtp as part of the names; an early naming convention was extreme programming, and it ended up in the name):

```
SELECT OBJECT_SCHEMA_NAME(object_id) + '.' +
       OBJECT_NAME(object_id) AS objectName,
           memory_allocated_for_table_kb,memory_used_by_table_kb,
           memory_allocated_for_indexes_kb,memory_used_by_indexes_kb
FROM sys.dm_db_xtp_table_memory_stats;
```

In the results, you can see in kilobytes how much memory is allocated to your objects and how much of that allocation is actually used from the tables and by the indexes. The next object is sys.dm_db_xtp_index_stats, and here is a basic query to use:

```
SELECT OBJECT_SCHEMA_NAME(ddxis.object_id) + '.' +
       OBJECT_NAME(ddxis.object_id) AS objectName,
           ISNULL(indexes.name,'BaseTable') AS indexName,
           scans_started, rows_returned, rows_touched,
           rows_expiring, rows_expired,
           rows_expired_removed, phantom_scans_started
           --and several other phantom columns
FROM    sys.dm_db_xtp_index_stats AS ddxis
                JOIN sys.indexes
                    ON indexes.index_id = ddxis.index_id
                        AND indexes.object_id = ddxis.object_id;
```

This gives us a couple of interesting details. The number of times the index was used is in scans_started, and the number of rows returned and the number of rows touched in queries are all documented objects. There are other internal columns listed that will show you some details about expiring rows and phantom scans. We will talk about phantom rows in the next chapter, but due to the way in-memory tables implement concurrency, if you are in SERIALIZABLE isolation level, a scan must be done at commit time to ensure nothing has changed so an index can be used for this and it shows up in this output as phantom_scans.

Finally, if you chose to use hash indexes, you would want to use sys.dm_db_xtp_ hash_index_stats to check up on their structures:

```
SELECT OBJECT_SCHEMA_NAME(ddxhis.object_id) + '.' +
       OBJECT_NAME(ddxhis.object_id) AS objectName,
           ISNULL(indexes.name,'BaseTable') AS indexName,
           ddxhis.total_bucket_count, ddxhis.empty_bucket_count,
           ddxhis.avg_chain_length, ddxhis.max_chain_length
FROM   sys.dm_db_xtp_hash_index_stats ddxhis
                JOIN sys.indexes
                    ON indexes.index_id = ddxhis.index_id
                        AND indexes.object_id = ddxhis.object_id;
```

This will return to you the bucket count as it was internally created (bucket counts are implemented in powers of 2), the number of empty buckets, average chain length (or number of rows that have pointers to each other), and max chain length. Let's use the RecordedWhen index on Warehouse.VehicleTemperatures we created earlier in the chapter:

total_bucket_count	empty_bucket_count	avg_chain_length	max_chain_length
65536	39594	2	10

We created 64,000 buckets, and it rounded up to 65,536. Of the 65,998 rows, there were 32,999 distinct values. An average chain length of 2 is good, and 10 rows max are typical in the cases I have seen, even with uniqueness constraint indexes.

Best Practices

Indexing is a complex subject, and even though this is not a short chapter, we've really only scratched the surface. Add in the newer memory-optimized technologies, and choices are numerous. The following best practices are foundational to what I use as a rule of thumb when creating new and adjusting existing databases. There are many many reasons to vary from these rules because no two systems are ever the same.

I assume in these best practices that you've applied PRIMARY KEY and UNIQUE constraints in all places where you have defined a uniqueness need. These constraints most likely should be there, even if they slow down your application (there are exceptions, but if a set of values needs to be unique, it is best to be sure). From there, every choice is a big trade-off of performance, maintenance, and cost. The first practice is the most important:

- *There are only a few reasons to add indexes to tables without testing*: Add non-constraint indexes to your tables only as needed to enhance performance. In many cases, it will turn out that no index is needed to achieve decent performance. Two caveats may be specific searches on values that are likely unique, but not guaranteed unique, and foreign key indexes, but in either case you should test and monitor to see if they are actually used, just as you should test to see what other indexes too add.

- *Choose clustered index keys wisely*: All nonclustered indexes will use the clustering key as their row locator, so the structure of the clustered index will affect all other index utilization. If the clustered index is poorly structured, it can affect the other indexes as well.

- *Keep indexes as thin as possible*: For all indexes of any types, only index the columns that are selective enough in the main part of the index. Use the INCLUDE clause on the CREATE INDEX statement if you want to include columns only to cover the data used by a query. Columnstore indexes can withstand much wider column counts, but if you will not use a column in a query, maybe not there either.

- *Consider several thin indexes rather than one or more monolithic indexes*: SQL Server can use multiple indexes in a query efficiently. This can be a good tool to support ad hoc access where the users can choose between multiple situations.

- *Be careful of the cost of adding an index*: When you insert, update, or delete rows from a table with an index, there's a definite cost to maintaining the index. New data added might require page splits, and inserts, updates, and deletes can cause a reshuffling of the index pages.

- UNIQUE *constraints are used to enforce uniqueness, not unique indexes*: Unique indexes are used to enhance performance by telling the optimizer that an index will only return one row in equality comparisons. Users shouldn't get error messages from a unique *index* violation (with the caveat of filtered unique indexes used to enforce selective uniqueness.).

- *Experiment with indexes to find the combination that gives the most benefit*: Using the missing index and index usage statistics dynamic management views, you can see what indexes the optimizer needed or try your own and then see if your choices were ever used by the queries that have been executed.

Apply indexes during your design in a targeted fashion, making sure not to overdesign for performance too early in the process. The normalization pattern is built to give great performance as long as you design for the needs of the users of the system, rather than in an academic manner taking things to the extreme that no one will ever use. The steps we have covered throughout this book for proper indexing are the following:

- Apply all the uniqueness constraints that are needed to enforce the integrity of the data (even if the indexes are never used for performance, though generally they will).

- Minimally, index all foreign key constraints where the parent table is likely to be the driving force behind fetching rows in the child (such as invoice to invoice line item) or there is regular removal of parent rows.

- Start performance testing early, running load tests to see how things perform.

- Identify queries that are slow, and consider the following:

  - Eliminate clustered index row lookups by covering queries where it makes sense, possibly using the INCLUDE keyword on indexes as much as you can without causing too much overhead on the server.

  - Work on data location strategies with filegroups, partitioning, and so on.

Summary

In the first ten chapters of this book, we worked largely as if the relational engine was magical like the hat that brought Frosty to life and that the engine could do almost anything as long as we followed the basic relational principles. Magic, however, is almost always an illusion facilitated by the hard work of someone trying to let you see only what you need to see. In this chapter, we left the world of relational programming and took a peek under the covers to see what makes the magic work, which turns out to be lots and lots of code that has been evolving more than 20 years (just counting from the major rewrite of SQL Server in version 7.0 and realizing that Microsoft just added the memory-optimized engine 8 years ago as I write this). Much of the T-SQL code written for version 1.0 (and almost everything from 2005) would STILL WORK TODAY with possibly only minor alterations. Take that, all other programmers. Most of it, with a little bit of translation, would even run using the new memory-optimized engine (if perhaps not taking full advantage, more of which I will cover in Chapter 13).

This is one of the reasons why, in this book on design, my goals for this chapter are not to make you an expert on the internals of SQL Server but rather to give you an overview of how SQL Server works enough to help guide your designs and understand the basics of performance.

We looked at the physical structure of how SQL Server persists data, which is separate from the database–schema–table–column model that is natural in the relational model. Physically speaking, for normal row data, database files are the base container. Files are grouped into filegroups, and filegroups are owned by databases. You can get some control over SQL Server I/O by where you place the files. When using memory-optimized objects, data is housed in-memory, but backed up with—you guessed it—files.

Indexing, like the entire gamut of performance-tuning topics, is hard to cover with any specificity on a written page (particularly not as a chapter of a larger book on design). I've given you some information about the mechanics of tables and indexes and a few best practices, but to be realistic, it's never going to be enough without you working with a realistic, active working test system.

Designing physical structures is an important step to building high-performance systems that must be done during multiple phases of the project, starting when you are still modeling and only being completed with performance testing and, honestly, continuing into production operation.

CHAPTER 12

Matters of Concurrency

Never be so busy as not to think of others.

—Mother Teresa, Humanitarian, from *The Joy in Loving:*
A Guide to Daily Living

Concurrency, in a strictly database sense, is the ability to have multiple users/ processes/ requests manipulate shared data resources at the same time while keeping everything secure, well maintained, and with proper integrity and not losing data in the process. The key is that when multiple processes or users are accessing the same resources, each user expects to see a consistent view of the data and certainly expects that other users will not be changing their results, at least not in ways that they have specified against. Fortunately, SQL Server's execution engine can give its full attention to a task as long as it needs to, even if that is minutes or microseconds, unlike most humans, as I've had to correct several mistakes I made as a result of trying to write this sentence as I was distracted by Twitter.

The topics of this chapter will center on understanding why and how you should design and write your database code and objects to make them accessible concurrently by as many users as you have in your system without data loss. While it may seem odd to be so late in the book, the entire book so far has been building up to this. The way we have formed the database so far has been leading up to a highly concurrent database where users are reading and modifying data simultaneously.

In this chapter, I'll discuss the following:

- *OS and hardware concerns*: I'll briefly discuss various issues that are out of the control of SQL code but can affect concurrency.

- *Transactions*: I'll give an overview of how transactions work and how to start and stop them in T-SQL code.

877

© Louis Davidson 2021
L. Davidson, *Pro SQL Server Relational Database Design and Implementation*,
https://doi.org/10.1007/978-1-4842-6497-3_12

- *SQL Server concurrency methods*: I'll explain the two major types of concurrency controls used in SQL Server—pessimistic (using locks) and optimistic (using versions of data). Included in this section are explanations and example of locks and isolation levels.

- *Coding for concurrency*: I'll discuss methods of coding data access to protect from users simultaneously making changes to data and placing data into less-than-adequate situations. You'll also learn how to deal with users stepping on one another and how to maximize concurrency.

Like the previous chapter, we will look at how the on-disk technologies contrast with the newer memory-optimized technologies. The most important difference between the two (once you get past some of the limitations of the memory-optimized engine, particularly coding limitations) is how each handles concurrency.

The key goal of this chapter is to acquaint you with many of the kinds of things SQL Server does to make it fast and safe to have multiple users doing the same sorts of tasks with the same resources and how you can optimize your code and the settings you need to use and then show how to test your concurrency settings. A secondary goal is to help you understand what you need to design into your code and structures to deal with what happens when two users' actions collide.

RESOURCE GOVERNOR

SQL Server has a feature called Resource Governor that is concurrency adjacent (especially as it relates to performance tuning), though it is more of a management tool than something that will affect your design. Resource Governor allows you to partition the workload of the entire server by specifying maximum and minimum resource allocations (memory, CPU, concurrent requests, IO, etc.) to users or groups of users. You can classify users into groups using a simple user-defined function that, in turn, takes advantage of the basic server-level functions you have for identifying users and applications (IS_SRVROLEMEMBER, APP_NAME, SYSTEM_USER, etc.).

For example, using Resource Governor, you can group and limit the users of a reporting application, Management Studio, or any other application to a specific percentage of the CPU, a certain percentage and number of processors, and limited requests at one time.

One nice thing about Resource Governor is that some settings only apply when the server is under a load. So, if the reporting user is the only active process, that user might get the entire server's power. But if the server is being heavily used, users would be limited to the configured amounts. I won't talk about Resource Governor any more in this book, but it is definitely a feature that you might want to consider if you are dealing with different types of user loads in your applications.

Because of the need to balance the amount of work with the user's perception of the amount of work being done, there are going to be the trade-offs:

- *Number of concurrent users*: How many users need to and can be served at the same time?

- *Overhead*: How complex are the algorithms to maintain concurrency?

- *Accuracy*: How correct must the results be? (This probably sounds really out of character for me to write, but some concurrency tuning techniques sacrifice data accuracy for performance.)

- *Performance*: How fast can each process finish?

- *Cost*: How much are you willing to spend on hardware and programming time?

If no one ever shared resources or tried to do more than one thing at a time on a computer, multitasking server operating systems would be unnecessary. All files could be placed on a user's local computer, and that would be enough. And if we could single-thread all activities on a server, more actual work on the server might be done, but just like the old days, people would sit around waiting for their turn (yes, with mainframes, people actually did that sort of thing). Internally, the situation is still technically the same in a way, as a computer cannot process more individual instructions than it has ability (and cores in its CPUs), but it can run and swap around fast enough to make hundreds or thousands of people feel like they are the only users. This is especially true if your system engineer builds computers that are good as SQL Server machines and the architects/programmers build systems that meet the requirements for a relational database and not just what seems cheapest/expedient at the time. More CPUs, fast storage, and lots of RAM that may not be used constantly are not an easy sale, but they can make the difference between slow performance and fast when needed. And the quicker queries perform, the less likely they are to need to compete for resources causing the concurrency issue I will cover in this chapter.

A common scenario for a multiuser database involves a sales and shipping application. You might have 50 salespeople in a call center trying to sell the last 25 closeout items that are in stock. In an ideal world, it isn't desirable to promise the last physical item accidentally to multiple customers, since multiple users might happen to read that it was available at the same time and all be allowed to place an order for it. In this case, stopping the first order wouldn't be necessary, but you would want to disallow or prevent the second (or subsequent) orders from being placed, since they cannot be fulfilled as would be expected, and telling them "tough luck" isn't going to induce them to make their next purchase from you.

Most programmers instinctively write code to check for this condition in the application and to try to make sure that this sort of thing doesn't happen. Code is generally written that does something along these lines:

- Check to make sure that there's adequate stock.

- Create an order row.

- Take payment.

- Create a shipment row.

That's simple enough, and it works 100% of the time on the dev computer and 99.9% of the time on prod. The problem with that .1% is what if one person checks to see if the product is available at the same time as another or even while setting up the details for that shipping row and then more orders are placed than you have adequate stock for? This is especially bad if we are talking about a highly sought-after item. Imagine if someone on eBay put up a signed Hamilton script, but there was no concurrency control at the end of the auction. Hundreds of people think they got the product and pay. Then there are hundreds of refunds to process, eating hard into the profits with time and bank fees (not to mention the uproar on social media causing bad publicity).

I should also note that the problems presented by concurrency aren't quite the same as those for *parallelism*, which is having one task split up and performed by multiple resources at the same time. Parallelism involves a whole different set of problems and luckily is more or less not your problem when writing and building T-SQL code. In T-SQL code, parallelism is done automatically at runtime, with tasks split among resources (sometimes, you will need to adjust just how many parallel operations can take place, but in practice, SQL Server does *most* of that work for you). When I refer to concurrency,

I generally mean having multiple *different* operations happening at the same time by different connections to shared SQL Server resources. Here are just a few of the questions you have to ask yourself:

- What effect will there be if a query modifies rows that have already been used by a query in a different batch?

- What if the other query creates new rows that would have been important to the other batch's query? What if the other query deletes others?

- Most importantly, can one query corrupt another's results?

You must consider a few more questions as well. Just how many concurrent users do you expect to have, and is it worth the cost to handle? The whole topic of concurrency is basically a set of trade-offs between performance, consistency, and the number of simultaneous users. In the end, it is a very good idea to know how many simultaneous requests of various types you can handle and limit the number of users to that number. So if you are selling event tickets to Disney World on the first day they are offered and you have tested for 10,000 simultaneous users, your application doesn't allow 100,000 in simultaneously, but rather queues users outside of the application's "door" and only allows in 10,000 at a time.

OS and Hardware Concerns

SQL Server is designed to run on a variety of hardware types, from a simple laptop with one processor (or even a Raspberry Pi with Azure SQL Edge) to massive machines with many processors (you can have a max of 64 sockets in Windows Server 2019, and the Xeon E7-8890 v5 can have 24 physical cores). What is amazing is that essentially the same basic code runs on a low-end computer as well as a clustered array of servers that rivals many supercomputers. Every machine running a version of SQL Server, from Express to Enterprise edition, plus the Azure SQL Database offerings can have a vastly different concurrency profiles with the same code. Each edition will also be able to support different amounts of hardware: Express supports up to 2 GB of RAM and one processor socket (with up to four cores, which is still more than our first SQL Server machine, which had one 486 processor and 16 MB of RAM), and at the other end of the spectrum, Enterprise edition can handle as much hardware as a manufacturer can stuff into one box. Generally speaking, though, in every version, the very same concerns exist about how SQL Server handles multiple users using the same resources seemingly simultaneously, whether it is two connections from the same user on that Raspberry Pi or 100,000+ on a 64-socket X 24-core Enterprise edition machine. In this section, I'll briefly touch on some of the issues governing concurrency that our T-SQL code needn't be concerned with, because concurrency is part of the environment we work in.

SQL Server and the OS balance all the different requests and needs for multiple users. My goal in this chapter isn't to delve too deeply into the gory hardware details, but it's important to mention that concurrency is heavily tied to hardware architecture. For example, consider the following subsystems:

- *Processor*: It controls the rest of the computer subsystems, as well as doing any calculations needed. If you have too few processors, less work can be done simultaneously, and excessive time can be wasted switching between requests. SQL Server breaks tasks up into work threads which get assigned to CPU threads in SQL Server's operating system. If you want to delve into how tasks are assigned in SQL Server, the Microsoft Docs article "Thread and Task Architecture Guide" goes much deeper than I will (`docs.microsoft.com/en-us/sql/relational-databases/thread-and-task-architecture-guide`).

- *Disk subsystem*: Disk is always the slowest part of the system (even with solid-state drives [SSDs] at this point being basically the status quo). A slow disk subsystem is the downfall of many systems, particularly because of the expense involved. Each drive can only read one piece of information at a time, so to access disks concurrently, it's necessary to have multiple disk drives and even multiple controllers or channels to disk drive arrays. I won't go any deeper into disk configuration because the tech changes faster than you can imagine, but even SSDs don't eliminate all IO waits.

- *Network interface*: Bandwidth to the users is critical but is often less of a problem than disk access. However, it's important to attempt to limit the number of roundtrips between the server and the client. This is highly dependent on whether the client is connecting over a slow wireless connection or a gigabit Ethernet (or even multiple network interface cards). Using SET NOCOUNT ON in all connections and coded objects, such as stored procedures and triggers, is a good first step, because otherwise, a message is sent to the client for each query executed, requiring bandwidth (and processing) to deal with them.

- *Memory*: One of the cheapest commodities that you can improve substantially on a computer is memory. SQL Server can use a tremendous amount of memory within the limits of the edition you use (and the amount of RAM will not affect your licensing costs like processor cores either). It is also important to tune the amount of RAM you allocate to SQL Server. For more information, check this article on Microsoft Docs: "Server memory configuration options" (`docs.microsoft.com/en-us/sql/database-engine/configure-windows/server-memory-server-configuration-options`).

Each of these subsystems needs to be in balance to work properly. You could theoretically have 128 CPUs and 1 TB of RAM, and your system could still be slow. In this case, a slow disk subsystem could be causing your issues (or just poor coding practices). The goal is to maximize utilization of *all* subsystems—the faster, the better—but it's not at all optimal to have super-fast CPUs with a super-slow disk subsystem. Ideally, as your load increases, disk, CPU, and memory usage would increase proportionally, though this is a heck of a hard thing to do. The bottom line is that the number of CPUs, disk drives, disk controllers, and network cards and the amount of RAM you have all affect concurrency.

For the rest of this chapter, I'm going to ignore these types of issues and leave them to others with a deeper hardware focus like Glenn Berry (`glennsqlperformance.com/glenns-blog/`). I'll be focusing on design- and coding-related issues pertaining to how to write better SQL code to manage concurrency between SQL Server processes.

Transactions

No discussion of concurrency can really have much meaning without an understanding of the transaction. *Transactions* are the mechanism that allows one or more T-SQL statements to be guaranteed either to be fully completed or to fail totally. It is an internal SQL Server mechanism that is used to keep the data that's written to and read from tables consistent throughout its duration, using criteria set by the user.

In this section, we will first discuss a few details about transactions, followed by an overview of the syntax involved with starting and ending transactions.

Transaction Overview

Whenever data is modified in the database, the changes are not written to the physical table structures directly, but first to a page in RAM; and then a log of every change is written to the transaction log immediately before the change is registered as complete (though you can change the log write to be asynchronous as well with the DELAYED DURABILITY database setting, and SQL Server 2019 provides support for persistent memory which can change this pattern somewhat as well (docs.microsoft.com/en-us/sql/database-engine/configure-windows/hybrid-buffer-pool)).

Later, the physical disk structure is written to asynchronously, hardening the data and making the page in-memory *clean* since it matches disk. Understanding the process of how modifications to data are made is essential, because while tuning your overall system, you have to be cognizant that when every modification operation is logged, you need to consider how large to make your transaction log, and when a database is written to frequently, the data files are often less important than the log files (and how important the data file's location is can be based on how much memory your server has and how much of your data you actually access.)

Beyond being a container for modification operations, transactions provide a container mechanism to provide boundaries that can be used to allow multiple processes access to the same data simultaneously while ensuring that logical operations are either carried out entirely or not at all, as well as defining boundaries for making sure one transaction's actions aren't affected by another more than is expected.

To explain the central purposes of transactions, there's an acronym: ACID. It stands for the following:

- *Atomicity*: Every operation within a transaction is treated to be a singular operation; either all its data modifications are performed, or none of them is performed. Atomicity has the same general meaning as we have used previously in that we are saying that we have decided that a set of operations are all part of one operation and cannot be separated and have the same meaning.

- *Consistency*: Once a transaction is completed (successfully or not), the system must be left in a consistent state. This means that all the constraints on the data that are part of the RDBMS definition must be honored and physical data written is as expected.

- *Isolation*: This means that the operations within a transaction must be suitably isolated from other transactions. In other words, the changes of other transactions must have only allowed effects on a transaction that is open. For example, a transaction generally should not see data in an intermediate state from another transaction. This is done by several methods, covered in the "SQL Server Concurrency Methods" section later in this chapter.

- *Durability*: Once a transaction is completed, all changes must be persisted if desired. The modifications should persist even in the event of a system failure. (Note that in addition to delayed durability, memory-optimized tables allow non-durable schema-only tables, which are emptied on a server restart).

Transactions have two benefits. The first is to provide the container for isolation between processes. Every DML and DDL statement, including INSERT, UPDATE, DELETE, CREATE TABLE, ALTER TABLE, CREATE INDEX, and even SELECT statements, that is executed in SQL Server is within a transaction. If you are in the middle of updating the data in a column of the table, you don't want another user to try to simultaneously change the datatype of the column. And if the operation within the transaction fails or if the user asks for an operation to be undone, SQL Server uses the transaction's log entries to undo the operations already performed.

Second, they batch together multiple operations into one logical unit of work. For example, if you write data to one table successfully and then try unsuccessfully to write to another table, the initial writes can be undone. This section will mostly be about defining and demonstrating this syntax. But even one single T-SQL statement like INSERT INTO Alt.SimplestTableEver (JustAColumn) VALUES ('1'); is more than just one simple operation. It requires several changes to memory at a minimum (the actual data and metadata of the row), and they have to complete successfully as a group or fail as a group as well.

The duration of how long the log rows are needed to be kept is affected by the recovery model under which your database is operating. There are three models:

- *Simple*: The log is maintained only until the operation is completed and a checkpoint is executed (manually using the CHECKPOINT statement or automatically by SQL Server). A checkpoint operation makes certain that the data has been written to the data files, so it is made durable.

885

- *Full*: The log is maintained until you explicitly clear it out. This is generally used so you can back up the transaction log for recovery. I don't talk about recovery in this book, but backup and recovery are very important. The log may also be used for replication, change tracking, etc.; so even backing up the log may not clear it out immediately.

- *Bulk logged*: This keeps a log much like the full recovery model but doesn't fully log some operations, such as SELECT INTO, bulk loads, index creations, or text operations. It just logs that the operation has taken place and the changed extents. When you back up the log, it will back up extents that were added during BULK operations, so you get full protection with quicker bulk operations, but you lose point in time recovery options when BULK operations occur.

Even in the simple model, you must be careful about log space, because if large numbers of changes are made in a single transaction or very rapidly, the log rows must be stored at least until all transactions are committed and a checkpoint takes place. This is clearly just a taste of transaction log management; for a more complete explanation, Microsoft Docs has good information about more of the details, starting with the article "The Transaction Log (SQL Server)" (docs.microsoft.com/en-us/sql/relational-databases/logs/the-transaction-log-sql-server).

Transaction Syntax

The syntax: to start and stop transactions is pretty simple. I'll cover the most common variants of the transaction syntax in this section, broken down into the following subsections

- *Transaction basics*: The syntax of how to start and complete a transaction.

- *Nested transactions*: How transactions are affected when one is started when another is already executing.

- *Autonomous transactions*: Transactions that are not a part of the primary transaction. SQL Server does not implement this as a user-defined tool, but certain operations behave as their own transaction not as part of the normal transaction.

- *Savepoints*: Used to selectively cancel part of a transaction.

- *Transaction state*: The different states a transaction can be in when errors occur and how to handle them.

- *Explicit vs. implicit transactions:* Whether or not you need to explicitly start a transaction vs. transactions starting implicitly when you do something in the database.

- *Distributed transactions*: Using transactions to control saving data on multiple SQL Servers.

These sections will give you the foundation needed to move ahead and start building proper code, ensuring that each modification is done properly, even when multiple SQL statements are necessary to form a single-user operation.

Transaction Basics

In transactions' basic form, three commands are required: BEGIN TRANSACTION (to start the transaction), then COMMIT TRANSACTION (to save the data), or ROLLBACK TRANSACTION (to undo the changes that were made). It's as simple as that.

For example, consider the case of building a stored procedure to modify two tables. Call these tables Table1 and Table2. You'll modify Table1, check the error status, and then modify Table2 (these aren't real tables, just syntax examples):

```
BEGIN TRY
   BEGIN TRANSACTION;
   UPDATE Table1
    SET Value = 'value';

   UPDATE Table2
    SET Value = 'value';
   COMMIT TRANSACTION;
END TRY
BEGIN CATCH
     --if an error occurs
     ROLLBACK TRANSACTION;
     THROW 50000,'An error occurred',16;
END CATCH;
```

Now, if some logical error (e.g., `'value'` is invalid for `Table2.Value`), some system error (e.g., the hard disk that all or part of the data needed for these queries failed), or even external error occurs (e.g., your dog unplugs your computer from the electricity for some reason, and battery backup won't help then) while updating either `Table1` or `Table2`, your database won't be left in the state where `Table1` is updated and `Table2` is not. It's also imperative not to forget to close the transaction (either save the changes with `COMMIT TRANSACTION` or undo the changes with `ROLLBACK TRANSACTION`), because the open transaction that contains your work is in a state of limbo, and if you don't either complete it or roll it back, it can cause a lot of issues just hanging around in an open state.

For example, if the transaction stays open and other operations are executed within that transaction, you might end up losing all work done on that connection (particularly since you don't realize it is still open). The open transaction may also prevent other connections from getting their work done, because each connection is isolated from one another messing up or looking at their unfinished work. Another user who needs the affected rows in `Table1` or `Table2` may have to wait (more on why this is throughout this chapter). The worst case of this I saw a number of years back, was a single connection that was open all day with a transaction open after a failure because there was no error handling on the transaction. We lost a day's work because we finally had to roll back the transactions when we killed the process (the connection was a pooled connection from a website that was not resetting between operations, so it was not a happy solution to management either).

Note   In versions of SQL Server prior to SQL Server 2019, rolling back large transactions could take as long as the data took to be created. SQL Server 2019 introduces a feature known as Accelerated Database Recovery which changes rollback operations to asynchronous using versioning, so you needn't wait for the undo work to occur and can get your transaction restarted quicker. See the Microsoft Docs article "Accelerated Database Recovery" for more details: `docs. microsoft.com/en-us/sql/relational-databases/accelerated-database-recovery-concepts`.

There's an additional setting for simple transactions known as *named transactions,* which I'll introduce for completeness. (Ironically, this explanation will take more ink than introducing the more useful transaction syntax, but it is something good to know and can be useful in rare circumstances!) You can extend the functionality of transactions by adding a transaction name, as shown:

```
BEGIN TRANSACTION <tranName> or <@tranvariable>;
```

This can be a confusing extension to the BEGIN TRANSACTION statement. It names the transaction to make sure you roll back or commit it, for example:

```
BEGIN TRANSACTION one;
ROLLBACK TRANSACTION one;
```

Only the first transaction mark is registered in the log, so the following code returns an error:

```
BEGIN TRANSACTION one;
BEGIN TRANSACTION two;
ROLLBACK TRANSACTION two;
```

The error message is as follows:

```
Msg 6401, Level 16, State 1, Line 7
Cannot roll back two. No transaction or savepoint of that name was found.
```

Unfortunately, after this error has occurred, the transaction is still left open (which you can tell by executing SELECT @@TRANCOUNT;—if that does not return 0, there is an open transaction). For this reason, it's seldom a good practice to use named transactions in your code unless you have a very specific purpose (it can be useful for making sure you don't roll back a transaction until a certain part of a process). Note too that ROLLBACK TRANSACTION, with no name, would not have received an error, which you will want to use if you are following along with the code so far.

The specific use that makes named transactions interesting is when named transactions use the WITH MARK setting. This allows putting a mark in the transaction log, which can be used when restoring a transaction log, instead of trying to figure out the date and time when an operation occurred. A common use of the marked transaction is to restore several databases back to the same condition and then restore all of the databases to a common mark.

The mark is only registered if data is modified within the transaction. A good example of its use might be to build a process that marks the transaction log every day before some daily batch process, perhaps one where a database is in single-user mode. The log is marked, and you run the process, and if there are any troubles, the database log can be restored to just before the mark in the log, no matter when the process was executed. Using the WideWorldImporters database, I'll demonstrate this capability.

We first set up the scenario by putting the WideWorldImporters database in full recovery model. The version I downloaded came with the SIMPLE recovery model:

```
USE Master;
GO

ALTER DATABASE WideWorldImporters
     SET RECOVERY FULL;
```

Next, we create a couple of backup devices to hold the backups we're going to do:

```
EXEC sp_addumpdevice 'disk', 'TestWideWorldImporters ',
                              'C:\temp\WideWorldImporters.bak';
EXEC sp_addumpdevice 'disk', 'TestWideWorldImportersLog',
                              'C:\temp\WideWorldImportersLog.bak';
```

Tip You can see the current setting of the recovery model and the backup devices on your server using the following code:

```
SELECT  recovery_model_desc
FROM    sys.databases
WHERE   name = 'WideWorldImporters';

SELECT name, type_desc, physical_name
FROM   sys.backup_devices;
```

If you need to delete the dump device for some reason, use

```
EXEC sys.sp_dropdevice @logicalname = '<name>', @delfile =
'DELFILE';
--DELFILE deletes the file too
```

Next, we back up the database to the dump device we created:

```
BACKUP DATABASE WideWorldImporters TO TestWideWorldImporters;
```

Now, we change to the WideWorldImporters database and delete some data from a table:

```
USE WideWorldImporters;
GO
SELECT COUNT(*)
FROM   Sales.SpecialDeals;

BEGIN TRANSACTION Test WITH MARK 'Test';
DELETE Sales.SpecialDeals;
COMMIT TRANSACTION;

SELECT COUNT(*)
FROM   Sales.SpecialDeals;
```

This returns 2 for the original amount of SpecialDeals rows. The second SELECT statement will return 0. Next, back up the transaction log to the other backup device:

```
BACKUP LOG WideWorldImporters TO TestWideWorldImportersLog;
```

Now, we can restore the database using the RESTORE DATABASE command (the NORECOVERY setting keeps the database in a state ready to add transaction logs). We apply the log with RESTORE LOG. For the example, we'll only restore up to before the mark that was placed, not the entire log:

```
USE Master
GO
RESTORE DATABASE WideWorldImporters FROM TestWideWorldImporters
                              WITH REPLACE, NORECOVERY;

RESTORE LOG WideWorldImporters FROM TestWideWorldImportersLog
                              WITH STOPBEFOREMARK = 'Test', RECOVERY;
```

If you have trouble restoring the database because the database is in use, you can use the following method of removing users:

```
--Set database into single user mode, and rollback all connections.
ALTER DATABASE WideWorldImporters SET SINGLE_USER WITH ROLLBACK IMMEDIATE;
--Then back into multi-user
ALTER DATABASE WideWorldImporters SET MULTI_USER;
```

After restoring the database, execute the counting query again, and you can see that the two rows are back in there:

```
USE WideWorldImporters;
GO
SELECT COUNT(*)
FROM    Sales.SpecialDeals;
```

STOPBEFOREMARK does not include the actions that took place in the transaction you commit with the mark. If you want to include the actions of the transaction that you have marked, use STOPATMARK instead of STOPBEFOREMARK. You can find the log marks that have been made in the MSDB database in the dbo.logmarkhistory table.

Nested Transactions

Every time I hear the term "nested" transactions, I envision Marlin Perkins in some exotic locale about to tell us the mating habits of transactions, but you already know that is not what this is about (and unless you are of a certain age, you probably need to hear it as Jack Hanna). I am referring to starting a transaction after another transaction has already been started. You can nest the starting of transactions like the following, allowing code to call other code that also starts a transaction:

```
BEGIN TRANSACTION;
    BEGIN TRANSACTION;
        BEGIN TRANSACTION;
```

In the engine, there is really only one transaction being started, but an internal counter is keeping up with how many logical transactions have been started. To commit the transactions, you have to execute the same number of COMMIT TRANSACTION commands as the number of BEGIN TRANSACTION commands that have been executed. To tell how many BEGIN TRANSACTION commands have been executed without being committed, use the @@TRANCOUNT global variable as previously mentioned. When it's equal to one, then one BEGIN TRANSACTION has been executed. If it's equal to two, then two have been executed, and so on. When @@TRANCOUNT equals zero, you are no longer within a transaction context.

The limit to the number of transactions that can be nested is extremely large. (In fact, I believe unlimited is probably right. I let some code run overnight to keep looping and starting transactions, on my i7 2.7 GHz Quad Core desktop, while I was writing this chapter... In 10 hours it had nested over 40 billion transactions. However, after 2,147,483,647 iterations, @@TRANCOUNT goes lower than 0 and becomes unstable). Clearly 2.147 billion nested transactions are far, far more than *any* process should ever need. If you have an actual use case needing more than a million, I would love to hear about it (louis@drsql.org)!

As an example, execute the following:

```
SELECT @@TRANCOUNT AS ZeroDeep;
BEGIN TRANSACTION;
SELECT @@TRANCOUNT AS OneDeep;
```

It returns the following results:

```
ZeroDeep
-----------
0
OneDeep
-----------
1
```

Then, nest another transaction, and check @@TRANCOUNT to see whether it has incremented. Afterward, commit that transaction, and check @@TRANCOUNT again:

```
BEGIN TRANSACTION;
SELECT @@TRANCOUNT AS TwoDeep;
COMMIT TRANSACTION; --commits previous transaction started with BEGIN
TRANSACTION
SELECT @@TRANCOUNT AS OneDeep;
```

This returns the following results:

TwoDeep

2

OneDeep

1

Finally, close the final transaction:

```
COMMIT TRANSACTION;
SELECT @@TRANCOUNT AS ZeroDeep;
```

This returns the following result:

ZeroDeep

0

As I mentioned earlier in this section, technically only one transaction is being started. Hence, it only takes one ROLLBACK TRANSACTION command to roll back as many transactions as you have nested. So, if you've coded up a set of statements that ends up nesting 100 transactions and you issue one ROLLBACK TRANSACTION, all transactions are rolled back—for example:

```
BEGIN TRANSACTION;
BEGIN TRANSACTION;
BEGIN TRANSACTION;
BEGIN TRANSACTION;
BEGIN TRANSACTION;
BEGIN TRANSACTION;
BEGIN TRANSACTION;
SELECT @@TRANCOUNT AS InTran;

ROLLBACK TRANSACTION;
SELECT @@TRANCOUNT AS OutTran;
```

This returns the following results:

```
InTran
-----------
7

OutTran
-----------
0
```

This is, by far, the trickiest part of using transactions in your code, leading to some messy error handling and code management. It's a bad idea to just issue a ROLLBACK TRANSACTION command without being cognizant of what will occur once you do—especially the command's influence on the code that follows. If code is written expecting to be within a transaction and it isn't, your data can get corrupted (and it will be your fault because SQL Server is doing what you told it to). In the previous chapter, we covered error handling with TRIGGER objects and constraints with transactions, noting how things can sometimes continue and sometimes stop depending on how you are error handling and how errors are occurring.

In the preceding example, if an UPDATE statement had been executed immediately after the ROLLBACK command, it wouldn't be executed within an explicit transaction. Also, if COMMIT TRANSACTION is executed immediately after the ROLLBACK command or anytime a transaction has not been started, an error will occur:

```
SELECT @@TRANCOUNT;
COMMIT TRANSACTION;
```

This will return

```
-----------
0

Msg 3902, Level 16, State 1, Line 2
The COMMIT TRANSACTION request has no corresponding BEGIN TRANSACTION.
```

Autonomous Transactions

The concept of an *autonomous transaction* is that a transaction can occur within another transaction and commit even if the external transaction does not. Sadly, for us developer types, SQL Server does not have the ability to do user-defined autonomous transactions, but there is one example of such a thing in SQL Server. Back in Chapter 7, I introduced the SEQUENCE object, as well as columns using the IDENTITY property. The transactions that these objects use operate as autonomous to the external transaction, but they are definitely transactions, as they have to do multiple operations to save the metadata of the operation that they are working on and keep other users from getting the same value. If you fetch a new SEQUENCE or IDENTITY value, but then ROLLBACK the external transaction, the generated value is lost.

As an example, consider the following SEQUENCE and TABLE objects (built in a database named Chapter12 in the downloads):

```
CREATE SCHEMA Magic;
GO
CREATE SEQUENCE Magic.Trick_SEQUENCE AS int START WITH 1;
GO
CREATE TABLE Magic.Trick
(
    TrickId int NOT NULL IDENTITY,
    Value int CONSTRAINT DFLTTrick_Value
                        DEFAULT (NEXT VALUE FOR Magic.Trick_SEQUENCE)
);
```

Now every time you execute the following code, you will get one row back, with incrementing numbers. You could run it on hundreds of connections, and you would get back two numbers that are growing larger and unique of each other:

```
BEGIN TRANSACTION;
--just use the default values from table
INSERT INTO Magic.Trick DEFAULT VALUES;
SELECT TrickId, Value FROM Magic.Trick;
ROLLBACK TRANSACTION;
```

There would never be more than one row in the output, but the values change. There are two transactions occurring for the IDENTITY and SEQUENCE, and those are not rolled back, only the INSERT operation. This is interesting because, as we will see later, when we look at isolation of connections, other connections will not need to wait to see if that value is used, because that autonomous transaction has been committed.

Savepoints

In the previous section, I explained that all open transactions are rolled back using a ROLLBACK TRANSACTION call. This isn't always desirable, so a tool is available to roll back only a fragment of a transaction: *savepoints*. Unfortunately, using savepoints can be a bit fragile if you are not sure of what your calling stack will be, but they can be very useful when you need to provide "selective" rollback in your code.

For this, from within a transaction, issue the following statement:

```
SAVE TRANSACTION <savePointName>; --savepoint names must follow the same
                              -- rules for identifiers as other objects
```

For example, I will use the following table:

```
CREATE SCHEMA Arts;
GO
CREATE TABLE Arts.Performer
(
    PerformerId int IDENTITY CONSTRAINT PKPeformer PRIMARY KEY,
    Name varchar(100) CONSTRAINT AKPerformer UNIQUE
);
```

Next, I will insert two different performers, one I like and one that should never have been included in my table of performers I am putting in my database:

```
BEGIN TRANSACTION;
INSERT INTO Arts.Performer(Name) VALUES ('Elvis Costello');

SAVE TRANSACTION SavePoint; --the savepoint name is case sensitive, even if
--instance is not.
--
--if you reuse a savepoint name, the rollback is to last

INSERT INTO Arts.Performer(Name) VALUES ('Air Supply');
```

```
--don't keep Air Supply, yuck! ...
ROLLBACK TRANSACTION SavePoint;

COMMIT TRANSACTION;

SELECT *
FROM Arts.Performer;
```

The output of this code is as follows:

```
PerformerId Name
----------- -------------------------
1           Elvis Costello
```

In the code, there were two INSERT statements within the transaction boundaries, but in the output, there's only one row. Obviously, the row that was rolled back to the savepoint wasn't persisted.

Note that you don't commit a savepoint; SQL Server simply places a mark in the transaction log to tell itself where to roll back to if the user asks for a rollback to the savepoint. The rest of the operations in the overall transaction aren't affected. Savepoints don't affect the value of @@TRANCOUNT, nor do they release any locks that might have been held by the operations that are rolled back, until all nested transactions have been committed or rolled back.

Note that you can't use savepoints when the transaction is enlisted into a distributed transaction.

Transaction State

There are three states that a transaction can be in, which can be detected by the return value from the XACT_STATE() system function:

- 1 *(active transaction)*: A transaction has been started. No indication of how many levels of transactions have been nested is provided, just that there is an active transaction. As mentioned earlier, use @@ TRANCOUNT for nested transaction count information.

- 0 *(no active transaction error handlers)*: The connection is not currently in the context of a transaction.

- -1 *(uncommittable transaction)*: Also known as a "doomed" transaction, something has occurred that makes the transaction still active but no longer able to be committed.

The first two states are just as we have discussed earlier, but the uncommittable transaction is a special case that is most commonly associated with error handling and XACT_ABORT (which stops the batch and rolls back the current transaction upon error) or certain trigger scenarios.

If you hit an error in a TRY...CATCH block while using XACT_ABORT or a TRIGGER object returns an error without rolling back, you can end up in an uncommittable state. As an example, let's create the following table:

```
CREATE SCHEMA Menu;
GO
CREATE TABLE Menu.FoodItem
(
    FoodItemId int NOT NULL IDENTITY(1,1)
        CONSTRAINT PKFoodItem PRIMARY KEY,
    Name varchar(30) NOT NULL
        CONSTRAINT AKFoodItem_Name UNIQUE,
    Description varchar(60) NOT NULL,
        CONSTRAINT CHKFoodItem_Name CHECK (LEN(Name) > 0),
        CONSTRAINT CHKFoodItem_Description CHECK (LEN(Description) > 0)
);
```

The constraints make certain that the length of the string columns is > 0. Now create a trigger that prevents someone from inserting 'Yucky' food in our database. Clearly this is not a complete solution, but it will cause the trigger to not let the insert occur:

```
CREATE TRIGGER Menu.FoodItem$InsertTrigger
ON Menu.FoodItem
AFTER INSERT
AS --Note, minimalist code for demo. Chapter 9 and Appendix B
   --have more details on complete trigger writing
```

```
BEGIN
   BEGIN TRY
        IF EXISTS (SELECT *
                    FROM Inserted
                    WHERE Description LIKE '%Yucky%')
          THROW 50000, 'No ''yucky'' food desired here',1;
   END TRY
   BEGIN CATCH
      IF XACT_STATE() <> 0
         ROLLBACK TRANSACTION;
      THROW;
   END CATCH;
END
GO
```

In this initial version of the trigger, we roll back the transaction on an error. Later in the section, we will remove the error handling from the trigger, as well as the ROLLBACK to see what occurs. To show how this works, we will use XACT_ABORT, which without error handling will stop the batch on error. It is a very useful tool when writing maintenance scripts or simple code where you don't need a lot of error handling or explanation in the code:

```
SET XACT_ABORT ON;

BEGIN TRY
    BEGIN TRANSACTION;

        --insert the row to be tested
        INSERT INTO Menu.FoodItem(Name, Description)
        VALUES ('Hot Chicken','Nashville specialty, super spicy');

        SELECT  XACT_STATE() AS [XACT_STATE],
                'Success, commit'  AS Description;
    COMMIT TRANSACTION;
END TRY
BEGIN CATCH
```

```
IF XACT_STATE() = -1 --transaction not doomed, but open
  BEGIN
        SELECT -1 AS [XACT_STATE],
                'Doomed transaction'  AS Description;
        ROLLBACK TRANSACTION;
  END
ELSE IF XACT_STATE() = 0 --transaction not doomed, but open
  BEGIN
        SELECT 0 AS [XACT_STATE],
                'No Transaction'  AS Description;;
  END
ELSE IF XACT_STATE() = 1 --transaction still active
  BEGIN
      SELECT 1 AS [XACT_STATE],
              'Transaction Still Active After Error'  AS Description;
        ROLLBACK TRANSACTION;
  END
END CATCH;
```

Since this INSERT statement met the requirements of all constraints, it succeeds:

```
XACT_STATE Description
---------- ----------------
1          Success, commit
```

Next, we will use the following INSERT statement (wrapped with the error handler from earlier) with an empty string for the description because, honestly, no words could adequately describe what that food probably would taste like:

```
INSERT INTO Menu.FoodItem(Name, Description)
VALUES ('Ethiopian Mexican Vegan Fusion','');
```

Because there was a constraint violated with XACT_ABORT on and a TRY...CATCH block, the transaction is doomed, so we get the following:

XACT_STATE	Description
-1	Doomed transaction

When the trigger does a ROLLBACK because of the string "yucky" being found

```
INSERT INTO Menu.FoodItem(Name, Description)
VALUES ('Vegan Cheese','Yucky imitation for the real thing');
```

we come out of the INSERT with no transaction:

XACT_STATE	Description
0	No Transaction

Finally, the last scenario I will show is the case where a TRIGGER object just returns an error and does not roll back:

```
ALTER TRIGGER Menu.FoodItem$InsertTrigger
ON Menu.FoodItem
AFTER INSERT
AS --Note, minimalist code for demo. Chapter 7 and Appendix B
   --have more details on complete trigger writing
BEGIN
        IF EXISTS (SELECT *
                   FROM Inserted
                   WHERE Description LIKE '%Yucky%')
            THROW 50000, 'No ''yucky'' food desired here',1;

END;
```

Now executing our 'Yucky' batch with XACT_ABORT either ON or OFF returns

XACT_STATE	Description
-1	Doomed transaction

Wow, so many different outcomes! When building error handlers for your code, you need to either make sure that every possible outcome is handled or do a very good job of standardizing code in triggers, constraints, and so on to work only in one desired manner, specifically so your clients will react and handle how transactions are managed when errors occur.

Explicit, Implicit, and Autocommit Transactions

I've alluded to the fact that every statement is executed in a transaction (again, this includes even SELECT, CREATE TABLE, ALTER INDEX, index reorganizations, etc.). This is an important point that must be understood when writing code. Internally, SQL Server starts a transaction every time a SQL statement is started. Even if a transaction isn't started explicitly with a BEGIN TRANSACTION statement, SQL Server automatically starts a new transaction whenever a statement starts; this is known as an *autocommit* transaction. The SQL Server engine commits the transactions it starts for each statement-level transaction automatically, known as an autocommit.

This is not the default behavior for some RDBMSs, so SQL Server gives us a setting to change this behavior: SET IMPLICIT_TRANSACTIONS. When this setting is turned on and the execution context isn't already within a transaction, BEGIN TRANSACTION is automatically (logically) executed when the connection is not already in a transaction context and any of the following statements are executed: INSERT, UPDATE, DELETE, SELECT (when it touches a table), TRUNCATE TABLE, DROP, ALTER TABLE, REVOKE, CREATE, GRANT, FETCH, or OPEN. This means that at least one COMMIT TRANSACTION or ROLLBACK TRANSACTION command has to be executed to end the transaction. Otherwise, once the connection terminates, all data is lost (and until the transaction terminates, locks that have been accumulated are held, other users are blocked, and pandemonium might occur).

SET IMPLICIT_TRANSACTIONS isn't a typical setting used by many SQL Server programmers or administrators that I have seen but is worth mentioning because if you change the setting of ANSI_DEFAULTS to ON, IMPLICIT_TRANSACTIONS will be enabled!

I've mentioned that every SELECT statement is executed within a transaction, but this deserves a bit more explanation. The entire process of rows being considered for output and then transporting them from the server to the client is contained inside a transaction. The SELECT statement isn't finished until the entire result set is exhausted (or the client cancels the fetching of rows), so the transaction doesn't end either. This is an important point that will come back up in the "Isolation Levels" section, as I discuss how this transaction can seriously affect concurrency based on how isolated you need your queries to be.

Distributed Transactions

It would be wrong not to at least bring up the subject of distributed transactions. Occasionally, you might need to view or update data on a server that's different from the one on which your code resides. The Microsoft Distributed Transaction Coordinator (MS DTC) service gives us this ability.

If your servers are running the MS DTC service, you can use the BEGIN DISTRIBUTED TRANSACTION command to start a transaction that covers the data residing on your server, as well as the remote server. If the server configuration 'remote proc trans' is set to 1, any transaction that touches a linked server will start a distributed transaction without actually calling the BEGIN DISTRIBUTED TRANSACTION command. However, I would strongly suggest you know if you will be using another server in a transaction (check sys.configurations for the current setting, and set the value using sp_configure). Note also that savepoints aren't supported for distributed transactions.

The following code is just pseudocode and won't run as is, but this is representative of the code needed to do a distributed transaction:

```
BEGIN TRY
    BEGIN DISTRIBUTED TRANSACTION;

    --remote server is a server set up as a linked server

    UPDATE RemoteServer.DbName.SchemaName.TableName
    SET Value = 'new value'
    WHERE KeyColumn = 'value';

    --local server
    UPDATE DbName.SchemaName.TableName
```

```
    SET Value = 'new value'
    WHERE KeyColumn = 'value';

    COMMIT TRANSACTION;
END TRY
BEGIN CATCH
    ROLLBACK TRANSACTION;
    DECLARE @ERRORMessage varchar(2000);
    SET @ERRORMessage = ERROR_MESSAGE();
    THROW 50000, @ERRORMessage,16;
END CATCH;
```

The distributed transaction syntax also covers the local transaction. As mentioned, setting the configuration option 'remote proc trans' automatically upgrades a BEGIN TRANSACTION command to a BEGIN DISTRIBUTED TRANSACTION command. This is useful if you frequently use distributed transactions. Without this setting, the remote command is executed, but it won't be a part of the current transaction.

SQL Server Concurrency Methods

Until SQL Server 2005, there was only one concurrency method implemented in SQL Server. This was the pessimistic concurrency mechanism using locks. If a user had control of a row, a lock was placed, and all users who wanted incompatible use of the row (e.g., two people can read a row simultaneously, but only one could change the row, and readers have to wait) were forced to wait. In 2005, a version of optimistic concurrency mechanisms was incorporated into the engine. Previous versions of data were written to tempdb to allow, when requested, a connection that would have been blocked from reading a row to see a version of the row that had been committed to be read. Writers could still block other users, and locks were still employed in all cases, but it was definitely better than strict pessimistic concurrency.

In SQL Server 2014, the new memory-optimized OLTP engine was implemented, which uses a complete optimistic concurrency mechanism, employing versions of rows rather than locks to manage concurrency. It is very different in many ways from what we have known of the engine for the past 20 years, which in most cases is a great thing. It is just different enough that one needs to understand what is going on first.

In SQL Server 2019, enabling the Accelerated Data Recovery feature changes where row versions are written to be the persistent version store in the local database rather than `tempdb`, but otherwise concurrency as the user will notice has not changed.

In this section, I will introduce the settings that define how much one transaction can affect another, known as *isolation levels.* Then I will explain and demonstrate how these work in pessimistic and optimistic concurrency enforcement.

What is interesting is that one transaction can mix different levels of concurrency implementation and locks. This will be particularly true when transactions enlist on-disk and memory-optimized tables but can be true of any combination of table access, even within the same query by using isolation level hints.

Isolation Levels

In this section, we will identify how one transaction might affect another's view of the world. Of course, the safest method to provide consistency in operations would be to take exclusive access to the entire database, do your operations, and then release control. Then the next user would do the same thing. Although this was relatively common in early file-based systems, it isn't a reasonable alternative when you need to support 20,000 concurrent users (or even 2).

Isolation levels generally control how isolated one connection is from another, in terms of a few phenomena that can occur. Take, for instance, this query on a given connection:

```
--CONNECTION A
BEGIN TRANSACTION;

UPDATE TableA
SET Status = 'UPDATED'
WHERE TableAId = 'value';
```

On another connection, we have

```
--CONNECTION B
BEGIN TRANSACTION;
INSERT TableA (TableAID, Status)
VALUES (100,'NEW');
```

Finally, we have

```
--CONNECTION C
BEGIN TRANSACTION;
SELECT *
FROM    TableA;
```

Consider the case that these statements are all executing simultaneously. They are all inside of transactions that say that they are not yet committed durably to the data structures. Will the SELECT statement see the new row? The changed row? The answer is "it depends." Timing plays a part as to which connection starts and finishes first, but isolation configuration does as well.

As we look at the concept of isolation, there are four specific phenomena that are necessary to understand to answer the preceding questions, as well as timing of which query commits or rolls back first.

The primary phenomena we are concerned with are

- *Dirty reads*: Seeing data that may never actually exist in the committed table rows. For example, when a second transaction retrieves a row that is in the process of being updated by a first transaction, the second transaction is reading data that has not been committed yet and may or may not be made durable by the first transaction.

- *Phantom rows*: Seeing new rows in the results. A phantom read occurs when rows have been inserted after a read operation and becomes visible in a follow-up read operation within the same transaction. Basically, once you have read data once, the next time you fetch what should be the rows, any new rows are phantom rows.

- *Nonrepeatable reads*: Occurs when data has been read in during a transaction and when reread, the data has changed or has been deleted.

- *Previously committed data*: Seeing data that no longer exists in the table as the connection sees it but was consistent at a point in time.

While you can't specify at a given level "I will accept dirty reads, but not previously committed data," there are five isolation levels that define an accepted set of phenomena for the different phenomena. All transactions will execute under one of these isolation levels, and you can change the isolation level mid-transaction or even for just one table in a query using isolation hints.

The following list describes the isolation levels to adjust how one connection can affect another:

- READ UNCOMMITTED: Allows dirty reads, phantom rows, and nonrepeatable reads. Shows you data as it is in memory, even if not fully committed, and as such it could change.

- READ COMMITTED: Allows phantom rows and nonrepeatable reads. So the same query could return different results in the same transaction, but you will not see uncommitted data.

- REPEATABLE READ: Allows phantom rows. New data is allowed to be added to the view of the query, but no data changes.

- SERIALIZABLE: Takes the protections of REPEATABLE READ and adds phantom protection so no new rows can come into view of the query either. As the name suggests, when using pessimistic locking, you are essentially serializing access through the use of this data for the purpose of changing the data. Using optimistic locking types, you never single-thread any access, but the SERIALIZABLE transaction will not be able to commit if rows it had read in have changed or been added to.

- SNAPSHOT: Lets you see rows as they existed when your transaction starts, even if changes have been made by other users during your transaction. Your view of the database will be constant, but things may have changed before you complete your transaction.

The syntax for setting the isolation level is as follows:

```
SET TRANSACTION ISOLATION LEVEL <level name>;
```

<level name> is any of the five preceding settings. The default isolation level for a typical SQL Server connection is READ COMMITTED and is a good balance between concurrency and integrity, but it does bear mentioning that READ COMMITTED isn't always the proper setting. Quite often, when only reading data, the SNAPSHOT isolation level gives the best results due to giving you a consistent view of data, with no blocking of other users. For example, say you are using the READ COMMITTED isolation level. You read

in all of the invoices, and before you have finished, invoices are deleted. You are reading in the invoice line items, and things don't quite match up. This scenario happens frequently in things like ETL where you are reading in lots of rows, but anything that easily happens in a large scale may still happen in a micro scale. If using the SNAPSHOT isolation level, you will see the data in a consistent state, even if it changes while you are reading it in.

When considering solutions, you must keep in mind isolation levels. As more and more critical solutions are being built on SQL Server, it's imperative to make absolutely sure to protect data at a level that's commensurate with the value of the data. If you are building procedures to support a system on a space shuttle or a life support system, this is generally more important than it would be in the case of a sales system, a pediatrician's schedule, or, like we set up in Chapter 6 and implemented in Chapter 7, a simple messaging system. In some cases, changes to data really don't matter. It is up to you when you are designing your system to truly understand that particular system's needs.

When you are coding or testing, checking to see what isolation level you are currently executing under can be useful. To do this, you can look at the results from sys.dm_exec_ sessions:

```
SELECT  CASE transaction_isolation_level
                WHEN 1 THEN 'Read Uncomitted'      WHEN 2 THEN 'Read Committed'
                WHEN 3 THEN 'Repeatable Read'      WHEN 4 THEN 'Serializable'
                WHEN 5 THEN 'Snapshot'             ELSE 'Something is afoot'
            END
FROM    sys.dm_exec_sessions
WHERE   session_id = @@spid;
```

Unless you have already changed it in a connection, the default isolation level (and what you should get from executing this query in your connection) is READ COMMITTED. Change the isolation level to SERIALIZABLE like so:

```
SET TRANSACTION ISOLATION LEVEL SERIALIZABLE;
```

Then, re-execute the query, and the results will now show that the isolation level is currently SERIALIZABLE. In the following sections, I will show you why you would want to change the isolation level at all:

```
SET TRANSACTION ISOLATION LEVEL READ COMMITTED;
```

Tip   I have included all of the code for these chapters in a single file, but you will want to start your own connections for CONNECTION A and CONNECTION B. Much of the following example code requires multiple connections to execute. Concurrency is the hardest thing to test in relational database code because issues can be very hard to replicate when they need to occur in a matter of microseconds. In our examples, we will look at how you use explicit transactions to help test, but once your code is deployed to production, a concurrency error may not happen for a year and then just happen with disastrous results.

The most common illustration of why transaction isolation is needed is called the *lost update*, as shown in Figure 12-1.

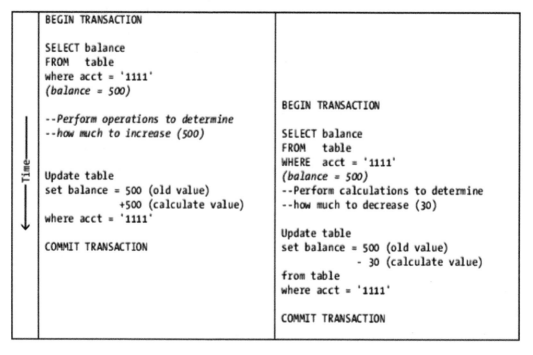

Figure 12-1. *A lost update illustration (probably one of the major inspirations for the other definition of multitasking: "screwing up everything simultaneously")*

The scenario in Figure 12-1 has two concurrent users. Each of these executes some SQL statements adding money to the balance, but in the end, the final value is going to be the wrong value, and that is not going to make anyone happy. Why? Because each user fetched a reality from the database that was correct at the time and then acted on it as if it would always be true. In the following two sections, we will look at the two major paradigms for isolation connections.

Pessimistic Concurrency Enforcement

Pessimistic concurrency enforcement is done by taking control of a resource when using it. Sometimes the control is exclusive, like when writing data, or shared, when simply viewing data. Control over a resource is achieved by using markers known as locks. *Locks* are tokens laid down by the SQL Server processes to stake their claims to the different resources available, so as to prevent one process from stomping on another and causing inconsistencies or prevent another process from seeing data that has not yet been verified by constraints or triggers. How long the locks are held will be controlled by what the connection is doing as well as the isolation level.

Every SQL Server process using an on-disk table applies locks to anything it is doing to ensure that that other user processes know what they are doing as well as what they are planning to do and to ensure that other processes don't get in its way. Minimally, a lock is always placed just to make sure that the database that is in use cannot be dropped.

Locks act as a message to other processes that a resource is being used or at least probably being used. Think of a railroad-crossing sign. When the bar crosses the road, it acts as a lock to tell you not to drive across the tracks because the train is going to use the resource. Even if the train stops and never reaches the road, the bar comes down, and the lights flash. This lock can be ignored (as can SQL Server locks), but it's generally not advisable to do so without a clear understanding of the situation, because if the train does come, your next trip to Disney World may be exclusively to the Haunted Mansion. (Ignoring locks is generally a bad practice, though not bad as blatantly ignoring a train-crossing signal unless your code is built to manage the train-crossing signals and you ignore the lock the train has placed on the tracks and put another train on the same tracks in a conflicting manner.)

In this section, we will look at a few characteristics of locks:

- *Type of lock*: Indicates what is being locked
- *Mode of lock*: Indicates how strong the lock is

Lock Types

If you've been around for a few versions of SQL Server, you probably know that since SQL Server 7.0, SQL Server primarily uses row-level locks when a process is reading some data. That is, a user locking some resource in SQL Server when executing a query does it on individual rows of data, rather than on pages of data or even on complete tables.

However, thinking that SQL Server only locks at the row level is misleading, as SQL Server can use several different types of locks to lock varying portions of the database, with the row being the finest type of lock, all the way up to a full database lock. And SQL Server uses each of them quite often. The list of lock types in Table 12-1 is not complete but is a sample of the common types of locks we will encounter in modifying data in tables.

Tip   Table 12-1 lists the lock types you will generally come in contact with in SQL Server, so these are all I'll cover. However, you should be aware that many more locks are in play, because SQL Server manages its hardware and internal needs as you execute queries. Hardware and internal resource locks are referred to as *latches*, and you'll occasionally see them referenced in many articles and Microsoft Docs, though the documentation is not terribly deep regarding them.

Table 12-1. Lock Types

Type of Lock	Granularity
Row or row identifier (RID)	A single row in a heap table.
Key	A single value in an index. (Note that a clustered table is represented as an index in all physical structures.)
Key range	A range of key values (e.g., to lock rows with values starting with the letter A, like from a query LIKE 'A%', even if no rows currently exist). Used for SERIALIZABLE isolation level.
Page	An 8 KB index or data page.
HoBT	An entire heap or B-tree structure.

(continued)

Table 12-1. *(continued)*

Type of Lock	Granularity
Table	An entire table, including all rows and indexes.
Application	A special type of lock that is user defined (will be covered in more detail later in this section)
Metadata	Metadata about the schema, such as catalog objects.
Database	The entire database.

At the point of request, SQL Server determines approximately how many of the database resources (a table, a row, a key, a key range, etc.) are needed to satisfy the request. This is calculated on the basis of several factors, the specifics of which are unpublished. Some of these factors incl",de the cost of acquiring the lock, the amount of resources needed, and how long the locks will be held on individual resources based on the isolation level. It's also possible for the query processor to upgrade the lock from a more granular lock to a less specific type if the query is unexpectedly taking up large quantities of resources. For example, if a large percentage of the rows in a table are locked with row locks, the query processor could switch to a table lock to finish out the process.

Lock Modes

Beyond the type of lock, the next concern is how tightly to lock the resource. For example, consider a construction site. Workers are generally allowed onto the site, but civilians who are not part of the process are not permitted. Sometimes, however, one of the workers might need exclusive use of the site to do something that would be dangerous for other people to be around (like using explosives).

Where the type of lock defines the amount of the database to lock, the mode of the lock refers to how strict the lock is and how protective the engine is when dealing with other locks. Table 12-2 lists these modes.

Table 12-2.   *Lock Modes*

Mode	Description
Shared	Grants access for reads only. It's generally used when users are looking at but not editing the data. It's called "shared" because multiple processes can have a shared lock on the same resource, allowing read-only access to the resource. However, sharing resources prevents other processes from modifying the resource.
Exclusive	Gives exclusive access to a resource and can be used during modification of data also. Only one process may have an active exclusive lock on a resource.
Update	Used to inform other processes that you're planning to modify the data but aren't quite ready to do so. Other connections may also issue shared, but not update or exclusive, locks while you're still preparing to do the modification. Update locks are used to prevent deadlocks (I'll cover them later in this section) by marking rows that a statement will possibly update, rather than upgrading directly from a shared lock to an exclusive one.
Intent	Communicates to other processes that taking one of the previously listed modes might be necessary. It establishes a lock hierarchy with taken locks, allowing processes that are trying to take a lock on a resource (like a table), that there are other connections with locks at a lower level such as a page. You might see this mode as intent shared, intent exclusive, or shared with intent exclusive.
Schema	Used to lock the structure of an object when it's in use, so you cannot alter a structure (like a table) when a user is reading data from it.
Bulk Update	Used when bulk copying data into a table, using one of the various tools like SSIS, BCP, or BULK INSERT in T-SQL, or when using the TABLOCK hint on some INSERT operations.

Each of these modes, coupled with the type/granularity, describes a locking situation. For example, an exclusive table lock would generally mean that no other user can access any data in the table. An update table lock would say that other users could look at the data in the table, but any statement that might modify data in the table would have to wait until after this process has been completed.

To determine which mode of a lock is compatible with another mode of lock, we need to consider *lock compatibility*. Each lock mode may or may not be compatible with the other lock mode on the same resource (or resource that contains other resources). If the types are compatible, two or more users may lock the same resource. Incompatible lock types would require that any additional users simply wait until all of the incompatible locks have been released.

Table 12-3 shows which types are compatible with others.

Table 12-3.   *Lock Compatibility Modes*

Mode	IS	S	U	IX	SIX	X
Intent shared (IS)	•	•	•	•	•	
Shared (S)	•	•	•			
Update (U)	•	•				
Intent exclusive (IX)	•			•		
Shared with intent exclusive (SIX)	•					
Exclusive (X)						

This is just an overview of the most common modes. In Microsoft Docs, for more details about lock compatibility, check their Transaction Locking and Row Versioning Guide at docs.microsoft.com/en-us/sql/relational-databases/sql-server-transaction-locking-and-row-versioning-guide#lock_compatibility.

Although locks are great for data consistency, as far as concurrency is considered, locked resources stink. Whenever a resource is locked with an incompatible lock type and another process cannot use it to complete its processing, concurrent throughput is lowered, because the process must wait for the other to complete before it can continue. This is referred to as *blocking*: one process is blocking another from doing something, so the blocked process must wait its turn, no matter how long it takes.

Simply put, locks allow consistent views of the data by only letting a single process modify a single resource at a time while allowing multiple viewers simultaneous utilization in read-only access. Locks are a necessary part of SQL Server's pessimistic concurrency architecture, as is blocking to honor those locks when needed, to make sure one user doesn't trample on another's data, resulting in invalid data in some cases.

In the next sections, I'll demonstrate the locking in each of the isolation levels, which in pessimistic schemes determines how long locks are held, depending on the protection that the isolation level affords. Executing SELECT * FROM sys.dm_os_waiting_tasks gives you a list of all processes that tells you if any users are blocking and which user is doing the blocking. Executing SELECT * FROM sys.dm_tran_locks; lets you see locks that are being held.

It's possible to instruct SQL Server to use a different type of lock than it might ordinarily choose by using *table hints* on your queries. For individual tables in a FROM clause, you can set the type of lock to be used for the single query like so:

```
FROM    table1 [WITH] (<tableHintList>)
            join table2 [WITH] (<tableHintList>)
```

Note that these hints work on all query types. In the case of locking, you can use quite a few. A partial list of the more common hints follows:

- PAGLOCK: Force the optimizer to choose page locks for the given table.

- NOLOCK: Leave no locks and honor no locks for the given table (other than schema locks, so objects in use cannot be modified), basically a synonym of READ UNCOMMITTED.

- ROWLOCK: Force row-level locks to be used for the table.

- TABLOCK: Go directly to table locks, rather than row or even page locks. This can speed some operations, but seriously lowers write concurrency.

- TABLOCX: This is the same as TABLOCK, but it always uses exclusive locks (whether it would have normally done so or not).

- XLOCK: Use exclusive locks.

- UPDLOCK: Use update locks.

Note that SQL Server can override your hints if necessary. For example, take the case where a query sets the table hint of NOLOCK, but then rows are modified in the table in the execution of the query. No shared locks are taken or honored, but exclusive locks are taken and held on the table for the rows that are modified, though not on rows that are only read (this is true even for resources that are read as part of a TRIGGER or CONSTRAINT object).

Of these, the TABLOCK and TABLOCKX are the two that you should most commonly be using. If you are loading a table, using TABLOCK to get a table lock or TABLOCKX to get an exclusive table lock will allow you to use bulk copy mode, and your transaction will be minimally logged if you are in simple or bulk logged recovery models.

Before moving to the examples, an important term to understand is "deadlock." A *deadlock* is a circumstance where two processes are trying to use the same objects, but neither will ever be able to complete because each is blocked by the other connection. For example, consider two processes (Processes 1 and 2) and two resources (Resources A and B). The following steps lead to a deadlock:

1. Process 1 takes a lock on Resource A, and at the same time, Process 2 takes a lock on Resource B.

2. Process 1 tries to get access to Resource B. Because it's locked by Process 2, Process 1 goes into a wait state.

3. Process 2 tries to get access to Resource A. Because it's locked by Process 1, Process 2 goes into a wait state.

At this point, there's no way to resolve this issue without ending one of the processes. SQL Server arbitrarily kills one of the processes, unless one of the processes has voluntarily raised or lowered the likelihood of being the killed process by setting DEADLOCK_PRIORITY to a lower value than the other. Values can be between integers –10 and 10 or LOW (equal to –5), NORMAL (0), or HIGH (5). SQL Server raises error 1205 to the client to tell the client that the process was stopped:

```
Msg 1205, Level 13, State 51, Line 242
Transaction (Process ID 66) was deadlocked on lock resources with another
process and has been chosen as the deadlock victim. Rerun the transaction
```

At this point, you could resubmit the request, as long as the call was coded such that the application knows when the transaction was started and what has occurred (something every application programmer ought to strive to do and, if done correctly, that will help you with dealing with optimistic concurrency issues).

Tip Proper deadlock handling requires that you build your applications in such a way that you can easily tell the entire stack of queries sent. This is done by proper use of transactions and batches. A good practice is to send one transaction per batch from a client application. Keep in mind that the engine views nested transactions as one transaction, so what I mean here is to start and complete one high-level transaction per batch.

A common trick to try to alleviate frequent deadlocks between pieces of code is to order object access in the same order in all code (so table dbo.Apple, dbo.Bananna, etc.) if possible. This way, locks are more likely to be taken in the same order, causing the lock to block earlier, so that the next process is blocked instead of deadlocked. For details about capturing deadlock information, see the Microsoft Docs article "Monitoring SQL Database Deadlocks" (docs.microsoft.com/en-us/dynamics365/business-central/dev-itpro/administration/monitor-database-deadlocks).

An important reality is that you really can't completely avoid deadlocks. But if you discover deadlocks occurring in the same parts of your code repeatedly, it can be indicative of a problem with your code, but often, if you are running a very busy server with concurrent connections, deadlocks happen, and the best thing to do is handle them by resubmitting the last transaction executed (too many applications just raise the deadlock as an error that sounds simply horrible to users: "chosen as deadlock victim"!).

The SNAPSHOT isolation level does not pertain to pessimistic concurrency controls, as it lets you see previous versions of data with the expectation that nothing will change. Readers don't block readers, so the examples will generally be along the lines of "make a change to the state of the database in an open transaction and then see what another connection can see when executing a statement of some sort in another connection."

Note   There's a file in the downloads that is a lock viewer that uses sys. dm_tran_locks to show you the locks held by a connection. If you are working through the examples, use this to see the locks held in given situations.

Isolation Levels and Locking

In the following sections, I will demonstrate how locks are taken and honored in the following isolation levels:

- READ UNCOMMITTED

- READ COMMITTED

- REPEATABLE READ

- SERIALIZABLE

In order to demonstrate pessimistic and optimistic concurrency enforcement, I'll briefly discuss the different isolation levels and demonstrate how they work using the following tables (and alternate versions using memory-optimized tables):

```
CREATE SCHEMA Art;
GO
CREATE TABLE Art.Artist
(
    ArtistId int CONSTRAINT PKArtist PRIMARY KEY
    ,Name varchar(30) --no key on value for demo purposes
    ,Padding char(4000)
        DEFAULT (REPLICATE('a',4000)) --so all rows not on single page
                --if all rows are on same page, some optimizations can
                --be made
);
INSERT INTO Art.Artist(ArtistId, Name)
VALUES (1,'da Vinci'),(2,'Micheangelo'), (3,'Donatello'),
       (4,'Picasso'),(5,'Dali'), (6,'Jones');
GO
CREATE TABLE Art.ArtWork
(
    ArtWorkId int CONSTRAINT PKArtWork PRIMARY KEY
    ,ArtistId int NOT NULL
            CONSTRAINT FKArtwork$wasDoneBy$Art_Artist
                                    REFERENCES Art.Artist (ArtistId)
    ,Name varchar(30)
    ,Padding char(4000) DEFAULT (REPLICATE('a',4000))
    ,CONSTRAINT AKArtwork UNIQUE (ArtistId, Name)
);
INSERT Art.Artwork (ArtworkId, ArtistId, Name)
VALUES (1,1,'Last Supper'),(2,1,'Mona Lisa'),(3,6,'Rabbit Fire');
```

READ UNCOMMITTED

A connection in READ UNCOMMITTED does not take locks on resources used (other than the database it is in) and does not honor locks by other connections other than metadata locks, such as a table that is in the process of being created. You do, of course, still get locks on any data you modify that are held until the transaction ends, which is true of all isolation levels.

READ UNCOMMITTED is generally the isolation level that you do not want to employ for production code. It is however a great tool when you need to see the state of a data operation in-flight. For example, if a transaction is loading a million rows into a table, instead of waiting for the transaction to complete, you can see the changes to the table. Another use of READ UNCOMMITTED is when you are the admin user and need to look at a production resource without blocking others. For example, say the following row is added to the Art.Artist table, but not committed yet:

```
--CONNECTION A
SET TRANSACTION ISOLATION LEVEL READ COMMITTED; --this is the default, just
                                                --setting for emphasis
BEGIN TRANSACTION;
INSERT INTO Art.Artist(ArtistId, Name)
VALUES (7, 'McCartney');
```

Then on a different connection, a user executes a query looking for that data:

```
--CONNECTION B
SET TRANSACTION ISOLATION LEVEL READ COMMITTED;
SELECT ArtistId, Name
FROM Art.Artist
WHERE Name = 'McCartney';
```

This will sit and not complete, because the row has not been committed. However, as an admin, I needed to see the data that had been added to the table before it was committed. Change this to READ UNCOMMITTED:

```
--CONNECTION B
SET TRANSACTION ISOLATION LEVEL READ UNCOMMITTED;
SELECT ArtistId, Name
FROM Art.Artist
WHERE Name = 'McCartney';
```

We will immediately get back the data that has been added:

ArtistId	Name
7	McCartney

The problem is, what happens if the process on Connection A decides to roll back their connection?

```
--CONNECTION A
ROLLBACK TRANSACTION;
```

Go back and execute that statement on connection B again and it is gone. Whether this is a problem or not is a matter for what the first half of the book was about: requirements. Too often though, if some process were to make some change (like perhaps applying uppercase on all of the names in this table) and another user saw the errant change and called the service desk, by the time they checked, all might be back to normal. While this might be a fun way to gaslight your service desk, it is not a good practice just to get slightly faster response times.

Being able to see locked data is quite valuable, especially when you're in the middle of a long-running process, because you won't block the process that's running, but you can see the data being modified. There is no guarantee that the data you see will be correct (it might fail checks and be rolled back), but for looking around and some reporting needs where you can accept this sort of issue, this data might be good enough.

Caution   Ignoring locks using READ UNCOMMITTED is almost never the right way to build highly concurrent database systems! Yes, it is possible to make your applications considerably faster, because they never have to wait for other processes. Yet there is a reason for this waiting. Consistency of the data you read is highly important and should not be taken lightly. Later in the "Optimistic Concurrency Enforcement" section, a feature can give you sort of the same performance without reading dirty data and possibly with no changes to your code.

READ COMMITTED

READ COMMITTED is the default isolation level as far as SQL Server is concerned, and as the name states, it only prevents you from seeing uncommitted data. Be careful that your toolset may or may not use it as its default (some toolsets use SERIALIZABLE as the default, which, as you will see, is pretty tight and is not great for concurrency). All shared and update locks are released as soon as the process is finished accessing a resource, which could be a single row before moving on to the next row in a SELECT statement. (Hence, if you are using 1,000 resources, it may take one lock, use a resource, release the lock, and access the next resource.)

However, understand that this isolation level isn't perfect, as there isn't protection for repeatable reads or phantom rows. This means that as the length of the transaction increases, there's a growing possibility that some data that was read during the first operations within a transaction might have been changed or deleted by the end of the transaction. As the data architect, you need to answer the question "What if data changes?" and see if this matters.

As an example, we will start a transaction and then view data in the Art.Artist table:

```
--CONNECTION A
SET TRANSACTION ISOLATION LEVEL READ COMMITTED;

BEGIN TRANSACTION;
SELECT ArtistId, Name FROM Art.Artist WHERE ArtistId = 7;
```

No rows are returned. Locks are only taken on resources as they are actually being used, so if you could run the lock viewer fast enough, you would just see one or so locks at a time. Check the lock viewer after the results have been retrieved, and you will only see a shared database lock.

Next, on a separate connection, we will add a new row to the table and commit it (I demonstrated in the previous section that we would be blocked from viewing the row in READ COMMITTED, since the row was in a dirty state, but here the transaction autocommits):

```
--CONNECTION B
INSERT INTO Art.Artist(ArtistId, Name)
VALUES (7, 'McCartney');
```

Going back to Connection A, we reselect the data, still in the same transaction:

```
--CONNECTION A
SELECT ArtistId, Name FROM Art.Artist WHERE ArtistId = 7;
```

It now returns

ArtistId	Name
7	McCartney

Update the row on Connection B:

```
--CONNECTION B
UPDATE Art.Artist SET Name = 'Starr' WHERE ArtistId = 7;
```

Then view and commit the transaction on the row again:

```
--CONNECTION A
SELECT ArtistId, Name FROM Art.Artist WHERE ArtistId = 7;
COMMIT TRANSACTION;
```

ArtistId	Name
7	Starr

The bottom line is that this isolation level is great for most cases, particularly when you are doing a single query. However, as the number of statements and complexity/length of transaction does too, it becomes less desirable. For example, consider what would have occurred if the process on Connection A had needed to confirm an artist named "McCartney" existed in the table. A transaction was started, to contain the operation, and the row was seen to exist. But after that the row changed to "Starr," so your query to check for that row has been invalidated, and the supposition you based following actions on might now be wrong.

Note   In Appendix B, available as a download, this is demonstrated for writing triggers, where you have to be careful of checking for some setting to exist in another table that you are not changing. If that value needs to be correct by the end of your transaction, using READ COMMITTED can be an issue.

The other process may have done its own checks to make sure it could update the rows, which may have been prevented by some step in your process that has not yet completed. This is to say this: concurrency can be complex, and it is very hard to test. The timing of the aforementioned scenario might be just microseconds, and it could actually happen simultaneously. It certainly is unlikely to occur on the developer's workstation, and unless you do massive amounts of highly concurrent testing, it may not occur in your test system either. But as Murphy's Law states, "Anything that can go wrong will go wrong," so you need to program defensively and consider "What if this happens?" Testing using extra BEGIN TRANSACTION and often WAITFOR statements can be very helpful in slowing down time enough to cause collisions that would rarely if ever occur. We will use WAITFOR to start two processes at the same point in time in tests later in the chapter.

The next two isolation levels will be particularly useful in dealing with data integrity checks, as we can hold locks on the rows we have accessed longer than just to make sure they are not changed as we return them.

REPEATABLE READ

The REPEATABLE READ isolation level includes protection from data being changed or deleted after you have accessed it in a transaction. Shared locks are now held during the entire transaction to prevent other users from modifying the data that has been read. You are most likely to use this isolation level if your concern is the absolute guarantee of existence of some data when you finish your operation.

As an example, execute the following statements on one connection:

```
--CONNECTION A
SET TRANSACTION ISOLATION LEVEL REPEATABLE READ;

BEGIN TRANSACTION;
SELECT ArtistId, Name FROM Art.Artist WHERE ArtistId >= 6;
```

This returns

ArtistId	Name
6	Jones
7	Starr

Then on another connection, execute the following:

```
--CONNECTION B
INSERT INTO Art.Artist(ArtistId, Name)
VALUES (8, 'McCartney');
```

If you go back to CONNECTION A and execute the SELECT again, you will see three rows. REPEATABLE READ doesn't protect against the phantom row, but if you try to delete the row with ArtistId = 6

```
--CONNECTION B
DELETE Art.Artist
WHERE  ArtistId = 6;
```

Connection B is now blocked. Connection A holds a shared key lock on the row with ArtistId = 6 (and 7 and 8 also since you have seen them), so that row cannot be deleted or updated, which would require an incompatible exclusive lock. Cancel the query on Connection B, and then COMMIT the transaction on Connection A to continue.

REPEATABLE READ isolation level is perfect for the cases where you want to make sure that some data still exists when your process has completed (like if you were implementing a foreign key–type check in code). I check to see if TableX.TableXId has a value of 1 in a row. If so, I make sure it does until I complete my process. Sure, the connection can delete it right after I commit, but it is expected that that connection will then have to check to see if there is a dependency on the value of 1 in the other table. Note that for on-disk tables, FOREIGN KEY constraints don't require REPEATABLE READ locking, as the constraint checks each direction for any modification or delete. This requirement will be different for memory-optimized tables.

This isolation level is not ideal for the situation where you want to maintain a balance (what if a negative value is inserted?) or where you want to limit the cardinality of a relationship (new rows are an issue because if the limit is two related rows, two connections that check the cardinality and insert new rows may not lock each other based on timing). We will explore how to deal with that situation in the next section.

One of the biggest concerns here is not so much that we might be locking rows we intended to touch, but if there is not an index on a column like `ArtistId` in this example, every row we touch in the query will be locked until the transaction ends. If we have to scan 100000 rows to look for ArtistId >= 6, all 100000 rows will be locked. If an index means we only have to touch 1 row, the other 99999 rows can be modified as desired. Hence, it is important to use proper indexing on columns that are used for such queries to avoid touching more data than is necessary.

SERIALIZABLE

`SERIALIZABLE` takes everything from `REPEATABLE READ` and adds in phantom row protection. SQL Server accomplishes this by taking locks not only on existing data that it has read but on any ranges of data that *could* match any SQL statement executed. This is the most restrictive isolation level and is the best in any case where the protections it provides are absolutely necessary. It can cause lots of blocking; for example, consider what would happen if you executed the following query under the `SERIALIZABLE` isolation level:

```
SELECT *
FROM Art.Artist;
```

For at least the duration of the query execution (and longer if in an explicit transaction), due to locks on all existing rows and range locks being taken on all keys in the range the query could have touched (in this case, an infinite number of values), no other user would be able to modify or add rows to the table until all rows have been returned and the transaction it was executing within has completed.

Note   Be careful. I said "No other user would be able to modify or add rows to the table…" I didn't say "read." Readers leave shared locks, not exclusive ones. This caveat is something that can be confusing at times when you are trying to write safe but concurrent SQL code. It is part of what leads to the lost update we discussed earlier in the chapter. Two connections fetch a balance, one updates, and the other does too but is blocked. When the blocking is over, the blocked connection is free to do their write, but could do so with stale data. We will look at techniques to avoid this issue later in this chapter as we discuss techniques to write our code to deal with concurrency.

If lots of users are viewing data in the table in the SERIALIZABLE isolation level, it can be difficult to get any modifications done. If you're going to use SERIALIZABLE, you need to be careful with your code and make sure it only uses the minimum number of rows needed.

As an example, execute this statement on a connection to simulate a user with a table locked:

```
--CONNECTION A
SET TRANSACTION ISOLATION LEVEL SERIALIZABLE;

BEGIN TRANSACTION;
SELECT ArtistId, Name FROM Art.Artist;
```

Then, try to add a new row to the table:

```
--CONNECTION B
INSERT INTO Art.Artist(ArtistId, Name)
VALUES (9, 'Vuurmann');
```

The INSERT statement is blocked. Commit the transaction on CONNECTION A:

```
--CONNECTION A
COMMIT TRANSACTION;
SELECT ArtistId, Name FROM Art.Artist;
```

This unblocks CONNECTION B, and you will see that the contents of the table are now the following:

ArtistId	Name
1	da Vinci
2	Micheangelo
3	Donatello
4	Picasso

5	Dali
6	Jones
7	Starr
8	McCartney
9	Vuurmann

It is important to be careful with the SERIALIZABLE isolation level. The name tells you that you will have single-threaded access to resources in this table, particularly when writing data to the table. I can't stress enough that while multiple readers can read the same data, no one can change it while others are reading. Too often, people take this to mean that they can read some data and be guaranteed that no other user might have read it also, leading occasionally to inconsistent results and more frequently to deadlocking issues.

Interesting Cases

In this section I will present a few interesting cases that are more than simple isolation, including foreign keys and application locks that can help us implement a critical section of code.

Locking and Foreign Keys

One of the interesting scenarios when working with locking involves FOREIGN KEY constraints. Consider our tables: Art.Artist and the child table Art.Artwork. When you insert a new row into the Art.Artwork table, it must check the Art.Artist table to see if the key exists:

```
--CONNECTION A
BEGIN TRANSACTION;
INSERT INTO Art.ArtWork(ArtWorkId, ArtistId, Name)
VALUES (4,9,'Revolver Album Cover');
```

Looking at the locks held using the Lock Viewer.sql file in the downloads, you will only see locks on the ArtWork table (on the two indexes, PKArtWork and AKArtWork). So it seems like there is no guarantee of the row for ArtistId = 9 being deleted. This is true in terms of locked resources, but FOREIGN KEY constraints protect both ways by executing code internally. So if on a different connection the following code is executed while this transaction is still open

```
--CONNECTION B
DELETE FROM Art.Artist WHERE ArtistId = 9;
```

this will be blocked from executing because while there are no rows currently that are committed that will cause the block, it needs to check the child row that has been created, but it still locked exclusively. You should see locks on a row and then intent locks on the page and object that contain the new row. In the resource_description column from sys.dm_tran_locks, you should see two hexadecimal values that are the same, one for the blocker and one for the blocked. This means that the new row will determine whether or not the artist can be deleted.

On Connection A, execute

```
-- CONNECTION A
COMMIT TRANSACTION;
```

Then, Connection B will complete with a delete reference error, since it now has child rows existing. However, to show that the Art.Artist row is not locked at any point in the process, you can update it:

```
--CONNECTION A
BEGIN TRANSACTION;
INSERT INTO Art.ArtWork(ArtWorkId, ArtistId, Name)
VALUES (5,9,'Liverpool Rascals');
```

Now, on Connection B execute

```
--CONNECTION B
UPDATE Art.Artist
SET  Name = 'Voorman'
WHERE ArtistId = 9;
```

It will succeed. Then back on Connection A, roll back the transaction, so that the new row is not added:

```
--CONNECTION A
ROLLBACK TRANSACTION;
SELECT * FROM Art.Artwork WHERE ArtistId = 9;
```

You will see just the one row returned. So what about cascading foreign keys? There are two different cases. If no child row exists, instead of taking no locks on the child table, an intent exclusive lock is placed on the table. This would keep anyone else from taking an exclusive lock on the table but would otherwise allow usage. If a user tries to insert or update a row that uses the deleted key, the FOREIGN KEY constraint checks would bump up against the locked row just as before.

If rows do exist in the child to be deleted, they will be exclusively locked just as if you did a delete, and a range exclusive lock is set to prevent anyone from inserting a row that might match the parent.

Foreign keys do slow down some operations in the execution of database code, but fortunately, when using the default isolation level, that effect is not necessarily long felt, even when a row references a value that exists in the other related table.

Application Locks

SQL Server has a built-in method you can use to implement a form of pessimistic locking: SQL Server *application locks*. The real downside is that enforcement and compliance are completely optional. If you write code that doesn't follow the rules and use the proper application lock, you will get no error letting you know. However, for the cases where you need to single-thread code for some reason, application locks are a great resource.

The commands that you have to work with application locks are as follows:

- sp_getAppLock: Use this to place a lock on an application resource. The programmer names an application resource, which can be named with any string value. In the string, you could name single values or even a range.

- sp_releaseAppLock: Use this to release locks taken inside a transaction.

- APPLOCK_MODE: Use this to check the mode of the application lock.

- APPLOCK_TEST: Use this to see if you could take an application lock before starting the lock and getting blocked.

As an example, we'll run the following code. We'll implement this on a resource named 'InvoiceId=1', which represents a logical invoice object. We'll set it as an exclusive lock so no other user can touch it. In one connection, we run the following code (note application locks are database specific, so you will need to be in the same database on Connections A and B). By default, applocks are associated with a transaction, so you will need to be in an explicit transaction. You can specify a parameter of @LockOwner of Session, and you will not need a transaction, but it will be around until you use sp_releaseAppLock or end the connection, which can be more difficult to manage.

```
--CONNECTION A

BEGIN TRANSACTION;
    DECLARE @result int;
    EXEC @result = sp_getapplock @Resource = 'InvoiceId=1',
                                 @LockMode = 'Exclusive';
    SELECT @result;
```

This returns 0, stating that the lock was taken successfully. Other possible output is shown here:

Value	Result
1	Lock granted after waiting for other locks
-1	Timed out
-2	Lock request cancelled
-3	Deadlock victim
999	Other error

You can see the type of applock taken by using APPLOCK_MODE():

```
--first parameter is a database principal, in this case public
SELECT APPLOCK_MODE('public','InvoiceId=1');
```

This returns the mode the lock was taken in, in our case Exclusive. Now, if another user tries to execute the same code to take the same lock, the second process has to wait until the first user has finished with the resource 'InvoiceId=1':

```
--CONNECTION B
BEGIN TRANSACTION;
    DECLARE @result int;
```

```
EXEC @result = sp_getapplock @Resource = 'InvoiceId=1',
                             @LockMode = 'Exclusive';
SELECT @result;
```

This transaction has to wait. Let's cancel the execution and then execute the following code using the APPLOCK_TEST() function (which has to be executed in a transaction context) to see if we can take the lock (allowing the application to check before taking the lock):

```
--CONNECTION B
BEGIN TRANSACTION;
SELECT  APPLOCK_TEST('Public','InvoiceId=1','Exclusive','Transaction')
                                                        AS CanTakeLock
ROLLBACK TRANSACTION;
```

This returns 0, meaning we cannot take this lock currently. The other output is 1, indicating the lock could be granted. APPLOCKs can be a great resource for building and implementing locks that are "larger" than just SQL Server objects. Later in this section, I will show you a very common and useful technique using APPLOCKs to create a pessimistic lock based on the application lock to single-thread access to a given block of code.

Application locks are particularly useful in cases where you want to single-thread a critical part of your code. For example, you might need to fetch a value, increment it, and keep the result unique among other callers that could be calling simultaneously (say you need to format the output beyond what a SEQUENCE object or a column with the IDENTITY property will not allow). The general solution to the single-threading problem is to exclusively lock the resources that you need to be able to work with, forcing all other users to wait even for reading and, more importantly, for a transaction to commit. In some cases, this technique will work great, but it can be troublesome in cases like the following:

- The code is part of a larger set of code that may have other code locked in a transaction, blocking users' access to more than you expect. You are allowed to release the application lock in the transaction to allow other callers to continue.

- Only one minor section of code needs to be single-threaded, and you can allow simultaneous access otherwise.

- The speed in which the data is accessed is so fast that two processes are likely to fetch the same data within microseconds of each other.

- The single-threading is not for a specific SQL Server resource. For example, you may want to write to a file of some sort or use some other resource that is not table based.

Tip   You can use application locks to implement more than just exclusive locks using different lock modes, but exclusive is the mode that I have used in all my cases. My most recent use of application locks was in a job system where one procedure checked to see what job could run next and another procedure set that a job was complete. By single-threading code through the two procedures, it was far easier to make sure that updates and reads were not interacting.

The following technique will leave the tables unlocked while manually single-threading access to a code block (in this case, getting and setting a value), using an application lock to lock a section of code.

To demonstrate a very common problem of building a unique value without using identities (e.g., if you have to create an account number with special formatting/processing), I have created the following table:

```
CREATE SCHEMA Demo;
GO
CREATE TABLE Demo.Applock
(
    ApplockId int CONSTRAINT PKApplock PRIMARY KEY,
                            --the value that we will be generating
                            --with the procedure
    ConnectionId int,       --holds the spid of the connection so you can
                            --who creates the row

    --the time the row was created, so you can see the progression
    InsertTime datetime2(3) DEFAULT (SYSDATETIME())

);
```

Next, a procedure that starts an application lock fetches some data from the table, increments the value, and stores it in a variable. I added a delay parameter, so you can tune up the problems by making the delay between incrementing and inserting more pronounced (slowing down operations to make sure they do incompatible things is essential to concurrency testing). There is also a parameter to turn on and off the application lock (noted as @UseApplockFlag in the parameters), and that parameter will help you test to see how it behaves with and without the application lock:

```
CREATE PROCEDURE Demo.Applock$Test
(
    @ConnectionId int,
    @UseApplockFlag bit = 1,
    @StepDelay varchar(10) = '00:00:00'
) AS
SET NOCOUNT ON;
BEGIN TRY
    BEGIN TRANSACTION;
        DECLARE @retval int = 1;
        IF @UseApplockFlag = 1 --turns on and off the applock for testing
            BEGIN
                EXEC @retval = sp_getAppLock @Resource = 'applock$test',
                                             @LockMode = 'exclusive';

                IF @retval < 0
                    BEGIN
                        DECLARE @errorMessage nvarchar(200);
                        SET @errorMessage =
                            CASE @retval
                                WHEN -1 THEN 'Applock request timed out.'
                                WHEN -2 THEN 'Applock request canceled.'
                                WHEN -3 THEN 'Applock involved in deadlock'
                                ELSE 'Parameter validation or other error.'
                            END;
                        THROW 50000,@errorMessage,16;
                    END;
            END;
```

```
--get the next primary key value. Add 1. Don't let value end in zero
--for demo reasons. The real need can be a lot more complex
DECLARE @ApplockId int;
SET @ApplockId = COALESCE((SELECT MAX(ApplockId) FROM Demo.Applock),0)
                                                              + 1;

IF @ApplockId % 10 = 0 SET @ApplockId = @ApplockId + 1;
--delay for parameterized amount of time to slow down operations
--and guarantee concurrency problems
WAITFOR DELAY @stepDelay;

--insert the next value
INSERT INTO Demo.Applock(ApplockId, connectionId)
VALUES (@ApplockId, @ConnectionId);

--won't have much effect on this code, since the row will now be
--exclusively locked, and the max will need to see the new row to
--be of any effect.

IF @useApplockFlag = 1 --turns on and off the applock for testing
    EXEC @retval = sp_releaseApplock @Resource = 'applock$test';

--this releases the applock too
COMMIT TRANSACTION;
END TRY
BEGIN CATCH
    --if there is an error, roll back and display it.
    IF XACT_STATE() <> 0
        ROLLBACK TRANSACTION;
    SELECT CAST(ERROR_NUMBER() as varchar(10)) + ':' + ERROR_MESSAGE();
END CATCH;
```

Now, you can set up a few connections using this stored procedure, attempting multiple connections first without the application lock and then with it. Since we're running the procedure in such a tight loop, it is not surprising that two connections will often get the same value and try to insert new rows using that value when not using the application lock:

```
--test on multiple connections
WAITFOR TIME '21:47';   --set for a time to run so multiple batches
                        --can simultaneously execute
go
EXEC Demo.Applock$Test @connectionId = @@spid
            ,@useApplockFlag = 0 -- <1=use applock, 0 = don't use applock>
            ,@stepDelay = '00:00:00.001';
            --'delay in hours:minutes:seconds.parts of seconds'
GO 10000 --runs the batch 10000 times in SSMS
```

You will probably be amazed at how many clashes you get (they will show up as errors) when you have application locks turned off. Doing 10,000 iterations of this procedure on three connections on an Intel NUC Quad Core i7, with 32 GB of RAM with 0 for the APPLOCK parameter, I got over 100 clashes pretty much constantly (evidenced by an error message: 2627:Violation of PRIMARY KEY constraint…Cannot insert duplicate key in object 'dbo.applock'...). With application locks turned on, all rows were inserted in slightly more time than the original time, without any clashes whatsoever.

To solidify the point that every connection has to follow the rules, turn off application locks on only a connection or two and see the havoc that will result. The critical section will now no longer be honored, and you will get tons of clashes quickly, especially if you use any delay.

This is not the only method of implementing the solution to the incrementing values problem. Another common method is to change the code where you get the maximum value to increment and apply locking hints:

```
SET @applockId =
     COALESCE((SELECT MAX(applockId)
                FROM APPLOCK WITH (UPDLOCK,PAGLOCK)),0) + 1;
```

Changing the code to do this will cause update locks to be held because of the UPDLOCK hint, and the PAGLOCK hint causes page locks to be held (SQL Server can ignore locks when a row is locked and it has not been modified, even if the row is exclusively locked).

The solution I presented is a very generic one for single-threading a code segment in T-SQL code, allowing that the one procedure is the only one single-threading. It does not take any locks that will block others until it needs to update the data (if there is no changing of data, it won't block any other users, *ever*). This works great for a hot spot where you can clearly cordon off the things being utilized at a given level, like in this example, where all users of this procedure are getting the maximum of the same rows.

Why Exclusive Locks Aren't Always Exclusive

In the introduction section covering locks and isolation levels, it was noted that exclusive locks "generally" block other access. However, exclusive locks are not actually exclusive in some cases. The name READ COMMITTED contains a clue that as to what may or may not be locked when you are reading data in a database.

If the page that a row sits on has not been actually dirtied (meaning the bit that tells SQL Server it needs to be saved to disk on the next checkpoint operation), it doesn't matter if it is locked with an exclusive lock. So you can execute the following code:

```
--Connection A
BEGIN TRANSACTION
SELECT *
FROM  Art.Artist WITH (XLOCK)
```

Then, without committing the transaction, you can execute the following statement on a different connection and can successfully query without being blocked:

```
--Connection B
SELECT Name
FROM   Art.Artist
WHERE  ArtistId = 1
```

This returns the data as it is in the table, which, at first glance, goes against logic:

```
Name
------------------------------
dah Vinci
```

Execute the lock query from the download, and you will see a lot of rows locked exclusively for the `Art.Artist` table. Now if you go back and execute this query back on Connection A

```
--Connection A
UPDATE Art.Artist
SET   Name = 'Dah Vinci'
WHERE  Artist.ArtistId = 1;
```

and then go back to Connection B and try to execute your statement again, then you will be blocked. The interesting scenario doesn't end there, however. Execute the following on Connection A:

```
--Connection A
ROLLBACK; --Close the transaction
BEGIN TRANSACTION --Start another one
SELECT *
FROM  Art.Artist WITH (XLOCK) --exclusively lock the rows again
```

Now, go back to Connection B and try to run the `SELECT` statement again. This time it may be blocked, without the `UPDATE` statement. This is because the data was dirtied by the first transaction, and it stays that way until a checkpoint flushes data to disk, which you can force with the `CHECKPOINT` command. (It can even be executed on Connection A or B while the transaction is still open or happens automatically.)

This is just one of the many optimizations that are done to try to avoid waiting on locks, and it is most interesting because users often try to use the `XLOCK` hint to keep users from accessing some data, not to realize that it does not have that effect.

Optimistic Concurrency Enforcement

While pessimistic concurrency is based on taking control of a resource by holding locks, generally from the expectation that multiple users will need to utilize the same resources and we need to order their utilization, optimistic concurrency is just the opposite. Optimistic concurrency control, generally speaking, assumes little overlap in incompatible usage and optimizes accordingly. And instead of locking resources, the idea is to give users access to previous versions of resources that have been or are being modified. If you are only reading data, just seeing data as it was when you started a transaction will not be a problem (and it will often make more sense to the user that doesn't have to wonder why there are child rows with no parent rows in the data they fetched). The outcome of not using locking is a tremendous reduction in most waiting times, though it is more work and, hence, a bit more costly, when incompatible concurrency collisions do occur.

Implemented in SQL Server 2005, there was one model of optimistic concurrency enforcement that was comingled with the locking we saw in the pessimistic locking scheme. This partial implementation did amazing things for performance, but still made use of locks to deal with direct write contention. It was not really used tremendously because the shift in paradigms felt complicated, but there was one feature that was highly used that does wonders to your lock contention issues which we will cover in the next section.

In SQL Server 2014, Microsoft added memory-optimized tables, which have a completely different concurrency model called multiversion concurrency control (MVCC), which is based completely on versions with no locks involved, other than locks purely for schema stability purposes. In Chapter 11, the structural differences between memory-optimized tables and on-disk ones were enumerated, but in this chapter, we will see them in use for concurrent access.

In the following sections, I will cover the on-disk implementation of optimistic concurrency, followed by coverage of memory-optimized tables.

Optimistic Concurrency Enforcement in On-Disk Tables

There are two main topics to look at when it comes to on-disk optimistic concurrency enforcement. The first is SNAPSHOT isolation level, which affects your connection at a transaction level (you get a consistent view of the database after you start your transaction), and second is the database setting READ COMMITTED SNAPSHOT, which affects queries at a statement level (much like READ COMMITTED does now, you can get completely different results on different executions in the same transaction). For SNAPSHOT isolation level, two executions of the same query will return the same results, unless you change the table in your connection.

SNAPSHOT Isolation Level

SNAPSHOT isolation lets you read the data as it was when the transaction started, regardless of any changes. No matter how much the data changes in the "real" world, your view stays the same. This makes it impossible to do things like check to see if a row exists in another table, since you will not be able to see it in your transaction if the row is changed or deleted before committing.

The largest downside is the effect SNAPSHOT isolation can have on performance if you are not prepared for it. This history data for on-disk tables is written not only to the log, but the data that will be used to support other users that are in a SNAPSHOT isolation level transaction is written to the tempdb (or to the current database if Accelerated Database Recovery is turned on in SQL Server 2019). Hence, if this server is going to be very active, you have to make sure that disk subsystems are up to the challenge, especially if you're supporting large numbers of concurrent users and some with long-running modification transactions.

The good news is that, if you employ a strategy of having readers use a versioning technology, data readers will no longer block data writers (no matter their isolation level), they will not be blocked by data writers, and they will always get a transactionally consistent view of the data. So, when the vice president of the company decides to write a 20-table join query to view corporate performance in the middle of the busiest part of the day, that query will never be blocked, and no other users will get stuck behind it either. The better news is that there will be no cases where the check constraint/ trigger hasn't had time to deny a mistaken $10 million entry that one of the data entry clerks added to the data yet (the vice president would have seen the error if you were using the READ UNCOMMITTED solution, which is the unfortunate choice of many novice performance tuners). The bad news is that eventually the vice president's query might take up all the resources and cause a major system slowdown, so it still isn't great to mix bad queries and highly active users in the same database. (Hey, if it was too easy, companies wouldn't need DBAs and programmers. And I, for one, wouldn't survive in a nontechnical field that did not include roller coasters.)

To use (and demonstrate) SNAPSHOT isolation level, you have to alter the database you're working with (you can even do this to tempdb):

```
ALTER DATABASE Chapter12
    SET ALLOW_SNAPSHOT_ISOLATION ON;
```

Now, the SNAPSHOT isolation level is available for queries. Let's look at an example. On the first connection, start a transaction and execute a SELECT statement that returns data from the Art.Artist table we used back in the "Pessimistic Concurrency Enforcement" section:

```
--CONNECTION A
SET TRANSACTION ISOLATION LEVEL SNAPSHOT;
BEGIN TRANSACTION;
SELECT ArtistId, Name FROM Art.Artist;
```

This returns the following results:

```
ArtistId    Name
----------- ------------------------------
1           da Vinci
2           Micheangelo
3           Donatello
4           Picasso
5           Dali
6           Jones
7           Starr
8           McCartney
9           Vuurmann
```

On a second connection, run the following:

```
--CONNECTION B
INSERT INTO Art.Artist(ArtistId, Name)
VALUES (10, 'Disney');
```

This executes with no waiting. Going back to Connection A, without ending the transaction, and re-executing the SELECT returns the same set of rows as before, so the results remain consistent. On Connection B, run the following DELETE statement:

```
--CONNECTION B
DELETE FROM Art.Artist
WHERE  ArtistId = 3;
```

This doesn't have to wait either. Going back to the other connection again, nothing has changed:

```
--CONNECTION A
SELECT ArtistId, Name FROM Art.Artist;
```

This still returns the same nine rows. Commit the transaction and check the differences:

```
--CONNECTION A
COMMIT TRANSACTION
SELECT ArtistId, Name FROM Art.Artist;
```

This now returns the changed set:

```
ArtistId     Name
----------   ------------------------------
1            da Vinci
2            Micheangelo
4            Picasso
5            Dali
6            Jones
7            Starr
8            McCartney
9            Vuurmann
10           Disney
```

So what about modifying data in SNAPSHOT isolation level? If no one else has modified the row, you can make any change:

```
--CONNECTION A
SET TRANSACTION ISOLATION LEVEL SNAPSHOT;
BEGIN TRANSACTION;

UPDATE Art.Artist
SET    Name = 'Duh Vinci'
WHERE  ArtistId = 1;

ROLLBACK;
```

But, if you have two connections competing and fetching/modifying the same row, you may get blocking. For example, say Connection B has a lock from a transaction in either a SNAPSHOT or a non-SNAPSHOT isolation level:

```
--CONNECTION B
BEGIN TRANSACTION

UPDATE Art.Artist
SET    Name = 'Dah Vinci'
WHERE  ArtistId = 1;
```

Then Connection A updates it while Connection B's transaction is still in force:

```
--CONNECTION A
SET TRANSACTION ISOLATION LEVEL SNAPSHOT;

UPDATE Art.Artist
SET    Name = 'Duh Vinci'
WHERE  ArtistId = 1;
```

You will find the query is blocked and the connection is forced to wait, because this row is modified and has an exclusive lock on it, and Connection B is not in the SNAPSHOT isolation level. When making changes to data in the SNAPSHOT isolation level, the changes still take locks, which will block any non-SNAPSHOT isolation transaction connection just like before. However, what is very different is how it deals with two SNAPSHOT isolation level connections modifying the same resource. There are two cases. First, if the row has not been yet cached, you can get blocked and wait until the other connection has completed.

In this next (quite typical) case (after rolling back the transactions from the previous example), Connection A caches the row, Connection B updates, and Connection A tries to update it also:

```
--CONNECTION A
SET TRANSACTION ISOLATION LEVEL SNAPSHOT;
BEGIN TRANSACTION;
SELECT *
FROM   Art.Artist;
```

Then execute the following on Connection B, to change the data. It is not in an explicit transaction:

```
--CONNECTION B
UPDATE Art.Artist
SET    Name = 'Dah Vinci'
WHERE  ArtistId = 1;
```

Now when you try to update the row that you think exists

```
--CONNECTION A
UPDATE Art.Artist
SET    Name = 'Duh Vinci'
WHERE  ArtistId = 1;
```

943

the following error message rears its ugly head because this row has been deleted by a different connection:

```
Msg 3960, Level 16, State 3, Line 586
Snapshot isolation transaction aborted due to update conflict. You cannot
use snapshot isolation to access table 'Art.Artist' directly or indirectly
in database 'Chapter13' to update, delete, or insert the row that has
been modified or deleted by another transaction. Retry the transaction or
change the isolation level for the update/delete statement.
```

For the most part, due to the way things work with SNAPSHOT intermingled with the pessimistic concurrency engine, it can be complex (or perhaps annoying is a better term) to work with. There is a key phrase in the error message: "retry the transaction." This was a theme from deadlocks and will be a major theme in the in-memory implementation of MVCC.

Of course, really this is a good thing. Since someone else has changed the data you are trying to modify in your transaction, it would behoove you to go out and check to see if anything has changed before resubmitting your modification statement.

READ COMMITTED SNAPSHOT (Database Setting)

The database setting READ_COMMITTED_SNAPSHOT changes the isolation level of READ COMMITTED to behave very much like SNAPSHOT isolation level on an individual *statement* level. It is a very powerful tool for performance tuning, but it should be noted that it changes the way the entire database processes READ COMMITTED transactions (there is no way to force one query to behave in the native manner either), and because data may be changing, it will behoove you to think deeply about how the code you write to check data integrity may be affected by changes that are in flight when you do your checks.

The important part to understand is that this works on a "statement" level and not a "transaction" level. In SNAPSHOT isolation level, once you start a transaction, you get a consistent view of the database *as it was* when the transaction started and you accessed data, until you end the transaction. READ_COMMITTED_SNAPSHOT gives you a consistent view of the database for a single statement. Set the database into this mode as follows:

```
--must be no active connections other than the connection executing
--this ALTER command
ALTER DATABASE Chapter12
    SET READ_COMMITTED_SNAPSHOT ON;
```

Or, if you want to do it immediately, killing existing users (like on a test server), you can force disconnect other users of the database with the WITH ROLLBACK IMMEDIATE clause of the ALTER DATABASE statement:

```
ALTER DATABASE Chapter13
    SET READ_COMMITTED_SNAPSHOT ON WITH ROLLBACK IMMEDIATE;
```

When you do this, every *statement* is now in SNAPSHOT isolation level by default. For example, imagine you're at the midpoint of the following pseudo-batch:

```
BEGIN TRANSACTION;
SELECT Column FROM Table1;
--midpoint
SELECT Column FROM Table1;
COMMIT TRANSACTION;
```

If you're in SNAPSHOT isolation level, Table1 could change completely—even get dropped—and you wouldn't be able to tell when you execute the second SELECT statement. You're given a consistent view of the database for reading. With the READ_COMMITTED_SNAPSHOT database setting turned on, in a READ COMMITTED isolation level transaction, your view of Table1 would be consistent with how it looked when you started reading, but when you started the second pass through the table, it might not match the data the first time you read through. This behavior is similar to plain READ COMMITTED, except that you don't wait for any in-process phantoms or nonrepeatable reads while retrieving rows produced during the individual statement (other users can delete and add rows while you scan through the table, but you won't be affected by the changes).

For places where you might need more safety, use the stronger isolation levels, such as REPEATABLE READ or SERIALIZABLE. They will continue to work with locking and blocking just as before. I would certainly suggest that, in TRIGGER objects and modification STORED PROCEDURE objects that you build using this isolation level change, you consider a stronger than default isolation level when validating data in other tables.

The best part is that basic readers who just want to see data for a query or report will not be affected like they are in the default implementation of READ COMMITTED, so the cost is far lower.

Note   READ COMMITTED SNAPSHOT is the feature that saved one of the major projects I worked on as version 2005 was released. We tried and tried to optimize the system under typical READ COMMITTED, but it was not possible, mostly because we had no control over the API building the queries that were used to access the database.

As an example, after setting the database setting, on Connection B we will add a new row in a transaction, but not commit it. On Connection A, we will fetch the rows of the table:

```
--CONNECTION A
SET TRANSACTION ISOLATION LEVEL READ COMMITTED;
BEGIN TRANSACTION;
SELECT ArtistId, Name FROM Art.Artist;
```

This returns the table as we had in the last section:

ArtistId	Name
1	da Vinci
2	Micheangelo
4	Picasso
5	Dali
6	Jones
7	Starr
8	McCartney
9	Vuurmann
10	Disney

```
--CONNECTION B
BEGIN TRANSACTION;
INSERT INTO Art.Artist (ArtistId, Name)
VALUES  (11, 'Freling');

--CONNECTION A
SELECT ArtistId, Name FROM Art.Artist;
```

The view on Connection A remains the same. Next, we update all of the rows, including the one we just added:

```
--CONNECTION B (still in a transaction)
UPDATE Art.Artist
SET  Name = UPPER(Name);

--CONNECTION A
SELECT ArtistId, Name FROM Art.Artist;
```

This still returns the same data. We could delete all of the rows in the transaction, and nothing would change until the transaction is committed. Commit the transaction on B; then go back and look at the data on Connection A:

```
--CONNECTION B
COMMIT;

--CONNECTION A
SELECT ArtistId, Name FROM Art.Artist;
COMMIT;
```

We see the changes in the data; then commit the transaction so we don't mess up the later demos:

```
ArtistId    Name
----------- -----------------------------
1           DAH VINCI
2           MICHEANGELO
4           PICASSO
5           DALI
6           JONES
```

7	STARR
8	MCCARTNEY
9	VOORMANN
10	DISNEY
11	FRELING

Optimistic Concurrency Enforcement in Memory-Optimized Tables

In the previous chapter, I discussed the differences between the on-disk and memory-optimized physical structures. In this chapter, we will take this farther and look at how code will be different for memory-optimized tables. While memory-optimized tables are generally meant to work with much the same code as their on-disk cousins, the internals, especially as it deals with concurrency, are quite different.

For an example, consider a table that has a column with the IDENTITY property and one that holds the country. When we first start the server and the memory-optimized tables are loaded, we have the structures like the following at timestamp 0:

TableNameId	Country	OtherColumns ...
1	USA	Values
2	USA	Values
3	Canada	Values

Next, Connection A starts a transaction at timestamp 50. Connection B starts a transaction and updates the row with TableNameId = 2 to have the Country = 'Canada'. Similar to how on-disk SNAPSHOT works and as discussed in Chapter 12, there can only be the one "dirty" row, so no other user could update that same row while Connection B is in the process. At timestamp 100, Connection B commits their transaction, but Connection A's transaction is held fast as the timestamp 50 version is still in use. So, while the live table looks like

TableNameId	Country	OtherColumns...
1	USA	Values
2	Canada	Values
3	Canada	Values

internally, there are four rows, as both views of the table that we have seen so far can be viewed by one or more users. The basic internal structure of this example is shown in Figure 12-2.

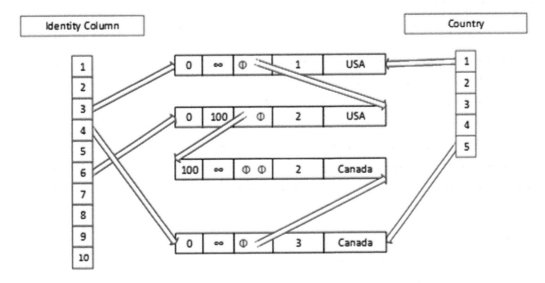

Figure 12-2. *Sample index structure at timestamp 100 and later*

Now if the user searches on Connection A, still stuck in timestamp 50 time, searching for Country = 'USA' will return two rows, and after timestamp 100, it will return one row. In these structures, Connection A will never be able to see what happens after timestamp 50, providing isolation that makes sure a user cannot change their view of the database. SNAPSHOT isolation is very similar to what we have already seen with on-disk tables, but in some cases, it is essential to be able to write code that can be affected by external transactions. Hence, there are two additional isolation levels supported: REPEATABLE READ and SERIALIZABLE. And while they provide the same phantom and repeatable read guarantees, they are implemented very differently than the on-disk version.

For reading data in REPEATABLE READ and SERIALIZABLE isolation levels, this is done at commit time to see if data has been modified or created that would change the view of the data in an incompatible way. So, if a row was deleted, it would fail at COMMIT time with an error that says there has been an isolation level issue.

Not being able to see what has occurred on other connections means that you will likely need to use the isolation levels stronger than SNAPSHOT more frequently. For example, say you want to check that a row of a certain type exists. It is impossible to know if the row is deleted or if one is inserted, and you cannot lock other users out in any manner making the impact on other connections likely to be less, since you will not be preventing them from using their view of the data. It will make certain sorts of implementations very undesirable, however. For example, implementing a queue could take lots of iterations in code, as you would have to fetch the row, do all of the work, and then roll back when you discover someone else has committed their changes using the same data.

For writing data, things get more interesting. You can only have one "dirty" version of a row that has been changed and is not committed (you can have virtually unlimited versions of committed rows with different start and stop timestamp values for users reading data). But if one connection updates a row, this row is in flux, and another connection cannot have the same situation. What this means is that something has to happen when a second connection tries to modify a row.

When multiple connections are trying to modify the same physical resource, and there can be only one, the user gets an immediate error (in the place where a pessimistic method would use blocking). Some collisions are logical in nature initially, and they are handled differently. For example, two connections insert the same value for a unique index. Until the values are actually added to the shared memory structure of the table, there is no physical collision. But when the insert occurs and the rows attempt to add duplicate values to the index, then it becomes a physical resource collision, and you will get an error. In the following sections, I will demonstrate each of these cases to make them clearer.

A term that should be introduced here is *cross-container*. The on-disk tables and in-memory tables are in the same database and can be enlisted in the same transaction, but the data for both are located in different "containers." Once you access resources in one container or another, it is part of a transaction. When you access resources in both containers (like accessing a memory-optimized table from interpreted T-SQL), it is considered cross-container. So the transaction timestamp will start once you access a memory-optimized table, not when you started your transaction, be it minutes or milliseconds ago.

For the examples, I will be using the same basic tables as we had in the previous sections on pessimistic concurrency control, but the schema will indicate that it is a memory-optimized table (note that this example only works on SQL Server 2016 or later and not the 2014 version of memory-optimized table due to multiple uniqueness constraints and foreign keys). First, add a memory-optimized filegroup to the Chapter13 database:

```
ALTER DATABASE Chapter12 ADD FILEGROUP [MemoryOptimizedFG]
                                CONTAINS MEMORY_OPTIMIZED_DATA;
ALTER DATABASE Chapter12
ADD FILE
(
   NAME= N'Chapter13_inmemFiles',
   --note, use a drive of your choice. Ideally not C: in production
   FILENAME = N'C:\temp\Chapter13InMemfiles'
)
TO FILEGROUP [MemoryOptimizedFG];
```

Then add the following new versions of the tables to the database:

```
CREATE SCHEMA Art_InMem;
GO
CREATE TABLE Art_InMem.Artist
(
    ArtistId int CONSTRAINT PKArtist PRIMARY KEY
                          NONCLUSTERED HASH  WITH (BUCKET_COUNT=100)

    --no key on value for demo purposes, just like on-disk example
    ,Name varchar(30)
    --can't use REPLICATE in memory optimized table, so will use in INSERT
    ,Padding char(4000)
) WITH ( MEMORY_OPTIMIZED = ON );

INSERT INTO Art_InMem.Artist(ArtistId, Name,Padding)
VALUES (1,'da Vinci',REPLICATE('a',4000)),
       (2,'Micheangelo',REPLICATE('a',4000)),
       (3,'Donatello',REPLICATE('a',4000)),
```

```
        (4,'Picasso',REPLICATE('a',4000)),
        (5,'Dali',REPLICATE('a',4000)),
        (6,'Jones',REPLICATE('a',4000));
GO

CREATE TABLE Art_InMem.ArtWork
(
    ArtWorkId int CONSTRAINT PKArtWork PRIMARY KEY
                            NONCLUSTERED HASH  WITH (BUCKET_COUNT=100)
    ,ArtistId int NOT NULL
        CONSTRAINT FKArtwork$wasDoneBy$Art_Artist
                            REFERENCES Art_InMem.Artist (ArtistId)
    ,Name varchar(30)
    ,Padding char(4000)
    ,CONSTRAINT AKArtwork UNIQUE NONCLUSTERED (ArtistId, Name)
) WITH ( MEMORY_OPTIMIZED = ON );

INSERT Art_InMem.Artwork (ArtworkId, ArtistId, Name,Padding)
VALUES (1,1,'Last Supper',REPLICATE('a',4000)),
        (2,1,'Mona Lisa',REPLICATE('a',4000)),
        (3,6,'Rabbit Fire',REPLICATE('a',4000));
```

We need to cover a few things before moving on. First, memory-optimized tables cannot be involved in a transaction that crosses database boundaries unless that database is tempdb or master (master in a read-only manner). So the following is prohibited:

```
INSERT INTO InMemTable
SELECT *
FROM DBOtherThanTempdb.SchemaName.Tablename;
```

This can make things interesting in some situations, particularly when building a demo database. I usually have a copy of the data held in a separate database so I can reload. But to move from a different database in T-SQL, you need to stage the data to your local database or tempdb first.

Second, when accessing memory-optimized tables in an explicit transaction, you generally need to specify the isolation level. For example, this works:

```
SELECT ArtistId, Name
FROM    Art_Inmem.Artist;
```

But if you access the object in an explicit transaction, the result will be different.

```
BEGIN TRANSACTION;
SELECT ArtistId, Name
FROM    Art_Inmem.Artist;
COMMIT TRANSACTION;
```

The following error occurs:

```
Msg 41368, Level 16, State 0, Line 667
Accessing memory optimized tables using the READ COMMITTED isolation level
is supported only for autocommit transactions. It is not supported for
explicit or implicit transactions. Provide a supported isolation level for
the memory optimized table using a table hint, such as WITH (SNAPSHOT).
```

You can allow this by using the following database level setting:

```
ALTER DATABASE Chapter12
    SET MEMORY_OPTIMIZED_ELEVATE_TO_SNAPSHOT ON;
```

However, I will for the most part (in the book and in real work) tend to specify the isolation level to make it clear and explicit, particularly when writing new code. This database setting is great when you are changing lots of code from on-disk to memory-optimized structures. There are still some limitations on what can be mixed also. For example, if you try to access the table when the connection isolation level is REPEATABLE READ

```
SET TRANSACTION ISOLATION LEVEL REPEATABLE READ
BEGIN TRANSACTION;
SELECT ArtistId, Name
FROM    Art_Inmem.Artist WITH (REPEATABLEREAD);
COMMIT TRANSACTION;
```

the following error occurs:

```
Msg 41333, Level 16, State 1, Line 684
The following transactions must access memory optimized tables and natively
compiled modules under snapshot isolation: RepeatableRead transactions,
Serializable transactions, and transactions that access tables that are not
memory optimized in RepeatableRead or Serializable isolation.
```

You need to specify the memory-optimized tables as SNAPSHOT for the on-disk engine to be using something other than READ COMMITTED, and you cannot access memory-optimized tables when in SNAPSHOT isolation level.

The following sections will first show how readers of data deal with changes to data by a different connection in SNAPSHOT, REPEATABLE READ, and SERIALIZABLE isolation levels and then show the different ways that one writer is isolated from another writer. Unlike the pessimistic strategy used for on-disk tables that almost always results in a blocking situation, there are several interesting differences in the way one writer may affect the action of another.

SNAPSHOT Isolation Level

When you read tables in SNAPSHOT isolation level, just like in the on-disk versions, no matter what happens in another connection, things just look to you like nothing ever changes.

To demonstrate, on CONNECTION A, start a transaction, and then on CONNECTION B, create a new row:

```
--CONNECTION A
BEGIN TRANSACTION;
```

```
--CONNECTION B
INSERT INTO Art_InMem.Artist(ArtistId, Name)
VALUES (7, 'McCartney');
```

Now on Connection A, look at the rows where ArtistId > 5:

```
--CONNECTION A
SELECT ArtistId, Name
FROM  Art_InMem.Artist WITH (SNAPSHOT)
WHERE ArtistId >= 5;
```

This returns the following, which matches the current state in the database. Note that McCartney was added after the transaction started, but since we had not touched data, our view of the data had not been set (or, in other words, our timestamp had not been set into the memory-optimized table's physical structure):

ArtistId	Name
7	McCartney
5	Dali
6	Jones

While the overall transaction container started when the BEGIN TRANSACTION started earlier, the memory-optimized transaction container starts when you cross the container barrier and then enlist in-memory resources. We started with three rows in Artist, so let's add a row to both tables on Connection B and delete where ArtistId = 5 and see what we can see:

```
--CONNECTION B
INSERT INTO Art_InMem.Artist(ArtistId, Name)
VALUES (8, 'Starr');

INSERT INTO Art_InMem.Artwork(ArtworkId, ArtistId, Name)
VALUES (4,7,'The Kiss');

DELETE FROM Art_InMem.Artist WHERE ArtistId = 5;
```

Back on CONNECTION A, if we read the data in the same transaction

```
--CONNECTION A
SELECT ArtistId, Name
FROM  Art_InMem.Artist WITH (SNAPSHOT)
WHERE ArtistId >= 5;

SELECT COUNT(*)
FROM  Art_InMem.Artwork WITH (SNAPSHOT);
```

the original view still persists:

```
ArtistId    Name

----------- ------------------------------

7           McCartney
5           Dali
6           Jones

-----------
3
```

If we COMMIT or ROLLBACK (we haven't made any changes, so the net effect is the same) the transaction on Connection A, our view of the data changes to what is current:

```
--CONNECTION A
COMMIT;

SELECT ArtistId, Name
FROM   Art_InMem.Artist WITH (SNAPSHOT)
WHERE  ArtistId >= 5;

SELECT COUNT(*)
FROM   Art_InMem.Artwork WITH (SNAPSHOT);
```

Our view is consistent with the current reality of three ArtistId values > 5 and four pieces of artwork in the database:

```
ArtistId    Name

----------- ------------------------------

7           McCartney
8           Starr
6           Jones

-----------
4
```

REPEATABLE READ Isolation Level

REPEATABLE READ isolation level provides the same protection using optimistic versions as it does with the pessimistic locking scheme. The difference is how you notice the change. Just like in the previous example, we will start with Connection A reading in a set of rows and then Connection B making a change. Connection B will add a row, which will cause a phantom row for Connection B, which is acceptable in REPEATABLE READ:

```
SET TRAN ISOLATION LEVEL READ COMMITTED;
--CONNECTION A
BEGIN TRANSACTION;
SELECT ArtistId, Name
FROM  Art_InMem.Artist WITH (REPEATABLEREAD)
WHERE ArtistId >= 8;
```

This returns the one row we knew existed:

ArtistId	Name
8	Starr

Now, on CONNECTION B, we insert a new row, not in an explicit transaction:

```
--CONNECTION B
INSERT INTO Art_InMem.Artist(ArtistId, Name)
VALUES (9,'Groening');
```

Then look at the row in the transaction context and commit the transaction and look again:

```
--CONNECTION A
SELECT ArtistId, Name
FROM  Art_InMem.Artist WITH (SNAPSHOT)
WHERE ArtistId >= 8;
COMMIT;

SELECT ArtistId, Name
FROM  Art_InMem.Artist WITH (SNAPSHOT)
WHERE ArtistId >= 8;
```

957

The first result set will return the same as before, but the second will have two rows. This is allowed, because phantom rows are allowed for REPEATABLE READ transactions:

ArtistId	Name
8	Starr
9	Groening

This time delete one of the rows after fetching it on CONNECTION A:

```
--CONNECTION A
BEGIN TRANSACTION;
SELECT ArtistId, Name
FROM   Art_InMem.Artist WITH (REPEATABLEREAD)
WHERE ArtistId >= 8;

--CONNECTION B
DELETE FROM Art_InMem.Artist WHERE ArtistId = 9; --Nothing against Matt!
```

No problem at all. But the problem is Connection A's view of the Artist table is not repeatable. This can be seen by the following batch:

```
--CONNECTION A
SELECT ArtistId, Name
FROM   Art_InMem.Artist WITH (SNAPSHOT)
WHERE ArtistId >= 8;
COMMIT;

SELECT ArtistId, Name
FROM   Art_InMem.Artist WITH (SNAPSHOT)
WHERE ArtistId >= 8;
```

We get two rows back, looking just like the data originally did and would as long as Connection A was in a transaction, but then we get an error message when trying to commit the transaction:

```
Msg 41305, Level 16, State 0, Line 775
The current transaction failed to commit due to a repeatable read
validation failure.
```

So, if our transaction had been open for 10 minutes, or 10 hours, the work that had been done is gone, and the entire transaction rolled back. Keeping transactions short can mitigate the cost of this, but it is certainly something to understand.

Note   When testing code in a MVCC, be careful to commit changes to check for errors. It is easy to fall into the habit from pessimistic locking methods to rollback changes and not realize that only a few situations will alert you to issues until you execute COMMIT TRANSACTION.

SERIALIZABLE Isolation Level

SERIALIZABLE isolation level behaves just like REPEATABLE READ, except that you get an error whether you are inserting, deleting, or updating a row. The following is a simple demonstration of just that:

```
--CONNECTION A
BEGIN TRANSACTION;
SELECT ArtistId, Name
FROM  Art_InMem.Artist WITH (SERIALIZABLE)
WHERE ArtistId >= 8;
```

This returns one row for 'Starr'. Add the one row on CONNECTION B:

```
--CONNECTION B
INSERT INTO Art_InMem.Artist(ArtistId, Name)
VALUES (9,'Groening'); --See, brought him back!
```

Then executing the following:

```
--CONNECTION A
SELECT ArtistId, Name
FROM  Art_InMem.Artist WITH (SNAPSHOT)
WHERE ArtistId >= 8;
COMMIT;
```

The result set will return the same one row, but the second call will fail:

```
Msg 41325, Level 16, State 0, Line 803
The current transaction failed to commit due to a serializable validation
failure.
```

Indexing is a big concern for concurrency, with memory-optimized tables as well as on-disk tables. When we created the table, we did not put a key on the Name column. What if this is a key column that you access single rows for, particularly for editing? Would this have an effect on concurrency? To see, let's fetch a row by name on Connection A:

```
--CONNECTION A
BEGIN TRANSACTION;
SELECT ArtistId, Name
FROM  Art_InMem.Artist WITH (SERIALIZABLE)
WHERE Name = 'Starr';
```

On a different connection, let's update a different row by name:

```
--CONNECTION B
UPDATE Art_InMem.Artist WITH (SNAPSHOT)
     --default to snapshot, but the change itself
     --behaves the same in any isolation level
SET    Padding = REPLICATE('a',4000) --just make a change
WHERE  Name = 'McCartney';
```

Going back to Connection A, if we try to commit

```
--CONNECTION A
COMMIT;
```

we see an error:

```
Msg 41305, Level 16, State 0, Line 825
The current transaction failed to commit due to a repeatable read
validation failure.
```

Note that the error is a repeatable read validation failure, not a serializable failure, since we updated a row. The message is a clue to what has gone wrong. If you inserted a row and there were no non-repeatable reads, the error would state the failure to be due to a serializable validation failure.

The big point, though, is that just like on-disk tables, is the rows it could touch that are serialized, not the rows that are actually returned. This is because a change to any of the rows scanned could change outcome. If you are using a column as a key, it will behoove you to add a key. This is also true of non-unique columns you frequently search with. Any chance to touch fewer rows means less likelihood of a collision and isolation validation failure:

```
ALTER TABLE Art_InMem.Artist
  ADD CONSTRAINT AKArtist UNIQUE NONCLUSTERED (Name) --A string column may
                    --be used to do ordered scans,particularly one like name
```

Repeat the experiment again, and you will see no error on the commit. While you won't see any blocking when using in-memory tables, you could see tons of issues that behave like deadlocks if you are not careful. And while deadlocks are not horrible for data integrity, they are not as great for performance as not having them.

Write Contention

In the previous sections, we looked at how readers and writers were isolated. The pattern was: read-only connections would never be blocked, would always see a consistent view of the database, and would fail at COMMIT if need be. In this section, we will now look at a less obvious set of cases that happens when a connection that is writing to the table (including updates and deletes) contends with another writing connection.

In the following examples, I will show several scenarios that will occasionally come up, such as

- Two users modify the same row.

- Two users insert a row with uniqueness collision.

- One user inserts a row that would collide with a deleted row.

Note that these are not all of scenarios that can occur, but there are some of the more interesting (and typical) things that we will see.

Two Users Delete the Same Row

When two users try to modify the same row, there is no blocking, but the method used to handle it is quick. The same effect occurs for deletes as well. For example, update the same row on Connection A and Connection B:

```
--CONNECTION A
BEGIN TRANSACTION;
UPDATE Art_InMem.Artist WITH (SNAPSHOT)
SET    Padding = REPLICATE('a',4000) --just make a change
WHERE  Name = 'McCartney';
```

Then as soon as we execute the same on Connection B (in or out of an explicit transaction)

```
--CONNECTION B
BEGIN TRANSACTION;
UPDATE Art_InMem.Artist WITH (SNAPSHOT)
SET    Padding = REPLICATE('a',4000) --just make a change
WHERE  Name = 'McCartney';
```

we are greeted with

```
Msg 41302, Level 16, State 110, Line 3
The current transaction attempted to update a record that has been updated
since this transaction started. The transaction was aborted.
Msg 3998, Level 16, State 1, Line 1
Uncommittable transaction is detected at the end of the batch. The
transaction is rolled back.
The statement has been terminated.
```

Only one "dirty" row version is allowed, so we get the immediate failure. Turns out that any combination of deletes and updates of the same physical resource will cause this to occur. Remember that a delete of a memory-optimized table row is not a removal of the resource immediately, but rather an update to the ending timestamp.

Two Users Insert a Row with Uniqueness Collision

Insert uniqueness collisions are also interesting because they are one of the few places where the issue cannot be detected until you commit because the detection of collisions is done on physical resources, not the values in data.

For example, on two connections, we will execute the following:

```
--CONNECTION A
ROLLBACK TRANSACTION --from previous example, with unique index on Name

BEGIN TRANSACTION
INSERT INTO Art_InMem.Artist (ArtistId, Name)
VALUES  (11,'Wright');

--CONNECTION B
BEGIN TRANSACTION;
INSERT INTO Art_InMem.Artist (ArtistId, Name)
VALUES  (11,'Wright');
```

Both of these actually succeed like everything is okay. Look at the data on either connection, and you will see a unique view of the data that looks essentially the same except for the surrogate key (and if the column had an IDENTITY-based column for the PRIMARY KEY column, each connection would have a different value due to autonomous transaction used for the IDENTITY value). So if two connections spin up and start inserting the same data in a large transaction, we could make a lot of new data, only to have the first connection succeed

```
--CONNECTION A
COMMIT;
```

and the second one:

```
--CONNECTION B
COMMIT;
```

Ends in a serializable failure (not a UNIQUE constraint collision, unfortunately, but it sees that there are issues of concurrency since there is a phantom row that has appeared that collides with your INSERT statement and alerts you to them). You will need to try that operation again to see that failure, after the row has been committed, and it exists when you start the transaction. If one connection never was terminated, other connections would continue to receive the row collision error message indefinitely.

One User Inserts a Row That Would Collide with a Deleted Row

The final case for this section is if one connection deletes a row, but hasn't committed, what happens if an INSERT tries to reinsert that row? This one goes against the grain of what we have seen so far, actually, but makes when compared to the previous section:

```
--CONNECTION A
BEGIN TRANSACTION;
DELETE FROM Art_InMem.Artist WITH (SNAPSHOT)
WHERE ArtistId = 4;
```

Then execute on a different connection, and insert with the same data:

```
--CONNECTION B same effect in or out of transaction, but transaction
--but transaction used later
BEGIN TRANSACTION;
INSERT INTO Art_InMem.Artist (ArtistId, Name)
VALUES (4,'Picasso');
```

This will result in a uniqueness violation, not a "Wait, someone is already working in this space" error. This is because the current, active row still exists and will until the COMMIT TRANSACTION on Connection A:

```
Msg 2627, Level 14, State 1, Line 2
Violation of UNIQUE KEY constraint 'AKArtist'. Cannot insert duplicate key
in object 'Artist'. The duplicate key value is (Picasso).
```

Now, commit Connection A's transaction, and still in a transaction for Connection B, retry the INSERT statement:

```
--CONNECTION A
COMMIT;
```

```
--CONNECTION B
INSERT INTO Art_InMem.Artist (ArtistId, Name)
VALUES (4,'Picasso');
```

Even though the row is gone from the table, you still get the UNIQUE KEY error, until you end your transaction and try again. When you end your transaction with a commit

```
--CONNECTION B
COMMIT;
```

it alerts you to the fact that your problems have been concurrency related:

```
Msg 41305, Level 16, State 0, Line 11
The current transaction failed to commit due to a repeatable read
validation failure.
```

Now on Connection B you can insert the data without problem:

```
--CONNECTION B
INSERT INTO Art_InMem.Artist (ArtistId, Name)
VALUES (4,'Picasso');--We like Picasso
```

As you can certainly see, the memory-optimized table implementation of concurrency is vastly different from the version we saw for the on-disk structures with a few interesting twists that can make multiple users affecting the same rows...tricky. However, the implementation does one thing completely different and much better than the on-disk implementation. Rather than blocking or being blocked by the other sessions, the memory-optimized engine validates data consistency at transaction commit time, throwing an exception and rolling back the transaction if rules are violated. This does, however, vastly reduce the possibility that you will stomp over changes and not realize it.

Foreign Keys

This section covers one last consideration of using the memory-optimized model of concurrency. You saw when dealing with on-disk structures that unless you were using CASCADE operations, no locks were held on the related table when you made changes. This is not the case for memory-optimized tables. When you insert a row and it checks the existence of the parent row (or vice versa), it behaves in a way that makes logical sense in that a REPEATABLE READ contract is started. However, this comes with the downside that if any part of the row is changed, you will get a failure.

For example, let's try to create a piece of artwork:

```
--CONNECTION A
BEGIN TRANSACTION
INSERT INTO Art_InMem.Artwork(ArtworkId, ArtistId, Name)
VALUES (5,4,'The Old Guitarist');
```

While we are out getting something to drink, another user changes a column on this artist row that would in no way change the meaning for our first query, because the key value still exists and has not been touched:

```
--CONNECTION B
UPDATE Art_InMem.Artist WITH (SNAPSHOT)
SET    Padding = REPLICATE('a',4000) --just make a change
WHERE ArtistId = 4;
```

Now we come back and COMMIT the transaction:

```
--CONNECTION A
COMMIT;
```

We get the following error:

```
Msg 41305, Level 16, State 0, Line 82
The current transaction failed to commit due to a repeatable read
validation failure.
```

SQL Server 2014 came out without foreign keys, because Microsoft didn't think that people who would employ such a feature made for high performance would use them. I somewhat agree, and this particular quirk in the version we have currently could make them less palatable. However, to implement your own foreign keys in code, you will need to either say "no deletes" or use REPEATABLE READ isolation level in the exact same manner. I suspect that many who need blazing performance will opt for the no delete policy, but data integrity, as I have said many times, is one of the most important considerations.

Coding for Asynchronous Contention

One of the most important considerations we need to make is how our software deals with the effects of delays in execution. So far in this chapter, I've discussed at length the different mechanisms, such as transactions, isolation levels, and so on, that SQL Server uses to protect one connection from another at a physical level. However, once your connections are not internally using the same resources, it is up to you as a programmer to make sure that the state of the data is the same when it executes as when you actually apply some changes. The time between this caching of rows could be microseconds in the case of two UPDATE statements that were blocking one another on the way to completion, or data may have been purposefully cached for days (e.g., a caching layer or just a user who opened a form made some changes and didn't click "save" until after they finished savoring their pepperoni Hot Pocket).

The general progression of events for most applications is the same: fetch some data for a user or a process to look at, operate on this data, and make changes to the data or make some decision based on the retrieved values. Once the users have performed their operations, they may make some additional database changes based on what they have seen.

For example, consider a customer row in a call center. It is a low probability that two people with access to the same account are calling into your sales call center on two lines talking to two different agents, making changes to the same account. But that low probability is not zero probability that two changes will be made to the same row simultaneously, perhaps by a system process. Another example is an inventory level. You check to see how many widgets are available and then offer to sell one to the customer. Even if there were 1,000 items there a moment before, you will still check as you save the order to ensure that is still the case.

The idea of optimistic change detection is basically the same as it is for SQL Server's MVCC mechanisms, except now we need to deal with asynchronous changes to data, not the synchronous ones that SQL Server handles. The problem for us programmers is that every synchronous contention issue turns into an asynchronous one. User A updates row R at the same time that User B updates row R, and one is turned away or blocked. Particularly when using locks, as User B was blocked, the person issuing the query would not ever know that the row had change, or even felt the latency if it lasted 10 milliseconds. But the row may have changed, and the second update could blow away the changes.

There are generally four ways this asynchronous timing issue is handled:

- *Chaos*: Just let it happen. If two users modify the same row in the database, the last user wins. This is not generally the best idea for most types of data, as the first user might have had something important to say and this method rejects the first user's changes. I won't cover this any further because it's straightforward and generally undesirable.

- *Row based*: Protect your data at the row level by checking to see if the rows being modified have the exact same values as in the table. If not, reject the operation, and have the interface refresh the data from the table, showing the user what was changed.

- *Logical unit of work*: A logical unit of work is used to group a parent row with all its child data to allow a single optimistic lock to cover multiple tables. For example, you'd group an invoice and the line items for that invoice. Treat modifications to the line items the same way as a modification to the invoice, for change detection purposes.

- *Reality/hybrid*: The reality of this situation is that if you are modifying many, perhaps even thousands of, rows, caching state, and then checking to see if you had the same thousands of rows, it may not always be reasonable to check. Most of the time this is a matter of performance in that adding another join to the cache of data isn't reasonable. In a true OLTP database, most large updates are done as maintenance during down time, so this may not be an issue. Using MVCC can also alleviate these issues because it will not let users change your data without failing in the end if you use the right isolation level.

Although it isn't typically a good idea to ignore the problem of users overwriting one another altogether, this is a commonly *decided*-upon method. Realistically, the best plan is optimally a mixture of the row-based solution for most tables and a logical unit of work for major groups of tables that make up some common object.

In the following sections, I'll cover row-based locking and the logical unit of work. The unchecked method ignores the concern that two people might modify the same row twice, so there's no coding (or thinking!) required.

Row-Based Change Detection

A row-based scheme is used to check every row as to whether or not the data that the user has retrieved is still the same as the one that's in the database. The order of events is fetch data to a cache, modify data in a cached copy, check to see that the row (or rows) of data is still the same as it was, and then commit the changes.

There are three common methods to implement row-based optimistic locking:

- *Check all columns in the row*: If you cannot modify the table structure, which the next two methods require, you can check to make sure that all the data you had fetched is still the same and then modify the data. This method is the most difficult, because any modification procedure you write must check previous values of the data, which can be tedious (particularly when NULL values are included). If you have any large datatypes with large values, this method can be terrifically slow. Checking all columns is typical when building bound data-grid types of applications, where there are direct updates to tables, especially if not all tables can follow the rather strict rules of the next two methods. Alternatively, using a hash or checksum of all the columns stored along with the data can be used as well.

- *Add a row-modified time column to the table*: Set the point in time value when the row is inserted and subsequently updated. Every update to the table is required to modify the value in the table to set the column that indicates when the row was last modified. Generally, it's best to use a trigger for keeping the column up to date (as done in Chapter 7), and often, it's nice to include a column to tell which user last modified the data (you need someone to blame in the "The row you are trying to modify has changed and was last modified by drsql").

- *Use a* rowversion *(previously known as* timestamp*) column*: In the previous method, a manually controlled value is used to manage the optimistic lock value. This method uses a column with a rowversion datatype. The rowversion datatype automatically gets a new value for every command used to modify a given row in a table. This is by far the easiest method of adding version checks to your data.

The next two sections cover adding the optimistic lock columns to your tables and then using them in your code.

Adding Validation Columns

In this section, we'll add a column to a table to support adding either the datetime2 column or the rowversion column. As an example, let's create a new simple table, Hr.Person. Here's the structure:

```
CREATE SCHEMA Hr;
GO
CREATE TABLE Hr.person
(
    PersonId int IDENTITY(1,1) CONSTRAINT PKPerson PRIMARY KEY,
    FirstName varchar(60) NOT NULL,
    MiddleName varchar(60) NOT NULL,
    LastName varchar(60) NOT NULL,

    DateOfBirth date NOT NULL,
    RowLastModifyTime datetime2(3) NOT NULL
        CONSTRAINT DFLTPerson_RowLastModifyTime DEFAULT (SYSDATETIME()),
    RowModifiedByUserIdentifier nvarchar(128) NOT NULL
        CONSTRAINT DFLTPerson_RowModifiedByUserIdentifier
                                            DEFAULT (SUSER_SNAME())
);
```

Note the two columns added for our optimistic lock, named RowLastModifyTime and RowModifiedByUserIdentifier. We'll use these to hold the last date and time of modification and the SQL Server's login name of the principal that changed the row. There are a couple ways to implement this:

- *Let the manipulation layer manage the value like any other column*:
  This is often what client programmers like to do, and it's acceptable, as long as you're using trusted computers to manage the timestamps. I feel it's inadvisable to allow workstations to set such values, because it can cause confusing results. For example, say your application displays a message stating that another user has made changes

and the time the changes were made is in the future, based on the client's computer. Then the user checks out their PC clock, and it's set perfectly.

- *Using SQL Server code*: For the most part, use a TRIGGER object to fire on any modification to data and set the values. It can be done in STORED PROCEDURE objects, but it must be meticulously managed and tested that changes occur far more than if done by triggers.

As an example of using SQL Server code (my general method of doing this), implement an INSTEAD OF trigger on the UPDATE of the Hr.Person table:

```
CREATE TRIGGER Hr.Person$InsteadOfUpdateTrigger
ON Hr.Person
INSTEAD OF UPDATE AS
BEGIN
   --stores the number of rows affected
  DECLARE @rowsAffected int = @@rowcount,
          @msg varchar(2000) = '';     --used to hold the error message

    --no need to continue on if no rows affected
  IF @rowsAffected = 0 RETURN;

  SET NOCOUNT ON; --to avoid the rowcount messages
  SET ROWCOUNT 0; --in case the client has modified the rowcount

  BEGIN TRY
          --[validation blocks]
          --[modification blocks]
          --remember to update ALL columns when building
          --instead of triggers
          UPDATE Hr.Person
          SET    FirstName = inserted.FirstName,
                 MiddleName = inserted.MiddleName,
                 LastName = inserted.LastName,
                 DateOfBirth = inserted.DateOfBirth,
                 -- set the values to the default
                 RowLastModifyTime = DEFAULT,
                 RowModifiedByUserIdentifier = DEFAULT
```

971

```
            FROM    Hr.Person
                        JOIN inserted
                                ON Person.PersonId = inserted.PersonId;
    END TRY
        BEGIN CATCH
                IF XACT_STATE() > 0
                    ROLLBACK TRANSACTION;
                THROW;
        END CATCH;
END;
```

Then, insert a row into the table:

```
INSERT INTO Hr.Person (FirstName, MiddleName, LastName, DateOfBirth)
VALUES ('Paige','O','Anxtent','19691212');

SELECT *
FROM    Hr.Person;
```

Now, you can see that the data has been created:

PersonId	FirstName	MiddleName	LastName	DateOfBirth
1	Paige	O	Anxtent	1969-12-12

RowLastModifyTime	RowModifiedByUserIdentifier
2020-06-18 23:08:10.526	SomeUserName

Next, update the row:

```
UPDATE Hr.Person
SET    MiddleName = 'Ona'
WHERE  PersonId = 1;

SELECT @@ROWCOUNT as RowsAffected; --if 0, then throw error to retry

SELECT RowLastModifyTime
FROM    Hr.Person;
```

You should see that the update date has changed:

```
RowsAffected
--------------------
1

RowLastModifyTime
--------------------
2020-06-18 23:09:12.453
```

If you want to set the value on INSERT or implement RowCreatedBy -Date or -UserIdentifier columns, the code would be similar. Because this has been implemented in an INSTEAD OF trigger, the user or even the programmer cannot overwrite the values, even if they include it in the column list of an UPDATE (typically I will add an INSTEAD OF INSERT TRIGGER, but will not for brevity, and I trust the programmer in this case to not set funky times for the insert).

Then check to see if the row has been modified and handle it if it hasn't, just as I will do in this next version using a rowversion column. In my opinion, this is the best way to go (note that the rowversion datatype is not supported in memory-optimized tables, and as I show in the downloads for Chapter 7, triggers are possible (if tricky) for memory-optimized tables for change detection columns), and I almost always use a rowversion when implementing an optimistic mechanism. I usually have the row modification time and user columns on tables as well, for the user's benefit. I find that the modification columns take on other uses (which I have suggested against several times in the book!) and tend to migrate to the control of the application developer, and rowversion columns never do. Plus, even if the triggers don't make it on the table for one reason or another, the rowversion column continues to work. Sometimes, you may be prohibited from using INSTEAD OF TRIGGER objects for some reason, but an AFTER TRIGGER object is usually not a problem (recently, I couldn't use them in a project I worked on because they invalidated the IDENTITY functions which were important to the programmers).

Let's add a rowversion column to our table to demonstrate using it as an optimistic lock:

```
ALTER TABLE Hr.person
     ADD RowVersion rowversion;
GO
SELECT PersonId, RowVersion
FROM   Hr.Person;
```

You can see now that the rowversion has been added and magically set:

PersonId	RowVersion
1	0x00000000000007D1

Now, when the row is updated, the rowversion is modified:

```
UPDATE  Hr.Person
SET     FirstName = 'Paige' --no actual change occurs
WHERE   PersonId = 1;
```

Then, looking at the output, you can see that the value of the rowversion has changed:

```
SELECT PersonId, RowVersion
FROM   Hr.Person;
```

This returns the following result:

PersonId	RowVersion
1	0x00000000000007D2

Caution   The rowversion datatype is an ever-increasing binary value, so it can be useful for determining changes in the database after a particular rowversion value.

Coding for Row-Level Change Detection

Next, let's look at the code to check for changes. Using the Hr.Person table previously created, the following code snippets will demonstrate each of the methods (note that I'll only use the optimistic locking columns germane to each example and won't include the others).

Check all the cached values for the columns:

```
UPDATE  Hr.Person
SET     FirstName = 'Headley'
WHERE   PersonId = 1
  --include the key, even when changing the key value if allowed
  --non-key columns
  and   FirstName = 'Paige' --Note, when columns allow NULL values, must
  and   MiddleName = 'ona'  --take extra precautions if using compiled code
  and   LastName = 'Anxtent'
  and   DateOfBirth = '19691212';
```

It's a good practice to check your @@ROWCOUNT value after an update with an optimistic lock to see how many rows have changed. If it is 0, you could check to see if the row exists with that primary key:

```
IF EXISTS ( SELECT *
            FROM   Hr.Person
            WHERE  PersonId = 1) --check for existence of the primary key
  --raise an error stating that the row no longer exists
ELSE
  --raise an error stating that another user has changed the row
```

Using the RowLastModifyTime datetime2 column, add it to the WHERE clause:

```
UPDATE  Hr.Person
SET     FirstName = 'Fred'
WHERE   PersonId = 1   --include the key
  AND   RowLastModifyTime = '2020-06-18 23:09:12.453';
```

Using a `rowversion` column, do the same, and add the `RowVersion` column to the WHERE clause:

```
UPDATE  Hr.Person
SET     FirstName = 'Fred'
WHERE   PersonId = 1
  and   RowVersion = 0x00000000000007D4;
```

Which is better performance-wise? One of these generally performs just as well as the other (unless you have very large columns in the first case!), because in all cases, you're going to be using the PRIMARY KEY index (usually clustered) to do the bulk of the work fetching the row and then your update.

Deletions use the same WHERE clause, because if another user has modified the row, it's probably a good idea to see if that user's changes make the row still valuable:

```
DELETE FROM Hr.Person
WHERE   PersonId = 1
  And   Rowversion = 0x00000000000007D5;
```

However, in each of these cases, if one of the indicators have changed since the last time the row was fetched, this would delete zero rows, since if someone has modified the rows since you last touched them, perhaps the deleted row now has value. I typically prefer using a `rowversion` column because it requires the least amount of work to always work perfectly. On the other hand, many client programmers prefer to have the manipulation layer of the application set a `datetime2` value, largely because the `datetime2` value has meaning to them to let them see when the row was last updated. Truthfully, I too like keeping these automatically modifying values in the table for diagnostic purposes. However, I prefer to rely on the `rowversion` column for checking for changes because it is far simpler and safer and cannot be overridden by any code, no matter how you implement the other columns.

Coding for Logical Unit of Work Change Detection

Although row-based optimistic change checks are helpful, they do have a slight downfall. In many cases, several tables together make one "object." A good example is an invoice with line items. The idea behind a logical unit of work is that, instead of having a row-based lock on the invoice and all the line items, you might only implement one on the invoice and use the same value for the line items. This strategy does require that the code always fetch not only the invoice line items but at least the invoice's timestamp into the client's cache when dealing with the invoice line items. Assuming you're using a rowversion column, I'd just use the same kind of logic as previously used on the Hr. Person table. In this example, we'll build the procedure to do the modifications.

When the user wants to insert, update, or delete line items for the invoice, the procedure requires the @ObjectVersion parameter and checks the value against the invoice, prior to update. Consider that there are two tables, minimally defined as follows:

```
CREATE SCHEMA Invoicing;
GO
--leaving off who invoice is for, like an account or person name
CREATE TABLE Invoicing.Invoice
(
    InvoiceId int IDENTITY(1,1),
    Number varchar(20) NOT NULL,
    ObjectVersion rowversion NOT NULL,
    CONSTRAINT PKInvoice PRIMARY KEY (InvoiceId)
);
--also ignoring what product that the line item is for
CREATE TABLE Invoicing.InvoiceLineItem

(
    InvoiceLineItemId int NOT NULL,
    InvoiceId int NOT NULL,
    ItemCount int NOT NULL,
    CostAmount int NOT NULL,
    CONSTRAINT PKInvoiceLineItem primary key (InvoiceLineItemId),
    CONSTRAINT FKInvoiceLineItem$references$Invoicing_Invoice
        FOREIGN KEY (InvoiceId) REFERENCES Invoicing.Invoice(InvoiceId)
);
```

For our delete procedure for the invoice line item, the parameters would have the key of the invoice and the line item, plus the rowversion value:

```
CREATE PROCEDURE InvoiceLineItem$Delete
(
    @InvoiceId int, --we pass this because the client should have it
                    --with the invoiceLineItem row
    @InvoiceLineItemId int,
    @ObjectVersion rowversion
) as
  BEGIN
    BEGIN TRY
        BEGIN TRANSACTION;

        --tweak the ObjectVersion on the Invoice Table
        UPDATE  Invoicing.Invoice
        SET     Number = Number
        WHERE   InvoiceId = @InvoiceId
          And   ObjectVersion = @ObjectVersion;

        IF @@ROWCOUNT = 0
          BEGIN
            IF NOT EXISTS ( SELECT *
            FROM   Invoicing.Invoice
            WHERE  InvoiceId = 1)
            THROW 50000,'The InvoiceId has been deleted',1;
ELSE
            THROW 50000,'The InvoiceId has been changed',1;

        DELETE  Invoicing.InvoiceLineItem
        FROM    InvoiceLineItem
        WHERE   InvoiceLineItemId = @InvoiceLineItemId;

        COMMIT TRANSACTION;

    END TRY
     BEGIN CATCH
          IF @@TRANCOUNT > 0
```

```
        ROLLBACK TRANSACTION;

        --will halt the batch or be caught by the caller's catch block
        THROW;
    END CATCH;
END;
```

Instead of checking the RowVersion on an InvoiceLineItem row, we check the RowVersion (in the ObjectVersion column) on the Invoice table. Additionally, we must update the RowVersion value on the Invoice table when we make our change, so we update the Invoice row, simply setting a single column to the same value. There's a bit more overhead when working this way, but it's normal to update multiple rows at a time from the client.

Best Practices

The number one issue when it comes to concurrency is data quality. Maintaining consistent data is why you go through the work of building a database in the first place. Generally speaking, if the only way to get consistent results was to have every call single-threaded, it would be worth it. Of course, we don't have to do that except in rare situations, and SQL Server gives us tools to make it happen with the isolation levels. Use them as needed. It's the data that matters.

- *Use transactions as liberally as needed*: It's important to protect your data, 100% of the time. Each time data is modified, enclosing the operation in an explicit transaction isn't a bad practice. This gives you a chance to check status, number of rows modified, and so on and, if necessary, to roll back the modification.

- *Keep transactions as short as possible*: The flip side to the previous bullet is to keep transactions short. The smaller the transaction, the less chance there is of it holding locks or causing optimistic locking collisions. Make sure that all table access within transactions is required to be executed as an atomic operation, or pull the code out of the transaction.

- *Recognize the difference between hardware limitations and SQL Server concurrency issues*: If the hardware is maxed out (excessive disk queuing, 90%-plus CPU usage, etc.), consider adding more hardware. However, if you're single-threading calls through your database because of locking issues (possibly due to doing too many un-indexed searches), you could add 20 processors and a terabyte of RAM and still see less improvement than adding a few indexes and changing some code.

- *Fetch all rows from a query as fast as possible*: Depending on the isolation level and editability of the rows being returned, locks held can interfere with other users' ability to modify or even read rows. Even when you are reading data in READ COMMITTED isolation level, there is locking overhead as each row is touched.

- *Make sure that all queries use reasonable execution plans*: The better all queries execute, the faster the queries will execute, and it follows that locks will be held for a shorter amount of time. Remember too that scans will generally require every row of a table or index to be locked at some point, whereas a seek will lock far fewer rows.

- *Use some form of optimistic locking mechanism in almost all of your code*: This is to handle when rows have changed between the time you cached it and the actual operation happens, preferably using a rowversion column, because it requires the smallest amount of coding and is managed entirely by SQL Server. Whether the difference in time is a millisecond or a day, it is important to make sure you are updating the row you expected.

- *Consider using some form of the* SNAPSHOT *isolation level*: For on-disk structures, either code all your optimistic-locked retrieval operations with SET SNAPSHOT ISOLATION LEVEL or change the database setting for READ_COMMITTED_SNAPSHOT to ON. This alters how the READ COMMITTED isolation level reads snapshot information at the statement level. All memory-optimized table access is in a flavor of snapshot. Be careful to test existing applications if you're going to make this change, because these settings do alter how SQL Server works and might negatively affect how your programs work.

Summary

Concurrency is a juggling act for SQL Server, Windows, the disk system, the CPUs, and so on. Making computer resources feel like multitudes of users are all important is hard. Concurrency is one of the fun jobs for a DBA, because it's truly a science that has a good deal of artsy qualities, and testing concurrency issues is complicated. You can predict only so much about how your user will use the system, and then experience comes in to tune queries, tune hardware, and tweak settings until you have them right.

I discussed some of the basics of how SQL Server implements controls to support concurrent programming, such that many users can be supported using the same data with locks and transactions. Then, I covered isolation levels and how they are implemented in each of the fundamental concurrency methods available to us in SQL Server. Understanding how to tweak the kinds of locks taken and how long they're held on a resource is important, in addition to understanding how adding in multiversion concurrency control (MVCC) in small doses or fully implemented changes how isolation is implemented, but does not change the fundamentals of isolation.

The most important thing to understand about concurrency was covered throughout the chapter, and that is understanding asynchronous change detection. It was covered in some detail in the section "Coding for Asynchronous Contention" and applies not only to when you explicitly implement optimistic locking but even in pessimistic locking as well. Because the trend for implementing systems is to use cached data sets, modify that set, and then flush it back, you must make sure that other users haven't made changes to the data while it's cached. But having two transactions modifying the same row, one modification blocked behind the changes of another modifier, is the exact same scenario. Are you modifying the same row you originally thought you were? It is essential to make sure for your data's sake.

CHAPTER 13

Coding Architecture

Architecture should speak of its time and place, but yearn for timelessness.

Frank Gehry, Architect

Here we are, at the end of the journey. So far in the book, we started with how one should design a database without regard for technology and then covered how one might implement, tune, and secure that database using much of what SQL Server has to offer. So far, the process has been one of building with one precept upon another. We have a database, and we know how to write T-SQL that is generally optimum for an OLTP system. In this chapter, I am going to approach the problem of how to put together a consistent, testable interface to deliver value to customers.

Hence, in this chapter, I am going to touch on a few final topics surrounding the process of building code to access the database and creating reusable components that can be used at the coding layer to make the process of accessing and using the database much easier:

- *Architecting your data access layer*: Or more generally, how best to architect your systems to provide the least amount of coupling with your application code.

- *Building reusable components*: Every database needs similar tools to do similar things. For example, a table of numbers can be very helpful. In this section, I will discuss how best to architect this sort of solution.

Following this chapter, in the epilogue, will be another set of topics that go beyond what I can cover in this book, in terms of releasing software and reporting on data. Those topics are so large as to fill entire books with more pages than I have in this book (not just to spare, in total).

© Louis Davidson 2021
L. Davidson, *Pro SQL Server Relational Database Design and Implementation*,
https://doi.org/10.1007/978-1-4842-6497-3_13

Building the Data Access Layer

After the database has been created and released into the wild for the programmers, the next thing that occurs is that a data access layer will be created. It is a really important choice that the data architect will ideally help guide, though it is rarely given much of a thought as to how to build this in the best way possible. Usually it will be defaulted to what is easiest or whatever the toolset the programmers know (or, worse yet, what each individual programmer knows) for creating an application. This won't necessarily be an immediate problem for smaller applications, but if you are pushing up on any limitations of size, hardware, and so on, the choice (or, at least, how well you implement the choice) becomes more crucial.

As an organization grows and more applications are created, there tends to be a proliferation of different ways the same kind of application is being created, and hence the more difficult they become to maintain. Perhaps even worse is when you have a standard that every application follows but have an application that actually would greatly benefit from a different development pattern. Yes, a lack of standardization is a serious problem as much as an unbending devotion to a standard.

This variance of needs is why it is essential for an architect to think about the architectural building blocks and make sure that a number of things are matched up when building any application:

- *Technical needs*: What does your application really need? Amazing throughput? Massive data quantities? Perfect data integrity? Ease of change?

- *Human abilities*: My personal feeling is to never limit what tech you use to the abilities of the staff that has been hired, but not everyone can do everything. Plus, some methods of architecting the code layer for a system are more time consuming, no matter the programmer.

- *Tools*: What tools will the programmers who are building the front end be using? Very few data architects will smile happily when the three letters ORM (object-relational mapping) are uttered, but ORM tools are popular and very useful if used correctly.

- *Existing standards*: Changing a standard for a special need can make maintenance more complex, so it is important to decide if it is worth the risk. However, as we have covered up to now in the book, particularly in chapters like the one on concurrency (Chapter 12), we must tailor our design to the need of the application, workload, and so on, and sometimes that means more work.

In this section, I will provide a brief overview of some of the architectural decisions you need to make when choosing how to architect your data layer, along with the pros and cons of the typical choices—in other words, "opinions" (technical-based opinions, but opinions nevertheless). Regardless of whether your application is an old-fashioned, client-server application or a multi-tier web application, based on an ORM technology, that uses some new application pattern that hasn't been created yet as this book goes to print or uses a pattern I simply haven't heard of, data must be stored in and retrieved from tables efficiently and with as much integrity as the situation requires.

In this section, I will present a number of my own opinions on how to use stored procedures and ad hoc SQL. Each of these opinions is based on years of experience working with SQL Server technologies, but I am not so set in my ways that I cannot see the point of the people on the other side of any fence—anyone whose mind cannot be changed is no longer learning. So, if you disagree with this chapter, feel free to email me at louis@drsql.org; you won't hurt my feelings, and if your mind is open to different ideas, we will both probably end up learning something in the process (and you may end up with a credit in the next edition of this book).

I will discuss the two high-level patterns of T-SQL application building:

- *Using ad hoc SQL*: Forming queries in the application's presentation and manipulation layer (typically procedural code stored in objects, such as .NET, Java, JavaScript, and so on, and run on a server or a client machine).

- *Using a T-SQL coded encapsulation layer*: Creating an interface between the presentation/manipulation layer and the data layer of the application. Typically, this would be mostly STORED PROCEDURE objects, which are what we will focus on, but it could be a layer of VIEW and TABLE-VALUED FUNCTION objects as well.

Each section will analyze some of the pros and cons of each approach, in terms of flexibility, security, performance, and so on. Along the way, I'll offer some personal opinions on optimal architecture and give advice on how best to implement both types of access.

Note   I previously mentioned ORM tools (examples of which include Hibernate, Spring, Entity Framework, etc.), so you might be thinking that I'm going to cover them in this chapter. In the end, these tools are typically using ad hoc access to the data in that they are generating T-SQL and executing it. For the sake of this book, they should be considered ad hoc SQL, unless they are used with STORED PROCEDURE objects (which is pretty rare).

The most difficult part of a discussion of this sort is that the actual arguments that go on are not so much about right and wrong, better and worse, but rather the question of which method is *easier* to program and maintain. Visual Studio .NET and other application development tools give you lots of handy-dandy tools to build your applications, mapping objects to data, and as the years pass, this becomes even truer.

The problem is that these tools don't always take enough advantage of SQL Server's best practices to build applications in their most common form of usage. Doing things in a best practice manner would mean doing a lot of coding manually, without the ease of simple, industry-standard automated tools to help you. Some organizations do this manual work with great results, but such work is rarely going to be popular with developers who have never had to support an application that is extremely hard to optimize once the system is in production. This is made even more problematic because early in the lifecycle of an application, when data size and user counts are reasonably low, the way an application behaves will be different than 5–10 years later, when you have many more users and 5–10 years more data accumulated.

A point that I really should make clear is that I feel that the choice of data access strategy shouldn't be linked to the methods used for data validation nor should it be linked to whether you use (or how much you use) FOREIGN KEY and CHECK constraints, TRIGGER objects, and the like. If you have read the entire book, you should be kind of tired of hearing how much I feel that you should do every possible data validation on the SQL Server data that can be done without making a maintenance nightmare. Fundamental data rules that are cast in stone should be done on the database server in constraints and triggers at all times so that these rules can be trusted by *any* user (e.g., an ETL process that doesn't use the custom-built UI). On the other hand, client code and perhaps stored procedures will be used to implement a lot of the same rules for ease of use, plus all of the mutable business rules too for the user's benefit.

In either situation, non–data-tier rules can be easily circumvented by using a different access path. Even database rules can be circumvented using bulk loading tools, so be careful there too.

Note   While I stand by all of the concepts and opinions in this entire book (typos not withstanding), I definitely do not suggest that your educational journey end here. Please read other people's work, try out everything, and form your own opinions. If someday you end up writing a competitive book to mine, the worst thing that happens is that people have another resource to turn to.

Using Ad Hoc SQL

Ad hoc SQL is sometimes referred to as "straight SQL" and generally refers to the formulation of DML statements such as `SELECT`, `INSERT`, `UPDATE`, and `DELETE` statements (as well as any DDL statements like `CREATE  TABLE`) in the client. These statements are then sent to SQL Server either individually or in batches of multiple statements to be syntax checked, compiled, optimized, and executed, usually letting some piece of software write queries. SQL Server may use a cached plan from a previous execution, but it will have to pretty much exactly match the text of one call to another to do so (the only difference can be some parameterization of literals, which we will discuss a little later in the chapter). The software can also compile the ad hoc SQL into a temporary reusable plan if it is going to be reusing that same query multiple times, more or less writing its own `STORED  PROCEDURE` object, though without formally doing so.

I will make no distinction between ad hoc calls that are generated manually and those that use a middleware setup like any ORM for this section's purpose: from SQL Server's standpoint, a string of characters is sent to the server by your code and interpreted (at least once) at runtime. So whether your method of generating these statements is good or poor is of no concern to me in *this* discussion, as long as the SQL generated is well formed and protected from users' malicious actions. For example, injection attacks are generally the biggest offender. The reason I don't care where the ad hoc statements come from is that the advantages and disadvantages for the database support professionals are pretty much the same, and in fact, statements generated from a middleware tool can be worse, because you may not be able to change the format or makeup of the statements, leaving you with no easy way to tune statements, even if you can modify the source code.

987

Sending queries as strings of text is the way that plenty of tools tend to converse with SQL Server and is, for example, how SSMS and other toolsets interact with the server metadata. (To be fair, that metadata is typically a layer of views on top of objects that are hidden from our view, so Microsoft can change the implementation without changing our view of the system metadata.) If you have never used Extended Events to watch the SQL that any of the management and development tools use, you should; just don't use it as your guide for building your OLTP system as it is some crazy code. It is, however, a good way to learn where some bits of metadata that you can't figure out come from.

There's no question that users will perform some ad hoc queries against your system, especially when you simply want to write a query and execute it just once. However, the more pertinent question is: should you be using ad hoc SQL when building the permanent interface to an OLTP system's data?

Note   This topic doesn't include ad hoc SQL statements executed from stored procedures (commonly called dynamic SQL), which I'll discuss in the section "Stored Procedure or Ad Hoc?"

Ad Hoc SQL Advantages

Using non-precompiled and non-pretested ad hoc SQL in application code has the following advantages over building compiled stored procedures:

- *Runtime control over queries*: Queries are built at runtime, without having to know every possible query that might be executed. This can lead to better performance as queries can be formed at runtime, meaning the query need only be as complex as it is, not as complex as the most complex case you are trying to solve. Additionally, you can retrieve only necessary data for SELECT queries or modify only data that's changed for UPDATE operations.

- *Flexibility over shared plans and parameterization*: Because you have control over the queries, you can more easily build queries at runtime that use the same plans and even can be parameterized as desired, based on the situation.

There is one more advantage that will not get its own section but is really the primary advantage: flexibility. The T-SQL needed to manipulate the database needn't be written; it can be generated by an application, saving a lot of up-front time.

Runtime Control over Queries

Unlike STORED PROCEDURE objects, which are prebuilt and stored in the SQL Server system tables, ad hoc SQL is formed at the time it's needed: at runtime. Hence, it doesn't suffer from some of the inflexible requirements of stored procedures. For example, say you want to build a user interface to a list of customers. You can add several columns to the SELECT clause, based on the tables listed in the FROM clause. It's simple to build a list of columns into the user interface that the user can use to customize their own list. Then the program can issue the list request with only the columns in the SELECT list that are requested by the user. Because some columns might be large and contain quite a bit of data, it's better to send back only the columns that the user really desires instead of a bunch of columns the user doesn't care about.

For instance, consider that you have the following table to document contacts to prospective customers (it's barebones for this example). In each query, you might return the primary key but show or not show it to the user based on whether the primary key is implemented as a surrogate or natural key—key type isn't important to our example either way. You can create this table in any database you like. In the sample code, I've created a database named Chapter13 in the downloads:

```
CREATE SCHEMA Sales;
GO
CREATE TABLE Sales.Contact
(
    ContactId   int NOT NULL CONSTRAINT PKContact PRIMARY KEY,
    FirstName   varchar(30) NOT NULL,
    LastName    varchar(30) NOT NULL,
    CompanyName varchar(100) NOT NULL,
    SalesLevelId  int NOT NULL, --real table would implement
                                --as a foreign key
    ContactNotes  varchar(max) NULL,
    CONSTRAINT AKContact UNIQUE (FirstName, LastName, CompanyName)
);
```

```
--a few rows to show some output from queries
INSERT INTO Sales.Contact
          (ContactId, FirstName, Lastname, CompanyName, SaleslevelId,
ContactNotes)
VALUES( 1,'Drue','Karry','SeeBeeEss',1,
          REPLICATE ('Blah...',10) + 'Called and discussed new ideas'),
      ( 2,'Jon','Rettre','Daughter Inc',2,
          REPLICATE ('Yada...',10) + 'Called, but he had passed on');
```

One user might want to see the person's name and the company, plus the end of the ContactNotes, in their view of the data:

```
SELECT  ContactId, FirstName, LastName, CompanyName,
        RIGHT(ContactNotes,28) AS NotesEnd
FROM    Sales.Contact;
```

So this is something like

ContactId	FirstName	LastName	CompanyName	NotesEnd
1	Drue	Karry	SeeBeeEss	lled and discussed new ideas
2	Jon	Rettre	Daughter Inc	Called, but he had passed on

Another user might want (or need) to see less:

```
SELECT ContactId, FirstName, LastName, CompanyName
FROM Sales.Contact;
```

This returns

ContactId	FirstName	LastName	CompanyName
1	Drue	Karry	SeeBeeEss
2	Jon	Rettre	Daughter Inc

And yet another user may want to see all columns in the table, plus maybe some additional information. Allowing the user to choose the columns for output can be useful. Consider how the file-listing dialog works in Windows, as shown in Figure 13-1.

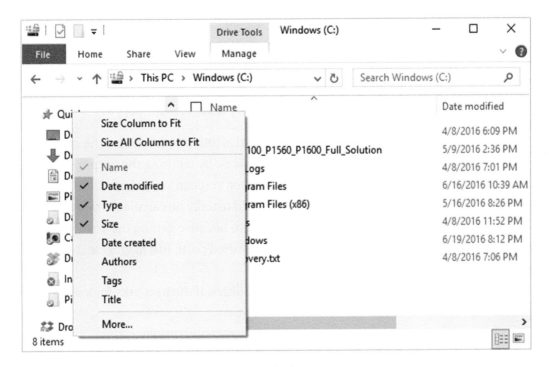

Figure 13-1. *The Windows file-listing dialog*

You can see as many or as few of the attributes of a file in the list as you like, based on some metadata you set on the directory. This is a useful method of letting the users choose what they want to see. But let's take this one step further. Consider that the Contact table is then related to a table that tells us if that contact has purchased something:

```
CREATE TABLE Sales.Purchase
(
    PurchaseId int  NOT NULL CONSTRAINT PKPurchase PRIMARY KEY,
    Amount numeric(10,2) NOT NULL,
    PurchaseDate date NOT NULL,
    ContactId   int NOT NULL
        CONSTRAINT FKContact$hasPurchasesIn$Sales_Purchase
            REFERENCES Sales.Contact(ContactId)
);
```

```
INSERT INTO Sales.Purchase(PurchaseId, Amount, PurchaseDate, ContactId)
VALUES (1,100.00,'2020-05-12',1),(2,200.00,'2020-05-10',1),
       (3,100.00,'2020-05-12',2),(4,300.00,'2020-05-12',1),
       (5,100.00,'2020-04-11',1),(6,5500.00,'2020-05-14',2),
       (7,100.00,'2020-04-01',1),(8,1020.00,'2020-06-03',2);
```

Now consider that you want to calculate the sales totals and dates for the contact and add these columns to the allowed pool of choices. By tailoring the output when transmitting the results of the query back to the user, you can save bandwidth, CPU, and disk I/O. As I've stressed, values such as this should usually be calculated rather than stored, especially when working on an OLTP system because getting the answer right is never a matter of whether some external code executed right. Just aggregate the data and present.

In this case, consider the following two possibilities. If the user asks for a sales summary column, the client will send the whole query:

```
SELECT  Contact.ContactId, Contact.FirstName, Contact.LastName
        ,Sales.YearToDateSales, Sales.LastSaleDate
FROM    Sales.Contact as Contact
           LEFT OUTER JOIN
               (SELECT ContactId,
                       SUM(Amount) AS YearToDateSales,
                       MAX(PurchaseDate) AS LastSaleDate
               FROM    Sales.Purchase
               WHERE   PurchaseDate >= --the first day of the current year
                           DATEADD(day, 0, DATEDIFF(day, 0, SYSDATETIME() )
                             - DATEPART(dayofyear,SYSDATETIME() ) + 1)
               GROUP   by ContactId) AS sales
               ON Contact.ContactId = Sales.ContactId
WHERE   Contact.LastName like 'Rett%';
```

This returns the following:

ContactId	FirstName	LastName	YearToDateSales	LastSaleDate
2	Jon	Rettre	6620.00	2020-06-03

If the user doesn't ask for a sales summary column, the client will send only the code that is not commented out in the following query:

```
SELECT  Contact.ContactId, Contact.FirstName, Contact.LastName
        --,Sales.YearToDateSales, Sales.LastSaleDate
FROM    Sales.Contact as Contact
            --LEFT OUTER JOIN
        --    (SELECT ContactId,
        --            SUM(Amount) AS YearToDateSales,
        --            MAX(PurchaseDate) AS LastSaleDate
        --    FROM   Sales.Purchase
        --    WHERE  PurchaseDate >= --the first day of the current year
        --            DATEADD(day, 0, DATEDIFF(day, 0, SYSDATETIME() )
        --            - DATEPART(dayofyear,SYSDATETIME() ) + 1)
        --    GROUP  by ContactId) AS sales
        --    ON Contact.ContactId = Sales.ContactId
WHERE   Contact.LastName like 'Karr%';
```

This returns only the following:

```
ContactId   FirstName     LastName
----------- ------------- ------------
1           Drue          Karry
```

Not wasting the resources to do calculations that aren't needed can save a lot of system resources if the aggregates in the derived table were very costly to execute. Even if it isn't terribly costly, it is still a waste of resources.

In the same vein, when using ad hoc calls, it's trivial (from a SQL standpoint) to build UPDATE statements that include only the columns that have changed in the set lists, rather than updating all columns, as can be necessary for a stored procedure. For example, take the customer columns from earlier: CustomerId, Name, and Number. You could just update all columns:

```
UPDATE Sales.Contact
SET    FirstName = 'Drew',
       LastName = 'Carey',
       SalesLevelId = 1, --no change
```

```
        CompanyName = 'CBS',
        ContactNotes = 'Blah...Blah...Blah...Blah...Blah...Blah...Blah...'
                    + 'Blah...Called and discussed new ideas'
WHERE ContactId = 1;
```

But what if only the `FirstName` and `LastName` values change? What if the `CompanyName` column is part of an index and it has data validations that take three seconds to execute? How do you deal with `varchar(max)` columns (or other long types)? Say the `ContactNotes` columns for the row with `ContactId = 1` contain 300 MB of `'Blah...Blah Blah'`. Execution could take far more time than is desirable if the application passes the entire value back and forth each time. Using ad hoc SQL, to update the `FirstName` and `LastName` columns only (which probably has less overhead than changing the `SalesLevelId` value that minimally has a foreign key), you can simply execute the following code:

```
UPDATE Sales.Contact
SET    FirstName = 'John',
       LastName = 'Ritter'
WHERE  ContactId = 2;
```

Some of this can be done with dynamic SQL calls built into a `STORED PROCEDURE` object, but it's far easier to know if data changed right at the source where the data is being edited, rather than having to check the data beforehand. For example, you could have every data-bound control implement a "data changed" property and perform a column update only when the original value doesn't match the value currently displayed. In a stored procedure–only architecture, having multiple update procedures is not necessarily out of the question, particularly when it is very costly to modify a given column, but it is certainly not as easy as

```
    IF TxtSalesLevel.Changed
    @SETClause = @SETClause + ",SalesLevelId = " + @NewSalesLevelValue
```

One place where using ad hoc SQL can produce more reasonable code is in the area of optional parameters. Say that, in your query to the `Sales.Contact` table, your UI allowed you to filter on either `FirstName`, `LastName`, or both. Take the following code to filter on both `FirstName` and `LastName`:

```
SELECT FirstName, LastName, CompanyName
FROM   Sales.Contact
WHERE  FirstName LIKE 'J%'
  AND  LastName LIKE  'R%';
```

What if the user only needed to filter by the LastName column value? Sending the '%' wildcard for FirstName could cause code to perform less than adequately, especially when the query is parameterized. (I'll cover query parameterization in the next section, "Performance.")

```
SELECT  FirstName, LastName, CompanyName
FROM    Sales.Contact
WHERE   FirstName LIKE '%'
  AND   LastName LIKE 'Carey%';
```

If you think this looks like a very silly query to execute, you are generally correct. If you were writing this query to be used repeatedly, you would write the more logical version of this query, without the superfluous condition:

```
SELECT  FirstName, LastName, CompanyName
FROM    Sales.Contact
WHERE   LastName LIKE 'Carey%';
```

This doesn't require any difficult coding. Just remove one of the criteria from the WHERE clause, and the optimizer needn't consider the other, and it can create a more meaningful plan without the extra, superfluous condition. What if you want to OR the criteria instead? Simply build the query with OR instead of AND. This kind of flexibility is one of the biggest positives to using ad hoc SQL calls.

Note The ability to change the statement programmatically will also play to the downside of any dynamically built statement. With just two parameters, we have three possible variants of the statement to be used, so we have to consider performance for all three when we are building our test cases; and when a query is slow, tuning all the possible permutations can be next to impossible.

For a stored procedure, you might need to write code that functionally works in a manner such as the following:

```
IF @FirstNameValue <> '%'
        SELECT  FirstName, LastName, CompanyName
        FROM    Sales.Contact
        WHERE   FirstName LIKE @FirstNameLike
          AND   LastName LIKE @LastNameLike;
```

```
ELSE
        SELECT FirstName, LastName, CompanyName
        FROM   Sales.Contact
        WHERE  FirstName LIKE @FirstNameLike;
```

This sort of code is generally a bad idea in T-SQL, as you ideally want to have every query in a procedure to execute or the generated plan can be suboptimal. Even worse, you can do something messy like the following in your WHERE clause so if any value is passed in, it uses it or uses '%' otherwise:

```
WHERE  FirstName LIKE ISNULL(NULLIF(LTRIM(@FirstNameLike)
                                      +'%','%'),FirstName)
  AND LastName LIKE ISNULL(NULLIF(LTRIM(@LastNameLike) +'%','%'),LastName)
```

Unfortunately though, this often does not optimize very well (particularly with a lot of data) because the optimizer has a hard time optimizing for factors that can change based on different values of a variable—leading to the need for the branching solution mentioned previously to optimize for specific parameter cases. A better way to do this with a STORED PROCEDURE object can be to create three—one as the primary driver procedure that chooses the scenario, then one with the first query, and another with the second query—especially if you need extremely high-performance access to the data. You'd change this to the following code in the driver stored procedure:

```
IF @FirstNameValue <> '%'
        EXECUTE Sales.Contact$Get @FirstNameLike, @LastNameLike;
ELSE
        EXECUTE Sales.Contact$GetByLastNameLike @LastNameLike;
```

You can do some of this kind of ad hoc SQL writing using dynamic SQL in stored procedures. However, you might have to do a good bit of these IF blocks to arrive at which parameters aren't applicable in various scenarios. Because a UI can know which parameters are applicable, handling this situation using ad hoc SQL can be far easier. Getting this kind of flexibility is the main reason that I use an ad hoc SQL call in an application: I can omit parts of queries that don't make sense in some cases, and it's easier to avoid executing unnecessary code.

Flexibility over Shared Plans and Parameterization

Queries formed at runtime, using proper techniques, can actually be better for performance in many ways than using STORED PROCEDURE objects for the same queries. Because you have control over the queries, you can more easily build queries at runtime that use the same plans and even can be parameterized as desired, based on the situation.

This is not to say that it is the most favorable way of implementing parameterization. (If you want to know the whole picture, you have to read this whole section on building the data access layer.) However, the fact is that ad hoc T-SQL access tends to get a bad reputation for something that Microsoft fixed many many versions back. In the following sections, "Shared Execution Plans" and "Parameterization," I will take a look at the good points and the caveats you will deal with when building ad hoc queries and executing them on the server.

Shared Execution Plans

The original primary reason that STORED PROCEDURE objects were sold as the only decent way to implement a SQL Server application was because the query processor cached their plans. Every time you executed a procedure, SQL Server didn't have to decide the best way to execute the query. As of SQL Server 7.0 (which was released in 1998 and was released before the first edition of this currently sixth edition book), cached plans were extended to include ad hoc SQL. However, the standard for what can be reused from the cache is far stricter than a STORED PROCEDURE object. For two calls to the server to use the same plan, the statements that are sent must be identical, except possibly for the literal values in search arguments. Identical means identical; add a comment, change the case, or even add a space character, and the plan will no longer match. SQL Server can build query plans that have parameters, which allow plan reuse by subsequent calls. However, overall, a STORED PROCEDURE object is better when it comes to using cached plans for performance, primarily because the matching and parameterization are easier for the optimizer to do, since it can be done by object_id, rather than having to match larger blobs of text.

A fairly major caveat is that for ad hoc queries to use the same plan, they must be exactly the same, other than any values that can be parameterized. For example, consider the following two queries. (I'm using WideWorldImporters tables for this example, as that database has a nice amount of data to work with.)

```
USE WideWorldImporters;
GO
SELECT People.FullName, Orders.OrderDate
FROM    Sales.Orders
          JOIN Application.People
              ON Orders.ContactPersonID = People.PersonID
WHERE   People.FullName = N'Bala Dixit';
```

Next, run the following query. See whether you can spot the difference between the two queries. Don't feel bad if you can't; the difference is very subtle, and I started to rewrite the queries because I thought I had made a mistake in a previous edition of the book:

```
SELECT People.FullName, Orders.OrderDate
FROM    Sales.Orders
          JOIN Application.People
              on Orders.ContactPersonID = People.PersonID
WHERE   People.FullName = N'Bala Dixit';
```

These queries can't share plans because ON in the first query's FROM clause is uppercase and on in the second query's FROM clause is lowercase. Using the sys.dm_exec_query_stats DMV, you can see that the case difference does cause two plans by running the following query:

```
SELECT  *
FROM    (SELECT qs.execution_count,
               SUBSTRING(st.text, (qs.statement_start_offset / 2) + 1,
                            ((CASE qs.statement_end_offset
                    WHEN -1 THEN DATALENGTH(st.text)
                    ELSE qs.statement_end_offset
               END - qs.statement_start_offset) / 2) + 1) AS statement_text
        FROM    sys.dm_exec_query_stats AS qs
                CROSS APPLY sys.dm_exec_sql_text(qs.sql_handle) AS st
        ) AS queryStats
WHERE   queryStats.statement_text
             LIKE 'SELECT People.FullName, Orders.OrderDate%';
```

This SELECT statement will return at least two rows, one for each query you have just executed. (It could be more depending on whether or not you have executed the statement more than two times and if you messed up entering/copying the query as I did a few times. Hence, trying to use some method to make sure that every query sent that is essentially the same query is formatted the same is important: queries must use the same format, capitalization, and so forth.

Parameterization

The next performance query plan topic is one we discussed back in Chapter 11 when we were looking at how indexes were applied to queries: parameterization. When a query is parameterized, only one version of the plan is needed to service several variations of a query. Stored procedures are parameterized in all cases where you don't force a recompile in the DDL, but SQL Server does also parameterize many ad hoc SQL statements. The rules for what can be parameterized generally limit the query to what is referred to a "simple" query in that it can only reference a single table. (You can get more details in Microsoft Docs, article "Query Processing Architecture Guide," "Simple Parameterization" section here: docs.microsoft.com/en-us/sql/relational-databases/query-processing-architecture-guide#SimpleParam) which is followed by a section on Forced Parameterization).

When the query meets the strict requirements, it changes each literal it finds in the query string into a parameter. The next time the query is executed with different literal values, the same plan can be used. For example, take this simpler form of the previous query:

```
SELECT People.FullName
FROM    Application.People
WHERE   People.FullName = N'Bala Dixit';
```

The plan (from using SHOWPLAN_TEXT ON in the manner we introduced in Chapter 11 as follows):

```
|--Index Seek(OBJECT:([WideWorldImporters].[Application].[People].
                            [IX_Application_People_FullName]),
    SEEK:([WideWorldImporters].[Application].[People].[FullName]
                            =[@1]) ORDERED FORWARD)
```

The value of N'Bala Dexit' has been changed to [@1] in the query plan, and the value is filled in from the literal at execute time. Of course, [@1] actually could be a column name, but that is how it shows up in the plan. Check the plan with a different value, either one from the table like N'Vlatka Duvnjak' or a less believable made-up name like N'Not Inthetable', and the plan will be the same. However, try executing this query that accesses two tables and joins the People table to the People_Archive table that is used for its temporal extensions:

```
SELECT People.FullName
FROM    Application.People
            JOIN Application.People_Archive
                ON People.PersonID = People_Archive.PersonId
WHERE   People.FullName =N'Lily Code';
```

The plan won't recognize the literal and parameterize it:

```
|--Hash Match(Inner Join, HASH:([WideWorldImporters].[Application].
         [People].[PersonID])=([WideWorldImporters].[Application].
                                    [People_Archive].[PersonID]))
     |--Index Seek(OBJECT:([WideWorldImporters].[Application].
                        [People].[IX_Application_People_FullName]),
            SEEK:([WideWorldImporters].[Application].[People].[FullName]
                                 =N'Lily Code') ORDERED FORWARD)
     |--Clustered Index Scan(OBJECT:([WideWorldImporters].
                 [Application].[People_Archive].[ix_People_Archive]))
```

Clearly it's no longer a "simple" plan, and the literal from the query is still in the plan as N'Lily Code' rather than a parameter. The plan is cached, but the next value passed in will not be used. In following calls, the plan won't be reused unless the precise literal value of N'Lily Code' is passed in:

If you want the optimizer to be more liberal in parameterizing all queries, you can use the ALTER DATABASE command to force the optimizer to parameterize:

```
ALTER DATABASE WideWorldImporters
    SET PARAMETERIZATION FORCED;
```

Try the plan of the query with the join (you may have to reconnect to the database). It now has replaced the N'Bala Dixit' with [@0], and the query processor can reuse this plan no matter what the value for the literal is. Note that there is a reason that more than simple plans are not parameterized by default. This *can* be a costly operation in comparison to normal, text-only plans, so not every system should use this setting. However, if your system is running the same, reasonably complex-looking queries over and over and is not doing any preparation of the queries being sent (which I will cover in a few pages), this can be a good setting to avoid the need to pay for the query optimization.

Not every query will be parameterized when forced parameterization is enabled. For example, change the equality to a LIKE comparison:

```
SELECT People.FullName
FROM    Application.People
            JOIN Application.People_Archive
                ON People.PersonID = People_Archive.PersonId
WHERE   People.FullName LIKE N'Lily Code';
```

The plan will contain the literal, rather than the parameter, because it cannot parameterize the second and third arguments of a LIKE operator comparison (the arguments of the LIKE operator are arg1 LIKE arg2 [ESCAPE arg3]; we are only using the first two in our example). The following is a partial plan, where you can see that it doesn't parameterize the LIKE expression, but it does recognize that it can use the index to seek to narrow what it has to compare. Try out 'Lily Code%' on your own to see the effect it has on the query (it is faint, but search for Lily Code), but it still definitely uses the query to narrow down the data to apply the LIKE expression on:

```
|--Index Seek(OBJECT:([WideWorldImporters].[Application].
                        [People].[IX_Application_People_FullName]),
SEEK:([WideWorldImporters].[Application].[People].[FullName]
                                            >= N'Lily Code'
  AND [WideWorldImporters].[Application].[People].[FullName]
                                            <= N'Lily
Code'),  WHERE:([WideWorldImporters].[Application].[People].[FullName]
                        like N'Lily Code') ORDERED FORWARD)
```

If you change the query to end with `WHERE N'Lily Code' LIKE People.FullName`, it would be parameterized, but that construct is rarely what is desired.

For your applications, another method is to parameterize your ad hoc query calls from the data access layer. Basically using ADO.NET, this would entail using T-SQL variables in your query strings, and then using a `SqlCommand` object and its `Parameters` collection. The plan that will be created from SQL is parameterized on the client and will in turn be parameterized in the plan that is saved.

The myth that performance is definitely worse with ad hoc calls is just not quite true. Performance when using ad hoc calls to the SQL Server in your applications can certainly be less of a worry than you might have been led to believe. However, don't stop reading here. While performance may not suffer tremendously, the inability to easily performance-tune queries is one of the pitfalls, since once you have compiled that query into your application, changing the query is never as easy as it might seem during the development cycle.

So far, we have just executed queries directly, but there is a better method when building your interfaces that allows you to parameterize queries in a very safe manner. Using `sp_executesql`, you can fashion your SQL statement using variables to parameterize the query. Check the plan (you will need to check the actual plan for queries using `sp_executesql`), and you will see `@FullName` parameterized in it:

```
DECLARE @FullName nvarchar(60) = N'Bala Dixit',
        @Query nvarchar(500),
        @Parameters nvarchar(500)

SET @Query= N'SELECT People.FullName, Orders.OrderDate
              FROM   Sales.Orders
                       JOIN Application.People
                         ON Orders.ContactPersonID = People.PersonID
              WHERE  People.FullName LIKE @FullName';
SET @Parameters = N'@FullName nvarchar(60)';

EXECUTE sp_executesql @Query, @Parameters, @FullName = @FullName;
```

Using `sp_executesql` is generally considered the safest way to parameterize ad hoc SQL queries because it does a proper job of parameterizing the query and avoids issues like SQL injection attacks, which I will cover later in this section when covering the disadvantages of ad hoc SQL.

Finally, if you know you need to reuse the query multiple times, you can compile it and save the plan for reuse. This is generally useful if you are going to have to call the same object over and over. Instead of sp_executesql, use sp_prepare to prepare the plan; only this time you won't use the actual value:

```
DECLARE @Query nvarchar(500),
        @Parameters nvarchar(500),
        @Handle int

SET @Query= N'SELECT People.FullName, Orders.OrderDate
              FROM    Sales.Orders
                        JOIN Application.People
                            ON Orders.ContactPersonID = People.PersonID
              WHERE   People.FullName LIKE @FullName';
SET @Parameters = N'@FullName nvarchar(60)';

EXECUTE sp_prepare @Handle output, @Parameters, @Query;
SELECT @handle;
```

That batch will return a value that corresponds to the prepared plan (in my case it was 1). This value is your handle to the plan that you can use with sp_execute on the same connection only. All you need to execute the query is the parameter values and the sp_execute statement, and you can use and reuse the plan as needed:

```
DECLARE  @FullName nvarchar(60) = N'Bala Dixit';
EXECUTE sp_execute 1, @FullName;

SET @FullName = N'Bala%';
EXECUTE sp_execute 1, @FullName;
```

You can unprepare the statement using sp_unprepare and the handle number. It is fairly rare that anyone will manually execute sp_prepare and sp_execute as we have in SSMS, but it is very frequently built into engines that are built to manage ad hoc access for you, particularly for queries that a system knows it will be running repeatedly. It can be good for performance, but it is a pain for troubleshooting because you have to decode what the handle 1 actually represents when you see it in a log of executed statements.

What you end up with is pretty much the same as a single statement STORED PROCEDURE object for performance, but it has to be done every time you run your app, and it is scoped to a connection, not shared on all connections (unlike the ad hoc query plans I showed in the previous section entitled "Shared Execution Plans"). The better solution, strictly from a parameterizing complex statements standpoint, is a STORED PROCEDURE object. Generally, the only way this makes sense as a best practice is when you have very flexible queries being executed (like in the first section of this section on ad hoc SQL or when you cannot use procedures, perhaps because of your tool choice) or using a third-party application. Why? Well, the fact is with stored procedures, the query code is stored on the server and is a layer of encapsulation that reduces coupling, but more on that in the "Stored Procedure or Ad Hoc?" section.

Ad Hoc SQL Disadvantages

Many applications are built generating SQL statements and sending them to SQL Server to execute the statements that are needed to manipulate data and data structures. It is not at all the worst possible scenario. However, there are many downsides to this path that I will discuss in the following sections:

- Low cohesion, high coupling
- Batches of statements
- Security issues
- SQL injection
- Performance-tuning difficulties

Generally speaking, if you have read the book so far, it probably will not come off as a surprise that the biggest advantage (that the application can do much of the up-front work, propelling application development work ahead rapidly) will turn out to be the leading cause of all these pitfalls as well.

Low Cohesion, High Coupling

The number one pitfall of using ad hoc SQL as your interface relates to what you ideally learned back in Programming 101: strive for high cohesion and low coupling. *Cohesion* means that the different parts of the system work together to form a meaningful unit. This is a good thing, as you don't want to include lots of irrelevant code in the system. On the other hand, *coupling* refers to how connected the different parts of a system are to one another. It's considered bad when a change in one part of a system breaks other parts of a system. (If you aren't too familiar with these terms, there is an interesting article in Microsoft Docs entitled "Patterns in Practice: Cohesion and Coupling" by Jeremy Miller (docs.microsoft.com/en-us/archive/msdn-magazine/2008/october/patterns-in-practice-cohesion-and-coupling)). You should build all the code you create with these concepts in mind.

When issuing T-SQL statements directly from the application, the structures in the database are tied directly to the client interface. This sounds perfectly normal and acceptable at the beginning of a project, but it means that any change in database structure might require a change in the user interface. This in turn means that making small changes to the system can be just as costly as making large ones, because a full testing cycle may be required.

When I started this section, I told you that I wouldn't make any distinction between toolsets used. This is still true. Whether you use a horribly, manually coded system or the best ORM, the fact that the application tier knows and is built specifically with knowledge of the base structure of the database is an example of the application and data tiers being highly coupled. Though stored procedures are similarly inflexible, they are stored with the data, allowing the disparate systems to be decoupled: the code on the database tier can be structurally dependent on the objects in the same tier without completely sacrificing loose coupling.

For example, consider that you've created an Employee table and you're storing the employee's spouse's name, as shown in Figure 13-2.

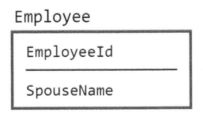

Figure 13-2.   *An employee table*

Now, some new regulation requires that you have to include the ability to have more than one spouse, which necessitates a new table, as shown in Figure 13-3.

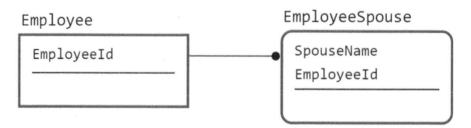

Figure 13-3.   *Adding the ability to have more than one spouse*

The user interface must immediately be morphed to deal with this case. In a scenario such as this, where the condition is quite rare (certainly almost everyone will have zero or one spouse), to handle this with minimal change to the application using ad hoc SQL is fairly difficult. Generally, because the UI and data structures are tightly coupled, a change to one structure is a change to the UI (and if there are more than one UI directly using tables, it can get even more complex).

Using a stored procedure, you could create the new table and initially just have the stored procedure take the one parameter that puts the value into the EmployeeSpouse table rather than the SpouseName column. Then as this and other UIs are ready to use it, an additional table-valued parameter for @MultipleSpouseList could be included that took one to many spouse names. The stored procedure code can handle the complexities of putting the data into multiple rows, and the UI can have an alternative view for the likely rare usage when > 1 spouse was used.

Batches of More Than One Statement

A major problem with ad hoc SQL access is that when you need to do multiple commands and treat them as a single operation, it becomes increasingly difficult to build the mechanisms in the application code to execute multiple statements as a batch, particularly when you need to group statements together in a transaction. When you have only individual statements, it's easy to manage ad hoc SQL for the most part. However, as complexity rises in the things you need to accomplish in a transaction, things get tougher. What about the case where you have 20 rows to insert, update, and/or delete at one time and all in one transaction?

The first way to deal with this situation is to start a transaction using procedural code. However, this is generally not considered ideal, because if something occurs during the execution of the object, you can still leave open transactions on the server. Many long-running transactions occur because a process starts a transaction and executes a statement, it fails, and the process just stops. The transaction is not rolled back, nor is the connection dropped. This is one of the reasons that a general best practice is if you send a BEGIN TRANSACTION command in a batch, include a COMMIT or ROLLBACK TRANSACTION command in the same batch. This isn't specifically a hard and fast rule and can be acceptable to do with a middle-tier object that requires no user interaction, as long as proper error handling is used and proper cleanup routines are in place.

The second way to deal with this is to build a batching mechanism for batching SQL calls. Basically, build a code-wrapping mechanism, using a template such as the following:

```
BEGIN TRY
BEGIN TRANSACTION;

    <-- statements go here

COMMIT TRANSACTION;
END TRY
BEGIN CATCH
    ROLLBACK TRANSACTION;
    THROW 50000, '<describe what happened>',16;
END CATCH;
```

For example, if you wanted to send a new invoice and line items, the application code would need to build a batch such as in the following code. Each of the SET @Action = ... and INSERT statements would be put into the batch by the application, with the rest being boilerplate code that is repeatable:

```
SET NOCOUNT ON;
BEGIN TRY
BEGIN TRANSACTION;

        DECLARE @Action nvarchar(200);

        SET @Action = 'Invoice Insert';
        INSERT Invoice (Columns) VALUES (Values);

        SET @Action = 'First InvoiceLineItem Insert';
        INSERT InvoiceLineItem (Columns) VALUES (Values);
```

```
        SET @Action = 'Second InvoiceLineItem Insert';
        INSERT InvoiceLineItem (Columns) VALUES (Values);

        SET @Action = 'Third InvoiceLineItem Insert';
        INSERT InvoiceLineItem (Columns) VALUES (Values);

COMMIT TRANSACTION;
END TRY
BEGIN CATCH
    IF @@TRANCOUNT <> 0
        ROLLBACK TRANSACTION;
    DECLARE @Msg nvarchar(4000);
    SET @Msg = @Action + ' : Error was: '
            + CAST(ERROR_NUMBER() AS varchar(10)) + ':' + ERROR_MESSAGE ();
    THROW 50000, @Msg,1;
END CATCH;
```

Executing multiple statements in a transaction in this manner is done on the server, and the transaction either completes or not. There's no chance that you'll end up with a transaction swinging in the wind, ready to block the next user who needs to access the locked row (even in a table scan for unrelated items). A downside is that it does stop you from using any interim values from your statements in your batch to set values in following statements (without some really tricky coding/forethought, as you are generating this code from other code), but starting transactions outside of the batch in which you commit them is asking for blocking and locking due to longer batch times.

Starting the transaction outside of the server using application code is likely easier, but building this sort of batching interface is the preferred way to go. First, it's better for concurrency, because only one batch needs to be executed instead of many little ones. Second, the execution of this batch won't have to wait on communications back and forth from the server before sending the next command. It's all there and happens in the single batch of statements. Bottom line: Keep transactions as short as possible, in a single batch if possible.

Note   The problem I have run into in almost all cases was that building a batch of multiple SQL statements is a very unnatural thing for the object-oriented or ORM-type coding tools to do. The way the code is generally set up is more one table to one object, where the `Invoice` and `InvoiceLineItem` objects have the responsibility of saving themselves. So either no overarching transaction is used, and a failure may end up leaving data in a messy state, or transactions are used, and a failure occurs but then a transaction is left hanging.

Security Issues

Security is one of the biggest downsides to using ad hoc access. For a user to use their own Windows login to access the server, you have to grant quite a few, possibly powerful, rights to the system, whereas with T-SQL coded objects, you can simply give access to specific coded objects to get very granular security. Using ad hoc T-SQL, you go with one of three possible security patterns, each with its own downsides:

- *Use one login for the application*: This, of course, means that you have to code your own security system for application access rather than using what SQL Server gives you. This even includes some form of login and password for application access, as well as individual object access.

- *Use application roles*: This is slightly better; while you have to implement security in your code since all application users will have the same database security, at the very least, you can let SQL server handle the data access via normal logins and passwords (ideally using Windows authentication). Using application roles can be a good way to let users use Windows Authentication, but still not have direct access to the system. The password for the application role is passed in clear text, so you should use an encrypted connection (truly this should be the de facto standard at this point in history).

- *Give the user direct access to the tables or possibly views*:
  Unfortunately, this opens up your tables to users who discover the
  magical world of Management Studio and Azure Data Tools, where
  they can open a table and immediately start editing it without any of
  those pesky UI data checks or business rules that only exist in your
  data access layer.

Usually, almost all applications follow the first of the three methods. Building your
own login and application security mechanisms is just considered a part of the process,
and just about as often, it is considered part of the user interface's responsibilities. At
the very least, by not giving *all* users direct access to the tables, the likelihood of them
mucking around in the tables editing data all willy-nilly is greatly minimized. With
procedures, you can give the users access just to stored procedures, which are not
natural for them to use and certainly would not allow them to accidentally delete data
from a table.

The other slight concern security-wise is basically performance related. SQL Server
must evaluate security for every object as it's used, rather than once at the object level
for stored procedures—that is, if the owner of the procedure owns all objects. This isn't
generally a big issue, but as your need for greater concurrency increases, everything can
become an issue!

Caution   If you use the single-application login method, make sure not to use an
account with system administration or database owner privileges. Doing so opens
up your application to programmers making mistakes, and if you miss something
that allows SQL injection attacks, which I describe in the next section, you could be
in a world of hurt.

SQL Injection

A big risk with ad hoc queries is being hacked by a SQL injection attack. Unless you
(and/or your toolset) program your ad hoc T-SQL intelligently and/or (mostly and) use
the parameterizing methods we discussed earlier in this section, a user could inject
something such as the following:

```
' + char(13) + char(10) + '''';SHUTDOWN WITH NOWAIT;' + '--'
```

In this case, the command might just shut down the server if the security context that executes the statements has rights, but you can probably see far greater attack possibilities. I'll discuss even more about injection attacks and how to avoid them in the "Stored Procedure or Ad Hoc?" section because they can have some of the same issues if using dynamic SQL. When using ad hoc SQL, you must be careful to avoid these types of issues for *every* call.

A SQL injection attack is not terribly hard to beat, but the fact is, for any user-enterable text where you don't use some form of parameterization, you have to make sure to escape any single-quote characters that a user passes in. For general text entry, like a name, commonly if the user passes in a string like "O'Malley," you must change this to 'O''Malley'. For example, consider the following batch, where the resulting query will fail. (I have to escape the single quote in the literal to allow the query to execute, but that only translates to a single quote in the EXECUTE statement.)

```
DECLARE @value varchar(40) = 'Smith';
SELECT 'SELECT '''+ @value + '''';
EXECUTE ('SELECT '''+ @value + '''');
```

This will return

```
----------------------------------------
SELECT 'Smith'

-----
Smith
```

All seems lovely, so you just continue on, not thinking of what happens when someone enters something a bit more inventive, such as

```
DECLARE @value varchar(40) = 'Smith''; SELECT ''What else could I do?';
```

In this value, the user terminated the string and then added in another statement. Uh-oh, this returns

```
--------------------------------------------------
SELECT 'Smith'; SELECT 'What else could I do?'

-----
Smith

--------------------
What else could I do?
```

Of course, this is the best possible case, but no self-respecting hacker is just going to stop with outputting some string data; they are going to start attempting to output some data, looking for common table names, going for system tables to see if you have used too high of a security level for the application user, and so on. The fact is, though, in no case should this ever be an issue because you should never allow a text entry value to not handle a single-quote character, so a name like O'Malley can be entered:

```
DECLARE @value varchar(40) = 'O''Malley';
```

How to handle this situation is right in the declaration in that you need to double up any single quotes. This makes the single quote a part of the string; otherwise, in the EXECUTE statement, you get the following error:

```
-------------------------------------------------
SELECT 'O'Malley'

Msg 105, Level 15, State 1, Line 1
Unclosed quotation mark after the character string ''.
```

This is a very common problem that arises, and all too often the result is that the user learns not to enter a single quote in the query parameter value. But you can make sure this doesn't occur by changing all single quotes in the value to double single quotes, like in the DECLARE @value statement. I will do this with a SCALAR USER DEFINED FUNCTION object that will be included as part of the major section "Building Reusable Components" later that does something similar to what QUOTENAME does, but is not limited to 128 character like it is:

```
CREATE SCHEMA Tools;
GO
CREATE OR ALTER FUNCTION Tools.String$EscapeString
(
     @inputString nvarchar(4000), --would work on varchar(max) too
     @character nchar(1) = N'''', --if you needed that
     @surroundOutputFlag bit = 1
)
RETURNS nvarchar(4000)
AS
  BEGIN
     RETURN (CASE WHEN @surroundOutputFlag = 1 THEN @character END
              +REPLACE(@inputString,@character,@character+@character)
              +CASE WHEN @surroundOutputFlag = 1 THEN @character END)
  END;
GO
```

Using this function, we can make sure that everything placed between the original two single-quote characters is safe to store and execute as it will be treated as a string:

```
DECLARE @value varchar(30) = 'O''Malley', @query nvarchar(300);
SELECT @query = 'SELECT ' +
                    Tools.String$EscapeString(@value,DEFAULT,DEFAULT);
SELECT @query;
EXECUTE (@query );
```

This returns

```
-------------------------------------------------
SELECT 'O''Malley'

--------
O'Malley
```

Now, if someone tries to put a single quote, semicolon, and some other statement in the value, it doesn't matter; it will always be treated as a literal string:

```
DECLARE @value varchar(40) = 'Smith''; SELECT ''What else could I do?',
        @query nvarchar(300);
SELECT @query = 'SELECT ' +
                        Tools.String$EscapeString(@value,DEFAULT,DEFAULT);
SELECT  @query;
EXECUTE (@query );
```

The query is now followed by the return:

```
----------------------------------------------------------
SELECT 'Smith''; SELECT ''What else could I do?'

-------------------------------------
Smith'; SELECT 'What else could I do?
```

However, what isn't quite so obvious is that you have to do this for *every single string*, even if the string value could never seemingly (due to application and constraints) have a single quote in it. If you don't double up on the quotes, the person could put in a single quote and then a string of SQL commands—this is where you get hit by the injection attack. And as I said before, the safest method of avoiding injection issues is to always parameterize your queries, though it can be very hard to use variable query conditions using the parameterized method, losing some of the value of using ad hoc SQL:

```
DECLARE @value varchar(30) = 'O''; SELECT ''badness',
        @query nvarchar(300),
        @parameters nvarchar(200) = N'@value varchar(30)';
SELECT @query = 'SELECT ' +
                        Tools.String$EscapeString(@value,DEFAULT,DEFAULT);
SELECT  @query;
EXECUTE sp_executesql @Query, @Parameters, @value = @value;
```

If you employ ad hoc SQL in your applications, I strongly suggest you do more reading on the subject of SQL injection and then go in and look at the places where SQL commands can be sent to the server to make sure you are covered. SQL injection is especially dangerous if the accounts being used by your application have too much power because you didn't set up particularly granular security.

Note that if all of this talk of parameterization sounds complicated, it's because it kind of is. Generally, there are two ways that parameterization happens well:

- By building a framework that forces you to follow the correct pattern (as do most object-relational tools, though they often force—or at least lead—you into suboptimal patterns of execution, like dealing with every statement separately without transactions).

- By using stored procedures. Stored procedures parameterize in a manner that is impervious to SQL injection (except when you use dynamic SQL, which, as I will discuss later, is subject to the same issues as ad hoc access from any client).

Difficulty Tuning for Performance

Performance tuning is generally the second most important part of any computer project, second only to getting the right answer. While ad hoc SQL has a few benefits for performance that we have already discussed, in far more cases than not, its Achilles' heel is that it is far more difficult to tune when having to deal with ad hoc requests, for a few reasons:

- *Unknown queries*: The application can be programmed to send any query it wants, in any way. Unless very extensive testing is done, slow or dangerous scenarios can slip through (accidentally or purposefully). With procedures, you have a tidy catalog of possible queries that might be executed, and these objects can be individually tested. This concern can be mitigated by having a single module where SQL code can be created and a method to list all possible queries that the application layer can execute, though that takes more discipline than most organizations have.

- *Often requires people from multiple teams*: It may seem silly, but when something is running slower, it is always SQL Server's fault (well, it is certainly blamed first in any case). With ad hoc calls, there are tools that the database administrator can use to help the query perform better, as I will discuss later in this section, but none as easy as using ALTER PROCEDURE to change the code to a better version of itself.

- *Front-end recompile required for changing queries*: If you want to change how a query works, the app likely needs to be rebuilt and redeployed. For stored procedures, you'd simply modify the query without the client knowing.

These reasons seem small during the development phase, but often they're the real killers for tuning, especially when you get a third-party application and its developers have implemented a dumb query that you could easily optimize, but since the code is hard-coded in the application, modification of the query isn't possible.

SQL Server 2005 gave us plan guides (and there are some improvements in their usability in later versions) that can be used to force a plan or even just add a hint for queries, ad hoc calls, and procedures when you have troublesome queries that don't optimize naturally. SQL Server 2016 and later have a feature called the Query Store that can help you see old plans and help to change the plan that is used. SQL Server 2017 and 2019 have greatly improved performance tuning with new features gathered under the heading of Intelligent Query Processing. Read more on this family of features in Microsoft Docs here: `docs.microsoft.com/en-us/sql/relational-databases/ performance/intelligent-query-processing`.

But the fact is going in and editing a query to tune is far easier than using either of these tools, particularly in light of how ad hoc SQL can change in a less manageable manner than a stored procedure.

Using a T-SQL Coded Encapsulation Layer

`STORED PROCEDURE` objects are compiled batches of SQL code that can be parameterized to allow for easy reuse. The basic structure of a typical interpreted `STORED PROCEDURE` object follows. For a complete reference, see the Microsoft Docs article "CREATE PROCEDURE (Transact-SQL)" (`docs.microsoft.com/en-us/sql/t-sql/statements/ create-procedure-transact-sql`):

```
CREATE PROCEDURE <procedureName>
[(
        @parameter1  <datatype> [ = <defaultvalue> [OUTPUT]]
        @parameter2  <datatype> [ = <defaultvalue> [OUTPUT]]
        ...
```

```
        @parameterN    <datatype> [ = <defaultvalue> [OUTPUT]]
)]
AS
<T-SQL statements>
```

You can put pretty much any statement that could have been sent as an ad hoc call into a STORED PROCEDURE object and call the code as a reusable unit. (Natively compiled procedures have far more limits, which I will cover in more detail in a later subsection of this section, but they are basically the same thing.) You can return an integer value from the procedure by using the RETURN statement or return almost any datatype by declaring one or more parameters as an OUTPUT parameter (other than text or image, though you should be using (max) datatypes because they have been deprecated and, perhaps more importantly, they are pretty horrible; you can also not return a table-valued parameter). After the AS, you can execute any T-SQL commands you need to, using the parameters just like variables (they are not read-only either). I will largely ignore natively compiled stored procedures for now, deferring discussion to the subsection "Advantages" that covers how using STORED PROCEDURE objects helps you make, or prepare to make, the most of the memory-optimized engine.

The following is an example of a basic STORED PROCEDURE object to retrieve rows from a table (continuing to use the WideWorldImporters database for these examples):

```
CREATE PROCEDURE Sales.Orders$Select
(
        @FullNameLike nvarchar(100) = '%',
        @OrderDateRangeStart date = '1900-01-01',
        @OrderDateRangeEnd date = '9999-12-31'
) AS
BEGIN
     SELECT People.FullName, Orders.OrderDate
     FROM    Sales.Orders
                JOIN Application.People
                    ON Orders.ContactPersonID = People.PersonID
     WHERE   People.FullName LIKE @FullNameLike
                --Inclusive since using Date type
        AND  OrderDate BETWEEN @OrderDateRangeStart
                                    AND @OrderDateRangeEnd;
END;
```

Now instead of having the client programs formulate a query by knowing the table structures, the client can simply issue a command, knowing a procedure name and the parameters. Clients can choose from four possible criteria to select the addresses they want. For example, they'd use the following if they want to find orders by Bala Dixit, leaving the other parameters to their default:

```
EXECUTE Sales.Orders$Select @FullNameLike = 'Bala Dixit';
```

Or they could use the other parameters:

```
EXECUTE Sales.Orders$Select @FullNameLike = 'Bala Dixit',
                    @OrderDateRangeStart = '2016-01-01',
                    @OrderDateRangeEnd = '2016-12-31';
```

The client doesn't know whether the database or the code is well built or less well built than ideal. Originally the name column might have been a part of the Orders table but changed to be in a customer table when an actual data architect was hired. Often, the tasks the client needs to do won't change based on the database structures, so why should the client need to know the database structures?

For much greater detail about how to write great T-SQL, consider the books *Beginning T-SQL* by Kathi Kellenberger (Apress, 2014) and *Learn T-SQL Querying: A guide to developing efficient and elegant T-SQL code* by Pedro Lopes and Pam Lahoud (Packt, 2019). In this section, I'll look at some of the advantages of using stored procedures as our primary interface between client and data, followed up by the disadvantages of such methods.

Advantages of T-SQL Object Layers

The advantages of using STORED PROCEDURE objects as your primary interface are considerable, and they are actually even more if you want to take full advantage of the memory-optimized table engine. I'll discuss the following topics:

- *Encapsulation*: Limits client knowledge of the database structure by providing a simple interface for known operations.

- *Dynamic procedures*: Gives the best of both worlds, allowing for ad hoc–style code without giving ad hoc access to the database.

- *Security*: Provides a well-formed interface for known operations that allows you to apply security only to this interface and disallow other access to the database. This way, even if a hacker gets access to your server via your application login, all they should be able to do is execute stored procedures, making it far more difficult to get data out of the system. Of course, this requires the application principal doing the execution is limited.

- *Performance*: Allows for efficient parameterization of any query, as well as tweaks to the performance of any query, without changes to the client interface.

- *Making full use of the memory-optimized engine:* Memory-optimized tables are great using interpreted code, but making full use of them requires use of natively compiled stored procedures. If your architecture is currently based on stored procedures, making this change will be far easier. I will describe a few of the limitations and differences between interpreted and natively compiled stored procedures.

Of course, your data access layer needn't be 100% STORED PROCEDURE object based to provide some of these benefits. For example, encapsulation can be achieved by using VIEW and FUNCTION objects. With these object types, you can produce an interface that looks like the structures you want the database to look like, but then the database itself may look completely different. Some of the security value can be achieved in the same way. However, the performance and controlled dynamic T-SQL benefits of STORED PROCEDURE objects would not be available. Hence, for most of this section, I will mostly cover STORED PROCEDURE objects.

Encapsulation

Encapsulation is, in my opinion, the primary reason for using objects other than directly accessing the TABLE objects directly. It will also be a little part of all the other advantage topics that I'll discuss. When talking about encapsulation, the idea is to hide the working details from processes that have no need to know about the details. Encapsulation is a large part of the desired "low coupling" of our code that I discussed in the pitfalls of ad hoc access. Some software is going to have to be coupled to the data structures, of course, but locating that code with the structures makes it easier to manage. Plus, the people who generally manage the SQL Server code on the server are not the same people who manage the compiled code.

For example, when we coded the `Sales.Orders$Select` procedure in the introduction to the "Using a T-SQL Coded Encapsulation Layer" section, it was unimportant to the client how the procedure was coded. We could have built it based on a VIEW object and selected from it, or the `STORED PROCEDURE` could call 16 different procedures to improve performance for different parameter combinations. We could even have used a horribly misguided cursor version that you find in some production systems:

```
--pseudocode:
CREATE PROCEDURE Sales.Orders$Select
...
Create temp table;
Declare cursor for (select all rows from the query table);
Fetch first row;
While not end of cursor (@@fetch_status)
 Begin
        Check columns for a match to parameters;
        If match, put into temp table;
        Fetch next row;
 End;
SELECT * FROM temp table;
```

This is horrible code to be sure. I didn't give real code so it wouldn't be confused for a positive example and imitated. However, it certainly could be built to return correct data and possibly could even be fast enough for smaller data sets. As they say, "Works on my machine!" Even better, if we do things right, when the client executes the following code, they get the same result, regardless of the internal code:

```
EXECUTE Sales.Orders$Select @FullNameLike = 'Bala Dixit',
                            @OrderDateRangeStart = '2016-01-01',
                            @OrderDateRangeEnd = '2016-12-31';
```

What makes a proper encapsulation layer great is that you can rewrite the guts of a module using the server's native language without any concern for breaking any client code. This means that anything can change, including table structures, column names, and coding method (cursor, join, etc.), and no client code needs to change as long as the inputs and outputs stay the same.

The only caveat to this is that you can get some metadata about procedures only when they are written using compiled SQL without conditionals (if condition select … else select…). For example, using sp_describe_first_result_set, you can get metadata about the procedure we wrote earlier:

```
EXECUTE sp_describe_first_result_set
        N'Sales.Orders$Select';
```

Or even with parameters:

```
EXECUTE sp_describe_first_result_set
        N'Sales.Orders$Select @FullNameLike = ''Bala Dixit''';
```

This returns metadata about what will be returned (this is just a small amount of what is returned in the columns):

column_ordinal	name	system_type_name
1	FullName	nvarchar(50)
2	OrderDate	date

For poorly formed procedures, even if it returns the exact same result set, you may not be as able to get the metadata from the procedure. For example, consider the following procedure:

```
CREATE PROCEDURE dbo.Test (@Value int = 1)
AS
IF @value = 1
    SELECT 'FRED' as Name;
ELSE
    SELECT 200 as Name;
```

If you run the procedure with 1 for the parameter, it will return FRED, and for any other value, it will return 200. Both are named "name," but they are not the same type. So checking the result se

```
EXECUTE sp_describe_first_result_set N'dbo.Test';
```

the output is this (actually quite) excellent error message, letting us know that the output of this procedure can't be determined because one call may have a varchar type and the next an integer:

```
Msg 11512, Level 16, State 1, Procedure sp_describe_first_result_set, Line 1
The metadata could not be determined because the statement 'SELECT 'FRED'
AS Name;' in procedure 'Test' is not compatible with the statement 'SELECT
200 AS Name;' in procedure 'Test'.
```

This concept of having easy access to the code may seem like an insignificant consideration, especially if you generally only work with limited-sized sets of data. The problem is, as data set sizes fluctuate, the types of queries that will work often vary greatly. When you start dealing with increasing orders of magnitude in the number of rows in your tables, queries that seemed just fine somewhere at N rows may start to fail to produce the kinds of performance that you need when you reach N * 10000, so you have to tweak the queries to get results in a reasonable amount of time. I will cover more details about performance tuning in a later section.

Note   Some of the benefits of building your objects in the way that I describe can also be achieved by building a solid middle-tier architecture with a data layer that is flexible enough to deal with change. However, I will always argue that it is easier to build your data access layer in the T-SQL code that is built specifically for data access. Unfortunately, it doesn't solve the code ownership issues (procedural vs. relational programmers).

Dynamic Procedures

You can dynamically create and execute code in a STORED PROCEDURE object, just as you can from the front end. Often, this is necessary when it's just too hard to get a good answer using the rigid requirements of a precompiled procedure. For example, say you need a procedure that requires a lot of optional parameters. It can be easier to include only parameters where the user passes in a value and let the compilation be done at execution time, especially if the procedure isn't used all that often. The same parameter sets will get their own plan saved in the plan cache anyhow, just like for typical ad hoc SQL.

Clearly, some of the problems of ad hoc SQL pertain here as well, most notably SQL injection. You must always make sure that no input that users can enter allows them to return their own results, allowing them to poke around your system without anyone knowing. As mentioned before, a common way to avoid this sort of thing is always to check the parameter values and immediately double up the single quotes so that the caller can't inject malicious code where it shouldn't be.

Make sure that any parameters that don't need quotes (such as numbers) are placed into the correct datatype. If you use a string value for a number, you can insert things such as 'novalue' and check for it in your code, but another user could put in the injection attack value and be in like Flynn. For example, take the sample STORED PROCEDURE from earlier, and let's turn it into the most obvious version of a dynamic SQL statement in a stored procedure:

```
ALTER PROCEDURE Sales.Orders$Select
(
        @FullNameLike nvarchar(100) = '%',
        @OrderDateRangeStart date = '1900-01-01',
        @OrderDateRangeEnd date = '9999-12-31'
) AS
BEGIN
        DECLARE @query varchar(max) =
        CONCAT('
          SELECT People.FullName, Orders.OrderDate
          FROM   Sales.Orders
                    JOIN Application.People
                      ON Orders.ContactPersonID = People.PersonID
          WHERE  OrderDate BETWEEN ''', @OrderDateRangeStart, '''
                       AND ''', @OrderDateRangeEnd,'''
            AND People.FullName LIKE ''', @FullNameLike, '''' );
        SELECT @query; --for testing
        EXECUTE (@query);
END;
```

There are two problems with this version of the procedure. The first is that you don't get the full benefit, because in the final query you can end up with useless parameters used as search arguments that make using indexes more difficult, which is one of the main reasons I use dynamic procedures. I'll fix that in the next iteration of the code, but the most important problem is the injection attack possibility. For example, let's assume that the user who's running the application has dbo powers or rights to sysusers (not as uncommon as you would hope). The user executes the following statement:

```
EXECUTE Sales.Orders$Select
        @FullNameLike = '~;''select name from sysusers--',
        @OrderDateRangeStart = '2016-01-01';
```

This returns three result sets: the two (including the code from the SELECT) from before plus a list of all of the users in the WideWorldImporters database. No rows will be returned to the proper result sets, because no address lines happen to be equal to '~', but the list of users is not a good thing because, with some work, a decent hacker could probably figure out how to use a UNION and get back the users as part of the normal result set.

Just as we did in the "Using Ad Hoc SQL" section earlier, fix this by doubling the single quotes in the query text string. I will do this using the Tools. String$EscapeString function built in the "SQL Injection" section earlier in the chapter (it needs to be added to the WideWorldImporters database) to make sure that all values that need to be surrounded by single quotes are formatted in such a way that no matter what a user sends to the parameter, it cannot cause a problem. Note that if you programmatically chose columns, you ought to use the QUOTENAME() function to insert the bracket around the name. SELECT QUOTENAME('FRED') returns [FRED].

This would look like (note that dynamic SQL STORED PROCEDURE objects never look as clearly written as proper objects, because they are basically code generators, not straightforward pieces of code)

```
ALTER PROCEDURE Sales.Orders$Select
(
        @FullNameLike nvarchar(100) = '%',
        @OrderDateRangeStart date = '1900-01-01',
        @OrderDateRangeEnd date = '9999-12-31'
) AS
BEGIN
        DECLARE @query varchar(max) =
        CONCAT('
    SELECT People.FullName, Orders.OrderDate
        FROM    Sales.Orders
                JOIN Application.People
```

```
                    ON Orders.ContactPersonID = People.PersonID
        WHERE   People.FullName LIKE ',
        Tools.String$EscapeString(@FullNameLike,DEFAULT,DEFAULT), '
                AND  OrderDate BETWEEN ''',
        @OrderDateRangeStart,''' AND ''', @OrderDateRangeEnd,'''');
        SELECT @query; --for testing
        EXECUTE (@query);
END;
```

In the next code block, I will change the procedure so instead of just blindly using the parameters, if the parameter value is the same as the default, I will leave off the values from the WHERE clause. Note that using sp_executesql and parameterizing will not be feasible if you want to do a variable WHERE or JOIN clause, so you have to take care to avoid SQL injection in the query itself:

```
ALTER PROCEDURE Sales.Orders$Select
(
        @FullNameLike nvarchar(100) = '%',
        @OrderDateRangeStart date = '1900-01-01',
        @OrderDateRangeEnd date = '9999-12-31'
) AS
BEGIN
        DECLARE @query varchar(max) =
        CONCAT('
          SELECT People.FullName, Orders.OrderDate
          FROM   Sales.Orders
                    JOIN Application.People
                        ON Orders.ContactPersonID = People.PersonID
          WHERE   1=1
          ',
          --ignore @FullNameLike parameter when it is set to all
          CASE WHEN @FullNameLike <> '%' THEN
                CONCAT(' AND  People.FullName LIKE ',
           Tools.String$EscapeString(@FullNameLike,DEFAULT,DEFAULT))
          ELSE '' END,
          --ignore @date parameters when it is set to all
```

```
        CASE WHEN @OrderDateRangeStart <> '1900-01-01' OR
                  @OrderDateRangeEnd <> '9999-12-31'
                    THEN
        --note, date values do not need to be escaped, because the
        --parameter will not accept a non-date value for a value
        CONCAT('AND  OrderDate BETWEEN ''', @OrderDateRangeStart, '''
                                    AND ''', @OrderDateRangeEnd,'''')
        ELSE '' END);
        SELECT @query; --for testing
        EXECUTE (@query);
END;
```

Now I might get a much better plan for some queries, especially if there are several useful indexes on the table. That's because SQL Server can make the determination of what indexes to use at runtime based on the parameters needed, rather than using a single stored plan for every possible combination of parameters. I also don't have to worry about injection attacks, because it's impossible to put something into any parameter that will be anything other than a search argument and that will execute any code other than what I expect. Basically, this version of a STORED PROCEDURE is the answer to the flexibility of using ad hoc SQL when the absolute need arises, though it is quite a bit messier to write. However, it is located right on the server where it can be tweaked as necessary.

Try executing the evil version of the query, and look at the WHERE clause it fashions:

```
WHERE    1=1
         AND People.FullName like '~''select name from sysusers--'
```

The query that is formed, when executed, will now just return two result sets (one for the query and one for the results) and no rows for the executed query. This is because you are looking for rows where People.FullName is like ~'select name from sysusers--. While not being exactly *impossible*, this is certainly very, very unlikely.

I should also note that in versions of SQL Server before 2005, using dynamic SQL procedures would always break the security chain, and you'd have to grant a lot of extra rights to objects just used in a stored procedure. This little fact was enough to make using dynamic SQL not a best practice for SQL Server 2000 and earlier versions. However, after SQL Server 2005, you no longer had to grant these extra rights, as I'll explain in the next section. (Hint: You can EXECUTE AS someone else.) If you are not already on 2005 or later...it might be time for a new employer.

Security

My second most favorite reason for using STORED PROCEDURE object access is security. You can grant access to just the STORED PROCEDURE objects, instead of giving users the rights to all the different resources used by the stored procedure. Granting rights to all the objects in the database gives them the ability to open SSMS or ADT and do the same things (and more) that the application allows them to do. This is rarely the desired effect, as an untrained user let loose on base tables can wreak havoc on the data. ("Oooh, I should change that. Oooh, I should delete that row. Hey, weren't there more rows in this table before?" or the ever classic "Oops!") I should note that if the database is properly designed, users can't violate core structural business rules, but they can circumvent business rules enforced strictly in the middle tier and can execute poorly formed queries that chew up important resources.

Note   In general, it is best to keep most of your users away from the power tools like SSMS in your production OLTP servers and keep them in a sandbox where even if they have advanced powers (like because they are CEO), they cannot accidentally see too much (and particularly modify and/or delete) data that they shouldn't. Provide tools that hold users' hands and keep them from shooting off their big toe (or really any toe for that matter).

There are techniques available to allow a user to look at your OLTP database directly without harming performance, for example, Always On readable secondary replica. For more details, see the Microsoft Docs article "Offload read-only workload to secondary replica of an Always On availability group" (`docs.microsoft.com/en-us/sql/database-engine/availability-groups/windows/active-secondaries-readable-secondary-replicas-always-on-availability-groups`).

With a STORED PROCEDURE object layer, you have a far clearer surface area with named actions that can be managed at pretty much any granularity desired, rather than tables, columns, and actions (SELECT, UPDATE, INSERT, DELETE), so you can give rights to just a single operation, in a single way. For example, the question of whether users should be able to delete a contact is wide open, but should they be able to delete their own contacts? Sure, you can do that with row-level security, but it can get

kind of complex to set up layers of block filters. If we create a stored procedure like
`Contact$DeletePersonal` (meaning a contact that the user owned), making this choice
easy would be based on how well you name your procedures. I use a naming convention
of `<tablename | subject area>$<action>` as you probably have witnessed throughout
the book. How you name objects is completely a personal choice, as long as you follow a
standard that is meaningful to you and others.

As discussed back in the "Using Ad Hoc SQL" section, a lot of architects simply
avoid this issue altogether (either by choice or as a result of political pressure) by letting
objects connect to the database as a single user, leaving it up to the application to handle
security. That can be an adequate method of implementing security, and the security
implications of this are the same for stored procedures or ad hoc usage.

The `EXECUTE AS` clause gives the programmer of the procedure the ability to build
procedures where the procedure caller has the same rights in the procedure code as the
owner of the procedure—or, if permissions have been granted, the same rights as any
user or login in the system.

For example, consider that you need to do a dynamic SQL call to a table. Note that
we covered this in more detail in Chapter 10, but I want to show a quick example here
as it pertains to the value of using objects for security encapsulation. First, create a test
user:

```
CREATE USER Fred WITHOUT LOGIN;
```

Next, create a simple stored procedure:

```
CREATE SCHEMA SecurityDemo;
GO
CREATE PROCEDURE SecurityDemo.TestChaining
AS
EXECUTE ('SELECT PersonId, FullName
         FROM   Application.People');
GO
GRANT EXECUTE ON SecurityDemo.TestChaining TO Fred;
```

Now execute the procedure (changing your security context to be this user):

```
EXECUTE AS USER = 'Fred';
EXECUTE SecurityDemo.TestChaining;
REVERT;
```

You're greeted with the following error:

```
Msg 229, Level 14, State 5, Line 1
The SELECT permission was denied on the object 'People', database
'WideWorldImporters', schema 'Application'.
```

You could grant rights to the user directly to the object, but this gives users more usage than just from this procedure, which is precisely what we are trying to avoid by using stored procedures! Now change the procedure to EXECUTE AS SELF:

```
ALTER PROCEDURE SecurityDemo.testChaining
WITH EXECUTE AS SELF
AS
EXECUTE ('SELECT PersonId, FullName
         FROM   Application.People');
```

Note   If you have restored this database from the Web, you may get an error message: Msg 15517, Cannot execute as the database principal because the principal "dbo" does not exist, this type of principal cannot be impersonated, or you do not have permission. This will occur if your database owner's sid is not correct for the instance you are working on. Use ALTER AUTHORIZATION ON DATABASE::WideWorldImporters to SA to set the owner to the SA account. Determine the database owner using this query: SELECT SUSER_SNAME(owner_sid) FROM sys.databases WHERE name = 'WideWorldImporters';.

Now, go back to the context of user Fred and try again. Just like if Fred had access directly, you get back data. You use SELF to set the context the same as the principal creating the procedure. OWNER is usually the same as SELF, and you can only specify a single user in the database (it can't be a role or a Windows group). Warning: The EXECUTE

AS clause can be abused if you are not extremely careful. Consider the following query, which is obviously a gross exaggeration of what you might hope to see but not beyond possibility:

```
CREATE PROCEDURE SecurityDemo.YouCanDoAnythingWithDynamicSQL_ButDontDoThis
(
    @query nvarchar(4000)
)
WITH EXECUTE AS SELF
AS
EXECUTE (@query);
```

This procedure gives the person who has access to execute it full access to the database. Bear in mind that *any* query can be executed (DROP TABLE? Sure, why not?), easily allowing improper code to be executed on the database. Now, consider a little math problem; add the following items:

- EXECUTE AS SELF

- Client executing code as the database owner (a very bad, yet very typical practice)

- The code for SecurityDemo.YouCanDoAnythingWithDynamicSQL_ ButDontDoThis

- An injection-susceptible procedure, with a parameter that can hold approximately 4000 characters

What do you get? If you guessed no danger at all, please email me your Social Security number, address, and major credit card details. If you realize that the only one that you really have control over is the fourth one and that hackers, once the SecurityDemo.YouCanDoAnythingWithDynamicSQL_ButDontDoThis procedure was created, could execute any code they wanted as the owner of the database, you get the gold star. So be careful to block code open to injection.

> **Tip**   I am not suggesting that you should avoid the EXECUTE AS setting completely, just that its use must be scrutinized a bit more than the average stored procedure along the lines of when a #temp table is used. Why was EXECUTE AS used? Is the use proper? You must be careful to understand that in the wrong hands this command can be harmful to security.

Performance

There are a couple of reasons why stored procedures are great for performance:

- Parameterization of complex plans is controlled by you at design time rather than controlled by the optimizer at compile time.

- You can performance-tune your queries without making invasive programmatic changes in any other layers of your system.

Parameterization of Complex Plans

Stored procedures, unlike ad hoc SQL, can always have parameterized plans for maximum plan reuse. This lets you avoid the cost of recompilation, as well as the costs of looking for parameters in the code. Any literals are always literal, and any variable is always a parameter. This can lead to some performance issues as well, as occasionally the plan for a stored procedure that gets picked by the optimizer might not be as good of a plan as might be picked for an ad hoc procedure. (This leads very well into the next subsection in this performance heading as well.)

The interesting thing here is that, although you can save the plan of a single query with ad hoc calls, with procedures you can save the plan for a large number of statements together as a package. With all the join types, temp tables, indexes, view text expansions, and so on, optimizing a query is a nontrivial task that might take quite a few milliseconds. As user counts go up, the amount of time begins to add up. With stored procedures, this has the potential to be done only once for each pre-known batch of queries. Parameterization will show up again under disadvantages in some ways, but it is by far a more valuable asset of procedures when used by someone who has a basic understanding of how they work.

Fine-Tuning Without Program Changes

Even if you didn't have the performance capabilities of parameterization for stored procedures (say every query in your procedure was forced to do dynamic SQL and recompile for each call), the ability to fine-tune the queries in the stored procedure without making any changes to the client code is of utmost value. Of course, this is the value of encapsulation, but again, fine-tuning is such an important thing.

Often, a third-party system is purchased that doesn't use stored procedures (it helps if you can blame someone you don't actually work with). If you're a support person for this type of application, you know that there's little you can do if any of the automatic tuning capabilities in SQL Server's Intelligent Query processing fails you, other than to add an index here and there. Then if that doesn't work, force a plan using Query Store or plan guides. For some more details, check out this blog from Grant Fritchey entitled "Query Hash Values, Plan Guides, and the Query Store" (`www.scarydba.com/2017/04/24/the-query-hash-plan-guides-and-the-query-store/`).

"But," you're probably thinking, "shouldn't the third party have planned for the amount of data I have in my table, since we pay them a lot of money?" That would be nice, but the answer is generally only "maybe." In general, the performance characteristics of a database implementation can vary wildly based on how it is actually used, as well as the hardware it is on and what other software is executing. And sometimes these companies make mistakes. While this can be somewhat excusable for a company delivering software to thousands of clients, why do this to yourself when implementing a new system?

By implementing the database access using STORED PROCEDURE objects, it's possible to tweak how queries are written very easily without making any other code changes as data set sizes change from small to massive. For example, I've seen many not so perfect queries that ran great with tens of thousands of rows, but when the needs grew to millions of rows, queries ran for hours. Rewriting the queries using proper query techniques, or sometimes breaking the query up into multiple queries using temporary tables as intermediate steps, gave performance that was many orders of magnitude better. And I have had the converse be true, where I have removed temporary tables and consolidated queries into a single statement to get better performance. The user of the procedures did not even know. We made the change, tested that the output was the same for the same inputs, and deployed.

Even following all of the rules of proper code management, your modify/test/ distribute cycle can be very fast and high quality. This is not because a STORED PROCEDURE object is so much better, but more that it is a fixed piece of code, rather than code that is generated by another piece of code that might optimize different for every execution (or change completely on the next release of the code generator it was implemented on).

For smaller organizations, it can be overly expensive to get a really good test area, so if the code doesn't work quite right in production, you can tune it easily then. Tuning a procedure is easy, even modification procedures; you can just execute the code in a transaction and roll it back. Keep changing the code until satisfied, compile the code in the production database, and move on to the next problem. (This is not best practice AT ALL, but it is something I have to do from time to time.)

Beyond performance, you can also fine-tune things about how the system works. For example, say you are receiving a lot of error messages, but are having a lot of trouble finding out where the error occurs. In the TRIGGER object templates, we include error logging that will capture the error that has occurred in a table. This can also be done in STORED PROCEDURE objects pretty easily.

The primary thing to realize is that the ability to fine-tune the data layer without affecting any changes to the other layers of code is a fantastic benefit. Of course, don't just do it without testing and proper source controls (or source control!) that you would have with any other changes. It is just quicker to regression test a single module, prove that you haven't changed the public interface (the inputs and outputs look exactly the same), and roll out to production.

Ability to Use the Memory-Optimized Engine to Its Fullest

Of all of the arguments I have made to this point of the section on building a data layer, this one can actually be one of the more compelling in my opinion and really goes hand in hand with the previous section. As discussed along in the latter half of the book, there are two engines in SQL Server for data storage, and there are two engines for executing SQL statements. The first is an interpreted engine that compiles your code into high-level commands that are executed and can be tweaked at runtime (hence the reason we have both an estimated plan and an actual plan we can look at when tuning queries). If you access memory-optimized tables using interpreted T-SQL, it accesses in interop mode. You still get the benefits of things like no locking or blocking or multiversion concurrency control, but statements are still interpreted at execution time.

However, if you want to get the full potential out of the memory-optimized engine, you need to use natively compiled objects. There are some very large differences between the two object types. Interpreted code is late bound. If you create an object and reference a name that doesn't exist, then in most cases it doesn't fail until you execute it. The procedure (or function/trigger) references objects by `object_id` in the plan, but if that `object_id` changes, it can recompile by the name.

Natively compiled objects are compiled into machine code, just like if you had written C# and compiled it (as are the tables you have created, by the way), and they reference all resources they use with strong connections. As such, natively compiled objects all must be created as `WITH SCHEMABINDING`, which tells you that the referenced object cannot change when this object is referencing it. (This can make altering objects much more difficult, so it makes source control and scripts far more important since you have to drop or recreate objects sans schema binding first.)

Every `STORED PROCEDURE` object you create natively has one other feature that is interesting. They all execute as an atomic block, which means that everything in the procedure completes or it all fails. You don't have to begin or commit a transaction, and how this occurs really depends on the type of error you receive.

The only real downside of natively compiled objects is the limitations on what they can do. First, they can only access natively compiled objects and in-memory tables. This is to be expected, as the code and objects are all compiled to machine code and are tightly linked together. Second, as of SQL Server 2019, the limitations on available syntax are still quite tremendous—limitations like not being able to use `LIKE, CASE, DELETE,` and `UPDATE with a FROM clause, APPLY, NEXT VALUE FOR` (sequences), and so on. For a more complete set of details about the features and limitations and so on, see the Microsoft Docs topic "Transact-SQL Constructs Not Supported by In-Memory OLTP" (`docs.microsoft.com/en-us/sql/relational-databases/in-memory-oltp/transact-sql-constructs-not-supported-by-in-memory-oltp`).

For examples, I will create two quick example procedures that show you the basic format of natively compiled objects and demonstrate the atomic block feature. This is not a programming book, so I will not dive too deep, but you should at least understand the basics so that you appreciate the discussion of the pros and cons of `STORED PROCEDURE` objects and why natively compiled objects can be tremendous for your performance—as long as you can live with the concurrency differences I discussed in Chapter 12 and the code limitations you can read about here: `docs.microsoft.com/en-us/sql/relational-databases/in-memory-oltp/supported-features-for-`

natively-compiled-t-sql-modules. (It is quite telling that the article is, as of 2019, titled "Supported Features for Natively Compiled T-SQL Modules" rather than referring to some limitations.)

The procedures I will build will use the Warehouse.VehicleTemperatures table in the WideWorldImporters database we have been using in previous chapters. The first, very simple STORED PROCEDURE object fetches and returns rows from the VehicleTemperatures table where a temperature is within a range, based on a couple of parameters:

```
USE WideWorldImporters;
GO
CREATE PROCEDURE Warehouse.VehicleTemperatures$Select
(
        @TemperatureLowRange decimal(10,2) = -99999999.99,
        @TemperatureHighRange decimal(10,2) = 99999999.99
)
WITH SCHEMABINDING, NATIVE_COMPILATION  AS
   BEGIN ATOMIC WITH (TRANSACTION ISOLATION LEVEL = SNAPSHOT,
                     LANGUAGE = N'us_english')
        SELECT VehicleTemperatureID, VehicleRegistration,
               RecordedWhen, Temperature
        FROM    Warehouse.VehicleTemperatures
        WHERE   Temperature BETWEEN @TemperatureLowRange
                                AND @TemperatureHighRange
        ORDER BY RecordedWhen DESC; --Most Recent First
   END;
```

There are a few interesting things to point out. I discussed SCHEMABINDING already, and NATIVE_COMPILATION is obviously telling the engine to use the native compilation engine. BEGIN ATOMIC is a new construct, and it basically says this entire object operates as an atomic unit. If one thing fails, the whole thing does. It is like BEGIN TRANSACTION and COMMIT or ROLLBACK TRANSACTION, but it is built into the module. You specify an isolation level for the atomic block, SNAPSHOT, REPEATABLE READ, or SERIALIZABLE, and they work just as described in Chapter 12. Finally, you have to give it a language to compile under, because it doesn't just default to the local language. This goes to the compiler, just as if you were building your own DLL in a less awesome language than T-SQL.

I compile this and then can execute the procedures just like any other stored procedure:

```
EXECUTE Warehouse.VehicleTemperatures$Select ;
EXECUTE Warehouse.VehicleTemperatures$Select @TemperatureLowRange = 4;
EXECUTE Warehouse.VehicleTemperatures$Select @TemperatureLowRange = 4.1,
                                      @TemperatureHighRange = 4.1;
```

Each of these calls will return a result set shaped like the following:

VehicleTemperatureID	VehicleRegistration	RecordedWhen	...
65270	WWI-321-A	2016-05-30 10:04:45.000000	...
65227	WWI-321-A	2016-05-30 09:18:14.000000	...
64942	WWI-321-A	2016-05-29 12:37:20.000000	...
64706	WWI-321-A	2016-05-29 07:44:12.000000	...
...	...	...	...

Next, I will build a STORED PROCEDURE object that will change a row of data, with a bit of trick code to cause an error if a 0 variable is passed in:

```
CREATE PROCEDURE Warehouse.VehicleTemperatures$FixTemperature
(
    @VehicleTemperatureID int,
    @Temperature decimal(10,2),
    @ThrowErrorFlag bit = 0
)
WITH SCHEMABINDING, NATIVE_COMPILATION AS
--Simulating a procedure you might write to fix a temperature that was
--found to be outside of reasonability
  BEGIN ATOMIC WITH (TRANSACTION ISOLATION LEVEL = SNAPSHOT,
                  LANGUAGE = N'us_english')
    BEGIN TRY
         --Update the temperature
         UPDATE Warehouse.VehicleTemperatures
         SET    Temperature = @Temperature
         WHERE  VehicleTemperatureID = @VehicleTemperatureID;
```

```
      --give the ability to crash the procedure for demo
      --Note, actually doing 1/0 is stopped by the compiler
      DECLARE @CauseFailure int
      SET @CauseFailure =  1/@Temperature;

      --return data if not a fail
      SELECT 'Success' AS Status, VehicleTemperatureID,
             Temperature
         FROM    Warehouse.VehicleTemperatures
         WHERE   VehicleTemperatureID = @VehicleTemperatureID;
      END TRY
      BEGIN CATCH
          --return data for the fail
          SELECT 'Failure' AS Status, VehicleTemperatureID,
                 Temperature
          FROM    Warehouse.VehicleTemperatures
          WHERE   VehicleTemperatureID = @VehicleTemperatureID;

                IF @ThrowErrorFlag = 1
              THROW; --This will cause the batch to stop, and will cause
this
                      --transaction to not be committed. Cannot use ROLLBACK
                      --does not necessarily end the transaction, even if it
                      --ends the batch.
          END CATCH;
    END;
```

I included the THROW in the CATCH block to show the state of the data and to show that the TRY...CATCH construct works, and you can try things like logging errors or whatever you want to try. To show it working, I can use the following batches:

```
--Show original value of temperature for a given row
SELECT Temperature
FROM    Warehouse.VehicleTemperatures
WHERE   VehicleTemperatureID = 65994;
```

This shows the original value:

```
Temperature
---------------------------------------
4.18
```

Now, I execute the procedure with a value that will work:

```
EXECUTE Warehouse.VehicleTemperatures$FixTemperature
                               @VehicleTemperatureId = 65994,
                               @Temperature = 4.2;
```

This will return

```
Status  VehicleTemperatureID Temperature
------- -------------------- -------------------
Success 65994                4.20
```

So that worked just fine. Now, I cause an error by sending a 0 value:

```
EXECUTE Warehouse.VehicleTemperatures$FixTemperature
                               @VehicleTemperatureId = 65994,
                               @Temperature = 0;
```

This causes the following error, though you can see the data was updated successfully:

```
Status  VehicleTemperatureID Temperature
------- -------------------- ---------------
Failure 65994                0.00

Msg 8134, Level 16, State 0, Procedure VehicleTemperatures$FixTemperature,
Line 18
Divide by zero error encountered.
```

Check the data in the table, and you will see that the data has not changed. The THROW caused the module to fail, so it was rolled back. Next, I use the ThrowErrorFlag to show what happens when I ignore the error:

```
EXECUTE Warehouse.VehicleTemperatures$FixTemperature
                            @VehicleTemperatureId = 65994,
                            @Temperature = 0,
                            @ThrowErrorFlag = 0;
```

It still says failure, but provides no error message:

```
Status   VehicleTemperatureID Temperature
-------  -------------------- ----------------
Failure 65994                 0.00
```

I check the actual value in the table, and it is 0.00. So the error from the THROW statement killed the batch and the transaction. Next, let's look at what happens inside a transaction. I start a transaction, let the error occur, and see if I am still in a transaction:

```
UPDATE VehicleTemperatures --Reset the value to the original value
SET     Temperature = 4.18
FROM    Warehouse.VehicleTemperatures
WHERE   VehicleTemperatureID = 65994;
GO
SELECT @@TRANCOUNT AS TranStart;
BEGIN TRANSACTION
EXECUTE Warehouse.VehicleTemperatures$FixTemperature
                            @VehicleTemperatureId = 65994,
                            @Temperature = 0,
                            @ThrowErrorFlag = 1;
GO
SELECT @@TRANCOUNT AS TranEnd;
GO
```

The data is updated. We don't roll back in the procedure, and we just throw an error. The transaction that is started externally is not rolled back:

```
TranStart
-----------
0
Status   VehicleTemperatureID Temperature
-------  -------------------- ----------------------------------------
Failure 65994                 0.00

Msg 8134, Level 16, State 0, Procedure VehicleTemperatures$FixTemperature,
Line 18
Divide by zero error encountered.

TranEnd
-----------
1
```

Now, before I have rollback, I check the value:

```
SELECT Temperature
FROM   Warehouse.VehicleTemperatures
WHERE  VehicleTemperatureID = 65994;
```

The value has not changed, because the error was thrown:

```
Temperature
----------------------------------------
4.18
```

If I make the procedure ignore the error, the data would be changed. I can then roll it back with the ROLLBACK TRANSACTION statement or use the COMMIT TRANSACTION statement to commit it.

So programming natively compiled code is very much the same as normal T-SQL, but there are some subtle, yet big differences you will need to contend with. For some things that you cannot use natively compiled code for, you can use a wrapper of interpreted code. For example, if you wanted to use a SEQUENCE object for a surrogate key, the pseudocode might be as follows:

```
CREATE PROCEDURE InterpretedCode
    @Columns datatype
AS --ignoring any transaction management\error handling you might do
    DECLARE @SurrogateKeyValue int = NEXT VALUE FOR NotNative_SEQUENCE;
    EXEC NativeCode @SurrogateKeyValue = @SurrogateKeyValue
                    @Columns = @Columns;
```

This way you can do as much natively as possible, but still use the constructs you need that are not currently supported. It is definitely a big change of paradigm with a lot of subtle and not so subtle differences, but you can use the memory-optimized engine to greatly improve your performance in ways that can be tremendous. The biggest problem is having the hardware to actually store all the data you need to.

Disadvantages of T-SQL Object Layers

So far, everything has seemingly been all sunshine and lollipops for using STORED PROCEDURE objects, but to be fair there are disadvantages as well. We need to consider the following disadvantages of this method:

- The high initial effort to create an object layer can be prohibitive vs. letting a tool just generate the calls.

- Complexities of implementing optional parameters in searches in an optimum manner.

- Complications of implementing parameterization due to different parameters being sent not being equally as useful.

- Difficulties affecting only certain columns in an operation.

Another pitfall, which I won't cover in detail here, is cross-platform coding. If you're going to build a data layer that needs to be portable to different platforms such as Oracle or MySQL, this need for cross-platform coding can complicate your effort, although it can still be worthwhile in some cases.

High Initial Effort

Of all the pros and cons, the high initial effort to create stored procedures is most often the straw that breaks the camel's proverbial back in the argument for or against building an object layer. For every time I've failed to get a T-SQL object access layer established as the method of access, this has been the reason given in almost every case. There are many tools out there that can map a database to objects or screens to reduce development time. The problem is that they suffer from some or all of the issues discussed in the ad hoc SQL pitfalls.

It's an indefensible stance that writing lots of stored procedures takes the same time up front—quite often, it takes quite a bit more time for initial development. Writing stored procedures is definitely an extra step in the process of getting an application up and running.

An extra step takes extra time, and extra time means extra money. You see where this is going, because customers generally like activities where they see results, not infrastructure. When a charismatic new programmer comes in and promises fantastical results, it can be hard to back up claims that "Down the road, this extra work will pay off." The best defense is knowing the pros and cons and, especially, understanding the application development infrastructure you'll be dealing with.

Difficulty Supporting Optional Parameters in Searches

I already mentioned something similar to optional parameters earlier when talking about dynamic SQL. In those examples, all of the parameters used simple LIKE parameters with character strings. But what about integer values? Or numeric ones? A common (yet ugly) solution is to pass NULL into the variable values by doing something along the lines of the following code:

```
WHERE  (IntegerColumn = @IntegerColumn OR @IntegerColumn IS NULL)
  AND  (NumericColumn = @NumericColumn OR @NumericColumn IS NULL)
  AND  (CharacterColumn LIKE @CharacterColumn);
```

Generally speaking, it's possible to come up with some scheme along these lines to implement optional parameters alongside the rigid needs of parameters in stored procedures. For character strings, while you can use LIKE '%', that isn't necessarily the best-performing construct, since a user could pass in '%value%' and then it would need to scan all rows, so the plan has to be ready to do "good enough." You can even use additional parameters to state @ReturnAllTypeFlag to return all rows of a certain type.

It isn't possible to come up with a perfect scheme, especially a scheme that can be optimized perfectly. However, you can always fall back on using dynamic SQL for these types of queries using optional parameters, just like I did in the "Using Ad Hoc SQL" section. One thing that can help this process is to add the WITH RECOMPILE clause to the stored procedure declaration. This tells the procedure to create a new plan for every execution of the procedure. The cost of compilation is high, but it does start fresh using the values you passed in as parameters.

Although I try to avoid dynamic SQL because of the coding complexity and maintenance difficulties, if the set of columns you need to deal with is large, dynamic SQL can be the best way to handle the situation. Using dynamically built stored procedures is generally the same speed as using ad hoc access from the client, so the benefits from encapsulation still exist.

Parameterization Complications

Stored procedure parameterization uses the variables that you pass the first time the procedure is called to create the plan. This process is known as *parameter sniffing*. (Natively compiled procedures do not do this; they always optimize for UNKNOWN unless you use the OPTIMIZE FOR hint). This is great, though sometimes you get in a situation where you have some values that will work nicely for one query but others that work pitifully. Two different values that are being searched for should end up creating two different plans, but the compiled plan is based on only one of those values.

For example, you might pass in one parameter value that causes the query to return no values, and SQL Server uses that value to build and store the plan. When you pass in another parameter value that causes the query to return more rows, perhaps millions of rows, it takes far too long to execute because the plan chosen was specifically chosen for cardinality of the original parameter value.

Using WITH RECOMPILE at the object level, or the WITH RECOMPILE statement-level hint can avoid the problems of parameter sniffing, but then you have to wait for the plan to be created for each execution, which can be costly if this is a procedure that is executed frequently, losing one of the primary advantages of a stored procedure in the first place. It's possible to branch the code out to allow for both cases, but this can get complicated if you have more than a few scenarios to deal with. Query Store can help mitigate things by watching and applying better plans, and in some cases, you can use an OPTIMIZE FOR hint to optimize for the common case when there are parameter values that produce less than adequate results, although presumably results that you can live with, not a plan that takes an hour or more to execute what normally takes milliseconds.

In some cases, the plan gets stale because of changes in the data or even changes in the structure of the table. In a STORED PROCEDURE object, SQL Server can recompile only the single statement in the plan that needs recompiled. While managing compilation and recompilation can seem a bit complicated, it really isn't; there certainly are a few caveats, but they are generally very few and far between (even less so as Microsoft advances the optimizer with features you can read about here in this Microsoft Docs article: "Intelligent query processing in SQL databases" (docs.microsoft.com/en-us/sql/relational-databases/performance/intelligent-query-processing)).

Difficulty Affecting Only Certain Columns in an Operation

When you're coding stored procedures without dynamic SQL, the code you'll write is going to be pretty rigid. If you want to write a stored procedure to modify a row in the table created earlier in the chapter—Sales.Contact—you'd write something along the lines of this skeleton procedure:

```
USE Chapter13;
GO
--table create is part of download

CREATE PROCEDURE Sales.Contact$Update
(
    @ContactId    int,
    @FirstName    varchar(30),
    @LastName     varchar(30),
    @CompanyName  varchar(100),
    @SalesLevelId int,
    @ContactNotes varchar(max)
)
AS
 BEGIN
    BEGIN TRY
          UPDATE Sales.Contact
          SET    FirstName = @FirstName,
```

```
                LastName = @LastName,
                CompanyName = @CompanyName,
                SalesLevelId = @SalesLevelId,
                ContactNotes = @ContactNotes
          WHERE   ContactId = @ContactId;
    END TRY
    BEGIN CATCH
      IF @@TRANCOUNT > 0
            ROLLBACK TRANSACTION;

      DECLARE @ERRORmessage nvarchar(4000)
      SET @ERRORmessage = 'Error occurred in procedure ''' +
                  OBJECT_NAME(@@procid) + ''', Original Message: '''
                  + ERROR_MESSAGE() + '''';
      THROW 50000,@ERRORmessage,1;
    END CATCH;
  END;
```

A procedure such as this is fine *most* of the time, because it usually isn't a big performance concern just to pass all values and modify those values, even setting them to the same value and revalidating. However, in some cases, validating every column can be a performance issue because not every validation is the same as the next.

For example, suppose that the SalesLevelId column is a very important column for the corporate sales process and needs to validate in the data if the customer should, in fact, actually be at the level assigned. A TRIGGER object might be created to do that validation, and it could take a relatively large amount of time. Note that when the average operation takes 1 millisecond, 100 milliseconds can actually be "a long time." It is all relative to what else is taking place and how many times a minute thing is occurring. You could easily turn this into a dynamic SQL procedure, though since you don't know if the value of SalesLevelId has changed, you will have to check that first:

```
ALTER PROCEDURE Sales.Contact$Update
(
    @ContactId   int,
    @FirstName   varchar(30),
    @LastName    varchar(30),
    @CompanyName varchar(100),
```

```
    @SalesLevelId   int,
    @ContactNotes   varchar(max)
)
WITH EXECUTE AS SELF
AS
  BEGIN
    DECLARE @EntryTrancount int = @@TRANCOUNT;

    BEGIN TRY
        --declare variable to use to tell whether to include the sales level
        DECLARE @SalesOrderIdChangedFlag bit =
                CASE WHEN (SELECT SalesLevelId
                           FROM   Sales.Contact
                           WHERE  ContactId = @ContactId) = @SalesLevelId
                      THEN 0 ELSE 1 END;

      DECLARE @query nvarchar(max);
        SET @query = '
        UPDATE Sales.Contact
        SET    FirstName = ' +
                  --Function created earlier in chapter
                  Tools.String$EscapeString(@FirstName,DEFAULT,DEFAULT) + ',
               LastName = ' +
                  Tools.String$EscapeString(@LastName,DEFAULT,DEFAULT) + ',
               CompanyName = ' +
               Tools.String$EscapeString(@CompanyName,DEFAULT,DEFAULT) + ',
                '+ CASE WHEN @salesOrderIdChangedFlag = 1 THEN
                'SalesLevelId = ' + CAST(@SalesLevelId AS varchar(10)) + ',
                ' else '' END + ',
               ContactNotes = ' +
               Tools.String$EscapeString(@ContactNotes,DEFAULT,DEFAULT) + '
        WHERE  ContactId = ' + CAST(@ContactId AS varchar(10)) ;
        EXECUTE (@query);
    END TRY
    BEGIN CATCH
      IF @@TRANCOUNT > 0
          ROLLBACK TRANSACTION;
```

```
    DECLARE @ERRORmessage nvarchar(4000)
    SET @ERRORmessage = 'Error occurred in procedure ''' +
                OBJECT_NAME(@@procid) + ''', Original Message: '''
                + ERROR_MESSAGE() + '''';
    THROW 50000,@ERRORmessage,1;
  END CATCH;
END;
```

This is a pretty simple example, and as you can see the code is already getting pretty darn ugly. Of course, the advantage of encapsulation is still intact, since the user will be able to do exactly the same operation as before with no change to the public interface, but the code is immediately less manageable at the module level.

An alternative you might consider would be an INSTEAD OF trigger to conditionally do the update on the column in question if the inserted and deleted columns don't match:

```
CREATE TRIGGER Sales.Contact$InsteadOfUpdate
ON Sales.Contact
INSTEAD OF UPDATE
AS
BEGIN
   SET NOCOUNT ON;
   SET ROWCOUNT 0; --in case the client has modified the rowcount
   --use inserted for insert or update trigger, deleted for update or
   --delete trigger count instead of @@rowcount due to merge behavior that
   --sets @@rowcount to a number that is equal to number of merged rows,
   --not rows being checked in trigger
   DECLARE @msg varchar(2000),    --used to hold the error message
   --use inserted for insert or update trigger, deleted for update or
   --delete trigger count instead of @@rowcount due to merge behavior that
   --sets @@rowcount to a number that is equal to number of merged rows,
   --not rows being checked in trigger
         @RowsAffected int = (SELECT COUNT(*) FROM inserted);

   --no need to continue on if no rows affected
   IF @RowsAffected = 0 RETURN;
```

```
BEGIN TRY
      --[validation blocks]
      --[modification blocks]
      --<perform action>

      UPDATE Contact
      SET    FirstName = inserted.FirstName,
             LastName = inserted.LastName,
             CompanyName = inserted.CompanyName,
             PersonalNotes = inserted.PersonalNotes,
             ContactNotes = inserted.ContactNotes
      FROM   Sales.Contact AS Contact
                 JOIN inserted
                     ON inserted.ContactId = Contact.ContactId

      IF UPDATE(SalesLevelId) --this column requires heavy validation
                             --only want to update if necessary
         UPDATE Contact
         SET    SalesLevelId = inserted.SalesLevelId
         FROM   Sales.Contact
                   JOIN inserted
                       ON inserted.ContactId = Contact.ContactId

         --this correlated subquery checks for values that
         --have changed
         WHERE  EXISTS (SELECT *
                        FROM   deleted
                        WHERE  deleted.ContactId =
                                           inserted.ContactId
                          AND  deleted.SalesLevelId <>
                                           inserted.SalesLevelId)
END TRY
BEGIN CATCH
     IF @@TRANCOUNT > 0
        ROLLBACK TRANSACTION;
```

```
        THROW;

    END CATCH
END;
```

This is a lot of code, but it's reasonably simple. Just update the simple columns all the time. Then verify whether or not the "high-cost" columns have been referenced in the UPDATE statement before updating them. The point of this is to note that the more encapsulated you get from the client, the more you can do in your code to modify the code to your needs. The stored procedure layer can be treated as a set of modules that return a set of data, save the state of some data, and so forth, without the client needing to know anything about the structure of anything other than the parameters and tabular data streams that are to be returned.

Stored Procedure or Ad Hoc?

If the opinions in the previous sections were not enough (and as an author, I will rarely provide definitive answers unless it is something 100% right or 100% wrong), this section summarizes my opinion on what is good and bad about using ad hoc SQL and stored procedures. As Oscar Wilde was quoted as saying, "It is only about things that do not interest one that one can give a really unbiased opinion, which is no doubt the reason why an unbiased opinion is always absolutely valueless." This is a topic that I care about, and I have firm feelings about what is right and wrong. Of course, it is also true that many viable, profitable, and stable systems don't follow any of these opinions. That said, let's recap the pros and cons I have given for the different approaches.

With no outside influence other than this list of pros and cons so far in this chapter and a lot of experience, I can state without hesitation that building a STORED PROCEDURE (or at least VIEW/TABLE-VALUED FUNCTION) layer is the way to go, if for no other reason than the encapsulation angle. By separating the database code from the client code, you get an effective separation of data manipulation code from presentation code. But "no outside influence" is a pipe dream, as developers will have their own ideas, and to be realistic, I am obviously open to the value of using an ORM-type tool that speeds up development time and encapsulates a lot of the work of application building. The important point is that we have to keep in mind that development costs will be dwarfed by maintenance costs not only over time, dealing with code optimization issues, but in simple downtime if the object layer code that generates SQL does so poorly for the amount of data you grow to have. People sitting around, not working, but still getting paid is not a great thing, though still better than 10s or 1000s of customers who can't spend money on the website because it is crashing.

I must also note that I'm not suggesting that *all* code and logic that works with data must, or even should, be encoded into STORED PROCEDURE objects. Too often when stored procedures are used as the complete data interface, the people doing the programming tend to start putting all sorts of procedural code in the procedures, making them hard to write and hard to maintain. The next step is moaning that procedures are terrible, slow, inflexible, and just too hard to code. This is often one of the sticking points between the two different opinions on how to do things. More or less, what's called for when building a user interface is to build STORED PROCEDURE objects that replace T-SQL statements that you would have built in an ad hoc manner, keeping T-SQL control of flow language at a minimum. Sometimes you will need a few statements to transform structures to make things work cleaner for the UI, but the goal is simplicity and tunability.

Several types of code act on data that shouldn't be in stored procedures or T-SQL:

- *Mutable business logic and rules*: T-SQL is a rigid language that can be difficult to work with to do complex logic. T-SQL should be used to manipulate and do calculations with data.

- *Formatting data*: When you want to present a value in some format, it's best to leave this to the presentation layer or user interface of the application. You should use SQL Server primarily to do set-based operations using basic DML and have as little of the T-SQL control of flow language as possible.

The bottom line is that what often tips the scales to using ad hoc access is just plain old up-front time. The initial effort required to build stored procedures is going to be increased over just using ad hoc SQL generated from a mapping layer. In fact, for every system I've been involved with where our access plan was to use ad hoc SQL, the primary factor was time: "It takes too long to build the procedures," or "It takes too long to develop code to access the stored procedures," or even "The tool we are using doesn't support stored procedures." All this inevitably swings to the statement that "The DBA is being too rigid. Why do we want to...?"

The complicated part of this argument is that their arguments have merit. If the code for the system is replaced every other year with new technology, the objects you create may be obviated the next year and need to be rewritten. The database design probably lives as is unless requirements change considerably, but paradigms to access the data can change quite rapidly. The more complicated part is that when a system is built that works well enough (which usually means taking your time and doing things in a best practice manner right), it may last for 10 years or more, through three or four new versions of SQL Server. Stored procedures can take advantage of new SQL features and be easily tested one by one.

This discussion responses are a large part of why this section of the chapter needed to be written. It's never good to state that ad hoc SQL is just plain wrong, because that's clearly not true. The issue is which is better in general circumstances, and stored procedures greatly tip the scale, at least until outside forces and developer talents are brought in.

Building Reusable Components

As we near the end of the database design process, the core database should be pretty much completed from a design standpoint. We have spent time looking at performance, concurrency, and security patterns, and so far in this chapter, we looked at patterns of development that you can follow to help implement the database in a manner that will work well under almost any typical OLTP-style load.

As you are coding, one thing you will start to notice is that you have bits of code that you use over and over, sometimes as utilities and sometimes as building blocks for other code. I already introduced one such tool when I built the `Tools.String$EscapeString` function that I used in several sections of the book to handle when you need to take a value like O'Rierdon and put that value into a variable/string safely as 'O''Rierdon'.

I introduced the concept of a contained database earlier to help maintain a secure and portable database. The concepts of this chapter are based on the idea that the fundamental goal is to make databases have all of the code they need inside them, for a couple of reasons:

- *Portability*: If the database has everything it needs to execute, you never have to be concerned if you have some other database available to reference.

- *Versioning*: If you need to break backward compatibility for some purpose, you can version a tool such that Database A has the new version and Database B can catch up whenever it can, but Database A needn't have to get a renamed version to get the new functionality, leading to a mess.

Naturally, the reality of database design is that most databases are rarely complete cookie-cutter affairs. Most companies, even when they buy a third-party package to implement some specific part of their business, are going to end up making (possibly substantial) customizations to the database to fit their needs. However, most projects will have many components that follow a common pattern that will look like something that has been done before (not at all unlike how SQL Server has many system objects that you can use to get things like the name of the server or database you are working on).

In this section, I want to explore a few database constructs that I find to be useful and almost always the same for every database I create (where I have complete control, obviously!). Not every database will need to contain all of what I will present, but when I need a common feature, I will use the exact same code in every database, installable just with a script that is version controlled first by itself and then the code again in the database where it is used.

Note   If you are dealing with a third-party system that forbids adding any of your own objects, even in a schema that is separated from the shipped schemas, don't think that everything I am saying here doesn't apply to you. All of the example code presented supposes a single-database approach, but if you cannot follow that approach, another common approach is to create a companion database where you locate code you need to access their code from the database tier. You would need to slightly rework some examples in this chapter to use that approach, but that rework would be minimal specifically to add three-part names and handle the cross-database security as discussed in Chapter 10.

Be aware though; it is great to build modules that you reuse, but care should be taken not to do a tremendous amount of modularization in your SQL code. Query optimization is a complex process, and when you start calling objects from objects from other objects, performance is probably going to start suffering pretty quickly. It may not be likely to be noticed when you are doing your initial development, but more once you have real customers on your site.

For the examples in this section, I am going to use a copy of the `WideWorldImporters` database (which we have used in previous sections of this chapter and others already) to stick to the supposition of the chapter that you should place the tables in the database with the data you are working with. The examples are easily ported to your own database or even older SQL Server example databases like `AdventureWorks` or even `Northwind`.

> **Note**   The code in this chapter will all be presented using on-disk tables. Some objects will have in-memory OLTP versions in the download.

Before digging into the specific examples, I should note that the goal of building reusable components I am covering is the building of objects that are needed in your database code, not management utilities like those you might use for checking who is active on your server like Adam Machanic's sp_whoisactive (whoisactive.com) or maintaining your server like Ola Hallengren's toolset (ola.hallengren.com). Utilities like that are typically installed in the master database. Another tool that I make use of are scripts that are stored in files (or Redgate's SQL Prompt snippet/template system) that I have available without trying to create objects that are permanently stored in a database. Utility code is far different from heavily repeated code such as what you use to build an OLTP or even report database from.

In this section, I will discuss and briefly demonstrate several modules, some of which will be available in the downloads for the book.

- *Numbers table*: A table of numbers, usually integers that can be used for a number of interesting uses (not many of them mathematics related).

- *Calendar table*: A table where every row represents a day, assisting in grouping data for queries, both for reports and operational usage.

- *Utility objects*: Utilities to monitor usage of the system and extended DDL to support operations that aren't part of the base DDL in T-SQL. Most programmers I know have utility objects/scripts that they use to make their job easier, and some just fit as permanent objects in the databases where they are usable.

- *Tools library*: There are lots of code that I regularly use, beyond the Numbers and Calendar tables, that are good to have in all databases I work with. In this section I will include the code for a few such items.

- *Logging objects*: Utilities to log the actions of users in the database, generally for system management reasons. A common use is an error log to capture when and where errors are occurring.

- *Data*: There is some data that is useful universally, such as geographic/demographic data. Having such data available in a versioned manner can be very useful.

The sky is the limit obviously; use your imagination as to how you can build up your code base in a way that is reusable and also will enhance your application's needs. The more controlled/repeatable your code is, the easier it will be to go from database to database and not have to relearn how each new system works.

My installable scripts will allow you to set the name of the schema you choose to put your code into, but I generally use Tools for stuff that general users can use, Utility for stuff that is very governed/dangerous (e.g., things like the ability to remove all of the constraints on a database), Monitor for monitoring tools, ErrorHandling for error management tools, and finally Reference for data and tools to manage reference data that is read-only to the user, but might contain the names of the countries in the world, states in the United States, and so on—still versioned because if a new country comes into being, not all applications may be able to use it immediately.

Note   In the downloads on GitHub (`github.com/drsqlgithub/dbdesignbook6`), there will be a set of "Useful Code" where these objects and others are included for download, along with the Chapter 13 file.

Numbers Table

A numbers table is a precalculated table of some numeric sequence, with the most typical being non-negative integers. The name "numbers" is pretty open ended, but getting so specific as CardinalNumber is going to subject you to ridicule by the other programmers on the playground. In earlier editions of the book, I had used the name sequence (which is truly a better name), but with the addition of the sequence object in SQL Server 2012, the name "numbers" was the next best thing. We will use the numbers table when we need to work with data in an ordered manner, particularly a given sequence of numbers. For example, if you needed a list of the top ten products sold and you only sold six, you would have to somehow manufacture four more rows for display. Having a table where you can easily output a sequence of numbers is going to be a very valuable asset at times indeed.

While you can make a numbers table contain any numbers you may need, usually it is just a simple table of non-negative integers from 0 to some reasonable limit, where *reasonable* is more or less how many you might possibly need. I generally load mine by default up to 999999 (999999 gives you full six digits and is a very convenient number for the query I will use to load the table). With the algorithm I will present, you can easily expand to create a sequence of numbers that is larger than you can store in SQL Server, even in a numeric datatype.

There are two really beautiful things behind this concept. First, the table of non-negative integers has some great uses dealing with text data, as well as doing all sorts of math with. Second, you can create additional columns or even other tables that you can use to represent other sets of numbers that you find useful or interesting, for example:

- Even or odd, prime, squares, cubes, and so on.

- Other ranges or even other grains of values, for example, -1, -.5, 0, .5, 1

- Some mathematical progression like the Fibonacci sequence (though the first two numbers are 1, but 1, 2, 3, 5, 8, 13, etc.) of square numbers (1, 4, 16, 25, 36, etc.). One of the examples in the downloads under the heading "Extended Examples" uses a mathematical equation to set a column and use it to do a stupid math trick.

In the examples in this section, we will look at a technique you may find useful and possibly quite often. The following code to generate a simple numbers table of integers is pretty simple, though it looks a bit daunting the first time you see it. It is quite fast to execute in this form, but no matter how fast it may seem, it is not going to be faster than querying from a table that has the sequence of numbers precalculated and stored ahead of time (not to mention if you want to add attributes that are not easily calculated):

```
CREATE TABLE Tools.Number
(
    I    int CONSTRAINT PKNumber PRIMARY KEY
);

--Load it with integers from 0 to 999999:
;WITH digits (I) AS (--set up a set of numbers from 0-9
        SELECT I
```

```
         FROM    (VALUES (0),(1),(2),(3),(4),(5),(6),(7),(8),(9)) AS digits (I))
--builds a table from 0 to 999999
,Integers (I) AS (
        --since you have every combinations of digits, This math turns it
        --into numbers since every combination of digits is present
        SELECT D1.I + (10*D2.I) + (100*D3.I) + (1000*D4.I) + (10000*D5.I)
                + (100000*D6.I)
        --gives us combinations of every digit
        FROM digits AS D1 CROSS JOIN digits AS D2 CROSS JOIN digits AS D3
                CROSS JOIN digits AS D4 CROSS JOIN digits AS D5
                CROSS JOIN digits AS D6 )
INSERT INTO Tools.Number(I)
SELECT I
FROM    Integers;
```

Now, look at the data, and you can see there are 999999 rows:

```
SELECT *
FROM    Tools.Number
ORDER BY I;
```

This code will return a set of 10,0000 rows as follows:

```
I
-----------
0
1
2
...
999998
999999
```

In the downloads, I will include several additional examples (including my favorite stupid math trick inspired by the *Futurama* TV show, but a simple and incredibly useful usage is when trying to find some character in a really long string of characters that are in multiple rows).

For example, say we want to find names with a certain character in the name. Sometimes when you execute a query and you expect to see data formatted in a specific way, it turns out that some data isn't quite right. Some data with a really large/odd Unicode value (like 20012, picking one randomly) that you didn't expect in your database of English-only words could cause issue with your programs.

Using the following technique, you don't have to go column by column/row by row looking for rows with this data; it can be done all at once, character by character. Using a relatively simple join, you can do this for a large number of rows at once, this time joining to a table in the WideWorldImporters database that can provide us with an easy example set.

The idea is that we join the Tools.Number table to the People table and use each number from 1—the length of the string to substring the value to get the output:

```
SELECT People.FullName, Number.I AS Position,
            SUBSTRING(People.FullName,Number.I,1) AS [Char],
            UNICODE(SUBSTRING(People.FullName, Number.I,1)) AS [Unicode]
FROM    Application.People
            JOIN Tools.Number
                ON Number.I <= LEN(People.FullName )
                    AND  UNICODE(SUBSTRING(People.FullName, Number.I,1))
                                                            IS NOT NULL

ORDER  BY FullName;
```

This returns 15128 rows (one for each character in every full name) in < 1 second on my desktop (which admittedly is pretty solid: i7, 32 GB, 1 TB NVMe, SSD):

FullName	Position	Char	Unicode
Aahlada Thota	1	A	65
Aahlada Thota	2	a	97
Aahlada Thota	3	h	104
Aahlada Thota	4	l	108
Aahlada Thota	5	a	97
Aahlada Thota	6	d	100
Aahlada Thota	7	a	97
Aahlada Thota	8		32
....	...	.	...

Aakarsha Nookala	1	A	65
Aakarsha Nookala	2	a	97
Aakarsha Nookala	3	k	107
Aakarsha Nookala	4	a	97
Aakarsha Nookala	5	r	114
Aakarsha Nookala	6	s	115
Aakarsha Nookala	7	h	104
Aakarsha Nookala	8	a	97
....	...	.	...

With that set, you can easily start eliminating known safe Unicode values with a simple WHERE clause and find your outlier that is causing some issue with some process. For example, you could find all names that include a character not in the range of A–Z, space, comma, or dash characters:

```
SELECT People.FullName, Number.I AS Position,
            SUBSTRING(People.FullName,Number.I,1) AS [Char],
            UNICODE(SUBSTRING(People.FullName, Number.I,1)) AS [Unicode]
FROM    Application.People
          JOIN Tools.Number
            ON Number.I <= LEN(People.FullName )
              AND  UNICODE(SUBSTRING(People.FullName, Number.I,1))
                                                            IS NOT NULL
WHERE   SUBSTRING(People.FullName, Number.I,1)
                  NOT LIKE '[a-zA-Z ~''~-]' ESCAPE '~'
ORDER   BY FullName;
```

This returns the following:

FullName	Position	Char	Unicode
Abhoy PrabhupÄda	15		129
BahadıÄ±r Korkmaz	7	±	177
Bimla PrabhupÄda	15		129
Deviprasad PrabhupÄda	20		129
Himadri PrabhupÄda	17		129
Ivica LuÄic	10		141

Malay PrabhupÄda	15		129
Sevim AydÄ±n	11	±	177
Taner YÄ±lmaz	9	±	177
Tereza PinÄakova	12		143
VÄ›ra Kopecka	3	›	8250
VÄ›ra Stejskalova	3	›	8250
Vicente ChÃ¡vez	12	¡	161

With just the simple numbers table, you can do this and many other sorts of calculations far easier.

Calendar Table

A common task that people want to know how to do is perform groupings and calculations with date values. For example, you might want sales grouped by month, week, year, or any other grouping. You can usually do this using the SQL Server date functions, but often can be costly or at least pretty messy or impossible if you want something more than a simple calendar year and month grouping (like if you want to group by times of corporate sales events and times when there is no sales event). What can truly help with this process is to use a table filled with date values, decorated with the common and not so common grouping values. This is generally called a calendar table. Using a calendar table is commonplace in business intelligence/OLAP implementations, but it certainly can be useful in OLTP databases when you get stuck doing a confusing date range query.

Using the same form of precalculated logic that we applied to the numbers table, we can create a table that contains one row per date. I will set the date as the primary key and then have data related to the date as columns. The following is the basis of the date table that I currently use. You can extend it as you want to include working days, holidays, special events, and so on, to filter/group in the same manner as you do with these columns, along with the others I will show you how to add later in the section (again, I am working in a copy of WideWorldImporters, bolting on my tools to make life easier):

```
CREATE TABLE Tools.Calendar
(
        DateValue date NOT NULL CONSTRAINT PKTools_Calendar PRIMARY KEY,
        DayName varchar(10) NOT NULL,
```

```
        MonthName varchar(10) NOT NULL,
        Year varchar(60) NOT NULL,
        Day tinyint NOT NULL,
        DayOfTheYear smallint NOT NULL,
        Month smallint NOT NULL,
        Quarter tinyint NOT NULL
);
```

Note that the name `Calendar` is not truly consistent with our names representing a single row, at least not in a natural way, but the other names that we might use (Date, DateValue, etc.) all sound equally forced or hokey. Since the table represents a calendar and a calendar item generally would logically represent a day, I went with it. A stretch perhaps, but naming is pretty difficult at times, especially when working in a namespace in which the real world and SQL Server have so many established names.

The next step is to load the table with values, which is pretty much a straightforward task using the `Numbers` table that we just finished creating in the previous section. Using the DATENAME and DATEPART functions and a few simple case expressions, you load the different values. I will make use of many of the functions in the examples, but most are very easy to understand:

```
--load up to the next 2 years
DECLARE @enddate date = CAST(YEAR(GETDATE() + 2) AS char(4)) + '0101';
WITH Dates (NewDateValue) AS (
        --pick some base date for your calendar, it doesn't really matter
        SELECT DATEADD(day,I,'19000101') AS NewDateValue
        FROM Tools.Number
)
INSERT Tools.Calendar
        (DateValue,DayName
        ,MonthName,Year,Day
        ,DayOfTheYear,Month,Quarter
)
SELECT
        Dates.NewDateValue as DateValue,
        DATENAME(dw,Dates.NewDateValue) AS DayName,
        DATENAME(mm,Dates.NewDateValue) AS MonthName,
        DATENAME(yy,Dates.NewDateValue) AS Year,
```

```
          DATEPART(day,Dates.NewDateValue) AS Day,
          DATEPART(dy,Dates.NewDateValue) AS DayOfTheYear,
          DATEPART(m,Dates.NewDateValue) AS Month,
          DATEPART(qq,Dates.NewDateValue) AS Quarter

FROM      Dates
WHERE     Dates.NewDateValue BETWEEN '20000101' AND @enddate
ORDER     BY DateValue;
```

Just like the numbers table, there are several commonly useful ways to use the calendar table. As an example of usage, say you want to know how many sales had been made during each year in the Sales.Order table in the WideWorldImporters database. This is why there is a Year column in the table:

```
SELECT Calendar.Year, COUNT(*) AS OrderCount
FROM    /*WideWorldImporters.*/ Sales.Orders
          JOIN Tools.Calendar
             ON Orders.OrderDate = Calendar.DateValue
                --OrderDate is a date type column
GROUP BY Calendar.Year
ORDER BY Calendar.Year;
```

This returns the following:

Year	OrderCount
2013	19450
2014	21199
2015	23329
2016	9617

The beauty of the calendar table is that you can easily group values that are not that simple to compute in a really obvious manner all while using a natural relational coding style/technique. An example is to count the sales on Tuesdays and Thursdays:

```
SELECT Calendar.DayName, COUNT(*) as OrderCount
FROM    /*WideWorldImporters.*/ Sales.Orders
          JOIN Tools.Calendar
```

```
            --note, the cast here could be a real performance killer
            --consider using date columns where possible
         ON CAST(Orders.OrderDate as date) = Calendar.DateValue
WHERE Calendar.DayName IN ('Tuesday','Thursday')
GROUP BY Calendar.DayName
ORDER BY Calendar.DayName;
```

This returns the following:

DayName	OrderCount
Thursday	13421
Tuesday	13737

In the downloads under "Extended Examples," I will extend the table to include fiscal years and even relative positioning columns that help you ask for the last N months using simple arithmetic.

Utility Objects

As you acquire more and more experience over the years (which is loosely synonymous with the many failures you will encounter), you will undoubtedly end up with a toolbox full of various tools that you find you use quite frequently. Some of these tools will be used in an ad hoc manner when you are dealing with the same problems over and over again.

In this section, I will cover a few types of utilities that I find useful in my databases I manage. I will present one example in each, though this is only just a start to whet your appetite to build more.

I will cover a few utilities in these categories:

- *Monitoring tools*: Tools to watch what is going on with the database, such as row counts, file sizes, and so forth.

- *Extended DDL utilities*: Tools used to make changes to the structure of the database, usually to remove keys or indexes for load processes, usually to do multiple DDL calls where SQL Server's DDL would require multiple calls.

Monitoring Objects

Keeping an eye on database usage is a very common need for the database administrator. A very typical question from upper management is to find out how much a system is used and particularly how much the database has grown over time. With a little bit of planning, it is easy to be prepared for these questions and others by doing a bit of monitoring.

In the example, I will build a table that will capture the row counts from all of the tables in the database (other than the sys schema), by running a stored procedure. It is set up to use the sys.partitions catalog view, because it gives a "good enough" count of the rows in all of the tables. If it is important to get extremely precise row counts, you could use a cursor and do a SELECT COUNT(*) from each table in the database as well. In my real systems, we have this sort of object, as well as many based on the dynamic management views (DMVs) that capture statistics about the database daily or sometimes hourly.

For monitoring data, I will create a Monitor schema. To this I will not give rights to anyone other than the db_owner users by default, as the Monitor schema will generally be for the DBA only to get a feel for system growth, not for general usage:

```
CREATE SCHEMA Monitor;
```

Next, I will create a table, with the grain of the data being at a daily level. The procedure will be created to allow you to capture row counts more than once a day if needed. Note too that the ObjectType column can have more than just tables, since it might be interesting to see if indexed views are also growing in size. I will include only clustered or heap structures so that we get only the base structures:

```
CREATE TABLE Monitor.TableRowCount
(
        SchemaName   sysname NOT NULL,
        TableName    sysname NOT NULL,
        CaptureDate AS (CAST(CaptureTime AS date)) PERSISTED NOT NULL,
        CaptureTime datetime2(0)    NOT NULL,
        Rows         int NOT NULL, --proper name, rowcount is reserved
        ObjectType   sysname NOT NULL,
        CONSTRAINT PKTableRowCount
            PRIMARY KEY (SchemaName, TableName, CaptureDate)
);
```

Then the following procedure will be scheduled to run daily:

```
CREATE OR ALTER PROCEDURE Monitor.TableRowCount$CaptureRowcounts
(
     @RecaptureTodaysValuesFlag bit = 0
)
AS
-- ------------------------------------------------------------------
-- Monitor the row counts of all tables in the database on a daily basis
-- Error handling not included for example clarity
--
-- NOTE: This code expects the Monitor.TableRowCount to be in the same
--        db as the  tables being monitored. Rework would be needed if this
--        is not a possibility
--
-- 2020 Louis Davidson - drsql@hotmail.com - drsql.org
-- ------------------------------------------------------------------

SET XACT_ABORT ON; --simple error handling, rollback on any error

BEGIN TRANSACTION;

IF RecaptureTodaysValuesFlag = 1
  DELETE
  FROM Monitor.TableRowCount
  WHERE CaptureDate = CAST(SYSDATETIME() AS date);

-- The CTE is used to set up the set of rows to put into the
--   Monitor.TableRowCount table
WITH CurrentRowcount AS (
SELECT OBJECT_SCHEMA_NAME(partitions.object_id) AS SchemaName,
       OBJECT_NAME(partitions.object_id) AS TableName,
       SYSDATETIME() AS CaptureTime,
       SUM(rows) AS Rows,
       objects.type_desc AS ObjectType
```

```
FROM    sys.partitions
          JOIN sys.objects
              ON partitions.object_id = objects.object_id
WHERE   index_id in (0,1) --Heap 0 or Clustered 1 "indexes"
AND     object_schema_name(partitions.object_id) NOT IN ('sys')
--the GROUP BY handles partitioned tables with > 1 partition
GROUP BY partitions.object_id, objects.type_desc)

--MERGE allows this procedure to be run > 1 a day without concern,
--it will update if the row for the day exists
MERGE  Monitor.TableRowCount
USING  (SELECT SchemaName, TableName, CaptureTime, Rows, ObjectType
        FROM CurrentRowcount) AS Source
              ON (Source.SchemaName = TableRowCount.SchemaName
                  AND Source.TableName = TableRowCount.TableName
                  AND CAST(Source.CaptureTime AS date) =
                                        TableRowCount.CaptureDate)
WHEN NOT MATCHED THEN
        INSERT (SchemaName, TableName, CaptureTime, Rows, ObjectType)
        VALUES (Source.SchemaName, Source.TableName, Source.CaptureTime,
                Source.Rows, Source.ObjectType);

COMMIT TRANSACTION;
```

Now, you execute the following procedure and check the results for the HumanResources schema in WideWorldImporters, where we have been working:

```
EXEC Monitor.TableRowCount$CaptureRowcounts;

SELECT *
FROM    Monitor.TableRowCount
WHERE   SchemaName = 'Purchasing'
ORDER BY SchemaName, TableName;
```

Then (assuming you are still in the pristine version of the WideWorldImporters database we are working on), the output of this batch will be as follows:

```
SchemaName   TableName                       CaptureDate  Rows   ObjectType
----------   ---------------------------     -----------  -----  ---------
Purchasing   PurchaseOrderLines              2020-06-15   8367   USER_TABLE
Purchasing   PurchaseOrders                  2020-06-15   2074   USER_TABLE
Purchasing   SupplierCategories              2020-06-15   9      USER_TABLE
Purchasing   SupplierCategories_Archive      2020-06-15   1      USER_TABLE
Purchasing   Suppliers                       2020-06-15   13     USER_TABLE
Purchasing   Suppliers_Archive               2020-06-15   13     USER_TABLE
Purchasing   SupplierTransactions            2020-06-15   2438   USER_TABLE
```

If you look at all of the rows in the table for the Monitor schema, you will see that they were 0, since it was checked before we added these rows. Run it again tomorrow, and you will notice that there is an increase of rows in the Monitor.TableRowCount table, notably the rows we just added. I tend to capture the row count of all tables in the Monitor and Tools database as well just to see the history of these values as well. In many cases, I will then add a procedure to check for abnormal growth of rows, or reduction in rows, in a table. For example, if the Calendar table changes rows (up or down at all most of the year or more than 366 at the end of the year), there could easily be an issue, since this table will generally grow once, at the end of each year. You might also write a query to make sure that the monitoring table rows are increasing and alert the admin if not.

Extended DDL Utilities

In a high number of the systems I work with, data is constantly being moved around, sometimes a very large amount. I almost always make sure that there are FOREIGN KEY, CHECK, UNIQUE constraints and so on in almost every database I build, even if it is just a replica of data from another database. This is a way to make sure that the data that is loaded meets the needed quality standards that the user demands.

However, constraints can really slow down the loading of data in bulk, so quite often the loading program (like SSIS) disables your constraints to make it load the data faster. Unfortunately SSIS, at least, doesn't re-enable the constraints after it is done loading the data, and often we wish for it to be increased later in the process. So I created the following procedure to re-enable the constraints in some or all of the tables in the database. I will put the procedure in a Utility schema and restrict access to only sysadmin users (even going so far as to use a DENY all permissions for non-sysadmin access):

```
CREATE SCHEMA Utility;
GO
CREATE PROCEDURE Utility.Constraints$ResetEnableAndTrustedStatus
(
    @table_name sysname = '%',
    @table_schema sysname = '%',
    @doFkFlag bit = 1,
    @doCkFlag bit = 1
) as
-- ----------------------------------------------------------------
-- Enables disabled foreign key and check constraints, and sets
-- trusted status so optimizer can use them
--
-- NOTE: This code expects the Monitor.TableRowCount to be in the
--same db as the tables being monitored. Rework would be needed
--if this is not a possibility
--
-- 2020 Louis Davidson - drsql@hotmail.com - drsql.org
-- ----------------------------------------------------------------
  BEGIN
        SET NOCOUNT ON;
        DECLARE @statements cursor; --use to loop through constraints to
                        -- execute one constraint for individual DDL calls
        SET @statements = CURSOR FOR
            WITH FKandCHK AS
                (SELECT OBJECT_SCHEMA_NAME(parent_object_id) AS  schemaName,
                        OBJECT_NAME(parent_object_id) AS tableName,
                        NAME AS constraintName, Type_desc AS constraintType,
                        is_disabled AS DisabledFlag,
                        (is_not_trusted + 1) % 2 AS TrustedFlag
```

1067

```
                FROM    sys.foreign_keys
                UNION ALL
                SELECT OBJECT_SCHEMA_NAME(parent_object_id) AS schemaName,
                        OBJECT_NAME(parent_object_id) AS tableName,
                        NAME AS constraintName, Type_desc AS constraintType,
                        is_disabled AS DisabledFlag,
                        (is_not_trusted + 1) % 2 AS TrustedFlag
                FROM    sys.check_constraints )
        SELECT schemaName, tableName, constraintName, constraintType,
                DisabledFlag, TrustedFlag
        FROM    FKandCHK
        WHERE   (TrustedFlag = 0 OR DisabledFlag = 1)
          AND   ((constraintType = 'FOREIGN_KEY_CONSTRAINT'
                                            AND @doFkFlag = 1)
                  OR (constraintType = 'CHECK_CONSTRAINT'
                                            AND @doCkFlag = 1))
          AND   schemaName LIKE @table_Schema
          AND   tableName LIKE @table_Name;

    OPEN @statements;

    DECLARE @statement varchar(1000), @schemaName sysname,
            @tableName sysname, @constraintName sysname,
            @constraintType sysname,@disabledFlag bit, @trustedFlag bit;

    WHILE 1=1
        BEGIN
            FETCH FROM @statements INTO @schemaName, @tableName,
                            @constraintName, @constraintType,
                            @disabledFlag, @trustedFlag;
            IF @@FETCH_STATUS <> 0
                BREAK;

            BEGIN TRY -- will output an error if it occurs but will keep
                      -- on going so other constraints will be adjusted
```

```
            IF @constraintType = 'CHECK_CONSTRAINT'
                    SELECT @statement = 'ALTER TABLE ' +
                            @schemaName + '.' + @tableName +
                            ' WITH CHECK CHECK CONSTRAINT '
                            + @constraintName;
            ELSE IF @constraintType = 'FOREIGN_KEY_CONSTRAINT'
                    SELECT @statement = 'ALTER TABLE ' +
                            @schemaName + '.' + @tableName +
                            ' WITH CHECK CHECK CONSTRAINT '
                            + @constraintName;
        EXEC (@statement);
    END TRY
    BEGIN CATCH --output statement that was executed along with
                --the error number
        SELECT 'Error occurred: ' +
                CAST(ERROR_NUMBER() AS varchar(10))+ ':' +
                error_message() + CHAR(13) + CHAR(10) +
                'Statement executed: ' +  @statement;
    END CATCH
  END;

END;
```

Another set of utility procedures I have available is to work with extended properties. I love extended properties, but remembering the hierarchical syntax is painful. So I have a set of utility procedures that I can install to a database to let extended properties be added, dropped, and modified using simple parameters. Here are examples of the add and drop procedures. I will use them in the next section along with a tool procedure to view a table's properties.

```
CREATE PROCEDURE Utility.Table$AddExtendedProperty
    @schema_name sysname,
    @table_name sysname,
    @property_name sysname,
    @property_value   sql_variant
AS
```

```
  BEGIN
      EXEC sys.sp_addextendedproperty @name = @property_name,
                                       @value = @property_value,
                                       @level0Type = 'Schema',
                                       @level0Name = @schema_name,
                                       @level1Type = 'Table',
                                       @level1Name = @table_name;
   END;
  GO

  CREATE OR ALTER PROCEDURE Utility.Table$DropExtendedProperty
      @schema_name sysname,
      @table_name sysname,
      @property_name sysname
 AS
  BEGIN
      EXEC sys.sp_dropextendedproperty @name = @property_name,
                                       @level0Type = 'Schema',
                                       @level0Name = @schema_name,
                                       @level1Type = 'Table',
                                       @level1Name = @table_name;
   END;
```

Now I don't have to remember all the different levels in the hierarchy (which can get pretty convoluted in some cases), and I can just use the natural names of things like schema and table.

The rest of these procedures I have created, and a few more of these utilities will be included in the Extended DDL Utilities.sql file in the "Useful Code" directory of the downloads.

Tools Library

One of the really useful sets of reusable objects are tools that you can give to the user that do things that a user may commonly need. In this section, I will show four such objects that I regularly find use for in a database (in addition to the Tools.String$EscapeString function we already built):

- *Tools.String$SplitPart*: Function to replicate a standard function in SQL that pulls out a value from a delimited string based on a position.

- *Tools.Table$ListExtendedProperties*: A user-oriented STORED PROCEDURE object companion to extended properties, to list all of the extended properties on one or more table objects

- *Tools.SystemSecurityName$Get*: A function that will give the executor their server principal they are executing as, including if they are impersonating another principal or using session context for security identification purposes

- *MemOptTools.String$Replicate*: A function that can be used in memory-optimized code to replicate the functionality of REPLICATE()

SQL Server provides many system functions that allow us to manipulate strings, but there always seems to be one or more essential functions that are missing from the product when you need them. One such example is the SPLIT_PART() function that doing a quick search of the Internet is a part of many other RDBMSs.

SPLIT_PART() is used to take a denormalized string like 'A,BEE,SEEME', and you can pass in the value, the delimiter (say comma in this case), and a position. If position = 2, the result would be BEE. The code follows, and it makes use of the Tools.Number table created earlier in the chapter as well:

```
CREATE OR ALTER FUNCTION Tools.String$SplitPart
(
    @inputValue nvarchar(4000),
    @delimiter  nchar(1) = ',',
    @position   int = 1
)
----------------------------------------------------------------------
-- Helps to normalize a delimited string by fetching one value from the
-- list. (note, can't use STRING_SPLIT because return order not guaranteed)
--
-- 2020 Louis Davidson - drsql@hotmail.com - drsql.org
----------------------------------------------------------------------
RETURNS nvarchar(4000)
```

```
WITH SCHEMABINDING, EXECUTE AS CALLER AS
BEGIN
        DECLARE @start int, @end int
        --add commas to end and start
        SET @inputValue = N',' + @inputValue + N',';

        WITH BaseRows AS (
            SELECT Number.I,
                    ROW_NUMBER() OVER (ORDER BY Number.I) AS StartPosition,
                    ROW_NUMBER() OVER (ORDER BY Number.I) - 1 AS EndPosition
            FROM    Tools.Number
            WHERE   Number.I <= LEN(@inputValue)
              AND   SUBSTRING(@inputValue,Number.I,1) = @delimiter
        )                       --+1 to deal with commas
        SELECT @start = (SELECT BaseRows.I + 1 FROM BaseRows
                        WHERE BaseRows.StartPosition = @Position),
               @end = (  SELECT BaseRows.I FROM BaseRows
                        WHERE BaseRows.EndPosition = @Position)

        RETURN SUBSTRING(@inputValue,@start,@end - @start)
  END;
```

To test this out, you can use a simple query like the following:

```
DECLARE @Value nvarchar(10) = 'a,b,c,d';
SELECT Tools.String$SplitPart(@Value,',',1) AS pt1,
       Tools.String$SplitPart(@Value,',',2) AS pt2,
       Tools.String$SplitPart(@Value,',',3) AS pt3,
       Tools.String$SplitPart(@Value,',',4) AS pt4,
       Tools.String$SplitPart(@Value,',',5) AS pt5;
```

This will return the following, since there are only four parts; part 5 returns a NULL value:

pt1	pt2	pt3	pt4	pt5
a	b	c	d	NULL

The next example is a procedure that will list the extended properties for a table:

```
CREATE OR ALTER PROCEDURE Tools.Table$ListExtendedProperties
     @schema_name_like sysname = '%',
     @table_name_like sysname = '%',
     @property_name_like sysname = '%'
-------------------------------------------------------------------------
-- List the extended property on tables, based on a set of like expressions
--
-- 2020 Louis Davidson - drsql@hotmail.com - drsql.org
-------------------------------------------------------------------------

WITH EXECUTE AS OWNER --need extra rights to view extended properties
AS
 BEGIN
     SELECT schemas.name AS schema_name,  tables.name AS table_name,
            extended_properties.name AS property_name,
               extended_properties.value AS property_value
     FROM   sys.extended_properties
                JOIN sys.tables
                    JOIN sys.schemas
                            ON tables.schema_id = schemas.schema_id
                  ON tables.object_id = extended_properties.major_id
     WHERE  extended_properties.class_desc = 'OBJECT_OR_COLUMN'
       AND  extended_properties.minor_id = 0
       AND  schemas.name LIKE @schema_name_like
       AND  tables.name LIKE @table_name_like
       AND  extended_properties.name LIKE @property_name_like
     ORDER BY schema_name, table_name, property_name;
  END
```

For example, using the procedure created in the "Utility Objects" section, let's add an extra extended property to the Sales.Invoices table:

```
EXECUTE Utility.Table$AddExtendedProperty @schema_name = 'Sales',
     @table_name = 'Invoices',          @property_name = 'DBDesignBook',
     @property_value = 'Tested';
```

Now you can list the extended properties on the Sales.Invoices table using the procedure we just created:

```
EXEC Tools.Table$ListExtendedProperties @schema_name_like = 'Sales',
    @table_name_like = 'Invoices';
```

This returns

schema_name	table_name	property_name	property_value
Sales	Invoices	DBDesignBook	Tested
Sales	Invoices	Description	Details of customer invoices

We can then drop the new property using the drop extended property procedure:

```
EXECUTE Utility.Table$DropExtendedProperty @schema_name = 'Sales',
    @table_name = 'Invoices',        @property_name = 'DBDesignBook';
```

For the last example, I will create a security-oriented function. While Microsoft provides a lot of security-oriented system functions for you to determine who the user is, sometimes they aren't enough. For some systems, I have employed a function in a schema named Tools.SystemSecurityName$Get() to allow for overriding the system context information when needed. The goal is that whenever you need to record what user is making changes to your system, you can call the Tools. SystemSecurityName$Get() function and know that it is doing the heavy lifting, either looking to the ORIGINAL_LOGIN() system function or SESSION_CONTEXT(), or you could even extend it using a custom-built security system. The following is the code for the object:

```
CREATE OR ALTER FUNCTION Tools.SystemSecurityName$Get
(
    @AllowSessionContext bit = 1,
    @IgnoreImpersonation bit = 0
)
--------------------------------------------------------------------
-- Get the user's security context, using SESSION_CONTEXT, SUSER_SNAME,
-- or ORIGINAL_LOGIN
```

```
--
-- 2020 Louis Davidson - drsql@hotmail.com - drsql.org
----------------------------------------------------------------------------
RETURNS sysname
AS
 BEGIN
    RETURN (
     CASE WHEN @AllowSessionContext = 1
                AND SESSION_CONTEXT(N'ApplicationUserName') IS NOT NULL
             THEN CAST(SESSION_CONTEXT(N'ApplicationUserName') AS sysname)
          WHEN @IgnoreImpersonation = 1
             THEN SUSER_SNAME()
          ELSE ORIGINAL_LOGIN() END)
 END;
```

To show this work, in the database you build this in (I am still in the WideWorldImporters database), grant this to the public role (There are not a lot of great reasons to use the public role, but tools which are basically extensions to the SQL language is not a terrible usage.):

```
GRANT EXECUTE ON Tools.SystemSecurityName$Get to Public;
```

To demonstrate, I will create a user and give it rights to access the database:

```
CREATE LOGIN Tester WITH PASSWORD = '820q0qjc,nm98ur';
CREATE USER Tester FOR LOGIN Tester;
EXECUTE AS Login = 'Tester';
```

Now, the user can execute the following query and see that the original login is me executing the query:

```
--allow session context and ignore impersonation
SELECT Tools.SystemSecurityName$Get(DEFAULT, DEFAULT) AS LoginName;
```

This returns the following:

```
LoginName
--------------------------------------------------
Domain\drsql
```

Then, you can set a session context value (basically setting a named-value pair value on the connection):

```
EXEC sys.sp_set_session_context @key = N'ApplicationUserName',
          @value = 'Louis';
```

Now, run the Tools.SystemSecurityName$Get function, and you get the name from the session context:

```
LoginName
-------------------------------------------------
Louis
```

Then, you can ignore session context and impersonation and see the user that is being impersonated:

```
SELECT Tools.SystemSecurityName$Get(0, 1) AS LoginName;
```

This returns the following:

```
LoginName
-------------------------------------------------
Tester
```

Then you can clean up after the example set up:

```
EXEC sys.sp_set_session_context
          @key = N'ApplicationUserName', @value = NULL;

REVERT;
DROP USER Tester;
DROP LOGIN Tester;
```

Finally, some tools may only be needed in rather special occasions. For example, if you are using memory-optimized tables and want to use the REPLICATE() system function to replicate some text (like in sample code where you want to make really large values), you would find that the function is not allowed in natively compiled modules or memory-optimized table constraints. So the following object could be used to give you that capability:

```
CREATE SCHEMA MemOptTools;
GO
CREATE OR ALTER FUNCTION MemOptTools.String$Replicate
(
    @inputString    nvarchar(1000),
    @replicateCount smallint
)
RETURNS nvarchar(1000)
WITH NATIVE_COMPILATION, SCHEMABINDING
AS
BEGIN ATOMIC WITH(TRANSACTION ISOLATION LEVEL = SNAPSHOT,
                  LANGUAGE = N'English')
    DECLARE @i int = 0, @output nvarchar(1000) = '';

    WHILE @i < @replicateCount
    BEGIN
        SET @output = @output + @inputString;
        SET @i = @i + 1;
    END;

    RETURN @output;
END;
```

Writing natively optimized code leads to code like this, because there is quite a bit of functionality that you cannot use. Some of it you can write yourself, and the code will often look pretty clunky. Note that since this is compiled to binary code, instead of interpreted at runtime, it will execute very fast (and the actual REPLICATE() function probably does the exact same thing internally anyhow).

Logging Objects

In many systems, you will find you need to watch the activities that are occurring in the database. Back in Chapter 10, we implemented an audit trail using the audit feature. In this section, the types of logging we will want to do are a more generic form of logging that is intended more for the DBAs to see what errors have been occurring.

As an example, one thing that we often may want to log is errors. A common goal is to make sure that no errors occur at the database level. Logging any errors that occur to a table can help to see where you have recurring issues. Probably the most interesting way this has ever helped me in my systems was once when a programmer had simply ignored all return values from SQL calls. So a large number of calls to the system were failing, but the client never realized it. (In Appendix B, available in the downloads, I will employ this functionality in the trigger templates that I provide.)

The `ErrorHandling.ErrorLog$Insert` procedure I will demonstrate is used to log the errors that occur in a table, to give you a history of errors that have occurred. I do this because, in almost every case, an error that occurs in a `TRIGGER` object is a bad thing that ought to be checked out later. The fact that the client sends data that might cause the trigger to fail should be fixed and treated as a bug. In stored procedures, this may or may not be the case, as stored procedures can be written to do things that may work or may fail in some situations. This is a very broad statement and in some cases may not be true, so you can adjust the code as fits your desires.

The DML for the table is as follows:

```
CREATE SCHEMA ErrorHandling;
GO
CREATE TABLE ErrorHandling.ErrorLog(
        ErrorLogId int NOT NULL IDENTITY CONSTRAINT PKErrorLog PRIMARY KEY,
                Number int NOT NULL,
        Location sysname NOT NULL,
        Message varchar(4000) NOT NULL,
        LogTime datetime2(3) NULL
                CONSTRAINT DFLTErrorLog_LogTime  DEFAULT (SYSDATETIME()),
        ServerPrincipal sysname NOT NULL
        --use original_login to capture the user name of the actual user
        --not a user they have impersonated
        CONSTRAINT DFLTErrorLog_ServerPrincipal DEFAULT (ORIGINAL_LOGIN())
);
```

Then we create the following procedure, which can be coded into other procedures and trigger whenever you need to log that an error occurred:

```
CREATE PROCEDURE ErrorHandling.ErrorLog$Insert
(
        @ERROR_NUMBER int,
        @ERROR_LOCATION sysname,
        @ERROR_MESSAGE nvarchar(4000)
) AS
```

```
-------------------------------------------------------------------------
-- Writes a row to the error log. If an error occurs in the call (such as a
-- NULL value) It writes a row to the error table. If that call fails an
-- error will be returned
--
-- 2020 Louis Davidson - drsql@hotmail.com - drsql.org
-------------------------------------------------------------------------

  BEGIN
        SET NOCOUNT ON;
        BEGIN TRY
           INSERT INTO ErrorHandling.ErrorLog(Number, Location,Message)
           SELECT @ERROR_NUMBER,
                  COALESCE(@ERROR_LOCATION, N'No Object'),@ERROR_MESSAGE;
        END TRY
        BEGIN CATCH
           INSERT INTO ErrorHandling.ErrorLog(Number, Location, Message)
           VALUES (-100, 'Utility.ErrorLog$Insert',
                    'An invalid call was made to the error log procedure ' +
                    ERROR_MESSAGE());
        END CATCH;
END;
```

Then we test the error handler with a simple test case, as follows:

```
--test the error block we will use
BEGIN TRY
    THROW 50000,'Test error',1;
END TRY
BEGIN CATCH
    IF @@TRANCOUNT > 0
        ROLLBACK TRANSACTION;

    --[Error logging section]
        DECLARE @ERROR_NUMBER int = ERROR_NUMBER(),
                @ERROR_PROCEDURE sysname = ERROR_PROCEDURE(),
                @ERROR_MESSAGE varchar(4000) = ERROR_MESSAGE();
```

```
    EXEC ErrorHandling.ErrorLog$Insert
                    @ERROR_NUMBER,@ERROR_PROCEDURE,@ERROR_MESSAGE;

  THROW; --will halt the batch or be caught by the caller's catch block

END CATCH;
```

This returns the error we threw:

```
Msg 50000, Level 16, State 1
Test error
```

And checking the ErrorLog

```
--Left off ServerPrincipal for space
SELECT ErrorLogId, Number, Location, Message, LogTime
FROM   ErrorHandling.ErrorLog;
```

you can see that the error is logged:

ErrorLogId	Number	Location	Message	LogTime
1	50000	No Object	Test error	2020-07-13 15:31:52.649

This basic error logging procedure can make it much easier to understand what has gone wrong when a user has an error (or see when hundreds of errors have occurred and the code has just TRY...CATCH hidden from the user). Expand your own system to meet your organization's needs, but having an audit trail will prove invaluable when you find out that certain types of errors have been going on for weeks and your users "assumed" you knew about it!

The only real downside to logging in this manner is transactions. You can log all you want, but if the log procedure is called in a transaction (not a problem with the TRIGGER object code since it logs the error directly after ROLLBACK TRANSACTION is executed) and that transaction is rolled back, the log row will also be rolled back. To write to a log that isn't affected by transactions, you can use the xp_logevent extended stored procedure in the error handler to write to the Windows Event Log. Using this method can be handy if you have deeply nested errors and are not building reasonably simple error handler stacks, in which all the `ErrorHandling.ErrorLog` rows get rolled back due to external transactions.

Best Practices

The first half of the chapter discussed the two primary methods of architecting a SQL Server application, either by using `STORED PROCEDURE` objects as the primary interface or by using ad hoc calls built outside the server. Either is acceptable, but as stated, my opinion is that it is best to use a set of `STORED PROCEDURE` objects as much as possible to provide a layer of abstraction between the physical structures and the way they are accessed. There are a few reasons:

- As precompiled batches of SQL statements that are known at design and implementation time, you get a great interface to the database that encapsulates the details of the database from the caller.

- They can be a performance boost, primarily because tuning is on a known set of queries and not just on any query that the programmer might have written that slips by untested (not generally maliciously, usually just being a bit of functionality that only gets used "occasionally" and didn't get caught during testing with enough data). The ability to parameterize and reuse query plans is also a solid performance gain most of the time but has its own set of concerns.

- They allow you to define a consistent interface for security that lets you give users access to a table in one situation but not in another. Plus, if procedures are consistently named, giving access to database resources is far easier.

However, not every system is written using stored procedures. Ad hoc access can serve to build a fine system as well. You certainly can build a flexible architecture, but it can also lead to harder-to-maintain code that ends up with the client tools being tightly coupled with the database structures. At the very least, if you balk at the use of procedures, make sure to architect in a manner that makes tuning your queries reasonable without full regression testing of the application.

I wish I could give you definitive best practices about how to architect your systems, but there are so many possibilities, and either method has pros and cons. (Plus, there would be a very nerdy mob with cell phone torches and pitchforks at my door, no matter how I said things must be done.) This topic will continue to be hotly contested, and rightly so. In each of the last few releases of SQL Server, Microsoft has continued to improve the optimizer in ways that will improve the use of ad hoc SQL, but it's still considered a best practice to use STORED PROCEDURE objects if you can. I realize that in a large percentage of systems that are created, such an interface is only used when there's an overwhelming reason to do so (like some complex SQL or perhaps to batch together statements for a transaction).

Whether or not you decide to use stored procedure access or use ad hoc calls instead, you'll probably want to code some reusable objects for use in the database. This is particularly true in the case of building a solid set of reusable component tables, functions, and stored procedures to allow you to do certain tasks and write certain types of code in pretty much every database. Still, be wary of over-modularization in T-SQL, because while it has been incrementally improved with SQL Server 2019's new scalar function inlining capabilities, this only helps in one specific case. It won't help if you start trying to write single function modules in your T-SQL and end up, for example, with views referencing views referencing even more views using functions that use tables. Some calculations can just be too much.

Summary

In this chapter rife with opinions, what's clear is that SQL Server has continued to increase the number of options for writing T-SQL to access data. I've covered two topics that you need to consider when architecting your relational database applications using SQL Server. Designing the structure of the database is (reasonably) easy enough no matter what kind of transaction processing database you are creating. Follow the principles set out by normalization to ensure that you have limited, if any, redundant data and limited anomalies when you modify or create data. On the other hand, once you have the database architected from an internal standpoint, you have to write code to access this data, and this is where you have a couple of seemingly difficult choices.

The primary thing to take from this chapter is that no matter how you access the data in your databases, it can be complicated either way. Use any code method of accessing your data poorly, and your results will be poor. Hopefully this advice will be of value to you, but as you were warned at the start of the chapter, a good amount of this chapter was opinion.

The secondary thing is that even if you never use a coded object as an interface, you can still extend what the database has to offer and maintain code libraries of utilities, tools, and so on to make coding easier. Doing the same thing over and over and having 20 versions of a piece of code that does the same thing is dumb, but equally dumb is having 20 databases dependent on external code stored in a central repository. Duplicating utility and tool code into each database where it is used means that you never have to worry if you upgrade to the `Tools.String$SplitPart` function for one database; it isn't going to break any other database code other than that in your database.

Note   A resource that I want to point out for further reading after this chapter is by Erland Sommarskog. His website (`www.sommarskog.se`) contains a plethora of information regarding many of the topics I have covered in this chapter—and in far deeper detail. I would consider most of what I have said the introductory-level course, while his papers are nearly graduate-level courses in the topics he covers.

In either case, the goal is now and should always be to make the database its own contained universe. The more contained you can keep your database, the easier it is to test, rebuild from code, and move to another server, even to an Azure SQL Database instance. The more of the queries that end up in the database as objects, the easier it will be to test that everything works and that a change in one system will have no effect on the other. That should mean fewer questions at 3:00 AM about why something failed because another database wasn't available when another needed it. That can't be a bad thing, can it?

Epilogue

We're just getting started. We're just beginning to meet what will be the future—we've got the Model T.

Grace Murray Hopper, American Computer Scientist, Navy Rear Admiral

Admiral Hopper was quoted as saying this about where computers were when she was asked if the computer revolution was over back in 1983 (which, if you recall, was before Edgar Codd wrote his papers outlining what would become relational databases like SQL Server). She was not wrong. (You can read more about her here: `president.yale.edu/biography-grace-murray-hopper`.) The same quote could come out of the mouth of so many people who work for technology companies today. Over the lifecycle of six editions of this book, things have changed so much it amazes me greatly. And by the time I consider a new edition of the book, I can't even predict where things will be by then.

In this epilogue, I wanted to point out a few concepts that a database programmer needs to know about that are beyond the design concepts that I have covered in my book and just don't have space to cover:

- *Source control*: Source control is a repository for holding the DDL of the database in, so you not only have a copy of the DDL of your current database but for all of the changes over time. There are various types of source control engines, but one of the more popular these days is Git, also GitHub which you can use for free (for a quick tutorial, visit `guides.github.com/activities/hello-world/`.) In any case, it is important to not just store your database code in the database as its only location.

- *DevOps*: This is a set of methods and practices for IT departments from developers to operations to work together through the process of deploying software. At the center of these practices are Continuous Deployment/Continuous Integration, allowing for even near-constant deployment of new software, but so much more than that. For more information, consider the book *DevOps for the Database* by Baron Schwartz, available for free here as of this book's printing: `www.solarwinds.com/resources/ebook/devops-for-database`. Further reading can be found in the books *DevOps for Developers* from Michael Hüttermann (`www.apress.com/gp/book/9781430245698`) and *DevOps on the Microsoft Stack* by Wouter de Kort (`www.apress.com/us/book/9781484214473`).

- *PolyBase in SQL Server 2019*: There was a really major feature added to SQL Server 2017 that was much enhanced in 2019 in a way that makes it useful for the average SQL Server developer called PolyBase. Using PolyBase, you can connect to external data sources (relational sources like SQL Server and Oracle, files in Azure Blog Storage and Azure Data Lake, and NoSQL-type sources like Hadoop) and report on disparate data sources in a very integrated manner using typical T-SQL syntax. (There is a feature called Big Data Clusters which builds even further on this concept as well.) For more details about PolyBase, see the Microsoft Docs entry "What is PolyBase?" (`docs.microsoft.com/en-us/sql/relational-databases/polybase/polybase-guide`).

- *Using other languages than T-SQL right in SQL Server:* In SQL Server 2017, Microsoft implemented the ability to use R and Python directly on the database server using SQL Server Language Extensions. In SQL Server 2019, Java was added. Using this technology, you can run code in these languages right from T-SQL. It is not exactly native utilization like using T-SQL, but it allows you to execute Machine Learning and other types of code locally in a repeatable fashion. For more details, Microsoft Docs has a good set of documents to cover this technology, starting with "What is SQL Server Language Extensions?" (`docs.microsoft.com/en-us/sql/language-extensions/language-extensions-overview`).

- *Dimensional design for reporting*: This is a technique that follows a different pattern of implementation that is made strictly for reporting. It eschews the concepts of normalization (except for the First Normal Form) and flattens tables into two kinds of tables: fact tables that have things that you measure activities and dimensions that have data to group those activities. It can be more complex than this, but this is the gist of dimensional modeling. The gold standard books about this topic are from the Kimball Group: `www.kimballgroup.com/data-warehouse-business-intelligence-resources/books/`. The chapter and material for a chapter on reporting design written by Jessica Moss for the previous two editions of the book is included in the downloads as Appendix C.

If this book on relational database design has only scratched the surface on the relational database design process, these few bullets are only scratching the surface on what is available and useful for to you to learn about building relational database systems. There is so much to learn out there and so many technologies at your disposal to expand the boundaries of what SQL Server can do and, by extension, what your customer can do with their data.

APPENDIX A

Scalar Datatype Reference

Choosing proper datatypes to match domains chosen during logical modeling is an important task. One datatype might be more efficient than another of a similar type. For example, you can store integer data in an int datatype, a numeric datatype, a floating-point datatype, a character type, or even a binary type, but these datatypes certainly aren't alike in implementation or performance.

In this appendix, I'll introduce you to all the relational intrinsic datatypes that Microsoft provides and discuss the situations where they're best used. The following is a list of the datatypes I'll cover. I'll discuss when to use them and, in some cases, why not to use them.

- *Precise numeric data*: Stores data with no loss of precision due to storage.

  - bit: Stores either 1, 0, or NULL. Used for Boolean-type columns

  - tinyint: Non-negative values between 0 and 255

  - smallint: Integers between -32,768 and 32,767

  - int: Integers between -2,147,483,648 and 2,147,483,647 (-2^{31} to $2^{31} - 1$)

  - bigint: Integers between 9,223,372,036,854,775,808 and 9,223,372,036,854,775,807 (-2^{63} to $2^{63} - 1$)

  - decimal: Values from $-10^{38} + 1$ through $10^{38} - 1$

  - money: Values from -922,337,203,685,477.5808 through 922,337,203,685,477.5807

  - smallmoney: Values from -214,748.3648 through +214,748.3647

© Louis Davidson 2021
L. Davidson, *Pro SQL Server Relational Database Design and Implementation*,
https://doi.org/10.1007/978-1-4842-6497-3

- *Approximate numeric data*: Stores approximations of numbers in an efficient manner that provides for a large range of values with enough precision for scientific uses.

    - `float (N)`: Values in the range from `-1.79E + 308` through `1.79E + 308`

    - `real`: Values in the range from `-3.40E + 38` through `3.40E + 38`. `real` is a synonym for a `float(24)` datatype.

- *Date and time*: Stores point in time values, including date, time of day, and a combination of both.

    - `date`: Date-only values from January 1, 0001, to December 31, 9999 (3 bytes).

    - `time`: Time of day–only values to 100 nanoseconds (3–5 bytes). Note that the range of this type is from 0:00 to 23:59:59 and some fraction of a second based on the precision you select.

    - `datetime2`: Despite the clunky name, this type will store dates from January 1, 0001, to December 31, 9999, to 100-nanosecond accuracy (6–8 bytes). The accuracy is based on the precision you select.

    - `datetimeoffset`: Same as `datetime2` but includes an offset from UTC (8–10 bytes).

    - `smalldatetime`: Dates from January 1, 1900, through June 6, 2079, with accuracy to 1 minute (4 bytes). (Note: It is suggested to phase out usage of this type and use the more standards-oriented `datetime2`, though `smalldatetime` is not technically deprecated and has an accuracy that cannot be easily reproduced.)

    - `datetime`: Dates from January 1, 1753, to December 31, 9999, with accuracy to ~3 milliseconds (stored in increments of .000, .003, or .007 second) (8 bytes). (Note: It is suggested to phase out usage of this type and use the more standards-oriented `datetime2`, though `datetime` is not technically deprecated).

- *Character (or string) data*: Used to store textual data, such as names, descriptions, notes, and so on.

- char: Fixed-length ASCII or UTF8 character data up to 8,000 characters long

- varchar: Variable-length character data up to 8,000 characters long

- varchar(max): Large variable-length character data; maximum length of $2^{31} - 1$ (2,147,483,647) bytes, or 2 GB

- text: Large text values; maximum length of $2^{31} - 1$ (2,147,483,647) bytes, or 2 GB (Note that this datatype is outdated, *officially* deprecated, and should be phased out in favor of the varchar(max) datatype.)

- nchar, nvarchar, ntext: Unicode UTF16 equivalents of char, varchar, and text (with the same deprecation warning for ntext as for text)

- *Binary data*: Data stored in bytes, rather than as human-readable values, for example, files or images.

  - binary: Fixed-length binary data up to 8,000 bytes long

  - varbinary: Variable-length binary data up to 8,000 bytes long

  - varbinary(max): Large binary data; maximum length of $2^{31} - 1$ (2,147,483,647) bytes, or 2 GB

  - image: Large binary data; maximum length of $2^{31} - 1$ (2,147,483,647) bytes, or 2 GB (Note that this datatype is outdated, officially deprecated, and should be phased out for the varbinary(max) datatype.)

- *Other scalar datatypes*: Datatypes that don't fit into any other groups nicely but are still very useful.

  - timestamp (or rowversion): Used for optimistic locking

  - uniqueidentifier: Stores a globally unique identifier (GUID) value

  - cursor: Datatype used to store a cursor reference in a variable. Cannot be used as a column in a table

- `table`: Used to hold a reference to a local temporary table. Cannot be used as a column in a table

- `sql_variant`: Stores data of almost any datatype

- *Not simply scalar*: For completeness, I mention these types, but they are not covered in any detail. These types are XML, `hierarchyId`, and the spatial types (geometry and geography).

Although we'll look at all these datatypes, this doesn't mean you'll ever have a need for all of them. Choosing a datatype is a specific task to meet the needs of the client with the proper datatype. You could just store everything in unlimited-length character strings (this was how some systems worked in the old days and how some systems improperly work today), but this is clearly not optimal. From the list, you'll choose the best datatype, and if you cannot find one good enough, you can use the CLR and implement your own (you can find more on this topic in the Microsoft Docs article "CLR User-Defined Types" (`docs.microsoft.com/en-us/sql/relational-databases/clr-integration-database-objects-user-defined-types/clr-user-defined-types`).

The proper datatype choice is the first step in making sure the data is stored for a column correctly and efficiently. (Using a `CHECK` constraint to narrow the domain of a column to exactly what the column actually means is very important too. For example, what actual real-world value has a domain of `-2,147,483,648` and `2,147,483,647`?)

Note   I include information in each section about how the types are affected by using compression. This information refers to how the value is affected by the row-level compression step of compression.

Numeric Data

You can store numeric data in many base datatypes, depending upon the actual need you are trying to fill. There are two different classes of numeric data: precise and approximate. The differences are important and must be well understood by any architect who's building a system that stores readings, measurements, or other numeric data.

Precise values have no error in the way they're stored, from whole numbers to fractional numbers, because they have a fixed number of digits before and after the decimal point (or *radix*).

Approximate datatypes don't always store exactly what you expect them to store. However, they are useful for scientific and other applications where the range of values varies greatly. The term approximate is important, and as I will demonstrate, in some cases, the value stored is not exactly what you will expect, but it is *close enough*.

The precise numeric values include the `bit`, `int`, `bigint`, `smallint`, `tinyint`, `decimal`, and money (`money` and `smallmoney`) datatypes. I'll break these down again into three additional subsections: integer numbers, precise decimal numbers, and approximate decimal numbers. This is done so we can isolate some of the discussion down to the values that allow fractional parts to be stored, because a few mathematical "quirks" need to be understood surrounding using those datatypes. I'll mention a few of these quirks, most notably with the `money` datatypes. However, when you do any math with computers, you must be careful how rounding is achieved and how this affects your results.

Integer Values

Integer numbers are, for the most part, whole numbers stored using base-2 bit values that are native to typical CPUs. You can do bitwise operations on them, though generally it's frowned upon in SQL for normalization reasons (each value should be scalar, and making the bits of a value have different meaning is worse than having each byte of a readable character string have specific meanings for usability). Math performed with integers is generally the fastest way to perform math because the CPU can perform it directly using registers. I'll cover four integer sizes: `tinyint`, `smallint`, `int`, and `bigint`.

The biggest thing that gets a lot of people in trouble using integers is integer math. Intuitively, when you see an expression like

```
SELECT 1/2;
```

you expect that the answer is .5. However, this is not the case, because integers don't work this way; integer math only returns precise answers, which means it only returns integer values.

Instead of rounding, integer math truncates values, because it performs math like you did back in elementary school. For example, consider the following equation, 305 divided by 100:

$$
\begin{array}{r}
3\ R\ 5 \\
100\ \overline{\smash)305} \\
-300 \\
\hline
5
\end{array}
$$

In a query, you get the whole number result using the division operator, and to get the remainder, you use the modulo operator (%). So you could execute the following query to get the division answer and the remainder:

```
SELECT 305 / 100, 305 % 100;
```

This returns 3 and 5. (The modulo operator is a very useful operator.) If you want the result to be able to be a non-whole number, you need to cast at least one of the values to a datatype with a fractional element, like numeric, either by using CAST() or CONVERT(), or a common method is to cast one of the factors to numeric, by simply multiplying a factor by 1.0:

```
SELECT  CAST(305 AS numeric)/ 100, (305 * 1.0) / 100;
```

These mathematical expressions now both return 3.050000, which is the value that most users are likely desiring to get from a typical math equation, much as the person dividing 1 by 2 expects to get .5. One additional intuitive leap you will probably make is that .5 should round up to 1, right? Nope, even the following query returns 0:

```
SELECT CAST(.99999999 AS integer);
```

tinyint

Domain: Non-negative whole numbers from 0 through 255.

Storage: 1 byte.

Discussion:

Used to store small non-negative integer values. Uses a single byte for storage. If the values you'll be dealing with are guaranteed always to be in this range, a tinyint is perfect. A great use for this is for the primary key of a domain table that can be guaranteed to have only a small number of values. The tinyint datatype is especially useful in a data warehouse to keep the surrogate keys small.

Row compression effect:

No effect, because 1 byte is the minimum for storing a number, other than bit.

smallint

Domain: Whole numbers from -32,768 through 32,767 (-2^{15} to $2^{15} - 1$).

Storage: 2 bytes.

Discussion:

If you can be guaranteed to need values only in this range, the smallint is very useful. It requires 2 bytes of storage.

One use of a smallint that crops up from time to time is as a Boolean. This is because some tools like Visual Basic store False as 0 and -1 for True (technically, VB would treat any nonzero value as True, but it used -1 for its representation of False). Storing data in this manner is not only a tremendous waste of space—2 bytes vs. potentially one-eighth of a byte for a bit or even a single byte for a char(1), 'Y' or 'N'. It's also confusing to all the other SQL Server programmers. ODBC and OLE DB drivers do this translation for you, but even if they didn't, it's worth the time to write a method or a function in VB to translate True to a value of 1.

Row compression effect:

The value will be stored in the smallest number of bytes required to represent the value. For example, if the value is 10, it would fit in a single byte; then it would use 1 byte, and so forth, up to 2 bytes.

int

Domain: Whole numbers from -2,147,483,648 to 2,147,483,647 (-2^{31} to $2^{31} - 1$).

Storage: 4 bytes.

Discussion:

The int datatype is frequently employed in the surrogate key of a table because it's small (it requires 4 bytes of storage), efficient to store and retrieve, and even just in the positive range of values. Two billion rows is generally a large enough table for most scenarios.

One downfall of the int datatype is that it doesn't include an unsigned version, which for a 32-bit version could store non-negative values from 0 to 4,294,967,296 (232). Because most primary key values start out at 1, this would give you more than 2 billion extra values for a primary key value without having to involve negative numbers that can be confusing to the user. This might seem unnecessary, but systems that have billions of rows are becoming increasingly common.

Row compression effect:

The value will be stored in the smallest number of bytes required to represent the value. For example, if the value is 10, it would fit in a single byte; then it would use 1 byte, and so forth, up to 4 bytes.

bigint

Domain: Whole numbers from -9,223,372,036,854,775,808 to 9,223,372,036,854,775,807 (that is, -2^{63} to $2^{63} - 1$).

Storage: 8 bytes.

Discussion:

One of the common reasons to use the 64-bit datatype is as a primary key for tables where you'll have more than 2 billion rows. Of course, there are some companies where a billion isn't really a very large number of things to store or count, so using a bigint will be commonplace to them. As usual, the important thing is to size your utilization of any type to the situation, not using too small or even too large of a type than is necessary.

Row compression effect:

The value will be stored in the smallest number of bytes required to represent the value. For example, if the value is 10, it would fit in a single byte; then it would use 1 byte, and so forth, up to 8 bytes.

Precise Numeric Values

The decimal datatype is precise in that whatever value you store, you can always retrieve it from the table exactly as you entered it. In the next major section "Approximate Numeric Data," this will not always be exactly the case (which is not as bad as it sounds). However, when you must store fractional values in precise datatypes, you pay a performance and storage cost in the way they're stored and dealt with. The reason for this is that you have to perform math with the precise decimal values using SQL

Server engine code. Math with the approximate numeric types uses IEEE floating-point values (the `float` and `real` datatypes) using the floating-point unit (FPU), which is part of the core processor in all modern computers. This isn't to say that the `decimal` type is slow, *per se*, but if you're dealing with data that doesn't require the perfect precision of the `decimal` type, it may be worth it to use the `float` datatype if you are doing heavy amounts of calculations.

decimal and numeric

Domain: All numeric data (including fractional parts) between $-10^{38} + 1$ and $10^{38} - 1$.

   Storage: Based on precision (the number of significant digits): 1–9 digits, 5 bytes; 10–19 digits, 9 bytes; 20–28 digits, 13 bytes; and 29–38 digits, 17 bytes.

   Discussion:

   The `decimal` and `numeric` datatypes are a precise datatype because data is stored in a manner that's like character data (as if the data had only 12 characters, 0–9 and the minus and decimal point symbols). With SQL Server, `decimal` and `numeric` types are functionally the same, but they are not technically the same datatype:

```
SELECT name, system_type_id
FROM   sys.types
WHERE  name IN ('decimal','numeric');
```

   This returns:

```
name        system_type_id
----------- --------------

decimal     106
numeric     108
```

   However, `decimal` and `numeric` datatypes both incur an additional cost in doing math on the values, because there's no hardware to do the mathematics.

   To specify a decimal number, you need to define the precision and the scale:

- *Precision* is the total number of significant digits in the number. For example, 10 would need a precision of 2, and 43.00000004 would need a precision of 10. The precision may be as small as 1 or as large as 38.

- *Scale* is the possible number of significant digits to the right of the decimal point. Reusing the previous example, 10 would require a scale of 0, and 43.00000004 would need 8.

Numeric datatypes are bound by this precision and scale to define how large the data is. For example, take the following declaration of a numeric variable:

```
DECLARE @testvar decimal(3,1);
```

This allows you to enter any numeric values greater than -99.94 and less than 99.94. Entering 99.949999 works, but entering 99.95 doesn't, because it's rounded up to 100.0, which can't be displayed by decimal(3,1). Take the following, for example:

```
SELECT @testvar = -10.155555555;
SELECT @testvar;
```

This returns the following result:

```
-------------------
-10.2
```

This rounding behavior is both a blessing and a curse. You must be careful when butting up to the edge of the datatype's allowable values. There is a setting—NUMERIC_ROUNDABORT—that when turned on causes an error to be generated when a loss of precision would occur from an implicit data conversion. That's kind of like what happens when you try to put too many characters into a character value.

Take the following code:

```
SET NUMERIC_ROUNDABORT ON;

DECLARE @testvar decimal(3,1);
SELECT @testvar = -10.155555555;

SET NUMERIC_ROUNDABORT OFF ;--this setting persists for a connection
```

This causes the following error:

```
Msg 8115, Level 16, State 7, Line 3
Arithmetic overflow error converting numeric to data type numeric.
```

SET NUMERIC_ROUNDABORT can be quite dangerous to use and might throw off applications using SQL Server if set to ON. However, if you need guaranteed prevention of implicit round-off due to system constraints, it's there.

As far as usage is concerned, you should generally use the decimal datatype as sparingly as possible, and I don't mean this negatively. There's nothing wrong with the type at all, but it does take that little bit more processing than integers or real data, and hence there's a performance hit. You should use it when you have specific values that you want to store where you can't accept any loss of precision or that are so huge they will not fit in a bigint. I'll deal more with the topic of loss of precision in more detail in the section "Approximate Numeric Data." The decimal type is commonly used as a replacement for the money type, because it has certain round-off issues that decimal does not.

Row compression effect:

The value will be stored in the smallest number of bytes necessary to provide the precision necessary, plus 2 bytes overhead per row. For example, if you are storing the value of 2 in a numeric(28,2) column, it needn't use all the possible space; it can use the space of a numeric(3,2), plus the 2 bytes overhead.

money and smallmoney

There are two intrinsic datatypes that are for storing monetary values. Both are based on the bigint and integer types, with fixed four decimal places. These types are as follows:

- money

  - *Domain*: -922,337,203,685,477.5808 to 922,337,203,685,477.5807

  - *Storage*: 8 bytes

- smallmoney

  - *Domain*: -214,748.3648 to 214,748.3647

  - *Storage*: 4 bytes

Despite the fact that they are based on integers and as such are faster because they can be manipulated with hardware, the money datatypes are generally considered a poor choice of datatype, even for storing monetary values, because they have a few inconsistencies that can cause a good deal of confusion. First is that while you can specify units, such as $ or £, the units are of no real value, for example:

```
CREATE TABLE dbo.TestMoney
(
    MoneyValue money
);
go

INSERT INTO dbo.TestMoney
VALUES ($100);
INSERT INTO dbo.TestMoney
VALUES (100);
INSERT INTO dbo.TestMoney
VALUES (£100);
GO
SELECT * FROM dbo.TestMoney WHERE MoneyValue = $100;
```

The query at the end of this code example returns the following results (each having the exact same value):

```
MoneyValue
--------------------
100.00
100.00
100.00
```

The second problem is that the money datatypes have well-known rounding issues with math. I mentioned that these types are based on integers (the range for smallmoney is -214,748.3648 to 214,748.3647, and the range for an integer is 2,147,483,648 to 2,147,483,647). Unfortunately, as I will demonstrate, intermediate results are stored in the same types, causing unexpected rounding errors, for example:

```
DECLARE @money1 money  = 1.00,
        @money2 money  = 800.00; --same result with one of these integer

SELECT CAST(@money1/@money2 AS money);
```

This returns the following result:

```
--------------------
0.0012
```

However, try the following code:

```
DECLARE @decimal1 decimal(19,4) = 1.00,
        @decimal2 decimal(19,4) = 800.00;

SELECT  CAST(@decimal1/@decimal2 AS decimal(19,4));
```

It returns the following result:

```
----------------
0.0013
```

Why? Because money uses only four decimal places for intermediate results, where decimal uses a much larger precision:

```
SELECT  @money1/@money2;
SELECT  @decimal1/@decimal2;
```

This code returns the following results:

```
--------------------
0.0012
------------------------------------------
0.0012500000000000000
```

That's why there are round-off issues. And if you turned SET NUMERIC_ROUNDABORT ON, the decimal example would fail, telling you that you were losing precision, whereas there is no way to stop the round-off from occurring with the money types. The general consensus among database architects is to avoid the money datatype and use a numeric type instead, because of the following reasons:

- Numeric types give the answers to math problems in the natural manner that's expected.

- Numeric types have no built-in units to confuse matters.

Using a decimal type instead gives you the precision needed for calculations. To replicate the range for money, use decimal(19,4) or, for smallmoney, use decimal(10,4). However, you needn't use such large values if you don't need them. Even if you happen to be calculating the national debt or my yearly gadget allowance, each could actually fit in a decimal(14,2) or (18,4). I also find that people I have worked with who are not accountants but do a lot of reporting on monetary value prefer to simply have two digits in their monetary values as well, rather than four decimal places (and you still get the proper results for math since numeric and decimal use as much precision as needed for calculations).

Row compression effect:

The money types are simply integer types with their decimal places shifted. As such, they are compressed in the same manner that integer types would be. However, since the values would be larger than they appear (because of the value 10 being stored as 10.000 or 10000 in the physical storage), the compression could be less than expected for an integer of the same magnitude.

Approximate Numeric Data

Approximate numeric values contain a decimal point and are stored in a format that's fast to manipulate but can be lossy (meaning data can be lost, giving imperfect, if satisfactory, results in some cases). They are called *floating point* because they have a fixed number of significant digits, but the placement of the decimal point "floats," allowing for extremely small numbers or extremely large numbers. Approximate numeric values have some important advantages, as you'll see later in this appendix.

Approximate is such a negative term, but it's technically proper. It refers to the real and float datatypes, which are IEEE 75454 standard single- and double-precision floating-point values. The number is stored as a 32-bit or 64-bit value, with four parts:

- *Sign*: Determines whether this is a positive or negative value

- *Exponent*: The exponent in base-2 of the mantissa

- *Mantissa*: Stores the actual number that's multiplied by the exponent (also known as the *coefficient* or *significand*)

- *Bias*: Determines whether the exponent is positive or negative

A complete description of how these datatypes are formed is beyond the scope of this book but may be obtained from the IEEE body at www.ieee.org or wikipedia.org/wiki/Floating-point_arithmetic#internal_representation.

- float [(N)]*Domain*: -1.79E + 308 through 1.79E + 308. The float datatype allows you to specify a certain number of bits to use in the mantissa, from 1 to 53. You specify this number of bits with the value in N. The default is 53.

  - *Storage*: See Table A-1.

- real

  - real is a synonym for float(24).

Table A-1. *Floating-Point Precision and Storage Requirements*

N (Number of Mantissa Bits for Float)	Precision	Storage Size
1–24	7	4 bytes
25–53	15	8 bytes

At this point, SQL Server rounds all values of N up to either 24 or 53. This is the reason that the storage and precision are the same for each of the values.

Discussion:

Using these datatypes, you can represent most values from -1.79E + 308 to 1.79E + 308 with a maximum of 15 significant digits (a value with 308 places before or after the decimal point). This isn't as many significant digits as the numeric datatypes can deal with, but the range is enormous and is plenty for almost any scientific application. These datatypes have a *much* larger range of values than any other datatype. This is because the decimal point isn't fixed in the representation. In exact numeric types, you always have a pattern such as NNNNNNN.DDDD for numbers. You can't store more digits than this to the left or right of the decimal point. However, with float values, you can have values that fit the following patterns (and much larger):

- 0.DDDDDDDDDDDDDDD

- NNNNN.DDDDDDDDD

- 0.00000000000000000000000000000DDDDDDDDDDDDDDD

- NNNNNNNNNNNNNNNN000000000000000000

So you have the ability to store tiny numbers or large ones. This is important for scientific applications where you need to store and do math on an extreme range of values. The float datatypes are well suited for this usage.

You can see the value of the float not storing the value exactly with the classic example of storing .1 in a float:

```
DECLARE @FirstApproximate REAL = 22.33
SELECT @FirstApproximate --sql server renders the view of output correctly
SELECT STR(@FirstApproximate,20,16) --but the whole value gets messy
```

The output of this is

```
-------------
22.33

--------------------
22.3299999999999980
```

That round-off is typically worth it when storing lots of scientific data, but less so when you are dealing with things like money where round-off errors can actually be a legal matter.

Row compression effect:

The least significant bytes with all zeros are not stored. This is applicable mostly to non-fractional values in the mantissa.

Date and Time Data

Almost every database and most tables are going to save some sort of point in time value. Ever since SQL Server 2008, when a set of new datatypes was added to the two datatypes for working with date and time values we originally had, datetime and smalldatetime, things have been a lot better, but a good deal more confusing. Those datatypes added were date, time, datetime2, and datetimeoffset; and it feels like they are *still* in the process of gaining appreciation 11 years later. These datatypes represented a leap of functionality in addition to the original datetime and smalldatetime, but there are a few tricks you can't do with them that some people won't let go of (like adding to them (e.g., @DateValue + 1) instead of using DATEADD(day,1,@DateValue)). For the most part, the new types cover the range of date and time values that could be represented in the original types, though only the smalldatetime type can easily represent a point in time to the minute.

date

Domain: Date-only values from January 1, 0001, to December 31, 9999.

Storage: 3-byte integer, storing the offset from January 1, 0001.

Accuracy: One day.

Discussion:

Of all the features that was added back in 2008, this one datatype was worth the price of the upgrade. The problem of how to store date-only values, or even remove time values from a datetime value, had plagued T-SQL programmers since the beginning of time (aka version 1.0). With this type, you are able to avoid the tricks you have needed to go through to ensure that date types had no time in order to store just a date value. Even removing the time part of a point in time value is as simple as CAST(<datevalue> as date).

Row compression effect:

Technically you get the same compression as for any integer value, but dates in the "normal" range require 3 bytes, meaning no compression is realized.

time [(*precision*)]

Domain: Time of day (note this is not a quantity of time, but rather is a point in time on the clock).

Storage: 3–5 bytes, depending on precision.

Accuracy: To 100 nanoseconds, depending on how it is declared. time(0) is accurate to 1 second, time(1) to .1 second, up to time(7) as .0000001. The default is time(7).

Discussion:

The time type is handy to have but generally less useful than it may seem. Initially it will seem like a good idea to store a point in time, only if the day is also known. Rather, for the most part when you want to store a time value, it is a point in time, and you need one of the date + time types.

The time value can be useful for storing a time for a recurring activity, for example, where the time is the same on multiple days rather than a single point in time.

Row compression effect:

Technically you get the same compression as for any integer value, but time values generally use most of the bytes of the integer storage, so very little compression should be expected for time values.

datetime2 [(*precision*)]

Domain: Dates from January 1, 0001, to December 31, 9999, with a time component.

Storage: Between 6 and 8 bytes. The first 4 bytes are used to store the date and the others an offset from midnight, depending on the accuracy.

Accuracy: To 100 nanoseconds, depending on how it is declared. `datetime2(0)` is accurate to 1 second, `datetime(1)` to .1 second, up to `datetime(7)` as .0000001. The default is 7 or datetime2(7).

Discussion:

This is a much better datatype than `datetime`. Technically, you get far better time support without being limited by the .003 accuracy issues that `datetime` has.

The best benefit of this type is to specify the amount of accuracy that your users actually desire. Most of the time a user doesn't desire fractional seconds, unless the purpose of the type is something scientific or very technical. With `datetime2`, you can choose 1-second accuracy. Also, if you really do want to store fractional sections, like for temporal data, you can store .999 second, unlike `datetime`, which would round .999 up to 1, and .998 would round down to .997.

Row compression effect:

For the date portion of the type, dates before 2079 can save 1 byte of the 4 bytes for the date. Little compression should be expected for the time portion.

datetimeoffset [(*precision*)]

The `datetimeoffset` datatype is the same as `datetime2` in terms of the date and time portion, but adds an offset from UTC (8–10 bytes).

Domain: Dates from January 1, 0001, to December 31, 9999, with a time component and offset from the UTC, in a format of [+|-] hh:mm. (Note that this is not time zone/Daylight Saving Time aware. It simply stores the offset at the time of storage.)

Storage: Between 8 and 10 bytes. The first 4 bytes are used to store the date, and just like `datetime2`, 2–4 bytes will be used for the time, depending on the accuracy. The UTC offset is stored in the additional 2 bytes.

Accuracy: To 100 nanoseconds, depending on how it is declared. `datetimeoffset(0)` is accurate to 1 second, `datetimeoffset (1)` to .1 second, up to `datetimeoffset (7)` as .0000001.

Discussion:

This datatype is the ideal datatype to use when you need to store an exact point in time. You can store data in your local time zone so your local users will not have to constantly do math, but with the time zone offset to know when it actually occurred in the world right in the datatype.

Note, however, that the offset might be more cumbersome than using two date columns, one for UTC and one for local (though this will save a bit of space). A useful operation is to translate the date from its local offset to UTC, like this:

```
DECLARE @LocalTime datetimeoffset;
SET @LocalTime = SYSDATETIMEOFFSET();
SELECT @LocalTime;
SELECT SWITCHOFFSET(@LocalTime, '+00:00') AS UTCTime;
```

The true downside is that it stores an offset, not the time zone, so Daylight Saving Time will still need to be handled manually.

Row compression effect:

For the date portion of the type, dates before 2079 can save 1 byte of the 4 bytes for the date. Little compression should be expected for the time portion.

smalldatetime

Domain: Date and time data values between January 1, 1900, and June 6, 2079.

Storage: 4 bytes (two 2-byte integers: one for the day offset from January 1, 1900, the other for the number of minutes past midnight).

Accuracy: 1 minute.

Discussion:

The `smalldatetime` datatype is accurate to 1 minute. It requires 4 bytes of storage. `smalldatetime` values are the best choice when you need to store the date and the time, of some event where accuracy of a minute isn't a problem. The biggest issue with smalldatetime is that 2079 is not as far off in the future as it seems, and it is not inconceivable that you start needing to store point in time values that are past that date in the near future.

The smalldatetime datatype is suggested to be phased out of designs and replaced with datetime2, though it is very pervasive and will probably be around for many versions of SQL Server yet to come. Unlike datetime, there is not a direct replacement in terms of accuracy, as minimum datetime2 accuracy is to the second.

Row compression effect:

When the time stored is midnight, 2 bytes can be saved, and times less than 4:00 AM can save 1 byte.

datetime

Domain: Date and time data values between January 1, 1753, and December 31, 9999.

Storage: 8 bytes (two 4-byte integers: one for the day offset from January 1, 1753, and the other for the number of 3.33-millisecond periods past midnight).

Accuracy: 3.33 milliseconds.

Discussion:

Using 8 bytes, datetime is a bit heavy on memory, especially considering datetime2 uses that at its max precision, but the biggest issue is regarding the precision. It is accurate to .003 second, leading to interesting round-off issues. For example, very often a person will write an expression such as

```
WHERE DatetimeValue <= '20110919 23:59:59.999'
```

This is used to avoid getting any values for the next day of '20110920 00:00:00.000'. However, because of the precision, when you write the following expression

```
SELECT CAST('20110919 23:59:59.999' AS datetime);
```

what actually will be returned is 2011-09-20 00:00:00.000. Instead, you will need to use

```
SELECT CAST('20110919 23:59:59.997' AS datetime);
```

And no matter how matter how many years I have done this, it is hard to remember to do that. datetime is suggested to be phased out of designs and replaced with datetime2, if for no other reason than datetime2 is just so much better.

Row compression effect:

For the date portion of the type, dates before 2079 can save 1 byte. For the time portion, 4 bytes are saved when the time is midnight, and it uses the first 2 bytes after the first 2 minutes and reaches the fourth byte after 4:00 AM. After 4:00 AM, compression can generally save 1 byte.

Note   Why January 1, 1753, was chosen for the starting date of the datetime datatype is not technical, but historical. For more details, read Kalen Delaney's article here: `www.itprotoday.com/sql-server/inside-datetime-data`.

Discussion on All Date Types

Date types are often some of the most troublesome types for people to deal with. In this section, I'll lightly address the following problem areas:

- Date ranges
- Representing dates in text formats

Date Ranges

This topic will probably seem really elementary, but the fact is that one of the largest blunders in the database implementation world is working with ranges of dates. The problem is that when you want to do inclusive ranges, you have always needed to consider the time in the equation. For example, consider the following criteria:

```
WHERE PointInTimeValue BETWEEN '2012-01-01' AND '2012-12-31'
```

This means something different based on whether the values stored in `PointInTimeValue` have, or do not have, a time part stored. The problem is that any value with the same date as the end value plus a time (such as `'2012-12-31 12:00:00'`) does not fit within the preceding selection criteria, because you will miss all the activity that occurred on December 31 that wasn't at midnight (`00:00:00`).

There are two ways to deal with this. Either code your WHERE clause like this:

```
WHERE PointInTimeValue >= '2012-01-01' AND pointInTimeValue < '2013-01-01'
```

Or translate point in time values in your tables to date-only values (possibly using a computed column like `DateValue AS CAST(PointInTimeValue AS date)`). Many times, the date value will come in handy for grouping activities by day as well. Having done that, a value such as `'2012-12-31 12:00:00'` will be truncated to `'2012-12-31'` which is equivalent to `'2012-12-31 00:00:00'`, and a row containing that value will be picked up by selection criteria such as this:

```
WHERE PointInTimeValue BETWEEN '2012-01-01' AND '2012-12-31'
```

A common solution that I don't generally suggest is to use a between range like this:

```
WHERE PointInTimeValue
        BETWEEN '2012-01-01' AND '2012-12-31 23:59:59.9999999'
```

The idea is that if the second value is less than the next day, values for the next day won't be returned. The major problem with this solution has to do with the conversion of `23:59:59.9999999` to one of the various date datatypes. Each of the types will round up, so you must match the number of fractional parts to the precision of the type. For datetime2(3), you would need `23:59:59.999`. If the `PointInTimeValue` column was of type datetime, you would need to use this:

```
WHERE PointInTimeValue BETWEEN '2009-01-01' AND '2009-12-31 23:59:59.997'
```

However, for a smalldatetime value, it would need to be this:

```
WHERE PointInTimeValue  BETWEEN '2009-01-01' AND '2009-12-31 23:59'
```

And so on, for all of the different date types, which gets complicated by the new types where you can specify precision. You might programmatically get it right, and anyone else is going to mess it up regularly.

Representing Dates in Text Formats

When working with date values in text, using a standard format is always best. There are many different formats used around the world for dates, most confusingly MMDDYYYY and DDMMYYYY (is 01022004 or 02012004 the same day or a different day?). Although SQL Server uses the locale information on your server to decide how to interpret your date input, using one of the standard formats ensures that SQL Server doesn't mistake the input for something different than you expect, regardless of where the value is entered.

Using a standard format prevents any issues when sharing data with international clients or even with sharing it with others on the Web when looking for help.

There are several standard formats that will work and be unambiguous:

- ANSI SQL standard

  - *No time zone offset*: `'YYYY-MM-DD HH:MM:SS'`

  - *With time zone*: `'YYYY-MM-DD HH:MM:SS -OH:OM'` (Z, for Zulu, can be used in place of the -0H:0M to indicate the time zone is the base time of 00:00 offset, otherwise known as GMT [Greenwich Mean Time], or the most standard/modern name is UTC [Coordinated Universal Time].)

- ISO 8601

  - *Unseparated*: `'YYYYMMDD'`

  - *Numeric*: `'YYYY-MM-DD'`

  - *Time*: `'HH:MM:SS.sssssss'` (SS and `.sssssss` are optional)

  - *Date and time*: `'YYYY-MM-DDTHH:MM:SS.sssssss'`

  - *Date and time with offset*: `'YYYY-MM-DDTHH:MM:SS.sssssss -OH:OM'`

- ODBC

  - *Date*: `{d 'YYYY-MM-DD'}`

  - *Time*: `{t 'HH:MM:SS'}`

  - *Date and time*: `{ts 'YYYY-MM-DD HH:MM:SS'}`

Using the ANSI SQL standard format or the ISO 8601 format is generally considered the best practice for specifying date values. It will definitely feel odd when you first begin typing `'2008-08-09'` for a date value, but once you get used to it, it will feel natural and clear (and the values sort better as text too!). Even the bank teller probably won't question it once you start writing the date on your deposit slip when you cash your birthday check from Grandma using a standard format.

The following are some examples using the ANSI and ISO formats:

```
SELECT CAST('2013-01-01' AS date) AS DateOnly;
SELECT CAST('2013-01-01 14:23:00.003' AS datetime) AS WithTime;
```

You might also see values that are close to this format, such as the following:

```
SELECT CAST ('20130101' AS date) AS DateOnly;
SELECT CAST('2013-01-01T14:23:00.120' AS datetime) AS WithTime;
```

For more information, check Microsoft Docs for "Supported String Literal Formats for datetime" (docs.microsoft.com/en-us/sql/t-sql/data-types/datetime-transact-sql#supported-string-literal-formats-for-datetime). Related to dates, the function FORMAT will help you output dates in any format you need to. As a very brief example, consider the following code snippet:

```
DECLARE @DateValue datetime2(3) = '2012-05-21 15:45:01.456'
SELECT @DateValue AS Unformatted,
       FORMAT(@DateValue,'yyyyMMdd') AS IsoUnseparated,
       FORMAT(@DateValue,'yyyy-MM-ddThh:mm:ss') AS IsoDateTime,
       FORMAT(@DateValue,'D','en-US') AS USRegional,
       FORMAT(@DateValue,'D','en-GB') AS GBRegional,
       FORMAT(@DateValue,'D','fr-fr') AS FRRegional;
```

This returns the following:

Unformatted	IsoUnseparated	IsoDateTime
2012-05-21 15:45:01.456	20120521	2012-05-21T03:45:01

USRegional	GBRegional	FRRegional
Monday, May 21, 2012	21 May 2012	lundi 21 mai 2012

The unformatted version is simply how it appears in SSMS using my local settings. The IsoUnseperated value was built using a format mask of yyyyMMdd and the IsoDateTime using a bit more interesting mask, each of which should be fairly obvious, but check the "FORMAT (Transact-SQL)" topic in Microsoft Docs (docs.microsoft.com/en-us/sql/t-sql/functions/format-transact-sql?view=sql-server-ver15) for a full rundown of features.

The last two examples format the date in the manner of a given region, each of which could come in very handy when building regionalized reports. Note that the Great Britain version doesn't list the day of the week, whereas the US and France versions do.

FORMAT does more than just date data, but this is where we have generally felt the most pain with data through the years, so I mentioned it here. Note that FORMAT can be reasonably slow as a function if you are processing a lot of rows, so if it is being called many many times, it could be a performance hit.

There is another handy function PARSE that will let you take a value in a given regional version and parse information out of a formatted string (as well as a few other datatypes). I won't demonstrate PARSE, but rather wanted to make you aware of more tools to work with date data here in this section of the appendix.

Character Strings

Most data that's stored in SQL Server uses a character datatype. Frequently, character columns are used to hold noncharacter data, such as numbers and dates. Although this might not be technically wrong, it isn't ideal. For starters, storing a number with eight digits in a character string requires at least 8 bytes, but as an integer it requires 4 bytes. Searching on integers is far easier because 1 always precedes 2, whereas 11 comes before 2 in character strings that aren't left padded, something that makes dealing with strings pretty awful. Additionally, integers are stored in a format that can be manipulated using intrinsic processor functions, as opposed to having SQL Server–specific functions deal with the data.

char[(*number of bytes*)]

Domain: Fixed-length ASCII or UTF8 characters, up to 8,000 characters long.

Storage: 1 byte × number of bytes.

Discussion:

The char datatype is used for fixed-length character data. Every value will be stored with the same number of characters, up to a maximum of 8,000 bytes. Storage is exactly the number of bytes as per the column definition, regardless of actual data stored; any remaining space to the right of the last character of the data is padded with spaces. The default size if not specified is 1 (it is best practice to include the size).

For most collations, every character in a char datatype will be stored in an ASCII format and will take 1 byte each. But for UTF8 collations, a character will be stored in Unicode format, which can be 1, 2, or 4 bytes. See Chapter 7 for more details on collations and their effects on storage and manipulation of data.

The maximum limit for a char is 8,000 bytes, but if you ever get within a mile of this limit for a fixed-width character value, you're possibly making a big design mistake because it's extremely rare to have massive character strings of exactly the same length. You should employ the char datatype only in cases where you're guaranteed to have exactly the same number of characters in every column value in each row.

The char datatype is most often used for codes and identifiers, such as customer numbers or invoice numbers where the number could logically include alpha characters as well as integer data. Often this might be a number, like 123, but left padded with zeros to fit the space, like 00000000123, if it was a char(11). An example is a vehicle identification number (VIN), which is stamped on most every vehicle produced around the world. Note that this is a composite attribute/smart key, because you can determine many things about the automobile from its VIN.

Another example where a char column is usually found is in American Social Security numbers (SSNs), which always have nine characters and two dashes embedded.

Note that the length is optional. When used in a variable or column declaration, such as DECLARE @column char, the max length is 1. When used in a CAST or CONVERT, such as CAST(@column AS char), the max length is 30. Best practice is to always specify a length because it is way too confusing to try to remember if what you just did defaults to 1 or 30.

Row compression effect:

Instead of storing the padding characters, it removes them for storage and adds them back whenever the data is actually used. The way the data behaves when you are using the values actually is still the same, however. You can see that in the following example:

```
--Create tables with the same datatype of char
--one with DATA_COMPRESSION

CREATE TABLE dbo.TestChar
(
      value char(100)
);

CREATE TABLE dbo.TestChar2
(
      value char(100)
)
WITH (DATA_COMPRESSION = PAGE);
GO
```

```
--insert the exact same data
INSERT INTO dbo.TestChar(value)
VALUES('1234567890');
INSERT INTO dbo.TestChar2(value)
VALUES('1234567890');
GO
--output the length of the text, and the amount of memory used
SELECT LEN(value), DATALENGTH(value)
FROM    dbo.TestChar;
SELECT LEN(value), DATALENGTH(value)
FROM    dbo.TestChar2;
```

The result is they are both the same:

```
----------- -----------
10          100

----------- -----------
10          100
```

Note   The setting ANSI_PADDING determines exactly how padding is handled. If this setting is ON, the table is as I've described; if not, data will be stored as I'll discuss in the "varchar(length)" section. It's best practice to leave this ANSI setting ON to keep your data behaving as is expected from char value.

---

varchar[(*number of bytes*)]

Domain: ASCII or UTF8 characters, up to 8,000 characters long.

    Storage: 1 byte × (declared number of bytes) + 2 bytes (for overhead).

    Discussion:

    For the varchar datatype, you choose the maximum length of the data you want to store, up to 8,000 bytes. The varchar datatype is far more useful than char, because the data doesn't have to be of the same length and SQL Server doesn't pad out excess memory with spaces. There's some reasonably minor overhead in storing variable-length data. First, it costs an additional 2 bytes per column. Second, it's a bit more costly to get to the data, because it isn't always in the same location of the physical record. The same caveats apply with varchar as char with collation and UTF8.

Use the varchar datatype when your character data varies in length. The good thing about varchar columns is that, no matter how long you make the maximum, the space used by the column is based on the actual size of the characters being stored plus the few extra bytes that specify how long the data is.

You'll generally want to choose a maximum limit for your datatype that's a reasonable value, large enough to handle all situations, but not too large as to be impractical to deal with in your applications and reports. For example, take people's first names. These obviously require the varchar type (or nvarchar, as we cover later, but in SQL Server 2019 with UTF8 available, it is not a given), but how long should you allow the data to be? First names tend to be around 15 characters long, though you generally would want to specify 50 characters for the unlikely exception. You would not want to choose 500, just in case, because you would then have to be able to put a name with 500 characters on every form that your company prints. If you were the DMV, everyone's driver's license might have to be 3 feet long...just in case.

The most prevalent storage type for non-key values that you'll use is varchar data, because, generally speaking, the size of the data is one of the most important factors in performance tuning. The smaller the amount of data, the less has to be read and written. This means less disk access, which is one of the two most important bottlenecks we have to deal with (networking speed is the other). Hence, if you can avoid Unicode values (e.g., for codes or names of products), it would be best to do so. Luckily in SQL Server 2019, we have UTF8 collations which you can convert your data to without changing the datatype, though changing collation is pretty much as much work as changing the datatype.

Note that just like for char, the length is optional. When used in a variable or column declaration, such as DECLARE @ColumnValue varchar;, the max length is 1. When used in a CAST or CONVERT, such as CAST(@column AS varchar), the max length is 30. Best practice is to always specify a length.

Row compression effect:
No effect.

varchar(max)

Domain: ASCII or UTF8 characters, up to $2^{31} - 1$ characters (that is a maximum of 2 GB worth of text!).

   Storage: Size is 2 bytes plus the actual size of the data. Where the data is stored is affected by the setting of the table option `'large value types out of row'`, which is set with the `sp_tableoption` system stored procedure:

- `OFF` or = 0: When the data for all the columns fits in a single row and the data is stored in the row with the same storage costs for non-max `varchar` values. Once the data is too big to fit in a single row, data is placed on more than one page. This is the default setting.

- `ON` or = 1: You store `varchar(max)` values using 16-byte pointers to separate pages that just hold large objects. Use this setting if the `varchar(max)` data will only seldom be used in queries.

Discussion:

   You can deal with `varchar(max)` values using mostly the same functions and methods that you use with normal `varchar` values. The same caveats apply with `varchar(max)` as `char` with collation and UTF8. There's a minor difference, though. As the size of your `varchar(max)` column grows toward the upper boundary, you likely aren't going to want to be sending the entire value back and forth over the network most of the time. I know that even on my 1000 MBit LAN, sending 2 GB is no instantaneous operation, for sure. "Chunked" writes are enabled using the .write method of a `varchar(max)` column, which lets you change only parts of a `varchar(max)` value.

   One word of warning for when your code mixes normal `varchar` and `varchar(max)` values in the same statement: Normal `varchar` values do not automatically change datatype to a `(max)` type when the data being manipulated grows beyond 8,000 characters. For example, write a statement such as the following:

```
DECLARE @value varchar(max) = REPLICATE('X',8000) + REPLICATE('X',8000);
SELECT LEN(@value);
```

   This returns the following result, which you would expect to be 16000, since you have two 8,000-character strings:

```
--------------------
8000
```

The reason is that the type of the REPLICATE function is varchar when replicating normal char values (even if you say REPLICATE('x',10000)). Adding two varchar values together doesn't result in a varchar(max) value. However, most of the functions return varchar(max) values when working with varchar(max) values, for example:

```
DECLARE @value varchar(max) = REPLICATE(CAST('X' AS varchar(max)),8000)
                            + REPLICATE(CAST('X' AS varchar(max)),8000);
SELECT LEN(@value);
```

This returns the following result:

```
--------------------
16000
```

> *Row compression effect:*
> No effect.

text

Don't use the text datatype for any reason in new designs. It might not exist in the next version of SQL Server (though I now have written that statement for many versions of this book). Worst of all, the text datatype is simply horrible to work with. Replace immediately with varchar(max) whenever you possibly can. See the Microsoft Docs topic "ntext, text and image (Transact-SQL)" (docs.microsoft.com/en-us/sql/t-sql/data-types/ntext-text-and-image-transact-sql) if you have questions about existing usage of the text or ntext datatype.

Unicode Character Strings: nchar(double byte length), nvarchar(double byte length), nvarchar(max), ntext

Domain: Unicode (UTF16) characters, up to $2^{31} - 1$ characters (2 GB of storage).

Storage: Same as other character datatypes, though space is declared in double bytes instead of single bytes. So an nvarchar(20) will require 40 bytes + 2 bytes for the variable character overhead.

The actual amount of space each character may take depends on the collation. See Chapter 7 for a discussion on collation for more details, but the typical Unicode character takes 2 bytes per character, up to 4 bytes per character.

Discussion:

The n-prefixed character types all store character strings encoded in UTF16. This specifies a 16-bit character format that can store characters beyond just the Latin character set. SQL Server supports the Unicode Standard, version 3.2.

If you want to specify a Unicode value in a string, you append an N (must be a capital N; a lowercase n will give you an error) to the front of the string, like so:

```
SELECT N'Unicode Value';
```

Tip   You should migrate away from ntext as a datatype just as you should for the text datatype.

Row compression effect:

Just like their ASCII counterparts for fixed-length types, it will not store trailing blanks for the fixed-length types. In all versions after SQL Server 2008R2, compression can compress Unicode values using what is known as the Standard Compression Scheme for Unicode (SCSU), which gives anywhere between 15% and 50% storage improvement depending on the character set. This is particularly interesting as a lot of third-party systems use Unicode storage "just in case," and it is becoming more and more the norm to use Unicode for pretty much everything in a system to allow for the future, even if you never make use of anything other than a standard ASCII character.

Binary Data

Binary data allows you to store a string of bytes. It's useful for storing just about anything, especially data from a client that might or might not fit into a character or numeric datatype. Binary values are essential to the process of storing encrypted values in SQL Server. In Chapter 10, we mentioned some of the ways you can encrypt data in SQL Server, and you can read a good deal more in Microsoft Docs in the "SQL Server Encryption" topic here: docs.microsoft.com/en-us/sql/relational-databases/security/encryption/sql-server-encryption.

One of the restrictions of binary datatypes is that they don't support bitwise operators, which would allow you to do some powerful bitmask storage by being able to compare two binary columns to see not only whether they differ but in which bytes they differ. The whole idea of the binary datatypes is that they store strings of bits. The bitwise operators can operate on integers, which are physically stored as bits. The reason for this inconsistency is fairly clear from the point of view of the internal query processor. The bitwise operators are handled in the processor, whereas the binary datatypes are SQL Server specific.

Binary literal values are specified hexadecimal literals such as 0xB1B2B3 . . . BN. 0x tells you that it's a hexadecimal value. B1 specifies the first single byte in hexadecimal.

binary[(*number of bytes*)]

Domain: Fixed-length binary data with a maximum length of 8,000 bytes.

Storage: Number of bytes the value is defined for. The default length is 1, if not specified (it is best practice to include a size).

Discussion:

The use of binary columns is fairly limited except for holding results of encryption due to their fixed length. You can use them to store any binary values that aren't dealt with by SQL Server. Data stored in binary is simply a string of bytes:

```
DECLARE @value binary(10)  = CAST('helloworld' AS binary(10));
SELECT @value;
```

This returns the following result:

```
----------------------
0x68656C6C6F776F726C64
```

Now you can reverse the process:

```
SELECT CAST(0x68656C6C6F776F726C64 AS varchar(10));
```

This returns the following result:

```
----------
helloworld
```

Note that casting the value HELLOWORLD gives you a different value:

```
--------------------
0x48454C4C4F574F524C44
```

This fact that these two binary values are different, even for textual data that would be considered equivalent on a case-insensitive collation, has been one use for the binary datatype: case-sensitive searches. This is generally not the best way to do a case-sensitive comparison, as it's far more efficient to use the COLLATE keyword and use a different collation if you want to do a case-insensitive comparison on string data.

Row compression effect:

Trailing zeros are not stored but are returned when the values are used.

varbinary[(*length*)]

Domain: Variable-length binary data with a maximum length of 8,000 bytes.

Storage: Number of bytes the value is defined for, plus 2 bytes for variable-length overhead. The default length is 1, if not specified (it is a best practice to include a size).

Discussion:

The usage is the same as binary, except the number of bytes is variable.

A very common use for varbinary data is when you are using encryption of some sort and it returns some binary value that is not of fixed length.

Row compression effect:

No effect.

varbinary(max)

Domain: Binary data, up to $2^{31} - 1$ bytes (up to 2 GB for storage) when data is stored in SQL Server files, up to the max of the storage for data stored in the filestream. For more information and examples about the filestream, check Chapter 9.

Storage: There are a couple of possibilities for storage based on whether the data is stored using the filestream setting, as well as the setting of the table option `'large value types out of row'`:

- `OFF`: If the data for all the columns fits in a single row, the data is stored in the row with the same storage costs for non-`max` `varchar` values. Once the data is too big to fit in a single page, data will be placed on greater than one page.

- `ON`: You always store `varbinary(max)` values using 16-byte pointers to separate pages outside the table. Use this setting if the `varchar(max)` data will only seldom be used in queries.

Discussion:

The `varbinary(max)` datatype provides the same kinds of benefits for large binary values as the `varchar(max)` does for text. Pretty much you can deal with `varbinary(max)` values using the same functions and the same methods as you do with the normal `varbinary` values.

What's cool is that you can store text, JPEG and GIF images, and even Word documents and Excel spreadsheets using the `varbinary(max)` type. On the other hand, it can be much slower and needs more programming work to use SQL Server as a storage mechanism for files, mostly because it's slow to retrieve really large values from the database as compared to from the file system. You can, however, use filestream and perhaps filetable access to get the best of both possible worlds by using Win32 access to a file in a directory within the context of a transaction. This approach is described in greater detail in Chapter 9 in the section on storing images and files.

Row compression effect:

No effect.

image

Just like the `text` datatype, the `image` datatype is deprecated. Don't use the `image` datatype in new designs if at all possible. It very well may not exist in the next version of SQL Server. Replace with `varbinary(max)` in any location you can. See the Microsoft Docs topic "ntext, text and image (Transact-SQL)" (`docs.microsoft.com/en-us/sql/t-sql/data-types/ntext-text-and-image-transact-sql`) for more information or if you have existing `image` column data that you need to manipulate.

Other Datatypes

The following datatypes are somewhat less easy to categorize but are still commonly employed in OLTP systems:

- `bit`
- `rowversion (timestamp)`
- `uniqueidentifier`
- `cursor`
- `table`
- `sql_variant`

bit

Domain: 0, 1, or NULL.

Storage: A `bit` column requires 1 byte of storage per up to eight instances in a table. Hence, having eight bit columns will cause your table to be no larger than if your table had only a single `bit` column, but far smaller than if you use an integer type to store a 1 and 0.

Discussion:

You use `bit` values as a kind of imitation Boolean value. A `bit` isn't a Boolean value in that it has values 0 and 1, not `True` and `False`. This is a minor distinction but one that needs to be made. You cannot execute code such as this:

```
IF (bitValue) DO SOMETHING;
```

A better term than a Boolean is a *flag*. A value of 1 means the flag has been set (such as a value that tells us that a customer does want email promotions). Many programmers like to use character values `'yes'` or `'no'` for this, because this can be easier for viewing, but it can be harder to program with using built-in programming methods. In fact, the use of the `bit` datatype as a Boolean value has occurred primarily because many programming languages usually use 0 for `False` and nonzero for `True` (some use 1 or –1 explicitly).

You can index a bit column, but usually it isn't of much value only to index it. Having only two distinct values in an index (technically three with NULL) typically makes for a poor index. (See Chapter 11 for more information about indexes. You may be able to use a filtered index to make some indexes on bit columns useful.) Clearly, a bit value most often should be indexed in conjunction with other columns.

Another limitation of the bit datatype is that you can't do math operations or some aggregates with bit columns. Math is somewhat expected, but there are certainly places where the MAX aggregate would be a very useful thing. You can cast the bit to a tinyint and use it in math/aggregates if you need to.

A relatively odd property of the bit datatype is that you can cast the string values 'True' and 'False' to bit values 1 and 0, respectively. So the following will work:

```
SELECT CAST ('True' AS bit) AS True, CAST('False' AS bit) AS False;
```

Spelling counts (though not case) and other text values will give you a type conversion error. Not even 'yes' and 'no' will work.

Row compression effect:

Depends on the number of bits in the row. For a single bit value, 4 bits will be needed because of the metadata overhead of compression.

Tip   There's typically a good deal of discussion about using the bit datatype. It's often asked why we don't have a Boolean datatype. This is largely because of the idea that datatypes need to support NULL in RDBMSs, and a Boolean datatype would have to support both UNKNOWN and NULL, resulting in four-valued logic tables that are difficult to contemplate (without taking a seriously long nap) and hard to deal with. So we have what we have, and it works well enough.

---

rowversion (aka timestamp)

The rowversion datatype is a database-wide unique number. When you have a rowversion column in a table, the value of the rowversion column changes for each modification to a row in an 8-byte binary value. The value in the rowversion column is guaranteed to be unique across all tables in the database. It's also known as a timestamp value, but it doesn't have any time implications—it's merely a unique value to tell you that your row has changed.

Tip   In the SQL standards, a timestamp datatype is equivalent to what you know as a datetime datatype. To avoid confusion, Microsoft has deprecated the name timestamp and now recommends that you use the name rowversion rather than timestamp, although you will notice that some of their examples and scripting tools will still reference the timestamp name. While I doubt they ever change this, you should still change columns to use rowversion whenever you get the chance (not as urgently as text and ntext, but still…).

The rowversion column of a table (you may have only one) is usually used for an optimistic locking mechanism. It's stored as an 8-byte varbinary value. Binary values aren't always easy to deal with, and their use depends on which mechanism you're using to access your data.

As an example of how the rowversion datatype works, consider the following batch:

```
SET NOCOUNT ON;
CREATE TABLE dbo.TestRowversion
(
    Value   varchar(20) NOT NULL,
    Auto_rv   rowversion NOT NULL
);

INSERT INTO dbo.TestRowversion (Value)
VALUES('Insert');

SELECT Value, Auto_rv
FROM dbo.testRowversion;

UPDATE dbo.TestRowversion
SET Value = 'First Update';

SELECT Value, Auto_rv
FROM dbo.TestRowversion;

UPDATE dbo.TestRowversion
SET Value = 'Last Update';

SELECT Value, auto_rv
FROM dbo.TestRowversion;
```

This batch returns the following results (your `Auto_rv` column values may vary, but they should still be hexadecimal representations):

Value	Auto_rv
Insert	0x00000000000007DA

Value	Auto_rv
First Update	0x00000000000007DB

Value	Auto_rv
Last Update	0x00000000000007DC

You didn't touch the `Auto_rv` column, and yet it incremented itself twice. You can't trust that `rowversion` values will be an unbroken sequence for changes in the same table, because updates of other tables will change the value as well. All `rowversion` values in a database draw from the same pool of values. You can however use the fact that the `rowversion` number is an incrementing value in your code if you want to discover everything in the database that has changed since a certain point in "time," that time being a value of a `rowversion` value.

You can create variables of the `rowversion` type for holding `rowversion` values, and you can retrieve the last-used `rowversion` via the `@@DBTS` configuration function. I use `rowversion` columns in Chapter 13 to demonstrate optimistic locking.

Row compression effect:

Uses a `bigint` structure representation of the value, using 8 bytes. Then it can be compressed just like the `bigint` type.

uniqueidentifier

Globally unique identifiers are a mainstay of Microsoft computing. The name says it all—these identifiers are values that are purportedly globally unique for each value you generate. According to the way that GUIDs are formed, the chance that there will ever be any duplication in their values is tremendously remote, as there are 2^{128} possible values (though if the *Hitchhiker's Guide to the Galaxy* teaches us one thing, it is that unless something is impossible, it is actually possible, so it is still best to protect against duplication using constraints). They're generated by a formula that includes the current date and time, a unique number from the CPU clock, and some other "magic numbers."

In your databases, these GUID values are stored in the `uniqueidentifier` type, which is implemented as a 16-byte binary value. An interesting use is to have a key value that's guaranteed to be unique across databases and servers. You can generate a GUID value in T-SQL using the `NEWID()` function:

```
DECLARE @guidVar uniqueidentifier = NEWID();

SELECT @guidVar AS GuidVar;
```

This returns (a similar value to) the following:

```
GuidVar
-----------------------------------------------------------
6C7119D5-D48F-475C-8B60-50D0C41B6EBFF
```

While GUIDs are stored as 16-byte binary values, they aren't exactly a straight binary value. You cannot put just any binary value into a `uniqueidentifier` column, because the value must meet the criteria for the generation of a GUID, which isn't exactly well documented. (For more information, a good resource is `en.wikipedia.org/wiki/guid`.)

If you need to create a `uniqueidentifier` column that's auto-generating, you can set a property in the `CREATE TABLE` statement (or `ALTER TABLE`, for that matter). It's the ROWGUIDCOL property, and it's used like so:

```
CREATE TABLE dbo.GuidPrimaryKey
(
    GuidPrimaryKeyId uniqueidentifier NOT NULL ROWGUIDCOL
    CONSTRAINT PKGuidPrimaryKey PRIMARY KEY
    CONSTRAINT DFLTGuidPrimaryKey_GuidPrimaryKeyId DEFAULT NEWID(),
    Value varchar(10)
);
```

Execute the following INSERT statement:

```
INSERT INTO dbo.GuidPrimaryKey(Value)
VALUES ('Test');
```

Then run the following command to view the data entered:

```
SELECT *
FROM   dbo.GuidPrimaryKey;
```

This returns the following result (though your key value will be different, or this would not be a GLOBALLY unique value, would it?):

GuidPrimaryKeyId	Value
490E8876-A695-4F5B-B53A-69109A28D493	Test

The ROWGUIDCOL property of a column built with the uniqueidentifier notifies the system that this value can be used to identify a row for the table in a way that can be applied in a standard way across multiple tools. Note that the ROWGUIDCOL property does not guarantee uniqueness. To provide such a guarantee, you need to implement your column using a PRIMARY KEY or UNIQUE constraint.

It would seem that the uniqueidentifier would be a better way of implementing primary keys, because when they're created, they're unique across all databases, servers, and platforms. However, there are two main reasons why you ideally won't use uniqueidentifier columns to implement all your primary keys:

- *Storage requirements*: Because they're 16 bytes in size, they're considerably more bloated than a typical integer column.

- *Typeability*: Because there are 36 characters in the textual version of the GUID, it's hard to type the value of the GUID into a query. There's a reason why phone numbers are not 36 characters long.

If you're using the GUID values for the primary key of a table and you're clustering on this value, you can use another function to generate the values: NEWSEQUENTIALID(). You can use this function only in a default constraint. It's used to guarantee that the next GUID chosen will be greater than the previous value:

```
DROP TABLE dbo.GuidPrimaryKey;
GO
CREATE TABLE dbo.GuidPrimaryKey
(
```

```
GuidPrimaryKeyId uniqueidentifier NOT NULL
        ROWGUIDCOL CONSTRAINT DFLTGuidPrimaryKey_GuidPrimaryKeyId
                            DEFAULT NEWSEQUENTIALID()
        CONSTRAINT PKGuidPrimaryKey PRIMARY KEY,
   Value varchar(10) NOT NULL
);
GO
INSERT INTO dbo.GuidPrimaryKey(value)
VALUES('Test'),
      ('Test1'),
      ('Test2');
GO

SELECT *
FROM   GuidPrimaryKey;
```

This returns something like the following, with a notable progression to the values of the GuidPrimaryKeyId column values:

GuidPrimaryKeyId	Value
18812704-49E3-E011-89D1-000C29992276	Test
19812704-49E3-E011-89D1-000C29992276	Test1
1A812704-49E3-E011-89D1-000C29992276	Test2

You may notice that the increasing value appears to be in the letters to the far left. To the naked eye, it would appear that we could be pretty close to running out of values, since the progression of 18, 19, 1A is going to run out pretty quickly. The fact is the values are not being sorted on the text representation of the GUID, but on the internal binary value. Note, however, the values are not guaranteed to remain sequential with existing data in the table after a Windows reboot, so it can become a bit of an issue.

Now, using a GUID for the primary key is just about as good as using an identity column or value from a SEQUENCE object for building a surrogate key, particularly one with a clustered index (they are still rather large at 16 bytes vs. 4 for an integer or even 8 for a bigint). That's because all new values will be added to the end of the index rather than randomly throughout the index. (Chapter 11 covers indexes, but be cognizant that a random value distributed throughout your rows can cause fragmentation unless you provide a fill factor that allows for adding rows to pages, but the leaving space via fill factor then bloats the size of your index.)

Values in the `uniqueidentifier` type will also still be four times as large as an `integer` column, hence requiring four times the storage space. This makes using a `uniqueidentifier` a less than favorable index candidate from the database storage layer's perspective. However, the fact that it can be generated by any client and be very likely to be unique is a major plus, rather than requiring you to generate them in a single-threaded manner to ensure uniqueness. (One of the tech editors for the book reported that he sees duplicated GUID values occasionally in a highly concurrent banking system that relies on them for surrogate keys—it is not impossible to have collisions.)

Row compression effect:
No effect.

cursor

A cursor is a mechanism that allows row-wise operations instead of using the normal set-wise way. You use the `cursor` datatype to hold a local reference to a SQL Server T-SQL cursor. You may not use a `cursor` datatype as a column in a table. Its only use is in T-SQL code to hold a reference to a cursor, which can be passed as a parameter to a stored procedure.

Row compression effect:
Not applicable.

table

The `table` type is kind of two different things. First, you have the `table` type that is essentially a temporary table that you can declare like a variable at runtime, and you can define its characteristics. Second, you have table types that are defined and stored for later use, for example, as table-valued parameters. I have broken these two different types of uses down into two sections. Neither usage is affected by row compression.

Table Variables

The table variable holds a reference to a result set. The name of the datatype is a pretty bad choice, because it will make functional programmers think that they can store a pointer to a table. It's actually used to store a result set as a temporary table. In fact, the table is very similary a temporary table in implementation. However, you don't get any kind of statistics on the table, nor are you able to index the table datatype, other than to apply PRIMARY KEY and UNIQUE constraints in the table declaration. You can also have CHECK and DEFAULT constraints.

The following is an example of the syntax needed to employ the table variable type:

```
DECLARE @tableVar TABLE
(
    Id int IDENTITY PRIMARY KEY,
    Value varchar(100)
);
INSERT INTO @tableVar (Value)
VALUES ('This is a cool test');

SELECT Id, Value
FROM    @tableVar;
```

This returns the following result:

```
id            value
-----------   --------------------------
1             This is a cool test
```

As with the cursor datatype, you may not use the table datatype as a column in a table, and it can be used only in T-SQL code to hold a set of data. One of the primary purposes for the table datatype is for returning a table from a user-defined function, as in the following example:

```
CREATE FUNCTION dbo.Table$TestFunction
(
    @returnValue varchar(100)
)
```

```
RETURNS @tableVar table
(
      Value varchar(100)
)
AS
BEGIN
   INSERT INTO @tableVar (Value)
   VALUES (@returnValue);

   RETURN;
END;
```

Once created, you can use the `table` datatype returned by the function using typical SELECT syntax:

```
SELECT *
FROM dbo.Table$testFunction('testValue');
```

This returns the following result:

```
Value
---------------------------------
testValue
```

One interesting thing about the `table` datatype is that the tables that are created as variables aren't subject to transactions, since they are variables, for example:

```
DECLARE @tableVar TABLE
(
   Id int IDENTITY,
   Value varchar(100)
);
BEGIN TRANSACTION;

INSERT INTO @tableVar (Value)
VALUES ('This will still be there');
```

```
ROLLBACK TRANSACTION;

SELECT Id, Value
FROM @tableVar;
```

This returns the following result:

```
Id          Value
----------- ------------------------------
1           This will still be there
```

For this reason, these tables are very useful for logging errors, because the data is still available after the ROLLBACK TRANSACTION.

Table-Valued Parameters

One of the oft-requested features for SQL Server over the years was the ability to pass in a table of values to a stored procedure. Using the table type, you can do this, but not in as free a manner as you probably would have initially hoped. Instead of being able to define your table on the fly, you are required to use a type that you predefine.

The table type you will define is the same as the datatype alias we discussed in Chapter 7, except you specify an entire table, with all of the same things that a table variable can have, including PRIMARY KEY, UNIQUE, CHECK, and DEFAULT constraints.

An example that I have used several times in real life is a generic table type with a list of integer values to pass as a parameter or to use in a query instead of an IN clause:

```
USE WideWorldImporters;
GO
CREATE TYPE GenericIdList AS TABLE
(
    Id Int PRIMARY KEY
);
```

You declare the table variable just like any other and then load and use the variable with data just like any other local variable table:

```
DECLARE @PeopleIdList GenericIdList;
INSERT INTO @PeopleIdList
VALUES (1),(2),(3),(4);
```

```
SELECT PersonId, FullName
FROM   Application.People
           JOIN @PeopleIdList AS list
               on People.PersonId = List.Id;
```

This returns the following:

PersonId	FullName
1	Data Conversion Only
2	Kayla Woodcock
3	Hudson Onslow
4	Isabella Rupp

And after 2014, you can use a memory-optimized TABLE type as well:

```
--database must support in-memory with in-mem filegroup
CREATE TYPE GenericIdList_InMem AS TABLE
(
    Id Int PRIMARY KEY NONCLUSTERED
    --Use nonclustered here,  as it should be fine for typical uses
) WITH (MEMORY_OPTIMIZED = ON);
```

This will execute the same way, though it can be a good bit faster in some scenarios (if the limitations are not a problem, like not being able to join across database containers):

```
DECLARE @PeopleIdList GenericIdList_InMem;
INSERT INTO @PeopleIdList
VALUES (2),(3),(4);

SELECT PersonId, FullName
FROM   Application.People
           JOIN @PeopleIdList AS list
               ON People.PersonId = List.Id;
```

Of course, you can then use either of the types in your STORED PROCEDURE object creation statements as well:

```
CREATE PROCEDURE Application.People$List
(
    @PeopleIdList GenericIdList READONLY
)
AS
SELECT PersonId, FullName
FROM   Application.People
         JOIN @PeopleIdList AS List
             ON People.PersonId = List.Id;
```

Unfortunately, you cannot pass a set of row constructors to the stored procedure; you will need to declare and load a table variable to use this construct from T-SQL:

```
DECLARE @PeopleIdList GenericIdList;

INSERT INTO @PeopleIdList
VALUES (2),(3),(4);

EXEC Application.People$List @PeopleIdList;
```

What makes this really nice is that in ADO.NET, you can declare a DataTable object and pass it to the procedure as a parameter, just like any other value. This will make the technique to insert multiple items at a time or SELECT multiple rows far easier than ever before. In the past, we used a kludgy, comma-delimited list or XML to do this, and it worked, but not in a natural manner we are accustomed to, not to mention being generally slow since you had to work to split the data up. This method works in a natural manner, allowing us to support multiple operations in a single transaction using an easy-to-build ADO.NET construct.

sql_variant

The catch-all datatype, the sql_variant type, allows you to store a value of almost any datatype that I've discussed. This ability allows you to create a column or variable where you don't know ahead of time exactly what kind of data will be stored. The sql_variant datatype allows you to store values of various SQL Server-supported datatypes, except for varchar(max), varbinary(max), xml, text, ntext, rowversion/timestamp, and sql_variant.

Note   Although the `rowversion` datatype cannot be stored directly in a `sql_variant`, a `rowversion` value can be stored in a `binary(8)` variable, which can in turn be stored in a `sql_variant` variable. Also, it might seem strange that you can't store a variant in a variant, but this is just saying that the `sql_variant` datatype doesn't exist as such—SQL Server chooses the best type of storage in which to store the value you give to it. Storing a `sql_variant` in a `sql_variant` would cause a logical endless loop.

Generally, `sql_variant` is a datatype to steer clear of unless you really cannot know the datatype of a given value until the user enters the value. I used the `sql_variant` in Chapter 9 when I implemented the user-specified data storage using the entity-attribute–value solution. This allows the user to enter any type of data and then have the system store the data in the most appropriate method. By not needing to know the type at design time, you can allow the user to insert any type of data that they might want. In that example, a good deal of the work was making sure the data the user saved was of the right datatype.

Any positives with `sql_variant` lead directly to the negatives of the type. Although simple storage and viewing of the data isn't too hard, it isn't easy to manipulate data once it has been stored in a `sql_variant` column. Some issues to consider are as follows:

- *Difficulties assigning data from a* `sql_variant` *column to a stronger-typed datatype*: You have to be careful, because the rules for casting a variable from one datatype to another are difficult and might cause errors if the data can't be cast. For example, you can't cast the `varchar(10)` value `'Not a Date'` to a `datetime` datatype. Such problems become an issue when you start to retrieve the `variant` data out of the `sql_variant` datatype and try to manipulate it unless you are quite careful with the data entry and typing of values (which kind of defeats the purpose!). Using the `TRY_CAST` function can be very useful when extracting data from a `sql_variant` column.

- `NULL` `sql_variant` *values are considered to have no datatype*: Hence, you'll have to deal with `sql_variant` `NULL` values differently from `NULL` values in other datatypes.

- *Comparisons of* variants *to other datatypes could cause difficult-to-catch programmatic errors, because of the* sql_variant *value instance's datatype:* Usually, the compiler will know whether you try to run a statement that compares two incompatible datatypes, such as @intVar = @varcharVar. However, if the two variables in question were defined as sql_variants and the datatypes are incompatible, then the values won't match and may give you errors.

When working with sql_variant variables or columns, you can use the SQL_VARIANT_PROPERTY function to discover the datatype of a given sql_variant value, for example:

```
DECLARE @varcharVariant sql_variant = '1234567890';

SELECT @varcharVariant AS VarcharVariant,
   SQL_VARIANT_PROPERTY(@varcharVariant,'BaseType') AS BaseType,
   SQL_VARIANT_PROPERTY(@varcharVariant,'MaxLength') AS MaxLength,
   SQL_VARIANT_PROPERTY(@varcharVariant,'Collation') AS Collation;
```

The preceding statements return the following result:

varcharVariant	baseType	maxLength	collation
1234567890	varchar	10	Latin1_General_100_CI_AS

For numeric data, you can also find the precision and scale:

```
DECLARE @numericVariant sql_variant = 123456.789;

SELECT @numericVariant AS NumericVariant,
   SQL_VARIANT_PROPERTY(@numericVariant,'BaseType') AS BaseType,
   SQL_VARIANT_PROPERTY(@numericVariant,'Precision') AS Precision,
   SQL_VARIANT_PROPERTY(@numericVariant,'Scale') AS Scale;
```

This returns the following result:

numericVariant	baseType	precision	scale
123456.789	numeric	9	3

As noted, comparisons may not work exactly as expected due to the way datatypes are handled. For example, consider this query:

```
DECLARE @varcharVariant int = 1234567890;
DECLARE @varcharVariant2 varchar(10) = '1234567890';

SELECT 'Value Matches'
WHERE  @varcharVariant = @varcharVariant2;
```

For this comparison, the varchar(10) is implicitly converted to an integer, and this query returns 'Value Matches'. But the next comparison fails:

```
DECLARE @varcharVariant sql_variant = 1234567890;
DECLARE @varcharVariant2 sql_variant = '1234567890';

SELECT 'Value Matches'
WHERE  @varcharVariant = @varcharVariant2;
```

This is because it compares the values as they are, and the first would be implicitly cast as the integer value 1234567890 and the other as the character value '1234567890' which are not the same.

Not Simply Scalar Datatypes

This section briefly notes the class of datatypes that have been implemented by Microsoft that aren't really scalar values. Another common term for these datatypes that have cropped up around the Internet is *beyond relational*, but to many people this is a confusing term.

The non-scalar types include the following:

- hierarchyId: Used to help build and manage a tree structure. It is very close to being a scalar type with several methods that can be applied to traverse and work with a hierarchy. For more details, see the Microsoft Docs article "Hierarchical Data (SQL Server)" (docs.microsoft.com/en-us/sql/relational-databases/hierarchical-data-sql-server).

- *Spatial types*: Geometry for dealing with planar/Euclidean (flat-Earth) data; geography for ellipsoidal (round-Earth) data, such as GPS longitude and latitude data. The spatial types technically hold arrays of values that represent sets on their own. For more details, see the Microsoft Docs article "Spatial Data (SQL Server)" (docs.microsoft.com/en-us/sql/relational-databases/spatial/spatial-data-sql-server).

- XML: Used to store and manipulate XML values. A single XML column can more or less implement a database almost on its own. For more details, see the Microsoft Docs article "XML Data (SQL Server)" (docs.microsoft.com/en-us/sql/relational-databases/xml/xml-data-sql-server).

Each of these types has some value to someone and fills a void that cannot be straightforwardly represented with the relational model, at least not as easily.

Index

A

Accelerated Database Recovery, 888, 940

Account model, 570

Acyclic graphs, 598, 604

Ad hoc SQL, 985
- batching mechanism
  - blocking/locking, 1008
  - code-wrapping mechanism, 1007
  - Invoice and InvoiceLineItem objects, 1009
  - new invoice/line items, 1007, 1008
  - single batch, 1008
  - transaction, 1006
- compilation, 987
- DML statements, 987
- injection attacks, 987
  - DECLARE @value statement, 1012
  - error, 1012
  - parameterized methods, 1010, 1014, 1015
  - SCALAR USER DEFINED FUNCTION object, 1012, 1013
  - single-quote characters, 1011–1013
  - string value, 1014
- low cohesion, high coupling, 1004
  - add ability, 1005, 1006
  - employee table, 1005
  - stored procedure, 1006
  - toolsets, 1005

- T-SQL statements, 1005
- user interface, 1006
- performance tuning, 1015, 1016
- queries, 988
- runtime control, queries, 988
  - Contact table, 991
  - ContactNotes, 990
  - create table, 989, 990
  - driver stored procedure, 996
  - inflexible requirements, 989
  - logical version, 995
  - modify column, 994
  - optimizer, 996
  - optional parameters, 994
  - SalesLevelId value, 994
  - sales summary column, 992
  - STORED PROCEDURE object, 994, 995
  - UPDATE statements, 993
  - WHERE clause, 996
  - Windows file-listing, 990, 991
- security issues, 1009, 1010
- shared execution plans, 988, 997, 999
- *vs.* stored procedures, 1049, 1050

Anti-patterns, 629–631
- generic key references, 637–641
- one-size-fits-all key domain, 633–636
- undecipherable data, 631, 632
- unstructured data, 641–643

© Louis Davidson 2021
L. Davidson, *Pro SQL Server Relational Database Design and Implementation,*
https://doi.org/10.1007/978-1-4842-6497-3

U, V, W, X, Y, Z

Printed by Printforce, the Netherlands